MW00561329

A COMMENTARY
on the
GOSPEL OF MATTHEW

A COMMENTARY
on the
GOSPEL OF MATTHEW

CRAIG S. KEENER

WILLIAM B. EERDMANS PUBLISHING COMPANY
GRAND RAPIDS, MICHIGAN / CAMBRIDGE, U.K.

255 Jefferson Ave. S.E., Grand Rapids, Michigan 49503 /
P.O. Box 163, Cambridge CB3 9PU U.K.

Printed in the United States of America

04 03 02 01 7 6 5 4 3 2

Library of Congress Cataloging-in-Publication Data

Keener, Craig S., 1960-
A commentary on the Gospel of Matthew / Craig S. Keener.
p. cm.
Includes indexes.
ISBN 0-8028-3821-9 (cloth: alk. paper)
1. Bible. N.T. Matthew — Commentaries.
2. Bible. N.T. Matthew — Socio-rhetorical criticism.
I. Title.
BS2575.3.K43 1999
226.2′077 — dc21 98-53605
CIP

To my parents,
John and Gail Keener
With love and gratitude

Contents

Acknowledgments

I appreciate the academic and faith communities that have afforded me the opportunity to explore Matthew with them, especially the students in my Matthew seminars at Eastern Baptist Theological Seminary in Philadelphia, the Center for Urban Theological Studies in Philadelphia, and Hood Theological Seminary in Salisbury, NC, and the members of Mt. Zion Baptist Church in Salisbury, NC. I am grateful to Ben Witherington of Asbury Seminary and John Simpson of Eerdmans for their guidance and support. I owe much gratitude to my copyeditor Milton Essenburg, who patiently and cheerfully worked through a long manuscript containing sometimes tedious notes. I am also grateful to Eerdmans and InterVarsity for allowing me the opportunity to present a much more academic version of my much more popular commentary published by the latter (1997a).

Abbreviations

General Abbreviations

A.D.	*anno Domini,* in the year of our Lord
Aram.	Aramaic
b.	Babylonian (Talmud)
bar.	baraita
B.C.	before Christ
bib.	bibliography
bk.	book
ca.	*circa,* around
cf.	*confer,* compare
ch.	chapter
cm.	centimeter
col.	column
comm.	commentary
DSS	Dead Sea Scrolls
ed.	edition
e.g.	*exempli gratia,* for example
Ep.	Epistle
fig.	figure
fr(g).	fragment
ft.	feet
Gk.	Greek
i.e.	*id est,* that is
incant.	incantation
inscr.	inscription
intro.	introduction
KJV	King James Version
lit.	literally
LXX	Septuagint

ABBREVIATIONS

m.	Mishnah
Midr.	Midrash
MSS	manuscripts
MT	Masoretic Text
n.	note
NIV	New International Version
NRSV	New Revised Standard Version
NT	New Testament
OT	Old Testament
p.	Palestinian (Talmud)
par.	paragraph
pp.	pages
pq.	pereq.
pref.	preface
prol.	prologue
Q	Quelle ("sayings" source for the Synoptic Gospels)
Rec.	Recension
rev.	revised
t.	Tosefta
trans.	translated by
UBS	United Bible Societies
v.	volume
vs.	versus

Apocrypha

Bar	Baruch
1-2 Esdr	1-2 Esdras
4 Ezra	4 Ezra
Jdt	Judith
Ep Jer	Epistle of Jeremiah
1-2-3-4 Macc	1-2-3-4 Maccabees
Pr Azar	Prayer of Azariah
Pr Man	Prayer of Manasseh
Sir	Sirach
Sus	Susanna
Tob	Tobit
Wis	Wisdom of Solomon

Old Testament Pseudepigrapha

Ahiqar	Ahiqar
Apoc. Abr.	Apocalypse of Abraham
Apoc Elijah	Apocalypse of Elijah
Apoc. Ezek.	Apocalypse of Ezekiel
Apoc. Mos.	Apocalypse of Moses

Apoc. Sedr.	Apocalypse of Sedrach
Apoc. Zeph.	Apocalypse of Zephaniah
Asc. Isa.	Ascension of Isaiah
Ass. Mos.	Assumption of Moses
2-3-4 Bar.	2-3-4 Baruch
1-2-3 Enoch	1-2-3 Enoch
Ezek. *Exag.*	Ezekiel *Exagōgē*
Jos. and Asen.	Joseph and Aseneth
Jub.	Jubilees
Mart. Is.	Martyrdom of Isaiah
Odes Sol.	Odes of Solomon
Ps-Philo	Pseudo-Philo
Ps-Phocyl.	Pseudo-Phocylides
Pss. Sol.	Psalms of Solomon
Sib. Or.	Sibylline Oracles
Test. Abr.	Testament of Abraham
Test. Adam	Testament of Adam
Test. 12 Patr.	Testaments of the Twelve Patriarchs
Test. Reub.	Testament of Reuben
Test. Sim.	Testament of Simeon
Test. Levi	Testament of Levi
Test Jud.	Testament of Judah
Test. Iss.	Testament of Issachar
Test. Zeb.	Testament of Zebulun
Test. Dan	Testament of Dan
Test. Naph.	Testament of Naphtali
Test. Gad	Testament of Gad
Test. Asher	Testament of Asher
Test. Jos.	Testament of Joseph
Test. Benj.	Testament of Benjamin
Test. Mos.	Testament of Moses
Test. Jacob	Testament of Jacob
Test. Job	Testament of Job
Test. Sol.	Testament of Solomon
Tr. Shem	Treatise of Shem

Early Christian Literature

Acts of Jn.	Acts of John
Acts Thom.	Acts of Thomas
Apoc. Pet.	Apocalypse of Peter
Apocr. Jn.	Apocryphon of John
Apost. Const.	Apostolic Constitutions
Athen.	Athenagoras
Barn.	Barnabas
1 Clem.	1 Clement
Clem. Alex. *Strom.*	Clement of Alexandria *Stromateis*

Did.	Didache
Ep. Arist.	Epistle of Aristeas
Ep. Diogn.	Epistle to Diognetus
Epiph. *Haer.*	Epiphanius *Haereses*
Euseb.	Eusebius
H.E.	*Historia Ecclesiastica*
Onom.	*Onomastica*
P.E.	*Praeparatio Evangelica*
Gos. Nic.	Gospel of Nicodemus
Gos. Peter	Gospel of Peter
Gos. Thom.	Gospel of Thomas
Herm.	Hermas
Com.	*Commands (Mandates)*
Sim.	*Similitudes*
Vis.	*Visions*
Ign.	Ignatius
Eph.	*Ephesians*
Magn.	*Magnesians*
Rom.	*Romans*
Trall.	*Trallians*
Iren. *Haer.*	Irenaeus *Adversus Omnes Haereses*
Jerome *Com. in Ep. ad Eph.*	Jerome *Commentary on the Epistle to the Ephesians*
Justin	Justin
1 Apol.	*First Apology*
Comm. Matt.	*Commentary on Matthew*
Dial.	*Dialogue with Trypho*
Mart. Pol.	Martyrdom of Polycarp
Origen *De Princ.*	Origen *De Principiis*
Pol. *Phil.*	Polycarp *Letter to the Philippians*
Sent. Sext.	Sentences of Sextus
Tert.	Tertullian
Apol.	*Apologeticus*
Spec.	*De Spectaculis*
Theoph.	Theophilus to Autolycus

Classical and Hellenistic Literature

Ach. Tat. *Clit.*	Achilles Tatius *Clitophon and Leucippe*
Ael. Arist.	Aelius Aristides
Or.	*Orations*
Plat. Disc.	*Discourses against Plato*
Anacharsis *Ep.*	*Epistle to Tereus*
Appian	
C.W.	*Civil War*
R.H.	*Roman History*
Ap. Rhod.	Apollonius Rhodius

ABBREVIATIONS

Apul. *Metam.*	Apuleius *Metamorphoses* (= *The Golden Ass*)
Arist.	Aristotle
De An. Hist.	*De Historia Animalium*
E.E.	*Ethica Eudemia*
Gen. Anim	*De Generatione Animalium*
N.E.	*Nicomachean Ethics*
Pol.	*Politica*
Rhet.	*Rhetorica*
V.V.	*On Virtues and Vices*
Aristophanes	
Acharn.	*Acharnians*
Lysist.	*Lysistrata*
Arrian	
Alex.	*Alexander*
Ind.	*Indica*
Artem. *Oneir.*	Artemidorus *Oneirocriticon*
Athenaeus *Deipn.*	Athenaeus *Deipnosophistae*
Aul. Gel.	Aulus Gellius *Noctes Attica*
Babrius	Babrius
Char. *Chaer.*	Chariton *Chaereas and Callirhoe*
Cic.	Cicero
De Divin.	*De Divinatione*
De Leg.	*De Legibus*
De Nat. Deor.	*De Natura Deorum*
De Offic.	*De Officiis*
De Orat.	*De Optimo Genere Oratorum*
De Re Publ.	*De Republica*
De Senec.	*De Senectute*
Lael.	*Laelius de Amicitia*
Par. Stoic.	*Paradoxa Stoicorum*
Tusc. Disp.	*Tusculanae Disputationes*
Verr.	*In Verrem*
Cod. Theod.	*Codex Theodosius*
Columella	
Rust.	*De Re Rustica*
Corn. Nep.	Cornelius Nepos *De Viris Illustribus*
Crates *Ep.*	*Crates Epistles*
Curt.	Curtius Rufus
Demosth. *2nd Olynth. Or.*	Demosthenes *Second Olynthiac Oration*
Dig.	*Digest*
Dio Cassius *R.H.*	*Roman History*
Dio Chrys. *Or.*	Dio Chrysostom *Orations*
Diod. Sic.	Diodorus Siculus, *Library of History*
Diog. *Ep.*	Diogenes *Epistles*
Diog. Laert.	Diogenes Laertius *Lives of Eminent Philosophers*
Dion Hal.	Dionysius of Halicarnassus *Roman Antiquities*
Epict.	Epictetus

ABBREVIATIONS

Disc.	*Discourses*
Encheir.	*Encheiridion*
Eurip.	Euripides
Androm.	*Andromache*
Bacch.	*Bacchae*
Hippol.	*Hippolytus*
Iph. Taur.	*Iphigenia Taurica*
Gaius *Inst.*	*Institutes*
Greek Anthol.	*Greek Anthology*
Herod. *Hist.*	Herodotus *History*
Hesiod	
Theog.	*Theogonia*
W.D.	*Works and Days*
Op.	*Opera et Dies* (= *Works and Days*)
Hom.	Homer
Il.	*Iliad*
Od.	*Odyssey*
Hor.	Horace
Carm.	*Carmina*
Ep.	*Epodes*
Sat.	*Satirae*
Iamb. *V.P.*	Iamblichus *De Vita Pythagorica*
Isoc.	Isocrates
Demon.	*Demonicus*
Nic./Cypr.	*Nicocles/Cyprians*
Paneg.	*Panegricus*
Jos.	Josephus
Ant.	*Antiquities of the Jews*
Apion	*Against Apion*
Life	*Life of Flavius Jesephus*
War	*The Jewish War*
Justin.	Justinian
Dig.	*Digest of Roman Law*
Inst.	*Institutions*
Juv. *Sat.*	Juvenal *Satires*
Livy	Livy *Annals of the Roman People*
Lucan *C.W.*	*Civil War*
Lucian	
Alex.	*Alexander the False Prophet*
Dial. of the Dead	*Dialogue of the Dead*
Lucretius *Nat.*	Lucretius *De Rerum Natura*
Macrob. *Sat.*	Macrobius *Saturnalia*
Malal. *Chron.*	Malalas *Chronographia*
Marc. Aur. *Med.*	Marcus Aurelius *Meditations*
Mart. *Epig.*	Martial *Epigrams*
Mus. Ruf.	Musonius Rufus
Oros.	Orosius
Ovid *Metam.*	Ovid *Metamorphoses*

ABBREVIATIONS

Parthenius *L.R.*	*Romantic Love (Erōtika Pathēmata)*
Paus.	Pausanias *Description of Greece*
Persius *Sat.*	*Satyra*
Petron. *Sat.*	Petronius *Satyricon*
Philo	
Abr.	*De Abrahamo*
Aet.	*De Aeternitate Mundi*
Agr.	*De Agricultura*
Cher.	*De Cherubim*
Conf.	*De Confusione Linguarum*
Cong.	*De Congressu Quaeredae Eruditionis Gratia*
Decal.	*De Decalogo*
Det.	*Quod Deterius Potiori Insidiari Soleat*
Ebr.	*De Ebrietate*
Flacc.	*In Flaccum*
Fug.	*De Fuga et Inventione*
Gig.	*De Gigantibus*
Immut.	*Quod Deus Immutabilis Sit*
Jos.	*De Josepho (On Joseph)*
Leg. Alleg.	*Legum Allegoriae*
Leg. Gai.	*De Legatione ad Gaium*
Migr. Abr.	*De Migratione Abrahami*
Mut.	*De Mutatione Nominum*
Omn. Prob. Lib.	*Quod Omnis Probus Liber Sit*
Op. Mund.	*De Opificio Mundi*
Plant.	*De Plantatione*
Post.	*De Posteritate Caini*
Praem.	*De Praemiis et Poenis*
Q. Ex.	*Questiones et Solutiones in Exodum*
Sac.	*De Sacrificiis Abelis et Caini*
Som.	*De Somnis*
Spec. Leg.	*De Specialibus Legibus*
Virt.	*De Virtutibus*
Vit. Con.	*De Vita Contemplativa*
Vit. Mos.	*De Vita Mosis*
Philost.	Philostratus
V.A.	*Vita Apollonii*
Pindar *Olym.*	Pindar *Olympic Odes*
Plato	
Alcib.	*Alcibiades*
Apol.	*Apology*
Crit.	*Crito*
Phaed.	*Phaedo*
Rep.	*Republic*
Symp.	*Symposium*
Tim.	*Timaeus*
Plaut.	Plautus
Mostell.	*Mostellaria*

Trin.	*Trinummus*
Pliny *N.H.*	*Natural History*
Plot.	Plotinus *Enneads*
Plut.	Plutarch
Alex.	*Alexander*
Brut.	*Brutus*
Cato Min.	*Cato Minor*
Educ.	*The Education of Children*
Fortune of Alex.	*Fortune of Alexander*
G.Q.	*Greek Questions*
Mor. Moralia	*Moralia*
Plat.Q.	*Platonic Questions*
Pomp.	*Pompey*
Praec. Ger. Deip.	*Praeceptae Gerendae Republicae*
R.Q.	*Roman Questions*
T-T	*Table-Talk*
Uneduc. Ruler	*Uneducated Ruler*
Polyb. *R.R.E.*	Polybius *Rise of the Roman Empire*
Polyc. *Ep.*	Polycrates *Epistles*
Porphyry	
Life of Pyth.	*Life of Pythagoras*
Vit. Plot.	*Life of Plotinus (Vita Plotini)*
Propertius *Eleg.*	Propertius *Elegies*
Ps-Demosthenes *Or.*	Pseudo-Demosthenes *Orations*
Ps-Philo	Pseudo-Philo *Biblical Antiquities*
Ps-Phocyl.	Pseudo-Phocylides
Pub. Syr.	Publilius Syrus
Pythag. Sent.	*Pythagorean Sentences*
Quint. *Inst. Or.*	Quintilian *Institutes of Oratory*
Rhet. ad Herenn.	*Rhetorica ad Herennium*
Sall.	Sallust
Catil.	*Bellum Catilinae*
Jug.	*Bellum Jugurthium*
Sen.	Seneca
Apocol.	*Apocolocyntosis*
Consol.	*De Consolatione*
De Benef.	*De Beneficiis*
Dial.	*Dialogues*
Ep. Lucil.	*Epistles to Lucilius*
Sext. Emp. *Pyrrh.*	Sextus Empiricus *Outlines of Pyrrhonism*
Socratics	
Ep.	*Epistles*
Sopatros *Rhet. Gr.*	*Greek Rhetoric*
Soph.	Sophocles
Antig.	*Antigone*
Oed. Col.	*Oedipus Coloneus*
Oed. Rex	*Oedipus Rex*
Philoct.	*Philoctetes*

Women Tr.	*Women of Trachis*
Strabo *Geog.*	Strabo *Geography*
Suet.	Suetonius
Aug.	*Augustus*
Calig.	*Caligula*
Claud.	*Claudius*
Dom.	*Domitian*
Gramm.	*De Grammaticis*
Tib.	*Tiberius*
Vesp.	*Vespasian*
Syr. Men. *Epit.*	Syriac Menander *Epitome*
Syr. Men. Sent.	Sentences of the Syriac Menander
Tac.	Tacitus
Ann.	*Annales*
Hist.	*Histories*
Theon *Progymn.*	Theon *Progymnasmata*
Val. Max. *Fact.*	Valerius Maximus *Factorum et Dictorum Memorabilium Libri*
Varro *Agric.*	Varro *Agriculture*
Virg.	Virgil
Aen.	*Aeneid*
Ecl.	*Eclogues*
Georg.	*Georgics*
Orph.	*Orpheus*
Priapea	*Priapea*
Xen. *Mem.*	Xenophon *Memorabilia Socratis*

Dead Sea Scrolls and Related Texts

CD	Cairo Damascus Document
1QapGen	Genesis Apocryphon from Qumran Cave 1
1QH	Thanksgiving Hymns *(Hôdāyôṭ)* from Cave 1
1QM	War Scroll *(Milḥāmāh)* from Cave 1
1QpHab	Pesher (Commentary) on Habakkuk from Cave 1
1QS	Manual of Discipline *(Serek hayyaḥad)* from Cave 1
1QSa	Appendix A (Rule of the Congregation) to 1QS
3Q	Cave 3
4QBeat	Beatitudes from Cave 4
4QFlor	Florilegium (Eschatological Midrashim) from Cave 4
4QpIsa	Pesher on Isaiah from Cave 4
4QMMT	*Miqsat Maʿaseh ha-Torah* from Cave 4
4QPBless	Patriarchal Blessings
4QpHos	Pesher on Hosea from Cave 4
4QpNah	Pesher on Nahum from Cave 4
4QpPs	Pesher on Psalms from Cave 4
4QPrNab	Prayer of Nabonidus from Cave 4
4QTest	Testimonia Text from Cave 4

11QMelch	Melchizedek from Cave 11
11QTemple	Temple Scroll from Cave 11

Orders and Tractates in Mishnaic and Related Literature

ʾAbot	ʾAbot
ʿArak.	ʿArakin
ʿAbod. Zar.	ʿAboda Zara
B. Bat.	Baba Batra
Bek.	Bekoret
Ber.	Berakot
Beṣa	Beṣa (= Yom Ṭob)
Bik.	Bikkurim
B. Meṣ.	Baba Meṣiʿa
B. Qam.	Baba Qamma
Dem.	Demai
ʿEd.	ʿEduyyot
ʿErub.	ʿErubin
Giṭ.	Giṭṭin
Ḥag.	Ḥagiga
Ḥal.	Ḥalla
Hor.	Horayot
Ḥul.	Ḥullin
Kelim	Kelim
Ker.	Keritot
Kil.	Kilʾayim
Kip.	Kippurim (= Yoma)
Maʿaś.	Maʿaśerot
Maʿaś. Sh.	Maʿaśer Sheni
Mak.	Makkot
Maksh.	Makshirin
Meg.	Megilla
Meʿil.	Meʿila
Menaḥ.	Menaḥot
Midd.	Middot
Miqw.	Miqwaʾot
Moʿed Qaṭ.	Moʿed Qaṭan
Nazir	Nazir
Ned.	Nedarim
Neg.	Negaʿim
Nez.	Neziqin
Nid.	Niddah
Ohol.	Oholot
ʿOr.	ʿOrla
Para	Para
Peʾa	Peʾa
Pesaḥ.	Pesaḥim

Qidd.	Qiddushin
Rosh Hash.	Rosh Hashshana
Sanh.	Sanhedrin
Shab.	Shabbat
Sheb.	Shebiʿit
Shebu.	Shebuʿot
Sheqal.	Sheqalim
Soṭa	Soṭa
Sukk.	Sukka
Taʿan.	Taʿanit
Tamid	Tamid
Tem.	Temura
Ter.	Terumot
Ṭohar.	Ṭoharot
ʿUq.	ʿUqṣin
Yad.	Yadayim
Yebam.	Yebamot
Yoma	Yoma (= Kippurim)
Zab.	Zabim

Other Rabbinic Works

ARN	ʾAbot de Rabbi Nathan
DE	Derek Ereṣ
Der. Er. Rab.	Derek Ereṣ Rabba
Der Er. Zut	Derek Ereṣ Zuṭa
Mek. Bah.	Mekilta Bahodesh
Mek. Shir.	Mekilta Shirata
Mek. Vay.	Mekilta Vayassa
Pesiq. R.	Pesiqta Rabbati
Pesiq. Rab Kah.	Pesiqta de Rab Kahana
Pirqe R. El.	Pirqe Rabbi Eliezer
Sifra A.M.	Sifra Aharé Mot
Sifra Behar	Sifra Behar
Sifra Behuq.	Sifra Behuqoti
Sifra Lev.	Sifra Leviticus
Sifra Mes.	Sifra Mesora
Sifra Qed.	Sifra Qedoshim
Sifra Shir.	Sifra Shirata
Sifra Taz.	Sifra Tazria Negaim
Sifra V. D. Deho.	Sifra Vayyiqra Dibura Dehobah
Sifra V. D. Den.	Sifra Vayyiqra Dibura Denedabah
Sifra Zab.	Sifra Zabim
Sifre Deut.	Sifra Deuteronomy
Sifre Num.	Sifre Numbers
Yalq. Ex.	Yalqut Exodus

ABBREVIATIONS

Targumic Material

Targ. Neof.	Targum Neofiti
Targ. Onq.	Targum Onqelos
Targ. Ps-J.	Targum Pseudo-Jonathan
Targ. Yer.	Targum Yerushalmi

Papyri

P. Amh.	*Amherst Papyri*
P. Cairo Zen.	*Zenon Papyri*
P. Eleph.	*Elephantine Papyri*
P. Enteuxis	*Enteuxis Papyri*
P. Fay.	*Fayyum Papyri*
P. Flor.	*Florentine Papyri*
P. Giess.	*Giessen Papyri*
P. Grenf.	*Grenfell Papyri*
P. Hal.	*Halensis Papyri*
P. Hamb.	*Hamburg Papyri*
P. Hib.	*Hibeh Papyri*
P. Lond.	*London Papyri*
P. Mich.	*Michigan Papyri*
P. Oxy.	*Oxyrhyncus Papyri*
P. Par.	*Paris Papyri*
P. Ryl.	*Rylands Papryi*
P. Sikaon	*Sikaon Papyri*
P. Strassb.	*Strassburg Papyri*
P. Tebt.	*Tebtunis Papyri*
P. Théad.	*Théadelphie Papyri*
P. Tor.	*Papyri graeci regii Taurinensis Musei Aegyptii*

Modern Publications

ACCS	*Ancient Christian Commentary on Scripture: Mark* (InterVarsity, 1998)
ANET	*Ancient Near Eastern Texts* (J. B. Pritchard, ed.)
BAGD	W. Bauer, W. F. Arndt, F. W. Gingrich, and F. W. Danker, *Greek-English Lexicon of the New Testament*
BCH	*Bulletin de Correspondance Hellénique*
B.G.U.	*Berliner Griechische Urkunden*
CIJ	*Corpus Inscriptionum Iudaicarum*
CIL	*Corpus Inscriptionum Latinarum*
CPJ	*Corpus Papyrorum Iudaicarum*
DJD	Discoveries in the Judaean Desert
ExpT	*Expository Times*
HUCA	*Hebrew Union College Annual*

ABBREVIATIONS

IG	*Inscriptiones Graecae*
IGRR	*Inscriptiones Graecae ad Res Romanes Pertinentes*
ILS	*Inscriptiones Latinae Selectae*
JE	*Jewish Encyclopedia*
JSJ	*Journal for the Study of Judaism*
KUB	*Keilschrifturkunden aus Boghazköi*
LCL	Loeb Classical Library
NHL	Nag Hammadi Library
NTA	*New Testament Abstracts*
OGIS	*Orientis Graeci Inscriptiones Selectae*
OPT	*Old Testament Pseudepigrapha*
PDM	*Papyri Demoticae Magicae*
PGM	*Papyri Graecae Magicae*
P.S.I.	*Pubblicazioni della Società Italiana*
SB	*Sammelbuch griechischer Urkunden aus Ägypten*
SEG	*Supplementum epigraphicum Graecum*
SIG	W. Dittenberger, *Sylloge Inscriptionum Graecarum*
SNTS	Society for New Testament Studies
W.Chr.	= *B.G.U.*
WO	*Die Welt des Orients*

Introduction

The Focus of This Commentary

Different commentaries emphasize differing primary concerns, such as redaction criticism (Gundry 1982), structuralism (Patte 1987), and the history of interpretation (Luz 1989; cf. idem 1994; Schnackenburg 1996). Without minimizing or excluding such concerns, this commentary focuses especially on two aspects of interpretation: analysis of the social-historical contexts of Matthew and his traditions on one hand, and pericope-by-pericope suggestions concerning the nature of Matthew's exhortations to his Christian audience on the other. The latter aspect can be helpful today in that most readers of Matthew commentaries use them not simply to reconstruct early Christian history but to attempt to reapply Matthew's instruction (or those of his traditions) to their own generation (or, in the case of scholars, often to teach those who will do so).

But if there is to be any degree of analogy between the early Christians' wisdom and that of their modern interpreters, we must take into account the historical context not only *in which* but also *to which* they communicated their message. Such a context naturally shaped the form of their message, suggesting the importance of my first focus for my second. Intrinsic study of the text is more essential to understanding the text than extrinsic analysis, but most users of commentaries will require more assistance with extrinsic data.[1] This social-historical study of Matthew will include some attention to the rhetoric both of his Gospel (especially in terms of genre, forms, and narrative techniques) and of its traditions, as well as to historical matters made relevant to a study of Matthew by Matthew's genre (see below).

1. Although narrative criticism rightly emphasizes intrinsic information, narratives generally assume rather than state some information shared by the implied author and implied audience (see, e.g., Powell 1993; Bauer 1996: 132). For important comments about the need for extrinsic methodology in NT scholarship, see Hengel 1994; idem 1996, both based on his 1993 SNTS presidential address.

Yet our information concerning the precise social situation the First Gospel addresses is quite limited.[2] For this reason, the social situation of the earliest traditions behind the Gospel sometimes provide more fertile ground for exploration. Even if we cannot reconstruct the precise social situation of Matthew or his traditions, the general social context is far more accessible for both. Most of Matthew's traditions probably reflect the same general eastern Mediterranean, perhaps Syrian, Jewish milieu as that in which Matthew writes. Comparing the issues Matthew addresses with what we know of the historical situation of Jewish-Christian relations in the late first century provides us a basic picture of what issues he must have considered relevant for his community, but to move too far beyond that basic picture into details is necessarily speculative.[3] Given modern readers' cultural remove from the first-century eastern Mediterranean world, however, background from the larger milieu remains helpful even where we cannot reconstruct more precisely the details of Matthew's particular situation.

A detailed analysis of how Matthew uses his tradition would require a full-scale commentary devoted largely to redaction-critical concerns (like Gundry's massive 1982 work), which is not the primary focus of this commentary. At the same time, given the Gospel's basic genre, Matthew's literary method is inseparable from his presuppositions as a biographer/historian, so I will often pause to explore historical questions behind particular Matthean sections or pericopes, interacting to some degree with contemporary Jesus research.

Because ancient biography normally included some level of historical intention, historical questions are relevant in evaluating the degree to which Matthew was able to achieve the intention his genre implies. This does not require us to demand a narrow precision regarding details, a precision foreign to ancient literature, but to evaluate the general fidelity of substance.[4] (Ironically, however, Matthew remains closer to the earliest sources than we are, so any attempt to evaluate his success demands some humility.)[5] My most striking discovery while writing this commentary was how often Matthew "re-Judaizes" his sources, probably mostly on the basis of concrete Palestinian, Jewish-Christian oral tradi-

2. Cf. Kingsbury 1991: 260, 262; Johnson 1996: 91; also the correct if overstated warning of Patte 1987: 13.

3. Although I here adopt the usual expression "Matthean community," Stanton 1992a; idem 1993: 50-51 is correct that Matthew must intend a wider circulation than a single house church of fifty or so members. How wide an audience Matthew intended is unclear, but within a few decades after publication his Gospel became a favorite in the Eastern churches.

4. Thus Dion. Hal. 7.1.6 permits prior historians a few years' latitude in their citation of dates but is quite annoyed with a historian who is two or more generations off due to failure to check his sources (7.1.4-6). Even the most accurate historians usually made some mistakes on details; e.g., Herodian 3.4.3; 3.9.3; likewise Dio Cassius *R.H.* 48.26.2 contradicts the earlier Jos. *Ant.* 14.13.9-10; *War* 1.13.9-11 and Dio Cassius himself in *R.H.* ch. 41 and 49.22.6 (see Dio Cassius LCL 5:272-73 n.1); historians also were normally ready to reveal errors once they were discovered (Diod. Sic. 4.56.7-8). Yet ancients could also affirm that histories that are true (Jos. *Apion* 1.15), like the Scriptures (*Apion* 1.37-38), should not contradict one another.

5. Cf. Wright 1992a: 106: modern scholarly constructions often proceed on the basis of hypotheses, but the Gospel writers had access to much more of the firsthand data.

tions. (This re-Judaizing is all the more noticeable in view of Matthew's frequent abridgment of Mark.) I suspect that Matthew remains closer to the earliest strata of tradition than has often been supposed.

The purpose of this commentary does not allow me to summarize and interact in detail with all secondary sources on Matthean research.[6] At the same time, to make this commentary as useful as possible to students who wish to pursue their own research further, I have cited as much of the secondary literature as is feasible where it proves most relevant.[7] The brevity with which I have cited many sources does not permit the fine nuancing of detailed interaction, nor in most cases the opportunity to list both strengths and weaknesses of various works. Nevertheless, I have provided them for the reader's further exploration. It should be understood that, as in most scholarly work, disagreement with any author on a particular point does not indicate criticism of that author's scholarship in general, nor is the reader obliged or expected to concur with all the exegetical decisions reflected in this commentary.

I have often chosen to include far more citations than necessary for the point in the text because scholars and seminarians who use this commentary will thereby have access to much more information, which they can then expand in research articles and papers, than I could include in other than such summary fashion. (In lecturing I prefer to illustrate my points with some concrete ancient examples, usually the more graphic or entertaining; but here I frequently list instead multiple references for those who may wish to investigate more sources for themselves.) Naturally those who wish to make use of a commentary without such documentation (like my lighter Matthew commentary for the InterVarsity New Testament Commentary series) will generally simply ignore it. Where possible, I have tried to provide primary sources that have not been available in other commentaries, although in the interest of thoroughness I have also followed other commentators at many points (noted in the commentary where space permits); because a significant percentage of my sources do not appear in earlier commentaries I hope that this commentary will contribute to further research.

The focus of this commentary will lie in understanding the lessons Matthew's Gospel may provide his first-century, predominantly Jewish-Christian community. That is, rather than merely providing various bits of information related to details in verses of Matthew's text, I will subsume as much of the detailed information as possible under the larger lessons or morals found in each of Matthew's narrative units. This attempt is somewhat more precarious and less certain than simply placing various items within the text in their social-historical context.

6. On recent Matthean scholarship, see especially Stanton 1995b.

7. To accomplish this purpose in the face of the ever-increasing number of secondary resources, I have made use of abstracts where necessary on numerous points not central to my examination, just as many commentaries list more works in their segmented bibliographies than they actually cite in their text. Although it is no longer possible to be exhaustive, my purpose here is to provide the reader with a brief idea of other resources she or he may pursue further.

Nevertheless, looking for the text's lessons fits the genre and purpose for which Matthew undoubtedly wrote it. Ancient narrators regularly sought to teach morals or lessons through their narratives;[8] some historians explicitly listed as central to their purposes for writing history both the desire to praise the virtuous and the urge to spur others to emulate them (Dion. Hal. 1.6.3-5). Others stated that history tells about a nation's greatness and provides models one may imitate (Livy 1, pref. 10). Understanding *why* events happened could allow statesmen to use such historical accounts as precedents or models (*paradeigasin* — Dion. Hal. 5.56.1),[9] just as early Christians (1 Cor 10:11) and other early Jews (Philo *Abr.* 4) used Israelite Scripture. Some biographers and historians emphasized moral lessons more than others, or even varied the level within their own works according to their sources.[10] But among the various overlapping purposes for biographies, praising the subject, using his life as an example, and teaching ethics were common. Many philosophers and politicians employed historical biographies as propaganda in apologetic or polemical situations (Burridge 1992: 80, 149-51, 185-88); official writers also tended to reflect positively on their political or economic patrons (cf. Josephus's pro-Flavian propaganda in, e.g., Saulnier 1991; cf. his portrayal of pagan rulers in Feldman 1993e; 1994a).

The Gospels demonstrate features consonant with such purposes, including the early Christian use of Jesus as a moral example (Phil 2:5; 1 Pet 2:21; 1 Jn 2:6). Matthew probably provides the clearest example of this purpose; his "intention to provide a 'paradigm' for discipleship is noted by many redaction critics" (Burridge 1992: 214-15).[11] Contemporary literary criticism has properly demonstrated the limitations of endeavoring to infer the author's "intention" from a text. At the same time, the implied author has given us enough explanations and

8. See, e.g., Aune 1987: 36; cf. Lyons 1985: 29-32; Feldman 1993b; Dihle 1991: 367-73. Sometimes writers explicitly stated these morals in narrative "asides" (e.g., Dio Cassius 1.5.4; Dion. Hal. 7.65.2-3; Arrian *Alex.* 4.10.8; Corn. Nep. 16 [Pelopidas], 3.1; as noted below, Matthew's explicit narrative asides are mainly fulfillment quotations).

9. Such moral examples regularly appeared in historically based exhortation (Sir 44:16; 4 Macc 1:7-8; 13:9; 2 Bar. 18:1; 1 Clem. 16–19; cf. *Rhet. ad Herenn.* 4.2.2; Plut. *Educ.* 14, *Mor.* 10BE; *Theseus* 11.1; Epict. *Disc.* 1.2.22; Diog. Laert. 7.1.10-11; Herodian 3.13.3; Gray 1987), in speeches (e.g., Isoc. *Demon.* 51, *Or.* 1; Dion. Hal. 6.80.1; cf. Kennedy 1980: 70), or to set precedent for case law (e.g., p. Yebam. 4:11, §8). One should imitate the virtuous rather than the wicked (Isoc. *To Nic.* 26, *Or.* 2; *Nic./Cypr.* 37, *Or.* 3.34; *Nic./Cypr.* 61, *Or.* 3.39; *Demon.* 9, 11, 36, *Or.* 1; Sen. *Dial.* 10.15.2; Epict. *Encheir.* 51.3; Marc. Aur. *Med.* 1.9; Socratics *Ep.* 28; Athenaeus *Deipn.* 13.611c; Ep. Arist. 280; Ps-Phocyl. 77; Test. Benj. 3:1; 4:1) or proficient (Cic. *De Oratore* 2.21.89–22.90; Plut. *Lectures* 6, *Mor.* 40B; Quint. 10.2.14; Theon *Progymn.* 1.81-83; 2.138-43; Kennedy 1980: 116-19); some moralists invited imitation of themselves (1 Cor 4:16; 11:1; Epict. *Disc.* 4.8.31; contrast Sen. *Dial.* 7.18.1). Classical Greek theories of artistic imitation of reality and appropriate limits (cf., e.g., Verdenius 1949: 17-18; Lodge 1953: 167-91; Warry 1962: 100-118) are more distantly related.

10. See, e.g., Burridge 1992: 68-69, comparing Plutarch's *Pompey* and *Cato,* sporting many morals, with *Caesar,* which emphasizes few.

11. Careful narrative criticism also points to Jesus as the primary model for discipleship in this Gospel (Howell 1990: 249-59). Because it possesses the omniscient narrator's commentary, the implied audience is superior to, though linked with, the narrative's disciples (Howell 1990: 248).

thematic clues throughout the narrative for us to observe his general didactic method.[12]

Thus, when I infer the lessons Matthew or his tradition may have been preaching from the stories and teachings in this Gospel, I extrapolate on the basis of his rhetorical method to the kinds of lessons I believe Matthew would at least affirm to be consistent with his purpose.[13] This step can help bridge the gap between traditional exegesis and modern sermon or Bible study preparation, which I suspect also returns more consistently to the purpose for which Matthew recorded his Gospel (cf. 28:19). That is, when we consider the contexts in which Matthew's exhortations find their greatest relevance, we are better positioned to hear the true force of his exhortations. Others will undoubtedly note didactic principles I have missed and question some of those that I think I have found; the historical question of what the writers intended and their audiences inferred is always more hypothetical than the much broader possibilities of what could be inferred in any given historical context. Nevertheless, I hope that this commentary will point readers toward further fruitful explorations of their own into Matthew's probable didactic methods.

Relevant Social Contexts

Because we cannot locate Matthew's community or communities with absolute certainty, reconstructing specific settings remains hypothetical. Where patterns emerge consistently in specifically Matthean emphases, we may infer the sorts of community needs Matthew was addressing, but the fruits of such inferences are usually more slender than a historian would like. Reconstructing the general milieu of the eastern Mediterranean, however, sheds much light on how Matthew's first readers (vis-à-vis modern readers) would approach his Gospel. Even if we knew the precise location, variables like social class and prevailing ideologies in the particular synagogue and church communities there might elude us, but a general knowledge of antiquity provides more of the data Matthew and his first audience would have assumed than a purely modern reading of the text would.

For such reasons as these, I have drawn from as wide a range of sources as possible.[14] Diverse Greek and Roman sources often attest to customs or

12. Cf. Burridge 1992: 125: ". . . the purpose of the author is essential to any concept of genre as a set of expectations or contract between the author and the reader or audience."

13. This approach would be even more to the point if Matthew's implied reader is not a specific late-first-century community but rather any disciple (Kingsbury 1988b), though even this premise (if accepted) would not obviate the need to understand the implied author's and audience's own social-historical location, which, intentionally or unintentionally, will inform the environment in which the Gospel is best understood.

14. Scholars who tend to favor some sources over others and criticize the use of other sources should note that if I am able to cite a variety of sources, I am also cognizant which of those sources are primarily Jewish, which are probably pre-Christian (e.g., the Scrolls and Josephus versus the rab-

ideas that had long before begun to permeate society in general. No one can read Josephus, Egyptian Jewish papyri, or many documents widely circulated among first-century Jews (like the Wisdom of Solomon or 2 Maccabees) without recognizing that Judaism, even Palestinian Judaism, was part of a broader Mediterranean social world. Although sources depicting Jewish life in Syria-Palestine may therefore be most directly helpful (especially when considering Jesus' Galilean ministry), other sources that place that life in its broader eastern Mediterranean context will also be helpful (especially when considering how Matthew's audience would have understood his work). A wide variety of ancient narratives, from distant genres like widely circulated epics of the past to nearer ones like history and especially biography, shed light on Matthew's narrative techniques.

None of the specific Jewish sources on which this commentary depends is without some problems. For example, Josephus, one of my most important sources, is early and adequately broad, but as frequently as possible he translates native Jewish ideas into broader hellenistic categories to make them more intelligible (and acceptable) to his milieu. (Philo carries this process still further, and, while providing one helpful perspective on how hellenistically educated aristocratic Jews in Alexandria could think, must be counterbalanced by other sources closer to Jesus' usual milieu.) The Dead Sea Scrolls are early, Palestinian, and in many respects analogous to early Christianity (although the latter never segregated themselves physically from the larger Jewish society), but they represent particular sectarian perspectives that do not always indicate the sentiments of common Judaism. Rabbinic texts preserve many customs and ideas that appear in the broader culture, but when unparalleled in other Jewish texts must be employed with greater caution because even the earliest texts stem from a period after their particular segment of Judaism had achieved some measure of power, in contradistinction to the first-century situation.[15]

Given the limitations of using any single pool of ancient data, the safest way to reconstruct a knowledge of the general milieu in which Jesus lived, in which Palestinian Jewish Christians transmitted the traditions, and in which Matthew wrote, is to look for customs and ideas within the widest possible frame of sources. Thus if third-century rabbis, the Qumran sect, and a second-century Roman novel all inadvertently attest a common practice, we may guess that some form of this practice widely permeated ancient Mediterranean society. Standard

bis), which are closer to the NT era (Tannaim versus Amoraim, earlier versus later collections), and so forth. But I choose to cite a greater amount of data that are possibly relevant, though preferring the data that are most relevant, rather than citing only the assured minimum of sources (which is sometimes not substantial). That is, because I differ methodologically from some other scholars does not imply that I am unaware of critical issues in the use of such sources.

15. I do not think, however, that their date lays most of them open to a great deal of Christian influence, except in plainly apologetic texts. Provided "we allow for the difference in social location and cultural background" (Horsley 1995: 198), I do not agree with those who wish to bracket rabbinic literature from consideration altogether (convenient as that omission would be for many NT scholars, given the special difficulties inherent in interpreting rabbinic texts).

logic can also be helpful; whereas some later Jewish texts contain likely Christian interpolations,[16] other texts bear no signs of direct or indirect Christian influence, suggesting that the Christian practice reflects the influence of the Jewish custom rather than the reverse. Thus dependence on the widest possible range of sources seems the safest method for reconstructing Matthew's general milieu (even if not always his local situation).

Nor is the function of a given "parallel" necessarily self-evident. Parallels in wording can represent coincidence (especially if one has large samples of nonparallel texts in the collection from which the parallel text derives), reflections of a common milieu, analogous function within a common milieu, linguistic influence, allusion, deliberate contrast, or deliberate quotation.[17] Thus, although I sometimes simply list citations to keep the commentary to a workable size, I usually endeavor to emphasize how they shed light on a Matthean text. At the same time, my attention to Matthew itself has not permitted me to digress here into questions of dating, textual problems, and so forth in each text I cite, because of the limits of a one-volume commentary.[18] Some sources are more valuable than others, but I have listed the broadest range of sources, trusting that those readers who pursue further work with those sources will already have or will acquire adequate competence in those sources.[19]

Questions of Interpretation

Before treating other questions, it is important to survey various methods traditionally employed in critical works on the Gospels. A brief treatment of these methods is relevant here because these methods inform this commentary to some degree, although the space limitations and purpose of this work have led me to

16. E.g., the Testaments of the Twelve Patriarchs and Sibylline Oracles include Christian interpolations; with less consensus, the Testament of Job and Joseph and Aseneth may also betray some Christian influence. Such sources nevertheless reflect a general cultural-philosophical milieu that is helpful for reconstructing early Jewish Christianity.

17. For a helpful and more detailed list of possibilities, see Boring 1995: 23-32.

18. For the same reason, I do not provide a running textual commentary on Matthew, although I will note the most important variants. As Stanton 1995a: 33-48 observes, the Gospels contain many textual variants, but we retain *essentially* the right text. A one-volume commentary on Matthew may explore only the larger issues, leaving the details to more detailed projects.

19. Some prefer to cite only the most relevant sources; I prefer to cite even less relevant sources but to leave conclusions more tentative when these constitute the only available evidence, except where parallels with NT tradition are very strong yet early Christianity is unlikely to have furnished the source of the tradition. Earlier rabbinic collections (Mishnah, Tosefta, and then Tannaitic Midrashim) reflect our earliest rabbinic sources; then baraitot, then citations attributed to Tannaim in Amoraic sources, and lastly Amoraic sources. Because this is a commentary on Matthew, however, reproducing all attributions in Amoraic sources (or exploring other issues in my cited texts) would drive this work to inordinate length, so I provide the late citations as secondary rather than central corroboration, for those who have space to explore them in greater detail.

focus especially on social-historical methods and social-historical information less accessible to most readers of commentaries.[20]

Source Criticism

As nineteenth- and early twentieth-century scholars sought to test the historical reliability of the Gospels, their attention naturally turned to source criticism.[21] Source criticism asks the question: What written sources might the author of a Gospel have used? Scholars who study Greco-Roman literature have increasingly recognized the weaknesses of traditional source criticism (e.g., Whittaker 1969: lxi-lxii), but the criteria appear somewhat more objective in Matthew, where we probably retain evidence for at least two of Matthew's sources. Although various source theories have come and gone, the majority of scholars today agree that Matthew used Mark, "Q" (i.e., a source shared by Luke), and some other material not employed by Mark or Luke. Scholars commonly call this view the "Two-Source Hypothesis."

While this remains the general consensus, however, scholars are no more unanimous on this subject than on most others. Following the older Griesbach Hypothesis, some able scholars have made a defensible case that Mark used Matthew rather than the reverse (e.g., Farmer 1964), and their case merits fair consideration in modern scholarship.[22] But because so much of Mark appears in Matthew and Luke, most scholars remain convinced that Matthew and Luke both used Mark and at least one other source they shared in common (see Senior 1983: 17-19; Davies and Allison 1988: 98-114). Consistent patterns appear in Matthew's abbreviation of Mark (Davies and Allison 1988: 73-74),[23] and Matthew uses an eclectic text-type for his Old Testament quotations *except* where he overlaps with Mark, in which case he tends to follow Mark in employing the Septuagint (see Gundry 1975: 9-28; cf. Stanton 1993: 353-63).[24]

20. For the history of interpretation of Matthew, see presently especially Luz 1989; idem 1994; for the earliest period, Massaux 1990-1993; in more detail, watch for the forthcoming project published by InterVarsity and edited by Thomas Oden.

21. For more detailed discussion, see, e.g., Duling and Perrin 1994: 11-16; France 1985: 34-38; Carson, Moo, and Morris 1992: 26-38; Stein 1992c.

22. Cf. Longstaff 1977: 218; Murray 1984. For proto-Matthew see Lowe and Flusser 1983; some have also contended for something like Lukan priority (e.g., Lindsey 1990: 84; Young 1989: 129-63; cf. Lindsey 1992-93), though this thesis has so far gained few adherents outside modern Israel (cf. Ådna 1992-93).

23. The abbreviation is, however, less often theologically motivated than supposed in the heyday of redaction criticism (e.g., Held 1963: 169; on expansion, 193-206).

24. Sometimes he follows the MT sequence but the LXX wording (e.g., in 19:18-19; cf. Hagner 1995: 557). Gundry 1975: 174-85 also argued that the eclectic text-types behind citations found in all three Gospels fit only the trilingual milieu of first-century Palestine; while I would contend for common oral tradition in the earliest community on this point, Gundry suggests that this material goes back to Matthew the tax collector's notes (xii). Rabbis also used eclectic text-types (see Goulder 1974: 27); they are most obvious where Matthew's redactional hand is clearest (see Soares Prabhu 1976: 63-106; cf. Cope 1976: 121-22). For a survey of views regarding the source of Matthew's quotations, see Hagner 1993: lvi.

Most scholars also agree that Matthew shared with Luke another source (e.g., Davies and Allison 1988: 115-24), which is nicknamed Q (probably from the German *Quelle,* "source," which Weiss abbreviated to "Q" in 1890) for lack of a better name (Stanton 1995a: 63). Here, too, scholarship lacks complete unanimity. Although some write as if they are very certain about the substance and extent of Q (e.g., Edwards 1975; Mack 1988: 84; idem 1993), most scholars express skepticism about the degree of certainty to which it can be reconstructed.[25] Still others have debated even its existence as a conplete document (e.g., Burkitt 1907: 123; Dodd 1961: 39; idem 1968: 70). While most view Q as a complete document (e.g., Schweizer 1971: 124-25; Tuckett 1996: 1-39), some envision it as purely oral tradition (e.g., Betz 1968: 22), and still others as a composite of sources (e.g., Petrie 1959; Perry 1920: 11). Some dispense with Q altogether, suggesting that Luke (some here add Mark) simply used Matthew;[26] this final view, however, remains a distinct (though respectable) minority position (see Martin 1956; Grant 1965; Tuckett 1984).[27] Q was probably also edited a number of times, and the Gospel writers probably employed Q in various stages of its editing (cf. Koester 1982: 2:46).

But since Matthew and Luke often follow Q in the same sequence (with Tuckett 1996: 34-39; the divergences to which Ellis 1991: 35 points are minor and explained by Matthew's penchant for rearrangement), I concur with the most common theory about Q: it probably represents a single prominent written source. Although I acknowledge weaknesses in this position (and probably interaction with continuing oral tradition at every stage of writing), this commentary will begin from the basic Two-Source Hypothesis. Because the Q collection was probably edited in the 40s, less than two decades after the events it describes (Theissen 1991: 203-34, especially 220-21, 230-32; pace Mack 1988: 84), we may assume a high degree of reliability for its traditions. In contrast to the arguments of some who radically distinguish Q from other elements of early Christianity, its theology resembles that of other early Christian documents (see, e.g., Meadors 1992; Keener 1995; for future eschatology, see Tuckett 1996: 139-63).

Because Matthew follows Mark and Q closely (by ancient literary standards) where we can check him, the assumption held by many scholars that he simply invents material where we *cannot* check him (traditionally loosely called "M" material, though no longer held to represent a single source) appears to be

25. Apart from many members of the "Q Seminar," this skepticism probably characterizes the majority of Gospels scholarship; see, e.g., Stanton 1974: 5; idem 1995: 73-74; Keck 1974: 448; Overman 1990a: 193; Theissen 1991: 204; Catchpole 1993: 6; Meier 1994: 177-80; Johnson 1996: 52-53.

26. A significant number of scholars, e.g., Drury 1976: xi, 121; Farrer 1956b: 247-48; Goulder 1978: 234; Gundry 1982: 5; Abogunrin 1987; Sanders and Davies 1989: 91, 112. Linnemann 1996: 7-11 provides a recent challenge to the Q hypothesis.

27. Cf. also the well-argued case against any literary dependence among the Gospels by Linnemann 1990; idem 1992. Nevertheless, I remain confident that the Synoptics share too much common ground with Mark, while simultaneously reflecting a far broader knowledge of abundant tradition outside Mark (cf. also Jn 21:25) to deny some measure of interdependence.

simply imagination run amuck.[28] His basically conservative editing at most points will impress one if one begins with neither a thoroughgoing skepticism nor a naive fundamentalism, but the standards of ancient texts in general. As Witherington puts it (1994: 214), Matthew

> takes over more than 90% of his Markan source (606 out of 661 Markan verses), while Luke takes over only a little over 50%. The difference in degree of word for word appropriation of Mark in the pericopes and sayings that Matthew and Luke take over is minimal. Luke uses about 53% of Mark's exact words in the material culled from that source, while the First Evangelist uses about 51% of Mark's exact words of the 606 verses he appropriates. This means that Luke and the First Evangelist are about equally likely to preserve the exact wording of their source, and they do so about half the time.

So "conservative" is Matthew's editing by ancient standards that Witherington suspects that Matthew "very likely saw himself as primarily an editor or redactor, not an author" (1994: 343).[29] Even if this suggestion overstates the case (Matthew edited his Gospel so tightly that it surely functions as a unified whole), many changes that Matthew makes in some of his sources depend on information his other sources supply.[30] Thus Matthew sometimes "corrects" ambiguities in Mark (e.g., Mt 12:3-4//Mk 2:25-26; Mt 3:3//Mk 1:2-3; Mt 14:1//Mk 6:14); sometimes he re-Judaizes his language ("kingdom of heaven/God"; Mt 19:3, 9//Mk 10:2, 11-12); and at least on some occasions he makes his changes because of early tradition older than Mark (Mt 12:28//Lk 11:20; missing in Mk 3:23-29).

At the same time, Matthew's relative conservatism need not render all his *sources* of equal historical worth; and where the sources were oral, Matthew may have exercised greater freedom in their retelling.[31] At any rate, Matthew's community certainly had other Palestinian traditions besides Mark and Q, and these traditions had undoubtedly been interacting with Mark and Q long before he wrote his Gospel (Meier in Brown and Meier 1983: 55).[32] From the earliest pe-

28. Commonalities between John and the Synoptic tradition besides Mark and Q also support the existence of oral traditions (see Stein 1992b). If the "M" material is oral, Matthew may be able to adapt it more freely, however (cf. Brooks 1987).

29. Cf. Johnston 1992, who even compares it to a manual produced by a committee; and Jones 1995: 36, who uses the dominance of tradition to question the current biographical, literary, wholistic approach to the Gospels. Jones 1995: 52-54 emphasizes Matthew's conservatism with his sources and failure to rewrite them, challenging traditional redaction-critical assumptions.

30. Diod. Sic. 1.37.4, 6; Dion. Hal. 1.6.1-3 explicitly note that they provide additional information from different sources that some previous historians lacked. Technical historians sometimes cite sources by name (e.g., Dion. Hal. 1.6.1); more popular-level Jewish sources generally do not, however, so from Matthew's silence we can infer nothing about Mark's or "Q's" anonymity.

31. See Hill 1972: 31-34; Davies and Allison 1988: 124-25; Luz 1989: 48; Brown 1994: 59-61.

32. The oral development of sources does not challenge the existence of written sources. Against the idea that an apocalyptic community like the earliest Christians would not care about writings (hence all written Gospel sources must be late), one need simply compare the early Qumran

riod, Mediterranean storytellers regularly drew on a much larger body of oral traditions; for example, though countless allusions in Homer (e.g., *Od.* 12.69-72) were developed later, they are often so incomplete by themselves that it is clear that Homer alludes to commonly known fuller stories that he does not record.

Form Criticism

Because the early Christians told and retold the stories about Jesus orally before writing Gospels, scholars also began to ask about the way the early Christians transmitted them, and developed form criticism (see, e.g., Duling and Perrin 1994: 16-20; Carson, Moo, and Morris 1992: 21-25). Many form critics noted that Jesus used teaching forms popular among his contemporaries (such as parables and witty sayings), and that early Christians transmitted Jesus' sayings and deeds in forms used by other biographers and storytellers of their day. Some form critics started with skeptical presuppositions and consequently produced studies with predictably skeptical conclusions (e.g., Bultmann 1968); others started with less skeptical premises and produced more favorable conclusions (e.g., Dibelius 1971; Jeremias 1971; Taylor 1935).

The conclusions differed in part because of the varying premises with which different scholars started, and in part because flaws existed in the standard methodology (see Sanders 1969). Some criteria for authenticity that form critics developed were, however, reasonable; for instance, a saying of Jesus attested in a variety of independent sources or which would not have been made up by the later church was probably authentic. At the same time, although these criteria could logically help to verify traditions, they could not logically help to falsify them; one could hardly assume that a saying of Jesus preserved only once or that his followers agreed with must be inauthentic! In other words, the best criteria of form criticism work much better to demonstrate the reliability of the Gospels than to argue the reverse (see France 1976).

The abuse of these criteria has led to pure speculation grounded only in preexisting theories about the development of early Christianity (so Wright 1992a: 341-42). In a post-Schweitzer period of skepticism about the historical Jesus, Bultmann and many other New Testament scholars focused on the early communities that transmitted reports about Jesus, which they thought might prove more fruitful historically. But this approach has proved ironic, for we know far less about the earliest transmitting communities than we know about the historical Jesus (Wright 1992a: 342).[33]

texts (cf. Boyd 1995: 125). Concern for history also makes sense in a Jewish covenant context in which people believed God had revealed himself in history (Wright 1992a: 426).

33. I will address some of the traditional criteria in more detail below, when asking how reliable Matthew and his traditions are.

Redaction Criticism

While source and form criticism were sometimes helpful in understanding the nature of Jesus' teachings and the way the Gospels are written, scholars asked these questions mainly to test the Gospel stories' reliability, not to understand the Gospels' message. Inevitably scholars began to ask, "Given that Matthew used Mark and Q, *why* does Matthew edit Mark and Q the way he does? What is Matthew's *point?*" This question became the focus of the editorial critics, generally called redaction critics.[34]

More sober controls eventually checked the early excesses of some redaction critics. Some early redaction critics assumed that any material Matthew or Luke added to their main sources was not historical; this view stemmed not from the method, however, but from some unlikely presuppositions, namely, that Matthew and Luke had no other information available except in Mark and Q, and that editing a source for literary style or theological emphasis renders one's information unhistorical.[35] The probable presence of substantial traditional material in Matthew besides Mark and Q weakens the premises of stylistic analysis (Jones 1995: 13-14).[36] Further, characteristic diction or style does not make elements ahistorical (see Payne 1983: 209); indeed, writers could openly acknowledge their stylistic redaction of earlier sources even for purely aesthetic reasons (Phaedrus 2, prol. 8-12). Current scholarship thus practices its redaction criticism more carefully, though it would be a mistake to abandon the method's insights altogether (Stanton 1993: 23).

Other redaction critics focused on the Gospel writers' theology, preferring more conservative historical conclusions or leaving historical questions aside (e.g., Marshall 1970; Martin 1972; cf. Osborne 1991: 169-70). By focusing on how Matthew consistently edits his sources, one can observe some of his emphases, which in turn helps one interpret more obscure passages in light of his whole Gospel (cf., e.g., Gundry 1982: 624-25). This tool can provide checks on scholarly imagination concerning Matthew's emphases (Jones 1995: 33). The Gospel writers' contemporaries, such as Josephus, noticeably exercised a degree of both freedom and fidelity in their handling of *biblical* history (see, e.g., Begg 1996), and one would expect the Gospels to represent the same mixture, albeit not nec-

34. For surveys, see, e.g., Duling and Perrin 1994: 20-23; Spivey and Smith 1982: 64-65; Carson, Moo, and Morris 1992: 38-45; Osborne 1992; Blomberg 1987: 35-43. In view of redaction criticism, a commentary might wish to speak of "Matthew's Jesus" rather than simply of "Jesus," but to avoid the cumbersome nature of that expression, I have followed the latter wording and trust readers to keep in mind the larger redactional framework I articulate elsewhere.

35. Dio Cassius *R.H.* 1.1.1-2 explicitly affirms the contrary. Thus, e.g., Matthew's account of Judas's death is so Matthean that Gundry 1982: 553 admits that one might think it Matthew's "wholesale creation" — were it not for Acts 1:15-20. For specific characteristics of Matthean style (useful for redaction criticism) see, e.g., Davies and Allison 1988: 74-96; but on the dangers of inaccurate use of style criteria, see Jones 1995: 12.

36. Jones introduces further complications: What if Matthew's version of Mark is an oral tradition based on but differing from our text of Mark (1995: 29-30, 39)?

essarily in the same degree of each. Luther apparently considered concern over divergences among the sources on points of detail a pedantic exercise (Stanton 1995a: 8); modern historians of the period regularly mine various ancient historians for data despite divergences among them (e.g., Whittaker 1969: xlv-lii).

Although I have exercised severe restraint in making redactional observations due to this commentary's focus and length and the potentially competing literary or theological explanations for most changes Matthew makes in his sources, one important social-rhetorical pattern has emerged. Where possible, Matthew has made Mark's Jesus "more Jewish." That is, where Mark adapted Jesus to a broader (more "universal") Greco-Roman audience, Matthew has consistently re-Judaized Jesus. In some cases, Matthew may have been following the rhetorical practices of speech-in-character and historical verisimilitude,[37] making Jesus fit what was known about him in general (e.g., as a Jewish teacher, he should have introduced parables with the sorts of formulas used by Jewish teachers; he may have used "kingdom of heaven"); and, given Matthew's proximity to Jesus' situation, his guesses are more apt to be correct than ours. In other cases, however, I am reasonably sure that Matthew has re-Judaized Jesus based on solid traditions available to him. Some of these may be more Palestinian (e.g., 27:51-53) but not necessarily more historical than Mark (so Brown 1994: 59-60); others may actually represent the original oral traditions behind Mark or some other materials shared with Luke. Thus the Didache regularly cites some of this pre-Matthean tradition, sometimes material attested nowhere else but in Matthew (e.g., Blomberg 1995: 42; cf. Draper 1984).[38]

Such revision should not surprise us; Matthew elsewhere "corrects" Mark's adaptations for Gentile readers to accord better with historical data available to him (see especially Theissen 1991: 88n.70, who concludes that Matthew here improves Mark's historical accuracy). Matthew and Luke occasionally add the same material from oral tradition or from Q where Mark has omitted something (e.g., Mt 12:28//Lk 11:20), further indicating Matthew's readiness to adapt Mark on the basis of prior tradition. At times Matthew also demonstrates a more sensitive understanding of Palestinian Jewish nuances than Luke or his tradition (Vermes 1993: 153-54; cf., e.g., Mt 19:3//Mk 10:2) or at least a more sensitive understanding of how his Jewish audience would be able to hear Jesus' original message as he has reconstructed it. (Omission of Mark's Aramaic might be for purely stylistic reasons, since some Roman teachers similarly often disapproved of including foreign terms in a Latin composition, e.g., [Virgil] *Catalepton* 7.)

37. Cf. Theon *Progymn.* 1.46-52; 2.79-81; 8.2-3; Arist. *Poetics* 15.4-6, 1454a; in a history, see, e.g., Dio Cassius *R.H.* 62.11.3-4.

38. Note further the Semitic parallelism pervading Jesus' sayings, probably more emphatic in Matthew (cf. Hagner 1993: xlviii). Held 1963: 242 argued that Matthew adapted healing stories to the form of scholastic controversy dialogues; Gundry 1982: 2 emphasizes the biblicizing style. Cf., e.g., the frequently Semitic "behold" (1:20, 23; 2:1, 9, 13; 3:16; 4:11; 8:2, 24, 29; 9:2; 10:18; 11:8, 19; 12:2, 10, 18, 41, 46, 47 MS, 49; 13:3; 15:22; 17:2; 19:16, 27; 20:18, 30; 21:5; 22:4; 23:38; 24:23; 25:6; 26:45, 51; 27:51; 28:2).

Vermes is thus correct to argue that Matthew has preserved much of the special Jewish coloring of Jesus, which fits with our picture of Jesus in undeniably authentic traditions (1993: 17-19).

At the same time, Matthew also fills the story of Jesus with fresh insights, interpreting the Jesus tradition with an abundance of intentional overt and covert biblical allusions (Allison 1993b: 139) that should have been intelligible to his Jewish audience (cf. Vermes 1993: 186). His explicit fulfillment quotations derive from whole sections of the Old Testament that early Christians had already applied to Jesus (Gundry 1975: 205-8), perhaps on principles drawn from Jesus' own teaching (Gundry 1975: 213-14; cf. Lk 24:25-27, 44-47). Matthew often builds on a typological scheme, recognizing analogies in God's work in history (see Longenecker 1975: 141-42). Nevertheless, it is more likely that Matthew generally finds such analogies already present in his tradition than that he creates them simply to fulfill the Old Testament; otherwise we would have to expect far more new fulfillment material than we in fact have, with far less of it beyond the special Matthean material overlapping with Mark and Luke. We would also expect his narratives to conform more closely to the citations and expect Matthew to have chosen more obvious citations (see comment on the infancy narratives).

Contemporary Literary Criticism

Because redaction criticism's focus was in locating the Gospel writers' emphasis, redaction-critical questions naturally led to a new set of questions that were more concerned with the points the Gospel writers sought to convey than with their historical accuracy or attempts to reconstruct a history of tradition behind an extant text. The 1970s began to expose more of the weaknesses of traditional redactional assumptions (e.g., that all changes were theologically motivated and that what writers change is more significant than what they retain), paving the way for a more wholistic interpretation of each Gospel (see Spencer 1993: 385-86; cf. Jones 1995: 7-16). Scholarship also increasingly recognized that the traditional redactional attempt to explain every emphasis in the Gospel by reconstructing hypothetical external referents represented simply a new form of allegorization (Anderson 1996: 248; Watson 1998).[39]

Redaction criticism thus gave way to "composition criticism," which examines themes that run through each Gospel and asks, "What does this Gospel mean as a whole?"[40] (Earlier formalist literary critics like T. S. Eliot and C. S. Lewis emphasized discovering meaning from the text itself rather than from

39. For other complaints about older redaction critics' assumption of transparency and failure "to distinguish sufficiently between the 'act of reading or hearing' and the 'act of historical reconstruction,'" between story world and real world, and between implied reader and intended reader, see especially Kingsbury 1988b: 458. On the limits of redaction criticism, see also Carter 1996: 275-76.

40. Perhaps the most thorough examination of repetition in Matthew's Gospel, including recent perspectives on narrative development, is Anderson 1994.

something extrinsic to it; unfortunately, Gospels scholarship had remained decades behind trends in literary criticism in general.) Narrative criticism adds characterization, plot, and perspective (matters that also concerned ancient readers, e.g., Arist. *Poetics* 15, 1454a) to the thematic pursuits of composition criticism (Powell 1992; Bauer and Powell 1996: 9-10).

More recent literary approaches such as structuralism and reader-response criticism have approached texts for their transcultural literary themes or to examine how current readers in various interpretive communities interpret texts.[41] Although various forms of literary criticism adopt different methodologies, they all point beyond layers of tradition behind the text, whether to the text itself (as in the older formalism) or to the act of reading the text from various social locations or interpretive frameworks (as in various reader-response orientations). In contrast to some modern literary critics, Matthean scholars usually embrace the various interpretive strategies as complementary rather than contradictory (Bauer and Powell 1996: 25).

But though literary questions are essential, not all literary approaches are equally helpful for a given purpose. My aim is to reconstruct as well as possible what Matthew endeavored to communicate to his readers in their shared historical and social context (which, on almost all views, is at least one important goal in interpretation — see Allison 1993b: 3; Ashton 1991: 113). Focusing on this approach is not intended to devalue other approaches that remain outside this focus. Thus, for example, as helpful as hearing a text from a first-time reader's perspective may be, it was probably not the dominant reading experienced in the earliest Christian communities. Matthew's audience probably knew Mark, and probably listened to Matthew in segments (Stanton 1993: 76), and Matthew probably expected his audience to hear his Gospel more than once. Reading Matthew as a narrative whole, however, is fully in keeping with his Gospel's biographical genre (Burridge 1998: 127).

Social-Historical and Sociological Interpretation

Although the extant evidence is incomplete, it is adequate to allow us to reconstruct a general first-century Mediterranean setting more relevant to the original constructions of Matthew than are our own contemporary settings, which we might otherwise presuppose. Asking social-historical questions is therefore essential, provided we acknowledge the requisite limitations imposed by incomplete knowledge of some matters.

This commentary involves less application of more direct social-sciences approaches, however, except in interacting with works that employ them as their

41. See, e.g., Patte 1976; Barton 1984: 104-39, 180-97; Tompkins 1980; see also Osborne 1991: 153-73, 366-96. When used as a descriptive tool, reader-response criticism can prove very valuable in reconstructing how various historical communities have understood texts (on a semipopular level, cf., e.g., Usry and Keener 1996: 98-109).

primary method. Such approaches can be quite helpful in reconstructing the social context by extrapolation (often on the basis of cultures with some social patterns more like the culture we study than our own is) where our evidence is limited. Nevertheless, the assurance of modern interpreters' conclusions must remain constrained to some degree by the limitations of our data. Current sociological and anthropological scholarship emphasizes that models must function heuristically, and be adjusted or discarded where they do not fit the hard data.[42] In all cases, then, I will give preference to hard data from archaeological or literary sources over extrapolations from models or generalized cultural patterns, helpful as the latter can sometimes be.

Above all, Matthew invites his audience to hear the Gospel in the context of the early Christian message: his central discourse is emphatic that only those who press close as persistent disciples of the kingdom can truly understand the message of the kingdom (13:11-23). Matthew's Jewish-Christian community, rooted both in the new message of the kingdom and the broader context of Israel's ancient kingdom story (13:52), held a special advantage.

Matthew as Biography

Readers approach different works with different expectations, which affect the meanings they construct on those texts (see Shuler 1982: 25-28; Hirsch 1967: 68-126). Expectations also affected the way ancient readers approached works, and many ancients no less than contemporary literary theorists recognized this principle. Thus ancient writers distinguished literary forms from one another (Theon *Progymn.* 2.5-33), and on a larger level one genre from another (see Burridge 1992: 27-29, 34), though then, as today, writers in practice mixed categories (Burridge 1992: 56-57, 61; Aune 1981: 10-11, 48; idem 1987: 83).

What kinds of questions would ancient readers expect a work like Matthew to answer? Scholars have offered various proposals concerning the genre into which a Gospel like Matthew falls. Some writers have said that the Gospels are "unique" (e.g., Hennecke 1963: 1:80; Riesenfeld 1970: 2), but in whatever sense this description might be true (cf. Jones 1995: 43, 169; Guelich 1991), it is not very helpful in informing us how the first readers would have approached them.[43] Indeed, while the Gospels are in some sense distinct from other kinds of

42. In personal conversation, my associates David Fraser in sociology and Marla Frederick in anthropology, both cognizant of some trends in biblical scholarship, have emphasized this contemporary approach. For a specific example of questions concerning some applications (while remaining largely favorable), see my review (Keener 1996b: 226).

43. It is unlikely that "gospel" in 24:14 and 26:13 identifies Matthew's genre (pace Stanton 1993: 16); although Mark may have applied the term to his document (Mk 1:1; cf. perhaps 14:9) as a title indicating that his task is proclamation, Matthew and Luke may have received this title simply by later association with Mark (see Gundry 1996). Some have argued that the language of "gospel" derives from LXX Is 52:7; 61:1-2 and Jesus' consequent "gospel of the kingdom," perhaps even in light of Is 52:13–53:12 (see Stuhlmacher 1991a; 1991b: 19-25; Betz 1991; cf. Hengel 1991: 244-48; Guelich 1991: 194-96).

narrative, they are also distinct from each other (Marxsen 1969: 150). K. L. Schmidt's view that the Gospels are popular or "folk literature" of the lower classes (Schmidt 1923; also, e.g., Kümmel 1965: 37) is equally unhelpful and at the same time inaccurate. Schmidt's "high" literature actually influenced "folk" literature, rendering clear-cut distinctions questionable (Burridge 1992: 11, 153; Aune 1987: 12, 63; Downing 1988c). Further, the Gospels themselves vary in levels of audience expectation (e.g., Luke is far more conscious of considerations of classical style than Mark — Koester 1982: 1:108). Finally, biographies appear at both ends of the continuum (Tacitus's *Agricola* versus the popular *Life of Aesop*).

Readers throughout most of history understood the Gospels as biographies (Stanton 1989a: 15-17), but after 1915 scholars tried to find some other classification for them, mainly because these scholars compared ancient and modern biography and noticed that the Gospels differed from the latter (Talbert 1977: 2-3; cf. Mack 1988: 16n.6).[44] The current trend, however, is again to recognize the Gospels as ancient biographies.[45] The most complete statement of the question to date comes from a Cambridge monograph by Richard A. Burridge. After carefully defining the criteria for evaluating genre (1992: 109-27) and establishing the characteristic features of Greco-Roman "lives" (128-90), he demonstrates how the canonical Gospels fit this genre (191-239). The trend to regard the Gospels as ancient biography is currently strong enough for British Matthew scholar Graham Stanton to characterize the skepticism of Bultmann and others about the biographical character of the Gospels as "surprisingly inaccurate" (1993: 63; idem 1995: 137).[46]

Ancient biographers did not write the way modern biographers do; they could start in the subject's adulthood (so Mark or *Life of Aesop*); they also had the freedom to rearrange their material topically rather than in chronological se-

44. For a complete history of the question, see Burridge 1992: 3-25.

45. See Aune 1987: 46-76; Stanton 1974: 117-36; idem 1992b; idem 1993: 64; Shuler 1982; Sanders and Davies 1989: 252-58; Burridge 1992; Robbins 1992: 2-3; Blomberg 1992a: 46-47; Hagner 1993: lvii.

46. Contrast Mack 1988: 322-23, who views Mark as fiction; for sound critiques of the novelistic genre as applied to earliest Christian historiography, see Burridge 1992: 245; Hengel 1991: 212, and (in this instance the Book of Acts), Bauckham 1993; Porter 1994: 548-58; cf. Palmer 1993, especially 3, 29 (though elements modern readers would consider fictitious elaborations could occur in some forms of biographies; cf. Chance 1991; cf. especially works about much earlier characters — e.g., Lefkowitz 1996: 82). Scholars debate the character of Matthean biography, however: Shuler 1982 finds laudatory biography (but most biography was by its nature epideictic in some sense, whether Tacitus's *Agricola,* Plutarch's *Lives,* or Josephus's *Life* [see Neyrey 1994], though some focused more on encomium and others on moral instruction; see Burridge 1992: 88); Robbins 1992: 10 focuses on biographies that addressed teachers and disciples. Modern research probably cannot assign a more specific category than "biography" (Stanton 1993: 64-65). The *apomnēmoneumata* with which early Christians compared the Gospels (Justin *Apol.* 66.3; 67.3; *Dial.* 103.8; 106.3) probably recall Xenophon's *Memorabilia,* his "life" of Socrates (Stanton 1993: 62-63; cf. Robbins 1992: 63-67); pace some recent proposals, these "memoirs" of the apostles clearly refer to our Gospels (see Abramowski 1991).

quence (4 Macc 12:7; Aune 1987: 31-32; Stanton 1974: 119-21). Further, like other writers they could expand or abridge accounts freely (2 Macc 2:24-25; Theon *Progymn.* 3.224-40; 4.37-42, 80-82).[47] Thus Matthew often abridges Mark, probably sometimes because of considerations of length.[48] Historians likewise wrote history differently than most historians do today. Where biographers and historians lacked access to definite historical sources, they simply tried to construct as reasonable an account as they could (Plut. *Theseus* 1.3; Aune 1987: 83). Nevertheless, it appears that even more frequently ancient writers, like modern ones, cited the divergent sources, sometimes preferring one source but at other times leaving the decision to the reader (Diog. Laert. 1.23; 6.113; 8.2.67-72; Paus. 2.5.5; 2.26.3-7; Plut. *Lycurgus* 1.1; Diod. Sic. 5.70.1; Dion. Hal. 1.84.4; 1.87.4; 3.35.1-4; 8.79.1; Suet. *Tib.* 5; Appian *R.H.* 11.9.56; 12.1.1; Livy 9.44.6; 23.19.17; 25.11.20; 25.17.1-6; 42.11.1; Arrian *Alex.* 1, pref. 1-3; 3.3.6; 4.9.2-3; 4.14.1-4; 5.3.1; 5.14.4; 6.2.4; 7.14.2; 7.27.1-3; Corn. Nep. 7 [Alcibiades], 11.1; 9 [Conon], 5.4; Herodian 7.9.4; 7.9.9; *Contest of Homer and Hesiod* 323; Parthenius *L.R.* 11.1-3; 14.5; p. Soṭa 9:13, §2). (That the Gospels do not list divergent sources may result from the recentness of the events they narrate, which have not yet generated such widely divergent traditions in the apostolic circle. This observation would be consistent with works reporting relatively recent events.) But though such historians did not always write the way we write history today, they were clearly concerned to write history as well as their resources allowed (Jos. *Ant.* 20.156-57; Arist. *Poetics* 9.2-3, 1451b; Diod. Sic. 21.17.1; Dion. Hal. 1.1.2-4; 1.2.1; 1.4.2; cf. Mosley 1965).[49]

Although the historical accuracy of biographers varied from one biographer to another, biographers intended biographies to be essentially historical works (see Aune 1988: 125; Witherington 1994: 339; cf. Polyb. 8.8).[50] Although the biographical genre differs from that of history, shared interests between them allow us some comparisons. Historians sought to make their accounts interesting

47. See further Sanders 1969: 19, 46-189, 272; Stein 1980: 238-40. The better historians opposed excessive amplification, however (e.g., Polyb. *R.R.E.* 15.33-34); thus the second-century rhetorician Lucian also objected to those historical writers who amplified and omitted merely for literary or encomiastic purposes (i.e., to make the character look better; Shuler 1982: 11-12). A writer could cite witnesses to support his accuracy while admitting that his account was incomplete (Jos. *Life* 365-67); early Christians also recognized the differences in sequence among their Gospels as inconsequential (Augustine *Harmony of Gospels* 21.51, *ACCS* 25).

48. Matthew probably abridges Mark less for theological reasons (contrast Held 1963: 168-92) than to keep his account concise and to fit all his narratives on one scroll! Greco-Roman readers may have appreciated conciseness (Theon *Progymn.* 5.39-43, 52-53); the Gospels and most ancient "lives" also fit the standard length for scrolls to be read in one "sitting" (Burridge 1998: 141).

49. See, e.g., Dion. Hal. 7.66.5; 11.1.1-6. There apparently were bad historians and biographers who made up stories, but they became objects of criticism for violating accepted standards (cf. Lucian *History* 12, 24-25).

50. Various genres, including biography and history, overlapped considerably in antiquity (see Burridge 1992: 63-69). Nevertheless, the Gospels are too brief to represent nonbiographical history (pace Dihle 1991: 379), and Suetonius did not originate historical biography (pace Dihle 1991: 383-84), as the value of Tacitus's *Agricola* from the same period indicates.

(2 Macc 2:24-25; Aune 1987: 80, 95) and had specific emphases in writing,[51] but these practices do not oppose historical interest.[52] Biographers shared some common interests with historians, though they focused more on the virtues of their chosen protagonists and generally intended their works for less technical audiences (Corn. Nep. 16 [Pelopidas], 1.1). Historians focused on events rather than persons (Lucian *How to Write History* 7), but even historians distinguished "history" from mere "chronicles" by the way one selected and arranged the material (Lucian *History* 4-6).

Yet to what extent their historical interest determined their historical accuracy varies from one writer to the next, depending on how they used their sources. Chronological distance from the events they report inevitably affected writers. Whereas biographers like Plutarch and Livy spice up their accounts and often depend on ancient legends, biographers like Tacitus and Suetonius are much more accurate and depend on information closer to their own time.[53] Many are freely skeptical of some earlier accounts (Diod. Sic. 1.6.2; 1.9.2; 4.8.4; Dion. Hal. 1.39.1; 1.41.1; Livy 6.1.2; 7.6.6; Arrian *Alex.* 4.28.1-2; Jos. *Apion* 1.15, 58; some, like Hesiod *W.D.* 158-60, 165; Arrian *Alex.* 5.1.2, allow for a supernatural element) but have a higher standard for the more recent period (Diod. Sic. 4.8.3; Livy 6.1.3), especially while eyewitnesses remain alive (Jos. *Life* 359-66; *Apion* 1.50).[54] Some report their sources but urge the reader to employ discretion in evaluating them (Livy 4.29.5-6; 23.47.8), evaluate the historical probability of their sources (Arrian *Alex.* 3.3.6), determine the historically probable nucleus of their sources (e.g., Livy 3.8.10), explain legendary material on rationalistic grounds (Arrian *Alex.* 2.16.6), or simply admit that they do not *know* how something happened (Sall. *Jug.* 67.3).

Despite Josephus's self-serving agendas (and sometimes reasonable self-

51. For further detail on this point see Momigliano 1977: 71-73; Mason 1992: 60-71, 77-81; Lyons 1985: 29-32; Robbins 1992: 110-11. For ancient historians suggesting inspired interpretation of the historical data, see especially Hall 1986: 13-46, particularly on Josephus.

52. On this point see Dio Cassius *R.H.* 1.1.1-2; Vermes 1984: 19-20; Lyons 1985: 66; cf. Davies 1966a: 115. Thus, e.g., Diodorus Siculus teaches morals in his history by reporting good, bad, and mixed characters (15.1.1; 37.4.1), yet tries to get them right; he elsewhere criticizes a historian who allowed "personal enmity" to distort his perspective (21.17.1, LCL 11:30-31; cf. Jos. *Life* 356). Dionysius of Halicarnassus teaches morals about divine activity (8.56.1), but criticizes historians who investigate their data inadequately (7.1.4).

53. Ancient historians recognized that they were less accurate in reporting the less documented, more distant past (Diod. Sic. 1.6.2; 1.9.2; 4.1.1; Dion. Hal. 1.12.3), and that the best one could sometimes do with the *prehistoric* past was write edifying fiction (Diod. Sic. 4.8.3-5).

54. Thus many historians were not shy about criticizing their predecessors' accounts of particular events, sometimes merely due to intrinsic improbabilities (Dion. Hal. 4.6.1; 9.22.1-5; Paus. 9.31.7; Arrian *Alex.* 6.28.2; Appian *R.H.* 11.7.41; Aul. Gel. 10.12.8-10; Plut. *Isis* 8, *Mor.* 353F) or that a tradition appealed only to local pride (Paus. 2.1.1), in other cases charging that they preferred flowery rhetoric to facts (Jos. *Apion* 1.24-25; Herodian 1.1.1-2). Most exposed predecessors' inadequacies (e.g., Diod. Sic. 1.3.1-2; Jos. *Life* 336-39, 359, 361; Sallust *War with Catiline* 3.2); others tactfully warned that they were not *criticizing* their predecessors (Dion. Hal. 1.1.1; 1.8.1; cf. Diod. Sic. 1.37.4, 6; Jos. *Life* 339).

defense — *Life* 336-67; Krieger 1994 may go too far), he gets correct many details now confirmed by archaeology (see Josephus 1982: passim; cf. Rajak 1983: 9-10; Sanders 1992: 6; Syon 1992; Cotton and Geiger 1989), though he remained quite capable of making mistakes (Fischer and Stein 1994).[55] N. T. Wright likewise notes that Josephus retells the same event differently in different books (comparing the ascension in Lk 24:51; Acts 1:3), but that this does not imply that the event "did not happen, only that he is presenting it from a different angle" (1992a: 378). However creative they may have been with many details,[56] even Plutarch and Livy apparently did not create for their accounts *events* from whole cloth.

Specifically Jewish biographies without Greco-Roman influence are more difficult to locate. Our best examples rarely represent biographies in the sense of entire books depicting the life of a main character. Traditional Jewish books surrounding central characters (Job, Ruth, Judith, Jonah, Esther, Daniel, and Tobit; see Hengel 1991: 219-20) were not strictly biographies, since they focused more on events than on persons (Stanton 1974: 126; though cf. Dihle 1991: 366-67); clear dependence on earlier sources is also missing. Nevertheless such works may provide our closest Jewish models widely circulated in Jesus' day, when they were usually treated as historical. Although the parallels in these sources may be inadequate, biographical information in rabbinic sources is still much more incidental (e.g., Neusner 1970: 8).

Jewish sources also reveal another range of writings that provides some overlap with historical or biographical sources, though the examples at the least historical extreme of the spectrum could be classified as historical novels. Palestinian Jewish storytellers gradually expanded biblical stories (especially from the Pentateuch) (e.g., Jubilees; Ps-Philo) and sometimes produced wholly new, novelistic accounts about the characters (1 Enoch; Life of Adam and Eve/Assumption of Moses; History of Joseph; Testaments of the Twelve Patriarchs; Testament of Abraham). Although works in the former category like Pseudo-Philo's *Biblical Antiquities* add many details (e.g., Murphy 1988), they may follow the biblical narrative closely (often virtually quoting it); works in the latter category, however, sometimes share with the Bible no more than the names of characters. Although these reworkings are not strictly midrash nor targum (Harrington 1986: 242), the writers employed some midrashic or haggadic principles in their composition (e.g., Johnson 1985: 252). Such works could involve rewritings of biblical narratives in ways relevant to their own audiences (Mendels 1988; Vander Kam 1992).

55. Although more apt to creativity in summary statements (e.g., *Ant.* 6.390-91), Josephus *usually* stays close to the biblical text he retells, e.g., in the David story (*Ant.* 6.156-392), even in recounting David's sin with Bathsheba (*Ant.* 7.130-31) and Uriah's murder (7.131-46), though he adds details and perspectives and modifies for encomiastic or apologetic purposes (cf., e.g., Begg 1988; 1993ab; 1994; 1995a-h; Levison 1991).

56. On the range of permissible rhetorical liberties, see, e.g., Diod. Sic. 20.1.1–2.2. Cf., e.g., Theissen 1991: 149, comparing Jos. *Ant.* 18.289-309 and Philo *Leg. Gai.* 261-336, although the primary problem on detail here may be, as Theissen suspects, an exaggerated Herodian source.

As in other Greco-Roman literature, ancient Jewish literature generally permitted variation in detail. Although amplification in matters of halakah was sometimes discouraged (e.g., ARN 1A), the practice was especially frequent in narratives, either to answer questions posed by a narrative[57] or to heighten the praise of God or the protagonist,[58] sometimes by fanciful midrash.[59] Similarly, negative incidents could be toned down,[60] omitted,[61] or justified[62] in the character's favor. This could range from the sort of "twist" on a narrative acceptable in modern journalism to fabricating details to explain what was not said. The way to distinguish Jewish works on this continuum between historical works and novels surrounding historical characters is to evaluate their degree of fidelity to prior sources (especially the Old Testament, which the Jewish works regarded as historically accurate — e.g., Philo *Creation* 1-2). In this respect, Matthew and Luke, whose fidelity we can test against some of their sources, rank high among ancient works.

All four Gospels, written in Greek and probably addressing audiences outside Palestine, are closer to the Greek model (Aune 1987: 22); but of course Jewish documents in Greek typically adopted hellenistic narrative techniques (Cohen 1987: 43; cf. van der Horst 1978). Most Jewish works in Greek (especially those from outside Palestine) followed Greek models to varying degrees. The *Lives of the Prophets* resembles the briefer Greek lives of the poets (Aune 1987:

57. E.g., Demetrius the Chronographer, *Fr.* 5 (Euseb. *P.E.* 9.29.16); Jub. 4:1, 9; 12:14; 13:11; 27:1, 4-5 (Esau and Jacob vs. Isaac and Jacob); p. Ketub. 12:4, §8. Sometimes details are added for literary purposes, to make a better story (Jub. 11:14-15, 13:18, 22); this includes names (Jub. 11:14-15; *Lives of the Prophets* 19 [Joad]; §30 in Schermann's Greek text; Jos. *Ant.* 8.231; Ps-Philo 40:1; in Ps-Philo in general, cf. Bauckham 1983: 67).

58. 2 Macc 2:1-8 (expanding Jeremiah's mission); Jub. 29:14-20 (rhetorically contrasts Jacob's respect for his parents with Esau's disrespect); Test. Job 9-15 (see *OTP* 1:832); Test. Jos. 3:1.

59. Pesiq. Rab Kah. 4:3 ("the rabbis" on Solomon); cf. Artapanus on Pharaoh's behavior toward Moses in light of 1 Sam 18:17, 21-25 (Euseb. *P.E.* 9.27.7). Genre conventions could also dictate amplifications; Joseph and Aseneth, a hellenistic romance, incorporates features ideal in such romances.

60. Ps-Philo 12:2-3 (Aaron's sin with the golden calf). Test. Job 39:12-13 *(OTP)*/39:9-10 (Kraft); 40:3/4 seems concerned to soften God's letting Job's children die for his test. Cf. Freund 1991.

61. Jub. 13:17-18 (conflict between Lot's and Abram's servants), 14:21–16:22 (omitting Sarah's problems with Hagar, though they surface in 17:4-14), 29:13 (omits Jacob's fear); Test. Zeb. 1:5-7 (Zebulun did not act against Joseph). In Jubilees (e.g., Abram passing off his sister as his wife), see Wintermute 1985: 35-36; Josephus, cf. Aune 1987: 108; in Greco-Roman literature, see Shuler 1982: 50 (following Cic. *De Partitione Oratoria* 22). The same tendency of tradition may be noted in the Chronicler's omission not only of David's but also Solomon's sins reported in Samuel-Kings (cf., e.g., Williamson 1982: 236).

62. CD 4.20–5.3 (David's polygamy); Jub. 19:15-16 (Rebekah, in light of current morality), 27:6-7 (how Jacob could leave his father), 28:6-7 (Jacob's sororal polygyny), 30:2-17 (Simeon and Levi), 41 (Judah and Tamar both made more innocent, though Tamar's deed is interpreted as deathworthy); 1QapGen 20.10-11 (Sarah rather than Abraham proposes the pretense that she is his sister); Jos. and Asen. 23 (Levi and Simeon); Test. Jud. 8–12 (whitewashing Judah, and to a lesser extent Tamar, though Judah confesses it as a lesser sin); Test. Iss. 3:1 (cf. Gen 49:15).

41-42). Philo follows hellenistic biographic conventions (cf. Canevet 1986), though like some traditional Greek biographers he writes lives of Abraham, Joseph, and Moses mainly to interpret them for lessons about virtue and adjusts details where necessary to accommodate his ideals (cf. Petit 1976; Stanton 1974: 127). Josephus follows hellenistic literary (both biographic and novelistic) conventions in describing the Aqedah, Joseph, Moses, Saul, and others.[63] Shaye Cohen in fact lists 2 Maccabees and Josephus among Jewish historical works owing "more to Herodotus, Thucydides, and hellenistic historiography than to Kings and Chronicles" (1987: 194).

Nevertheless, the language and thought of the Greek version of the Old Testament pervades the Gospels, and Matthew and John stand closer to Palestinian Jewish biographical forms than Mark and Luke do.[64] Thus, while adapting the genre of the hellenistic *bios,* or "life," the Gospel writers developed a style steeped in Old Testament historiography (Luz 1989: 44-45).

For this reason, some writers have suggested that Matthew "midrashically" expanded elements in his tradition's story of Jesus. There is probably some measure of truth in this proposal, but it must not be pressed too far. That Matthew interprets Jesus in light of the Old Testament is clear, but Matthew also interprets the Old Testament record in light of Jesus; indeed, had Matthew been creating infancy narratives about Jesus to match Old Testament messianic texts, he usually could have chosen better texts to start with and created stories that matched them better (cf. Soares Prabhu 1976: 159-60). Matthew customizes his account to show fulfillment of prophecy, but this is not the same as creating events from whole cloth. Like *most* Greek-speaking Jewish biographers, Matthew is more interested in interpreting tradition than in creating it.[65] Many scholars thus point out, against other scholars, that it is too simplistic to define Matthew's narratives as midrash and to define midrash as historically inaccurate embellishment (see Payne 1983; Cunningham and Bock 1987; Blomberg 1987: 43-53).[66]

Whether one reads Greek-speaking Jewish historical writers or Roman historians, one must evaluate the degree of fidelity to a writer's sources by comparing the sources. A Gospel writer like Luke was among the most accurate of ancient historians, if we may judge from his use of Mark (see Marshall 1978; idem 1991) and his historiography in Acts (cf., e.g., Sherwin-White 1978; Gill and Gempf 1994). Luke clearly had both written (Lk 1:1) and oral (1:2) sources

63. See Veldhuizen 1985; Silver 1973; Rajak 1978; Feldman 1982; Feldman 1985; cf. Runnalls 1983; Amaru 1988; Feldman 1988ab; 1989b; 1992a-h; 1993a; Begg 1989b.

64. Different perspectives on history were not necessarily mutually exclusive regarding the data; thus Dion. Hal. 5.56.1 proposes to investigate the causes (hence meaning) of events rather than merely the facts; cf. the ancient Christian dictum that John was a "spiritual" Gospel.

65. E.g., Jones 1995: 41 points out that Goulder's midrashic expansion thesis fails the test in the parables.

66. Goulder, who regards Matthew as a midrash on Mark (1974: 32-34), also puts forth the hypothesis that Matthew is arranged around lectionary readings (1974: 171-201; cf. 202-473); but this suggestion falters still more on inadequate evidence and undue speculation (cf. Aune 1987: 26; Talbert 1977: 15).

available, and his literary patron Theophilus already knew much of this Christian tradition (1:4), which would exclude Luke's widespread invention of new material.[67] Luke undoubtedly researched this material (1:3)[68] during his (on my view) probable sojourn with Paul in Palestine (Acts 21:17; 27:1; on the "we-narratives," cf., e.g., Maddox 1982: 7).[69] Although Luke writes more in the Greco-Roman historiographic tradition than Matthew does, Matthew's normally relatively conservative use of Mark likewise suggests a high degree of historical trustworthiness behind his accounts.

Matthew did not write his Gospel without forethought; he was a historian-biographer and interpreter and not just a storyteller. Just as speech writers carefully premeditated their works (Quint. *Inst. Or.* 10.6.1-2), writers of narratives began with a rough draft, then revised and polished it (Aune 1987: 82, 128; cf. Hata 1975; Krieger 1992a).[70] Like other writers, Matthew would follow one main source (in this case Mark) and weave his other sources around it.[71] Matthew also had to plan the length of his Gospel; the Gospels conform to the stan-

67. Pointing out that one was appealing to facts already known to one's hearers was an effective rhetorical technique (Dion. Hal. 7.43.2); Josephus explicitly appeals to public knowledge shared by all the people (*Apion* 2.107) and to witnesses who could have been consulted (*Apion* 1.50-52); he regards history dependent on public records as more reliable (*Apion* 1.20, 23, 28-29).

68. For a comparable claim of extensive investigation see Diod. Sic. 1.4.1; 1.4.4-5, though his geography, unlike Luke's in Acts, may suggest that he overstated his case, especially with regard to Mesopotamia; cf. also Appian *R.H.,* pref. 12; Herodian 1.1.3. For criticism of inadequate travel research, see Arrian *Indica* 7.1.

69. "We" appears in fictitious narratives (Dibelius 1956: 202-3), but fiction customarily used the same vocabulary as history did, and hundreds of other words are shared by both, too. "We" appears in historical narratives no less, and only historical works, not novels, had historical prologues like that of Luke (Aune 1987: 124). Further, the "we" leaves off in one city as Paul moves on (Acts 16:12-18), and picks up there again after Paul returns (Acts 20:1-6; Philippi was in Macedonia), which seems to me more difficult to explain as a literary device. On a more common view, Luke is simply using someone else's earlier travel journal (e.g., Foakes Jackson and Lake 1979b: 158-59; Morton and MacGregor 1964: 41; Cadbury 1968: 60-61). The travel journal itself is extremely precise: the number of days he reports from one port to the next is exactly the number of days it would take for a boat in his time to make those ports under the weather conditions he describes, and the titles of local officials, which in his day varied from city to city and decade to decade, are exactly correct. Clearly the travel narrative is reliable, and reflects the experience of someone who traveled with Paul as he was planting churches (and everyone agrees the churches got there somehow). That Luke employs a meticulous travel journal is likely, but that it was not his own is not likely: Luke writes some of the most polished Greek in the NT, and he puts his sources in Acts into his own words so thoroughly that we cannot distinguish different sources there. If this is the case in the rest of Acts, it would be remarkable if he left the "we" of someone else's travel journal in without changing it to "they."

70. Few scholars today agree with the older views of published proto-Gospels (Streeter 1925: 199-222; Taylor 1935: 6), but knowing how ancient narratives were written may suggest that such documents existed at least temporarily! Josephus secured help editing his materials after first taking notes and then arranging them (*Apion* 1.49-50).

71. See Aune 1987: 65, 139; cf. Downing 1988a; idem 1991; Burridge 1992: 204-5; Meier 1979: 7. For traditions and arguments for Mark's use of Petrine material, see *ACCS,* xxi-xxviii; Hengel 1991: 238-43; cf. Feldmeier 1991: 252-56.

dardized lengths of the scrolls on which they are written, all of which fall into the appropriate range for ancient biography (Burridge 1992: 118, 199, 225-26).[72]

If Matthew's basic genre suggests historical *intention,* his relatively conservative use of sources (where we can check them, especially Mark) indicates that Matthew's other purposes did not obscure an essential historical intention. My survey of data below suggests that the sources on which Matthew depends also preserved a substantially reliable picture of Jesus, the tradition being "carefully transmitted and relatively stable" as well as quite close in time to the events described (Hagner 1993: xliii).

How Reliable Are Jesus' Teachings in Matthew?

My own judgment, after working through the Synoptic pericopes and comparing how Matthew and Luke adapt Mark, supports this assignment of the burden of proof to those skeptical of Matthew's historical accomplishment. Nevertheless, in many cases inadequate historical evidence remains to make a clear historical judgment in either direction. Needless to say, therefore, scholars who start with the working assumption that material is likely inauthentic till proven otherwise are apt to arrive at conclusions quite different from those who start with the opposite assumption. For that reason it is important to form the most reasonable assumptions possible before approaching the material. While genre provides a very general framework for forming accurate critical assumptions, it is only an introductory step.

Although our survey of matters of genre suggests that Matthew has followed his sources about Jesus in a substantially accurate manner, "substantial accuracy" only minimally circumscribes freedom in matters of detail. Further, even if the Gospel writers simply transcribed their sources verbatim (and they did not), this transcription would not guarantee the accuracy of their sources. Critical scholars have sometimes followed traditions about what is or is not historically accurate (note Meier 1994: 2), but scholars increasingly recognize that on historical grounds issues must be decided case by case (hence the historical comments in this commentary). The most one can say from the above study is that in any given instance the burden of proof weighs on those who deny, rather than on those who affirm, historical authenticity.[73] The burden of proof shapes one's

72. Thus Luke, Acts, and Matthew are about the same length; John is close to three-quarters of this length, and Mark is about half that length (Morton and MacGregor 1964: 16; Metzger 1968: 5-6; cf. F. F. Bruce 1963: 12; Palmer 1993: 5). For scroll length forcing abbreviation, see, e.g., Jos. *Apion* 1.320; Corn. Nep. 15 (Epaminondas), 4.6; for length determining genre, see Arist. *Poetics* 24.4, 1459b.

73. Pace Mack 1993: 198, "speeches-in-character" would not be relevant to Synoptic composition (although one might consider them for Johannine tradition and speeches in Acts); prosopopoeia normally applies to composing discourses, not to the transmission of individual sayings (Theon *Progymn.* 1.46-52; 2.79-81; 8.2-3; cf. Isoc. *Nic./Cypr., Or.* 3; Diog. Laert. *Lives* 3.62). Even with most speeches, however (possibly excepting Josephus — Gempf 1993: 289-90; Rajak 1983: 80-82), there were limits (see Gempf 1993: passim, especially 264, 272, 283-84).

general approach to the material, but it does not invite one to neglect more specific historical data where available.

The Importance of Such a Question for Matthew

As noted above, ancient biographers often arranged their material topically; a good disciple could also arrange his teacher's sayings for relevance to the issues that he felt compelled to address.[74] With his five major blocks of Jesus' sayings (Mt 5–7; 10; 13; 18; 23–25), Matthew clearly wants to emphasize Jesus' teachings (28:19). Many scholars even suggest that Matthew intended Christian scribes to use the collections of Jesus' teachings in his Gospel as a teaching manual, the way later rabbis and probably earlier scribes provided running commentary on Scripture (28:19; cf. Bultmann 1968: 356; F. F. Bruce 1972a: 62-63; Sandmel 1958: 180). The manual may offensively support the church's missionary task, but it may also function defensively as an apologetic tool to equip new disciples for challenges from hostile synagogue leaders (cf. Blomberg 1992a: 34-35).

Matthew's emphasis highlights one of Jesus' historical activities. Whatever Jesus' other roles, he was undoubtedly a sage as well; I will discuss this issue in more detail under Jesus' identity, below. Matthew is not the only Gospel to portray people asking Jesus legal questions, faith questions, or difficult riddles (e.g., Mk 10:2, 17; 12:18-23, 28; Lk 12:13). Matthew deepens this emphasis, however, so that the wording of Jesus' teachings in his Gospel comes closer to Jewish rabbis' formulations than does the way Mark and Luke put Jesus' teachings.[75]

The Rhetoric of Jesus

Returning to the historical question, how accurately does Matthew preserve Jesus' teachings? How accurately would Jesus' followers still remember his teachings? As a Jewish teacher, Jesus used parables, graphic illustrations, hyperbole, and other standard rhetorical techniques to communicate points to his readers (see Stein 1978; Tannehill 1975; Funk 1993: 28, 31). Further, although reconstructing the Aramaic behind the Gospel traditions is more complex than often allowed, some have argued that the Aramaic original of as much as 80 percent of the Synoptic sayings material appears to fit a poetic or rhythmic form helpful for memorization (Witherington 1990: 16-17; Riesner 1982b: 507).

These standard Jewish rhetorical forms helped Jesus communicate his point, but they also made it easier for disciples to remember their teachers' say-

74. Cf., e.g., repeated citations of earlier rabbis in halakic texts; less randomly, Pirqe 'Abot or Arrian's *Encheiridion* of Epictetus.

75. It may be true in Matthew that Pharisees and strangers rather than Jesus' disciples except Judas call him "teacher," and that Matthew prefers for Jesus the divine title "Lord" (Bornkamm 1963a: 41-43). But this preference is because Matthew views Jesus as more than a teacher, not less than a teacher.

ings, and (as we argue further below) it is quite likely that Jesus' disciples accurately remembered and transmitted his teachings.

Later Revision by the Church?

Clearly the early Christians resisted the temptation to read major issues of their day (such as the debate about Gentile circumcision) into Gospel materials (Stein 1980: 225-28; Wright 1992a: 421; Stanton 1995a: 60-61).[76] Some of Paul's occasional letters also inadvertently attest the accuracy of elements of the Jesus tradition (1 Cor 7:10-12; 11:23; 15:3; 1 Thess 4:15), whereas the Jesus tradition in the Gospels exhibits little Pauline influence (Gundry 1975: 191; cf. Pfitzner 1979; Thompson 1991; Richardson and Gooch 1984: 52). That Paul does not quote the Jesus tradition frequently should not surprise us any more than the lack of quotations from the Fourth Gospel in the Johannine Epistles; the specific genre of apostolic letters differs considerably from gospels and "calls specifically for only occasional or incidental reference to the Jesus-tradition" (Stuhlmacher 1991b: 16-19, especially 18; cf. Gerhardsson 1991.)

Indeed, many sayings in the tradition imply a setting relevant only to Palestine and/or the specific time of Jesus (see Theissen 1991: 25-59). More to the point, written Gospels were appearing within three decades of Jesus' ministry, while eyewitnesses maintained positions of prominence in the church;[77] Luke attests his reader's awareness of many existing written sources (Lk 1:1-4). Had early traditioners and writers indulged in free invention in various communities, we could have expected Gospels much more diverse than our Synoptics are (Gundry 1975: 191) — more like the later Gnostic materials formed under such conditions (e.g., Hill 1979: 163, 172; cf. *P. Oxy.* 1 in Jeremias 1964c: 106-11).

Discerning "tradition" on the basis of spontaneous revelation (cf. Acts of Paul 3:1; Thecla 1) also appears to be a later practice. Although all concur that the early Christians prophesied, it is highly unlikely, as suggested by some scholars,[78]

76. They also avoided harmonizing their portrayal of early Christianity. As Wright 1992a: 454 notes, after recounting Luke's recital of Ananias and Sapphira, church divisions, and the separation of Paul and Barnabas, the mythical claim to early Christian uniformity was the invention of Eusebius, not of first-century Christians still close to the events.

77. Davids 1980: 89-90; France 1986: 100-101; cf. Blomberg 1995: 22; pace Koester 1990; idem 1994. Ancients also regarded eyewitnesses as generally more reliable (e.g., Jos. *Life* 357; *War* 1.2-3; *Apion* 1.46-49; Arrian *Alex.* 6.11.8; *Indica* 15.7; Corn. Nep. 23 [Hannibal], 13.3; 25 [Atticus], 13.7; 17.1), especially if they knew both sides of the story (Jos. *Apion* 1.49, 56).

78. Pace Beare 1967: 181; Bultmann 1968: 163; Boring 1972: 501-2; Boring 1982; Miller 1988. Boring 1982: 77 thinks that prophets contributed to the Jesus tradition because they valued it; yet the opposite is far more likely: they valued it enough to retain it as a distinct standard for evaluating prophecies. Boring 1982: 110 may be less far afield when he contends that early Christian prophets often adapted rather than simply created Jesus material (cf. Hill 1979: 163); but lack of adequate formal criteria undercuts his attempts to argue that Christian prophets transmitted and adapted Jesus material. As he himself concedes, some prophetic material must stem from Jesus the prophet (1982: 138-39).

that many "sayings of the risen Jesus" were attributed to the historical Jesus.[79] The few clear examples of prophecies we have in the New Testament are always explicitly identified as such (cf., e.g., Hill 1979: 160-170; Aune 1983: 243-44; Stanton 1995a: 97),[80] and again, issues of the later church rarely appear in collections of Jesus' teachings (see Witherington 1990: 3-7). Jesus was a prophet who launched a prophetic movement (see below); but he was also a sage who taught his disciples to preserve and expound his teachings. The disciples probably were communicating the substance of Jesus' teaching even during his lifetime, if (as I argue in my comments on Mt 10) even a historical kernel lies behind Jesus' sending the Twelve in his lifetime (Witherington 1990: 181).

Written and Oral Tradition

It is unlikely that the early Christians depended only on the memories of those who knew Jesus. Disciples of Greek teachers normally took notes on what their teachers said (Stowers 1988: 74; Gempf 1993: 299; cf. Diog. Laert. 6.1.5), and sometimes published them afterward (Kennedy 1980: 19). Such notes often reflected the teacher's own style (Epict. *Disc.* 1, pref.), and the teachers themselves might later attest the accuracy of the notes (Quint. *Inst. Or.* 1, pref. 7-8; cf. Diod. Sic. 40.8.1); some also gathered other forms of research in copious written notes (Aul. Gel., pref. 2, 22). Jewish students emphasized oral transmission far more than Greek students did, but they could also take some notes to help prod them in memorizing larger bodies of oral tradition (Gerhardsson 1961: 160-62; cf. Safrai 1974/1976a: 966). Eventually many sayings were gathered into collections (e.g., Proverbs; 'Abot; cf. Diog. Laert. 2.18-47; Plut. *Sayings of Kings, Mor.* 172B-194E).

Even without notes, however, disciples' memories in the first generation should have preserved Jesus' teachings quite accurately.[81] Some more skeptical scholars have depended on studies of oral tradition that focused on modern folklore transmission in limited regions like the Balkans (see Witherington 1990: 17-18), but their conclusions underestimate Palestinian Jewish education (especially

79. See Aune 1983; Hill 1979; Hill 1974; Bauckham 1976-77; Dunn 1978a. See Sanders 1993: 62-63 for the view that it occurred occasionally but rarely. This position sounds more conservative than the language in Sanders 1969: 27-28.

80. The prejudice against anonymous oracles also counts against the prophetic generation of Synoptic Jesus material, as does the relative scarceness of material attributed to Jesus outside the Gospels (Stanton 1989a: 159). Given his prophetic activity, could not Jesus himself be responsible for genuinely prophetic material in the tradition (cf. Hill 1979: 180-81)?

81. Greek writers like Pausanias might even depend on a tradition circulated purely orally for half a millennium (Paus. 1.23.2); in such cases skepticism might be more warranted. Ancients themselves recognized that centuries of oral transmission could introduce variants (Jos. *Apion* 1.12 and Diog. Laert. 9.12.113 on Homer; cf. Gen. Rab. 49:7), though Jewish people insisted they were meticulously careful with their own Scriptures (Jos. *Apion* 1.28-36; p. Sanh. 2:6, §3; Gen. Rab. 36:8).

its emphasis on learning Scripture — Jos. *Apion* 1.60; 2.204),[82] assume a much longer period of transmission than is possible before the Gospels were written, compare accounts whose historical rootage is quite different, and fail to explain the preservation of so many elements in Jesus' teachings uncomfortable to the later church (Witherington 1990: 8, 19-20).[83]

While some cultures have shown rapid adaptation of oral traditions, methods of transmission in many other cultures have proven substantially accurate and enduring even over centuries (e.g., African traditions confirmed by European travelers' accounts — Lewis 1975: 43; for a humorous European example, see Lampe and Luz 1991: 404). Ancient Mediterranean society as a whole also emphasized memory. Thus, for example, Roman orators regularly memorized their speeches even when these were several hours long (Quint. *Inst. Or.* 11.2.1-51); *memoria,* "learning the speech by heart in preparation for delivery," was one of the orator's five primary tasks (Satterthwaite 1993: 344). More relevant here, members of Greek schools passed on sayings of founders from one generation to the next (Culpepper 1975: 193; cf. Diog. Laert. 10.1.12; Diod. Sic. 10.5.1; Aul. Gel. 7.10.1; Socrates *Ep.* 20); inattentive students could warrant public rebukes (Aul. Gel. 8.3). Although this practice could introduce error over a number of generations, the first generations should have preserved the teacher's message accurately. Greco-Roman education as a whole emphasized memorization (Quint. *Inst. Or.* 1.3.1; 2.4.15; Isoc. *Demon.* 18, Or. 1; Seneca *Controversies* 1.pref., 2; Plut. *Educ.* 13, *Mor.* 9E; Koester 1982: 1:93; Ferguson 1987: 84), and Jewish education[84] was no exception (Jos. *Life* 8; m. 'Abot 6:6; Gerhardsson 1961: 124-25; Riesner 1982a: 51-64).[85] Given the breadth of evidence, it is

82. Cf., e.g., Jos. *Ant.* 4.211; m. 'Abot 5:12. If this was purely propaganda, it proved more effective than most; despite prevalent anti-Judaism, many Greeks viewed the Jews as a "nation of philosophers" (Gager 1983: 39; Stern 1974: 8-11, 46, 50; cf. Mayer 1972: 125-26). The view that the Greeks borrowed from the Jews (e.g., Aristobulus, *Fr.* 3-4 in Euseb. *P.E.* 13.12.1-8; Ep. Arist. 312-16; Justin *1 Apol.* 59; Stern 1974: 93-96) was more often mere propaganda, although Thales and Pythagoras may have had geographic links with Syro-Palestine (Green 1991-92). The specific examples of Jewish education undoubtedly apply best to the educated class (Horsley 1995: 246), but the evidence seems to imply greater facility in the national traditions than was common in most ancient cultures. Although scholars debate whether Jewish disciples in this period would treat the traditions of their sages as equivalent to Scripture, disciples who came to acknowledge their teacher as "Messiah" and "Lord" surely might do so.

83. The original data can also be understood in a much more positive direction; see Blomberg 1987: 28-31; Boyd 1995: 122.

84. Despite Philo's Aristotelian language concerning memory (Boccaccini 1991: 192-94), he draws on Jewish tradition such as the Epistle of Aristeas (194-98), recalling God's acts in history (197).

85. Riesner 1984a has refined and corrected Gerhardsson's overstatements, especially by drawing on nonrabbinic sources (cf. Boyd 1995: 121-22); indeed, if understood as simply making an analogy between early Christian and later rabbinic transmission, Gerhardsson's views are now becoming mainstream (see Neusner 1998). As against Bultmann's informal uncontrolled tradition and Gerhardsson's formal controlled tradition, Bailey 1991 makes a good case for informal controlled tradition, noting that most elements preserved in the Synoptic tradition were those most apt to be transmitted orally.

highly unlikely that the basic models of transmission later attested in rabbinic sources arose only in a later period (Hagner 1993: xlix).

At least by the second century and probably earlier, rabbis expected disciples to memorize their teachings through repeated practice (e.g., Sifre Deut. 48.1.1-4; 48.2.3; 306.19.3; Goodman 1983: 79). Although over the passage of generations disciples undoubtedly conflated and confused some sayings, rabbis highly valued careful transmission (t. Yebam. 3:1; Mek. Pisha 1.135-36; ARN 24 A). Of course, students regularly paraphrased sayings of teachers; paraphrase was in fact a standard school exercise in Greco-Roman education (Theon *Progymn.* 1.93-171; cf. Gerhardsson 1961: 136-48), and it was the "gist" rather than the verbatim precision that ancients valued (Small 1995). Scholars from across the theological spectrum thus acknowledge that Jewish and Christian sources alike both preserved and adapted earlier tradition (Davies 1967b: 156; Draper 1984: 269-87).

Some scholars argue that ancient writers may have modified written texts more often than oral traditions; hence Matthew may have adapted Mark more freely than the whole process of oral tradition modified Jesus' sayings (Gundry 1974: 102; Witherington 1990: 22; cf. Diog. Laert. 1.48). This is one reason that redaction criticism (examining how the Gospel writers adapted earlier sources) can help us examine historical tradition as well as a specific Gospel writer's emphases.

The burden of proof thus rests with New Testament scholars who betray an unduly skeptical bias toward the Gospel accounts (on the question of the burden of proof, cf. Goetz and Blomberg 1981: 39-63); such scholars must imply that disciples who considered Jesus Lord were far more careless with his words in the earliest generations of Christianity than first- and second-generation students of most other ancient teachers were (see Davies 1966a: 115-16; Benoit 1973/1974: 1:33). Especially given how much of Jesus' teaching was disseminated in public during his lifetime, the sort of "radical amnesia" this skepticism requires of Jesus' first followers (Witherington 1990: 14) is certainly not typical of schools of other early sages.

Some Form-Critical Issues

Form critics earlier in the century established some criteria that remain helpful today, although form criticism's serious weaknesses have rendered most contemporary scholars skeptical about the degree to which it remains valuable (e.g., Hill 1972: 58; Stuhlmacher 1991b: 2-12; more forcefully, Theissen 1991: 5).[86] One criterion, that of dissimilarity, has fallen on hard times; used to exclude Jesus tradition, the criterion excludes the likelihood of Jesus having a high degree of continuity with his Jewish contemporaries and the likelihood of his disciples' having

86. Recent scholars have critiqued even the criterion of coherence (e.g., Johnson 1996: 130), though it was used even by ancients (Arrian *Alex.* 7.14.4-6). Although less warranted than criticism of the dissimilarity criterion, the critique is at least somewhat deserved, given the unsystematic and sagelike character of Jesus' teaching.

a high degree of continuity with his teachings. From what we know of ancient schools, the reverse is far more likely; hence the criterion is useful only in its positive role: what later Christians would not have invented is authentic tradition (this resembles what scholars currently call the criterion of embarrassment). Further, the criterion of Palestinian Jewish environment makes far more sense than the criterion of dissimilarity and frequently cancels it out.[87] In recent years scholars have thus seriously critiqued the negative use of this criterion and urged special caution (see, e.g., Meier 1991a: 173; Brown 1994: 19; Stanton 1995a: 143; Young 1995: 257; cf. Mealand 1978a; Mack 1993: 193).[88]

Aramaic figures of speech also tend to suggest authentic Jesus material (Witherington 1990: 11; cf. Barrett 1967: 6), especially if the first translators into Greek frequently sought word-for-word fidelity, as some suggest (Young 1989: 180). Aramaic was probably the first language of most Galileans outside the urban centers, even in Lower Galilee (see Horsley 1995: 247-49). Greek was nevertheless quite widespread in the land (e.g., Mussies 1983; cf. p. Soṭa 7:1, §4); even in Jewish Palestine, as many as two-thirds of known funerary inscriptions are in Greek (van der Horst 1992; cf. Leon 1960: 75), though more in some areas and later periods.[89] Semitic remains prevail primarily in part of heavily traditional Upper Galilee (cf. Meyers 1988: 74), but Aramaic inscriptions are common around villages of Jesus' Lower Galilee as well (Horsley 1995: 249). Despite its use as a holy language (e.g., Jub. 12:25-27), and hence its significance in developed scribal settings (attested in the Mishnah and many Qumran scrolls) and its value for nationalistic fervor (attested in the Bar Kokhba materials — Carmon 1973: 73), Hebrew was probably not a primary spoken language among the common people (pace Safrai 1991ab; Ep. Arist. 11, 30, 38; Sifre Deut. 46.1.2); epigraphic data and coins indicate that, as a common language, Aramaic had long before begun to supplant it (Neh 13:24; Bright 1981: 411).

Because most of Jesus' teachings in the Synoptics appear to have been delivered to Galilean villagers, they probably reflect Aramaic (Meier 1991a: 267-68; Deissmann 1978: 64; Black 1957: 305; Jeremias 1971: 4) rather than Greek originals. Because he also taught in urban Jerusalem, the scholars who suggest that he sometimes taught in Greek (Porter 1993; cf. Argyle 1956; pace Draper 1956) are also likely correct.[90]

87. Ancient historians could also test a report's probability according to coherency with known customs of the report's day (e.g., Dion. Hal. 9.22.1-5).

88. The older liberal view that the earliest Christology evolved from a Palestinian Jewish apocalyptist to a hellenistic divine man does not fit all the evidence, but it certainly fits better than the contemporary "Jesus Seminar's" reversal of the sequence, which contends that later Christians Judaized Jesus (Blomberg 1995: 22), a thesis that makes no sense in view of Roman anti-Judaism and the growing influence of Diaspora Christianity as years passed. Paul shares an apocalyptic worldview with much of Palestinian Judaism as much as two decades before Mark (Overman 1990a: 194).

89. Claims about Greek use based on the hellenized cities, however, should not be extrapolated to all Palestine, as Schwank 1987 does.

90. A Semiticist as early as Dalman already recognized the use of Greek in Jerusalem (1929: 3). For discussion of Jesus' language through Dalman, see Schweitzer 1968: 270-78.

It is quite true that the earliest church, like Jesus, often spoke Aramaic; the bilingual milieu of the Syrian and Palestinian churches undoubtedly facilitated the ready translation on a popular level of Jesus' sayings from Aramaic to Greek, sometimes in diverse forms (Dibelius 1949: 25). Some might therefore charge that the earliest Christians could have invented some sayings attributed to Jesus in this period (Meier 1991a: 178-80). But given all we know of Jewish and (for that matter) Greco-Roman traditioning and the growth of legends (see discussion above), this would be the *least* likely period in which sayings or stories would be invented.[91] (Paul attests two of the leading eyewitnesses — Peter and John — plus Jesus' brother in positions of leadership in the Jerusalem church — Gal 2:9; cf. 1 Cor 15:7.) At the same time, the early Christians wrote our Gospels and probably their direct sources in Greek, and just as Matthew frequently adjusts Mark's Greek, his sources may also have adapted earlier language. So Aramaisms suggest traditions stemming from the earliest (hence most reliable) community; but (pace Burkitt 1910: 20) good Greek is not a mark *against* the reliability of the traditions (especially if most Palestinian Jews were bilingual, as is probably the case; see Meier 1991a: 255-68; cf. Argyle 1973).[92]

Conclusions regarding the Sayings Material

Matthew's method may be, if anything, more conservative than that of many of his predecessors in preserving what he believes to be the substance of Jesus' teaching, although he freely rearranges and midrashically adapts that teaching. As E. P. Sanders observes (1993: 193):

> The gospel writers did not wildly invent material. They developed it, shaped it and directed it in the ways they wished. But even Matthew did not create a sizeable body of material in favour of the Gentile mission, though he seems to have enhanced what he had.

One need only read afresh Jesus' sayings in many Matthean discourses to see that they represent collections of isolated sayings or groups of sayings that Matthew has arranged as topically as possible, often even without literarily adequate explanatory transitions. Had Matthew wished to create teaching material for Jesus (apart from minor transitions), the importance of his work's literary unity would have provided him plenty of incentive to do so. But the evidence of Matthew's

91. More adaptation might occur in the "translation" into Greek (although Josephus claims in *Apion* 1.1 that he "translated" his *Antiquities* from the Hebrew Bible, he clearly exercised stylistic and apologetic freedom where he felt necessary; the degree of "translation" is not quite clear — e.g., Jos. *War* 1.3; cf. *Ant.* 1.7; 20.263-64; see Townsend 1971: 148; Hata 1975).

92. Horsley's case (Horsley 1989: 5-40) against Nigel Turner's "Jewish Greek" (Turner 1964: 46-47; cf. Nock 1933b: 138-39; Malherbe 1983: 35-36) does not dispute the presence of Semitisms or other features of bilingualism, but that a separate dialect is in view (6, 40). Most bilinguals are less fluent in their second language, which may be the culture's dominant language (Horsley 1989: 23-24).

text suggests not merely his freedom to rearrange sayings but also his conservatism in reporting rather than inventing them.

How Accurate Are Matthew's Narratives?

Ancient biographers generally felt that a record of the subject's deeds and words revealed the person's character far better than editorial comments might (Stanton 1995a: 139). Jewish disciples cared about their teacher's lifestyle, which they normally sought to imitate (Jos. *Life* 11; among later rabbis, cf., e.g., b. Ber. 62a; Kirschner 1986), and which later might even function as legal precedent (t. Piska 2:15-16; Sifre Deut 221.1.1; p. B. Meṣ. 2:11, §1; Nid. 1:4, §2; Sanh. 7:2, §4; Yebam. 4:11, §8). Jewish children learned by practice and imitation as well as by memorization (Jos. *Apion* 2.171, 173-74, 204).[93] In Greek as well as Jewish culture, students were eager to preserve the *deeds* and character of their masters as well as their teachings (cf. Liefeld 1967: 223; Robbins 1992: 64). Although the early Christians undoubtedly retold the stories in a variety of ways, the most common form of Synoptic pericopes suggests that the early Christians adopted the sort of short narratives typically used to recount the deeds and deed-related sayings of famous teachers.

Form-Critical Considerations

Although we have our present Gospels as finished literary works intended to be read as such, they still reflect some of the process of oral tradition that stands behind their sources. For instance, many of our stories in the Synoptic Gospels (Matthew, Mark, and Luke) are brief accounts of events in Jesus' ministry, often with a minimum of chronological links to their context. On average these Synoptic accounts resemble *chreiai,* brief examples (often of heroes of history) recounted, memorized, and paraphrased in regular school exercises in the ancient Mediterranean world.[94] (The length and form of *chreiai* admittedly varied — cf.

93. To a lesser degree, cf. the broader Greco-Roman principle of imitation among disciples (Quint. 1.2.26; Philost. *V.A.* 5, §21) and children (Isoc. *Nic./Cypr.* 57, *Or.* 3.37; Quint. 1.1.5; 1.3.1-3; 1 Cor 4:16). For the importance of imitating virtuous fathers or elder brothers in Judaism, see, e.g., Ps-Philo 20:6; 4 Macc 9:23.

94. Disciples could readily adapt both the Jesus tradition and Cynic tradition, both highly critical of the social establishment, to fit this form (cf. Theissen 1991: 115; Wright 1992a: 427-35), but this does not imply that *chreiai* represent a strictly Cynic form or that the stories were composed under Cynic influence. Synoptic pericopes fit both Greco-Roman and Jewish forms (Theissen 1991: 120-22, especially 120n.143; cf. Guenther 1989, though Greek rhetorical forms may have prevailed less in first-century Palestine than he thinks); the specifically Cynic position of Mack 1988: 179, 186-87 is thus too narrow, as is his attribution of Q to "Cynic-like" circles (1988: 69, 84; cf. Downing 1988b; idem 1991; but also the critique in Overman 1990a: 193; Tuckett 1988; Witherington 1990: 184; Blomberg 1995: 21; Boyd 1995: 160).

Robbins 1988: 3; Mack and Robbins 1989: 196-97. Jewish forms of transmitting tradition often closely resembled broader Greco-Roman patterns.) It was natural for Jesus' disciples and their first hearers to remember stories about Jesus in the same way they were accustomed to remember stories about other important figures. The combination of such narratives with anecdotes, teaching material (sayings and speeches), and an extended account of the protagonist's end characterizes ancient biography in general (Burridge 1992: 203).

In the first half of the twentieth century form critics pointed out some particular patterns in the Synoptic Gospels' accounts about Jesus. Some form critics called one recurrent pattern "controversy narratives," paragraphs in which Jesus debates with his opponents and proves his case. Although we may guess that the social repercussions of these debates continued long after the recorded narratives end, such narratives typically close with a rejoinder or quip from Jesus (what contemporary North Americans would call a "slam") that silences and shames his opponents. Some form critics called narratives concluding with Jesus' witty retorts "pronouncement stories." Such stories about teachers were common in antiquity,[95] suggesting that Jesus shamed his opponents in a way understood by his disciples from their culture.[96] The use of such accounts also suggests why the disciples would have transmitted the stories as they did. Occasions on which restraint is shown in describing miracles (e.g., Mk 9:26) suggest controls on these traditions similar to those on the sayings traditions (e.g., Gundry 1975: 190).

Because Jesus authored the sayings material but not the narratives about him, his disciples presumably transmitted the sayings more carefully and the narratives more in their own words (e.g., Witherington 1990: 28-29; Pesch 1991: 107; Theissen 1991: 60); hence Aramaisms predominate in the former. Other ancient writers also seem to have adapted narratives with some degree of freedom. Like historians today, ancient historians could abridge accounts; one Jewish document claims to be a careful abridgment of another five-volume work, observing that the writer followed the "rules" of abridgment (2 Macc 2:24-25, 28). But in

95. See, e.g., Plut. *Agesilaus* 21.4-5; Alsup 1981; Robbins 1981; Poulos 1981; Barrett 1981: 119-26; in Jewish contexts, cf., e.g., 1 Kings 3:16-28; 10:3; t. ʿAbod. Zar. 6:7; Sanh. 13:5.

96. These seem to have been substantially more rare in strictly Jewish works, perhaps due to the genres involved; cf. VanderKam 1981 (19 examples, mainly in Test. Job and Ahiqar); Greenspoon 1981; and especially Porton 1981, who alone deals with the Jewish equivalent of "sage" narratives found in the Greek parallels. Yet Porton may underestimate the value of the rabbinic texts, which cite Scripture as in the Gospel narratives (see Theissen 1991: 120n.143). These do admittedly become dominant, especially in the Amoraic period, however, probably due to the primarily halakic character of Tannaitic texts preserved. In rabbinic controversy-dialogues (e.g., b. Rosh. Hash. 32b), the rabbis debate pagan interlocutors in general (e.g., b. Bek. 8b; Sanh. 39a; p. Meg. 1:11, §3; 3:2, §3; Pesiq. Rab Kah. 1:2; 4:7; Num. Rab. 4:9; 9:48; Qoh. Rab. 2:8, §2) and pagan philosophers (t. ʿAbod. Zar. 6:7; b. ʿAbod. Zar. 54b, bar.; Bek. 8b-9a; cf. b. Sanh. 39a), including "Epicureans" (possibly used in its general denigrating sense of those who denied divine providence and judgment; t. Sanh. 13:5; p. Sanh. 10:1, §7; cf. m. 'Abot 2:14, expounded in b. Sanh. 38b), Sadducees (b. ʿErub. 101a), Samaritans (p. Yebam. 1:6, §1), and *minim* (schismatics) in general (b. Sanh. 38b, 39a; 43a; b. Ḥul. 84a; perhaps b. Yoma 56b-57a; Herford 1966: 226-27 also lists Qoh. Rab. 30:9, 53cd; b. Ḥul. 87a; Shab. 152b; Sukk. 48b; cf. Bagatti 1971: 98ff.

antiquity one could "expand" accounts as well; Theon advised students to "expand" or "condense" fables by elaborating speeches or descriptive details (*Progymn.* 4.37-42, 80-82). One could of course edit historical stories interfering with historical details less than one might render fables. While he may add details known from other sources and add some description that is either implicit in the narrative or inherently probable in itself, Theon's example for expanding a *chreia* does not change its basic meaning much (*Progymn.* 3.224-40; cf. 2.115-23; Longinus *On the Sublime* 11.1). Similarly, while Matthew often abridges Markan accounts, possibly for the sake of space, and sometimes adds what fits his theological interests (Stanton 1991: 259-71), expansion was more characteristic of the apocryphal Gospels (although some later accounts also abridge the early Gospels; cf. Carmignac 1980: 411-15; Blomberg 1984: 195).

Did the Earliest Christians Reject Narrative?

Some contemporary scholars, however, are highly suspicious of early Christian narrative. They have questioned whether the Gospel narratives and sayings are compatible, as well as whether the eschatological and wisdom sayings are compatible (e.g., Crossan 1991a: 265-306).[97] In both matters, they employ forced-choice logic. On the latter, for instance, the Similitudes of Enoch freely mixes wisdom and apocalyptic thought; no necessary boundary in antiquity rendered these categories mutually exclusive (Witherington 1990: 243; on 4Q300, see Schiffman 1993).[98] Although most modern scholars recognize the apocalyptic eschatological element in Jesus' teaching, a few scholars, eager to eliminate that element, have tried to read second-century Gnosticism back into Palestinian Judaism and make Jesus the precursor of Gnostic teachers.

The same move supports the suspicion of narrative. Noting that the second-century Gnostic Gospels are mainly sayings traditions, such scholars have also suggested that some Gospels, such as the Gnostic Gospels, represent the original Gospels, and that the first Gospels (which were "antinarrative") included only sayings. This idea, however, goes against all the extant evidence.[99] While say-

97. Perhaps especially by way of protest oracles, hellenism probably exerted significant influence on Jewish eschatological thought (cf. Glasson 1961, though overstated); Roman yearning for a new golden era in Augustan propaganda may have also contributed (Virg. *Ecl.* 4.4-25; 8.27-28). Nevertheless, the Egyptian Potter's Oracle and prior Egyptian and Asian models for apocalyptic suggest that the influence moved more from east to west (cf. also Baker 1963). In our period, eschatological material would reflect more a definite Jewish than a purely hellenistic milieu.

98. Pace Crossan 1991a: 288-91, who cites only extremely hellenized sources. Crossan likewise contrasts Paul's apocalyptic Jesus with the Corinthians' sapiential one (228-30), but Paul hardly rejects the sapiential (1 Cor 1:30; 8:5-6); nor does Jesus' beginning a ministry distinct from that of John the Baptist support Crossan's conclusion that Jesus must have rejected John's apocalypticism (230-38). Even Koester allows that Jesus' message probably contained eschatological elements (see 1992).

99. In more detail, see Keener 1995.

ings collections, like narratives, could be either early or late, both the Gnostic texts and the more "orthodox" apocryphal Gospels are clearly later, expansive, and considerably farther removed from the Palestinian Jesus tradition than the canonical Gospels are, as the mainstream of New Testament scholarship currently recognizes (see Meier 1991a: 114-39; Sanders 1993: 64; Stanton 1995a: 77-95).[100] It is, moreover, clear that, excepting some Jewish-Christian Gospels (Nazarenes, Ebionites, and Hebrews), sayings "gospels" and infancy "gospels" do not even represent the basic biographical genre of the canonical Gospels, rendering comparisons strained (Burridge 1992: 249-50).

Further, though his disciples probably remembered some of Jesus' teachings in collections of short, pithy sayings like Proverbs and Pirqe 'Abot (Vermes 1973: 27),[101] the earliest Christian "sayings collections" were not opposed to the inclusion of narrative; they regularly included some. The very early Gospel source Q was probably not, as many have argued, purely a collection of Jesus' sayings and nothing else; although it emphasizes sayings, the material Matthew and Luke share in sequence includes some narrative (e.g., Mt 3:1-12; 4:1-11; 8:5-13; 11:1-19//Lk 3:3-18; 4:1-13; 7:1-10; 7:18-35). (Eliminating narrative in Q to preserve the hypothesis that Q lacked narrative is not an argument; it is assuming what one hopes to prove.)

Rather than regarding sayings and narrative as mutually opposed, biographers like Diogenes Laertius typically included both kinds of sources in their biographies. Ancient writers regularly reported sayings and narrative separately or combined them at will: although teachers of rhetoric formally distinguished sayings *chreiai* and action *chreiai,* they also formally recognized mixed *chreiai,* which included both (Theon *Progymn.* 3.22-23); sayings *chreiai* could also include both statement and response (*Progymn.* 3.27-28). Biographers regularly reported sayings from separate sources after narrating a "life," without implying that the two genres were contradictory (e.g., Plut. *Timoleon* 15.1); Ahiqar's wisdom sayings and narrative were probably already combined more than half a millennium before the Gospels were written.

Outside of sayings collections, sayings were often transmitted apart from one another (e.g., Aune 1987: 34). Ancient readers considered inserting sayings from sayings collections into narratives, or from narratives into sayings, a matter

100. For most reconstructions this includes the Gospel of Thomas (e.g., Meier 1991a: 139; Wright 1992: 437-43; Blomberg 1995: 23-24; Stanton 1995a: 84-93; Johnson 1996: 89 on the evidence and current consensus), but especially the Secret Gospel of Mark (Brown 1994: 297; Stanton 1995a: 93-95) and the Gospel of Peter (Meier 1991a: 117; Brown 1994: 1317-49; Stanton 1995a: 78-81), against current uses by Crossan, Koester, and others. Some even regard Secret Mark as a scholarly forgery (Neusner 1998: xxvii, calling it a "scholarly fraud"). Ancient fiction writers sometimes pretended that they were translating "ancient writings that no one but themselves had seen" (Lefkowitz 1996: 111). Preserved agrapha appear of such varying quality as to underline the comparative value of our written Gospels as more dependable sources for Jesus' teaching (see Hofius 1991).

101. Similar sayings of the wise appear, e.g., in Ben Sira. In a Roman context, one may compare, e.g., the poetry of Publilius Syrus, which greatly resembles wisdom sayings of the Egyptian and Israelite traditions.

of arrangement, not of fabrication (Theon *Progymn.* 4.73-79; cf. 5.388-441). The alternative to such combined narratives was simply to relate narratives in episodic fashion, as Mark sometimes does; although this practice did not conform to established literary tastes, most readers found it acceptable alongside the more approved method (Drury 1976: 30).

Structure, Authorship, Provenance, and Date

Whereas we have focused on general observations based on literary type and traditions, questions about structure are more difficult, and specific questions concerning authorship, provenance, and date may never be resolved with certainty unless excavations bring unexpected new evidence to light.

Structure

Matthew's arrangement coheres with basic principles of ancient rhetoric and biography (cf. Kennedy 1984: 101-2).[102] As noted above, many biographers arranged their material topically;[103] Matthew arranges even many sayings thematically (see Davies and Allison 1988: 87-88). In part because various outlines of Matthew abound[104] and in part because his favorite points recur, some are reticent to outline this Gospel (Gundry 1982: 10; cf. Davies and Allison 1988: 61; Guthrie 1990: 43).[105] Yet we should not despair of structural clues altogether; later rabbis whose thought-world may be similar to Matthew's repeatedly emphasized their points, though their edited literature betrays substantial structural forethought (cf. Daube 1973: 64-65).

This Gospel may divide chronologically into three sections (Kingsbury 1975: 7-25);[106] the teaching material divides topically into five. Whereas Luke

102. Kennedy thinks that 1:1-17 function as the proem, chs. 1–4 as the narration, and the Sermon on the Mount as the proposition, with the examples in chs. 1–4 providing the basis for chs. 5–7 (1984: 103-4). Matthew may not have thought in these precise terms, but his neat division of material lends itself to such observations.

103. Among the rabbis, whose literature includes little biography, one notes the penchant for arrangement, even into tractates, by the time of the Mishnah (cf. Goulder 1974: 27). Still, Josephus is concerned lest some stricter Jews misunderstand his reason for rearranging some of Moses' laws (*Ant.* 4.197).

104. For a full survey of views, see Bauer 1988: 21-55. Bauer's own outline arises from internal features, particularly various forms of repetition developed throughout the Gospel (see especially 57-128).

105. Some others overzealously locate structural clues, e.g., the overstated evidence for inclusio in Ellis 1974: 98 (this "rabbinic habit" is also less common in Matthew than Goulder 1974: 27 supposes).

106. Cf. Plummer 1910: xviii, using "from then on" in 4:17; 16:21; 26:16; but cf. the warning of Neirynck 1988 on the inadequacy of this common expression for a structuring schema. Strecker's threefold schema for Matthean salvation history (1995) is probably overdependent on Conzelmann's schema for Luke (see Stanton 1995b: 9).

provides (or preserves) settings for more of his teaching material from Q, as was common in biographies, Matthew gathers it primarily in topical sections (Burridge 1992: 196-97). Most scholars identify five discourses by the closing formula "when he had finished speaking" in 7:28; 11:1; 13:53; 19:1; 26:1.[107] Although some scholars object that chapter 23 is a discourse distinct from that in chapters 24–25 (Kingsbury 1975: 4-5; Senior 1983: 21),[108] their theme of judgment on the religious establishment binds them together (see my comments loc. cit.). Others object by citing 11:7-30 as another section of Matthew with extended discourse (Senior 1983: 21), but this passage is much shorter than the others, especially when one accounts for Jesus' sayings directly connected with the preceding narrative about the Baptist. Some narrative critics have claimed that Matthew is only a plot and reject the older division by discourse sections. Yet if Matthew is *only* a story, "it is a rather dull one for several long stretches, where the disciples basically sit around while Jesus talks." Hence we should take note of the discourse sections in addition to the broader narrative structure that provides their final context (Smith 1997: 541). One need not choose between these two most common alternatives; the threefold chronological narrative structure and the fivefold discourse structure are not incompatible (Senior 1983: 26-27; Blomberg 1992a: 24-25). Ultimately, a more detailed confluence of structural elements is probably unnecessary, especially if Matthew intended his Gospel for oral performance in shorter sections (Justin *1 Apol.* 67; Stanton 1993: 75).

Some scholars have compared Matthew's five discourse sections to the five books of the Pentateuch (e.g., F. F. Bruce 1980a: 41; F. F. Bruce 1972a: 62-63; Ellis 1974: 10; Sandmel 1978a: 51), a view that originated with Papias in the early second century and was revived by B. W. Bacon early in the twentieth (Davies 1966b: 6). Most contemporary scholars who recognize five discourse sections nevertheless remain skeptical about an implied parallel with the Pentateuch (e.g., Davies and Allison 1988: 61; Hagner 1993: li). Some ancient works did have five divisions (Psalms; Proverbs; Ecclesiastes; Megilloth; the prototype of 2 Maccabees; 1 Enoch;[109] 2 Enoch; Pirqe 'Abot; cf. Strack 1969: 53; Charlesworth 1981: 104); but it is not clear how many of their editors consciously modeled this number after the number of books in the Pentateuch (cf. Davies 1966b: 6; Dimant 1983).[110] Because only Matthew's discourse sections (not the Gospel

107. See, e.g., Gundry 1982: 10; Aune 1987: 19, 49; Kee 1980: 141; Jeremias 1963: 13-14; Argyle 1963: 64; Beare 1981: 200; Thompson 1970: 1; Luz 1989: 43-44. For such a completion formula accompanying divine revelations in the OT, cf. Gen 17:22; 18:33; Ex 31:18; but the particular LXX wording differs and the phrase is idiomatic Hebrew.

108. Keegan 1982 finds five discourses but omits ch. 23 on the basis of "key" *introductory* words, but the words he finds characteristic of Matthean speech introductions are too typical of Matthew's narratives in general to count for much. Guelich finds five closing formulas but six discourses, counting ch. 23 separately from chs. 24–25 (1982: 55).

109. The structure may follow Enoch's biography in Jub. 4:16-25 rather than the Pentateuch (Dimant 1983), but the fivefold division may remain significant (Milik preserves it though substituting the Book of Giants for the Similitudes).

110. Rabbis did sometimes read "five" as symbolic for the Pentateuch (e.g., Gen. Rab. 64:8).

as a whole) divide into five parts and because no correspondence with specific Pentateuchal books is obvious, one must either dismiss the theory (so Kingsbury 1975: 5) or, more likely, accept it as correct but not particularly useful in the interpretation of Matthew's structure. Even if Matthew views himself as passing down Jesus' words as a sort of "oral law" (which is possible, but scholars currently debate how early that phrase appears in early Judaism), he may have arranged the sayings into five sections simply to emphasize that point, without assuming any correspondence between his discourses and particular books of the Pentateuch. While some reject the traditional Jewish image of the new Moses in Matthew (Filson 1960: 29; Albright and Mann 1971: 49 et passim), some examples of this possibly related motif do appear (e.g., 2:16; 4:2; cf. 5:1; see especially Allison 1993b).

Authorship

Like modern critics, ancient writers often questioned traditional attributions of various works (e.g., Jos. *Apion* 1.221; Arrian *Alex.* 5.6.5). The minority of scholars favoring Matthean authorship have marshaled important arguments and provided answers to those more skeptical that Matthew wrote this Gospel (Gundry 1982: 609-22; cf. Guthrie 1990: 43-53). Yet while Matthew is the best individual *named* candidate offered, the lack of evidence for any other particular suggestion does not necessarily make the limited evidence for Matthean authorship compelling. In favor of Matthean authorship, the titles of the Gospels were unanimously accepted over a large geographical region in the second century (see Hengel 1985: 81-82). Papias in the very early second century preferred oral tradition, but reported attributions for the Gospels he believed accurate (Hengel 1991: 232-38). Because travelers networked early Christian assemblies throughout the Empire and word traveled quickly among them (cf., e.g., Aune 1983: 215-16),[111] early traditions concerning the authors of popular Christian works' are probably generally correct.

External evidence (church tradition) stemming from Papias in the early second century and confirmed by the unanimous title (added after early Christians identified the extant Gospels as one genre, though possibly before they were collected)[112] sup-

111. On this networking, see, e.g., Stuhlmacher 1991b: 16; Bauckham 1998a: 33-36 (for letters and messengers between churches, see 37-44; for the network implied in Ignatius's letters, see 40-42); and especially Thompson 1998: 49-70. Travelers regularly networked the Pauline churches (e.g., 1 Cor 1:11; 11:16; 14:33; 16:12, 19; 2 Cor 9:2), and any Pauline scholar approaching Gospels research will be astounded at the lack of networking Gospels scholars sometimes assume among the early churches. Pauline scholars in this case work with a much more solid base of explicit data than Gospels scholars do.

112. Sanders 1993: 64 does not believe the Gospels were titled before our first clear evidence for their titles ca. 180, but one wonders whether second-century Christians (less organized than their immediate descendants) would have achieved unanimity over a wide geographical area so quickly without prior tradition. Stanton 1995a: 16-18 provides evidence for four-Gospel codices, hence the use of collections containing exactly four Gospels, by the end of the second century.

ports Matthean authorship.[113] But these arguments depend on early church tradition, not on the earliest text of the Gospel itself; and in this instance, the argument from tradition may be suspect. If Papias is wrong that Matthew wrote in Hebrew or Aramaic (the most natural way to take his words; cf. Hagner 1993: xliv-xlv)[114] and wrong that Matthew wrote before Mark did,[115] he may also be mistaken that Matthew wrote the extant Gospel of Matthew (though he could be mistaken about one while correct about the other). Even if Matthew wrote at one stage of the tradition (say, an early version of Q—the version behind Matthew and Luke was probably already in Greek—Tuckett 1996: 84; for the Aramaic original, see Polag 1991: 99), we have no guarantee that the finished product is largely from Matthew's hand. Matthew's use of Mark also may speak against the author's having been a firsthand witness of the events he describes (Luz 1989: 94), as much as the church would have liked him to have been (where we can check him, the writer of the Fourth Gospel, who claims eyewitness information, is not as dependent on sources like Mark as Matthew appears to be).[116] This point may make Matthew's claim to authorship on any level the weakest among the four canonical Gospels, a claim which I at one time therefore dismissed without further consideration.

Still, Papias's tradition probably dates to within half a century of Matthew's publication, and no one in the years surrounding Papias's testimony challenged Matthean authorship; nor was Matthew the most obvious name to attach to the Gospel (apostles like Peter, Andrew, and perhaps even Thomas might commend themselves with greater authority; cf. Carson 1984b: 17-19; Blomberg 1992a: 44; Hagner 1993: lxxvi).[117] Many thus accept a Matthean tradition edited

113. Papias in Euseb. *H.E.* 3.39; probably followed by Iren. *Haer.* 3.1.1, also cited in Euseb. 5.8.2 (Davies and Allison 1988: 8). The variants Davies and Allison mention in Matthew's title (1988: 7-8) are irrelevant to the issue of authorship.

114. Our current Gospel of Matthew was clearly written in Greek (see Horbury 1997 against an early dating of Shem Tob's Hebrew Matthew, though cf. Shedinger 1997), but I intend this as an evaluation of Papias's claim, not an argument against Matthean authorship based on the quality of the Greek. On Josephus's fluency in Greek (on a more sophisticated level), see Rajak 1983: 46-64. Some also read Papias's "Hebrew dialect" as "with Jewish rhetorical forms" (Stanton 1993: 116, following Kürzinger 1963).

115. It is also possible that Papias's tradition, or Papias himself before being distorted by later tradition, may have meant simply that Matthew wrote the *logia* of Q, as many hold (e.g., Hill 1972: 23-27, 53; F. F. Bruce 1980a: 40; Hagner 1993: xliv cites also F. Schleiermacher, T. W. Manson, M. Black, and B. de Solages); Papias does, however, elsewhere apply *logia* to Markan narrative as well as sayings (Stanton 1993: 117n.1). Cf. similarly the suggestion of Matthew's "notes" as "the basis for the apostolic gospel tradition" (Gundry 1975: 182, following A. T. Robertson and E. J. Goodspeed).

116. The usual reply in favor of Matthean authorship is that Matthew was supplying a catechetical manual for new disciples already aware of Mark and other early traditions (e.g., Mounce 1985: xiv). This reply functions as a better argument than suggesting that Mark may have depended on Peter's dependence on Matthew's notes anyway (Gundry 1975: 184), which, if true, might make Matthew's dependence on Mark *more* difficult to fathom.

117. A pun on the disciple's name with the similar Greek term for "disciple" is not impossible, fitting the way a haggadist might have solved the Gospel's anonymity, but it does not commend itself as the most probable origin of the Gospel's title.

among a community of Matthew's disciples or by one of his disciples (e.g., Hagner 1993: lxxvii; cf. Hill 1972: 55).[118]

In contrast to my earlier opinion (1993: 43), and as a result of reevaluating the earliest patristic materials that depend most heavily on apostolic Christianity, I am currently inclined to give more weight to the voice of early Christian tradition than I did previously. The break between the first and second century, or between "apostolic" and "subapostolic," was not complete; oral tradition, in some circles still frequently reliable, remained important in the late first (Jn 21:25) and into the second century (Hengel 1991: 213). Confusion might reign on a number of issues in the tradition, but authorship would be the *last* point forgotten. Further, that this Gospel originally circulated without oral knowledge of its author is unlikely; as an anonymous work it would not have quickly commanded wide acceptance, and authors of biographies of this length normally were named (though persecution could have demanded a special case of anonymity here).[119] The early second-century church cited the "Gospels" alongside traditional Jewish Scripture, and Matthew was the most popular of the Gospels in circulation by this period (Stanton 1995a: 98).

I am therefore presently inclined to accept the possibility of Matthean authorship on some level, although with admitted uncertainty. Perhaps the most probable scenario that incorporates the best of all the currently available evidence is the presence of at least a significant deposit of Matthean tradition in this Gospel, edited by the sort of Matthean school scholars have often suggested (though I believe the final product is the work of a single author, not a "committee").

Yet the discussion of this Gospel's authorship ultimately involves neither the authority nor accuracy of the Gospel, because it does not name its author (the titles were added to all four Gospels later). Thus even most of the more conservative scholarly commentators, while varying in their views of Matthean authorship or influence, acknowledge that the matter is uncertain (Carson 1984b: 19; France 1985: 34; Blomberg 1992a: 43-44; McKnight 1992: 528). Likewise, some scholars who reject Matthean authorship are troubled by the antiquity of the Gospel titles and the tradition of authorship; Luz complains that too many scholars simply ignore these difficulties (1989: 94-95).

Yet what we *do* conclude about the author does affect our understanding of the Gospel. Matthew is clearly Jewish, in dialogue with contemporary Jewish thought, and skilled in traditional Jewish interpretation of the Old Testament (Iren. *Fr.* 29).[120] Matthew also knows the context of his citations much better

118. Nepper-Christensen 1991 is even willing to look for elements of the apostle Matthew's original Hebrew Gospel in our current First Gospel.

119. Sanders 1993: 66 seeks to turn anonymity to advantage, but this would have been the exception among ancient historical works rather than the rule, unless we are to accept the Gospels as purely cultic aretalogies (which is unlikely; against the aretalogy proposal, see Burridge 1992: 18-19).

120. Many scholars concur here, in the 1970s (e.g., Hill 1972: 39, 43; Ellis 1974: 3), 1980s (Carson 1984b: 18; Davies and Allison 1988: 17-58; Senior 1983: 11-12; Luz 1989: 79-82), and

than many modern readers have supposed (Gundry 1975; Ellis 1974: 22), and he demonstrates familiarity with a variety of text-types (see above).[121]

Location of Origin

Scholars have proposed a variety of places of writing for the first Gospel. Brandon's suggestion of Alexandria (1967: 290-91) runs counter to our evidence for the character of Jewish thought in first-century Alexandria. Osborne argues for the relatively obscure Edessa based on various Eastern parallels (Osborne 1973), but Palestinian Jewish parallels seem far stronger. Most scholars, however, accept a Syrian provenance for Matthew, most commonly (but not exclusively) Antioch,[122] in part due to Matthew's influence on Ignatius and the Didache in that region. Matthew emphasizes locations in Syria (4:24-25), background that may fit only Syria (17:24-27), and advocates a Gentile mission that the Syrian Jewish church had first embraced (Gundry 1982: 609; Theissen 1991: 250, 258). Apostolic tradition would naturally center in and a published Gospel naturally spread most rapidly from an urban center like Antioch; possibly the church in Antioch would also have preserved data about Peter such as we find in Matthew that is not included in Mark (Hengel 1980: 98).[123] In contrast to Alexandria, Antioch recognized the citizenship of its Jewish population (Jos. *Apion* 2.39); the largest concentration of Jewish people outside Palestine was also in Syria, especially in Antioch (Jos. *War* 7.43; cf. Levinskaya 1996: 128-32).

Other scholars prefer a provenance in rural rather than urban Syria, perhaps nearer Galilee or the Decapolis; after all, Antioch had embraced the Gentile mission from the start (Theissen 1991: 251, also comparing the water shortage of Did. 7:2-3). Some have suggested that Matthew wrote this Gospel in Palestine (Viviano 1979; Hengel 1974a: 1:105); Overman 1996: 16-19 is among recent authors making a sound case for Galilee (which the Gospel certainly does emphasize); he favors especially Sepphoris or Tiberias or their outskirts (18).

1990s (Kingsbury 1991: 264; Stanton 1993: 131-39); yet von Dobschütz suggested Matthew as a rabbi as early as 1928 (reprinted 1995); see further below. We thus disagree with Nepper-Christensen 1958; Meier 1979: 17-25; idem 1980: xi; cf. Van Tilborg 1972b: 96-97. Schoedel 1991 is concerned how Ignatius's Gentile-Christian community could make such heavy use of Matthew, suggesting that he also employed M traditions; Meier 1991b argues that Ignatius probably just used the Gospel.

121. For his precision in his use of various fulfillment formulas, see Soares Prabhu 1976: 48-58. See also the extensive treatment of OT citations in Matthew in Stendahl 1968 (who sees a scribal community at work); Cope 1976: 11-83 (on what he views as key texts placed in the middle of sections); cf. Jn 12:38.

122. E.g., Goppelt 1962: 198; Hill 1972: 50-52; Ellis 1974: 6; Zumstein 1980; Hengel 1980: 98; Senior 1983: 12-14; Meier in Brown and Meier 1983: 15-27; Mounce 1985: xiv; Davies and Allison 1988: 138-47; Blomberg 1992a: 37; cf. Hagner 1993: lxxv; Schweizer 1995: 149-50.

123. Cf. Gal 2:11-14 and the uncertain but interesting thesis of Brown and Meier 1983, that Petrine tradition was used to "domesticate" the Pauline tradition, bringing it more in line with traditional Jewish Christianity.

In view of all the evidence (which is admittedly more meager than we would like, as Luz 1989: 90-91 notes), I would prefer an urban center in Syro-Palestine that spoke Greek, included a sizeable Jewish community residentially segregated from Gentiles, probably remained bitter against the Romans for the recent massacres of 66-70, and remained in touch with rising currents in Judea. Although any proposal ultimately remains a guess, a community in Antioch appears more likely than the alternatives if, despite its heritage in the Gentile mission, it has recently shifted toward embracing more conservative Jewish-Christian traditions in the wake of the bitter Jewish-Roman war of 66-73.[124] But no evidence limits the provenance specifically to Antioch, and wherever Matthew's specific provenance, he was probably within range of the emerging sphere of rabbinic or rabbinic-like scribal influence, hence probably somewhere in Syro-Palestine.

Date

Although some scholars have made a good case that Matthew could precede A.D. 70,[125] the contents of the book may suggest a date after 70, perhaps as late as the 80s[126] (though a date after the end of the first century is untenable).[127] As noted above, this does not imply that Matthew is inaccurate; he depends on earlier traditions. But like preachers today, Matthew emphasized those features of his tradition that best addressed the pastoral situation of his readers. Especially the following evidence seems to favor a date after A.D. 70:

(1) More than Mark or Luke (but much less exclusively than John, who writes in the 90s), Matthew particularly engages Pharisaism, which became a dominant element in early Syro-Palestinian Christians' primary opposition mainly after 70. Indeed, Pharisees may have been much less hostile toward law-keeping Jewish Christians in the 60s (cf. Acts 23:6-9; Jos. *Ant.* 20.200-3).[128]

124. Hagner 1996 explains the tension between ethnic particularism and universalism (29-32) in terms of tension between the early Christians and Judaism (32-45), but he may postulate a more severe break than we might suspect in this period.

125. E.g., Gundry 1982: 599-608; Robinson 1977: 76-78; France 1986: 121; cf. tentatively France 1989: 82-91; Blomberg 1992a: 41-42; Hagner 1993: lxxiv.

126. E.g., Ellis 1974: 5; F. F. Bruce 1980a: 40; Senior 1983: 13-14; Mounce 1985: xv; Davies and Allison 1988: 127-38; Duling and Perrin 1994: 333.

127. A date after the end of the first century is untenable; pace Koester, the second-century citations clearly represent our extant First Gospel (Davies and Allison 1988: 130). Even a suggestion of the 90s is probably too late (White 1991: 241 dates it between 70 and 132, but thinks that the period near Agrippa II's death, ca. 92-93, most likely; but his evidence is hardly compelling by itself, and other evidence for an earlier date, plus a situation less advanced than in the Fourth Gospel, outweighs it).

128. Overman 1996: 12-13, 15 rightly notes that the Gospel portrays the "Pharisees" and "scribes" as Jesus' primary opponents, and that elements of these groups achieved considerable influence in the post-70 "leadership coalition."

(2) Matthew reflects a Jewish worldview closer to that of the rabbis than any other writer in the New Testament (although many other parts of the New Testament are equally Jewish). But the rabbinic movement began achieving prominence only after 70 (and even then, most common Galileans seem to have remained unaware of most of its views).
(3) Matthew and Luke both probably depend on Mark, which probably derives from the mid-60s and may have addressed the church in Rome. The early church was well networked, so Mark may have circulated and become a standard work among many (cf. Lk 1:1) quickly; nevertheless, Matthew must have read and assimilated Mark, then invested a great deal of time arranging, drafting, and polishing his own Gospel. All this evidence suggests a date sometime after 70.[129] (This argument of course falters if, with many conservative scholars, one dates Mark before the 60s. Contrary to accepted scholarly tradition, we lack definite reason to date it to the 60s or early 70s, and our assumption of a date for Mark no earlier than the mid-60s largely represents deference to consensus. Evidence for dating Mark before the 60s, however, seems to me no more definite.)
(4) Matthew more clearly separates the disciples' questions about the temple's destruction and the world's end for his readers than Mark does (Mt 24:3// Mk 13:2-4), even though Matthew's Jewish readers would have been more familiar with the traditional prophetic perspective that arranged events according to their kind rather than according to their timing.

Other supporting evidence, such as the fire of Matthew 22:7, offers some support but is not as critical to the discussion. Those who argue for an earlier date dispute each of the above points. They also provide counterarguments, such as early Christian tradition, or suppose that practices related to the temple are less relevant after A.D. 70 (e.g., 5:23-24; 23:16-17), although one might reply that Matthew preserves many other authentic Jesus traditions whose details remained local or outdated when the principles remained valid. That Matthew's own redaction seems to announce Jesus' return "immediately" after the temple's destruction (24:29) may also strongly support a pre-70 date (Hagner 1995: 712), unless (as I think) Matthew merely echoes a recent expectation that caused confusion in the first years after 70, a confusion he has sought to counter in 24:2-3. Within the present space constraints I can offer only a tentative case consistent with my reading of the Gospel as a whole.

129. Hagner objects that Mark need have been in circulation only a short time before Matthew could use it (1993: lxxiv), but with all the other traditions Matthew had and presumably other Gospels in circulation (Lk 1:1), it is doubtful that Matthew would have depended so *heavily* on Mark unless Mark had become a standard in the church. Even if the early church was well networked by travelers (which I regard as almost certain based on Paul and on analogous Jewish material), if Mark derives from Syria (which is possible) and if he had a wealthy patron with many scribes functioning as an ancient equivalent of a "printing press" (which is less likely), Mark's popularity presupposes a number of years after its initial publication, perhaps as much as a decade.

The weight of some of the strongest arguments, including the situation the Gospel addresses, initially suggested to me a date as late as the mid-80s, making it (in my opinion) later than both Mark and Luke, but with a polemic less developed (and with opponents less powerful and less targeted) than in the Fourth Gospel in the 90s. Yet because I believe some post-70 bitterness toward Gentiles informs the need for stressing the Gentile mission (especially for those who would place this Gospel or its author in Antioch, a home of that mission),[130] and because I believe other recollections of the trauma of 70 remain quite relevant to the church (including perhaps false teachers claiming a false parousia during the war),[131] I am inclined to lower the date by perhaps half a decade and guess that Matthew was written in the late 70s.[132] (In addition, one should not place the Gospel too late in the first century, for example, around 90, since by the early second century Matthew already appears as the favorite Gospel.)[133]

Again, I have chosen to favor internal evidence (in a case where the available external evidence is inadequate to be decisive) over second-century tradition (that the apostle Matthew wrote before Mark), a move some more conservative scholars would dispute. But I readily concede that arguments for a pre-70 date merit more consideration than they have often received. And as R. T. France, a British scholar who tentatively advances a pre-70 date, rightly warns, our proposed dates "depend on the relative dating of various writings and events . . . there are few fixed points." Thus, "any 'publication date' can be advanced only very tentatively" (1985: 30), whether that date is "early" or "late." Despite our best attempts to pinpoint a precise date, Luke Timothy Johnson is correct when he observes, "The dating of the four canonical Gospels is entirely a matter of scholarly deduction based on arguments concerning literary dependence" (1996: 90). Uncertainty about the date also affects the degree of precision to which our attempts to reconstruct the historical situation addressed can be successful.

130. Given the frequency of Gentile adherents in Mediterranean Jewish communities, Overman 1996: 33 is skeptical about the significance of Gentiles for an implied "Gentile mission" in Matthew; but the issue was certainly central in the church earlier (e.g., Acts 11:18; 15:28-29; Rom 15:7-29) and can only have been intensified in the wake of A.D. 70.

131. Matthew's "apocalyptic eschatology" also fits this situation (see Sim 1996), though there is no reason to *limit* such eschatology to this situation or period.

132. Despite Matthew's emphasis on the Gentile mission, judgment on the Judean religious establishment takes precedence where the two themes might compete (cf. Mt 21:13 with Mk 11:17). This also suggests fresh hostility with Judean religious leaders and exultation over the temple's ruin, but a Syrian Jewish Christian community could have faced such situations anywhere in the 70s or 80s.

133. Not only mainstream Jewish and Gentile Christians but also Gnostics apparently made early use of this Gospel (Stanton 1993: 256-77). By contrast, it is possible that John's relative lateness (along with its adoption by some Gnostics) may have delayed its widespread acceptance among the orthodox as belonging to the same category as the Synoptics.

The Situation Matthew Addresses

A recent collection of essays argues that the canonical Gospels were written for the whole of ancient Mediterranean Christianity rather than for specific communities (see Bauckham 1998b). As biographers, the Gospel writers most likely sought wider circulation than letter-writers normally did (Burridge 1998: 113-45). Gospels are more "open texts," requiring less locally specific information for correct understanding by implied readers, than are epistles (Bauckham 1998a: 48). Their written publication extended their audience beyond the previous oral setting (Alexander 1998: 90). This view is a helpful and necessary corrective to previous reconstructions of hypothetical communities, many of which piled guess upon guess about specific matters for which no data remain. Certainly Luke writes for an audience that is specific yet also knows many circulated gospels (Lk 1:1).

Nevertheless, at least some Gospel writers seem to have addressed primarily a particular range of ideal audience within the ancient Mediterranean world; even the necessity of understanding Greek would restrict the Gospels' immediate accessibility in some parts of the Roman empire. Matthew includes recurrent emphases (e.g., the Gentile mission) and appears to presuppose a largely Jewish ideal audience who will understand many of his allusions. But looking for Gospel audiences and their locations is not the same as reconstructing detailed "communities" (Barton 1998: 194); seeking to ascertain Matthew's ideal audience is more like "our modern concept of 'target audience' or 'market niche'" than traditional redactional assumptions (Burridge 1998: 143). When we use the traditional language of "community," we mean not a single house-church nor even a movement within a particular city; even if we suspected a narrower audience, we could in any case infer only the broadest judgments about the author's ideal audience based on the gospel itself. But whoever else was invited to listen in, Matthew probably addressed most fully and deliberately those parts of the church he knew best.

Although Matthew's dependence on earlier tradition prevents him from adapting everything in his Gospel to his readers' situation, enough of his emphases remain and fit what we know of the issues of his day.[134] Matthew's plot, like that of the other Gospels, focuses on conflict (Kingsbury 1992). While conflict could simply imply a good story, if *anything* can be clear from the issues Matthew addresses in his Gospel, then Matthew is engaged in some sort of polemic against the Jewish authorities, as scholars commonly contend.[135] Jesus' popular-

134. Patte 1987: 13 is more skeptical about historical reconstruction than necessary, though caution is needed; Stanton 1993: 45 strikes the right balance.

135. This view was already widespread in the 1970s (e.g., Van Tilborg 1972b; Ellis 1974: 4-6; Cope 1976: 126), and continued in the 1980s (e.g., Meeks 1986: 137; Harrington 1980: 97; Senior 1983: 6-10) and 1990s (e.g., Segal 1991: 35-37; White 1991: 240; Duling and Perrin 1994: 335). Yet as Stanton 1993: 26 observes, this common current view was earlier and independently advanced by A. Schlatter (*Der Evangelist Matthäus,* Stuttgart: Calwer, 1929).

ity with the masses in Matthew, uncommitted as they may prove to be either for or against him, weighs against the possibility that the main source of opposition his Jewish Christian communities faced was on the popular level; more than likely it stemmed instead primarily from the minority that wielded more intellectual influence in the community.

As noted above, Matthew's special target appears to be the successors of the scribes and Pharisees, the founders of the rabbinic movement at Jamnia and whatever Jewish leaders throughout Syro-Palestine may have been aligned with or influenced by them.[136] Like his teacher Jesus, Matthew agrees with some of these Pharisees' teaching (23:2-3), but he resents their behavior and opposition to the truth of Jesus and his followers (23:29-37; note Bornkamm 1963a: 31; Barth 1963: 89, but contrast Barth 1963: 103). Probably the Jerusalem Christians and the Pharisees were getting along reasonably well in the 60s (Acts 15:5; cf. Acts 23:6) when, led by James, the Jerusalem church was known for its piety in the law (Acts 21:20). Given Josephus's regular association of the Pharisees with observance of the law, those who most firmly protested James's unjust execution as a transgressor of the law (Jos. *Ant.* 20.200-201) may also have been Pharisees (traditionally known for leniency in any case — *Ant.* 13.294). But when most of the Jerusalem Christians abandoned Jerusalem (cf. 24:15-16), willing to flee if necessary even on the Sabbath (24:20), they may have incurred more suspicion. And if, as is likely, aristocratic elements dominated the new coalition of leadership at Jamnia, class issues may have joined competition and the new leadership's attempts to consolidate influence to foster a difficult breach between the Jamnian alliance (probably dominated in some measure by well-to-do Pharisees) and Jewish Christians.

The current consensus is that the first generations of rabbis exercised little direct power in Palestine (e.g., Horsley 1995: 98, 103-5). Yet evidence within Matthew itself suggests a specifically Pharisaic component of some sort in the community's opposition, likely competing with the early Christians for influence over popular thought.[137] The conflict Matthew addresses need not involve the oft-cited Birkath ha-Minim, the curse against schismatics (e.g., Ellis 1974: 5; Burridge 1994: 91),[138] usually dated ca. 85, although that probably provides one

136. For more details, see the discussion in Overman 1990b: 35-71.

137. As far as particular *sects* are concerned, the Pharisees would remain the primary competition after A.D. 70 (Schiffman 1985: 52). Matthew exhibits far less concern regarding the Sadducees, a group that had ceased to provide much of a threat after A.D. 70 (cf. Van Tilborg 1972b: 2); nor is Matthew's Jewish world of thought primarily that of the Qumran sectarians (Ito 1992). Bultmann 1968: 52 may be correct that even Mark emphasizes particularly Pharisaic and scribal opposition.

138. Some doubt that the Christians are primarily in view (Stemberger 1977; Finkel 1981). But Jewish Christians seem to have understood the malediction as aimed at them: Justin, a Gentile Christian raised in Palestine, half a century later seems to take the same curse (the Amida was the only thrice-daily prayer — Schiffman 1981: 151) as specifically anti-Christian (Horbury 1982: 19; Barnard 1964: 400; idem 1967: 44-45; Shotwell 1965: 83-84; Williams 1930: xxxii; pace Kimelman 1981: 235-38). Schäfer suggests that the primary point of the malediction is deliverance from political oppression; while it would also have terminated the unpopular schismatics' participation in the di-

extant illustration of the tensions characterizing the period.[139] Even if the curse had been quickly disseminated among many synagogues outside Judea (which is unlikely),[140] the polemic of the First Gospel can be accounted for easily enough in broader tensions already building in the years after 70.[141] (Indeed, the conflicts had begun well before 70 and continued long after it could be remembered as only one conflict among many.)[142] Previous generations of scholars overestimated rabbinic power and underestimated Judaism's diversity in late first-century Palestine. I suspect that contemporary scholarship, in evaluating Jewish and Christian texts from diverse communities, underestimates the oral networks of frequent travelers connecting these communities, as well as these communities' knowledge of one another.[143] I also suspect that the status of the emerging leadership coalition in Judea may have been analogous to the role of the scribes and Pharisees before 70 and many prominent social groups today: widely known and respected in Judea (and perhaps Galilee) on those occasions when people

---

vine service, this was not its primary goal (1975: 61). But its title suggests a different emphasis, a secondary emphasis would have been an emphasis nonetheless, and even had its framers intended no harm against the sectarians (which is unlikely), the sectarians would have suspected malicious intent (cf. Whitacre 1982: 8). *Nozrim* may have been added to *minim* later (so Urbach 1981: 288; Jocz 1979: 54-57; Flusser 1988: 638; Marmorstein 1923: 389; pace Schoeps 1961a: 55-56; Moore 1911: 111-12), but the numerous Jewish Christians probably provided the primary original object of the *minim*.

139. With Davies and Allison 1988: 136. Stanton 1993: 142-44, 281 allows that although the curse may have been a factor in the separation and Matthew probably contended with the Jamnian academy's agendas, "we cannot say more." Evidence for a unified prayer liturgy throughout the synagogues is disputed even in Palestine; its pervasive use in the Diaspora by the end of the first century is highly questionable. For evidence that does not suggest a common liturgy, cf. Levine 1986: 19-20; Cohen 1986: 175; Sanders 1992: 205-7; for evidence that could favor some common Jewish liturgy, cf. Schiffman 1986; Goodman 1983: 86. (Jos. *Life* 277, 290-295 probably reflects a more common custom of synagogue prayers, but not necessarily common recitation.) Some common prayer probably did exist at least in Palestine, however; cf. purportedly Tannaitic traditions in b. Ber. 28b, 29a and Herford's possible case regarding Samuel haKaton (1966: 129-32).

140. In my commentary on John (with Hendrickson Publishers) scheduled for publication shortly after this one, I allow for more tradition flowing from the conflict with Jamnia, both because of the later date and because of internal evidence in the Fourth Gospel; but even there the Birkath probably functions more as an example of conflict than its cause.

141. The Birkath would not itself accomplish a formal excommunication (Katz 1984: 46-49), though early evidence seems to exist for the full *ḥerem*: see Horbury 1985: 13-38; cf. R. Eliezer in p. Moʿed Qat. 3:1, §6. (In later times, rabbinic grounds for excommunication could include casting doubt on a ruling of the sages, even if one did so on the basis of the sages' words — p. Moʿed Qat. 3:1, §§7, 9.) The nature of any attempts to drive schismatics from synagogues would also have varied from place to place in the early period (see also Overman 1990b: 53). But such a curse would have made most "schismatics" feel unwelcome (Katz 1984: 51; Hare 1967: 56).

142. Hagner 1996: 41-42, 64 cites, e.g., Hebrews and material in Dunn 1983: 10; see also France 1989: 101.

143. See Stuhlmacher 1991b: 16; Bauckham 1998a: 33-36, for early Christians. Davies and Allison 1997: 700 complain that modern scholars underestimate the impact of larger changes on local communities, noting that first-century couriers could get a letter from Rome to London in a week; the seventeenth-century doctrine of Sabbatai Zevi spread throughout all Europe in less than three years; and the Reformation's most significant impact spread through much of Europe in five years.

thought of them, even though most of the common people did not know or attend to the intricacies of their scribal conclusions.

Some scholars have regarded Matthew as anti-Jewish (Cook 1983; cf. van Tilborg 1972b: 96-97), but their position needs to be qualified or rejected.[144] One need survey only some of the genuine anti-Judaism of Matthew's Gentile contemporaries (e.g., claims recorded in Jos. *Apion* 2.145: Moses was a deceiver and Jewish laws promoted immorality) to recognize the difference. Matthew writes as a Jewish Christian critiquing other Jews, especially the leadership, just as Israel's prophets critiqued Israel from within. Amy-Jill Levine's observations are apropos (1988: 99):

> . . . to claim that the entire Jewish world has aligned itself against Jesus and his church is incorrect. The Jewish leaders are most accurately to be compared not with coreligionists such as the sinners, prostitutes, and lepers lacking full or equal participation in the cultus but with members of other elite, exploitive groups: the Roman rulers, those who attempt to control the church through domination rather than those who guide through service, even the disciples of Jesus and of John who on occasion perceive themselves to be better than those more distanced from the prophetic figures.

Matthew provides positive historical precedents for the Gentile mission in Jesus' life and ministry, but rarely at the expense of his own people's identity. Matthew may emphasize divine judgment on Jerusalem, but this no more constitutes a repudiation of Israel or of his own Jewish heritage than the same theme in 4 Ezra or 2 Baruch does (Davies and Allison 1997: 202).

A majority of commentators believe that Matthew's audience had already decisively broken with the synagogue when the Gospel was written, although the Gospel preserves traces of earlier conflict.[145] Yet an increasing number of scholars doubt that Matthew's audience had completely ruptured with the synagogues[146] or question whether the evidence is decisive in either direction.[147] Some differences between the two positions may be semantic; the Matthean Christians clearly held their own structures distinguishable from the synagogue

144. As many scholars recognize; see Stanton 1984; idem 1993: 146-68; cf. Harrington 1980: 13, 95-97; idem 1989a; Niedner 1989. This is not to deny Matthew's later exploitation by anti-Semites (e.g., Hare 1979: 27).

145. E.g., Strecker 1966; Meier 1979: 15-17; Meier in Brown and Meier 1983: 49; Meeks 1986: 137; Gundry 1991; Stanton 1993: 6-7, 124-31.

146. E.g., Hummel 1963; Saldarini 1991; idem 1994; White 1991: 217; cf. Kingsbury 1991: 265.

147. Cf. Hagner 1993: lxviii. Overman 1989: 338 thinks that the Matthean community view themselves as a persecuted minority withdrawing from the world (for the Gospel's providing cohesion for a persecuted sectarian group cf. also Stanton 1992a; idem 1993: 91-98). Various scholars also point to "their" synagogues in 4:23; 9:35; 13:54, as distinct perhaps from "ours"; but this argument's weight is questionable, since one cannot explain Mk 1:39's identical phrase on the basis of Mark's "sectarian" Judaism. On "Q" Christians still seeing themselves as part of Judaism, see Tuckett 1993.

communities (Stanton 1993: 130); but this concession to the majority view need in no way suggest that they had broken with their own ethnic heritage.

Concurring with the perspectives of what is still probably the minority view, I find in the Gospel an author and audience intensely committed to their heritage in Judaism while struggling with those they believe to be its illegitimate spokespersons.[148] On this reading, Matthew writes to Jewish Christians who, in addition to being part of their assemblies as believers in Jesus, are fighting to remain part of their local synagogue communities.[149] Even if local authorities or Judean leaders with influence in the local situation have sought to expel them, they have not yet (and perhaps never did) ceased to regard themselves as Jewish by culture and faith. Nor is it easily conceivable (except to later Gentile Christians) that first- or second-generation Jewish Christians would have abandoned ethnic ties merely in reaction to those whom they considered illegitimate guardians of their heritage.[150] As Davies and Allison complain (1997: 695),

> Modern scholars sometimes leave the impression that a Jewish believer in Jesus could leave Judaism as easily as a person can today leave, let us say, the Methodist Church for the Episcopalian. . . . But . . . to leave Judaism meant . . . to move from one society to another: it involved the painful severing not only of family and cultic ties but being cut off from the whole life of a community upon which one was socially and economically dependent.

Thus I concur with Overman's claim (1996: 10): Matthew does not represent a conflict between Jews and "Christians" as mutually exclusive groups, but "details the tensions and issues that existed between different Judaisms at the close of the first century C.E. in Palestine."

Claiming that Matthew's primary audience is essentially Jewish Christian does not imply that it excluded Gentile converts;[151] it suggests only that those Gentile converts recognized that in converting to Christianity they were adopting a Jewish faith and with it some elements of the Jewish culture that had brought it

148. Boccaccini 1991: 16-19 views early Christianity as a whole as a form of early Judaism, a thesis that accurately reflects earliest Christianity's self-perception.

149. By "synagogue communities" I mean the social ties within the local communities, rather than only Sabbath prayer services. But even in the case of Sabbath gatherings, if Jewish Christians met early on Sunday mornings (cf. Acts 20:7) they would remain free to attend Sabbath services in the synagogues. It is highly doubtful that early Jewish Christians, unlike later Gentile Christians, believed the Sabbath had been changed to Sunday (a change lacking in first-century attestation). (*Minim* emphasize the holiness of Sunday in b. Ta'an. 27b, but this is the third century, and it is doubtful that most Jewish Christians would have accepted an eighth-day Sabbath based on the Epistle of Barnabas.)

150. Horsley may well be right that a Galilean Christianity *external* to Judaism does not predate Constantine (1995: 105-6).

151. Schnackenburg 1985: 10 contends that Matthew's audience includes Gentile as well as Jewish Christians, but that Matthew himself is more at home in Jewish views and modes of expression.

to them.[152] As far apart as Jewish Christians and many non-Christian synagogue leaders may have felt themselves, to outsiders a sect that claimed the one God of Israel and Israel's Bible and that originated in a messianic matrix on Jewish soil could not have appeared far from Judaism. That sort of distinction could take place only after Gentile Christianity became a sufficiently dominant force to influence public perceptions and discourse concerning it.[153] Further, even in most Diaspora cities where Jews and Gentiles shared the same city, Jews (like other ethnic minorities) most often congregated in their own parts of the city. House churches within walking distance for most members would therefore most often involve their own ethnic community (although exceptions in some cities, like Corinth, are likely).

Of all four Gospels, the language and method of Matthew most closely resemble those of the part of Pharisaic scribalism growing into the emerging rabbinic movement.[154] Noting the similarities, Overman even sees early rabbinic Judaism and Matthean Christianity as "fraternal twins" (1990b: 160). Whether Matthew reflects some "rabbinic" thought or simply more popular Jewish scribal currents also found in early rabbinic traditions, the parallels are noteworthy. Some scholars have rightly pointed out the evidence of Christian scribes in Matthew (13:52; 23:34; see Stendahl 1968; Cope 1976), people ready to make disciples of the Gentiles (28:19; cf. Harrington 1980: 96). Probably Matthew responds to Jewish charges that Christians oppose the law, a charge his Gospel therefore emphatically denies (5:17-20; cf. Smalley 1977: 185).[155] Thus as early as the sixteenth century Sebastian Münster called Matthew a "new Torah" (Lapide 1984: 55).

Of course, Matthew's readers are not so fortunate as to be facing only one problem (cf. also Stanton 1993: 3). Scholars who suggest that false teachers provide a threat to his community are undoubtedly also correct (cf. Thompson 1970: 258-64). One may note that condemnations of the scribes and Pharisees (3:7-10;

152. As Overman 1996: 229 notes, other early Diaspora Christians (e.g., Acts 15:1-20; Rom 9:25-30) and Jews (Philo *Mos.* 2.43; *Spec.* 1.97; 2.165-67; *Praem.* 114) also discussed how Gentiles could become part of their Jewish communities. That Matthew does so less than some others (Overman 1996: 230-31) stems from his scope as a biographer of Jesus, for Luke may emphasize it less than Matthew, yet Luke authored Acts. The Pauline position that such Jewish culture was not normative for Gentile converts is more nuanced, but if that debate had ever been part of the Matthean communities (as one would expect if they grew near Antioch), it does not clearly register in Matthew's Gospel. Perhaps some compromise position was deemed acceptable, as in Acts 15:20 or as in the case of Gentile God-fearers in the synagogues, except that they would be accepted as full members. Gentiles could have converted as they normally would to Judaism, but had these been the circles of Matthew's Gospel, it would be more difficult to explain its Gentile mission and especially its early acceptance by catholic Gentile Christendom.

153. Thus Schiffman dates the separation of Jewish Christians from Judaism to the Bar Kochba period and the major influx of Gentile Christians into Palestine (1985: 75-78). Even then, I suspect that many Jewish Christians marginalized from Gentile Christianity remained faithful to their heritage in Judaism.

154. Compare also Goulder 1974; Bonnard 1963; Ellis 1974: 3; Gundry 1982: 606; cf. Vermes 1993: 73.

155. Matthew is not reacting against Paul (cf. Davies 1967a: 27-28).

12:24, 33-34) coalesce with warnings regarding false charismatic prophets (7:15-23; 24:24). Likewise, judgments against the false religious leaders of Jesus' day (23:13-29) serve as a warning to religious leaders of the end-time generations (24:45-51).[156] But most of all, Matthew probably functions as a discipling manual, a "handbook" of Jesus' basic life and teaching, relevant to a Jewish-Christian community engaged in the Gentile mission and deadlocked in scriptural polemic with their local synagogue communities.

Matthew and "Historical Jesus" Research

A central character's "great deeds" generally comprise the bulk of an ancient biographical narrative, and the Gospels fit this prediction (Burridge 1992: 208). In other words, biographies were *about* someone in particular. Aside from the 42.5 percent of Matthew's verbs that appear directly in Jesus' teaching, Jesus himself is the subject of 17.2 percent of Matthew's verbs; the disciples, 8.8 percent; those to whom Jesus ministers, 4.4 percent; and the religious establishment, 4.4 percent. Even in his absence he often remains the subject of others' discussions (14:1-2; 26:3-5). Thus, as was common in ancient biographies (and no other genre), at least half of Matthew's verbs involve the central figure's "words and deeds" (Burridge 1992: 196-97, 202). The entire point of using this genre is that it focuses on Jesus himself, not simply on early Christian experience (Burridge 1992: 256-58).[157] Thus it is consonant with Matthew's purpose to inquire, to the extent the extant evidence will allow, into the degree to which his portrait of Jesus coheres with historical data.

Nevertheless, the available data for such an inquiry lend themselves to a variety of interpretations, depending on one's interpretive grid. History has passed a negative verdict on most of the past two centuries of "historical Jesus" research.[158]

156. Matthew's own community was probably more susceptible to false charismatics precisely because he and his community were charismatic, not because they were anticharismatic (cf. 5:12; 23:34; Michaels 1976: 309-10).

157. Ancient biographies included both "flat" and "round" characters (Burridge 1992: 182-84); rather than directly analyzing character, ancient biographers more often displayed "character through deeds and words" (Burridge 1992: 205, 208; e.g., Mt 8:27; 9:36). Lucian criticizes historians who merely praise their own leaders and slander the enemy (*History* 7-8). Although some characters were wholly good (like Matthew's Jesus; cf. Josephus's Moses or Josiah, Feldman 1992f; 1993d) or bad (like Matthew's religious leaders; cf. Josephus's Jeroboam, Feldman 1993c), ancient biographers and historians reported various character traits (Corn. Nep. 4 [Pausanias], 1.1; 11 [Iphicrates], 3.2) and often rounded characters on both sides of a conflict (e.g., Dion. Hal. 9.39.1-6; Feldman 1994c), including their heroes (Dion. Hal. 8.60.1-2; 8.61.1-3; Arrian *Alex.* 3.18.12; 4.7.4; 4.8.1–4.9.6; Lavery 1994). Reporting fears and motives on both sides in a conflict of the distant past increases suspense and praise for the victor, while augmenting the enemy's nobility deepens tragic pathos (e.g., the Albans in Dion. Hal. bk. 3).

158. Crossan 1991a: xxvii-xxviii puts the matter quite well (cf. similarly Meier 1991a: 3), but he then proposes a methodology to circumvent the impasse (xxviii-xxix) that in my opinion fails for lack of adequate attention to the Jewish and, despite his claim, Greco-Roman context.

While quests for the historical Jesus have started with the reasonable assumption that later orthodox Christology should not be read into our earliest accounts of Jesus, they have almost invariably read Jesus in light of too narrow a background (e.g., a revolutionary, a teacher, a prophet, or otherwise, but rarely more than one at a time) or as a reflection of their own values.[159] Unfortunately, some quests have also ignored basic historical constraints — such as the radically eschatological predecessor (John the Baptist) and followers of Jesus who make a noneschatological Jesus highly improbable (Johnson 1996: 25). Although scholars after Schweitzer for a time gave up the picture of Jesus as a comfortable, noneschatological sage, some have returned to this position, prompting one critic to remark, "There is something disturbingly familiar about a mildly reforming, sagacious teacher, who . . . does not use language and imagery that promises the reversal of the rulers of the world" (Overman 1990a: 195). As Meier complains (1991a: 177):

> A tweady poetaster who spent his time spinning out parables and Japanese koans, a literary aesthete who toyed with 1st-century deconstructionism, or a bland Jesus who simply told people to look at the lilies of the field — such a Jesus would threaten no one, just as the university professors who create him threaten no one.

It is hard to explain how the harmless, noneschatological sage of the Jesus Seminar, Crossan, Mack, and others, like that of the nineteenth-century lives of Jesus, would get himself crucified (cf. Meier 1991a: 177; Stanton 1995a: 177).[160] Admittedly, the historical method can give us only a partial picture of the Jesus who lived in history (Meier 1991a: 21-31); but the broader the base of evidence, the fuller the picture we can likely construct.

Because the commentary proper cannot provide as much background as I would like for recurrent themes every time they occur, I will provide a brief treatment of some of Matthew's primary christological motifs here. Further, because the commentary must focus especially on social-historical interpretation rather than investigating the historical reliability of Matthew's traditions (though I will not neglect that investigation entirely), I will address the historical roots of Matthew's christological motifs most fully here.

I am working from two basic methodological assumptions. First, much evidence suggests that Palestinian Judaism was very hellenized, although the Greco-Roman world on the whole was far less Judaized (e.g., Hengel 1974a; Lieberman 1962). Second, and consequently, a confluence of Jewish and helle-

159. Since Schweitzer 1968, scholars have periodically remarked on how frequently presuppositions shape one's conclusions in Jesus research (e.g., Stanton 1995a: 145), a practice to which even the Jesus Seminar objects in principle (Funk 1993: 5). For summaries of the first quest, see Schweitzer 1968; for the first and second quests, Thompson 1985: 90-111; for all three, briefly Wright 1992b: 1-18; for the third quest, see especially Witherington 1995.

160. Johnson 1996: 41 challenges the Jesus Seminar's claim to be representative of mainstream Gospels scholarship in its skepticism concerning Jesus' eschatology. For a full refutation of those who doubt Jesus' eschatological orientation, see Allison 1998: 95-130.

nistic motifs is Jewish, and cannot be purely hellenistic with no regard for traditional Jewish components. Thus I reject the view that Jesus, though Jewish by birth, was more "hellenistic" in his behavior (Mack 1988: 87n.7).

Jesus as a Teacher and Prophet

Jesus as a Teacher

Matthew portrays Jesus in a variety of ways that neither he nor his audience would have regarded as mutually exclusive. First, he portrays Jesus as a teacher, for example, in the Sermon on the Mount; others, including Jesus' enemies, also recognized that he filled this role, inadequate as it was to describe him fully (9:11; 12:38; 17:24; 22:16, 24, 36).[161] Perhaps because Matthew heavily emphasizes teaching, "understanding" also becomes a central motif in his Gospel (9:13; 12:7; 13:14-15, 23, 51; 15:10, 16; 16:9, 11-12; 17:13; 22:29; 24:15, 39). Matthew could simply have derived this motif from Mark, who also emphasizes it (Mk 4:12-13, 33-34; 6:52; 7:14, 18; 8:17, 21; 9:31),[162] but he sometimes adds it to Mark or develops it (e.g., Mt 13:23, 51).[163]

The available evidence clearly indicates (and few would dispute) that Matthew is historically correct: Jesus was a teacher. Although scribes in the ancient Mediterranean world in general were executors of legal documents (e.g., *CPJ* 1:12, 18, 21, 70, etc.; Goodman 1983: 59), a position that sometimes included high status (e.g., *B.G.U.* 1256.1-2; *P. Tebt.* 39.1), a more significant role traditionally befell some Jewish scribes in Palestine (cf. Ezra 7:6; 1 Macc 5:42; 1 Enoch 12:4; 92:1; Test. Abr. 11 B). Many scribes in Jewish Palestine also educated local children in the law, and the most skilled would have trained disciples to become scribes as well (Keener 1991a: 23, 145-46; cf. Stambaugh and Balch 1986: 99). Given their economic situation and religious education, probably a disproportionate number of priests became scribes (Sanders 1992: 170-71). Although a wide gap exists between prototypical sages of traditional wisdom like Joshua ben Sira on the one hand and local legal experts on the other (many, like Witherington 1994: 345-46, rank Jesus among the former), many people apparently expected popular teachers to straddle the continuum, and many teachers accommodated such expectations (see, e.g., m. 'Abot 1–3).

Some scholars, emphasizing that Jesus was a charismatic leader of some

161. Developing and perhaps more fully re-Judaizing Mark, who also presents Jesus as a teacher (on which see Robbins 1992: 82).

162. Robbins 1992: 167-68 finds in "understanding" a typically Greek pattern of thought, but many of his points here (e.g., rejection of the protagonist by authorities; cf. Jer 7:27; 11:18-23; 15:10, 21; 18:18-23; 20:2, 10; 29:26-27; 36:5-26; 37:1–38:13) could as easily be explained on Jewish grounds.

163. Cf. Luz 1995: 119, who suggests that Matthew reduces the Markan disciples' misunderstanding.

sort, are reticent to call Jesus a teacher of the law.[164] It is true that Jesus was not part of what later became the rabbinic movement, nor was he *merely* a Jewish scribe or ancient Near Eastern wisdom sage.[165] But many early sages traveled,[166] and it is unlikely that most Galilean Jews who saw themselves as faithful to God's law would have sharply contrasted charismatic teachers from other teachers of the law as if the former lacked legal wisdom (cf. Meeks 1986: 117; Hengel 1981b: 55-56). Although others besides scribes undoubtedly expounded Scripture in first-century synagogues,[167] Jesus' frequent teaching in synagogues suggests that many viewed him as an authoritative teacher, though not an ordained rabbi in the later sense (Hill 1979: 50). Most scholars note that many characteristics of Jesus' ministry fit expectations for sages and scribes, and whatever else Jesus may have been, he was clearly a Jewish teacher of one or both types as well.[168]

Each teacher had some unique or characteristic elements in his style (e.g., Tarfon's "May I bury my sons," t. Ḥag. 3:33; Shab. 13:5; Sifra V. D. Deho. par. 4.7.3.2; b. Shab. 16b-17a; 116a), and many scholars have commented on specific characteristics of Jesus' teaching style, some unique to him and others common to ancient Jewish teachers in general (see Jeremias 1971: 22-37; Stein 1978: 13-32; Tannehill 1975). For instance, few if any other teachers sometimes prefaced their words with, "Amen [Truly], I tell you."[169]

By contrast, other elements of Jesus' style are characteristic of his contemporaries in general. Most rhetorical forms in biblical wisdom literature, such as prov-

164. E.g., Freyne 1988: 249-50; Hengel 1981b: 42-50; Smith 1978: 22-23.

165. E.g., Jeremias 1971: 77; Vermes 1984: 30-31; cf. Borg 1987: 97-124. Vermes 1993: 54 doubts that Jesus would have used implicit quotations, opining that few Galileans would have been educated enough to catch them. Yet this misrepresents the educational status of the Galileans (perhaps acceding to Judean propaganda in early rabbinic sources), and Jesus' contemporaries did not shun such allusions aimed at those who would catch them (cf. Jos. *Apion* 2.178; Philo *Leg. Gai.* 115, 210, cited by Vermes himself, 1993: 186); further, can we suppose that later *Gentile* Christians added the allusions? Yet even Vermes would differ from Mack 1988: 64, who (exhibiting little feeling for first-century Palestinian Judaism) suggests that Jesus employed only wisdom thought and may have been as conversant in the Cynic thought of Meleager as in the Bible. Wright 1992a: 104n.41 correctly notes Mack's book as one "modern example of a hypothesis which constantly dismembers the evidence in the interests of a broad overall scheme."

166. Safrai 1974/76a: 965; cf. 1974/76b: 762; Sifre Deut. 43.3.7; 48.2.4, 6; Liefeld 1967: 89-133. Cf. the related Greek tradition of traveling philosophers (see Diog. Laert. *Lives* 2.22; Liefeld 1967: 26-59). Liefeld uncovers little evidence for itinerant rabbis before A.D. 70 (119), but this is hardly surprising given the scarcity of evidence for rabbis before A.D. 70 in general. Georgi sought Diaspora Jewish parallels for Cynic-Stoic itinerancy and various ancient missionary religions (1986: 99-101, 111-12).

167. Although elders and synagogue "rulers" undoubtedly welcomed scribal exposition when available (cf. Acts 13:15), in Galilee probably these leaders were frequently simply the village equivalent of municipal aristocracies, the most respected community leaders (see comment on synagogue "rulers" [9:23-26]).

168. See Davies 1964: 422-25; Davies 1966: 134; Stein 1978: 1-3; Carlston 1980; Meeks 1986: 117; Cohen 1987: 122; Vermes 1993: 50-70, 76-119.

169. Scholars often comment on the meaning of this distinctive trait; see Jeremias 1971: 35-36; cf. Hill 1979: 64-66; Aune 1983: 164-65; Witherington 1990: 186-88; Marshall 1990: 43-44.

erbs and riddles, continued among sages of Jesus' day (cf. Gottlieb 1990). Jewish teachers typically employed the rhetorical techniques of hyperbole and rhetorical overstatement (e.g., m. 'Abot 2:8; ARN 36 A); Greek and Roman readers were also comfortable with such figures of speech (cf. *Rhet. ad Herenn.* 4.33.44; Quint. *Inst. Or.* 8.6.73-76; Arist. *Rhet.* 3.11.15; Demetrius *On Style* 2.124-27; 3.161), a rhetoric disseminated perhaps most commonly in the marketplace (cf., e.g., *PGM* 36.69, 134, 211-12, 320). Jesus employed the same method, in each teaching seeking to evoke specific responses rather than provide direct proof-texts for subsequent theological systems (cf. Stein 1978: 8-12). It is particularly important for modern interpreters to remember this characteristic of Jesus' teaching, or we will find contradictions among his teachings precisely because we have not read his teachings carefully enough to learn to understand them as catchy figures of Jewish speech rather than developed doctrinal pronouncements. Like other sages, Jesus employed riddles, parables, and other figures of speech as evocative language forcing the hearer to contemplate his message (Witherington 1994: 3).

Jesus as a Prophet

Second, and closely connected with Jesus' teaching role, Matthew presents Jesus as a prophet like Jeremiah (Mt 16:14; 21:12; 23:29-32; cf. Zucker 1990: 292) and especially a prophet-healer like Elijah and Elisha (e.g., the healings of Mt 8–9; Mark especially develops this signs-prophet Christology).[170] That a follower of John should have been considered a prophet is hardly surprising (cf. Vermes 1993: 73-74). The Gospel tradition identifies John as the expected Elijah at various points (e.g., 17:10-13; Mk 1:6; Lk 1:17), elsewhere reserving this image, alongside that of the new Moses, for Jesus (e.g., Lk 4:24-27; 9:8, 30-35, 61-62; Jn 1:21; 6:14-15; cf. Robbins 1992: 54).[171] Unlike the Baptist, Jesus apparently claimed that his ministry was actually introducing (not merely presaging) the kingdom, and all strata of Gospel tradition confirm that Jesus performed miracles like those of Elijah and Elisha (cf. Meier 1994: 1044-45).[172]

170. On the new Moses motif, besides what appears briefly below under eschatological prophets, see especially Allison 1993b and comments on the relevant passages in the Gospel loc. cit.; in early Judaism, e.g., Knowles 1989; for greater detail see my forthcoming commentary on John (see also Glasson 1963a; Teeple 1957), though in that Gospel it is subordinate to divine Christology.

171. Nortjé 1989 may be correct in harmonizing these images by viewing Jesus as a John redivivus: John and Jesus may both have carried on functions of the eschatological Elijah. Roth 1992 may also be correct that Mark emphasizes Jesus as one greater than Elijah, whereas Matthew emphasizes the comparison with Moses. Comparison *(synkrisis)* was a standard rhetorical technique of the period (e.g., Demosthenes *On the Embassy* 174; Stanton 1993: 83).

172. See Jos. *Ant.* 18.63 (comparing the language for Elisha in *Ant.* 9.182) and (in a negative vein) the rabbinic sources also preserve this tradition of Jesus as miracle worker (Meier 1994: 621; Vermes 1993: 5), making it one of the best-attested features of Jesus' ministry. In view of Q tradition (Mt 11:4-5//Lk 7:22), Jesus probably viewed his miracles as special eschatological signs fulfilling Scripture (especially Is 35; see, e.g., Witherington 1990: 171; Sanders 1993: 167-68).

Those who insist that because Jesus was a sage he was not a prophet (e.g., Mack 1988: 57, 87n.7; cf. idem 1993: 31-32) assume exclusive modern categories that would not have held among Jesus' contemporaries. Some popular charismatic teachers looked more like prophets, and despite more scribal teachers' objections, the line between popular teachers and prophets may have remained thin for the masses. Some scholars have proposed that Jesus resembled an ancient magician (Smith 1978); this proposal falters because it ignores the lack of techiques that normally characterized magicians, whereas what Jesus shared with magicians he also shared with other categories of wonder workers.[173] More popular was the comparison of Jesus with hellenistic "divine men." Because the disparate details of the latter portrait paralleling Jesus were assembled only long after the Gospels, however, the latter view has fallen from favor.[174]

One need not look to purely Greek sources for charismatic healers; Palestinian Judaism had more orthodox healers, like Hanina ben Dosa. While Vermes may go too far in thinking that Galileans of Jesus' era listened to holy men like Hanina ben Dosa more than to priests or scribes, he rightly emphasizes that many people would have followed such charismatic leaders (cf. Vermes 1984: 5; cf. Hengel 1981b).[175] Although scholars increasingly concur that the historical Jesus was a "charismatic leader" in some sense, they dispute whether he was "(with Vermes) a charismatic healer like Hanina ben Dosa and Honi the Circle-Drawer or (with Hengel, Theissen and others) a charismatic prophet" (Sanders 1990: 3).[176] Given the fluidity of such distinctions in antiquity and the Gospel portrayal of Jesus as a legal teacher, healer, and prophet, one must ask why we are forced to choose among these options. Observers probably approached him in terms of whichever role they needed him to fill, although this probably meant in practice that most people approached him as a charismatic signs-prophet (cf. Mt 4:24-25; 16:14; 21:11, 46; Lk 24:19).[177]

173. See, e.g., Yamauchi 1986; Meier 1994: 537-52; Twelftree 1993: 190-207; Witherington 1990: 202, following Goergen 1986: 173-75. Few have followed Smith here, and some are scathing (Neusner 1998: xxvii).

174. See, e.g., Blackburn 1986; Tiede 1972; Holladay 1977; Pilgaard 1997; cf. Lown 1986.

175. Horsley 1995: 152-55 also suspects the Galileans' loyalty to Torah. From a Pharisaic standpoint such suspicions would be justified, but most Galileans undoubtedly saw themselves as loyal to Torah as they understood it.

176. Borg 1987: 15 correctly acknowledges that Jesus was "a charismatic who was a healer, sage, prophet, and revitalization movement founder"; yet he denies that Jesus was an *eschatological* prophet (ibid., 14, but based primarily on a very selective poll — 20n.25). For a critique of Vermes and Borg on the "close" relevance of charismatic teachers like Hanina and Honi, see Witherington 1990: 153, 182-83; Chilton 1994: 45. On Jesus as a prophet, see, e.g., Jeremias 1971: 78-80; Hill 1979: 50-69; Aune 1983: 153-69; Borg 1987: 150-71; Harvey 1982: 36-65.

177. Thus, e.g., Sigal 1986: 154 sees Jesus as both a proto-rabbi and "a charismatic prophet-figure."

Excursus: Early Disciples as Wandering Prophets?

Theissen creates and overemphasizes the type of early Christian "wandering prophets" (cf. Theissen 1978: 8-16; Gager 1979: 176).[178] Wandering charismatics may appear at times in early Christianity, such as in Acts 11:27-28;[179] the Didache;[180] and, if the prophetic element is dominant enough, in the activities of both Paul and some of his opponents (2 Cor 11:22-27). Elsewhere in antiquity, wandering prophets often traveled outside their land, preserving collections of oracles (Collins 1972: 6). But itinerancy marked teachers at least as much as prophets (cf. Dio Chrys. passim, e.g., *Or.* 3; 4; 80; Socrates *Ep.* 2 to Xenophon; Diog. Laert. *Lives* 2.22; Sent. Sext. 18-19; Liefeld 1967: 26-133; Bowers 1980: 318-19), and the landless commonly wandered as well (Goodman 1983: 39). In other words, mobility characterized first-century Roman society in general, rather than merely prophets in particular (Aune 1983: 211-12; cf. Boyd 1995: 122-23).[181]

The Jesus tradition, while charismatic, provides no evidence that specifically links him or his disciples with the wandering prophets proposed by Theissen (cf. Boring 1982: 59-61; Fiorenza 1983: 74). Paul himself provides our best concrete *evidence* for the lifestyle commitment commanded in the Gospels (e.g., 1 Cor 4:9-13),[182] and he is as much a teacher as a prophet. The travels of Samuel, Elijah, and Elisha indeed provide the strongest Palestinian models for Jesus' itinerancy, but these otherwise dominant models in the Jesus tradition make the lack of clear evidence for groups of itinerant followers of Jesus after the resurrection all the more striking.

178. Some evidence supports traveling Galilean teachers at this time, although it is probably exceptional rather than the norm (Vermes 1993: 46). For a critique of Theissen's "wandering charismatic" thesis, see Witherington 1990: 249. Galilee was small enough that Jesus could have traveled without spending most nights away from home (Overman 1990a: 194). For further discussion, see comment on 4:18-22.

179. All three NT cases of traveling prophets represent a specific purpose, not aimless itinerancy, and probably the prophets returned to their sending communities when they finished their mission (Acts 11:27-28; 21:8-11; 15:32; Aune 1983: 212).

180. Aune 1983: 213, however, notes that visiting teachers (11.1-2; 13.2) and apostles (11.3-6) are more prominent in the Didache than are itinerant prophets (13.1); Harnack overstated the itinerant nature of early Christian prophecy (Aune 1983: 202, 211). NT itinerancy (Philip, John) more often resembles the apostolic model (Aune 1983: 215); some cultists of the mysteries were itinerant (Burkert 1987: 31); and Theissen himself (1978: 14-15) parallels Cynics in the Greek tradition.

181. Aune 1983: 214 is too generous; he regards Theissen as basically convincing, but after undercutting both the prophetic composition of sayings for Jesus and the idea that such sayings reflect the social reality of those among whom they circulated, he has dismantled the whole foundation for the thesis.

182. Many of Jesus' radical sayings are hyperbolic (see Tannehill 1975: 73-76, 139-40), but even if they are to be taken literally, they may function as much as a critique of the community as a description of it (see Keck 1974: 450; Aune 1983: 243). Cf. the proposed competition of local and translocal traditions in Scroggs 1980: 172.

Further, one should not exclude all signs-prophets from being viewed as messianic (hence in some sense end-time) figures as well. First-century Jewish Palestine's most popular figures were probably the prophets of deliverance, leading messianic movements and modeling their ministries after Moses and Joshua.[183] These were signs-prophets like Theudas, who tried to part the Jordan, and the Egyptian false prophet who expected Jerusalem's walls to collapse before him, both seeking to anticipate eschatological deliverance by working Moses- or Joshua-like miracles.[184] Some of these signs-prophets may have envisioned themselves as possible messiahs; Josephus, who tells us of them, had good reasons to play down messianic claims (although he does fail to brand them "brigands" as he normally does revolutionaries).[185] Some of their followers undoubtedly understood them in such terms, and they could not help but recognize that their followers did so.[186]

Modern scholars who insist that if Jesus were a sage he could not be an eschatological figure ignore the intensely eschatological orientation of Palestinian Judaism as a whole in Jesus' day (cf. Horsley and Hanson 1985: 25); nor can teachers and revolutionaries always be distinguished (cf. Horsley and Hanson 1985: 119). Most of this forced-choice logic represents the strict imposition of modern categories on much more fluid concepts of charismatic leaders held by people in first-century Jewish Palestine.[187]

Excursus: "Zealots" and Revolutionaries

Evidence seems to tell against a *unified* revolutionary movement in first-century Palestine.[188] The term "Zealots" applies strictly only to some rather than to most early Jewish revolutionaries; Josephus seems to reserve the title for a limited group.[189]

183. Besides popular Judaism, the Mosaic prophet was important to the Essenes (Villalón 1972: 62-63; cf. Teeple 1957: 51-52) and apparently to the Samaritans (F. F. Bruce 1978: 39; Simon 1958: 61, 73).

184. Cf. Sanders 1985: 138, 171; Meeks 1967: 163-64; Horsley 1985.

185. See Hill 1979: 28-29; cf. Betz 1968: 68. Crossan puts Josephus's bias best (1991a: 93): "Nobody from the highest aristocracy on either side is guilty of anything."

186. The portrayal of at least some of the apparent revolutionaries in first-century Palestine as "social bandits" has much to commend it (see below). Although general studies of peasant culture shed some light on Galilean agriculturalists (cf., e.g., Malina 1981: 71; Scott 1989: 85-86, 92; Oakman 1992: 117-18), however, the picture of Jesus as a "peasant" (e.g., Oakman 1992: 120-21) is not very nuanced, being dependent on a rather broad definition of "peasant" (cf. Vermes 1993: 6; Witherington 1990: 75). Particularly objectionable is Crossan's characterization of Jesus as a "peasant Jewish Cynic" (1991a: 421-22; cf. 1991b), a type that one may claim with confidence never existed (Cynics were characteristically urban, while peasants in the strict sense were rural, and very few Jews adopted Cynicism).

187. Cf. Robbins 1992: 114; Sanders 1993: 153; Witherington 1994: 201.

188. Mason 1992: 206; Borg 1984: 27-28; idem 1987: 90; cf. Kingdon 1972.

189. Now widely held: Horsley and Hanson 1985: 214-17; cf. 190-243; Baumbach 1965; Smith 1971; Borg 1971; Sanders 1992: 281-83; Borg 1984: 35-36.

Horsley and Hanson 1985: 220-41 see the Zealots as peasant brigands in contrast to more educated groups of resisters (cf. Crossan 1991a: 217).

Josephus portrays the revolutionaries as "brigands," endeavoring to marginalize them from the mainstream Jewish population. Some modern scholars view the brigands before the Jewish revolt in the light of modern studies of social bandits.[190] The revolutionaries and bandits of Jesus' day may have had some support from Galilean villagers; at least Cumanus thought so (Jos. *War* 2.228-29; note, however, that the villagers *could* not have caught everyone — cf. Deut 21:1). But it is not clear to what extent Galilean peasants really supported the goals of such bandits, especially in the Lower Galilee from which Jesus came (see comment on 26:69);[191] one should also allow for the impact of a certain degree of urban unrest (cf. Donaldson 1990). Nevertheless, many bandits may have circulated among the peasantry (cf. Horsley and Hanson 1985: 77-85).

Much of this brigandage before the first revolt may have been "prepolitical" rather than aimed at an overthrow of Roman domination, as the objective became toward the beginning of the Jewish War.[192] Brigandage was common in antiquity and inevitably warranted execution if the brigands were captured (Lewis 1983: 204). Yet revolution was always a possibility. Many dissatisfied persons opted to work within the system, but many likewise hoped for its overthrow, eschatologically or otherwise (Sanders 1992: 35-43). Even Josephus informs us that some of these fancied themselves kings (Jos. *Ant.* 17.285), suggesting that the authorities could view the line between revolutionary and messianic sentiment as thin (see Mt 27:11-14, 37).

Although some Pharisees may have opposed the Zealot ideal (Davies 1967a), the Zealots, while distinct from other Pharisees, seem to have carried out a basic Pharisaic ideology in a more militant manner (Simon 1967: 44; cf. Neusner 1984: 26-27; see especially Jos. *Ant.* 18.4, 23-25).[193] Sanders (1992: 13-14; cf. pp. 280-84, 408-11) is surely right that the "Fourth Philosophy" was "largely Pharisaic in opinion, but whose members would accept no master but God (*Antiq.* 18.23; *War*

190. Horsley and Hanson 1985: 190 distinguish the Sicarii themselves from peasants and social bandits, relating them to a line of teachers of resistance (194-97). They suspect that Judas the Galilean may have advocated martyrdom rather than violence (197-98), but this is unclear.

191. Pace Crossan 1991a: 304-5; Horsley and Hanson 1985: 48-50, 69-70; Oakman 1992: 131. Horsley and Hanson 1985: 71 contend that the common people asked for justice against Herod when he killed the bandits, citing Jos. *Ant.* 14.168, but Josephus seems to refer to *relatives.* Villagers did protect bandits who robbed a servant of Caesar (72, citing Jos. *Ant.* 20.113-17; *War* 2.228-31), and *War* 2.253 may also be relevant, but Josephus himself does not indicate that the "inhabitants" ravaged by the brigands were nobles. The drowning of nobles is significant (*War* 1.314-16, 326; *Ant.* 14.431-33), but *Ant.* 20.255-56 does not explicitly differentiate "Jews" as gentry from the "masses." Jos. *War* 2.235-38 may well be relevant, but one wonders whether the elders in *Ant.* 14.167 are peasants since the speaker is a Pharisee. The nuancing of Crossan 1991a: 170 (their social location between the powerful and powerless) may be helpful.

192. Horsley and Hanson 1985: xiii-xiv, 250-51; Crossan 1991a: 194; Horsley 1995: 259. Josephus's sources regarding brigands appear weak for 6-44, though he reports some uprisings (cf. also Mk 15:27); but after 44 he supplies many reports of bandits with heavy followings (*War* 2.228, 235, 238, 253; *Ant.* 20.121, 124, 161; Horsley and Hanson 1985: 66-69).

193. Falk 1985: 57-58, 120-25 even decides (too narrowly) that the Zealots were Shammaites.

2.118)."[194] Most of their ideas were probably widespread in early Judaism (Horsley and Hanson 1985: xv), and eschatological expectation probably fueled all levels of Jewish resistance (cf. Horsley and Hanson 1985: 19, 76). Both resentment against Rome (Horsley and Hanson 1985: xv; Borg 1984: 36-47) and confidence that God would defend those loyal to him (Sanders 1992: 241) were also widespread. Josephus disparages "brigands" of all sorts except in the one case in which he need not do so, the speech he creates for Eleazar (Sanders 1992: 6-7).

Witherington 1990: 83 points out that some Pharisees did "basic training" (Jos. *Life* 11–21) and that revolutionary leaders could send Pharisees in charge of military contingents (Jos. *Life* 197).[195] In the earlier *Wars,* when the material is still sensitive, Josephus plays down both Pharisaic involvement in the revolt and Jewish involvement more generally, but in the later *Antiquities* a revolt as early as A.D. 6 appears to be part of a larger movement toward the revolution (Jos. *Ant.* 18.9-10, 23-25; Acts 5:34-35). Menahem of the revolt of 66-70 was descended from Judas the Galilean of the earlier revolt (Jos. *War* 2.433), and Josephus admits the revolutionaries' theological commitments (Jos. *Ant.* 18.4-5, 23); the evidence may not entirely support the early use of the title "Zealot," but it does support the continuing existence of simmering revolutionary sentiments through the early first century (Wright 1992: 179-80; Witherington 1990: 84-87, against Horsley and Hanson).

Was Jesus a revolutionary? Against Brandon (e.g., 1967: 283),[196] little evidence connects Jesus with insurrectionary activity; one can unfortunately argue almost any case when one rejects as unreliable the only historical evidence we have (cf. Harvey 1982: 14-15). Nevertheless, it is not difficult to see how some would have understood his popular appeal to the masses and open challenges to social customs as potential political threats. Yet Jesus comes closer to another paradigm of his day, namely, the paradigm that depended on God to intervene supernaturally to bring history to a close. Sanders 1993: 262 cites the repeated expectation in some strands of early Jewish literature that God would bring down a new temple (1 Enoch 90:28-29; 11QTemple 29:8-10) or fight for Israel and bring in the kingdom by his own power (1QM; Ps. Sol. 17:33-34). Some scholars think that Jesus went to the cross as a deluded visionary, hoping to provoke God's hand; Christian scholars more often affirm instead that he accomplished exactly what he intended.

---

194. Hengel 1961 saw them as a religiously motivated movement; Giblet 1974 believes that they saw themselves as more religious than political. While assuming specific religious beliefs, the nationalists did not represent an organized religious group (Salomonsen 1964). Applebaum 1971 regarded the revolutionary movement as a natural response to the Roman situation. Evidence at Masada indicates the Sicarii's religious commitment (Josephus 1982: 489, 499).

195. Josephus may have assumed command of many brigands himself; see the evidence in Horsley 1995: 266-67.

196. For the history of the revolutionary thesis, see Bammel 1984d: 11-68. For critiques of Brandon (and implicitly his first predecessor Reimarus), see, e.g., Cullmann 1956b: 8-49; Hengel 1969; Sweet 1984; Anderson 1976: 41-42; some even contend that the charge of sorcery was a greater issue (Horbury 1984: 183-95). Note also Stanton 1995a: 176 (Q's "love your enemies" is probably authentic). Sanders 1985: 68 regards Brandon as adequately refuted; see his own case on 231-32.

Jesus as Messiah/King

More important than his portrayals of Jesus as a teacher and prophet, Matthew hails Jesus as the true king of Israel (2:2; 21:5-9; 25:34; 27:11, 29, 42; of God in 22:2), that is, the Messiah (Christ; 16:16-20). Jesus' teachings have such special authority for Matthew's Jewish-Christian audience precisely because he is God's appointed king. (Witherington 1990: 180 provides sufficient evidence for the overlap of messianic and sage categories in early Judaism.)

Messianic Categories in Early Judaism

Israel's prophets had promised a final king and/or dynasty descended from David (e.g., Is 9:7; Jer 23:5), a theme that continued in early Judaism (e.g., Ps. Sol. 17:21; Fitzmyer 1974: 113-26). Because the king was the "anointed one," Jewish people often labeled this ultimate king "the anointed one," or "the Messiah," which the Greek translation of the Hebrew Bible regularly renders "the Christ." The timing of Daniel 9:24-27 had probably increased messianic expectation in the decades immediately preceding Jesus' ministry (see Beckwith 1981: 521-42).

Later Christians and Jews outside Palestine were far less interested in a "Messiah" than the Gospels were, which indicates how unlikely it would have been for the Gospel writers simply to have invented the tradition of Jesus' Messiahship (pace Mack 1993: 4-5). (That Greek Christians seem to have used "Christ" as Jesus' surname certainly suggests that the title did not originate among them!) Of course, the Gospels may simplify matters for their readers when they provide the impression that Palestinian Jews in general understood the term "Messiah" and expected his coming. Although most Jews who read the Old Testament believed in a Messiah, not all Jews had the same ideas concerning what he would be like.[197]

The Dead Sea Scrolls, for instance, may report a priestly community's expectations of two "anointed ones, a Davidic ruler and a priest rivaling his prestige (both priests and kings were anointed for office). The Zadokite priests who founded the Qumran community rejected the Hasmonean combination of priesthood and kingship in the same person (1 Macc 14:41-42; 1QpHab 8.8-10; 9.4-7; 11.5-6; 12.5); like some others, they anticipated a future priest (cf. Test. Reub. 6:8; Test. Jud. 21:1-2; Zech 4:14; 6:13). In time, some scholars contend, these sectarians believed in two or three Messiahs (e.g., Aune 1983: 123),[198] though others hold that they accepted one Messiah (Higgins 1953: 333),[199] that Qumran sectarians varied among themselves (Smith 1959), or that the documents in ques-

197. Cf., e.g., Villiers 1978; Goldstein 1984-85; Glasson 1963b: 8-13.

198. Also Villalón 1972: 63; Burrows 1958: 297-311; de Jonge 1966: 141-42; Brown 1957: 54-66.

199. Also idem 1966-67: 215-19; Laurin 1963: 52; cf. possible conflation in García Martínez 1993.

tion represent different stages in the community's development of thought (Longenecker 1981: 114).[200] The texts probably do imply diverse views (e.g., 1QS 9.11; CD 12.23–13.1; 14.19; 20.1; 1QM 11.7-8), but once we recognize that "anointed one" can mean anyone anointed for a leading office, the apparent conflict diminishes (LaSor 1956: 429; Gaster 1976: 392). The two "anointed ones" refer to "the anointed high priest" (in contrast to the wicked one in the temple) and "the anointed king of Israel" (cf. Silberman 1955: 82). Still, the Qumran emphasis on the anointed priest shows how a sectarian community could come up with very different ideas of the messianic era.

Probably more relevant on the popular level were deliverance movements surrounding prophetic messiahs (Horsley 1993b). Some of Josephus's "false prophets" must have been would-be messiahs of various sorts, though Josephus carefully avoids talk that would sound revolutionary to his Roman readers.[201] After the failed Bar Kochba revolt of A.D. 132-35 and the execution of rabbis who had supported him, rabbis, too, grew more cautious in their messianic expectations (Moore 1971: 2:346), though they still maintained messianic hopes afterward (e.g., Sifre Deut. 34.4.3; p. Ketub. 12:3, §13). In a first-century environment, however, the masses would surely interpret messianically one who promised an imminent kingdom and the meek inheriting the land, as well as implied a central role for himself in its inauguration (Witherington 1990: 272-73; cf. Marshall 1990: 54-56).

The pseudepigraphic Psalms of Solomon, which may be Pharisaic but probably reflect popular Jewish thought, expected a Davidic warrior Messiah (17:21-25, 32) similar to the one expected by the disciples in the Gospels. This view of a warrior Messiah was surely one of the most popular among the masses (cf. 1QM for a related picture). The very concept of the Messiah normally at least connoted a divinely ordained future ruler with political (not merely spiritual) rule (a criterion that many Jewish people felt Jesus had failed to satisfy).[202]

Evidence for Jesus' Messianic Claim

Even the earliest strands of Gospel tradition, however, indicate that Jesus taught that his disciples would have a role in the messianic kingdom, which would natu-

200. Also Driver 1965: 468-69; Priest 1962: 55-61. Qumran may have developed the Chronicler's dual leadership as well as reacting against the Hasmonean conflation of the two (Schniedewind 1994).

201. Cf. Kraeling 1951: 52; Freyne 1988: 194-95; Witherington 1990: 83; Josephus may have even toned down the biblical portrait of David for his Roman audience (Feldman 1989a). Peasants and slaves throughout the Mediterranean were especially open to enthroning prophets (Diod. Sic. 34/35.2.5-6; 34/35.2.22); leaders of such movements usually met swift retribution from the authorities (Diod. Sic. 34/35.2.22-23).

202. See Wächter 1976; Berger and Wyschogrod 1978: 18-19; Borowitz 1980: 21. Among some later rabbis, apparently any Davidic descendant who fulfilled the role properly could "become" the eschatological Messiah; cf. R. Joshua bar Levi concerning Hezekiah (Song Rab. 4:8, §3).

rally imply that he attributed to himself the role of Israel's king (Sanders 1985: 234). Despite the subsequent course of events (not conforming to any contemporary pattern for the Messiah's career), his disciples claimed that he was the Messiah, and his execution as king indicates that others believed that he considered himself king, despite his reticence to employ the title "Messiah" publicly.[203] One might add to this case other factors such as the Palestinian features of the Triumphal Entry narrative (such as the Hallel) that suggest the authenticity of the Entry, when Jesus approached Jerusalem as a king (cf. Sanders 1993: 242), especially because Mark does not explicitly cite Zechariah 9:9, which Jesus may have consciously fulfilled (see comment on Mt 21:1-9). E. P. Sanders thus thinks that many scholars have been too cautious about assuming that Jesus believed he was a king (1985: 307):

> Jesus taught about the *kingdom;* he was executed as would-be *king;* and his disciples, after his death, expected him to return to establish the *kingdom.* These points are indisputable. Almost equally indisputable is the fact that the disciples thought that they would have some role in the kingdom. We should, I think, accept the obvious: Jesus taught his disciples that he himself would play the principal role in the kingdom.

Sanders allows a potential distinction between the image of king here and the traditional title of Messiah, but only to elevate the claim still further (1993: 242).

Yet the Gospels provide ample reason why Jesus would limit public testimony to his messiahship.[204] Contemporary messianic figures *usually* avoided claiming their own messiahship, depending instead on others to acclaim them (Witherington 1990: 265-67). Also significant from a theological standpoint, his mission redefined the meaning of the term (cf. Marshall 1990: 89-90). Perhaps equally significant on a practical level, deferring messianic acclamation could delay the political consequences of such an acclamation — and hence control the timing of his own execution (on the "messianic secret," see further comment on 8:4). After examining evidence for Jesus' Messiahship (1994: 473-80), Brown concludes (1994: 480):

> . . . I judge it plausible that during Jesus' lifetime some of his followers thought him to be the Messiah, i.e., the expected anointed king of the House of David who would rule over God's people. Jesus, confronted with this identification, responded ambivalently because associated with that role were features that he rejected, and also because God had yet to define the role that he would play in

203. Sanders 1985: 307; cf. Chilton 1981: 168; Witherington 1990: 104; Stanton 1995a: 173-87. Fredriksen 1988: 123 regards as ambiguous evidence for whether Jesus claimed to be messiah, but notes that "he certainly died as if he had."

204. This is not to deny that he may have also drawn on 2 Sam 7:4-17 and Is 61:1-4 (Davies and Allison 1991: 600). Despite brilliant aspects of Wrede's thesis of Mark's combination of messianic and nonmessianic traditions (Wrede 1971: 228), its internal inconsistencies have rendered it untenable (Wright 1992a: 104; Burkill 1972: 1-38).

> the kingdom beyond what he was already doing. Such an indefinite and ambivalent answer could have constituted the basis on which his enemies gave him over to the Romans as would-be king.

At least very soon after his death, his disciples understood his kingdom in a manner quite different from typical messianic expectations of their contemporaries. Pilate had Jesus executed as a would-be king, but the messianic movement that followed him did not pursue military or political power; Jesus had planted in them an expectation for a messiahship "not of this world" (Sanders 1985: 294).[205]

Son of God

Matthew also frequently employs the expression "Son of God," which he regards as virtually interchangeable with "Christ" (cf. 16:16 with Mk 8:29). Kingsbury may very well be correct that this represents Matthew's primary christological title (1975: 40-83; cf. Thiemann 1989: 322-38), although others have challenged this contention (Hill 1980 thinks that "servant" defines Sonship, and Meier 1979: 218-19 thinks that Son of Man is as prominent as Son of God). At any rate, it represents an important title expressing Jesus' authority under the Father. The Aramaic expression in Mark 14:36 indicates that Jesus historically did call God his Father, but people employed the expression "son of God" in various ways.

How might the first disciples have understood the term? Various people in the Greek world employed the expression loosely for heroes (e.g., Grant 1986: 68-69), sorcerers (Smith 1978: 101; but cf. Blackburn 1986: 189), philosophers (e.g., Epict. *Disc.* 1.9.6), or reigning emperors (e.g., Sherk 1988: passim). But no less a scholar of hellenistic antiquity than Arthur Darby Nock long ago demonstrated that the early Christian usage of "God's Son" has little in common with hellenistic usage; the closest parallels function only by way of contrast (1964a: 45). Early Christian usage bears this out: Paul emphasized Christ's Lordship far more than his Sonship, perhaps to *avoid* specifically hellenistic associations of the term (Hengel 1976: 7). Further, not only does every known stratum of Gospel tradition and redaction portray Jesus as God's "Son" at least occasionally; the title occurs in one saying of Jesus that is nearly impossible to attribute to early Christianity (Mk 13:30). Matthew stresses it more than Mark and Luke do, and John, who stresses it most, is just as Jewish as Matthew (see Longenecker 1981: 98). Further, in extant Gospel tradition, Jesus is not merely *a* son of God, but *the* Son of God, his beloved and unique Son (see Hengel 1976: 24).

The Old Testament and Jewish tradition apply the title to the righteous (Vermes 1973: 195-97), those who belong to God (Hengel 1976: 21-23), and es-

205. Without immediate political repercussions, it is not surprising that the earliest Jesus movement does not spring quickly into the purview of Rome's historians; even Herod the Great finds little space in Dio Cassius (49.22.6; 54.9.3). Josephus happily compares Herodotus's neglect of Judea (*Apion* 1.60-65) with his neglect of Rome (*Apion* 1.66).

pecially to Israel (see Longenecker 1981: 97); but Matthew's identification of Jesus with Israel is not thoroughgoing enough to account for this title in his Gospel, and the Jesus of our sources is again not merely one son of God among many. While other figurative nuances of sonship like obedience, intimacy, and delegated authority (all natural aspects of the metaphor in a Jewish context) also apply, the ultimate Old Testament example of a special son of God was the Davidic dynasty (e.g., 2 Sam 7:14; 1 Chron 22:10; Ps 2:7), and at least some Jews still used the title this way in Jesus' day (4QFlor 1.10-11; 1QSa 2.11-12; perhaps 4Q246; in Longenecker 1981: 95; Stanton 1989a: 225; idem 1995: 154-55; Collins 1993; but on 4Q246 cf. Fabry 1993; Fitzmyer 1993). But our Gospel evidence does indicate that, at the earliest stage, Jesus allowed others to voice the claim rather than embracing the title for himself (Vermes 1993: 168), fitting the "messianic secret" noted above.

Other Christological Issues

Son of Man

"Son of Man" represents another important christological term for Matthew, although he borrows it from sources like Mark, who develops an eschatological Christology related to the son of man in Daniel 7 (cf. Manson 1961: 72-73; Longenecker 1981: 82-92).[206] Because "son of man" can mean a "human being" (and perhaps occasionally function as "I"), some scholars reject its eschatological sense in the Gospels.[207] Most, however, recognize that at least some of the "Son of Man" sayings use the title eschatologically, whether they derive the title's background from Daniel or, less likely, from the uncertainly dated Similitudes of 1 Enoch (Burkitt 1910: 66-68),[208] a usage perhaps also reflected in 4 Ezra (cf. 13:1-56; Boring 1995: 143; J. Collins 1992). When the Pharisees think that Jesus "blasphemes" because he forgives sins, Jesus demonstrates the "Son of Man's authority on earth" (Mt 9:6; Mk 2:10); he likewise claims authority for the Son of Man as "Lord of the Sabbath" (Mt 12:8; Mk 2:28). But Jesus' allusion to Daniel 7:13-14 becomes most explicit in Matthew 24:30//Mark 13:26 (to Jesus' disciples) and in Matthew 26:64//Mark 14:62 (to Jesus' opponents, ending Mark's "messianic secret").

206. While the allusion in Mt 28:18-20 suggests the importance of the passage for Matthew, Ellis 1974: 24-25 probably goes too far in building the whole structure of Matthew around Dan 7:13-14. At the same time, Donahue is wrong to suppose that Matthew rejects Mark's eschatological orientation (1973: 234-35).

207. Vermes 1973: 160-91; Leivestad 1972: 266-67; cf. Cullmann 1959: 138; Chilton 1994: 75-109. "That man" can function periphrastically (Pesiq. Rab Kah. 9:1; p. Ḥag. 2:1, §9; Ketub. 4:14, §1; Sukk. 5:1, §7; Ta'an. 1:4, §1; 4:5, §1).

208. Also, e.g., Tödt 1965; Ladd 1974b: 145-58; Lindars 1975; idem 1983: 99; Boccaccini 1991: 219. Glasson 1976 argues fully for an early date.

Although some scholars have argued that the later church created many or all of Jesus' "Son of Man" sayings,[209] "Son of Man" in early Christian texts appears almost exclusively on Jesus' lips. The proper, positive use of the criterion of dissimilarity thus would suggest that if *any* title of Jesus is authentic, this one is.[210] Although many scholars agree that Jesus used the title, they dispute the authenticity of one or more groups of sayings in which the title is used (especially the future "Son of Man" sayings). Yet if the title is authentic and barely used by anyone except Jesus, one should not a priori exclude any of the uses; and if Jesus proclaimed a kingdom and implied his Messiahship, one especially need not exclude the eschatological sayings. If the Gospels provide any indication at all, Jesus apparently defined his mission — both its suffering and exaltation — in terms of the son of man of Daniel 7:13-14.[211] For Matthew's source Mark, the Son of Man who suffered before his exaltation is the forerunner of the community of faith, his readers, now suffering great tribulation at the hands of hostile world-rulers (cf. Dan 7:21-22, 25-27). Matthew likewise interprets the title in view of Daniel 7 (see Davies and Allison 1991: 50-52). Yet because of its more common idiomatic associations, "Son of Man" retains an ambiguity that "Son of God" as a title for a specific person would lack. Thus Kingsbury suggests that "Son of God" reveals Jesus' identity in Matthew, whereas "Son of Man" is his public title, emphasizing how Jesus must relate to a world that rejects him as God's Son: "conflict" and "vindication" (Kingsbury 1984: 31-32; though contrast Hill 1984: 50-51).

Judge, Lord, and Mediator of the Divine Presence

In the Q traditions Jesus portrays himself not as a mere human teacher but as judge in the day of judgment who will be addressed as "Lord, Lord" (Mt 7:21//Lk 13:25; Mt 7:24-27//Lk 6:46-49; Tuckett 1996: 209-82 focuses on Jesus as Son of Man and Wisdom's suffering envoy in Q). Even John the Baptist recognizes the Coming One as greater than a merely human, natural messiah or teacher. He presents Jesus as one whose sandals he is unworthy to unloose or carry (Mt 3:11; Lk 3:16) — that is, as one whose servant he is unworthy to be (see comment on Mt 3:11). This supernatural figure would not baptize in mere water, but in the Spirit of God (for the righteous) and fire (for the wicked); he would likewise perform the divine role of judge, separating the righteous for eternal life and the wicked for damnation (Mt 3:11-12; Lk 3:16-17). If Matthew and Luke believed Jesus to be a merely natural messiah, they both did an inexpli-

209. E.g., Higgins 1964; Borg 1987: 14; idem 1984: 221-27; Boring 1982: 239-50.

210. Many scholars have concluded this; cf., e.g., Bowman 1943: 125-42; Jeremias 1971: 260-76; Kümmel 1973: 106; Gerhardsson 1979: 57; Riesenfeld 1964: 94-95; Marshall 1966; idem 1990: 63-82; Davies and Allison 1991: 43-50; Witherington 1992: 170.

211. Cf. Stanton 1974: 160-61; Witherington 1990: 234-45; Brown 1994: 509-14; pace Crossan 1991a: 238-55.

cably sloppy job of editing Q. One may dispute the witness of Q and other early evidence for a "high" Christology, but one should be clear about what one is doing: dismissing early parts of the evidence that do not fit traditional critical theories and then reconstructing a more favorable portrait with what remains.

Early Christian writers preferred to make their case through a variety of images rather than to focus on answering a small number of precise christological questions no one was yet asking in their century; but their images from the start include a superhuman role subordinate to the authority of the Father (e.g., Mt 25:31-34). Later Christian vocabulary has tended to follow the language of the creeds, but the Gospel writers had much more creative liberty and drew from a vast reservoir of biblical images for God and God's agents in history. A degree of subtlety and connection with prior biblical history and established Jewish categories of divine leadership may also reflect the apologetic context of early Christianity: whereas the masses were probably uncomfortable with the Jesus movement's portrait of a divine Christ, like the "crowds" in the Gospels they undoubtedly thought very highly of the signs-prophet and teacher from Nazareth. Thus the Synoptic writers, less concerned with lower-Christology schismatics than the Johannine community encountered, may have preferred to recount stories of a prophet-teacher who only occasionally revealed his higher identity. In this the Gospels likely follow their tradition; one may suspect that if the prophet-teacher from Nazareth thought himself to be more than a prophet-teacher, he might have followed the same strategy for communicating it in such a public context.

Matthew, like John, represents a strain of Jewish Christianity less hellenized than that of Mark or Luke; and like John, Matthew emphasizes Jesus' deity to monotheistic readers.[212] Whereas John uses especially the image of Wisdom to develop his Christology, however, Matthew also focuses on the Shekinah. Although Matthew elsewhere articulates Wisdom Christology (cf. Suggs 1970; Deutsch 1990; Johnson 1986: 189-90), he frames his Gospel with the portrait of Jesus as the present, saving God. Jesus is not only God present with his people (1:23), after his exaltation as Son of Man (28:18) equal to the Father and divine Spirit (28:19) and virtually omnipresent (28:20); Jesus is God's presence among his people (18:20), fulfilling a function Jewish teachers ascribed to the Shekinah, God's presence.

Yet for all this "high" Christology, it is hardly Matthew's emphasis (cf.

212. On Jesus' deity in Matthew, cf. comment on 1:23; Danker 1992. Witherington 1994: 336-37 rightly suggests that Matthew and John arose in the same sort of milieu, with Jewish Christian teachers "being trained in a school setting where sapiential thinking and Wisdom literature are important formative influences." He is also undoubtedly right (201-8) that Jesus presented himself on some occasions as divine Wisdom, and (339-40) that the Wisdom Christology in Matthew and John may account for the increase in Father/Son language already present in earlier strata of the tradition. (John seems to develop his sources in light of this pervasive Wisdom theme more freely.) Others have also concluded that the early Christians worshiped Jesus from the start (Wright 1992: 362; cf. Pliny *Ep.* 10.96).

Pregeant 1996); Matthew devotes far more space to Jesus as authoritative teacher, Messiah (rightful King of Israel), the fulfillment of ancient Israel's history and prophecies, and so forth (on Matthew's Christology, see especially Kingsbury 1975). One of the most prominent characteristics of Matthew's Jesus is how he fulfills Scripture, sometimes literally and sometimes as the embodiment of Israel's history (passim below). Matthew is clear that Jesus is the goal of the law and prophets, hence anyone faithful to the heritage and Bible of Israel must recognize and follow him.

The Kingdom of Heaven

With but four exceptions, Matthew employs the phrase "kingdom of heaven" rather than the phrase "kingdom of God" found elsewhere in the New Testament, including all other material from the Gospel tradition. Some other Jewish texts use "kingdom of heaven" as a periphrasis for "kingdom of God" (e.g., Sifra Qed. pq. 9.207.2.13; p. Qidd. 1:2, §24).[213] Matthew, preferring a usage that would communicate better in the Pharisaic-type circles he was engaging, naturally preferred this synonymous expression (Goulder 1974: 63; Jeremias 1971: 97; contrast Guelich 1982: 77).

The Hebrew, Aramaic, and Greek terms here translated "kingdom" usually signify the concept "reign" or "authority" or "rule."[214] Like the Old Testament (e.g., Is 6:5), Jewish teachers could speak of God's present rule (especially among the people who obeyed his law; see, e.g., m. Ber. 2:2; Sifra A.M. pq. 13.194.2.1; Sifre Deut. 313.1.3; 323.1.2; see Bonsirven 1964: 176; cf. Ps 145:2; 146:10). But the Jewish people also looked for the kingdom as God's future rule, when he would reign unchallenged (e.g., Is 9:6-7; 24:23; 52:7; Zech 14:9; Wis 5:16; Jub. 1:28; Mek. Shir. 10.42-45; Sifra Behuq. pq. 8.269.2.3),[215] as attested in regular Jewish prayers (see, e.g., Oesterley 1925: 65, 70). Jesus' picture of the kingdom, as well as of the Son of Man, may derive especially from Daniel 7, a passage less frequently mined by Jesus' followers (Witherington 1990: 242).

Because virtually every stratum of Gospel tradition testifies that Jesus regularly announced the kingdom, there should be no doubt that this was a characteristic emphasis of Jesus' teaching (Sanders 1985: 139-40). Scholars have sometimes debated whether Jesus emphasized a present or future kingdom, however. More clear evidence seems to favor Jesus announcing a future (impending) kingdom.[216]

213. This is commonly pointed out, both by scholars of Judaism (e.g., Bonsirven 1964: 7; Marmorstein 1968b: 93; Moore 1971: 1:119) and of the NT (e.g., Goppelt 1981/82: 1:44).

214. Frequently acknowledged by scholars, e.g., Dodd 1961: 34; Perrin 1963: 24; Betz 1968: 33; Boring 1995: 54; but contrast Aalen 1962.

215. For further data, cf. Moore 1971: 1:423; 2:309; Bonsirven 1964:176-77; Laurin 1958; Young 1989: 193; Targ. Ezek 7:7, 10 in Boring 1995: 53.

216. So, e.g., Sanders 1985: 151-54, 231-32; Allison 1994; cf. Burkitt 1910: 69; Schweitzer 1968: 223-397.

Yet many have noted an emphasis on the presence of the kingdom in the Gospels, especially in the kingdom parables and sayings like the one about entering the kingdom as a child.[217] If one examines the total picture of the Gospels, the kingdom is both present and future, as is widely recognized today.[218] It was only natural for Jesus and his first followers, once they recognized that Jesus would need to come again to establish his kingdom fully, to recognize that the anticipated kingdom would arrive in two stages corresponding to Jesus' first and second comings. If one does not arbitrarily exclude either set of evidence by virtue of posing a contradiction that the first generations of disciples would not have seen as a contradiction, both sets of evidence fit together adequately. As noted above, in the Gospel tradition Jesus implied his Messiahship, spoke of a Son of Man, and was introduced by John's prophecy of the Coming One; we may thus assume that when he announced the kingdom, he undoubtedly announced God's imminent rule in the final sense (rather than simply God's providential rule over creation or over Israel through the law, as above). But in his own person, the kingdom was present in a hidden, obscure way, just as the anticipated destiny of a mustard bush was implicitly present in a mustard seed (Mt 13:32).

Early Christians (most notably in the Pauline circle) continued the present and future tension in eschatology required by a Messiah who had not yet visibly completed Israel's eschatological hopes. As Jesus' resurrection is the first installment on the future resurrection of the righteous, guaranteeing that it will occur (1 Cor 15:20), so Jesus' demonstrations of God's rule at his first coming foreshadow the completed revelation of his rule when he returns. In the interim, according to the distinctive perspective probably shared by most early Christians, believers enjoy the Spirit as the "down payment" of their future hope (Rom 8:23; 2 Cor 1:22; 5:5; Eph 1:13-14; Heb 6:4-5). In short, the present significance of the future kingdom in early Christian teaching was thus that God's people in the present age were citizens of the coming age, people whose identity was determined by what Jesus had done and what they would be, not by what they had been or by their status in the world.

Some scholars, who maintain that Jesus' future kingdom is an unrealistic hope for modern people, label the kingdom a myth and translate it into existential language more appropriate for their own academic circles of thought.[219] But their position presupposes modern contempt for apocalyptic thought rather than

217. So, e.g., Dodd 1961; Jeremias 1972; Young 1989: 221; Vermes 1993: 147-49.

218. E.g., Stein 1978: 60-79; Ladd 1974b: 70-80; Aune 1972: 3-4; Dunn 1975: 89; Harvey 1982: 91; Davies and Allison 1988: 389; Witherington 1992: 51-74; Blomberg 1992a: 74; Meier 1994: 10, 289-506. Sanders 1993: 177-78 grudgingly concedes this possibility, but he remains doubtful that any authentic passage clearly teaches the kingdom's presence. But especially odd here is Mack 1993: 126, who thinks the authentic kingdom sayings in Q simply match the Cynic use of a philosopher reigning as king (in contrast to the LXX and other Jewish traditions of the reign of Israel's one God!); pace Mack, though the kingdom is not dominant in early Jewish texts, it is quite frequent (see Meier 1994: 240-69; cf. Vermes 1993: 127-30).

219. E.g., Bultmann 1951: 1:24; Perrin 1963; Tannehill 1975: 56; Borg 1984: 248-63; cf. Bultmann 1984: 137-38.

a detailed historical argument (see Sanders 1985: 7, 27, 125-27; cf. also Meier 1994: 242). Further, the future kingdom is hardly irrelevant to the persecuted and oppressed, who nurture hope that God's justice will ultimately triumph and vindicate them (cf. also Thompson 1985: 95; Thurman 1981: 20-27).[220]

Conclusion

Matthew's portrait of Jesus recognizes Jesus' role as the supreme teacher (23:8-10), for whose teachings his disciples must make more disciples (28:19). But Jesus' teaching is supremely authoritative precisely because he is the rightful ruler of Israel, God's Son the Messiah (16:16-17), who will return to judge the world (3:12; 25:31-32). Matthew derives each aspect of his portrait of Jesus from earlier, substantially accurate historical traditions, but emphasizes these particular aspects to address the concrete situation of his audience.

Internal evidence from Matthew and John supports the notion that Jesus remained a popular figure, and Jewish Christians maintained a measure of respect among many of their Galilean siblings; the threat to them is not yet a populist one. But Matthew and John both focus on the threat from the leadership, particularly the Pharisees (a tendency even clearer in John, perhaps a decade or more later than Matthew). After A.D. 70, one relatively small group of Pharisees and some allies in many synagogues may have become a dominant influence in Syro-Palestinian Judaism. According to the emerging consensus from archaeological sources, it appears unlikely that this group had yet achieved much influence on the popular level, but internal evidence from both Matthew and John, alongside exaggerated later views of the rabbis, suggests the possibility that this group maintained enough influence with the intelligentsia — the minority who would ultimately wield the most social power — to make the more popular Jewish Christians feel threatened.

This group of predominantly Pharisaic scribes and some synagogue leaders allied with their agendas may have set out to define Judaism according to their traditions, bringing them into direct conflict with the mission of the more numerous but less socially powerful Jewish Christians. Matthew writes to equip his readers in their responses to the Jewish legal scholars who challenged them, and also to call them to look beyond the horizons of Israel to another mission that had to be completed before Israel as a whole would come to repentance, that is, the mission to the Gentiles (24:14; 28:19). The Christians faced persecution (10:17; 24:9), counterfeit prophets (7:22; 24:11, 24), apostasy (13:21-22; 24:10, 12), and an incurable need for more laborers with Jesus' heart (9:37) — in short, the hostility of their society and the apparent inadequacy of their church to transform the situation for good.

220. Sim 1996 finds Matthew's "apocalyptic eschatology" appropriate to a sectarian community in crisis and conflict after A.D. 70.

CONCLUSION

Matthew counters these challenges with the call of Jesus to radical discipleship (8:20-22; 16:24-27; 24:13), Jesus' demand for obedient and holy living (chs. 5–7), and Jesus' promise of ultimate success in their mission (24:14; 28:19-20), albeit probably at the cost of most of their lives (10:17-39). But above all the teaching towers the figure of Jesus himself: King, Messiah, Son of Man, the rightful Lord of Israel whom their people would one day acknowledge (1:21; 23:39). The final judge, the true revelation of the Father (11:27), was the meek and lowly One who had walked among the first disciples and died for his people (11:29; 20:28; 21:5), the One who would also empower Matthew's readers to fulfill the task he had given them (10:19-20; 11:28-30).

Commentary

Matthew 1:1-17: Jesus' Background in Israel's History

Cf. Lk 3:23-38. Although their works were not always strictly chronological, ancient biographers often "began with matters such as birth, parents, ancestors, and subprenatal prophecies" (Aune 1987: 32). They frequently emphasized their subjects' ancestry, sometimes (as in Nepos and Plutarch) opening with it (Burridge 1992: 146, 178, 194; Jos. *Life* 3-6). Such ancestry could help praise the subject by evoking what was known about the character of the subject's predecessors (cf. Ex 6:12-30).[1] Matthew opens his Gospel by showing both Jesus' historic inseparability from the history of Israel and his inseparability from the Gentile mission already implicit in that history. He does this by listing Jesus' ancestors who evoke Israel's rich Old Testament heritage and by listing four Gentiles in Jesus' ancestry who came to participate in that heritage. In literary terms, he connects his plot with the broader plot of Israel's history (Wright 1992a: 385).[2] The opening verse of the Gospel introduces two ancestors who become pivotal characters in the genealogy: Jesus is the son of Abraham (the ideal Jew) and the son of David (the Messiah).

Son of David and Abraham (1:1). In this genealogy Matthew explicitly emphasizes Jesus' descent from David and Abraham.[3] Matthew first calls Jesus

1. Garland 1993: 14-15 rightly cites Quint. *Inst. Or.* 3.7.10 here. Considering the broader context, Overman 1996: 30 points out the importance of origin stories in Greco-Roman antiquity (e.g., the *Aeneid*).

2. One could extend this principle further, e.g., in the Lukan perspective of the Gentile mission rooted in Israel's faith; at least some historians explicitly noted that history set individual lives in a broader context (Diod. Sic. 1.2.3).

3. The chiastic appearance of Abraham and David in the genealogy (cf. Bauer 1996: 141) may reinforce this emphasis, although a nonchiastic parallelism could have accomplished the same, and Matthew may mention David first to recognize Jesus' unique messianic status not shared with Israel.

the "son of Abraham." Although some regard "son of Abraham" as a messianic title (Argyle 1963: 25; cf. Gordon 1965b: 143n.2), it is the "son of David" title that performs the messianic function here (1:20; 9:27; 12:23; 15:22; 20:30-31; 21:9, 15; cf. 12:3; 22:42). "Son of Abraham" instead refers to the status Jewish people saw for themselves (e.g., 3:9; 8:11-12; 4 Macc 6:17, 22; 18:1; t. Ned. 2:5; Sifre Deut. 311.1.1; 313.1.3; ARN 23, §46B), and evokes the promise to Abraham (cf. Meier 1980: 4) and the history of Israel. Not only this opening verse but the structure of the genealogy evokes Israel's history; following narratives further identify Jesus with Israel as its representative, the epitome of its history (e.g., 2:15; 4:2).[4] Jesus is thus the heir of Abraham par excellence, who can communicate Abraham's promised blessings to his people.[5]

Second, Jesus is the "son of David," a title of the rightful heir to Israel's throne (e.g., Jer 23:5; 33:15; Ps. Sol. 17:21-23; 4QFlor; p. Ḥag. 2:2, §2; cf. Fitzmyer 1974: 113-26; Nickelsburg 1981: 304; Rogers 1993; Kaufmann 1994). Many scholars have even seen an allusion to David in the number of generations Matthew enumerates in three sets of names; "fourteen" is the total numerical value of the three letters of David's name in Hebrew.[6] This numerical allusion, like some other proposed reasons for the use of fourteen here,[7] may be questionable; perhaps fourteen was simply Matthew's average estimate of the generations from one period in Israel's history to the next. Matthew preferred a round number for each set of generations, perhaps for ease of memorization (cf. 2 Macc 2:25); some argue that occasional Talmudic lists also edited lists to fourteen elements (Valler 1995). But he probably did so especially to imply that, as in the case of the new Elijah of Matthew 3:4, Israel was due for its Messiah to come when Jesus was born (cf. also Hagner 1993: 7).[8]

4. Cf. Kingsbury 1975: 12; Longenecker 1975: 141-43; F. F. Bruce 1972a: 64-65.

5. Later Jewish teachers (especially in those circles that later produced rabbinic Judaism) not only regarded Abraham as the ideal Israelite (even the model Pharisee in p. Soṭa 5:5, §2) but also as the first Gentile convert to Judaism (Pesiq. R. 11:4; Montefiore 1979: 43; Urbach 1979: 1:32; Sandmel 1978b: 181; cf. also on his proselytization of others, e.g., ARN 12A; 26, §54). Given Matthew's emphases in this genealogy, he could appeal to either or both nuances, though the Israelite nuance is stronger. Second-century rabbis may have toned down messianic speculation, hence the Son of David image (widespread in some parts of Judaism) after Bar Kochba, but even here it reemerged in later sources; cf. b. Sanh. 97b-98a; p. Sukk. 5:1, §7; Gen. Rab. 88:7; Song Rab. 2:13, §4; Pesiq. R. 15:14/15.

6. Many scholars favor this view: see, e.g., Martin 1977: 246; Davies 1966b: 14-15; Argyle 1963: 24; Meier 1980: 4; Gundry 1982: 13, 19; Davies and Allison 1988: 161-65; Lachs 1987: 3. Numbers could be used symbolically to spell names (e.g., Lucian *Alex. False Prophet* in LCL 4:190-91); on gematria see, e.g., Russell 1993; N. Cohen 1992; Lieberman 1987.

7. Some find six weeks of generations preparing for an eschatological sabbath (e.g., Foresti 1984; cf. Meier 1980: 3); other interpreters (e.g., Lake and Cadbury 1979: 151; see Johnson 1988: 200) detect three 490-year periods. If the traditions behind 2 Bar. 53–54 existed in Matthew's day, 14 may have appealed to Matthew from its use there.

8. However one counts, not all Matthew's sets come to precisely 14; but Jewish interpreters did not expect numerical exactitude (cf. the more than three sayings of R. Eliezer b. Hyrcanus in m. 'Abot. 2:10), and ancients could vary between inclusive and exclusive counting (Blomberg 1992a: 53 cites m. 'Abot 5:1-6). Fourteen was a reasonable round number of generations (cf. 16 in Dion. Hal. 1.9.4).

At any rate, the report is also appropriate for Matthew as biographer: there is little doubt that Jesus' family historically stemmed from Davidic lineage.[9] All clear early Christian sources attest it (e.g., Rom 1:3); Hegesippus reports a Palestinian tradition in which Roman authorities interrogated Jesus' brother's grandsons for Davidic descent (Euseb. *H.E.* 3.20); Julius Africanus attests Jesus' relatives claiming Davidic descent *(Letter to Aristides);* and, probably more significantly, non-Christian Jewish polemicists never bothered to try to refute it (Jeremias 1969: 291). Jesus' relatives known in the early church seem to have raised no objection to the claim of their family's background (Brown 1977: 507). Thus Matthew opens and closes the genealogy with a title for Jesus significant but rare in his Gospel: "Jesus Christ" (1:1, 18; against Fenton 1977: 42).

The character of Matthew's genealogy (1:2-17). That Matthew's attribution of Davidic sonship to Jesus appears historically reliable does not imply that Matthew writes Jesus' genealogy the way modern Westerners would try to write their family trees today. Matthew does have to omit some unhelpful generations and otherwise adjust the genealogy to fit his scheme.[10] But skipping some generations was common enough in ancient genealogies, and Matthew would have seen no harm in approximating generations, since generations had to be reckoned in approximate time rather than in exact years anyway.

More problematic to most commentators is the striking conflict between the genealogies in Matthew and Luke. Scholars have offered various proposals to address the discrepancy. Luther suggested that Matthew offered Joseph's ancestry, whereas Luke provided Mary's;[11] his grammatical evidence for the position is not compelling, however (Johnson 1988: 143-44). By utilizing levirate marriages, Africanus harmonized Matthew's genealogy (Joseph's biological ancestry) with Luke's (Joseph's legal ancestry by inheritance; Euseb. *H.E.* 1.7; Johnson 1988: 141). Modern scholars more frequently argue that Matthew provides the legal line of royal inheritance; but those who wish can connect this lineage with Luke's physical line by means of two adoptions.[12] The best alternative to

9. This is generally accepted, even if cautiously (e.g., Meier 1991a: 216-19). B. Sanh. 43a, bar., may preserve a tradition that Jesus was of royal lineage (unless it suggests connections with the Herodian or Roman rulers, or that he was about to take control of the people; both views are unlikely).

10. Albright and Mann 1971: 4 are surely correct that at least one and possibly more of the omissions stem from Matthew's use of the Greek version of the Old Testament here (1 Chron 3:11 LXX; see also Johnson 1988: 186). But because Matthew must have counted as well as transcribed the names from the Chronicler, it is unlikely that he skipped three generations by having his eye slip a line (ibid.). Either he adjusted the numerical scheme (as I think more likely) or his manuscript of Chronicles had already made the error Albright and Mann suggest.

11. Cf. also Feuillet 1988. Although we lack definite proof, preference for clan-based endogamous marriages (cf. Malina and Rohrbaugh 1992: 100) plus some archaeological evidence for group migrations from Judea to the Nazareth area could allow the possibility that both are from the Davidic line.

12. Johnson 1988: 142 summarizes their position. Nettelhorst 1988 suggests that Luke traces the lineage via Joseph's father, Matthew via Joseph's maternal grandfather.

harmonizing the lists is to suggest that Matthew emphasizes the nature of Jesus' lineage as royalty rather than trying to formulate a biologically precise list (contrast possibly Luke), to which he did not have access.

The question of historical detail cannot be settled merely on the thesis that people did not keep track of their ancestries, however. Priestly families' genealogies remained in public records before 70 (Jos. *Life* 6; *Apion* 1.31, 36), but because evidence for preserving lay genealogies in the temple is ambiguous, some doubt that most genealogies were accurate more than a few generations back, aside from one's clan (Johnson 1988: 99-108; cf. Safrai 1974/1976b: 753). Yet families interested in their lineage undoubtedly preserved their own ancestry, whether or not it was officially registered in the temple records (cf., e.g., Cotton 1995). Taxation status at times required peoples elsewhere in the Empire to be able to trace their lineage back as many as seven generations (see Lewis 1983: 41-42, citing *P. Oxy.* 109-21 and other texts), and a Roman of noble birth could disdain to marry his daughter to a man unable to "trace his family back even five generations" (Dion Hal. 4.47.4, LCL 2:427). If Luke traveled with Paul (see the Introduction) and could have interviewed James the Lord's brother in Jerusalem, he would likely have had access to the family's tradition (cf. Feuillet 1988, though Mary may have been deceased by that time).

But what about Matthew? None of Johnson's examples of midrashic reworking of genealogies (1988: 109-10) predates A.D. 70 or applies to living people who might recount their own heritage; nor were fanciful predictions of the Messiah's lineage (1988: 111-12, 115-38) ever based on a particular living individual held to be the Messiah. That Matthew does not simply fabricate a fourteenth generation to add to his thirteen in the final segment of his genealogy may also suggest that he is bound to some prior source (Davies and Allison 1988: 186; contrast Meier 1980: 5).

Matthew may thus preserve accurate historical information in this genealogy. Still, Matthew's list is plainly incomplete; for the five centuries between Zerubbabel and Joseph, he lists about nine names, whereas Luke lists eighteen (Davies and Allison 1988: 181). Further, it is clear that Matthew takes some liberties with his genealogy and expects his readers to notice that he has done so. Matthew especially follows the listing in Chronicles where possible (Gundry 1982: 14-15; Jeremias 1969: 280n.26). Yet many commentators on the Greek text of Matthew note that he makes a few theologically significant adjustments to Chronicles: Asa and Amon become the more righteous Israelite figures Asaph (the psalmist, 1 Chron 25:1; superscriptions in Ps 50; 73–83) and Amos (the prophet).[13] Just as Matthew traces Jesus' line from David's royal house via Solomon (cf. 12:42; contrast Lk 3:31), by subtle midrashic allusions he connects Je-

13. See Schweizer 1975: 24; Gundry 1982: 15-16; Davies and Allison 1988: 175. Taken collectively, these changes cannot be viewed as merely orthographic, pace Johnson 1988: 182. By contrast, Josephus presents Asa largely positively and even tones down Manasseh's idolatry; cf. Feldman 1994b; 1991.

sus to priestly and prophetic threads in Israel's history.[14] (Ancient writers could use genealogies to account for a descendant's character — see Ex 6:10-30; Aune 1987: 53. Similarly, Greek writers often connected their protagonists to past heroes characterizing ideal virtues — cf. Aune 1987: 84-85.) The possibility of Old Testament allusions in the genealogy's postexilic names like Zadok, Eleazar, and Jacob father of Joseph[15] is less clear.[16] But Matthew's contemporaries might not read all his possible allusions favorably: in 1:3-4 "Ram" becomes "Aram," reflecting the one spelling of the name in the Septuagint (1 Chron 2:9-10; contrast Ruth 4:19; 1 Chron 2:9 [another reference], 25, 27) that could also possibly be used to allude to the Gentile mission (cf. Is 7:1, 2, 5, 8).

The purpose of Matthew's genealogy (1:2-17). While scholars may debate how thoroughly Matthew has adapted available sources, exclusive attention to that discussion risks missing Matthew's real point. Even had Matthew taken his list unchanged from a complete and precise genealogy scroll, Jesus' spiritual ancestry is more critical for Matthew than his genetic ancestry (cf. Meier 1980: 3; Johnson 1988: 209-10). The names in Matthew's genealogy — like Judah, Ruth, David, Uzziah, Hezekiah, Josiah — would immediately evoke for Matthew's readers a whole range of stories they had learned about their heritage from the time of their childhood. Genealogies provided family honor, defining also in-groups and inheritance rights (Hanson and Oakman, 1998: 28-29, who argue that the apical ancestors Abraham and David provide honor in this genealogy — 52-55). By evoking great heroes of the past like David and Josiah, Matthew points his readers to the ultimate hero to whom all those other stories pointed. For Matthew and his circle of Jewish Christians, Jesus was not an afterthought to Judaism, a distinct and unexpected addition to God's plan in the Old Testament. Jesus was the goal to which Israel's lovingly remembered history pointed. Matthew thus establishes rhetorical community with his audience in his proem; proems typically appealed to audience sympathy (Kennedy 1984: 102).

Matthew makes this point clear in the opening words of his genealogy: the "book of the genesis of Jesus Christ" (1:1).[17] That Matthew starts with Jesus'

14. Even in Israel's exile he will find messianic significance (2:17-18).

15. One might wonder, though one cannot test, whether Joseph is the son of "Jacob" to allude to the climactic hero of the Genesis story (Gen 37–50; cf. Lk 3:23).

16. Jer. 22:24-30 could suggest that Jeconiah's line was unfit for royal heirs, but already in the OT his line was restored (1 Chron 3:17-19; cf. 2 Kings 25:27-30; Jer 52:33; Hag 2:23; cf. the ration tablets in *ANET* 308). Possibly Jeconiah repented (cf. 2 Chron 33:12-13; Jer. 18:5-10); this was also the rabbis' explanation of his restoration (Johnson 1988: 184, following Strack-Billerbeck). That Zerubbabel (exalted as a deliverer in 1 Esdr. 3–4) is listed as Shealtiel's son indicates that he inherited through the royal line of the firstborn; perhaps Shealtiel died without offspring (see 1 Chron 3:17-19; cf. Deut 25:5-10). Some later traditions are confused; despite Ezra's priestly lineage in Ezra 7:1-5, 4 Ezra 3:1 identifies him with Shealtiel. For comments on the textual problem, see Hagner 1993: 6.

17. Greek readers knew the first book of the Bible as "Genesis" (its title in the LXX). The phrase "the book of" could introduce an entire book (e.g., Tob 1:1; Rev 1:1; cf. *PGM* 13.343). But in light of the inclusio in 1:1, 18 and Genesis's application of the term to genealogies (in 2:4; 5:1; cf. 10:1), most scholars concur that this title applies to the genealogy, not to the whole Gospel (e.g.,

earliest ancestors and proceeds to his latest ancestors fits Old Testament (rather than Luke's and Greek) genealogies (Aune 1987: 121), but Matthew's use of "the book of the generations of" contrasts starkly with the use of that phrase in Old Testament genealogies. Most scholars agree that Matthew's phrase depends here on the expression in the genealogies of Genesis (e.g., Allen 1977: 1; Meeks 1986: 140; Johnson 1988: 186). Yet genealogies like those in Genesis typically list a person's *descendants* after this phrase, rather than a person's ancestors (Gen 5:1; 10:1). Matthew's point here is profound: so much is Jesus the focal point of history that his ancestors depend on him for their meaning. In other words, God sovereignly directed the history of Israel and preserved the Davidic line because of his plan to send Jesus (Gundry 1982: 10, 13; Patte 1987: 18).

Many people regarded ancestry and couples joining as a sign of divine rule (e.g., Hierocles in Malherbe 1986: 100; Epict. *Disc.* 1.12.28-29; Char. *Chaer.* 1.1.6). Jewish people in particular believed that bringing all husbands and wives together represented an act of divine providence (e.g., Pesiq. Rab Kah. 23:8; cf. Tob 6:17; Mt 19:6); some later rabbis even called it a miracle as great as the parting of the Red Sea (b. Sanh. 22a; Gen. Rab. 68:4; Pesiq. Rab Kah. 2:4; cf. Lev. Rab. 8:1; Num. Rab. 3:6). Because the Jewish people viewed history in these terms, genealogies could represent to them a testimony of God's providence in their ancestry, and Matthew's genealogy climaxing in Jesus would testify still more eloquently concerning God's sovereign plan for history in Christ. As the genealogies of Genesis 5 and 11 unify history between major figures (Adam, Noah, and Abraham; cf. Johnson 1988: 78), Matthew's genealogy unifies the defining periods of Israel's history and points them to Jesus.

Mixed marriages and the Gentile mission (1:3, 5-6). While Matthew's most obvious point is the connection of Jesus with Israel's history, however, another point would also probably strike his biblically sensitive ideal readers forcefully. Genealogies need include only men (cf., e.g., 1 Chron passim), so the unexpected appearance of four women draws attention to them (so, e.g., Edwards 1985: 11; Johnson 1988: 153). (So often were women's names lost that later Jewish haggadists sometimes had to make up names for important women characters, e.g., 1 Enoch 85:3.)

Gentiles in Jesus' ancestry. Had Matthew merely meant to evoke the history of Israel in a general way, one would have expected him to have named the matriarchs of Israel: Sarah, Rebekah, Leah, and Rachel.[18] Instead he names four

---

Kingsbury 1975: 10; Meier 1980: 4; Gundry 1982: 13; Stanton 1993: 12-13; Nolland 1996: 469-70), although in view of strong pointers in both directions Davies and Allison 1988: 150-53 ultimately contend for a double entendre (cf. Bauer 1988: 73-77 for the proposal that it applies to the section 1:1–4:16). Malina and Rohrbaugh 1992: 24 and Bauer 1996: 159 connect the "genesis" allusion here with the "end of the age" passage in 28:18-20, the former also noting parallels there with the edict that probably closes the Hebrew canon (2 Chron 36:23; but stronger parallels exist).

18. Later teachers often praised these matriarchs (Jub. 36:23-24; Pesiq. Rab Kah. 11:6; see also Kaunfer 1995), e.g., Sarah (1QapGen 20.2-10; Test. Abr. 3, 5, 6A; ARN 26, §54B; Gen. Rab. 20:6; 41:2; Num. Rab. 14:11; Pesiq. Rab Kah. 22:1; Pesiq. R. 43:4); for the popularity of her name, cf. Tob 3:7; *CIJ* 1:402, §543; 1:431, §593; 1:437, §608; 2:141, §942; 2:205, §§1124-25, 2:218, §1169; *CPJ* 1:169, §26; 1:187-88, §41; 2:124, §§179-80.

women whose primary common link is their Gentile ancestry: Tamar of Canaan, Rahab of Jericho (whom Matthew weaves into the Old Testament line here),[19] Ruth the Moabitess, and the ex-wife of Uriah the Hittite.[20] Indeed, most Jewish tradition subsequent to the Old Testament amplifies the record of their Gentile character (e.g., Gen. Rab. 50:10; 85:6; 88:7; cf. Zakowitch 1975; Jeremias 1958: 13-14; Johnson 1988: 167-70; Bamberger 1968: 193-95). Thus, for instance, Ps-Philo (9:5) praises Tamar's refusal to return to the Gentiles, and the Testament of Judah (10:6), against the natural reading of Genesis, manages to deny that Tamar is Canaanite while allowing her to remain a Gentile.[21]

Not all commentators regard these women as representative Gentiles. Many commentators instead link them to charges of either sinfulness or irregular births, suggesting that their names prepare readers for the scandal of the virgin birth in 1:18-25 or counter slanders of Mary's infidelity; as God vindicated these women of old, he would also vindicate Mary.[22] The "irregular" birth interpretation is possible (and not necessarily inconsistent with the interpretation of the Gentile mission above — Davies and Allison 1988: 170-71; Hagner 1993: 10), but if that were his main point, why would he choose these four women over Sarah, Rebekah, and Rachel, whose wombs God opened? The latter are more prominent and would provide better examples of "irregular" births in the miraculous sense he intends for the virgin birth. The scandal interpretation is more problematic. If Matthew were defending Mary against slanders of infidelity, why would he choose Tamar and Bathsheba, both of whom did in fact act immorally by the standards of his Jewish contemporaries? It is true that Jewish tradition exculpates Rahab and Tamar; Ruth is already innocent in the Hebrew Bible (e.g., Luz 1989: 109-10). Yet one would expect Matthew to use scandalous conceptions like Bathsheba's only if he actually believed the slanders of Mary's immorality rather than the virgin birth he recounts in the next paragraph![23] The whole point of Matthew's defending Mary might be moot anyway; some scholars suspect that the Jewish calumnies about the virgin birth arose after the time of Matthew (Davies

19. This particular element of the genealogy appears without biblical precedent (Rahab and Salmon were as many as two centuries apart) and, as far as we know, Jewish tradition (Davies and Allison 1988: 173; though some later depict her as ancestor of priests and prophets — Ruth Rab. 2.1); she may represent Matthew's way of drawing attention to and emphasizing his point by working another prominent Gentile woman into the narrative (cf. 15:22).

20. Schweizer 1975: 25; Reicke 1974: 118; F. F. Bruce 1972a: 65; Gundry 1982: 15; Garland 1993: 18; Reeves 1993: 93. Nolland 1997: 537-39 is cautious about linking Bathsheba with the other women, because she is mentioned only by her former husband's name.

21. A.-J. Levine (1988: 71-80) and others have raised reasoned objections to the Gentile interpretation, but Bauer 1996: 148-49 provides a sufficient response.

22. Brown 1977: 71-74; Stendahl 1995: 74; Stauffer 1960: 17; Tasker 1961: 32; Smith 1978: 26, 66-67; Laws 1980: 137; Harrington 1982: 13-14; Edwards 1985: 11; Freed 1987; Blomberg 1991; idem 1992a: 55-56; cf. A. B. Bruce 1979: 62-63; Lachs 1987: 2; Heil 1991.

23. The late tradition in b. Shab. 56a attributes some guilt to Uriah, but to soften David's; especially after rabbinic patriarchs claimed a Davidic heritage, many sages exonerated David in the affair (Shimoff 1993). The earliest tradition does not emphasize Rahab as a "prostitute" (see Lane 1991: 379; Johnson 1988: 162; Jos. *Ant.* 5.9).

1966b: 11; Johnson 1988: 158-59). Nor should one argue that Matthew merely wishes to present women in a bad light by his selection of the more unsavory examples early in his Gospel; the rest of his Gospel suggests otherwise (cf. 1:18; 15:28; 28:5-8) and favors instead an allusion to the Gentile mission (2:1-2; 24:14; 28:19), which speaks to disciples of their responsibility to cross cultural boundaries to spread Christ's gospel.[24]

Genealogies and pure lineage. The Jewish people regarded genealogies as important to establish the purity of their lineage (Jos. *Apion* 1.30; cf. b. Pesaḥ. 62b; p. Ter. 7:1; Johnson 1988: 88-95). Priestly genealogies were preserved in the temple records before their destruction in A.D. 70, those of aristocratic priests reportedly being traced into the preexilic period (cf. Jos. *Apion* 1.31-33, 36; Jeremias 1969: 280-90; Stauffer 1960: 14), and purity in priestly lineage was essential (1 Esdr 5:39-40; cf. t. Ḥag. 2:9; 7:1; p. Ketub. 1:9, §1). One presumes that other Jews who could would have taken pride in the purity of their Jewish lineage.[25] Yet Matthew seems to highlight the *mixed* nature of Jesus' lineage purposely! Admittedly Matthew probably believes this to be Jesus' legal rather than blood line (1:18-25), but such an observation in no way detracts from the importance of that line; Matthew lived in a world where adoption lines were significant and frequently qualified sons for royalty (e.g., Augustus with Tiberius, Suet. *Tib.* 23).

When Matthew cites these four women, he is probably reminding his readers that three ancestors of King David and the mother of King Solomon were *Gentiles.*[26] The Bible that accepted David's mixed race also implied it for the messianic King; Matthew thus declares that the Gentiles were never an afterthought in God's plan, but had been part of his work in history from the beginning. One who traces Matthew's treatment of Gentiles through the Gospel, from the Magi who sought Jesus in chapter 2 through the concluding commission to disciple the nations in 28:19, will understand Matthew's point in emphasizing this. Matthew exhorts his readers that as much as Jesus is connected with the her-

24. The view that these women were sinful or scandalous further fails to explain virtuous Ruth, whose most notable literary characteristic for Jewish readers was simply her ethnic alienation from Israel. Josephus draws a moral for his Gentile readers from this ancestor of David being so lowly (*Ant.* 5.337). But Jewish readers recalled especially her Moabite ancestry. Although a Moabite was not officially permitted to marry into Israel (Deut 23:3), God accepted Ruth the Moabitess because she followed him at a cost to herself (Ruth 1:16). (Jewish interpreters generally argued instead that Deuteronomy intended to exclude only male Moabites — m. Yebam. 8:3; Sifre Deut. 249.1.1-2; Pesiq. R. 49:2.) Subsequent Jewish tradition praised Ruth, Rahab, and Tamar (e.g., Ps-Philo 9:5; ARN 45, §125 B; Pesiq. R. 40:3/4; 49:2; Bamberger 1968: 195-99; Johnson 1988: 159-66; cf. Heb 11:31; b. B. Bat. 91a; Daube 1973: 33); in some traditions many prophets descended from Rahab (Sifre Deut. 357.2.1; cf. Pesiq. Rab Kah. 13:5).

25. One could deride another person by ridiculing his low birth, e.g., Josephus's employing common anti-Egyptian sentiment (*Apion* 2.41). Marrying an unconverted Gentile was reprehensible (e.g., Gen. Rab. 65:2).

26. Some later rabbis also tried to whitewash Solomon's intermarriages with pagans by suggesting that they were for proselytization (e.g., p. Sanh. 2:6, §2), but 1 Kings 11:1-13 clearly portrays Solomon's actions in a negative light; the wives influenced Solomon more than the reverse.

itage of Israel, he is for all peoples as well, and his disciples have a responsibility to let everyone know about him.

Excursus: Matthew's Infancy Narratives (1:18–2:23)

Like many ancient biographers, Matthew and Luke include information about Jesus' ancestry and infancy, here supplementing Mark (Burridge 1992: 249).[27] That most of the Gospel addresses Jesus' public ministry, providing comparatively little on the introductory matters of his early life, also fits the common pattern of Greco-Roman biographies (Burridge 1992: 197-98). Against this general, common pattern, what remains striking is that Matthew has constructed almost every paragraph following the genealogy and until the Sermon on the Mount around at least one text of Scripture. He thus invites his ideal audience to read Jesus in light of Scripture and Scripture in light of Jesus — to recognize that the person and work of Jesus are central to Scripture's character.

Are the infancy narratives historical? Because Matthew builds each pericope around Scripture, these passages naturally contain midrashic elements, but various reasons prevent us from assuming a priori that these passages are therefore necessarily unhistorical (cf. Hagner 1993: lviii; against Bourke 1960; Beare 1981: 82).[28] First, while midrash can lead to fanciful elaborations of biblical accounts, it need not do so; midrash essentially involves merely reflection on Scripture. Second, were Matthew embroidering the stories of Jesus' birth, one might expect him to do so far more thoroughly, as various Jewish accounts embroidered biblical births (e.g., 1 Enoch 106:2-3) or later apocryphal infancy Gospels (e.g., trans. O. Cullmann and A. J. B. Higgins, in Hennecke 1963: 1:363-417) embroidered Jesus' childhood.[29]

27. From Jesus' baptism to his resurrection, Matthew largely follows Mark's basic chronological and geographical framework (Schnackenburg 1985: 29).

28. Hill 1972: 77 prefers to speak in terms of haggadic elaboration rather than pure midrashic creation. Such haggadic elaboration or deletion could be used to answer questions posed by a narrative (e.g., Demetrius the Chronographer *Fr.* 5 in Euseb. *P.E.* 9.29.16; Jub. 4:1, 9; 12:14, 13:11, 27:1, 4-5; p. Ketub. 12:4, §8); to make a better story (Jub. 11:14-15, 13:18, 22), e.g., by adding names (Jub. 11:14-15; *Lives of the Prophets* 19, Joad [§30 in Schermann]; Ps-Philo 40:1; Rook 1990); to heighten the praise of God or the protagonist (e.g., 2 Macc 2:1-8; Jub. 29:14-20; Test. Job 9-15; Test. Jos. 3:1), albeit sometimes by fanciful midrash (Pesiq. Rab Kah. 4:3; cf. Artapanus on Pharaoh's behavior toward Moses in light of 1 Sam 18:17, 21-25 in Euseb. *P.E.* 9.27.7). Similarly, negative incidents could be toned down (Ps-Philo 12:2-3; Test. Job 39:12-13 (*OTP*)/39:9-10; 40:3/4), omitted (e.g., Jub. 13:17-18; 14:21–16:22; 29:13; Test. Zeb. 1:5-7), or justified (CD 4:20–5:3; Jub. 19:15-16; 27:6-7; 28:6-7; 30:2-17, 41; 1QapGen 20.10-11; Jos. and Asen. 23; Test. Jud. 8-12; Test. Iss. 3:1) in the character's favor. Viviano 1990a suspects that 1 Tim 1:4 polemicizes against narratives like Matthew's infancy narratives as "myths and genealogies." Yet the argument works only on the prior assumption that Matthew's material is mythical; further, the narratives' theology as a whole hardly fits the object of that epistle's polemic (cf. 1 Tim 1:6; 4:3; 6:5).

29. Noah's infant glory (1 Enoch 106:2-3; 1QapGen col. 2; cf. Fitzmyer 1965; idem 1971: 77-79; Brown 1966: 51) may resemble Greek myths in which lightning flashes from a divine or

Third, many texts Matthew cites are hardly obvious ones if Matthew started with texts and then created stories around them (stories that sometimes do not fit very well); while ignoring obvious messianic texts, however, he selects other texts that his contemporaries did not regard as messianic (Gundry 1975: 194, contrary to his later view).[30] This suggests that Matthew started with the infancy traditions and found biblical texts that fit (albeit adjusting the telling of both in the process). As one commentator observes, "The only conceivable reason for introducing these texts is that it was already known that Jesus went to Egypt, that there was a slaughter of children, and that Jesus' home was in Nazareth, and that scriptural justification was desired for these elements in his background" (France 1985: 71). Although we lack definite evidence that these events happened, it seems quite likely that Matthew believed prior, perhaps first-generation reports that these events happened.

Fourth, scholars concerned to trace each detail of their narrative to extant sources can easily abuse midrash. Whereas some Matthew scholars suggest that some of Matthew's infancy material is midrash on traditions later incorporated into Luke (e.g., Gundry 1982: 20), some Lukan scholars suggest that Luke has midrashically interpreted Matthew (Drury 1976: 123-25); without objective controls, one can view any independent materials thus. Fifth, the infancy narratives' vocabulary is not much more characteristically Matthean than the rest of the Gospel (Soares Prabhu 1976: 167-70). Indeed, substantial evidence supports the possibility that pre-Matthean narratives stand behind Matthew's infancy stories (Davies and Allison 1988: 190-95). Finally, midrashic elements do not make these accounts strictly midrash in themselves (see Wright 1966: 454-56). Given the literary unity and occasional Lukan confirmation of Matthew's birth narratives apart from these Old Testament citations, Matthew probably added the quotations to the narratives or traditions rather than simply the reverse (Down 1978; cf. Soares Prabhu 1976: 159-60, 165).[31]

Although inadequate evidence remains to "prove" the historical reliability of the infancy narratives, arguments against the narratives' reliability appear no more

---

semidivine infant (e.g., Asclepius in Paus. 2.26.5). Later tradition amplified Moses' birth (Bowman 1977: 284-97; contrast Jub. 47:1-8; Ezek *Exag.* 12-31), especially claiming that he was born circumcised (Ps-Philo 9:13; ARN 2A; b. Soṭa 12a; Lev. Rab. 20:1), a rare phenomenon (p. Yebam. 8:1, §12; Gen. Rab. 26:3; 46:12; 84:6). Such Moses traditions likely stemmed from exegetical inference from Ex 2:2 (cf. Philo *Mos.* 1.9; Jos. *Ant.* 2.230-31), but some rabbis may have polemicized against what they considered undue exaltation of Noah (cf. Gen. Rab. 28:8; 29:1, 3; 26:6; 36:3), also the ancestor of the Gentiles, which may explain the unexpected dearth of haggadic expansion about his birth in these sources.

30. Sanders 1993: 88-89 believes that Matthew and Luke mined the OT to fill in incomplete information for the infancy stories (so also Meier 1991a: 213), but acknowledges "limits," as in other Jewish texts and as evidenced by lack of assimilation to David and limits to assimilation with Moses.

31. Von Dobschütz 1995: 34 saw in the quotations evidence of Matthew's scribal method. Some think the fulfillment quotations, which vary from what they take to be Matthew's characteristic use of the LXX, derive from scribes in his community (e.g., Luz 1989: 78). But Matthew's mixed-type citations may reflect his own style and themes (Stanton 1993: 358-63), and the formula quotations function as theological "asides" (Stanton 1993: 346). Some writers' narrative asides include the fulfillment of prophetic oracles (e.g., Diod. Sic. 31.10.2), but virtually all of Matthew's explicit asides are fulfillment quotations.

substantive (France 1981b). Because we have no access to Matthew's sources for these narratives we lack much concrete evidence either way. In the absence of evidence to the contrary, however, we should assume that Matthew uses his sources in this part of his Gospel as carefully as he uses Mark and Q elsewhere. Elsewhere, while Matthew surely arranges and edits his material, he nevertheless derives it from prior tradition. Further, the details we find in these texts fit what we know of contemporary history (e.g., the character of Herod and Archelaus), in contrast to some historical novels depicting earlier periods (e.g., Tobit, Judith, most apocryphal Gospels and apocryphal Acts). Had Luke reported the same undoubtedly pre-Matthean traditions, many scholars would be inclined to accept their historical core on the basis of multiple attestation or at least a pre-Synoptic tradition. Luke's and Matthew's divergences do help us historically in one way, however. Because these infancy narratives are independent (so also, e.g., Hagner 1993: 14-15), the points where they *do* overlap do provide independent attestation for pre-Synoptic tradition.

Excursus: Debates about the Virgin Birth

Matthew and Luke independently attest the prior tradition of the virgin birth. More skeptical scholars have offered various alternative explanations of the virgin birth. Some Jews did apply the term "virgin" loosely to a wife during her first marriage (Vermes 1973: 218; Leon 1960: 232), following the looser Greek sense of the term,[32] though the term more often simply meant "virgin" (e.g., Eurip. *Electra* 270; Ap. Rhod. 1.671). But these data are not relevant to Jesus' birth; the whole point of the Christian accounts is that God miraculously made Mary pregnant apart from sexual means (Mt 1:18, 20, 25; Lk 1:34-35; cf. Justin *1 Apol.* 21, 33, 46; *Dial.* 43, 66, 77–78; Iren. *Haer.* 1.26.1; Test. Jud. 19:8). It is not likely that this tradition would have arisen in pre-Synoptic tradition, while members of Jesus' family remained in positions of prominence (1 Cor 15:7; Gal 1:19; 2:9), merely on the basis of a misinterpreted Greek word.

Gordon offers parallels for his proposal that one could have a human father and yet derive one's status from a divine paternity (Gordon 1977: 101; idem 1978a: 26-27). Greeks sometimes called their human heroes "Zeus-born" or "Zeus-nurtured" in a purely figurative sense (e.g., Hom. *Il.* 16.49, 126, 707; 17.34, 238, 685, 702; 21.75). The parallels seem questionable, but in any case only indirectly illumine the early Christian "son of God" title, and a virgin birth (on which divine Sonship was not predicated; see the Introduction) not at all. Bultmann asserts that the virgin birth must be a hellenistic addition to the story (1968: 291). Yet most alleged parallels to the virgin

32. See Liddell and Scott 1968: 1339; Moulton and Milligan 1976: 494; Delling 1967: 828-30; Ford 1966; cf. Carmignac 1977; P.Oxy. 3177.2-3 in Horsley 1981: 71. Ilan 1996: 98 suggests that the story reflects the Jewish use of virginity as "a symbol of purity and innocence"; her evidence (funerary inscriptions citing virginity), however, is inadequate (the inscriptions invite pathos; see comment on 9:18-26).

birth (see Allen 1977: 19; Soares Prabhu 1976: 5-6; cf. Grant 1986: 64) are hopelessly distant, at best representing supernatural births of some kind (Barrett 1966: 6-10; Brown 1977: 522-23; Davies and Allison 1988: 214-15; Hagner 1993: 17; even further are ancient biological views, e.g., Arist. *Gen. An.* 3.6.5; Ep. Arist. 165). Certainly pagan stories of divine impregnation, which typically involve seduction (e.g., Ovid *Metam.* 3.260-61) or rape (Ovid *Metam.* 3.1-2), bear no resemblance to a *virgin* birth.

Even most proposed Jewish parallels (Daube 1973: 6-9; cf. also 2 Enoch 71; Gen. Rab. 53:6) are too late or on closer examination have little merit (cf. Brown 1977: 523-24); Philo's claims that God supernaturally opened wombs (Schweizer 1975: 33; cf. Vermes 1973: 220) probably simply imply that only God can provide conception (cf. Gen 30:2; cf. Meier 1991a: 221-22). Although no direct Old Testament precedent existed for virgin births, supernatural births (e.g., Gen 21:2; 25:21; 30:6, 17; Judg 13:3; cf. Maillot 1978) and prenatal annunciations (e.g., Gen 16:11; Judg 13:3-14; cf. 1 Enoch 107:3) abounded, and the biblical language is much closer to Matthew 1:21 (modeled on Is 7:14 in Mt 1:23) than pagan and most other Jewish accounts are. Because Matthew's contemporaries do not seem to have interpreted Isaiah 7 messianically, however, there is no reason to suppose that early Christians composed the doctrine on the basis of the text, either (Davies and Allison 1988: 214).

It is difficult for those who accept Matthew as Scripture to reject the event of the virgin birth as history; Matthew derives theological capital from both the fulfillment of Scripture and the miracle. If Matthew's point rests on a fiction, it offers little genuine support for his premise about God's plan. Matthew's perspective challenges the Enlightenment compromise that the essential point of the virgin birth is its "meaning" and not its historicity (against, e.g., Fuller 1956). Ultimately, the historical plausibility of this particular account rests on one's presuppositions (Wilkinson 1964). Would anyone whose logic was not shaped by Enlightenment thought doubt that of all the miraculous births of history, the supreme prophet's might be the most miraculous? One cannot deny testimony for a miracle by dismissing it on the grounds that miracles cannot happen.[33]

We must evaluate the function and reliability of the virgin birth story by tools more reliable than culturally and historically shaped philosophical presuppositions. On the one hand, ancient writers did prefer to depict miraculous births when possible. Greco-Roman biographies, or "lives," frequently included birth narratives (Aune 1987: 65; Burridge 1992: 249), including miraculous signs like dreams when appropriate (Shuler 1982: 94).[34] Thus it is not surprising that Matthew would focus on

33. See Craig 1986; cf. Goppelt 1981/82: 1:145; France 1976: 105-7; Borg 1987: 33-34; on antisupernaturalism regarding the infancy narratives in general, see Young 1992; on the historical context of modern skepticism, cf. Benoit 1973/1974: 1:39; Kee 1983: 3-16; Bockmuehl 1988.

34. For announcement by a dream, cf., e.g., Plut. *Alex.* 2.1–3.2 (Boring 1995: 37-38); for miraculous omens, cf., e.g., Suet. *Augustus* 94 (Boring 1995: 43-44); Aul. Gel. 6.1.2-4. For supernatural births of famous philosophers, Diog. Laert. *Lives* 3.1-2, 45; Iamblichus *Life of Pythagoras* 2.3-5; Diod. Sic. *Library of History* 4.9.1-10 (Boring 1995: 33-35, though every one of these sources for supernatural births derives from at least half a millennium after the persons they depict). Davies 1993: 31-32 cites examples of miraculous births in hellenistic biographies (including Plut. *Romulus* 2; *Alex.* 2), but notes

such events, although other scholars are also correct that his birth narratives do not perfectly fit this genre, lacking the structure of miracle stories (see Theissen 1991: 123). Matthew's infancy narratives set the stage for Jesus' ministry depicted in the rest of the Gospel, "defining his origin and goal" (Meier 1980: 1-2). Miracles were especially appropriate in connection with Jesus' birth; Greek literature conferred "miraculous birth stories" only on sages considered divine, to confirm their divine origin (Aune 1987: 34; cf. Paus. 2.26.5; Aune 1987: 30, 65, citing Diod. Sic. 16.1; 19.2.1-7; Menander Rhetor 371.3-14).

Yet, on the other hand, an inclination to report a kind of event does not render evidence for that event unhistorical. The basic account of the virgin birth predates both Gospels that open with Jesus' infancy; neither Gospel is clearly dependent on the other (see Meier 1980: 17; Brown 1977: 162; pace Drury 1976: 123-25). The tradition stems from a period when Jesus' *brother* led the church in Jerusalem. Reliable sources also stand behind many details of the accounts; Jesus' birth would likely be one of the stories whose reliability Luke investigated (Lk 1:3; see Introduction), since, on our reading of his "we-narratives" (see Introduction), he implies that he had direct access to a younger son of Mary (Acts 21:18; 27:1).

Possibly if Mary's family was from Bethlehem or certainly if Luke's genealogy is hers, Mary could have been of Davidic descent; otherwise perhaps she was a Levite (Lk 1:36; Stauffer 1960: 45). Nor should we doubt that Joseph was Mary's husband; that early Christians called Jesus the "son of Joseph" to correspond with the rabbis' suffering "Messiah ben Joseph" (Gordon in Isbell 1975: 130) is unlikely. That rabbinic tradition probably dates to the century after the canonical Gospels were completed (Vermes 1973: 140; Yamauchi 1978: 165-66); further, the early Christian sources are unanimous on the name of Mary's husband, despite the cognitive dissonance such memories could generate for those struggling with the issue of his divine Sonship.

Some scholars, however, have appealed to evidence that is probably unreliable. Lacking first-generation incentive to have gathered or preserved reliable accounts, later rabbinic tradition about Mary (properly "Miriam"; see Dalman 1973: 31) probably depends on and garbles early Christian sources. The context of such traditions is probably the view that immoral circumstances of conception incline the child toward apostasy (see Stauffer 1960: 207-8). Probably due to a Hebrew wordplay and confusion with Mary Magdalene, it often calls Mary a "hairdresser" (Herford 1966: 40-41). Most Greek and Roman women would not have regarded hairdressing as an ignoble occupation (e.g., *ILS* 9727, 9730, and 9732 in Lefkowitz and Fant 1982: 170); but given the role of hair in seduction (Keener 1992: 29, 53), the rabbis may have associated her alleged profession with the tradition that Mary was immoral.[35] The rabbinic tradition that Mary conceived Jesus by a Roman soldier may involve a wordplay between *pandera* (for the soldier) and the Greek term for

---

that these stories presuppose sexually active deities producing semidivine heroes, and that Matthew drew not on that Greek tradition but on the biblical tradition of God as creator. One might also think of Gen 2:21-22: as God formed Eve from Adam, he could form Jesus from Mary's ovum.

35. Hairdressers were not always associated with immorality, though they catered to people of means; cf. Ilan 1996: 188.

"virgin" *(parthenos)* rather than a carefully solicited slander from Mary's hometown concerning Mary's prenuptial pregnancy.[36] None of these traditions has historical merit, but they do indicate how easily both the circumstances of Jesus' birth and some people's animosity toward Jesus could reflect on his parents, underlining the courage of Joseph and Mary revealed in the infancy narratives.

The Virgin Gives Birth (Matthew 1:18-25)

Cf. Lk 2:1-7. That early Christian traditions should have preserved less of Jesus' early life than of his ministry is not surprising: it fits (1) the primary significance of his ministry to his first followers; (2) their eyewitness attestation of the ministry (as opposed to most of his childhood); and (3) standard rhetorical form in passing quickly over material less relevant to one's purpose (cf. Lucian *How to Write History* 56-57; Satterthwaite 1993: 345). Ancient biographies could focus on the public portion of a person's life, addressing only in cursory fashion the most relevant features of a person's childhood. Thus, for example, Josephus summarizes the first thirty years of his life in *Life* 1-16 (around 4 percent of the *Life,* considerably less than Matthew allots in his introduction to Jesus' public ministry). Yet even some of this introductory material in Josephus's *Life* (especially *Life* 13-16) prepares his readers for his role in the war. One may likewise expect many features of Matthew's infancy narratives to prepare his audience for themes dominant throughout the Gospel.

If the genealogy indicates that Joseph descended from King David, this narrative explains in what sense this son of David (1:20) became Jesus' legal father by adoption, given the already existing tradition of the virgin birth in the early church.[37] Matthew may also indicate that the one empowered by the Spirit (3:16) was born from the Spirit (1:18, 20).[38] In this brief narrative, Matthew provides not

36. Klausner 1979b: 23-24, 48-51; cf. Goguel 1948: 74; Stauffer 1960: 16-17; Herford 1966: 35-50; Maier 1978: 198-200; Origen *Contra Celsum* 1.28, 32, 33, 39. Later rabbinic sources also reserved tortures for a particular Miriam hanging by her breasts in hell (e.g., t. Sukk. 4:28; p. Ḥag. 2:2, §5; Sanh. 6:6, §2). Insulting another's mother's sexuality was one of the deepest and most punishable insults (e.g., Jos. *Ant.* 13.292, 293-95). Hanson and Oakman 1998: 57 thus take too seriously the occurrence of one tombstone of a soldier in Syria named Pantera; even were the story true, the odds of chance preservation of precisely the right tombstone are minimal.

37. Cf. also A. B. Bruce 1979: 66; Harrington 1982: 14; Meier 1980: 9; Garland 1993: 21. Ancients did not hesitate to speak of a mortal "father" who raised a child despite its being reportedly conceived by a deity (cf. Diog. Laert. *Lives* 3.1-2, 45, in Boring 1995: 33-34; Eurip. *Madness of Heracles* 587, 1192). By his faith in God's promise concerning a supernaturally born son, Joseph may also act as a "son of Abraham" (1:1), but too few clues in the narrative support such a connection for it to be more than conjectural.

38. Proposed parallels to divine "spirits" *impregnating* humans or organisms (Plut. *Numa* 4.2-4; *Table-Talk* 8.1-3; Boring 1995: 38-39) are not close, and such thoughts would have been out of the question for Jewish readers. More helpfully, cf. comments on the Spirit and creation (e.g., Hill 1972: 78), an ancient Israelite connection (Gen 1:2; Job 33:4; Ps 104:30).

only an account of the virgin birth but reinforcement of the Christian view of Scripture, Christ, and various principles of ethics for disciples of the kingdom.

Jesus' birth fulfills Scripture (1:22-23). Matthew emphasizes various points for his community, one of the most prominent being the authority of Scripture, which God fulfills with or without mortals' cooperation. For whatever other reasons God incarnated Jesus through a virgin, the only reason Matthew lists is "that Scripture might be fulfilled" (1:22).

This basic point is clearer than the actual nature of Matthew's argument from Isaiah. The Hebrew term *'almah* in Isaiah 7:14 need not always mean "virgin" (on *bethulah,* see m. Nid. 1:4); thus most Jewish interpreters reject the messianic interpretation of this text (Berger and Wyschogrod 1978: 41). Indeed, because the earlier Greek version's term for young woman usually (albeit not always) meant "virgin," as in Matthew (cf. Benoit 1973/74: 1:5-7), later Jewish translators into Greek insisted on translating the term "young woman" (Longenecker 1975: 144n.25). Matthew, who regularly blends Greek and Hebrew text-types, must have known the possible ambiguity in Isaiah (rabbis often selected whichever textual tradition suited their argument at the moment).

Yet Matthew may not be claiming a simplistic correspondence with the Isaiah text anyway (see Willis 1978; Brennan 1964). Clearly the child of Isaiah 7:14 was an urgent sign to Ahaz and would still be young when the kings oppressing Ahaz were carried into captivity (Is 7:7-25); some have thus applied the prophecy to Hezekiah (Trypho in Justin *Dial.* 67, 77; Shotwell 1965: 75; Barnard 1967: 25; Kronholm 1989; cf. Bright 1981: 291). In the immediate context, however, Isaiah probably referred to his own son "Swift Is the Plunder, Speedy Is the Loot," who would perform exactly the same function as Immanuel (8:1-4). But because Isaiah's children were for "signs" (8:18), it was reasonable for Matthew to see in Immanuel (cf. 8:8) a sign pointing to the ultimate presence of God and triumph for Judah in the Davidic Messiah who would be born to Israel (9:1-7; see, independently, Blomberg 1992a: 60; Keener 1993: 48). Matthew's use of other texts in Isaiah 6–9 suggests that he may have in view the entire section from which he is citing (Ellis 1977: 201).[39] Whatever Matthew's exegesis, his primary point is clear enough: Scripture reveals the divine plan, and those who trust its authority need doubt no miracle it promises.

Lessons from a righteous man's obedience (1:19, 24-25). But this pericope emphasizes another series of points no less clearly.

The model of Joseph's behavior here provides a number of exhortations for Matthew's audience. But Matthew's narrative may on the whole serve a more apologetic than ethically didactic function: by underlining the moral nobility of Joseph and Mary, he defends the purity of Jesus' origin and the piety of Jesus'

39. Matthew may have the whole section of Is 7–9 in view. Ellis admits that Matthew lacks evidence for testimonia in the sense of an apologetic book, but he does seem to work from a set of passages (Ellis 1977: 201; cf. Lindars 1961: 13-14; Longenecker 1975: 89-90; Stendahl 1968: 207-17). The Dead Sea Scrolls contain some possibly analogous collections of eschatological texts (cf. Allegro 1956b; Fitzmyer 1974: 59-89; in the rabbis, cf. Urbach 1979: 1:686).

upbringing; not only in biography (e.g., Jos. *Life* 7) but in speeches of praise and blame one's background could shed light on one's character. This apologetic strategy functions adequately because Matthew can presuppose a shared moral world with his community's opponents on the ethical matters in question. Biographies sometimes opened with the protagonist's parents or noble family background (e.g., Corn. Nep. 2 [Themistocles], 1.2; 7 [Alcibiades], 1.2); although such background did not always shape how a child turned out (Sall. *Catil.* 5.1; cf. 2 Chron 28:1; 29:2; 33:3; 34:2; 36:5), one's background could help define a hero's character (e.g., Hom. *Il.* 20.215-41). One could insult parents by reviling their children or children by reviling their parents (e.g., Ps-Cicero *Invective against Sallust* 5.13: your father injured the nation by begetting you).

Still, one of Matthew's purposes in his Gospel is to transmit Jesus' ethics (28:19), and Jewish teachers taught by example as well as by words. Ancient biographers often taught positive or negative moral lessons by the characters they depicted (e.g., Diod. Sic. 15.1.1; 37.4.1; Aune 1987: 36; cf. Lyons 1985: 29-32);[40] Matthew here portrays a righteous young man and woman as models for Christian living. Whereas Luke focuses more on Mary's experience (Lk 1:27-56; 2:19), Matthew confronts us directly with Joseph's.

First, in a culture that valued the wisdom of age, Joseph and Mary's youth makes their piety all the more striking. Although the point is less clear than in Luke (who plainly contrasts Mary with Zechariah in Lk 1:5-38), Matthew's selection of this young couple as his Gospel's first narrative protagonists is consonant with Matthew's confidence that the young and obscure could effectively model Christian virtue (18:2-6; 19:14; 21:15-16). Their youth is not stated, but Matthew's audience would probably assume it unless explicitly informed otherwise. Jewish teachers stressed the importance of marrying young, often to avoid temptation (see Keener 1991a: 73-74, 177-78). If rabbinic texts reflect the wider custom here, Jewish men in Joseph's day probably often married around the age of eighteen or twenty (m. 'Abot 5:21, 32; b. Qidd. 29b-30a; Qoh. Rab. 3:2, §3; cf. Davis 1958; Jeremias 1972: 129; also elsewhere, e.g., Lewis 1983: 55, though the Diaspora Jew in *CIJ* 1:409, §553 marries around 22). Jewish women often married as young as twelve or fourteen, upon reaching puberty (Gen. Rab. 95 MSV; Pesiq. Rab Kah. 11:6; Jeremias 1969: 365),[41] though some were older than

40. Although Boring 1995: 89 cites the moral in Aesop *Fables* 172 to illustrate the way ancients might have approached Jesus' parables, I suspect it works much better for nonparabolic narratives. (On the special hermeneutic for parables, see under Mt 13.) Eighteenth-century English historiography also followed this Greek and Roman historical tradition (Frei 1989: 56).

41. Among Gentiles, cf. Epict. *Encheir.* 40; for young brides cf. also, e.g., Plut. *Bride* 2, *Mor.* 138D; Quint. *Preface* 4; *Ninus Romance* fr. 1, A.3; 13 in Ovid *Metam.* 9.714. This was often 13 to 16 among Greeks and Romans (Friedländer 4:123-31; Lewis 1983: 55; cf. Pleket 10 in Lefkowitz and Fant 1982: 136; Pomeroy 1975: 41, 118, 164; Boer 1979: 39, 269; Verner 1983: 41), though 18 may have been most common (cf. Hesiod *W.D.* 698). In inscriptions in Gardner 1986: 39, about 40 percent of the women studied married before age 15 and almost 75 percent before age 19; in Egyptian census declarations, however, only 10 percent were married before age 15, suggesting some geographical variation; see more fully Rawson 1986b: 21-22; *CIL* 6.

twenty.[42] Young men were expected to begin adult responsibilities around age thirteen,[43] so Joseph at eighteen or twenty had already begun to fill that role and had likely already saved some money for his marriage.

Second, Matthew portrays a couple who, far from being immoral before marriage, model sexual restraint (cf. 5:27-30). In contrast to false assumptions opponents of Christianity might draw (and some eventually did draw) from the story of the virgin birth, Matthew wants his audience to know that Mary and Joseph, like most of their Jewish contemporaries, practiced sexual restraint before their marriage.

A couple normally would marry a year after their betrothal,[44] but restraint was normal and expected in that society, and it is unclear how long Joseph and Mary have been engaged. In any case, Joseph apparently married Mary immediately after the angelic announcement, perhaps to minimize her shame (though cf. the longer account in Lk 2:5). A godly man would not sleep with his fiancée before marriage (Jos. and Asen. 21:1/20:8; contrast, e.g., *P. Ryl.* 154.4); despite their marriage, however, they refrained from marital relations until Jesus' birth (1:25),[45] not consummating their marriage according to ancient custom (cf. Ach. Tat. 5.20.5; 21.1).[46] It is this point that would elicit the appreciation of ancient hearers because of its restraint. Even in many Middle Eastern societies outsiders assume that "if a man and woman are alone together for more than twenty minutes they have had in-

42. Ilan 1996: 67-69 notes that women usually married in their teens (at ages like 13 or 16), but some married even older than 20.

43. Cf. m. 'Abot 5:21; ARN 16A; Pesiq. Rab Kah. Sup. 3:2; Gen. Rab. 63:10; probably Lk 2:42 and Jos. *Ant.* 10.50 (not yet adult); cf. adulthood at 12 in 1 Esdr 5:41. Egyptian males entered adulthood at 14 (Lewis 1983: 156), as did Roman males (Gaius *Inst.* 1.196; 2.113; 3.208; Gardner 1986: 14); cf. also Jos. *Life* 9. The basic matter was achieving puberty (e.g., Gaius *Inst.* 1.196; Gen. Rab. 91:3; p. Ter. 1:3), as in many traditional societies (Mbiti 1970: 158-73; Eliade 1958: 41; Dawson 1964: 309). Men could marry as young as puberty or 14 (Gardner 1986: 38); in the Greek world, however, men traditionally married in their 30s (Hesiod *W.D.* 695-97; Pomeroy 1975: 118). Roman men were generally a decade older than their brides (Shaw 1987).

44. M. Ketub. 5:2; Ned. 10:5; Song Rab. 4:8, §1; Safrai 1974/76b: 757; Davies and Allison 1988: 199. From the time of Augustus (who desired to replenish especially the aristocracy), Roman law required marriage within two years (Dio Cassius *R.H.* 54.16.7).

45. The wording in 1:25 may argue against perpetual virginity, i.e., after Jesus' birth (Davies and Allison 1988: 219), a doctrine probably initially derived from the *Protevangelium of James* 19:3 (Blomberg 1992a: 57; cf. Lk 2:7, 23). Luz 1989: 124-25 contends that the grammar cannot *disprove* perpetual virginity here, but that the concept is alien to Matthew's community and would therefore have had to have been expressed explicitly if Matthew wished to communicate it.

46. Matthew probably records Joseph's sexual restraint with Mary before Jesus' birth to underline Mary's virginity and Joseph's self-control, rather than from fear that a nonvirgin birth would contaminate a virgin conception. Although some of his ancient readers may have thought that women could conceive during pregnancy, apparently few felt that this conception mixed new paternal heritage into the first fetus (Gardner 1986: 53, citing Arist. *Gen. Anim.* 553a). But the couple's restraint also demanded Mary's trust in Joseph: the wedding night would provide no proof of her virginity, hence there would be neither current vindication nor subsequent legal protection for her should Joseph ever reject her (cf. Deut 22:13-19; in modern times, see Eickelman 1989: 174). But second-century rabbis required claims against a bride's virginity either immediately or within a month after the wedding (p. Ketub. 1:4, §4).

tercourse" (Delaney 1987: 41); Jewish people expected immorality from Gentiles alone with a Jewish woman (m. ʿAbod. Zar. 2:1). Jewish tradition before and after this period especially celebrated the sexual example of the biblical Joseph (Jub. 39:5-8; p. Hor. 2:6, §4; Gen. Rab. 87:6, 8; Lev. Rab. 23:10; Song Rab. 4:12, §1; cf. Teugels 1991); some later rabbis went even further with a story of a man forced by pagans to sleep with his betrothed his whole life, who never touched her because they lacked a valid Jewish marriage contract (b. Giṭ. 57a). Under appropriate circumstances, pagan Gentiles could also respect the noble character implied in such abstention (Eurip. *Electra* 43-44, 255-61).

Especially because they were probably a poor couple (cf. Lk 2:24; Lev 12:8), we may assume that Joseph and Mary shared the same bed in the same room (cf. Tob 7:16; Goodman 1983: 30-31; Stambaugh and Balch 1986: 83).[47] Married though they were, they controlled their passions for the honor of God's Messiah (cf. 19:12). Matthew may imply that they restrain themselves in obedience to Scripture, to fulfill literalistically Isaiah's promise that a virgin would both conceive and *bear* (1:22-23). By waiting till after Jesus' birth to have intercourse, hence failing to provide the bloody sheet that proved Mary's virginity on the wedding night (Deut 22:15; cf. p. Ketub. 1:1, §§7-8; Eickelman 1989: 174),[48] Mary and Joseph also chose to confirm their shame in order to preserve the sanctity of God's call.

Third, while Matthew allows that divorce is just under some circumstances (cf. 5:32), he shares the Jewish and biblical view that infidelity is always unjust. By calling Joseph "righteous," Matthew invites his audience to learn from Joseph's character about fidelity, discipline, and preferring God's honor above one's own. Given the economic agreement involved, Jewish people rarely ended betrothals lightly (cf. perhaps Jos. and Asen. 23:3), and Joseph plans to do so only under the severest of circumstances.

For Joseph to "put Mary away" (1:19) meant that he would divorce her. To explain the necessity of divorce to end a betrothal, one must understand the significance of betrothal. As elsewhere in the Mediterranean world (e.g., Hom. *Od.* 4.5-12; Ovid *Metam.* 4.60-61; 9.715; Longus 3.30-31; 4.36; *Ninus Romance* fr. 1, A.1), fathers were guardians of their daughters' virginity, arranged their marriages, and "gave" them to their husbands (with some measure of barter in either direction; cf. Tob 7:13-15; Sir 7:24-25; Jub. 28:6-7).[49] Witnesses and a sym-

47. For more endowed homes, see later sources in Safrai 1974/76b: 736. Some Jewish circles (e.g., Essenes) apparently allowed intercourse only for procreation, but other circles (including most later rabbis) allowed married couples to practice it for pleasure if they wished (Ilan 1996: 107-11).

48. Later rabbis, undoubtedly following the lenient Pharisaic tradition, invariably ruled in favor of women when they claimed exceptional reasons for a hymen not bleeding when married (Ilan 1996: 98-99). Obviously a pregnancy before marriage would not lend itself to such an explanation.

49. Llewelyn 1992: 14 correctly notes (citing m. Qidd. 4:9; t. Yebam. 13:1; DJD 2.19.6-7; but also cf. m. Giṭ. 9:3) that adult women could refuse marriage; Ilan 1996: 84 specifies the decease of the woman's father. Most Jewish marriages involved young virgins (who were preferred; Jos. *Ant.* 4.244; cf. *Life* 414) rather than adults (who were usually divorcées or widows); see Keener 1991a: 72-78; children nevertheless often could influence betrothal plans (Parthenius *L.R.* 1.2).

bolic act were essential for *erusin,* or Jewish betrothal;[50] although Romans sometimes used "engagement rings," Judaism seems to have adopted this custom only later (Safrai 1974/76b: 756). Betrothal's function was primarily commercial (Finkelstein 1962: 1:46), but it was quite serious legally: dissolved only through divorce if both partners lived, betrothal similarly left the survivor of the man's death a widow (m. Ketub. 1:2; Yebam. 4:10; 6:4).[51] Although a betrothed couple like Joseph and Mary did not live together or have intercourse, their union was as binding as marriage.[52]

The issue is not that Joseph fears to wed Mary because he recognizes the virgin conception (pace Gundry 1982: 22);[53] the angel has not yet informed him that the Holy Spirit is the cause of her pregnancy (Mt 1:20), and he considers a divorce less shameful for her rather than more (1:19). Joseph plans to divorce Mary not because he believes that God caused her to conceive but because he assumes her to be guilty of unfaithfulness.

In contrast to most of modern Western culture, Joseph lived in a society where he had no option of giving Mary a second chance, even if he wanted to (which he presumably would not have). Jewish, Greek, and Roman law all demanded that a man divorce his wife if she were guilty of adultery (Keener 1991a: 31, 156; Gardner 1986: 89; Bockmuehl 1989; Justinian, *Digest* 48.5.1, pref.; Demosth. *Against Neaera* 87).[54] Jewish law demanded that a man charge his wife immediately on discovery that she had not been a virgin (cf. p. Ketub. 1.4, §4); Roman law actually treated a husband who failed to divorce an unfaithful wife as a panderer exploiting his wife as a prostitute (Gardner 1986: 131-32; Richlin 1981: 227; cf. Ps-Phocyl. 177-78). Mediterranean society viewed with contempt the weakness of a man who let his love for his wife outweigh his appropriate honor in repudiating her (e.g., Diod. Sic. 32.10.9).

Perhaps Mary's family would have wished to have sent her away to prevent others from learning of her pregnancy (cf. Lk 1:39); the corruption of a virgin shamed her father, especially if she were betrothed (Parthenius *L.R.* 35.1, 3-4; Lev 21:9). But if Joseph knew, he was probably not alone, and word could spread quickly in a small town like Nazareth (cf. Lk 1:26) or Bethlehem. If Joseph married Mary and it was clear to anyone besides himself that she was pregnant, others would assume that *he* must have gotten her pregnant; otherwise, they would reason, he would surely divorce her for being unfaithful to him! While his town would not have viewed a betrothed couple's intercourse as seriously as

50. Cohen 1966: 292, 298; on Roman betrothal, cf. Paulus *Opinions* 2.1-9; Cohen 1966: 279-347; Gardner 1986: 45-47.

51. Writers regularly point this out (Argyle 1963: 27; Sandmel 1978b: 194; Gundry 1982: 21; Belkin 1940: 250; Davies and Allison 1988: 199).

52. M. Giṭ. 6:2; Ketub. 1:2; 4:2; Yebam. 2:6; b. Giṭ. 26b; Montefiore 1968: 2:5; Davies and Allison 1988: 199.

53. The exhortation not to fear means not to fear to do God's will; cf. 8:26; 9:2; 10:26; 14:27; 17:7; 28:5, 10. Joseph would soon have a different reason to fear (2:22).

54. For an example of divorce for adultery, see, e.g., Apul. *Metam.* 9.27-29.

adultery (cf. Deut. 22:14, 22), townspeople would have questioned the moral commitment of both parties.

Further, Joseph had little reason to trust Mary's innocence. On the historical level, to be sure, Joseph probably did not know Mary well and had little reason to trust her innocence. Jewish texts suggest that Galilean couples were allowed no privacy (hence neither chance for intercourse nor private conversation) together until the wedding (Safrai 1974/76b: 756-57; Finkelstein 1962: 1:45).[55] Yet while we believe Luke preserves reliable information that Mary and Joseph were living in Galilee (Lk 1:26; see the Introduction on Luke's special sources), one reading Matthew without other tradition would assume that Jesus was probably conceived in Bethlehem (Mt 2:1). Matthew's omission of more specific information does not contradict the Lukan account, but members of his audience unaware of other traditions would probably hear the story as if Jesus were conceived in Judea, and might not even know the cultural differences traditionally posited between the two. Nevertheless, since a virgin birth had never before happened, Mary had not claimed rape, and Joseph had not had intercourse with her, he could assume only that she had had intercourse with another man. Thus he faced the pain of apparent betrayal in a world that considered adultery the ultimate theft — the stealing of another man's most precious possession, the undivided affection of his wife (Ps-Phocyl. 3; Keener 1991a: 31, 155); the emotional response to such betrayal was often quite serious (e.g., Parthenius *L.R.* 5.3). Because a wife's adultery could imply the husband's inadequacy or his family's poor choice of a mate, it shamed the husband as well (e.g., 2 Enoch 71:6-11; cf. Gilmore 1987: 4; Ps-Herodotus *Life of Homer* in Boring 1995: 40-41). From Joseph's standpoint within the narrative at this point, Mary's apparent betrayal had brought him shame.

Under these circumstances, Joseph was righteous in divorcing Mary; to fail to do so would violate law and custom, would bring enduring reproach on his household, and would constitute embracing as his wife one who had betrayed him in the worst manner conceivable in his culture. Given Jewish law and custom Matthew's readers would expect Joseph to remarry, and Matthew's words later in the Gospel support this probability (5:32; 19:9; cf. Keener1991a: 36-37; Allison 1993a).

Fourth, Joseph models the principle of justice tempered by compassion. This is a principle that Matthew regards as central to the interpretive conflict between the ethics of Jesus and those of his followers' opponents (cf. 9:13). Matthew does not state that Joseph was righteous *because* he was divorcing Mary (though he makes clear that Joseph was not unrighteous for doing so). Rather, he

55. Judeans, reportedly less careful (Ilan 1996: 100 even cites a recently discovered marriage contract indicating prior cohabitation), also assumed a greater likelihood that the woman would get pregnant before the wedding. Even today, some Middle Eastern villages assume that any woman alone with a man for over 20 minutes has had intercourse with him (Delaney 1987: 41). The circumstances are thus quite different from those portrayed where a Greek loyally defends his fiancée's honor even to death (Soph. *Antig.* 631-765, 1221-43).

emphasizes that Joseph was righteous for divorcing Mary *privately* — that is, for not bringing unnecessary shame on her.[56]

Jewish courts in this period could not execute capital sentences[57] and would not have carried out the death penalty even though Jewish law prescribed it for sexual unfaithfulness (Deut 22:21-24; Jub. 30:8-9; Ps-Philo 25:10; Jos. *Apion* 2.201; Sifre Deut. 242.1.6; Sifra Qed. pq. 10.208.2.4; ARN 2 A; b. Sanh. 50b). Nor would such behavior likely provoke an illegal lynching in Jewish Palestine (in contrast to some traditional societies; cf. Delaney 1987: 42).[58] Nevertheless, the shame would be intense and deliberate (cf., e.g., Demosth. *Against Neaera* 86; Sen. *Dial.* 2.18.2; Plut. *G.Q.* 2, *Mor.* 291F; b. Soṭa 8b). Thus a zealously virtuous ancient Mediterranean family might even prefer their daughter's death to her defilement (Diod. Sic. 12.24.3-4; Dion. Hal. 11.37.5; Livy 3.44.4–3.48.9), and an ancient Mediterranean audience might consider virtuous a woman who, defiled against her will, preferred death to living with dishonor (*Contest of Homer and Hesiod* 323; Livy 1.58.12; Diod. Sic. 10.19.3; 15.54.3; Dion. Hal. 4.66.2-4; 4.67.1; 4.82.3; Dio Cassius *R.H.* 2.11.16-19). The more public the knowledge of her deed, the more public the humiliation of Mary and her family. Her premarital pregnancy had likely ruined any chance of her ever marrying (cf. Delaney 1987: 42), a horrible fate in an economically male-centered society where a woman's honor depended on her status vis-à-vis a man.

Yet Joseph might have profited from divorcing her publicly. By taking her to court Joseph could have impounded her dowry — the total assets she brought into the marriage[59] — and perhaps recouped the bride price if he had paid one at

56. Cf. Allen 1977: 9; Tosato 1979; contrast Romaniuk 1980, who takes the participle as concessive.

57. Jos. *War* 2.117; Sherwin-White 1978: 32-45; Stewart 1975; O'Rourke 1971: 174-75. For debate on appropriate penalties for adultery in Palestinian Jewish sources, see Ilan 1996: 135-41.

58. Many traditional societies prohibit or limit adultery, though the behavior of the wife is more at issue than that of the husband (e.g., Firth 1963: 119, 475-77; Stephens 1963: 245; Schapera 1966: 204-7; Barnouw 1955: 23; Wilson 1957: 134, 258, 262; Mbiti 1971: 193, 268-69, 275; for allegedly harsher penalties for adulterous women than men in early Judaism, cf. Swidler 1976: 148-54). Romans executed Vestal Virgins who had intercourse (Plut. *R.Q.* 96, *Mor.* 286EF; Dion. Hal. 1.78.5); husbands or fathers who caught adulterers in the act could under specific circumstances kill them (Aul. Gel. *Attic Nights* 10.23; Quint. 7.1.7; Plut. *Solon* 23.1; Diog. Laert. 6.1.4; b. Ned. 91b; cf. Char. *Chaer.* 1.4.7, 11-12), and other legal punishments for adultery existed (Sen. *De Benef.* 6.32.1; Mart. *Epig.* 2.60; 2.83; 3.85; Ach. Tat. 6.5.3-4; O'Rourke 1971: 181-82; in classical Greece, Dover 1984: 146; though cf. Epict. *Disc.* 1.18.5-6, 11-12). What mortals could not avenge, God would (cf. Sib. Or. 3:764-66; 5:430; Test. Abr. 12 B; Acts of John 35), also by bestowing public shame (Sir 23:21; Ps. Sol. 8:8-10; Num. Rab. 9:1).

59. "Like the dowry in Ptolemaic Egypt, the *kethubah* was used to penalise the spouse who was either at fault or initiated the divorce (e.g., *m. Ket.* 5.7, 7.6, *t. Ket.* 12.1)" (Llewelyn 1992: 12-13). For the Greek dowry, cf., e.g., Plut. *Bride* 12, *Mor.* 139DE; Diod. Sic. 32.10.2; for parallels between the Jewish and pagan customs, see Cohen 1966: 348-76; among the hellenized Herodians, see Hanson 1990. Divorces normally required repayment of the dowry (cf. *P. Tebt.* 104.12, 31-33, 37-38; *P. Oxy.* 1273.5-20; *B.G.U.* 1103.10-14); rather than risk having to repay high dowries, some men preferred to marry poorer women (Ps-Phocyl. 199-200; Jos. *Apion* 2.200; cf. Plut. *Bride* 22, *Mor.* 141AB; *Educ.* 19, *Mor.* 13F–14A), but this view was not universal (Ovid *Metam.* 4.704-5).

betrothal (cf., e.g., *B.G.U.* 1052; P. Eleph. 1.6-8; Quint. *Inst. Or.* 7.4.11; Safrai 1974/76b: 790; Ferguson 1987: 55).[60] In contrast, by forfeiting this economic reimbursement he could instead simply provide her a certificate of divorce in front of two or three witnesses[61] — and so minimize her public dishonor. Even though Jewish tradition ruled that a wife could lose her dowry for infidelity or for as little as scolding her husband (m. Ketub. 7:6), in normal divorces where the wife was not charged she kept her dowry (Lewis 1983: 56).[62] Although ancient readers would assume Joseph deeply wounded by what he believed to be Mary's betrayal (cf., e.g., Char. *Chaer.* 1.4.7), he acted out of compassion for this woman he cared about rather than from a zeal for vengeance or even economic remuneration (see 9:13; 12:7; cf. p. Ketub. 11:3, §2).

Fifth, Joseph values obedience to God above his own honor (cf. 7:21-27; 23:5-11). When God reveals the truth to Joseph, he immediately believes and obeys God's will, unbelievable as the truth would seem without a deep trust in God's power. Joseph's response to God's revelation reveals the depth of his trust in God, especially since the revelation was limited to a dream.[63] Joseph was convinced enough by the revelation to believe what was on natural terms impossible (cf. Lk 1:37), and to obey God. This example, too, summons the reader to trust and obey God, responding differently than those who do not trust his word.[64] Because Joseph alone received this revelation, outsiders in the story world would still think that he had gotten Mary pregnant before the wedding. He would remain an object of shame in a society dominated by the value

60. He may have paid a "bride price" if the "reforms" suggested by Ilan 1996: 90-91 (cf. also a rule in m. Soṭa 1:5) were not as pervasive in Galilee, and perhaps not in Judea, in this period as rabbinic tradition might imply (the sources suggest that they were instituted only by the first-century Pharisaic "schools"). After the reforms, a Jewish man might marry young and pay off the bride price only in the case of divorce; he had to continue supporting her until he finished paying off the bride price (p. B. Meṣ. 1:5, §4). In many traditional cultures bride prices represent a significant investment, testifying to how much the groom and bridal family value the wife; sometimes the groom might not even finish paying (cf. Eickelman 1989: 173 on wealthier Middle Eastern families today). In some societies the amount of money involved depended partly on the bride's physical attractiveness (Ps.-Demosth. *Or.* 59, *Against Neaera* 113); Mediterranean peoples often viewed lack of monetary bride price as unusual (Arrian *Indica* 17.4).

61. M. Giṭ. 2:5; 9:3, 4, 8. Cf. most commentators (Hill 1972: 78; Carson 1984b: 75; Tosato 1979; Derrett 1973: 38; France 1985: 77; Davies and Allison 1988: 204-5); pace Gundry 1982: 21-22.

62. A *git,* or certificate of divorce, could provide the husband possession of the dowry (cf. *B.G.U.* 1103, in Sherk 1988: 246), but the more complex the certificate the more necessary the aid of a village scribe, hence publication of the news.

63. The mention of Joseph's anxiety probably has more to do with the story line than with the frequency of citing mental states when relating dreams (cited by Davies and Allison 1988: 206; Plut. *Brut.* 36.4; Jos. *Ant.* 11.334; Philost. *V.A.* 4.34). We may infer the centrality of the dream to Matthew's account by the supernatural guidance (dreams — 2:12, 13, 19, 22; cf. Acts 2:17 — or the star — 2:2, 9) represented in every paragraph from 1:18-25 to the end of the second chapter.

64. Some ancient readers *might* also think Joseph regretful for having mistrusted Mary (cf. Ach. Tat. 5.19.6, which may also suggest suspense here), but at any rate readers would recognize that God vindicated Mary in her betrothed husband's eyes.

of honor.[65] Joseph's obedience to God cost him the right to value his own reputation.

Excursus on Dreams (1:20)

Dreams were often, though not always, regarded as sufficient grounds for faith. Whether in Greece and Macedonia (Hom. *Il.* 1.63; 5.150; Virg. *Aen.* 4.556-57; 7.415-20; Ovid *Metam.* 9.685-701; 15.653-54; Paus. 4.19.5-6; 9.26.4; Longus 1.7; 2.23, 26-27; 3.27; 4.35; Appian *R.H.* 11.9.56; 12.12.83; Arrian *Alex.* 2.18.1; Babrius 136.3-4; Ach. Tat. 1.3.2; 4.1.4; 7.12.4; Char. *Chaer.* 1.12.5; 2.9.6; 3.7.4; 4.1.2; 5.5.5-7; 6.2.2; 6.8.3; cf. Orphic Hymn 85-87; Epidauros inscriptions; Hadas 1951: 184-85; Reinhold 1983: 35; Oberhelman 1979; Hanson 1980; Martin 1987: 48-50; Martin 1991), Rome (Tac. *Ann.* 2.14; Marc. Aur. *Med.* 1.17.8; van der Horst 1973: 221-22), Egypt (Ezek. *Exag.* 68-89; Sib. Or. 3.293; Philo *Mig.* 190; Deissmann 1978: 154; Lewis 1983: 99), Carthage (Dio Cass. bk. 13, fr. in Zonaras 8.22), the East (Herod. *Hist.* 1.34, 107, 127), Palestine (Jos. *War* 1.328; 2.116; *Life* 208-10), among later rabbis (ARN 40 A; 46, §§128-29 B; b. B. Bat. 10a; Ber. 55a-58a; Ḥag. 14b; Gen. Rab. 17:5; 44:17; 89:5-6, 8; Lev. Rab. 3:5; 34:12; Qoh. Rab. 1:1, §1; 3:2, §2; 5:2, §1; 5:6, §1; Lam. Rab. 1.1.16-18; Zeitlin 1975; Alexander 1995), or in magical papyri (*PGM* 4.2076-80, 2444-45, 2625, 3172; *PDM Sup.* 117-30), people believed that dreams conveyed divine messages. So compelling was trust in dreams' warnings that a fabricated dream reportedly precipitated an innocent man's execution (Dio Cassius *R.H.* 60.14.4–15.1; cf. Appian *R.H.* 12.2.9), and some warned of false dream-tellers and interpreters (Juv. *Sat.* 6.542-47; Lam. Rab. 1:1, §14-15; cf. Virg. *Aen.* 5.636).

God revealed things to biblical heroes in Jewish tradition as well (e.g., Gen 28:12; 37:5-9; Dan 2:19; cf. Jos. *Ant.* 2.13-16, 63-73), and later stories amplified the frequency of such revelations (1QapGen 19.14-23; Jub. 27:1-3; 32:1; 41:24; Ezek. *Exag.* 68-89; Jos. *Ant.* 6.38; 7.147; Ps-Philo 9:10; 42:3; 4 Ezra 10:59; Test. Abr. 4 A; 4, 6 B; Life of Adam 23:2/Apoc. Mos. 2:2; Endres 1987: 207). Perhaps most to the point here, God promised Moses' father in a dream that he would keep the infant Moses safe (Jos. *Ant.* 2.216-19).

Some dreams were especially believed to be sacred, namely, those experienced in a sacred place. The ancient Near Eastern practice of incubation — receiving a dream by sleeping in a temple (cf. Gen 15:12-13; 1 Sam 3:3-4; 1 Kings 3:4-5; Keret in *ANET* 143, KRT A i; Aqhat in *ANET* 150, AQHT A i) — continued in the hellenistic and Roman periods (e.g., Diod. Sic. 1.25.3-4; 1.53.8; Paus. 1.34.5; 2.27.2; Herodian 4.8.3; Grant 1953: 16, 38; Oepke 1967: 223-24; Grant 1986: 66-67; cf. Rousselle 1985; in Josephus, Gnuse 1993). Later rabbis believed that revelatory

65. One who denounced his new bride as not being a virgin was normally presumed honest, given the price of the wedding banquet (p. Ketub. 1:1, §7; though cf. differences on the burden of proof in m. Ketub. 1:6); exceptions were made if she had bled earlier (p. Ketub. 1:1, §4).

dreams could be secured through fasting (p. Ketub. 12.3, §7) or their ill pronouncements revoked through fasting (Pesiq. Rab Kah. 28:2). Still, people realized that not all dreams were divine revelations, and those who were more skeptical dismissed most dreams from being revelations (Sir 34/31:1-8; Ep. Arist. 213-16; Jos. *Apion* 1.207-8; Hom. *Od.* 19.559-67; Herod. *Hist.* 7.12-19; Arist. *Soul; Prophecy in Sleep;* Artem. *Oneir.* 1.1; Herodian 2.9.3; cf. b. Hor. 13b; Cic. *De Divin.* 2.58.119–72.150; Diog. Laert. 6.2.43). Some dreams were even intended or regarded as divine deceptions (Hom. *Il.* 2.20-21; Virg. *Aen.* 5.893-96; *P. Par.* 47).

Of all New Testament writers, especially Matthew stresses revelation through dreams (2:12, 13, 19, 22; 27:19). The character of the dream is noteworthy. Pagan (e.g., Hom. *Il.* 23.65, 83-85; Eurip. *Hecuba* 30-34, 703-6; Virg. *Aen.* 1.353-54; 2.268-97, 772-94; 4.351-52; 5.721-23; Ovid *Metam.*11.586-88, 635, 650-73; Apul. *Metam.* 8.8; 9.31; Plut. *Bravery of Women, Mor.* 252F; cf. Hom. *Od.* 4.795-839; 19.546-49; Appian *R.H.* 8.1.1; Arrian *Alex.* 7.30.2) and Jewish (ARN 40A; Pesiq. Rab. Kah. 11:23; p. Ḥag. 2:2, §5; Ketub. 12:3, §7; Sanh. 6:6, §2; Qoh. Rab. 9:10, §1; the earliest Christian example is Acts of Paul 11:6) dreams often included apparitions of deceased persons; like the biblical tradition, however, Matthew limited apparitions to angels (in Matthew's narrative, the angel of the Lord appears only in dreams until the appearance in 28:2); this account also lacks typical postbiblical expansions (see France 1985: 78).[66]

Jesus is the Savior (1:20-21). But while Matthew emphasizes the authority of Scripture through his citation of Isaiah and fidelity, commitment, and obedience through the example of Joseph, he also provides teaching about salvation through Christ. Even while Jesus is in Mary's womb, the angel declares that his name will be *Yeshua* (here in its Greek form *Iēsous,* generally translated "Joshua" in the English Old Testament and "Jesus" in the New), which means "God is salvation" (e.g., Fenton 1977: 43; cf. Bultmann 1968: 291).[67] Like "Joseph" and "John," "Yeshua" is among the common Jewish names attested on inscriptions from this period (cf. Ilan 1987). But the symbolic use of names was

66. Miller 1990 thinks that early Judaism blurred the older distinction between night visions and dreams; Gnuse 1990 favors the OT dream genre here (standard revelations such as those to Jacob, not like Joseph's or Daniel's). Josephus hellenizes some of his dream reports (see Gnuse 1989)

67. Later rabbis shortened Jesus' name (but not that of other Yeshuas) to Yeshu, possibly to avoid this meaning of his name (Blinzler 1959: 24-25). The rabbinic tradition of the Messiah's naming before the world's creation (Hagner 1993: 19 cites b. Pesaḥ. 54a, bar.; one might add b. Ned. 39b, bar.; Gen. Rab. 1:4; Lev. Rab. 14:1 — his spirit; Pesiq. R. 33:6; Midr. Ps. 72:17; in Lev. Rab. 30:16 the Messiah himself appears preexistent) may not have been prominent enough in Matthew's day to have been obvious for interpreting this passage (though cf. perhaps 1 Enoch 46:1-2; 48:2-3; 62:7; 4 Ezra 12:32; 13:26); it might even respond to Christian polemic (Montefiore and Loewe 1974: 586). The Tannaitic Mek. Pisha 1.54-56 fails to presuppose the tradition, so even if it existed this early it was probably not prominent even in rabbis' thinking. More relevant, early tradition reports that Moses' name fit an Egyptian verb for "save" (Jos. *Ant.* 2.228; cf. *Apion* 1.286; Allison 1993b: 144-45).

common in the biblical tradition (e.g., Gen 41:51-52; Hos 1:4, 6, 9; Greeks also played on names, e.g., Hom. *Od.* 1.62; 5.340), and Jesus would bear this name because he would save his people from their sins (1:21). Jesus' other acts of "salvation"[68] point to his ultimate redemption of "his people," which for Matthew still means Israel (e.g., 2:4, 6; 4:16, 23; 21:23; 27:64; cf. 10:6; 19:28; Lk 1:10; 2:10), echoing earlier biblical usage (e.g., 13:15; 15:8; also in early Jewish usage, e.g., *Lives of the Prophets* 2:1 [25 in Schermann, on Jeremiah]). Many of the quotations in Matthew's infancy narratives derive from passages stressing God's deliverance of his people from slavery (cf. Willis 1993). Matthew speaks of more than personal repentance; he evokes the Old Testament hope of the salvation of God's people, including the justice and peace of God's kingdom.

More than anything Matthew's narrative of the virgin birth, like every other event in Matthew, explains and exalts the character of the Lord he regularly worships. If Matthew finds implicit truth about Jesus throughout Israel's Bible, he expects his audience even more fully to hear what his own narratives declare about Jesus explicitly. In view of Matthew 18:20 and 28:20, Matthew clearly understands "God with us" in Isaiah 7:14 to mean that Jesus is truly God (Mt 1:23; Ridderbos 1974: 102).[69] But as God "with us," Jesus is also the fully human one who "saves his people" by the cross. Matthew thus invites his audience to consider and worship the God who accepted the ultimate vulnerability, born as an infant to humiliated and probably relatively poor parents into a world hostile to his presence (cf. 2:1-16).

Pagans Worship Jesus (Matthew 2:1-12)

(Cf. perhaps Lk 2:8-20, although the accounts are probably unrelated.) Matthew confronts his audience in this passage with a summons to personal decision by contrasting the main characters, a practice that constituted a standard ancient literary device (*synkrisis;* cf., e.g., Shuler 1982: 50; Stanton 1993: 77-80, 83; in rhetoric, e.g., Demosthenes *On the Embassy* 174). The Magi and scribes function as composite characters, like the chorus in a Greek drama (Arist. *Poetics* 18.19, 1456a). The pagan astrologers worship Jesus; Israel's ruler seeks his death, acting like a pagan king; Jerusalem's religious elite — forerunners of Matthew's readers' opponents — take Jesus for granted. Matthew forces his audience to

68. 8:25, though not in Mk 4:38; Mt 9:22; 14:36. In the eschatological sense, cf. 10:22; 16:25; 19:25; probably 21:9; the Greek term is broad in meaning. Early Christians continued the Jewish story of salvation in history (Wright 1992a: 458).

69. Cf. Ellis 1974: 28; Danker 1992; Sib. Or. 8.456-79; Apoc. Adam 7:9; Test. Sol. 6:8; pace Harris 1992: 256-58. Given the emperor's role as Jupiter's agent in Flavian imperial theology, Jesus' role as the agent of God's presence and reign (see Carter 1998b) would have implications far beyond Palestine. Allison 1993b: 154-55 observes that Moses acted as a god to Pharaoh (Ex 4:16; 7:1) and tentatively asks if new Moses imagery might be in view; nevertheless, the reference to omnipresence in 18:20 (see comment there) demands a higher Christology than this.

identify with the pagan Magi rather than with Herod or Jerusalem's religious elite, and hence to recognize God's interest in the Gentile mission. The God who sought servants from the pagan west like the Roman centurion (8:5-13) also sought previously pagan servants "from the east" (2:1; cf. Is 2:6) like the Magi (see 8:11).

Some see the passage as substantially reliable historically, leaving the burden of proof with the questioners (Hagner 1993: 25); others doubt even the birth at Bethlehem (e.g., Meier 1991a: 216), despite its attestation in both Gospels with infancy narratives, as well as (possibly derivative) echoes in early rabbinic disputes (Herford 1966: 253-55).[70] Matthew's method elsewhere leads us to accept his dependence on the substance of his source; his source, however, is not available for more detailed historical examination.[71]

The Magi's identity may support the narrative's essential reliability: given the rampant attraction to astrology in their culture and official Jewish polemic against it, Matthew and his Jewish church would probably not have made up the story about Magi believing in Jesus (see Davies 1966b: 12), though they might put a preexisting story to good use. Given its probable earliness, the story more likely than not preserves a historical core; but with insufficient historical evidence to offer a further judgment, I will focus primarily on the narrative's theology, which is Matthew's focus in any case.

Matthew challenges prejudice against pagans (2:1-2). This narrative fits Matthew's theme of the Gentile mission (e.g., 1:3, 5-6; 3:9; 4:15; 8:10-12, 28). The first story after Jesus' birth opens with Magi who have traveled a long distance to offer homage to a new king born in Judea. Leaders in some realms often dispatched official representatives to congratulate new leaders in other realms (e.g., Jos. *War* 2.309; 4.498-501; Acts 25:13).[72] The Magi enter Jerusalem with a large enough caravan to attract the city's attention (2:3; cf. Ruth 1:19) and to sustain them in comfort during the long journey from the East (cf. 2:16). (Caravans normally provided protection from robbers and evil spirits, especially at night; see, e.g., t. ʿAbod. Zar. 1:16.) The Magi must have assumed that they would find the newborn king in Herod's palace in Jerusalem.

Magi were Persian astrologers, and that they would respond to celestial phenomena in the manner in which the text depicts is not implausible (A. B. Bruce 1979: 1:71; Allen 1977: 14).

70. In view of the unlikelihood that John is unfamiliar with the Bethlehem tradition, Jn 7:42 either represents polemic against it (for its Judean connections) or, more likely in our view, assumes it as common knowledge among his audience, ironically polemicizing against the ignorance of the Judean elite.

71. For one hypothetical reconstruction of Matthew's source, see Brown 1977: 116-17. It is highly unlikely that Matthew has transformed Luke's shepherds (pace Gundry 1982: 26): although developing traditions could transform other people into rulers (e.g., LXX Job 2:11; Test. Job 3:7/6; later tradition on the Magi), this story has little in common with Luke; even the timing (2:16) is quite different.

72. Friedländer 1965: 1:211; O'Toole 1978: 16-17. Overman 1996: 44 points to the broader category of "embassy" of which our examples represent a more specific kind.

Excursus on Magi

Against some unlikely alternative proposals,[73] most scholars recognize that these Magi belonged to a priestly caste of Eastern astrologers.[74] In most accounts Magi hail from Persia or Babylon (e.g., Cic. *De Leg.* 2.10.26; Philo *Spec.* 3.100; *Prob.* 74; Dio Chrys. *Or.* 36; Lucian *Runaways* 8; Diog. Laert. 8.1.3; Char. *Chaer.* 5.9.4; Philost. *V.A.* 1.24).[75]

The Chaldeans or Persians were known for divination (Apul. *Metam.* 2.12; Arrian *Alex.* 7.18.2, 4) and astrology (Diod. Sic. 1.81.6; 2.31.8; Juv. *Sat.* 6.553-64; Aul. Gel. 1.9.6; 14.1; Philo *Dreams* 1.53; Sib. Or. 3.227; Pesiq. R. 14:8) and the Greeks and Romans regularly associated Chaldean Magi with magical powers (Char. *Chaer.* 5.9.4), prediction of the future (Marc. Aur. *Med.* 3.3.1; Arrian *Alex.* 7.16.5), dream interpretation (Herod. *Hist.* 1.107, 127; 7.12-19; cf. Jos. *Ant.* 10.195-203; Cic. *Divin.* 1.46), or specially regarded wisdom (Diog. Laert. 8.1.3; 9.11.61; Dio Chrys. *Or.* 36.38-48; Lucian *Runaways* 8; cf. Cic. *De Leg.* 2.10.26; Philo *Prob.* 74; *Spec.* 3.100; Philost. *V.A.* 1.24).[76] Roman officials are known to have received Magi with honor (Albright and Mann 1971: 14; Schweizer 1975: 37), and Herod was typically generous to pagan cities (see Josephus 1982: 90-93). A star allegedly guided Aeneas to the place where he was to found Rome (Virg. *Aen.* 2.694; Hagner 1993: 25), and a goddess caused a trail of heavenly light or fire to guide the Argonauts as long as they needed it (Ap. Rhod. 294-97, 301-2).

Whatever these Magi's religious commitments, Matthew's audience would probably recall the Magi of their Greek translation of the OT: they were Daniel's enemies, whom Daniel's narratives portray in a negative light as selfish, incompetent, and brutal pagans (cf. Dan 2:2, 10). This is even clearer in some later Greek versions of the Old Testament (Theodotion: Dan 1:20; 2:2, 10, 27; 4:7; 5:7, 11, 15; Aquila: Deut 18:11; 1 Sam 28:3, 7-9; 2 Kings 21:6; 23:24; Is 29:4); see also Josephus *Ant.* 10.195-203. Here a group of people who were part of the court of the Persian ruler, whose role included honoring his reign ("king of kings," Suet. *Caligula* 5; Plut. *Pompey* 38.2; Arrian *Alex.* 6.29.11; Deissmann 1978: 363), honor Jesus instead (Horsley 1993a: 58-59).[77]

73. McNamara 1968; Charbel 1983; Custance 1975: 19-20; Davies and Allison 1988: 228. Schnackenburg 1985: 23 is uncommitted. Biblical tradition called Arabia "East," but this is hardly a frequent location for Magi.

74. F. F. Bruce 1951: 184; Hagner 1993: 27; cf. Argyle 1963: 30; Liddell and Scott 1968: 1071; Montefiore 1968: 2:9.

75. On the Magi of Persia, see further Olmstead 1959: 28-29, 196, 251, 372, 449, 477-78, 496, 517.

76. Magi were not, however, positive in all cases; cf., e.g., Herod. *Hist.* 3.79-80. Jews may have also viewed their association with dreams as a divine accommodation to pagan inability to hear more clearly (cf. Gnuse 1990b).

77. Earlier texts apply "King of kings" to the Babylonian ruler (Ezra 7:12; Ezek 26:7; Dan 2:37),

Without condoning astrology, Matthew's narrative challenges his audience's prejudice against outsiders to their faith (cf. also 8:5-13; 15:21-28): even the most pagan of pagans may respond to Jesus if given the opportunity (cf. Jonah 1:13-16; 3:6–4:1, 10-11). For one special event in history, the God who rules the heavens chose to reveal himself where pagans were looking (cf. Acts 19:12, 15-20; A. B. Bruce 1979: 1:70). Yet even supernatural guidance like that of the star can take the astrologers only so far; for more specific direction they must ask the leaders in Jerusalem where the king is to be born (2:2). That is, their celestial revelation was only partial; they must finally submit to God's revelation in the Scriptures, preserved by the Jewish people (cf. Meier 1980: 11).

Matthew challenges prejudice that unjustly accommodates political power (2:3, 7-8). The issues implied in this passage are not merely ethnic; they also address social stratification. Magi held a significant political role in Persia (Horsley 1993a: 53-54), but this would probably not be their characteristic that would be first evident to Matthew's audience.[78] By contrast, many would remember Herod as a client-king of the Romans (Horsley 1993a: 40-44); if Persius *Sat.* 5.180 refers to Herod the Great (so LCL 386-87n.4), Herod's power was recalled as far away as Rome in the second half of the first century. Herod's oppressive taxation and tyranny (Horsley 1993a: 44-45) had invited resistance, hence longing for the coming of Israel's rightful ruler (Horsley 1993a: 46-49). Likewise the priests and scribes of Herod's late reign represent the ruling class, whose interests were allied with those of Herod (Horsley 1993a: 51).

That Herod is dismayed by the Magi's announcement is not surprising (2:3); astrology was widespread, especially in Greco-Roman paganism.[79] The

---

other texts to any great king (Test. Jud. 3:7), some Greeks to Zeus or the supreme deity (Dio Chrys. *Second Disc. on Kingship* 75; *PGM* 4.1201-2); magical papyri often employ the expression imprecisely (e.g., *PGM* 2.53-54; 4.640-44). Jewish texts most often apply the title (sometimes "king of kings of kings") to the supreme God, whether in hellenistic (3 Macc 5:35; Philo *Decal.* 41; *Spec.* 1.18; *PGM* 13.605; cf. Egyptian Book of the Dead, spell 185Eb, part S-1), nonrabbinic Semitic (1 Enoch 9:4; 84:2; 3 Enoch 22:15; 25:4; Aramaic incant. text 67:2), or rabbinic texts, both tannaitic (m. 'Abot 3:1; t. Sanh. 8:9; Sifra Sav Mekhilta DeMiluim 98.8.5; ARN 25; 27A; 1, §1; 27, §56; 29, §61B) and later (b. Ber. 28b; 32b-33a; 62b; Sanh. 38a; Gen. Rab. 8:7; 12:1; 14:1; Ex. Rab. 2:2; 6:1; 20:1; Lev. Rab. 18:1; 33:3; Num. Rab. 1:4; 4:1, 20; 8:3; 14:3; 15:3; 18:22; Ruth 2:3; Esth. Rab. 3:15; Qoh. Rab. 2:12, §1; 4:17, §1; 5:10, §2; 9:15, §7; 9:18, §2; 12:1, §1; 12:7, §1; Song Rab. 1:12, §1; 7:5, §3; Lam. Rab. 1:16, §50; Pesiq. R. 13:7; 15, preamble; 23:8); as well as in early Christian texts (1 Tim 6:15; Rev 17:14; 19:16). This application may continue an earlier adaptation of the royal title in "God of gods" (Deut 10:17; Ps 136:3; cf. *PGM* 5.468-69; 22b.20; 62.24; *PDM* 14.684), but derivation from secular imagery may have marred the title's sacredness for a few interpreters (p. Meg. 1:9, §17).

78. His audience might, however, associate them with Parthia and hence with opposition to Rome, the power with which Herod was allied and which crushed Jerusalem in 66-70 (see Horsley 1993a: 56).

79. E.g., Horace *Ode* 2.17.17-25; Petron. *Sat.* 76; Mart. *Epig.* 9.82.1; Juv. *Sat.* 6.579; Artem. *Oneir.* 2.36; Vettius Valens *Anthologies* 5.9.2; Stobaeus *Eclogae* 1.5.14; *P. Tebt.* 276; *PGM* 4.651; 13.709-11; 36.330-32; 62.52-75; *PDM Sup.* 183-84. In more detail, see MacMullen 1966: 128-62; Friedländer 1965: 1:185-88; Winslow 1971: 243-44. The Greeks had borrowed the practice from the East (cf. Rochberg-Halton 1984; Rochberg-Halton 1988; Rochberg-Halton 1989 [including comment on nativity omens]; Grant 1953: 60; *ANET* 333). For skepticism concerning astrology, see, e.g., Epicurus in Long 1974: 41-42; as well as Pliny *N.H.* 2.6.28-30; Sextus Empiricus *Against the Professors* 5.

Roman world respected astrological confirmations of its rulers (cf. Oster 1982), and emperors feared astrological predictions of their demise (Tac. *Ann.* 14.22; Suet. *Nero* 36). Although the Hebrew Bible forbade divination (Deut 18:9-13), including astrology (Is 47:13; cf. Deut 4:19), it had infiltrated much of Jewish thought and practice by this period. Although all observant Jews affirmed that God was sovereign over the stars (Jos. *Ant.* 1.156; Philo *Op. Mund.* 46; *Spec. Leg.* 1.13), some accepted the stars' relative authority over the nations (later, e.g., Test. Sol. 8:2-4). Many more, whether or not they regarded astrology as sinful, accepted astrology's accuracy in prediction, at least for the nations (e.g., Jos. *Ant.* 1.69; 18.216-17; Philo *Creation* 58-59; t. Qidd. 5.17; Cohen 1982). Thus, despite opposition to astrology,[80] most Jewish people seem to have acquiesced to its pervasive influence in late antiquity.[81] Herod thus had every reason to believe the astrologers' report (2:3).

Believing it led to his dismay, for there was little room for two kings in his realm: though he was Idumean by birth (Jos. *War* 1.123; 1.313), he considered himself "king of the Jews."[82] A cosmic signal of another ruler would thus necessarily indicate his own demise. Comets (like Halley's, ca. 12 B.C.) and analogous celestial signs usually signaled the death of one ruler and the consequent rise of another (e.g., Suet. *Vesp.* 23; Lucan *C.W.* 1.529; cf. Pliny *N.H.* 2.23.92 in Malina and Rohrbaugh 1992: 32; Artem. *Oneir.* 2.36; on ancient comet interpretation, see Keyser 1994). Thus tradition declared that a constellation informed Magi of Alexander the Great's birth as future ruler of Asia (Allen 1977: 14), and other sources contend that the heavens offered similar predictions for Mithridates and Abraham (Albright and Mann 1971: 14; cf. Montefiore 1968: 2:9).[83] Contempo-

80. Cf., e.g., 1 Enoch 6:7, MSS; 8:3; Jub. 8:3; 12:17; 13:16-18; Philo *Praem.* 58; Syr. Men. Sent. 292-93; Sib. Or. 3:221-22, 227-29; Sifra Qed. pq. 6.203.2.1; Sifre Deut. 171.4.1; Did. 3:4.

81. Mek. Pisha 2.44-46; in more detail, see Charlesworth 1977; cf. Allegro 1964; Mayer 1972: 123-25; Siker 1987; Stieglitz 1981; contrast Lehmann 1975. First-century writers even interpreted elements of the temple (Jos. *War* 5.214, 217; cf. Philo *Q. Ex.* 2.79) accordingly. Later Judaism became even more open to these influences (Wächter 1969; cf. Goldstein and Pingree 1979), and later synagogues adopted the Greek zodiac to symbolize God's rule over the cosmos (May 1944: 9; Goodenough 1953/68: 8:167-218; Hachlili 1977; Meyers 1980: 106; Narkiss 1986: 185-86; Shanks 1984; *CIJ* 2:212-13, 240-42); but astrology permeated the Mediterranean world even more in those centuries, e.g., in relation to Mithraism (cf., e.g., Beck 1976abc; Campbell 1968: 44-180) and Gnosticism (Burkitt 1932: 30-33). Pagans could also accept prediction without causation (e.g., the late writer Plotinus 2.3.1).

82. Though Judeans had reason to resent a foreigner's reign (Deut 17:15), it was known that the Idumeans had converted to Judean customs (Strabo *Geog.* 16.2.34); in favor of Herod's claim to be religiously Jewish, see Hadas-Lebel 1993. Nevertheless, it was also known that Herod the Great built pagan temples for Gentiles (e.g., Jos. *Ant.* 15.298; 16.147; on his attempts to achieve honor through benefaction in general, see Jacobson 1988). For Matthew, Jesus is the rightful king (21:5).

83. Some see in the star a symbolic reference to Num. 24:17 (Meier 1980: 11; Harrington 1982: 17; Albright and Mann 1971: 14; cf. Test. Levi 18.3; Hagner 1993: 25); Davies and Allison 1988: 235 suggest that Matthew fails to cite it because his formula quotations in 2:1-23 have a geographical focus. (Far less plausible is the suggestion that this verse was excised from Matthew's text by an anti-Gnostic redactor — Albright and Mann 1971: 15-16; it lacks textual support, dates

rary writers often noted heavenly signs portending major events (e.g., Tac. *Ann.* 14.22; *Hist.* 5.13; Suet. *Vesp.* 23; Sib. Or. 3.334-37; 5.155-56); Matthew himself may draw a parallel here with the sign of Jesus' coming kingdom (24:29-30).[84] Magi reportedly predicted the rise of other rulers (Pliny *N.H.* 1.47; 30.6; Boring 1995: 42). Nor need this have been Herod's first encounter with supernatural signals of competition; other peoples in the East anticipated a coming king who would begin an age of universal peace (cf. Schweizer 1975: 38).

News of a star signaling a new ruler in his realm would thus undoubtedly trouble a ruler as paranoid as Herod (compare Suet. *Nero* 36); other rulers also proved paranoid about astrologers (e.g., MacMullen 1966: 133; Kee 1980: 71), and some had been ready to kill their own descendants to keep the throne (Herod. *Hist.* 1.107-10; see comment below on 2:16).[85] That the Magi seek one "*born* King of the Jews" may further underline the challenge to Herod, who was widely known to have achieved rule by warfare and politics, not by birth (Overman 1996: 43). If Herod had actually permitted some to hail him as a deity (cf. *OGIS* 415) and, more likely, had rewarded prophets who appeared to validate his reign (Jos. *Ant.* 15.373-79; Witherington 1990: 93 suggests that this validation was intended in a messianic sense) or otherwise revealed messianic aspirations (Agourides 1992), one can understand just what sort of threat the Magi's announcement represented to him. That all Jerusalem was troubled with him (a strong term; cf. 14:26) may indicate the degree to which they felt threatened by the possibility of political instability more than they longed for a deliverer.

In Jewish tradition, both Pharaoh and his people feared when they learned in advance of the coming of Israel's deliverer (Jos. *Ant.* 2.206; Allison 1993b: 146) — again casting Judea's leadership as equivalent to the oppressors of Is-

---

Gnosticism too early, and ignores Matthew's usual practice of citing only one primary text per passage in the infancy narratives.) Further, Bar Kochba provides early second-century evidence for the assumption of star or "son of a star" as a messianic title (Albright and Mann 1971: 15). But in Mt 2:1-12 the star signals Jesus' coming rather than represents the Messiah (Soares Prabhu 1976: 9).

84. Kepler suggested a temporary light from a nova or supernova (Sachs and Walker 1984); some later scholars have suggested in his name that the event was historically a conjunction of Jupiter and Saturn in 7 B.C. (Stauffer 1960: 32-34; Harrington 1982: 16-17), or a conjunction of Jupiter, Saturn, and Mars followed by a temporary bright star in 7-6 B.C. (Ramsay 1898: 215-17), a suggestion Babylonian astronomical texts may disconfirm (Sachs and Walker 1984). Chinese astronomers observed a nova for 70 days in 5/4 B.C. (the 1977 *Quarterly Journal of the Royal Astronomy Society,* cited in France 1985: 82; see Humphreys 1992). Luz 1989: 132 surveys various proposals, but, given Luke's failure to mention the star and Jesus' parents' apparent lack of knowledge (Mk 3:31-35), doubts even a historical nucleus here. Clear astronomical evidence for a historical nucleus may be questionable here, but the counterarguments are also weaker than they might first appear: Luke's birth narratives do not extend to Jesus' second year, as here, and the Gospel tradition gives other examples that miracles were less than coercive (e.g., the probably reliable Q tradition in Mt 11:3-6). Allison 1993c argues that the star represents an angel; given the angelic character of stars in Jewish thought this is reasonable, though it does not fit the imagery of the current narrative.

85. Küchler 1989 thinks that Jesus here replaces Augustus as rightful emperor because the star could symbolize Augustus; but such an interpretation would better suit Luke's presentation of Jesus' nativity.

rael's true remnant.[86] Matthew's community probably was still struggling with people of whom Herod and the Jerusalemites would remind them — people too concerned about their own political and religious status or stability to acknowledge Jesus as rightful ruler over their people.

Matthew challenges what he regards as spiritual complacency. Not knowing himself where the king would be born, Herod gathers the religious experts (2:4), most of whom by this period were loyal to his agendas (cf. Jos. *Ant.* 15.2, 5). The successors of these experts, the chief priests (cf. 16:21; 21:15, 23, 45; 26:3; 27:41, 62; 28:11) and scribes (cf. 7:29; 15:1; 17:10; 21:15; 23:2; 26:3; 27:41), in the following generation frequently become Jesus' enemies; someone hearing the Gospel more than once would therefore view this group negatively.

These experts immediately identify the place where the Messiah will be born on the basis of Micah 5:2 (Mt 2:5-6).[87] Contemporary Judaism had not forgotten Micah's indication that the Messiah would hail from Bethlehem (Jn 7:42; Edgar 1958: 48; cf. Jeremias 1969: 277; Justin *1 Apol.* 34); those who later polemicized against the Christian appeal to the Bethlehem prophecy did so on other grounds (Gen. Rab. 82:10; cf. Herford 1966: 253-55; Bagatti 1971: 15). Nor did Matthew's opponents deny that Jesus had been born there (Stauffer 1960: 20); as early as the second century Bethlehemites knew the exact cave where Jesus had reportedly been born in Luke's manger (cf. Jerome *Letter 58 to Paulinus* 3; Paulinus of Nola *Epistle* 31.3; Stauffer 1960: 21; Finegan 1969: 20-23).[88]

But while the religious leaders know where the Messiah will be born, they do not join the Magi in their quest (cf. also Filson 1960: 57). These were the religious leaders, but they failed to act on their most critical biblical knowledge. Although these authorities did not desire to kill Jesus as Herod did, their successors a generation later did seek his death (26:57, 59), and their Judean successors in

86. The significance of this portrayal becomes all the starker when we recall the role this particular enemy played in Jewish thought; Egypt is virtually Israel's only enemy in rabbinic parables (Johnston 1977b: 626). For Philo's Greek dislike of native Egyptians, cf. Goodenough 1962: 132.

87. Micah's Ephratah is the Ephrath of Gen. 35 with a *he* directional, i.e., "Bethlehem *toward* Ephrath." Matthew probably omits the detail as irrelevant for his readers, substituting the more helpful "in Judah." The "shepherd" statement alludes to Mic 5:4; Matthew also changes the "least" to "not the least" (see Gundry 1982: 29 for targumic parallels; cf. 20:26). The weaving in of a clause from the Davidic 2 Sam 5:2 is also significant (Gundry 1975: 207). For studies of Matthew's interpretation of the text here, see France 1981a; Petrotta 1985; idem 1990.

88. Later generations may have connected the grotto of Jesus' birth with the Mithraic cave (Gervers 1979; cf. Campbell 1968: 6-11; for Mithraism borrowing Christian symbolism, cf. Latourette 1970: 247), but the tradition of Jesus' birth, and certainly Bethlehem's caves, predates the primary spread of Mithraism in the Roman world in the second century (cf. Grant 1986: 40-41). Pace Boring 1995: 42-43, it is unlikely that the Tammuz grove indicates a pagan cultic site before the Christian site; Bethlehem was a Jewish town, and the supposition of a pre-Hadrianic pagan grove there overstates the paganization of Judea near Jerusalem. (Sacred groves were, however, common; see, e.g., Deut 16:21; Paus. 5.10.1; 8.38.2, 5; Lucan *C.W.* 3.399-425.) For the tradition of the cave, see also Justin *Dial.* 78; Origen *Contra Celsum* 1.51; and later Euseb. *Life of Constantine* 3.43 (Finegan 1969: 20).

Matthew's day apparently resent Jesus' followers. As I argue in my comments on chapter 23, Matthew also intended his vehemence against the religious establishment of his day as a warning to his fellow disciples. Matthew is emphatic that the sin of taking Jesus for granted, like the sin of wishing him dead, is a sin that can especially characterize those who claim to be God's servants.

The pagans worship Jesus (2:9-11). A road led south to Bethlehem, which was about six miles from Jerusalem (cf. Monson 1979: 1-1; Gardner 1981: 172-73). Without a tail extending to earth as suggested in some modern artistic portrayals of the event, a celestial light could have pointed them only in the most general way or by symbolic means toward Judea, and could now "move" before them to Bethlehem (2:9-10) only in the sense that stationary objects in the sky appeared to move as travelers did. Why then does Matthew describe the star's "movement" in these terms? Possibly the moving star in Matthew alludes to the pillar of cloud guiding Israel in the wilderness (Soares Prabhu 1976: 280), suggesting that however the astrologers viewed the star, God used it in a manner reminiscent of Israel's salvation history.[89]

They find Jesus in Bethlehem, probably in a house.[90] That the Magi offer Jesus both homage and standard gifts from the East (2:11) fits Eastern practices (Montefiore 1968: 2:9; cf. *ANET* 286; contrast Bultmann 1968: 292); frankincense and myrrh were often used in royal courts (Van Beek 1960; cf. Fenton 1977: 47; Argyle 1963: 31); they were items of great cost (Rev 18:13; Test. Job 32:10/11; Ps 45:8; Song 3:6; 4:6).[91] Joy was customary at special public events (1 Sam 18:6; 2 Chron 30:26), such as the birth or accession of a ruler (1 Kings 1:40; 2 Kings 11:20), which may be relevant at Jesus' resurrection (28:8); Matthew might then be alluding to the good news to Israel in the first line of Zechariah 9:9, although he omits this in 21:5 (cf. Zeph 3:14). For Matthew, joy is the appropriate response to the kingdom (5:12; 13:44; 25:21, 23), although it carries no guarantee of perseverance (13:20-21).

Some scholars find in the Magi's homage to Jesus a reflection of biblical language alluding to the pilgrimage and homage of nations in Psalm 72:10 and/

89. Early Christian readers sometimes connected the star with a "pillar of light"; see the Syrian *Chronicle of Zuqnin,* redacted ca. A.D. 775, in Boring 1995: 41. For Matthew's probable adaptation of this pillar by way of Wis 10:17; 18:3, see Viviano 1996.

90. After what could have been as long as two years (cf. 2:16) Jesus was certainly no longer in the manger of Lk 2:7, 13; that accommodation was probably only a temporary measure due to crowding in the family house (see Bishop 1964; Danker 1972: 25; Bailey 1979; Byrne 1982; Kipgen 1983; cf. LaVerdiere 1985; Ottey 1986).

91. Of course, these items had other functions in other contexts (e.g., 1 Enoch 29:2). The Egyptians used myrrh for embalming with any spices except frankincense (Herod. *Hist.* 2.86); the Essenes cleansed clothes for the Sabbath with frankincense (*libona,* CD 11.4). It grew in Syria (Stern 1974/84: 1:15), among other places. Perhaps more significantly, they were used with some offerings (e.g., Ex 30:23, 34; Lev 2:1-2, 15-16; 5:11; 6:15; 24:7; Num 5:15 LXX; Jub. 3:27; 6:3; 16:24). Because most frankincense and myrrh derived from South Arabia and Somaliland, they were quite expensive (Pliny *N.H.* 12.65; Virg. *Georg.* 2.117; *P. Tebt.* 35; Horsley 1987: 129-31). Babylonian Magi burned frankincense on silver altars (Olmstead 1959: 517 cites Arrian *Anab.* 3.16.3; Curt. 5.1.19ff; Marmor Parium B, 6).

or Isaiah 60:6,[92] or to the Queen of Sheba visiting Solomon (1 Kings 10:1-13), or to all three texts (Soares Prabhu 1976: 281; Gundry 1982: 32). A late midrash on the Queen of Sheba story includes a miraculous star (Bruns 1961). If Matthew has Psalm 72 or 1 Kings 10 in mind, his narrative would portray Jesus as King Solomon's greatest son (cf. Mt 1:6-7; 12:42).[93]

At any rate, the threefold repetition of homage (2:2, 8, 11) reinforces the point of the narrative: if Israel will not honor Jesus, the Gentiles will (Harrington 1982: 17). Homage to Jesus also reflects some recognition of his identity (e.g., 8:2; 9:18; 14:33; 15:25), climaxing in the homage of 28:9, 17, a context that declares Jesus' royal authority equivalent to the Father's (28:18-20; cf. 4:10; Meier 1980: 11; Edwards 1987).[94] Prostration was standard before Eastern rulers (Char. *Chaer.* 5.2.2), and Diaspora Jews considered it an appropriate gesture of respect before officials (3 Macc 5:50; Test. Jos. 13:5; cf. Jos. and Asen. 5:7/10); but Matthew implies more than this. Probably the Magi narrative already implies divine honor of some sort; if anything, Persians would have a greater tendency to see obeisance as more than mortal respect more fully than Palestinian Jews would (cf. Arrian *Alex.* 4.11.8; Corn. Nep. 9 [Conon], 3.3; Esth 3:2).[95]

That the Magi needed a supernatural revelation to warn them not to return by way of Jerusalem (2:12) suggests their innocent naiveté.[96] Even had the Magi (or, less likely, Matthew's audience) known nothing of Herod's character (see comment on 2:16), few kings would be ready to surrender their own rule to one whom some foreigners hailed as king! Herod's "secret" meeting with them (2:7; in a positive sense, cf. 1:19) should have been as suspicious as the Sanhedrin's secret meeting in 26:3-5 (Gundry 1982: 30; cf. Prov 17:7). Their innocence compared to Herod's murderous shrewdness again reminds Matthew's readers not to prejudge the appropriate recipients of the gospel (cf. 13:3-23).

92. Widely held; see, e.g., Brown 1977: 187-88; Argyle 1963: 31; Meier 1980: 12; Davies and Allison 1988: 228, 253; Davies 1993: 36; cf. Montefiore 1968: 2:9.

93. Lachs 1987: 10 cites various rabbinic sources (generally late) to illustrate the gifts both Jew and Gentile would offer the Messiah (b. Pesiq. 118b; Esth. Rab. 1:1; Tanchuma Shoftim 19; Midr. Ps. 87.6, 189b; Gen. Rab. 78:16; Ex. Rab. 35:5).

94. One would "fall" to worship in the more technical sense but also to make entreaty (8:2; 15:25; 17:6, 14; 18:26; 20:20; 26:39; Jos. *Life* 138; sometimes with clasping knees, e.g., Eurip. *Orestes* 382). Respect for a deity could include looking at its feet (*PGM* 13.704-5).

95. If these Magi were Zoroastrian (see, e.g., b. Sanh. 39a; cf. Frye 1996: 67-74), they were dualists rather than traditional polytheists (pure Zoroastrians were monotheistic dualists, but in practice paganism had sometimes filtered into Zoroastrianism over time — see Olmstead 1959: 475); but most of Matthew's audience would grasp only the narrative's emphasis that they were pagan astrologers, especially given their probable primary reliance on the Daniel narratives.

96. This naiveté might reflect or conflict with popular stereotypes. Those in the Mediterranean world generally thought some Eastern "barbarians," particularly the Scythians, to be savage and murderous (2 Macc 4:47; 3 Macc 7:5; 4 Macc 10:7; Jos. *Apion* 2.269; Herod. *Hist.* 1.15; 4.66, 76; Diog. Laert. 1.102; Hor. *Ode* 4.5.25; Sen. *Dial.* 4.15.1; Plut. *Fortune of Alex.* 1.5, *Mor.* 328C; Char. *Chaer.* 2.9.3; Sext. Emp. *Pyrrh.* 1.149; 3.208, 210); but some viewed the Scythians as noble barbarians (e.g., Anacharsis to Croesus *Ep.* 9; Strabo 7.3.7; cf. *Greek Anth.* 7.92). But widely known Greek experience with the Persians had revealed a powerful civilization quite in contrast with the Scythians.

The Persecuted Child (Matthew 2:13-18)

Little evidence sheds light on the correspondence between Matthew's account here and the historical data behind it. Specific arguments both for and against its reliability are weak and rest primarily on one's broader critical presuppositions. I will summarize here what little extant historical evidence could possibly prove relevant to this pericope.

Second-century Jewish tradition, perhaps based on Christian claims (besides Matthew, compare later "infancy Gospels" in Hennecke 1963: 410-13), mentions Jesus' stay in Egypt, which it associates with the sorcery Jewish people felt prevailed there (Dalman 1973: 33; Plummer 1910: 17).[97] Egyptian Christians undoubtedly developed eagerly the tradition of Jesus' stay there, but a first-century origin for their tradition is likely. In the first century Egypt boasted a large Jewish population, including perhaps one-third of Alexandria (cf. Stambaugh and Balch 1986: 165-67; see *CPJ,* passim), and in this period many other Jews sought refuge there (Harrington 1982: 18; cf. 1 Kings 11:17, 40; Jer 26:21).[98] But early in the second century the Jewish community in Egypt, already unpopular with the Greeks (Jos. *Apion* 2.32), was virtually annihilated or exiled in response to a Jewish uprising; by the mid-second century, with memories of Egyptian Jewry fading, creation of a Jewish-Christian tradition there would be less likely. At the same time, their first-century source could simply be Matthew's Gospel. It was surely circulating in Egypt by then and could have provided the basis for the tradition; further, Egypt's large first-century Jewish population lacked reason to preserve a tradition about one more immigrant family.[99]

One can more easily venture comment, however, on Matthew's literary agenda.

God protects Jesus and his family. Matthew here narrates God's protec-

97. Luz 1989: 145 thinks the oldest form of the rabbinic traditions does not depend on Matthew here, and thus may attest that Jesus actually stayed in Egypt (certainly not that Matthew seeks to refute the magician libel, pace Lachs 1987: 11). On sorcery in Egypt, see, e.g., ARN 28A; 48, §132B; b. Qidd. 49b; Gen. Rab. 86:5; Exod. Rab. 9:6; 20:19; cf. Achtemeier 1976: 156; the prefect's circular in Horsley 1981: 47-51; Hom. *Od.* 4.228-34; Dauphin 1993; Frankfurter 1994. Perhaps the demon in Tob 8:3 flees to remote regions of Egypt to escape civilization, but it may simply be fleeing as far as possible from the fish-liver smoke.

98. Herod had no formal extradition treaty with the Roman authorities in Egypt, even if he knew where the family had fled or suspected (as he probably did not, in the logic of the story) that the object of his pursuit had escaped. Further, the family would easily have blended into the large Jewish community in Egypt, and if Jesus was born around 7 B.C., Herod sought his life roughly two years later (2:16), and Herod died in 4 B.C., then Jesus probably remained there little more than a year. Popular arguments concerning Jesus' "missing years" neglect that his contemporaries called him Jesus "of Nazareth," ignore his carpentry work (cf. on 13:53-58), and so on.

99. Arguments against the account based on treating summaries as detailed observations, however, are liable to stray from the mark. Thus one should no more press the grammar of Lk 2:39 to contradict the historical plausibility of Matthew's account (pace Gundry 1982: 36-37) than one should read Acts 9:19-26 against Gal 1:17-18; Luke has no more reason than other writers, ancient or modern, to detail points that do not concern him.

tion for Jesus (2:13-15) and Herod's brutal massacre of other children (2:16-18). Divine protection could function as divine vindication in ancient narratives;[100] a similar narrative about Moses likewise exalted him (Jos. *Ant.* 2.205-37).

This narrative may first imply that Jesus identifies with his people's heritage (2:13-15). Jesus appears as the promised one greater than Moses (Deut 18:18; cf. Mt 4:2; 17:2) and the heir of God's call to Israel.[101] Ancient literature is replete with stories of divine children overcoming superhuman opposition (see Caird 1966: 147-48; Beasley-Murray 1974: 192-94), as well as of other babies (e.g., Cyrus and Romulus) miraculously preserved by fate for their future destiny (e.g., Appian *R.H.* 1.1.2; for a listing, see Bultmann 1968: 293).[102] In a world of superhuman tragedies and human brutality (emphasized in texts influenced by the Greek tragic genre), the story of a divinely protected fugitive who will ultimately triumph over those forces nurtures hope.

But this narrative most closely recalls the story of Moses. Some have seen in Herod's desire to kill Jesus a parallel with Laban's desire to kill Jacob in Jewish tradition (Tuñí 1972; cf. Meier 1980: 13), but a parallel between Moses and Jesus is much clearer (Davies 1966b: 15; Gundry 1975: 209; cf. Ellis 1974: 29). Some points in Matthew's story parallel extrabiblical Jewish tradition about Moses' birth as well: a "scribe" predicted to Pharaoh the birth of Israel's deliverer, but a dream warned Moses' father to protect him (see Jos. *Ant.* 2.205-17, 234-36).[103] Jesus goes to Egypt like Israel under the first "Joseph" (so Patte 1982: 37; Goulder 1964: 3; Gundry 1982: 33), and, like Pharaoh, Herod slays male Israelite children (Ex 1:16–2:5; Ps-Philo 9:1).[104]

The Greek version of the Old Testament first uses Matthew's word for "fled" in Exodus 2:15, when Moses fled from Pharaoh in Egypt (cf. Fenton

100. Cf., e.g., Brawley 1987: 57; Ladouceur 1980; Aune 1987: 130; Char. *Chaer.* 3.4.9-10, 18; 8.4.2.

101. Besides repeating Goulder's examples of earlier Moses typology (1 Macc 2:1, 14, 26, 49ff.; 3:4, 8; Allison 1993b: 309), Allison 1993b: 11-95 provides numerous other examples of earlier Moses typology (some of them, including those in the Hebrew Bible, strong); for the prophet like Moses, see 73-84; for the Mosaic Messiah, 85-90; for other parallels between Jesus and Moses, cf. Kensky 1993. For Matthean echoes of the Exodus narrative, see also Goldberg 1989: 355-56, though he disagrees with Matthew's understanding. Such "comparison" was a typical rhetorical technique (Stanton 1993: 77-80). Wright 1992a: 388 views the new exodus as a central Matthean theme.

102. For a thorough chart providing comparisons to the story of the persecuted royal child (Moses, Abraham, Rev. 12, Cypselus, Mithridates, Romulus and Remus, Augustus, Nero, Gilgamesh, Sargon I, Cyrus, Zoroaster, Frêdun, Krishna), some fuller than others, plus still remoter parallels, see Luz 1989: 152-55. Cf. also Soph. *Oed. Rex* 1022-34. Nevertheless, cultural tendencies dominant in various cultures should not mute the extent to which Matthew's story may actually critique similar hero stories (see Horsley 1993a: 162-72).

103. Noted in Crossan 1986; Soares Prabhu 1976: 289-90; Brown 1977: 114-15; France 1985: 85; Meier 1980: 13; Overman 1990b: 77-78. In rabbinic tradition astrologers foretell Moses' birth (b. Sanh. 101a; Soṭa 12b; Ex. Rab. on 1:22), and the Jerusalem Targ. Ex. 1:15 calls them "magicians" (Allison 1993b: 145).

104. Also Davies 1966b: 15; Gundry 1982: 34; Teeple 1957: 74. In some Jewish traditions, Pharaoh went so far as to slay even Egyptian children to protect his throne (Lachs 1987: 12-13 cites b. Soṭa 12a; Ex. Rab. 1:18), but these are probably too late to prove relevant here.

1977: 48). Infanticide (Boer 1979: 98-99, 113, 116; Rawson 1986a: 172) and, more frequently, child abandonment (Soph. *Oed. Rex* 717-19; Quint. *Inst. Or.* 7.1.14; Juv. *Sat.* 6.602-9; Gardner 1986: 6) constituted typically pagan offenses that the Jewish people despised (e.g., Wis 12:5-6; 14:23; Ps-Philo 2:10; 4:16). In their tradition only such pagan evildoers as Antiochus Epiphanes had repeated Pharaoh's murder of Israelite babies (1 Macc 1:60-61; 2 Macc 6:10; 8:4). Part of the moral of the story is therefore how it reflects on rulers among God's people: if a "king of the Jews" can be a new Pharaoh, Matthew's community is right not to trust all the community leaders of its day. Perhaps the same reality may challenge his audience's prejudice against Gentiles, reminding his audience of their opposition from fellow Jews. It is also possible, though less certain, that Herod's behavior may summon them to examine the sins of their own people first (cf. 7:1-5); pagan Magi act like God's servants, whereas the ruler of God's people acts like a pagan tyrant. Yet if the text looks back to Exodus, it also looks forward to the flight of 10:23 (cf. 24:16): the suffering of the persecuted church committed to proclaiming the gospel.[105]

Most significantly, Matthew teaches in this passage that in Jesus the anticipated salvation of God's people has begun. In Hosea, the past exodus with which Jesus identified (Hos 11:1) was the historic sign of the covenant anticipating a new exodus (Hos 11:11). By quoting the beginning of the passage, Matthew evokes the passage as a whole and shows how Jesus is the forerunner of the new exodus, the time of ultimate salvation. Jesus has cut a new way through the wilderness to the land of promise. Because Matthew's audience's opponents defined them as schismatics, it was easy for the disciples to become a defensive minority with a sectarian mind-set. Instead, Matthew uses God's pattern in history to remind them that their call and destiny must define them: they are the people of the new exodus, the people of the kingdom.

Matthew declares (2:15) that Jesus' sojourn in Egypt fulfills Hosea's prophecy, "Out of Egypt I called my son" (11:1).[106] But this second line in Hosea's verse directly parallels the first, "When Israel was young I loved him." The Scriptures often called Israel God's son (e.g., Ex 4:22) or children (e.g., Deut 32:19), and both the early versions and the rabbis understood the text as referring to Israel (cf., e.g., Daube 1973: 191). Matthew's ability to quote Scripture accurately (here he ignores what was probably the most common Greek version's interpretive translation — "his children" — and translates the Hebrew directly) suggests that he and his community knew the context very well. If our later evidence is relevant, those who quoted Scriptures generally alluded to the context of

105. Stanton 1993: 201-2 curiously accepts the flight of the Magi as paradigmatic for the readers but rejects the flight of Jesus as such. Yet Jesus' sufferings in the Gospel typically foreshadow those of the disciples (e.g., 10:22-25; 16:24).

106. Soares Prabhu 1976: 227-28, who thinks the narrative may contain historical reminiscences, suggests that Hos 11:1, in contrast to the other formula quotations in the infancy narratives, may even have been in Matthew's source. Whether or not the text is preredactional, it certainly fits Matthew's Israel typology well.

those texts in the memories of the hearers (e.g., m. 'Abot. 3:2; p. Qidd. 4:1, §2). Matthew's allusions in the context (e.g., the departure at night may recall Jewish Passover tradition, Patte 1987: 37) suggest that Matthew understood Hosea 11:1 as a reference to the exodus as well.[107]

Matthew expects all his readers to understand the primacy of Scripture and the centrality of Christ's mission in Scripture; but he expects his more sophisticated readers to catch his allusion to Israel's history as well. Contemporary commentators thus generally recognize that by citing Hosea 11:1, Matthew evokes the new exodus in Jesus, who embodies Israel's purpose and mission.[108] Matthew emphasizes Jesus' solidarity with Israel elsewhere as well (cf. 1:1; 4:2); like the messianic servant (Is 49:5-7; 52:13–53:12) who fulfills the mission Israel had failed (Is 42:18-22), Jesus fulfills Israel's call (cf. Is 42:1-4; 43:10; 49:1-3). But like Stephen in Acts 7, Matthew emphasizes another point as well: God declares Jesus' Sonship in his return from Egypt, that is, outside the Promised Land (Patte 1987: 38). Jesus is not for Judea alone, but for all peoples.

Yet Matthew also teaches that Jesus was a refugee (2:13-14). Jesus' miraculous escape here should not lead us to overlook the nature of his deliverance (cf., e.g., 1 Kings 17:2-6). Jesus and his family survived, but they survived as refugees, abandoning any livelihood Joseph may have developed in Bethlehem and undoubtedly traveling lightly. The passage thus foreshadows Jesus' rejection as an adult: the Son of Man already lacked a place to lay his head (8:20; so also Davies and Allison 1988: 259). Although travel within Egypt was easy for visitors with means (Casson 1974: 257), many Judeans had traditionally regarded refuge in Egypt as a last resort (2 Macc 5:8-9). Most importantly, God commanded Israel not to oppress refugees, remembering that they had been refugees in Egypt (Ex 23:9).

Like other episodes in Matthew's first narrative section (1:18–4:25), the accounts of Jesus' childhood fulfill Scripture, with at least one explicit quotation per section. But all four stories in chapter 2 also surround place names rooted in Scripture; Jesus is "forced to wander from place to place," king of a world hostile to him (Schweizer 1975: 41, 45; cf. Harrington 1982: 16).[109] The world's treatment of Jesus likewise promises little better for his followers (10:23-25); they must expect hostility, false accusations, and even death for Jesus' name (10:17-39; 13:21; 16:24-27; 24:9-14; cf. 1 Thess 3:3; 1 Pet 4:12-13). This also fits the motif of withdrawal from opposition that characterizes Matthew's narrative and undoubtedly instructs his community.[110]

107. It is true that they are not *leaving* Egypt here (as in 2:21; Davies and Allison 1993: 261); yet this divergence is intentional, for by presenting Herod as a new Pharaoh Matthew has purposely and ironically inverted the ethnic perspective of the tradition.

108. A frequent view; see, e.g., Davies 1966b: 15; Longenecker 1975: 144-45; Meier 1979: 55; F. F. Bruce 1980a: 41; Patte 1987: 37; Gundry 1982: 34; Blomberg 1992a: 67; Hagner 1993: 36-37.

109. That two citations address the locations indicates the centrality of these four place names for Matthew (Stendahl 1995: 71-72).

110. Good 1990, citing also 2:21-23; 4:12; 12:14-15; 14:12-13; 15:21 and following the tradition of Wisdom's withdrawal in 1 Enoch 42 and elsewhere. For earlier biblical precedent, cf., e.g., Gen 26:17, 21.

Matthew denounces a ruler's injustice (2:16-17). The narrative reveals the severity of political conflict, a conflict actually escalated by Jesus' presence (cf. Horsley 1988). Matthew's narrative world testifies to God's intervention on behalf of his plan, but it does not encourage a utopian idealism that ignores the fact that God often does not intervene in behalf of his own (cf. Tupper 1991; Erickson 1996). The narrative laments injustice (2:18) rather than creates an ideal story world in which it does not exist. Five times Matthew mentions "the child and his mother," thereby underlining the senselessness of Herod's paranoid brutality (cf. Stanton 1993: 182); texts sometimes emphasized the physical powerlessness of the oppressed to underline the act's heinousness (cf., e.g., the murdered emperors as "old men" in Herodian 8.8.6). Matthew's mention of the child's "mother" may also help him highlight the virgin birth, though given Joseph's role as the one who raised Jesus, ancients would have understood the title "father" as applied to him despite the virgin birth (Eurip. *Madness of Heracles* 587, 1192; *Select Papyri* 3.476-77, §116.7; Lk 2:27, 41).

We lack a concrete historical record for the episode of the infants' slaughter (except a garbled and probably derivative account from Macrobius; Ramsay 1898: 219), but it certainly fits Herod's character (France 1979; cf. Plummer 1910: 16; Soares Prabhu 1976: 227-28; Stauffer 1960: 35-41). When Herod's young brother-in-law was becoming too popular, he had a "drowning accident" in what archaeology shows was a rather shallow pool (cf. Jos. *War* 1.437); later, Herod had falsely suspected officials cudgeled to death (*War* 1.550-51). Wrongly suspecting two of his sons of plotting against him, he had them strangled (*Ant.* 16.394; *War* 1.550-51; though such palace intrigues were not limited to the Herod family — Livy 40.56.9). Likewise, five days before his own death Herod, on his own deathbed, had a more treacherous, Absalom-like son executed (*Ant.* 17.187, 191; *War* 1.664-65). Thus many modern writers repeat the probably apocryphal story that Augustus remarked, "Better to be Herod's pig than his son" (e.g., Ramsay 1898: 219-20).[111]

Nor were Herod's atrocities limited to contenders for his throne. In a fit of jealous rage (which he later regretted) he had his favorite wife strangled (*War* 1.443-44); she turned out to be innocent of the crime of which he had accused her. He had religious men who had tampered with his golden eagle burned alive, and many thought his own increased physical agony afterward was judgment for this act (*War* 1.655-56; *Ant.* 17.167-69). Fearing lest his people would not mourn at his death, he reportedly ordered that nobles from throughout the land be executed when he died to ensure mourning on that day (*Ant.* 17.174-79; *War* 1.659-60). (Instead they were freed, leading to rejoicing — *War* 1.666.) It is possible that he also engaged in persecutions outside the scope of Josephus's sources, as

111. Macrob. *Sat.* 2.4.11 (cf., e.g., in Van der Horst 1973: 222; Reinhold 1983: 100) probably reflects tradition springing from the Gospel itself (Smallwood 1976: 104n.156), although it may follow a standard style of rhetorical insult (Diog. Laert. 6.2.41); Ass. Mos. 6:6, which compares Herod to the Egyptians, may also reflect Christian influence, and Gk. Ezra 4:11 clearly does. For relations in the Herodian family, see Hanson 1989.

in the repression of the wilderness Essenes (Fritsch 1956: 23-24). In an era of many, highly placed political murders, the execution of perhaps twenty children in a small town would warrant little attention (see France 1979: 114-19).[112]

Although Josephus readily lists Herod's atrocities, most of his reports surround the royal house or events known on a national scale; it is not improbable that Herod was no less brutal when acting out of range of Josephus's sources (cf., e.g., Carson 1984b: 94; pace Mason 1992: 97). Herod could even have personally dispatched soldiers from his fortress-palace called the Herodium (on which see Jos. *War* 1.419-20; Netzer 1983; Vardaman 1975; Corbo 1989; Netzer 1989); this fortress was four miles southeast of Bethlehem and visible from there (cf. Finegan 1969: 18). The event is thus neither historically documented nor historically implausible.

Matthew does not simply report this act of injustice dispassionately, any more than later rabbis who recounted the horrors at Bethar and thereby expressed hatred toward Rome and lamentation for their people (e.g., p. Ta'an. 4:5, §10: Lam. Rab. 2:2, §4). Ancient rhetoric urged careful selection of explanatory texts, and Matthew chooses an ancient lament from one of the most sorrowful times of his people's history. Jeremiah 31:15 spoke of Rachel weeping for her children, poetically describing the favored mother of Benjamin (standing for all Judah) mourning because her descendants were led into exile (cf. Montefiore 1968: 2:10-11).[113] Rachel had been buried in Bethlehem (Gen 35:19), some six miles south of Jerusalem; Ramah was roughly six miles to the north of Jerusalem, on the road by which the Babylonians would lead the captive Judeans from their land (cf. Fenton 1977: 49). Some later rabbis even said that Jacob buried Rachel in Bethlehem so that she could pray for the exiles when they later passed that way (Gen. Rab. 82:10; 97 MSV; Pesiq. R. 3:4; cf. Lam. Rab. Proem 24). Matthew may connect the two passages (Gen 35:19; Jer 31:15) by using "Rachel" as a common link (using the Jewish interpretive method *gezerah shewah*). Rachel, who wept from her grave in Bethlehem during the captivity, was now weeping at another, nearer crisis significant in salvation history (cf. 1:12, 17; cf. Longenecker 1975: 145).

More important than the specific nuances that recall Jesus' identification with the time of Israel's exile, the context in Jeremiah 31 also implies future hope.[114] Rachel weeps for her children, but God comforts her, promising the restoration of his people (Jer 31:15-17), because Israel is "my dear son, the child in

112. Some view both Matthew's account and part of the material in Josephus as tyrant-legends (Smallwood 1976: 103-4; cf. Mason 1992: 97); first-century-B.C. posthumous criticism of Herod certainly abounded (cf. Test. Mos., ch. 6). But Josephus reports such misdeeds of Herod in his *War* as well as in his *Antiquities,* though the former tends to be more positive toward Herod (cf. Mason 1992: 90-96).

113. For later Jewish traditions on this passage, see Zatelli 1991. In Pesiq. Rab Kah. Sup. 5:2, many ancestors lamented from their graves over the exile. Matthew adapts the language of the quotation slightly (see Charlesworth 1985: 72); but this was customary in Jewish citations.

114. Cf. also Davies and Allison 1988: 269, more tentatively, and citing in support Mek. Pisḥa 1 (Laut. 1:5-6) on Ex 12:1.

whom I delight" (31:20; cf. again Mt 2:15). This time of new salvation would be the time of a new covenant (31:31-34). The painful events of Jesus' persecuted childhood are the anvil on which God would forge the fulfillment of his promises to his people, just as the cross would usher in the new covenant (26:28).

Although Jesus, like Jeremiah (Jer 40:1-6), was not an object of judgment and the text applies to Israel as a whole, this text shows that God called his son Jesus to identify with the suffering and exile of his people (cf. 1:12, 17; cf. Jer 43:5-7) as he identified with their exodus (Mt 2:15). Israel's history points to Jesus, and God declares Jesus' solidarity with Israel's history, an important fact to Matthew's readers. Even when Israel was disobedient and merited judgment from oppressors, God's servants lamented and God reserved a promise of hope for his people.

Settling in Nazareth (2:19-23)

Cf. Lk 2:39-40. Whereas modern Western readers are most interested in a series of neat, concise theological statements, Matthew's contemporaries could learn no less about Jesus' character and how to defend their faith on the basis of more concrete historical forms.

God grants a temporary respite from trouble (2:19-20). Although Jesus would face more persecution in his adult years, Herod's death granted him a time of relative respite until his public ministry.[115] Although Matthew mentions Herod's murder of the children, he notes Herod's own death three times — indicating that God alone holds the ultimate power of life and death (Patte 1987: 36). To oppressed disciples, whether persecuted for their faith (Mt 10:22; 1 Pet 4:13-14) or repressed for other unjust reasons (Mt 5:39-41; Jas 5:1-7), this reminder of the oppressors' mortality is a reminder that all trials are temporary and that their loving Father is in control (Mt 10:28-31; cf. 1 Pet 5:10).

The angelic orders to return to Eretz-Israel because those seeking the child's life were dead (2:19-21) explicitly recall Exodus 4:19-20, as scholars generally observe (Argyle 1963: 33; Montefiore 1968: 2:11; Soares Prabhu 1976: 212-13; Allison 1993b: 142-44).[116] All Jewish hearers remotely familiar with the Moses story would have recognized the allusion; like Moses, Jesus had outlived his persecutor and would lead his people to salvation (cf. 1:21; Acts 7:35).

115. If Jesus was born around 6 or 7 B.C., as many scholars think (cf. Stauffer 1960:32-34; Harrington 1982: 16-17, and discussion above; Dionysius Exiguus was slightly off on his sixth-century calendar), his family may have brought him back to the land of Israel when he was about 3, since Herod died in 4 B.C. (Against Thorley 1981, we cannot date Herod's death after 4 B.C.; cf. Bernegger 1983.) Since Jesus had been less than two years old when his family left Palestine (2:16), they may have remained in Egypt for only a year.

116. It is doubtful that the plural ("those who sought") alludes specifically to Antipater as well as Herod (pace Wojciechowski 1988); though they died only five days apart, the former is not mentioned in the narrative and would probably not have been prominent in the tradition.

God provides wisdom to guard the family from a potential danger (2:21-22). A few days before Herod's death, Archelaus, his son by a Samaritan wife (Jos. *Ant.* 17.20), was named ruler (Schürer 1961: 158). Sharing all his father's negative qualities while lacking his administrative abilities, he quickly provoked the opposition of many of the people (Suet. *Tib.* 8; Jos. *Ant.* 17.311-17). Although he maintained his position as ethnarch for some time, the opposition of A.D. 6 led to his banishment to Vienna in Gaul (Strabo *Geog.* 16.2.46; Jos. *Ant.* 17.342-44; Dio Cassius *R.H.* 55.27.6; cf. F. F. Bruce 1972b: 24; Hoehner 1972: 103-5). Given Archelaus's character, Joseph was wise to avoid Judea (cf. Prov 22:3; 27:12); God responded to Joseph's fear with another revelation (Mt 2:22). Meier argues that whereas Luke has Joseph's family migrate to Judea for Jesus' birth, Bethlehem was Jesus' home in Matthew; he thus ministered in exile in Galilee and returned home only to die in the Passion Narrative (Meier 1980: 16).

It is God's plan, not an accident, that they settle in an obscure place (2:23). Matthew does not report why the family chose to settle in Nazareth in particular; Luke indicates that they were originally from there (Lk 2:39-40; archaeological data suggest that many Judeans had settled in the Nazareth area). Matthew is more interested in the ultimate significance of their choice of Nazareth.

Nazareth was politically insignificant. In contrast to the two major cities of Galilee, Sepphoris and Tiberias,[117] Nazareth was, though located near Sepphoris and major trade routes, "a tiny agricultural village," like many Galilean towns. According to the high, earlier estimates it boasted a population of as many as 1,600-2,000 inhabitants.[118] The more recent and probably more reliable estimates suggest perhaps five hundred inhabitants (Stanton 1993: 112; Horsley 1995: 193); in any case, a village of fewer than two thousand people would be quite small by modern urban standards.[119] Because it was an uneventful town, urbanites would regard it an inappropriate place of origin for a Messiah (also France 1985: 71, 89); civic rivalry, which was common in antiquity (e.g., Acts 21:39; MacMullen 1974: 58-59; Yamauchi 1980: 164-65), may also have led to the envy of Galileans from other towns (cf. Jn 1:46; Barnett 1986: 64). Nazareth's insignificance undoubtedly pressured early Jewish Christians to provide biblical rationale (such as this verse provides) for why Jesus settled there (Davies and Allison 1988: 274).

Nazareth was divinely significant. Matthew, however, turns this objection

117. Recent estimates suggest a population around 15,000 for Sepphoris, halving some previous estimates (Horsley 1995: 166).

118. Meyers and Strange 1981: 27, 56; cf. Finkelstein 1962: 1:41; Stauffer 1960: 54.

119. Malina and Rohrbaugh 1992: 37, by contrast, place the size at "a hundred or so," which is probably too small. Egyptian tax records indicate that hamlets that small did exist; at the same time, however, large villages could hold 3,000 to 6,000 inhabitants (Lewis 1983: 67-68, citing *W. Chr.* 63; *P. Mich.* 224; *P.S.I.* 101-2). Nathanael's tone is dismissive (Jn 1:46), but at least he has *heard* of the place (though it is also true that the likeliest site for Cana — cf. Jn 21:2 — was only about nine miles from Nazareth).

around by showing divine significance in the choice of Nazareth as Jesus' hometown. Matthew accomplishes this exercise by a wordplay (cf. Ellis 1977: 202), a standard and accepted form of argumentation in both Jewish and Greco-Roman rhetoric (Keener 1992: 54n.101). Jewish exegesis commonly revocalized and repunctuated texts to yield new interpretations (cf., e.g., Patte 1975: 55-56; for a later period, Jacobs 1973: 2).

That Matthew is making a play on the name Nazareth is far easier to recognize than the specific word with which he is playing, however, and scholars are divided in their opinions here. Those who believe that Matthew would not use a wordplay that worked only in Hebrew usually hold that Matthew intended "Nazirite" (cf. Patte 1987: 39-40; Meier 1979: 57; Meier 1980: 16; Garland 1993: 31). The language indeed bears some resemblance to a birth oracle like Judges 13:5 (cf. also 16:17 LXX). But scholars who argue this position typically assume that Matthew drew a typological application from Samson in Judges (part of the former prophets) that he attributed for some reason to the Messiah. A more likely alternative would be to assume that Matthew reads the Hebrew *nazir* in light of Jesus, hence "holy to God" (cf. Soares Prabhu 1976: 205-6).

But whereas Matthew's less skillful readers would have to have satisfied themselves that the text was in their Bible somewhere, those skillful enough to recognize no single text that said this would also recognize Matthew's method; many might also know Hebrew. (That Matthew alludes to more than a single text may be implied by his use of his "through the prophets" rather than "through the prophet." Blending of texts was common; see, e.g., 4Q266, 270, in Baumgarten 1992.) Some, noting that the Septuagint (probably testifying to a Jewish usage) substitutes "Nazirite" for "one set apart" or "holy one," have suggested Isaiah 4:3 (Davies and Allison 1988: 276-80), but the few matching words and the distance of the equation make it too obscure. Other scholars suggest that Matthew plays here on the Hebrew for "watchmen" in Jeremiah 31:6 (Zolli 1958; Albright and Mann 1971: 20-22), which occurs in a context frequently mined by early Christian writers.

Because the reason for applying this single text to the Messiah is relatively obscure, however, the much more common appeal to the prophets' messianic title "the branch" (Is 11:1; cf. Is 4:2; Jer 23:5; 33:15; Zech 3:8; 6:12; cf. Test. Jud. 24:4, if not an interpolation) bears more weight.[120] It is true that of the messianic branch passages only Isaiah 11 uses *nezer* (Soares Prabhu 1976: 204), but even if it fits only one primary text this title remains more clearly messianic than "Nazirite." Further, *nezer* recurs in the Dead Sea Scrolls as a messianic title (1QH 6.15; 7.19; 8.6, 8, 10) and may be associated with Jesus in later rabbinic texts (b. Sanh. 43a, bar.; cf. Herford 1966: 95-96). Jewish teachers used wordplays so frequently (with Nazirite, cf. Gen. Rab. 98:20) that

120. Cf. Walker 1963: 392-93; Black 1967: 198; Fenton 1977: 51; Pritz 1988: 12; idem 1991; Filson 1960: 62; Lachs 1987: 14; Hagner 1993: 41-42.

Matthew may have left the matter ambiguous to draw on various connotations (Patte 1987: 30).

Even without the possibly debatable archaeological evidence in favor of the family settling in Nazareth (Finegan 1969: 28-33; cf. de Nazareth 1956), little doubt exists that Jesus' family settled there. Archaeology attests that Nazareth was settled by this period (Finegan 1969: 27), and, as noted above, later Christians would hardly have made up such an obscure place of origin for their Messiah, especially given Jesus' more significant links with Bethlehem and Capernaum. Undoubtedly the epithet "of Nazareth" (21:11; Mk 1:24; Acts 10:38) followed Jesus from the beginning of his ministry outside that town. Likewise, that Joseph took up work as a carpenter in Nazareth is almost beyond dispute (see comment on 13:55). After neighboring Sepphoris was burned to the ground early in Jesus' childhood (Jos. *War* 2.68), Antipas began rebuilding it, requiring carpenters from outlying areas.

Nazareth would have been as traditional a place to grow up as any other Galilean town. The lack of iconography and the settling of one of the priestly courses there after A.D. 70 indicate that Nazareth itself was religious and ritually pure.[121] It existed in the shadow of the wealthy, hellenized Jewish city of Sepphoris (for archaeological and literary data on the city, including claims of a later Christian presence there, see Meyers, Netzer, and Meyers 1986; idem 1988; Crocker 1987; Weiss and Netzer 1991; cf. Boelter 1977); yet Galilean villages and towns were not severely dependent economically on the two hellenized cities (Goodman 1983: 27, 60), and though Sepphoris's theater seated 4,000-5,000 (Freyne 1988: 138), that would not seat all the adults of Sepphoris, much less rural "tourists" (Horsley 1995: 250-51).[122] Further, despite Sepphoris's hellenization in many respects (cf., e.g., Josephus 1982: 216) and unwillingness to participate in the revolt of A.D. 66 (Jos. *Life* 30), even it remained faithful to Judaism as its inhabitants understood it (see Avi-Yonah 1974/76b: 105; cf. Meyers 1988: 76).[123] Later rabbis emphasize (perhaps partly for propagandistic reasons, given their own work there) that Sepphoris was particular about the purity of Israelite lineage (m. Qidd. 4:5, implying that Galilean records had been kept there) and acknowledge the surrounding region to be Jewish (p. Sanh. 5:1, §3). Rabbis also attest the presence of later followers of Jesus in Sepphoris (b. ʿAbod. Zar. 17a; cf. Herford 1966: 115).

121. Meyers and Strange 1981: 27; Finegan 1969: 29; Lachs 1987: 14; cf. perhaps Vermes 1973: 72. Pottery fragments also suggest an earlier history as part of ancient Israel (Horsley 1995: 193). For a later dating of priestly settlement in Galilee, however, see Trifon 1989.

122. The limited trade connections (for agriculture, cooking ware, and storage containers, see Adan-Bayewitz and Perlman 1990) do not suggest a religiocultural continuum (see Freyne 1994; Horsley 1995: 250-51). Sepphoris was the most pro-Roman city in Galilee (Jos. *Life* 346-48; cf. 30, 38, 124, 232); for rural Galilean hatred toward these cities, see Jos. *Life* 373-75, 382-84.

123. Note also careful observation of the Sabbath in the other hellenized city, Tiberias (Jos. *Life* 275, 279).

Warnings of a Wilderness Prophet (3:1-12)

Cf. Mk 1:2-8; Lk 3:1-9, 16-17; Jn 1:19-23, 26-27.[124] Q probably opens with John, like other gospel traditions (Mk 1:1-4; Jn 1:19-20; Acts 10:37; 13:24-25). Although Josephus presents the Baptist's mission as that of a moralizing philosopher for his hellenized audience (see Meier 1992: 234; cf. Liefeld 1967: 146n.31), the Gospel accounts preserve a greater ring of authenticity concerning the Baptist's own milieu: John was a wilderness prophet proclaiming impending judgment. Repentance (3:2, 6, 8) was the only appropriate response to the coming kingdom (3:2), fiery judgment (3:7, 10-12), and the final judge, who would be more than a merely political Messiah (3:11-12). Given the widespread view in early Judaism that prophets in the formal sense had ceased (Keener 1991b: 77-91), John's appearance naturally drew crowds (3:5).

The warnings in this passage serve a twofold function: judgment against persecutors vindicates the righteous they oppress, but judgment also warns the righteous not to become wicked (Ezek 18:21-24). Matthew retains and amplifies Mark's accounts of the opposition of the Pharisees (5:20; 12:38; 15:1; 16:1; 19:3; 21:45; 22:15; 23:2; 27:62) and sometimes Sadducees (16:1; 22:23). By narrowing Q's "crowds" to "Pharisees and Sadducees" (3:7; cf. Lk 3:7; Kraeling 1951: 46-47; pace Witherington 1990: 39; Blomberg 1992a: 77), Matthew thus provides in the coming judgment special encouragement to his community: their Pharisaic opponents, for all their claims to represent the truest form of Judaism, were spiritual Gentiles (3:6, 9).[125] Yet Matthew also expects his community to recognize that they, too, can become like these Pharisees (24:48-51; cf. Amos 5:18-20).

John's lifestyle (3:1, 3-4). Biographers normally described their subjects' appearance only if they had good reason to do so (Drury 1976: 29); thus, for example, Mark and Matthew describe John but not Jesus. John's location, garb, and diet suggest a radical servant of God whose lifestyle would challenge the values of our society even more than it did his own (on his lifestyle as a model for Christian discipline, see Jerome *Letters,* To Rusticus 125.7, *ACCS* 6-7).

First, *John's location* suggests that the biblical prophets' promise of a new exodus was about to take place in Jesus.[126] So significant is the wilderness (3:1) to John's mission that all four Gospels justify it from Scripture (3:3; Mk 1:3; Lk 3:4); some even suspect that John himself used this text (Is 40:3) to explain his

124. Some material from chs. 3, 4, and 12, though originally prepared for this commentary (in late 1994), was used in earlier form in Keener 1997b: 91-134.

125. Vengeance and consolation remain central to "apocalyptic eschatology," including that of Matthew's possibly sectarian community in conflict after 70 (Sim 1996: 227-35).

126. Because John's agricultural images suit the period in and shortly after April (Ramsay 1908: 227) and because the Jordan was deeper and warmer after the rainy season (Malina and Rohrbaugh 1992: 39), some scholars seek to pinpoint the season as well as the location, but this is more problematic. One is not restricted to citing metaphors current only at the season; likewise, the Jordan's depth varies by location and the basin can remain warmer than the Judean hills (recall, e.g., nearby Jericho's palms).

own sense of mission (Jn 1:23; Robinson 1962: 13).[127] The meaning of John's location would not be lost on Syro-Palestinian Jews. Israel's prophets had predicted a new exodus in the wilderness (Hos 2:14-15; Is 40:3; later interpreters properly understood such passages as applicable to the time of Israel's restoration — e.g., Ps. Sol. 11:1). Jewish people in John's day acknowledged this as the appropriate place not only for renewal movements (cf. Theissen 1978: 48-50) but for prophets and Messiahs (24:26; Acts 21:38; Jos. *Ant.* 20.189; *War* 2.259, 261-62; cf. Beasley-Murray 1957: 84).

Further, the Qumran community applied the same Isaiah text to their own mission in the wilderness (1QS 8.13-14; cf. Brownlee 1950: 71; Brown 1972: 4), especially to their knowledge of the law (1QS 8.15-16). If John was aware that others used the text, however, he undoubtedly felt that it applied better to himself. Rather than separating himself totally from Israel as the Qumran community did (1QS 8.13-14; 9.19-20; F. F. Bruce 1956: 177; Witherington 1990: 36; cf. Scobie 1969: 68; van der Minde 1988), he preached directly to the crowds that came to him there (3:5). Many commonalities John shared with Qumran probably reflect wider patterns in pietist Judaism (cf. Taylor 1997: 15-48).[128]

No less important to John's mission, the wilderness was likewise a natural place for fugitives from a hostile society (e.g., Heb. 11:38; Rev. 12:6; Ps. Sol. 17:17; Song Rab. 2:13, §4; Tac. *Ann.* 14.23), including prophets like Elijah (1 Kings 17:2-6; 2 Kings 6:1-2). The Gospels may emphasize the Baptist's wilderness existence partly to prefigure Jesus' location of testing (Kelber 1979: 17; Mauser 1963: 90)[129] and even partly to emphasize the fulfillment of Isaiah 40:3 (Marxsen 1969: 37; Bultmann 1968: 246), but all the evidence also supports John's literal sojourn there. He could have safely drawn crowds (3:5) there as he could have nowhere else (cf. Jos. *Ant.* 18.118), and it provided him the best ac-

127. Although Mark freely blends texts (Is 40:3; Mal 3:1) in the standard Jewish manner (linking them by means of the common phrase "prepare the way," Longenecker 1975: 138), naming the more well-known prophet in his composite quotation, Matthew simplifies Mark's citation by including only the quotation actually from Isaiah (cf. Meier 1980: 23; composite quotations provide one primary reason for postulating the early Christian use of testimonia — Fitzmyer 1974: 65). The formula in 3:3 fits contemporary Scripture citations (Davies and Allison 1988: 292 compare CD 10.16; 16.15; 11QMelch 2.14). Fitzmyer 1961 argues that in general early Christian quotations are closer in form to Qumran than rabbinic citations; still, fulfillment formulas may appear less in the Qumran Scrolls (Fitzmyer 1974: 55; idem 1966: 253), though they become common in Targumim (McNamara 1983: 220).

128. Josephus also portrays the Essenes as ascetics (*War* 2.120), and evidence suggests that John baptized near them (see Jeremias 1971: 43). But if John was ever an Essene (Betz 1990), it was not during his public ministry — the Essenes did not accept those who differed from them in any respect (see Pryke 1964). That John historically baptized in the wilderness (Mk 1:4-5) is clearly early tradition, presupposing a geographical situation (the narrow Jordan Valley in the wilderness) that obtained only in Palestine (Theissen 1991: 39). Theologically, Israel was "initiated" into the land through the Jordan (Josh 3–4); prophets in Elisha's day also gathered near the Jordan (2 Kings 6:2, 4; cf. "baptism" in 5:10).

129. For Matthew's various literary parallels between John and Jesus, see Allison 1993b: 137-38; Stanton 1993: 81. On the historical level, Jesus' baptism by John presumably implies Jesus' agreement with John's message (Sanders 1993: 94; pace Crossan 1991a: 230-38).

commodations for public baptisms that symbolically challenged the hegemony of establishment leaders (see Jos. *Ant.* 18.117). Thus John's location symbolizes the coming of a new exodus, the final time of salvation, and the price a true prophet of God must be willing to pay for his or her call: total exclusion from all that society values — its comforts, status symbols, and even basic necessities (cf. 8:20; 1 Kings 13:8-9, 22; 20:37; Is 20:2; Jer 15:15-18; 16:1-9; 1 Cor 4:8-13). The restrictions on Jesus' messengers in 10:9-10 (cf. 10:40-42) suggest that Matthew himself affirms this second lesson as well as the first.

John's garment (3:4) in general resembled the typical garb of the poor (Wright 1962: 191-92), as would befit a wilderness prophet cut off from all of society's amenities (cf. Heb 11:37). Camels were common enough in Palestine (cf. 19:24; 23:24), and camel's hair garments fit the rugged lifestyle of desert nomads.[130] But his clothing specifically evokes that of the Israelite prophet Elijah (2 Kings 1:8 LXX), as many commentators recognize.[131] Malachi promised Elijah's return (4:5-6), a promise that subsequent Jewish tradition developed (e.g., Sir 48:10).[132] Although Matthew did not regard John as Elijah *literally* (17:3; cf. Lk 1:17), he believed that John had fulfilled Malachi's prophecy of Elijah's mission (Mt 11:14-15; 17:11-13).

John's garb tells Matthew's community two things: first, their Lord arrived exactly on schedule, following the promised end-time prophet; and second, John had to be a wilderness prophet like Elijah. Although true prophets could function within society during the reigns of godly kings (e.g., 2 Sam 12:1-25; 24:11-12), in evil times mainly corrupt prophets remained in royal courts (1 Kings 22:6-28; cf. Mt 11:8), God's true messengers being forced into exile (1 Kings 17:3; 18:13). Most Jewish people in the first century practiced their religion seriously; but the religious establishment could not accommodate a prophet like John whose lifestyle dramatically challenged the status quo, any more than the religious establishment of most of Christendom could today.

John's diet also provides Matthew's community a model of commitment. Some other poor people in antiquity also ate locusts (3:4),[133] and honey was the

130. E.g., Gnilka 1997: 75. Cf. the vegetable clothing of Bannus in Jos. *Life* 11. Davies and Allison 1988: 295 cite Jos. *War* 1.480 (though it lacks direct bearing on desert nomads) and modern bedouins. The Judean wilderness today is even sparser than then, rarely providing even locusts and honey (Hepper 1992: 54-55).

131. E.g., Jerome *Homily* 91, on the Exodus (*ACCS,* 7); Hooker 1983: 9; Lane 1974a: 51; Ladd 1974b: 35; Hengel 1981b: 36. The Synoptic miracle traditions and passages like Lk 9:61-62 (cf. 1 Kings 19:20; Lk 10:4 — cf. 2 Kings 4:29) transferred some Elijah images to Jesus, but for Jesus these were inadequate (cf. Lk 9:8, 19-20, 33-35). The antiquity of the eschatological Elijah tradition is guaranteed, though scholars still dispute the antiquity of his messianic forerunner role; see, e.g., Milikowsky 1982-83; Schneider 1962: 169; Faierstein 1981: 86; Fitzmyer 1985; Allison 1984.

132. Cf. 4 Ezra 6:26; t. 'Ed. 3:4; Sifre Deut. 41.4.3; 342.5.2; see Teeple 1957: 4-8; Lane 1974a: 324.

133. See A. B. Bruce 1979: 80; Argyle 1963: 36; Davies and Allison 1988: 296 cite Lev 11:20-23; Pliny *N.H.* 6.35; 7.2; 11QTemple 4; m. Ḥul. 3:7; Ter. 10:9; and modern bedouin practice as well as that of the poor in "Arabia, Africa, and Syria." Cf. also Qoh. Rab. 10:8, §1 (different in Esth. Rab. 3:7); etc.

regular sweetener in the Palestinian diet,[134] readily available to the poor (Judg 14:8; 1 Sam 14:25; Is 7:22). It was widely used in the ancient Mediterranean world (see Cary and Haarhoff 1946: 112), typically produced by domestic beekeepers (e.g., m. B. Bat. 5:3; Virg. *Georg.* 4.1-558; Columella *Rust.* 9); Attic honey was the favorite (Aristoph. *Peace* 252-54; *P. Cairo Zen.* 59426.6; Petron. *Sat.* 38). John may have acquired wild honey by smoking bees out and breaking the honeycomb (cf. m. ʿUq. 3:11; Sheb. 10:7; Ap. Rhod. 2.130-34; for wild bees, see Virg. *Aen.* 12.586-87).[135]

But locusts sweetened with honey constituted John's *entire* diet. The sort of pietists that lived in the wilderness and dressed simply normally ate only the kind of food that grew by itself (2 Macc 5:27; Jos. *Life* 11). In the wilderness, both refugees (Qoh. Rab. 10:8, §1) and pietists with special kosher requirements (CD 12.14; 11QTemple 48.1-5; cf. Davies 1983) might subsist on locusts. Matthew is explaining that John lived simply — with only the barest forms of necessary sustenance.[136] This was not the only lifestyle to which God called his servants, but Matthew believed that God called some disciples to it (Mt 11:18-19), and their lifestyle challenges all disciples to consider whether they have staked everything on the kingdom (13:46; cf. the emphasis in Lk 3:11; 12:33; 14:33; Acts 2:44-45; 4:32-35).

John's mission to Israel (3:5-6, 8-9).[137] Although some Jewish traditions denied that the righteous like Abraham needed repentance (Pr Man 3:8; cf. Test. Abr. 10A; ARN 14A), most acknowledged that all people have sinned[138] and all need repentance (Sanders 1977: 174-80; Montefiore and Loewe 1974: 315-33).

134. E.g., Ex 3:8; 13:5; Prov 24:13; 25:16, 27; 27:7; Jub. 1:7; Sir. 11:3; 24:20; Ep. Arist. 112; t. B. Bat. 1:9; Bek. 1:8.

135. Ancients thought that bees recycled flowers into honeycombs — Ovid *Metam.* 13.928; Arist. *De An. Hist.* 5.22.4. Though some have thought of vegetable honey (A. B. Bruce 1979: 80; cf. Kraeling 1951: 195n.11; Jos. *War* 4.468; Aelian *Animals* 5.42), this proposal is improbable here (Davies and Allison 1988: 296, citing Diod. Sic. 19.94; b. Ber. 38a; Ketub. 111b; cf. Jos. *War* 4.469); since date honey is more obscure, it would need to be explicitly indicated. The spiritual honey of Jos. and Asen. 16.14/7-8 and the abundance of honey in the new era (Sib. Or. 3.622) are probably also irrelevant.

136. Jos. *Ant.* 18.12 praises the Pharisees for their simple diet; John's diet is far simpler, and an ancient audience that understood Josephus's praise would also understand that of Mark and Matthew.

137. The Q material in 3:7-10 (Meier 1994: 27-31) and 3:11-12 (Meier 1994: 32-33), none of which bears marks of Christian christological revision, has strong claim to authenticity; both Jesus (as is often suggested; see, e.g., Meier 1994: 116-30) and some of his disciples may once have followed John. Although others knew of John the prophet (Jos. *Ant.* 18.116-19), it was especially his adherents who retained his teachings (see Theissen 1991: 60). That during his ministry Jesus did not "baptize" anyone "in the Spirit" may support the authenticity of the prophecy as well (Witherington 1990: 38, 41-42).

138. 1 Kings 8:46; 1 Esdr 4:37-38; Sir 8:5; Test. Abr. 9A; 1 Enoch 40:9; 4 Ezra 8:35; see further Moore 1971: 467-69; Bonsirven 1964: 114. One might repent one day before death, hence should do it daily (m. 'Abot 2:10; ARN 15A; 29, §62B; Shab. 153a; Midr. Ps. 90:12). Some later Amoraim observed that repentance even one day before death could spare the wicked hell (Ruth Rab. 3:3; Qoh. Rab. 1:15, §1).

The fifth benediction of the Amida requests that God turn Israel to repentance (Oesterley 1925: 63).[139]

"Repentance" in the Gospels recalls not the "change of mind" earlier etymological interpreters sometimes supposed (cf. Char. *Chaer.* 3.3.11; Marc. Aur. *Med.* 8.10; often in LXX), but the biblical concept of "turning" or "returning" to God (Is 31:6; 45:22; 55:7; Jer 3:7, 10, 14, 22; 4:1; 8:5; 18:11; 24:7; 25:5; 26:3; 35:15; 36:7; 44:5; Lam 3:40; Ezek 13:22; 14:6; 18:23, 30; 33:9, 11; Hos 11:5; 12:6; 14:1-2; Joel 2:12-13; Zech 1:3-4; Mal 3:7). The idea of repentance as returning to God was pervasive in early Judaism (see Petuchowski 1968) but foreign to Greek religion (Burkert 1987: 14). Sages extolled repentance (Sir. 44:16; b. B. Meṣ. 59a; Rosh Hash. 16b; Yoma 86a; Pesiq. Rab Kah. 24; cf. Herm. 2.4.2), some later rabbis even claiming its preexistence (Gen. Rab. 1:4; Midr. Ps. 90:3; 93:2) or its association with the Messiah's mission (Song Rab. 7:5, §3). It is efficacious (Sir 17:24; 18:21; Pr Man 1:7; Ps. Sol. 9:7; 1 En. 50:3-5; Jos. and Asen. 15:7/6-7; Sifre Deut. 30.1.2; ARN 12; Pesiq. Rab Kah. Sup. 3:2), though in rabbinic tradition it merely suspends judgment until the Day of Atonement may remove it (m. Yoma 8:8; t. Kip. 4:7; ARN 39), and beyond a certain limit is not efficacious for the person who premeditates sin in hopes of repenting afterward (m. Yoma 8:9; ARN 39-40A). Yet John's call is more radical; his "repentance" refers not to a regular turning from sin after a specific act, but to a once-for-all repentance, the kind of turning from an old way of life to a new that Judaism associated with Gentiles converting to Judaism (as in Jos. and Asen. 9:2; 15:7; Pesiq. Rab Kah. 12:20; Acts 14:15; 1 Thess 1:9), here in view of the impending day of judgment (cf. 4:17; 11:20; 12:41; Acts 17:30-31; Rom 2:4). His call to repentance recalls a familiar summons in the biblical prophets (see Bowman 1943: 231; cf. 4 Bar. 8:12). In various ways John warns his hearers against depending on the special privileges of their heritage. (For John's message of repentance, see more fully Taylor 1997: 106-11.)

First, *John's baptism* confirms that he is calling for a once-for-all turning from the old way of life to the new, as when Gentiles convert to Judaism. None of the other sorts of regular ceremonial washings can qualify as background for John's baptism.[140] In antiquity, only the baptism of Gentiles into Judaism

139. Vermes 1993: 192 suggests that John's and Jesus' repentance was personal as opposed to the corporate repentance found in Qumran liturgy (e.g., 1QS 1.24-26), but the personal decision on entrance into that community (e.g., 1QS 3.9-11; 5.8, 13-14; acknowleged in 1993: 192n.8) is actually more analogous. For eschatological associations with repentance in some circles and probably John's proclamation, see Sanders 1985: 92, 106-7.

140. Ancient Near Eastern societies from Egypt (e.g., Book of the Dead, spell 20) and Mesopotamia (Moyer 1969: 130) to the Hittites (Moyer 1969: 132; *ANET* 207, 209) required ritual washings; indeed, many unrelated cultures do the same (Fallaize 1918: 455-66; Mbiti 1970: 169, 172; Fry et al. 1984: 61). Various Greek cults employed lustrations as preliminary purifications in their initiatory rites (e.g., Apul. *Metam.* 11.1; Mylonas 1961: 248; Wild 1981: 129-48), although scholars have rightly pointed out that such acts were simply preliminary washings, and never initiatory of themselves (Wagner 1967: 71-72, 102-3; Burkert 1987: 101;

signified the kind of radical change the Gospels report that John was demanding.[141] This "proselyte baptism" appears at an early period in our extant sources[142] and was known outside Palestine (Epict. *Disc.* 2.9.20; probably Juv. *Sat.* 14.104; Sib. Or. 4.162-65). Further, it is highly unlikely that Jewish people would admit Gentiles into the covenant without ritual cleansing from their former state of impurity,[143] and still more unlikely that second-century Judaism would have adopted the practice from Christians (see, e.g., Rowley 1940: 313; Schiffman 1985: 26-30).[144] If this is the case, John was treating his fellow Jews as if they were spiritually Gentiles, calling them to turn to God on the same terms they believed God demanded of Gentiles. As F. F. Bruce puts it, "If John's baptism was an extension of proselyte baptism to the chosen people, then his baptism, like his preaching, meant that even the descendants of Ab-

---

Nock 1964a: 60-62, 133). Jewish people had long used pools for ritual immersion (see, e.g., Yadin 1966: 164; Pearlman 1867: 179; Avigad 1980: 139-43; Reich 1984). Some have suggested immersions at the Qumran community as background for John's baptism and/or Christian baptism (e.g., Thiering 1980; idem 1981b; Smith 1982; Taylor 1997: 76-88, though cf. also 99). But while Qumran may have practiced an initial washing preceded by repentance (1QS 5:8-23; Black 1961: 94, 100-101), this washing, too, was simply the first among many washings for a monastic community following a reformed priesthood (cf., e.g., Jos. *War* 2.150; Driver 1965: 496-506; Ringgren 1963: 221; Milik 1959: 102-3; Pryke 1964; Sutcliffe 1960a). Just as most Jews would assume a commitment to purity among those immersing themselves for a ritual bath (cf. b. Ta'an. 16a; Pesiq. R. 44:1), initiatory immersion demanded sincerity to function efficaciously (cf. 1QS 3.4-9; 5.13-14). Although some argue against proselyte baptism as a source (Beasley-Murray 1962: 18-31), scholarly opinion is increasingly shifting in the direction of recognizing it as a source, with whatever modifications (e.g., Abrahams 1917: 42; Montefiore 1968: 1:8; Kraeling 1951: 99-100; White 1960: 78-79, 320; F. F. Bruce 1972b: 156; Ladd 1974: 41; Goppelt 1981/82: 1:37; Meeks 1983: 150; LaSor 1987).

141. One may note several differences between proselyte baptism as known from the sources and John's baptism, especially the latter's eschatological character and application to Jews (Rowley 1940: 333-34), but these differences do not undercut the likelihood of proselyte baptism as the basic model that John has adapted (Rowley 1940: 313-14).

142. E.g., m. Pesaḥ. 8:8; t. 'Abod. Zar. 3:11; Pusey 1984; contrast Taylor 1956; Légasse 1976. See further below.

143. According to a tradition stemming from second-century Palestinian rabbis, idolaters (most Gentiles) were impure enough to render common contact with them or their homes contaminating (e.g., m. Pesaḥ. 8:8; ARN 8 A; b. 'Abod. Zar. 8b; Pesaḥ. 9a). Other forms of washing were common even for minor impurities (e.g., Jos. *War* 2.129; *Ant.* 6.235; 18.19; m. Miqw.; Para 11:6; t. Miqw.; ARN 8, 25A), even of objects (e.g., CD 11.3-4; m. Maksh. 4:6; Miqw. 9:5-7, 10; Sifra Shir. pq. 9.115.1.6-8; p. Ḥag. 3:8, §§1-3; cf. Mart. *Epig.* 3.47); well-to-do families on the Temple Mount even had their own mikvaot (Avigad 1980: 142; Sanders 1992: 223-25). That ritually impure Gentiles could enter Judaism without cleansing is inconceivable.

144. Meier 1994: 52 objects that proselyte baptism does not appear in Josephus, Philo, the NT, or Joseph and Aseneth, whereas circumcision appears in Jos. *Ant.* 20.34-48 and the NT. But initiatory washings were common in many cultures (e.g., *IG* 2 [2].1366 in Horsley 1983: 23; *PGM* 1.54; Epict. *Disc.* 3.21.14; Plut. *Isis* 75, *Mor.* 381D; Iamb. *V.P.* 71-74; Diog. Laert. 7.1.119; 8.1.33; Ach. Tat. 8.3.2; Apul. *Metam.* 11.1, 23; cf. Wild 1981: 129-48) and left no physical marks, hence they would not be controversial and not require mention; Philo and the NT do not *describe* conversions to *Judaism,* and as a post-OT practice *tebillah* may not be universal, though it was surely used in Palestine (see more fully Keener 1997b: 63-64, 146-49).

raham must . . . enter . . . by repentance and baptism just as Gentiles had to do . . ." (1978: 61).[145]

Although Josephus does not explain that John's baptism was this radical, he does confirm the image of John as a wilderness reformer, who sought to purify those who had first purified their souls (*Ant.* 18.117, corresponding to the Gospels' picture of a baptism "of repentance," though in more hellenistic language). This fits the Gospel image of them "confessing their sins" (cf. Lev 5:5; 16:21; Ps 32:3, 5; Prov 28:13; 1 Jn 1:9; for Yom Kippur, see Lachs 1987: 38) as a prerequisite for acceptable baptism (Carson 1984b: 102; Witherington 1990: 37; cf. 1QS 3.4-7; 5.13-14; Pesiq. Rab Kah. 12:20). In addition to public confession of general sin in later synagogue liturgy, communal confession probably appears in the Qumran Scrolls (4Q393 in Falk 1994); here public acknowledgment of personal sins (cf. Taylor 1997: 111-12) may contribute to Israel's repentance.

Second, *John did not regard his hearers as good descendants of their ancestors anyway.* "Viper" was certainly an insult (BAGD 331b cites negative Greek usage; cf. Kraeling 1951: 48); vipers were a horrifying image (e.g., Ovid *Metam.* 4.454, 475, 491-99, 617-20), and a viper could hide in the house and suck a person's blood (Soph. *Antig.* 531-32). But "children of vipers" carries the insult further, as I will argue below. Contemporary scholars sometimes read "offspring of vipers" (3:7; 12:34; 23:33; cf. Lk 3:7; Is 1:4; 57:4) as "offspring of Satan" (Manson 1979: 40) — even though Matthew's source has the plural and avoids Genesis's term for "serpent." Others have suggested a mistranslation of an Aramaic original for a leopard or hyena, outwardly attractive but inwardly detestable (Lachs 1987: 42), but such animals are not necessarily more natural candidates for use in an insult than serpents.

More likely, Matthew may allude to a fairly widespread ancient view that vipers were mother killers. In the fifth century B.C. Herodotus declared that newborn Arabian vipers chewed their way out of their mothers' wombs, killing their mothers in the process.[146] Herodotus believed that they did so to avenge their fathers, who were slain by the mothers during procreation (Herod. *Hist.* 3.109); later writers applied his words to serpents everywhere (Aelian *On Animals* 1.24; Pliny *N.H.* 10.170; Plutarch *Divine Vengeance* 32, *Mor.* 567F). Perhaps in line with such thought a widely influential Greek drama had included the insult, "mother-killing dragon" (Eurip. *Orestes* 479); more distantly but still relevant to the image of familial strife, a stepmother hostile to the children of the former wife is a "viper" to them (Eurip. *Alcestis* 310). Calling his hearers vipers may have been an insult, but calling them "offspring of vipers" accused them of kill-

145. Kraeling 1951: 103 thinks that John merely requires Abraham's descendants to live like Abraham, rather than that he expects them to approach God on the same terms as Gentiles; but this disallows for John the "originality" Kraeling elsewhere allows in some measure for the nature of his baptism (p. 110), and thus misses Qumran evidence (and cf. Amos 9:7).

146. This was probably the same sort of fanciful biology in which Egyptian cats jumped into crocodiles' mouths, then clawed their way out unscathed, killing their host (Strabo 17.1.39; Diod. Sic. 1.87.5).

ing their own mothers,[147] indicating the utmost moral depravity.[148] The image of vipers fleeing wrath[149] may derive from serpents fleeing the stubble set on fire to ready the fields for winter sowing (A. B. Bruce 1979: 82) or a tree-serpent fleeing those who will destroy the forest (Jer 46:21-23; France 1985: 92).[150] One may guess that opponents of the Matthean community would bristle at the depiction of their predecessors in such terms.

Third, employing the image of a tree's fruit, both John and Jesus demand that *a professedly repentant person's life match one's profession* (3:8; 7:16-17; 12:33; 13:22-23; 21:34, 43; cf. 15:13; 21:19; Jn 15:6; Jude 12).[151] John's more mainstream contemporaries also insisted that repentance be demonstrated practically (Sir 31:26; m. Yoma 8:8-9; Montefiore 1968: 2:15). But John drives home the point that the nation as a whole stands under impending judgment, and that one could not simply appeal to one's ethnic character or descent from Abraham to be exempted from it (cf. Deut 26:5; Jn 8:33-41; Rom 4:1–5:11). Biblical tradition had already applied the image of a tree being cut down (Ezek 31:12-18; Dan 4:23) or burned (Ps 80:16; Jer 11:16; cf. 2 Sam 23:6-7) to the judgment of a nation. Although Jewish people used trees symbolically in a variety of ways, some have cited the specific Jewish symbol of trees to stand for nations — in this case,

147. In the fourth century B.C., Aristotle declared that vipers produce eggs internally but bring forth their young alive; he made no comments on the nature of their delivery, however (Arist. *Gen. Anim.* 1.10, 718b-30). Likewise Strabo altogether omits discussions of Indian vipers' birth (Strabo *Geog.* 15.1.45). Not all writers in subsequent centuries agreed with Herodotus; in the second or third century A.D. Aelian, following a work of Aristotle's successor Theophrastus no longer extant, at one point agrees that the mother's womb bursts, but argues that it is through no malice of the offspring (Aelian *On Animals* 15.16); but he elsewhere concurs with and elaborates on Herodotus's account, as noted above. Clawing out of the womb expresses evil in Gen. Rab. 34:10.

148. Aelian regards the hippopotamus as the most ungodly of creatures because it eats its father (*On Animals* 7.19). Ancient Mediterranean peoples considered parent-murder one of the most hideous crimes conceivable (e.g., Soph. *Oed. Rex* 1440-41; Corn. Nep. 15 [Epaminondas], 6.2; Diod. Sic. 1.77.8; Dion. Hal. 8.80.1; Seneca *De Clementia* 1.23.1; Epict. *Disc.* 1.7.31-33; Plutarch *Romulus* 22.4; Marc. Aur. *Med.* 6.34; Apuleius *Metam.* 10.8; Diog. Laert. *Lives* 1.59; 1 Tim 1:9), despite occasional just cause (Hom. *Il.* 9.461; Soph. *Electra* 1411-16), and continued to recall Nero's matricide (Mart. *Epig.* 4.63.3-4; Sib. Or. 4:121, 5:30, 8:71). Most people believed that even children who justly avenged their fathers (cf. Orestes in Hom. *Od.* 3.196-98, 310) erred in carrying out revenge against their mothers, and thus the Furies would torment them (e.g., Eurip. *Electra* 1238-91; *Orestes* 531-32, 549-63; Soph. *Oed. Col.* 1299, 1434; Ovid *Metam.* 9.407-10).

149. One could seek to flee from wrath rightly (Is 26:20-21; Zeph 2:3; 1 Thess 1:10) or wrongly (Is 2:10, 19-22; Hos 10:8; Rom 2:3; 4 Macc 9:32). John's opponents' attempt to flee would prove vain.

150. The tradition that Arabian vipers nested especially under balsam trees (e.g., Paus. 9.28.3-4) might have smoothed the connection between the images of vipers and trees in Mt 3:7-10, though this is at most speculation.

151. Q follows the literal Semitic and LXX idiom "make fruit" here (Black 1967: 138-39). Fruit appears as moral behavior or acts in Jewish texts, e.g., Is 5:2; Hos 10:1, 12-13; 4 Ezra 3:20; cf. Prov 11:30; Jas 3:18; Apoc. Sedr. 12:5 (Davies and Allison 1988: 305 also cite Ps 1:3; Prov 1:31; Is 3:10; Sir 23:25; Jos. *Ant.* 20.48; 2 Bar. 32:1; Apoc. Adam 6:1; b. Qidd. 40a; and even the genetically unrelated Buddhist text *Dhammapada* 5); fruit appears in various other senses as well, a naturally multivalent image in an agrarian society.

Israel (Rom 11:16-17; Ps 80:14; Jer 11:16; cf. Mussner 1960; more narrowly Kraeling 1951: 43-44); if they are correct, this would further drive home the point.[152]

In any case, his judgment metaphor could not be more transparent. Some suggest that Palestinians would use wood from such a tree "for domestic and manufacturing purposes" (Kraeling 1951: 44), but most small trees that could not bear fruit would be especially useful for firewood (see Lewis 1983: 139). Because cutting down trees with the sort of axes the average farmer would own required considerable labor, we should think here especially of dead trees and of small trees bearing little fruit (Hepper 1992: 41).

Fourth, that *God could raise up children for Abraham from stones* (cf. Gen 1:24; 2:19-22) warns John's hearers not to take their status as God's people for granted. Jewish people believed they were chosen in Abraham (cf. Neh 9:7; Mic 7:20; Sanders 1977: 87-101; Borg 1984: 207), but John responds that this ethnic chosenness is insufficient to guarantee salvation unless it is accompanied by righteousness (cf. Amos 3:2; 9:7).[153] Pagans had stories of people formed from stones (e.g., Ovid *Metam.* 1.393-94, 400-415) or dragon's teeth (Ap. Rhod. 3.1355-57; Ovid. *Metam.* 3.101-30; 7.121-30), as well as many people turned into stones by gods (Hom. *Il.* 24.611; *The Great Eoiae* 16; Ovid *Metam.* 2.696, 705-7, 830-32; 4.276-78, 551-60; 10.241-42) or even by fear (Ovid *Metam.* 9.224-25, in contrast to Soph. *Women of Trachis*; 10.67-68), for example, by seeing the Gorgon (Ovid *Metam.* 4.180-209, 230-35, 248-49, 655-60). Other creatures also were changed into stone (Ovid *Metam.* 11.59-60, 404; 12.22-23; 14.72-74). (Given Ovid's subject matter — *Metam.* 1.1-2 — he probably does introduce some of these "metamorphoses" into tradition.) Being sprung from a stone or an oak may have been an ancient Mediterranean idiom for not being well-born (Hom. *Od.* 19.163; cf. LCL 2:246-47, n. *a,* citing Hom. *Il.* 22.126; Hesiod *Theog.* 35; Plato *Apol.* 34D; *Rep.* 8.544D); this image might be more relevant, except that it is not clear how widely the idiom circulated outside classical and literary Greek.

152. Rabbinic parables use trees to symbolize "contrasting types of men" (m. 'Abot 3:18; Qidd. 40b; ARN 39:1; Johnston 1977b: 596). Jewish teachers often portrayed Israel (Jub. 1:16; 36:6; 1QS 8.5; 11.8; CD 1.7; 4 Ezra 5:23; Ps-Philo 12:8-9; 23:12; 28:4; b. Ḥul. 92a; Gen. Rab. 88:5; 98:9; Lev. Rab. 30:12; Esth. Rab. 9:2) or the patriarchs (1QapGen 19.14-23; Pesiq. Rab Kah. 15:5; 27:9; Gen. Rab. 53:3) as trees or plants; cf. also references in Mussner 1960; Gaster 1976: 352; Fujita 1976; Wirgin 1965: 22-26. In view of Mt 3:9, it may be noteworthy that the Gentiles might be "engrafted" (Rom 11:16-17; b. Yebam. 63a; cf. Riggans 1987), a practice often noted in ancient texts (e.g., Plut. *Table-Talk* 2.6.1-3, *Mor.* 640B-641A; Marc. Aur. 11.8; m. Sheb. 2:6; Sifra Qed. par. 3.202.1.5; b. Shab. 73b; Gen. Rab. 41:1; Num. Rab. 3:1; Ramsay 1906: 221-29). Cf. the church as a tree in Hermas 3.8.

153. That this passage repeats the Targumic image of Abraham making converts (Delcor 1971) seems less likely. Jewish people regularly viewed themselves as "the children of Abraham" (e.g., 4 Macc 6:17, 22; 18:1; b. Ber. 6b). Recognizing Abraham's intercessory power (e.g., Gk. Ezra 2:5; Test. Abr. 14A; Gen. Rab. 35:2), third-century traditions attribute to his intercession the protection of Israelites from Gehenna (b. 'Erub. 19a; Gen. Rab. 48:8 — third-century tradition; cf. 2 Macc 1:2; Justin *Dial.* 44.1; m. Sanh. 10:1; Song Rab. 8:9, §3; contrast Lk 16:24-26!).

But John's words make the best sense in his own setting in Jewish Palestine: prophets were not above using witty wordplays at times (Amos 8:1-2; Mic 1:10-15; Jer 1:11-12), and "children" and "stones" probably represent a wordplay in Aramaic, as commentators frequently observe.[154] Scripture had long used stones to symbolize God's people (Ex 24:4; 28:9-12; Josh 4:20-21; 1 Kings 18:31; cf. Gen. Rab. 68:11) or covenants (Gen 31:46; Josh 4:20-24); John's hearers thus should have understood his language clearly; he savaged their sense of security. Other early Jewish Christian texts echo this view that God is so sovereign that he can choose the elect even on a basis that contradicts Israel's view of the covenant (cf. Rom 9:6-29). In its Matthean context, Matthew may be emphasizing that God wanted children who would truly follow the patriarchs' ways, not prophet killers like vipers who murdered their parents (cf. 23:30-36; Jn 8:39-40).

Excursus: Personal and Ancestral Merits in Jewish Texts

Although "works" appears elsewhere, the "doctrine of merits" appears particularly in rabbinic literature dating long after the time of Jesus. Some discussions, such as whether God redeemed Israel from Egypt on account of her own merits or those of her ancestors, may date from the first century; evidence for most of the material is much later. But in any case, inferences about legalism drawn by some earlier New Testament scholars do not correspond with the evidence of the texts themselves. I will now survey very briefly some of the evidence, including samples of both relatively early (by rabbinic standards) and later texts. Because different teachers expressed different views, what follows is merely a summary of some views, not an attempt at a comprehensive "theology" of merits in all periods of rabbinic literature.

One could accrue merits (cf., e.g., CD 5.5; 3 Bar. 14:2) for doing good works (t. Pe'a 1:2; 3:8; Sifre Deut. 229.4.1; 252.1.2; 283.7.1; b. Soṭa 6a, 21a; Gen. Rab. 9:9; 68:6; Ex. Rab. 34:2; Lev. Rab. 25:1; Qoh. Rab. 5:6, §1; 11:1, §1; 3 Enoch 18:17). In some texts God provided commandments so that Israel could obtain merit (m. 'Abot 6:11; Mak. 3:16; Mek. 12:6; Num. Rab. 15:2; Ruth Rab. 6:11). Circumcision was meritorious (Mek. Pisha 16.169-70; Ruth Rab. 6:10), as were Torah study (e.g., b. Ber. 8a; Ḥag. 15b; p. Meg. 3:6, §2; Ta'an. 4:2, §13; Num. Rab. 12:4; Song Rab. 3:10, §§2-3), faith (Gen. Rab. 74:12; Marmorstein 1968a: 175-76), and pure lineage (Num. Rab. 9:7).

Merits of special individuals often brought corporate benefits. God had often acted on account of Israel's merit (Sifra Behuq. pq. 13.277.1.14; Sifre Deut. 57.1.1; 176.1.1; 176.2.2; Deut. Rab. 2:31; 7:9; Pesiq. R. 47:4), and Israel suffered (Sifre Deut. 2.1.1-4) or required mercy (Mek. Shir. 9.24ff; Ex. Rab. 1:35; Pesiq. R. 49:4; for God's showing mercy to the righteous who humbly confess their need for it, see, e.g.,

154. Manson 1979: 40; Argyle 1963: 36; Fenton 1977: 56; Gundry 1982: 47; Mounce 1985: 22; Hagner 1993: 50.

Ps. Sol. 3:5-8; 10:1-3; 13:6-11) for lack of merit. But he also acted on account of Moses, Aaron, and Miriam (Ex. Rab. 15:3; Num. Rab. 3:12; 3 Enoch 1:3; cf. Jos. *Ant.* 3.322; the Samaritan prayer in Bowman 1977: 335), or some other righteous person (e.g., 2 Bar. 2:1; Pesiq. Rab Kah. 2:5).

In a view that frequently prevailed in later texts (for exceptions, see, e.g., ARN 12, §30B; Ex. Rab. 1:28; 16:1; 23:5; Lev. Rab. 28:4; Num. Rab. 20:22), the merits of the ancestors brought salvation in the exodus (Mek. Pisḥa 16.165-68; Beshallah 4.52ff.; Sifre Deut. 8.1.1; p. Taʿan. 1:1, §8; Gen. Rab. 23:6; 55:8; 74:12; 76:5; 84:5; 87:8; Ex. Rab. 2:4; 15:4, 10; 31:2; Lev. Rab. 34:8, bar.; Num. Rab. 3:6, bar.; 13:20; Deut. Rab. 2:23; Song Rab. 4:4, §4; Pesiq. R. 10:9). Ancestral merits also helped in other respects (Sifra Behuq. pq. 8.269.2.5; p. Sanh. 10:1, §6; Taʿan. 4:1, §14; Pesiq. Rab Kah. 1:1; 2:5; 22:4; Pesiq. Rab Kah. Sup. 5:2; Gen. Rab. 39:3; 44:16; 49:11; 60:2; 63:2; Ex. Rab. 1:4; Lev. Rab. 9:2; 31:4; 36:5; Song Rab. 3:6, §3; Pesiq. R. 15:9; 27/28:1; cf. the first benediction in the Amida; *Three Hebrew Children* 11; Test. Levi 15:4; depending on the sense in which it means "patriarchs"; see also *CIJ* 1.519, §719).[155]

Thus in some texts Israel was forgiven on account of the patriarchs (e.g., Ex. Rab. 44:5; Lev. Rab. 29:7; Deut. Rab. 3:15; Song Rab. 1:2, §3); God might withhold judgment for one's father's righteousness (Gen. Rab. 63:1). Some felt that Abraham's merit guaranteed the salvation of all Israelites (Pesiq. Rab Kah. 23:8), whereas others acknowledged that limits existed to the effectiveness of ancestral piety, at least regarding Ishmael and Esau (Sifre Deut. 329.3.1; cf. Rom 9:6-13; Ps-Philo 33:5; 2 Enoch 53:1). Further, one could make do without them (ARN 12, §30B), and proselytes had to do so (Num. Rab. 8:9). In some texts, redemption in the exodus was conditional on future obedience (Sifra Qed. pq. 8.205.2.6; Emor pq. 7.227.1.6; Behar 5.255.1.10). But rabbinic texts are more apt to criticize than to praise a bookkeeping sort of legalism (m. 'Abot 1:3; p. Qidd. 1:7, §9; Soṭa 5:5, §2); pure works salvation was not rabbinic, though it appears elsewhere (4 Ezra, in Sanders 1977: 409-27; 2 Bar. 51:7) and enters Christianity as early as the second century (Hermas 2.4.3). (Some have compared the rabbinic conception of ancestral merit with the later Catholic idea of the treasury of the church that probably drew on it, cf. Maher 1979; but for the denial that merits are supererogatory in rabbinic texts, see Sanders 1977: 183ff.; Carson 1981: 87-88.) Despite some attempts to qualify the still more distorted works of his predecessors, Bultmann's portrayal of "legalistic" rabbinic Judaism thus remains a total misrepresentation of Jewish piety (1958: 67-73). Especially in the early texts the image is usually one of reckoning reward (e.g., m. 'Abot 2:2; ARN 22, §46B) rather than of achieving eschatological salvation (for exceptions, cf. perhaps 2 Bar. 14:12; b. ʿAbod. Zar. 4b; Pesiq. Rab Kah. 10:2; Gen. Rab. 70:8). Jesus, too, spoke of heavenly reward (see, e.g., Mt 5:12; 6:1).

Some broader comments about early Jewish soteriology may be in order. The

155. One may also note the specific and different merit of the "matriarchs" in some late texts (Pesiq. Rab Kah. 11:6; Ex. Rab. 1:12; Lev. Rab. 21:11; 36:5; Num. Rab. 11:2; Pesiq. R. 12:5; 15:9; cf. Pesiq. Rab Kah. 2:5).

rabbis used the terminology of "righteousness" primarily to describe God's ethical demands rather than a saving gift (see Przybylski 1980: 39-76), but also heavily emphasized grace (Sanders 1992: 275-78; Limbeck 1971; cf. idem 1970). Grace is likewise prominent in the earlier hellenistic Jewish Epistle of Aristeas (Boccaccini 1991: 171-74). The Dead Sea Scrolls emphasize both aspects of righteousness (Przybylski 1980: 13-38). The Psalms of Solomon stress both trust in God and dependence on one's works (Lane 1982). Is it not possible that much of early Judaism, like many contemporary Christians, was inconsistent in its soteriology, reflecting various approaches that most people allowed to coexist side by side?[156]

John's message of the coming judge and judgment (3:2, 7-12). In all four Gospels, John thought himself and his own baptism miniscule compared with the Coming One and his baptism. In three successive paragraphs Mark depicts God anointing Jesus with the Spirit at baptism (Mk 1:10), thereby qualifying Jesus to bestow the same Spirit on others (1:8) and indicating that participation in his baptism includes sharing his sufferings (1:12; cf. Robinson 1982: 76-77; Keener 1997b: 49-90). In contrast to this abbreviated program in Mark's introduction, however, Matthew and Luke follow a longer form of the Baptist's saying in a fuller context that speaks of a judgment-baptism in fire as well as in the Spirit (cf. also Lk 12:49-50 in light of Mk 10:38-39; cf. Menzies 1991: 137-44).[157] Although Matthew and Luke retain Mark's emphasis on the Spirit — possibly de-

156. Evidence for works-righteousness in early Judaism (e.g., Scott 1995: 274-76) should therefore be used to *qualify* Sanders's thesis (1977), not to *deny* its corrective value vis-à-vis earlier distortions (cf. the balance in Boccaccini 1991: 218-20). Just as modern Christian soteriology on a popular level is rarely consistent, one need not expect full consistency in the diversity of early Judaism.

157. The Qumran Scrolls also link the eschatological outpouring of the Spirit and end-time judgment (1QS 4.12-13, 21; Gnilka 1997: 74). Some think that John's original proclamation addressed only the threshing floor image of wind blowing the chaff so that it could be separated from the wheat and burned (cf. Lev. Rab. 28:2; Qoh. Rab. 5:15, §1). In this case, John would have thought not of the "Holy Spirit" but of a "purifying wind," which would be translated much the same way (A. B. Bruce 1979: 84; Flowers 1953; cf. Dunn 1978b: 695; Is 4:4; Mal 3:2; Barnard 1957: 107 suggests the image of a fiery stream). But four reasons militate against taking John's original words as merely "wind and fire": Jewish people usually understood "holy spirit" as a reference to God's Spirit; wind, like fire, can represent God's purifying Spirit in the OT; many — especially John's contemporaries in the wilderness — associated the Spirit with purification (see Keener 1991b: 65-69); and all extant traditions apply the saying to God's Spirit (cf. F. F. Bruce 1966: 50; Aune 1983: 132). Thus it is more likely that John offered another wordplay (cf. 3:9); he announced the promised outpouring (a water image) of God's Spirit for the end time (e.g., Joel 2:28-29; Is 44:3; Ezek 39:29) as an agent separating the wicked from the righteous for judgment; and only water could douse fire. Meier 1994: 32-33, conversely, thinks "Spirit" but not "fire" is authentic, but I think that Mark abbreviates Q for his preface (on Mark's use of Q, cf., e.g., Catchpole 1992) and that the Fourth Gospel's author omits "fire" because his eschatology is primarily realized. Since Jesus did *not* historically baptize with fire, the prophecy is hardly a "prophecy after the event." The combination of "fire" and "wind/spirit" in *PGM* 4.618 (where "fire" relates to stars); 62.24 is probably coincidence.

rived from Q to begin with — they report more of John's preaching of judgment. Especially given John's audience in Matthew (3:7), we should not suppose that all receive a positive baptism.

Matthew and Luke also qualify John's preaching of judgment with a later Q narrative. John is a reliable character in Matthew's Gospel, performing his promised function as a forerunner (3:3). Nevertheless, Matthew does ultimately qualify his portrait of John's eschatological proclamation about the Coming One: John needed to recognize that the first stage of Jesus' kingdom, in contrast to its future revelation, would come in a more obscure form (11:2-6). Baptism in the Spirit and in fire belonged to separate phases of Jesus' work. In this context, baptism in the Spirit must include a salvific element due to its contrast with fire baptism; it likely also includes prophetic empowerment, however (Joel 2:28-29; cf. Is 42:1; 43:10-12; 44:3, 8-9; 59:21; 61:1; perhaps 1 Enoch 91:1; for these categories, see Keener 1997b: 6-48).

The kingdom is coming. In Matthew's summary of their preaching, both John and Jesus announce the same message: "Repent, for the kingdom of heaven is at hand!" (3:2; 4:17).[158] Matthew intends his community to see in Jesus' and John's preaching a model for the community's preaching as well (10:7). Such a message would encourage the righteous and warn the wicked: the Lord is not looking the other way in a world of injustice, but he will come someday to set matters straight. Therefore those who believe his warnings must get their lives in order! John combines images of harvest with the coming of God's kingdom (3:2), impending wrath (3:8), and eternally destructive fire (3:10-12; cf., e.g., 4 Macc 12:12; Jub. 36:10).

Most Jewish people in Palestine expected a time of impending judgment against the wicked and deliverance for the righteous (on "kingdom of heaven," see the Introduction to this commentary).[159] But many expected judgment on other peoples and only on the most wicked in Israel (cf. Sanders 1985: 96).[160] John's challenge to religious and ethnic self-assurance is reminiscent of that of some of his biblical predecessors (cf. Amos 3:1-2; 5:18).

Farmers destroy useless products after the harvest. Earlier biblical writers had employed the natural agricultural image of harvest and the threshing floor (3:8, 10, 12) as judgment and/or end-time imagery;[161] the image also recurs else-

158. On Matthew's assimilation of John to Jesus, see, e.g., Wink 1968: 33-35 (for radical distinctions, see 36-39); for further examination of the content of the proclamation, see comment on 4:17.

159. Some hellenized Jews like Philo stressed judgment far more rarely; e.g., *Cong.* 171-72 says: God, being good, would not literally send famine or death (but contrast Ep. Arist. 131; Sib. Or. 3.34).

160. According to a common belief, "all" Israel would be saved, with specific exceptions (m. Sanh. 10:1; b. Ḥag. 15b; Sanh. 110b, bar.; Num. Rab. 14:1; Song Rab. 1:1, §5; cf. b. Sanh. 103a, where even Manasseh, or Pesiq. R. 1:5, where even Jeroboam ben Nebat, may be saved). Justin in the second century contends that only the repentant remnant of Israel will be saved (*Dial.* 26, 28, 118); he is apparently more skeptical than Paul (Rom 11:25-26) about a mass turning of Israel. Cf. also 1QM, where the righteous remnant of Israel is arrayed against the wicked nations and the vast number of apostate Jews.

where in Jesus' sayings (Mt 9:38; 13:39; 21:34) and in early Judaism (4 Ezra 4:30-32; Jub. 36:10)[162] and Christianity (Jas 5:7-8; Rev 14:15);[163] the wicked are destroyed "like straw in fire" (1 Enoch 48:9). Fire naturally symbolized future judgment (e.g., Is 26:11; 66:15-16, 24; CD 2.4-6; 1QpHab 10.13; 1 Enoch 103:8; Sib. Or. 4.43, 161, 176-78; 2 Thess 1:6-7; Ex. Rab. 15:27).[164]

The imagery is realistic to a point. Villagers carried grain to village threshing floors, though large estates worked by tenants would have their own (Lewis 1983: 123). Archaeologists have recovered winnowing shovels, and the procedure is well known (see Hepper 1992: 90-91). People used chaff for various purposes, of which the most prominent was fuel (*CPJ* 1:199; Gen. Rab. 83:5; cf. Hepper 1992: 41; cf. straw in Pesiq. R. 10:4; straw was otherwise worthless, Num. Rab. 18:17). But where the imagery departs from realism, it most starkly underlines the point. Chaff did not burn eternally (Kraeling 1951: 42; Ladd 1974b: 37; cf. Is 29:5-6; 33:11), but John depicts the wicked's fire as "unquenchable." John does not simply echo the Jewish consensus of his day, because opinions divided on the character of hell (e.g., ARN 41 A; cf. also 36 A).[165] He specifically affirmed the harshest image of his day: divine judgment involved

161. E.g., Ps 1:4; Is 17:5-6, 13; 29:5-6; 33:11; 41:15-16; Jer 15:7; Hos 13:3; Joel 3:13; Zeph 2:2; cf. Ex 15:7; Jer 4:11-13; 13:24; Amos 8:1-2.

162. Compare further 1QM 14.1; Test. Abr. 12A; Sib. Or. 3.760-61; 5.274; Num. Rab. 4:1; cf. Sifre Deut. 312.1.1; 343.5.2.

163. In this context, the Tannaitic tradition that Ishmael and Esau were chaff from Abraham and Isaac, but that Jacob produced no chaff (Sifre Deut. 312.1.1; 343.5.2), may be relevant; but if influence exists either way, the rabbinic tradition might indicate polemic against the Christian teaching (cf. Rom 9:7-13) rather than the reverse.

164. Cf. also the references in Davies and Allison 1988: 310; Keener 1993: 599. For the conflation of water ("baptism") and fire metaphors, see the many references in Davies and Allison 1988: 316, who also cite texts linking fire and water in judgment (Ps 66:10-12; Is 30:27-28; 43:2; 66:15-16; Sib. Or. 3.689-92; Jos. *Ant.* 1.70) and as a river or flood of fire (e.g., Dan 7:10; 1QH 3.29-36; 1 Enoch 67.13; Sib. Or. 2.196-205, 252-54; 3.54, 84-87; 4 Ezra 13:10-11). The river of fire image is also Greek and Roman (e.g., Virg. *Aen.* 6.735-42), where it can depict torment in Tartarus (e.g., Virg. *Aen.* 6.551). At the very time salvation comes for some (Israel), judgment (often fiery hell) comes for others (e.g., 1 Enoch 96:1-3; Sifre Deut. 307.3.2; 324.1.5; Ex. Rab. 30:24; cf. Sib. Or. 4.42).

165. Many believed that it was eternal for at least the worst sinners (4 Macc 9:9; 12:12; t. Sanh. 13:5; probably 1 Enoch 103:8; 108:5-6; Ps-Philo 38:4; Asc. Isa. 1:2; 3 Enoch 44:3; t. Ber. 5:31; b. Rosh Hash. 17a; p. Ḥag. 2:2, §5; Sanh. 6:6, §2; cf. Diod. Sic. 4.69.5; Plut. *Divine Vengeance* 31, *Mor.* 567DE; for Gehenna's vast size, note b. Pesaḥ. 94a; Ta'an. 10a; Song Rab. 6:9, §3; cf. Virg. *Aen.* 6.577-79). But in what may be the most common early Jewish view, most sinners endure hell at most only temporarily and are then destroyed (cf. 1QS 4.13-14; Ps. Sol. 13:11; Gen. Rab. 6:6; most sinners in t. Sanh. 13:3, 4; Pesiq. Rab Kah. 10:4; Pesiq. R. 11:5; cf. 2 Macc 12:43-45) or released (Num. Rab. 18:20; other texts are unclear, e.g., Sir 7:16; Sifre Num. 40.1.9; Sifre Deut. 311.3.1; 357.6.7; ARN 16 A; 32, §69 B; 37, §95 B); twelve months is a familiar duration (b. Shab. 33b; Lam. Rab. 1:11-12, §40). Many Jewish storytellers conflated Gehenna with the Greek Tartarus (e.g., Sib. Or. 1:10, 101-3, 119; 4.186; 5.178; 11.138; cf. Gk. Ezra 4:22; b. Giṭ. 56b-57a; p. Ḥag. 2:2, §5; Sanh. 6:6, §2; Apoc. Pet. 5-12). Although Luke does not reject future eschatology in his effort to contextualize for Greek readers (Acts 17:31-32; 23:6; 24:15; contrast, e.g., Jos. *Ant.* 18.14, 18; *War* 2.163; Philo *Sacr. Abel. et Cain.* 5, 8), Matthew's emphases retain more of their original Jewish flavor (cf. Milikowsky 1988; Goulder 1974: 63).

eternal torment (cf. also other early Christian sources, e.g., 25:41; Mk 9:43, 48; Jude 7; Mart. Pol. 11.2; later, Gregory of Nyssa *Address on Religious Instruction, ACCS,* 132).

The coming judge is incomparably powerful. Judgment is coming, but what is the identity of this coming judge whom John announces (3:11-12)? Although the Spirit would rest on the Davidic Messiah (Is 11:1-2; cf. 42:1; 61:1), no mere mortal could pour out the Spirit; this was the gift of God alone (Is 44:3; 59:21; Ezek 36:27; 37:14; 39:29; Joel 2:29; Zech 12:10), just as no mere mortal would baptize in fire (which in this context must mean judge the wicked).[166] Whereas Israel's prophets had called themselves "servants of God" (e.g., 2 Kings 9:7, 36; Jer 7:25; Dan 9:6, 10; Amos 3:7),[167] John declares himself unworthy even to be the coming judge's slave (e.g., Anderson 1976: 72-73; Taylor 1952: 157)! (The narrator also approves of John's self-abasement; cf. the positive claim of unworthiness in 8:8.)

In ancient Mediterranean thought, a household servant's most base tasks involved his master's feet, such as washing his feet, carrying his sandals, or unfastening his sandals' thongs (cf., e.g., Diog. Laert. *Lives* 6.2.44; b. B. Bat. 53b).[168] Although ancient teachers usually expected disciples to function as servants,[169] later rabbis made one exception explicit: disciples did not tend to the teacher's sandals (b. Ketub. 96a, cited in Davies 1966b: 135; cf. Daube 1973: 266). "Loosening" (Mk 1:7; Lk 3:16) and "carrying" (Mt 3:11) the sandals convey the same sense of servility, and hence communicate the same point despite the variation in wording (cf. data in Daube 1973: 266; they may also reflect the

166. In John's image, the judge burns chaff already separated from the wheat; thus Webb 1991 suggests that John saw his ministry as already having separated the two.

167. For the prophets in general, see, e.g., 2 Kings 9:7, 36; 10:10; 14:25; 17:13, 23; 21:10; 24:2; Ezra 9:11; Is 20:3; Jer 7:25; 25:4; 26:5; 29:19; 35:15; 44:4; Dan 3:28; 6:20; 9:6, 10; Amos 3:7; Zech 1:6; cf. ARN 37, §95 B; for David, see 2 Sam 3:18; 7:5, 8, 19-21, 25-29; 1 Kings 3:6; 8:24-26, 66; 11:13, 32, 34, 36, 38; 14:8; 2 Kings 8:19; 19:34; 20:6; 1 Chron 17:4, 7, 17-19, 23-27; 2 Chron 6:15-21, 42; Ps 78:70; 89:3, 20; 132:10; 144:10; Is 37:35; Jer 33:21-22, 26; Ezek 34:23-24; 37:24-25; cf. ARN 43, §121 B; for Moses, see Ex 14:31; Num 12:7-8; Deut 34:5; Josh 1:1-2, 7, 13, 15; 8:31, 33; 9:24; 11:12, 15; 12:6; 13:8; 14:7; 18:7; 22:2, 4-5; 1 Kings 8:53, 56; 2 Kings 18:12; 21:8; 1 Chron 6:49; 2 Chron 1:3; 24:6, 9; Neh 1:7-8; 9:14; 10:29; Ps 105:26; Dan 9:11; Mal 4:4; cf. Ps-Philo 30:2, *famulum;* ARN 43, §121 B. Cf. also the patriarchs (Gen 26:24; Ex 32:13; Deut 9:27; Ps 105:6; 2 Macc 1:2; Jub. 31:25; 45:3; Test. Abr. 9 A; 2 Bar. 4:4; ARN 43, §121 B) and Israel as a whole (Lev 25:42, 55; Deut 32:43; Is 41:8-9; 42:1, 19; 43:10; 44:1-2, 21; 45:4; 48:20; 49:3; Jer 30:10; 46:27-28; Ezek 28:25; 37:25; 2 Bar. 44:4; t. B. Qam. 7:5; ARN 43, §121 B; Gen. Rab. 96 NV; p. Qidd. 1:2, §24; cf. Tob 4:14 MSS). Being the slave of a deity represented high status; see the inscription in Grant 1953: 122; Martin 1990: xiv-xvi (citing Soph. *Oed. Rex* 410; Plato *Phaedo* 85B; Apul. *Metam.* 11.15; inscriptions), 46, 49; cf. Rom 1:1. Slaves of rulers exercised high status; see, e.g., Epict. *Disc.* 1.19.19; 4.7.23; Sherk 1988: 89-90; Deissmann 1978: 325ff. passim; Suet. *Gramm.* 21 (in Dixon 1988: 19); *P. Oxy.* 3312.99-100 (in Horsley 1983: 7-9); cf. Char. *Chaer.* 5.2.2.

168. Davies and Allison 1988: 315 cite also b. Qidd. 22b, bar.; Pesaḥ. 4a; Sifre Num. 15:41; Plaut. *Trin.* 2.1; Lachs 1987: 45 adds Mek. Ex. 21:2; b. B. Meṣ. 41a; ʿErub. 27b; Ketub. 96a; p. B. Meṣ. 7:9, plus Roman custom.

169. E.g., Ex 24:13; 33:11; Deut 1:38; 2 Kings 2:2-6; 3:11; 4:12, 43; 5:20; 6:3, 15, 17; 8:4; Diog. Laert. *Lives* 7.1.12; 7.5.170; t. B. Meṣ. 2:30; ARN 25A; b. Ber. 7b; Gen. Rab. 22:2; 100:10.

same Aramaic verb — cf. Manson 1979: 40). Not only John's later doubts about Jesus (11:3//Lk 7:19) but also his proclamation of a coming king (e.g., Is 9:6-7; Jer 23:5-6) who would also function as judge (perhaps Dan 7:10, 13-14) make good historical sense — the proclamation because of Scripture and the doubts because of the proclamation!

Indeed, the text that introduces John in Matthew (3:3) and Mark (1:2-3) is instructive concerning the Christology they learn from John's mission: the One whose way John prepares is none other than the "Lord" himself (Is 40:3);[170] Matthew's readers would not need to know Hebrew to realize that John was preparing the way for "God with us" (1:23). It is against this backdrop of John's proclamation of a judge whose slave he was unworthy to be that his reticence to baptize Jesus, and God's testimony to Jesus' identity, appears in 3:13-17.

The Baptism of God's Son (3:13-17)

Cf. Mk 1:9-11; Lk 3:21-22; Jn 1:29-34. Although Jesus alone did not need John's baptism — he was the giver of the true baptism (3:11) — he submitted to it to fulfill God's plan (3:14-15). In a traditional Mediterranean culture where society stressed honor and shame, Jesus relinquishes his rightful honor to embrace others' shame. After Jesus' public act of humility, God publicly identified Jesus as his own son (3:16-17; cf. 2:15) — that is, as the mightier One whose coming to bestow the Spirit John had prophesied (3:11-12). It was established rhetorical practice to hurry most quickly over points that might disturb the audience (Lucian *History* 6; Theon *Progymn.* 5.52-56). Matthew thus appropriately hastens over the baptism itself in a participle ("having been baptized," which the NIV properly fleshes out as "as soon as Jesus was baptized") to his main point: God's vindication of Jesus, who accepted the humiliation of baptism.

John recognizes Jesus as the ultimate baptizer (3:14). Given the embarrassment of some early Christian traditions (both in the canonical Gospels and the early Gospel of the Nazoreans) that Jesus accepted baptism from one of lower status than he, it is now inconceivable that the early Christians made up the story of John's baptizing Jesus (Sanders 1985: 11; idem 1993: 94; Fredricksen 1988: 97-98; Meier 1994: 100-105; Stanton 1995a: 164-66; pace Bultmann 1968: 251).[171] That John himself would admit Jesus' greater status and object to baptizing Jesus as in 3:14 is not unreasonable (against Dibelius 1949: 77) and fits the narrative's logic, given John's witness to a mightier one (3:11-12), subsequent witness to the Spirit descending on Jesus (3:16-17), and subsequent witness that he had at least initially assumed that Jesus was the Christ (11:3). Why

170. Isaiah 40:3-5 depict readying roads for the king's arrival, hence the coming of God's kingship (cf. 52:7); heralds would go before him announcing the good news as he led his people forth (60:6; 61:1).

171. Although Matthew and Luke could draw from Mark, this narrative is probably also in Q (Meier 1994: 103), and Mark may well have drawn from it.

would the fire-baptizer seek baptism like an ordinary mortal (Bowman 1943: 33-34; Meier 1980: 26; Hagner 1993: 55)? Whereas John recognizes Jesus' superiority, however, Jesus humbly identifies himself with John's mission: "it is proper for *us* to do this to fulfill all righteousness" (Meier 1980: 26-27).[172]

Although Judaism recognized the biblical teaching that the Spirit enabled prophets to prophesy and John would therefore acknowledge the Spirit's empowerment in his own ministry (cf. Keener 1991b: 69-77), John recognized that Jesus had come to bestow the Spirit in fuller measure than even he as a prophet had received, and he desired this baptism (3:11; cf. 11:11-13).

Jesus "fulfills all righteousness" by identifying with his people (3:15). Since "fulfilling righteousness" elsewhere in Matthew may pertain to obeying the principles of the law (1:19; 5:17, 20; cf., e.g., Sib. Or. 3.246) as well as to the mission of Jesus and his followers (5:10; 11:19; 27:19), Jesus probably here expresses his obedience to God's plan revealed in the Scriptures. Matthew's readers familiar with the Scriptures would already understand that Jesus sometimes "fulfilled" the prophetic Scriptures by identifying with Israel's history and completing Israel's mission (2:15, 18). This baptism hence represents Jesus' ultimate identification with Israel at the climactic stage in her history: confessing her sins to prepare for the kingdom (3:2, 6). Jesus' baptism, like his impending death (cf. Mk 10:38-39 with Mk 14:23-24, 36), would be vicarious, embraced on behalf of others with whom the Father had called him to identify.[173] This experience prepares Jesus for testing by the devil (4:1-11) — perhaps part of what it means for Jesus to fulfill all righteousness. No less plainly, this text makes Jesus an example of humility (cf. 11:29; 12:19; 21:5).

In this passage, God declares his approval of Jesus in several ways (3:16-17). First, *the heavens part,* reflecting biblical language for God's revelation or future deliverance (Is 64:1 [LXX 63:19]; Ezek. 1:1; Kingsbury 1983: 64; Schweizer 1970: 37; cf. Jos. and Asen. 14:2/3), probably also intelligible to pagans further removed from the religious presuppositions shared by Matthew and his ideal audience (cf. Virg. *Aen.* 9.20-21).[174]

Second, *Jesus witnesses the Spirit descending on him like a dove.* The background for this sign of God's approval may require further comment. Despite the multiplicity of proposals,[175] Genesis 8:8-12 may provide the most suit-

172. Matthew describes John's "consent" in the same language as the devil's departure (4:11), suggesting that John unwittingly had taken the devil's side in seeking to deter Jesus' mission (Blomberg 1992a: 86n.82; cf. similarly 4:10; 16:23).

173. E.g., Lampe 1951: 39; cf. Barth 1963: 138; Uprichard 1981; cf. Mk 10:38-39; Robinson 1962: 160-61; Lane 1974a: 380.

174. Davies and Allison 1988: 329 cite further references for eschatological expectation (Job 14:12 LXX; Ps 102:26; Is 64:1; Hag 2:6, 21; Sib. Or. 3.82; 8.233, 413; Mt 24:29; 2 Pet 3:10; Rev 6:14), which I take as more influential here, although they prefer the more frequently Christian reading of personal revelation (e.g., Ezek 1:1; Jn 1:51; Acts 7:56; 10:11; Rev 11:19; 19:11 [should be eschatological]; 2 Bar. 22:1; Test. Abr. 7; Herm. 5.1.1.4; Apocr. Jn 1). Taking Jesus' "going up" from the water (3:16) as a type of his ascension (Robinson 1962: 162-63n.7) probably reads too much into the phrase, especially outside Luke, since Matthew never so much as narrates the ascension.

able background (cf. 4 Bar. 7:8): here the dove appears as the harbinger of the new world after the flood, which other early Christian literature employs as a prototype of the coming age (24:38; 1 Pet 3:20-21; 2 Pet 3:6-7).[176] (Pagan tradition also recognized birds functioning as favorable omens from deities; see, e.g., Hom. *Il.* 10.274-75.) Matthew may also see in the Spirit "upon" Jesus an echo of the servant's mission (12:18).

Third, God shows his approval of Jesus by *a "heavenly voice,"* a concept with which Matthew's Jewish readers were undoubtedly familiar.[177] Some scholars deny that the Jewish tradition of the heavenly voice could be in view here, since the *bath qol* was a second-class substitute for the Spirit of prophecy (Song Rab. 8:9, §3; Hooker 1983: 12-13; Gundry 1982: 53; cf. Burge 1987: 52), but provided one allows the broader concept that the rabbinic phrase attests,[178] this objection is untenable. First, the *bath qol* was by definition a heavenly voice more than it was a substitute for prophecy; second, the same body of sources reports that the *bath qol* became active before the Spirit of prophecy departed from

175. Although some alternative flying creatures that could land on people (such as bats or locusts) would be inappropriate symbols of the Spirit, one must ask why God uses a dove rather than some other birds. Matthew 10:16 (contrast Lk 9:3) does not seem helpful here (though patristic sources viewed this dove as a symbol of innocence — Origen *Homilies on Luke,* Homily 27; Tert. *On Baptism* 8; or gentleness — Chrys. *Matthew* 12.3, *ACCS,* 13). Jewish use of the dove to symbolize God's Spirit (Abrahams 1917: 48-49; Barrett 1966: 38; cf. Odes Sol. 24:1; 28:1) is both rare and late; so also the rabbinic comparison with the dove of the brooding Spirit in Gen 1 (Taylor 1952: 160-61; cf. Davies and Allison 1988: 331-34; Allison 1992) and the divine voice (b. Ber. 3a); the eagle comparison (t. Ḥag. 2:5; p. Ḥag. 2:1; Lachs 1987: 47) is probably irrelevant. Judaism more frequently used the dove to represent Israel (e.g., Ps-Philo 39:5; b. Ber. 53b; Shab. 49a; 130a; Ex. Rab. 20:6; Song Rab. 1:15, §2; 2:14, §§1-2; 4:1, §2; cf. Goodenough 1953/68: 8:41-46; Johnston 1977b: 595 finds this figure in Mek. Beshallah 3.86ff.; 7.27ff., but doubts whether it is frequent enough to constitute a standard metaphor). Some commentators think that this last source reinforces the image of Jesus as the ideal Israelite (Lane 1974a: 57). But the Gospel passages portray the Spirit, not Jesus, as a dove. Associations with Aphrodite (Plut. *Isis, Mor.* 379D; Ovid *Metam.* 13.673-74; cf. Sophia in Schroer 1986; perhaps Lucian *Syrian Goddess* 54) or other deities (Hom. *Od.* 3.371-72; 22.239-40; cf. *Il.* 7.58-59) or comparisons with deities' speed (Hom. *Il.* 21.493) or inconspicuousness (Hom. *Il.* 5.778) are even farther from the mark.

176. Gregory Thaumaturgus (*Fourth Homily,* On the Holy Theophany, or Of Christ's Baptism, *ACCS,* 12) felt that the dove identified Jesus as a new Noah. Though elsewhere as well doves brought objects (Hom. *Od.* 12.62-63), Garnet 1980 rightly links the dove with Noah; but his linking of Noah, Enoch, and the Son of Man are too tenuous to make the case. One could note that Sib. Or. 1.242-52 uses for Noah's doves a term related to the prophetic doves of Dodona (cf. Liddell and Scott; Herod. *Hist.* 2.57), but this connection, too, is less than obvious (since Matthew applies a different term). The parallel in Test. Jud. 24:2-3 is *too* close, probably representing a Christian interpolation.

177. Rabbinic literature frequently mentions the *Bath Qol,* or "daughter of a voice" (e.g., b. 'Abot 6:2; B. Bat. 73b, 85b; Mak. 23b; 'Erub. 54b; Shab. 33b; 88a; Soṭa 33a; p. Soṭa 7:5, §5; Pesiq. Rab Kah. 15:5; Lev. Rab. 19:5-6; Deut. Rab. 11:10; Lam. Rab. Proem 2, 23; Lam. Rab. 1:16, §50; Ruth Rab. 6:4; Qoh. Rab. 7:12, §1; Pesiq. Rab Kah. 11:16).

178. See nonrabbinic conceptual parallels in Dan 4:31; Jos. *Ant.* 13.282-83; Artapanus in Euseb. *P.E.* 9.27.36; Sib. Or. 1.127, 267, 275; Dion. Hal. 1.56.3; 5.16.2-3; 8.56.2-3; Arrian *Alex.* 3.3.5; Lucan *C.W.* 1.569-70; Plutarch *Isis* 12, *Mor.* 355E; *Mart. Pol.* 9; cf. Johnson 1948: 62-63.

Israel (b. Pesaḥ. 94a; Ḥag. 13a; Sanh. 39b); third, a few late sources give it future ramifications as well (Lev. Rab. 27:2; Pesiq. Rab Kah. 17:5). Most important, however, many considered the *bath qol* the primary source of revelation apart from Scripture exposition while the Spirit of prophecy was quenched.

The Synoptic tradition contends that three voices — Scripture, a prophet's voice in the wilderness, and the heavenly voice — all attest Jesus' identity. The heavenly voice alone would have been inadequate, for Jewish tradition allowed that it testified of others as well[179] and that it remained subordinate to Scripture (b. Ḥul. 44a = Pesaḥ. 114a; p. Moʿed Qaṭ. 3:1, §6), but here it confirms the witness of Scripture and a prophet. For Matthew and his sources, Jesus is not a mere prophet but the subject of other prophets' messages.

Although many scholars doubt that the crowds heard the heavenly voice,[180] Matthew's alteration of Mark here suggests that he viewed the parting of the heavens as an objective experience and not merely Jesus' vision. Further, his change of Mark's "You are my Son" to "This is my Son" suggests a public theophany and testimony to Jesus (Meier 1979: 58).[181] Unlike many Israelite biblical narratives, Matthew rarely portrays God's direct action in the narrative, focusing instead on Jesus. The two exceptions are the heavenly voices of 3:17 and 17:5, which provide adequate divine authorization (see Thiemann 1989: 338-39). The Gospel writers seem most concerned, however, that their *readers* have heard God's pronouncement (Quesnell 1969: 132).

The fact of the voice is important, but *what the voice says is most important, for this is what declares Jesus' identity to the reader.*[182] Pagan sources speak of both divine and human sons of deities, sometimes "specially loved sons" (e.g., Hom. *Il.* 5.314, 318; 14.338; 16.460; *Od.* 5.28), but the nature of deity and sonship is quite different from that in early Judaism and the Jesus tradition (see the

179. E.g., Sifre Deut. 357.10.3; b. Ber. 61b; B. Bat. 58a; Ketub. 104a; Soṭa 21a, 48b; p. ʿAbod. Zar. 3:1, §2; Hor. 3:5, §3; Soṭa 9:16, §2; Pesiq. Rab Kah. 9:2.

180. E.g., Kingsbury 1975: 14; Hill 1979: 59; Kelber 1979: 18-19; Cranfield 1955: 58; Borg 1987: 41, 53n.19; Witherington 1990: 150-51.

181. This functions as an annunciation formula (cf. 27:37; its "this is" is lacking in Mk 15:26). On the form as a recognition oracle, see Aune 1983: 68-70, 272.

182. Some contend that an original ambiguous *pais* ("servant" or "son") underlies the Gospels' *huios* ("son"), referring to the servant rather than to the "Son" (Marshall 1969: 327 summarizes the arguments, which he rejects). But Mark, emphasizing suffering, would not have dismissed potential servant language (Mk 10:45; 14:24), and Q apparently carries the same sense. The word order of Ps 2:7 LXX differs from that of Mark (Cranfield 1955: 61), but the voice may place "Son" later to keep the added "beloved" with "in whom I am well pleased"; the early Christians used Ps 2 for Jesus regularly (e.g., Acts 13:32-33 and Heb. 1:5); see Marshall 1969: 332-33. More scholars find Is 42 in Mk 1:11 than find Gen 22:2 there, but in Mark the Genesis allusion is probably paramount (cf. Best 1983: 81; Stegner 1985; Suder 1982); the Greek version sometimes uses "beloved" to translate *yaḥid* (an *only* son), among other places in Gen 22 (Dodd 1961: 130n.1), increasing the pathos of the sacrifice; cf. Mk 14:36; 15:39. God's voice also spoke "from heaven" at the sacrifice of Isaac (Gen 22:11-12; cf. the Christian interpretation in Test. Levi 18:4-12), though one could also use the dove to appeal to a voice in Noah's time (cf. Gen 9:1; Sib. Or. 1:127, 267). At the binding of Isaac, see also Isaac's vision of heavenly angels attesting his obedience in Targ. Ps-J. Gen 22:10 (Boring 1995: 51).

Introduction; Gk. Ezra 4:35 depends on Christian tradition). The idea of heroes loved by gods (Hom. *Il.* 1.74, 86; Plut. *Lycurgus* 5.3; cf. Apoc. Sedr. 3:1) is even more distant; "beloved sons" of mortals (Jub. 19:27; 4 Bar. 7:24) provides only the general image that informs all the others. Rather, the voice rehearses ancient biblical language, as some ancient teachers apparently expected heavenly voices to do on occasion (b. Sanh. 104b; Yoma 22b; p. Taʿan. 4:5, §10; Song Rab. 1:1, §5). Scholars generally agree that one text here is Psalm 2:7 ("You are my Son"). Psalm 2 was originally an enthronement psalm (Bright 1981: 225-26; Harrelson 1969: 86-87; de Vaux 1961: 109), reinterpreted eschatologically in early Judaism (cf. Bons 1995) and here probably employed as a proleptic enthronement fulfilled after the resurrection (cf. Kingsbury 1983: 66; Kim 1978: 92).

The second proposed biblical allusion here, Isaiah 42:1, is more controversial, despite its many proponents.[183] Mark's wording differs entirely from the Greek version of Isaiah (Hooker 1959: 72); further, other biblical passages besides Isaiah 42:1 employed "Son," "beloved," and "pleasing" together (Hooker 1959: 72-73); nor is Isaiah 42 alone in speaking of the Spirit's conferral (cf. Schweizer 1975: 38). But however Mark and his tradition may have interpreted the phrase, Matthew 12:18 suggests that Matthew read Isaiah's servant into the heavenly voice, for he reads the voice's recognition oracle into his own translation of Isaiah. It is not impossible (though not likely) that Mark's probable allusion to Genesis 22:2 retains some force; because Jesus is the son of Abraham as well as the son of David (Mt 1:1), Jesus' mission includes suffering as well as reigning. But the servant allusion makes that claim no less boldly, and Matthew instructs his community that they, too, must suffer as well as reign (5:11-12; 10:22; 16:24-27; 19:27-29; 24:9-13).

Matthew's audience could have inferred a number of principles from the Father's acclamation of the Son. First, *if Jesus is central to the Father's love and his plan for history,* their opponents could not reject Jesus and simultaneously please God the Father, as they claimed. For Matthew and most of early Christianity, Jesus was not one prophet among many but God's ultimate revelation (16:14-16; cf. Acts 4:12; Jn 14:6). Jewish traditions often emphasized God's special love for Israel (e.g., Jub. 31:15, 20); to the early Christians, Jesus was an even more special focus of the Father's love (e.g., Jn 1:14; Eph 1:6).

Second, they could infer that *Jesus is the ultimate ruler who will usher in justice and peace,* providing a persecuted church hope for the future.

Finally, this text might remind them that Jesus was *the Son obedient to the point of death.* He willingly divested himself of his proper honor by identifying with his people in baptism and death. This could encourage fidelity to him and the sacrificial cost of emulating his mission.

183. For proponents see, e.g., Marshall 1969: 335; Jeremias 1971: 53-54; Kingsbury 1983: 40, 65; Schweizer 1975: 37.

Jesus Passes the Test (4:1-11)

Cf. Mk 1:12-13; Lk 4:1-13. Given the early church's lack of political temptation, many scholars argue that Jesus himself must have communicated the temptation narrative to his disciples, at least as a spiritual reality or in parabolic form.[184] If this argument for the narrative's authenticity lacks much conviction (and it does), the argument against it, depicting the narrative necessarily as only myth or legend, is evidentially weaker, based merely on modern cultural assumptions dismissing the reality of the demonic rather than on formal grounds.

At bare minimum historically, Jesus undoubtedly sometimes felt tempted, sometimes sought to get alone to pray, and probably would have fasted before starting his public ministry (Sanders 1993: 112). Since he used "twelve" symbolically in calling disciples, Jesus may well have also used "forty" days to refer to Israel's forty years in the desert (Sanders 1993: 112-13)[185] or Moses' forty-day fast there (Ex 24:18; 34:28; Deut 9:9, 11, 18, 25; 10:10; b. Shab. 89a). Elements of the narrative are consistent with Jesus' known practice (e.g., his refusal to accommodate his enemies' demands for a sign — Sanders 1993: 117). Whether the Q narrative represents a "mythological" elaboration of such an experience (so Sanders 1993: 117) may hinge partly on how one defines "mythological elaboration." At the very least, this narrative, like much of Q, is probably early, perhaps less than two decades after the events it depicts.[186]

Those who propose a Buddhist (Thapar 1966: 119; cf. Montefiore 1968: 2:19, 21; Manson 1979: 45)[187] or even general Greco-Roman (e.g., Barrett 1966: 52; Dibelius 1971: 245) background for the account miss the clearer background

184. See Jeremias 1972: 123; idem 1971: 71-72; Manson 1961: 55; Dupont 1966; Riesenfeld 1970: 75-76; Feuillet 1979; Michaels 1981: 63. Gerhardsson 1966: 11 views the Q testing narrative as "haggadic midrash," expanding its core in relation to Deut 6–8 (71).

185. Although the number has symbolic significance, I think that it is likely that Jesus literally fasted 40 days to provide the symbol rather than offered a shorter fast that he then portrayed symbolically as 40 days. This may seem more plausible to me in part because I have devout friends who engage in 40-day fasts.

186. Some of Theissen's arguments in favor of a date in the 40s (1991: 207-15) are speculative; the figure he finds most relevant in the reign of Caligula appears in Daniel and Psalms of Solomon, and the imperial cult was an issue both before and after Caligula. But given some of his stronger arguments for the antiquity of Q (Theissen 1991: 203-34, passim), of which I believe the testing narrative a part (rather than merely a late addition to Q, as if the written scroll was undergoing regular redaction), his date in the 40s is very likely correct.

187. Trade connections existed with India in this period (e.g., Paus. 3.12.4; Petron. *Sat.* 38; Mart. *Epig.* 4.28.4; cf. Sib. Or. 11:299; Wheeler 1971: 115-71; Charlesworth 1970: 57-73; for Sri Lanka, Pliny *N.H.* 6.84-85), and some Greek thinkers interacted with Indian thought (Juv. *Sat.* 6.585; Diog. Laert. 9.11.61; Philost. *V.A.* bks. 2 and 3; Finegan 1952: 149), some of it likely Buddhist in this period (cf. Scott 1986). But such connections are certainly negligible (cf. Delaygue 1995) compared with closer Greco-Roman and particularly Jewish biblical contexts, so some proposed echoes of Buddhist sources in Jewish texts are unlikely (e.g., Stehly 1975; probably likewise other Indian sources in Flusser 1986).

in Israel's testing in the wilderness, which is widely recognized.[188] Matthew makes this biblical background clear even in simple ways like saying the Spirit "led" Jesus into the wilderness (following Q; Mark employs a much stronger "impelled," Mk 1:12), reflecting a common biblical motif of God guiding his people in the wilderness (e.g., Ps 107:7; Is 63:14).[189] Jesus, like John, had to exit the confines of society for his supernatural encounter (see comment on 3:1).[190]

Scholars' interpretations broadly fall into three primary categories (Theissen 1991: 218-19): (1) A salvation-historical interpretation, in which Jesus' testing recalls that of Israel in the wilderness; (2) a christological interpretation, which affirms a correct understanding of Jesus' messiahship as against contemporary political or militaristic interpretations; and (3) a parenetic interpretation, in which Jesus provides a model for tested believers. Clues within the narrative (e.g., 4:2) and the rest of Matthew (e.g., 6:13; 26:41; 27:42-43) indicate that for Matthew as well as for the traditioning community that preceded him, the narrative functions in all three ways.[191]

In this drama, the devil (*diabolos,* "slanderer," by which the Greek version of the Old Testament translates the Hebrew "Satan") plays himself. Especially after the exile, Israel began to recognize Satan's activity as a prosecuting attorney against them (1 Chron 21:1; Zech 3:1); originally "Satan" functioned as his title rather than as a name (in Job, "the *satan,*" or adversary).[192] The biblical and

188. E.g., Teeple 1957: 75-76; Dunn 1970a: 30; Riesenfeld 1970: 76; Albright and Mann 1971: 36; Collins 1974; Meier 1979: 59-61; Gundry 1982: 53; France 1985: 98; Stegner 1990. Gerhardsson 1966 also finds in the threefold test an allusion to the Jewish interpretation of the three demands for loving God in the Shema, but the links are too speculative (see Davies and Allison 1988: 353).

189. God led his people (e.g., Ps 80:1; 143:10), especially in the exodus: Ex 13:18, 21; 15:13, 22; Deut 8:2; Neh 9:12; Ps 77:20; 78:14, 52; 106:9; 136:16; Is 48:21; Jer 2:6, 17; 23:8; Hos 11:2-4; Amos 2:10; Acts 13:17; Bar 2:11; 1 Enoch 89:22; 4 Ezra 14:4; Sib. Or. 3.255; Pesiq. R. 12:8; for his leading in the new exodus, cf., e.g., Rom 8:14; Ps. Sol. 17:40-41; Pesiq. R. 30:2. The Bible also connected the Spirit's presence with the exodus (Is 63:10-11, 14; Hag 2:5). Buse 1956 even sees Is 63 in the background of Mk 1's baptism narrative, though he probably goes too far.

190. Some also believed the wilderness to be a special haunt of demons (see comment on 12:43; cf. Is 13:21; 24:14 LXX; 1 Enoch 10:4; 4 Macc 18:8; Alexander 1980: 29; Jeremias 1971: 69; Davies and Allison 1988: 354 cite also Targ. Yer. I to Deut 32:10). Apart from a few rugged people like John who made the "wilderness" between the Jordan Valley and Judean hills their home, it represented a dangerous and inhospitable setting. One had to return to the Jordan Valley for food and water, and the rugged terrain made injury easy (Sanders 1993: 113).

191. Luz 1989: 185-86 thinks that the christological interpretation is more central in Matthew than a parenetic one. While the christological interpretation is probably central, the recurrent motif of believers' tests in this Gospel prohibits us from rejecting the parenetic focus altogether, however.

192. Jewish literature in the time of Jesus and succeeding centuries still recognized his roles as accuser (Rev 12:10; Jub. 1:20; 48:18; 1 Enoch 40:7; 3 Enoch 14:2; 26:12; b. Yoma 20a; Gen. Rab. 38:7; 84:2; Lev. Rab. 21:4; Num. Rab. 18:21; Qoh. Rab. 3:2, §2; Pesiq. R. 47:4), deceiver (Jn 8:44; CD 4.15-17; 1 Enoch 54:6; Test. Job 3:6/5; 6:4/3; 17:2/1; 23:1; Test. Abr. 16 A; Apoc. Mos. 17:1; cf. Pesiq. Rab Kah. 26:2), and tempter (Jub. 17:15-18; b. Qidd. 81ab; Ex. Rab. 19:2; Best 1965: 53; Garrett 1998: 32-42), sometimes to turn biblical heroes from their God-appointed tasks (Pesiq. R. 40:6).

standard Jewish picture of Satan was that the devil must answer to God, and God can turn Satan's evil into good. The Bible usually makes God the author of "testing" (Gen 22:1; Deut 13:3; Ps 81:7), but in the sense that he proves the depth of a person's commitment (translated "trial"), not in the sense of seeking to make a person fall (translated "temptation"; cf. Best 1965: 49-50).[193]

God's calling must be tested and his servants must pass the test (4:1-3, 6). In this narrative Matthew presents Jesus as Israel's — and Jesus' followers' — champion, the one who succeeded in the wilderness where Israel had failed. (A champion was one who fought another on behalf of and as a representative of his people; epic literature included various illustrations of this practice; see, e.g., 1 Sam 17; 2 Sam 2:14-16; Hom. *Il.* 3.69-70, 86-94, 253-55; 7.66-91, 244-73; Virg. *Aen.* 10.439-509; 11.115-18, 217-21; 12.723-952; Aul. Gel. 9.13.10.) If John had been a model of sacrificial obedience for living in the wilderness and subsisting on locusts, Jesus, who *fasts* in the wilderness, is even more so.[194] (His fast especially recalls that of Moses in Ex 24:18; 34:28, as does that of Elijah in 1 Kings 19:8.)[195] Like most of his heroic predecessors in biblical history (Abraham, Joseph, Moses, David, Job), Jesus had to pass the period of testing before beginning his public ministry; earlier tests prepare one for future ones (cf. 1 Sam 17:34-37; Dan 1:12-17; 3:12; Pub. Syr. 218). When biblical heroes had matured through the time of testing, they knew the depth of God's grace that had sustained them. Some of his predecessors almost snapped under pressure, restrained only by God's favor (e.g., 1 Sam 25:13-34; 1 Kings 19:4; Jer 20:7-18); Jesus provides the perfect model for triumphing in testing.

193. Contemporary and later Jewish literature also recognized that God sent testing (e.g., Jub. 17:17; Sir 2:1; 36:1; Wis 3:5-6; 10:10; 11:9; Jdt 8:25; 3 Macc 2:6; Ps. Sol. 16:12-15; Gen. Rab. 55:2; Num. Rab. 17:2; cf. Jub. 19:3), but viewed as evil testing whose goal was stumbling (4 Macc 9:7; 1QS 11.9-22). Jewish sources praised those who had endured testing, such as Abraham (e.g., m. 'Abot 5:3).

194. Although Jewish tradition sometimes conjoined fasting with visions or revelations (2 Bar. 20:5; 43:3; cf. Col 2:18; Herm. 1.2.2; 1.3.1, 10, 13; 3.5.1), no such connection is likely here (pace Hagner 1993: 63). It more frequently accompanied repentance or mourning (Sir 31:26; Bar 1:5; 2 Bar. 5:7; 9:2; 12:5; Test. Zeb. 4:1-3; Apul. *Metam.* 2.24; Did. 7.4) and prayer (Tob 12:8; Bar 1:5; 2 Macc 13:12; Test. Benj. 1:4-5; cf. Acts 13:2; Did. 1.3; 8.1-2; Test. Jacob 7:17), often with weeping (Bar 1:5; 2 Macc 13:12). Whereas Greeks could use fasting for purificatory initiation (Mylonas 1961: 241-43, 258-59), Judaism forbade ascetic or unhealthy fasting (t. Kip. 4:1-2; Ta'an. 2:12, 14; p. Ta'an. 3:11, §3), though many of the pious engaged in much fasting (p. Ned. 8:1, §1; Ta'an. 4:3, §2). To the earliest Gospel audiences, Satan was literally capable of the sorts of tests mounted here (Job 1:6–2:10; cf. Sanders 1993: 114).

195. Many recognize the Moses allusion (e.g., Gundry 1982: 55; France 1985: 98; Allison 1993b: 165-72; cf. 2:16, 20), although the Scripture *citations* allude to Israel as a whole. Although normal fasts were typically from one sunset to the next (e.g., p. Ned. 8:1, §6), later Jewish literature had others repeat Moses' 40-day fast, e.g., Adam in the Life of Adam and Eve 6:1. Cf. Zosimus's fast from wine and bread for 40 years in the desert in History of the Rechabites 1:1 (possibly dependent on Christian desert monasticism); contrast Abaris's continual magical fast (Blackburn 1986: 191) and Baruch's seven-day fast that did not make him hungry (2 Bar. 21:1; contrast Mt 4:2). Ancients also recognized that 40 days without food could precipitate death by starvation (Diog. Laert. 8.1.40).

Further, the Spirit, having empowered Jesus for his mission as God's Son (3:16-17), now is the one who leads him into the wilderness where his call must be tested (4:1, 3, 6). Matthew expressly informs his audience that the purpose of the Spirit's first leading of God's Son was that he might be tested. Matthew's audience might infer two primary lessons from this narrative. *First, the narrative presents Jesus as the vicarious advocate for his people, relinquishing his own power for his mission to save them from their sins.*

But second, no less than Matthew's discourse sections (28:19), *this narrative provides a model for them* (6:13), for Jewish teachers instructed by example as well as by word.[196] Jesus had to be tested and overcome the tester before he could do anything else (cf. Schlier 1961: 40). Disciples are destined for testing (6:13; 26:41), but Jesus their forerunner has gone before them and shown them how to overcome.

The devil invites Jesus to abuse his power for personal ends rather than his Father's purposes (4:3, 5-6, 8-9). For Jewish Christians perhaps accused in some circles of antinomianism (cf. comment on 5:17-20), models of their teacher's obedience to the Father's will (e.g., 3:15) would be important. Scholars have suggested various connections between the temptation narrative and its context (e.g., Przybylski 1974). But whatever Matthew's other connections, both he and his source clearly develop the narrative of Jesus' call in 3:16-17. In 3:16-17, God declares Jesus as his Son; the devil here challenges not the fact but the nature of Jesus' Sonship; "Since [more likely than "if"] you are God's Son," he declares, act according to various worldly expectations for that role (cf. Gundry 1982: 55; Danker 1972: 55; Test. Job 37:8 MSS).

In this passage *the devil seeks to redefine Jesus' call; by appealing to various culturally prevalent models of power to suggest how Jesus should use his God-given power.* The devil tests Jesus with three roles into which other Palestinian charismatic leaders had fallen — from the generally despised and crassly demonic sorcerer's role to those that some Jews justified as pious. Jesus' refusal in each case allows Matthew to define Jesus' call over against the charges of his opponents (12:24; 26:55; 27:11, 40-43).

First, Jesus was not a magician (4:3). Magicians typically sought to transform one substance into another to demonstrate their power over nature (e.g., Hom. *Od.* 10.239-40; Ovid *Metam.* 14.414-15; p. Ḥag. 2:2, §5; Sanh. 6:6, §2). Such magical practices could be understood as usurping or manipulating divine prerogatives, for in pagan tradition it was deities that metamorphosed a substance (Hom. *Od.* 13.162-63) or person (besides references on 3:9, see, e.g., Hesiod *Astronomy, Fr.* 3; *Aegimius* 3 in Apollodorus 2.1.3.1; Eurip. *Bacch.* 1330-32; Longus 1.27) into something else, or sometimes transformed them-

196. Biographies often recounted the protagonist's refusal to turn from a heroic vocation for other temptations (Shuler 1982: 96). Jewish teachers sometimes told stories of their predecessors' invulnerability to sexual or other temptations (ARN 16 A), although other stories illustrated their predecessors' vulnerability to temptation (e.g., b. Qidd. 81a in Urbach 1979: 1:480)

selves (Hom. *Od.* 4.417-18; Ovid *Metam.* 1.548-52).[197] Jesus' opponents cannot deny his power but wish to attribute it to Satan, as if he were a magician (12:24; cf. Bultmann 1968: 255-57; Smith 1978: 105); many Jews associated demons with the worst kind of sorcery (Ps-Philo 34.2-3; b. Sanh. 67b; Smith 1978: 97-99; Arnold 1989: 18). Unlike most of Jesus' religious contemporaries, however, the reader knows the true story and just how false the charge of Jesus' association with magic was. Even after a forty-day fast, Jesus resisted the temptation to turn stones into bread. Even to a person much less hungry (cf. Gen 3:6; Ex 16:2-3; Ps 78:18), the temptation could seem a natural one: John has been talking about *God's* transforming rocks (3:9), but Jesus will not usurp the Father's prerogatives. Still, like some Old Testament prophets, Jesus fed multitudes (14:13-21; 15:29-38; 16:9-10; cf. 1 Kings 17:14-16; 2 Kings 4:3-6, 42-44) and certainly could have used his God-given power to feed himself; hunger was not in itself a bad motivation (21:18; cf. 12:3; 25:35). But Jesus instead waits on God to act for him (4:11; 6:11); he will use his power only at his Father's bidding. He knows that his Father will give him bread, not stones (7:9).

Magicians manipulated spiritual power and formulas, but Jesus acted from an intimate, obedient personal relationship with his Father (6:7-9). Like a father disciplining his children, God humbled Israel in the wilderness, teaching his people that he would provide their bread while they were unemployed if they would just look to him (Deut 8:1-5; cf. Robinson 1962: 54; Barrett 1966: 51-52). Jesus accepts his Father's call in the wilderness and waits for his Father to act.

Second, Jesus was not a deluded visionary (4:5-6) like Josephus's "false prophets" who wrongly expected God to back up their miraculous claims (e.g., Jos. *Ant.* 20.168; *War* 2.259).[198] By wanting Jesus to jump over an abyss (per-

197. Magicians also sometimes metamorphosed themselves or others (Apul. *Metam.* 1.9; 2.1, 5, 30; 3.21-25; 6.22; Blackburn 1986: 190, 193; in modern times, cf. Mbiti 1970: 220, 256-58; Nanan 1994), and were known for attempting invisibility (e.g., *PGM* 1.222-31, 247-62, 256-57; cf. Smith 1978: 120, though this feat sometimes simply represented divine help — see, e.g., Hom. *Il.* 20.321, 443-46; 21.597-98; Eurip. *Helen* 44-45; *Iph. Taur.* 27-30; *Or.* 1629-36). Some may have been skeptical of such alleged metamorphoses (Paus. 1.41.9), and some later Jewish teachers denied that demons could create (Alexander 1980: 33 cites b. Ḥul. 105b, probably following Edersheim), but some rabbis believed that they themselves had harnessed God's creative power (e.g., ARN 25 A), and in later texts some even understood God's activity in analogy with that of magicians (Hayman 1989); some Jews felt they could harness demons to do their bidding (e.g., Test. Sol. 7:8). Magic was widespread, yet not only in Palestinian Judaism (e.g., Wis 17:7; m. Sanh. 6:4; 7:11; Ps-Phocyl. 149), but even among Greeks and Romans, the charge of sorcery was a serious one (cf., e.g., Apuleius's defense; Kee 1983: 213; Smith 1978: 75-76; Theissen 1983: 239-42).

198. Interestingly, Young 1995: 31-32 cites a tradition in which the Messiah would announce redemption from atop the temple (Pesiq. R. 36; also Lachs 1987: 51); a link is possible, but the tradition is unfortunately not demonstrably early (nor is Jos. *War* 7.27-30, which he also cites, necessarily relevant). Smith 1978: 105 and others point out that claims to be able to fly also characterized magicians; early Christianity's closest parallel to this claim (Acts 8:39) is not analogous (cf. Keener 1993: 346-47). Cf. also the first-century false prophets who falsely promised the pious Jerusalemites the deliverance they wanted to hear (e.g., Jos. *War* 6.285-87). Albert Schweitzer in effect revived the deluded visionary hypothesis for the twentieth century by applying it to Jesus, albeit more sympathetically.

haps on the southeast corner of the temple area overlooking the Kidron Valley) known to invite certain death without God's intervention (cf. Jos. *Ant.* 15.412; perhaps *War* 4.343),[199] the devil wants Jesus to presume upon his relationship with God, to act as if God is there to serve his Son, rather than the reverse. (Some magicians claimed the ability to fly as well, though dependence on angels to carry them may render an allusion to magic in this temptation more doubtful.) Leading religious teachers echo Satan's theology at the cross: if Jesus is God's Son, let God rescue him from the cross (27:40-43). They might think they echo a wisdom saying in a book appended to the Greek version of the Bible: "For if the righteous man is a son of God, God will help him, and deliver him from the hand of those who resist him" (Wis 2:18); instead, they merely echoed the devil. The context of the wisdom saying depicted the situation more accurately: the wicked want to condemn the righteous to death unjustly because he claims to be a child of God and to have a good future (Wis 2:16-20).

Jesus understood Scripture accurately and alluded not only to the passage he cited but its context. When he warns against "putting God to the test" (Deut 6:16) he alludes to Israel's dissatisfaction in the wilderness (e.g., Ex 17:2-3, 7). Although God was supplying their needs, they demanded more than their needs, forgetting how much God had delivered them from. Yet Jesus did not get himself into testing presumptuously; like Elijah of old, he did what he did at God's command (1 Kings 18:36; Mt 26:42).

Finally, Jesus was not a political revolutionary, contrary to the assumptions and charges of the Jewish aristocracy (26:55, 61; 27:11-12; cf. Ellis 1974: 108; Jn 18:36).[200] The devil took Jesus to a "high mountain," whether a visionary, mythical mountain[201] or a literal one that provided a good representative sampling of the nearer kingdoms (Gen 13:14-15; Deut 34:1-4).[202] Many inhabitants of the Roman Empire felt that Rome ruled the earth's kingdoms (e.g., Rev 17:18; Jos. *War* 2.361; 3.473; Sall. *Catil.* 36.4; Ovid *Metam.* 15.758-59, 859-60; Corn. Nep. 23 [Hannibal], 8.3); to rule the earth would include the subjection of the Roman emperor. Although most Jewish people agreed that evil angels ruled

199. Matthew has "holy city" (4:5) for Luke's "Jerusalem" (Lk 4:9; Luke emphasizes Jerusalem, possibly suggesting that Matthew altered Q here); Matthew seems to regard the city as holy on account of its heritage (5:35; 27:53), though it has been defiled (23:32-38; 24:15).

200. In hellenistic circles, being a son of Zeus could also entitle one to rule humankind, as in the account in which the oracle of Ammon addressed Alexander of Macedon (cf. Diod. Sic. 17.51.1-2; Olmstead 1959: 511). Alexander yearned to rule the entire world (Dio Chrys. *4th Discourse on Kingship* 49).

201. Manson 1979: 44, cites 1 Enoch 24–25; 2 Bar. 76:3. Cf. Meier 1980: 30; France 1985: 99; Blomberg 1992a: 85n.81; Lucian *Charon*. Cf. the mountaintop between earth, sky, and sea, where all is visible, in Ovid *Metam.* 12.39-43.

202. Mount Nebo allowed Moses to survey the land (Deut 34:1-4) and look "every direction" (Deut 3:27), which the rabbis understood as viewing the whole earth (Hagner 1993: 68). Jub. 4:26 lists Eden, the "mountain of the East," Sinai, and Zion as God's holy places. Theissen 1991: 233 suspects that Mount Hermon provided the literal basis for the mythical mountain.

the nations (Dan 10:13, 20-21),[203] it was a delegated authority (cf. Jn 12:31; 16:11; 2 Cor 4:4; 1 Jn 5:19; Test. Sol. 1:12); despite the devil's claims (cf. also Lk 4:6), God, not Satan, had *ultimate* authority over the world's kingdoms (Dan 4:25; cf. m. 'Abot 3:15).[204] By resisting the devil's offer of the glory of the world's kingdoms (4:8), Jesus perseveres for a kingdom with greater glory (25:31). Contrary to some polemic against Jesus, he was not usurping God's role, but acknowledged one God (4:10; Deut 6:13; cf. Mk 12:29; Jn 5:18-47), as did his Jewish contemporaries (Deut 6:4; Jos. *Ant.* 3.91).

This test may have appealed especially to disciples (though they lacked political power outside the church, some gained it inside the church — 24:45-51); in this instance not Jesus' opponents but his own star disciple Peter echoes Satan's theology exactly: the messianic kingdom without the cross (16:22). (Attempts to dissuade from martyrdom contribute to the martyr's resolve in analogous texts, e.g., 2 Macc 6:21-22; Mart. Pol. 9-11; Acts 21:12-14; Socrates.) Jesus likewise pushes Peter away in disgust[205] as he had Satan — even to the point of calling Peter "Satan" (16:23; cf. 4:10). A disciple seeking to defend Jesus later struck with the sword (26:51), but Jesus informed him that God does not need his servants' violence to defend his purposes; retaliation only breeds more violence (26:52), and God is able to defend his purposes by himself when he wishes to do so (26:53; cf. Sider 1979: 23-24). Jesus' mission involved the cross (26:54), and so does the mission of Jesus' true disciples (16:23-26).

Because Luke frequently follows the order of his sources exactly, Matthew may purposely choose this temptation to climax the narrative:[206] Jesus, son of

203. E.g., Jub. 15:21-32, 35:17, 49:2-4; 1 Enoch 40:9; 61:10; 2 Enoch 20:1 (longer version); Mek. Shir. 2:112ff.; Sifre Deut. 315.2.1; b. Ber. 16b-17a; Yoma 77a; 3 Enoch 26:12; 29:1; 30:1-2; Test. Levi 3:8; Test. Job 49:2; Test. Sol. 6:4, 8:10; Asc. Isa. 1:3; 2:2 (but 1:4 sounds suspiciously Christianized); 3 Bar. 12:3; in early Gnostic texts, e.g., Apoc. Adam 1:4; Hypostasis of the Archons; on LXX Deut, see, e.g., Dodd 1935: 18-19; cf. the sun and moon in Gen. Rab. 6:9. Cf. more fully Keener 1992: 64-65.

204. Although the NT and some Jewish tradition portray Satan as the ruler of this age (Jn 12:31; 14:30; Eph 2:2), Jewish tradition rightly recognized the biblical notion that God was king of the universe, ruler of the world (2 Macc 7:9; Sifre Deut. 27.2.1; ARN 24, §51B); though angels could be "princes" (the "prince of light," CD 5.18; 1QM 13.10) and the present age was evil, the "ruler of the world" could be a positive title (3 Enoch 1:4; 30:2); but cf. also the prince who rules over the evil ones (1QS 2.5; CD 12.2; 1QM 1.15; 13.2, 4; 15.2-3; 17.5-6; 18.6; Asc. Isa. 2:4; Test. Benj. 6:1; Pesiq. R. 20:2; 53:2; "Prince Mastema" in Jub. 11:11; 17:16; 18:9, 12; 48:2, 9, 12, 15), which is what the NT means. On the title, cf. most thoroughly Segal 1981.

205. "Get away from me!" indicates disgust; cf. Is 30:22 MT; m. 'Abod. Zar. 3:6; Shab. 9:1; God thus addresses Satan in Pesiq. R. 20:2. Cf. also "Go!" in the exorcism in 8:32. The relationship, hence the sense, is quite different in the magician's polite dismissal of an angel once finished with it (*PGM* 1.185). The story line of a deity offering a mortal reward (e.g., Lucian *Judgment of the Goddesses,* LCL 3:400-401, Hera's promise to Paris) is no closer than that of kings promising their subjects great rewards (e.g., Mk 6:23). Serving God "alone" recalls the LXX and some Jewish literature (Flusser 1989).

206. Many scholars, however, suggest that Luke changes the original order here (e.g., Gundry 1982: 56; Carson 1984b: 111; France 1985: 97; Theissen 1991: 207; Blomberg 1992a: 84); Luke climaxes with the temple, which is admittedly characteristically Lukan, and Matthew's climax may repeat the original point in Q.

David, must take the kingdom God's way, through first transforming a remnant of sinful people into fit subjects for the kingdom (cf. 4:17-22). Matthew's readers probably knew how Roman forces had slaughtered the Jewish revolutionaries, and how resounding defeat had dashed their people's hopes for a worldly kingdom. They would thus take notice that Jesus humbled himself and waited for God's exaltation.

People can use Scripture for righteous or unrighteous causes (4:4, 6, 7, 10). Given their debates with Pharisees or leaders moving in their general circle, Matthew's community was well aware of the potential for interpreting texts in widely divergent manners. In form this narrative is closest to a "controversy dialogue" (Travis 1977: 69), and in fact it resembles the kind of debate one expects from two experts in the law (e.g., Jeremias 1971: 158; Davies and Allison 1988: 352).[207]

Jesus and the devil argue Scripture, and both are adept at it, though the devil quotes Scripture out of context and so values its wording over its meaning. Psalm 91:3-10 addresses protection from dangers that approach the righteous, not testing God to see if he will really do what Scripture promises (cf. Ps 78:18; Patte 1987: 54); although some applied Psalm 91:10 specifically to the evil impulse (b. Sanh. 103a), later Jewish teachers generally opposed such presumption (Moore 1971: 1:379). Jewish tradition did recognize the activity of guardian angels (see comment on 18:10) and found in Psalm 91:10 the principle that angels accompanied the righteous (see t. ʿAbod. Zar. 1:17; Shab. 17:2) and protect them from demons (Sifre Num. 40.1.5). In this passage Jesus, like a good Jewish teacher, refutes Satan's proof-text with a more appropriate text (4:7), and in the end the angels do minister to Jesus (4:11).

One need not look far to guess how Matthew and his community apply the principles of this narrative to their own day. Religious leaders in 27:40 become mouthpieces for the devil's lie in 4:3, and Jesus' leading disciple in 16:22 echoes 4:8-9. Matthew's audience may thus apply the narrative by picturing Jesus, their champion, engaged in intellectual battle with the devil they believed stood behind their Torah-educated scribal opponents.

But the devil's and the community's opponents' abuse of Scripture does not for a moment suggest to Matthew or his community that they neglect Scripture's real power when rightly interpreted and applied. Their Lord himself submitted his life to its claims (cf. 3:15) and calls his followers to do the same (5:17-20). Jesus' three responses in this testing narrative share the phrase, "It has been written" (4:4, 7, 10).[208] It comes as no surprise that Jesus' first citation declares

207. Some later texts playfully recount such debates with learned demons (Alexander 1980: 36; cf. b. Sanh. 89b; Schechter 1961: 252; Edersheim: 645; the conflict in Test. Job in Nickelsburg 1981: 243). The more frequent challenge-riposte sequence of an honor-shame culture is undoubtedly more relevant, however (see Malina and Rohrbaugh 1992: 41-42). Later rabbis recommended use of Torah to overcome temptation (Gen. Rab. 22:6).

208. For the formula "It is written" elsewhere, cf., e.g., 2:5; CD 1.13; 5.1; 7.10-11; 11.18, 20; 1QS 5.15, 17; 8.14; m. Giṭ. 9:10; Sanh. 10:1; Mek. Pisḥa 1.76; Sifre Deut. 56.1.2; p. Meg. 1:5, §1;

the primacy of God's words to his people, upon which they should feed as on necessary food (4:4; cf. Jer 15:16). While the devil trotted forth worldly categories of sonship, once even justifying them by Scripture, Jesus felt that God's will revealed in Scripture defined the character of his call. Jesus found in three texts from Deuteronomy part of Israel's mission that children of Abraham — not only himself but his followers — must fulfill.[209] If the texts applied to Israel God's son, then *qal waḥomer* (how much more — a common reasoning technique; e.g., 7:11) God's eschatological Son. Jesus' specific Spirit-led behavior in this model is significant: he already knew God's commands and their context, and for him to know was to obey; he adds no reasoning to God's simple commands (cf. Ps 119:11). Because Jesus functions as a model, Matthew's hearers ought to prove no less submissive (5:6; 6:10).

Finally, God promises triumph to those who persevere in testing (4:11). Matthew is far more specific than Mark's compressed description here (in which angels, like the tempter, could have been with Jesus all forty days); *without* Jesus' submitting to the devil (cf. 4:6: "his angels . . . will lift you up"), God's agents provide for Jesus' needs as soon as he has vanquished his foe. (Some Jewish traditions report the devil's jealousy of angels that prepared food for Adam — ARN 1A; a later tradition notes that he departs when his temptation is finished — Gen. Rab. 70:8.) After three high-stake tests the devil left, so that Jesus could later say that he was freeing Satan's possessions because he had already bound the strong man (12:29). Other than that later claim, however, Jesus does not cite his fast or his triumph over the devil publicly because he does his deeds in secret (6:18); his works in driving out demons testify concerning his own victory.

The temptation narrative might evoke readers' disgust for magicians as much as praise for a new Moses providing bread for his people (cf. Teeple 1957: 76). But Jesus is the new Moses who will provide bread for his people (see on 14:13-21; 15:29-38), whom God would deliver by the resurrection, and who would eventually rule the nations (Ps 2:7, cited by God in Mt 3:17). According to Jesus' call, all these things belonged to him; but the ends of God's call in the long term did not justify inappropriate means in the short term.

Sukk. 2:10, §1; 3:5, §1; Ta'an. 3:11, §5; Gen. Rab. 1:4; Num. Rab. 19:8; 3 Enoch 2:4 MSS; 5:14; 18:7, 18; 28:4, 9, 10; 31:2 (perhaps a nonscripture formula in 1QM 15.5-6, but the text is incomplete); in hellenistic papyri, see Deissmann 1923: 249-50; cf. "as it is said" (CD 19.15, B; m. 'Abot 1:18; 2:13; ARN 36A); "it/he says" (CD 4.19-20; 7.14; 9.8-9; 10.16; 1QpHab 6.2; Mek. Pisha 1.70-71; cf. CD 7.8); God "says" (CD 4.13; 6.13; 8.9; cf. Ep. Arist. 155; Mt 15:4; 19:4-5); Moses "said" (CD 5.8; 8.14); the prophet "said" (CD 6.7-8); God "taught" (1QM 11.5-6; cf. CD 9.7). Scripture itself spoke, adapted expressions, etc. (Mek. Shir. 6 in Laut. 2:43-44). Ancient writers could also cite passages directly without noting they were quoting (Plut. *Brutus* 23.3), and pagans, like Jews, cited past experts as authorities (e.g., Quint. 4.1.12).

209. The Gospels suggest the same central texts found among some of their contemporaries: if Cave 4 provides a fair cross-section of the most popular biblical books for the Qumran sectarians, they are first Deuteronomy, then Isaiah, then Psalms (Cross 1980: 43).

Moving to Capernaum (4:12-16)

Cf. Mk 1:21; Lk 4:31; Jn 2:12. John's imprisonment — which foreshadows Jesus' own suffering — becomes the signal for Jesus to begin public ministry (4:12; cf. Jn 3:23-30; Soares Prabhu 1976: 135); the forerunner has completed his mission of "preparing the way" (3:3). That Jesus "withdraws" to Galilee may indicate that he had been tested in the wilderness near Perea, where John was arrested. Since, however, much of Matthew's audience would probably not know these geographical details, the primary point is probably simply that Galilee must be the focus of Jesus' public ministry.

Matthew may address three issues in Jesus' move to Capernaum. *First, the move* immediately precedes the inauguration of Jesus' public ministry, and hence *may imply a concerted missions strategy.* Although Jesus had grown up in a relatively unpretentious town (see on 2:23), the time had come for him to find a more suitable base for his urgent mission. Thus he found a town with more people (cf. Malina 1993: 91; France 1985: 101),[210] with greater notoriety, and from which news would spread quickly around the perimeters of the lake of Galilee (by the roads there — see Liefeld 1967: 141-42; or fishing boats) and perhaps also via the nearby trade route (cf. Alexander 1980: 104). Capernaum was walking distance from both Perea and Philip's territories across the Jordan (Stanton 1995a: 115). Further, Nazareth was not going to accept his message (13:54-57), but Capernaum would be more responsive by comparison (cf. 9:1-2; 11:23).[211]

Still, Capernaum was not a Sepphoris or Tiberias, and would hardly be a town to be invented as the site for much of Jesus' ministry by later Diaspora Christians. Further, although Jesus continued to be identified by his place of supposed origin (Nazareth), as was customary, Jewish tradition supports the notion that even outsiders could in time come to view him as a resident of Capernaum (m. B. Bat. 1:5; Davies and Allison 1988: 378). That Capernaum appears in later rabbinic accounts solely in connection with "schismatics," presumably Jesus' followers (Theissen 1991: 50), suggests that Jesus' missionary strategy was ultimately successful. This model might have implications for the Matthean community (28:19), though the next point is more likely Matthew's emphasis.

Besides suggesting Jesus' own mission strategy, Matthew may also stress Jesus' Galilean ministry base for two other reasons more directly relevant to his audience. *The second issue is that Matthew's Pharisaic opponents, still centered*

210. Estimates have ranged as high as 12,000 (Davies and Allison 1988: 378, following Meyers and Strange 1981: 58), but the current estimate is closer to 1,000-2,000 people (Sanders 1993: 103; Stanton 1995a: 115; Horsley 1995: 194), hence not much larger than higher, older estimates for Nazareth. The more current, lower estimates appear to be more likely (this village is no more well known to Josephus' readers in *Life* 403 than any other in the vicinity), but the debate has not yet closed.

211. Häfner 1993 suggests an inclusio with Nazareth in 2:23, thereby connecting the passages and including both in Matthew's "prologue"; a similar inclusio may connect the proclamations of John and Jesus in 3:2; 4:17.

in Judea in this period, undoubtedly criticized the Jesus movement's Galilean origins. Matthew thus cites Scripture about a messianic role in Galilee to counter regional prejudice against the gospel. Galilee's positive theological role in the Gospels (Freyne 1988: 50-68, 82-90, 103-15; cf. Mt 26:32; 28:7; perhaps ironically 26:69) may reflect the strength of the Christian movement in the region where Jesus had ministered.[212]

But the Gospels may have praised Galilee largely because Judean opponents, including Matthew's opponents, ridiculed the Jesus movement's Galilean origins. Later Babylonian rabbis complained about the Galileans (Freyne 1988: 216-17) after their competitors — Palestinian rabbis — had settled in Galilee; but some earlier Palestinian rabbis also question the Galileans' observance of the law (m. Ned. 2:4; cf. t. Dem. 1:10). This was simply regional prejudice: sources contemporary with Jesus indicate the Galileans' essential loyalty to the law as they understood it[213] and may have been more strict with respect to some traditional customs than Judea was (m. Pesaḥ. 4:5; cf. especially in upper Galilee — Meyers 1976). Galileans were generally loyal to the Jerusalem temple and its priesthood (Freyne 1987; Freyne 1988: 178-90), and Jerusalem's status as Judaism's center gave it special influence (Freyne 1988: 150-52).

But regardless of their loyalty to the temple, first-century Galileans may have felt free to ignore predominantly Judean Pharisees and their successors (cf. Freyne 1981). The Pharisees on the whole were probably centered in Jerusalem rather than in Galilee (Vermes 1973: 56-57; Neusner 1975: 38; but cf. perhaps Jos. *Ant.* 20.43), and their successors settled in Jamnia, which was also in Judea. Likewise the Pharisees seem to have been primarily an urban movement (cf. also perhaps Jos. *Ant.* 18.15), whereas the Jesus movement began as a primarily rural movement (becoming urbanized shortly after the resurrection and only later penetrating the rural areas outside Palestine; cf. Judge 1960: 60-61; Schmeller 1992). Even in the second century, Galilee apparently rejected Pharisaic leadership (Goodman 1983: 93-118; Freyne 1981), even in purely religious matters (Goodman 1983: 107). The rabbis' idealism concerning tithes may well also not have commended itself to more agrarian peasants (Goodman 1983: 178).

Third, and probably most important, what Isaiah says about Galilee foreshadows the Gentile mission that Matthew keeps urging on his audience (4:14; cf. Kingsbury 1975: 23-24). Jesus again acts in obedience to Scripture (4:14-15; cf. Conzelmann 1969: 144), and this passage (Is 9:1-2; cf. Lk 1:79) — which clearly addresses the work of the Davidic Messiah (Is 9:6-7) — indicates that he would work in Galilee "of the Gentiles." This is not to say that Jesus directed his own ministry to Gentiles; the text merely foreshadows outreach to the nations. Galilee was more Jewish than Gentile in Matthew's day, against those earlier German scholars who contended that most Galileans were not fully Jewish (by

212. See Saunders 1977; Meyers 1988: 69, 71; cf. Julian in Stern 1974/84: 502-72; Epict. *Disc.* 4.7.6.

213. Malinowski 1980; cf. Mayer 1981; Meyers and Strange 1981: 37-38, 45.

1941 Grundmann even argued that Jesus was not Jewish — Freyne 1988: 2). Whereas Jewish texts depict the Idumeans as half-Jews, they depict the Galileans as Jews (Freyne 1988: 169). Archaeology indicates that Galilee was rather sparsely populated until *Judeans* resettled it after the Hasmonean conquests, implying substantial ethnically Jewish ancestry (Freyne 1988: 170).[214] Gentile cities surrounded Galilee (Freyne 1988: 143-44), and Galilee had some social intercourse with Gentiles (Goodman 1983: 41-53). But urban Jerusalem probably had greater contact with Gentiles than did Galilean towns.

Nevertheless, many Gentiles continued to live in towns and presumably in the two large cities in Galilee in Matthew's day (cf. 10:5; Wilkinson 1978: 23-24; Grant 1959: 99; Horsley 1995: 104); memory of Galilee's Gentile connections (cf. 1 Macc 5:15) probably remained strong as well. Jesus himself restricted his ministry almost entirely to the Jewish parts of Galilee, apparently avoiding even the two more hellenized Jewish cities Tiberias and Sepphoris (cf. Jeremias 1958: 35).[215] But Matthew sees in Jesus' fulfillment of Isaiah's mention of a Gentile region an advance notice of further ministry to the Gentiles (cf. Is 42:6; 49:6; 52:15).

Matthew has thus found a text that illumines Jesus' Galilean ministry in a general way. In medieval times the trade route through this region came to be called the "way of the sea";[216] Matthew may have simply applied Isaiah's less than technical expression to the trade route passing from Damascus by Capernaum and Sepphoris to the Judean coast. Capernaum was actually in Naphtali's territory, not directly Zebulun's (Meier 1980: 32); yet Zebulun, sometimes associated with the fishing industry (cf. Gen 49:13; Test. Zeb. 5:5), was not far off. At any rate, this Isaiah text would refute the claims of scribes who insisted that a Messiah must hail only from Bethlehem (2:5-6; Jn 7:42).

214. Whereas Upper Galilee had quite strong commercial ties with Tyre (Vale 1987), Lower Galilee was almost completely Jewish by Jesus' day (Goodman 1983: 31-32). Although hellenized art and speech may especially have impacted the latter through its two large cities (cf. Meyers 1976), in many respects it was probably no more hellenized (cf. Goodman 1983: 88-89). Literary and archaeological sources both suggest a cultural distinction between upper Galilee (the Golan) and lower Galilee. The latter included larger and more culturally mixed urban areas; although most of its inhabitants lived in villages, Galilee's cities, which reflected a larger cultural continuum, influenced the villages continuously (Freyne 1988: 171). Nevertheless, archaeological and literary evidence confirms that the heavy population of lower Galilee was primarily rural and agricultural (Freyne 1988: 144-45; cf. idem 1980), and villages, despite cultural influences, were mainly autonomous politically and economically (Goodman 1983: 120). Differences and hence misunderstandings between rural and urban culture were pronounced in antiquity (Finley 1973: 123-49; MacMullen 1974: 15, 30, 32; cf. idem 1966: 163-91; Applebaum 1974/76a: 663-64), despite the influence of the latter on the former (cf. Millar 1981). This clash between urban and rural life undoubtedly obtained in Galilee as well (cf. Freyne 1988: 146-47; Eddy 1996: 465).

215. Those who wish to place Jesus in a specifically hellenistic context have inappropriately exaggerated the cultural influence of these two cities on the surrounding countryside; see more correctly Horsley 1995: 174-81, who rightly cites Jos. *Life* 374-75, 384 and other evidence.

216. Avi-Yonah 1974/76b: 110; Beitzel 1991; cf. Meyers and Strange 1981: 43; Reicke 1974: 117; Hagner 1993: 73.

Calling Fishers of People (4:17-22)

Cf. Mk 1:14-20; Lk 4:15; 5:1-11; Jn 1:35-51. The essential material in this section seems to reflect genuine Jesus tradition (cf., e.g., Sanders 1993: 119). Once Jesus has moved to Capernaum (4:12-16), he will naturally come into contact with fishermen. Although the evangelists have tersely summarized Jesus' message in 4:17 (cf. Mk 1:15), it functions as an adequate summary of his call to Israel to return to God's path.[217] Davies and Allison (1991: 393-94) list a number of points favoring the historical tradition behind the section, which I have adapted only slightly below:

(1) The Synoptics and John independently attest that Peter and Andrew followed Jesus in Galilee.
(2) Other Q narratives confirm that Jesus, in contrast to most rabbis, called his own disciples (8:19-22//Lk 9:57-62), probably following the model of Elijah (1 Kings 19:19-21), which plays very little role in rabbinic texts.[218]
(3) The tradition of the Twelve attests that Jesus did choose disciples whom he expected to aid his mission (like other teachers, he expected disciples to propagate the work)
(4) The structure of Mark 1:17//Matthew 4:19 is "recognizably Semitic," and the saying makes sense only as part of the narrative.
(5) No one had reason to invent the four's occupation as fishermen, and Andrew, who is not central in Synoptic or Pauline tradition, must appear for more historical reasons.

Witherington also observes that "fishers of humans" is hardly a later Christian image for mission, but the metaphor makes sense if some of Jesus' earliest disciples were fishermen. The narrative also hardly drew the image of Jesus recruiting disciples from Jewish practice; finally (though less clearly), Luke 5:10 attests the "fishers of humans" saying in a different context and form, perhaps support-

217. Sanders doubts that repentance was as central to Jesus' teaching as John's (1993: 231-32; cf. idem 1985: 109, 203, 206), but the same word statistics could deny the centrality of love in his message despite 22:37-40; although Jesus may have used the *term* less than John, examples of radical conversion show the centrality of the concept in his ministry (e.g., Mk 2:14-17), and Luke's emphasis does not negate the occasional use of "repentance" earlier in the tradition (Mt 11:20-21 Q); and the idea that Jesus did not set out many "stipulations and conditions" for the kingdom (1993: 234) needs serious nuancing (cf., e.g., Mt 5:32). John undoubtedly influenced Jesus (see Michaels 1981: 1-24), and Sanders himself accepts that Jesus must have mostly agreed with the message of the prophet who baptized him (1993: 94; see further Chilton 1988).

218. Cf. also Lachs 1987: 58. Wilkins 1995: 43-91 finds characteristics of master-disciple relationships in some OT relationships, most convincingly the prophetic groups (Samuel's and Elisha's mentorship) and, less demonstrably, the scribal tradition (for prophets, cf. CD 8.20-21; Mek. Pisḥa 1.150-53; ARN 11, §28B). The Greek term *mathētēs* originally meant both "learner" and, in more technical contexts, "adherent" of a master or school, but by Jesus' day it meant especially the latter (Wilkins 1995: 42).

ing the saying's authenticity by means of multiple attestation (Witherington 1990: 129-30).

Once God had commissioned Jesus (3:17), the devil had tested him (4:3-11), the forerunner had completed his mission (4:12), and Jesus had settled in Capernaum (4:12-16), he was ready to begin his public ministry ("from that time on," 4:17). That Jesus "began" his public ministry here might recall the language of the early Christian summary of Jesus' mission, which usually began with his public ministry (Mk 1:1; Acts 10:37; cf. Robinson 1982: 69). Matthew opens this section with a summary of Jesus' message (4:17), which is spelled out more fully in subsequent discourse material (the repentant lifestyle that serves as a prerequisite for the kingdom appears in chs. 5–7); an opening summary of a teacher's message sometimes preceded the description of his ministry (Robbins 1992: 86). For Matthew, the message for both Galilean Jews (10:5-7) and eventually Gentiles (24:14; 28:18-19) is the same as John the Baptist's (3:2) and that of Jesus (13:19): Get your lives in order, for God's kingdom is coming (4:17). Jesus' proclamation probably implies that the kingdom "has drawn near"[219] rather than "has arrived,"[220] but in either case the sense of its intrusive imminence compels an immediate response (26:45-46; see France 1985: 90). Somewhat analogous warnings in biblical prophets (Is 13:6, 9; Ezek 30:3; Joel 1:15; 3:14; Obad 1:15; Zeph 1:7, 14) may connote a prophetic eschatological enthusiasm, but in context it can also indicate that nearer judgments foreshadow the imminent end (e.g., Joel's locusts). Jesus clearly was not interested only in encouraging disciples; his message was for the whole people (Borg 1984: 70; contrast Sanders 1985: 112-13, but cf. ibid.: 118).

As this message summarizes Jesus' proclamation of God's authority, so 4:18-22 demonstrate people's proper response to God's rule (also Patte 1987: 57); 4:23-25 demonstrates God's rule over sickness and demons; and chapters 5–7 flesh out the nature of the ethic of repentance (the values of the future kingdom) one must live to be prepared in advance for the kingdom. Just as Jesus' message concurred with that of John, so the message of Jesus' followers must accord with that of Jesus. They must proclaim the imminence of the kingdom (10:7; cf. 28:18), demonstrate God's rule over sickness and demons (10:8), and pass on the master's teachings (28:19). Following a teacher would include imitating his example (Betz 1968: 76; Jos. *Life* 11).

In 4:18-22 the one whom the Father called in 3:17 now calls others who will advance his mission. Jesus' call to leave profession and family was radical, the sort of demand that only the most radical teacher would make. This text provides Matthew's community several examples of servant leadership and radical discipleship. It also suggests that while Jesus was a traditional Jewish teacher in some respects (Bultmann 1958: 58), he was not *merely* a traditional teacher (see

219. E.g., Kümmel 1957: 19-25; Black 1967: 208-11; Nineham 1977: 69; cf. Carson 1984b: 117.

220. E.g., Dodd 1961: 44; idem 1961: 29; Argyle 1963: 42; though cf. Mt 21:34.

Hengel 1981b: 1-2, 27-33; in Matthew, see Kingsbury 1975: 33). As Schweizer observes, no one can question that Jesus called disciples (Schweizer 1955: 88; cf. Sanders 1985: 11); but the evidence indicates that, unlike other teachers, he never trained his disciples fully to replace him.[221] If Jesus is not an ordinary teacher, neither dare his disciples be ordinary disciples (cf. 5:20; 23:8).

First, Jesus took the initiative to call a nucleus of disciples. Greek teachers had disciples (e.g., Diog. Laert. 9.1.4-5; Pythagoras had about eighty — Diog. Laert. 8.1.39), and Jewish sages, including Pharisaic sages (Jos. *Ant.* 15.3, 370), heavily emphasized making disciples (m. 'Abot 1:1; cf. Hor. 3:5), who were to repeat back what they learned (Sifre Deut. 48.2.6). Some scholars make much of Jesus' calling his own disciples rather than waiting for them to come to him, noting that disciples normally chose their teachers rather than the reverse.[222] Early Jewish and Greek tradition most frequently assumes that disciples are responsible for acquiring their own teachers of the law or philosophy (m. 'Abot 1:6, 16; ARN 3, 8 A; Socrates *Ep.* 4; Diog. Laert. 7.1.3). Despite exceptions, some of the more radical teachers who, like Jesus, sometimes even rejected prospective disciples (see comment on Mt 19:21-22), may have considered the disciple's responsibility so weighty that some of them would have felt it dishonorable for the teacher to seek out the disciple.

Jesus' seeking out disciples himself may thus represent a serious breach of custom (Malina 1981: 78; but cf., e.g., Jer 1:4-10), "coming down to their level" socially. (Compare later rabbis' stereotype of the elitist academicians of Jesus' day, the Shammaites, who allegedly wanted to educate only the well-to-do of honorable birth: ARN 3 A; 4, §14 B.) Although discipleship language in the Gospels is roughly the same as in other extant streams of Jewish tradition (Culpepper 1975: 222), some of Jesus' methods mark him out as a radical teacher on the periphery of the more usual social institution. Probably Jesus selects as his model the prophetic way of choosing one's successor found in 1 Kings 19:19-21, as the Gospel tradition may have recognized (cf. Lk 9:61-62). As "fishers of people," their mission was primarily to "win back" the lost sheep of Israel (cf. 10:6; 18:15; Witherington 1990: 131), that is, to serve as the nucleus for Jesus' renewal movement.

221. Schweizer 1955: 88; cf. Ladd 1974b: 107; Betz 1968: 71; see Mt 23:8-10.

222. Davies 1966b: 133; Kingsbury 1975: 62; Gundry 1982: 62; Garland 1993: 48. Examples of teachers seeking disciples appear more frequently in the Greek tradition (e.g., Aul. Gel. 5.3.6); but these examples are of "radical" teachers, exceptions to the customary Greek as well as Jewish tradition. Robbins 1992: 89-94 cites helpful Greek examples (Plato *Theaetetus* 144D; *Charmides* 155A-58E; *Alcibiades Major* 135D; Aristophanes *Clouds* 497-517; Diog. Laert. 2.48). Finding little rabbinic precedent for summoning disciples or promising to make disciples into something they are not (1992: 104), Robbins locates the Jewish component of those elements' origin here especially in the divine call in biblical tradition (e.g., 115, citing Gen 12:1-2), alongside the Socratic model in Greek tradition (1992: 117-18). Philo (1992: 94-95) and Josephus (1992: 97, closer to the Gospels) apply typical Greek school language to the biblical tradition, suggesting the influence of such hellenistic models by this period. It is said that Hillel pursued laborers to get them to study Torah (not just as disciples to become rabbis, however) and receive eternal life (ARN 26, §54B); the earliest sages probably also had more independence than their later counterparts (cf., e.g., p. Sanh. 1:2, §13).

Second, consistent with Jesus' rhetoric elsewhere, he teaches his hearers in terms they can understand. Although most scholars agree that Matthew's community included Christian scribes (13:52; 23:34), Matthew and his sources are clear that Jesus did not call professionally trained rabbis (who might have much to *unlearn* first) to be his disciples. He called artisans and encouraged them that the skills they already had were serviceable in the kingdom. If God called shepherds like Moses and David to shepherd his people Israel, Jesus could call fishermen to be gatherers of people; other writers could likewise use fish as an analogy for people (e.g., Babrius 4.5-8).[223] (Commercial fishermen used nets — see, e.g., Babrius 4.1; 9.6; Ovid *Metam.* 13.922; Nun 1993; one should thus not think in terms of the modern leisure fisherman's bait or tackle, although poorer persons might engage in subsistence fishing in this manner — e.g., Babrius 6.1-4; Ovid *Metam.* 13.923.)

Third, Jesus' call was costly economically, involving downward mobility. Although artisans made far less than the wealthy (who comprised perhaps one percent of the ancient population), they were not among the roughly 90 percent of the ancient population we may call peasants, either.[224] Fishermen, like tax gatherers, were "among the more economically mobile of the village culture" (Freyne 1988: 241).[225] Although the primary occupation even on the lake of Galilee was agricultural (Horsley 1995: 194), fishing remained a major industry there (Safrai 1974/76b: 747),[226] and fish was a primary staple of the first-century Palestinian diet (Neusner 1984: 23), as elsewhere in Mediterranean antiquity (Horsley 1989: 99).[227] Workers processed fish to preserve them, then transported

223. Some scholars favor an OT background for "fishers of people" (Hab 1:15; Jer 16:16; Mt 13:47; cf. Ezek 47:10; later, CD 4.15-17; 1QH 5.7-8; Ps-Philo 3:11; Strauss 1973); see Jeremias 1971: 132-33; Fenton 1977: 73; Gundry 1982: 62; Lane 1974a: 67-68; MacLaurin 1978b; Derrett 1980. But the OT use is a judgment metaphor (Jos. and Asen. 21:21 MSS would be closer), so the image is questionable unless Jesus provocatively pictured those who should "trap" people for the kingdom (as suggested by Davies and Allison 1988: 398) or intended the allusion by way of contrast (cf. Vermes 1993: 102n.27). Jesus more likely called them to be "fishers of people" primarily because fishing was their prior profession, as the text indicates. A bilingual milieu may also help explain Jesus' use of the figure, since "catch" (Heb. *ṣud,* Aram. *tzadē*) could apply both to physical catching and to winning others by deception or debate (Lachs 1987: 58-59); the image also appears in Greek (Boring 1995: 55).

224. Greek sources suggest that fishermen may not always have been of the highest reputation (Horsley 1989: 100), although around the Lake of Galilee the demands of the local economy probably would outweigh any influence from imported perspectives.

225. Cf. *ILS* 7486; Wilkinson 1978: 29-30; Hengel 1974b: 27; Stanton 1989a: 186.

226. Cf. fishing implements found in Bethsaida (Arav 1991). Cf. also the abundance of small boats available for crossing the sea from one town to another (Jos. *Life* 163-64); on the recovered Galilean fishing boat (26.5 by 7.5 by 4.5 feet), see Riesner 1987; Wachsmann 1988; Stone 1989; Andiñach 1990; Peachey 1990.

227. Among the poor elsewhere, smoked fish could rank "the most popular item" in a general market's sales for a day (*P. Oxy.* 520; Lewis 1983: 136). Rarer, luxury fish (Dupont 1992: 277) and the complex market system in second-century Roman legislation cited by Malina and Rohrbaugh 1992: 44-45 are probably less relevant to the towns of lakeside Galilee (excepting urban Sepphoris and Tiberias), where the market was not far from the industry. A custom of eating fish on the Sabbath

them "as cured, pickled, salted, or dried (*m. Ned.* 6.4); and wine could be mixed in with fish-brine (*m. Ter.* 11.1)." They could be eaten "broiled or roasted" (Lk 24:42; Jn 21:9; Tob 6:5); "minced (*m. 'Abod. Zar.* 2.6), cooked with leeks (*m. Ma'as. Sh.* 2.1), with an egg (*m. Besa* 2.1), or in milk (*m. Hul.* 8.1). Fish oil could also be used as fuel for lamps (*m. Shabb.* 2.2) and as a medicine" (Hanson and Oakman 1998: 109). Family businesses, of course, would have been common (see Malina 1993: 151); keeping money in the family was economically as well as socially profitable. Luke even indicates that the two families had formed a fishing cooperative (Lk 5:10; cf. Stambaugh and Balch 1986: 69; Applebaum 1974/76a: 685), and Mark declares that Zebedee's (biblical Zabdi; cf. Jos. *Ant.* 5.33) family employed "hired servants" (Mk 1:20; Hengel 1974b: 27).[228] Thus these fishermen had much to lose economically by leaving their businesses.

Most first-century teachers had no formal schoolhouses for their academies except their own homes or those of their disciples; Jesus also seems to have used local homes (8:14-16; 13:1; cf. Mk 2:1-2; Riesner 1984a: 438-39) and recommended that his followers breaking new spiritual ground do the same (Mt 10:11-13). But while it was not the norm (most scribes simply dealt with legal documents and taught local children; see Keener 1991a: 23), some teachers traveled, sometimes with their disciples (Safrai 1974/76b: 762).[229]

Jesus had a base of operations in Capernaum (Mt 8:5, 14; 9:1, 9; 17:24), but he also made a broader circuit of ministry that required his disciples to be away from their homes and livelihoods for substantial periods of time (8:18, 28; 9:35; 10:11, 23; 11:1; 14:13, 21; 16:13; 17:1; 19:1). When apostles traveled later they took their spouses with them (1 Cor 9:5), but the list of women following the company (27:55-56; Mk 15:40-41; Lk 8:1-3) provides no indication that spouses were traveling with the disciples during the initial period of discipleship. Although I regard it as unlikely, it is possible that Jesus' ministry was seasonal and that the disciples returned to support their families part of the year. Seasonal study was not unknown; the Greek school year ran from October to June (Ferguson 1987: 83). Further, weather conditions may have limited the travels of Jesus' group. Rains in Galilee fell on average thirty to fifty days a year, concentrated in the four months from early December to early March, which would make travel during those periods more difficult (though tempera-

---

(Safrai 1974/76b: 747) may have obtained this early, though Galileans near the lake surely ate fish much more regularly. For fishermen's livelihoods depending on the sea, see, e.g., Ps-Theocritus *The Fishermen* (*Greek Bucolic Poets,* LCL 246-53).

228. Jewish Palestine may not have employed economic structures more complex than fishing cooperatives, but other parts of the Empire, such as Ephesus, knew influential fishing guilds (see Horsley 1989: 101-7; cf. *P. Oxy.* 3270.5, 8 in Horsley 1983: 18).

229. Traveling teachers were not the norm in Judea and, though attested, apparently remained rare even in Galilee (cf. Vermes 1993: 46, citing b. Ḥul. 27b; Sanh. 70a), but also not as uncommon (and Greek) as Robbins 1992: xxi, 101-5 and others have supposed (Greek examples may be significant but exceptional as well; cf., e.g., Hock 1980: 27-28); see the evidence for perambulatory or traveling lectures in Koenig 1985: 17; Young 1989: 234n.87 (e.g., m. 'Abot 3:7; Sifre Deut. 305; ARN 4A).

tures on the lake in January average between 50 and 65 degrees Fahrenheit; Sanders 1993: 110).

Nevertheless, disciples could not easily return to abandoned businesses. Adult agrarian workers could perhaps afford to be away between sowing and harvest, but for most workers in the artisan class like fishermen even seasonal departure from their families and livelihoods would be costly (though better than being away the entire year). Further, actual seasonal absence would be unnecessary: weather conditions would have limited travel only over long distances; while the disciples undoubtedly spent some nights away from home (especially when they traversed the lake), the Gospel itineraries suggest that they often ministered within walking distance of Capernaum or Bethsaida.

Such abandonment of full-time livelihood is significant. Jewish sages told stories of pagans relinquishing their wealth on converting to Judaism (Sifre Num. 115.5.7), and Greek philosophers told stories of converts to philosophy who abandoned wealth to become disciples (Diog. Laert. 6.5.87; Diogenes *Ep.* 38);[230] such stories reflected well on the teacher the students left all to follow (e.g., Diogenes *Ep.* 9).These stories demonstrate not only the relative worthlessness of possessions, but the incomparable value of what the converts gained (for God's care for proselytes, cf., e.g., Pesiq. Rab Kah. 10:10). For Matthew, the kingdom is like a precious treasure, worth the abandonment of all other treasures (13:44-46).

Fourth, Jesus' call cost comfort, challenged the priority of family, and was probably therefore scandalous. Matthew's narrative not only reports the historical activity of the first disciples, but he also presents it as a model of discipleship for his own audience (Wilkins 1995: 171-72; cf. Tert. *On Idolatry* 12; Basil *The Long Rules, Question 8, ACCS,* 19-20). James and John abandoned not only the boat — representing their livelihood — but their father and the family business (4:22). In a society where teachers normally stressed no higher responsibility than honor of parents (Jos. *Apion* 2.206; Keener 1991a: 98, 197), including economic responsibility for them (see comment on 15:4-6), some people would view such behavior as scandalous. (Torah teachers, however, did praise those who honored Torah above their families; see ARN 6 A; 13, §30 B.) Jesus elsewhere affirms the importance of marriage (19:9) and filial (15:4-6) relationships; Matthew does not find in Jesus' teaching an excuse to downplay one's responsibilities to one's family (see Keener 1991a: 98-99, 102). At the same time, God's call requires true disciples to value the demands of God's kingdom — announcing its good news — more highly than the public shame it

230. Boring 1995: 54-55 adds Aristotle *On Philosophy* 1.53. Davies and Allison 1988: 400 also cite among Jewish accounts Jos. and Asen. 13 and parallels in the sacrifices of the Essenes and Therapeutae (1QS 1.11-13; 6.20-23) found praiseworthy in hellenistic Jewish apologetic (Philo *Omn. Prob. Lib.* 76-77, 85; *Vit. Con.* 25-31; Jos. *War* 2.122; *Ant.* 18.20); Davies and Allison 1997: 46 add Philost. *V.A.* 1.13; Porphyry *Vit. Plot.* 7. Ancient sages commended those who paid a price for being disciples of the sages, including, apparently, the disdain of some common people more interested in other pursuits (ARN 11A).

brings on their families or the way they feel toward that shame (10:35-37). It is not hard to understand why some might feel more comfortable remaining unattached (19:11-12)!

Although disciples of rabbis normally remained with their wives during study (cf. Safrai 1974/76a: 965), the rabbis praised those said to have endured hardship for Torah study (e.g., Hillel), including those who stayed away from home for years of Torah study.[231] The stories are probably fictitious — many Jewish teachers forbade leaving one's wife for more than thirty days to engage in Torah study (m. Ketub. 5:6; Safrai 1974/76b: 763) — but the stories would not even make sense unless some Jewish men went away from home to study with famous teachers of the law (cf. Sifre Deut. 48.2.4, 6). Jesus apparently demanded more in this way than the vast majority of Bible teachers in his day. In the context of relationship with a person, such reports would indicate intense commitment (cf. 19:27); one would leave family only for a greater love (e.g., Ovid *Metam.* 7.72-73, 170). Thus one letter of recommendation from the second century A.D. passionately praises a friend who left family, property, and livelihood to care for the letter's writer (*P. Oxy.* 32.10-12).

Some have compared Jesus' demands on disciples to those of wandering Cynics (Hengel 1981b: 27-33; Theissen 1978: 14-15; cf. Kee 1980: 68). The comparison of Cynics to the early Jesus movement (often negatively by outsiders) is not unreasonable; missionaries like Paul (see Bowers 1980: 318-19; Scroggs 1980: 172) may have helped make this model acceptable to later monasticizing streams of Christian thought (Sent. Sext. 18-19). Yet Jesus' itinerant ministry is hardly distinctly Cynic (even in Luke, who is most apt to present Jesus to his readers in such culturally relevant terms; cf. Fiorenza 1983: 74; Witherington 1994: 117-45; Eddy 1996). As we have seen, Jesus maintained a base of operation in Capernaum (from which most of Galilee was in walking distance — Overman 1996: 67) and did not reject property altogether (cf. also 2 Kings 5:9). Further, Cynics were not the only Greek philosophers who traveled (e.g., Diog. Laert. 2.22); likewise, Torah teachers could also travel "from place to place to speak" (Safrai 1974/76b: 762).[232] Most telling, Cynics were surely too rare in Jewish Palestine to provide the primary model (e.g., Boyd 1995: 151-58; Eddy 1996: 463-67).

But Cynics and other radical teachers nevertheless shared with Jesus a notable departure from established societal roles. Those most apt to wander from town to town were socially dislocated people, such as landless persons seeking work (see Goodman 1983: 39). Although wandering prophets existed in the ancient world (J. Collins 1972: 6; Burkert 1987: 31), itinerancy — perhaps a feature of ancient mobility in general — was hardly a central feature of

231. On Aqiba, Sandmel 1978b: 246-47; Witherington 1984: 10; others, Gen. Rab. 95 MSV. Later teachers assumed such long separations to be consensual (p. Ketub. 5:7, §2; cf. Qoh. Rab. 7:6, §2); they also had to explain what happened to Aqiba's additional disciples acquired during this period (e.g., Qoh. Rab. 11:6, §1).

232. See also Safrai 1974/76a: 965; Sifre Deut. 43.3.7.

early Christian prophecy (Boring 1982: 59-61; cf. Aune 1983: 211-14; pace Harnack; Theissen).[233] Nevertheless, the best background for Jesus' itinerant mission widely known in Jewish Palestine is that of the Old Testament prophets (1 Sam 7:16-17; 2 Kings 4:8-10; cf. Hengel 1981b: 16-24; Culpepper 1975: 227).

Jesus Demonstrates God's Reign with Power (4:23-25)

Cf. Mk 1:39; 3:7-10; Lk 4:44; 6:17-18. Before both of the first two discourse sections (4:23-25; 9:35), Matthew includes a summary of Jesus' kingdom works.[234] Jesus was preaching and teaching the good news of the kingdom: teaching generally involved ethical or apologetic instruction (more scribal activity, as in 23:3; Ezra 7:10), whereas preaching was primarily proclamation aimed at bringing about conversion (Dodd 1980: 7-8; cf. Guelich 1982: 43).[235]

Yet Jesus not only proclaimed and explained the kingdom; he demonstrated God's authority by healing the sick and expelling demons (Ladd 1978a: 47).[236] The language of "healing" could include exorcism in ancient Jewish circles (Tob 12:3, 14). From Strauss onward, exorcism may have been the most frequently accepted feature of Jesus' miracle stories (Dunn 1975: 44). No less an authority than E. P. Sanders declares it an "almost indisputable" historical fact that "Jesus was a Galilean who preached and healed" (1985: 11), and that "The sheer volume of evidence makes it extremely likely that Jesus actually had a reputation as an exorcist" (1993: 149).[237] If the record does not always make the boundary between exorcism and healing clear, it at least does indicate a differ-

233. Strangely, Gerd Theissen contends that wandering Palestinian charismatics known from the Jesus tradition were Paul's opponents; yet Paul himself constitutes our best concrete *evidence* for a literal practice of this lifestyle. Many arguments for continuing itinerant prophets in the Gospels themselves are tenuous (cf., e.g., Tannehill 1975: 139-40; Hill 1979: 154; Aune 1983: 211-16, 243; Stambaugh and Balch 1986: 105).

234. On summary reports in ancient literature, see Aune 1987: 54; in the biblical Kings narratives, see, e.g., 1 Kings 14:19-20, 31; 15:8, 24; Rosner 1993: 76.

235. Grassi 1989 suggests that Matthew saw his own work as a "gospel of the kingdom," the way Deuteronomy repeated the earlier Torah; this view may be correct even if not demonstrable from 4:23. "Gospel" had a widespread secular usage (see Diogenes *Ep.* 23 to Lacydes; Milligan 1908: 141-44; Horsley 1983: 10-15, citing *P. Oxy.* 3313; Longus 3.33 for wedding announcements; in the LXX, e.g., Jer 20:15), but the early Christian usage echoes particularly LXX Isaiah (e.g., Is 40:9; 52:7; 60:6; 61:1; cf. Ps. Sol. 11:1). Some older authors wrongly associated the term too particularly with hellenistic cults (Nock 1933b: 132; e.g., Epict. *Disc.* 3.21.13).

236. At least one other ancient Jewish source invoked God's reign in exorcism (4Q510 1.4; Vermes 1993: 130), though this practice makes good sense; for more general observations on exorcism, see comment on 8:17.

237. Although skeptical of the story of the Syro-Phoenician woman (which he surprisingly thinks created to illustrate the early Christian view of missions), Meier 1994: 646-77 decides in favor of the authenticity of some specific exorcism accounts, thus also accepting the category as a whole as probable.

ence between the two.[238] That he healed "all" diseases (4:23) may mean every kind of sickness rather than every sick person, since the "all" of v. 24 is necessarily hyperbole; surely suppliants did not bring *every* sick person in Syria to him (Blomberg 1992a: 92n.5)![239]

Significantly, Jesus taught in the synagogues, the educational and community centers of the day (4:23).

Excursus: Synagogues

By "synagogues" I mean local gatherings, formal or informal, usually in regular meeting places (the community, not the edifice, as Frey notes in *CIJ* 1:lxx). In the Diaspora these gathering places were called *proseuchai,* that is, "places of prayer" well before the first century B.C. (e.g., *CPJ* 1:239-40, §129; 1:247-49, §134; 2:368, §1441; 2:370-71, §1443-44; 2:375-76, §1449).[240] Pagan literature also takes note of them (Juv. *Sat.* 3.296); in the Diaspora they functioned as *collegia* (corporations) on the model of other hellenistic social and religious associations (Jos. *Ant.* 14.258, 260; Philo *Leg. Gai.* 311-15; Mantel 1967: 75-91). Many were small and simple, like the first-century-B.C. structure on Delos (Stambaugh and Balch 1986: 48); the characteristic activity, rather than a particular structure, defined the site (cf. Acts 1:14; 16:13-16).

Some have argued that the assembly halls common in the Diaspora and attested in Jerusalem may have been less common in Galilee (see Horsley 1995: 222-33). Others contend that the reason few pre-70 Palestinian synagogues have been uncovered is simply that those building later synagogues completely demolished earlier ones on the same site; all three probable pre-70 synagogues that have been discovered are from sites not resettled after their destruction (Sanders 1992: 200; idem 1990: 77; cf. May 1944: 3). With the loss of the temple, synagogues also grew more ornate after A.D. 70.[241]

238. Although some attributed sickness, especially epilepsy, to demonic sources (e.g., Aramaic Incantation Text 53:12; Jub. 10:12; cf. Yamauchi 1986: 100-113), Matthew distinguishes the two in 4:24 (cf. Alexander 1980: 32, 63). He may think demonization could at times produce epileptic behavior (17:15), but his term for epilepsy did have a broader usage than epilepsy alone (cf. Ross 1978; Yamauchi 1986: 129).

239. Though some objected to this use of "all" (*Rhet. ad Herenn.* 2.20.32-33, 21.33), the hyperbolic "all" appears in Josephus, for whom "all Galilee" may refer to the Galilean aristocracy (*War* 1.291; *Ant.* 14.295; Horsley 1995: 56), and for whom "all" Balaam's predictions were fulfilled, but the others that have not been will be (*Ant.* 4.125).

240. For later examples, see, e.g., *CIJ* 1:476, §662; 1:495, §683; 1:497, §684; 2:367, §1440; 2:369, §1442; perhaps 1:525, §726; 2:360, §1432; 2:361, §1433. Jos. *Life* 277 also freely applies the hellenistic title to a Galilean structure; the favored title seems to have varied geographically (Applebaum 1974/76b: 490), perhaps until rabbinic influence became more widespread (Schubert 1981).

241. From the earliest period (well before A.D. 70) writers associated the synagogues with the Jerusalem temple (Cohen 1986: 163). The associations grew after 70, however, and probably still further under later Byzantine influence (Levine 1996: 446-47).

But even if one assumes the lack of formal structures functioning through the week as religious and community centers,[242] one should not suppose that observant Galileans failed to assemble (cf. Sir 1:30). While smaller towns may have lacked the resources for such formal structures,[243] Josephus reflects the interpretation that the law required Jews to assemble each Sabbath to study Torah (*Apion* 2.175) and pray (*Apion* 1.209).[244] A public place of prayer in Tiberias (one of Galilee's two large cities) functioned as the meeting place for the entire citizen assembly (*Life* 277-78).

Regardless of the kind of building, the assembly places were not restricted to what Western society would call religious functions as many modern Western churches are. To be sure, they remained houses of study (e.g., *CIJ* 2:333, §1404), but as Levine 1986: 14 summarizes, they also functioned as community courts (like the "gates" of biblical tradition; 10:17; 23:34; Acts 22:19; m. Mak. 3:12; though Urman 1993 argues for a distinction between synagogues and community centers in this period), gathering sites for charity (Mt 6:2; t. B. Bat. 8:14; Shab. 16:22; Ter. 1:10), places to raise funds for the temple (Philo *Leg. Gai.* 156; *Ant.* 16.167-68; 14.215), hostels (Theodotus inscription); and banquet halls (Jos. *Ant.* 14.214-16; 16.164). Further, both synagogue designs (e.g., May 1944: 9; Hachlili 1977; Narkiss 1986: 185-86; Levine 1996: 444) and comments of later rabbis (e.g., t. B. Meṣ. 11:23; Ṭohar. 8:11) show us that the local communities, not representatives of the rabbinic academy, controlled synagogues in the second century and later.[245] Seats face one another in the pre-70 synagogue at Gamla, suggesting interaction in Galilean assemblies (Freyne 1988: 152-53). Members of the community may have gathered at such assembly halls for special events during the week, such as the visit of a traveling teacher like Jesus. In many places the respected elders probably allowed any guests with a reputation as teachers to speak (cf. Sanders 1990: 80-81).

Once Jesus' reputation spread, people would have flocked to synagogues to hear him teach (on gossip networks, see Malina and Rohrbaugh 1992: 45); in the be-

242. No form was mandatory; various architectural types existed through the medieval period (Meyers 1986: 128-32); on pre-70 Judean types, see Chen 1980.

243. Well-to-do persons sometimes donated synagogues (Lk 7:5; *CIJ* 2:8, §738; Theodotus inscription). Some synagogues probably met in well-to-do patrons' homes, as house churches later did (Meyers and Strange 1981: 141); a private home lies beneath the later Capernaum synagogue (Strange and Shanks 1982: 29-30).

244. Cf. also Jos. *War* 2.289; *Ant.* 16.43. As Sanders 1992: 199 points out, Philo recognizes a "house of prayer" (*Embassy* 132), and Jews learned Torah in an assembly on the Sabbath (*Hypothetica* 7.12-13; cf. *Spec. Leg.* 2.62-63; *Every Good Man Is Free* 81). First-century Jews believed that Moses required this (Philo *Hypothetica* 7.12-13; Jos. *Apion* 2.175; Ps-Philo 11:8; Sanders 1990: 78).

245. Synagogues nevertheless regularly appear as positive places of worship in rabbinic texts; see, e.g., t. Sukk. 4:6; b. Meg. 28ab; p. Ta'an. 3:11, §4. Later rabbis both projected the institution anachronistically into the distant past (e.g., Lam. Rab. Proem 2) and exaggerated their numbers in the more recent past (e.g., Lam. Rab. 3:51, §9).

ginning he might have informally engaged others learned in Torah in discussion (cf. the synagogue seating plan in Sanders 1993: 100-101).[246] Other Jewish texts speak of people running to hear a popular teacher (e.g., p. Hor. 3:4, §4; B. Meṣ. 2:11, §1). Once word of Jesus as *healer* spread, however, one cannot doubt that people throughout Galilee would flock to him (cf. Sanders 1993: 154, who thinks it "fairly certain" that "healing, especially exorcism," was the basis for his fame; cf. Theissen 1983: 72); people in antiquity traveled long distances to reach healing sanctuaries (Casson 1974: 130-35, 193-94), and one may compare the masses flocking to the hot springs at Tiberias[247] and similar sites[248] to recover their health.[249]

Matthew also wants his readers to know how *widely* word about Jesus spread (4:24-25). Ancient narratives about popular teachers (as opposed to more aristocratic figures who often disdained the masses)[250] praised them by emphasizing their popularity (e.g., Philost. *V.A.* 1.40; Robbins 1992: 122n.74; cf. Ovid *Metam.* 3.339-40, 511-12); though an aristocrat, Josephus also appeals to his populist support (*Life* 250, 300-303). Matthew, however, is also interested in the geographical distribution of this popularity. Josephus indicates that many Jews lived in Syria in Jesus' day (e.g., Jos. *War* 2.461-68); if Matthew writes to believers in Syria (see Meier 1980: 36; cf. the Introduction), he may use the mention of Jewish followers from Syria to encourage his own readers. By "Syria" Matthew probably means not the entire official province, but the region to the north-northeast of Palestine.[251] Although many Jews lived in the Decapolis, these Jews' hearing of Jesus in a predominantly Gentile region[252] allows Matthew to

246. On Capernaum's synagogue, see Strange and Shanks 1983, although the remains of this structure may be later than they think (cf. Chen 1980: 38; idem 1986); less recently, Goodenough 1953-68: 1:181-92. Although the third-century synagogue was 65 feet long and two stories high (resembling some other magnificent synagogues of the period), its first-century predecessor was likely smaller (Sanders 1993: 103)

247. See, e.g., Jos. *War* 2.614; 4.11; *Life* 85; Pliny *N.H.* 5.15.71; Pesiq. Rab Kah. 11:16; Qoh. Rab. 10:8, §1.

248. Jos. *War* 1.657; Pliny *N.H.* 2.95.208; 5.15.72; Hirschfeld and Solar 1980; idem 1984; Schürer 1961: 157.

249. The springs of Tiberias were well known (e.g., b. Sanh. 93a; 108a; Shab. 40b; 147a; p. Ned. 6:1, §2; Gen. Rab. 76:5; other references in Urbach 1979: 1:393; Sandmel 1978b: 201; for the synagogue there, see Goodenough 1953/68: 1:214-16; Shanks 1984). Prayer for healing was common (cf. b. Ber. 60b), and appears in the 'Amida (p. Ta'an. 2:2, §7).

250. For aristocratic disdain of the masses and their demagogues, see Isoc. *To Nic.* 48-49, *Or.* 2; *Areopagiticus;* Arist. *Pol.* 3.6.4-13, 1281q-82b; 3.7.7-9, 1283ab; 3.12.1, 1288a; 4.4.4-7, 1292a; 5.4.1-2, 1304b; 5.5.4-5, 1305b; 6.2.10-12, 1319b; Arius Didymus *Epitome* (Malherbe 1986: 145); Polyb. 6.3-4; Plut. *Praising Inoffensivly* 16, *Mor.* 545C; Dion. Hal. 7.8.1; 7.31.1; 7.56.2; 8.31.4; 10.18.3; Diod. Sic. 10.7.3; 15.58.3; Diog. Laert. 6.42; Diog. *Ep.* 11; Philo *Creation* 171; cf. Gardner 1974: 27-59. The masses' support, however, could prove critical in some situations (Dion. Hal. 7.45.4).

251. So Davies and Allison 1988: 417, citing mishnaic usage: m. Dem. 6:11; B. Qam. 7:7; Rosh Hash. 1:4; 'Ed. 7:7; 'Abod. Zar. 1:8; Sheb. 6:2, 5, 6; Ma'aś. Sh. 5:5; Ḥal. 4:7, 11; 'Or. 3:9; Ohol. 18:7.

252. Cf., e.g., Parker 1975; Smith, McNicoll, and Hennessey 1981; Beare 1981: 122.

point his readers to a geographically expansive Gentile mission. Given his other lessons of desperate faith (e.g., 9:20; 20:31), it is not unlikely that the distance the sick people travel to find help from Jesus indicates their sacrificial faith as well. Such summary statements could praise Solomon's widespread popularity among surrounding nations (Jos. *Ant.* 8.182).

In its larger context, this narrative indicates that Jesus had awaited God's time for him to minister (4:12); now word was spreading quickly. Subsequent narratives, however, also warn that momentary popularity is just an opportunity to convey the message to those who really have ears to hear, only some of whom will become disciples.[253] Although the "crowds" remain more positive toward Jesus than do Jerusalem's leaders (see Van Tilborg 1972b: 142-65), popularity does not always translate into deep commitment in the end (27:20). Although they remain "available to Jesus as followers" in much of the Gospel, they sometimes become hostile under traditional leaders' influence. This mixed picture of easily influenced crowds probably reflects not only aristocratic wisdom (Ps-Phocyl. 95-96; Meeks 1986: 57) but also sociological reality: a few influential people shaped the views of the lower-class masses of antiquity (Saldarini 1994: 38). But this uncertainty also performs a function in Matthew's narrative, a lesson to the Matthean community. One's knowledge of God's mission must go unshakably deeper than public approval (3:16–4:11).

253. Some early Jewish Christians had experienced this temporary acceptability among their contemporaries; cf. Acts 21:20-21; Jos. *Ant.* 20.200-203. Possibly the general acceptability continued at the time of writing, but Matthew finds in Pharisaic opposition an ominous warning that the future may prove different.

The Sermon on the Mount (Matthew 5–7)

The sermon's message. Given the great variety of views on the sermon's message (more than thirty-six discrete views exist, depending on how one counts them), one might well be tempted to follow commentaries as notable as Davies and Allison in omitting a survey of views. Although I will interact briefly with some views below, I repeat here one recent summary of the most critical (Blomberg 1992a: 94-95): (1) The predominant medieval view, reserving a higher ethic for clergy, especially in monastic orders; (2) Luther's view that the sermon represents an impossible demand like the law; (3) the Anabaptist view, which applies the teachings literally for the civil sphere; (4) the traditional liberal social gospel position; (5) existentialist interpreters' application of the sermon's specific moral demands as a more general challenge to decision; (6) Schweitzer's view that the sermon embodies an interim ethic rooted in the mistaken expectation of imminent eschatology; (7) the traditional dispensational application to a future millennial kingdom; and (8) Blomberg's and others' view of an "inaugurated eschatology," "in which the sermon's ethic remains the ideal or goal . . . but which will never be fully realized until the consummation of the kingdom. . . ." Elements of different views listed above may be combined in different ways to produce further variations.[1]

Matthew's longest discourse sections are his first (Mt 5–7, on the ethics of the kingdom) and his last (Mt 23–25, on the consummation of the kingdom). Having summarized Jesus' message as repentance in view of the coming kingdom (4:17; cf. Is 56:1; Joel 1:13-15), Matthew now collects Jesus' teachings that explain how a repentant person ready for God's rule should live. The discourse suggests that only those submitted to God's reign in the present era are truly prepared for the time when Jesus will judge the world and reign there unchallenged (5:3, 10, 20; 7:24-27). This is not to say that Jesus' ethics represent only a brief "interim ethic" (pace Schweitzer) until the imminent end of the age, unsatisfactory for a longer period. Although these ethics cover the interim period,[2] they are

1. See Guelich 1982: 14-22 for a fuller history of interpretation; more recently, Durston 1988; Cranford 1992; Allen 1992; Stanton 1993: 289-97.

2. One might apply the same interim image to the ethics of the Qumran community (see Harris 1965), but even in Qumran and other Jewish eschatological texts the interim "ethic is, though provisional, nevertheless intended to be an infusion of the future light into the present darkness" (Meeks 1986: 102).

not merely the conditional ethics of the present interim state but the ideal ethics of the kingdom that its citizens must exemplify in advance (6:10; cf. Albright 1946: 303; Guelich 1982: 31).

Some modern Protestant interpreters, conditioned by their heritage to contrast naked ethical demands with grace, have stressed aspects of the sermon's theology that are peripheral to its thrust. Thus some emphasize that all fall short of its demands and require God's mercy (Hunter 1966: 86-88; cf. 6:12-15; 18:10-35). Those who take this approach to the extreme (reading Jesus in light of Paul rather than the reverse) characterize Jesus' sermon as an impossible ideal meant only to drive disciples to grace, not to instruct their behavior (Jeremias 1963: 8-9 summarizes and opposes this position). Others have applied its salvific demands primarily to God's offer of the kingdom to Israel, regarding applications of the ethics to Christians as secondary (Pentecost 1958).

Yet by contrast Matthew declares that Jesus addressed disciples (5:1-2), and Jesus' own statements suggest that he addressed those persecuted for his name (5:10-12; cf. 7:14-23; see Fuller 1980: 156-57). Although Jesus' teaching techniques here are specifically Jewish (Kennedy 1980: 126; cf. Songer 1992; Stevens 1992), it is helpful to recognize that even Greco-Roman rhetoricians would have classified the sermon as "deliberative" rhetoric — that is, instruction on how to behave (Kennedy 1984: 39-72, especially 66). The earliest Christians, whose interpretations appear in New Testament epistles and documents like the Didache and the writings of church fathers, demand obedience to Jesus' teachings recorded in this sermon (Grant 1978). Jesus himself apparently expected full compliance with his teaching, not in the legalistic or ascetic ways he himself condemns, "but as signs of God's Kingdom" (Dibelius 1949: 122; cf. Soares Prabhu 1980; Hauerwas 1988), expressions of submission to God's reign over the lives of his followers.

To capture the offensiveness of his message in his milieu, modern interpreters must let Jesus' radical demands confront us with all the unnerving ferocity with which they would have struck their first hearers. At the same time, the rest of the Gospel narrative,[3] where Jesus does not repudiate disciples who miserably fail yet repent, does season his teachings with grace (26:31-32); as Luz points out, grace is implicit because "the Sermon on the Mount is embedded in the history of God's action with Jesus" (1989: 215).[4] Most Jewish people understood the commandments in the context of grace (Sanders 1977); given Jesus' demands for greater grace in practice (including in material that appears specifically Matthean: 9:13; 12:7; 18:21-35), he undoubtedly intended the kingdom demands in light of grace (cf. Mt 6:12//Lk 11:4; Mk 11:25//Mt 6:14-15; Mk 10:15). In the Gospel narratives Jesus embraces those who humble themselves, acknowledging God's right to rule, even if in practice they fall short of the goal of moral

3. Conversely, the Sermon on the Mount also invites Matthew's audience to evaluate the characters in his narratives in its light (Anderson 1996).

4. Stassen 1992 is right to find grace in the Is 61 allusions, but makes that passage too central in the full scheme of Jesus' sermon.

perfection (5:48). But the kingdom grace Jesus proclaimed was not the workless grace of much of Western Christendom; in the Gospels the kingdom message transforms those who meekly embrace it, just as it crushes the arrogant, the religiously and socially satisfied.

Some interpreters have sought to preserve the sermon's ethics, which they regard as central, while rejecting its claims for Jesus' identity (Klausner 1979b: 414). But a central point of the sermon is Jesus' unique authority as the supreme expositor of the law's message, a new Moses (cf. Davies 1966b: 14-93). Both Jesus' climactic claim to unique authority by which he concludes the sermon (7:21-27) and the crowd's response (7:28-29) demonstrate that Matthew's discourse sections, like his narratives, stress Christology as well as ethics (see Guelich 1982); indeed, the ethics flow from the former, dependent on Jesus' authority. These teachings do not represent an ethical outline for humanity or nation-states, but for Jesus' disciples alone, for citizens of the future kingdom (cf. France 1985: 106).

The sermon's structure. Luke and Matthew are both aware of a sermon at this point in their source, and Matthew employs the occasion to gather a variety of Jesus' teachings on related topics, albeit gathered around many of the topics already present in the source (France 1985: 105-6; pace Carson 1984b: 122-25). As noted in the Introduction, ancient writers exercised the freedom to rearrange sayings, often topically. Writers who collected such sayings summarizing the thrust of a famous teacher's message (such as Epictetus's *Encheiridion,* Menander's epitome, or the Qumran Temple Scroll) called their collections "epitomes"; Matthew has exercised an analogous literary liberty,[5] collecting many of Jesus' sayings on the topic of ethics, even if the precise comparison with Greek "epitomes" may be overstated.[6] (The shorter parallels in rabbinic literature cited by Smith 1951: 103 are less convincing.) Evidence within the sermon itself suggesting various audiences (5:1; 7:28) may also support the view that the sermon is composite (Plummer 1910: 54). Matthew thus adds considerable material to the earlier compilation on which Luke also draws (see Gundry 1982: 65), just as various recensions of rabbinic collections could vary on details (e.g., ARN A and B).[7]

5. Betz 1979; Meeks 1986: 138; Malherbe 1986: 85, 105.

6. Stanton 1993: 310-11 is right that the Sermon on the Mount is not an epitome in the exact sense of Epictetus's *Encheiridion* or the unstructured *Kyriai Doxai* of Epicurus; the general analogy nevertheless remains helpful as an analogy for such a sayings collection.

7. Kennedy 1984: 68 suggests that Jesus, who traveled from synagogue to synagogue, probably delivered the same basic speech "in slightly different versions" on different occasions, and in view of ancient rhetorical conventions few of his disciples should "have had difficulty in dictating a version at some later time for readers who had not personally heard Jesus. Matthew's version might thus represent what was remembered from several occasions and not what Jesus said verbatim at any one delivery; but in the same sense it could represent a relatively full version of what he was remembered as saying at one period of his ministry." Kennedy may be correct, but Matthew elsewhere rearranges elements of his tradition from Mark or Q where he needs to do so. See Stanton 1993: 310-25 for a refutation of Betz's view that Matthew takes over the sermon intact from prior tradition (especially 318-25, emphasizing the typical Matthean redaction).

Interpreters have proposed various structures for the sermon. Patte suggests a chiasmus (Patte 1987: 65), but the asymmetry of its proportions would likely have hopelessly obscured this proposed structure to its first readers. An inclusio framing the sermon with blessings and warnings (Trites 1992) is more persuasive, although had this been Matthew's purpose one wonders why he does not conclude with some "woes" used in Matthew 23.[8] Davies used a random statement of Simeon the Just to divide the sermon into sections on law (5:17-48), worship (6:1-18), and deeds of loving-kindness (6:19–7:27; Davies 1966b: 88-89). Jeremias somewhat more convincingly divides the sermon on the basis of its audiences implied in the thesis statement, 5:20: theologians (5:17-48), pious laypersons (6:1-18), and disciples (6:19–7:27; Jeremias 1963: 22-23). Stefanovio 1992 finds the key in divisions of the synagogue service (blessings, elaboration on the Bible, and, in chs. 6–7, the sermon). Kennedy 1984: 55 likewise suggests a rhetorical structure suitable for deliberative speeches (with some plausibility, though perhaps obscured by the sermon's composite nature): proem (the beatitudes), proposition (5:17-20), explanation of "Jesus' view of the principle of the law" (5:21-48), and explanation of 5:20's "righteousness" in 6:1-18.[9] McEleney proposes that 5:21-48 expand on 5:17, while 6:1–7:12 expand 5:20 (1979). Bornkamm suggests three sections, the central and largest of which (6:1–7:12) expounds elements of the prayer in 6:9-13 (Bornkamm 1978). Guelich contends that the sections in 6:19–7:12 follow elements of that prayer (1982: 363-81). Despite exceptions, however, ancient writers were not generally concerned to provide prefatory statements delineating the precise outline of their epitomes, so one need not force the sermon into an unnatural structure, as most of these proposals do. Some discernible structure exists, however; at the least, clearly 5:17-48, 6:1-18, and 6:19-34 provide the largest complete units.

Kingdom Blessings for the Repentant (5:1-12)

Cf. Mk 3:13; Lk 6:17, 20-23.

The setting of Jesus' sermon (5:1-2). Various features of the setting contribute to Matthew's portrait of Jesus. *First, Matthew's "mountain"* (15:29; 28:16; probably not 4:8) is usually significant (see Kingsbury 1975: 56); this is especially the case in 5:1 and 17:1. Luke, by contrast, is content to depict this sermon's setting as a "level place." Level places and mountains were not geographically incompatible — the region is so mountainous that one might translate "mountain" as "hill country," as in the popular Aramaic idiom of Galilee (cf. Guelich 1982: 51-52; Carson 1984b: 129), and Luke's "plain" often meant "a

8. Wright 1992a: 387 regards that placement as strategic: blessings open his first discourse (5:3-12) and woes his last (23:13-33), reflecting the covenantal blessings and curses of Deut 27–30.

9. He admits that 6:19–7:20 do not fit the structure per se (59: "not anticipated quite as specifically . . . but still inherent in the injunction of 5:20"), but he is probably right that 5:17-20 dominate the discourse (see comment on 7:12).

plateau in mountainous regions" (Carson 1984a: 43). Matthew may elsewhere apply the term to "hill country" (14:23; 15:29), and a plateau on a hillside overlooking the lake both fits the traditional site and provides good acoustics (Blomberg 1992a: 97).

But since Luke had no reason to play down the mountain (pace Mánek 1967) and since Matthew elsewhere adds mountains to Markan material, we may suspect that Matthew chose to emphasize the presence of a mountain, and probably not for matters of purely topographic interest. Many scholars think that Matthew here recalls Moses' revelation on Mount Sinai (Ex 19:3; 24:13, 18).[10] If so, Jesus' superior revelation also makes him superior to those who "sit in Moses' seat" (23:2; Patte 1987: 61-62, 68); Jewish teachers advised one to receive a Torah scholar's words with fear and trembling as if one received them from Sinai (ARN 6 A). The one greater than Moses (cf. Is 2:3; 33:22), first encountered in 2:13-20, has begun his mission. In this period many sages lectured outside in places like vineyards and under trees, not merely in schoolhouses (Safrai 1974/1976a: 965).

Second, Matthew's depiction of Jesus' teaching is appropriate. That Jesus sat to teach (5:1; cf. 13:1-2; 23:2; 26:55) fits expected patterns of Jewish instruction. Teachers normally stood to read (Lk 4:16; Dalman 1929: 45) and sat to teach (Lk 4:20; Pesiq. Rab Kah. 18:5);[11] Jesus follows this appropriate cultural pattern in this passage. (Although we cannot define how early the practice is, some later texts indicate that only ordained rabbis sat to teach, whereas disciples stood; ARN 6A; Gen. Rab. 98:11. But if Jesus "studied" as a disciple, it was with the prophet John, not with a traditional sage.)[12] Thus Jesus takes the role of the scribes, but Matthew also indicates that Jesus is greater than the scribes (7:29; Patte 1987: 61). That Jesus "opens his mouth" represents a Semitic idiom,[13] although it may also recall Jesus' citation of Deuteronomy 8:3 in Matthew 4:4: a person lives by "every word that comes from the mouth of God" (Gundry 1982: 67; cf. Lk 4:4). That he begins with beatitudes may reflect the broader Greco-Roman practice of a proem warming up an audience (Kennedy 1984: 51), though

10. Montefiore 1968: 2:29; Davies 1966b: 17; Seitz 1969: 39; Fenton 1977: 77; F. F. Bruce 1972a: 67; Allison 1987b; idem 1993: 172-80; Davies and Allison 1988: 423-24; Hagner 1993: 86; cf. Meier 1980: 38; contrast Guelich 1982: 52; France 1985: 107.

11. Cf. further Dalman 1929: 45-46; Safrai 1974/76a: 968; Davies 1964: 423; cf. b. Meg. 21a, bar. Some differences in practice may have existed among Pharisees of Jesus' day (t. Ber. 1:3; Sifre Deut. 34.5.3; cf. Acts 2:14; 13:16).

12. Disciples regularly sat at their teachers' feet (m. 'Abot 1:4; ARN 6; 38A; 11, §28B; b. Pesaḥ. 3b; p. Sanh. 10:1, §8), so much so that "sitting" can represent "schooling" (m. 'Abot 2:7, attributed to Hillel). Lachs 1987: 67-68 emphasizes that rabbis sat in Matthew's day (p. Sheqal. 2:5; b. Beṣa 15b; Pesaḥ. 26b; Sanh. 99b), but cites one tradition to argue that in Jesus' day they learned Torah standing (b. Meg. 21a), hence challenging the verisimilitude of Matthew's portrayal. This argument fails for three reasons: first, disciples might learn one way while rabbis taught another (as suggested above); second, the single tradition favoring the change is late, much later than Matthew's evidence to the contrary; finally, had teaching sitting been a recent innovation in Matthew's day, he surely would have preferred to ascribe to Jesus what he knew to be the older practice.

13. Gundry 1982: 67; Guelich 1982: 54, cite, e.g., Job 3:1; Dan 10:16; especially Ps 78:2 in Mt 13:35.

the content (beatitudes) is Jewish and the form is not inappropriate to traditional Jewish settings (e.g., Ps 1:1, which would have held a notable place in Jewish worship, opens with a beatitude). Other features also reflect ancient rhetorical sensitivity to sound (in Greek, the object of praise in the first four beatitudes begins in each case with *p*).[14]

Jesus' sayings here make good sense in a Palestinian Jewish milieu. For instance, "God is merciful to the merciful" was an accepted principle in Judaism (Test. Zeb. 8:1; Dalman 1929: 226). The same saying translated back into Aramaic reflects a three-beat rhythm (Jeremias 1971: 24). Some of the verbal differences between Matthew's and Luke's beatitudes also reflect different ways of translating Aramaic expressions into Greek (see Jeremias 1963: 15-16). Sayings like 5:14 and 6:27, 24 resemble the traditional Israelite *mashal,* or proverb (Bultmann 1968: 81; see our comments on 5:32).

Finally, Jesus' stated audience also invites the attention of Matthew's audience. The crowds (4:25–5:1) following Jesus function as at least potential disciples (Patte 1987: 62), so far neither fully disciples nor committed enemies (see Guelich 1982: 420-21). The positive characteristics of the disciples in the Gospel function paradigmatically for subsequent generations of Jesus' disciples (Guelich 1982: 53), though the implied audience is superior to the narrative's disciples (Howell 1990: 248). Matthew explicitly indicates that Jesus taught his disciples (5:1-2), but also that the crowds were present (5:1; 7:28-29), implying that he wanted both to hear, calling both to decision (cf. 7:24-27; cf. Guelich 1982: 60).

The reward of the Kingdom (5:3-12). The beatitudes indicate that one who truly repents in light of the coming kingdom will treat one's neighbors rightly. No one who has humbled himself or herself before God, depending on the just judge to vindicate them in his coming day of judgment, can act with wanton self-interest in relationships.

Jesus employs a standard Old Testament (e.g., Ps 1:1), subsequent Jewish and, to a lesser extent, Greek literary form to express this point, a beatitude: "It will go well with the one who . . . for that one shall receive. . . ."[15] ("Fortunate" or "it will be

14. See Scott and Dean 1996: 322. As a further mark of careful arrangement, both the first and second groups of four beatitudes close with "righteousness."

15. Beatitudes appear in the OT (e.g., Ps 2:12; 32:1-2; 40:4; 41:1; 65:4; 84:4-5, 12; 94:12; 112:1; 119:1-2; 128:1; Prov 8:34; Is 56:2; Jer 17:7; Dan 12:12), Apocrypha (Bar 4:4; Sir 25:8-9), subsequent Jewish (e.g., Ps. Sol. 4:23; 5:16; 6:1; 10:1; Jos. and Asen. 16:14/7; 1 Enoch 99:10; 2 Enoch 42.6-14; 44:5; Sifra V. D. Deho. par. 5.44.1.1; b. Ber. 61b; Ḥag. 14b; Hor. 10b, bar.; cf. 4QBeat, 4Q525 in Brooke 1989; Viviano 1992; idem 1993ab), early Christian (e.g., Rom 14:22; Jas 1:12; for Jesus in Matthew, see Mt 11:6; 13:16; 16:17; 24:46), and occasionally Greco-Roman (*Contest of Homer and Hesiod* 322; *Homeric Hymn* 25.4-5; Babrius 103.20-21; Aune 1983: 61, 64; Guelich 1982: 63-66) literature; for fuller treatment, see Davies and Allison 1988: 431-34. Jesus may originally have given these blessings together with woes, as in Lk 6:20-26 (cf. Mt 23:13-29; on the conjunction of blessings with curses, cf. Gen 27:27-29, 39-40; Deut 28; a beatitude with woes, 1 Enoch 99:10-15), but the proposed detailed parallels of Fenton 1977: 368 are too ingenious, arbitrarily selecting specific aspects of imagery. Later Christians occasionally adopted the form from the Gospels

well with" may convey the point of the Hebrew *'ashre* and its Greek translation *makarios* better than "blessed" or "happy.") In this context Jesus' beatitudes mean that it will ultimately be well with those who seek first God's kingdom (6:33).

The blessings of the beatitudes are for a people ready for the kingdom's coming. The inclusio in 5:3 and 5:10 frames the bulk of this section with "theirs is the kingdom of heaven" (also Patte 1987: 66; 5:11-12 continue the thought of 5:10, modifying "theirs is" to "yours is").[16] All the blessings listed are blessings of the kingdom time; although beatitudes did not by their nature always specify eschatological blessing, this was a natural way to employ the term *makarios* and its cognates (e.g., 4 Macc 17:18). God would comfort his people at the final restoration of Israel (Is 40:1; 49:13; 51:3, 12; 52:9; 54:11; 57:18; 66:13; Bar 4:29-30; Pesiq. Rab Kah. 16:1, 6, 8; Gen. Rab. 100:9; Pesiq. R. 21:15; 29/30A; 34:1; cf. 1 Enoch 107:3; Lk 2:25); Jesus probably refers especially to Isaiah 61:2, which refers to the time when God will "comfort all who mourn" in Zion. (Some later Jewish traditions also view the eschatological Messiah as a comforter — Num. Rab. 13:5; Lam. Rab. 1:16, §51.) Then he would satisfy the hunger and thirst of his people (6:11; 8:11; 22:2; 26:29; Is 25:6; 55:1; Rev 2:17; 2 Bar. 29:8), as in the first exodus (Deut 6:11; 8:17; Is 41:17-18; see Mek. Vay. 3.42-46; 5.63-65; b. Sanh. 98b).

The ultimate mercy of the God whose character is mercy (Mic 7:18; Sir 5:1-7; cf. Mt 9:27; 18:33; 20:31) would be revealed on the day of judgment (1 Enoch 5:5; 12:6; 92:4; Ps. Sol. 16:15).[17] At that time he would ultimately declare the righteous (cf. 5:44-48) to be his children (Rom 8:19, 23; Rev 21:7; Jub. 1:24; Ps. Sol. 17:30; Sib. Or. 3.702-4), as he had to a lesser degree at the first exodus (Ex 4:22). God was technically invisible (1QS 11.20; 2 Enoch 48:5; Jos. *Apion* 2.22, §191; Sib. Or. 3:12, 17; *Fr.* 1, lines 8-11; ARN 2, 39 A; Sifra V. D. Den. pq. 2.2.3.2-3; Rom 1:20; 1 Tim 1:17),[18] but Jewish literature acknowledged

---

(Acts of Paul 3:5-6; cf. Pol. *Phil.* 2). Blessings and curses wielded prophetic force (e.g., Gen 9:25-27; 24:60; 27:27-29, 37-40; 49:1). Hanson 1994 relates the concept to the honor/shame character of ancient Mediterranean society.

16. Young 1989: 205, with Albright and Mann, prefers a partitive genitive (the kingdom consists of them) here to a possessive genitive (the kingdom belongs to them), but this is unlikely given 5:5 and its background in the Psalms. Matthew probably changed most of the second-person beatitudes to third-person beatitudes (as he adjusted Mk 1:11 in Mt 3:17) to fit LXX style (Gundry 1982: 67).

17. Later Jewish teachers emphasized mercy as one of God's primary attributes, e.g., in 3 Enoch 31:1; Sifra V. D. Deho. par. 12.65.2.4; Sifre Num. 8.8.2; Sifre Deut. 26.5.1; b. 'Abod. Zar. 3b; Ber. 7a; p. Ta'an. 2:1, §12; Gen. Rab. 12:15; 21:7; 26:6; 33:3; 73:3; 78:8; Ex. Rab. 3:7; 6:1, 3; 45:6; Lev. Rab. 29:4; 29:6, 9; Num. Rab. 9:18; 19:4; Qoh. Rab. 4:1, §1; 8:1, §1; Song Rab. 2:17, §1; Pesiq. R. 39:1; 40:2; cf. Dahl and Segal 1978. God's mercy was only for the merciful (Test. Zeb. 5:3; 8:3; Sifre Deut. 96.2.2; p. B. Qam. 8:7, §1; Pesiq. R. 38; cf. 1 Enoch 92:4; Test. Abr. 10 B).

18. Even in Philo: *Mut.* 2, §7 (see further Hagner 1971: 82-84; Isaacs 1976: 30; Lee 1962: 17; citing *Cher.* 101; *Mut.* 2, 9-10; *Praem.* 40, 44; *Som.* 1.67; *Immut.* 56; *Leg. Alleg.* 2.36); cf. also Aristobulus *Fr.* 4 in Euseb. *P.E.* 13.13.5; Orphic long version 11-12 in *OTP* 2:799; Ps-Euripides in *OTP* 2:828. Greek views seem to have varied (cf. Epict. *Disc.* 1.6.19; Plut. *Isis* 9, *Mor.* 354D; *Isis* 75, *Mor.* 381B; Char. *Chaer.* 1.14.1; Maximus of Tyre *Oration* 8.10 in Grant 1953: 168; Magical Papyrus 13.62 in Grant 1953: 47; cf. Plut. *Isis* 78, *Mor.* 383A).

that there were senses in which the righteous could see him. Although the righteous had seen a foretaste of God's glory in the exodus (Ex 24:10-11)[19] and those influenced by Greek philosophy or some conceptions of biblical prophetism sought the mystic vision of God in the present (1 Enoch 14:19, 21; Isaacs 1976: 50; Albright and Mann 1971: 47; cf. Jos. *Apion* 1.232-34), only in the end time (or, in some versions, after death) would the righteous fully see God (*CIJ* 1:452, §634; *CIJ* 1:509, §696; 1 Enoch 90:35; ARN 1 A; Sifra Behuq. pq. 3.263.1.5; Sifra V. D. Den. pq. 2.2.3.2; Sifre Deut. 310.6.1; 357.19.1; Marmorstein 1968c: 95-99; Kirk 1934: 14-15; cf. Mt 24:30). These are kingdom blessings, appropriate only for the people who will inherit the kingdom.

These blessings come only by God's intervention. The "divine passives" in each of these blessings suggest that God will provide these rewards directly: he will comfort them, bestow the earth, satisfy his people, show mercy, reveal himself, and call the righteous his children (see Jeremias 1971: 10; cf. Guelich 1982: 92). Affirming God's justice, most Jewish teachers stressed rewards for righteousness (e.g., Wis 5:15; m. 'Abot 2:2; Sifra A.M. par. 8.193.1.11; Sifra Behuq. pq. 2.262.1.9; b. Qidd. 39b; Pesiq. Rab Kah. Sup. 2:1; Deut. Rab. 7:9; see Smith 1951: 163-84), although advising that one do good for its own sake and not for reward (Sifre Deut. 48.6-7; see Brocke 1967). Likewise, Jesus emphasizes rewards for righteousness (e.g., 5:11, 46; 6:1; 10:41-42) reserved in heaven (cf. 6:19-21; 19:21). When Jewish people thought of the meek "inheriting the earth," they went beyond the minimal interpretation of Psalm 37:9, 11, 29 (where those who hope in God alone will "inherit the land"; cf. 25:13) and thought of inheriting the entire world (Rom 4:13; Jub. 32:19; 4QPs 37; 2 Bar. 51:3).[20] But because for Matthew and early Christianity as a whole the future kingdom is in some sense present in Jesus who provides bread (14:19-20) and comforts the brokenhearted (14:14; cf. 2:18; Lk 4:18), disciples participate in the *spiritual* down payment of these blessings in Christ in the present (cf. Gal 3:14; Guelich 1982: 111).

The prerequisites for the Kingdom (5:3-12). This passage articulates what kingdom-ready people should be like. *First, they are not those who try to force God's will on a world unprepared for it.* Social conditions in first-century Palestine inclined many people to suppose that revolutionary violence was the

19. Jewish writers still affirmed Scripture's teachings both that God spoke with Moses face to face (Ps-Philo 11:14; cf. Sifra V. D. Den. pq. 2.2.3.3) and that Moses could not see all God's glory; for Philo, Moses saw because he went beyond mortal vision (*Mut.* 8) and because he sought a revelation of God (*Spec.* 1.41; cf. Jn 14:8). One could see God in some sense yet remain alive (Gen. 32:30; Asc. Isa. 3:8-10), or in some traditions be spared temporarily by God's mercy (Gen. Rab. 65:10).

20. Cf. also, e.g., Mek. Beshallah 7.139-40; b. 'Abod. Zar. 35b; Ber. 4b; Gen. Rab. 11:7; Ex. Rab. 15:31. As the Israelites "inherited" the promised land, so they expected to "inherit" that land and the coming world in the future; cf., e.g., 21:38; 25:34; Ps 25:13; 37:9, 11; Is 57:13; 60:21; 61:7; Jub. 32:19; 1 Enoch 5:7; 2 Enoch 50:2; Rom 8:17; Eph 1:14; 4 Ezra 6:59; 7:96; 2 Bar. 51:3; Mek. Beshallah 7.139-40; b. Qidd. 40b; Ex. Rab. 2:6; 20:4. Cf. also 11QTemple 59.11-13; 4QpPs a 2.9-12; m. Qidd. 1:10, in Davies and Allison 1988: 450; eschatological or spiritual inheritance in Wis 3:14; 5:5; 2 Enoch 55:2. Losada 1979 connects the land to the land God promised Israel; Croatto 1979 emphasizes that this promise belonged to the oppressed *'anāwim*.

appropriate response to the violence of oppression they experienced. Because most Jews expected a final war against the Gentiles to culminate this age and inaugurate their redemption, many would have thought of the kingdom as belonging to the justly violent, what some call social bandits (cf. 11:12). Although the Essenes probably did not participate in revolts (pace Simon 1967: 62-65), even they clearly anticipated a final war in which they would participate (1QM). But Jesus promises the kingdom not to those who try to force God's hand in their time, but to those who patiently and humbly wait for it, people of peace (cf. Is 25:6-9; 26:8; 30:15, 18; 40:30-31; 49:23; 50:10-11; 57:13; 64:4; Lam 3:22-26; Mic 7:7; Jas 5:7-9).[21] Jesus and those of the Pharisees who advocated peace rather than revolution were ultimately vindicated when Rome brutally crushed Jewish hopes in 66-73 (Craigie 1978: 32; cf. Hagner 1993: 94; Mt 26:52), a point no doubt not lost on Matthew's audience.

Second, God favors the humble, who trust in him rather than in their own strength (5:3-9). a. These are people not easily provoked to anger. These are the "poor in spirit," "the meek" (5:3, 5; both terms possibly reflecting the same Semitic term *ʿanāwim*),[22] which also represents humility in Sirach, the Dead Sea Scrolls, and the rabbis (Dawes 1991). Some in the Greek world praised the generosity of leaders as "meekness" (Schweizer 1975: 89; Babrius 102.3; Plut. *Brutus* 29.2) and valued meekness in the sense of gentleness,[23] but the concept of humility often connoted the proper attitude only toward those of inferior rank and status.[24] Judaism, however, valued humility highly (Ps 72:2; Prov 3:34).[25] It also condemned the wicked who trod the lowly underfoot (1 Enoch 96:5; cf. 4 Ezra 11:42).

The expression "poor in spirit" (5:5) refers not to those with a deficit of moral righteousness (see 5:20), but reflects Matthew's explanation of the sense of Q's "poor" (Lk 6:20; see further Gundry 1982: 67).[26] Because the oppressed poor became wholly dependent on God (Jas 2:5), some Jewish people used the ti-

21. In military and political contexts "mercy" was a praiseworthy characteristic of victors (cf., e.g., Jos. *Life* 353; Sifre Deut. 323.4.1; see comment on 9:27).

22. With Ladd 1967: 95; Meier 1980: 39; Guelich 1982: 82; cf. Gundry 1982: 69. Diaspora Judaism sometimes used "spirit" for disposition (see Isaacs 1976: 71).

23. Davies and Allison 1988: 449 cite Plato *Crit.* 120E; *Rep.* 2.375C; Lucian *Somnium* 10; Ep. Arist. 257, 263; Philo *Vit. Mos.* 2.279; Jos. *Ant.* 19.330.

24. Cf. Marc. Aur. 9.40; Epict. *Disc.* 1.9.33; 3.24.75; Davids 1982: 150; Mounce 1985: 108; Blomberg 1992a: 99.

25. See further Zeph 2:3; Zech 9:9; Sir 3:17; Jos. *Ant.* 3.212; Moore 1971: 2:275; Sifre Deut. 38.1.4; ARN 38A; 29§§60-62; 41, §114B; b. Soṭa 4b-5a, 32b, bar.; p. Sanh. 6:6, §2; Taʿan. 4:1, §14; 4:2, §8; Gen. Rab. 33:3; Maher 1983; Young 1989: 245-51.

26. The Qumran scrolls provide striking parallels to Matthew's phrase (1QM 14:7; 1QH 14:3; often noted, e.g., by Brown 1972: 3-4; Schnackenburg 1985: 47). Citing such parallels, Young 1989: 204 surmises that Matthew preserves Jesus' Semitic idiom, which Luke adjusted to simplify the Greek construction, thereby limiting its sense; from the same parallels Vermes 1993: 143 draws the opposite conclusion. In any case, it is unlikely that Matthew intended, "poor by means of [God's] Spirit" (pace Jörns 1987). On "the poor" (especially Isaiah's usage), see Guelich 1982: 68-72; for Jesus' special concern for the poor in the tradition, cf., e.g., Ambrozic 1990.

tle as a positive religious as well as economic designation (1QM 11.9, 13; 13.14; 14.7; 1QpHab 12.3, 6, 10; 4QpPs 37 fr. 1, 2.10).[27] Thus it refers not merely to the materially poor and oppressed, but to those "who have taken that condition to their very heart, by not allowing themselves to be deceived by the attraction of wealth" (Freyne 1988: 72). Although Matthew does not stress renunciation of possessions to the same degree as Luke, for him as well the kingdom belongs to the powerless of the world, to the oppressed who embrace the poverty of their condition by trusting in God rather than favors from the powerful for their deliverance.

The "merciful" (5:7; Jas 3:17) again are those who would not harm others but would show compassion toward their need (cf., e.g., Test. Jud. 18:3-4; Epict. *Disc.* 1.18.4); this fits Matthew's love ethic (Mohrlang 1984: 94-96; contrast the rarer use by some philosophers, who regarded such compassion as weakness, Epict. *Disc.* 2.21.3; 4.6.1). The active expression of this virtue may include not only abstaining from hurt but also helping the needy (see Hagner 1993: 93; Test. Benj. 4:4); "almsgiving" (6:2) is a cognate term that probably called the concept to mind. The kingdom also belonged to the "peacemakers" (5:9; Jas 3:17-18), a virtue that other Jewish people urging peace with Rome also highly extolled (e.g., ARN 4A; 6, §19B).[28] Some other Jewish teachers also promised eternal reward for peacemaking (m. 'Abot 2:8; Pe'a 1:1; ARN 40A). But when Jewish teachers spoke of "peace," they thought on an interpersonal level in general, not just among nations (e.g., ARN 28 A; Deut. Rab. 5:15), and Jesus' demand does not merely challenge the bloodshed of revolution. Further, "peacemakers" means not only living at peace, but bringing harmony among others; the rare Greek term actually applied most often to emperors (Hill 1972: 113); it implies seeking where possible to reconcile those at enmity. While employing the traditional beatitude form, Jesus subverts its customary use: not the self-satisfied religious person, but the needy person solely dependent on God is blessed (Ray 1992).

b. These humble people are also those who yearn for God above all else (cf. Zeph 2:3). Matthew emphasizes the moral side of another Q saying in 5:6, so that those who hunger physically (Lk 6:21, fitting Luke's expected emphasis, and probably in Q) yearn for God's righteousness more than for food and drink. In this context, hungering for righteousness probably includes yearning for

27. See further Flusser 1960; Minear 1960: 63-64; Danker 1972: 81; also Ex. Rab. 31:13; Pesiq. R. 9:2; but cf. m. 'Abot 3:17. Some also find it in early Christianity; see Fitzmyer 1966: 244; Hengel 1974b: 34; idem 1980: 118; contrast Keck 1966.

28. Philosophers and moralists generally counseled peace (e.g., Sen. *Dial.* 3.14.1). Like some Greek rhetoricians (e.g., Isoc. *On Peace, Or.* 8), the rabbis — at least partly descended from those Pharisees who survived the wars with Rome — especially praised peace: e.g., m. 'Abot 1:12; t. Sanh. 1:2; Sifra Behuq. pq. 1.261.1.14; Sifre Num. 42.2.3; Sifre Deut. 199.3.1; ARN 4A; 6, §19; 48, §134B; b. Ber. 64a; Ḥul. 141a; Qidd. 39b; Tamid 32b; Yebam. 65b, bar.; Yoma 71b; Gen. Rab. 38:6; 48:18; 100:8; Lev. Rab. 9:9; Num. Rab. 11:7; 12:4; 21:1; Deut. Rab. 5:1; cf. Genot-Bismuth 1981 (though this is too monolithic on Pharisaism). Still, clearly not all Pharisees opposed war with Rome (see Sanders 1990: 86, 324); nor did advocacy of peace amount to nonresistance (cf., e.g., Num. Rab. 21:4).

God's justice, for his vindication of the oppressed (see Gundry 1982: 70); this context also implies that it includes yearning to do God's will (5:20; 6:33; 21:32; 23:29; Przybylski 1980: 98; cf. b. Sanh. 100a). (The term "righteousness" had a fairly broad range of meaning; in the various Dead Sea Scrolls, see Przybylski 1980: 13-38.) Hungering for God might imply fasting as well (6:16-18; cf. Fenton 1977: 81), which the Old Testament sometimes conjoined with mourning, including the mourning of repentance (e.g., Joel 1:14; 2:15; Jonah 3:5; cf. Test. Reub. 1:10). This passage reflects biblical images of passion for God, longing for him more than for daily food or drink (Job 23:12; Ps 42:1-2; 63:1, 5; Jer 15:16; cf. Mt 4:4). In biblical piety, God and his word should constitute the ultimate object of true disciples' longing (Ps 119:40, 47, 70, 92, 97, 103).

"Mourners" here (5:4) may thus refer especially to the repentant (Joel 1:13; cf. Jas 4:9-10; Lev 23:29; 26:41), those who grieve over their people's sin (Tob 13:14; Pesiq. R. 28:3). Given the promise of comfort, however, the term probably also applies more broadly to all those who are broken, who suffer or have sustained personal grief and responded humbly (cf. Fenton 1977: 368; France 1985: 109; Gen. Rab. 100:13). God is near the brokenhearted (Ps 51:17) and will comfort those who mourn (Is 61:1-3);[29] all the people of the kingdom are the humble, not the arrogant. The "pure in heart" (5:8; cf. 2 Bar. 9:1; 2 Enoch 45:3 J; Test. Jos. 4:6; Benj. 8:2; Vermes 1993: 143 cites 4QBeat) in Ps 73:1 refer to those who recognize that God alone is their hope (Ps 73:2-28).[30] Because a "pure" heart before God means a heart of unmixed devotion to God, James (who appears dependent on an early version of the Matthean Sermon on the Mount traditions) can relate purity to being peacemakers, merciful, gentle, and so forth (Jas 3:17-18).

c. This lifestyle of meekness Jesus teaches not only addresses Jewish revolutionaries, but challenges disciples in their daily lives. If disciples are to walk in love toward their enemies (5:43), how much more toward those closest them? If even sinners and outright pagans love their families and those who love them (5:46-47), disciples must strive to reconcile all conflicts as humbly and lovingly as possible. For Jesus' whole depiction of the meek lifestyle of the kingdom here is summarized in what he called the greatest commandments of the law: love of God and others (22:36-40). In general, Christians in "developing nations" have grasped and illustrated these biblical principles far better than Christians in the affluent West.

29. In the Scrolls, one should not "comfort" the wicked till they "turn," i.e., repent, a common reason for mourning (1QS 10.21). Noting Matthew's redaction of the beatitudes in light of biblical language, especially Is 61, Guelich 1982: 37-38 thinks that Matthew's focus is "christological and eschatological" rather than "ethicizing"; but if Matthew's focus here is christological, it is far too subtle to appear such to most readers and cannot be separated from the ethics in the context (5:17-20). Many scholars note the allusion to Is 61:1-2 (e.g., Kertelge 1991; Stassen 1992).

30. Gnilka 1988 finds the background of "pure in heart" especially in Ps 24:3-6; Cary and Haarhoff 1946: 335 compare Sen. *Ep. Lucil.* 87.21 on purity and vision of God. Jas 3:17 employs a different term in the context of peacemakers but may reflect the same Aramaic original.

Third, Jesus addresses those who endure persecution for the gospel (5:10-12; cf. 10:23; 13:21; 23:34). Lists of beatitudes sometimes closed with a formally different conclusion (Daube 1973: 196-98). Whereas the rest of Jesus' blessings in this section could apply to almost any Jewish audience in first-century Palestine, Jesus' conclusion in 5:10-12 specifically addresses his disciples. They were to submit to unjust suffering in hope of future vindication (cf. 2 Sam 16:12; Is 51:7-8; 1 Pet 4:14; 5:6, 10). Jesus' contemporaries also spoke of persecution for righteousness' sake (5:10; 4 Macc 9:29; 18:3; 2 Bar. 52:6; cf. 2 Macc 7:9; 14:38; Sen. *Dial.* 1.3.10), but here "for the sake of righteousness" (what Jesus preaches, 5:6, 20; 6:33) parallels persecution "on account of me" (5:11; cf. 10:18, 39; 16:25; 19:29; 24:9; cf. Jn 15:21; Acts 5:41; 1 Pet 4:14). Jesus' words demand far more than those of his contemporaries.[31] Jewish teachers typically counseled students to avoid unnecessary suffering that was not for the honor of God and his law. Although they would expect students to suffer for God's name (Ps 44:22; 69:7; Is 51:7; 2 Enoch 50:3-4; cf. Herm. 1.3.2), they would not have called students to suffer for their own names (see Jacobs 1957).

Here also Jesus takes his ethic of nonretaliation (5:38-47) to its furthest possible length: a disciple not only refuses to strike back, but rejoices when persecuted. The persecution itself confirms one's trust in God's promise of reward, because the prophets suffered likewise (13:57; 23:37; 26:68; Jer 26:11, 23; 1 Kings 18:4; 19:10; 2 Chron 36:15-16; Neh 9:26), as Jewish tradition also acknowledged.[32] Although the importance of a good report was widely stressed (Jdt 9:8; Acts 2:47; 1 Tim 3:7), not only Jesus (Lk 6:26) but some other ancient teachers recognized that one who earns the favor of the morally reprobate is probably morally dysfunctional oneself (e.g., Antisthenes in Diog. Laert. 6.5); likewise that it is a privilege to suffer others' evil reports (Diog. Laert. 6.1.3, 11; Plut. *Sayings of Kings,* Alexander 32, *Mor.* 181F; Epict. *Disc.* 3.12.10; cf. 1 Enoch 108:10; b. Shab. 88b, bar.).

In Matthew's wording (perhaps as opposed to Q's wording in Lk 6:23),[33] Jesus thus compares his own disciples with the biblical prophets and their persecutors with those who killed the prophets (Acts 7:51-53). The prophetic role of a disciple is analogous to (10:41-42; 23:34) and greater than (11:9, 11; 13:17) that of an Old Testament prophet.

31. Suffering "on account of" one need not imply that one's deity (e.g., Char. *Chaer.* 4.3.10), but suffering on account of one's "name" in a Jewish context most readily points in that direction. Some scholars (e.g., Lachs 1987: 78) see here the rejection of Jewish Christians by the larger Jewish community, exemplified particularly in the *birkat haminim.* Although the Jesus tradition includes early warnings of persecution, Matthew's audience may be suffering rejection of the sort that ultimately led to the *birkat haminim;* but see the Introduction. "Blessedness" *(makarios)* was appropriate to martyrs in general (4 Macc 17:18).

32. See Michel 1932; Schoeps 1950; Hare 1967: 137-38; Jeremias 1971: 280; Amaru 1983; also Davies and Allison 1988: 465, citing, e.g., *Lives of the Prophets* passim (such as 2:1, Schermann 25 p. 81; 6:1, Schermann 17 p. 60; 7:1-2, Schermann 14 p. 51); Jub. 1:12; 4QpHos a 2.3-6; Jos. *Ant.* 10.38; Asc. Isa. 2.16; 5.1-14; Targ. Is. 28:1; also 4 Bar. 9:31; Pesiq. R. 26:1/2.

33. Cf. Boring 1982: 43; Gundry 1982: 74; but cf. Theissen 1991: 52.

But Matthew is summoning his community to an honor far higher than merely filling the role of Old Testament prophets; he summons them to bear the name — the honor — of Jesus, who is greater than those prophets (16:14-17; cf. 13:57). To suffer for righteousness' sake is to suffer for Jesus' name (5:10-11), because the characteristics Jesus lists as belonging to the people of the kingdom are also those Jesus himself exemplifies as the leading servant of the kingdom and son par excellence of the Father (11:27; 20:28). The Gospel portrays Jesus as meek and lowly in heart (11:29), as mourning over the unrepentant cities of the land (11:20-24), as showing mercy (9:13, 27; 12:7; 20:30), as being a peacemaker (5:43-45; 26:52), and as being ridiculed as a false prophet (26:68). If Jesus the supreme teacher is meek and lowly, how much more must be his disciples who are to imitate his ways (10:24-25; 23:8-12) — in contrast to worldly paradigms for religious celebrities (23:5-7). By living this lifestyle of humble nonresistance and trust in God (5:38-44), disciples show themselves to be children of the Father (5:45).[34]

Worthless Disciples (5:13-16)

Cf. Mk 4:21; 9:50; Lk 14:34-35; 8:16. Having described the appropriate lifestyle of disciples, Jesus now explains that a "disciple" who does not live this lifestyle of the kingdom is worth about as much as tasteless salt or invisible light — nothing. Nominal disciples who do not live a life of discipleship will be "thrown out and trampled underfoot" (5:13; the phrase is intentionally graphic — cf. 1 Enoch 99:2; 108:10).

Jesus refers here to more than good deeds; he refers to a good character (7:17-20; 12:33-37; elsewhere he indicates that this demand depends on embracing God's kingship as a gift, e.g., 10:40; 18:4, 12-14, 27). The images of salt and light evoke consideration less of what one does than of what one is (cf. Aalen 1957/58). Moreover, the sphere in which disciples' lives must testify of God's kingship represents all humanity ("earth," world" — Schweizer 1975: 100; does Col 4:6 reflect this tradition?) If only true disciples count before God (5:13-16) and true discipleship means treating both friends and enemies kindly (5:3-12), the salt-and-light paragraph becomes a resounding warning to heed Jesus' teaching on meekness in the preceding pericope.

A disciple who rejects the values exemplified in the beatitudes is like tasteless salt: worthless (5:13). Commentators attribute to salt a variety of uses: preservative (Diog. Laert. 8.1.3; cf. a similar Pythagorean *akousma* in Thom 1994: 110); flavoring agent; a substance to treat wineskins (Aristophanes *Clouds* 1237); and an agent to retard fermentation in manure, which was used as fertilizer (cf. the last-resort function in Lk 14:34-35; see A. B. Bruce 1979: 101;

34. The christological interpretation of the beatitudes appears at least as early as Origen (Luz 1989: 244).

Danker 1972: 168; Gundry 1982: 76).[35] In the last instance, some suggest an Aramaic wordplay between *tabbala* (seasoning) and *zabbala* (manure; Manson 1979: 132). After listing eleven views, Davies and Allison 1988: 472-73 prudently conclude that the saying may play on salt's many uses rather than a particular one (similarly Hagner 1993: 99). In this context, however, taste may well be in view, as often in contemporary literature (b. Ber. 34a, bar.; Plut. *Isis* 5, *Mor.* 352F; *Table-Talk* 4.4.3, *Mor.* 669B); this might be the most obvious function to the Galileans who would constitute Jesus' primary audience.

In any case, the point is: what is to be done with salt that no longer functions as salt should?[36] Some commentators note that the salt deposits of the Dead Sea are so impure that they leave unsalty "salt" when the the real salt eventually dissolves, or that salt could be mixed with so many impurities "as to become useless" (Davies and Allison 1988: 473 on Pliny *N.H.* 31.82).[37] But Jesus may refer here to a more graphic, inconceivable situation of real salt's losing its taste (cf. Hill 1972: 115; Vermes 1993: 83). No true disciple *could* be merely nominal and remain a true disciple!

A later Jewish story illustrates how first-century hearers would have grasped Jesus' point. An inquirer reportedly asked a late-first-century rabbi what to salt tasteless salt with; he responded, "The afterbirth of a mule" (b. Bek. 8b).[38] In that society everyone knew that mules are half-breeds (Babrius 62) and sterile (e.g., Livy 26.23.5; Appian *C.W.* 1.9.83; 2.5.36; Sifre Deut. 119.2.3; Gen. Rab. 41:6); the point is: "You ask a stupid question, you get a stupid answer. Salt can't stop being salt!" But of course if it were to do so, it would no longer be of any value as salt. Although some suggest that this story challenges the view of Israel as salt (Manson 1979: 132; cf. Dodd 1961: 142) or cite the rabbinic image of the law as salt (cf. Schweizer 1975: 101), in this context Jesus challenges his disciples: tasteless salt lacks value, and so does a professed disciple who lacks genuine commitment (cf. Argyle 1963: 46; Dodd 1961: 140-42).

A disciple whose life reveals none of the Father's works is like invisible light for vision: useless (5:14-16). *In this passage, Jesus reinforces his point with various images.* A disciple should be as obvious as a city set on a hill (as most cities were), and a light in a home should be no easier to hide than a torchlit city at night (5:14-15; most homes had only one room). The light of this passage may even represent that of the brightness of a typically elevated ancient city at night (cf. Grant 1959: 97; possibly Ahiqar 159, §68), perhaps

35. Malina and Rohrbaugh 1992: 50 also suggest "an outdoor, earthen oven" using salted dung for fuel; salt plates functioned as a catalyst to make dung burn (Lk 14:34-35), but exhausted salt plates no longer could fulfill this function.

36. An Aramaic verb means both "to become foolish" and to "lose its saltiness," as in the case of impure salt deposits described in the paragraph above (France 1985: 112; Hagner 1993: 99). Early bilingual Christians seem to have understood the Greek verb in both senses as well (Gundry 1982: 76), suggesting that his readers may have caught Jesus' original wordplay (cf. also 5:22).

37. Cf. Hellestam 1990: one could accidentally get magnesium salt with one's cooking salt; the former tasted bitter and was used only on roads to hold down weeds and dust.

38. Noted also by Dalman 1929: 229; Lachs 1987: 82; Vermes 1993: 83.

Jerusalem.[39] But Matthew probably simply blends various images emphasizing the same point: a nominal disciple who does not function like one is worthless to the kingdom.

That the light material is longer than the salt material would not strike ancient hearers as asymmetrical and hence incongruous; rhetoricians typically "amplified," dwelling on a particular point to emphasize it (Kennedy 1984: 53). One commentator ingeniously suggests that Jesus' lamp in 5:15 is a Hanukkah lamp: Jewish custom forbade extinguishing the lamp during Hanukkah, but one could conceal its light (Derrett 1966; idem 1970: 191-92); a more obvious suggestion would be the weekly Sabbath lamp (e.g., m. Shab. 2).[40] But Jesus' point in this passage is the opposite: he refers to the pointlessness, under normal conditions, of lighting a lamp one then obscures from being visible.[41] As a popular sage had put it, "What is the value of concealed wisdom, any more than of treasure that is invisible?" (Sir 41:14; cf. the later proverb in Bultmann 1968: 108).

Jesus depicts his disciples' mission in stark biblical terms traditionally used for the mission of Israel. Ancient texts used light in a variety of symbolic fashions. Jewish texts often portray good and evil as light and darkness respectively (e.g., 1QS 3.3, 19-22; 1QM 13.5-6, 14-15; Test. Job 43:6/4; Sib. Or. fr. 1.26-27; cf. Enz 1976). Later Jewish teachers applied the image to the primeval light before or from the creation (2 Enoch 24:4; Gen. Rab. 3:6; Urbach 1979: 208-10) and suggested the restoration of this light in the end time (e.g., b. Ḥag. 12a; Gen. Rab. 11:2; 42:3); other texts likewise connect it with biblical images of future glory such as the righteous in the end time (e.g., Mt 13:43; Rev 22:5; Wis 3:7-8; 1 Enoch 1:8; 5:7; 108:11-14; 1QM 17.6-7; 4 Ezra 7:97; Sifre Deut. 47.2.1-2; ARN 37, §95B). Sages and philosophers often opined that light derived from true knowledge (Sir 31:17; Sen. *Ep. Lucil.* 48.8; Plut. *Lectures* 17, *Mor.* 47C). Jewish literature further portrays both Wisdom (e.g., Prov 6:23; Wis 6:12; 7:26, 29-30; 1QS 2.3; 11.5-6; 1QM 1.8; 4 Ezra 14:20-21; cf. Jn 1:4; 8:12) and Torah (Ps 119:105; Bar 4:2; *CIJ* 1:409, §554; Ps-Philo 9:8; 11:1-2; 15:6; 19:4, 6; 23:10; 33:3; 51:3; 2 Bar. 17:4; 18:1-2; 59:2; Sifre Num. 41.1.2) as light.

More to the point here, the Old Testament already speaks of God's people as lights to the the nations (e.g., Is 42:6; 49:6), that is, the whole "world" (cf. Mt 18:7). Jewish teachers applied the image to especially pious sages (e.g., Sir 50:6-

39. Cf. Campbell 1978: 346; Jeremias 1958: 66; idem 1963: 33; idem 1972: 217. A lighthouse would have been an equally intelligible image (e.g., Herodian 4.28) but less relevant for most Palestinian Jews.

40. On Hanukkah lamps, see, e.g., b. B. Qam. 30a; 62b; B. Mes. 118b; Shab. 21b; Sukk. 46a; p. Sukk. 3:4, §3; Pesiq. R. 2:1; 3:1; 6:1; 8:1; Goodenough 1953/68: 1:152; on Sabbath lamps, see, e.g., m. Shab. 2; b. Shab. 21a; Gen. Rab. 11:2; 12:6; Pesiq. R. 23:6. Vermes 1993: 83 contrasts with 5:15 the emphasis on the relative smallness of a lamp's light in Mek. Amalek 4 on Ex 18:27 (in Lauterbach 2.185-86), but the two texts share no point of comparison except the metaphor of a lamp.

41. Hand-held Herodian lamps generated barely enough light for the home (Safrai 1974/76b: 745-46; cf. Lk 15:8; Danker 1972: 104) and would easily be obscured (indeed, small lamps were easily extinguished — e.g., Babrius 114 — and a measuring container placed over one might extinguish it!).

7; Ps-Philo 51:4; ARN 25A; 13, §32B; cf. Jn 5:35), as well as to heroes such as Adam (ARN 9, §25 B), Abraham (Test. Abr. 7B; Gen. Rab. 2:3; 30:10), Moses (Sifre Num. 93.1.3; b. Soṭa 12a; 13a), the Messiah (1 Enoch 48:4; Pesiq. Rab Kah. Sup. 6:5; Gen. Rab. 1:6; 85:1), and ultimately God himself (1QH 7.24-25; 4 Bar. 9:3; Philo *Som.* 1.75; Ps-Philo 12:9; Life of Adam 28:2; Sifre Num. 41.1.1; see Ps 27:1). But they also applied this image more generally to Israel (Sir 17:19; Pesiq. Rab Kah. Sup. 5:1), Jerusalem (Pesiq. Rab Kah. 21:4; Gen. Rab. 59:5), and the temple (Pesiq. Rab Kah. 21:5, bar.; Gen. Rab. 2:5; 3:4).

But Isaiah 42:6 and 49:6 may well be Jesus' primary source for his saying: he himself would fulfill the servant's mission (Mt 12:17-21), but expected his disciples to assume the same responsibility (20:26-28). If Jesus is the prophesied light (4:16; Is 9:2; cf. Mt 17:2), so are his representatives (Mt 10:40-42). As Jewish teachers believed that it was Israel's mission to reach the nations (cf. Jeremias 1958: 12-13; De Ridder 1971ab), so the disciples are to shine to all peoples. It should come as no surprise that the light image becomes prominent in early Christian literature (Minear 1960: 128; Eph 5:8), some texts possibly reflecting knowledge of this saying of Jesus (Phil 2:15; cf. Rom 2:19 with Mt 15:14). Disciples are light because their destiny (13:43) rather than their past or environment must define them.

But disciples cannot be content to remain the world's light in a merely theoretical sense; they must "be what they are," letting their light shine for their Father's honor (5:16). While Jesus is opposed to doing good works publicly for one's own honor (6:1, "to be seen" by people), he exhorts his disciples to do those good works publicly for *God's* honor (5:16; cf. 6:9).[42] This distinction — underlined by contrasting wording in the same Matthean sermon ("glorifying" or honoring God vs. self-glorification — 5:16; 6:2) — is undoubtedly intentional. Jesus' works in this Gospel "glorify" God (9:8; 15:31).

Disciples Must Obey God's Law (5:17-20)

Cf. Lk 16:16-17. As if his words in 5:3-16 were not strong enough, Matthew's Jesus presents even more stringent demands of the kingdom in these verses. Matthew uses Jesus' words here as a thesis statement for the whole of 5:21-48 that follows.[43] Jesus essentially warns prospective followers, "My demands are more stringent than other interpretations of the law." For Matthew's community, perhaps concerned by some reports that many Gentile Christians neglected biblical teach-

42. Lachs 1987: 85 notes that good works honor God's name in other Jewish texts as well (citing, e.g., Sifra Lev. 19:1; Sifre Deut. 319); one might also cite, e.g., m. 'Abot 1:11; 2:2, 12; Pesiq. Rab Kah. 22:1; p. B. Meṣ. 2:5, §2.

43. Kennedy 1984: 54 sees these verses as "the proposition of the sermon" as a whole; I would apply it especially to 5:21-48. At least some of Jesus' words here seem to have appeared together earlier in a teaching on the kingdom law being more radical than it had been under Moses (Lk 16:16-18; see Schürmann 1960).

ings (Acts 21:21; Rom 3:8), their recollection of Jesus' fidelity to the law constituted an important part of their conscious identification with their culture. Matthew's Gospel is very positive toward Torah, provided the law is interpreted rightly (Segal 1991: 4-8; Overman 1990b: 86-89; Deutsch 1991; Müller 1992; Snodgrass 1992; idem 1996; Hagner 1997; Kosch 1997). It may be intermediate between the Petrine and Pauline positions on Torah at Antioch (Segal 1991: 21).[44]

Jesus demands wholehearted commitment to himself and his teachings. Like other Jewish teachers, Jesus demanded total obedience to the Scriptures (5:18-19);[45] unlike most of his contemporaries, he was not satisfied with the performance of the scribes and Pharisees, observing that this fell short even of the demands of salvation (5:20; cf. Harvey 1982: 36-65). After grabbing his hearers' attention with such a statement, Jesus goes on to define God's law not simply in terms of how people behave, but in terms of who they are (5:21-48; Ladd 1978: 83).

Jesus confronted the charge of antinomianism (12:2) and could conceivably have responded in terms such as those depicted in 5:17-20. Matthew may have needed to stress this point to counter antinomian teaching in the church (e.g., Charles 1992) or, more likely, continued accusations of immorality from his opponents (cf. Stanton 1993: 49).[46] Some radically contrast Matthew's teachings here with Paul's (Case 1975: 173); but while the two writers clearly address some different issues, the conflict has been overstated (see Przybylski 1980: 107; Marguerat 1982). Although Paul also affirmed his Jewish people's right to maintain the customs of their heritage (1 Cor 9:20; Acts 18:18; 21:23-27), accepted only faith demonstrated by obedience (Rom 1:5; 6:16; 16:26; for this sense of faith in the Synoptics, see Benoit 1973: 71-86), and spoke of the right approach to God's law for believers (Rom 3:27, 31; 8:2; 9:31–10:13), some of his contemporaries parodied or exploited various Pauline catchphrases, just as some antinomians continue to do today (Rom 3:8; Acts 21:21-22; cf. Bultmann 1968: 163).[47] Other Jewish

44. On a literary Matthean level, the Matthean Pharisees' approach to Torah yields "hypocrisy," whereas Jesus' yields "righteousness" (Rhoads 1992).

45. This is often acknowledged; see, e.g., Moore 1971: 2:9; Bultmann 1958: 61-62; Klausner 1979b: 77; Bornkamm 1963a: 24; Vermes 1993: 13.

46. By the early third century, the rabbis accused the *minim,* or schismatics (in Amoraic texts possibly applied to Gentile Christians as well), of keeping Sunday as a holy day (b. Ta'an. 27b). Rabbis often portrayed the *minim* as having a low view of the law (Justin *Dial.* 10; b. Ber. 10a; Shab. 31a; Ex. Rab. 47:1; but cf. b. 'Abod. Zar. 4a; Gen. Rab. 61:7); their Torah scrolls were invalid (b. Menaḥ. 42b); some accused them of holding only to the Ten Commandments (b. Ber. 12a). Torah-keeping Jewish Christians probably received bad press because of the polemics of Gentile Christians; cf. Pritz 1988: 58, 110. Although "suppose" (*nomisēte,* 5:17) does not always reflect a contrary-to-fact supposition (1 Cor 7:26, 36), it certainly does here (10:34; cf. 20:10; Lk 2:44; Test. Judah 19:4).

47. Matthew need not respond to this directly or indirectly; 5:17 is non-Pauline, but not anti-Pauline (Stanton 1993: 312-14), though Paul probably takes the love command's qualification of other laws farther than Matthew would (Mohrlang 1984: 45). Some think Jas 2:14-26 responds to Paul (Kee 1980: 150) or, more likely, to a perversion of Pauline teaching (F. F. Bruce 1972a: 90; Ladd 1974b: 592), but the allusion even there is not clear (with Reicke 1964: 5); they address different issues (e.g., Walker 1964).

people consequently charged the early Christians with antinomianism (cf. Justin *Dial.* 10; b. Shab. 31a; Ex. Rab. 47:1); thus Jesus' words in 5:17-20 would provide reassurance to Jewish Christians locked in polemic with synagogue leaders. Many commentators[48] note here that Jesus comes not to abolish the law,[49] but to expound its true sense, to fulfill its spirit.[50]

In affirming Scripture's authority, Jesus used but did not simply accommodate the rhetoric of his culture. In sharing his contemporaries' generally high view of Scripture, Jesus affirms it for his followers rather than simply employing it in public or polemical situations.[51] *First, Jesus' language clearly affirms his commitment to the law of Moses.* When Jesus says that he came not to "abolish" the law and prophets[52] but to "fulfill," he uses terms that would have conveyed his faithfulness to the Scriptures. To "fulfill" God's law was to "confirm" it by obedience and demonstrating that one's teaching accorded with it; to "annul" it was to cast off its yoke, treating God's law as void.[53] Jeremias even suggests that the rhythm of Jesus' Aramaic wording here is the meter used in lamentation at funerals, which may suggest that he originally uttered these lines with strong emotion (Jeremias 1971: 26-27).

Second, Jesus illustrates the eternality of God's law with a popular story line from contemporary Jewish teachers (5:18). Although the prophets had already affirmed the immutability of God's word (Is 40:8; Zech 1:5-6), Jesus here

48. E.g., Longenecker 1976: 139; Charette 1992b: 166; Allison 1993b: 232; Hagner 1993: lxii; Young 1995: 262; cf. Nickelsburg 1981: 304; Honeyman 1954: 141; McConnell 1969: 6-58.

49. Balch 1991: 68-84 suggests that Matthew here develops a Greek topos as early as Protagoras and Plato that Jewish writers had taken over (84: Dionysius of Halicarnassus and Josephus "claim not to be abolishing Romulus's or Moses' laws" and, like Matthew, share narrative contexts). Kennedy 1984: 43-44 depicts Matthew here as anticipating objections (a practice known among rhetoricians as *prokatalepsis*): to avoid appearing defensive, Jesus speaks authoritatively and positively, not "specifying how he may be thought to contravene" Torah.

50. Some claim here that Jesus was reinterpreting the law "in a more spiritual direction" (Taylor 1935: 97; cf. Jeremias 1971: 207); this statement might be better nuanced if phrased to allow Jesus to draw out implications already present in the law (the usual understanding of "midrash," Jewish interpretation of the time). At any rate, whether or not Matthew has followed a preexisting structure (Flusser 1988: 494), plainly none of the material in 5:17-20 originated in a hellenistic milieu (also Bultmann 1968: 138). For various interpretations, see, e.g., Senior 1983: 47-55.

51. Wenham 1977: 21; Wenham 1979a argues that Jesus' view of Scripture should be authoritative for Jesus' followers. Certainly this was Matthew's view, and at least 5:18 derives from Q material with the same thesis (Lk 16:16-18).

52. I.e., the Scriptures: 7:12; 11:13 (also Q: Lk 16:16); 2 Macc 15:9; Jn 1:45; Rom 3:21; Davies and Allison 1988: 484 cite also 4 Macc 18:10; t. B. Meṣ. 11:23. Cf. also the threefold division in Lk 24:44 (more popular among the sages — Sirach prologue; ARN 14A; b. ʿAbod. Zar. 19b; B. Bat. 13b, bar.; B. Qam. 92b; Mak. 10b; Sanh. 90b, Gamaliel II; 106a; p. Meg. 1:5, §3; Ned. 3:9, §3; Pesiq. Rab Kah. 12:13; Gen. Rab. 76:5; cf. Philo *Vit. Con.* 25). For weekly readings from both law and prophets in the second century, cf. m. Meg. 4:1-6. Snodgrass 1996: 107 suggests that "prophets" here qualifies law with a prophetic reading, as in 9:13; in this context it might also encourage persecuted disciples that the fruit of their labor would endure (5:12).

53. See Daube 1973: 60; Dalman 1929: 57; Longenecker 1976: 140; Flusser 1988: 495; cf. Sandmel 1978b: 356; Rom 3:31; Test. Naph. 8:7; b. Sanh. 90a, bar.

underlines this point in a graphic, hyperbolic manner (5:18; cf. 24:34-35). Jesus' "letter" (NRSV), "smallest letter" (NIV) or "jot" (KJV) undoubtedly refers to the Hebrew letter *yodh* (Manson 1979: 154; Vermes 1993: 19-20n.11), which Jewish teachers said would not pass from the law. They said that when Sarai's name was changed to Sarah, the *yodh* removed from her name cried out from one generation to another, protesting its removal from Scripture, until finally, when Moses changed Oshea's name to Joshua, the *yodh* was returned to Scripture. "So you see," the teachers would say, "not even this smallest letter can pass from the Bible" (b. Sanh. 107ab; p. Sanh. 2:6, §2; Gen. Rab. 47:1; Lev. Rab. 19:2; Num. Rab. 18:21; Song Rab. 5:11, §§3-4). Likewise, sages declared that when Solomon threatened to uproot a *yodh* from the law, God responded that he would uproot a thousand Solomons rather than a word of his law (p. Sanh. 2:6, §2; cf. Ex. Rab. 6:1).[54] Jesus makes the same point from this tradition that later rabbis did: even the smallest details of God's law are essential (cf. Barth 1963: 65).

Matthew declares that nothing will pass from the law "until all is accomplished" (5:18), meaning until the consummation of the kingdom, when heaven and earth pass away (24:34-35; cf. Jer 31:35-37; Ps-Philo 11:5; Sib. Or. 3:570-72). The idea that Jesus' death and resurrection is the "goal of the world," thus allowing the law to be set aside as fulfilled,[55] violates the whole thrust of the passage (Mohrlang 1984: 8); Overman 1996: 77 rightly calls "such hermeneutical gymnastics . . . excessive . . . tortured" and "contrived." And though the passage fits Matthew's Jewish Christian theology quite well, it is clearly dominical teaching; though perhaps limiting its force for his Gentile audience by other means, Luke preserves the saying intact (Lk 16:17; Vermes 1993: 19).

Third, Jesus declares that people will be judged by their response to God's Word, thus providing another graphic example of its authority (5:19). He claims that one who keeps, and leads others to keep,[56] the least commandment will be greatest in the kingdom (in the Greek of this period, "great" could mean "greatest," as translators frequently recognize in rendering 22:36; cf. Mussies 1976: 1042). Jesus again employs hyperbolic rhetoric characteristic of sages: his words do not envision the possibility of many who would keep or break the least commandment, hence vie for the same status, nor of some who would break some commandments while keeping others. Jewish teachers typically depicted various

54. The Greek letter *iota* used here might be a rough equivalent; cf. the play on the Latin "i" in Mart. *Epig.* 2.93 (at the end of bk. II, he suggests Regulus may wish to make it bk. I by subtracting an *iota*). Cf. the *yodh*'s significance in b. Menaḥ. 29b because of what it can spell; cf. Pesiq. R. 11:7. No one dare alter a word (Jos. *Apion* 1.42; Pesiq. Rab Kah. Sup. 1:8). Rulers were known to prescribe a capital sentence against those found chiseling out a single letter of their inscriptions (Dio Chrys. *31st Disc., Rhodian Oration* 86 in Boring 1995: 57); the 22 letters of the alphabet were prepared to testify against Israel's transgressions of Torah (Lam. Rab. Proem 24).

55. E.g., Meier 1980: 47; France 1985: 115; cf. Meier 1976: 168-69. Cf. likewise the proposal that Jesus refers to only one kind of law (Guelich 1982: 139-40, 148, 155).

56. Davies and Allison 1988: 498 suggest that Matthew possibly places doing before teaching in agreement with the Shammaite emphasis on deeds over study, in contrast to the Hillelites (citing m. 'Abot 1:15, 17; 3:10).

persons as "greatest"; the emphasis was not on numerical precision but on praising worthy people (e.g., m. 'Abot 2:8). When Jesus speaks of the "least" commandment, he also reflects Jewish legal language. Jewish teachers regularly distinguished "light" and "heavy" commandments (e.g., Sifra V. D. Deho. par. 1.34.1.3; 12.65.1.3; Dalman 1929: 64; Flusser 1988: 496; cf. Mt 23:23), and in fact determined which commandments were the "least" and "greatest."

Noting that both the "greatest" commandment about honoring parents (Ex 20:12; Deut 5:16) and the "least" commandment about the bird's nest (Deut 22:6-7) bore the same promise, "Do this and you will live," some later rabbis decided that "live" meant "in the world to come," and said that God would reward equally for any commandment. One who kept the law regulating the bird's nest merited eternal life, whereas one who broke it merited damnation (e.g., Urbach 1979: 1:350; Keener 1991a: 116; see Johnston 1982). In Hebrew parlance, to "break" one of the commandments meant to "relax" it, to tone it down "either by allowing what it forbids or by exempting men from some of its positive requirements" (Manson 1979: 154; cf. Sandmel 1978b: 356n.18); the opposite was "confirming Scripture by teaching so as to uphold it (e.g., Mek. Pisḥa 1.124; Gerhardsson 1961: 287). Jesus at first sight appears more merciful than the rabbis: one who breaks the commandment is least in the kingdom rather than excluded from it altogether (5:19); yet his following words show that those who merely honored the highest standards of their religion fell short of entering the kingdom at all (5:20; for "entering" the kingdom, cf. 7:21; 18:3; 19:23; 23:13; cf. 7:13; 25:10; Jn 3:5).

Fourth, Jesus' point in 5:19 is the same as that of other Bible teachers in his day: one cannot pick and choose among the commandments but must obey them all. As some teachers put it, one should be as "careful with regard to a light commandment as you would be with a heavy one, since you do not know the allotment of the reward" (m. 'Abot 2:1; cf. Sifre Deut. 96.3.2; 115.1.2; ARN 2 A). Likewise one who keeps a single commandment keeps his life, but one who neglects such a commandment neglects his life (ARN 35, §77 B; Sifre Deut. 48.1.3; cf. m. Qidd. 1:10; ARN 28 A). The sages were not suggesting that they never broke commandments (see Moore 1971: 1:467-68), but rather felt that one who cast off any commandment or principle of the law was discarding the authority of the law as a whole (m. Hor. 1:3; Sifre Deut. 54.3.2; ARN 27 A; 1, §8 B; cf. Jas 2:10; Test. Asher 2.2-8). Likewise, accepting some commandments implied recognizing the validity of them all (Sifra Qed. pq. 8.205.2.6; Behuq. par. 5.255.1.10; more fully, Keener 1991a: 115-17). Jesus concurs: God does not allow his servants to embrace his prohibition against murder while rejecting his teaching about adultery or fornication. To refuse his right to rule any of one's ethics or behavior is to deny God's lordship.

God will punish teachers who undermine students' obedience to any portion of the Bible (5:19). This text addresses not only obedience to the commandments, but how one teaches others ("and teaches others to do the same," 5:19; cf. Jas 3:1; b. Rosh Hash. 17a). This accords with the Jewish teaching that

God rewards or judges the teacher for the deeds of his pupils (ARN 24, 40 A; cf. b. Yoma 87a; contrast t. Sanh. 14:12) and that a court is responsible for ruling in error (m. Hor. 1:1-2).

Despite their commitment to Scripture, religious people without transformed hearts will have no place in the kingdom (5:20). Like John the Baptist in 3:7-12, Jesus savages the false security of the religious establishment (Edwards 1985: 23); in reality, they are "lawless" (23:28). By comparing the disciples with the religious establishment, Matthew employs a standard rhetorical technique (Stanton 1993: 81), but not for epideictic purposes (as in some texts, e.g., 3:14; 11:11; 12:6, 41-42). His purposes here are entirely deliberative, to exhort his disciples to a higher, more inward standard.

Throughout the ancient Mediterranean, "scribes" were executors of legal documents, those most knowledgeable in writing and the law; in Jewish Palestine scribes also taught children, and the most advanced of them were rabbis with adult disciples (Keener 1991a: 23; see the excursus on Mt 23). A contemporary equivalent might be religious educators, whereas one might compare the Pharisees with the most pious, Bible-believing laypeople in mainstream society (cf. Jeremias 1963: 22; many may have also been aristocratic — see the excursus on Mt 23). Pharisaic ethics emphasized "inwardness" as much as Jesus did,[57] but Jesus and Matthew challenge not Pharisaic ethics but the actual condition of the Pharisees' and others' hearts (Odeberg 1964). Jesus goes on to charge them with lawlessness and only a pretense of righteousness (23:28; cf. Acts 23:3), and indicates that the very best of human piety is inadequate for salvation.[58]

Jesus Applies the Principles of God's Law (5:21-48)

This section contains much material that is indisputably authentic (the substance of the divorce saying, for instance, is attested not only in Mark and Q but also in Paul; that the early Christians had to adjust the teaching to live with it also suggests that it did not originate with them — Sanders 1993: 200). The structure of the passage, however, may be Matthew's own way of underlining and rendering more cohesive the point he finds in the material. Although we lack firm evidence for a pre-Matthean structure of "You have heard it said . . . but I say," the partial antithesis in the parallel section in Luke 6:27 supports the likelihood that Mat-

57. E.g., m. 'Abot 2:9; b. Ber. 13a; compare rabbinic discussions of *kavanah* (on which see Bonsirven 1964: 95; Montefiore and Loewe 1974: 272-94; Pawlikowski 1970); cf. Jos. *Apion* 2.183, 217 in Vermes 1993: 32. Rabbinic documents may appear more legalistic because they are *legal* documents, but this does not represent all of rabbinic, Pharisaic, or Jewish ethics (Davies 1967b: 127; Vermes 1993: 195); the covenantal perspective is better represented in early Jewish prayers (Segal 1985). Vermes (1993: 195) thinks that Jesus exaggerated the inward and causal aspects of behavior far more than the rabbis, but this may be partly because he excludes as inauthentic more law material regarding Jesus than is necessary.

58. Onwu 1988 suggests that the standard of "righteousness" Jesus demands as a prerequisite for entering the kingdom is the eschatological righteousness to be lived out in the kingdom; cf. 4:17.

thew did not create them from nothing (Dunn 1975: 42).[59] Matthew surely preserves the general sense of Jesus' teaching, and it is not against biblical law (cf. Vermes 1993: 30-37).

Once Jesus has made it clear that he is not opposing the law but interpreting it, he shows how the customary practice of the law in his day is inadequate (cf. Westerholm 1982). Various first-century Jewish groups competed to win their contemporaries to their interpretations of the right way to observe the law; specific ways one should observe the law constituted a public, political issue, but one on which there was no absolute consensus (Saldarini 1994: 124-25). The passage challenges human hearts (cf. Mk 7:21), however, not traditional ethics. Although expositors of Jewish law naturally focused on legal questions, they also discussed ethical concerns (Sanders 1977: 69-84). Jesus' interpretations and later Jewish tradition share substantial points of contact (e.g., Sanders 1985: 55; Manns 1978). This is significant for modern Christian readers because it means that they cannot dismiss Jesus' critique as relevant only for a first-century Jewish sect, but must acknowledge that it remains relevant for anyone who shares Jesus' ethics (23:3).

In 5:21-48, Jesus explains six legal texts from the Old Testament, interpreting as a good Jewish scholar of his day would (e.g., Flusser 1988: 494; cf. Sanders 1985: 9-10, 56-57).[60] Some contend that Jesus challenges the law in 5:21-48, and hence regard Jesus' six interpretations as "antitheses" (Bultmann 1958: 89-90; cf. Strecker 1978: 71). Other scholars rightly object that prior theological commitments rather than solid exegesis of the passage demand that line of interpretation.[61] Although another word for "but" implies strong contrast *(alla),* our passage uses a weak form of "but" that often even means "and" *(de).* If anything, given the context of 5:17-20, Jesus makes the law more stringent in this passage, not less, and Jewish people never considered tightening the law to be disrespecting it (cf. Sanders 1985: 9-10, 256-57, 260). Jewish teachers, in fact, generally advocated building a "fence around the law," making it stricter, to make sure one did not violate its intention accidentally (e.g., ARN 2; 3 A; see Przybylski 1980: 81).

Some read "Amen, I say to you" as more radical than the prophetic "Thus says the LORD."[62] The prefatory "Amen," guaranteeing the veracity of what follows, was an extremely rare expression,[63] and may tend in this direction. But the

59. For differing views of which of the "antitheses" are redactional, see Luz 1989: 274-76 (who himself accepts only the first and second as original).

60. 5:21-48 seem to illustrate the principle of 5:17 (cf., e.g., Hort 1894: 18). Goulder 1974 compares the practice attributed to Hillel of following the principle with cases; so here, the principle (5:17) is illustrated with six examples (cf. also the thesis in 6:1, followed by three illustrations).

61. See Keener 1991a: 113-20; Przybylski 1980: 83; Gundry 1982: 83; Harrington 1989; Broer 1993a; Stanton 1993: 301-2; Overman 1996: 81.

62. E.g., Ladd 1974: 124-25; Robinson 1977: 104; Hill 1979: 68; cf. Berger and Wyschogrod 1978: 31.

63. Dalman 1929: 30; Jeremias 1969: 112; Ladd 1967: 96 Daube 1973: 388; see the Introduction.

"I say to you," while authoritative,[64] is more didactic than prophetic. Other Jewish teachers also offered phrases like "You have heard . . . , but I say to you" when expounding Scripture. Paul, in fact, uses exactly the same formula when applying one of Jesus' sayings in this context to a new situation (1 Cor 7:10-12). When Jewish teachers said things like this they did not see themselves as contradicting the law, but rather explaining it (sometimes vis-à-vis the majority view of their contemporaries), so we might read the passage thus: "You understand the Bible to mean only this, but I offer a fuller interpretation."[65]

At the same time, Jesus does not speak with merely scribal authority (7:28-29); there is no academic debate or citation of other teachers, but instead solemn pronouncements (Daube 1973: 58-59). Jesus upholds the law (5:17-19) but is the decisive arbiter of its meaning, not one scholar among many (Daube 1973: 59-60; cf. Guelich 1976: 455; idem 1982: 185). Matthew 5:21-48 provide concrete examples of the "greater righteousness" of 5:20 (Guelich 1973: 52).

Angry Enough to Kill (5:21-26)

Cf. Lk 12:57-59. This text addresses not just how one acts but who one is, that is, one's character. Earthly courts generally could not judge such offenses as displays of anger (except in tightly controlled communities like Qumran — 1QS 7.5; CD 9.3-6; cf. Davies 1966b: 82; France 1985: 120; Roman law also penalized defamatory words — Gaius *Inst.* 3.220).[66] But God's heavenly court would judge all such offenses (5:25-26; see more fully Keener 1987; idem 1991: 14-16).[67]

64. "I say to you" may imply the speaker's greater status, at least academically and momentarily (cf. Prov 4:10, 20; Hagner 1993: 111; Davies and Allison 1988: 490 cite, e.g., Jub. 36:11; 1 Enoch 92:18; 94:1; 99:13; Mt 3:9; Acts 5:38; Rom 11:13; though they may find in it *more* authority than it claims). "The ancients" (5:21, 33; probably assumed in the other "you heard it said" statements) probably refers to the wilderness generation (with Davies and Allison 1988: 511, though Jos. *Ant.* 13.292 does not support their position; cf. Sir 39:1; Test. Zeb. 9:5; pace Du Plessis 1967: 18), though "ancients were a regular object of appeal" (e.g., Cornutus 1.p.2.17-18 in Van der Horst 1981: 168; Epict. *Disc.* 1.18.17; Crates *Ep.* 35, to Aper; Babrius 47.1).

65. For full documentation, see Schechter 1900: 427; Abrahams 1917: 16; Smith 1951: 28-30; Daube 1973: 55-58; Urbach 1979: 1:294; Boxel 1988; Sanders 1990: 93; Keener 1991a: 119, 209; cf., e.g., Mek. Pisḥa 1.58, 62; Sifre Num. 112.1.2; b. Ber. 63a.

66. Lachs 1987: 92 indicates that Jewish courts could levy fines for offenses like slander and shaming another, but that name calling did not fit these categories (cf. m. B. Qam. 8:6; b. B. Qam. 86a-87a). Insulting a teacher could warrant both legal and postmortem punishment (see b. Ber. 19a).

67. On the heavenly court in Jewish texts (rooted in the biblical court of Yahweh related to the Canaanite court of El — Bright 1981: 158-59), generally comprised of either scholars or angels, see, e.g., ARN 32A; b. ʿAbod. Zar. 36a; Ber. 18b; 64a; B. Meṣ. 75a; 85b; 86a; Giṭ. 68a; Mak. 13b; Pesaḥ. 53b; Shab. 129b; p. Sanh. 1:1, §4; 11:5, §1; Gen. Rab. 49:2; 64:4; Ex. Rab. 12:4; 30:18; Lev. Rab. 11:8; 24:2; 29:1, 4; Num. Rab. 3:4; 18:4; 19:3; Ruth Rab. 4:3, 5; Qoh. Rab. 1:11, §1; 2:12, §1; 5:11, §5; Song Rab. 3:11, §2; 8:9, §2; Pesiq. Rab Kah. 23:4; 24:11; Pesiq. R. 15:19; cf. 11QMelch in Kobelski 1978:123; Test. Abr. 12A; 10B; 3 Enoch 2:4; 5:10-12; 16:1; 18:16; 28:8; 29:1; 30:1-2; Couturier 1984; for the Greek image, e.g., Char. *Chaer.* 5.4.6. On the links between heavenly and earthly, cf., e.g., Lincoln 1990: 157; Pesiq. Rab Kah. 1:3; Qoh. Rab. 3:14, §1; heavenly tablets in Jub. 3:10,

Jesus begins by citing the crime of murder in Exodus 20:13, for which biblical law required a Jewish court to execute the sentence of death (Gen 9:5-6; Deut 21:1-9; Jewish traditions naturally applied to it the punishment of Gehenna — Gen. Rab. 97 NV; 2 Enoch 60:1).[68] But Jesus presses beyond behavior specifically punished by law to the kind of heart that generates such behavior. Anger that would generate murder if unimpeded is the spiritual equivalent of murder (1 Jn 3:15; cf. Test. Gad 1:9; 4:4; Sen. *Benef.* 5.14.2; Davies and Allison 1988: 509 cite Targ. Ps-J. and Targ. Onq. on Gen 9:6; Der. Er. Rab. 11:13).[69] God never wanted people merely to obey rules; he wanted them to be holy as he is, to value what he values. Greco-Roman (Demosth. *Against Meidias* 43-44; *Against Aristocrates* 73; Gaius *Inst.* 3.208), Israelite (Num 35:20), and Jewish law (t. Rosh Hash. 2:7; Cohen 1966: 65-121; Jackson 1971) weighed an overt offense by a person's intention; would God himself do less?[70] One would instead expect God to judge even intentions one could not carry out, for God desired devoted hearts (e.g., Deut 5:29; 30:6).

The heavenly court will judge all offenses of intention. Although many scholars suggest that the offenses and punishments of 5:22 (Filson 1960: 85), or at least its offenses (Jeremias 1971: 149), are in ascending order of severity, Je-

---

31; 4:32; 5:13; 6:17, 29, 35; 15:25; 16:3, 9, 28-29; 18:19; 19:9; 23:32; 24:33; 28:6; 30:9, 18-23; 31:32; 32:10, 21, 28; 33:10; 49:8; 1 Enoch 81:1-2; 93:2-3; 103:2-3; 106:19; 107:1; 108:7; Noack 1957-58: 200; probably "les tables précieuses" in 4QTestuz in Testuz 1955; perhaps CD 3.3-4; Jub. 50:13 (cf. Roman eternal tables of the fates, e.g., in Ovid *Metam.* 15.809-15). Similarly, in the ancient Near East curses provided divine sanctions against lawlessness where courts could not enforce the laws (Assmann 1992).

68. Matthew nowhere shrinks from strong language such as "Gehenna" (e.g., 5:30; 10:28; 23:15) or "fire" (e.g., 3:10; 18:8; 25:41).

69. In ancient moral teaching, anger easily leads to murder (Demosth. *Against Conon* 19; Sir 8:16; Ps-Phocyl. 57-58; Did. 3.2; cf. Hor. *Epodes* 1.2.59-62; Boring 1995: 57 cites Plut. *Uneduc. Ruler* 6, *Mor.*). On the dangers of anger and the need to control it, see outside strictly Jewish texts Ahiqar 189, §91; Arist. *N.E.* 7.6.1, 1149a; Isoc. *To Nic.* 23, *Or.* 2; *Demon.* 31; Pub. Syr. 87, 88, 184, 214, 241, 311, 628, 643, 695; Cato *Collection of Distichs* 45; Hor. *Sat.* 1.3.76-77; Eph 4:26; Epict. *Disc.* 1.15.1-5; 2.19.26; Sen. *Dial.* 3–5; *Ep. Lucil.* 18.14; Plut. *Educ.* 14, *Mor.* 10B; *Bride* 38, *Mor.* 143D; Cato the Elder 16 in Plut. *Sayings of Romans, Mor.* 199A; Plut. *On Control of Anger, Mor.* 452F-464D; *On Rage* (fr. 148 in LCL 15:274-77); *Solon* 21.1; *Brutus* 29.2; Marc. Aur. *Med.* 6.26; Diog. Laert. *Lives* 1.70; 7.1.114; 8.1.23. In Jewish texts, see Sir 20:3; Jos. *War* 2.135; Test. Dan 2–4, especially 2:2; 3:6; m. 'Abot 2:10; Sib. Or. 3.377; b. Qidd. 40b-41a; Pesaḥ. 113b; Shab. 31a; p. Ta'an. 3:11, §4; Gen. Rab. 49:8; Lachs 1987: 91 adds Sifre Deut. 186-87; b. B. Meṣ. 58b. "Brother" in 5:22 may mean "neighbor" or "fellow citizen" (5:23), though it can mean more specifically "fellow-disciple" (5:9; 18:15; 23:8; 28:10).

70. Intention is important in nonlegal ethics as well; in philosophers, cf. Arist. *N.E.* 3.1.13-19, 1110b-1111a; *Rhet.* 2.19.21, 1392b; Sen. *Benef.* 5.14.1-2; Sent. Sext. 181; Phaedrus 5.3.11-13. In Judaism, see Ps-Phocyl. 51-52, 135-36; Jos. *Apion* 2.217; t. Pe'a 3:8; Sifre Deut. 252.1.2; 283.7.1; Maher 1981. Humanly enforced law could not push the issue of intention too far, however; cf., e.g., t. Pe'a 1:4; Urbach 1979: 1:382. Black 1988 contends that "without cause" belongs to the original text of 5:22; it may, however, represent a legitimate interpretation of Jesus' more graphic statement, which may have circulated orally in both forms (on the possible conditional Aramaic original, see Wernberg-Møller 1956-57: 72; for a comparison with Aristotelian and Stoic ethics, see Wolbert 1988).

sus probably simply repeated the same concept in three different ways: anger and calling someone a fool or an "emptyhead" are roughly equivalent (e.g., Köhler 1919: 91-95).[71] By the same token, if Jesus reads the "judgment" of 5:21 as the day of God's judgment (cf. 7:1; since Jewish courts could not execute capital sentences in his time), he probably means "the Sanhedrin" as God's heavenly court (Lachs 1987: 92-94; Keener 1987; cf. France 1985: 120), also portrayed as the Sanhedrin in Jewish texts,[72] and both as equivalent to the sentence to be decreed there: damnation to eternal hell (on which see comment on 3:12).[73] Because every word is uttered before the heavenly court, slandering another person merits for the accuser the eternal punishment that would have been due the accused (cf. 12:35-37; Deut 19:16-19; 11QTemple 61.7-11; Sus 62; Jos. *Ant.* 4.219; among Gentiles, Isoc. *Nic.* 29, *Or.* 2; Ferguson 1987: 51). The parable in 5:25-26 graphically expounds this point about the heavenly court's judgment; this principle also casts its shadow over the earthly Sanhedrin's false sentence against Jesus in 26:66.[74]

Jesus' prohibition of acting in anger is a general principle. As in each of his six examples, Jesus graphically portrays a general principle, although some of these principles (like anger and divorce) must be qualified in specific circumstances. Most hearers understood that such general principles expressed in proverbs and similar sayings needed to be qualified in specific situations (see Du Plessis 1967: 17; Keener 1991a: 22-28); most legal interpreters also recognized that even biblical laws had to be qualified under some circumstances (1 Macc 2:34-41; t. Sheb. 8:7-10; Sifre Deut. 175.1.3; 221.1.1; cf. Borg 1984: 76-77; Greene 1976), and Jesus takes this form of interpretation farther than most of his contemporaries (e.g., 12:3-8). Although condemning anger and in-

71. Since *raka* is Aramaic for "empty[head]" (e.g., b. B. Bat. 75a; Ber. 22a; Lachs 1987: 92 cites Targ. Onq. Gen. 37:14; b. Ber. 32a; Ned. 65a; Sanh. 100a; Ta'an. 20b; for "empty craniums" and "empty minds" in Greek, cf., e.g., Soph. *Electra* 403; Sib. Or. 3.430, 590; Ep. Arist. 8), some scholars propose that *mōre,* "fool," also bears nuances of a Semitic term for "rebel" (cf. ARN 32, §69 B; Pesiq. Rab Kah. 14:5; see Manson 1979: 156; Albright and Mann 1971: 61; cf. Smith 1951: 2). But *moros* is perfectly good Greek for "fool" (e.g., 7:26; 23:17; Sir 19:11; Lam. Rab. Proem 31), so this suggestion is questionable. Biblical tradition viewed concepts related to "folly" in a moral light (e.g., Deut 22:21; Judg 19:23-24; 1 Sam 25:25; Ps 14:1; 53:1; Prov 10:18, 23; 14:16, 29; 15:5; 20:3; 29:11; Is 32:6; Jer 17:11), and the Greek term "fool" was also quite harsh (Epict. *Disc.* 2.21.2; 2.22.4-5).

72. Lachs 1987: 92, 94; Keener 1987; additional documentation in idem 1991a: 141n.14; see much more fully note 67. Overman 1996: 85-86 suggests the five Roman *synedria* or courts in Palestine in 55 B.C. (Jos. *War* 1.170; *Ant.* 14.91); did these remain in effect a century later?

73. Thus the "twofold gloss" of Moule 1939 is unnecessary, as is his later attempt to view it as rhetorical heightening (Moule 1969: 11; cf. Gundry 1982: 85), what Meier 1979: 244-45; idem 1980: 51 sees as "mock . . . casuistry." *Krisis* can refer to coming to trial (*CPJ* 1:239-40, §129.7), but no less easily to divine judgment (e.g., Jub. 4:31; Sib. Or. 1.274; 3.34, 56, 91; Gk. Ezra 1:24); what escaped human judgment would face God's (Sib. Or. 3.258-60); for eschatological *krisis* against the "empty thinkers," see Sib. Or. 3.670.

74. That this text addresses not the kind of rhetorical condemnation Jesus elsewhere employed (23:17; see below) but perjury before the heavenly court or the broader society fits what we know of Jewish law (Matthews and Benjamin 1991b; Keener 1991a: 15-16); cf. slander as a sin against both humans and God in Qoh. Rab. 9:12.

sults, Jesus himself expressed grieved indignation and called people "fools" under appropriate circumstances (21:12; 23:17; cf. 23:13-33).[75] Yet he acted on behalf of God's agendas, humbly accepting suffering for himself.

A disciple's relationship with God is partly contingent on how the disciple treats others. God will not accept one's gift at the altar until one reconciles (cf. 18:15) with one's neighbor (cf. similarly m. Yoma 8:9).[76] Again Jesus depicts the situation graphically, since his Galilean hearers might have to travel a considerable distance to leave the Jerusalem temple and then return (5:23-24; see Stein 1978: 11).[77]

Jesus' following crisis parable (cf. Caird 1965; Jeremias 1972: 96; cf. the graphic parable in Sifre Deut. 309.1.1) shows how urgent the situation is (5:25-26). Given the prejudice against the poor in lawsuits in the Empire (Petron. *Sat.* 14; Gaius *Inst.* 4.183; Stambaugh and Balch 1986: 113; contrast Pub. Syr. 98; ARN 33, §73), the parable would appeal to the fears of Jesus' hearers. Imprisonment was generally a temporary holding place until punishment (or, if one lacked bail and the case were serious, until trial — Lewis 1983: 187-88); here, however, a longer penalty is envisaged. "The last *quadrans*" refers to the second-smallest Roman coin,[78] which represented one sixty-fourth of a denarius, hence only a few minutes' wages for even a day laborer. While Gentiles sometimes sold debtors into slavery to pay off a debt (cf. 18:25), sometimes the debtor was imprisoned until relatives and friends could come up with the shameful payment, as here (cf. 18:34; Malina and Rohrbaugh 1992: 55). Jewish people considered imprisonment for debt a horrible punishment characteristic of Gentiles (Jeremias 1972: 180); Rome abolished the practice in 326 B.C. (Livy 8.28.1). Through a variety of terrible, graphic images, Jesus indicates that when one damages one's relationships with others one damages one's relationship with God, leading to eternal punishment (cf. 18:21-35).

75. The title was standard rhetorical practice toward one's opponents or imaginary interlocutors in public debate and diatribe, both Jewish (e.g., Sifre Deut. 309.1.1; 309.2.1; b. B. Bat. 115b, end; Ber. 10a; 'Erub. 101a; Yebam. 102b) and more broadly (e.g., 1 Cor 15:36; Philo *Cher.* 75; Epict. *Disc.* 2.16.13; 2.21.2; 2.22.4-5; 3.13.17; 3.22.85; Marc. Aur. *Med.* 5.36.1; Phaedrus 3.15.2; on Epicureans, Plut. *Pleasant Life Impossible* 2, *Mor.* 1086EF; Diog. Laert. *Lives* 10.1.7-8), as well as challenge and insults (e.g., Mart. *Epig.* 10.100.1; Epict. *Disc.* 1.18.10; cf. in the judgment: Lk 12:20; b. 'Abod. Zar. 3a; Ruth Rab. 3:3; Qoh. Rab. 1:15, §1).

76. Cf. further p. B. Qam. 8:7, §1; Bonsirven 1964: 116-17; Hagner 1993: 117; Chilton 1994: 115; Boring 1995: 115-16; Sanders 1985: 249 cites Sifra Ahare Mot pq. 8.1; Sifre Zuta to Num 6:26; cf. Lev 6:5; Gen. Rab. 98:19. Some Greek communal ethics also stressed reconciliation with fellow citizens (e.g., Diod. Sic. 12.20.2), perhaps most popularly exemplified in the rhetoricians' *homonoia* speeches (e.g., Demosth. *Letter* 1.5-6).

77. Vermes 1993: 155n.2 doubts that this interest in the sanctuary would stem from Jesus and suspects that it is Matthew's creation; against this, cf. the cultic requirement in 8:4, which derives from Mk 1:44 (and is certainly not a creation of Mark or his community; cf. Mk 7:15, 19). Jesus' requirement here fits his Jewish context and biblical tradition (Davies and Allison 1988: 518 recall the biblical refrain that moral piety precedes ritual) and contrasts starkly with the Pythagorean view (Thom 1994: 106). The single judge of the parable may accurately depict pre-70 conditions (Vermes 1993: 111).

78. Technically it may have been the smallest Roman coin (Hor. *Sat.* 2.3.93; Juv. *Sat.* 7.8), but in Palestine the *lepton* was smaller (Mk 12:42; Lk 12:59; Wheaton 1982: 792).

Do Not Covet Others Sexually (5:27-30)

Cf. Mk 9:43-48.

Jesus' warning against lust would have challenged some ancient hearers' values. Although some philosophers, especially Stoics, opposed lust because it meant that pleasure rather than virtue dominated one's thoughts (e.g., Epict. *Disc.* 2.18.15-18; 3.2.8; 4.9.3; Marc. Aur. 2.10; 3.2.2; 9.40; cf. Nock 1964a: 19),[79] many men in the ancient Mediterranean thought lust a healthy and normal practice (e.g., Ach. Tat. *Clit.* 1.4-6; Apul. *Metam.* 2.8; Diog. Laert. 6.2.46, 69; Diog. *Ep.* 35 to Sopolis; Artem. *Oneir.* 1.78). Among the common magical spells used to secure love (e.g., *PGM* 13.304; 32.1-19; 36.69-133, 187-210, 295-311, 333-60; 62.1-24; 101.1-53; Theocritus *The Spell,* in *Greek Bucolic Poets,* LCL 26-39; the charm in Horsley 1981: 33-34), some magical spells describe self-stimulation as a way to secure intercourse with the object of one's desire (*PGM* 36.291-94), even if she was married (*PDM* 61.197-216 = *PGM* 61.39-71; cf. Eurip. *Hippol.* 513-16).

Jewish writers, however, viewed lust far more harshly (e.g., Job 31:1, 9; Sir 9:8; 23:5; 41:21; Sus 8; 1QS 1.6-7; 4.10; CD 2.16; 11QSTemple 59.14; 1QpHab 5.7).[80] Some, in fact, viewed it as visual fornication or adultery (Test. Iss. 7:2; Reub. 4:8; b. Nid. 13b, bar.; Shab. 64ab; Lev. Rab. 23:12; Pesiq. R. 24:2; see Keener 1991a: 16-17), as have Christian readers of Matthew (Justin *1 Apol.* 15; Sent. Sext. 233; Tert. *Apol.* 46.11-12; cf. Herm. 1.1.1). Likewise, other Jewish teachers employed the hyperbolic rhetoric that equated the thought with the act or treated the former as worse (b. Qidd. 81b; Lachs 1987: 96-97, citing b. Ned. 13b; Yom. 29a; Num. Rab. 8:5). Yet Jesus was not challenging his hearers' ethics; had he been doing so, he might have provided more scripture texts to prove his case to them. In this instance the scribes and Pharisees, like most of

79. For diverse views on self-stimulation, see Sext. Emp. *Pyrrh.* 3.206. Cf. Luz 1989: 295 for Stoic influence on hellenistic Judaism, citing Philo *Op. Mund.* 152; *Omn. Prob. Lib.* 159; *Spec. Leg.* 4.84; *Decal.* 142; Life of Adam 19; Rom 7:7; Jas 1:15; he also parallels the rabbinic use of the *yeser hara'.* Greek philosophers often felt that thoughts and intentions, not merely deeds, could be evil (Boring 1995: 58 cites Aelian *Variae historiae* 14.28, 42; Epict. *Fr.* 100; Diog. Laert. *Lives* 1.36; Plut. *On Being a Busybody* 13; Cic. *Goods and Evils* 3.9.32; Arist. *Magna Moralia*).

80. See further 1 Enoch 67:8; Sib. Or. 4.33-34; Ps. Sol. 4:4; Test. Iss. 3:5; 4:4; Reub. 4:1; 6:1-3; Jud. 17:1; m. Nid. 2:1; ARN 2A; 2, §9B; b. Ber. 20a; Yebam. 63b; p. Ḥag. 2:2, §4; Gen. Rab. 32:7; Pesiq. Rab Kah. Sup. 3:2; cf. Bonsirven 1964: 113; Schechter 1961: 225; Vermes 1993: 32-33; Ilan 1996: 127-28. Some Greek philosophers also acknowledged that the gods knew one's thoughts (e.g., Thales in Diog. Laert. *Lives* 1.36); even those who otherwise thought lust acceptable disapproved if the woman were betrothed or married (cf. Ach. Tat. 4.3.1-2 in context; Char. *Chaer.* 2.2.8), though it was not legally punishable (Char. *Chaer.* 5.7.5-6; 8.8.8). Seneca condemned as impious a woman whose virtue stemmed merely from fear (*Benef.* 4.14.1). Jewish writers also condemned *contemplating* evil (e.g., Ep. Arist. 132-33; though contrast b. Ḥul. 142a; and avoiding sin in one's thoughts was a high standard, Test. Zeb. 1:4); later rabbis went so far as to praise a predecessor who had never *looked* at his own private parts (p. Sanh. 10:5, §2). On lust, see also C. S. Keener, "Marriage, Divorce and Adultery," 712-17 in *Dictionary of the Later New Testament and Its Developments,* ed. R. P. Martin and P. H. Davids (Downers Grove: InterVarsity, 1997), 714-16.

Matthew's community, may have agreed with his basic premise, as Matthew's audience probably knew, but Jesus challenges their hearts, not just their doctrine. (Thus Jesus can condemn the whole generation as "adulterous" — 12:39; 16:4, though these texts refer primarily to spiritual adultery.)

But Jesus is offering an implicit argument from Scripture, not just a cultural critique. Although the seventh of the ten commandments declared, "You shall not commit adultery" (Ex 20:14), the tenth commandment declared, "You shall not covet," that is, desire, anything that belongs to your neighbor (Ex 20:17). In the popular Greek version of his day, the tenth commandment began, "You shall not covet your neighbor's wife," and used the same word for "covet" that Jesus uses here for "lust" (cf. also, e.g., Guelich 1982: 193; Carson 1984b: 151). In other words, Jesus reads the humanly unenforceable tenth commandment as if it matters as much as the other, more humanly enforceable commandments. In Matthean ethics, if one does not break the letter of the other commandments, but one *wants* to do so, one is guilty.

Jesus does, however, go beyond his contemporaries' customary views on lust. Jewish men expected married Jewish women to wear head coverings to prevent lust (single women were exempt, since they needed to find a husband).[81] Jewish writers often warned of women as dangerous because they could invite lust (e.g., Sir 25:21; 26:9; Ps. Sol. 16:7-8; Test. Reub. 3.11-12; 5.1-5; 6:1; Jos. *War* 2.121; *Ant.* 7.130; b. Taʿan. 24a),[82] but Jesus placed the responsibility for lust on the person doing the lusting (5:28; Witherington 1984: 28). He treats lust as if it is exclusively a sin of the lusting heart, not a sin of letting hair out from under one's covering (on head coverings in antiquity and early Christianity, see Keener 1992: 19-69).

Although Matthew retains the Markan context of causing others to stumble (Mk 9:42-48; Mt 18:7-9), he here uses Jesus' hyperbolic sayings about sacrificing limbs to underline the urgency of rejecting sin. (Cf. similarly a writer like Sen. *Ep. Lucil.* 51.13, who advises that if one cannot rid one's heart of vice in any other manner, one should rip out one's heart. One should not think of the Jesus tradition and Seneca anywhere following a common source, but they might employ common rhetorical conventions. Cf. also Philo *Som.* 2.68-69; Sen. *Dial.* 1.3.2; Gen. Rab. 55:4. Jesus says that it is better to suffer corporal punishment in the present — amputating one's lustful eye or other offending appendages — than to spend eternity in hell after the resurrection of the damned (5:29-30; 18:8-

81. See Keener 1992: 27-31; cf., e.g., Diod. Sic. 17.35.5; Charillus 2 in Plut. *Sayings of Spartans, Mor.* 232C; Petron. *Sat.* 14, 16; Dio Cassius 42.11.2-3; Apul. *Metam.* 2.8-9; Sus 32; 3 Macc 4:6; m. B. Qam. 8:6; Ketub. 7:6; Sifre Num. 11.2.1-3; ARN 3A; 14, §35B. In addition to ancient sources, one may compare the analogous use of headcoverings in Islamic Middle Eastern societies (e.g., Delaney 1987: 42; Eickelman 1989: 165), of which I was unaware when I wrote Keener 1992.

82. Greeks also suspected women's special weakness and consequent propensity for infidelity and other moral vice (cf., e.g., Eurip. *Androm.* 218-21; Diod. Sic. 1.59.3-4; Pub. Syr. 20, 365, 376; Juv. *Sat.* 6.242-43; Plut. *Bride* 48, *Mor.* 145DE; Char. *Chaer.* 1.4.1-2; among Jews, Sir 42:12-14; Test. Abr. 9B; Philo *Prob.* 117; m. 'Abot 2:7; b. Ber. 53a; Pesaḥ. 111a; Shab. 33b; Gen. Rab. 17:6; 45:5; 80:5; cf. Delaney 1987: 41; Eickelman 1989: 205-6).

9).[83] (Many Jewish teachers believed that one would initially rise in the form in which one died — 2 Bar. 50:2-4; Gen. Rab. 95:1; Qoh. Rab. 1:4, §2. Nevertheless, most Jewish people believed that amputated limbs would be restored at the resurrection of the righteous — 2 Macc 7:11.) A bad foot or eye could cause one to stumble literally, but stumbling here (cf. 13:41; 16:23; 17:27; 18:6, 8; 26:31) is a transparent metaphor for sin or apostasy (Ezek 14:3-7; Sir 34:7, 17; 35:15; 39:24; Jn 6:61; Rom 11:11; 1 Cor 8:9; Jas 2:10; 3:2; 1QS 2.12; 3.24; 1QpHab 11.7-8; b. Sanh. 55b; as a metaphor in Greek and Roman literature, cf. Plut. *Cato the Younger* 30.2; Marc. Aur. 7.22; Babrius 103.20); some texts (including, e.g., Sir 9:5; 25:21; b. Soṭa 22a) apply it specifically to sexual sin. Because the "right" side was normally preferred (cf. comment on 25:33), Matthew's note that it is the "right" hand or eye that is lost makes the image more emphatic and graphic (Tannehill 1975: 187n.14; Guelich 1982: 195).

Jesus is saying that lust, as a form of adultery, merits a capital sentence before the heavenly court: eternal damnation.[84] Thus it is better to tear out one's eye than to keep lusting (5:29). Of course, thrusting out one's eye cannot stop lust; even emasculation did not automatically stop that (Sir 20:4; 30:20; Epict. *Disc.* 2.20.19; Philost. *V.A.* 1.33, 36; Acts of John 53; though perhaps Philo *Deterius* 176 thought it would).[85] In this context, the hand might refer to self-stimulation, as in similar Jewish texts concerning lust as adultery (cf. Deming 1990), though it cannot be limited to this (cf. Blomberg 1992a: 109). But the same caveat remains as regards the eye (cf. 6:22; 7:3). Jesus is declaring in a graphic manner that by whatever means necessary, one should cast off this sin (Col 3:5 seems to interpret Jesus' amputation saying thus). One must repent to be ready for the kingdom of heaven (4:17).

83. For willingness to experience amputations to secure a greater good, see Plato *Symp.* 204CE (Boring 1995: 113-14); contrast Epict. *Disc.* 1.2.25. Corporal punishment was already known in the Middle East (Deut 25:11-12; Jos. *War* 2.642-44; *Life* 147, 177-78; Albright and Mann 1971: 63-64) and a favorable alternative to execution (Jos. *Life* 173), and Jesus' use of irony and hyperbole rule out the need to attribute the saying to Neopythagorean sources (as Schattenmann 1979 does). This passage indicates Jesus' belief in the bodily resurrection of the damned for torment; see Gundry 1976: 24 (the imprisonment parable need not; cf. Plato *Cratylus* 400C; Sen. *Dial.* 11.9.3; 12.9.7; and other Greek and Roman examples of *sōma-sēma*). Basser 1985b: 149-50 believes that he finds allusions to this amputation image in Gen. Rab. 11 and b. Shab. 116b (though less graphic language of "cutting off" evils appears elsewhere, e.g., Sib. Or. 1.154); citing 19:12, Lachs 1987: 97 thinks the "hand" here represents a Jewish euphemism for the male organ.

84. Adultery was punishable by death under Israelite law (Lev 20:10; Deut 22:22; Jos. *Apion* 2.215); and hell by God (b. Soṭa 4b); some rabbis claimed that lust would lead to hell (b. Ber. 16a, bar.). On punishments for adultery in Mediterranean antiquity, see, e.g., Demosth. *Against Neaera* 86, *Or.* 59; Richlin 1981; on the permissible range of vengeance for aggrieved husbands, including permissible killings, see, e.g., Demosth. *Against Neaera* 66; Quint. 7.1.7. See more fully our comment on 1:19.

85. Thus Tertullian warns that Christians need not blind themselves as Democritus did, but simply guard their minds, and contends that "The Christian is born masculine for his wife and for no other woman" (*Apol.* 46.11). Lachs 1989: 97 cites Jewish texts figuratively blaming the eye for leading men into sin, especially sexually (e.g., Num 15:39; Prov 21:4; Ezek 6:9; 18:6; 20:7-8; 23:27; Qoh. 11:9; Sifre Num. 115; b. Ber. 12b; Soṭa 8a; 45a; p. Ber. 9:2; cf. also Prov 6:13, 17; 16:30; Eccl 4:8; Ezek 33:25; 1 Jn 2:16).

Herod Antipas, controlled by lust (14:6), ended up murdering a prophet (14:10; cf. 5:11-12), illustrating the principle of both this paragraph and the preceding one (5:21-30), as well as the prohibition of oaths (5:33-37; 14:7). A primary difference between Herod and most readers of Matthew was that Antipas had the power over others to carry out what was in his heart; but for Matthew, desiring that power is bad enough. How different the model of Joseph and Mary (1:25) and virtuous single persons like John the Baptist and Jesus, who suffered persecution for righteousness!

Jesus teaches in a graphic manner the value that God places on marital and premarital fidelity (cf. 1:19). By saying "adultery" Jesus technically addresses only lust for married women (Gundry 1982: 88; Guelich 1982: 193);[86] but this is an example that should provoke its hearers to consider related moral issues. Thus, for example, it rules out "fornication of the heart" as well; Israelite law treated premarital sex in part as an offense against one's future spouse and one's partner's future spouse (Deut 22:13-21).

Jesus does not, of course, refer here to passing attraction, "but the deliberate harboring of desire for an illicit relationship" (France 1985: 121; cf. Blomberg 1992a: 109; Is 33:15). The Greek present tense often bears a continuous sense, and probably does so here: Jesus refers not to *noticing* a person's beauty, but to imbibing it, meditating on it, seeking to possess it. Paul and most of his Jewish contemporaries prescribed marriage as a helpful antidote to this sin (Keener 1991a: 72-74, 79-82).

Do Not Betray Your Spouse by Divorce (5:31-32)

Cf. Lk 16:18; see more detailed comment under Mt 19:1-9. In Matthew's ethics, adultery is unfaithfulness to one's spouse or accommodating another person's unfaithfulness to that person's spouse. Lust is one form of such unfaithfulness; divorce is another. In Jesus' teaching, the man[87] who betrays his spouse by divorce is no less unfaithful to his marriage than the adulterer or lustful person and presumably warrants the same punishment prescribed by the preceding passage — damnation (5:29-30). Because sages tried to build a "fence around the law" stricter than the law itself, his hearers could not regard Jesus' opposition to Mo-

86. Noting other occasions on which Matthew applies *pros* with the infinitive to intention rather than result, Luz 1989: 294 narrows the exact sense still further: the verse addresses "intentional looking with the aim of breaking the marriage of another man."

87. Mark, addressing a broader Greco-Roman context, rightly adds, "*her* spouse," bringing out the implications of Jesus' teaching in a different cultural setting (Mk 10:12). In broader Greco-Roman culture (which Paul addresses in 1 Cor 7:10-16) either the husband or the wife could unilaterally divorce the other without the other's consent (Cary and Haarhoff 1946: 144; O'Rourke 1971: 181). In terms of Palestinian Jewish law, even if a man remained married to his first wife his subsequent unions would not be adulterous because Jewish law permitted polygyny; Jesus here eliminates the double standard, perhaps rejecting polygyny as (at least hyperbolically) adulterous in the same way Jewish law would have viewed polyandry (Sigal 1986: 93-94, 157).

saic divorce as unbiblical (see above; for other modifications in the law, cf. Sanders 1985: 248-49; idem 1990: 127; idem 1993: 211; Cohen 1987: 181).

In principle, remarriage is adulterous because God rejects the validity of divorce. Employing the same teaching technique of rhetorical overstatement that pervades the context (e.g., 5:18-19, 29-30; 6:3),[88] Jesus declares that God does not accept divorce, hence a divorced woman remains married to her first husband and her remarriage is adulterous (5:32).[89] Precisely because the very term for legal "divorce" meant freedom to remarry, everyone understood that a woman without a valid certificate of divorce was not free to remarry (e.g., m. Giṭ. 2:1); Jesus declares that if God does not accept the divorce as valid, remarriage is adulterous (19:6, 9; cf. similarly France 1985: 123).[90] "Adultery" meant unfaithfulness to one's spouse, and remarriage is adulterous here precisely because in God's sight the original couple remains married. The moral issue of the image, however, is not remarriage but the validity of the divorce; Jesus is prohibiting divorce (hence implying the importance of marriage) in an incomparably graphic fashion (Keener 1991a: 34-40, 43-44; cf. idem 1992a: 34; Stein 1979).

Matthew specifically states an exception. When Jesus offered a proverbial saying stating a general principle (Mk 10:11; Lk 16:18), ancient hearers understood that such sayings needed to be qualified for specific situations (Keener 1991a: 22-25; cf. Tannehill 1975: 95-98; Stein 1978: 11).[91] Indeed, such general

88. So also Stein 1978: 8-12; idem 1979: 119; idem 1992: 198; Efird 1985: 57; Keener 1991a: 12-25; cf. Malina 1981: 120. Rhetorical overstatement and hyperbole were common Jewish teaching techniques (e.g., m. 'Abot 2:8; ARN 36A) and appear elsewhere in the ancient Mediterranean as well (e.g., Arist. *Rhet.* 3.11.15, 1413a; *Rhet. ad Herenn.* 4.33.44; Quint. 8.6.73-76); in Jesus' teaching, see especially Tannehill 1975.

89. See Keener 1991a: 22-24; cf., e.g., Davies 1993: 54; Mounce 1985: 44; Llewelyn 1992: 16. The image (which on my view assumes the hyperbole that marriage is indissoluble) presumably addresses the woman because Jewish law in Matthew's milieu permitted men to marry more than one wife anyway, but the sharing of a woman involved adultery (Keener 1991a: 35, 47-48; Easton 1940: 82; Guelich 1982: 200-201; but cf. somewhat differently, Luck 1987: 103-7; even near Palestine, many Jewish practices resembled those of Gentile neighbors — Wasserstein 1989). Malina and Rohrbaugh 1992: 53 suggest that a husband "makes her an adulteress" because one offers her "for sexual union with other males," and thus acts as "a pimp" (which is how ancient law viewed a man who retained, hence tolerated, an adulterous wife; see Gardner 1986: 131-32; Richlin 1981: 227). The text undoubtedly does not mean "cause adultery" literally (as in the case of Messalina in Dio Cassius *R.H.* 60.18.1-2).

90. Paul did not take this saying literally (1 Cor 7:15; nor, it appears, did John — Jn 4:18). As common as divorce and remarriage were in antiquity (Carcopino 1940: 95-100; cf. Jos. *Life* 415, 426), Paul's letters would surely have reflected it had he been spending time breaking up new converts' second and third marriages. The Roman authorities, already concerned about subversive religious groups disrupting families (Keener 1992: 139-42), would also have noticed and acted swiftly!

91. Maxims and proverbs, general statements of principle requiring qualification (cf., e.g., Prov 18:22 with 11:22; 12:4; 21:9; others in Keener 1993: 235), were common throughout the ancient Mediterranean (Isoc. *Demon.* 12, *Or.* 1; Arist. *Rhet.* 2.21.1-2, 12-15, 1394a-95b; *Rhet. ad Herenn.* 4.17.24-25; Petron. *Sat.* 4; Plut. *Poetry* 14, *Mor.* 35EF; cf. Diog. Laert. 2.18-47; 8.1.17-18; 9.1.7; Pythagorean Sentences passim; *Select Papyri* 3:440-43; Appian *R.H.* 4.11; cf. also Sinclair 1993) and in other societies (Mbiti 1970: 2). Legal principles also had to be qualified (Quint. 7.6.1, 5;

principles could conflict among themselves if applied beyond the situation to which they most clearly applied (e.g., Prov 26:4-5).[92] Two similar divorce sayings in different contexts, both with good claim to be genuine sayings of Jesus, actually conflict if pressed literally: Mark 10:9 assumes that divorce should not but can occur; the Q saying in Matthew 5:32//Luke 16:18 assumes that marriage is indissoluble and a genuine divorce *cannot* occur. But the conflict arises from ignoring Jesus' teaching style (Catchpole 1993: 238): "that disharmony simply means that each saying must be read as a demand rather than a law, and that the overarching social function of both must be recognized. That function is a call for absolute faithfulness in and to marriage."

To put the matter differently, Jesus "probably intended [this saying] to be more haggadic than halakhic; that is, its purpose was not to lay down the law but to reassert an ideal and make divorce a sin, thereby disturbing then current complacency" (Davies and Allison 1988: 532).[93] In practice, the early Christians immediately began to qualify Jesus' divorce saying; other principles of Jesus, such as not condemning the innocent (12:7) or the principle of mercy (23:23), would have forced them to do so in some circumstances. For instance, when confronted by Christians wanting to divorce unbelieving spouses, Paul used Jesus' saying to forbid their design, but noted that if instead the spouse left, the believer was "not bound" (1 Cor 7:15).[94] Paul's words recall the *exact* language for freedom to remarry in ancient divorce contracts, and his ancient readers, unable to be confused by modern writers' debates on the subject, would have understood his words thus (e.g., m. Giṭ. 9:3; *CPJ* 2:10-12, §144; Carmon 1973: 90-91, 200-201, §189; Harrell 1967: 71; Keener 1991a: 61-62).[95] The exception Matthew states is the spouse's unfaithfulness to the marriage (for the full argument, see comment on 19:9).

Paul's and Matthew's exceptions (Mt 5:32; 19:9; 1 Cor 7:15, 27-28) constitute two-thirds of the extant first-century Christian references to divorce, and both point to the same kind of exception: the person whose marriage is ended against his or her will.[96] In other words, Jesus' exceptions do not constitute an

---

cf. Arist. *Rhet.* 1.17.1354a; frequently in rabbinic texts), which is how Tannehill 1975: 72-73 takes this saying (and with whom we would agree in its Matthean form). Even the brief quips concluding many controversy-*chreiai,* as in Mt 19:9, functioned in this manner (cf., e.g., Plut. *Agesilaus* 21.4-5; *Statecraft* 7, *Mor.* 803CD; *Sayings of Spartan Women,* passim; Diog. Laert. 1.35; 2.72; 6.2.51).

92. Thus similarly tears of entreaty might generally fail (Pub. Syr. 128, 200), but those of a wife would succeed (Pub. Syr. 19, 153, 384); deliberation is both good and bad, depending on the situation (Pub. Syr. 162-63, 178); honor rarely returns to one who loses it, and one who truly has honor never loses it (Pub. Syr. 211-12). The genre naturally accommodates considerable paradox.

93. Cf. likewise Down 1984; Molldrem 1991; Parker 1993; Hagner 1995: 551.

94. Some works too recent for citation in Keener 1991a also view Paul's exception as implying that Jesus' prohibition is "not comprehensive" (Blomberg 1992a: 111-12; Vermes 1993: 34n.34).

95. In 1 Cor 7:27-28, the NIV mistranslates: rightly noting that one who is married should not "seek a divorce" (7:27a), they translate the same Greek word for divorce as "unmarried" in the next line, where remarriage is permitted (7:27b-28).

96. As Blomberg 1992a: 293 reasons, other exceptions probably exist, but they must be governed by the principle that unites the two biblical exceptions: (1) both infidelity and abandonment de-

excuse to escape a difficult marriage (cf. 1 Cor 7:10-14); they exonerate those who genuinely wished to save their marriage but were unable to do so because their spouse's unrepentant adultery, abandonment, or abuse de facto destroyed the marriage bonds.

Jesus used hyperbole to underline graphically a controversial point. Palestinian Jewish husbands could divorce for virtually any reason (Jos. *Ant.* 4.253), explicitly including their wives' disobedience (Sir 25:26; ARN 1A; Jos. *Life* 426, the latter apparently including something beyond her control) or for burning the bread (m. Giṭ. 9:10; Sifre Deut. 269.1.1). By removing the right of divorce, Jesus is probably protecting a wife from being betrayed by her husband (Kysar 1978: 43; Davies 1993: 54).

Although the thrust of this passage is faithfulness to one's marriage, Matthew's exception clause does not allow his readers to apply his rhetorical overstatement legalistically. Indeed, to read the Sermon on the Mount "legalistically as a set of rules is to miss the point; it represents a demand more radical than any legislator could conceive" (France 1985: 106), still less enforce. Jesus' central point, which the hyperbolic image is meant to evoke, is the sanctity of marriage (cf. 19:4-6; Efird 1985: 57-59). Addressing the hardness of legal interpreters' hearts (19:8), Jesus opposed divorce to protect marriage and family, thereby seeking to prevent the betrayal of innocent spouses.

Oaths are a Poor Substitute for Integrity (5:33-37)

Cf. Jas 5:12. When Jesus cites his Bible as prohibiting false vows and other oaths (Deut 23:23),[97] he probably also has in view the Decalogue, as in Matthew 5:21 and 27. In this case he alludes to the third commandment in the Decalogue: a false oath "misuses" or takes in vain God's name, because oaths by definition called on a deity to witness them (Ex 20:7; Hom. *Il.* 1.273; 14.158; Soph. *Oed. Rex* 646-48).[98] Breaking an oath was dangerous, for in all societies oaths contained curses that deities would avenge if the person who swore by them broke

---

stroy one of the basic components of marriage; (2) "Both leave one party without any other options if attempts at reconciliation are spurned"; and (3) both use divorce "as a last resort." That some will abuse this freedom (as he also warns) cannot make us insensitive to the innocent party who genuinely needs that freedom.

97. By the time of Tannaitic writings, many used *neder* (vow) and *shevu'ah* (oath) interchangeably, or (as in m. Ned. 2:2) with differences only in technical, theoretical discussions (Lachs 1987: 100-101).

98. The ancient world in general regarded keeping vows as pious (e.g., Isoc. *Demon.* 13, *Or.* 1) and oath violation as wicked (Hesiod *W.D.* 190, 194); oaths were considered sacred (e.g., Aul. Gel. 6.18; though pagan deities might break them — Hom. *Il.* 15.36-44); some were considered morally helpful (Num. Rab. 15:16; Ruth Rab. 6:4). One normally swore an oath by a deity (e.g., Apul. *Metam.* 2.5), and a false oath profaned God's name (e.g., Ex 20:7; Sifra Qed. par. 2.199.1.6). A very early Jewish teacher allegedly made people accountable to God for vows merely offered in one's heart (p. Sanh. 6:6, §2); God would also punish breaking one's word (b. B. Meṣ. 49a, bar.).

the oath (e.g., Hom. *Il.* 3.276-80; Hesiod *Theog.* 231; Eurip. *Medea* 752-55; Demosth. *Against Timocrates* 151; Dion. Hal. 7.43.1; Paus. 2.2.1; Livy 10.38.10; 21.10.9; Corn. Nep. 17 [Agesilaus], 2.5; Babrius 50.17; Deut 5:11; p. Giṭ. 4:3, §1);[99] Jewish legal experts also demanded punishment of those who swore oaths they could not keep (p. Sukk. 5:2, §1). The Bible's *point* in prohibiting false oaths, however, was that one should tell the truth and keep one's promises. The Hebrew Bible approved of some oaths and vows (e.g., Num 5:19-22; 6:2), but Jesus again summons his disciples beyond the law's letter to its intention.[100] His own point is not so much that oaths are evil as that the motivation for engaging in them is; one should simply tell the truth (5:37).[101]

Although Jesus' position on oaths is not wholly unique, it was rare enough to be distinctive. Following the line of reasoning in Ecclesiastes 5:4 (cf. also Sir 23:9-13), some Jewish teachers warned against customary oath taking, but others disagreed (Sifre Deut. 265.1.1; ARN 26A; 32, §72B), and nearly all accepted oath taking as valid (though limited in its application, e.g., Jos. *Ant.* 15.370; 17.42; Sanders 1990: 53); in daily life, the practice was surely common in the marketplace (Malina and Rohrbaugh 1992: 55), among other places. While a priest of Jupiter, one was not permitted to swear oaths (Livy 31.49.7). Some groups of Essenes may have also avoided oaths altogether (Jos. *War* 2.135; *Ant.* 15.370-71), except their initiatory oath for joining the sect (Jos. *War* 2.139-42; cf. 1QS 5.8; Black 1961: 94, 120).[102] Josephus declares that one could trust an Essene's word more than an oath, however (*War* 2.135). Philo indicates that their abstention from oaths declared their commitment to truth (*Every Good Man Is Free* 84; also Vermes 1993: 35), thus affirming that keeping one's oath was good, but that not swearing because one's word was as good as an oath was even better (*Decal.* 84-85).

Jesus and the Essenes probably intended the same as Pythagoras: let one's word carry such conviction that one need not call deities to witness (Diog. Laert. 8.1.22; cf. Diod. Sic. 10.9.2). The Jewish philosopher Philo declared that an honorable man's word should be as truthful as any oath (Philo *Spec.* 2.2). Because oath taking in a deity's name was so serious, others also discouraged it except under the most extreme circumstances (Isoc. *Demon.* 23, *Or.* 1). One should so consistently tell the truth that hearers would value one's word more highly than other people's oaths (Isoc. *Nic.* 22, *Or.* 2; cf. Kollmann 1996 for other parallels).

99. See further Sanders 1990: 51; Ferguson 1987: 117, 184; Mbiti 1970: 277.

100. This "You heard it said" statement may actually be a Targumic sort of conflation of Lev 19:12 with Deut 23:24, hence not a verbatim quotation of the Torah itself (Vermes 1993: 34).

101. The parallel in Jas 5:12 supports pre-Matthean tradition (cf., e.g., Blank 1989); for a response to arguments against authenticity, see Ito 1991.

102. The Scrolls themselves indicate that some Essenes continued to take some kinds of oaths (Sanders 1990: 53; McNamara 1983: 197). Other groups were also joined by oaths (e.g., Jos. *Ant.* 15.282; Angus 1925: 78-79; in other societies, e.g., Mbiti 1970: 276); Martin relates Jas 5:12 to Zealot initiatory oaths (1988: lxix; cf. Acts 23:12, 14). Emperors (Jos. *Ant.* 18.124; 19.247; Epict. *Disc.* 1.14.15; Judge 1960: 34), rulers like Herod (Jos. *Ant.* 15.370), and the military (Livy 6.38.8; 10.4.3) also demanded oaths of loyalty.

The point of this passage is integrity. Letting one's "yes" function as a "yes" and "no" as a "no" seems to employ ancient Jewish figures of speech simply to demand that one be as good as one's word, that one keep one's word.[103] Jesus observes that since God witnesses every word one says anyway, one should be able to tell the truth without having to call God to witness by a formal oath (cf. Harrington 1982: 30; Jeremias 1971: 220; Manson 1979: 158-59).[104]

Jesus addresses a popular abuse of oaths in his day. To protect the sanctity of the divine name against inadvertent oath-breaking, common Jewish practice introduced *kinnuyim,* surrogate objects by which to swear (Vermes 1993: 34-35). Some people apparently thought it harmless to deceive if they swore oaths by something like their right hand (t. Ned. 1:1; cf. its use in agreements, e.g., Jos. *War* 2.451). Others took all oaths more seriously, but specifically warned against using God's name lest if one break the oath one profane God's name (Philo *Spec.* 2.4-5; cf. 1 Enoch 69:13-16; Pesiq. R. 22:6); sometimes vows could not be fulfilled (m. Ned. 3:1). Jewish teachers had to arbitrate which oaths were actually binding as allusions to God's name (m. Shebu. 4:13; cf. CD 15.1-5; Smith 1951: 136). The further removed the oath was from the actual name of God, the less danger they faced for violating it (Schiffman 1983: 137-38; Sanders 1990: 53-54). Some later teachers had to insist that all roundabout substitutes for vows were equivalent to vows (m. Ned. 1:1; Nazir 1:1). Sages undoubtedly had to evaluate vows' validity frequently because they had acquired the role of canceling bad vows (e.g., t. Pisha 2:16), extending an Old Testament privilege accorded male guardians of unattached women (Num 30:3-15).

Thus people swore by heaven and earth (many cite Philo *Spec.* 2.5; m. Shebu. 4:13), Jerusalem (many cite m. Ned. 1:3; others in Lachs 1987: 102), one's head (m. Sanh. 3:2), God's throne (Apoc. Mos. 19.2) and the temple service (Sifre Deut. 1.3.2). Jesus teaches that all oaths invoke God's witness equally. Just as heaven, earth (Is 66:1-2), and Jerusalem (Ps 48:2; Mt 4:5; 27:53) belong to God (5:34-35), so do the hairs on one's head (5:36; cf. 10:30); one has no genuine control over their aging (cf. 6:27; Pub. Syr. 215). (The assumption

103. Vermes 1993: 35 cites a rabbinic tradition (Mek. Baḥodesh 5 on Ex 20:2 in Lauterbach 2:229-30) in which the Israelites accepted Torah with a "yes" or a "yes yes" (the double "yes" presumably being a stronger formula); with many, Vermes takes this as a formula meant to function with an oath's force. I am more skeptical of the relevance of the parallel; "Let your yes prove a yes and your no a no" may be more appropriate (Lachs 1987: 102 cites b. B. Meṣ. 49a; Sheb. 36a; Ruth Rab. 3:18; Der. Er. Rab. 5.1). Cf. Gen. Rab. 73:9; 74:3, 11; Lachs 1987: 101; Boring 1995: 59 cite 2 Enoch 49:1 as a parallel, but it sounds dependent on Matthew.

104. The language of the passage probably reflects Jesus' own idiom; aspects of Matthew's version of the saying are more Semitic than the form in Jas 5:12 (Laws 1980: 222-23; Davids 1982: 190), though some elements in James's wording may be more original (Ropes 1916: 301). The expression "Let your 'yes' be 'yes'" as an exhortation to be sure of one's words would have made sense to Jesus' first hearers (cf. m. Giṭ. 7:1; Jeremias 1971: 220). Some contend that it may even have functioned as an oath-formula itself (Manson 1979: 159; Dibelius 1976: 250), but probably it is just a Semitic expression meaning something like one should let one's response be emphatic (Meier 1980: 53; Gundry 1982: 93; Guelich 1982: 218; Davids 1982: 190).

would have been that hair was black and turned white with age — Soph. *Antig.* 1092-93; Phaedrus 2.2.9-10; Babrius 22.2-3. Only deities and magicians could change colors — cf. Ovid *Metam.* 11.314.) All oaths implicitly call God to witness because everything that exists was made by him. This implies that for Jesus God was actively involved in all aspects of life; no part of life except sin was purely secular.

Avoiding oaths is thus inadequate; the issue is telling the truth because God witnesses every word one speaks. Human cultures developed oaths because people could not trust their neighbors without calling an avenging deity to witness; but those who recognize that God witnesses every word must speak and act from integrity of heart that transcends such formalities. Herod Antipas trapped himself by a foolish oath (14:7), people cheat their parents by wrongful vows of dedication (15:5), and Peter betrayed Jesus with false oaths (26:72, 74). Jesus, however, avoided formal oaths. Even when he made a vow of abstinence (26:29) — vows were normally confirmed with an appeal to the deity — he swore only by affirming, "I tell you." When the high priest "adjured" him, that is, put him under oath, he responded, "You said it" (26:64; see Gundry 1982: 93; Brant 1996: 19). Although his followers continued to call on God to witness the truth of some of their statements, apparently taking his words as rhetorical overstatement (e.g., Rom 1:9; 9:1; Gal 1:20), they seem to have refrained from more overt oaths (2 Cor 1:17, whose "yes, yes . . . no, no" probably reflects this Jesus tradition; Jas 5:12, also reflecting this Jesus tradition). Oaths that invite penalties on oneself for violating them (cf. today's "Cross my heart and hope to die") are not necessary for people of truth.

Avoid Retribution and Resistance (5:38-42)

Cf. Lk 6:29-30; Rom 12:14, 17-21; 1 Pet 2:23. Jesus here warns against legal retribution (5:38-39) and goes so far as to undercut legal resistance altogether with a verse that, if followed literally, would leave most disciples stark naked (5:40). He also advocates not only compliance but cooperation with a member of the occupying army who might be borrowing a worker from his livelihood (5:41), as well as helping the beggar or others who seek the disciple's help (5:42). To deny that Jesus here literally advocates nudity (an offense to Jewish culture that would surely have called for comment in the other sources!) and living on the street — that is, to affirm that Jesus is speaking the language of rhetorical overstatement (5:18-19, 29-32; 6:3) — is not to tone down the seriousness of his demand. Jesus produced hyperbole precisely to challenge his hearers, to force them to think about what they valued. Jesus' words in this case strike at the very core of human selfishness, summoning his disciples to value others above themselves in concrete and consistent ways. They have no honor or property worth defending compared with the opportunity to show how much they love God and everyone else. Nonretaliation appears unrealistic and may invite further aggression, but Jesus' way scorns the world's honor. It is the lifestyle of those who expect his coming kingdom (4:17).[105]

Jesus' first illustration challenges the desire for personal vindication — that is, revenge (5:38). "An eye for an eye" never meant that a person could exact vengeance directly for his or her own eye; it meant that one should take the offender to court where the sentence could be executed legally. Modern readers sometimes cite this example as a case of Jesus disagreeing with the Old Testament.[106] But Jesus is not so much revoking a standard for justice as calling his followers not to make use of it; they qualify justice with mercy because they do not need to avenge their honor.

"An eye for an eye and a tooth for a tooth" (Ex 21:23-25; Deut 19:21) was standard ancient Near Eastern law (e.g., Hammurabi 196-97, 200; Diod. Sic. 12.17.4), except that most legal collections besides the Old Testament varied the punishments according to one's social class (e.g., Hammurabi 196-223). This "eye for eye" form of law, called *lex talionis,* provides the foundation for legal ethics by making the punishment commensurate with the offense (Jeremias 1963: 28; Meier 1979: 261; Guelich 1982: 224). In the classless Old Testament version these laws made a just point: each person must recognize that another person's life and members were worth no less than one's own. But whereas some Israelite laws could serve as deterrents (cf. Deut 19:20; 21:21) or provide benefit for the person injured (Ex 21:19, 26-27), the *lex talionis* regulations primarily avenged the person's honor, vindicating the person by punishing the assailant. Contemporary Jewish law sought to remedy this weakness by providing monetary restitution as an alternative to maiming the offender: Jos. *Ant.* 4.280; cf. Cohen 1966: 1:18; Belkin 1940: 97-103; Vermes 1993: 36; cf. b. Ketub. 32ab.[107]

A society could, however, recognize the justice of "eye for eye" while its sages warned against bringing oneself down to one's oppressors' moral level by fighting evil with evil (Akkadian wisdom in *ANET* 426; cf. Phaedrus 1.29.10-11). Plato portrays Socrates as warning against returning evil for evil since one should never do evil at all (*Crito* 49B), and some Greek and Roman philosophers opposed vengeance, for example, because the body mattered little or for the sake of societal harmony (Sen. *Dial.* 3.6.5; 4.32.1; Fitzgerald 1988: 103-4).[108] Al-

105. For the history of the practice of this passage, including its use in the Acts of Martyrs, see Broer 1993c.

106. By contrast, Rathey 1991 suggests that this passage in fact *radicalizes* the OT by having the oppressed renounce revenge and allowing the enemy to take revenge instead. The passage renounces the right to restitution as well as revenge (cf. Schwienhorst-Schönberger 1990).

107. The penalty may remain literal in Jubilees (Grintz 1972: 325 if he is correct; the retribution there is divine, and appropriateness of divine retribution coexisted with monetary penalties in the rabbis); Falk 1985: 118 suggests that the Shammaites also held the literal view (based solely on R. Eliezer in b. B. Qam. 84A). But some ancient Near Eastern societies had already preferred monetary payments (e.g., Eshnunna 42-43).

108. On Plato *Crito* 47c-49d; *Rep.* 1.331e-336a, see Gill 1991; for Sen. *On Anger* 2.34.1 and Diog. Laert. 2.21, see Boring 1995: 59-60. The same principle carried over into persuasive rhetoric (Dion. Hal. 6.80.4). For not defending oneself in court, see Epict. *Disc.* 2.2.20.

though it was never the corporate norm (1 Macc 2:67; cf. Test. Levi 5:3), both ancient Israel (Ex 23:4-5; Lev 19:18; Job 31:29-30; Prov 24:17-18, 29; 25:21-22) and later Judaism (Sir 28:1-8; 1QS 10.17-19; CD 9.3-6; Ps-Phocyl. 77; Jos. and Asen. 23.9; 29.3; Ps-Philo 8:10; b. Ber. 17a; Shab. 88b, bar.; Yoma 23a; Flusser 1988: 506; cf. Rom 12:17-20; 2 Enoch 50:3-4) advocated nonresistance at times.[109] Sometimes such admonitions cover overt behavior more than attitudes (1QS 10.19-21), address only the treatment of fellow Jews (Sifra Qed. pq. 4.200.3.6), or prefer but do not demand nonviolence (Ps-Phocyl. 32-34, 151), but those Jewish pietists who could release pursuit of their own honor could do so precisely because they left their vindication with God (1QS 11.1-2; Jos. *War* 5.377) and his day of justice (Rom 12:19; 1QS 10.19-20; 2 Enoch 50:4; cf. Stendahl 1962; the Pythagorean idea in Thom 1994: 111, citing Iamb. *VP* 155, 179).[110] Jesus calls for this humble response of faith in God; God alone is the center of existence and the final arbiter of justice.

Turning the other cheek summons disciples to neglect their honor and let God vindicate them when he wills (5:39). As in much of Jesus' (and Matthew's) teaching, pressing the illustration the wrong way may obscure the point, reading Scripture the very way he elsewhere warned against (12:2-5; 19:7-8): if someone strikes a disciple in the nose (rather than on the cheek), or has already struck both cheeks, is a disciple free to hit back? But Jesus provides a radical example to teach the principle of nonretaliation, not so disciples will explore the limits of his example (cf. Tannehill 1975: 73).[111]

A backhanded blow to the right cheek did not imply shattered teeth ("tooth for tooth" was a separate statement); it was an insult, the severest public affront to a person's dignity (Job 16:10; Lam 3:30; m. B. Qam. 8:6; Plut. *Platonic Questions* 9.4, *Mor.* 1010F).[112] God's prophets had sometimes suffered such ill-treatment (1 Kings 22:24; 2 Chron 18:23; Is 50:6; Jeremias 1963: 29), as Jesus would himself (26:67; cf. Mic 5:1). Yet though this was more an affront to honor, a challenge, than a physical injury, ancient Near Eastern societies typically pro-

109. Others allowed but qualified resistance: Josephus tells Gentiles that Jews cannot plunder their enemies (Jos. *Life* 128). Some read Matthew's nonresistance teaching as an inaccurate critique of contemporary Judaism (Broer 1994), but it is quite unlikely that Matthew, immersed in Jewish thought, would be unaware that many of his contemporaries did teach nonresistance on some level.

110. God is the avenger in Jdt 9:2; 1 Enoch 54:6; Jub. 48:14; 1QS 1.11; 2.6, 9; 4.12; 9.23; *CIJ* 1:385, §526; p. Qidd. 4:1, §2; an angel in 1 Enoch 20:4; some Greek deities in Barthell 1971: 25-26; Diogenes *Ep.* 45.

111. Some also misread this text as if it forbids one to oppose injustice; what it really says, however, is that one should be so unselfish and trust God so much that one leaves one's vindication with him. (The Greek phrase in 5:39 probably warns against resisting "an evil person," not against resisting evil itself — Tasker 1961: 70.)

112. Jeremias 1963: 28; idem 1971: 239; Moore 1971: 2:151n.3; Daube 1973: 260-61; Malina 1981: 35; Lachs 1987: 106 cites Sifra Lev. 24:19; t. B. Qam. 9:29; b. B. Meṣ. 59b; Sanh. 58b. Resistance to unjust arrest, by contrast, might involve physically harsher blows in the face with one's fists (Dion. Hal. 9.39.3); severer beatings also involved shame (e.g., Hom. *Il.* 2.265-70; 1 Thess 2:2).

vided legal recourse for this offense within the *lex talionis* regulations (e.g., Hammurabi 202-6; cf. Gaius *Inst.* 3.220).[113]

In the case of an offense to one's personal dignity, Jesus not only warns the offended disciple not to retaliate, but suggests that the disciple indulge the offender further. By freely offering one's other cheek, one demonstrates that one does not value human honor. In a sense, this could constitute a form of resistance by showing contempt for the value of the insulter's (and perhaps the onlookers') opinions (Sall. *Invective against Marcus Tullius* 1; Diog. Laert. 6.2.58; Diogenes *Ep.* 20). Thus philosophers sometimes declared that the best vengeance on one's opponents was to avoid behaving foolishly as they did (Marc. Aur. 6.6). Even in a society obsessed with honor and shame (e.g., Sir 1:30), a disciple must be so secure in his or her status before God that he or she can dispense with human honor. Such a person need not avenge lost honor because this person seeks God's honor rather than his or her own (5:16; 6:1-18). If their lives are forfeit when they begin to follow Jesus (16:24-27), they have no honor of their own to lose.

Jesus takes this image of **legal nonresistance farther by saying that rather than trying to get one's inner garment back by legal recourse, one should relinquish the outer one, too (5:40).** This practice would lead to nudity (see also Stein 1978: 10), an intolerable dishonor in Palestinian Jewish society (e.g., Gen 3:7, 10-11; 9:22; Jub. 3:21-22, 30-31; 7:8-10, 20; 1QS 7.12; Sifre Deut. 320.5.2). Many peasants (at least in poorer areas like Egypt) had only one outer cloak (e.g., Hom. *Od.* 14.513-14; Babrius 131.10-11) and pursued whatever legal recourse necessary to get it back if it were seized (*CPJ* 1:239-40, §129.5); without the cloak a person would be naked and cold (e.g., Babrius 131.14). Because the outer cloak doubled as a poor man's bedding, biblical law permitted no one to take it even as a pledge overnight (Ex 22:26-27; Deut 24:12-13); Jesus demands that one surrender the one possession the law explicitly protects from legal seizure (Guelich 1982: 222).[114] Jesus provides a shockingly graphic, almost humorous, illustration of what he means by nonresistance to force his hearers to consider their values. They value honor and *things* more than they value the kingdom.

113. On this and other ancient Near Eastern laws missing in the OT but preserved in the rabbis, cf. Greengus 1991. One might be levied a fine for humiliating an honorable person not only with a blow (e.g., m. B. Qam. 8:6) but also without one (the heavy fine for humiliating a sage in p. B. Qam. 8:6, §1); in third-century-B.C. Egypt the fine for one blow was over one-third of a year's average wages (*P. Hal.* 1.203-5). Malina and Rohrbaugh 1992: 55 suggest that in Mediterranean cultures friends will break up a public fight; by deferring to one's friends' intervention rather than avenging one's own honor, one allows the door of reconciliation with the offender to remain open. The situation depicted in the text, however, is an act of insult, not a physical brawl, though the same might apply.

114. Luke's form of the saying, in which the outer garment is seized first, pictures robbery (various commentators, e.g., Stein 1978: 151n.8; Gundry 1982: 95; Davies and Allison 1988: 545; the latter may well be correct that Matthew's form is more original, though Gundry argues the opposite), which was a common feature of village life in Egypt, where our records are most complete (Lewis 1983: 77).

This passage is a graphic image, but if pressed literally, it implies that disciples should never take anyone to court. This may be hyperbole, but again it challenges disciples to value the kingdom above anything the world can take from them.[115] (Ancient Mediterranean society, particularly urban Roman society, had become quite litigious; see Hor. *Sat.* 1.9; Dio Cassius 60.28.6; MacMullen 1974: 64-65.) One may compare the Stoic philosopher Epictetus, a former slave: one should surrender one's cloak or even one's body to those who demand it, for none of these things belongs to one anyway (*Disc.* 1.24.11-14; 1.25.21; cf. 1.18.16; 2.2.20).[116] One must thus love one's enemies and seek to turn them into friends, as many moralists pointed out.[117] Of course, one can do so only insofar as that is possible (Rom 12:18; cf. Sir 9:14); yet even when it is not possible, those who act justly and mercifully may trust God's vindication in the end.

The principle challenges any prior loyalties, not only to possessions but to one's people. In the context of recent violent resistance against Rome, the message of 5:38-42 probably also had "pacifistic implications" (Davies and Allison 1988: 542, though their wording may be a bit strong for the 30s of the first century).

Jesus commands disciples to love even their oppressors (5:41). Because tax revenues did not cover all the Roman army's needs, soldiers could requisition what they required (Lewis 1985: 172-73; *Dig.* 50.4.18.4; 50.5.10.2-3; 50.5.11; *Cod. Theod.* 8 *passim* in Rapske 1994: 14; Sall. *Jug.* 75.4) and legally demand local inhabitants to provide forced labor (27:32).[118] Throughout the duration of Roman rule soldiers were known to sometimes abuse this privilege, often annoying the senate as well as local residents (Livy 43.7.11; 43.8.1-10; Apul. *Metam.* 9.39; Herodian 2.3.4; 2.5.1; *P. Lond.* 3.1171, *IGLS* 5.1998 = *SEG* 17.755 in Sherk 1988: 89, 136; *P.S.I.* 446; Jones 1970: 197; Llewelyn 1994: 80-85; cf. *P. Hal.* 1.166-85); later rabbis told of Romans forcing Jews to carry burdens on the Sabbath during Hadrian's oppression (p. Ḥag. 2:1, §8). Writers frequently employed this verse's term "forces" in this sense,[119] and it is probably no coinci-

115. Cf. also 1 Cor 6:1-8, perhaps dependent on Jesus' teaching. When Paul wrote that passage, believers were a persecuted minority in the Empire, and bad press about internal dissension was the last thing they needed. The Romans allowed synagogues to function as courts for local Jewish communities, arbitrating cases within their own communities, and churches could function analogously (cf. Hare 1967: 102; Grant 1977: 38).

116. Not all Greek philosophers responded as graciously as Epictetus. Diogenes the Cynic, who had but one cloak, reportedly refused to give his up, claiming that it was in use (Diog. Laert. 6.2.62).

117. Rom 12:21; Ep. Arist. 227; Ps-Phocyl. 142; Test. Benj. 4:3; Diog. Laert. 8.1.23; Hierocles *Duties. Fraternal Love* 4.27.20; Ariston 1 in Plut. *Sayings of Spartans, Mor.* 218A; Pub. Syr. 142; b. Ber. 17a.

118. On the Roman administration's use of local transport services, see, e.g., the *kanōn* in Horsley 1981: 36-45; most fully, Llewelyn 1994: 58-92.

119. Cf. Deissmann 1923: 86-87; Manson 1979: 160; Hill 1972: 128; Fenton 1977: 93; France 1985: 127.

dence that Matthew uses for a measure of distance the originally Latin term "mile" (Sider 1979: 26-27; somewhat shorter than our mile). Thus Matthew presumably means submission to a Roman soldier's demands (Fuller 1980: 157; Derrett 1973: 89; Guelich 1982: 222-23; Llewelyn 1994: 86-87), a necessity to which some other non-Romans acceded (others cite Epict. *Disc.* 4.1.79; m. 'Abot 3:17). Yet "going the *extra* mile" is not only a case of submitting to unjust demands but also of exceeding them — showing love to one's oppressor, although one's associates may wrongly view this love as collaboration with the enemy occupation. It is bending over backward to show that one loves and takes no offense.

Jesus and Paul responded firmly to unjust blows in the face (Jn 18:22-23; Acts 23:2-5) and in other circumstances (Jn 8:40-44; Acts 16:37; 22:25; 25:11; 26:25) without retaliating in their own interests; the text need not rule out all forms of resistance (cf. Clavier 1957; France 1985: 126; Vermes 1993: 36). Certainly Matthew would affirm, however, that those experiencing persecution for their faith should not retaliate (some think that this is the primary focus of the passage: Jeremias 1963: 28-29; idem 1971: 239; Danker 1972: 84-85). Jesus himself lashed out against the spiritual oppressors of his day (Mt 23), perhaps out of compassion for those the religious leaders oppressed (Mt 12:7; 23:4-13), taking a prophetic stance against shepherds unconcerned for God's wounded and broken sheep (Ezek 34:2-6; cf. Manson 1979: 52-53). But in any case, the purpose for resistance against injustice on behalf of others or speaking for justice on one's own behalf is not the defense of one's honor; and Jesus requires those who work for justice to do so without the weapon of hate (cf. Thurman 1981: 88).

Some rightly observe that Jesus' warnings against resistance address personal resistance rather than nations at war (Neil 1976: 160-62; for other views, see Luz 1989: 457-59); it is unlikely that Jesus or Matthew envisioned nations adjusting to the notion of Christian self-sacrifice. Yet prohibiting personal involvement in violence hardly seems irrelevant to disciples' active participation in national wars (cf. Sider 1979). Even just wars such as international police actions do invariably kill unwilling participants unjustly; to what extent would Matthew, had he anticipated the question, felt disciples could participate in such wars and to what extent would it be appropriate to wait for God to raise up others, like the Babylonians or Assyrians of old, to do the job? Some Christian interpreters respond that God's kingdom is no longer tied with the nation-state as in the Old Testament (Craigie 1978: 102, 110-11), and Christians going to war for one country or tribe now may kill Christians warring for another country or tribe. The text was not designed to answer such questions; the early Christians apparently saw themselves as a persecuted minority sect until their Lord's imminent return and left little direct counsel for a world in which Christians could feel at home without compromise.

Social conditions differ from one place and era to another, and even the nature of protest differs today from a situation envisioned by the early Christians. In first-century Palestine, few "safe" vehicles existed for nonviolent social protest against the Romans; the Romans viewed most public protest as linked with revolution, and punished it accordingly. In a society like ours where Christian egalitarianism has helped shape conceptions of justice, nonviolent protest stands a much better chance of working. How far did Jesus and Matthew expect disciples to carry nonviolence? In Matthew, Jesus himself exemplifies the meekness he prescribes (11:29). When the time appointed by his Father arrived, Jesus allowed people to crucify him, trusting his Father's coming vindication to raise him from the dead (17:11; 20:18-19; 26:52-53). He was too meek to cry out or bruise a reed until the time would come to bring "justice to victory" (12:19-20). Yet he would proclaim justice (12:18), openly denounced the unjust (23:13-36), and actively, even violently (but nonlethally), protested unrighteousness although he knew what it would cost him (21:12-13). He called his disciples to be both harmless as doves and wise as serpents (10:16) — in short, to be ruled by the law of love (22:39). Love of neighbor not only does no harm to one's neighbor, but bids disciples place themselves in harm's way to protect their neighbors. Jesus modeled a prophetic activism inseparable from martyrdom.

One must surrender one's possessions to whoever requests them (5:42). Judaism recognized giving to beggars who requested alms as a moral though not legal obligation (Guelich 1982: 223). It stressed both charity and a high work ethic; most beggars genuinely had no alternative means of income.[120] Still, giving *anything* requested to whoever asks for it (cf. Corn. Nep 5 [Cimon], 4.2, perhaps a rhetorical overstatement) would quickly leave the giver a beggar, too, once word of one's limitless generosity spread; this practice would quickly reduce one to the possessionless lifestyle of Cynic mendicants (cf. Schweizer 1975: 130).

Some Jewish teachers also urged lending to those who wished to borrow (Moore 1971: 2:168; Bonsirven 1964: 152-53) or reproved those who would too quickly demand repayment (Sir 20:15); others, however, warned of the danger of losses (Sir 19:4; Syr. Men. Sent. 181-88). Likewise, although some sages considered usury the severest of sins (e.g., Tannaim in b. B. Meṣ. 71a; cf. Jos. *Apion* 2.208; *Ant.* 4.266; Ex. Rab. 31:13), businessmen found ways to get around biblical laws against usury (Gamoran 1976), and Gentile creditors (who naturally expected repayment, e.g., Mart. *Epig.* 2.3; 3.40) were more than ready to seize property to recover outstanding debts (*P. Cairo Zen.* 59001.39-43; *P. Amh.* 50; *P. Oxy.* 269).[121] Further, despite pietists' warnings against pursuing debts ruthlessly

120. In a society dominated by honor and shame, some considered it better to die than to beg (Sir 40:28-30; cf. Diog. *Ep.* 34); few would resort to that lifestyle unnecessarily. Work generally generated more income than begging anyway; especially among Gentiles, begging usually met refusal (Diog. *Ep.* 11; Diog. Laert. 6.2.49). Jewish sages might limit recipients to the godly (Sir 12:1-2, 4, 7), to needy Israelites (Sifra Qed. pq. 3.198.1.5).

121. Interest rates were high among Israel's neighbors (e.g., Eshnunna 18A; Albright 1968: 181; De Vaux 1961: 171). Reportedly Greek and Roman law had originally opposed usury but gradually acquiesced to it (Appian *C.W.* 1.6.54; cf. Hladik 1992); thus although a few ancient Greek sages regarded usury as unnatural (Arist. *Pol.* 1.3.23, 1258b), interest rates continued to run high (*P. Cairo Zen.* 59001.34), in the Roman world averaging around 12% and known to rise as high as nearly 50%

(Ps-Phocyl. 83; p. Ta῾an. 3:11, §4), Jewish teachers also expected repayment (cf., e.g., Sir 8:12) and even devised ways to guarantee it, lest people quit lending (cf. Sanders 1992: 427-28). Whereas some teachers wanted to impose limits on charity (roughly 20 percent beyond tithes) lest one impoverish oneself out of well-intentioned devotion (Hengel 1974b: 20; cf. Jeremias 1969: 127), Jesus places no cap on giving. Yet while Jesus lived simply, especially once he began his itinerant ministry, Matthew implies that he did have a home (4:13). But if Jesus merely counseled, "Live simply," without confronting his disciples with forceful images, they might define simplicity in terms of their desires rather than in terms of the world's needs; his forceful rhetoric demands that his disciples contemplate his intention.

Again Jesus invites his hearers to grapple with his point, to which he will return with far greater force in 6:19-34. If nonresistance means disdaining one's right to one's own honor (5:38-39), one's most basic possessions (5:40), and one's labor and time (5:41) when others seek them by force, one must also disdain these things in view of the needs of the poor (5:42). When the kingdom comes, one's deeds rather than one's wealth will matter (6:19-21; cf. 25:34-46); in the meantime those who disdain everything else for the kingdom (13:44-45) must do with these other possessions what Jesus wills: give them to those who need them more (19:21). One's "vested interests" must be in heaven, not on earth (6:19-21); if one cannot value the kingdom that much, one has no place in it (19:29-30).

Love Your Enemies (5:43-48)

Cf. Lk 6:27-28, 32-36; Rom 12:20-21. Jesus not only demands nonresistance toward evil people assaulting one's honor or possessions (5:38-42; cf. Jas 5:6), but that one go so far as actively to love one's enemies.[122] Luke's version of this command is fuller, but Matthew's is clear enough. Jesus' teaching here develops a principle already present in the law: one should not allow personal animosity to prevent acts of kindness or justice (Ex 23:5; b. B. Meṣ. 32b).

(Grant 1977: 80; Oakman 1991: 157). Egyptian villagers had to borrow money to pay taxes, the debts to be repaid at harvest at 50% interest; debts were inherited if the father died (Lewis 1983: 71, 218n.9; cf. Grant 1992: 90). Warnings about the danger of borrowing money at high interest rates or that would otherwise be difficult to repay constituted a commonplace (e.g., Demosth. *On the Embassy* 99; Pub. Syr. 11; Petron. *Sat.* 57; Plut. *Love of Wealth* 2, *Mor.* 523F-24A; *That We Ought Not to Borrow, Mor.* 827D-32A; Ahiqar 111, saying 29; 130-31, saying 43; Sir 18:33; m. 'Abot 2:9; b. Sanh. 22a). Judaism regarded as pious forgiving those who could not repay (Test. Job 11:11/10).

122. The preceding paragraph already began to imply this (e.g., 5:41); in Luke both teachings belong to the same paragraph (Lk 6:27-36). Wink 1991 defends the authenticity of this teaching on the basis of dissimilarity: who else taught defying one's oppressors by exceeding their demands? One sets the terms for the oppressor rather than the reverse, forcing them to make the next choice, thus actively rather than passively confronting them (Wink 1992; cf. idem 1993). Buddhism and Taoism teach loving one's enemies (Gnilka 1997: 226-27), but geographically represent an unlikely source for Jesus' teaching.

Jesus probably addresses all kinds of enemies. When Jesus explains his final quotation from the Torah, "Love your neighbors," he adds to the quotation an implication some of his contemporaries found there: "Hate your enemies." Perhaps because public greetings were so important (see on 23:7), some teachers defined as a personal enemy a person who had not spoken to you for a month (Abrahams 1924: 213). Jesus could certainly have addressed personal enmity in the setting of Galilean villages (Horsley 1986a; Freyne 1988: 154).

Jesus' contemporaries might, however, perhaps have thought less of Scripture advocating hatred toward a personal enemy than toward a corporate threat to Israel or the moral fabric of the community (cf. Borg 1987: 139), such as "outsiders" to Israel (Vermes 1993: 157). Whereas the biblical command to love neighbors (Lev 19:18) included foreigners in the land (Lev 19:33-34; cf. Lk 10:27-37) and implied doing right even to one's personal enemy (Ex 23:4-5), other texts revered a passionate devotion to God's cause that bred hatred of those who opposed it (Ps 139:21-22; cf. 137:7-9).[123] Popular piety, exemplified in the Qumran community's oath to "hate the children of darkness" (cf. Jos. *War* 2.139; cf. 1QS 1.3-4; 9.16, 21-22), may have extended such biblical ideology in Jesus' day.[124] The Qumran community was certainly not alone, of course (cf. Guelich 1982: 226; Gundry 1982: 96); as well as loving friends and hating enemies fits human self-interest, we should not be surprised to find the dictum and/or practice elsewhere.[125] Probably both personal and corporate enemies are in view (Moulder 1978).

Jesus argues his case by appealing to a positive and negative example. Examples, both positive and negative, were a standard part of ancient argumentation. First Jesus provides the ultimate moral example: God. Jesus chooses a line of argument that would not have been controversial among ancient hearers. Jewish teachers generally recognized, like Jesus, that God was gracious to all humanity, including the morally undeserving (Sifre Deut. 43.3.6; Bonsirven 1964: 13-14; cf. Test. Jud. 21:6; Tit 3:4); some Greek sages declared the same (Epict.

123. Lachs 1987: 107 suggests that later rabbinic haggadah recognized the universal application, whereas halakic texts restricted the principle to fellow Israelites (citing Mek. Nezikin 4, Laut. 3:37, on Ex. 21:14; Sifre Deut. 112; 266).

124. On holy war in the OT and the Qumran Scrolls, see Nielsen 1961. Cf. Sutcliffe 1960; Seitz 1969: 51; F. F. Bruce 1969: 74; Yamauchi 1972: 144; Sanders 1993: 211; on hating the *minim,* schismatics, cf. Sifre Deut. 331.1.2; ARN 16A. Given the lack of significant parallels from Qumran and rabbinic sources, some here claim that the criterion of dissimilarity supports the authenticity of Jesus' teaching to love one's enemies (Q material; see Lk 6:27, 35); see Merkel 1984: 144; Stanton 1995a: 176.

125. Others have suggested that Jesus by "hate" means "love less" (cf. Mt 10:37 with Lk 14:26) and that he insists on favoring one's enemy *over* one's neighbor (cf. Linton 1964); this suggestion is unlikely, though it would be quite appropriate to Jesus' practice of rhetorical overstatement in the context, because it would have been more characteristic of Jesus to make such overstatement explicit. Hatred of enemies appears frequently outside Judaism (Davies and Allison 1988: 549 cite Polyb. 18.37.7; Hesiod *Op.* 342-43; Solon *Fr.* 1.3-5; Plato *Tim.* 17d-18a; *Rep.* 375C; *Meno* 71E; Tac. *Hist.* 5.5.-6); on Hesiod *Works and Days* 342-43, 352-56 see Bouttier 1978. Perhaps speaking more generally, some contended that true goodness must be shown without prejudice to all (Pub. Syr. 99).

Disc. 1.6.42; Marc. Aur. 7.70; cf. Petron. *Sat.* 100). Jewish sages saw rain as one of God's universal signs of beneficence.[126] Like Jesus in this passage, other moralists sometimes invited their hearers to show mercy to all as God did to them (Test. Zeb. 7:2; Marc. Aur. 9.11), and not to repay evil for evil (Ex. Rab. 26:2). Jewish teachers also recognized that those who imitated God's kindness were truly his children (Sir 4:10; Montefiore 1968: 2:81).

After adducing the ultimate moral example, Jesus offers an example from the opposite end of his hearers' moral spectrum: even those they considered the most immoral met the standard of righteousness practiced by Jesus' most pious hearers. Jesus thus provokes his hearers to shame by comparing their ability to obey the love commandment with that of tax gatherers and non-Jews (the latter were generally idolaters), the epitome of moral reprobates (Mt 6:7; 18:17; 20:25; cf., e.g., Sifre Deut. 43.16.1; Gen. Rab. 60:5; some other teachers also shamed hearers by such examples; see, e.g., b. Qidd. 31a). Most people would have agreed that everyone, including sinners, loved those who loved them (cf. Sifre Deut. 24.3.1). Indeed, both Jewish (Ps-Phocyl. 152; Test. Benj. 4:2; Flusser 1988: 506; Sanders 1992: 234-35) and Greek (Diog. Laert. 1.78; 6.1.12; cf. Plut. *Profit by Enemies, Mor.* 86B-92F; Pub. Syr. 188) sages sometimes admonished against hating one's enemies, although the more common sentiment in practice — then as today — was to make sure you did your enemies more harm than they did to you (Isoc. *Demon.* 26, *Or.* 1). One whose righteousness would surpass that of the scribes and Pharisees (5:20) must exemplify a higher standard of righteousness than loving those friendly to one's own interests.

Jesus builds a fence around the law of love (22:39), amplifying it to its ultimate conclusion (cf. Ex 23:4-5). In so doing, he makes demands more stringent than the law itself. One may similarly compare Jesus' command to pray for those who persecute one (5:44); he hardly has in mind the sort of prayer for vengeance characteristic of earlier biblical tradition (2 Chron 24:22; Jer 15:15; cf. Syr. Men. Sent. 126-32)![127] But again, his words are graphic pictures that force his followers to probe their hearts; they do not cancel the Hebrew Bible's trust in divine

126. Jewish sages saw God's gift of rain as one of his ultimate acts of power and beneficence (b. Ber. 33a; Ta'an. 2ab, 7a; p. Ta'an. 1:1, §2; Lev. Rab. 35:8; Flusser 1988: 482; cf. 1 Enoch 2:3; 6:7; Mbiti 1970: 47, 53, 234-37), and recognized it as for all people, worthy or unworthy (p. B. Meṣ. 2:5, §2; 9:5, §1; Gen. Rab. 13:6, 15; Pesiq. R. 48:4; Flusser 1988: 490-91). This generally remained true even when they said it came only on Israel's account (Gen. Rab. 66:2; cf. b. Ta'an. 19b, bar.) or through the intercessions of the righteous (Jas 5:17-18; Jos. *Ant.* 8.343-46; 14.22; m. Ta'an. 3:8; ARN 6A; b. Ta'an. 8a, 23a-26a; p. Ta'an. 1:4, §1; 3:9, §§6-8; 3:11, §4; cf. Diog. Laert. 8.2.59-60) or that it rained more in righteous generations (Sifra Behuq. pq. 1.261.1.4; cf. Deut 28:12; 1 Enoch 101:2; Ps. Sol. 17:18; Sifre Deut. 37.3.2; 41.6.4). That all share the same blessing (or fate — Sir 8:7) was an appropriate basis for calling one not to despise others.

127. Cf. also the summons to pray for persecutors (Lk 6:28), which, while in Q, is emphasized more by Luke-Acts (Lk 23:34; Acts 7:60; cf. Did. 1.3; Pol. *Phil.* 12; Acts of Peter 28; Acts of John 81; Test. Jos. 18:2). Some second-century Jewish sources prefer prayer for one's enemies' repentance to prayer for their judgment (R. Meir in b. Ber. 10a in Lachs 1987: 108; Test. Abr. 10:12-15 A).

vindication (23:33, 38; cf. 2 Tim 4:14; Rev 6:10-11), but they summon disciples to leave their vindication with God and seek others' best interests in love.

Jesus demands that disciples be perfect like God (5:48). What Jesus illustrated by graphic, concrete examples earlier in the sermon (5:21-47) he now epitomizes in a summary statement that forces his hearers to go beyond mere examples. For example, loving one's enemy is an example of a principle of perfect love for all people (Davies and Allison 1988: 561-63). For Matthew, one can appeal to no law to prove that one is now righteous enough — that would be legalism. Instead, one must desire God's will so much that one seeks to please him in every area of one's life — that is holiness. Matthew wants disciples to follow God's law, but teaches that God's law was never about mere rules; instead God desires complete righteousness of the heart, total devotion to God's purposes in this world.

Matthew 5:48 ("be perfect"; cf. 19:21) and Luke 6:36 ("be merciful") probably represent two ways to translate a single Aramaic term that Jesus used meaning "whole" or "complete" (Robinson 1977: 32). As the Qumran sectarians measured perfection in terms of the law as their community interpreted it (cf. 1QS 1.8-9, 13; 2.1-2; 4.22-23; 8.9-10; Carson 1984b: 161), in the context of 5:17-47 "perfection" means full allegiance to God's will in the Mosaic law as Jesus has interpreted it (Hagner 1993: 135).[128] That God becomes the standard of comparison suggests that this is exhortation, setting a goal, not assuming a state to which the hearers have already come. Other Jewish teachers also advocated being merciful as God is (Ep. Arist. 208; Dalman 1929: 226; McNamara 1972: 118). But to be morally complete "as God is" is no small feat, nor was it a new commandment. As God told his people in earlier times, warning them not to compromise with pagan behavior, "You shall be perfect with the LORD your God" (Deut 18:13; see Grant 1943: 220-22; Gundry 1982: 100). He further admonished them to cleave to his values rather than those of the world by demanding: "Be holy, for I am holy" (Lev 11:44-45; 19:2; 20:26). Although his Jewish hearers might not have thought about God's being the moral standard in this context, they would have understood it quite well; moralists throughout the ancient world emphasized it.[129] Further, Jesus had just made the point in 5:45. As long as God represents the moral standard, no one has room to boast; all disciples must strive together for God's kingdom and righteousness.

128. Many also see 5:48 as the conclusion of the sixth "antithesis" (Lachs 1987; cf. 5:45); while this is true, it also functions as the conclusion to this section of the sermon.

129. Many Greco-Roman (Cic. *Tusc. Disp.* 5.25.70; Heraclitus *Ep.* 5; Plut. *Borrowing* 7, *Mor.* 830B; Sen. *Dial.* 1.1.5; Epict. *Disc.* 2.14.12-13; cf. Rutenbar 1946: chs. 2–3), Greco-Jewish and -Christian (Ep. Arist. 188, 190, 192, 208-10, 254, 281; Philo *Creation* 139; Eph 5:1; Test. Asher 4:3; Sent. Sext. 44-45), and later Jewish (Mek. Shir. 3.43-44; Sifra Qed. par. 1.195.1.3; on the rabbinic doctrine of imitating God in Tannaitic and Amoraic texts, see further Vermes 1993: 201-4; cf. idem 1984: 52; Veghazi 1979; in a broad Mediterranean context, Crouzel 1978) teachers also acknowledged the principle of imitating God. (For another general parallel, see Musonius Rufus 17 in Van der Horst 1974: 307, though it is not extremely close.)

Showing Only God One's Righteousness (6:1-18)

Matthew begins this section of Jesus' teaching with a thesis statement summarizing his point: Do your righteousness for God to see you, not others (6:1).[130] He then illustrates his point with the examples of secret charity (6:2-4), prayer (6:5-15), and fasting (6:16-18). The middle section, dealing with prayer, is the longest (Matthew may have inserted the Lord's Prayer from a different context; cf. Lk 11:1-4), perhaps in part because prayer constitutes the mark of piety least separable from public religion. As I point out in Matthew 23, Matthew intends these ethical applications not only for Jesus' contemporaries but also for his own audience that follows Jesus' teachings. I should add several observations concerning the teachings of 6:1-18 before approaching the distinct paragraphs of the passage in more detail.

First, disciples must impress God alone. In all three examples, Jesus warns his followers not to be like the "hypocrites" (6:2, 5, 16; 7:5; 15:7; 22:18; 23:13-29; 24:51). This term originally designated actors in the theater (e.g., Arist. *Poetics* 18.19, 1456a; Diod. Sic. 37.12.1; Herodian 3.8.9),[131] a profession Roman law treated like prostitutes (Gardner 1986: 32), so some have suspected that the theater in Sepphoris may have influenced Jesus' usage as he was growing up (Theissen 1991: 13, tentatively following Batey). But Jewish texts had already borrowed the literal use long before this period (Ep. Arist. 219), and, more significantly, both Greek and Roman (Epict. *Disc.* 2.9.20; Plut. *Educ.* 17, *Mor.* 13B; Appian *R.H.* 12.8.55; Marc. Aur. *Med.* 1.11; 3.7; 9.2; Malherbe 1986: 40; Van Tilborg 1972b: 13) and Jewish (Sir 1:29; 35:15; 36:2; cf. Gal 2:13; 1 Tim 4:2; ARN 48, §132B) writers frequently used this and cognate terms for moral pretense. Jewish teachers regularly expected God's judgment on practitioners of "hypocrisy" (Ps. Sol. 4:6, 20; see comment on 23:1-12).[132]

Jesus' warning does not, of course, preclude public acts of righteousness — even with the knowledge that such acts will draw attention — as long as the disciple seeks to be seen for God's glory rather than his or her own (5:16). One does righteousness "in secret" here lest one be praised, but for *God's* glory "a city set on a hill cannot be concealed" (5:14, using a cognate expression). This text warns disciples, however, how easy it is to justify one's own desire to impress others as merely "being a light."

Second, Jesus demands more than assent to ethical propositions. On many ethical points in this section Jesus and his leading contemporaries agreed.

130. Other Jewish teachers also sometimes started with a principle then illustrated with examples; cf. Goulder 1974: 24-25, citing Hillel's *'abh wetholedot.* On the strong symmetry of this section (6:1-18), see, e.g., Minear 1972: 47-48.

131. As often emphasized: Beare 1981: 165; Patte 1987: 86; Batey 1984; Stock 1986; on the masks, cf. Frontisi-Ducroux and Vernant 1983.

132. In Matthew, a "hypocrite" may be one who praises the opposite of God's will as if it were God's will, himself too ignorant of God's will in Torah to know the difference (Van Tilborg 1972b: 8-26).

Although as far as we can tell (sometimes perhaps due to the limitations of our extant data) few sages seem to have provided such a thoroughgoing and frequent critique of human pride, many expressed sentiments quite like Jesus'. A late second-century teacher warned that one should let one's secret behavior be like one's public behavior because people pass on secrets (ARN 28A). Other Jewish teachers emphasized that the proper motivation was to obey God's commandments because he had commanded it, whereas doing them to be called a scholar was wickedness (ARN 46, §129B; m. 'Abot 2:8; p. Ḥag. 2:1, §12). One should not do good deeds to earn others' praise; God will reward only those whose motives are pure (ARN 40A; cf. Sen. *Ep. Lucil.* 5.1-2).[133] Jesus' contemporaries would also have resonated with his appeal to a reward in heaven to be awarded on the day of judgment.[134] As often, Jesus here challenges not so much his hearers' ethical doctrine as their behavior. Thus, for example, in practice some influential persons could employ public fasts to manipulate the people, forcing others to comply with such false piety for the sake of appearance (Jos. *Life* 290-91). In other words, Jesus was not satisfied that someone claimed to *agree* with his ethics; he wanted people to behave accordingly.

Third, Jesus' three examples are random; he intends secrecy to apply to all acts of righteousness. Although Jesus may have taken his three examples from a list in Tobit 12:8 (in which "righteousness" appears as a fourth; cf. Sir 7:10; 2 Clem. 16), such lists were never more than random examples; Judaism viewed each of these examples as extremely important but did not usually list the three as standard examples together (Wimmer 1982: 54-56; though cf. later Qoh. Rab. 5:6, §1). Another early teacher lists the three basic deeds as Torah observance, temple service, and charity (m. 'Abot 1:2; cf. ARN 31, §67B); still another, judgment, truth, and peace (m. 'Abot 1:18); later teachers would list prayer, charity, and repentance (p. Taʿan. 2:1, §9; Pesiq. Rab Kah. 28:2; Qoh. Rab. 7:14, §1), but even these later teachers did not explicitly define repentance only as fasting. Lists of three (m. 'Abot 2:1; 3:1; ARN 4, §17; 31, §68B; cf. Goulder 1974: 26) and sets of three admonitions (e.g., m. 'Abot 1:1, 4-8, 10, 15-17; 2:10) were common for other issues as well. For instance, some teachers considered works such as visiting the sick, hospitality, and comforting the bereaved more meritorious than charity because they required personal involvement (Van Unnik 1954: 96-97). Matthew thus intended his audience to apply Jesus' principle (6:1) not only to the specific cases by which he illustrates it (6:2-18) but to all acts of righteousness.

Fourth, Jesus promises eternal reward for those who seek to please

133. Some later rabbis did emphasize that obedience even with the wrong motives could eventually lead to purer motives (b. Sanh. 105b), an insight modern psychological studies may confirm (cf. 1 Cor 4:3-5).

134. Christians who likewise believe in reward (e.g., Rev 11:18; 22:12) should not consider ancient Judaism a legalistic religion for emphasizing reward (see Odeberg 1964: 32-33; Sanders 1977: passim); reward was never to be one's primary motivation (m. 'Abot 1:3). For a full survey of Tannaitic teaching on reward, including 117 concrete examples, see Smith 1951: 163-84.

God rather than humans. Jesus concludes each of his warnings with another graphic image: businessmen regularly wrote the phrase "received their reward in full" (6:2, 5, 16) on receipts to indicate that no further payment was required (Deissmann 1923: 229; idem 1978: 110; Ladd 1967: 90).[135] This may recall the Jewish doctrine that the heavenly court would avenge what the earthly court could not (Keener 1987; cf. Midr. Ps. 72, §3; 1 Tim 5:24). Jesus is saying that those who give for others' approval and pray and fast to people rather than to God already have what they wanted, others' approval. They will not be rewarded for the deeds again on the day of judgment. Religious as they appear to be outwardly, they have lived for human approval rather than God's.

Doing Charity Secretly (6:2-4)

Jesus again employs hyperbole in his descriptions (cf. 5:19, 29-30), adding graphic force to his warnings. Perhaps alluding figuratively to the trumpet-shaped charity boxes in the temple and provinces (m. Sheqal. 2:1; 6:1, 5; cf. McEleney 1985; Lachs 1987: 112-13) or hyperbolically to trumpets calling assemblies for prayer or Sabbath worship (CD 11.21-22), Jesus condemns those who sound trumpets when they give alms. Though some scholars have argued that people actually blew trumpets during giving in the synagogues (Friedrich 1971: 86), Jesus probably uses this image simply to reinforce his point, as when picturing the Pharisees who swallow a camel whole but strain out a mere gnat (23:24; cf. Num 10:10; Gundry 1982: 102).[136]

Jesus adds to this stark image still another: one should be so secretive in giving that one should not let one's left hand know what one's right hand is doing (6:3). Everyone would recognize the hyperbole — since both hands belonged to the same person the image is patently impossible in the literal sense — but it impresses on the hearer just how private one's giving should be. Others used such images ("do not let your own ear hear you" — Marc. Aur. 8.9) to reinforce their point graphically.[137] As Paul put it, "I do not even judge [evaluate] myself," for

135. God's "repayment" also employs language used elsewhere in Matthew for the repayment of debts (cf. Weber 1992); if Matthew employs this image here, he may borrow it from the OT (cf. Prov 19:17; cf. Tob 4:14). Cic. *Rep.* 6.23 contends that one should prefer one's heavenly home to earthly fame, but the idea there is that virtue causes the soul to ascend — quite different from here (Boring 1995: 61).

136. While Davies and Allison 1988: 579 concur, they note the trumpets blown on fast days (Joel 2:15; m. Ta'an. 2:5) when alms came to be requested (cf. b. Ber. 6b; Sanh. 35a), allowing for a custom possibly unknown to us. Trumpets were probably used more widely than our scattered sources indicate; e.g., Babylonian Judaism included horn-blowing to announce funeral processions (b. Mo'ed Qaṭ. 27b; Safrai 1974/76b: 778).

137. Argyle 1963: 55 appeals to the Arab use of the right hand's relation to the left as an image of intimate fellowship, hence "do not let even your closest friend know about your generosity!" While he may be correct (few Arabic sources exist for the early Christian period), the nature of hyperbole invites the "impossible" reading I have suggested above. Cf. perhaps Jonah 4:11.

only God's evaluation on the day of judgment would count (1 Cor 4:3-5). Jesus challenges his hearers about the danger of public piety with such forceful language precisely "because our assurance that such hypocrisy is no great problem with us is a major part of the problem" (Tannehill 1975: 85).

Jesus emphasizes future reward for those who forgo present honor (6:1, 2, 4, end). Jesus undoubtedly meant the promise of divine reward literally, as did most of his contemporaries. Jewish teachers often felt that charity delivers the giver from death and stores up treasure in heaven (Tob 4:10; 12:8; 14:10; t. Pe'a 4:21; Pesiq. R. 25:2).[138] Jesus likewise emphasized heavenly reward for serving those truly in need (6:19-21; see comment there).

The phrase "when you give to the needy" (6:2) implies the expectation, standard in Judaism, that **one would care for the needs of the poor** (Tob 4:7), just as the phrase "when you pray" (6:5) takes for granted that the hearer would pray (m. 'Abot 2:10).[139] Greek culture did not emphasize charity to the same extent (cf. Artem. *Oneir.* 3.53), except in the sense that rich benefactors contributed to public works and were requited by honor from the populace (Stambaugh and Balch 1986: 64; Tarn 1974: 108; cf. Ps-Phocyl. 80; Boer 1979: 34-36).[140] Jesus' Jewish contemporaries emphasized charity heavily, as even Gentiles recognized (Jos. *Apion* 2.283).[141] Sages declared that one should treat the poor as members of one's own family (m. 'Abot 1:5). Texts speak of specifically assigned persons who locally collect and distribute charity (CD 14.13-16; t. B. Qam. 11:3; B. Meṣ. 3:9; Dem. 3:16; cf. Acts 4:35; 6:2-3; the date of the rabbinic practice is unclear — cf. Seccombe 1978), although late texts sometimes also warn against their oppressing the poor by demanding funds from them for the collections (b. B. Bat. 8b; Pesiq. R. 51:1; Lev. Rab. 30:1).

Yet they would have agreed with him not only that charity was one of the primary obligations of God's people, but that one must give charity from the

138. Jewish teachers sometimes went so far as to say that acts of charity brought Israel's salvation nearer or brought a person life (Tob 4:7-11; 12:8; b. B. Bat. 10ab); they felt that charity atones for sins (Sir 3:30; cf. b. B. Bat. 10a) and invites God's protection from harm (Sir 29:12-13; cf. ARN 3A; b. B. Bat. 10a; Ex. Rab. 30:24). They regarded withholding charity from the needy as a sin (Bonsirven 1964: 152; cf. Num. Rab. 5:2; Ruth Rab. 5:9), one that characterized wicked pagans (t. Pe'a 4:20) like those of Sodom (Gen. Rab. 49:6; cf. Ezek 16:49). Treasure "in heaven" here means "with God" (Jeremias 1971: 9); see below.

139. For social justice issues in general in Matthew, see especially Powell 1995: 113-48.

140. For exceptions, see, e.g., Pub. Syr. 274; Corn. Nep. 5 (Cimon), 4.1-2; cf. Hesiod *W.D.* 354 (give to the generous; cf. perhaps Prov 11:25; 22:16); Romans also praised those who used their resources to serve the needy rather than profiting from their office (Dion. Hal. 12.1.7).

141. Both earlier (e.g., Prov 29:7; Ezek 16:49; Tob 1:3; 2:14; Sir 4:1-8; 17:22) and later (Test. Job chs. 9–12; 15:1; Test. Iss. 3:8; Ps-Phocyl. 29; Jos. and Asen. 10:11/12; cf. Did. 1) Jewish writers emphasized charity, and the rabbis continued to elaborate the issue (e.g., m. Dem.; t. B. Qam. 11:3; Dem. 3:16; ARN 3, 7A; 14, §33B; b. Ta'an. 21a; Montefiore and Loewe 1974: 412-39). Judaism in the Diaspora articulated it as plainly as in Palestine (*CIJ* 1:142, §203). A Jewish-Christian writer claimed that charity was more meritorious than fasting or prayer (2 Clem. 16), fitting a Jewish teaching that it outweighed all other commandments (t. Pe'a 4:19; b. B. Bat. 9a); on Christian charity in the patristic period, see Grant 1977: 124-45.

right kind of heart (m. 'Abot 5:13; Bonsirven 1964: 67; cf. Eth. Apoc. Peter 11). Indeed, some Jewish teachers also praised secret charity and objected to ostentation in charity (Test. Job 9:7-8; m. Sheqal. 5:6; t. Pe'a 4:19-21; Sheqal. 2:16; b. B. Bat. 9b; Pesaḥ. 113a).[142] Probably most of the scribes and Pharisees Jesus and Matthew address were just as pious theologically as the later Jewish teachers on whom we depend for this information (5:20).

Praying Secretly (6:5-8, 14-15)

Three times in this section Jesus repeats the phrase "when you pray" (6:5, 6, 7; cf. Mk 11:25), creating the following four-part structure:

A	When you pray, do not . . .	v. 5
	B When you pray, (do) . . .	v. 6
A′	When you pray, do not . . .	v. 7
	B′ Pray like this	v. 9

Jesus emphasizes that one should not pray "like the hypocrites," to be seen by others (6:5); instead one should pray privately (6:6). He also emphasizes that one should not pray "like the pagans," that is, Gentiles, expecting to manipulate an answer from their deities (6:7); instead, one should pray a simple prayer to one's Father (6:8-13). Technically the "Lord's Prayer" (6:9-13) is a digression in Matthew's passage on secret prayer;[143] I will treat it in a section distinct from this one only so that I can explore each line in greater detail.

Jesus stresses that one must also pray in secret. He seizes the hearers' attention with forceful language, warning against seeking to pray in the synagogues (where prayers were customarily offered throughout the Mediterranean — e.g., Jos. *Life* 277; *CPJ* 1:239-40, 247-49, 476, 495; 2:367-71, 375-76; Juv. *Sat.* 3.296) and in the most visible location, the streets (Tannehill 1975: 82; cf. 12:19).[144] One should thus enter into a private room, but this is not "your room" (NRSV; NIV), for most Galilean homes had one or at the most two rooms (Horsley 1995: 192), and the only room in the average Palestinian home that had its own door would be the much smaller "closet" (KJV) or "storeroom" (Schweizer 1975: 145; Hagner 1993: 142; cf. Lk 12:24).[145] By detailing stages of the action

142. See further Abrahams 1924: 125; Odeberg 1964: 84-85; Bonsirven 1964: 153; Beare 1981: 166; Lachs 1987: 113; Vermes 1993: 196.

143. Digressions were common in ancient writings (Aune 1987: 30), e.g., Josephus's defense against the charges of Justus (*Life* 336-67).

144. "Standing" was, as here, the customary Jewish posture in prayer; Lachs 1987: 115 cites, e.g., Lk 18:11, 13; m. Ber. 4:5; b. Ber. 10b; 26b; 30a; p. Ber. 4:1; Midr. Ps. 4:9; Targ. Esth. 4:1; cf. also 1 Chron 23:30; 35:5; Ps 24:3; 135:2. "In the street" can mean "before the public notary" (e.g., *P. Oxy.* 261.8-9; 266.7; 270.7), but prayer "in the streets" probably suggests persons stopping to pray wherever they were at the regular times of prayer (Lachs 1987: 115 cites b. Ber. 3a; Meg. 26a).

145. Jeremias 1971 contends that it is an ordinary room and that Jesus may allude to Is 26:20

(enter room, shut door, pray, 6:6) the text follows the typical rhetorical practice of *ap' archēs achri telous,* "from beginning to end"; like the doubling (synagogues and streets, 6:5) this practice creates *enargeia,* "a vivid picture of the action" (Kennedy 1984: 58).

Jewish people did not normally pray in the street, but Jesus again reduces the questionable behavior to the absurd by graphically depicting a worst-case scenario: a person who craves notice so much that he arranges to find himself in the street during the regular daily prayer times (cf. Jeremias 1971: 187; France 1985: 132). Yet some Jewish laborers might actually have no choice at times, and Jesus' demand for privacy would make prayer difficult (Tannehill 1975: 82). This illustration, like Jesus' preceding one (6:2-3), involves a humorous hyperbole; none of our reports of Jesus' private prayer takes place in a storeroom (14:23; 26:36-44). This text precludes not public prayer (18:19-20; 21:13; cf. 1 Tim 2:8) but prayer to be seen and glorified by others.

We should note, however, that whereas the text's language is hyperbolic, it conveys a point that is quite literal. Some other noted pious men in Jewish tradition sought solitary places for prayer (Vermes 1993: 195-96n.11; cf. t. Ber. 3:5). When Jesus prayed privately, he normally sought a place more secluded than a storeroom, going into the Galilean hills (14:23). Because people arose at daybreak for work, Jesus had to arise before dawn if he wished to retreat to a private place for prayer (Mk 1:35; many Jewish people would have recited the Shema and other prayers upon rising). Because Galilean homes were often crowded (Mk 2:2),[146] were closely packed together,[147] and villages and towns in the Galilean countryside also often lay close together,[148] one might not get time alone with God and away from all others' gazes without retreating into the hills.[149] Even there, his disciples finally could find him (Mk 1:36-37).[150]

The issue is not supposed impiety in the Jewish prayer tradition. Contemporary Judaism emphasized regular, efficacious prayer far more than modern

---

in view of the impending catastrophe (cf. also 1 Kings 22:25). But Jesus more probably alludes to a common feature of architecture relevant to daily life. Any "room" could be in view (cf. Tob 7:16), but privacy and the door suggest a storeroom within the home or on the roof. In 24:26 the chamber is very private, opposed to the wilderness; in Luke 12:3, private as opposed to a housetop.

146. See data in Wilkinson 1978: 28; Meyers and Strange 1981: 58-59; Goodman 1983: 31; Stambaugh and Balch 1986: 83; MacMullen 1974: 13-14.

147. See data in Wilkinson 1978: 29; Goodman 1983: 30-31; Freyne 1988: 153; Lewis 1983: 65, 67; for cities of the Empire in general, see MacMullen 1974: 63, 68.

148. See Goodman 1983: 29; Horsley 1995: 190.

149. Crowding was standard throughout urban centers in the Empire (Meeks 1983: 28-29; cf. Friedländer 1965: 1:211).

150. Vermes 1993: 14-15, 195 takes Jesus too literally here, urging that one never finds Jesus engaged in public prayer, in contrast to his followers (Acts 2:46; 3:1; 22:17); but he argues this thesis from silence. Jesus seems to have known and approved prayers that had corporate implications (the Kaddish — Mt 6:9-10; Vermes himself accepts the Lord's Prayer as corporate — 1993: 165), and together with his disciples he recited the Passover Hallel (26:30); further, the Acts texts he cites reflect particularly Lukan emphasis on prayer and the early Christians' identification with the temple and Israel.

Western Christians do (see Sir 7:14; Montefiore and Loewe 1974: 342-81; Jeremias 1971: 170n.4). Those who conveniently assume that Jesus' target is specifically Jewish ethnically rather than a temptation also available to Jesus' disciples miss his point; for example, do not pray like the "hypocrites," but pray the Lord's Prayer three times a day (Did. 8.2).

Some interpreters imply that Jesus opposes the formalism of Jewish ritual prayers. It *is* possible that Jesus implies preference for prayer in the vernacular language (Aramaic) rather than in the synagogue's traditional Hebrew.[151] But the text gives no indication that Jesus opposes Jewish ritual here. First, in this early period various Jewish teachers still debated among themselves whether fixed prayer could become too mechanical, and some advocated spontaneous prayers from the heart (m. 'Abot 2:13; Ber. 4:4).[152] Second, it is pagan rather than Jewish wordiness that Jesus critiques when he addresses verbiage (6:7).[153] And third, Jesus does not himself hesitate to offer his disciples a sample prayer (6:9-13).[154]

Jesus' point of contention with his Jewish contemporaries was not the *form* of their prayers (which his own prayer in 6:9-13 closely matches) but their *motivation.* Again, such words strike not at a practice limited to Jesus' contemporaries, but at the very heart of outward piety in general, a temptation the reality of which most religious people can attest. Jesus rejected lengthy prayers designed to impress others (see also Mk 12:38-40; Lk 20:46-47). Nor should one suppose that the longevity of one's prayer earns a response (as in, e.g., Life of Adam 6/ Apoc. Mos. 29; Life of Adam 41:1);[155] faith's object must be God rather than one's own eloquence.

But **Jesus** not only warns against the "hypocrites'" prayers that invite human rather than divine attention; he **criticizes pagan prayers designed to manipulate their deities.** Pagans piled up as many names of the deity they were en-

151. Suggested by Dalman 1929: 18-21; Jeremias 1971: 188-89; idem 1964: 92-94; cf. Vermes 1993: 164 on 6:9-13.

152. See further Sandmel 1978b: 152; Moore 1971: 2:220-21; Abrahams 1924: 84; Johnson 1948: 61.

153. The precise sense of "babble" is unclear (Carson 1984b: 166); but if it refers to useless verbosity, perhaps Sir 7:14 may also warn against thinking it efficacious to add words to one's prayer. Pagan texts sometimes make fun of prayer traditions, as when one prays for rain while another prays for dry weather (Aesop *Fables* 299 in Boring 1995: 90); a few questioned the value of petitionary prayer (van der Horst 1995), but it was widespread. Greeks and Romans frequently mistrusted the motives behind silent prayers (van der Horst 1994; cf. 1 Sam 1:12-16).

154. Admittedly Jesus offers it as a structural model rather than a verbatim liturgy to be recited (Albright and Mann 1971: 75). Jewish flexibility in the use of model prayers at this time may be one reason why the Lord's Prayer appears in different versions in Matthew and Luke.

155. Davies and Allison 1988: 589 also cite *Sepher Ha-Razim* 5.37; Lachs 1987: 116-17 adds, e.g., m. Yoma 5:1; Sifre Num. 105; Mek. Vay. 1 (Laut. 2.91) on Ex 15:25; b. Ber. 5b; 34a; 61a; Shab. 10a; Soṭa 37a; Yoma 53b. Luz 1989: 365n.11 helpfully compares ancient warnings against tiring the deities (citing Sen. *Ep. Lucil.* 31.5; Horatius Flaccus *Carm.* 1.2.26) and other exhortations to pray concisely (Plautus *Poenulus* 1.2.203; Marc. Aur. *Med.* 5.7). Tannaim apparently valued and expected God to reveal secret prayer openly (Mek. Baḥodesh 1, Laut. 2:196 on Ex 19:2 in Lachs 1987: 114, though this is weak).

treating as possible (e.g., Hom. *Il.* 1.37-38, 451-52; 2.412; *PGM* 4.2916-27; Cleanthes' *Hymn to Zeus;* more restrained, *ILS* 190),[156] hoping at least one would be effective (Burkert 1985: 74); this may be the import of "many words" (6:7; Gundry 1982: 103-4). Roman magistrates read prayers exactly as they had been handed down through tradition; "if one syllable or one ritual gesture was performed incorrectly, the prayer might well be invalid" (Stambaugh and Balch 1986: 129). Pagans also reminded a deity of favors owed, seeking an answer on contractual grounds, as many ancient texts attest (e.g., Hom. *Il.* 1.39-41; 10.291-94; *Od.* 1.61-62, 66-67; 4.762-64; 17.240-42; Ap. Rhod. 1.417-19; Virg. *Aen.* 12.778) and historians often remark (Burkert 1985: 74-75; Ferguson 1987: 118, 147-48; Stambaugh and Balch 1986: 129; Malherbe 1967: 20).[157]

To compare Jewish hearers' behavior with that of pagans would have shamed them deeply (6:7; pace Meier 1980: 59). Matthew (5:47; 6:32; 18:17; 20:25), his Bible (Lev 18:3, 24-25; 20:23; Deut 18:9; Jer 10:2), and other early Jewish sources (Jub. 21:21; Test. Dan 5:5) contain warnings not to be like the pagans. One should pray not because one thinks that one's prayers or formulas earn God's favor, but as an expression of trust in a Father who already knows one's need and merely waits for his children to express their dependence on him (6:8, 32).[158] Some other Jewish writers, like Philo, also defined prayer in terms of dependence on God (see Dowd 1983). Although Judaism recognized a variety of ways of appealing to God, not all of which fit Scripture equally well (see Johnson 1948: 38-60), many stressed that prayer involved a heartfelt relationship with God and not just petition (Abelson 1969: 325).

156. Garland 1993: 79 notes that after Catullus piles up titles of Diana, he concludes, "whatever name you prefer" (*Poems* 34). "Not like others" was acceptable comparative language (*Rhet. ad Herenn.* 3.7.14).

157. Cf. also threats that one would view gods as impotent if they fail to deliver (Eurip. *Cyclops* 606-7). One may note that whereas ancient Israel shared with its neighbors thank offerings, atonement offerings, and so forth, Israel had no sacrifices to secure rain or any favors from God; God gave these only in response to Israel's obedience to his covenant (Deut 27–28). This is not to deny that people eventually created traditions to that end, e.g., the water ritual at Sukkoth meant to secure rain (cf. m. Ta'an. 1:1; t. Sukk. 3:18; Sifre Deut. 40.4.2; b. B. Meṣ. 28a; Ta'an. 25b; p. Rosh Hash. 1:3, §§43-46; Ta'an. 1:1, §§1-10; Pesiq. Rab Kah. Sup. 7:2; Qoh. Rab. 7:14, §3; Song Rab. 7:2, §2; cf. Moore 1971: 2:44-45; Harrelson 1969: 69).

158. Vermes 1993: 155n.3 compares miracle-workers who foreknow petitioners' needs (cf. also Jos. and Asen. 6:6; 23:8; 26:6; 2 Enoch 40:1-2; 3 Enoch 11:1-3; *Lives of the Prophets* 17, Nathan.2/Scherman §28; p. Ḥag. 2:2, §5; Rosh Hash. 1:3, §§39-42; Sanh. 6:6, §2; Diog. Laert. 9.7.42; *PGM* 3.479-94; the Messiah in Ps. Sol. 17:25; demons in Test. Sol. 20), but the best parallels are the much more common texts about God's omniscience (Jn 2:24-25; Rom 8:27; 1 Jn 3:20; Acts of Paul 3.24; 2 Macc 7:35; Sir 39:19; Bar 3:32; Sus 42; Jub. 15:30; 16:26; 1 Enoch 9:5; 39:11; 84:3; CD 2.9-10; Ep. Arist. 132-33, 210; Ps. Sol. 9:3; 14:8; 2 Bar. 21:8; Sib. Or. 1.151; 3:12; fr. 1.4; Test. Jud. 20:3-4; Zeb. 5:2; Naph. 2:4-5; m. 'Abot 2:1; t. B. Qam. 7:2; Sanh. 8:3; b. Ber. 58a; Ex. Rab. 21:3; 43:3; 46:3; *PGM* 4.3046-48; cf. Plut. *Isis* 1, *Mor.* 351E; *Isis* 51, *Mor.* 371E; Epict. *Disc.* 1.30.1; 2.14.11; Diog. Laert. 9.2.19); on God as "overseer," see Wis 1:6; 7:23; Ep. Arist. 16; 4 Bar. 7:35; Sib. Or. 1.152; 2.177; fr. 1.3; Test. Benj. 4:3; 6:6 (the language is hellenistic; cf., e.g., Theon *Progymn.* 11.194; Epict. *Disc.* 1.14.1, 9). This contrasts with pagan prayers that required the suppliant to describe the request precisely "lest the deity grant the wrong favor" (Malina and Rohrbaugh 1992: 59).

In 6:14-15, Jesus concludes his words on prayer by returning to the warning implicit in 6:12: **those who do not forgive will not be forgiven** (cf. Mk 11:25). Jesus again accords with one stream of Jewish wisdom tradition (Sir 28:1-8), albeit one that not all Jews necessarily accepted (Syr. Men. Sent. 345-46; p. B. Qam. 8:7, §1). Some other sages also praised forgiveness in more moderate language (Cato the Elder in Plut. *Sayings of Romans, Mor.* 198E; p. Qidd. 4:1, §2). From the similar parable of 18:21-35 we learn that grace preceded this demand; but a forgiven person who could not forgive would lose the status of being forgiven (Jeremias 1963: 26; cf. Ezek 18:24). Other early Christians also recognized that poor relationships with others hindered one's relationship with God, hence his accessibility in prayer (1 Pet 3:7, 12).

The Kingdom Prayer (6:9-13)

Cf. Lk 11:2-4. Versions of this prayer appear in both Matthew (6:9-13) and Luke (11:2-4). Matthew's structure for the prayer is clearer than Luke's, and probably reflects Matthew's penchant for systematic arrangement. Matthew's version of the Lord's Prayer may contain two equal sets of petitions containing three petitions each (or the second stanza may contain an extra line, reflecting an asymmetric balance as in some psalms): three "Thou-petitions" addressing God's honor and three or four "we-petitions" addressing the suppliant's needs. Some commentators have compared here the two sections of the Decalogue and the two great commandments (Plummer 1910: 96).

Some writers suggest that Jesus offered variant forms of the same prayer twice (Botha 1967: 46). Although this suggestion is plausible, Luke and Matthew regularly rework their narratives (e.g., the centurion's servant in Mt 8:5-13//Lk 7:1-10), and Matthew has almost certainly constructed the structure of the context in which his form of the prayer appears. If Jesus did not offer the prayer twice, Luke's basic form of the prayer is probably generally older (Dibelius 1949: 120; Bandstra 1981: 36).[159] Later copyists presumably expanded Luke's form to fit Matthew's longer one (hence the reading in the Byzantine Text followed in the KJV; cf. Bandstra 1981: 25-30; Metzger 1968: 121). Because early Christians would have used and adapted the prayer in the liturgies of their various communities (fragments later turn up even in *PGM* 83.14-15 among various Jewish quotations), Matthew may not derive this prayer from the Q source (Hagner 1993: 145); given some variant adaptations of the Aramaic in Matthew and Luke, an oral source is more probable than Q here.

Most scholars accept the prayer in its pre-Synoptic form as authentic (Witherington 1990: 204). A minority of scholars, like Crossan, deny the authen-

159. Luke's version of the prayer's setting may address Gentile Christians learning how to pray to Israel's God; Matthew's version of the setting addresses Jewish Christians learning how not to pray (Jeremias 1963: 21).

ticity of the Prayer, suggesting that if Jesus taught this prayer to his followers it should show up in more than two Gospels and in "a more uniform version" (Crossan 1991a: 294).[160] Yet *how* wide the attestation we should expect for any given tradition is a rather subjective judgment; indeed, we should count ourselves fortunate to have any attestation for the prayer since we have no early Christian hymnbook: Qumran hymns from the Teacher of Righteousness (the community's founder) only rarely turn up outside Qumran's liturgical documents. Yet Crossan needs the prayer to be inauthentic, or at least (as he says) for none of it to be eschatological, to defend his argument that Jesus did not teach a future kingdom (1991a: 293-95). Jesus would have been at least as likely to adapt a traditional Jewish prayer as his followers would, however, and the Jewish prayer he adapted in reference to the coming kingdom was clearly eschatological (future-oriented).

The Lord's Prayer is thoroughly Jewish in its content, form, and language (cf. Lapide 1991). Early Christians sometimes adapted Jewish prayers; the eucharistic thanksgiving in the Didache, for instance, borrows language from the Jewish Kiddush blessing (Did. 9:2-4). The Lord's Prayer itself came to be prayed three times daily, like the Amida (Did. 8:3). Most scholars recognize that Jesus here probably adapts an early form of what became a basic synagogue prayer, the Kaddish.[161] At least some people probably already used the basic form of the Kaddish in Jesus' day (cf. Oesterley 1925: 72); it is quite difficult to believe that the Kaddish adapted the Lord's Prayer instead![162] Jeremias quotes what he believes to be the prayer's earliest form (1964: 98; cf. Oesterley 1925: 73; Bonsirven 1964: 133):

> Exalted and hallowed be his great name
> in the world which he created according to his will.

160. Arguments that Matthew simply created the Lord's Prayer and Luke followed him (Goulder 1963: 45; Van Tilborg 1972a: 104-5) can array little specific support (see C. Brown 1976: 869-73). Some allow that Jesus prayed component parts but wisdom followers assembled them (e.g., Taussig 1988; O'Neill 1993), but this view fails to account for the coherence of the prayer as a whole against the background of Jewish liturgy; its appearance as a whole in Matthew, Luke, and the Didache; the possibility that Jesus would have taught his followers a specific prayer; and the lack of most of its constituent parts to appear as prayers elsewhere in the tradition. Walker (1982) suggests that Jn 17 draws on the Lord's Prayer or on a source that used it, but given the recurrence of these motifs in early Jewish prayers his parallels are not impressive (Carson 1980: 174 argues that the parallels suggest the same author).

161. Bonsirven 1964: 133; Jeremias 1964b: 98; idem 1971: 21; Moore 1971: 2:213; Smith 1951: 136; Hill 1972: 136-37; Perrin 1976b: 28-29; Vermes 1984: 43; Davies and Allison 1988: 595; Luz 1989: 371; pace Meier 1994: 361-62n.36; Lachs 1987: 118.

162. Although the overall links between the Lord's Prayer and the Kaddish are too close for coincidence, they do contain many individual features that were standard among Jewish prayers in general, such as in the Eighteen Benedictions. (Bivin 1992 suggests that it is a shortened substitute for the Benedictions, which could be abbreviated in emergencies — m. Ber. 4:4.) Prayers often link God's Fatherhood and reign (Vermes 1993: 152), the latter also being common in prayers (see b. Ber. 40b; Davies and Allison 1988: 603). For further comparisons, cf. Petuchowski and Brocke 1978.

May he let his kingdom rule
in your lifetime and in your days and in the lifetime
of the whole house of Israel, speedily and soon.
And to this, say: amen.

The parallel between the Kaddish and the first stanza of Jesus' model prayer was so obvious that an eighth-century translation of the Lord's Prayer from Latin into Hebrew borrows some of its wording directly from the Kaddish (Lapide 1984: 8).

Although Jesus' ministry sets the elements of the prayer in a new context — the future kingdom is present in a hidden way in the future King, Jesus of Nazareth (8:29; 13:31-33) — the disciples must have heard in Jesus' words an exhortation to seek God's coming kingdom (4:17; 6:33) by praying for it to come.[163] Neither the Kaddish nor Jesus' sample prayer suits a complacent person satisfied with the treasures of this age. This is a prayer for the desperate, who recognize that this world is not as it should be and that only God can set things straight — the broken to whom Jesus promises the blessings of the kingdom (5:3-12).

Various features of this prayer are significant. **First, Jesus predicates it on the basis of an intimate relationship with God: "Father."** This is a relationship that denotes both respectful dependence and affectionate intimacy as well as obedience. *One must understand what God's "fatherhood" would have meant to most of Jesus' hearers.* In first-century Jewish Palestine, children were powerless social dependents and fathers were viewed as strong providers and examples on whom their children could depend (in contrast to many homes in contemporary Western society; cf. 7:7-11; Heb 12:5-11). Jesus summons his disciples to pray not like the pagans (6:7), but with a dependence on God as their Father (6:8-9) who watches over them (Deut 8:3-5, in Mt 4:4).

Perhaps more significantly, the context (6:7-8) indicates that intimate communion is implicit in "our Father"; effective prayer is not a complex ritual but a simple cry of faith predicated on an assured relationship (7:7-11). The earnest brevity and simplicity of this prayer contradict human pride (6:7); this is the prayer of those who know they must depend on God for their daily provision, who need their debts forgiven, who need his protection from the testing all around them.[164] This is not the prayer of the complacent and the self-satisfied, but of the humble, the lowly, the broken, the desperate. This is the prayer of those who have nowhere to turn but to God — the "meek" who will "inherit the earth" (5:5).

163. Many scholars see all the petitions as addressing the time of the kingdom (e.g., Meier 1980: 62; tentatively, Davies and Allison 1988: 594); while there is evidence to support this, I see the "Thou-petitions" as primarily eschatological and the "we-petitions" (which incidentally do not belong to the Kaddish parallel) as primarily directed toward present needs (cf. also Gerhardsson 1978).

164. Bultmann, too, notes the brevity, which he distinguishes from piling up predicates of God (in addition to Father) in extant synagogue prayers (1956: 77; but contrast b. Ber. 33b; cf. Sanders 1990: 76). Bultmann's insight may have merit, but we should keep in mind that extant synagogue prayers performed a different function than originally private prayers (cf. the Qumran hymns).

One cannot assert, as some have, that "father" was a solely Jewish or Christian title for God; Greek references to the chief deity as "father" are abundant (e.g., Hom. *Il.* 3.276, 320, 350, 365; 10.154; 11.56, 80, 182, 201, 544; 16.253; 17.46; *Od.* 14.440; 15.341; 16.260; 24.518; Hesiod *W.D.* 169; Eurip. *Medea* 1352; Aristophanes *Clouds* 1468-69). More specifically, from the earliest written period Greek religion and from an early period Roman religion recognized Zeus or Jupiter as "father of gods and men" (Hom. *Il.* 1.544; 4.68; 5.426; 8.49, 132; 12.445; 15.12, 47; 16.458; 20.56; 22.167; *Od.* 1.28; Hesiod *Theog.* 457, 468, 542; *Shield of Heracles* 27; *W.D.* 59; Phaedrus 3.17.10; Ovid *Metam.* 2.848; 14.807), "father of gods and king of men" (Virg. *Aen.* 1.65; 2.648; 10.2); "father of gods" (Hom. *Il.* 1.503, 534, 578-79; Virg. *Aen.* 9.495; Ovid *Metam.* 9.245; Phaedrus 1.2.13), "father" of the rest of creation (Babrius 142.3), "omnipotent father" (Virg. *Aen.* 1.60; 3.251; 4.25; 6.592; 7.141, 770; 8.398; 10.100; 12.178; Ovid *Metam.* 1.154; 2.304, 401; 3.336; 9.271), or simply "the father" or "Zeus father" (Hom. *Il.* 8.69, 245, 397; 14.352; 15.637; 16.250; 22.60, 209; *Od.* 12.63; 13.51; Virg. *Aen.* 2.691; *Georg.* 1.121, 283, 328, 353; 2.325).[165]

Thus both the Olympian deities (Hom. *Il.* 8.31; 22.178; 24.473; *Od.* 1.45, 81; 5.7; 8.306; 12.377; Aristoph. *Wasps* 652; even those not descended from him like his siblings — Hom. *Il.* 5.757, 762; 19.121; *Od.* 13.128) and mortals (Hom. *Il.* 2.371; 7.179, 202, 446; 8.236; 12.164; 13.631; 15.372; 17.19, 645; 19.270; 21.273; 24.461; *Od.* 12.371; Cleanthes' *Hymn to Zeus;* Soph. *Oed. Rex* 202; Aristoph. *Acharn.* 223-25; Ap. Rhod. 4.1673; Plut. *R.Q.* 40, *Mor.* 274B; Longinus *Sublime* 9.10) frequently addressed him as "father." In these images, the chief deity is the supreme patriarch and ruler of the cosmos, the same way the emperor could be hailed as "father" of the Roman state (Herodian 2.2.9; 2.6.2).

By Jesus' day, however, a nearer context for a Galilean teacher was certainly early Judaism, and whatever the measure of Greek influence on its preference for the language, its most direct source was the Hebrew Bible. The Hebrew Bible recognized God as Israel's father by adoption in redemption (Jeremias 1964b: 12), and Jewish literature in general continued this tradition (e.g., Wis 2:16; 3 Macc 5:7; 7:6), also in prayer, though in a relatively restrained manner (3 Macc 6:8; Jeremias 1964b: 15-16; idem 1965: 14).[166] But the form of synagogue Judaism we know from later rabbinic literature commonly calls God "our Father in heaven" (m. Soṭa 9:15; t. Ber. 3:14; B. Qam. 7:6; Ḥag. 2:1; Pe'a 4:21;

165. The deity is in a number of cases "father" as "creator" or progenitor (e.g., Soph. *Ajax* 387); most of the Latin references above are to *pater,* but Jupiter is also called *genitor* (see, e.g., Virg. *Aen.* 12.843). Sometimes "father Zeus" is also listed alongside Athene and Apollo, as in Hom. *Od.* 4.340; 7.311; 17.132; 18.235; 24.376.

166. The Greeks may not have employed the title as pervasively as Judaism and in contrast to Judaism applied the image to the deity's power rather than his intimacy with Israel (cf. Johnson 1948: 61). Jewish literature regularly calls God Israel's (occasionally in Diaspora Judaism humanity's) "father" (Jub. 1:25, 28; Wis 11:10; Tob 13:4; Jos. and Asen. 12:14 MSS; Apoc. Mos. 35:2; Test. Job 33:3 MSS, 9; Test. Abr. 16, 20A; cf. Prayer of Joseph 1). In Jesus' teaching, "Father" applies to the disciples, not to all humanity (pace Montefiore 1956; Acts 17:28 represents a different and far rarer NT usage, accommodating that of Greco-Roman paganism and Jewish apologetic).

Sifra Qed. pq. 9.207.2.13; Behuq. pq. 8.269.2.15; Sifre Deut. 352.1.2),[167] as scholars conversant in the material regularly point out (e.g., Marmorstein 1968b: 56-60; Moore 1971: 2:204-9; McNamara 1972: 116-18).[168] Contrary to some scholars' views, the importance of Jesus' teachings do not rise or fall on their uniqueness; Judaism stressed that God as the Father of his people exhibited special love toward them, a view drawn from the Hebrew Bible with which Jesus agreed.

Jesus' recognition of God as his own Father goes beyond the usual synagogue usage, however (cf. Klausner 1979b: 378); even Jewish texts not intended for corporate use only rarely designate God as personally "my Father" (Sir 23:1, 4; Wis 2:16; cf. Jeremias 1964b: 26, homiletically overstating the case), whereas Jesus nearly always did (Jeremias 1965: 17; cf. idem 1964b: 29-31; see comment on Mt 26:39). When Jewish people called God by the Old Testament title "Father," they used a title of intimacy as well as respect and dependence; Jesus summons his disciples to appropriate this intimacy still more deeply (cf. Mk 14:36; Rom 8:16; Gal 4:6).[169]

Second, the prayer seeks first God's glory, not the petitioner's own needs (cf. Sifre Deut. 343.1.1-2). The "Thou-petitions," for God's kingdom and glory, precede the "we-petitions" for the community's own needs. That each of the first three petitions in Greek concludes with "your" in the emphatic, final position leaves no doubt that the prayer emphasizes seeking God's kingdom first (6:33).[170]

167. Outside as well as within rabbinic texts, Judaism frequently associates God with "heaven" (e.g. 1 Esdr 4:58; Tob 10:13; Jdt 6:19; 1 Macc 3:18, 50, 60; 4:24; 3 Macc 7:6; 1 Enoch 83:9; 91:7; Test. Abr. 2A; Philo *Creation* 82; Sib. Or. 1.158, 165; 3.247, 286; "the heavenly deity" in Sib. Or. 4.51). Greeks also attempted to define their deity's location in prayer (Burkert 1985: 74), sometimes in heaven (Zeus in Ach. Tat. 5.2.2; cf. Sen. *Dial.* 12.8.5); many religions associate God with the sky (cf. Mbiti 1970: 42, 67-68). "Heaven" was also a Jewish periphrasis for God (e.g., Dan 4:26; Lk 15:18, 21; Rom 1:18; 1 Enoch 6:2; 13:8; 1QM 12.5; 3 Macc 4:21; m. 'Abot 1:3, 11; 2:2, 12; t. B. Qam. 7:5; Sifra Behuq. pq. 6.267.2.1; Sifre Deut. 79.1.1; 96.2.2; b. ʿAbod. Zar. 18a, bar.; B. Qam. 76a; Moʿed Qaṭ. 17a; Nid. 45a, bar.; Pesaḥ. 66b; Taʿan. 14b; Num. Rab. 7:5; 8:4; Ruth Rab. 7:1; Qoh. Rab. 7:8, §1; 7:27, §1; 9:12, §1; this circumlocution probably also stands behind the misunderstanding in Diod. Sic. 40.3.4). For the polarization between heavenly and earthly realities in Matthew, cf. Syreeni 1990.

168. The title is even more common in later sources (e.g., b. Ber. 30a, bar.; p. Sanh. 10:2, §8; Pesiq. Rab Kah. 24:9; Lev. Rab. 1:3; 7:1; 35:10; Song Rab. 7:11, §1). Jeremias contends that "Father" is rarely attributed to rabbis before the decades immediately preceding Matthew's Gospel, most of the many references being later (1964: 16-17); but this observation omits some evidence (Vermes 1984: 40) and fails to take into account the sparseness of rabbinic attributions *in general* in the earlier period. Chilton 1994: 59 cites "Father" as a prayer invocation in Test. Job and (probably later) in the Targumim; cf. 42. Evidence for the use of an "our Father" as far away as Pompeii by A.D. 79 is, however, unlikely (Baines 1987; pace Botha 1967).

169. "Father in heaven" appears frequently in Matthew (e.g., 5:16, 45; 6:1, 14, 26, 32; 7:11; 12:50; 15:13; 16:17; 18:10, 19, 35; 23:9), as does "my Father" (7:21; 10:32; 11:27; 12:50; 15:13; 16:17; 18:10, 19, 35; 20:23; 25:34; 26:29, 39, 53) and "your Father" (e.g., 6:8; 10:20, 29; 18:14; cf. "their Father," 13:43).

170. Cf. Jos. *Apion* 2.196: Jews pray for others' welfare before their own.

What did it mean in a first-century Jewish context for God's name to be hallowed in the future? Although many profaned God's name — his honor — in this age (acting as if it were unholy, Ex 20:7; Jer 34:16; Ezek 29:14), God would see to it that his name would be hallowed in the coming time of the kingdom (Is 5:16; 29:23; Ezek 38:23; 39:7, 27; 1QM 11.15; cf. Zech 14:9 with Deut 6:4), just as God had sanctified his name when he had acted in the past (e.g., 1QM 17.2). A benediction in one standard Jewish prayer acknowledged the holiness of God's name in the present (the Amida — m. Rosh Hash. 4:5; Sifra Emor par. 11.234.2.3; cf. Bowman 1977: 328), but Jesus' prayer, like the Kaddish (cited above; cf. Sanders 1985: 7-8; Deut. Rab. 7:6), yearns for the day when God's name alone will be hallowed, that is, sanctified or shown holy, special above every other name. (On the sanctity of God's honor, see also comment on 5:33-37.)

Yet Jesus' Jewish hearers would have understood the implications of the prayer for present existence as well, for one could ask with integrity for the future hallowing of God's name only if one lived in the present as if one valued it. Hallowing God's name *(kiddush ha-Shem)* was "the most characteristic feature of Jewish ethics," along with its opposite, profaning the name (Moore 1971: 2:101; Urbach 1980/82: 1:357-60, 507, 2:283-84; cf., e.g., Sifre Deut. 221.6.1; b. Shab. 89b; p. Sanh. 3:5, §2); everything is forgiveable, said some teachers, except profaning the Name (Sifre Deut. 328.1.5), an offense that required not only the Day of Atonement and repentance but also the offender's death (ARN 29A). Scripture already warned against profaning God's name by evil behavior (Lev 22:32; Jer 34:16; Ezek 13:19; 20:9, 14, 22, 27, 39; 22:16; 36:20; 39:7). Jewish teachers believed that one's motivation in doing good should be "for the name of heaven," that is, for God's honor (m. 'Abot 2:2, 12; cf. Num. Rab. 8:4; 15:12). Acts of charity or otherwise seeing to it that God's will is carried out in the world sanctifies God's name; disobeying God's will or misrepresenting it through false teaching profanes it (e.g., m. 'Abot 1:11; Num. Rab. 7:5; 8:4; Pesiq. R. 22:2; Moore 1971: 2:104-5). Later rabbis said, for instance, that a Bible teacher who does not pay his bills on time profanes God's name (Montefiore and Loewe 1974: 397). One might have to "sanctify" or show holy God's name by kindness to unbelievers (Pes. Rab Kah. 22:1; p. B. Meṣ. 2:5, §2; cf. 2 Bar. 1:4; Urbach 1981: 283-84), by suffering for the name (b. Pesaḥ. 53b; Num. Rab. 4:6; Song Rab. 2:7, §1; Pesiq. Rab Kah. 11:14; Montefiore 1979: 63), or by other forms of obedience (e.g., Num. Rab. 12:21); one must never profane God's name before Gentiles (CD 12.6-8; t. B. Meṣ. 5:18; p. Sanh. 3:5, §2; Gen. Rab. 39:7). Some went so far as to say that if a Jew *must* sin, he ought to go somewhere where no one knows him and pretend to be a Gentile, lest he bring reproach on God's name (b. Ḥag. 16a; Qidd. 40a). Scandals among God's people that bring dishonor on the name of the God they purport to represent are reprehensible (cf. Rom 2:24; Test. Levi 14:1; 16:1; b. Yoma 86b; Ruth Rab. 7:1); one might need to expose or excommunicate hypocrites to prevent God's name from being profaned (b. Yoma 86b; p. Ta'an. 3:10, §1).

Third, disciples long for the coming of God's kingdom and the doing of

his will (6:9-10). The hallowing of God's name, the consummation of his reign, and the doing of his will are all variant versions of the same end-time promise: everything will be set right someday. Not only the Kaddish but other Jewish prayers like the Amida as well expressed yearning for the time of the future kingdom (cf. Bultmann 1958: 42; Guelich 1982: 285; Wilson 1978: 16). Jewish tradition did not normally speak of the kingdom "coming"; the prayer probably combines the eschatological reign of God with God's eschatological "coming" (Davies and Allison 1988: 604, citing, e.g., Zech 14:5; 1 Enoch 1:3-9; 25:3; Jub. 1:22-28; Targ. Zech. 2:14-15).

Jesus' prayer here is not just a prayer of submission to God's will in this age, as in 8:2 and 26:39 (cf. also 1 Macc 3:59-60), although it also implies that. The Kaddish mentions God's will in the original creation, but Jesus' kingdom prayer even more explicitly reminds us that God in the kingdom will restore the perfect purpose for which he formed the world in the beginning (cf. Moore 1971: 2:309; Goppelt 1981/82: 1:70).[171] Those who long for God's will on earth in the future should live consistently with that longing in the present, working for God's righteousness and seeking his will here (6:33; 26:39).[172] Indeed, only those who bring forth the fruit of repentance, showing themselves ready for the kingdom, dare genuinely pray for his kingdom to come (cf. 3:2, 8).

The Lord's Prayer concludes with three "Thou-petitions" (strictly four petitions, the last two of which are synonymous). **The fourth petition expresses dependence on God for daily sustenance (6:11).** While in this context the text clearly

171. Jewish texts especially emphasized God's "will" in ethical terms (e.g., t. Ber. 3:7), but present ethics and future eschatology are hardly incompatible (Davies and Allison 1988: 605). Scholars propose various primary backgrounds, e.g., Dan 4:32 (Philonenko 1992); others note that various Jewish texts affirm the submission of heavenly bodies to God (Davies and Allison 1988: 606 cite Sir 43:6-10; Ps. Sol. 18:10-12; 1 Enoch 41:5, though some of their other texts speak of God's sovereignty over the earth, too: Sir 16:18-29; 1 Enoch 2:1-2). God's will was known to be done in heaven. Ancients viewed the heavenly bodies as angels (1QM 10.11-12; 2 Enoch 4:1; 29:3A; 3 Enoch 46:1; 2 Bar. 51:10; Ps-Phocyl. 71; Pesiq. Rab Kah. 1:3; Ex. Rab. 15:6; Philo *Plant.* 12, 14) or deities (1 Enoch 80:7; Lev. Rab. 31:9; Cic. *De Re Publ.* 6.15.15; *De Nat. Deor.* 2.15.39-40; Sen. *Ben.* 4.23.4; Apul. *Metam.* 11.22; cf. souls in Plato *Timaeus* 41E-42A; 4 Macc 17:5; Philo *Giants* 7-8; demons in Test. Sol. 2:2; 4:6; 5:4; 6:7; 7:6; 8:4; ch. 18). The highest heavens were pure, the proper realm of virtuous souls, in Greek thought (e.g., Plato *Phaedrus* 248AB, 248E-249A; Pythagoras in Diog. Laert. 8.1.27, 31; Plotinus *Ennead* 2.1; 3.4.6; cf. Cic. *De Re Publ.* 6.14.14-15; 6.17.17; 6.18.18-19; 6.26.29; *Tusc. Disp.* 1.19.43-44; 1.31.75; Sen. *Dial.* 5.6.1; 12.11.6; Lucian *Dance* in LCL 5:220) and Jewish circles influenced by it (cf., e.g., Test. Job 36:3; 48–50). Spirits lived in the heavens (e.g., Test. Sol. 2:3), and angels ruled each of the heavens (*PGM* 35.1-7), which might be seven in number (2 Enoch 20:1-3; 27:31J; 3 Enoch 1:2; 17:1, 3; Jos. and Asen. 22:9, MSS; Asc. Isa. 7; Apoc. Mos. 35:2; Pesiq. Rab Kah. 1:1; 23:10; b. Ḥag. 12b; 13a; Pesiq. R. 20:4; Iren. *Haer.* 1.30.12; *Greek Anth.* 1.19; Qur'an Sûra 2.29), but sometimes three (Test. Levi 2–3; cf. 2 Cor 12:2; Apoc. Mos. 37:5) or other numbers.

172. If the kingdom were wholly future, one might despair of accomplishing any justice now; if one supposed that it were wholly present, the realities of this age would quickly terminate disciples' illusive utopianism. But because the Gospels affirm that in Jesus the kingdom is present in a hidden way, believers in him can begin to make a difference in their world now, contending for the reality to be consummated at Christ's return (see Grenz 1992; cf. Lk 18:5-8).

indicates trust in God for sustenance (see 6:25-34; cf. "bread" in 4:3; 7:9; 12:4; 14:19; 15:26, 36; 16:5), scholars still debate some points, particularly the meaning of the phrase "daily bread." The most common proposed meanings are "daily rations," "essential for survival," and (most commonly) "bread for tomorrow."

The single alleged occurrence of the rare term for "daily" as "daily rations" (F. F. Bruce 1963: 69) is rightly disputed (Metzger 1957: 53-54). A few scholars object that the phrase simply means "sufficient" bread (ten Kate 1978; cf. Patte 1987: 104). More scholars marshal substantial evidence that the expression probably means "tomorrow's bread," possibly meaning the bread of the coming age.[173] Many read "tomorrow's bread" simply as rations "for the coming day," that is, adequate provision for the next day's work.[174] Other interpreters read "bread for tomorrow" as the bread of the future age (Jeremias 1964b: 100-101; Fenton 1977: 101; Meier 1980: 61), although the arguments for this position have been seriously challenged (Young 1989: 31-33). Jesus clearly shared his contemporaries' belief in the future gift of bread for God's people (cf. 5:6), but it is not clear that he alludes to that concept here. Nor would a nuance of future bread necessarily exclude the nuance of present bread.

Whether one asks for "today's" bread or "tomorrow's," the prayer stresses that the requester needs it "today" (in Greek, "today" appears in an emphatic position), and all ancient Mediterranean peoples acknowledged their need for daily bread (Yamauchi 1966: 148-53).[175] They must seek a "day's" supply because that is all one needs (6:30, 34; cf. Prov 30:8).[176] Jesus may instruct his followers to seek the future kingdom, but they also needed bread in the present, as he well knew (6:31-33; 7:9; 15:32; cf. Pesiq. R. 33:5).

The most obvious source for the "daily bread" image is manna (e.g., Grelot

173. For "tomorrow's bread," Leaney 1958: 185; Hemer 1984 point to Greek lexical evidence, and Jeremias 1964b: 100-101 to evidence for the original Aramaic word *mahar.* Although Matthew spiritualized the beatitudes in some sense (5:3, 6), it remains unlikely in this context that Jesus includes spiritual bread (cf. 15:26) or emphasizes the Eucharist (pace Bourgoin 1979; Dewailley 1980ab; Jeremias 1964b: 102), except in the sense that both foreshadow the eschatological manna. One scholar combines the manna allusion with "bread for tomorrow," finding an allusion to the double portion of manna preceding the Sabbath (Eisler in Hoskyns 1947: 294; Ex 16:22); some view earthly bread in *anticipation* of the future banquet (Aleixandre 1987). Ramaroson 1991 reads "bread that comes" as bread "falling to one's lot," exhorting trust that God will supply.

174. E.g., Manson 1979: 169; Filson 1960: 96; Botha 1967; Gundry 1982: 107; Luz 1989: 382-83; Blomberg 1992a: 119.

175. On ancient Mediterranean breads (some barley but wheat preferred), see Malina and Rohrbaugh 1992: 62. Papyri reveal the deprivation in Egypt, and the available intake per person suggested by m. Ketub. 5:8-9 may indicate that even in Palestine most people had less available food than basics assumed by modern Western societies (Malina and Rohrbaugh 1992: 95, 133, probably taking into account that these are the wife's rations; but did they account for first-century Palestinian Jews being smaller than most Westerners today? But even in Rome, cf. Dupont 1992: 272; for physically active legionaries, ibid., 125).

176. The suggestion that Matthew's version ("tomorrow's bread") reflects the situation of itinerant charismatics but Luke's ("each day") a more economically stable community (Bindemann 1991) is plausible but too speculative.

1979).[177] Jewish people remembered how God supplied bread daily while they were in the wilderness, and hoped for that manna again in the future (Mek. Vay. 3.42-46; 5.63-65; cf. 5:6; Sib. Or. 7.149).[178] Some could also remark that God provided Israel's manna daily so they would depend on him as on a heavenly father (reportedly second-century source in b. Yoma 76a; cf. Mt 6:8; Deut 8:2-5). As Jesus resisted the first temptation, trusting only God to supply his bread in the wilderness (4:3-4, 11; cf. Barrett 1966: 51-52), so also must his followers. This prayer fits the audience of the rest of the sermon; a prayer expressing dependence on God for daily bread and asking only for bread was the prayer of a person willing to live simply, satisfied with the basics (Prov 30:8-9; cf. 1 Tim 6:8). Like many of the other petitions, this one is most naturally uttered by the poor of this world, a condition that characterized many Galilean peasants and (by Western standards of poverty) artisans who followed Jesus (see comment on 5:3).

The fifth petition entreats God to release the community's debts before him (6:12). This line of Jesus' prayer, too, would remind his hearers of a standard Jewish prayer: the sixth of the Eighteen Benedictions entreated God's forgiveness (though without, as Davies and Allison 1988: 610 note, the condition). Yet one who has truly embraced the principle of grace in God's forgiveness must also extend it to one's fellow servants who are of equal worth in his sight (18:35; Pol. *Phil.* 2, 6). Many Jewish teachers also acknowledged that God will only forgive the debts of those who forgive the debts of others (see especially Sir 28:1-8; cf. Derrett 1970: 46; Montefiore 1968: 2:103); human forgiveness is modeled after God's (Abrahams 1917: 150-67).

The image of debts was a graphic one to most of Jesus' contemporaries. Human debts usually involve money; farmers often needed to borrow to sow crops, and many Jewish merchants would also extend credit to regular customers (Goodman 1983: 55). Thus some have suggested that this petition is directed against the practice of debt-enslavement (Fensham 1960) or, more likely in first-century Palestine, repudiating the *prosbul,* the Pharisaic way around the periodic release of all debts prescribed in the Bible (Deut 15:1-3; Lev 25; see Lachs 1975a).[179] Because biblical law prohibited charging interest, however, "the loan

177. Cf. Ex 16:4, *devar-yom beyomo,* "the [bread] of that day in its [proper] day"; cf. LXX: *to tēs hēmeras eis hēmeran.* Some Gentile readers, especially in Rome, may have heard in it the broader practice of daily grain distribution (cf. Heinen 1990).

178. Jewish people also anticipated the promised messianic banquet in the time to come (Is 25:6-8; cf. the discussions on a Qumran text in Priest 1963; Smith 1958-59: 224), a doctrine rabbinic literature emphasizes (m. 'Abot 3:16; 4:16; b. Ber. 34b; Sanh. 98b; Gen. Rab. 51:8; 62:2; Ruth Rab. 5:6; Marmorstein 1968a: 46, 59, 120, 135). On eschatological manna or bread, see as above Mek. Vay. 3.42-45; 5.63-65; cf. Kuzenzama 1980; Christian material in Sib. Or. 7.149; on the hidden manna in the ark to be restored, see 2 Macc 2:4-7; 2 Bar. 29:8; 4 Bar. 3:10, 19; *Lives of the Prophets* 2.15/Schermann 25; t. Kip. 2:15; cf. Gangemi 1977; among Samaritans, McDonald 1964: 365; M. F. Collins 1972.

179. Because the OT taught forgiving debts (Jos. *Ant.* 3.281-83 *may* suggest that the Jubilee continued in his day) and some lenders were tempted to quit lending, Jewish teachers by Jesus' day found ways to get around biblical laws about forgiving debts in the seventh year (Sanders 1992: 427-

itself was regarded as an act of kindness, but the lender did expect repayment" (Lachs 1975a: 6-7; cf. Ps 112:5, 9). Creditors by definition would exact payment (m. B. Qam. 9:9-10), but Jesus forbids caring about possessions even this much (Mt 5:42; cf. Lk 6:30, 35).

While debts include money, however, most of Jesus' hearers would have been borrowers rather than lenders, so Jesus probably includes more than merely economic debts. *It is clear that "debts" before God represent "sins,"* as they normally did both in Jewish teaching (e.g., Gen. Rab. 85:2; 92:9; Ex. Rab. 25:6; 31:1; Pesiq. R. 11:23; 51:8; McNamara 1972: 120) and in the Aramaic term used for both concepts (*hoba,* Black 1967: 140; Jeremias 1971: 6n.15, 196), and as Luke or his source interprets the tradition (Lk 11:4). Some Jewish writers recognized that human life was itself but a loan from God (Ps-Phocyl. 106; Jos. *War* 3.374; m. 'Abot 3:16). The analogy with God's forgiveness and the parable in 18:21-35 indicates that one must forgive anyone any way they have hurt one (cf. similarly among other Jewish teachers, Sir 28:1-8; Montefiore 1968: 2:103).[180] The text promises grace commensurate with one's obedience in forgiving.

The final petitions plead for God's protection in testing (6:13). *"Temptation" here means "testing," as in trials of suffering;* the English word "temptation," which includes the connotation that the tester seeks the person's fall through the trials, is too narrow unless the context warrants it (as in Jas 1:13-18; Sir 2:1-6; cf. Best 1965: 59). In this context the person is praying precisely that the testing will not lead to falling: testing with a view to bringing people to succumb was the business of the "evil one" (6:13b), a characteristic Matthean title for the devil.[181] The primary test that the early Christians would face and that the heroes Jesus' hearers revered had faced was persecution, the temptation to apostasy (Manson 1979: 170; cf. 1 Pet 5:8-9; 1QS 11.13). Jewish teachers came to regard martyrdom or perseverance in dangerous tests as the ultimate way to "hallow God's name" (6:9; Moore 1971: 2:105-7). This test, like Jesus' test, may

---

28). Contrary to its intention, the *prosbul,* which perhaps originally reflects a hellenistic legal context (Llewelyn 1994: 225-32), probably perpetuated indebtedness (Horsley and Hanson 1985: 60). Debt enslavement (e.g., Amos 2:6; 8:6) provided a vivid metaphor for the danger of debt (Prov 22:7; Pub. Syr. 11). Although people often hated creditors (Herodian 7.7.3; Jer 15:10), aristocrats despised "demagogues" who proposed abolishing debts (Dion. Hal. 7.8.1; Appian *R.H.* 2.9; but cf. the popular move in Arrian *Alex.* 7.5.1-3); they felt that the poor might by necessity receive "grace" *(chariti),* but should not seek to get free forcibly (Dion. Hal. 6.81.3).

180. The underlying Aramaic perfect tense could function as a present, "herewith we forgive our debtors," i.e., one releases one's debts during the prayer, hence the present tense of Lk 11:4 (Jeremias 1971: 201). This would have been less clear to most readers approaching Matthew in Greek, but Matthew's sequence appears in 18:27-35. At any rate, the passage teaches that continuance in God's grace demands mercy toward others (also 5:7).

181. Cf. 13:19 with Mk 4:15; Lk 8:12; Jub. 50:5; Grelot 1989. Cf. also 5:37; 13:38; probably 1 Jn 5:18. I prefer this interpretation to the generic sense "evil" (certainly an "evil person" in general, the sense in 5:39, is not in view, despite prayers in the Psalms for deliverance from one's enemies; cf. also 1QM 14.10), though some prayed for God to protect his people from sin (Jub. 1:19) and, in later texts, for eschatological deliverance from the evil impulse (Ex. Rab. 46:4).

represent a challenge to the disciples' commitment to their call as their Lord wished to define it (4:1-11; cf. Patte 1987: 105).

Those inclined to see all the petitions as addressing the end time usually see the "temptation" or "test" here as the final period of testing Jewish people anticipated before the kingdom.[182] This eschatological interpretation makes good sense of the whole context of the sermon: one must get right in view of the coming kingdom (4:17). Most Jewish people also expected a period of suffering before the time of the kingdom (1QH 3), and some prayed for protection for that time (b. Pesaḥ. 118a).[183] Scholars rightly note the prominence of the final tribulation in the Gospels (Albright and Mann 1971: 76-77) and that one cannot distinguish between the present and future time of testing in the Dead Sea Scrolls (Perrin 1963: 197-98) or in the New Testament (1 Cor 7:26; Davies and Allison 1988: 613-14).

Jesus probably does not refer exclusively to a specific future period of testing, however; the very lack of distinction between present and future testing means that an eschatological community would regard whatever remains of the present era as the time of tribulation (cf. perhaps CD 20.14-15). While the omission of the Greek definite article may not constitute a decisive argument against interpretation in terms of the future,[184] the conjunction of "lead us not into testing" with "deliver us from the evil one" (possibly a Matthean antithesis — Goulder 1974: 41) suggests that present trials are in view (cf. 13:19; Gundry 1982: 109; Luz 1989: 384).

Most other Jewish prayers that requested protection from temptation referred to testing in the present time (Montefiore 1968: 2:103; cf. Abrahams 1924: 101; Jeremias 1964b: 105; b. Ber. 60b; Sanh. 64a; God could deliver people over to their sins, e.g., Jub. 21:22). Further, the future cast of the first petitions need not support the future cast for this "test"; the first petitions refer to the coming kingdom, not to the tribulation that precedes it. "Watching" to be ready for testing (26:41) might even prefigure watching for the ultimate test: not the tribulation, but the judgment at the Son of Man's coming (24:42–25:13).[185] In the

182. E.g., Schweitzer 1968: 364; Jeremias 1964b: 105-6; Tasker 1961: 74; George 1966; Brown 1972: 4; Meier 1980: 62.

183. The antiquity of the specific phrase "birth pangs of the Messiah" has been questioned, but a Qumran hymn suggests that it may already have been in use (1QH 3.1-18; for various interpretations, see Baumgarten and Mansoor 1955; Brown 1957; S. Brown 1968; Gordis 1957; Silberman 1956; Brownlee 1956-57b; cf. Allegro 1956a: 95); certainly it was a general enough image of judgment in the OT (e.g., Is 26:17-19; Jer 4:31; 6:24; 13:21; Hos 13:13; Keener 1993: 594) and appears in early Christianity from the start (24:8; 1 Thess 5:3). Pace Sanders 1985: 23, the view that such testing was coming is widespread, however (e.g., Jub. 23.13; 1QM 15.1; Sib. Or. 3.213-15, 635-56; 4 Ezra 6:24; 7:29; 8:63–9:8; 2 Bar. chs. 26–30; Test. Mos. 7-8; often in later rabbinic texts, e.g., m. Soṭa 9:15; b. Sanh. 97a), regardless of the frequency of that *phrase*.

184. Cf. Carson 1984a: 83; pace Schweizer 1975: 156; Moule 1974: 66-67; Marshall 1978: 461; idem 1974: 68.

185. Cf. Cameron 1990, who suggests that the test here is a judicial test in God's court (cf. Ps 26:2): "Do not judge us as we deserve"; but this suggestion would not fit Matthew's parallelism with deliverance from the evil one nor the sense of the most common Jewish prayer language relevant here; cf. also the critique of Moore 1991.

whole context of Matthew, "testing" here probably includes the final tribulation but is not limited to it; thus this petition is not strictly eschatological. If a specific allusion is intended in this context, it may be to the time of the exodus. God released his people from slavery (cf. perhaps 6:12) and fed them with manna (6:11), and they, like Jesus, were tested in the wilderness (6:13; cf. 4:1-2).[186]

In either case Jesus is calling his disciples to pray for deliverance from and protection in testing, not proposing that his disciples can avoid tests of their faith. A prayer suggesting that one could avoid tests of faith would contradict God's dealings with his people in ancient Israel (Gen 22:1; Deut 13:3) and the model of Jesus (4:1). The Aramaic might have had a permissive sense, "Do not let me succumb to the test" or "fall prey to" it (Jeremias 1971: 202; cf. Willis 1975; but contrast Moule 1974: 72-73). A more substantial argument may be that the disciples would have heard the prayer as something like the kind of prayer later standardized in daily Jewish liturgies (b. Ber. 60b in Jeremias 1964b: 105; idem 1971: 202):

> Lead my foot not into the power of sin,
> And bring me not into the power of iniquity,
> And not into the power of temptation,
> And not into the power of anything shameful.

Testing itself was inevitable, but petitioners sought protection in testing (cf. 1 Cor 10:13); sages in Jesus' day continued the Old Testament wisdom tradition that testing was good for a person, provided they endured it and so passed the test (Sir 4:17; 21:1-6). But if Matthew's first readers wondered at all whether or not "lead us not into temptation" meant "let us not succumb to testing," Matthew 26:41 would have settled the matter (cf. also the connection in Pol. *Phil.* 7); this is a closer parallel than 26:39 (pace Moule 1974: 74-75). Jesus warns them to watch and pray lest they "fall [literally, enter] into temptation," but in the context testing is already inevitably on the way (26:45). The issue is not whether testing will come, but whether it will find the disciples unprepared (it did). Scholars thus generally concur that this is a prayer that God bring one safely through testing (cf., e.g., Ps 141:3-4; Is 63:17; 64:7 NRSV; Rev 3:10; Jub. 11:17; 21:22; 22:23), rather than deliver one from experiencing it (e.g., Dahms 1974; though contrast Garland 1993: 81).

The familiar doxology closing the modern version of the Lord's Prayer appears in a textual note in many translations because the earliest manuscripts of Matthew do not include it (most scholars, e.g., Bandstra 1981: 18-25). But the early Christians adopted many Jewish worship practices, and Jewish prayers typically closed with words of praise (Bonsirven 1964: 134); Jewish worshipers often closed regular prayers with spontaneous doxologies (Jeremias 1964b: 106).

186. Houk 1966 and Lewis 1974 may be correct in finding an allusion to the exodus narrative, but find more than Matthew's language warrants in reading, "lest we test *God*" (Ex 17:1-7; Houk 1966: 223; more tentatively Lewis 1974: 43; cf. Walker 1962; Grayston 1993).

Some parallel this doxology quite closely (cf. 1QM 18.13; Smith 1951: 137). The earliest Christians added a doxology like this one when praying the Lord's Prayer in public (Did. 8, 10), and naturally later added this liturgical feature (perhaps from the Didache) to the text of Matthew. Although its content, like that of most Jewish prayers, comported well with the Hebrew Bible, it is not part of the original text of Matthew.

Finally, we should note that **the kingdom prayer is a communal prayer.** The plural pronouns ("give *us,*" etc.; especially prominent in Matthew's version: "*Our* Father") remind Jesus' hearers that those who approach God as their Father must remember God's other children. Although scholars currently dispute how common communal prayers were in first-century Palestine,[187] most extant Jewish liturgies recognized the needs of the whole community, and Jesus' prayer is no exception.

Christians Should Fast in Secret (6:16-18)

In this case (contrast 6:2) the "hypocrites" who "disfigure their faces" may well evoke the original sense of "hypocrites" as actors in the theater (see above); actors typically wore large theatrical masks over their faces. The term for "disfigure" is also quite strong ("ruin") and is the opposite of the term the NRSV and NIV translate "to show," suggesting hyperbole for the sake of rhetorical effect (Tannehill 1975: 82-83). Fasting accompanied grief (e.g., Judg 20:26; 2 Sam 3:35; Esth 4:3; 9:31; Ps 35:13-14; 2 Macc 18:12; Test. Zeb. 4:1-3; Hom. *Il.* 19.156, 206-14; Dion. Hal. 3.22.1; Arrian *Alex.* 4.9.4; 7.14.8; Apul. *Metam.* 2.24), and Jewish piety sometimes conjoined fasting with the sorrow of penitence or judgment (Neh 1:4-7; 9:1-2; Zech 7:5; Sir 31:26; Jdt 4:9-13; Bar 1:5; 2 Bar. 5:7; 9:2; 12:5; Test. Reub. 1:10; Test. Jud. 15:4; Did. 7.4), but as Schweizer notes, humans are so perverse that they "can take pleasure in the pain of their own penance" (Schweizer 1975: 146). Yet as Joel put it, the true penitent must rend one's heart and not one's garments (2:13); Isaiah declared that the true fast was to act for justice (Is 58:6-10; cf. the inadequate fast in Jer 36:9). Some Jewish traditions also emphasize fasting in secret (cf. Test. Jos. 3:4-5); one later rabbi told of a woman hanged by her breasts in hell because she told people about her fast (p. Ḥag. 2:2, §5). A Greek philosopher also had to warn against trying to impress people by one's simple diet of water (Epict. *Disc.* 3.14.4-6).[188]

187. Sanders 1990: 73-76; idem 1992: 205-7 may overemphasize their rareness; but cf. the note in the Introduction in the section addressing the Birkath ha-Minim.

188. Sanders 1985: 263 doubts that 6:16-18 fit the historical Jesus, whose disciples did not fast (Mk 2:18-22) and who was accused of being lax in asceticism (Mt 11:19). But while Jesus' disciples fasted less than the Pharisees, Mark cannot mean that they never fasted (omission of the biblical fast, Yom Kippur, would have yielded serious charges of which the Gospels provide no hint); further, Judaism repudiated purely *ascetic* fasting (see above) and the charge in Mt 11 addresses eating with sinners, not failing to fast (see loc. cit.). The particular construction, of course, probably remains Matthean (Gundry 1982: 110).

In biblical and Jewish tradition, fasting was a time of drawing close to God by demonstrating one's commitment to him; most fasts ran from sundown to sundown (p. Ned. 8:1, §6). Other Mediterranean religions observed some fast days as well (Hor. *Sat.* 2.3.280-81; Aristoph. *Thesmophoriazusae* 984; Mylonas 1961: 241, 258), as in various religions today (cf., e.g., Eliade 1958: 67; Fox 1964: 181). Normally coupled with prayer in the New Testament (Acts 9:9; 13:2-3; 14:23; cf. 1 Cor 7:5 MSS; Mk 9:29 MSS) and some other sources (e.g., Ezra 8:23; Neh 1:4; Jos. *Life* 290-95; Bar 1:5; 2 Macc 13:12; Test. Benj. 1:4-5; Did. 1.3), such fasting is not asceticism for asceticism's sake (cf. Col 2:18-23; Lohse 1971: 115; Francis 1973: 168-69).[189] Many Pharisees may have fasted twice a week as a mark of piety (Lk 18:12; b. Taʿan. 12a; Gen. Rab. 76:3; Safrai 1974/76c: 816; cf. b. Taʿan. 27b, bar.; Did. 8.1; Borg 1984: 108; pace Abrahams 1917: 125); but one suspects that some early Christians missed the point of this passage when they insisted that one should not fast on Mondays and Thursdays like the "hypocrites," but rather on Wednesdays and Fridays (Did. 8:1).

Under normal circumstances people trimmed beards or changed clothes before appearing in public (cf. Gen 41:14); one would also wash one's face (e.g., b. Shab. 31a; 39b) if one had been weeping (Gen 43:30-31), as would be the case with mourning, including penitence. They also anointed themselves as a matter of regular course along with washing (Hom. *Od.* 4.49, 252; 6.219-20, 227; 8.364-65, 454; 10.364, 450; 17.88; 18.179; 19.320, 505; 23.154; b. Shab. 61a), especially if they intended to present themselves publicly (Qoh. Rab. 9:8, §1). One rabbi went so far as to say that a person who bathes without anointing has wasted the bath (b. Shab. 41a). Because many Westerners of northern European descent do not anoint their dry skin with oil (most try to wash excess grease from their skin or hair) the practice of anointing may invite some explanation. Greeks regularly oiled their bodies before exercises, afterward scraping "the dirt and sweat off with the oil by means of a curved metal instrument called a strigil" (Ferguson 1987: 76; cf. Virg. *Aen.* 3.281; Crates 20, to Metrocles; Diogenes 35, to Sopolis; Epict. *Disc.* 3.22.88); some inhabitants of Palestine seem to have used the practice (see Reich 1991). Probably more to the point, Palestinian Jews used oil to clean and anoint their skin, especially on their heads (t. Sheb. 6:9; ARN 3A; b. Sanh. 101a; Yoma 35b; Safrai 1974/76b: 743; cf. Ruth 3:3; 2 Sam 12:20; Ps 23:5; 141:5; Eccl 9:8; Ezek 16:9; Lk 7:46), probably to lubricate dry

189. Davies and Allison 1988: 618 also cite 1 Sam 7:5-6; Tob 12:8; Philo *Spec. Leg.* 2.203; Pol. *Phil.* 7; Apoc. Zeph. 7:6; Test. Jacob 7:17 as coupling prayer with fasting; the last text is exorcistic and probably depends on Mk 9:29 MSS; on fasting for revelations, see, e.g., 2 Bar. 20:5; 43:3; Herm. 1.2.2; 1.3.1; 1.3.10; Lincoln 1981: 111. Later Jewish teachers viewed penitential fasting as a form of sacrifice (Abrahams 1917: 123; Urbach 1979: 1:434-35). Although later Jewish teachers generally scorned fasting for merely ascetic purposes (see b. Taʿan. 11a; p. Taʿan. 3:11, §3; 4:3, §2; Bonsirven 1964: 142), some appear to have practiced it (Safrai 1974/76c: 816; cf. p. Ned. 8:1, §1). Rabbis likewise warned against fasts that would endanger a weakened person's (b. Taʿan. 14a, bar.) or (in view of high infant mortality) pregnant or nursing mother's (t. Taʿan. 2:14) or child's (t. Kip. 4:1-2) health, or one's safety (t. Taʿan. 2:12).

scalps.[190] Mediterranean peoples sometimes employed anointing oil on special occasions (Mart. *Epig.* 3.12; Jos. *Ant.* 19.239; *Life* 74; b. Ketub. 17b).

Because penitent fasting included "afflicting oneself" (Lev 23:32), for most Jewish people the most extreme fasts included not only abstention from food but other forms of self-abasement like not shaving, washing one's clothes, anointing, or having intercourse (m. Taʿan. 1:6; 4:7; Yoma 8:1; p. Rosh Hash. 1:3, §27; Taʿan. 1.6, §5; Sanders 1990: 83; idem 1992: 141); they could even involve social isolation (4 Ezra 5:19-20; 2 Bar. 20:5). (More dangerous for one's health, fasts typically meant avoidance of water as well — e.g., m. Yoma 8:1; 2 Bar. 20:5.) (Those in mourning, such as a husband longing for his wife, might likewise forgo anointing and bathing; see, e.g., *P. Oxy.* 528.9-11; cf. also Jdt 10:3; Lucan *C.W.* 2.375-76.) Jesus thus prohibits some practices that normally accompanied religious fasting in his day. Jesus is thus so concerned with keeping one's righteousness private that he contravenes customary features of what his contemporaries considered a strict fast (Tannehill 1975: 83).[191] Perhaps the insistence on absolute secrecy may be hyperbolic, too — it would be difficult to conceal from one's family that one was not sharing the meal — but observing Jesus' warning as literally as possible might help guard one's motives before God.

Do Not Value Possessions (6:19-34)

Cf. Lk 11:34-36; 12:22-34; 16:13.[192] Jesus exhorts his followers not to value possessions enough to seek them (6:19-24); yet he also exhorts them not to value possessions enough to worry about them (6:25-34). His words strike at the core of human selfishness, challenging both the well-to-do who have possessions to guard and the poor who wish they could acquire them. So uncomfortable are his words that among his professed followers today it appears far more common to explain away his radical teachings here than to consider how to apply them.

190. The Essenes' reported aversion to oil is noted as exceptional (Jos. *War* 2.123). Oil was a basic staple (Sib. Or. 3.243), especially for such reasons. But it was also essential for lamps (25:3-4, 8; Ex 27:20; b. Shab. 26a), and could be used to anoint the sick (Life of Adam 40:1; Apoc. Moses 13:1; Mk 6:13; Jas 5:14), especially their wounds (m. Shab. 14:4; t. Shab. 12:12; Lk 10:34); or to anoint kings (1 Sam 10:1; Jos. *Ant.* 9.106) or priests (Ex 29:7; b. Ker. 5ab, bar.). In some sources, the ultimate healing oil would come only eschatologically (Life of Adam 41-42; Apoc. Mos. 13:2).

191. Pilch 1992: 130 considers this activity deception; Guelich 1982: 299-300 denies it. The difference may be semantic; by suppressing activities normally associated with fasting, the passage expects disciples to lead others to believe that they are not fasting, though not explicitly denying that they are fasting.

192. Matthew probably rearranges disparate Q material freely to emphasize his point, as rabbis would pull together various biblical citations; cf. Matthew's double use of Mk 9:42-48 in Mt 5:29-30 and 18:8-9.

Do Not Value Possessions Enough to Seek Them (6:19-24)

So prominent in Jesus' parables and wisdom sayings are his emphasis on utter faith in God and relinquishment of possessions that Vermes 1993: 148 considers "detachment from possessions, unquestioning trust in God and absolute submission to him" as the central thrust of Jesus' teaching. Paul S. Minear declared that it was no wonder that those with vested economic and political interests hated Jesus; "So insidious was [his] attack upon earthly treasures that he became, according to Kierkegaard, a 'far more terrible robber' than those who assault travelers along a highway. Jesus assaulted the whole human race at the point where that race is most sensitive: its desire for security and superiority" (Minear 1954: 133).[193] What do Jesus and Matthew say about possessions?

Excursus: Some Contemporary Views on Wealth

Greek and Roman sages often claimed that wealth could be used positively (Plato *Laws* 9.870AB; Diog. Laert. 6.6.95; Sen. *De Benef.* 6.3.1-2), but many praised the moral blessing of poverty (Diod. Sic. 10.7.1; Sen. *Ep. Lucil.* 4; 17:4-5; *Dial.* 2.13.3; 5.2.1; 12.10.10–11.2; Diog. Laert. 6.9.104; Aul. Gel. 9.8),[194] and condemned the danger of wealth (Lucretius *Nat.* 5.1105-42; Cato *Distichs* 4.1; Pub. Syr. 58; Sen. *Dial.* 5.33.1; Lucian *Wisdom of Nigrinus;* Heraclitus 8, to Hermodorus; Plut. *Educ.* 8, *Mor.* 5D; Phaedrus 4.12.5-8; Sall. *Catil.* 5.8; 52.7; *Jug.* 6.1). Wealth is worthless compared to knowledge (Dio Chrys. *79th Disc.* §6; Diog. Laert. 2.115) or virtue (Hor. *Ep.* 1.1.52). Most philosophers and moralists stressed the virtue of contentment (Horace *Ode* 2.18; 3.16; Mart. *Epig.* 4.77.2; Juv. *Sat.* 14.303-4; Cicero *Tusc. Disp.* 5.31-32; Diogenes 46, to Plato; Pub. Syr. 626; Sen. *Ep. Lucil.* 61.4; Plut. *Love of Wealth, Mor.* 523C-28B; Diog. Laert. 6.1.11; 10.1.11; Dio Chrys. *6th Disc.;* Marc. Aur. 5.1, 14; 8.45.1; Jos. *Apion* 2.291-92). Wealth caused anxiety (Plut. *Love of Wealth* 1-2, *Mor.* 523DE; Diog. Laert. 4.48; cf. likewise m. 'Abot 2:7, atttributed to Hillel). In general, Greeks and Romans seem to have preserved respect for the old-fashioned virtues of military discipline and rustic simplicity (e.g., Diod. Sic. 33.7.1-5; 37.2.1; 38/39.9.1; Dion. Hal. 6.94.2; 6.96.2; Livy 21.4.5-7; 39.40.10-11; Aul. Gel. 1.14; 2.24; 13.24; 15.12.1-4; Corn. Nep. 3 [Aristides], 3.2; 19 [Phocion], 1.3-4; 25 [Atticus], 13.6-7; 14.3; 22.4; Sall. *Catil.* 54.4-5; *Jug.* 85.33); they certainly condemned greed (e.g., Herodian 3.8.8) and praised gererosity (e.g., Arist. *N.E.* 4.1.6-14, 1120a).

193. Those who wish to grapple with how Jesus' teaching might apply today might consult Sider 1990, a book Gordon Fee once declared "every American Christian should read," or, on a broader economic level, Economic Justice 1986. Far more radical in some respects are many works by Wesley, Finney, and others; cf., e.g., Jennings 1990.

194. Also Musonius Rufus *On Clothing and Shelter* 19 in Boring 1995: 81-82; Pythagoras in Malherbe 1986: 110.

Jewish views on wealth varied similarly, usually depending on how people used wealth: some could regard wealth positively, as a sign of blessing (Sib. Or. 3.783; Ep. Arist. 204-5; m. 'Abot 4:9; Qidd. 4:14; cf. Sifre Deut. 352.1.1); yet many also acknowledged the spiritual dangers of wealth (1 Enoch 63:10; 94:8; 96:4; 97:8; 1QS 10.18-19; 11.2; CD 4.17; 8.7; Sir 31:8-11; Ep. Arist. 211; Jos. *War* 2.250; *Ant.* 4.190; m. 'Abot 2:7; Sifre Deut. 43.3.1-2, 5; 318.1.1-4) and "love of gain" (Sib. Or. 3.189, 234-36, 640-42; Ps-Phocyl. 42-47; 1 Enoch 108:8; Test. Levi 17.11; Jud. 17.1; 18.2; 19.1; Sir 31:5-8; Philo *Spec.* 1.281), a vice also found in Greek tradition (Isoc. *Demon.* 9, 27-28, *Or.* 1; Plato *Hipparchus,* 225A-32C; Plut. *Bravery of Women: Chiomara, Mor.* 258E; Diog. Laert. 4.48; 6.2.50; Theon *Progymn.* 3.91-92). Sometimes Jewish writers even oppose the uselessness of worldly wealth with the true treasure of the world to come: 1 Enoch 100:6; m. 'Abot 4:1; 6:9; b. B. Meṣ. 114b; Gen. Rab. 67:5; cf. Herm. 1.1.1. True wealth could thus include contentment (m. 'Abot 4:1; Finkelstein 1970: 187).

Views on wealth varied among thinkers in the Greco-Roman world, but most people then like most people today pursued whatever material advancement was available. For the wealthy, that meant greater wealth; for most of the Empire, it meant continued subsistence. Those who would associate Jesus' views strictly with those of Cynic philosophers miss the diversity in both Greek and Jewish thought on wealth. A number of ancient writers expressed the worthlessness of wealth, although some such critics (like Seneca and Philo) apparently ignored their own possession of it.[195] Jesus' Jewish emphasis on depending on God also differs considerably in content from a Cynic emphasis on self-dependence (Witherington 1994: 124). But Jesus lived simply (8:20), and most inhabitants of the Roman Empire would have considered this call to abandon valuing possessions as unduly radical. While uncomfortable with those preaching universal abandonment of possessions, however, ancients might respect those who, like the Essenes, abandoned their own (Jos. *War* 2.122-27; *Ant.* 18.20, 22; Philo *Every Good Man Is Free* 76-87; *Hypothetica* 11.4; Pliny *N.H.* 5.15.73; cf. Philo *Vit. Con.* 34-39).

If disciples *really* trust God, they will live as if treasure in heaven is what matters (6:19-21; cf. 13:52; 19:21; 1 Tim 6:8-10). Although only the more radical sages of antiquity shared Jesus' view that earthly possessions were essentially worthless, his *illustrations* of the point may not have surprised his hearers as starkly original. In 6:19-20 Jesus' illustration follows a rhythmic pattern that reinforces his point (Tannehill 1975: 48; cf. Kennedy 1984: 60 on the "gnomic effect" of the repetitive "treasuring treasure"). Because people often kept all their monetary savings in strongboxes in their own homes or buried beneath their floor, the danger of thieves and corruption was quite real (Stambaugh and Balch

195. On Philo, cf. Schmidt 1983; Downing 1985; Mealand 1978b; idem 1985.

1986: 73; cf. 24:43).[196] Precious apparel, considered a treasure (Josh 7:21; 2 Kings 5:22-23; 7:8), could be corrupted by moth (Gundry 1982: 112), whereas precious metals would be corrupted by rust. Idols made of precious materials would succumb to rust and moth alike (Ep Jer 12). What good was wealth if one kept it buried in the ground for fear of thieves (Hor. *Sat.* 1.1.41-42)? Ancients often acknowledged the corruptibility of wealth (Sir 34:5; m. 'Abot 2:8); Ben Sira admonishes his hearer to use money for a friend in need rather than letting it rust, for one would thereby lay up treasures according to God's commandments (Sir 29:10-11).

Jesus' contemporaries often stressed that obedience on earth led to treasure in heaven (4 Ezra 7:77; 2 Bar. 14:12; 24:1; 44:14).[197] Second-century tradition declared that a first-century king who gave to the poor dispensed with earthly treasures to gain heavenly ones (t. Pe'a 4:18). A later teacher insisted that if his disciples sought wealth in this world they would lose their reward in the world to come, where alone their labor in the law would be rewarded (Montefiore and Loewe 1974: 205-6). Yet for Jesus, the treasure is not merely *in* heaven (19:21); it represents the kingdom of heaven (13:44). Idolaters who value Mammon too highly to abandon it for what Jesus values will have no place in his kingdom (19:21-30; cf. Lk 14:33).

One first-century Jewish teacher insisted that one should value one's neighbor's property as highly as one's own (m. 'Abot 2:12; cf. Ex 22:6; 23:4-5; Deut 22:1-4). But nearly all Jesus' extant statements on wealth go beyond the rabbinic model; some scholars thus suggest that "closer to Qumran, Jesus disdains all earthly wealth" (Meier 1980: 65; cf. Flusser 1988: 194-95). Qumran, however, practiced a rigid communalism (1QS 6.22-23; Jos. *Ant.* 18.20; *War* 2.122; Philo *Prob.* 85-86; *Hypothetica* 11.4-5; Mealand 1975), whereas the early Christians shared possessions voluntarily as the needs arose (Acts 2:45; 4:32-35; see Fitzmyer 1966: 243).[198] Jesus did not establish a council to enforce his teachings on possessions as at Qumran, but his views were no less countercultural and radical than Qumran's.

Some other countercultural sages in antiquity also advocated lack of attachment to material possessions. One sage remarked that you can lose only what you

196. Various commentators, following literally the Greek wording here, note that thieves would easily "dig" through mud-brick walls (e.g., Hagner 1993: 157, citing Job 24:16; cf. Test. Abr. 10A). Because such an invasion at night would be loud and slow, hence dangerous (especially given Ex 22:2-3), I regard Jesus' language as graphic but probably not literal. By this period the term also meant "breaking and entering" (Luz 1989: 395).

197. Cf. further Tob 4:8-10; 12:8; Test. Levi 13:5; Gen. Rab. 9:9; 53:5; Ex. Rab. 31:2; 45:6; Lev. Rab. 34:16; Qoh. Rab. 1:3, §1; Song Rab. 7:14, §1; Marmorstein 1968a: 20; Sandmel 1978b: 190-91; Guelich 1982: 327; cf. Col 1:5; 1 Pet 1:4; Gk. Ezra 1:14. For "treasuries" in heaven in a more cosmic sense, cf., e.g., 2 Enoch 5:1-2; 6; 3 Enoch 10:6; 2 Bar. 10:11.

198. Scholars propose various reasons why Jesus' rhetoric in Luke is stronger than the church's behavior in Acts (Arai 1983; Kraybill and Sweetland 1983), but given Jesus' own home base in Capernaum (Mt 4:13) and earlier in Nazareth (2:23), Jesus' rhetoric may be radical not so that all believers immediately sell all possessions on conversion, but that they relinquish all valuing and ownership of them, hence stop acquiring possessions of merely personal value.

have, so if you had had more, you would have lost more; had you had less to lose, you would have complained about not having much (Epict. *Disc.* 1.18.15-16). Unlike some philosophers, however, Jesus is not against possessions because he supposes them evil (cf. Lucretius *Nat.* 5.1105-42; Sen. *Dial.* 5.33.1); the issue is not that possessions themselves are bad, but that a higher priority demands people's resources. If they value what God values rather than what most societies value, they must value the basic needs of others without adequate resources above the accumulation of possessions beyond basic needs (19:21; cf. Lk 3:11; 12:33-34).

The person whose perspectives are distorted by materialism is blind to God's truth (6:22-23).[199] Other ancient sages also naturally employed illustrations comparing the eye to one's will (Marc. Aur. 10.35). Those who justify their pursuit of material possessions by comparing themselves with others will blind themselves (cf. 7:3-5) to the truth of their disobedience and affect their whole relationship with God.

Jesus' illustration about the "single" (NRSV: "healthy"; NIV: "good") eye and the evil eye would immediately make sense to his hearers: a "good" eye was literally a healthy eye, but figuratively also an eye that looked on others generously (Sir 32:8).[200] In the Greek text of the Gospels, Jesus literally calls the eye a "single" eye, which is a wordplay: the Greek version of the Hebrew Bible also uses this word for "single" to translate the Hebrew term for "perfect," that is, "single-minded" devotion to God, setting one's heart on God alone. Jesus' contemporaries also used the expression for righteousness (1 Macc 2:60; Test. Iss. 3:5 MSS; Eph 6:5; cf. perhaps "simplicity" or "integrity" in Marc. Aur. 6.30; 7.31; 10.1; 10.9.2; 10.32) and generosity (Albright and Mann 1971: 81; cf. Ps 119:113; Rom 12:8; Jas 1:8). An "evil eye," conversely, was a stingy, jealous, or greedy eye (Deut 15:9; Prov. 23:6; 28:22; Sir 14:8-10; 34:13; Tob 4:7, 16; m. 'Abot 2:9, 11; 5:19; cf. also Roberts 1963); yet it also signifies here a "bad eye," one that cannot see properly.[201] Jesus used the "single" eye as a transition

199. Davies and Allison 1988: 641 contend for the authenticity of 6:22-23 because it (1) retranslates into Aramaic or Hebrew; (2) contains nothing distinctively Christian; (3) coheres with Jesus' correlation of inner and outer; (4) fits Jesus' appreciation for riddles and parables; and (5) exhibits the same formal structure as 6:24, which is likely authentic.

200. Ancients differed as to whether external objects impressed the eyes or the eyes emitted light (cf. Arist. *On Sense and Sensible Objects* 2, 438ab; Aul. Gel. 5:16; Diog. Laert. 9.7.44; Plut. *Table-Talk* 1.8.4, *Mor.* 626C; Jos. and Asen. 6:6/3; Allison 1987a), and many scholars find reference to the latter view in Matthew or the Lukan parallel (e.g., Davies and Allison 1988: 635-36), although the body being enlightened may indicate that the eyes here *admit* light. In the figurative language of the day, light in the eye could symbolize the proportion of good or evil (Vermes 1993: 82); Philo uses the eye as an analogy for the mind (*Creation* 53, 66).

201. Some spoke of the "evil eye" as not only jealous or stingy but opening up the way for magical dangers *(baskainein)* against its victims (cf. Deut 28:54, 56; Prov 23:6; 28:22 LXX; Test. Sol. 18:39; b. B. Meṣ. 85a; Gen. Rab. 84:10; Deut. Rab. 6:8; *P. Oxy.* 292.11-12; *Select Papyri* 1.318-19; Aul. Gel. 9.4.8; Plut. *Table-Talk* 5.7.1, *Mor.* 680C; *Pleasant Life Impossible* 5, *Mor.* 1090C; Aelian *Animals* 11.18; different references in Guelich 1982: 331; Elliott 1988; Kern-Ulmer 1991; Dickie 1991); cf. the principle in other cultures in Prince 1964: 92; Madson 1964: 426-27; Mbiti 1970: 269. The magical sense is generally absent in biblical occurrence (see Fensham 1967).

to his next point, for the "single" eye is literally undivided, seeing the whole picture: thus one is not divided between two masters, as the text goes on to explain (6:24).[202]

One must love either God or money; the professed lover of both is an idolater (6:24). One must serve someone, but a person whose service is divided will love one master and hate the other. Jewish law addressed possibly theoretical cases of persons who were half-slave and half-free or jointly owned by two persons (m. ʿEd. 1:13; Giṭ. 4:5; Pesaḥ. 8:1; t. Ker. 1:17; b. ʿArak. 2b; B. Qam. 90a; Giṭ. 43a; Ḥag. 2a; Qidd. 90a; Yebam. 66a); divisions of estates at inheritances could encourage such situations (cf. *P. Grenf.* 1.21). This seems to have been an uncommon situation (cf. Acts 16:16), but Jesus' observation seems to have obtained accurately: the slave naturally preferred one master to the other (Groenewald 1967; Beare 1981: 183).[203] Jesus warns his audience that one must choose which master one will serve: those who work for possessions will end up hating God; those who work for God will end up hating possessions.[204]

"Mammon" here was a common Aramaic term for money or property,[205] but its contrast with God as an object of service here suggests that it has been deified as well as personified (cf. Sir 34:7; Meier 1982: 66). For Jews, the "worship" of money functioned as a *reductio ad absurdum*; indeed, even Gentiles would ridicule one who "worshiped" money (Eurip. *Cyclops* 316). The early Christians extended the principle of not serving two masters to avoiding theaters (where humans were routinely slaughtered for public entertainment, akin to much modern entertainment except that it was not fictitious; Tert. *Spec.* 26) and to gaining the world and thereby forfeiting one's soul (2 Clem. 6). But Jesus here applies the principle to one of the greatest temptations: the idolatry of materialism (cf. possibly Col 3:5, though there it may refer to sexual desire).

For those interested in how the text's radical demands might sound in our culture, I pause here to repeat the lament of North American scholar Craig Blomberg 1992a: 124: "Many perceptive observers have sensed that the greatest danger to Western Christianity is not, as is sometimes alleged, prevailing ideolo-

202. Some scholars miss the wordplay in 6:22, arguing for *either* "single" eye or "generous" eye (Manson 1979: 93; cf. Schweizer 1975: 163) rather than both (France 1985: 139); but wordplays were common for advancing an argument (see on 2:23). 6:24 may have followed 6:22-23 directly in the tradition, since Pauline Christians applied "singleness" (6:22) to devotion to God as Christian slaves' true Lord (Eph 6:5; Col 3:22). Matthew reports sayings about slaves of God (18:23; 21:34; cf. 20:27, of one another) and of Jesus (10:24; 24:45; 25:14). Others also condemned the hypocrisy of those with "two hearts" or "faces" or "mouths" (1 Enoch 91:4; Test. Asher 3:1-2; 4:1-2; Benj. 6:5-7), who have divided interests (Epict. *Disc.* 3.15.13; 4.10.25; cf. 2.1.28).

203. The parallel to 6:24 that Safrai and Flusser cite — humans are slaves to both God and the evil impulse until they die (Safrai and Flusser 1976; Flusser 1988: 169-70) — misses Jesus' point that one *should* not and ultimately *cannot* have two masters.

204. "Hate" could mean "love less," i.e., hate by comparison to one's love for something else (10:37//Lk 14:26; Gundry 1982: 115 cites Gen 29:30, 33).

205. See Black 1967: 139-40; Hengel 1974b: 24; Jeremias 1971: 6 n.2; Flusser 1988: 153; Davies and Allison 1988: 643.

gies such as Marxism, Islam, the New Age movement or humanism but rather the all-pervasive materialism of our affluent culture." Pointing out that the New Testament also summons churches in one part of the world to look out for the needs of churches elsewhere (2 Cor 8:13-15), Blomberg further reminds readers that because "over 50 percent of all believers now live in the Two-Thirds World . . . a huge challenge to First-World Christianity emerges. Without a doubt, most individual and church budgets need drastic realignment" (Blomberg 1992a: 126-27; cf. also idem 1992b; Schmidt 1988; Hagner 1995: 562).

Do Not Value Possessions Enough to Worry about Them (6:25-34)

Jesus' message here picks up his earlier discussion of secret charity (6:1-4). Christians must not seek material gain (6:19-24), but should trust God's power to provide for genuine needs (6:25-34). Jesus' culture, of course, defined need quite differently from modern Western society. If God sustains life and protects the bodies of those who serve him, they should not complain if he provides without honoring the symbols of status their culture values (6:25). If he feeds his children like the birds (6:26; cf. 1 Kings 17:6) or clothes them like the flowers (6:28), he will have provided more than what human cultures value, not less (6:29). Yet if God provides for birds and flowers, he will also provide for his children (6:30).[206]

God promises the basics (6:25-26, 28-30). Jesus twice uses a standard type of Jewish argument traditionally called *qal waḥomer:* "how much more?" (6:26, 30).[207] If God cares for birds and for perishable flowers, how much more for people in his image and for his own beloved children (cf. 6:8, 32)? Unlike most modern biologists, ancient naturalists were sometimes also sages, who regarded all God's creation as a legitimate field for inquiry. Wisdom sayings often addressed nature (e.g., 1 Kings 4:33; Ahiqar col. 6; Sir 43:33; Plut. *Cleverness of Animals, Mor.* 959B-985C).[208] Philosophers regularly drew lessons from nature (see Keener 1992: 42-43, 66), sometimes including that people should "merely . . . avert hunger, thirst, and cold" (Seneca *Ep. to Lucil.* 4, LCL 19) or should not

206. Jeremias (1963: 25; idem 1972: 215; 1971: 236) suggests that Jesus addressed these words to the departing missionaries (cf. 10:9-10); Theissen 1978: 13 associates these words specifically with wandering charismatics; others see the lifestyle depicted as appropriate only for peasants who have few material possessions to begin with (cf. Pilch 1991: 188). Given contemporary models in Jewish Palestine, however, he probably addresses all would-be disciples to a radical lifestyle relinquishing dependence on possessions, while not necessarily relinquishing all possessions (see comment on Mt 4:20; cf. Acts 2:44-45; 4:32-35). At least ideally, Matthew's *whole* community remains a missionary community (24:14; 28:19).

207. Matthew 6:25-33 employs both arguments *a maiori ad minus* and *a minori ad maius* (see Dillon 1991).

208. Cf. also Aesop's *Fables* and the subsequent genre, e.g., Avianus *Fables* intro. 8-9. On God's fatherly care for creation, see, e.g., Philo *Creation* 10, 172.

borrow (Plut. *Borrowing* 7, *Mor.* 830 B), though unlike animals we do need clothing (Epict. *Disc.* 1.16.1). They also recognized humanity's inherent superiority to other animals (Epict. *Disc.* 1.16.2; 4.7.7).

Jesus draws a lesson from God's care for birds and flowers (6:26, 30). Although later Jewish teachers prohibited prayers for birds, considering this a trivialization of prayer (m. Ber. 5:3; Jeremias 1971: 182; Urbach 1979: 1:383), they did recognize God's provision for creatures (cf. Ps 104:24-27; Langer 1991) and that people were worth much more than birds. Jewish people recognized that God knew the exact number of raindrops he caused to fall (2 Bar. 21:8; cf. Mt 10:29). Teachers recognized God's care for animals in Scripture (Deut 25:4) and sometimes reasoned from this observation to God's care for people (Cohen 1966: 63; cf. Jos. *Apion* 2.213; 1 Cor 9:9-10); some emphasized mercy to animals (Test. Zeb. 5:1; Gen. Rab. 33:3; Pesiq. R. 48:2, 4). A late-second-century sage allegedly learned that not a single bird hunted by a fowler died or escaped apart from a heavenly decree, and decided that therefore he should emerge from hiding, trusting God to protect him as well (Pesiq. Rab Kah. 11:16; Gen. Rab. 79:6; cf. Mt 10:29). Another early teacher observed that just as animals and birds, created to serve humanity, did not toil, people, created to serve God, would not have had to toil had they not sinned (m. Qidd. 4:14).[209] Jesus, who regards God's original purpose at creation as still valid (19:4-6), believes that the God who cares for unemployed animals will care still more for his children regardless of their economic situation.

Sheep were the most common grazing animal in the ancient Mediterranean world, so clothes were commonly made of wool, or of linen made from flax; only the rich wore silk, and cotton was not widely used. Poor people often wore wool undyed or, when possible, stained with cheap, dark dye producing a grey or dull brown cloak; for dressier occasions (cf. 22:11) they might wear brighter colors from vegetable dyes, though only the rich could afford the various shades of purple (Cary and Haarhoff 1946: 96-97). People considered their cloaks essential, and the law in fact took this for granted (Ex 22:26-27; Guelich 1982: 339). John had rugged clothing, but at least he had some (3:4). Some early Christians (less given to hyperbole than their Palestinian masters) declared that Christians need nothing more than food and clothing (1 Tim 6:8). But Jesus declares that God can provide for his children adequately even if they *lack* clothing (cf. also 5:40)! He appeals to the splendor of the fields, whose vegetation is nevertheless used as

209. Vermes 1993: 85-86 elaborates the contrast between Jesus and Simeon ben Eleazar here; but Jewish teaching certain presupposed God's provision for his people (see, e.g., Davies and Allison 1988: 645, 650). Vermes 1993: 156n.4 thinks Matthew's Semitic "birds of the air" more original than Luke's "ravens" (Mt 6:31-32//Lk 12:24); he may be correct, but cf. 1 Kings 17:6, on which either Jesus or Luke may have drawn (often recalled, e.g., in Lev. Rab. 19:1; that pagans associated ravens with prophecy — Phaedrus 3.18.12 — is not likely relevant). Healey 1989 points here to a non-Masoretic variant on Proverbs 6:7 that does not seem to praise animals' (ants') industry; but such a model is too distant for the background of Jesus' saying in 6:26 (praise of ants' industry was also more widespread than Proverbs; cf. Virg. *Aen.* 4.402-7; Ovid *Metam.* 7.624-26, 655-57; Babrius 140; Phaedrus 4.25; cf. bees in Virg. *Aen.* 1.430-36; *Georg.* 4.156-57).

fuel for baking bread (Blomberg 1992a: 125; cf. Ps 104:27-36); were not people, to whom God gave such use of his creation, more valuable to him than these flowers? Since 6:30 identifies "lilies" (6:28) with "grass," the term probably refers in a general way to any of Jewish Palestine's wildflowers (Guelich 1982: 339; France 1985: 141), although some identify them with anemones, which were purple as one might imagine Solomon's royal apparel to be (6:29; Gundry 1982: 117; Jeremias 1972: 215; for royal purple, cf., e.g., 1 Macc 10:20, 62, 64; 14:43-44). Solomon's splendor had become proverbial (*CIJ* 2:83, §837; Jos. *Ant.* 8.35-41; m. B. Meṣ. 7:1; Guelich 1982: 340; Vermes 1993: 87n.11), but it remained miniscule compared to the splendor of God's creation (cf. Ps 8:1-9). In one ancient story, a powerful king asked a sage if he had witnessed any sight as lovely as the king's array; the sage responded that he had seen pheasants and peacocks far more beautiful, "for they shine in nature's colours, which are ten thousand times more beautiful" (Diog. Laert. 1.51, LCL 1:53). A Jewish teacher similarly reminded his hearers that no matter how much wealth a king possessed, only God could send him the rain to produce sustenance (Sifre Deut. 42.1.5). Health matters more than wealth (Sir 30:14-16), as the body matters more than clothing (Mt 6:25). In the end, Jesus teaches here, wealth does not matter, but God's blessing does, and he will provide it.

Jesus again shames his hearers by reminding them that even Gentiles seek material things (6:31-33; cf. 5:47; 6:7). Pagans seek (NRSV: "strive for"; NIV: "run after") their own needs (6:31-32); God's children should seek instead God's agendas, assured that God will care for them in the process (6:33). Even in Jesus' model prayer, his disciples seek God's kingdom first (6:9-10; on seeking God and his Torah, see, e.g., Ps 9:10; 27:8; 34:10; 119:2, 45; Sir 35:15; 51:13-14, 21; Wis 1:1-2; CD 1.10). The faith Jesus taught was not an intricate ritual to get what one desired, as in later magical texts; his teaching of faith meant obeying God's will with the assurance that God would ultimately fulfill the best interests of his children. In the Gospel tradition, that kind of faith grows only in the context of an intimate relationship of love between the heavenly Father and his children, the kind of relationship Jesus had with his Father and modeled for his disciples in his relationship with them.

Apart from a few philosophers who advocated concern for only one matter (e.g., Epict. *Disc.* 1.14), to the average Roman citizen of means, material advancement constituted a basic goal, as it does for most Western Christians (White 1971: 233). Yet nearly all Gentiles, especially the vast majority who were peasants working feudal estates, sought the basics, and some Greek-speaking Jewish writers, eager to perpetuate the notion that the Jews were a nation of philosophers, contrasted themselves with the Gentiles on this point. Other nations "are men of food and drink and raiment, for their whole disposition has recourse to these things," whereas the Jews disdained such concerns and contemplated only God's reign over the world (Ep. Arist. 140-41, trans. Hadas 1951: 157).

Jesus not only failed to associate faith with being able to obtain possessions from God, but Jesus did not even associate it with diligently *seeking* basic needs from God. Pagans seek those things, he warned (6:32); you should seek instead God's kingdom and his righteous will (6:33; cf. Clement of Alexandria's report of Jesus' saying in Jeremias 1964c: 99). Seeking God's kingdom means valuing what God values and obeying his commands: it is when his people care for others in need among them that God supplies the needs of his people as a whole, perhaps because then he can best trust them to use his gifts righteously (Deut 15:1-11; Blomberg 1992a: 126).[210]

Jewish people recognized that in calling them to love him with their whole heart and soul, God demanded that they care for him more than for their life or possessions (Sifre Deut. 32.4.2). Jesus and the prophets had faith in the Hebrew sense of *'emunah* — a firm, persevering trust (cf. Vermes 1984: 49). Modern readers who wish to hear the text as Matthew's first audience would have should listen to the text's demand in its radical fulness.

Anxiety does no good (6:27, 34). Anxiety will not add even the smallest unit of time to one's life. Some translations read as if one added a cubit to one's height (Schwarz 1980, speculatively retroverting into Aramaic; cf. Tert. *Spec.* 23), but the adjective "single" in the phrase "a single cubit" militates against this interpretation. Jesus in 6:27 refers not to adding a "mere" cubit to one's height — which would be a considerable addition! — but to adding a "mere" cubit to one's longevity (see Schweizer 1975: 165; Filson 1960: 101; France 1985: 140; cf. Ps 39:5), thus the NRSV translation, "a single hour." (Though a graphic image, a cubit as a metaphorical time unit was intelligible; cf., e.g., Ap. Rhod. 4.1510.) Jesus may employ intentional understatement here (rhetoricians would have called his figure "catachresis," whereby a related term substitutes for a more precise one, such as "short power" or "small height" — *Rhet. ad Herenn.* 4.33.45). Not only is it true that one cannot extend one's life by worrying; daily experience in our comparatively fast-paced culture confirms the wisdom of an earlier Jewish sage who observed that worry and a troubled heart actually shorten life (Sir 30:19-24; cf. Pub. Syr. 187). If much study is wearying to the flesh (Eccl 12:12), "worry" about wealth also banishes sleep and destroys the flesh (Sir 34:1).

Greek philosophers sometimes disdained such bodily needs altogether, complaining that their bodies were prisons because they were dependent on food and drink (Epict. *Disc.* 1.9.12) and advising that one turn one's mind to higher pursuits (Marc. Aur. 7.16). A Greek sage like Epictetus insisted that God would take care of good men, who ought not worry about food (*Disc.* 3.26.27), although he added that it was no major loss should God fail to provide and the good man die (*Disc.* 3.26.29; cf. 1.9.19-20)! Jesus never condemns people for recognizing these basic needs; their Father *knows* that they need food and clothing. Yet he calls them to depend on God for their daily sustenance, a provision that Jewish people considered one of God's greatest miracles (e.g., Gen. Rab. 20:9; 97:3; Pesiq. R. 33:5), and the most peasants could consistently hope for (cf. Oakman

210. The implied subject of the passive "shall be added" is God, as frequently in Jewish texts (Guelich 1982: 348).

1992: 118). Jewish teachers often insisted that God cared for Israel's needs, but only when Israel performed his will (Sifre Deut. 42.3.3). Those who could trust their heavenly Father to care for them (as most first-century Jewish children could depend on their earthly fathers) need not be anxious concerning clothes or food (Ep. Diogn. 9 follows Jesus here).

Unlike some early Christian writers, Jesus makes his point in graphic word pictures; his is the language of the oral literary artist. Like a typical sage, Jesus finally notes that one has enough to worry about for the day without adding tomorrow's worries (6:34; cf. Prov 27:1; b. Ber. 9b; Sanh. 100b; Yebam. 63b; Epict. *Disc.* 3.24.26).[211] There was no way to predict which of today's ventures would render success on the next day (Abrahams 1924: 209, citing Eccl 11:1-6 and b. Ber. 9b). Employing the typical rhetorical technique of personification (Kennedy 1984: 60; cf. *Rhet. ad Herenn.* 4.53.66; Cic. *De Nat. Deor.* 2.23.60-62), Jesus further admonishes his hearers to let "Tomorrow" worry about itself, the sort of admonition that also suits the graphic language of sages (Marc. Aur. *Med.* 7.16; cf. 12.1.1). Essene law forbade talk about the following day's work on the Sabbath (CD 10.19), but Jesus' rest requires continually leaving tomorrow with God, fulfilling God's true purpose for the Sabbath — rest (11:28-30), just as those who sought Wisdom would quickly be freed from care (Wis 6:15; cf. 7:23; m. 'Abot 3:5).

Yet when Jesus graphically forbids his disciples to worry about tomorrow (6:34; cf. "worries" also in 10:19; 13:22; Phil 4:6), this does not suggest that he expects them to ignore whatever concerns arise. Rather, he expects them to express dependence on God in each of these concerns, praying for their genuine needs (6:11), provided they pray for God's kingdom most of all (6:9-10; most of Paul's "concerns" fit this category — 2 Cor 11:28; 1 Thess 3:1-5). Whether or not "bread for tomorrow" is the correct interpretation of the petition in 6:11, Jesus' exhortation in 6:34 would not prohibit prayer for tomorrow's bread. Thus another early Jewish teacher could on the one hand daily utter the Jewish prayer called the Amida, the ninth benediction of which sought God for a good harvest, while contending on the other hand, "Whoever has a morsel in his basket and says What shall I eat tomorrow? is among those of little faith" (b. Soṭa 48b in Abrahams 1924: 106; cf. Mek. 16:4 in Smith 1951: 137).[212] True disciples can show God their love for him by trusting his loving purposes for them and leaving the future with him.

211. Frequently noted; see, e.g., Bultmann 1968: 106-7; Davies 1980: 221; Abrahams 1924: 208-9; Jeremias 1971: 18; Vermes 1993: 167n.21.

212. Some other later Jewish and Christian sages chided those of "little faith" (e.g., Mek. Vay. 5.11-14, 84; b. Pesaḥ. 24b; 118b; Soṭa 48b; Sent. Sext. 6; cf. Abrahams 1924: 191; Held 1963: 293; Lachs 1987: 133). "Of little faith" is acceptable Greek, but the term appears only in Semitic literature before the Gospels (Jeremias 1971: 161; Black 1967: 132), suggesting either that even the term was early in the Jesus tradition (see Lk 12:28) and/or that it reflects Matthew's Semitic world of thought (Mt 8:26; 14:31; 16:8; 17:20); it reduces the harshness of "no faith" (Mk 4:40).

Do Not Judge (7:1-6)

Cf. Mk 4:24-25; Lk 6:37-42; 8:18. The rhetoric of this section, like many of Jesus' other sayings, employs familiar techniques like hyperbole that may have moved an ancient audience to laughter. In this case, Jesus would have been employing such Middle Eastern humor (cf. Pilch 1995) to disarm his audience and communicate his message with intensity.

Matthew continues to arrange Jesus' teaching in a relevant, pastoral way to his readers. Jesus probably followed many topics at some length in his teaching before changing the subject, and the oral tradition of his teaching probably continued the process of arrangement. But Matthew has a special penchant for arranging Jesus' sayings, so it helps us to notice how he ties different blocks of Jesus' teaching together in the Sermon on the Mount. He retains at least 7:1-5, 12, 15-27 from the extant version of Jesus' sermon on this occasion (cf. Lk 6:31, 37-38, 41-49), which provides an extended sample of his teaching.

But both these and other teachings obtain special nuances by their context in Matthew's whole sermon. Thus, just as outward acts of righteousness can be misleading (6:1-18), disciples should avoid external evaluations of individuals altogether (7:1-5) and certainly not trust all religious claims (7:15-23). Just as Matthew's promise concerning giving (6:19-34; cf. Lk 11:34-36, 12:22-34) picks up his earlier discussion of private charity (6:1-4), his promise concerning prayer (7:7-11; cf. Lk 11:2-13, which includes the prayer of Mt 6:9-13) expands his earlier discussion of private prayer (6:5-15) and probably "seeking" the kingdom first (6:32-33). Jesus' admonition to self-examination (7:1-5), warning that few will enter God's kingdom (7:13-14), observation that one's behavior reveals one's character (7:15-20), and caution that one's life and not just lips must acknowledge Christ (7:21-23) suitably climax in his final warning that only those who obey his teaching will endure the judgment (7:24-27).[213]

Paul seems to allude to this judgment saying in Romans 2:1 (cf. 14:1, 10, 13; also Hagner 1993: 169); James 5:9 may also allude to it. Warnings about judging or accusing God's servants are, of course, much more ancient (Ps 109:6, 20, 29). The principle of reciprocity in 7:12 apparently forms an inclusio (a framing device; cf. 5:3, 10) with 7:1 (the NIV's "so" in 7:12 means "therefore," connecting it with its preceding context): since what you do will be returned to you, make sure you do what you would like to have done to you. In the context in Luke, who includes more sayings on the subject, giving and receiving God's mercy includes being like God (6:35-36; cf. Mt 5:45, 48). In both Matthew and Luke, this text reminds the sermon's readers that one cannot take the kingdom's demands seriously without also embracing grace.

Judging assumes a divine prerogative. The second line of 7:1 declares

213. Patte 1987: 95 connects this section with the preceding context thus: as "disciples should not have a negative attitude (anxiety) toward their own situation" in 6:25-34, "so they should not have a negative attitude toward others" in 7:1.

that the person judging "will be judged." It is not impossible that when Jesus first taught the crowds, he offered a proverb about human reciprocity: people will think ill of a critical, judgmental person (cf. 7:12). But another reading fits as well, and in this context, commentators are correct to read this line as a future divine passive indicating that God will judge conclusively on the day of judgment (Gundry 1982: 120-21; France 1985: 142; see 7:13-14, 25-27). The final judgment belongs to God alone, and those who seek to judge others now usurp God's position.

By this point in the sermon, a disciple who has been taking the Matthean Jesus' words seriously might well be too introspective to focus on judging others anyway. The graphic language of Jesus' teaching so far (5:3–6:34) challenges its hearers to a radical personal commitment to God's kingdom and righteousness that should scare them into attending to themselves. But just in case the hearers had been too obtuse to grasp that point in 5:3–6:34, Matthew renders it explicit in 7:1-5. One dare not assume God's prerogatives by withholding forgiveness (6:12-15) or judging (7:1-5). Disciples are instead objects of God's evaluation, and God evaluates most graciously the meek, who recognize God alone as God and judge. One should note, however, that Jesus warns against assuming God's prerogative to condemn the guilty, not against disciples' discerning truth from error (7:15-23). Further, Jesus does not oppose offering correction, but only offering correction in the wrong spirit (7:5; cf. 18:15-17; Gal 6:1-5).

The discourse recognizes that right beliefs about judging are inadequate. Although Jesus regards scribal and Pharisaic righteousness as inadequate (5:20), it is not because the scribes and Pharisees *professed* the wrong doctrine on this issue. The popular early sage Ben Sira warned that if one takes vengeance, God will take vengeance for one's sins (Sir 28:1), if one forgives others one will be forgiven by God (28:2), if one hates others one does not merit God's pardon (28:3). Another early sage, Hillel, reportedly declared, "Do not judge your neighbor until you have been in his situation [lit., 'his place']" (m. 'Abot 2:4/5).[214] Other early sages also insisted that one should assume the best of any person (ARN 19, §41B; cf. b. Shab. 127b).

As noted above, the issue is not failure to discern, but hypocrisy in judging others for one's own faults. Later rabbis declared that one should "remove [one's] own blemish first," giving the example of a rabbi who deferred a case to correct his own behavior before he ruled that another must do the same (Abrahams 1924: 118; see other examples in Bultmann 1968: 107; cf. b. Rosh Hash. 16b; Gen. Rab. 98:4). Greek and Roman sages offered similar wisdom: for example, one must solve one's own problems, and only then may one turn to crit-

214. Cf. admonitions to proper judgment in m. 'Abot 1:6, 8. The principle, "Judge not alone" (m. 'Abot 4:8; cf. Deut. Rab. 1:10), reflects mistrust for human fairness (cf. Vermes 1993: 159; he does not regard single judges as the Galilean practice in Jesus' day, however — 111-12; for Jewish priests as judges, cf. Diod. Sic. 40.3.5). Cf. the admonition to minimal judging *(minime iudice)* in Cato *Collection of Distichs* 53. For God's mercy to the merciful, see also texts in Davies and Allison 1988: 669; Lachs 1987: 136.

icizing others accurately (Demosth. *2d Olyn. Or.* 27); we see others' faults more quickly than our own (Longinus *Sublime* 4.1; Phaedrus 4.10; Babrius 66; Sen. *Dial.* 4.28.6-8). Likewise, "Practice nothing in your deeds for which you condemn others in your words" (Isoc. *Nic./Cypr.* 61, *Or.* 3.39, LCL 1:110-13),[215] which seems to have become part of common moral wisdom (cf., e.g., Juv. *Sat.* 2.9-10, 20-21; 14.38-40; Plut. *Profit by Enemies* 5, *Mor.* 88F-89A).

Not only the basic principle but the very image of measuring back what one measures out (7:2; what goes around comes around) was proverbial wisdom. In the marketplace one would measure out to others the appropriate portions of what they were purchasing (e.g., m. Beṣa 3:8). This image had become a Jewish maxim, however: "By the measure by which a man metes it is measured to him" (judgment in the present era in m. Soṭa 1:7; b. Soṭa 8b).[216] Perhaps only one stream of Jewish tradition applied it to the day of judgment as Jesus does (cf. Rüger 1969), but it is at least implied elsewhere: a person judged mercifully by another ("with the scale weighted in my favor") prayed that God would also judge the other mercifully at the judgment (ARN 8A). Jesus' contemporaries often affirmed his principle and even used the same kind of illustrations, but Jesus demands more than agreement from disciples: he demands *obedience* (7:24-27).

One blinds oneself by rationalizing away one's guilt (7:3-5; also 6:22-23; cf. Rom 2:1-3; Tert. *Apol.* 39.14). A splinter or wood chip in one's eye might render one blind, but a plank imbedded in one's eye would certainly render one blind. The image (possibly borrowed from a carpenter's workplace — France 1985: 143) is graphic, even hyperbolic (Tannehill 1975: 114-18):[217] consider the absurdity of one's walking around with a thick roof beam protruding from one's eye (as if either end of it would even fit!), totally ignorant of one's impossibly grotesque state. Just as one would not want someone blind leading one into a pit (15:14; 23:16), one would not want a blind eye surgeon operating on one's eyes.[218] Only one who sees well is competent to heal others' source of blindness (cf. 9:27-31; 20:29-34); thus one must "pluck out" (cf. 5:30) any impediments to sight.

215. Cf. similarly Isoc. *Demon.* 17, 48, *Or.* 1; Sen. *Ep. Lucil.* 20.1-2; Diog. Laert. *Lives* 6.2.28; probably Catonian lines in Columbanus 27 in *Minor Latin Poets* 1:630-31; Manson 1979: 58 cites Democritus.

216. See at least four different early sources, plus later ones, in Smith 1951: 135; Dalman 1929: 225; Davies and Allison 1988: 670; Bivin 1991.

217. Cf. possible parallels in Renehan 1973: 19; Hagner 1993: 169. The Talmud complains of those who resent "the mildest criticism. If someone is told, 'Take the chip out of your eye!' he retorts, 'Take the beam out of yours!' (b. ʿArak. 16b; b. B. Bat. 15b)" (Vermes 1993: 80; other texts in Lachs 1987: 137); if this is not a polemical distortion of Jesus' saying, it probably reflects a common figure of speech, in which case Jesus is graphically saying that those who resent our criticism have a point until we get our lives in order.

218. This would especially be the case if the surgeon's eyes had been removed for ruining someone else's in an earlier surgery (5:38; cf. similar penalties in some cultures, e.g., Hammurabi 218-20). Eye surgery sometimes involved lancing the eye (Epict. *Disc.* 1.25.32), a delicate operation. Crocker 1991 notes the use of bone rather than metal spatulas in removing articles from one's eye.

Even when one is right, one should not impose the truth on others against their will (7:6). Jesus' saying in 7:6 is certainly authentic; although unattested elsewhere, it is inconceivable that Matthew would simply create a saying that fits his context with such difficulty (also in favor of authenticity, cf. the Aramaic rhythm in Jeremias 1971: 25). Its meaning is unfortunately less clear than its authenticity; as Schnackenburg puts it, the saying is "rätselhafter" and "dunkel" (1985: 72-73). Perhaps because the saying seems to make such little sense in its Matthean context, interpretations of 7:6 abound.

Some think that the "dogs" here are the Gentiles (15:26) and the pearl the gospel of the kingdom (13:45-46; see Meier 1980: 69-70).[219] The specific connection between dogs and Gentiles some have drawn in other Jewish texts (Manson 1979: 174 cites especially 1 Enoch 89) appears but is not well-attested enough (given other usages) to insure this meaning, however (Abrahams 1924: 195; Johnston 1977b: 596; Vermes 1993: 89). The image of dogs even in 15:26 is not quite as wholly negative and demeaning as it is here (see comment there), so it is unlikely that the saying ever applied to the Gentile mission (see Jeremias 1958: 20n.8), despite other possible limitations on that mission in the history of the Matthean community (perhaps 10:5). Certainly *Matthew* would not have understood the saying as prohibiting the Gentile mission, because he views Jesus' teaching in the Sermon on the Mount as applicable in his own day (7:21-27; 28:19), whereas the prohibition of preaching the kingdom to Gentiles (10:5) was restricted to the time of Jesus' earthly ministry (28:19). Had Matthew had an isolated saying that his readers might have understood as prohibiting the Gentile mission, he surely would have placed it in the context of 10:5-6, not here. Other attempts to narrow the saying's object to prohibiting sinners from the Eucharist, as in the Didache (9.5; cf. Llewelyn 1989 on the redactional level; rejected in Fenton 1977: 110) also exceed our evidence.[220]

Nevertheless, Matthew's audience, hearing the Gospel more than once, might interpret this saying in the light of 15:26. In that case, the saying might warn against giving miracles (cf. 7:7-11) to those unwilling to be part of the family, just as Jesus demands faith and submission rather than bestowing his power like magic (15:22-28). In this case the saying forces people to press in to become disciples (13:10-12); it would qualify both the following context about prayer and the preceding prohibition against "judging," inviting disciples to discern

219. Lachs 1987: 138-40 notes rabbinic warnings against teaching Torah to Gentiles (e.g., b. Ḥag. 13a), the figurative use of pearls for clever teaching (t. Soṭa 7; Mek. on Ex 13:2; ARN 18; b. Ḥag. 3a), and dogs and pigs as Gentiles (b. Shab. 188a; Yoma 29a); yet curiously he concludes that here dogs represent Samaritans (Gen. Rab. 81:3) and pigs, Rome.

220. Many think the text contains an allusion to dogs disdaining holy things like sacrificial food (Smith 1951: 146; Kahane 1957; Gundry 1982: 123; France 1985: 143); one writer less reasonably suggests that a scribe altered the text to read thus (Maxwell-Stuart 1979; but cf. Llewelyn 1989, who suggests an intentional reapplication). People threw dogs meat (Gen. Rab. 57:4; meat torn by animals was always to be left for the dogs — Ex 22:31; Ps-Phocyl. 147-48; contrast von Lips 1988), but Aseneth felt it better to throw sacrificial meat to street dogs (scavengers) than to her pets (Jos. and Asen. 10:13).

"dogs" from God's children. Still, both 7:6 and 15:26 appear preredactional, and it is possible that Matthew intended no connection; had Matthew intended an obvious connection, 7:6 would have fit better closer to the pericope of the Canaanite woman.

In its most general sense the logion probably was simply a wisdom saying like Proverbs 23:9: "Do not speak in the hearing of a fool, who will only despise the wisdom of your words" (NRSV; cf. also Syr. Men. Sent. 328-32). Some thus suspect that Matthew has apostate Christians in view (Meier 1980: 69-70; Guelich 1982: 354). Dogs may refer to the wicked or oppressors more generally (cf. Ps 22:16, 20; 59:6, 14-15; Prov 26:11; Gen. Rab. 63:8; 65:1; Ex. Rab. 9:2).[221] It was also commonly known that stray scavenger dogs — the main kind encountered in the towns of Jewish Palestine (Tob 5:16 probably reflects Diaspora thought) — growled at those feeding them as much as at passing strangers (Isoc. *Demon.* 29, *Or.* 1). Clearly these are people who do not value what disciples have to offer them, like swine who find what looked like peas or acorns to be inedible instead (A. B. Bruce 1979: 129-30). Swine proverbially lacked appreciation of value (Prov 11:22), and even people "trampled underfoot" what they viewed as worthless (Mt 5:13).

Its possible sense in its present Matthean context has provoked a variety of proposals; after all, Matthew had some reason for including the saying where he did, even if it is not a perfect fit.[222] Some therefore connect the saying to the preceding context by suggesting that it means that it is worthless to try to correct (7:1-5) someone unwilling to listen (cf. Sen. *Ep. Lucil.* 29.2-3); one should let the person be as a Gentile (18:17, assuming again the identification of dogs and Gentiles; cf. van Zyl 1982). But in this case, given the possibility that the self-evaluated person would evaluate others in verse 4, one would expect verse 6 to contain some note of disjunction (Schweizer 1975: 170-71). Others note that while disciples should not judge (7:1-5), some people should be avoided (A. B. Bruce 1979: 129-30) and disciples must exercise discernment (Guelich 1982: 353; France 1985: 144); these suggestions are noteworthy but likewise fail to explain the lack of disjunction. Still others contend that 7:6 functions as an illustration of 7:1-2: judging others is like giving food to dogs, and being judged like one's gifts and oneself being trampled (Bennett 1987).

221. Jewish texts considered dogs evil (e.g., Sifre Deut. 81.4.2) and regarded them as unclean and scavengers (cf., e.g., b. Sanh. 108b, bar.; Shab. 121b, 128a) alongside pigs (for pigs' uncleanness, cf., e.g., Jos. *War* 1.34; b. Ber. 25a; Qidd. 49b; Gen. Rab. 63:8; probably Mt 8:31; Aelian *Animals* 7.19); one early Christian text links apostate Christians in this capacity with both dogs and swine (2 Pet 2:22); probably because they both liked unclean surroundings, some other texts also link them (e.g., Aristoph. *Peace* 24; Hor. *Epodes* 1.2.25-26; Davies and Allison 1988: 677 cite also 1 Enoch 89:42; *P. Oxy.* 5.840.33; b. Shab. 155b; Hor. *Epodes* 2.2.75, of varying value). For pigs' uncleanness in ancient Egypt, cf. *ANET* 10; Herod. *Hist.* 2.47; Plut. *Isis* , *Mor.* 353CF; Jos. *Apion* 2.141; for chthonic deities, *ANET* 209, 351; Moyer 1969: 29, 96 (citing, e.g., *KUB* 17.28.4-5; 36.83.3, 7); Aristophanes *Peace* 1.372; Ferguson 1987: 202.

222. By contrast, Luz 1989: 419 altogether abandons reading it in its Matthean context, suggesting (probably rightly) that its original, proverbial sense in Q allowed multivalent usage.

Most likely, 7:6 provides a transition between the preceding and following contexts. One commentator suggests that just as people are careful how they measure and to whom they give (7:1-6; cf. Hesiod *W.D.* 354: Give only to one who gives), God will do likewise, giving only to those willing to receive from him, forgiving the forgivers and being merciful to the merciful (7:7-11; Fenton 1977: 110). A similar interpretation might combine the strengths of several of the above proposals: correcting those who will not receive correction is futile (7:1-5; Prov 9:8; 23:9); one should discerningly continue to offer wisdom or the gift of the kingdom (cf. 13:45-46) only to those willing to receive what one offers, just as God does (7:7-11). In this case the text sounds a note of reciprocity to be repeated in 7:12 (Keener 1993: 64). If 7:6 means something along these lines, it does not allow one to prejudge who may receive one's message (13:3-23), but does forbid one to try to force it on those who show no inclination to accept it (10:13-16; cf. Carson 1984b: 185; Blomberg 1992a: 128-29; Hagner 1993: 172).[223]

Good Gifts Guaranteed (7:7-11)

Cf. Lk 11:9-13. Jesus' call to prayer in this passage opens with a typically Semitic step parallelism (Bailey 1976: 48; cf. Manson 1979: 32; Jeremias 1971: 25; Tannehill 1975: 46-47):

A Ask, and it will be given you
  B Seek and you will find
    C Knock and it will be opened to you
A′ For everyone who asks receives
  B′ And the one who seeks finds
    C′ And to the one who knocks it will be opened

Matthew did not elect to place this passage on prayer in his longer section on the subject in 6:5-15, but the present passage fulfills important functions in its immediate context. The image behind "asking" is that of a dependent child making a request of his or her father (6:8-9; cf. 21:22); the image of giving a gift may continue the thought of 7:6 suggested above.[224] Contextually, the supreme object of "seeking" is the kingdom (6:33; for the food he mentions, cf. also 8:11; on "finding," cf. 10:39; 11:29; 13:44; 16:25); though disciples ask God to supply their material needs (6:11), they do not "seek" them zealously (6:32-33; cf. 1

223. Cf. the Pythagorean *akousma,* "Do not throw bread into a chamber pot," which was understood as, "Do not try to teach those who are unfit to receive your teachings" (Thom 1994: 109).

224. Jeremias wrongly construes the asking of 7:7 more narrowly than I have as the image of the asking of beggars (1971: 191). Although he is correct that beggars learned the lesson of persistence, Jesus contextually refers only to children asking from fathers (7:11), a relationship that undoubtedly yielded more answered requests!

Tim 6:5-11). The door to be opened is the gate of salvation (7:13; contrast Lk 11:5-13). Thus it is possible that Matthew's emphasis in this section is prayer for God's rule (cf. 6:9-10).[225] Another possible sense of the context is that if one should not judge others (7:1-5), one may nevertheless pray for them (cf. 18:15-20). In either case, the specific application of the saying in a given context depends on its more general principle concerning how God hears prayers of faith (21:21-22; cf. 14:28-31). That Matthew and Luke felt free to reapply the pericope in various ways suggests that the tradition already applied it in a general manner, probably in accord with Jesus' teaching to his disciples on faith.

God can supply anything to the righteous who seek his purposes (7:7-10). This pericope emphasizes some important lessons: *First, Jesus promises his disciples extraordinary power with God, like that of Elijah of old.* In this case, the Gospel narratives and other "charismatic" sayings (e.g., Mk 9:23; 11:22-25; Jn 14:13-14; 15:7; 16:23-27; cf. Jas 1:5) demonstrate that Jesus was not speaking figuratively, but training disciples to express bold faith (cf. 6:8; 18:19; 20:20; 21:21). Early Jewish teaching did celebrate God's kindness in answering prayer (Hagner 1993: 174), but rarely promises such universal answers to prayer to all of God's people as the language here suggests.[226] Only a small number of sages were considered pious enough to have such power with God. Judaism had a tradition concerning men of God with holy chutzpah, or boldness, who could request and receive anything they asked from God (e.g., Lachs 1987: 171-80; Keener 1991b: 138-39; Vermes 1993: 198; citing, e.g., b. Ta'an. 25b; 26b; Pesiq. Rab Kah. 22:2). Both the Hebrew Bible (e.g., Gen 32:26-30; Ex 33:12–34:9; 1 Kings 18:36-37, 41-46; 2 Kings 2:2, 4, 6, 9; 4:14-28) and the Gospel tradition (Mk 5:27-34; 7:24-30; 10:46-52; Mt 8:7-13; Jn 2:3-5) provide examples of such bold faith. Greek tradition sometimes valued sages' impudence (e.g., Diog. Laert. 6.2.34), and Jewish sages also respected persistence (e.g., Pesiq. Rab Kah. 22:2). But Vermes and others have drawn attention especially to a tradition of Jewish holy men like Honi the Circle-Drawer and Hanina ben Dosa, who could pray and receive almost anything from God. The most crucial model for such holy men is probably Elijah, who despite his human frailty (1 Kings 19:4) could summon fire from heaven against those potentially threatening his life simply by declaring, "If I am a man of God, may fire come down from heaven" (2 Kings 1:10, 12-15). James, a sage who may move in the general Matthean circle, likewise tells us that Elijah was a person of flesh and blood just like his audience,

225. Compare Luke's parallel section, in which the Lord's Prayer and this connected exhortation address prayer for Spirit-empowerment (Lk 11:13; this is probably Lukan redaction, with Menzies 1991: 181; Witherington 1994: 243; pace Gundry 1982: 124; cf. Jas 1:17). (Compare Wis 6:14: whoever seeks Wisdom will find her.)

226. For exceptions, cf., e.g., Pesiq. Rab Kah. 28:2; Pesiq. R. 23:9 (God answers the prayers of those who delight in the Sabbath); third-century Test. Adam 1:10 (if one prays at the right time of night); Ep. Arist. 18 (not a promise, but a hope that God hears prayers motivated by righteousness; cf. Ep. Arist. 192). Cf. also Herm. 2.9. Though Goodenough 1953/68: 2:160 wrongly relates the promise in Jn 14:13 to magical name invocation (cf. Keener 1993: 299-300), he observes that it exceeds anything "claimed for most charms."

who through faith could have access to the kind of miracles that Elijah had (Jas 5:16-18).

Second, it presupposes that the petitioners will be as committed to God's purposes as Elijah and like-minded servants of God were. Such a call to believing prayer supposes a heart of piety submitted to God's will; although Jesus states the promise graphically, he implicitly addresses only disciples, who will seek the good of God's kingdom and provision for their basic needs (6:11, 19-34). Jesus' promise is for the righteous — people who share kingdom values in 6:19-34, who ask God to supply their basic needs and requests concerning the kingdom. But beyond this significant limitation, Jesus' promise might have amazed and troubled his first hearers (most proposed parallels in Dalman 1929: 230; Smith 1951: 137-38 resemble the wording only, not the concept). Jesus' disciples were to be prophets (5:12) and holy persons whose requests God would hear, like Elijah or Honi of old.

Third, this passage's context suggests the kinds of prayers Matthew intends such righteous people to offer. They seek first the purposes of God's kingdom (6:9-10, 31-33; cf. Ps 9:10; 24:6; 27:4, 8; 34:14; 63:1; 69:6, 32; 70:4; 119:45; 122:6-9; and especially Prov 2:4-5; 8:17; Is 55:6; Jer 29:13) and provision for their own basic needs (6:11). "Good things" (7:11) is not very specific; it sometimes referred to agricultural produce that the righteous would then share with others (Test. Iss. 3:7-8), and at other times to prosperity more generally (Sib. Or. 3.659-60, 750; cf. Test. Jos. 2:7). Some traditions (probably foreign to both Jesus and Matthew) suggested prayers for "good things" in general because one could not know what was good, for any specific gift one might seek could produce harm (Pythagoras in Diod. Sic. 10.9.8; Diog. Laert. *Lives* 8.1.9; contrast Mt 6:11-13).[227] Yet the specific examples Jesus gives that children would request are basic staples in the Palestinian diet — bread and fish (meat was a rare luxury; see Safrai 1974/76b: 747).[228] Of course such requests fit the image in the parable; often such staples might be all that Palestinian Jewish fathers could provide their children on a regular basis.[229] But they also indicate the sort of range Jesus'

227. This may stem from the commonplace that in some cases humanity has corrupted everything good (e.g., Diod. Sic. 12.1.1). Cf. Diog. Laert. *Lives* 6.2.42: Diogenes "would rebuke men in general with regard to their prayers, declaring that they asked for those things which seemed to them to be good, not for such as are truly good" (LCL 2:44-45); or Diog. Laert. *Lives* 2.136: when Menedemus heard one claim "that the greatest good was to get all you want, he rejoined, 'To want the right things is a far greater good'" (LCL 1:266-67; cf. also Sent. Sext. 88). In Jos. *Apion* 2.197, God has given what is good, so prayer is securing it.

228. Neusner 1984: 23; cf. Pliny *N.H.* 22.68.138; Sib. Or. 3.243; in more detail Lewis 1983: 68. Ancients typically regarded wheat as the most important kind of food besides wine (e.g., Diod. Sic. 4.3.5).

229. Giving bread as an act of kindness might be contrasted with casting stones (Phaedrus 3.2.17-18). That a loaf of peasant bread could appear as a stone and one variety of local catfish looked like a snake (Jeremias 1972: 226; Meier 1980: 70; France 1985: 144) is probably irrelevant since that kind of fish was unclean and fathers would not serve it anyway (cf. Jeremias 1972: 226). That women often cooked bread on hot, flat stones and that small pieces of stone sometimes invaded the flour (Hepper 1992: 92) is probably also irrelevant, except for possible associations of image.

promise includes: the basics he had already promised his hearers (6:25-34). Jesus later provided bread and fish for his followers (14:19-20; 15:36-37), encouraging Matthew's audience that the risen Lord would also hear their requests for provision for their lives and the work of the kingdom (6:11; 10:8-13, 40-42).

God's Fatherly care for his children is their assurance that he will answer them (7:11; cf. 6:8). God, who gives "good gifts" to his children, may not grant a child's request for something harmful (in contrast to some pagan expectations concerning misplaced prayers — Ovid *Metam.* 2.44-102; 3.287-98, 308-9; 11.100-105; 14.129-53),[230] but he will not withhold any good thing from those who desire and seek what is right (Ps 37:4; 84:11). Jewish scholars typically argued by means of "how much more" arguments *(qal waḥomer):*[231] if a principle is true in the lesser case, how much more in the greater.[232] Thus another sage perhaps a century after Jesus taught, "If a member of a man's household is well-treated, how much more a member of the Creator's household?" (Sifre Num. 88, cited in Smith 1951: 138; Lachs 1987: 142). As Tannehill points out, "The vivid oddness of considering whether we fathers might respond to the needs of our children in a harmful or capricious way makes distrust of the heavenly Father appear unnatural" in 7:7-10, which the "how much more" of 7:11 reinforces (Tannehill 1975: 133).

Reciprocate good deeds in faith (7:12). Cf. Lk 6:31. If those who con-

230. Although Jesus commonly uses the divine passive, Blomberg 1992a: 130 thinks that this without a subject allows the notion here that God will decide what is best when "(it) is given" to you. God was known for his beneficence of good gifts for his people (Tob 4:19; Philo *Creation* 77-78; Gen. Rab. 13:15; 1 Tim 4:4; Jas 1:17; in paganism, Cleanthes' *Hymn to Zeus* in Stobaeus *Eclogae* 1.1.12).

231. *Qal waḥomer* is *extremely* frequent in rabbinic texts, e.g., m. 'Abot 1:15 (on an extrabiblical saying!); t. Ber. 4:16, 17; 6:19; Pe'a 3:8; Ter. 6:4; Kil. 5:6; Ma'aś. 2:2; Shab. 15:16; B. Qam. 7:6; 'Ed. 3:4; Mek. Pisha 1.38; 2.36-37; 7.48, 61; 9.45; 13.105; 16.119, 126; Beshallah 1.54; 2.73; 7.128; Bahodesh 5.90; 11.64, 109; Nez. 1.101; 2.17; 3.43, 69, 128; 10.47, 67; 12.5; 16.92; 18.79, 80, 83, 97; Kaspa 2.26; 5.51, 80, 103; Shabbata 1.14; 2.41; Sifra V. D. Den. par. 2.3.4.3; par. 3.5.3.2; par. 5.10.1.1; V. D. Deho. pq. 12.53.1.3; Sifra Sav pq. 8.80.1.2; par. 9.90.1.3, 8; pq. 17.96.1.1; Sav Mekilta DeMiluim par. 98.8.5, 7; 98.9.5; Shemini Mekilta deMiluim 99.3.9; Sifra Shir. par. 1.100.3.1; pq. 3.104.1.3; pq. 4.105.2.2; 3.2; pq. 6.99.3.7, 8; pq. 9.115.7, 8; Neg. pq. 1.127.2.1; 127.3.11; par. 3.131.1.1; pq. 8.139.1.1; Mes. par. 2.150.1.2, 5, 10; Zab. par. 1.160.2.1; pq. 1.161.4; par. 2.163.1.1; pq. 3.164.2.2; par. 3.166.2.1; Qed. pq. 11.209.1.7; Emor par. 1.211.1.8; par. 12.236.1.2; Behuq. par. 1.260.1.1; pq. 2.262.1.9; pq. 12.276.3.13; Sifre Num. 1.4.1; 1.6.3; 8.1.1; 15.1.1; 15.2.2; 16.3.1; 18.1.1; 23.1.1; 25.7.1; 26.6.1; 28.2.2; 29.1.1; 30.1.1; 30.2.1; 31.3.2; 31.4.1; 35.1.2; 42.1.1; 42.2.3; 78.1.1; 78.4.1; 92.4.1; 99.2.2; 103.1.1; 104.1.1; 105.1.1; 107.3.2, 3; 111.5.3; 112.2.3; 115.3.2; Sifre Deut. 1.8.2-3; 18.2.2; 26.1.1; 27.2.1; 32.5.1, 4; 34.2.1; 35.1.2; 37.1.2, 5; 37.2.1; 38.1.4; 38.2.3; 47.3.1-2; b. Ber. 62b; B. Meṣ. 2b; 3ab; Ḥag. 27a; Shab. 143b; Ter. 16a; Gen. Rab. 60:7; 73:5; 81:4; 82:14; 92:7; 100:6, bar.; Lev. Rab. 25:6; 31:2; Pesiq. Rab Kah. 12:16. For Hillel's seven rules, cf., e.g., t. Sanh. 7:11; ARN 37A; Beraita DeRabbi Ishmael Pereq 1.8; for Ishmael's thirteen, e.g., Beraita DeRabbi Ishmael Parashah 1.1; b. Ḥul. 115b.

232. This is hardly the only example in Jesus' teaching (pace Bultmann 1968: 185; cf., e.g., 6:30; 10:25), though it is often implicit (e.g., Lk 18:6-7). This traditional Jewish feature could represent a mark of authenticity, though the matter is not so readily decided (the same form appears outside Jewish Palestine; cf. Aristotle in Kennedy 1980: 71). Some take the rare "Who among you?" formulation as a sign that the saying is authentic; see Aune 1983: 165.

demn others are condemned (7:1-5), God clearly operates on a principle of reciprocity; thus one must do good to people *in advance* of their doing good to one, trusting God to reward one later. The principle in this context is: as one gives, it will be given to one by God in the day of judgment (cf. also Test. Zeb. 5:3). If God is the example of giving (7:7-11), one should give whatever people need (5:42). How one treats others (7:12) reveals one's character (7:16-20), hence one's eternal destiny (7:13-14, 21-23).[233]

This golden rule was a widespread principle of ancient ethics.[234] This principle coopts the principle of retaliation (Judg 15:11; Prov 24:29); in societies where honor was rewarded and shame avenged, one who did harm to others invited harm in return (cf. Num 35:16-25; Judg 1:7, 9, 24, 56; Ps-Philo 11:10-13; Hesiod *W.D.* 709-12; Diog. Laert. 1.69; Phaedrus 1.26; Gen. Rab. 96 MSV). Such a context naturally invited meditation on the fact that one ought to treat others as one wished to be treated (the positive form of the rule) and not treat others as one did not wish to be treated (the negative form of the rule). The positive form of the rule appears as early as Homer and recurs in Herodotus, Isocrates, and Seneca (Danker 1972: 86; Meier 1980: 70); the negative form appears in Tobit 4:15 ("And what you hate, do not do to anyone") and in Philo (*Hypothetica* 7.6).[235]

Another early Jewish work employed a form that straddled both, advising a king: "Just as you do not wish evils to befall you, but to participate in all that is good, so you should deal with those subject to you and with offenders" (Ep. Aristeas 207; trans. Hadas 1951: 181). Although some commentators have tried to disparage the negative form by contrast with the positive (seeking to make Jesus' rule here more distinctive), they mean essentially the same thing; both biblical law (Lev 19:18) and Paul (Rom 13:10) define the positive commandment of love by means of negative commandments (Sanders 1992: 258-59; cf. Guelich 1982: 360-61).

Apart from its function as an epitome of the law, the saying was probably a proverb before Hillel (Moore 1971: 2:87), as its earlier occurrence in Tobit and

233. At least since a sermon of John Wesley in 1750, this has been called the "Golden Rule" (Guy 1959); over a millennium earlier, a Christian Roman emperor allegedly engraved the saying on his wall in gold (France 1985: 145).

234. Ancient wisdom also included the more familiar political strategy of today: Do to others what they would do to you if they could before they can (Demosth. *1st Olynthiac Oration* 24).

235. One may compare Isoc. *Demon.* 21, *Or.* 1; *To Nic.* 38, *Or.* 2; *Nic./Cypr.* 49, 3.37; Sen. *Ep. Lucil.* 47.11; Diog. Laert. 1.36, 59 (Thales, Solon); Syr. Men. Sent. 245-51; Pub. Syr. 2; cf. Arist. *Rhet.* 1.5.16, 1361b. For Stoic parallels to the Golden Rule, cf. Epict. *Disc.* 1.11.25; Hierocles *Duties. Fraternal Love* 4.27.20; see van der Horst 1975: 157; early Christian philosophers carried on the thought (Sent. Sext. 179-80); cf. also Gos. Thom. 6.3 (a derivative form; see Chilton 1994: 123-49). Although the *idea* in the positive form existed in Judaism (Sir 31/34:15; ARN 26A; 29, §60B; Targ. Ps-J. on Lev 19:18), the lack of the form suggests to Vermes the authenticity of Jesus' saying by the criterion of dissimilarity (1993: 41). One could as easily argue that hellenistic Christians adapted its form, but the presence of the idea in Judaism makes the small change in form relatively simple and the common property of sages.

its later appearance without citation in a story of an early second-century rabbi indicate (see Dalman 1929: 226; Montefiore and Loewe 1974: 172-73). The principle that God requites what people have sown is also ancient (e.g., Judg 1:7; 9:24, 56).

One who observes this basic principle will fulfill all the basic principles of the law the way God intended them (cf. 5:21-48; 22:37-40). Later Jewish tradition declares that the sage Hillel, who taught before Jesus did, had already seen this rule as "the heart of the law," as Jesus also put it (possibly drawing on contemporary Greek concepts of the unwritten law — Jeremias 1963: 3). As the story goes, a Gentile approached both Hillel and his rival sage, promising each that he would convert to Judaism if the sage could teach it to him concisely ("while standing on one foot," which was proverbial for doing something with ease, e.g., Hor. *Sat.* 1.4.10; plausibly but less likely, Jospe 1990 prefers reading *rgl* as the Latin "rule"). Hillel declared, "Do not do to your fellow what you hate to have done to you. This is the whole Law, entire; the rest is explanation. Go, learn!" (b. Shab. 31a as quoted in Moore 1971: 2:86-87).[236] By echoing the Matthean phrase "law and prophets" in 5:17, this epitome joins that statement as pivotal expressions of the sermon's ethics (see Luz 1989: 429-30).

This principle must guide one's daily treatment of others. The principle is so natural that it appears in cultures totally isolated from the ancient Mediterranean, including Confucian teaching from sixth-century-B.C. China (verbally almost identical to the negative formulation above; see Jochim 1986: 125). The commonness of this principle should not surprise us because one of the most natural rules of ethics is that a person extrapolates from his or her own worth to that of others, and hence values others as oneself (cf., e.g., Sir 31:15); thus every person is morally responsible to recognize how he or she ought to treat every other person.

In Matthew's ethics, no one so insensitive as to demean another human being on account of that person's social station (e.g., a child — 18:3-4; 19:14; 21:16) warrants God's mercy (5:7; 6:14-15; 7:1-5). This is the law of love, the principle by which Jesus epitomizes the entire humanward aspect of God's law (22:39-40; cf. Jn 13:34-35), a principle Jesus' earliest followers never forgot (Rom 13:8-10; Gal 5:14; 6:2; Jas 2:8) What is distinctive about Matthew's citation of the principle is its relation to the day of judgment in this context (7:1-2, 13-14; contrast Lk 6:31, where it naturally fits the flow of Lk 6:27-36//Mt 5:38-48).

236. Because the evidence for Hillel's saying is so late (Sanders 1992: 258), one could argue that Matthew's use of the phrase as a legal epitome may have influenced his contemporaries; but it was clearly in vogue by the early second century (ARN 25, §53B). Jewish teachers also produced other epitomes of the law, however (ARN 27A; 24, §49B; Philo *Decal.* 154; 4 Macc 2:7-9; cf. Epict. *Disc.* 1.20.14-15; Diog. Laert. 6.1.11); a general summary of principles was an important practice of Jewish law (Goulder 1974: 25; Vermes 1993: 44).

Present Claims versus Future Judgment (7:13-23)

Cf. Lk 6:43-46; 13:23-27. Most first-century Jewish people believed that they were saved by virtue of descent from Abraham (3:9). Yet Jesus regards the assumption of salvation as a deception; most of his contemporaries were unsaved (7:13-14). Those who led them showed by their lives that they were not God's true representatives (7:15-20); indeed, professing servants of Christ would themselves be banished from God's presence in the judgment (7:21-23), for only those who truly obeyed Jesus' teaching would stand (7:24-27). Matthew intends this part of the discourse not only to challenge his community's opponents but to prevent his community from becoming like that of those opponents.

The way of salvation is narrower than Jesus' hearers think (7:13-14). Greek and Roman writers fairly often employed the image of the two paths in life (Sen. *Ep. Lucil.* 8.3; 27.4; Diogenes 30 to Hicetas; Aune 1987: 197; cf. the Pythagorean version of a narrower way in Athenaeus *Deipn.* 10.77; Porphyry *Vit. Pyth.* 42; Thom 1994: 106) or two ways after death (Virg. *Aen.* 6.540-43; Cic. *Tusc. Disp.* 1.30.72). Jewish pietists also stressed the two moral ways (Deut 30:15; Ps 1:1; m. 'Abot 2:9; Test. Asher 1:3, 5);[237] early Christian literature developed it further (cf. Did. 1:1–6:2; Barn. 18:1–21:9; see Kraft 1965: 134-62), and those particularly concerned with the future judgment especially employed the image of the two ways, the narrow one leading to life (cf. 19:17) and the broad one to destruction (4 Ezra 7:3-16, 60-61; 8:1-3; Test. Abr. 11A; 8B).[238] The story is told of a pious first-century teacher, Johanan ben Zakkai, unsure on his deathbed whether he will proceed on the road to paradise or the one to Gehenna (ARN 25A; b. Ber. 28b; Gen. Rab. 100:2; cf. Gen. Rab. 96:5); other accounts similarly depict those two roads after death (ARN 25A; Pesiq. Rab Kah. 27:2; cf. Gen. Rab. 59:6; 69:7).[239]

To enter the narrow gate of the kingdom one must knock — that is, request that God make one a citizen of his kingdom (7:7-8).[240] The difficulty of Jesus'

237. Also Qoh. Rab. 1:14, §1; Lev. Rab. 30:2; Deut. Rab. 4:3; Song Rab. 1:9, §2. In Proverbs, see Bricker 1995; see further Young 1989: 242, especially on Sifre Deut. 53. The weighing of souls in Test. Abr. 12-13 may reflect an Egyptian image (Ellul 1990).

238. Cf. Sib. Or. 2:150; Ex. Rab. 30:20; Nickelsburg 1972: 27-29; for Qumran cf. Robinson 1962: 20; for the rabbis, Davies 1980: 315-16; Flusser 1988: 500.

239. In Lk 13:22-27, the sayings about few being saved (there a question, probably provoked by sectarian ideas such as later appear in 4 Ezra) and the gate (Mt 7:13-14) appear directly before the damnation of evildoers who claimed to know Jesus (Mt 7:21-23); Matthew inserts other material from the appropriate place in the Q sermon (Lk 6:43-45) directly into this sequence (Mt 7:15-20; cf. 12:33). It is possible that Luke has rearranged some material; clearly 13:30 derives from Mk 10:31, where Luke (18:30; contrast Mt 19:30; 20:16) omits it. Lk 13:25-27 resembles Mt 25:10-13 and Lk 13:28-29 resembles Mt 8:11-12, but whether Q read like Matthew or Luke in these cases is unclear. Each may have drawn on different recensions of Q (Stanton 1993: 287).

240. Though cf. Guelich 1982: 357: "This command most likely functions metaphorically here for prayer as it also did at times in Judaism (Str-B 1:458-59) rather than allegorically referring to entrance into the Kingdom. . . ." Lachs 1987: 141 cites, e.g., b. Meg. 12b; p. Ber. 1. On gates of the kingdom, see comment on 16:18-19.

way is that it includes persecution (5:10-12).[241] As in the first chapter of the Didache, the narrow way of life includes the ethics taught in Matthew 5.

Most Jewish people in Jesus' day were religious; respecting God and keeping his commandments were important parts of their culture. These would be the "many" people of whom Jesus' hearers would think when they heard him. Yet Jesus, like a few of his more scrupulous contemporaries (4 Ezra 7:45-61; 8:1-3; cf. b. Sukk. 45b), declared that most people were lost.[242] (In Luke, many Gentiles enter in while many of Abraham's descendants are excluded — Lk 13:22-30; cf. Mt 8:11-12.) Matthew does not want his audience to devise methods for calculating who is more likely to "make it in" (7:1-5); they already know that they are a minority. Yet such words might jar even them from complacency, recalling Jesus' teachings about temper, mental chastity, integrity, and so forth (cf. 5:21-48).

True prophets obey Jesus' teachings (7:15-23). Jesus urges his followers here to "take heed" (7:15; cf. 6:1; 10:17; 16:6, 11; customary hortatory language, e.g., Marc. Aur. 10.8.1; Tob 4:12, 14; Test. Dan 1:2), and surrounds the basic warning with an inclusio ("know them," 7:16, 20; cf. 7:23). Like the false prophets of old (Jer 5:31; 6:13-14; 8:11; 23:13-17; Ezek 13:1-16; Mic 3:5-8), those against whom Matthew warns in the context of 7:15 probably proclaim a gospel of false peace, setting forth an easy way that neglects God's true demands (7:13-14; France 1985: 147; cf. Hill 1972: 151). Matthew elsewhere warns against false prophets (7:22; 24:5, 24) and apostate Christians and leaders in the church (24:12, 48-51). Jesus elsewhere applies the present denunciations of fruitless trees against the religious leaders of his day (12:33; cf. 3:8, 10; 21:19; 23:3; for earlier agricultural images see, e.g., Is 5:2; Hos 10:1, 12-13), but because his words in this context address prophets one suspects that Matthew wants his own generation to take notice (cf. Meier 1980: 73-74).[243]

Prophets falsely promising swift messianic deliverance remained inside Jerusalem after the Christians left in A.D. 66 (Jos. *War* 6.285-88), and possibly reputedly Christian prophets claimed to portend Jesus' return in the years surrounding A.D. 70, when it seemed that the second coming was about to be ful-

241. Cf. Mattill 1979b: 546, who may overexegete in associating the way with the final tribulation, as Derrett 1982 overexegetes in his merchant interpretation.

242. Davies and Allison 1988: 700-701 point out that rabbis exhorted one to treat each commandment as if it alone merited salvation or damnation, and therefore suggest that one should "act *as if* only a very few will enter." This fits both rabbinic homiletic damnation (Sanders 1977: 141) and Jesus' style of rhetoric (5:18-19), but falters here in that the nearer verbal parallels appear in apocalyptic texts like 4 Ezra that *do* exude soteriological pessimism.

243. Hill 1976 sees Mt 7:15 as addressing Jewish religious leaders and 7:22 disobedient Christian prophets; but Matthew probably connects the two in this context, reapplying a meaning from Jesus' life-setting to his own. Thus Jesus' criticism of religious leaders in 23:25 *(esōthen/harpages)* fits his depiction of false prophets in 7:15 (cf. also "lawlessness" in 7:23; 23:28); but the early Christians probably reapplied more generally his image of fruit consistent with the tree (e.g., Jas 3:12, perhaps in line with a more general figure; see Davids 1982: 148). Daniel 1969: 51-55 contends that of the Jewish sects only the Essenes could qualify as "prophets," but their relative obscurity in daily life made them unlikely targets of Jesus' historical polemic. Smith 1992a; idem 1992b goes too far in seeing the Gospel's opponents as only Christian prophets (not synagogue leaders as well).

filled (24:34). Jesus' words are not only polemic against enemies of the faith from the outside; they are also warnings to those who claim to be his followers. The reader dare not restrict the title "hypocrites" to Jesus' religious contemporaries (6:2, 5, 16; pace Did. 8.1-2); Matthew clearly warns that God's subsequent servants may share the same fate (24:51).[244] This passage presents his audience with several lessons.

One must evaluate prophets by their fruits, not by their spiritual gifts (7:15-23). Although the term for "do" is very common, the language of the passage may establish an implicit contrast between merely doing" miracles (7:22) and "doing" the Father's will (7:21). More plainly, these false prophets (7:15) claim to have prophesied, exorcised, and effected miracles by Jesus' name (7:22; cf. perhaps 24:5). Although one could find in this passage Jewish exorcists' attempts to use God's sacred name (12:27; Jos. *Ant.* 8.47; cf. m. Sanh. 10:1; Bietenhard 1967: 243; *PGM* 1.168) — as yet unaware of their judge's identity as Jesus (cf. 25:31) — it almost certainly refers instead to false Christian charismatics whose disobedience Christ finally reveals (10:26; Aune 1983: 223). "In his name" means "as his representatives" (e.g., 10:41-42; 18:5; cf. 21:9) rather than implying the use of magical techniques by which ancient exorcists invoked names of higher spirits to expel lower ones (cf. Acts 19:13-16). Although some could prophesy and work signs by demonic power (in conjunction with Jewish beliefs on false prophets, cf., e.g., 24:24; Jer 2:8; 23:13; especially 2 Thess 2:9; Rev 13:13-16), biblical precedent warned that one could prophesy and yet be lost (1 Sam 19:24).

Matthew is not anticharismatic — that he must warn his community against the wrong kind of prophets, yet fails to attack prophetism in general, strongly suggests that he and his community both accept some prophets as genuine (5:12; 10:8, 40-42; 23:34; cf. Michaels 1976; Hill 1979: 156; Aune 1983: 215; Schweizer 1995: 151). The Didache similarly provides moral tests for prophets precisely because its community accepts the validity of prophets (e.g., Did. 11.3-12). NRSV's "evildoers" in 7:23 is literally "workers of lawlessness," those who violate God's law articulated in 5:17-20 (lawbreakers rather than libertines; cf. 23:28; Ps. Sol. 1:8; 17:18; Meier 1980: 73-74; Gundry 1980: 132-33; Davison 1985). Jesus' words about fruit thus refer to repentant works (7:21; 3:8, 10), recalling Jesus' ethical teachings in 5:21–7:12.[245] Jesus uses a word for bad fruit that often means "rotten," though here the meaning is "worthless" (Manson

244. Stanton 1993: 101-2 correctly applies social conflict theory to 7:19-23; 24:51: the "internal enemy" (i.e., misbehaving Christians) warrants treatment no less severe than external enemies. Nevertheless, even apart from the human tendency to judge more strictly views in closer proximity to one's own, the false Christian prophets may pose a significant threat to the stability of the community. Stanton also correctly warns (1993: 3, 47-49) against finding internal opponents or antinomians on the basis of mirror-reading; nevertheless, the text itself suggests that Matthew wishes to reapply Jesus' condemnation of leaders in Jesus' day to deviant or potentially deviant Christians in his own.

245. Paul similarly subordinates the gifts of the Spirit to the "fruit" of the Spirit (1 Cor 13; cf. Gal 5:22-23) and submission to Jesus' Lordship (1 Cor 12:1-3).

1979: 32). Many ancients recognized that, despite all pretense, an evil person's nature was bound to emerge (Livy 3.36.1; Prov 27:22; 1 Tim 5:24-25); the Greek sage Antisthenes had reportedly complained that states will perish once they prove incapable of discerning good and bad people (Diog. Laert. 6.1.5).

Once inside the church, false prophets and their teaching will cost the spiritual lives of some disciples (7:15). Although people disguising themselves in sheepskins could sometimes pass as stray dogs or other animals temporarily (Jos. *War* 3.192), Jesus is employing graphic hyperbole here (wolves do not wear clothes, and changing one's hide was a metaphor for the impossible — Jer 13:23; Jub. 37:20). By coming in sheep's clothing, the false prophets pretended to be sheep (7:15; Acts 20:29-30; and perhaps Sib. Or. 7.134-35 echo this saying), though they were in fact hungry wolves who had come to prey upon sheep (cf. 10:16); ancients viewed wolves quite negatively (e.g., Epict. *Disc.* 1.3.7; 2.4.11), and the enmity of lambs and wolves was by now proverbial (e.g., Is 11:6; 65:25; 1 Enoch 89:15, 55; Jub. 37:21; Hor. *Epode* 4.1-2; cf. Hom. *Il.* 22.263; Virg. *Aen.* 9.566; Ovid *Metam.* 1.505; 5.626-27; 6.527-28; Phaedrus 1.1; Babrius 89; 102.8). Others naturally compared stealthy, nocturnal human predators to wolves (Ovid *Metam.* 14.778) or employed "hungry wolves" as a metaphor for warriors (Hom. *Il.* 16.156-57, 352). Further, the image of a human trying to sneak forward disguised in a wolfskin (Eurip. *Rhesus* 209-15; Longus 1.21) or sealskin (Hom. *Od.* 4.435-55) or hidden beneath sheep (Odysseus's men slipping past Polyphemus in Hom. *Od.*) was widely known in the Greek world, and Aesop's fable of the wolf in sheep's clothing may have been this early and may have circulated in Palestine (some of his fables influenced some rabbinic texts; Davies and Allison 1988: 704, following Schwartzbaum).[246]

God will expose the true state of people's hearts on the day of judgment (7:19, 21-23). "On that day" (7:22) refers to the final "day of the Lord" (cf., e.g., 10:15; 24:36; Is 2:11, 17, 20; 11:10-11; Joel 1:15; 3:18; 2 Thess 1:10; Kingsbury 1975: 27).[247] Some people may have claimed that they accepted Jesus as a great teacher, yet no more than a teacher. Yet a central component of Jesus' teaching (here from Q material) is the revelation of his identity, admittedly in veiled terms at first. In this passage, as in Matthew 25:31-46, Jesus claims the role of final judge (Argyle 1963: 63; France 1985: 149). Whether suppliants may have

246. The story lines probably became standard. Cf. also the natural hungry wolf image later employed in Avianus *Fable* 1 or the donkey in lion's skin, who fooled other animals but not his owner (Avianus *Fable* 5; Babrius 139); wolves were reputed for their ferocity and mercilessness (Aelian *Animals* 7.20) and their deceit (Phaedrus 1.8.5-12; 1.10.9). Cf. their attacks on sheep (Ap. Rhod. 2.123-24; Virg. *Ecl.* 3.80; 5.60; 8.52; Ovid *Metam.* 1.232-37, 304; Longus 1.11, 22; Babrius 93; 105.1; 113; 4 Ezra 5:18) and other animals (Virg. *Ecl.* 2.63; *Aen.* 11.811; Ovid *Metam.* 11.366-75; Diog. Laert. 6.5.92; Longus 2.16, 22; 4.15; Phaedrus 1.8; Babrius 16) among wolves.

247. Davies and Allison 1988: 714 also cite Is 10:20; Hos 1:5; 2:21 LXX; Amos 9:11; Zeph 1:15; Zech 12:3-11; 13:1-4; 14:4, 6, 8, 9, 13, 20; 1 Enoch 45:3; Lk 17:31; 21:34; 2 Thess 1:10; 2 Tim 4:8, noting that rabbis by contrast usually applied the expression to the messianic period or the world to come (following Strack-Billerbeck 1:468). On 2 Thess 1:10, cf. Milligan 1908: 92; F. F. Bruce 1982: 153. For the pervasiveness of judgment scenes in Matthew, see Gnilka 1997: 159.

greeted Jesus with "Lord, Lord" (7:21) during his earthly ministry (Cullmann 1959: 202), other teachers did not suppose that God would judge hearers primarily on the basis of their words (cf. Lk 6:46-49; Mt 25:11; 2 Clem. 4); indeed, "Lord, Lord" could function as a divine address (Test. Abr. 9; 10A; but doubling names is particularly characteristic of that document — 14, 15A; cf. Jub. 18:1, 10; 23:3).[248] Luke's version of the judgment scene (Lk 13:25-27) likewise indicates that the judge on the final day will be Jesus who ate and drank with them, a connection that his former associates will vainly endeavor to exploit in a manner customary of Near Eastern hospitality (Lk 13:26).

Not those who claim to "know" or be "known by" Jesus, but only those who do the Father's will (cf. 6:10; 18:14; 21:31; 26:42), have any in-group claim on Jesus (12:50). Jesus thus borrows biblical language for righteous enmity toward the wicked (Ps 6:8; 119:115; 139:19) to banish them from his presence (7:23; cf. 25:41). "I never knew you" is a formal repudiation of the person (25:12; cf. 10:33; 26:70, 72, 74; France 1985: 149); also used in mild rabbinic bans, it is far more serious here (b. ʿErub. 53a; Moʿed. Qaṭ. 16a; p. Moʿed. Qaṭ. 3:8; Carson 1984b: 193; Lachs 1987: 150).[249]

Obeying Jesus' Words (7:24-27)

Cf. Lk 6:47-49. Jesus' sermon concluded with this final parable before Matthew edited it (see Lk 6:46-49); both in the source and in Matthew, Jesus' sermon on ethics climaxes with Christology, which provides the authority for his ethics.[250] Earlier in the sermon disciples suffer persecution on account of Jesus (5:11; cf. 10:18), and Jesus "fulfills" Torah (5:17); here he appears as the eschatological judge (7:21-23; cf. 3:11-12; 16:27; 19:28; 25:31-46; Stanton 1993: 320).

Jesus again employs typical wisdom language familiar to Jewish sages (e.g., Tuttle 1977), but Jesus is clearly more than a sage here. Although some Jewish teachers debated whether knowing or obeying the law was more important, since one could not obey it without knowing it (m. 'Abot 1:17; 3:9, 17; 5:14;

248. Davies and Allison 1988: 712 thus cite Esth 4:17 LXX; Ps 108:21 LXX; 140:8 LXX; Mt 25:11; b. Mak. 24a; Ḥul. 139b.

249. Jewish texts insist equally firmly on doing the Father's will (e.g., CD 3.15-16; Jub. 21:2-3, 23; m. 'Abot 5:20 MSS; Sifre Num. 42.1.2; Sifre Deut. 47.2.9; 306.28.2; among Greeks, cf. Socrates *Ep.* 1); Israel faces judgments in the present when they disobey God's will (Sifre Deut. 40.4.1; 40.6.1; 305.2.1; cf. 114.1.1; 118.1.1; ARN 34A). Lucian depicts philosophers casting away their later followers who corrupted their teachings (Lucian *Dead to Life/Fishermen;* LCL 3:76-77), and others ridiculed those who entreated deities without obeying their dictates (Dio Chrys. fg. in LCL 5:350-51).

250. For the connection with the preceding context, cf., e.g., the opening "everyone who" in 7:21, 24 (cf. v. 19). But one often recapitulated one's central thesis toward the end of one's speech (cf., e.g., Demosthenes' restatement of charges in *On the Embassy* 177, though the speech runs to 343). Kennedy 1984: 62 regards 7:21-27 as the sermon's epilogue, which, like typical ancient epilogues, both recapitulates the central point (7:21-23) and stirs the audience to respond (7:24-27).

Sifra Behuq. par. 2.264.1.4; Sifre Deut. 41.2.5-6; b. Qidd. 40b; p. Ḥag. 1:7, §4; Pesiq. Rab Kah. 12:10; Song Rab. 2:14, §5; Dalman 1929: 64),[251] nearly all agreed that obedience was essential (e.g., ARN 24A; b. Sanh. 106b; Yoma 86a; Pesiq. Rab Kah. 27:9; Lev. Rab. 35:7; Num. Rab. 14:10; cf. Ep. Arist. 127; contrast p. Ḥag. 2:1, §§10-11; Ruth Rab. 6:4). Some held that knowing without obeying led to judgment (Sifre Deut. 32.5.12; b. Sanh. 106b; Yoma 86a; Deut. Rab. 7:4; cf. Jas 1:22).[252]

One early second-century teacher, while illustrating this point with many examples, went so far as to say that one who studies Torah and has good works "may be likened to" one who lays a foundation of stones and then of bricks, so that rising water or rain cannot overturn it. But one who studies Torah and has no good works is like one who builds with bricks on the bottom, so that even a small amount of water overturns it (ARN 24A; a similar example is found in Bultmann 1968: 202). The language of this example is almost as similar to Matthew's as Luke's version of the parable is (cf. Gundry 1982: 135).

Jesus here refers to his own words as Jewish teachers generally referred to God's law (Jeremias 1972: 194; Argyle 1963: 64; Luz 1989: 452). The label "sectarian" (a demand to follow Jesus rather than other teachers; Meeks 1986: 138) may therefore constitute an understatement! The language at least implies that Jesus is God's prophetic spokesperson (Ezek 33:32-33) but is more authoritative than is typical even for prophets; in this context (7:21-23; cf. 18:20), the claim is far higher. Neither Matthew nor his tradition allows a reader to be content with calling Jesus a great teacher or prophet (16:13-16); one must either accept all his teachings, including those that demand submission to his Lordship, or reject him altogether. For the early Christians, Jesus was not one way among many; he was the standard of judgment.

The Hebrew Bible often employed the rock image for the security Israel had in God if they obeyed him (e.g., Deut 32:4, 18, 31; Ps 18:2, 31, 46; 19:14), as in a time of flood and disaster (Is 28:14-19); other biblical images may also be indirectly relevant (see on Mt 16:18): a house was built by wisdom (Prov 24:3; cf. Ps 127:1; Jer 22:13). The storm could represent any test,[253] but in this context it surely points especially to the final test, the day of judgment (e.g., Jeremias

251. According to one tradition, study of Torah equaled or exceeded study of the other commandments; see m. Pe'a 1:1; ARN 40A; b. Qidd. 39b.

252. Ancient moralists typically coupled the necessity of deeds with words (in Jewish sources, see Wis 1:16; Test. Abr. 9A; Test. Gad 6:1; 1 Jn 3:18). Philosophers emphasized practice as well as learning, deeds as well as words: Maximus of Tyre *Discourse* 36.55 in Malherbe 1986: 78; Pythag. *Sent.* 14 in ibid. 110; Isoc. *Nic./Cypr.* 61, *Or.* 3.39; Sen. *Ep. Lucil.* 20.1-2; Diog. Laert. 6.2.64; 6.3.82; Epict. *Disc.* 1.25.11; 2.9.13. Such advice was an ancient commonplace (Demosth. *3d Olynthiac* 14; *2d Philippic* 1; *3d Philippic* 15; Diod. Sic. 9.9.1; Dion. Hal. 7.33.3; 9.10.3; 9.47.4; 11.1.4; 11.58.3; Quint. 1, pref. 14). Biblical prophets had also emphasized the necessity of acting on the Lord's message (Ezek 33:32-33).

253. This would fit the general language of wisdom tradition, hence the "wise" person; but Jesus could speak of the "wise person" in eschatological contexts as well (e.g., 10:16; 24:45; 25:2). The image of "falling" also worked in other eschatological contexts (e.g., 21:44, if original in Matthew).

1963: 8-9; Heil 1998: 23-35; cf. the test of the final tribulation in Jeremias 1972: 169). The ultimate storm here may recall the flood that Jesus elsewhere uses to prefigure the final day (24:37-39; Schweizer 1975: 191, citing also Ezek 13:10-16; cf. 1 Enoch 94:7). One commentator wryly observes that the Hebrew Torah "ended with blessings and curses; so much the more, the 'Torah' of Jesus!" (Meier 1980: 75).

Jesus' clear assurance of deliverance in the final test contrasts with the fears of some of his contemporaries. Many Greeks had little certainty of the afterlife (Plato *Apol.* 29AB; *Phaedo* 64A; Lucian *Demonax* 43). According to later accounts, the great teacher Johanan ben Zakkai was unsure which of the two ways he would take when he died (Bonsirven 1964: 167-68; Sandmel 1978b: 202; cf. fear of death in Test. Abr. 1.10A). The tellers of these accounts probably intended to emphasize Johanan's humility (Sanders 1977: 228; Sandmel 1978b: 244), and some later teachers proved considerably more self-assured, even possessed of holy chutzpah (Gen. Rab. 62:2; 92:2). After all, Judaism believed that Jews by virtue of their Jewishness would inherit God's kingdom unless they broke covenant with God by casting off the law (cf. 3:9). Nevertheless, no disciple could long utter ben Zakkai's words, for then they would be doubting Jesus' promise (cf. 2 Clem. 18:1-2). The bold promise and warning that Jesus offers here, and especially what the text implies about his identity, exceeded the bounds of academic propriety observed by most ancient scholars, especially in the stream that became the rabbinic movement. Jesus spoke publicly with unparalleled authority (7:28-29; cf. 8:9; 9:6; 21:23).

Jesus' Hearers Recognize His Claims to Authority (7:28-29)

Cf. Mk 1:21-22; Lk 7:1; Jn 7:46. Each of Jesus' five major discourses in Matthew concludes with the formula, "And when Jesus had finished speaking these words" (or, in 13:53, "these parables"), which was a relatively natural way to conclude a section (Ex 34:33; Jub. 32:20; 50:13; Allison 1993b: 192-93 compares Deut 31:1, 24; 32:45). Four of the five discourses also close with a parable that invites continued reflection (Jones 1995: 173).[254] The crowds respond to Jesus' teaching as disciples and groups of people often responded to his other acts: with awe (8:27; 9:8; 12:23; 22:33; cf. Jn 7:46). What amazed them so much about Jesus' teaching was not his use of proverbs, parables, hyperboles, and other standard pedagogic devices of his day; what astonished them was his claim to authority, a theme that climaxes in 28:18.[255] Other Jewish teachers regularly

254. Although Jones 1995 does not believe that all the closing parables summarize or exhibit identical character (280), he notes that this parable, like the final parable in the final Matthean discourse (25:31-46), addresses future judgment (189).

255. Davies suggests that Matthew omits Mark's claim that Jesus' teaching was "new" to fit his emphasis on the continuity of the law (Mt 5:17-20; Davies 1966b: 28-29; cf. Vermes 1993: 72). Some scholars argue that the crowds marveled because Jesus gave "new" interpretations of the law

cited earlier sages' opinions (cf. Meier 1980: 76; Gundry 1982: 137; Morris 1974: 109), and though later teachers sometimes came to regard their tradition as tantamount to God's word, Jesus' contemporaries never would have said, like Jesus, that people would be judged according to how they treated a particular teacher's words.[256] With greater authority than the scribes who expound the law, greater authority than Moses who gave it (5:1), the authority indeed of the one who will judge humanity on the final day (7:21-23), Jesus declares God's word, and the people recognize that he speaks with authority unlike their other teachers.

---

like those of an ordained rabbi rather than a "mere" scribe (Daube 1973: 206-14); but this distinction between scribes and ordained rabbis may represent a development long after Jesus' earthly ministry and the writing of Mark (Mk 1:27, which connects the "new teaching with authority" to Jesus' power to expel demons with a word). "Authority" as used here may exceed the scribal category altogether (cf. Argyle 1969).

256. From at least the early second century on, some rabbis identified earlier traditions with the law itself as a sort of "oral law" (ARN 15 A; 29, §§61-62 B; Sifra Behuq. pq. 8.269.2.14; Sifre Deut. 306.25.1; 351.1.2, 3) and eventually viewed oral tradition as greater than written Torah (e.g., p. Sanh. 11:4, §1; ʿAbod. Zar. 2:7, §3; Hor. 3:5, §3; b. ʿAbod. Zar. 35a; ʿErub. 21b) because oral law encompassed and explained written law (e.g., Sifre Deut. 313.2.4). The words of the scribes were nearly always on a lower level than the words of Torah in the earliest rabbinic sources, however (Sanders 1990: 115-25), and the identification of the two may not have been widespread in the early period (Sanders 1990: 97-130). Like the Samaritans (Bowman 1977: v-vi), many non-Pharisaic Jews regarded the written Torah as sufficient, while filling in its gaps that they did not admit existed.

Examples of Jesus' Miracles (8:1–9:38)

After completing Jesus' sermon, Matthew begins recounting signs reported in both Mark and some other source(s) Matthew shares with Luke. Thus, for example, he begins with the first miracle story he reports from Mark (8:1-4//Mk 1:40-45) and proceeds next to the first miracle story following Luke's Sermon on the Plain (8:5-13; Lk 7:1-10).[1] Matthew has saved these examples for this section of his Gospel, having narrated previously only a general summary of miracles (4:23-25). He arranges this material in a special way, and scholars generally accept one of two views about this section's arrangement, or both.

Scholars frequently count the narration of ten specific miracles in this section, although others insist that Matthew was not counting (Gundry 1982: 138). Some scholars emphasize that this points to the ten signs of a new Moses (Teeple 1957: 82; cf. Sanders 1993: 146). It may be significant that Matthew opens this section with the descent from the mountain (8:1; Ex 19:14; Gundry 1982: 138), although perhaps merely Matthew's special setting for the sermon of chs. 5–7 may have demanded the geographical transition. Others may count ten specific miracles (e.g., Kingsbury 1975: 63), but emphasize the section's structure as a whole: because two of the miracles appear in one miracle story, Matthew narrates a total of nine miracle stories (Meier 1980: 79). These nine stories break into sets of threes, separated by blocks of Jesus' teaching (Meier 1979: 67; idem 1980: 80). Davies and Allison 1991: 4 attribute this merely to Matthew's love for triads. Interestingly, however, Exodus also arranges all but the last of Moses' ten plagues in three sets of three (Allison 1993b: 211).

Matthew 8:1-17 shows Jesus' authority over sickness; 8:23-28 shows his authority over nature, demons, and paralysis; and 9:18-34 demonstrates his authority over disabilities and death.[2] Whereas these narratives demonstrate how much authority Jesus has in creation, the intervening sections teach that people — the only ones with a choice — should acknowledge Jesus' rightful authority over them (8:18-22; 9:9-17). The concluding summary of miracles (9:35) contains another declaration of Christ's authority: disciples must ask the Lord to send out workers to demonstrate Jesus' authority over these needs (9:36-37).

1. The term "build" in Lk 7:5 might suggest the close connection between this story and its preceding context in Luke (6:48).

2. Cf. Empedocles, who claims "power over sickness, nature, and even death" (Empedocles *On Nature* fr.; in Boring 1995: 79-80).

This becomes the bridge to the following section when Jesus sends out his disciples to demonstrate the reality of his kingship (10:7-8).[3]

Jesus' Willingness to Cleanse a Leper (8:1-4)

Cf. Mk 1:40-45; Lk 5:12-16. As Davies and Allison 1991: 9 point out, arguments against the historical kernel of this passage are not compelling; the narrative also fits Jesus' own testimony that he healed lepers (11:5, with a strong case for authenticity) and other evidence that Jesus "lived his life within the confines of the Torah."

Even the best of ancient historians was interested in the meaning of history, its moral, as well as its data; most biographers especially explored their characters as positive or negative examples. (Ancient writers, unlike many modern ones, had a sense of responsibility to their societies; many also included remarks more cynical about the depravity of their own time than this parenthetical comment.) The Gospel writers are interested in more than listing all Jesus' deeds (as if that were possible anyway — cf. Jn 21:25); they select examples from their materials to emphasize relevant points for their own readers (cf. Jn 20:30-31). In narrating events like Jesus healing people, Matthew encourages his audience that the Lord to whom they pray for provision for their needs in the present demonstrated his ability to meet those needs during his earthly ministry. Matthew's narratives call not only for obedience to lists of ethical demands but also for active faith. While Matthew addresses particularly trusting Jesus to heal, the principles can apply to other desperate needs among the members of his community.[4]

They might hear in this narrative various principles, especially about prayer. **First,** like many other suppliants whose faith is praised in the narratives (e.g., 9:2, 18, 20), the leper was not approaching Jesus with merely cavalier interest. **The leper was in a desperate and apparently permanent situation.** Biblical leprosy was probably not what we call leprosy today (Hansen's disease, caused by *Mycobacterium leprae*), but an assortment of serious skin problems that isolated the leper from the rest of society (Trapnell 1982: 459; Gundry 1982: 139; Matthews and Benjamin 1991a; Mull 1992; Malina 1993: 14; but for the view that this disease did exist in Jesus' day, see Zias 1989; on skin diseases in the Qumran Scrolls, see Baumgarten 1990). Social isolation may have consti-

3. Kingsbury 1978 suggests that 8:1-17 address Christology; 8:18-34 discipleship; 9:1-17 separation from Israel; and 9:18-34 faith. Moiser 1985b suggests that Mt 8–9 reflects the same basic structure as the Sermon on the Mount (possibly stretching in both cases).

4. Pagan aretalogies and other lists of healing miracles (e.g., in Horsley 1982: 21-25; Epidauros inscriptions; Paus. 2.27.3) generally served to reinforce suppliants' faith for experiencing miracles themselves. The late fourth-century-A.D. Epidauros inscriptions clearly postdate many of the accounts they include, some of which contain significant legendary accretions (Boring 1995: 65); but the period of oral transmission is much longer than for the Gospel accounts.

tuted one of the most painful components of the disease, a custom among Gentiles as well as Jews (cf. Jos. *Apion* 1.229, 233). Leprosy was incurable apart from God's intervention (cf. Num 12:12-14; 2 Kings 5:14; Ex. Rab. 1:23), and was compared with the uncleanness of death (Jos. *Ant.* 3.264; b. Sanh. 47a; Gen. Rab. 71:6; Ex. Rab. 5:4; inferred from Num 12:12; 2 Kings 5:6-7). The leper's desperation contributes to the picture of holy chutzpah that may appear more clearly in some other texts (cf. 9:20-21).[5]

Second, the leper approaches Jesus with perfect trust in his power. He knows Jesus is *able* to make him clean if he wants to (8:2); this is not a false sort of faith that uses "if God wills" as an excuse to evade genuine trust (cf., e.g., Is 7:12), but the sort of genuine yet humble confidence in God's power that Matthew's community knew from the biblical record (e.g., 2 Kings 19:15-19). That the language resembles that of Jesus' submission to the Father's will (26:39; cf. 6:10) indicates Matthew's approval of this prayer. Yet while the text teaches the leper's faith, it distinguishes trust in Jesus' power from presumption.

Third, the leper approaches Jesus with humility and the acknowledgment that the choice belongs to Jesus (8:2). Bowing down before another person was an act of respect for the other's dignity or power to deliver one from urgent distress (e.g., Diod. Sic. 36.15.2; Hom. *Il.* 1.427; Herodian 7.5.4), especially for a Jewish person (e.g., Test. Abr. 3-4, 9, 16A). In biblical tradition, acknowledging that God has the right to grant or refuse a request is not lack of faith (cf., e.g., Gen 18:27, 30-32; 2 Sam. 10:12; Dan 3:18; even at times in paganism, *PGM* 4.648-49: "If it is your will"; cf. regrets at answered prayers in Babrius 23.8-10); it is the ultimate act of dependence on God's compassion, which takes great trust and commitment for a desperate person to utter.

Fourth, Matthew teaches his community about Jesus' character: Jesus *wanted* to make the man whole **(8:3).** Although Matthew, in abbreviating Mark's account, omits mention of Jesus' "compassion" here (Mk 1:41), he plainly views compassion as a primary motivation in Jesus' acts of healing (Mt 9:36). In 8:17 Matthew will develop this theme: Jesus was ready to pay a high price himself to bring healing for his people.

Fifth, Jesus is prepared not only to heal but to touch the untouchable, though in the eyes of others this meant he shared the leper's uncleanness (8:3). Although large crowds followed Jesus (8:1) — the sort of circumstance that would draw the attention of the Romans' aristocratic agents (e.g., Jos. *War* 2.259-60) — Matthew focuses not on the masses but on a desperate man excluded from society. Jewish law forbade touching lepers (Lev 5:3) and quarantined lepers from regular society (Lev 13:45-46; Jos. *Ant.* 3.261, 264), and people avoided contact with them (2 Kings 7:3; Jos. *Ant.* 9.74; *Apion* 1.229, 233,

5. Desperation in other cases drove suppliants to their knees before those whom they thought could grant miracles; see, e.g., Tac. *Hist.* 4.81 and other sources in Theissen 1983: 53. Seeking healing from a sage also appears in Jewish tradition, as in the biblical Elijah and Elisha accounts and b. B. Bat. 116a (Lachs 1987: 155).

281; Sifra Neg.; Sifra Mes. par. 1-5).[6] Some ruled that the defilement of leprosy was one of the greatest defilements, for a leper could communicate it even by entering a house (m. Kelim 1:4; cf. Num. Rab. 7:8). By the third century one rabbi even warned against coming within a hundred cubits downwind of a leper, lest one contract defilement (Lev. Rab. 16:3).

It is thus no small matter for Jesus compassionately to touch the man (Patte 1987: 113; Gundry 1982: 139; Lane 1974a: 87), as he likewise touches some others who are unclean (e.g., 8:15; 9:21-22, 25).[7] Yet by touching Jesus does not actually undermine the law of Moses, but fulfills its purpose by providing cleansing (5:17-48; cf. Lev 13:3, 8, 10, 13, 17; Gundry 1982: 140). Like many religious people in most cultures, some ancient Jews probably needed theological rationalizations for others' misfortune so that they could exempt themselves from the fear that they, too, were vulnerable; hence some later teachers decided that leprosy was divine punishment (m. Sheqal. 5:3; Lev. Rab. 17:3; Num. Rab. 7:5), especially for slander (Sifre Deut. 275.1.1; ARN 9A; 16, §36; 41, §116B; b. ʿArak. 16a; Ex. Rab. 3:13; Lev. Rab. 16:6-7; Num. Rab. 7:4; 16:6; Deut. Rab. 6:8; see Bonsirven 1964: 109; Urbach 1979: 1:372 for earlier sources).[8]

Sixth, Jesus does not seek human honor for himself (8:4). This healing would be viewed as no small miracle. As noted above, some Jewish teachers, following Numbers 12:12 and 2 Kings 5:7, regarded leprosy as akin to death, and cleansing a leper as akin to raising the dead (b. Sanh. 47a; cf. Jos. *Ant.* 3.264). Moreover, whereas some contemporary holy men effected healing by prayer, Jesus cleansed directly, evidencing greater authority (Davies and Allison 1991: 13, citing b. Ber. 34b). Yet Jesus not only refuses to take advantage of the opportunity for publicity; he attempts to suppress it.

Various reasons have been offered for the messianic secret in the Gospels

6. Following m. Negaʿim passim, Davies and Allison 1991: 11 show that their isolation was not total; they also suggest (from a targum and 11QTemple 46:16-18) that they may have congregated in leper "colonies" as in the Middle Ages, though this is unclear. (Sometimes, at least, they traveled in bands — 2 Kings 7:3; Lk 17:12 — probably a corollary of their general isolation.)

7. Some early Gentile commentators opined that Jesus touched the leper to show that he was not bound by the law (Chrysostom *Gospel of Matthew,* Homily 25.2; cf. Ephrem the Syrian, *Commentary on Tatian's Diatessaron, ACCS,* 26) or externals (Origen *Healing of the Leper, ACCS* 25-26). Touching is common in other early Christian healing accounts (Theissen 1983: 62) and could also symbolize healing in a few other ancient traditions (see Tac. *Hist.* 4.81; Bultmann 1968: 222); for other parts of the body, cf. Theissen 1983: 62), but it was usually associated only with deities, not human miracle workers (cf. Aune 1980: 1533; Gen. Apoc. 20.21-22 and b. Ber. 5b are exceptions). Boring 1995: 78 notes that people wanted to touch rulers to share in their good fortune (Plut. *Life of Sulla* 35, 474c; Arrian *Anab.* 6.13.3). Some also believed that particles emanated from people for good or harm (Boring 1995: 78-79 cites Plut. *T-T* 5.7.1-2, *Mor.;* cf. commentaries on Lk 8:44; Acts 5:15), but one could also simply accept a suppliant by giving one's hand (Dion. Hal. 8.2.1); for this gesture as a greeting, alliance, or agreement, see, e.g., Ezra 10:19 LXX; 2 Macc 12:12; Ep. Arist. 179; Jos. and Asen. 5:7/11; Gal 2:9; Dion. Hal. 6.84.4; Diog. *Ep.* 33 (further, it could function therapeutically nonmagically, as in modern medicine — Yamauchi 1986: 135-36).

8. Herod. *Hist.* 1.138 indicates that the Persians and probably some other peoples also viewed lepers as unclean because of some fault on their part (Boring 1995: 64).

(it is most prominent in Mark).[9] Wrede contended that Mark invented the messianic secret to explain why some traditions denied that Jesus claimed Messiahship (Wrede 1971: 17-18, 228), but most scholars today judge this thesis to be inadequate because it dismisses too much of the data.[10] Others suggest that Jesus rejects the title initially due to its military connotations (Cullmann 1956b: 26); no public acclamation of Jesus' Messiahship could be understood accurately until after the crucifixion and resurrection (Mk 15:26; Hurtado 1983: xxiii; Marshall 1990: 89-90). Indeed, some scholars argue that Jesus was only Messiah-designate till after the resurrection anyway (Longenecker 1981: 68-73). Thus messianic acclamations could and did lead the authorities wrongly to classify Jesus as a revolutionary and seek his execution; Jesus delays his death until the appropriate time by seeking to reduce publicity. Undue publicity drew uncontrollable crowds (e.g., Mk 1:45; 2:2; 3:9-10, 20); the crowds and the rumors they might spread could invite further "incriminating charges" that Jesus sought to delay until the appropriate time (see Rhoads and Michie 1982: 87; cf. Augustine *Tractates on John,* Tractate 113, *ACCS,* 55).[11]

Wrede's thesis falters not only on literary-critical grounds but also from comparative studies. Contemporary messianic figures *usually* avoided claiming their own messiahship, depending instead on others to acclaim them (Witherington 1990: 265-67). In the broader culture, self-testimony may have seemed inappropriate, especially in view of the sentiment against self-boasting in the first-century Mediterranean world (cf. Isoc. *Nic./Cypr.* 46, *Or.* 3.36; Plut. *Praising Oneself Inoffensively, Mor.* 539A-547F, especially 15, *Mor.* 544D; Quint. *Inst. Or.* 11.1.17-19; Lyons 1985: 44-45, 68-69). Some prominent biblical prophets often worked clandestinely, endeavoring to accomplish their mission without seeking their own honor (e.g., 1 Kings 11:29; 13:8-9; 21:18; 2 Kings 9:1-10), partly because they were investing their time especially in a small circle of disciples they were training (1 Sam 19:20; 2 Kings 4:38; 6:1-3; Keener 1993: 134).

But because the "secrets" of the kingdom extend far beyond Jesus' Messiahship (13:11), solutions addressing only a "messianic secret" may be too narrow.[12]

9. That one should not communicate secret magical formulae (e.g., *PGM* 1.130-32, 192-94; cf. Acts 19:18; Theissen 1983: 68-69, 141-42) is probably irrelevant (Boring 1995: 64); so also commands to keep the secrets of the Mysteries (Lucian *Lexiphanes* 10; Apul. *Metam.* 11.23) or some other kinds of divine encounters (*PGM* 4.2474-90; Orphic Hymn 30.3, 7; Philost. *V.A.* 1.1; Philo *Det.* 175-76; *Cher.* 48; Jos. *Apion* 2.94; 2 Cor 12:4) secret.

10. E.g., Ellis 1975; Burkill 1972: 1-38; idem 1960; Anderson 1976: 46; Wright 1992a: 104.

11. On a literary level, one may add the obduracy of disciples, particularly in Mark, as a foil for Jesus (in John, cf. Braun 1956). This pattern appeared elsewhere in ancient texts (e.g., 4 Ezra 5:34-35; Herm. *Vis.* 3.6, 10; *Comm.* 12.4; *Sim.* 9.12); see further Robbins 1992: 167-68; Aune 1987: 34, 55-56; Lemcio 1978.

12. Compare "mysteries" in apocalyptic texts, especially in Daniel and the Dead Sea Scrolls (e.g., 1QS 5.11-12; 9.18; 11.3-5; 1QM 3.9; 14.14; 17.9; 1QpHab 7.4-5, 8, 13-14; 1QH 2.13; 9.23-24; 11.9-10, 16-17; 12.11-13, 20; 13.2, 13-14); cf. 4 Ezra 14:45-47; etc. For the sake of brevity here, I refer to Gibbard 1956: 109-11; Brown 1959; Ellis 1977: 208; Longenecker 1975: 41-42; and most thoroughly Caragounis 1977.

One may further consider an apologetic literary function: if Jesus is the Messiah, why did Israel as a whole not embrace him (cf. Rom 9:6)? Mark emphasizes that Jesus' identity is hidden to those who fail to believe (Hooker 1983: 61); Jesus' works testified of him (cf. Jn 5:36; 10:25, 37-38; 14:10-12; 15:24), but God allowed Israel to be blinded through their hardness of heart (cf. Rom 11:25). Whatever the other reasons, Jesus is not interested in getting "credit" with others for his power with God (cf. 6:1-18).

Finally, Jesus honors the requirements of the law of Moses (8:4). Although this testimony comes to Matthew from earlier tradition (Mk 1:44), it accords well with his own emphasis that Jesus upholds the law (Mt 5:17-20): the law commanded lepers who thought they were cleansed to submit to priestly inspection and offer sacrifice to thank God (Lev 14:1-9; CD 13.6-7; Jos. *Ant.* 3.264; m. Neg.; cf. b. Yoma 30b).[13] Jesus may not seek "credit" for the miracle, but his faithfulness to the law takes precedence over his personal prohibition against announcing the work. It is possible that the man's obedience required two separate steps. Priests lived throughout Palestine and came to Jerusalem only during their courses (Lk 1:8; Sandmel 1978: 133; Jeremias 1969: 72, 199); some Jewish traditions thus expect a leper to submit to local priests' inspection (cf. Jeremias 1969: 206) before offering the sacrifice in the temple (Lev 14:2-3). Miracle stories often concluded by sending the healed person away (Theissen 1983: 67-68).

A Roman Exception (8:5-13)

Cf. Mk 2:1; Lk 7:1-10.The motif of one entreating on another's behalf occurs in various ancient healing stories (see Theissen 1983: 49); Jn 4:46-54 bears some resemblance to the present account but is most likely a different story.

The Gentile mission was at most peripheral to Jesus' earthly ministry: he did not actively seek out Gentiles for ministry (10:5), and both Gentiles he heals are from a distance (8:13; 15:28; Blauw 1962). The Gentile mission became central to the early church, however, and early Christians naturally looked to the Jesus tradition for what examples of ministry to the Gentiles they could find there (cf. 1:3, 5-6; 2:1-2, 11; 3:9; 4:15). When the Gospel writers seek examples for the Gentile mission in Jesus' ministry, however, they have available only two healing stories to which they may turn (with the possible exception of Mk 5:1-20; Matt 8:28-34; Lk 8:26-39); although all three Synoptic Gospels emphasize the Gentile mission (Mt 28:19; Mk 13:10; Lk 24:47), only Matthew includes both full stories (8:5-13; 15:21-28; Mk 7:24-30; Lk 7:2-10).

The account of the Roman centurion constitutes the only clear miracle

13. The testimony could be "against" them (23:31), but in view of the language from Leviticus it almost certainly simply means "to" them (10:18). "Go" sounds redundant to contemporary ears but was common then and is typical of Matthean diction (cf., e.g., 8:13; 19:21; 21:28; 27:65; 28:10).

story in Q. If, as Theissen thinks, Q was edited in the 40s, the story of the Syrian legate Petronius's dangerous intervention on behalf of the temple may have rendered the story of a "good" Roman officer more palatable than at some other times (Theissen 1991: 226). But why would Q, which is not against Jesus' miracles (cf. 11:5-6) but normally expends no space recounting them, include this particular narrative?[14] Although the healing of the centurion's servant is a miracle story, Jesus' climactic pronouncement about Israel's privilege in 8:11-12 is more critical to this account than the healing itself (with Bultmann 1968: 209).

To comprehend the full significance of the passage one must grasp some basic information about Roman centurions and what they represented to Jewish people in the first century. In this period, soldiers in the Roman legions served twenty years (Ferguson 1987: 39) and could not join unless they were Roman citizens (noncitizens could work as auxiliaries — Jones 1971: 205-6; Stambaugh and Balch 1986: 31). Unlike aristocrats who immediately could become tribunes or higher, most centurions achieved their position from the ranks and became members of the equestrian (knight) class when they retired (Jones 1971: 201-3; Friedländer 1965: 1:194); demotion was a grievous insult (Dion. Hal. 9.39.1). Each of the ten cohorts in a legion included six centurions (Ferguson 1987: 38), each of them commanding a "century" of roughly eighty troops (Jones 1971: 194; cf. *B.G.U.* 696.11-15).[15] Roman soldiers participated in pagan religious oaths to the divine emperor (Jones 1971: 212).

Matthew here demonstrates that properly discipling the nations (28:19) demands a prior abandonment of ethnic and cultural prejudice (cf. 5:44). When

14. Manson 1979: 63 suspects that only the dialogue was present in Q, and Matthew and Luke overlap otherwise through oral tradition; France 1977: 253-54 suspects dependence on oral tradition. I believe that Q included more than Jesus' sayings (Mt 3:7–4:11//Lk 3:7–4:13), that the location of the pericope in both Matthew and Luke indicates a written source, and that the writers simply felt more freedom to diverge in retelling the story than in recounting their master's words. Luke structures his account to parallel that of Cornelius in Acts 10–11, whether by adding details (Wilson 1973: 31) or simply by including them (cf. F. F. Bruce 1977a: 215; had Matthew and Luke felt free to modify the story radically, would they have retained Jesus' initial resistance to the Gentile's request?). Matthew typically abbreviates — a standard rhetorical practice — by omitting intermediaries like messengers (Mt 9:18//Mk 5:35; pace Gagnon 1994), though they were intrinsically likely (Plut. *Consolation to Wife* 1, *Mor.* 608B). This was typical ancient writing style (see the example in Gundry 1982: 141).

15. A similar first-century structure stands beneath a second- or third-century Roman bathhouse in Capernaum (Horsley 1995: 193-94; cf. a late second-century Roman villa near Jerusalem in Edelstein 1990), and we now appear to have evidence for a Roman presence in first-century Capernaum (Stanton 1995a: 115; Laughlin 1993; earlier doubted, cf. Sanders 1990: 15). Yet even if we lacked this evidence we should not argue from silence against the presence of some Romans. Although no legions were stationed in Palestine in Jesus' day, we know of contingents of soldiers in Caesarea and Jerusalem (we also know of places where soldiers passed through; cf. Dar and Kokkinos 1992; and of pagan presence in Jewish areas; see, e.g., di Segni 1991). Capernaum, being a customs station, may have included some military personnel as well (Reicke 1974: 117; Gundry 1982: 141), if Antipas had arranged this with the Roman prefect. One could suppose a *retired* centurion with a land grant there, but his title and probable lack of family militate against this suggestion.

Matthew is writing (especially if somewhere in the decade following 70), his Jewish readers in the vicinity of Syria or Palestine would be tempted to hate Romans passionately, especially Roman soldiers, and perhaps especially their basic officers. (Centurions were the officers ordinary citizens of other lands most frequently had to confront; e.g., *CIJ* 2:132, §920; Sifre Deut. 309.1.1.) This situation would be harshest in the two decades immediately after A.D. 66, however. Many in Matthew's audience undoubtedly had relatives or knew of close relatives of friends who had died in the siege of Jerusalem or whom the Romans enslaved after Jerusalem's fall.[16]

Jesus' teaching about not resisting a Roman soldier's unjust request (5:41), paying taxes to a pagan state that used the funds in part for armies (22:21), or paying a temple tax that the Romans now confiscated for pagan worship (17:24-27) would seem intolerable to anyone whose allegiance to Christ was not greater than one's allegiance to all the people one knew and cared about. But Jesus is unsatisfied that a disciple should treat an enemy respectfully; he demands that one actually *love* that enemy (5:44). No one challenges prejudices — and sometimes provokes antagonism — more than a "good" member of a group that has unjustly treated one's people. This narrative challenges such prejudice in a number of ways.

First, the centurion humbles himself before Jesus not on behalf of himself but for a servant. For Matthew's audience, the servant's social status might be akin to that of some Jews enslaved after A.D. 70.[17] Luke paints the picture of

16. As early as the Maccabean period texts indicate resentment toward Gentiles in general, not merely Rome (cf. Goodman 1987: 76-108); but Jewish literature is also replete with complaints about Roman oppression (e.g., rabbinic complaints about the "four kingdoms"). The object of the Kittim in the Qumran scrolls (1QM 1.2, 6, 10, 12; 15.2; 16.3; 18.2-3; 1QpHab 2.12-14; 3.4, 9; 4.5, 10; 5.1-2; 6.1, 10; 9.7; 4QpNah 1.3; Jub. 24:28-29; cf. Silberman 1961-62: 342) is debated and may have changed from one period to the next (some contend for the Romans — e.g., Burrows 1955: 123-42; idem 1958: 194-203; Rabin 1956; others, perhaps less plausibly, for Greeks or Seleucids — cf. Avi-Yonah 1952: 5; Michel 1954; Rowley 1956b; Treves 1958: 420; for "sons of darkness" in general, North 1958: 86-87; Carmignac 1955: 748; van der Ploeg 1959: 24-25; cf. Yadin 1962: 25), but the Romans are clearly in view in the latest texts. Early Jewish texts portrayed Rome as Babylon, the place of the new captivity (Sib. Or. 5.143, 159; 2 Bar. 11:1; 67:7; 4 Ezra 3:1-2, 28; Rev 14:8), and the Amoraim frequently nicknamed Rome "Edom" (e.g., b. Mak. 12a; Gen. Rab. 37:2; 44:15, 17; 63:7; 76:6; Ex. Rab. 1:26; 18:12; 23:6; 31:17; 35:5; Lev. Rab. 13:5; 23:6; Num. Rab. 11:1; 14:1; 15:17; Deut. Rab. 1:16; Qoh. Rab. 5:7, §1; 11:1, §1; 11:5, §1; Pesiq. Rab Kah. 5:14; Pesiq. R. 10:1; 13:2; 14:15; 15:20; cf. Hadas-Lebel 1984).

17. Bultmann claims that the term here means "son" in contrast to "servant" in Lk 7:2 (cf., e.g., *CIJ* 1.369-70, §505; Char. *Chaer.* 3.5.4; for the ambiguity, see Theon *Progymn* 5.104-6), but of 24 uses in the NT, the present term means "servant" in all but one (France 1977: 256; pace also Hagner 1993: 204, though he is more tentative). Matthew does use *pais* for "son" in his source in 17:18 (Mk 9:17//Lk 9:38), but Luke's *doulos* makes it impossible for "son" to stand explicitly in Matthew's source here, suggesting that Matthew simply liked the former term. Matthew depicts some elements of the illness missing in Luke and perhaps in Q, possibly to connect this narrative with that concerning the paralytic (9:2) as well as the general crowds in 4:24. Thus this man provides an illustration of miracles demonstrating the kingdom (4:24) and (as in 9:1-8) an example of the faith of others (8:10; 9:2) leading to forgiveness.

ethnic reconciliation even more clearly (Lk 7:4-5),[18] but even in Matthew this Roman soldier was one that Jewish people would have to count as an exception. As in the case of the synagogue leader (9:18), one with societal power must humble himself before Jesus as a patron or advocate for one with little social power (cf. Levine 1996: 395).

This slave was probably the centurion's entire "family" (ancients reckoned household slaves as part of their household; see, e.g., Barrow 1968: 22-64; Verner 1983: 30, 33).[19] Roman soldiers were not permitted to have legal families during their two decades of military service (see, e.g., Jones 1970: 155-56; Llewelyn 1992: 148). Although many soldiers took unofficial concubines (e.g., Fabius Maximus 4 in Plut. *Sayings of Romans, Mor.* 195EF; *B.G.U.* 140.10-33; Livy 43.3.2; Herodian 3.8.5; Gardner 1986: 58, 143; O'Rourke 1971: 182), centurions were frequently transferred from one legion to another, preventing permanent ties with local women (cf. Jones 1971: 203); a code of dignity may also have lessened the likelihood of their liaisons with concubines (among higher officers, cf. Scipio the Elder 2, Plut. *Sayings of Romans, Mor.* 196B). But this centurion regards the servant as perhaps the only member of his family in this land. His interest in the servant's welfare is certainly not merely ecomonic: whereas the average slave would have cost roughly one-third of the annual pay of the highest paid legionary (Verner 1983: 61; cf. Speidel 1992; data in Lewis 1983: 208 may suggest a significantly higher percentage for the average legionary), the base pay of a centurion was fifteen times that of a rank-and-file soldier, and a senior centurion *(pilus primus)* made some four times that base pay (Jones 1971: 202-3).

Second, the centurion humbles himself by acknowledging his inferior status as a Gentile (8:8; cf. 15:27). The centurion's initial announcement of the need (8:6) is an oblique form of request; one rarely simply presumed on others' favor (cf. Lk 24:28-29; Jn 1:38-39), and one of higher social status rarely would utter a direct request unless desperate (cf. Jn 2:3). But Jesus forces the centurion to admit his status as a suppliant.

The emphatic Greek "I" in 8:7 suggests that Jesus' words there are probably better translated as a question: "Shall *I* come and heal him?"[20] Most Palestinian Jews, after all, considered entering Gentile homes questionable (cf. Acts 10:28; m. Pesaḥ. 8:8; Ohol. 18:7; Jos. *War* 2.150; Safrai 1974/76c: 829; Wright 1992a: 239-40), though this custom primarily grew from the hatred of idolatry

18. On the centurion's patronal role in the synagogue community, see Moxnes 1991: 252; Overman 1996: 115; cf. the praise accorded to synagogue sponsors (e.g., *CIJ* 2:99-100, §861) and the analogous role of the *archisynagōgos* in some communities (*CIJ* 1:522, §722; 2:332-35, §1404).

19. The exception would be if the "centurion" were retired; veterans tended to get land grants in colonies (e.g., *ILS* 9059; *CIL* 16.146 in Sherk 1988: 145-46, 161; Ferguson 1987: 32; O'Rourke 1971: 175) or in larger, wealthier settlements where they outranked most locals in status and wealth (Lewis 1983: 22, 24). This would also explain why he was not stationed in Caesarea; but one might perhaps then expect more qualification of the title "centurion."

20. Often noted, e.g., in Jeremias 1958: 30; Martin 1978: 15; France 1977: 257; Carson 1984b: 201.

(cf. ARN 8A; b. Pesaḥ. 9a). In this case, Jesus erects a barrier between the centurion and himself as he does with the Canaanite woman (15:24, 26); an outsider who would entreat his favor must first acknowledge the privilege of Israel, whom their peoples had oppressed or disregarded (cf. Jn 4:22). Such initial rejection was a not uncommon ploy for demanding greater commitment (see comment on 19:16-22). One might implicitly demand (Judg 11:7) and the suppliant accept the demand (11:8) to humble oneself and reverse a previous allegiance, and the obstacle or test might include an emphatic "I" (11:9).

Rather than protesting, the centurion acknowledges his questionable merit before Jesus (cf. Lk 7:4, 6), adopting the appropriate role of a suppliant totally dependent on a patron's benefaction, a role centurions often filled for local populations (Malina 1981: 78; Malina and Rohrbaugh 1992: 70). If we do not read 8:7 as a question (so Meier 1980: 83), the point remains much the same, except that the centurion offers the act of faith without Jesus' provocation: he recognizes that it is inappropriate for Jesus to enter his home as long as the centurion remains a Gentile who has not become Jewish. One might question whether some guest was worthy of full hospitality (cf. 2 Jn 10), but in this case the centurion, conscious of his Gentile status, questions whether he is worthy to show hospitality to Jesus (cf. 10:8). Jesus' only reported long-distance healings are with two Gentiles (8:13; 15:28) and with an aristocratic partisan of Rome or Herod whom Jesus also initially rejects (Jn 4:49-53; France 1977: 258).

Third, the centurion recognizes Jesus' unlimited authority to heal, even from a distance (8:8-9). The centurion clearly has heard of Jesus, along with most of Capernaum, and respects him. The title with which he greets Jesus, "Lord" (8:6, 8; cf. 8:2), can read as weakly as "Sir" (e.g., *P. Giess.* bib. 21.11; *P. Oxy.* 123.1, 26; *Select Papyri* 1:338-39; Test. Abr. 2, 15, 18A; 8B) or as strongly as deity; in this context, the centurion at the least acknowledges Jesus as one of authority superior to his own in the matter at hand (France 1977: 255; Ladd 1974: 171; Charlesworth 1985: 88; for the comparable Latin expression, Friedländer 1965: 4:81-87). Despite Matthew's emphasis on Jesus as a teacher, only his enemies call him this (26:25, 48); others grant him the greater title that Matthew's community would understand retrospectively as "Lord" (Meier 1979: 49).

The man shows faith not only by acknowledging his own unworthiness but also by recognizing that Jesus' power is so great that this request is nevertheless small to him. Most of the centurion's contemporaries would have balked at such faith. Jewish people considered long-distance miracles especially difficult and rare, the domain of only the most powerful holy men like Hanina ben Dosa (Bonsirven 1964: 128-29; Manson 1979: 65; Vermes 1984: 7-8; cf. b. Ber. 34b). Stories of sages who could simply speak a decree and it happened (e.g., Pesiq. Rab Kah. 11:16; cf. Mt 21:21; Bultmann 1968: 222) were rare (for deities, e.g., Virg. *Aen.* 1.142).

The centurion reasons, however, from what he knows: he himself can issue commands and receive obedience because he is "under authority," that is, backed by the full authority of the Roman Empire that he represents to his troops (cf. Haslam 1985); cf. Plut. *Praec. Ger. Reip.* 813EF: those taking office must remind themselves that they, too, are subjects, governing under the authority of Caesar's agents. In the same way, the authority of Israel's God backs Jesus, and a mere command from his lips banishes powers in subjection under him, such as sickness. (Saying "Go," and one goes, and "Come," and one comes, was a standard summary statement of one's authority — Epict. *Disc.* 1.25.10-11.)[21] This principle of delegated authority stands behind the ministry of the disciples as well (10:8, 40).

Fourth, Jesus accepts this attitude as one of faith — greater than the faith of his own people (8:10). This text provides a twofold lesson: a general lesson about the nature of faith (the centurion recognized Jesus' unlimited authority and Jesus did heal the servant — 8:13) and a lesson about prejudices that seemed justly founded. Surrounding narratives rehearse the first lesson repeatedly (8:13; 9:2, 22; 15:28; 18:6; 21:21; unbelief in 6:30; 13:58; 14:31; 17:17; 23:23; 27:42). Some ancient miracle stories emphasized faith (e.g., Epidauros inscriptions 3-4 in Grant 1953: 56-57); but it is far more common in Matthew. (That the Synoptics address faith directly less than any other part of the New Testament except Revelation does, however, renders doubtful the idea that Matthew's emphasis on faith is purely redactional; see Jeremias 1971: 160-61.) The recurrent theme of the Gentile mission in Matthew reinforces the second theme, which bears more special comment here.

Matthew, who writes for Jewish Christians, expresses Jesus' response toward Israel more harshly than Luke does. In Luke, Jesus has not found such faith "even" in Israel, where he expected it (Lk 7:9); Matthew omits the concession "even," emphasizing the raw charge in Jesus' words (France 1977: 259; Martin 1978: 18). Jesus "marvels" (NRSV "was amazed"; NIV "was astonished") only twice in the Gospel traditions, here at a Gentile's faith (8:10) and in Mark 6:6 at his hometown's unbelief (France 1977: 259).[22] In Matthew's theology, those closest to the truth often take it for granted whereas those who have had the least exposure to it often recognize its power (2:1-12).

Finally, Jesus regards this exceptional Gentile as the promise of more Gentiles to come (8:11-12). Strong evidence supports 8:11-12 as an authentic saying of Jesus (Semitisms and background in Jeremias 1958: 55-62). Matthew may draw Jesus' words here from another context (Lk 13:28-29) to reinforce the

21. Jeremias's reconstruction of the Aramaic so that the centurion speaks of his own authority over troops (1958: 30) misses the mark; unless the centurion were a Syrian recruit, Jesus undoubtedly speaks with him in Greek, the common language of the eastern Mediterranean (Hooke 1957). Closer is the concept of spoken blessings and curses by God's authorized agents in the Hebrew Bible (in Jewish tradition, cf. Moore 1971: 1:414).

22. On the criterion of embarrassment, Meier 1994: 725 thinks that this element of the Q tradition is probably authentic. While he may well be right (if it was not simply the tradition's inference from Jesus' words), so palpably quantifiable a nonverbal expression would have had to have made a profound impression on the earliest disciples from whom the tradition stems.

point that this story prefigures the Gentile mission, which Jesus endorsed in advance (France 1977: 260).

"Sons of the kingdom" (cf. 13:38; 23:15) refers to Jewish people — those who expected salvation based on their descent from Abraham (3:9); "sons of" sometimes means "those destined for" (France 1977: 262; Abrahams 1924: 187). Outer darkness plainly signified damnation (13:42; 22:13; 25:30; 1 Enoch 10:4-6; 62:11; 63:6, 11; 92:5; 108:14; 2 Enoch 25:4-5; 26:3; Ex. Rab. 14:3; Sib. Or. 2:291-92; cf. Ps. Sol. 14:9; 15:10), and sometimes is conjoined with burning (1QS 4.12-13; Sib. Or. 4.43; 1 Enoch 103:8; 2 Enoch 10:2; Apoc. Peter Eth. 9/Akhmim 27; cf. Ex. Rab. 14:2);[23] a Greek reader might also think here of eternal separation from all other people (cf. Diog. Laert. 8.1.31). Weeping indicates mourning over damnation (Jdt 16:17; Test. Jud. 25:5; cf. Mt 13:42; 22:13); gnashing of teeth might indicate anger or strong emotion similar to it (e.g., Ps 112:10; Acts 7:54; Edersheim: 253), but it probably signifies primarily anguish (Sib. Or. 2:203, 305; 8.86, 105, 125; Ex. Rab. 31:5; Qoh. Rab. 1:15, §1; cf. Derrett 1973: 70; Mt 13:42, 50; 22:13; 24:51; 25:30; Lk 13:28).[24] The damnation of those who thought themselves destined for the kingdom sounded a sober warning to nationalist Jews of Matthew's day, just as it would sound a warning to complacent Christians today (Goldingay 1977: 254).[25]

Jesus could originally have referred to Diaspora Jews as those who would come from the east and the west (Sanders 1985: 220; Allison 1989), but given the pointed theological contrast with his hearers, he more likely refers to the eschatological ingathering of Gentiles promised in the prophets (Is 56:3-8; see more fully data in Jeremias 1958: 56-61; Sanders 1985: 213-15), especially if

23. Lachs 1987: 156 also finds the "darkness" of Gehenna in the late Ex. Rab. 14:2; Lev. Rab. 27; one may add Pesiq. Rab Kah. 9:1; pagans typically associated darkness with the realm of the dead (e.g., Virg. *Aen.* 6.545; *Georg.* 4.497; Ovid *Metam.* 10.54). God would reward Israel with eschatological separation from the Gentiles (e.g., Sifre Deut. 315.1.1).

24. People in the ancient Mediterranean sometimes expressed their anguish by painful gestures such as tearing out of hair (e.g., Hom. *Il.* 22.77, 405-7).

25. On the lostness (Jdt 16:17; 1 Enoch 99:4; 1QM 11.12-13; 14.7; 15.1-2; 17.1-2; t. Sanh. 13:2; b. Rosh Hash. 17a; Lev. Rab. 13:2; Num. Rab. 19:32; Qoh. Rab. 1:9, §1; Pesiq. R. 10:5; 11:5) and evil (e.g., 1 Macc 5; Jub. 1:9; 15:34; 22:16-18, 20-22; 23:24; 24:25-33; 4QpNah 1.1; Ps-Philo 7:3; 12:4; m. ʿAbod. Zar. 2:1; t. ʿAbod. Zar. 8:5; Sifre Deut. 213.1.1; Gen. Rab. 80:7) of the Gentiles in some Jewish traditions and the emphasis on the righteous Gentiles (e.g., Ep. Arist. 279; Sifra A.M. pq. 13.194.2.15; b. Ḥul. 92a; Yoma 71b; Lev. Rab. 1:3) and hope for them (1QH 6.12-14; 1QM 12.14; Sib. Or. 1.129; 3.710-26; Ps. Sol. 17:30; Test. Zeb. 9:8 MS; t. Ber. 6:2; Sifre Deut. 307.4.2; Sanh. 13:2; Num. Rab. 1:3) in others, see the data summarized in Keener 1997b: 62-63, 84-85; Sanders 1977: 206-12; idem 1985: 214-15; Bonsirven 1964: 65-68. Jeremias 1958: 40 may be too severe. In practice, probably few Gentiles met the criterion of "righteous" (Sanders 1992: 270), but undoubtedly Jewish teachers generously hoped for more. Positive treatment of Gentiles was partly for witness's sake (Tob 13:3; CD 12.6-8; Qoh. Rab. 11:1 §1, cf. Ps-Phocyl. 39-40; Isoc. *To Nic.* 22, *Or.* 2). Views varied considerably from hellenistic Jewish writers such as Josephus, Philo, and Aristeas to more rigid sectarian sources like the Qumran Scrolls (Boccaccini 1991: 176-79, 251-65).

Isaiah 25:6-8 is in view (Sanders 1993: 185).[26] Jesus necessarily knew this promise in the Bible even if he were isolated from other Jewish speculation that developed it, and such attitudes on his part would more readily explain why his followers within a matter of decades began a Gentile mission on terms that quickly transcended those of other Jewish groups (e.g., Acts 11:20-21; 15:14-21). Because no one questioned whether Diaspora Jews as a whole would inherit the kingdom, they would make little sense in "an example of surprising inclusion in contrast with surprising exclusion" (Gundry 1982: 145).

Whereas we can affirm that Jesus very probably meant Gentiles, that *Matthew* means the Gentiles is clear: Rome was the great power that lay to the west, and Matthew had earlier illustrated the coming of pagans from the east (2:1). These would recline at table (the standard posture for feasts and banquets, e.g., in Qoh. Rab. 9:8, §1) in the kingdom with the patriarchs — the messianic banquet Israel expected for themselves (5:6; 22:2; Lk 16:23; 4 Macc 13:17; 1 Enoch 70:4; 3 Enoch 48A:10; Test. Asher 7:7; Test. Benj. 10:6-9; p. Taʿan. 4:2, §12; cf. Koenig 1985: 16). The key to the request, as for many healings, was the man's faith (cf. 9:29; 15:28), the characteristic that also gained him entrance into the kingdom. As the first converts of a province might embody hope for that region (1 Cor 16:15; Minear 1960: 112), so this Gentile functions as a foretaste of the fruits of the Gentile mission yet to come. His audience for now must love their enemies (5:44-45; cf. 5:44; 22:21).

Jesus the Healer (8:14-17)

Cf. Mk 1:29-34; Lk 4:38-41. Although Matthew employs Jesus' past healings as an apologetic, as a proof of Jesus' messianic claim, he undoubtedly regarded the continuing signs of his community's missionaries as apologetic testimony as well (see comment on 12:24). Matthew spends much of his narrative presenting Jesus as a healer because he expects his audience to experience Jesus as a continuing healer, as one who now holds all authority in heaven and on earth (28:18; cf. 9:35-38; 10:1; Rom 15:19; 1 Cor 12:9; 2 Cor 12:12; Gal 3:5; Jas 5:14-15).

First, Jesus healed not only in the course of public ministry but also when needs arose in daily situations (8:14). Jesus healed not just in synagogues but also in home settings, in this case one posed by fairly typical living arrangements for the family of one of his disciples. Despite ancient mother-in-law comedies (e.g., Terence *The Mother-in-Law,* second century B.C.; cf. Juv. *Sat.* 6.231-32), ancient Jewish literature presupposes close ties with one's in-laws (e.g., p. Moʿed Qaṭ. 3:5, §28), and concern for Peter would

26. Davies and Allison 1991: 27-28 tentatively object that no passage in the Hebrew Bible has both nations coming to Zion (Is 2:2-4) and banqueting (25:6-8). This objection, however, ignores the synthetic way Jesus and others read Isaiah; even if he drew from only a single text, his understanding of that text would be informed by others. Theissen 1991: 45 suggests uncertainly that both Diaspora Jews and Gentiles could be involved.

carry over to concern for his household (cf. Malina 1993: 67). Newlyweds might initially live with the husband's family (Derrett 1973: 38; Blue 1994: 185n.255),[27] sometimes in a second-story room atop their roof; apparently Peter, away from his native Bethsaida (Jn 1:44), is now well enough established to own his own home.[28] But this would not mean that only his nuclear family could live with him. Fathers were normally older than their wives to begin with (admittedly less so in Palestine), and often died early in their offspring's adulthood (Saller 1987). If a father died, children might need to take in an aged mother (cf. 15:5-6; 1 Tim 5:4, 8; Hierocles *Duties. Marriage* 4.22.21-24; *Duties. Conduct toward Parents* 4.25.53; Quint. 6.6.5; Sir 3:16; Sib. Or. 2.273-75; Moore 1971: 2:170), as Peter has done with his mother-in-law here. Some archaeologists think they have found relatively secure evidence for Peter's house in Capernaum, where this and other miracles (Mk 2:1-2) probably occurred.[29]

Hagner 1993: 208-9 points out a minor chiastic structure in 8:14-15, in which Jesus first ministers to Peter's wife's mother, and she in turn ministers to him.[30] This structure may make emphatic the model for discipleship: after Jesus transforms a person, the person serves him. If so, this is not the only text where Matthew chooses women disciples as a paradigm for discipleship in general (27:55-61; 28:1-10). That Jesus touches her to cure her may also indicate the way he values people over traditions, given the reported prejudice against touching people with fevers (Witherington 1984: 67; Hagner 1993: 209; Carson 1984b: 204; following Strack-Billerbeck 1:479-80); cf. 8:3; 9:20, 25.[31]

Second, as word of the healing spread, others came seeking healing, and Jesus healed all who came (8:16). Ancient Mediterranean culture valued

27. The practice was clearest in Egypt (Horsley 1987: 92). Then again, unusual circumstances are possible: Peter might have moved from Bethsaida (Jn 1:44) to Capernaum to work in his wife's family business or if his father-in-law had passed without sons; the husband and bride's father decide the new marital residence in *P. Eleph.* 1.5-6 (311 B.C.). Village endogamy was probably common, but cementing relations with a nearby town was no less feasible (Horsley 1995: 199; cf. Ilan 1996: 75-79; Hanson and Oakman 1998: 32-34).

28. His own home may be another sign of his relatively comfortable economic status (see comment on 4:18-22); impoverished peasants in places like rural Egypt, e.g., might still be renting very cramped, small homes at age 50, which for them might be near the end of life (see Lewis 1983: 70, on one Kronion in A.D. 114; on the severe cramping and sometimes renting fractions of one-room dwellings, see Lewis 1983: 53, 65, 67, citing, e.g., *B.G.U.* 115 = *W. Chr.* 203). Peter's wife appears in 1 Cor 9:5, his alleged daughter in the first section of Acts of Peter.

29. Cf. Loffreda 1971; Strange and Shanks 1982: 26-37; Hengel 1974b: 27; Blue 1994: 138. The relatively late date of the evidence might bring this conclusion into question (Taylor 1989).

30. Though Pilch 1989 may also be correct that healing signified appropriate state of being more than, as today, restored ability to work. Carson 1984b: 204 suggests that the fever might be malaria, but notes that the text speaks of "fever" because people considered it a disease itself at the time (cf. also Trapnell 1982: 459). B. Shab. 66b-67a lists various cures (mainly magical) for fevers (Davies and Allison 1991: 35).

31. A later rabbinic tradition emphasizes that divine intervention to heal fever is greater than protecting God's servants in the fiery furnace (b. Ned. 41a in Boring 1995: 64-65).

openness or harmlessness exhibited by having a home always open to others in the community (Malina 1981: 78). Although their arrival in the evening may have interfered with Jesus' early sleep, Mark informs us that the suppliants had to await sunset because the day had been the Sabbath (Mk 1:21, 29, 32). Matthew's abbreviating technique leads him to omit this law-honoring detail, though he also omits the more offensive healing of Peter's mother-in-law and her serving them on the Sabbath. Further, Matthew is more explicit than Mark that Jesus healed all who came to him (Filson 1960: 112). Having heard of his power, those who were diligent enough to come to him at evening undoubtedly had faith, removing the primary obstacle to his healing activity (cf. 13:58). As throughout the Book of Acts (and in many Jewish and pagan miracle traditions), signs both met people's needs directly and drew public attention to the message the signs attested.

Third, that Jesus healed and expelled demons with a mere word demonstrates his incomparable power (8:17). Like people in many non-Western cultures, Jesus' contemporaries recognized the reality of spirit-possession (for examples, cf. Kiev 1964, passim; Goodman 1988), but sought to relieve it by means of incantations, pain compliance techniques like smelly roots, or invoking higher spirits to get rid of lower ones (Tob 6:7-8, 16-17; 8:2-3; Jos. *Ant.* 8.45-49; Jub. 10:10-13; Apul. *Metam.* 3.15).[32] Jesus instead expelled demons simply by his word (8:16; cf. Twelftree 1986: 383; Vermes 1973: 23, 63-65), fitting the picture of Jesus' absolute authority Matthew's reader has just encountered (his "word" in 7:24; 8:8; cf. 8:13, 16, 22, 32; 9:9; 28:19).

Although the miracles of Elijah and Elisha provide the role model for many of Jesus' miracles, the closest Old Testament model for exorcisms would be David in 1 Samuel 16:14-23 (cf. Betz 1968: 66; Barrett 1966: 53; Ps-Philo 60); early Judaism viewed David's son Solomon as exorcist par excellence (e.g., Test. Sol. 5.10; Aramaic incantation text 47:1-2; p. Ketub. 12:3, §11; Pesiq. Rab Kah. 5:3). Curing disease with a mere word (8:3, 8) was also quite unusual, contrasting with most of the popular magicians of the day (Anderson 1976: 97; cf. some threats against demons in Theissen 1983: 63-64).

32. On the magical practice in Tob 8:2-3, see Kollmann 1994. Other texts concerning the magical expulsion of demons include late rabbinic sources purporting to depict an account of Johanan ben Zakkai (Num. Rab. 19:8; Pesiq. R. 14:14). For other accounts, cf. 1QapGen 20; Justin *Dial.* 85; Test. Sol. 5:13; for name invocation of spirits to counter other spirits, as in pagan magical texts, cf. *PGM* 101.38-39; Aramaic incantation text 3.8-9; 50.7-8; Test. Sol. 2.4; 5.5; 8.5-11; ch. 18; on named demons in 4Q560, see Penney and Wise 1994. For more detail, see Alexander 1980: 126-28; from a purely anthropological standpoint, Goodman 1988: 125 comments that exorcism actually is the one effective transcultural method for relieving spirit-possession. On demons as "spirits" Davies and Allison 1991: 36 cite 1 Sam 16:23 LXX; CD 12.2; 1 Enoch 15:4–16:1; 99:7; Ps-Philo 60. Certainly Jewish consciousness of demons had developed considerably beyond anything found in the Hebrew Bible (perhaps stimulated by Persian thought — cf. Olmstead 1959: 18, 53, 96, 195, 232); one conservative scholar suggests that in view of the predicted nearness of the kingdom, Satan's kingdom had initiated a counteroffensive raising the visibility of demon-possession in this period (Alexander 1980: 249).

Finally, Matthew informs his audience that healing was part of Jesus' mission, which God provided at great cost to Jesus (8:17). Matthew bypasses the spiritualized reading in the Greek version and translates the Isaiah passage directly from the Hebrew.[33] The context in Isaiah 53 suggests that the servant's death would heal the nation from its sin (53:4-6, 8-9; cf. 1 Pet 2:22-25), a figurative usage (along with judgment) frequent in the prophets (13:15; Is 6:10; 57:18; Jer 3:22; 6:14; 8:11; 14:19; Hos 14:4; cf. 1QH 2.8-9; Sir 28:3; Pesiq. R. 44:8). But the broader context of Isaiah (assuming either Isaiah's unity, as Matthew's own audience would, or that a later "Isaiah" drew on the earlier one, as some contemporary scholars think) shows God's eschatological concern for his people's complete wellness (29:18; 32:3-4; 35:5-6), suggesting secondary nuances of physical healing in 53:4-5 as well (Gundry 1982: 150; cf. France 1985: 158). The servant's suffering would restore to Israel eschatologically the benefits lost through sin (cf. Deut 27–28). Thus Matthew cites Isaiah 53:4 to demonstrate that Jesus' mission of healing fulfills the character of the mission of the servant, who at the ultimate cost of his own life would reveal God's concern for a broken humanity. Matthew himself also recognizes that genuine physical healings can illustrate principles about spiritual healing (9:5-7, 12; 13:15). (On the servant, see comment on Mt 12:18-21.)[34] Jesus' sacrifice to bear others' infirmities may also provide a model for his disciples; it appears elsewhere in early Christian parenesis (Rom 15:1-3; 1 Pet 2:20-24).

Following Where Jesus Leads (8:18-22)

Cf. Mk 4:35; Lk 9:57-62. The key discipleship term "follow" (4:20; 9:9; 10:38; 16:24; 19:21; 20:34; 27:55; cf. the crowds in 4:25; 8:1, 10; 12:15; 19:2; 20:29; 21:9; Diog. Laert. 7.1.3) connects the two short pericopes of 8:18-20 and 8:21-22, demonstrating that not all would-be followers of Jesus (even "disciples," 8:21) have yet counted the genuine cost of being Jesus' followers. The same Jesus who has authority over nature (8:23-27), demons (8:28-34), and paralysis (9:2-8) is the one whose authority his disciples must acknowledge over their lives.[35]

Jesus' encounters here fit the logic of their Matthean context: Jesus is lead-

33. Longenecker 1975: 147-48; Best 1965: 107; Meier 1980: 85; Gundry 1982: 150.

34. Carson 1984b: 207 provides insights for those who wish to apply the text: "This text and others clearly teach that there is healing in the Atonement; but similarly there is the promise of a resurrection body in the Atonement, even if believers do not inherit it until the Parousia . . . this does not mean that all such benefits can be secured at the present time on demand" (cf. similarly Blomberg 1992a: 145). Ancient readers would more likely take the text as a general principle than as a contractual certainty (cf. Mek. Vay. 1.172ff. in Laut. 2.96-97).

35. The form of a series of questions and responses (cf. Diog. Laert. 1.36-37) is probably original, but Matthew and Luke develop it differently (Mack and Robbins 1989: 83-84). Matthew 8:20 has the three-beat Aramaic rhythm Jesus and other sages used to emphasize important maxims (Jeremias 1971: 23). Theissen 1978: 10 suggests that 8:20 addressed "wandering charismatics," but see comments above on 4:17-22.

ing his disciples to a boat for their journey when one wishes to "absent himself temporarily" to bury his father. Jesus, however, expects the man to "follow" him — beginning by boarding the boat with him (8:23; Kingsbury 1988a: 56).

First, following Jesus may cost a disciple even the most basic security such as a place to live (8:18-20). A "scribe" (Matthew's clarification; cf. Lk 9:57) no doubt supposes that he is paying a high price in volunteering to follow Jesus; such a decision will cost popularity in some circles, and going through the process of discipleship after already being a scribe would be a humbling and time-consuming experience.

Jesus, however, warns his prospective disciple that even such a sacrifice may well prove inadequate. Jesus is, after all, the "son of man" who must suffer before his exaltation (cf. Dan 7:13-22; pace Bultmann 1958: 49). As the Arab Christian commentator Ibn Sa'id remarked on this passage, the disciple "does not understand that 'follow' means Gethsemane, and Golgotha, and the tomb" (Bailey 1980: 24). Although Jesus presumably had made a good wage as a carpenter before he began itinerant ministry (cf. Freyne 1988: 241) and still retained a home base in Capernaum (4:13), his traveling ministry left him and his disciples at the mercy of others' hospitality. In practice, then, Jesus was essentially homeless (regarded by some as the hardest of sufferings for humans — Hom. *Od.* 15.343), even more dependent on others than were the Levites in biblical law. In contrast to antisocial persons such as the Cynics or prophetic figures like John, mainstream society normally regarded such a lifestyle as wretched (e.g., Pub. Syr. 182), though it was sometimes depicted as the temporary lot of righteous heroes (e.g., Eurip. *Electra* 202-6, 234-36). Anyone who followed Jesus full-time during his earthly ministry would find himself or herself in the same situation. Jesus may employ biblicizing language, like the righteous sufferer who must flee like a bird (Ps 11:1; cf. 84:3; 102:6-7; 124:7) or perhaps foxes who lurk in desolate places (Lam 5:18: Ezek 13:4), but if he intends any specific allusion, it is most likely to David's attempt to send away a volunteer lest he become a wanderer with him (2 Sam 15:19-20); the proper response, however, is for the volunteer to follow anyway (2 Sam 15:21-22).[36] Matthew records Jesus' words not merely as a matter of historical interest but as a call to his own generation: were they ready to follow Jesus even at the cost of all securities (10:5-14; cf. Heb 11:38)?

Yet while Jesus' traveling ministry identified him in one sense with the

36. Radical philosophers also demanded readiness to abandon possessions (Epict. *Disc.* 2.2.15; 4.8.31); the destitute peasants had little choice (cf. again Kronion in Lewis 1983: 70). The founder of the Qumran community mourned that enemies had banished him into the wilderness "like a bird out of the nest" (Betz 1968: 72; cf. Prov 27:8). Following E. Nestle, Bultmann and Hagner suggest a popular proverb in Plut. *Tiberius Gracchus* 9.4-5, but the parallel is not close enough to warrant assuming it is a proverb (Marshall 1978: 410). If "son of man" means generic person here, Jesus would be commenting cynically on God's provision for the animals, but that people, including himself, were often rootless (Chilton 1994: 91, 97-98; cf. Vermes 1993: 87). A generic usage, however, does not cohere well with his usual use of "Son of Man" (see the Introduction or his teaching in 6:25-30).

homeless, hence of low status in the eyes of others, his depiction of his ministry might also allude to rejected divine Wisdom without a dwelling place on earth (1 Enoch 42:2; Marshall 1978: 410; Witherington 1990: 52-53). If so, Jesus' words to this scribe, like his words to the would-be disciple in Matthew's following lines, imply a status higher than the society would grant to a mortal teacher.

Second, following Jesus takes precedence over all social obligations, even those family obligations one's society and religion declare to be ultimate (8:21-22).[37] "Let the dead bury their dead" may represent a typically sagelike sort of catchy saying (cf. Ps-Phocyl. 147-48) probably meaning, "Let the 'spiritually dead' (cf. Lk 15:24, 32; p. Taʿan. 3:8, §2; see further Hengel 1981b: 7-8; Davies and Allison 1991: 56n.168; Vermes 1993: 29) see to such concerns."[38] Others suggest, "Let the other physically dead in your father's tomb see to your physically dead father," a manifest impossibility characteristic of Jesus' typically shocking and graphic style to emphasize that this is no business of the living disciple's (cf. Gundry 1982: 153; McCane 1990: 41).[39]

Jesus' demand may prove less harsh in some respects than it sounds at first. The "disciple" (he has already acknowledged Jesus as his teacher; cf. Lk 9:59; by calling him "disciple" Matthew makes the narrative explicitly relevant for his community's commitment) is probably not asking permission to attend his father's funeral later that day; his father more likely either was not yet dead or, most likely, had been buried once already. When a person died, mourners would gather, the body would be prepared, and a funeral procession would take the body to the tomb immediately (cf. 27:59-60; Mk 5:35, 38; Lk 7:12), leaving no time for family members to be away talking with rabbis; for a week afterward, the family would remain mourning at home and not go out in public (Sir 22:12; Jdt 16:24; Safrai 1974/76b: 782; Apoc. Mos. 43:3; cf. b. Sanh. 47b; Jn 11:19-20; Sandmel 1978b: 200-201; though cf. Life of Adam 51:2).[40] But father and son

37. 8:21-22 are widely accepted as authentic (Hengel 1981b: 13-15; Sanders 1985: 252, 254, who interpret the passage quite differently), particularly due to the positive application of the criterion of dissimilarity; it does not fit the mainstream of early Judaism, Christianity, or Greco-Roman thought. (Witherington 1990: 118 does, however, see a parallel in Iamb. *Pythag.* 17.73.) Hengel envisions an eschatological context for the demand (cf. Mt 10:34-35; Hengel 1981b: 13); McCane briefly suggests an imminent eschatology in the direction of Schweitzer (1990: 42-43).

38. Ancient texts can refer to the severely deprived as virtually dead (Dio Cassius *R.H.* 45.47.5; b. Beṣa 32b, bar.; Ex. Rab. 5:4; see comment on 8:1-4). More significantly, "dead" is analogous to "fool" in Sir 22:11-12, and elsewhere it functions as a spiritual or moral analogy (Lucretius *Nat.* 3.1046; Epict. *Disc.* 1.5.4; Jos. and Asen. 8:9/11; 4 Ezra 7:92; Eph 2:1). A sentence of death hung over the disobedient (Gen 2:17; 9:4-5; Deut 4:1), so that the wicked were as dead already (Gen. Rab. 39:7; Qoh. Rab. 9:5, §1; cf. Epict. 1.13.5; Diog. Laert. 2.35; Buchanan 1970: 201; Sanders 1977: 317).

39. The suggestion of an original mistranslation from the Aramaic such as "Let the waverers or gravediggers bury their dead" (Abrahams 1924: 183; Black 1967: 207-8; Schwarz 1981), perhaps based on public responsibility for the burial of the poor or unidentified (cf. Moore 1971: 2:176), is improbable; cf. Gundry 1982: 154. Hengel 1981b: 7 and Sanders 1985: 254 take the saying as eschatologically conditioned rather than proverbial.

40. Whereas Jewish mourners completed their mourning that year, the more somber Romans *prohibited* even women from mourning longer than this (Sen. *Ep. Lucil.* 63.13).

might wish to be together before the father died (Jos. *Life* 204), and current Semitic idioms show that "I must first bury my father" can function as a request to wait until one's father dies — perhaps for years — so that one may fulfill the ultimate filial obligation before leaving home (Bailey 1980: 26; cf. Vermes 1993: 29).[41]

A custom practiced only in the decades immediately surrounding the time of Jesus may illumine this passage more directly, however. In Jesus' day the eldest son would return to the tomb a year after the father's death to "rebury" his father by neatly arranging his now bare bones in a container and sliding it into a slot on the wall. If the father has died, this young man cannot refer to his father's initial burial, and hence must be asking for as much as a year's delay for a secondary burial (see McCane 1990).[42]

Then again, Jesus' demand also proves harsher than it sounds to us at first. The offense lies not in the immediacy of the demand but in the priority the demand takes over family obligations (10:21, 35-37; cf. Hengel 1981b: 13), the kind of demand God made of biblical prophets (Hengel 1981b: 11-12). Many Jewish people considered honoring parents the supreme commandment (Ep. Arist. 228; Jos. *Apion* 2.206; Ps-Phocyl. 8; Moore 1971: 2:132), and regarded burial of one's parents as one of the most important implications of that commandment regardless of the circumstances (Tob 4:3-4; 6:14; 1 Macc 2:70; 4 Macc 16:11).[43] A few teachers did insist that one should honor one's teacher above one's parents (m. B. Meṣ. 2:11; p. Ḥag. 2:1, §10),[44] but for a young man in his thirties (as Jesus apparently was; Lk 3:23) to seek such honor would be considered presumptuous and shameful (Bailey 1980: 29).[45] When sages figuratively placed demands for the honor of sages higher than those of one's parents, it was to emphasize the importance of Torah study, but they would never have placed even the urgency of Torah study above the urgency

41. Cf. similarly the curse in *PGM* 40.3-4 against a father who apparently robbed his own daughter's tomb: "May he not . . . bury his parents," i.e., may he die before them; a parent's final request might be burial by her son (thereby guaranteeing that he outlived her, Ap. Rhod. 1.280-83). Cf. also Char. *Chaer.* 3.5.4-6; 8.6.10, requesting the son not to depart until the father has died. For burial as a metonymy for death, Pesiq. R. 22:6.

42. On reburial after the wasting of the flesh, see further m. Moʿed Qaṭ. 1:5; Pesaḥ. 8:8; Sanh. 6:6; Meyers and Strange 1981: 29; Finegan 1969: 217. McCane 1991 contrasts Jewish ossuaries and later Christian reliquaries. A year's mourning period also appears in Eurip. *Alcestis* 336 (cf. 430-31).

43. Cf. Test. Job 39:10/39:7; Hengel 1981b: 8; Sanders 1985: 253-55; Harvey 1982: 60; compare also Beare 1981: 214. Burial of the dead was an urgent duty throughout Mediterranean antiquity (e.g., Tob 1:17-20; 2:7-10; 2 Macc 4:49; 13:7; 1QM 7:2; Ps-Phocyl. 99-101; 1 Enoch 98:13; Jos. *Apion* 2.201; Eurip. *Suppliants* passim; Plut. *Nicias* 6.5-6; Epict. *Disc.* 4.7.31; Diog. Laert. *Lives* 6.2.52; Char. *Chaer.* 1.5.25; 4.1.3), and failure to bury one's father was a heinous offense (Demosth. *Against Aristogeiton* 54). Even a priest should bury a corpse if no one else was available to bury it (Sanders 1993: 225-26).

44. Cf. Diod. Sic. 10.3.4. Also, when no son was available, a leading disciple would bury a teacher, as with John's disciples in 14:12: Diog. Laert. *Lives* 6.2.78; Diod. Sic. 10.3.4. That one should honor one's teacher as one honors God (m. 'Abot 4:12) was a graphic way of increasing the honor due a teacher without diminishing that due God (as with disciples, etc., in the same saying).

45. Josephus claims that his command of Galilee at the young age of 30 aroused envy (*Life* 80).

of burying a parent who had died (cf., e.g., m. Ber. 3:1), and presumably would have avoided dishonoring or disobeying living parents by any means possible (see references on 15:4-6).

In most current interpretations of biblical law, only one person's honor took precedence over the honor shown to parents: God's (Deut 13:6; 4 Macc 2:10-12; Jos. *Apion* 2.206; Ps-Phocyl. 8; b. Meg. 3b). Jesus does insist on honoring parents (15:4-6); yet he demands greater affection toward himself. A disciple cannot simply "move on" from him after several years as with some other teachers and count it a profitable learning experience (Jos. *Life* 12). Jesus scandalously claims the supreme position of attention in his followers' lives. And lest anyone doubt that Jesus could demand the sort of immediate abandonment of family obligations so that this passage need not imply, Luke adds a third account that requires just that (Lk 9:61-62; cf. Keener 1993: 215; Meier 1980: 87).

Third, Jesus' purpose is to weed out would-be disciples who are weak in commitment. Jesus wanted people to follow him and welcomed the masses; nor did Jesus actually want prospective disciples to abandon him. Mark reports that Jesus loved a prospective disciple (Mk 10:21) — just before he effectively discouraged the man from following him (Mk 10:22). But those who would genuinely be disciples of the king must count the cost before they begin following him (Lk 14:26-35). (Parallels from some other radical ancient teachers demonstrate that commitment rather than harshness was Jesus' intent; see comments on Mt 19:16-22.)

Jesus' Authority over Nature (8:23-27)

Cf. Mk 4:36-41; Lk 8:22-25. This passage affirms Jesus' authority over nature (8:26). Yet if we are right in thinking that Matthew addressed a predominantly Jewish urban congregation, most of his readers rarely faced life-threatening storms at sea. Matthew may encourage his readers that as Jesus has power over nature, so he has power over whatever natural crises they may face, whether persecution (10:28-31), provision (14:32-38), the winds of eschatological judgment (7:25), or anything else; compare the similar example of Elijah in James 5:14-18. (In this case we ask how Matthew's audience might apply the story, rather than suggesting that he allegorizes it, against Bornkamm or Borg.)[46]

46. It is doubtful that the story should be explained or allegorized in terms of the Qumran hymns' ship's facing the storm, depicting the sufferings of the elect in the end time, but if this image were familiar it would encourage Matthew's audience to identify with the struggle of those in the boat in view of their own situation (cf. Davies and Allison 1991: 69; for figurative uses see Plut. *Chance* 2, *Mor.* 97F; *Precepts of Statecraft* 19, *Mor.*). "Waves" also had a figurative usage (Davies and Allison 1991: 71 cite Is 57:20; Wis 14:1; 1QH 2.12-13, 27-28; 6.23; Jude 13; positively, cf. Plut. *Oracles at Delphi* 21, *Mor.* 404E). Matthew also introduces the term "earthquake" (8:24), which sometimes was used for storms at sea and is a term he likes (24:7; 27:51, 54; 28:2; Hagner 1993: 221; for specifying earthquakes, see Jos. *Ant.* 6.27).

The tradition behind this particular story is very likely Palestinian, describing in traditional Galilean (but contrary to foreign) fashion the Lake of Galilee as a "sea" (v. 24; see Mk 4:39; also Theissen 1991: 105-8). The story's setting is also plausible. Over six hundred feet below sea level, the Lake of Galilee is surrounded by ravine-marked hills that can abruptly pull strong winds onto the lake, leading to unexpected storms (Mounce 1985: 75; Paterson 1982: 404). Galilean fishing boats were on average small, holding only a few men (cf. Jos. *War* 3.523; Sanders 1993: 102). Contracts show that those renting boats agreed to return them undamaged except in acts of God beyond their control such as storms (Llewelyn 1992: 82-83). The account of disciples being caught in a storm is not, therefore, implausible; whether one deems the rest of the story plausible involves one's presuppositions about Jesus and about what is possible.

Most scholars today recognize that Jesus performed healings and exorcisms (often because they wish to explain them psychosomatically) but view the nature miracles as legendary embellishments.[47] But most legendary miracle stories in antiquity (cf., e.g., Smith 1978: 119) surrounded characters of the distant past (Grant 1986: 62) rather than arising when eyewitnesses remained. The Western prejudice against nature miracles, like the increasingly less common prejudice against miracles in general, may reveal more about the Enlightenment presuppositions of many twentieth-century Western academicians than about first-century history.[48] Nor would the tradition have taken note of a mere customary stirring of the sea stopping in a customary manner at the moment Jesus "coincidentally" ordered it to do so (Klausner 1979b: 269). Those of us who move in circles where we have witnessed significant miraculous acts (including some nature miracles) are much more disposed to accept the biblical accounts as reasonable as they stand than are those whose Enlightenment skepticism of such phenomena remains absolute.

First, Jesus reproves the disciples for their fear (8:26). Jesus' peace (8:24) contrasts starkly with the disciples' fear (8:25); they are "of little faith" (8:26), just like those who are anxious for tomorrow (6:30) or who doubt his power to work extraordinary miracles (14:31; 16:8; 17:20). Ability to sleep during trouble was often

47. E.g., Taylor 1952: 141; cf. Crossan 1991a: 404; see summary in Aune 1980: 1524. Even Meier 1994: 874-1038 is skeptical of the nature miracles, although this may in part be because, having parceled them into four other categories (877-78), he has too few remaining to defend them on grounds of multiple attestation (contrast Habermas 1995: 129, listing a broader range of sources, but therefore with less substantial evidence). He doubts the authenticity of this particular story because of the prominence of OT themes here to articulate Christology (1994: 924-33). Yet I would suggest that a genuine miracle of this magnitude would have lent itself to christological development in light of the Hebrew Bible, and that if the miracle is authentic, Jesus may stand behind the Christology as well.

48. For questions about Enlightenment philosophical presuppositions concerning miracles see Craig 1986: 43; Benoit 1973/74: 1:39; France 1976: 105-7; cf. Abogunrin 1980; Kee 1983: 3-12; Goppelt 1981/82: 1:145; Borg 1987: 33-34; Davies 1991: 62-65; Meier 1994: 11, 519-21; Brown 1994: 143-44; Boyd 1995: 113-28). Cf. Johnson 1996: 145: "For those living in a community where 'signs and wonders' done in the name of Jesus are a regular occurrence, hearing of such deeds attributed to Jesus in the Gospel narratives is no surprise or scandal."

a sign of faith in God (Ps 3:5; 4:8; Anderson 1976: 144), and Greeks also praised philosophers who demonstrated consistency with their teaching by maintaining a serene attitude during a storm (Diog. Laert. 1.86; 2.71; 9.11.68; Aul. Gel. 1.2.11; 19.1.4-6, 11-21; Brawley 1987: 56). Just as Jesus expects his disciples to trust God for material provision (6:25-34), he expects them to trust him for safety (cf. 10:29-31).[49] By this point in the narrative, the disciples appear without excuse for their unbelief (cf. Rhoads and Michie 1982: 93), like Israel in the wilderness; "Jesus expects them to have taken charge of the storm themselves" (Rhoads and Michie 1982: 90). Yet the narrative also indicates that when their faith remained imperfect, Jesus nevertheless responded to their need.

Second, this account reminds Matthew's community of Jesus' power and consequently Jesus' identity. Against Bornkamm (1963b: 57), who focuses on discipleship here, the primary function of this narrative is christological (Feiler 1983).[50] Surely the disciples did not expect the boat to sink with this mighty teacher aboard who had not yet completed his mission? Faith in Jesus' authority flows from conviction concerning his true identity (cf. 8:8; 9:6). His power over the sea, however, forces them to grapple afresh with that question (8:27). Jesus' true identity and works repeatedly exceeded his contemporaries' expectations for him (7:28; 9:9; 12:23; 22:33).

Some stories about nature miracles circulated in antiquity, although they were less frequent than healing stories. The Pythagorean Empedocles could reportedly control winds and rain (Diog. Laert. 8.2.59); Orpheus, Abaris, Epimenides, Pythagoras, Apollonius, and others were also said to do such works (Porphyry *Life of Pythagoras* 29; Iamb. *Pythagoras* 135; Philost. *Apoll.* 4.13; Blackburn 1986: 190; Boring 1995: 67). A number of charismatic Jewish sages also were able to produce rain (e.g., t. Taʿan. 2:13; cf. Paus. 2.29.8), and some later traditions recount storms becoming calm at sea (e.g., b. B. Bat. 73a; B. Meṣ. 59b; p. Ber. 9:1; Urbach 1979: 1:126; Lohse 1976: 178; Boring 1995: 66, 68). Most of these accounts are considerably later than the characters they depict, however, and when pagans spoke of contemporary nature miracles, they nearly always ascribed them directly to the gods, especially Zeus (Grant 1986: 62).[51]

49. Early Christians probably continued to trust God for "nature miracles" when necessary (cf. Jas 5:16-18; Mk 11:23), but unlike Jesus, they apparently did not view their authority in such situations as automatic or unlimited (see Acts 27:10-26; because Luke-Acts heavily emphasizes signs, it is unlikely that Luke would tone down a stronger early Christian emphasis on nature miracles).

50. In general Held 1963 thinks that Matthew often redacted Mark to present more christological and other theological interpretations of the miracles. But in this narrative Mark's focus is also christological.

51. Pagans often ascribed safety at sea to the Dioscuri (Varro *Latin Language* 5.10.58; Plut. *Pleasant Life Impossible* 23, *Mor.* 1103C; Lucian *Ship/Wishes* 9; Epict. *Disc.* 2.18.29; Artem. *Oneir.* 2.37; *Greek Anthology* 6.149; Acts 28:11), who appear abundantly in ancient literature (e.g., Euhemerus *Sacred History* 6; Hor. *Ode* 3.3.9-10; 4.5.35-36; *Epode* 17.40-44; Paus. 3.13.6; 3.16.2-3; 4.3.1; 5.15.5; Persius *Sat.* 5.49; *Greek Anth.* 4.1.24). When in trouble at sea, one might call on Poseidon (Ach. Tat. *Clit.* 3.4; cf. Virg. *Aen.* 1.142; Boring 1995: 69); in this narrative, however, Jesus does not call on the Lord but acts *as* the Lord.

Parallels to the Jonah story (Cope 1976: 96-98) can link the disciples' amazement at Jesus' stilling of the storm to God's stilling the storm in the Jonah story (Jonah 1:15-16); other backgrounds in the Hebrew Bible also point to Jesus' identity with God (cf. in Lane 1974a: 176). In biblical tradition, it was God whom the seas obeyed (e.g., Job 38:8-11; Ps 65:5-8; 89:8-9; France 1985: 162).[52] The astonishment of Jesus' disciples at his nature miracles is therefore understandable (Mk 4:41; 6:51; cf. a similar response to Apollonius in Greek tradition in Robbins 1992: 149; amazement at miracles, wonders, or deity is standard; see, e.g., *P. Lond.* 1912.8-9; 1 Enoch 26:6; Sib. Or. 1.32; Test. Abr. 3; 6A).

Their cry for Jesus to "save" them (8:25; not in Mk 4:38; cf. Mt 1:21; 9:21-22; 14:36) reflects a perfectly good use of the Greek term "save" ("deliver safely" — Keener 1992: 130-31n.124; sometimes addressed to deities at sea — cf. 14:30; Acts 27:20, 31; Diod. Sic. 4.43.1; Ach. Tat. 3.5),[53] but it probably also alludes on a literary, Matthean level to Jesus' broader mission (1:21). It may also reflect the biblical motif of people crying out to the Lord in distress (Ps 44:23; 78:65), including when he would still a storm for them (Ps 107:25-30; cf. Hooker 1983: 44). Jesus "rebukes" the sea (8:26) just as he would any spirit (17:18).[54]

Third, Jesus' exhausted slumber in the boat passage incidentally illustrates Jesus' statement that the Son of Man has nowhere to lay his head (8:20). Jesus had been a refugee from his early youth (2:13-23), and his ministry now demanded the same lack of security. As if to underline the point, Matthew's omission of Mark's mention of the makeshift cushion (Mk 4:38; for sleeping in the higher stern, cf. Virg. *Aen.* 4.554-55) may represent more than his usual ab-

52. Davies and Allison 1991: 70 compare both Greco-Roman (Herod. 7.191; Virg. *Aen.* 4.553-83; Pliny *N.H.* 37.142, 155; Plut. *Caesar* 38; Ael. Arist. *Or.* 42.10; 45.29, 33; Philost. *V.A.* 4.13; Clem. Alex. *Strom.* 6.3; Iamb. *Vit. Pyth.* 135) and Jewish (ARN 3; b. B. Meṣ. 59b, noting that Bultmann 1968: 237-38 favors a Palestinian origin) sea miracles and deliverances, but argue that the closest parallels are those of the Jonah story, originally emphasizing that Jesus was "one greater than Jonah" (Mt 12:41). They note that Jesus acts not as a mere prophet, but as Yahweh (citing Ps 65:7; 89:8-9; 93:3-4; 106:8-9; 107:23-32; Is 51:9-10; 2 Macc 9:8; 4Q381).

53. For "salvation" in terms of physical rescues from distress in Greek, see, e.g., LXX Ex. 14:13, 30; Sir 46:1; Jdt 8:17; 9:1; 11:3; 1 Macc 4:25; Ps. Sol. 16:5; Jos. *Ant.* 2.339; 3.1; 11.282; *War* 5.415; 6.310; *Life* 244, 259; Philo *Decal.* 53, 60, 155; 4 Macc. 15:8; Test. Job 19:2/1; Demosth. *On the Crown* 324; *Or.* 60, *Funeral Speech* 10, 23; *Letter* 1, §2; Diod. Sic. 11.24.2; Dion. Hal. 12.1.8; Apul. *Metam.* 6.28; Char. *Chaer.* 2.7.6; 2.8.1. For Greek deities and the emperor as "saviors," see, e.g., Sall. *Letter to Caesar* 13.6; Arrian *Indica* 21.2; 36.3; Paus. 1.40.3; 2.20.6; 4.34.6; 8.31.2; 9.26.8; Plut. *On Borrowing* 7, *Mor.* 830B; Epict. *Disc.* 1.22.16; Athenaeus 7.288F; *Orphic Hymns* 14.8; 27.12; 74.4; inscription in Grant 1953: 30. For rulers, including emperors, Mart. *Epig.* 2.91; *CPJ* 1:185-86, §38; 2:31, §151; *SEG* 11.923 in Sherk 1988: 58; *SB* 3924 in ibid.: 61; *OGIS* 90 in Grant 1953: 68; for Israel's God, see, e.g., 1 Macc 4:30; Sib. Or. 1:73, 152, 167; 2:28; 3:35; Odes Sol. 5:11; Nock 1933b: 132; Longenecker 1981:142-43 (cf. Test. Dan 5:10, of a messianic figure). Note especially the Jewish inscription praising God for deliverance at sea in Horsley 1987: 113. There is thus no need to allegorize the text.

54. This need not imply that he addressed the angel over the sea (as in Jub. 2:2; 1QM 10.11-12; 1 Enoch 66:2; 2 Enoch 19.3-4; b. Pesaḥ. 118b), although it is interesting that in later tradition God slew that angel during the exodus (b. B. Bat. 74b; Num. Rab. 18:22). The term for "rebuke" here expresses authority in a different manner in 12:16, and negatively in 16:22; 20:31.

breviation technique. Matthew also purposely emphasizes that his true disciples "followed" him (8:23).

Jesus' Authority over Demons (8:28-34)

Cf. Mk 5:1-20; Lk 8:26-39. Although Matthew, abbreviating his accounts to get all of them onto his single scroll, omits many details concerning the "strong man" that "no one could bind" from Mark 5:1-20 (cf. Mk 3:27), his account nevertheless makes clear that Jesus overcomes extremely powerful demoniacs ("no one could pass that way" — 8:28; for unnatural strength involved in some possession trances, see, e.g., Murphy 1964: 58; for demonstrable physiological changes during possession trance, see Goodman 1988: 20, 126). Such suspense-building techniques were as common in exorcism stories (Theissen 1983: 52) as in other stories.

Details in the story both build suspense and bring out the significance of Jesus' power. Matthew's readers may also have heard of the healing sanctuary at Gadara (Wilkinson 1978: 102) — which clearly had not done these demoniacs much good. That tombs (in this region, see A. B. Bruce 1979: 145) were unclean (e.g., m. Nazir 3:5; 7:3; t. B. Bat. 1:10-11; Kelim B. Qam. 3:7; Sheb. 3:13; Mek. Pisha 1.83-84; ARN 41A) and considered usual haunts of demons and magic (*PGM* 101.1-3; Nineham 1977: 153; Alexander 1980: 29; cf. Jub. 22:17; ARN 3A; b. Ber. 18b; Test. Sol. 8:9; Apul. *Metam.* 2.20; Lewis 1983: 96) increases the audience's suspicion that these demons are inordinately powerful — hence the narrative's opening suspense and christological impact.[55]

Matthew also clarifies Jesus' power against potential magical misinterpretations of Mark (Gundry 1982: 159) and adds a note of eschatological conquest: "before the appointed time" (8:29). Ascertaining a demon's name was important in magical exorcism (Test. Sol. 5:2, 6-7, 9; cf. 11:5), but Matthew omits the words in Mark that could be thus interpreted (Mk 5:9). In 8:29 Matthew omits Mark's *horkizō* ("implore," Mk 5:7), though adding the cognate *exorkizō* in 26:63, perhaps because oath invocations had magical associations in other exorcisms — *PGM* 1.80-82, 167; 36.307, 347-48; 39.19-20; Test. Sol. 11:6; cf. the inscription in Kotansky 1995. "Go" (8:32) may bear verbal reminiscence to formulas used by other exorcists (Bultmann 1968: 232; "come out from" in Barrett

55. Exorcisms served the epideictic purposes of much biography by emphasizing the exorcist's authority (cf., e.g., the third-century Philost. *V.A.* 4.20), but both the christological context and the intensity of demonic bondage here allow Matthew to imply more for Jesus than for another exorcist. The LXX sometimes associates demons with idolatry, further increasing Jewish apprehension of Jesus' encounter with spirits in Gentile territory (Deut 32:17; Ps 96:5 [LXX 95:5]; 106:37 [LXX 105:37]; Bar 4:7). Matthew omits Mark's description of their masochism (Mk 5:5), which seems to have characterized some eastern Mediterranean rites (1 Kings 18:28; Roberts 1970; Sen. *Dial.* 7.26.8; references to the Galli in Keener 1991a: 175 n. 21) and other religions (e.g., Jochim 1986: 154; Mbiti 1970: 106, 225-26). For spirit-possession and trance behavior see, e.g., Henney 1974; Pressel 1974; Goodman 1974.

1961: 34; "rebuke" in Kee 1968: 246; it was, after all, a common goal to get the spirit to depart), but the other parallels generally derive from contexts of lengthy magical incantations, whereas Jesus casts out spirits merely "with a word" (8:16).[56]

Two minor critical issues warrant comment. Matthew's "Gadarenes" (8:28) represents a different city than Mark's "Gerasenes" (Mk 5:1). Historians freely corrected earlier historical claims in light of better geographical evidence (Diod. Sic. 4.56.7-8), and some suppose that Matthew does so with Mark here. Gerasa was larger and more powerful in Mark's time,[57] hence Mark used the more prominent city to identify the region (cf. Vander Broek 1983: 89-102); Matthew, probably writing to Christians in Syria who knew the region better, clarifies the matter by naming the prominent city nearer the lake itself (six miles away as opposed to thirty — Anderson 1976: 147-48).[58] In both Gospels, the writer is simply identifying the region; Gadara and Gerasa were both parts of the Decapolis, a primarily Gentile area with a large Jewish population (Jos. *War* 1.155; cf. *Ant.* 15.354; Gen. Rab. 65:20; not the Perean Gadara of Jos. *War* 4.413-15). It probably had connections with the east as well as with Greek culture (Bowsher 1987). The presence of pigs further underlines the Gentile character of the region, since observant Jews would avoid raising pigs (e.g., Lev 11:7; Deut 14:8; m. B. Qam. 7:7). The largely Gentile location fits Matthew's emphasis on the Gentile mission, though he develops it less than one might expect.

The other issue is that Matthew doubles Mark's demoniacs (Mt 8:28//Mk 5:2), as he later doubles his blind men (Mt 9:27-31; 20:29-34//Mk 10:46-52; cf. perhaps 21:2; 26:60). That doubling is a Matthean stylistic feature thus follows (Meier 1980: 230), but one must ask *why* it is a Matthean characteristic. Some propose that he desires two witnesses to fulfill the requirements of Jewish law (26:60; France 1985: 163), but this proposal would render doubtful why he does not double characters more consistently. In both other instances of doubling he has omitted one of Mark's accounts (the demoniac of Mk 1:23-26; the blind man of Mk 8:22-26), hence he feels justified compensating here; such a literary practice would not have been unusual in his day (cf. Holtzmann in A. B. Bruce 1979: 145; Goulder 1974: 44-45; Gundry 1982: 158).

56. Yamauchi 1986: 133. For parallels with contemporary exorcists and differences (especially regarding his distinctive expressions of authority), see Twelftree 1993: 172-73.

57. It grew tremendously between A.D. 22 and 76, and may even have served as the capital of the Decapolis for awhile (Theissen 1991:109), hence an understandable way to identify the region. Despite what he takes to be Mark's geographical error, Theissen concludes that the story "fits well within the tensions between the Decapolis and its Jewish neighbors," hence undoubtedly circulated originally in a Palestinian milieu (Theissen 1991: 109; but would not a southerly Syrian milieu be just as effective?). Some suggest that Mark intended not Gerasa (modern Jerash) but a relatively insignificant Gergesa identified with modern Kursi, which lies directly on the lake (Finegan 1969: 62; France 1985: 162), a view already held by third-century-A.D. Christians (Tzaferis 1989).

58. Gadara in the Decapolis was also near the river Yarmak (Pliny *N.H.* 5.16.74), hence connecting it directly to the lake. Some scholars have disputed its proposed "colony" status (cf. Dvorjetski and Last 1991).

Excursus: On Demons and Exorcism

Greeks could picture gods (Hom. *Il.* 17.210-11) or other spirits (Epict. *Disc.* 1.14.14) entering a person, but the Greek term translated "demon" is not in itself negative, although at times it could refer to an evil spirit (e.g., *P. Grenf.* 2.76.3-4, but this is A.D. 305-6), to the spirits of the dead (*PGM* 4.1965-69), or to one touched by madness (also among Persians; cf. Olmstead 1959: 53). Greeks often applied it to deities or demigods, ranging from Olympians to suprahuman spirits (Hom. *Il.* 1.561; Ps-Plato *Epinomis* 984DE; Dion. Hal. 1.31.1; Plut. *Isis* 26, *Mor.* 361A; *Obsolescence of Oracles* 10-22, *Mor.* 415B-422C; *Sign of Socrates* 10, 24, *Mor.* 580C, 593D; Socrates *Ep.* 1; Epict. *Disc.* 3.22.53; Ach. Tat. *Clit.* 3.10.1; *Orphic Hymn* 17.8; 50.2; 73.1-2; Paus. 9.22.7), and sometimes even the equivalent of the Roman *genius* (Epict. *Disc.* 1.14.12). Not everyone concurred with this intermediary category between gods and mortals, but it was widely held (Dion. Hal. 1.77.3). Josephus freely employs this hellenistic language for the divine (Isaacs 1976: 33-34).

But Persian demonology bears some resemblance to the Jewish and Christian perspective (Olmstead 1959: 18, 96, 195, 232), and on a popular level Greeks close to the early Christian period applied the term increasingly often to the many forces between gods and nature (see Nilsson 1948: 170-72; Puiggali 1983; Sánchez 1976). Many Jewish people believed that the gods of the pagans were demons in any case (Bar 4:7; 1 Enoch 19:1; Jub. 22:17; Test. Sol. 5:5; 6:4; Sifre Deut. 318.2.1-2); some Middle Eastern religions demonized the deities of those they supplanted (Gordon 1965b: 246-47; Alexander 1980: 19; for fallen angels, cf. the fallen gods of Enuma Elish, the Greek Titanomachy, and the Hittite account in Gurney 1977: 15). Such demons could prove hostile (cf. Char. *Chaer.* 3.1.4; 6.2.9, though these may be divine). From such demons even pagans recognized the need for exorcism (*PGM* 4.3007-86; see Ferguson 1987: 185; comment on 8:16-17). Exorcism was common in early Judaism (Jos. *Ant.* 8.46-48; accepted at Qumran, 4QNab 1.4; Kirchschläger 1976). It might involve smoking a demon out with a special substance (Tob 6:7-8, 16-17; 8:2-3; cf. Test. Sol. 5:13; Parshall 1983: 85), invoking other spirits to expel it (incantation text 3.8-9; 50.7-8; Test. Sol. 2:4; 5:5; 8:5-11; 18), or even laying on one's hands in prayer (1QapGen 20). As in paganism, the visible proof of departure by some outward act often remained important (Jos. *Ant.* 8.48; in modern times, Hes 1964: 376). Various forms of exorcism have continued among some traditional Jewish groups into the modern period (cf., e.g., Hes 1964: 376, 380), as in many cultures (Kaplan and Johnson 1964: 211; Fuchs 1964: 135-37; Mbiti 1970: 106).

A variety of Jewish conceptions of demonology developed, probably most of them overlapping in popular religion, although it is difficult to know at what period various strands originated. Some Jewish traditions adapted Greek concepts, such as reference to avenging spirits resembling the Greek Furies (Sir 39:28); elsewhere, however, angels of destruction appear to be spirits serving the evil prince of darkness (1QM 13.11-12; perhaps p. Shebu. 6:6, §3). A few later texts may also reflect the late

Platonic notion (cf. Dillon 1977: 317-19) of demons as disembodied (or in this case, simply nonembodied) souls (Gen. Rab. 7:5). Magical texts reflecting some folk religion specify among other types of demons groups such as "liliths" (Aramaic incantation texts 1.6, 8; 3.14; 6.11; 10.2; 11.1-3, 9; 12.2, 8; cf. 2 Bar. 10:8; Hes 1964: 376; in older Canaanite religion, see Kaiser 1973: 131); others might expect deceased giants to remain on earth as evil spirits (1 Enoch 15:9). Some texts also call demons "unclean spirits" (Test. Sol. 3:7; cf. Jub. 10:1), as at times in the Gospels (10:1; 12:43; Mk 1:23-27; "unclean" might indicate "evil," as apparently in 1QpHab 8.13). Demons also occasionally are associated with particular sins, like demons of deceit associated with witchcraft and divination (Test. Jud. 23:1). Named demons appear early (4Q560; Penney and Wise 1994; cf. Mk 5:9).

Demons could also cause physical afflictions (Test. Sol. 1:1-4; 18), as at times in the Gospels. Some sources suggest a special unleashing of demons in the eschatological time before the end (2 Bar. 27:9), perhaps relevant to the views concerning their prevalence in the time of Jesus; for the possible linking of exorcism with eschatology, cf. Test. Sim. 6:6; with the kingdom, see 4Q510, 1.4 (Vermes 1993: 130).

In popular culture people sought various means of protection from hostile spirits; though much of our documentation comes from one or more centuries after the first century when these means became pervasive, enough attests that demons were a matter of practical concern to popular folk religion already by the first century. Amulets were widespread (see MacMullen 1966: 103-4); common enough in the Republic (Varro 7.6.107), they became even more widespread under the Empire (Nilsson 1948: 167; cf. Greek magic against demons in Betz 1980). Magical practices designed to protect against the influence of demons in Sassanian Babylonia (third to seventh centuries) crossed religious boundaries, as popular syncretism typically does (Gordon 1978b: 231). Superstition readily crossed folk boundaries and from there would naturally permeate more sophisticated systems as well; for example, Mesopotamian rabbis' fears about even numbers rendering one susceptible to demons (b. B. Meṣ. 86a; Qidd. 29b; Pesaḥ. 110a, bar.) reflect a broader ancient superstition (Virg. *Ecl.* 8.75; Plut. *R.Q.* 102, *Mor.* 288D).

Later magical amulets in Israel (e.g., Rahmani 1981) and incantation texts guaranteeing protection from specific demons (texts 17.1-2; 19.2; 34.1, 6; 47.1) indicate how widespread such views became: beginning no later than the third century many rabbis thought that the very air around them was crowded with demons (b. Ber. 6a; Deut. Rab. 4:4; Midr. Ps 17:8). Demons were thought to attack people (1 Enoch 69:12; Tr. Shem 2:9), but at least the rabbis usually viewed them as mortal (b. Pesaḥ. 111b). Before the first century some Jews believed particular medicines could protect people from evil spirits (Jub. 10:10-13), and later rabbis used various folk remedies to ward off such spirits (b. Ber. 6a); some might even hope for warriors to protect them (Song Rab. 3:7, §5; Pesiq. R. 15:3).

Sages came to urge proper precautions against demonic assaults. Drinking water at night rendered one susceptible to demons (b. ʿAbod. Zar. 12b, bar.); going out on particular nights of the week was dangerous (b. Pesaḥ. 112b, bar.; other peoples also recognized unlucky days, e.g., Aul. Gel. 5.17); different demons exercised their dangers during different times of the year (Num. Rab. 12:3). One kind of evil spirit dwelt in reed stalks (Gen. Rab. 56:6), and others might be found in palm and other trees (b. Pesaḥ. 111a, bar.; 111ab); various trees and bushes harbored various sorts of demons (b. Pesaḥ. 111b), as did most vegetables (b. Sanh. 101a, bar.). Rabbis reportedly learned some of these traditions from reports offered by demons themselves (b. Pesaḥ. 110ab), a source, one might think, of dubitable veracity, however firsthand its information (though perhaps obtained by interrogation; cf. Fuchs 1964: 135-36).

Demons might be found in ruins (b. Ber. 3ab), in bathhouses (t. Ber. 6:25; b. Ber. 62a; Qidd. 39b-40a; Shab. 67a; Qoh. Rab. 2:8, §1; Song Rab. 3:7, §5), and elsewhere; because of their association with the dead, spirits remain associated with burial grounds in some cultures today (Schmidt 1964: 147). Rabbinic piety suggested that prayer could render many demons impotent or destroy them, though dealing with them was never pleasant (b. Qidd. 29b). Other pious acts, like the erection of the tabernacle, could destroy demons (Num. Rab. 12:3; Pesiq. R. 5:10); fear of God could protect one from them (Gen. Rab. 36:1). Later rabbis thought that some kinds of demons could look like people (b. Giṭ. 66a). Some even felt that particular demons might prove helpful (b. Meʿil. 17b; Gen. Rab. 24:6; 63:8). But of course such spirits were subject to and recognized God's sovereignty (Jub. 49:2; CD 8.2-3; 1QapGen 20.16-17; 1QM 14.9-10; Test. Adam 1:1; Num. Rab. 14:3; cf. VanderKam 1978: 245). Perhaps relevant to the crowds' application of "son of David" to Jesus in Mt 12:23 (perhaps also 15:22) is the longstanding association between Solomon and exorcism (Jos. *Ant.* 8.45-49; *CIJ* 1:394, §534; 2:374, §1448; *PGM* 4.850-929, 3039-41; Test. Sol. Greek title; 5:10; incantation text 47.1-3; 48.4-5; Pesiq. R. 5:3; cf. p. Ketub. 12:3, §11); for David himself, see Ps-Philo 60 (cf. 1 Sam 16:23).

Although many modern students of the Gospels doubt the reality of spirit-possession, they admit that the ancients believed it and acted accordingly, as in many gospel accounts (Wrede 1971: 26-27); others challenge the presuppositions that produce skepticism toward such phenomena (Yamauchi 1986: 142-47; cf. Borg 1987: 62, 72n.16). (Some explain the deviant possession phenomena in terms of their social function; cf. Hollenbach 1981; Crossan 1991a: 318; but the phenomena seem too widespread in too many cultures to allow a reductionist interpretation.) Anthropologists note spirit-possession in many unrelated cultures (see Crapanzaro and Garrison 1977: 7; Goodman 1988: 1-24, 126; Mbiti 1970: 106, 111, 113, 249-50; Lewis 1971; Alexander 1980: 105-6). In various cultures where it has been observed in the modern world, spirit-possession sometimes yields superhuman strength that makes restraint difficult or impossible (e.g., Kaplan and Johnson 1964: 208; cf. Mk 5:4) and often yields destructiveness (Eliade 1958: 71; Gelfand 1964: 165, 170; Schmidt 1964: 145; Kaplan and Johnson 1964: 227; Mt 8:28), including at times self-laceration (Fox 1964: 185; Mk 5:5; 1 Kings 18:28).

Most scholars concur that Jesus historically gained a reputation as an exorcist (Sanders 1993: 149, 154; Meier 1994: 646-77; Dunn 1975: 44; Michaels 1981: 174; Twelftree 1986). The lack of most contemporary magical techniques such as rings, roots, incantations, and so forth is noteworthy (Justin *Dial.* 85; Kee 1968: 239;

Vermes 1973: 23, 65; Twelftree 1986: 383-84; Witherington 1990: 159), though a few later rabbis were said to have expelled demons with commands (Vermes 1973: 66; cf. Kee 1968: 246). The form of many of the exorcism accounts resembles many miracle stories (cf. Guillemette 1980).

The narrative articulates various principles for Matthew's missionary community. **First, even demons are sensitive enough to know who their Lord and Judge is (8:28-30).** In Matthew's larger narrative structure, this implies that disciples, who receive positive benefits for obedience, should obey willingly (8:18-22; 9:9-13, 37-38). Whereas demons confess from fear, others (16:16) confess from faith or love (Augustine *On the Psalms* 50.2, *ACCS,* 40). The demoniacs ran to him (8:28), and the demons protested his coming to torture them (cf. Test. Sol. 5:5) in advance (8:29). Jesus' presence also reduced them to entreating permission just to enter some pigs (8:30). Supernatural beings alone recognize Jesus' true identity, which fits the Matthean and Markan story worlds (Kingsbury 1983: 86-87), but also the language of ancient magical texts (Witherington 1990: 170, citing, e.g., *PGM* 8.13). In ancient texts, demons who encountered someone more powerful would plead for mercy (Test. Sol. 2:6; Twelftree 1986: 381; Theissen 1983: 57) and might scream as here (Test. Sol. 1:12; 3:4); they also appear to have preferred to remain in the same region where they had been active, as here (Tob 8:3; Twelftree 1986: 381). "What is there between us and you?" (8:29) reflects a Semitic idiom creating or recognizing distance between the speaker and addressee (e.g., Judg 11:2; 2 Sam 19:22; 1 Kings 17:18; cf. also Epict. *Disc.* 2.19.16, 20.11; Mart. *Epig.* 1.76.11-12).[59]

Second, the kingdom is "already" as well as "not yet" (8:29). Matthew's redaction ("before the time," missing in Mark) allows him to underline this point. Because the king of the future age arrived almost unannounced before the future age, his kingdom also invaded the present age in a way hidden to people but recognized by the evil one and his forces (cf. Cullmann 1950: 71). Demons who believed they were free to torment people until the final day (references in Gundry 1982: 159; cf. Test. Sim. 6:6) and expected eternal torment only in the day of judgment recognized that their judge had appeared ahead of schedule.[60] While Matthew's community awaited God's ultimate intervention, they could still depend on his power over the evil one in the present transitional period.

Third, Jesus values people more than property (8:30-32). In ancient ex-

59. For demons speaking through humans, see, e.g., Philost. *V.A.* 3.38; cf. 1 Sam 18:10; 1 Kings 22:22.

60. In various traditions the fallen angels were presently tormented while awaiting the final judgment or free to roam while awaiting the final judgment, or some were assigned to each station (e.g., 1 Enoch 10:4-6, 12-13; 15–16; 19:1; 69:28; Jub. 5:6, 10; 10:8-9; Ps-Philo 60:3; Test. Sol. 6:3; Hagner 1993: 227). Augustine *Tractate on John* 7.6.2 suggests that demons knew that Jesus would eventually come, from prophets and angels (*ACCS,* 21).

orcism traditions demons typically made a scene when they departed, melodramatically indicating their protest and the exorcist's power (e.g., Jos. *Ant.* 8.48-49; Philost. *V.A.* 4.20; Alexander 1980: 144; Theissen 1983: 66-67); but rarely did they make *this* much of a scene! Although most Jewish traditions about demons spoke of binding them in a pit (see on 12:29), others suggested the destructibility of some kinds of demons (e.g., ARN 37A; Aramaic incantation text 3.17; Alexander 1980: 33), and many of Matthew's Jewish readers may have interpreted this narrative accordingly. That the demons who lived in humans were willing to subsist in pigs (for parallels, see Bultmann 1968: 225) suggests that they preferred a domicile of some sort to simply wandering; this preference in turn suggests that the destruction of the herd was Jesus' idea, not theirs (cf. Gundry 1982: 160), although the act may have employed and revealed their own destructive impulses (cf. Mk 5:5; Lane 1974a: 186; Chrysostom *Discourse Against Judaizing Christians* 8:6, *ACCS,* 70-71). Pigs could normally swim for some distance if necessary (Alexander 1980: 214); some demons reportedly feared water (Test. Sol. 5:11-12), but others could reportedly survive there (Test. Sol. 25:7) or even live there (Twelftree 1986: 382). Perhaps the demons were thus banished to hell (cf. Gundry 1982: 160); at the very least this account suggests that they were disabled. In some Jewish traditions they were mortal (e.g., Aramaic incantation text 3.17; Jub. 10:5; ARN 37A).[61]

The earliest Jewish hearers of this story would have nodded knowingly that demons wished to enter unclean pigs and that Jesus let the herd perish,[62] but to the owners of the swine the destruction of their herd meant serious financial loss. The deliverance of the demoniacs mattered more to Jesus than the fate of the swine (also Jerome *Homily* 54, *ACCS,* 70; Hooker 1983: 39).[63]

Fourth, one should expect opposition for such priorities, because most people value property more than they value God's delivering activity (8:33-34). Gentile wonder-workers were often "magicians," whose power others perceived as malevolent more often than not (e.g., Apul. *Metam.* 2.5, 20, 30; 3.16-18; 9.30).[64] Ig-

61. For questions about the mortal status of some partly divine beings in Greek thought, see, e.g., Eurip. *Cyclops* 231, 321; Ap. Rhod. 4.1679-80; even Ares in Hom. *Il.* 5.385-91. An allusion to Ex 14–15 (Derrett 1979a) is possible (albeit not likely) in Mark, but Matthew omits many of the allusions that would even make the suggestion plausible in his account.

62. Jewish distaste for pigs was widely known and disdained (e.g., Juv. *Sat.* 6.160), even though various other cultures also held food taboos (*ANET* 391; Herod. *Hist.* 2.41; Diod. Sic. 1.11.4; 2.4.3). The Egyptians may have also abstained from swine (*ANET* 10; Herod. *Hist.* 2.47; Plut. *Isis and Osiris, Mor.* 353F; Jos. *Apion* 2.141), though swine were used in other cults, especially for underworld deities (*ANET* 351; Aristophanes *Peace* 1.372; Moyer 1969: 96, 127; but even here, see *ANET* 209; Moyer 1969 106; idem 1983: 29).

63. Given the direct relevance of exorcism to a first-century missionary audience, connecting the "legion" (which shows the demons' numerical strength, Mk 5:9) and the pigs (unclean animals, many of which would be raised in this area) with the Syrian tenth legion Fretensis, whose insignia included (among other things) the image of a boar, is stretching the evidence (pace, e.g., Theissen 1991: 110). Twelftree 1993: 72-87 argues that Mark probably preserved the story in close to its original form.

64. Cf. further Smith 1978: 75-76; Theissen 1983: 239-42; Yamauchi 1986: 90; Schmidt 1982; Remus 1982; Raynor 1984: 225.

noring the men's deliverance and focusing on the destruction of the property, the Gadarenes viewed Jesus as dangerous to their interests.[65] Though pigs normally grazed without much oversight (Cary and Haarhoff 1946: 109), at least some herdsmen were likely (8:33); such herdsmen, responsible to the owners for the safety of their pigs, would naturally prove particularly hostile (cf. Eurip. *Iphig. Taur.* 296-310). (Perhaps merely due to abbreviating the narrative, Matthew omits Jesus' commissioning the man to return to his Gentile community and set the record straight — Mk 5:19; cf. Mt 10:5.)

Since miracles could conceivably derive from more than one source (9:34; 12:24; 24:24), they may draw attention without demonstrating the authenticity of their worker (thus Aristotle distinguished between witnesses to facts and those who understood the point of the facts — Trites 1977: 178); but, probably like some witnesses of the Matthean missionaries' signs, the nearby community exhibits no interest in exploring matters further. Early Christians sometimes faced a backlash due to the economic consequences of their activity (Acts 19:23-28; Pliny *Ep.* 10.96). Jesus apparently withdraws without protest (8:34; cf. 12:19-20).[66]

Authority to Forgive Sins (9:1-8)

Cf. Mk 2:1-12; Lk 5:17-26. The "boat" (9:1) connects this narrative with preceding paragraphs (8:18, 23, 28; Fenton 1977: 134). In abbreviating Mark, Matthew omits the memorable event of letting the paralytic through the roof, possibly the very reason tradition had preserved this story.67 Nevertheless, Matthew preserves the main *point* of the story: Jesus' authority to heal the body testifies to his authority to forgive (9:6-7; cf. 9:12). Jesus' "authority" (9:6, 8) is a central focus of the context (7:29; 8:9, 27; cf. 28:18). This narrative presents a number of lessons.

First, Jesus is moved by suppliants' faith, even on behalf of others (9:2). The paralytic was not alone in his faith; his friends who brought him believed, too.[68] The narrative hints at a theology of intercession also assumed by

65. The pre-Christian Callimachus *Aitia* 3.75 does, however, report the transfer of epilepsy from a woman to wild goats (Boring 1995: 72-73); but Jesus had transferred demons to domestic stock.

66. Overman 1996: 120 suggests that Jesus is accommodating the colonial situation; Jews in the Decapolis had to remain careful in their relations with their neighbors (cf. Jos. *War* 2.461, 466-68).

67. The proposal that "letting down through the roof" has a Greco-Roman milieu related to those once thought dead not entering through the door (Boring 1995: 73-74, citing Plut. *R.Q.* 5, *Mor.*) is farfetched; one might as well parallel the Pharisees' letting down their companions to remove Herod's eagle (Jos. *War* 1.651). Luke's "tiles" portray northern Mediterranean roofs (Lk 5:19), despite their incompatibility with the story (such a roof would collapse — cf. Aristoph. *Clouds* 1486-89)!

68. Some have applied the principle in this text to infant baptism (e.g., Richardson 1958: 360-62); others would be more skeptical of that application unless more explicit apostolic evidence supports it.

their contemporaries: disciples may pray for others, not merely for themselves. Mark's fuller narrative recounts the character of their faith: they were so persistent and determined to reach Jesus, so confident that their friend would be healed if they reached him, that they dug through the roof (Mk 2:4-5). But by this point in Matthew, Matthew's readers also know that genuine faith is a very serious matter, involving humble commitment (8:8-10, 20-22, 26).

Second, Jesus knows that suppliants need forgiveness even more than physical healing (9:2). Although Jesus' miracles teach about his power to heal physically, these signs are especially meant to turn attention to the kingdom of God (6:33; 9:12). Similarly, in the Book of Acts signs and wonders constitute the primary method of drawing attention to the claims of the gospel, but it is the gospel itself that is paramount (e.g., Acts 14:3). In this narrative, physical healing certainly draws the crowd's attention (9:8), as miracles in miracle stories normally did (e.g., 8:27, 34; 9:26, 31, 33).

Thus Jesus turns his attention to forgiveness first. The Gospels do not argue that sickness was always a direct personal result of sin (2 Kings 13:14; Jn 9:3), as many people in Jesus' day, both Jewish (Ps 103:3; Jn 9:2; 4Q510; 4QPrNab; m. 'Abot 2:7; t. Ber. 6:3; Mek. Nez. 18.55-58; Abrahams 1917: 108-12; Lachs 1987: 166; Davies and Allison 1991: 89) and Gentile (Plut. *Profit by Enemies* 5, *Mor.* 88F; van der Horst 1975: 157-58), thought. That Jesus did not always pause to forgive sins shows that he did not always connect disease and sin in a causal relationship (pace Montefiore 1968: 1:43; cf. Dibelius 1949: 112-13); but Jesus' healing of the human body also functions as a dramatic illustration of healing for the human character (13:15). The Gospels do, however, suggest that when these problems are intertwined, God wishes to deal with both (Jas 5:14-16).

Third, Matthew may warn that speaking for God usually invites opposition, especially from others who wrongly suppose that speaking for God has been *their* role (9:3). Jesus' unique authority on earth to forgive sins sets him apart from other people, a claim that disturbed the "teachers of the law" (9:3). One rare sectarian document reports an exorcist "forgiving sins" (4QNab 1.4; cf. Vermes 1984: 10; Sanders 1985: 273), and priests may have exercised delegated authority to pronounce forgiveness of sins (Sanders 1990: 62; idem 1985: 240); Jesus' passive voice also declares that it is God rather than Jesus himself who is forgiving the man's sins (Sanders 1990: 61; Vermes 1993: 192). But Jesus not only speaks on God's behalf to forgive sins for which no clear atonement has been made — an act the teachers present could equate with impious presumption (Sanders 1990: 62-63), but before the narrative concludes he proceeds to announce publicly that he has authority from the Father to forgive sins, an attribute Jewish people did not even associate with the Messiah (Gundry 1982: 163).

Thus the scholars decided that Jesus was "blaspheming," which in the general sense simply meant "reviling (in this case, God)," and in the most technical sense meant "using God's name in vain." Although Matthew omits Mark's "only

God can forgive sins," in this instance the religious teachers probably use "blaspheme" in an intermediate way: Jesus brings reproach on God's name by usurping divine prerogatives for himself (cf. Sanders 1990: 58-60; Lane 1974a: 95).[69] This assumes, of course, that God did not delegate his authority to Jesus (cf. 28:18), an assumption the narrative suggests is unlikely by the fact that Jesus knows their thoughts (9:4; cf. 12:25). Jewish people believed that only God knew everything about human hearts (e.g., Jub. 15:30; 1 Enoch 84:3; Ps. Sol. 9:3; 14:8; Ep. Arist. 132-33; Test. Zeb. 5:2; m. 'Abot 2:1; t. B. Qam. 7:2; Sanh. 8:3), and that he shared only some of that knowledge with great prophets (Jos. and Asen. 23:8; 26:6; *Lives of the Prophets* 17.2; p. Ḥag. 2:2, §5; Sanh. 6:6, §2; cf. the Messiah in Ps. Sol. 17:25).[70] The opposition Jesus' act generates will be familiar to audiences familiar with either the biblical prophets or the Socratic tradition of hellenistic philosophers, leading the way to the teacher's martyrdom (cf. Robbins 1992: 109, 147). Yet the reader will ultimately find these leaders' charge ironic, for soon Matthew informs his audience that the leaders' opposition to Jesus itself is blasphemous (cf. 12:31).

Fourth, Jesus' authority to heal demonstrates his authority to forgive (9:6-7). Because healing as opposed to forgiveness is empirically verifiable, the teachers of the law would conclude that it is easier to *say,* "Your sins are forgiven" (Meier 1980: 91). By performing a sign that is empirically verifiable, however, Jesus argues that he is God's authorized agent and therefore has authority to forgive sins. The argument runs like a traditional Jewish *qal waḥomer* argument: if God would authorize Jesus visibly to heal the effects of humanity's fallenness, would he not send him to combat that fallenness itself? Jesus implies that his mission is so dramatic by alluding to Daniel 7:13, the "Son of Man's authority" (Hamerton-Kelly 1973: 62); but if his adversaries recognized the allusion, it nevertheless remained subtle enough to sabotage attempts at public retaliation (cf. Rhoads and Michie 1982: 84-85).[71] In the broader Matthean context,

69. Sanders 1993: 214 doubts that the claim to know God's mind would be particularly offensive, but cites Honi the Circle-Drawer to make his case. Whereas the rabbis accepted rare accounts of supernatural knowledge within their own circles (t. Pisha 2:15), various tales express some suspicion toward the less traditional works of Hanina and Honi. According to later tradition, some wanted to place Honi under the ban for his use of God's name (Boring 1995: 76-77, citing b. Taʿan. 23a).

70. To "say in one's heart" was good Semitic idiom for thinking, and Jewish people generally located "thoughts" in the heart, as here (e.g., Jub. 12:16-17; cf. Sib. Or. 1:134; internal "reasonings" in 1 Macc 2:63; Test. Job 2:3-4). "Evil" (9:4) often applies to the leaders in Matthew (12:33-35, 38-45; 16:1-4; 22:18; Van Tilborg 1972b: 27-38). Many church fathers thought that Jesus' forgiveness of sins here identified him as divine (Iren. *Haer.* 5.17; Novatian *The Trinity* 13; Chrysostom *The Paralytic Let Down through the Roof* 6, *ACCS,* 27-28), which differs from a mere Christian pastor pronouncing forgiveness in the name of the Godhead rather than his own (Ambrose *The Holy Spirit* 3.18.137). Chrysostom saw Jesus' knowledge of the scribes' hearts, like his authority to forgive sin, as a demonstration of deity (*Gospel of St. Matthew,* Homily 29.1, *ACCS,* 28).

71. "Son of man" can mean human being generically, although in this context it must mean more than that (Kümmel 1957: 46n.93; pace Montefiore 1968: 1:44). Hagner 1993: 234 suggests that as Son of Man Jesus brings the blessings of the eschatological time, which include forgiveness (Is 33:24; Jer 31:34; CD 14.19; 11QMelch 4–9).

Jesus' authority "on earth" in this passage prepares the way for his universal authority in 28:18.

Finally, in the end Jesus' signs of authority brought God glory, despite the opposition (9:8).[72] God vindicated his work despite opposition (cf. 7:28; 8:27; 9:33; 12:23).

Sinners Need a Physician (9:9-13)

Cf. Mk 2:13-17; Lk 5:27-32. On a positive use of the criterion of dissimilarity (see Sanders 1985: 174), most scholars concur that Jesus sometimes ate with those whom others considered sinful.[73] While scholarly reconstructions diverge at this point (e.g., whether the "sinners" were, with Jeremias, the *'am haareṣ* or, as most scholars hold today, were more actively outside the scope of the biblical commandments), most scholars concur that Jesus' actions would have struck his contemporaries as radical (R. Zera in b. Sanh. 37a is exceptional).

Whereas the preceding narrative introduces the notion that forgiveness is a primary focus of Jesus' mission (9:9), this narrative carries that point further and uses Jesus' healing ministry as an acted parable of his most important mission: repairing lives broken by sin (9:12). (Matthew also retains Mark's use of "save" for rescue and healing in the Greek text of 8:25 and 9:22; the term's familiar theological nuances from 1:21 reinforce the notion of parabolic action here.) Matthew's more biblically literate readers would already have caught the connection in Matthew's dependence on Isaiah 53 in 8:17.

Surrounding narratives also demonstrate that it is the broken, such as paralytics, blind people, lepers, and those in mourning, who recognize their need for God's help (cf. 11:5). Matthew here seems to imply that the morally and socially reprobate also often humble themselves more readily than religious people.

First, Jesus was not ashamed to call to be a disciple a probable collaborator with Palestinian Jewry's common enemy (9:9). Jesus' call to follow was a

72. Matthew and Luke both change Mark's word for "bed," perhaps independently due to its colloquial overtones (Thiselton 1977: 93). (Without questioning Markan priority, the other options are that Mark modified a source like Q or, not at all likely, that Matthew and Luke here used an earlier version of Mark.) The Markan term can denote "a 'poor man's bed'" (Horsley 1982: 15).

73. Mack 1988: 80 is exceptional, thinking the meal stories derive from an etiological legend based on the Christ cult ritual outside the Q community. His supposition that a later hellenistic meal is read into the narratives fails to explain (1) why hellenistic storytellers would have done so much research to construct Palestinian Jewish details for the Last Supper (see comment on 26:17-30); (2) why the narratives, which make sense in their own milieu given the frequency of discussions during meals, focus on conflicts but provide little more detail on the meal settings themselves except that people ate there; (3) why one should appeal to meals as a common gathering in hellenistic culture (Mack 1988: 81) but not in Jewish Palestine; and (4), given the commonness of banquets, why even a Greek meal connoted a cultic focus. A better case could be made for Luke's hellenistic construction of his symposium section (Lk 14:1-24), to which Luke connects eating with sinners (Lk 15:1), but even this is not cultic per se.

call to be his disciple, that is, a future teacher in training (4:19; 8:22; 10:38; 16:24; 19:21). But whereas Jesus warned a scribe who was a would-be follower about the cost (8:19-20), he openly invited a despised tax gatherer to join his circle (cf. 18:17)! *The common people and nonaristocratic pietists despised tax gatherers as agents of the Romans and their aristocratic pawns* (Sanders 1985: 178; cf. Capito in Philo *Leg. Gai.* 199-202), perhaps — though usually to a lesser extent — like the hatred the Dutch or French felt toward local collaborators with the Nazis or Africans felt toward the *slatees,* African assistants to European slave traders.[74]

Rabbinic texts contrast tax gatherers and Pharisees, the least and most pious people one might expect to meet in daily life (e.g., t. Dem. 2:17; 3:4; b. Bek. 31a, bar.). Later rabbinic tradition continues the common people's disdain for the profession (b. Sanh. 25b; p. Ḥag. 2:2, §5; Abrahams 1917: 54; Jeremias 1971: 110; idem 1969: 311); they were as unclean as lepers, communicating impurity to a house by entering it (p. Ḥag. 3:6, §1; cf. b. Ḥag. 26a).[75] Perhaps not surprisingly, those directly involved with taxation were not popular elsewhere in the Empire either (Cic. *De Offic.* 1.42.150; Diogenes *Ep.* 36 to Timomachus; Epict. *Disc.* 3.15.12).[76]

The average Jewish person in ancient Palestine had several reasons to dislike tax gatherers. First, Palestine's local Jewish aristocracies undoubtedly arranged for this tax collection (Sanders 1990: 46-47; see Jos. *War* 2.405; cf. Herrenbrück 1981; Hoehner 1972: 77-78).[77] *Second,* that the Empire sometimes had to take precautions against tax gatherers' overcharging people (Lk 3:12-13; Carmon 1973: 105, 226) suggests that some tax gatherers did just that (Hoehner 1972: 78; cf. Philo *Leg. Gai.* 199). Abuses by tax farmers before and during this period in rural Egypt reportedly included torturing and killing for the sake of locating tax fugitives (Philo *Spec. Leg.* 3.30; Lewis 1983: 161) or beating an old woman because her relatives were behind on taxes (*B.G.U.* 515, A.D. 193). Extant documents indicate that to avoid such problems people sometimes paid tax gatherers bribes, in one case as high as 2,200 drachmas "for extortion" (Lewis 1983: 161-63; a drachma was close to an average worker's daily wage).[78]

74. Thus, e.g., ancients might slay fellow citizens who had allied themselves with enemy conquerors (Diod. Sic. 19.66.6).

75. Malina and Rohrbaugh 1992: 83 point out that though tax gatherers render a Pharisee's house unclean (m. Ṭohar. 7:6), so would *any* nonobservant person who handled things in the person's home (in this case, to assess wealth).

76. MacMullen 1974: 16; Best 1965: 139. Overman 1996: 126 includes some of our references plus Dio Chrys. *Or.* 14.14 and, among Jewish sources, m. Ned. 3:4; Ṭohar. 7:6.

77. KJV's "publicans" is a mistranslation, since the Romans rarely still collected taxes in the provinces through *publicanoi,* well-to-do Roman businessmen (Ramsay 1904b: 394; Stambaugh and Balch 1986: 77-78; Badian 1972: 11; White 1971: 230). In some areas of Palestine much of the grain (or perhaps the land on which it was grown) belonged to Caesar (Jos. *Life* 71, Upper Galilee); some tax gatherers belonged to members of the aristocracy like Bernice (*Life* 118-19).

78. Interestingly, the problem continued into the Byzantine period, when Copts fled exorbitant taxes by joining monasteries; see Bianquis 1988: 164. For further examples of abuse and corruption, see Llewelyn 1998: 68-74, §4.

Further, nearly all scholars concur that taxes were exorbitant even without overcharging; many contend that those who paid both taxes and tithes were paying between 30 and 40 percent (Stern 1974/76: 332; Neusner 1984: 22; F. F. Bruce 1972: 40; Hoehner 1972: 75-77; Wilkinson 1978: 25; Borg 1984: 31-32; idem 1987: 84-85). In some parts of the Empire taxation was so oppressive that laborers fled their land, at times depopulating entire villages (*P. Graux* 2; *P. Théad.* 17; Lewis 1983: 164-64, citing *P. Oxy.* 2669; *P. Ryl.* 595; *SB* 7462, and most significantly *PSI* 101, 102; Llewelyn 1998: 97-105, §6). Most would not have time, but traditional tax farmers could legally search almost anything but the person of a Roman matron, and seize undeclared property (Quint. *Declamations* 359; Lewis 1983: 142).

Matthew's office would have made him locally prominent, possibly as a customs official. Matthew probably either taxed local fishermen or acted as a customs agent charging levies on merchandise that was leaving Philip's tetrarchy and entering that of Herod Antipas (Gundry 1982: 166). Because Capernaum was ideally located for significant customs revenue, many commentators today lean toward the view that Matthew here is a customs officer.[79] Not only ports but boundaries of cities and tetrarchies charged customs duties, raising the price of imported goods (Applebaum 1974/76a: 686; Lewis 1983: 140; *IGRR* 1.1183). Tolls and customs tariffs were usually less than 3 percent for a given city, and the money collected went not to Rome itself but to municipal treasuries overseen by the municipal aristocracies with whom Rome was allied (Stambaugh and Balch 1986: 74; cf. Lewis 1983: 141). Customs officers demanded written declarations of travelers' possessions, searched baggage (Casson 1974: 290-91), and may have collected some other government revenues as well (Stern 1974/76b: 333). Jewish texts condemn customs officers as well as other tax gatherers (cf. Edersheim: 236), though some appear to have become benefactors to local populations (Jos. *War* 2.287-88), and they probably were not considered collaborators with the Romans to the extent other tax collectors were.[80]

Eating with sinners connoted approval of them; by contrast, a pious person normally preferred to eat with scholars (cf. Jeremias 1966a: 236).[81]

79. E.g., Stern 1974/76: 333; Manson 1979: 253-54; Lane 1974a: 101-2; Anderson 1976: 104; Witherington 1990: 78; contrast Ramsay 1904: 394, who reasonably doubts that customs officers would incur such hatred. For customs toll receipts, cf., e.g., *P. Grenf.* 2.50 c; *P. Ryl.* 197 a; *Select Papyri* 2:28-29. Hanson and Oakman 1998: 106 suggest that *telōnai* means "brokers," who bought fishing rights from local rulers and contracted with fishers.

80. Building on Jos. *War* 2.285-88, Sanders 1993: 228-29 rightly notes that people would not have viewed customs officers as negatively as other tax collectors, but in view of the Gospels' portrayal of pietists' reactions (9:11; 21:31-32), he may infer too much from this single passage (indeed, John had much to lose, and is mentioned in *addition* to the leading men). Galilean townspeople undoubtedly preferred their municipal aristocracies to Rome and resented direct taxation of their resources far more than commercial tolls that profited Galilee, but those inclined to accept no ruler but God may have classed them together; the Gospels' terminology certainly does not differentiate them.

81. Inviting scholars for dinner was good — one would be blessed on their account (ARN 11, §27B; p. Ter. 8:7; Urbach 1979: 1:434; Jeremias 1972: 126). Some think that Matthew changed

Excursus: Who Were the "Sinners"?

Some take "sinners" here to mean the *ʿam haareṣ,* common people whom the Pharisees despised for their lack of adherence to Pharisaic food laws (e.g., Jeremias 1972: 132; Lane 1974a: 103). Others respond that the Pharisees did not despise the common people, at least not as sinners (Sanders 1985: 176-99; Witherington 1990: 73). Later rabbis did look askance at them (m. ʾAbot 3:11; b. Pesaḥ. 49b) and apparently felt that they communicated uncleanness to scrupulous Pharisees (m. Demai 2:2; Maʿaś. Sh. 3:3; Ḥag. 2:7; Ṭohar. 4:5, 8:3, 5; t. Ahilot 5:11; p. Ḥag. 2:6, §13; Lev. Rab. 18:1). Conversely, the rabbis tolerated them (m. Giṭ. 5:9; Urbach 1979: 1:632-34) and viewed them negatively primarily in relation to the law as the rabbis had come to understand it (Urbach 1979: 1:633). Some scholars believe that the Pharisees considered them "sinners" (Jeremias 1971: 118; idem 1972: 132), and they certainly did fail to tithe according to the standards of the Pharisaic fence around the law.[82]

The nonpejorative biblical sense of *ʿamme haareṣ* (cf. de Vaux 1961: 70-71; Nicholson 1965) had changed considerably by this period, at least among the voices reported in rabbinic sources. So great was the division between *haberim,* who observed (probably Pharisaic) scruples about purity and tithing, and the nonobservant *ʿamme haareṣ,* that the distinction overrode class distinctions (m. Hor. 3:8; Goodman 1983: 77). Later rabbis felt that a scrupulous person should not eat with a priest of the *ʿamme haareṣ* lest he provide unconsecrated food (ARN 32, §72B). The primary problems with *ʿamme haareṣ* involved their lack of scrupulousness in purity concerning food, tithes, and other matters (t. ʿAbod. Zar. 3:8, 10; Dem. 2:14-15; Maʿaś. 2:5; ARN 41A; b. ʿAbod. Zar. 69a; Ber. 47b, bar.; Pesaḥ. 42b). An *ʿam haareṣ* could become scrupulous, but would be accepted by Pharisaic standards only if he embraced all the standards of the Pharisees (t. Dem. 2:5; this must mean in principle, since Pharisees themselves debated details — see comment on 23:23). Some texts report that some later rabbis wished to limit business and banquet dealings with *ʿamme haareṣ* (m. Dem. 2:2; 4:5; Maʿaś. 5:3; Maʿaś. Sh. 3:3; b. Ned. 20a).

Hillel reportedly doubted their piety (m. ʾAbot 2:5). Perhaps because all were expected to study Torah (Sifre Deut. 48.4.1), at least some later rabbis felt they were ignorant of Scripture (b. Ber. 61a), probably the same way many members of the educated religious elite today feel about the religious masses (but it is possible that the

Mark's "Levi" (Mk 2:14) to "Matthew," one of the Twelve (Mk 3:18; Mt 10:3), because his Gospel was associated with that person (Meier 1980: 93-94) or for a wordplay with the Greek words for "disciple" and "learn" (9:10-11, 13; Kiley 1984). But many people in antiquity had double names (see Acts 1:23; *CIJ* 1:24, §30; 2:111, §879; *CPJ* 2:143, §261; 2:151, §298; 3:9, §453; cf. Leon 1960: 107, 111-13), including double Semitic names (France 1985: 166), and the tradition may have preserved its author's other name (especially if this Gospel is associated in any way with Matthew, as later tradition suggests); see especially Gundry 1982: 166.

82. Exorbitant tithes were probably favored by the priestly aristocracy and others besides Pharisees; cf., e.g., Jos. *Ant.* 4.240. Taxes rendered tithes more difficult (Pesiq. Rab Kah. Sup. 4:2), and teachers became particularly adamant against eating untithed food even inadvertently (e.g., Gen. Rab. 60:8; Lam. Rab. 1:3, §28).

'amme haareṣ also include wealthy but less scrupulous landholders — Smith 1963: 172). Some said that sitting among them would deprive one from the coming world (m. 'Abot 3:10/11; cf. ARN 36A; b. Ber. 43b). Nevertheless, the later isolated claim that it was permissible to "stab" an *'am haareṣ* even on a doubly holy day (b. Pesaḥ. 49b, with other harsh reports) is, of course, hyperbole; *'amme haareṣ* may not be scrupulous in purity by what became rabbinic standards, but one should still treat them properly (p. Ter. 6:1).

The view of total separation between the Pharisees and other members of Palestinian Jewish society, however, is a modern construct, suited more for the wilderness Essenes than for the Pharisees or the *haberim.* Pharisees must have done business with *'amme haareṣ,* or they would not have had to rule concerning what to do with *demai,* untithed produce (Sanders 1990: 238). Members of the *'amme haareṣ* could work for or be apprenticed to a scrupulous person and be trusted under his supervision (t. Dem. 2:19); the wife of a *haber* may share appliances and work in company with the wife of an *'am haareṣ* for the sake of communal peace (m. Giṭ. 5:9). A father could also have some children who were *'amme haareṣ* and bequeath some things to them (t. Dem. 6:8, giving no indication of disowning them; though in marriage, cf. p. Ketub. 7:6, §1). *Haberim* would want to supervise purity at any banquet sponsored by an *'am haareṣ* (t. Dem. 3:6); scrupulous people might attend the banquets of the nonscrupulous, but would need to take proper precautions against their own impurity (t. Dem. 3:7). Even in later times, an *'am haareṣ* could listen to and learn from rabbis (Gen. Rab. 78:12); an *'am haareṣ* and a Samaritan were more trustworthy than a Gentile (b. Bek. 11b). One must not hate them, though one should hate apostates and sectarians (ARN 16A); some texts explicitly distinguish an *'am haareṣ* from the wicked (ARN 40A). The *'amme haareṣ* were probably often religious by their own standards and surely identified with their national heritage (even their detractors do not report any mass apostasy to paganism), whatever the *haberim* may have thought of them. Many of them apparently also tithed, at least by their own standards (cf. b. Beṣa 35b; a minority opinion in Ned. 84b).

If the *'am haareṣ* comprised the vast majority of Palestinian Jewry in the first century (Simon 1967: 15; cf. m. Qidd. 4:14), the Pharisees could hardly have viewed them as excluded from the covenant (m. Sanh. 10:1). While the Pharisees probably looked down on those uneducated in the law no less than much of the modern intellgentsia tends to be impatient with the "masses" (cf. m. 'Abot 2:6, 3:11; ARN 36A; b. Ber. 61a; Pesaḥ. 49b, including bar.), however, there is no reason to assume that "sinners" bears such a narrow meaning here; the term more likely specifies blatant violators of the law (Tob 4:17, MSS; Ps. Sol. 2:34; 13:1; 14:6-7; Sib. Or. 3.304). (Though it can include any human who sins, as in, for example, Test. Abr. 9A; 4 Ezra 7:138-40, Pharisaic opposition in this context demands a stronger sense of the term here.). Further, Mark leaves the general title "sinners" for his partly or largely Gentile Roman readers who would not naturally grasp this sense of "sinner" (2:17; see Best 1965: 139), rather than availing himself of an opportunity to portray the Pharisees explicitly as class-conscious snobs (a portrayal that might have put off Mark's readers and thus suited Mark's purpose well). In any case, Pharisees were concerned about with whom they ate, and if they were careful merely about meals with *ʿam haareṣ,* one can be certain that they would suspect a teacher who ate with blatant "sinners."[83]

Second, Matthew indicates that the collaborator was ready to follow Jesus (9:9) and other sinners were ready to listen to him (9:10). Jesus, for his part, was ready to eat with people with whom many pious Jews would not associate; widespread attestation and the criterion of dissimilarity strongly favor that Jesus did eat with those the Pharisees and other pietists considered sinners (Sanders 1985: 174-75).[84] Indeed, the term "recline" indicates that this was no ordinary meal (Palestinian Jews normally sat on chairs) but a banquet (when people reclined), probably in the teacher's honor (cf. Jeremias 1966a: 20-21). There are many people with whom most Christians today would not eat (for reasons of either spiritual or social incompatibility); the Pharisees went even farther in having special rules governing with whom they would eat (e.g., ARN 31, §68; 32, §72B). By emphasizing again the inclusion of outsiders, Matthew may support the Gentile mission while undermining the status of his community's prestigious opponents.

Third, religious people complained when Jesus brought into the kingdom people whose faith they did not trust (9:11). Jesus was eating with sinners, which to his contemporaries signified acceptance of them (Borg 1987: 101); the Pharisees, for whom pure table fellowship was a primary defining characteristic (Goodman 1983: 77),[85] would have been most disturbed by one claiming greater powers than they who nevertheless ignored their traditions. This thoroughly violated his contemporaries' understanding of holiness (Syr. Men. Sent. 148-53, 333-35; cf. Sir 12:4, 7; Borg 1984: 78-95). Jewish literature indicates that, for all of early Judaism's heavy emphasis on repentance and divine mercy (e.g., ARN 39A; b. Ber. 34b; Pesaḥ. 54; Sanh. 99a; 103a; Pesiq. Rab Kah. 25:3;

83. Although evidence clearly indicates that the Pharisees were careful with whom they ate (e.g., some references above), the idea that they ate food in priestly purity is a different matter; Sanders 1990: 166-84 makes a good case that the latter thesis overstates the case.

84. Sanders 1985: 205 suggests that this may represent "the priority of grace to repentance," but insists that Pharisaic distaste for the practice would not be strong enough to seek his death. None of Jesus' deeds or teachings should have provoked his death according to Pharisaic ethics, but we may suspect that many Pharisees, like many unregenerate Christians, do not always live the values they profess (12:14). While the conflict stories in their current form may represent later developments (Sanders 1985: 265) and Markan arrangement (Hooker 1983: 22; Dewey 1973: 400; idem 1980: 115-16), Christian origins are not comprehensible without some such conflicts (cf. Gal 1:13-14; 1 Thess 2:14-15; Montefiore 1968: 1:42); in these narratives Jesus clashed with the Pharisees over issues that were defining features of Pharisaism (Stambaugh and Balch 1986: 100-101); and first-century Palestinian Jewish groups frequently clashed seriously (albeit generally not violently).

85. I do not argue here that they intended to follow a *priestly* level of purity, as some have argued; see Sanders 1990: 131-254.

Deut Rab. 2:24; in Joseph and Aseneth, see Dschulnigg 1989), Jesus' act of actively *pursuing* sinners as a human teacher was unheard of (Ladd 1974: 83).

The sages desired edifying talk (Sir 9:15; m. 'Abot 3:2; ARN 26, 29A; 32, §68B; 35, §81; p. Taʿan. 3:11, §4),[86] including at meals (Ps 154:14; p. Ḥag. 2:1, §9; 2:2, §5; Safrai 1974/76a: 968-69). Discussion was a common feature of banquets (e.g., Jos. *Life* 222), though most banquets emphasized music over lectures (Sir 35:3-4; cf. Hom. *Od.* 1.153-55, 325-26; 9.3-6; 17.270-71; Plut. *Table-Talk* 1.1.5, *Mor.* 614F-615A). Some sages recognized that one would either conform to the social intercourse at banquets or conform others to one's own practice (e.g., Epict. *Disc.* 3.16; 4.2; *Encheir.* 33.6).

The Bible had clearly stated that one should not fellowship with sinners (Ps 1:1; 119:63; Prov 13:20; 14:7; 28:7); the point in each instance was to warn against being influenced by sinners. Jewish tradition properly developed this warning against improper association with the wicked (Sir 6:7-12; 12:13-18; 13:1; Ep. Arist. 130; m. 'Abot 1:6-7; 2:9; Sifre Deut. 286.11.4; ARN 16, §36B; Ps-Phocyl. 134; 1 Cor 15:33).[87] Yet in Jesus' case the influence was going one way — from Jesus to the sinners (9:9, 13; Lk 15:1; cf. Ps 25:8); and as an early Cynic philosopher reportedly explained when charged with visiting unclean places, "the sun too visits cesspools without being defiled" (Diog. Laert. 6.2.63, LCL 2:64-65; contrast Mek. Pisha 1.40-41). Those who controlled society in David's day had forced him to keep such company as well (1 Sam 22:1-2).

Although later Jewish tradition remarks that it would be difficult for a publican to repent (because it would be hard to make restitution; see, e.g., t. B. Meṣ. 8:26), it allowed that God can forgive this sin like any other (Abrahams 1917: 58) and emphasized God's love toward the repentant (Pesiq. Rab Kah. 24:12; Young 1995: 145); Jewish tradition already warned not to reproach one who had turned from sin (Sir 8:5). But Pharisees, like modern churchgoers, were presumably not always what their official ethics called them to be. In the total context of Matthew's Gospel, the informed reader ultimately recognizes that the religious establishment themselves are "sinners" (26:45; though the term could refer to Gentiles, its immediate contextual referent is probably the priestly aristocracy).

Finally, Jesus declared that his mission was to reach only those who acknowledged their sinfulness (9:12-13; cf. Jer 2:35). In an honor-and-shame based culture like the ancient Mediterranean, a public complaint such as the one the Pharisees had issued constituted a challenge. Quick repartee in the face of such a challenge would not only silence the challenge but shame the challengers (e.g., Plut. *Agesilaus* 21.4-5; Diog. Laert. 6.2.33; for quick re-

86. The Essenes took the matter further (cf., e.g., CD 11.4; Jos. *War* 2.128, 132-33; Philo *Every Good Man Is Free* 76, 81-82).

87. For the warning in Greco-Roman tradition, see, e.g., *Gnomologium Vaticanum* 460 in Malherbe 1986: 110; Crates *Ep.* 12; Socratics *Ep.* 24; Diod. Sic. 12.12.3; 12.14.1; Diog. Laert. 1.60; Babrius 9-12; in terms of skill rather than ethics, cf. Isoc. *Demon.* 20, *Or.* 1; Plut. *Educ.* 6, *Mor* 4A.

sponse, cf. also Ep. Arist. 295-96); despite the potential to alienate further the object of one's satire, radical Greek teachers, including Cynics, used humor, shock, and incongruity to hold attention (see Branham 1993); so did the biblical prophets. *Jesus shames his opponents with some traditional and biblical wisdom.* Jewish teachers often exhorted hearers to "Go and find," that is, search the Scripture for examples (Sifre Num. 76.2.1), or "Go and learn," that is, understand the point of a given text (Sifre Num. 115.5.6; cf. Sib. Or. 3.562-63; Stendahl 1968: 129; cf. Epict. *Disc.* 1.20.14). But when Jesus introduces his quote from Hosea with "Go and learn" in the context of a response to a challenge, he is insultingly suggesting his interlocutors' ignorance of the point of Scripture; he implies that perhaps they have never even *read* Hosea (cf. 12:5; Ex. Rab. 21:6). Hosea addressed a people satisfied with their ritual but displeasing to God (cf. Hos. 6:3-6; 8:2-3).

Jesus' response would have been clear enough. Jesus' many acts of healing made him a "physician," but sometimes he applied the language of healing figuratively (13:15). Others in the ancient Mediterranean also used health as a metaphor for spiritual or moral wholeness and disease as a metaphor for vice or folly (Plato *Rep.* 4.444E; Diog. Laert. 10.138; Epict. *Disc.* 4.8.29; Diog. *Ep.* 29); philosophers and teachers saw themselves as physicians of the soul (Anacharsis to Croesus 9; Crates *Ep.* 17; Diog. *Ep.* 49; Lucian *Demonax* 7; Diog. Laert. 2.70; 6.1.4; 6.2.30; Livy 42.40.3; Diod. Sic. 12.13.4; Cic. *Tusc. Disp.* 3.3.5; 3.10.22; 4.13.28; Epict. *Disc.* 2.14.21; Philo *Prob.* 12; Malherbe 1970: 207n.6; Tiede 1972: 47); statesmen might also view themselves as curers of their society's sickness (Dion. Hal. 9.53.3). Some Jewish teachers apparently viewed their work in similar terms (ARN 23A; p. Ketub. 7:7, §3; Qidd. 4:12, §2), although they could also apply the image in other ways (Johnston 1977b: 593). Thus it was not unusual for the image to become proverbial (Lane 1974a: 104n.43; Witherington 1990: 77).[88] Mere decades after Matthew's writing, Dio Chrysostom indicated that as the "good physician" goes where he is most needed, so does the sage go where fools are most abundant (*8th Disc., On Virtue* 5). Writing after the spread of Christianity, Diogenes Laertius reports a much earlier philosopher who, "when he was censured for keeping company with evil men," responded, "physicians are in attendance on their patients without getting the fever themselves" (Diog. Laert. 6.1.6, LCL 6-9).

Jesus came to "call" sinners — that is, to "invite" them to God's final banquet (22:3, 14), a foretaste of which the present table fellowship with them may have represented (cf. Lk 14:13-14, 23; as is often held; see, e.g., Becker 1978). Jesus' demand for mercy (translating directly the Hebrew of Hos 6:6; cf. Burkitt

88. Rhetoricians could also compare themselves with physicians (among other analogies; Quint. 2.17.25), especially if they were moralists (Isoc. *Peace* 39, *Or.* 8.167); the image applied also to a general (Appian *R.H.* 6.14.87) or anyone who provided aid (Eurip. *Electra* 70). Jewish people could use a physician as a metaphor for God as well (p. Ta'an. 3:6, §1). In biblical tradition, see the spiritual use of "physician" and "sickness" in, e.g., Jer 8:22; 46:11; 51:8; see further references under Mt 8:17. Literal physicians appear negatively, however, in m. Qidd. 4:14; b. Pesaḥ. 113a.

1910: 23) is so critical that it recurs in 12:7 (cf. 23:23).[89] This was not a repudiation of physical sacrifice, for Jesus elsewhere assumes that practice, and his earliest followers continued it (5:23-24; Acts 21:26; Sanders 1985: 67; pace Meier 1980: 94). Many of Jesus' contemporaries who offered sacrifice also emphasized the priority of mercy over physical sacrifice (e.g., Sir 35:1-7; Pr Azar 16–17; cf. Davies 1966b: 88; Hill 1977: 119; Sanders 1990: 42-43); later rabbis emphasized the virtue of mercy as well (e.g., p. Ketub. 11:3, §2). Borg argues that Jesus' mercy paradigm replaces the holiness paradigm of the Pharisees (1984: 123-43; cf. Patte 1987: 129; Snodgrass 1996: 125); yet the Pharisees would have agreed with the principle of mercy in theory, and particularly the school of Hillel emphasized it in legal interpretation. That Jesus' opponents agreed with his principle in theory yet invited his reprimand (cf. 23:3-4) suggests that Matthew wished not merely to condemn opponents but to warn his community against being like them. If Matthew writes to a community in or near Antioch, we should recall that the Jerusalem hard-liners had clashed with progressives there several decades before; probably following Jesus' precedent, Paul had insisted on continuing table fellowship with Gentile "sinners" (Gal 2:11-16; Stanton 1995a: 149).

A Time for Everything (9:14-17)

Cf. Mk 2:18-22; Lk 5:33-39. Some members of the socioreligious elite were disturbed that Jesus would eat with sinners (9:11); other religiously committed persons were disturbed that he *ate* (9:14) — or more particularly, that they did not observe his disciples fasting. For some, holiness meant avoiding eating with ungodly people; for others, holiness meant religious practices of self-discipline like fasting. For both, Jesus undoubtedly appeared self-indulgent (11:19). Thus Jesus responds with three illustrations about appropriateness: it is rude for the wedding party to fast during a wedding banquet when they must share the groom's joy; likewise, though new cloth and wine are good, they are inappropriate for vessels they will not fit. The celebration of sinners returning to God through Jesus' ministry is an inappropriate time for fasting.[90]

First, Jesus stands up for his disciples (9:14-15). Ancient literature regularly assumes that teachers had to answer for the behavior of their disciples (e.g.,

89. Goulder 1974: 37 also notes rabbinic use of repetition for reinforcement. "Doublets" more likely represent an authorial strategy than layers of sources, as Genesis scholarship has also concluded (Satterthwaite 1993: 363). Cope 1976: 127 thinks that Matthew here uses Scripture to justify the apparent unorthodoxy in Torah of Jesus in his tradition. Matthew frequently emphasizes "mercy" (9:27; 12:7; 15:22; 17:15; 20:30; 23:23), just as historians and biographers regularly praised the clemency of rulers toward vanquished foes (e.g., 1 Macc 2:57; Dion. Hal. 3.54.2; Arrian *Alex.* 1.17.12; 4.19.6; Appian *R.H.* 10.4.24; Corn. Nep. 8 [Thrasybulus], 2.6; Herodian 1.2.4; cf. also Jos. *Life* 353; Sifre Deut. 323.4.1; despite Achilles' usual demeanor, Hom. *Il.* 24.507-8, 665-70).

90. Whereas Mark has Pharisees and John's disciples together approach Jesus, Matthew allows only John's disciples to approach Jesus, though mentioning Pharisaic practice; the Pharisees may be too remote from the Matthean community for the community to picture dialogue with them.

Socrates for Alcibiades; Daube 1972: 3-4). Jesus also had to defend his disciples on other occasions (12:2-3). Early Christians probably took courage from this model of Jesus' advocacy when they faced persecution (cf., e.g., 10:18-20; Jn 9:34-41; 16:7-11; Acts 7:55-56).

Second, while fasting is good, there are appropriate times for everything (9:15-17). Rather than appealing to his own fast (4:1-11), Jesus avoids risking human honor for what he did before God in secret (6:16-18), and makes his point instead by three illustrations. Jesus had also taught his disciples to fast privately (6:16-18), behavior that may have led to the assumption that they did not fast at all (cf. Pilch 1992: 130).[91] Jesus responds not by citing his fast, but by noting that some times were inappropriate for fasting, which frequently connoted mourning.

It was inappropriate for groomsmen to fast until after the wedding banquet had ended. Weddings generally lasted seven days, and participants — the NRSV's "wedding guests" and the NIV's "guests of the bridegroom" means either the groomsmen (cf. Jn 3:29) or the guests (Edersheim: 306; Nineham 1977: 103) — were expected to participate joyfully. Everyone was expected to be joyful and to bring joy to the couple being married (p. Ketub. 1:1, §6; Safrai 1974/76b: 759); indeed, weddings took precedence over many religious obligations (m. Ber. 2:5, 8; t. Ber. 2:10; b. Sukk. 25b; p. Sukk. 2:5, §1), and sages were said frequently to interrupt their schools to hail passing bridal processions (ARN 4A). Weddings were a matter of joy with which any signs of sorrow seemed conspicuously incongruent (1 Macc 1:27, 39; 9:39-41; 3 Macc 4:6; Test Abr. 10A; Jos. *War.* 6.301; b. Ber. 6b, 30b-31a; Lev. Rab. 20:3; Qoh. Rab. 2:2, §4; Appian *R.H.* 3.4.7). The Gospels' readers would probably catch an allusion that Jesus' first hearers missed:[92] Jesus is the groom of God's people in the coming messianic banquet foreshadowed in their table fellowship (22:2; 25:10-13).[93] The "taking" of the bridegroom, of course, is a veiled reference to the impending crucifixion.[94]

New cloth had not yet shrunk, and when it began to shrink after being patched onto a garment that had finished its shrinking, the patch would tear loose

91. Lachs 1987: 169 reports without comment Zeitlin's view that Jesus could make national fast days no longer mandatory, since Zechariah promised that they would be turned to joy (Zech 7:3; 8:19). Even if this suggestion concerning corporate fasts proves relevant, however, one cannot doubt that the early Christians continued to fast at times (Acts 13:2); the issue remained appropriateness (cf. 1 Sam 14:28-30).

92. Because Mark does not avail himself of the opportunity to make the connection explicit, Witherington suggests that he authentically preserves a saying of Jesus (1990: 72). In Jewish texts, the "bridegroom" was most often God himself (Hos 2:16-23; Payne 1981: 11-12; Blomberg 1992a: 158).

93. Cf. Wrede 1971: 21-22; Anderson 1976: 107-8; Meier 1980: 95; Kingsbury 1983: 15-16; Wimmer 1982: 101; Ziesler 1973a; Batey 1971: 67; France 1985: 169.

94. Although most scholars concur that Jesus' disciples were charged with not fasting (Safrai 1974/76c: 816; Via 1975: 102) and that the core saying is authentic (Burkill 1972: 39-47), many speculate that the evangelists added features like the disciples' later fasting (e.g., Via 1975: 102) and perhaps the conjunction of Pharisees with John's disciples (Burkill 1972: 47). These features are, however, possible in Jesus' life-setting, rendering such suspicions somewhat speculative.

from the garment, "making the tear worse" (9:16; Hurtado 1983: 31; cf. Steinhauser 1976). In the same way, *old wineskins* had been stretched to the limit as wine had fermented and expanded in them. Because old wineskins had already been stretched to the limit, if they were filled with new wine it would ultimately burst them when it expanded (Hurtado 1983: 31-32).[95] (People regularly used animal skins, especially goatskins, for liquid containers, normally sewing two or three skins together — Lewis 1983: 132. Bedouins in the Negev still use goatskins for fluid containers today; see Glueck 1960: 232 and fig. 4.)

Luke adds the commonplace that people prefer old, that is, aged wine (Lk 5:39; cf. Sir 9:10; m. 'Abot 4:20; ARN 35, §§89-90B; but both old and new were better than medium wine — Aul. Gel. 13.31.14-17), perhaps to explain why traditionalists could not consider Jesus' new ways. Matthew, however, adapts the tradition in a different direction; whereas in Mark failure spells the loss of both the new wine and the old wineskin (Mk 2:22), Matthew develops the corollary: success spells the preservation of both (9:17; Hagner 1993: 244). Matthew's community hears in the newness an appreciation for the climactic salvation-historical event in Christ, not a denigration of the old (cf. 13:52; 26:29).[96] Matthew will not allow Jesus' words to be appropriated in an antinomian direction, whether by Jesus' followers or by their opponents (5:17).

Extraordinary Miracles of Compassion (9:18-26)

Cf. Mk 5:21-43; Lk 8:40-56. When Jesus allows a ritually impure woman to touch him and touches the hand of a corpse, he appears to contract ritual impurity under the law (Lev 15:19-33; Num 19:11-12).[97] One might argue that Jesus contracted no uncleanness in actuality; as in the case of his contact with sinners, the influence moved from him to them rather than the reverse (9:11-13). Yet in the eyes of those present, Jesus assumes the status of uncleanness (see the fuller account in Mk 5:33, where Jesus even invites public attestation of the touch). He is

95. Most other interpretations of either parable are too obscure, e.g., that the Gospels allude to Qumran's new wine festival versus old wineskins as regular religious observances (Brooke 1984). The evidence for the allegorical interpretation in Jeremias 1972: 117-18 likewise will not bear its weight. The difficulty of reconstructing its sense in this context might support the thesis that the tradition in Mt 9:16-17//Mk 2:21-22 was originally independent of the narrative (Witherington 1990: 71).

96. Some comment that the term for "new" in wine means "recent in vintage," whereas the different terms for "new" in wineskins mean "fresh, new in quality, previously unused" (Richardson 1958: 244-45; Barclay 1978: 76); but the Gospel tradition may vary the terms for variety's sake (variation being a standard literary device — Cadbury 1980: 92). A survey of the abundant use of "new" with "wine" in the papyri (courtesy of Duke's computer concordance of papyri) also indicates that one term was nearly always used with wine and thus was simply part of the idiom (also Sir 9:10).

97. Menstruation also produced ceremonial impurity in other traditions, e.g., a stele of Isis and Sarapis regarding a sanctuary (in Horsley 1987: 110). Cf. spirit-induced corpse-uncleanness in traditional Polynesia (Radcliffe-Brown 1965: 73, 75). Nevertheless, various Jewish groups, including the Sadducees, appear to have rejected Pharisaic strictness on the issue (see Ilan 1996: 100-105, 227).

willing to share suppliants' brokenness that they might be made whole (cf. the vicarious mission indicated in 8:17, an editorial aside).[98]

We should also note that many of the evangelists' positive stories surround women whose faith exceeded that of the male disciples.[99] In a world where women were generally second-class citizens and where women who were trotted forth as examples of heroism were viewed as exceptions (e.g., Plut. *Bravery of Women*), the greater balance in the Gospels is intriguing. Yet this balance fits what we know of women's status in antiquity, Jesus' teaching, and an emphasis in Matthew's Gospel: it was the socially powerless who most readily embraced him.

First, Matthew again emphasizes Jesus' willingness to heal and even to restore to life (9:18-19).[100] Mark tells us that the father did not yet know that his daughter had died; again Matthew abbreviates the account, omitting intermediaries (cf. Mt 8:5//Lk 7:3; Marshall 1977: 131), but this does not materially affect the main point of the text.[101]

Second, he presents the woman with the flow of blood positively as an example of scandalous faith (9:20-21). Because Matthew's language probably alludes to the Scriptures, he probably assumes that his audience will immediately think of the woman's impurity under levitical law.[102] Because of

98. Meier 1994: 777-88 argues from various criteria for the authenticity of this narrative in pre-Markan tradition. One might also suggest that early Jewish-Christian traditionaries, accustomed to linking biblical texts with keywords (what the rabbis called *gezerah shewah*), would originally have enmeshed the two stories homiletically here on the basis of their common "twelve years" (Mk 5:25, 42). The tradition preserved the duration of sickness, however, to emphasize the power of the healer (e.g., Jn 5:5; Acts 4:22; Test. Job 26:1; 27:6/9; 28:1; further references in Lake and Cadbury 1979: 45; Theissen 1983: 51-52), and, in the girl's case, possibly to emphasize pathos for her dying unmarried (tomb inscription in Lefkowitz and Fant 1982: 11, §21; Judg 11:37-39; Soph. *Antig.* 891; Eurip. *Hecuba* 416; *Children of Heracles* 579-80, 591-92; Hipponax, *Fr.* 68, in ibid.: 16, §31; Paus. 3.19.4; for young men, cf., e.g., Lk 7:12; Demosth. *Against Leochares* 18).

99. Cf. also Schierling 1980; Selvidge 1984; Borsch 1990; Kopas 1990; Schineller 1992; cf. Schottroff 1991 on Q.

100. Multiple attestation from Mark, Q (Mt 11:5//Lk 7:22), and John suggest that Jesus and his followers did believe that he raised the dead (Meier 1994: 773-873). Resuscitation stories also appear in Greco-Roman sources (e.g., Paus. 2.26.5; 2.27.4), sometimes in a hesitant or skeptical vein, and, without the skepticism, in the Elijah-Elisha cycles in the Hebrew Bible (Meier 1994: 773).

101. Nor does Matthew's omission of Mark's Aramaic (Mk 5:41) suggest that his community is Gentile (pace Meier 1980: 98, especially if one accepts Matthew's likely Syrian provenance); Matthew simply abbreviates as thoroughly as possible and may simplify his style (cf. [Virgil] *Catalepton* 7). (Both Jesus and the family may have spoken Aramaic as a first language — cf. Goodman 1983: 66; Mark's preservation of Aramaic does not represent magical words — Aune 1980: 1534-35; Riesenfeld 1970: 23; pace Smith 1978: 95; Theissen 1983: 61.) Omanson 1991 thus rightly critiques the 1973 NIV's original harmonization ("at the point of death").

102. Levine 1996: 384 doubts that Matthew indicates or implies *vaginal* bleeding, noting that Mark's language is closer to the LXX. While Matthew could have revised Mark to avoid the impression that Jesus violated ritual law (cf. 15:1-20), however, Matthew does not believe that even Jesus' direct touch violated that law (8:3). Mark's *pēgē tou haimatos* (5:29) in the LXX is clearly genital in every occurrence (Lev 12:7; 20:18), as is his *rysei haimatos* (Mk 5:25; Lev 15:19, 25; 20:18). But

her continual flow of blood (the medical term is menorrhagia — Tasker 1961: 102), she was not permitted to move about in crowds; anyone she touched or whose cloak she touched became unclean. Those who were most pious seem to have been most concerned to avoid unnecessarily exposing themselves to impurity (e.g., m. Nid.), even if it was impossible for married men to avoid that totally (Sanders 1992: 228-29).[103] Still abbreviating, Matthew omits Mark's crowds (Mk 5:27), but retains the woman's intention: she is so desperate that she will touch the teacher, knowing full well that under the law this will make him unclean (Lev 15:25-27). Indeed, at least in theory any strict Jewish man must learn whether a woman who touched his clothing or sat in a boat with him was unclean and therefore had rendered him unclean (m. Ṭohar. 5:8). (Despite his abbreviation elsewhere, Matthew clarifies her touch of Jesus' cloak; she touched his "fringe," which appears in the LXX of the Pentateuch only at Num 15:38-39; Deut 22:12, as a reminder to observant Israelites of God's commandments; see comment on 23:5.)[104] Seizing the edge of someone's robe was a gesture of fervent entreaty in biblical and Near Eastern tradition (Hutter 1984; 1 Sam 15:27).

Her condition is desperate both for medical reasons and because of its social consequences; her partial ostracism would extend especially to her private life.[105] Her ailment probably had kept her from marriage if it started at puberty, and almost surely would have led to her divorce if it began after she was married (which would have been within a few years after puberty), since intercourse was

---

though Matthew abbreviates the narrative considerably (omitting the phrase from Mk 5:29 and reducing the phrase in Mk 5:25 to one word), his *haimorroeō* (Matt 9:20) appears only once in the LXX (with no cognates), plainly vaginal (Lev 15:33). When the two Hebrew terms for "flow" appear with "blood" or are limited to women, they apply almost exclusively to genital flows. Pace Levine 1996: 383, the implied author need not state explicitly social conventions he shared with his audience, and Lev 15, like the rest of written Torah, would be among their most fundamental shared assumptions. Given their ingrained distaste for menstrual blood (illustrated, e.g., in the later text, Pesiq. Rab Kah. 17:6), disgust would probably be among their first reactions.

103. Cf. Jos. *Ant.* 3.261. Davies and Allison 1991: 128 list Jewish texts displaying restriction or abhorrence regarding women's menstruation (Ezek 36:17; CD 4.12–5.17; 11Q Temple 48.15-17; Jos. *War* 5.227; *Apion* 2.103-4; m. Zab. 4:1). Levine 1996: 386-88 contends that because uncleanness was so pervasive and inevitable, first-century Jews probably did not attend much to the matter; but even if we lacked other explicit documentation, the plain statements of Lev 15 (regardless of their earliest social context, which would be foreign to first-century interpreters) suggest that it can be assumed and that lack of attention to the matter, rather than more attention, is what would require explicit documentation.

104. The "edge of his cloak" she touches would have included a tassel in accordance with Jewish custom — 14:36; 23:5; Num 15:37-41; Deut 22:12; cf. Ep. Arist. 158; t. Ber. 6:10; Pesiq. R. 29/30A:3; Safrai 1974/76c: 797-98; M. Cohen 1992. Vermes 1993: 16n.6 perhaps relevantly compares the insistence of children seizing the fringe of Hanan's garment (perhaps because they could reach it); his other example, however, is *not* a "miraculous intervention," but a praise of tassels.

105. Levine 1996: 389-90 is right to challenge the view that menstruation required quarantine, and rightly notes lenient texts permitting participation in some activities of the synagogue. Nevertheless, the requirements for washing in Lev 15:19-27 surely suggest that those who were "clean" would seek to avoid *unnecessary* direct physical contact with the unclean.

prohibited under such circumstances (Lev 18:19) and childlessness normally led to divorce (Keener 1991a: 75). The stigma of childlessness (cf. Lk 1:24-25; 1 Enoch 98:5), the pain of feeling "left over" (although Palestine did not have a surplus of marriageable men as Greece did, neither did they have a shortage of men), the economic consequences of being unable to earn sufficient income, yet having neither husband nor children for long-term support, probably would have made her condition seem almost unbearable. Still, her desperation also begets a confidence that Jesus is an absolutely certain source of her healing. In desperation, she presses her way to Jesus with the determination of faith, regardless of the consequences.

Third, Jesus embraced her need (9:22). Both by calling her "daughter" (perhaps welcoming her as a dependent — 9:18; cf. 15:22) and by his following word of encouragement (*tharsei,* which the NRSV renders "Take heart"), he addresses her fear.[106] More critically, he acknowledges her act as an act of faith. By failing to offer a rebuke he demonstrated both that the healing came by God's power and not automatic magic (Hooker 1983: 61; cf. Lane 1974b: 160-61), and that he was unashamed to be identified with her uncleanness (more clearly in Mk 5:30-34), which her touch would have communicated in the eyes of the public. This fits Matthew's portrait of Jesus (cf. 8:17), who embraced humanity's ultimate humiliation and shame on the cross (3:15), perhaps refusing even a simple narcotic to deaden the pain (27:34).

Fourth, Jesus exercises authority over even death itself (9:23-26).[107] Children often died young (e.g., *CIJ* 1:308, §399; Plut. *Consolation to Wife, Mor.* 608C, 609D, 611D; Dixon 1988: 113); in poorer parts of the Empire perhaps half of the live births did not survive past their mid-teens (cf. Lewis 1983: 54; Malina and Rohrbaugh 1992: 84; in other traditional societies, cf. Mbiti 1970: 153). Mourning was of great importance (e.g., Gen. Rab. 100:4, 7; Virg. *Aen.* 11.148-50), and because bodies decomposed rapidly, mourners gathered quickly (e.g., b. Sanh. 47a). Women mourners (according to the rabbis; Jos. *War* 3.437 includes male keeners) were hired to display grief as ostentatiously as possible (e.g., Jos. *War* 2.6; *Ant.* 4.320; b. Meg. 3b; Sanh. 47a; Pesiq. Rab Kah. 15:4; Lam. Rab. Proem 2; Safrai 1974/76b: 778; cf. women's lamentation in Hom. *Il.* 18.30-31, 50-51; 19.284-85), and flutists normally accompanied them (11:17; Jos. *War* 3.437; m. Ketub. 4:4), as Matthew adds here (Hill 1972: 179, citing also b. Ketub. 7a). Later texts probably reflect the earlier view of many religious people in regarding at least two or three mourners (two flutists and one professional mourning woman) mandatory for the funerals of the poorest person, but a prominent local person like this "ruler" (9:18) would probably be able to afford more

106. Sages sometimes addressed disciples as "sons," and elders could view those who were younger in such terms (see comment on 23:9), but the broader cultural concepts of patronage and dependency may be close at hand even in these cases.

107. Levine 1996: 396 points to literary connections between this account and 14:1-12, where a different authority figure responds differently to a "girl," there producing death as this narrative leads to life.

(m. Ketub. 4:4; Gundry 1982: 175; France 1985: 171).[108] His wealth and status contrast him starkly with the ailing woman earlier in the story, but his grief has reduced him to the same position of dependence on Jesus.

If Jesus intended his assertion that the girl was merely asleep (9:24) to keep word about her resucitation from spreading, the tactic failed (9:26). "Sleep" was a common euphemism for death in antiquity (e.g., 1 Thess 4:13; Hom. *Il.* 14.231; Soph. *Oed. Col.* 1578; Plut. *Condolence to Apollonius* 12, *Mor.* 107D; Jub. 23:1; 36:18; Ps. Sol. 2:31; 4 Ezra 7:31-32; 2 Bar. 11:4; 21:25; 36:11; *CIJ* 1:8, 12, 17-19 and passim; b. Shab. 30b) as in many other cultures (Mbiti 1970: 204-5), but Jesus' contrast between sleep and death here suggests that he wished them to understand that she was not truly dead. Long-term professional mourners would recognize the difference, however (Harris 1986: 309),[109] so they seem not to have believed him (9:26).[110] That their grief quickly turns to the laughter of derision (9:24) *need* not underline their insincerity, but given the striking contrast between the two emotional states, it might suggest it (cf. ridicule of pretended grief in Mart. *Epig.* 1.33).

Corpse-uncleanness was the most serious uncleanness anyone could contract, rendering a person unclean for seven days (Num 19:11; see further Sanders 1990: 184-92); Jesus thus showed his exceptional kindness and commitment to help by taking the girl's hand when he raised her up.[111]

Astonishing Cures for Disabilities (9:27-34)

Cf. 12:22-24; 20:29-34; Mk 3:22; 10:46-52; Lk 11:14-15; 18:35-43. The tradition behind this narrative can make a good claim for authenticity.[112] Many educated

108. Such "rulers of the synagogue," a post frequent in the Diaspora (*CIJ* 1:xcvii-xcix; 1:187-88, §265; 1:297-98, §383; 1:369, §504; 1:409, §553; 1:428, §584; 1:433, §596; 1:457, §638; 1:492, §681; 1:522, §722; 2:10, §741; 2:12, §744; 2:27-28, §766; 2:55-56, §803-4; 2:175, §991; 2:332-35, §1404; 2:339, §1414; Leon 1960: 171-72), often became prominent because of their wealth and benefactions for the community (cf. Goodman 1983: 119, 123; Rajak and Noy 1993). This *rosh ha-knesset* was often the highest office in the synagogue (Applebaum 1974/76b: 492). Pace Bultmann 1968: 241, in Matthew the tradition omits rather than adds a name (in Mark, the fairly common "Jairus" — *CIJ* 2:312-13, §1367-68).

109. One doubts that certification of death was quite as emphatic as with the taxation bureaucracy in Egypt, however, where as many as four physicians would attest a person's death (Horsley 1982: 16). That she was truly dead differs from the story line of one stopping the premature burial of one not truly dead (Celsus *On Medicine* 2.6; cf. Pliny *N.H.* 7.37; 26.8; Apul. *Florida* 19; Boring 1995: 79).

110. Matthew stresses the spread of news about Jesus (9:26), probably drawing on Mk 1:28, 45, as Gundry notes (1982: 176); Goulder considers the borrowing of features from one narrative for another to be midrashic practice (e.g., 1974: 37). Matthew also omits here some details important to Mark's "secret" motif, such as taking only a select group with him and the charge to silence.

111. Levine 1996: 385 doubts that corpse-uncleanness is in view because Matthew does not mention it. While a purely formalist reading could settle for only textual clues, however, the implied author and audience share fundamental common assumptions of a shared milieu, particularly their knowledge of Torah, including Num 19 (cf., e.g., Jos. *Ant.* 3.262; *Apion* 2.205).

112. See Meier 1994: 686-90. One particularly cogent argument for pre-Markan tradition is

writers ridiculed gullibility about supernatural stories (cf. Petron. *Sat.* 62-63) and doubted the authenticity of some miracles (Plut. *Isis* 8, *Mor.* 353F), but those skeptical about most or all miracles (Lucian *Alex.;* Marc. Aur. 1.5; Diog. Laert. 8.1.41) were far fewer in antiquity than they are in modern Western society. Most ancients would have regarded substantial cures like opening blind eyes as of the highest evidential value (e.g., Jn 9:32; Epidauros inscr. 9); thus the crowds react with amazement (Mt 9:31, 33), and members of the religious elite redouble their efforts to prove that Jesus' genuine miracles are not of God (9:34).[113]

First, Jesus responds to faith (9:27-31). Their initial act of faith was approaching Jesus with a plea for mercy (5:7; 20:31; Mk 10:47; cf. Test. Zeb. 2:2; Test. Sol. 20:1; Gk. Ezra 1:8-10; Epict. LCL: xxvi; healing in Tob 8:17; 11:15), recognizing that they were dependent on his kindness rather than on any merit of their own (contrast much Greek prayer — comment on 6:7). Their initial faith also includes a recognition of Jesus' identity. By moving their acknowledgment of Jesus as "Son of David" forward to this point in the narrative (20:31; Mk 10:47), Matthew allows two blind beggars (the usual occupation of blind men) to confess Jesus' messianic identity before Peter does (16:16; cf. Jn 4:25-26). (Charlesworth 1997 thinks that the blind suppliant in Mk 10:47 means, not "Messiah" but one like Solomon, who was probably associated with exorcism of demons that could cause sickness, including blindness. These associations are reasonable but probably not what Matthew's audience would first assume — cf. 1:1.) But while Mark also reports how crucial faith was to their healing (Mk 10:52 = Mt 9:29), Matthew emphasizes it further (9:28; drawing from the Jesus tradition — cf., e.g., Mk 5:34; 9:23; 11:23). Despite their initial acts of faith, Jesus forces them to clarify that they not only seek his help and recognize his identity, but acknowledge his ability to heal this otherwise irreversible disability (9:28). Jesus refuses to heal without faith; he is not a magician, but one who seeks to glorify his Father (cf. 13:58).

This account in Matthew occurs at a different point in the story in Mark (10:46-52); Matthew preserves that story in the appropriate place as well (Mt 20:29-34; on the literary function of "doublets" see Satterthwaite 1993: 363), but repeats it here to list it among Jesus' ten signs.[114] This repetition, like Matthew's others, reinforces the point he wishes to make (cf. Anderson 1985). He probably

---

the fact that Mark must *explain* "Bar Timaeus" (Mk 10:46; Meier 1994: 688). Witherington 1990: 170 argues that multiple attestation supports Jesus' healings of the blind: Mark (8:22-26; 10:46-52); Matthew (15:30, but this summary could derive from his use of Markan accounts); John (ch. 9); and Q (Mt 11:5//Lk 7:22, alluding to Is 35 and 61).

113. See Hom. *Il.* 6.139; Davies and Allison 1991: 135 for examples in ancient literature of blindness as a punishment. Whereas pagan sources sometimes recount healers of blindness (e.g., Tac. *Hist.* 4.81 and Suet. *Vesp.* 7, of Vespasian; but also by deities, e.g., *SIG* 3.1168 in Asclepius' temple), Davies and Allison note (ibid.) that Jewish reports of analogous healings (Tob 2:10; 3:16-17; 11:10-14; Ep. Arist. 316; Ps-Philo 25:12; b. B. Meṣ. 85b) never include a personal intermediary. This may be coincidence, but it does suggest how dramatic the miracle appeared.

114. Matthew's doublets may follow the midrashic principle of borrowing features from one narrative and repeating them in a similar narrative (Goulder 1974: 36-38).

doubles the healings of the blind men for the same reason that he doubled the demoniacs delivered in 8:28 (cf. Mk 5:2); he had omitted one elsewhere (Mk 8:22-26) as part of his abbreviating technique and so compensates by simply adding one in this story (Harrington 1982: 43; Meier 1980: 99; cf. Goulder 1974: 44-45). Matthew elsewhere emphasizes spreading the word (4:24; 9:26, 31; 14:35; cf. 28:19), a motif rooted securely in the Jesus tradition (e.g., Mk 1:28, 37, 45; 3:8; 5:20); the messianic secret here (Mt 9:30) comes from Mark 8:26. (Matthew omits it in 20:34, following Mk 10:52; but here the secondary allusion to the healing of Mk 8 takes precedence.)

Second, Jesus has adequate authority to cure any ailment. This includes both natural ailments (9:27-30) and demonically induced ailments (9:32-33), which in the Gospels are not always distinguishable on the basis of symptoms alone. Jewish law went beyond that of many other societies in protecting weak members of society, such as deaf-mutes and minors (m. B. Qam. 8:4), but Jesus could actually strengthen the weak. Matthew probably relates these narratives in large measure to encourage his audience concerning the character and power of their Lord.

Third, ridicule was the only tactic left to Jesus' opponents (9:34). Not all responses to Jesus' ministry were favorable (9:33). Jewish wisdom recognized that a person without a more adequate answer might resort to simple ridicule or slander (Prov 29:9), and in Matthew's view Jesus' most religiously committed contemporaries were reduced to explaining his works as emanating from a source other than God (12:24; cf. Mk 3:22; Jn 7:20; 8:48, 52; 10:20). Matthew not only writes to encourage his community that Jesus can meet their needs, but to remind them that the opposition they were facing was not new; Jesus himself had to confront it. That Matthew reports this charge in the direct context of the disciples' carrying on Jesus' mission (9:35–11:1) and again (12:24) shortly after the Pharisees had criticized Jesus' disciples (12:1-2) suggests that he sees the charge as relevant to his own community. (Matthew brackets the entire section from 9:32 to 12:24 with the Pharisaic charge in response to Jesus' healing a mute demoniac.)

Even aside from Euhemerus and others who denied supernatural activity altogether, many ancient rationalists preferred nonsupernatural explanations when they were possible (e.g., Diod. Sic. 4.47.3-4). But the Pharisees were hardly modern antisupernaturalists; they believed miracles could happen. The consensus seems to have arisen, however, that though some might seek to adduce miracles in support of their claims (e.g., b. B. Meṣ. 59b; p. Sanh. 6:6, §2; Baumgarten 1983), scholarly tradition took precedence over miracles (t. Yebam. 14:6; cf. p. Sanh. 11:4, §1; Vermes 1973: 80-81); the Matthean community itself recognized that charlatans and false prophets could also perform signs and wonders (24:24). If they were like many of their modern counterparts, one can understand the religious people's sentiments in Jesus' day; after all, if God were still doing miracles like those he had done through Elijah and Elisha, surely he would have been doing it through *them.* Were they not the ones with correct doctrine? Matthew's community probably experiences analogous opposition from their contemporaries.

More Laborers for the Harvest (9:35-38)

Cf. Mk 6:6, 34; Lk 8:1; 10:2; Jn 4:35. Matthew adds a summary statement similar to 4:23-25 (which also precedes a kingdom discourse), making clear that the incidents he has reported are merely prominent examples of Jesus' many works and teachings. At this strategic point, however, Matthew also emphasizes that Jesus' mission is not his alone. On the historical level, Jesus' ministry to Galilean villages (9:35) undoubtedly paved the way for his disciples' subsequent Galilean mission by providing Galilee a positive foretaste of his ministry (cf., e.g., Acts 9:32-43). On the historical level, Jesus' ministry must also have prepared his disciples to carry on that ministry by example; such were the customary roles of teachers and disciples.

This section, which introduces Jesus' mission discourse in chapter 10, places in parallel Jesus and his disciples who must carry on his works.[115] As Jesus perpetuated John's message concerning the kingdom (3:2; 4:17, 23; 11:1; cf. chs. 5–7), his followers will do the same (10:7). As Jesus demonstrated the kingdom by compassionately healing (9:35; cf. chs. 8–9), his disciples must do the same (10:8). In short, this is the point in the Gospel at which Matthew clarifies the suggestion of 3:11 and 16 that much of Jesus' mission is likewise the church's mission. Matthew rearranges material from various sections of his sources in chapter 10 not merely to emphasize a past, historical mission with little current significance, but to provide a model for his audience (cf. S. Brown 1978).[116] If Matthew purposely adapts Mark's "in Christ's name" (Mk 9:41) to "in a *disciple's* name" (Mt 10:42), he underlines further the need for the mission to continue in his own day (cf. Overman 1990b: 120-21).

First, Matthew teaches that Jesus' motivation was compassion (9:36). Although some commentators press the literal sense of "had compassion" as "he was moved inwardly," "his bowels were moved," the metaphoric associations of the term had long since vanished and by the first century it simply represented compassion (Thiselton 1977: 81). "Compassion" reflected Jesus' character (14:14; 15:32; 18:27; 20:34; cf. Phil 2:1).[117]

When lacking God-appointed leaders God's people are often presented in the Hebrew Bible as "sheep without a shepherd" (Num 27:17; 1 Kings 22:17;

115. This principle is often noted; cf., e.g., Carson 1987: 119; Davies and Allison 1991: 411-12; Allison 1993b: 138-39; Stanton 1993: 81.

116. Grassi 1977 is probably correct that 9:35–11:1 reflects "succession" language, but the specifically testamentary background he suggests, and especially the suggestion of rooting it in Gen 49:1-33, is too narrow; better, though still too narrow, is the suggestion of Morosco 1984, which roots it in Moses' commission in Ex 3–4 (see, e.g., the critique of Allison 1993b: 217). Some Jewish teachers stressed that disciples must do some of the master's works during his lifetime lest they face undue hostility later (Sifre Deut. 305.1.1).

117. Malina 1993: 24-25 points out that showing emotion fits honor in the Mediterranean world, citing as examples Plut. *Caesar* 5.2; 11.3; 41.1; 48.2; *Cicero* 47.2; cf. also Test. Abr. 3; 5A; 3B. (These examples are more relevant than the philosophical model I previously cited in Keener 1993: 385.)

2 Chron 18:16; Ezek 34:5; cf. Mt 26:31; 4 Ezra 5:18), inviting the compassionate Lord to shepherd his people himself (Ezek 34:11-16) by feeding them (Ezek 34:2-3; Mt 14:19-20), healing them (Ezek 34:4; Mt 9:35; cf. "torn" in 9:36), and bringing the lost sheep back (34:4-6; Mt 18:12-14) — performing miracles for them as at the first exodus (Mic 7:14-15). Matthew's audience already knows that Jesus fulfills this mission (Mt 2:6; Mic 5:2; cf. Mt 25:32). This implies that the religious leaders of Israel who purported to be their shepherds had failed to obey God's commission (Ezek 34:2-10; Mt 23). The disciples (sheep themselves; cf. 7:15; 10:16) will carry on Jesus' mission to these sheep (10:6).[118]

Second, Matthew emphasizes the need for more workers to complete Jesus' mission (9:37). Jewish teachers understood that they each could handle only so many students by themselves, even if the students were yet minors (Safrai 1974/76a: 957). Miracle-working teachers sometimes expected their disciples to work miracles, although the disciples were not always successful (p. Taʿan. 3:8, §2; cf. 2 Kings 2:14; 4:31); Jesus' disciples sometimes fell short of their teacher, too (17:16; Malina 1993: 131). The term Jesus uses for "workers" here recurs in 10:10 (cf. 20:1), indicating that the workers Jesus wished to send forth into the harvest were his own disciples. Gathering the wheat in the harvest has eschatological ramifications in view of the approaching kingdom (3:12; 13:30), and the urgency of harvest (often emphasized in ancient texts, e.g., Babrius 88.11-19) was a potent image that provided other Jewish teachers similar analogies (a late first-century teacher made nearly the same statement in m. ʾAbot 2:15, probably concerning study and teaching of Torah, m. ʾAbot 2:16).[119]

Third, before Jesus sends laborers out he summons them to pray that he will raise up laborers (9:38). After commissioning them to pray for "workers," Jesus commissioned them as "workers" (10:10). Some have argued that the "master of the harvest" is God (Weaver 1990: 79), which would fit comparable Jewish parables; it is interesting, however, that it is Jesus who sends the workers forth (10:5; cf. 13:37-43).

118. The shepherd motif in Matthew (2:6; 9:36; 10:6, 16; 15:24; 18:12-14; 25:32; 26:31) may draw especially on images from Ezek 34 (see especially Heil 1993), though Matthew midrashically weaves various other biblical passages into this framework (Mic 5:2; Zech 13:7).

119. R. Tarfon's saying may have been understood eschatologically until Bar Kochba (Silberman 1989). Flusser's parallel from Hippocrates, fifth century B.C. (Young 1989: 36), may suggest a proverb, though the language may be coincidental, based on an idea natural to the urgency of harvest. Rabbinic tradition often recalls Jesus' followers, as well as Jesus himself, as miracle-workers (cf. e.g., Lachs 1987: 178).

Jesus Commissions His Representatives (10:1-4)

Cf. Mk 3:16-19; 6:7; Lk 6:13-16; 9:1; Acts 1:13.

Jesus authorizes the Twelve to expel demons and heal (10:1).[1] Jesus assigns the Twelve to carry on his own mission of healing (9:35) because the laborers were so few (9:37); he is multiplying the laborers. The text explicitly recounts that Jesus' mission included not only proclaiming the kingdom but also demonstrating it (see comment on 4:23-25). The model of training other miracle-workers fits the ancient Israelite model of prophetic guilds: Elijah trained Elisha and also apparently led a revival of wilderness prophets (cf. 2 Kings 2:3-18); Samuel also was training a prophetic movement that had not existed when God first began calling him (1 Sam 3:1; 19:20-24).

The number of disciples signifies a mission to Israel (10:1). That the title "twelve" remained even after Judas's death (1 Cor 15:5) suggests a representative function for the number (Jeremias 1971: 234; Sanders 1985: 99-101). Twelve naturally could symbolize the twelve tribes of Israel, and many contemporary interpreters understood other references to "twelve" in this manner (perhaps even the twelve signs of the zodiac! — e.g., Pesiq. Rab Kah. 16:5; Pesiq. R. 4:1; 29/30A:6; cf. Jos. *War* 5.217). The Qumran community included a leadership of twelve special officers, a number that comported well with their vision of themselves as the true remnant of Israel (1QS 8.1-2; F. F. Bruce 1969: 76). Although Jesus had many disciples, he apparently selected a core group of twelve (e.g., Mk 3:16; 1 Cor 15:5) to make a statement similar to that of the Qumran community (F. F. Bruce 1969: 75; Sanders 1985: 104): Jesus' disciples were the leaders of the true remnant of God's people (19:28). The spiritual community built on this foundation of the twelve leaders of Israel's remnant represents the true heir of God's ancient promises.[2]

1. Some documents emphasize "authority" over demons in contexts referring to commanding them or manipulating them for magical purposes (e.g., Test. Sol. 1:5), but Jesus and his disciples just silenced them and cast them out (e.g., Mk 1:22-27).

2. The tradition of the Twelve — which is older than any given list of the names themselves — is a nearly certain bedrock tradition going back to the historical Jesus (Sanders 1985: 11, 98-101; Witherington 1990: 126-27). (In contrast to the slight variations in the canonical lists, one may compare the forms in the Apostolic Church Orders and the Epistola Apostolorum — Lake 1979b: 41.) Most Jewish people expected an eschatological restoration of the lost tribes (e.g., Tob 13:6; 2 Macc 2:18; Ps. Sol. 8:28; Test. Benj. 9:2; Pesiq. Rab Kah. Sup. 5:3; Gen. Rab. 98:9; Sanders 1985: 96-97; for their mythical place of exile, cf. 4 Ezra 13:40; Gen. Rab. 73:6; Pesiq. R. 31:10), though some dissent seems to have arisen (m. Sanh. 10:5; t. Sanh. 13:12).

Jesus chose a band of disciples that was in some respects diverse to reach all Israel (10:2-4). Ancient literature provides many lists of heroes or those who do exploits (e.g., 2 Sam 23:8-39; 1 Chron 25:1-7; Hom. *Il.* 3.161-242; Ap. Rhod. 1.23-228); more critically, lists of disciples seem to have been conventional (though not mandatory) in Jewish literature (Davies and Allison 1991: 150 cite m. 'Abot 2:8; Diog. Laert. 8.46) and may stem from an early stage of the tradition, despite variations in our extant sources. For effectiveness in reaching Israel, Jesus naturally limited his disciples to free male Jews; perhaps due to the pool of available disciples, he also seems to have selected mainly Galileans. Of the roughly half his disciples whose occupations we know, all were drawn from middle-income professions in which less than 10 percent of Jewish Palestine's population engaged (fishermen and tax gatherers), perhaps to give emphasis to more socially prominent individuals who were nevertheless unassociated with any religious or social elite, hence who would be respected by most people. The Gospels may also report only those more noteworthy professions (a tax gatherer and fishers). (Later commentators often emphasized instead the lack of aristocratic presence, thus that he chose common people — Euseb. *P.E.* 3.7 — and uneducated people — Origen *First Principles* 4.1.2; Euseb. *P.E.* 3.7; *ACCS,* 18-19.)

Despite the commonalities among the disciples, however, the list also indicates some diversity. That Jesus included in the same band of disciples a "tax gatherer" on one hand (10:3) and on the other possibly a revolutionary, but certainly one zealous for Israel's ancestral law (10:4), is striking. That Simon was a "revolutionary" is not absolutely clear. Luke's "Zealot" translates Matthew's and Mark's *Kananaios,* an Aramaic word for "zealous one" spelled in Greek letters.[3] But whereas "zealot" could mean a particular kind of "revolutionary" to writers after the first Jewish revolt (66-70), it is doubtful whether most people employed the term this way in the earliest period of the church when Aramaic was the primary language of faith (Horsley and Hanson 1985: passim; Davies and Allison 1991: 156; cf. Witherington 1990: 97-98). Whether the nickname implies exceptional zeal for the law (no one else in the list receives the title) or some sort of revolutionary patriotism (or social banditry),[4] however, a "zealot" would hardly be predisposed toward favorable relations with a tax gatherer.

At least four of the other disciples were fishermen (4:18-22). The mention of Peter first suggests his influential position (cf. 16:16-17).[5] The meaning of

3. Most scholars acknowledge this: e.g., Gundry 1982: 183; Smith 1951: 1; Cullmann 1956b: 15; idem 1953: 22n.24; F. F. Bruce 1972b: 93; Filson 1964: 52; Klausner 1979b: 284n.11. The rabbis used *qannaim* more broadly than for Zealots only (cf. Salomonsen 1966).

4. The epithet must be significant in some respect because Simon alone receives it (Witherington 1990: 98); France thinks that, while the term did not connote a revolutionary this early, it might have already depicted the sort of zeal for God's rule that led to the later party (1985: 177), perhaps rooted in the model of Phinehas (Num 25:7-13; 1 Macc 2:23-27, 50; cf. Ps 106:28-31; 1QH 14.13-15).

5. Some go so far as to argue Peter's primacy in Matthew from this position in the list, comparing the position of the firstborn in OT genealogies (Salerno 1980); since this list is not a geneal-

"Iscariot" is unclear,[6] but the title's most important original function among the disciples was probably to distinguish Judas from another of Jesus' disciples (Lk 6:16; Jn 14:22; Acts 1:13), though he may bear the name "Thaddeus" in Matthew's list for this reason (following Mark; also Jeremias 1971: 232). Hebrew burial inscriptions attest that biblical names were common in this period, hence Jesus' circle included three persons named James (literally "Jacob"), four Simons, three Judases, and so forth (Dalman 1929: 28).[7] Both nicknames (e.g., p. Soṭa 9:13, §2; Dion. Hal. 7.2.4; Hachlili and Killebrew 1983b) and double names (e.g., *CIJ* 1:24, §30; 2:111, §879; *CPJ* 2:143, §261; Leon 1960: 107, 111; Acts 1:23; Wilkinson 1978: 47-48) were fairly common.

The Mission of Jesus' Agents (10:5-15)

Cf. Mk 6:8-11; Lk 9:2-5. Jesus' instructions here show that the disciples would carry on most aspects of his mission (9:35-38). A historical basis surely stands behind the account of Jesus sending his disciples; teachers could train disciples in part by giving them practice among themselves and with others, and that Jesus did so best explains the disciples' rapid imitation of his miraculous ministry in the years immediately following the resurrection (cf. 2 Cor 12:12).[8] Historical data clearly limit Matthew's freedom to adjust the account; although Matthew stresses the Gentile mission (28:19), his Jewish-Christian audience remains well

---

ogy, one should not press nuances of the "firstborn," but the parallel is instructive in informing us that the sequence is significant. In this case even Overman 1990b: 136-40 may read too much into "first" to think it suggests development of authority within the community (against which Matthew must work in 23:7-8). For Peter's title, see comment on 16:17-18.

6. Cullmann 1956b: 15; idem 1953: 22n.25 relates it to "Sicarius," hence a revolutionary, but this is too early for this title and he surely was not the *son* of a *sicarius* as well (Jn 6:71; 13:26; Witherington 1990: 98; Brown 1994: 1414-15); Filson 1964: 52 and others suggest "man of Kerioth," perhaps in southern Judea (Josh 15:25). After Brown 1994: 1413-16 surveys the major proposals and the evidence against them, he concludes that the specific meaning had probably been forgotten even by the time of the evangelists.

7. Simon was perhaps the most popular name of the period (Fitzmyer 1974: 105-12), requiring a distinguishing name to accompany it ("Peter," "son on Jonah," etc.). Although a Greek name, it functioned as the equivalent for the biblical and Jewish "Simeon" (Brown 1994: 915) and was common for Jews (*CIJ* 1:117, §165; 2:117, §890; 2:126, §905; *CPJ* 1:29; 3:191-92). Given the few extant traditions about most of the disciples, the production of two similarly named persons to harmonize divergent traditions (as in Diod. Sic. 4.4.1-5; Arrian *Alex.* 2.16.1-3; 4.28.2; *Indica* 5.13) is unlikely here.

8. Sanders 1993: 123-24 doubts that the disciples were as misunderstanding as the Second Gospel implies or as independent as this passage implies; otherwise it would be difficult to reconcile the two pictures. Yet even in Mark Jesus *expects* the disciples to exercise more faith, and it is only the especially difficult cases (like Mk 9:18-19, 28-29//Mt 17:16-20) that stump them. Disciples were sometimes known to fall short of their masters' faith (cf. 2 Kings 5:20; 6:15-17; the later story about Levi ben Sisi and two generations after him in p. Taʿan. 3:8, §2). Since Matthew does not report the results of their mission, it would actually be Mark (if either of them) who would be exaggerating their success (Mk 6:13; cf. Malina 1993: 131).

aware that before the cross Jesus sent his disciples only to Israel (10:5-6). Yet Matthew provides these instructions not merely as a matter of historical interest — had Matthew's interest been *merely* historical he would not have rearranged this section so thoroughly to be relevant to his communities — but as a living message to his own audience.

Thus he includes some material strictly irrelevant to the first mission but which his community would recognize as particularly relevant in their own day, including prosecution before synagogue and pagan courts (10:17-18).[9] Likewise, Matthew 11:1 does not actually report the disciples' mission (contrast Mk 6:12-13) because for Matthew the mission must continue in his own generation. Summoning his community to greater commitment to the Gentile mission, he provides instructions for those who would go forth to evangelize, and in more general ways for the churches that send them.

First, Jesus "sent," or "apostled" these disciples (10:5; cf. Hunter 1944: 63). Thus he provides a relevant model for his appointed agents in subsequent generations (whether they are "apostles" in the narrower sense or not); the "Twelve" constituted only some of the apostles (for distinctions between the groups, see Acts 14:4; 1 Cor 9:5-6; 15:5, 7; Gal 1:19; Sanders 1985: 105). Although verbs do not always recall their cognate nouns (the noun does not appear in the Septuagint), the language used here for "sending" probably connotes commissioning agents with delegated authority (in recent studies, e.g., Witherington 1990: 133-35; Davies and Allison 1991: 153; Hagner 1993: 265; cf. Mt 2:16). This recalls a wider spectrum of ancient practices. The verb applies to anyone sent, but in the case of a kingdom "sending" representatives it applied particularly to "ambassadors" (Diod. Sic. 40.1.1). Surrounding cultures had long used heralds and ambassadors, the latter acting on the sender's authority and responsible to carry out his wishes (e.g., Demosth. *On the Embassy* 4; Dion. Hal. 6.88.2; Jos. *Ant.* 4.296; 18.1, 265; Pliny *Ep.* 10.18.190-91; cf. 2 Cor 5:20); philosophers could likewise send disciples to teach in their stead and act as their representatives (e.g., Diog. Laert. *Lives* 7.1.9).[10] Ancient Israelite circles also used formal agents or messengers (e.g., Prov 10:26; 13:17; 22:21; 25:13; 26:6). Agency eventually became a legal custom so pervasive that both Roman and Jewish law recognized the use of agents, or intermediary marriage-brokers, in betrothals (Cohen 1966: 295-96).

Later sources suggest that an agent *(shaliaḥ)* did not necessarily have high legal status (b. Ketub. 99b-100a); even slaves were permitted to fill the position (b. Giṭ. 23a). Yet agents carried delegated authority, because they acted on the

9. Matthew's application for his own generation is often acknowledged; see, e.g., F. F. Bruce 1972a: 68; Morosco 1979; Beare 1981: 252; Edersheim: 295; Meier 1980: 102-3; Theissen 1991: 55; Bartnicki 1988; Doohan 1988; pace Schweitzer 1968: 361; Wilkinson 1974b. Meier 1980: 102 notes that Matthew also meshes Mark and Q material (the latter found in Lk 10:1-20).

10. Similarly, the Jewish aristocracy (Jos. *Life* 28-29) clearly used such agents (Jos. *Life* 65, 196-98), who commanded widespread respect (*Life* 72-73). Nevertheless, this background by itself would be too narrow to explain "apostleship" (contrast De Ridder 1971b: 124-26).

authority of the one who sent them. Thus later teachers commonly remarked that a person's agent is "equivalent to the person himself" (t. Ta'an. 3:2; m. Ber. 5:5). How one treats Jesus' messengers or heralds therefore represents how one treats Jesus himself (10:40-42; cf. Did. 11.4); similarly, mistreating a people's envoys was the epitome of treachery, warranting severe punishment (Polyb. *R.R.E.* 15.2; Diod. Sic. 36.15.1-2; Dion. Hal. 8.43.4; Appian *R.H.* 3.6.1-2; 4.11; 8.8.53). Treatment of representatives (e.g., Jos. *Ant.* 8.220-21; Dio Cassius *R.H.* 19.61; Diod. Sic. 4.10.3-4), including God's representatives (e.g., Moses in Jos. *Ant.* 3.85-87; 4.329; Boring 1995: 83), reflected one's feelings toward the one who sent them, though some ancient characters distinguished between the feelings of messengers and the one who sent them (Hom. *Il.* 1.334-36).[11] Because the agent had to be trustworthy to carry out his mission, teachers sometimes debated the character the pious should require of such agents (m. Dem. 4:5; t. Dem. 2:20; cf. Plato *Laws* 12.941A; Demosth. *On the Embassy* 4-5). This also implies, of course, that a *shaliaḥ*'s authority was entirely limited to the extent of his commission and the fidelity with which he carried it out. That Jesus authorizes disciples to perform acts of compassion (9:36) in his name does not authorize them to use his power to get whatever they want (4:3).

While some scholars reject the "agent" background for early Christian apostles (e.g., Malan 1976: 57; Ehrhardt 1958: 5), the early and broad Mediterranean parallels for the general concept support the idea (cf., e.g., Rengstorf 1969: 27; Dix 1947: 228-30), and it was accepted as early as Jerome (*Comm. in Ep. ad Gal.* 1.1, in Dix), long before it was advocated by Lightfoot in the last century (Lightfoot 1869: 93-94, citing Epiph. *Haer.* 30). The concept of agency informs the early Christian idea of apostleship in a general way (see Lake 1979b), but differences also exist (Käsemann 1980: 5-6; Kirk 1975: 252).[12] These differences point us to a specific *kind* of "agent" in this passage: in biblical history, *God's* agents were the prophets. The connections in this text between Jesus' commissioned messengers and prophets should not be overlooked (10:41; cf. Boring 1982: 89).[13] When Jesus "sends" disciples (10:5, 16; cf. 22:3; 23:34, 37), the dis-

11. Pagans had also long observed the sancitity, hence inviolability, of heralds (e.g., Hom. *Il.* 1.334; 7.274-82; 8.517; Eurip. *Children of Heracles* 272; Herodian 6.4.6), and demanded accuracy of them (e.g., Eurip. *Children of Heracles* 292-93). Letters of recommendation frequently identify the sender with one he recommended (Malherbe 1983: 102-3).

12. Schmithals 1969: 108 objects that the evidence for sending agents by twos (Mk 6:7; Lk 10:1: Acts 13) is late and rare; but while most rabbinic evidence is by its nature late, it is abundant (cf. p. Rosh Hash. 2:8, §4; quite abundantly, Liefeld 1967: 225-27; cf. Jeremias 1971: 235). He further neglects the historic model of paired heralds traversing a distance (e.g., Hom. *Il.* 1.320; see Gordon 1965a: 110) as well as the frequent custom of disciples (Stambaugh and Balch 1986: 144; Safrai 1974/76a: 968). Matthew's arrangement of the disciples' names by twos may hint at Mark's pairs (Hill 1972: 183).

13. Some Jewish teachers viewed as agents Moses (Sifra Behuq. pq. 13.277.1.13-14; ARN 1 A, MSS), Aaron (Sifra Sav Mekhilta DeMiluim 98.9.6), the Old Testament prophets (Mek. Pisha 1.87; ARN 37, §95 B; as ambassadors, see ARN 34A), or, most generally, anyone who carried out God's will (Sifra Sav Mekhilta DeMiluim 98.9.5). Jewish teachers who saw the prophets as God's

ciples stand in the tradition of the prophets (21:34, 36; 23:37), John (11:10), and Jesus himself (15:24; 21:37).

Second, Jesus limited his disciples' initial mission to Israel (10:5-6). This limitation fits the historic priority of Israel in salvation history (cf. Rom 1:16; 2:9-10; 15:8-9), was practical (these disciples were not yet equipped to cross such cultural boundaries), and would undoubtedly not have been objectionable to the first disciples themselves (cf. Acts 10:28). The saying is undoubtedly authentic: even those early Jewish Christians least inclined to cross ethnic barriers would probably not have invented such a mission saying for Jesus themselves, since Judaism did not oppose making proselytes (Witherington 1990: 124). Further, the prohibition fits a short-term mission during Jesus' ministry. Jesus undoubtedly did see a future hope for the Gentiles in the Scriptures (see comment on 8:11-12), involving the kingdom that his ministry was introducing (see comment on 4:17). Nevertheless, Jesus historically limited his own mission primarily or exclusively to Israel (Sanders 1985: 11; Ellis 1974: 49). Perhaps the Hebrew Bible's emphasis on blessing the nations through Abraham stood behind his interest in first establishing a renewed remnant within Israel from which to reach the nations (cf. Scott 1990).

Jesus' concern for the "lost sheep" of Israel (10:6; 15:24) echoes his complaint that his people were "helpless" like "sheep without a shepherd" (9:36; cf. 10:16).[14] The biblical prophets complained that the irresponsibility of Israel's shepherds allowed the sheep to go astray (Jer 50:6; Ezek 34:5); Jesus may also have recalled the price God would pay through him to restore the "lost sheep" (Is 53:6). Jewish people often thought that ten of the twelve tribes were lost and would be restored only in the end time (Jeremias 1971: 235; Sanders 1985: 96-97; Esth. Rab. 2:14; though contrast some in m. Sanh. 10:5; t. Sanh. 13:12); Jesus' choice of "twelve" apostles signified the imminence of the end-time regathering of God's scattered people (10:1; cf. Jeremias 1971: 235; Sanders 1985: 98-106).

Nevertheless, Jesus' orders address geography *more* than ethnicity. "Way of the Gentiles" (NRSV's "among the Gentiles" is interpretive and probably mistaken) merely prohibited taking any of the roads leading to hellenistic cities in Palestine (Manson 1979: 179; cf. Jeremias 1958: 19n.3, who renders the phrase "toward" Gentile populations). Since Samaria and Gentile territories surrounded

---

commissioned messengers were consistent with the portrait of prophets in their Scriptures; Israel's prophetic messenger formulas echo ancient Near Eastern royal messenger formulas such as, "Thus says the great king," often addressing Israel's vassal kings for the suzerain king Yahweh (Holladay 1970: 31-34; Rabe 1976: 127; cf. Judg 11:15; 2 Kings 18:19). OT perspectives on prophets inform the early Christian view of apostleship (Grudem 1982: 43-54), although they do not exhaust its meaning (cf. Hill 1979: 116-17); early Christianity clearly maintained the continuance of the prophetic office (Acts 11:27; 21:10; 1 Cor 12:28), while seeming to apply to apostles the special sort of position accorded only certain prophets in the OT (such as prophet-judges like Deborah and Samuel, and other leaders of prophetic schools like Elijah and Elisha).

14. Concern for the marginalized of Israel, as against the elite rulers, may also be implicit in Matthew's understanding of the "lost sheep"; see Levine 1988: 56.

Galilee, Jesus' orders de facto limited his disciples' mission geographically, restricting their activity to Galilee (see Gundry 1982: 185). Because Jesus' earliest followers extended this prohibition beyond its minimal sense, it undoubtedly remained in the background of early Christian opposition to the Gentile mission (cf. Acts 11:3; Meier 1980: 106-7).

In contrast to Jesus' treatment of other commandments in this chapter, however, Matthew indicates that Jesus later revokes this one, specifically clarifying that this one command was a temporary measure during his earthly ministry. For Matthew, the critical prerequisite for the end that the church can affect is world evangelization (24:14); his Gospel's climactic conclusion is likewise the commission to disciple *all* nations until the end of the age (28:19-20). Indeed, the contextual literary function of 10:5 may best explain why Matthew both retains and emphasizes it: by highlighting that the gospel's recipients are Jewish, hence that even *Jewish* people may reject the kingdom and be treated as Gentiles (10:14-15), this verse implies for Matthew a supraethnic view of the covenant that ultimately necessitates the Gentile mission. Whatever the saying might have meant in previous contexts, its sense in Matthew's Gospel cannot undermine the Gentile mission; Matthew places the saying in the context of a mission discourse that includes testimony before Gentile authorities (10:18; Stanton 1993: 140).[15]

Third, their message is the good news of God's impending kingdom (10:7). That Matthew intends this proclamation to remain the church's message (cf. Acts 8:12; 20:24-25; 28:31) is clear not only from the fact that Matthew nowhere revokes it but from the parallel formulation in his Gospel's conclusion: "as you go" (not the imperative "go" as in the NRSV rendering of 28:19) is a participle in both instances (though 10:7 is present and 28:19 aorist). That Jesus has all authority in the universe (28:18) and appears alongside the Father and the Spirit (28:19) indicates his rule or kingdom, especially in view of the allusion to Daniel 7:13-14 in Matthew 28:18. To make disciples for this king is to proclaim the good news that God's future kingdom is already active in this age (cf. 28:20).

Fourth, both for Jesus and for the Matthean community, signs constitute one critical authentication of the kingdom message (10:8). "The disciples' mission (vv. 7-8) replicates and extends the mission of Jesus in preaching the coming of God's kingdom and in healing the sick (see 4:23)" (Harrington 1982: 45; cf. Stanton 1993: 81; on Mark, cf. Delorme 1974). Cleansing lepers, for instance, extends Jesus' own ministry (cf. 8:1-4; 11:5). Jesus' commands in 10:8 are all sharp, parallel statements that would communicate emphasis in both Aramaic and Greek (Jeremias 1971: 21-22; they need not represent prophetic speech, pace Boring 1982: 145-46). Although hard-hearted people would never be satisfied with signs (15:37–16:1; cf. Jn 11:47-48; 12:10-11; Acts 4:16-17), signs could draw other people's attention to the gospel of the kingdom (11:3-6,

15. Perhaps Matthew prepared for this saying in advance by using Jesus as a model in 4:15, which purposely locates him on a "way" near Gentiles. In the context of his whole Gospel, Mark's account of the sending of the Twelve (Mk 6:7-13) may also imply a universal commission; cf. Anthonysamy 1980.

21, 23; cf. Jn 2:11; Acts 9:35, 42). Matthew again emphasizes a point not merely for historical interest, but for the missionary activity of his community.

Fifth, Jesus' agents live simply (10:8-10). Manson remarks that the disciples here depend on the people of the land, "like an invading army" (1979: 181). In a traditional Jewish proverb of uncertain date God commissioned Torah teachers to offer Torah freely as he did (b. Bek. 29a; *D.E.* 2.4; Dalman 1929: 226; Lachs 1987: 180; cf. m. 'Abot 1:3; Sifre Deut. 48.2.7; p. Ned. 4:4); some early Jewish teachers prohibited accepting pay for teaching (Jeremias 1969: 112; Gundry 1982: 187).

A more general backdrop for Jesus' command is not difficult to envision. Peasants, at least in the poorest parts of the Empire like Egypt, often owned only one cloak (cf. 5:40; Theissen 1978: 34-35). Cynics voluntarily limited themselves to a single cloak; they chose a simple and toilsome lifestyle living on the street (unlike Jesus' disciples here) to prepare themselves for hardships (Crates *Ep.* 18, 30). Since some Cynics were known in hellenistic cities of Syria (Freyne 1988: 241), a distant and indirect Cynic connection is not impossible, though they are unattested in Jewish Palestine (and certainly in the traditional towns Jesus frequented). Cynics were hardly alone, in any case; other ancient Mediterranean people, probably especially the Romans, valued such harsh lifestyles for purposes of discipline (e.g., Livy 21.4.5-7; Plut. *Dinner of Seven Wise Men* 12, *Mor.* 155; see more fully the excursus on Mt 6:19-24). Yet more to the point, some Jews known as Essenes showed their devotion to God by a simple lifestyle, those who lived in the wilderness devoting all their goods to the community (1QS 1.11-13; 6.22-23; Jos. *Ant.* 18.20; *War* 2.122; Philo *Prob.* 76; *Hypothetica* 11.4-5; Fitzmyer 1966: 243; Mealand 1975; cf. Fabry 1977). Josephus also indicates that the Essenes did not take provisions when they traveled, expecting hospitality from fellow Essenes in every city (*War* 2.124-25). Even disciples of rabbis often lived sacrificially to achieve their education (e.g., ARN 11A).

Perhaps most relevant is the model of Israel's ancient prophets in times of national apostasy (e.g., 1 Kings 18:13; 2 Kings 4:38; 6:1; cf. Meeks 1986: 106). One may recall Elisha's unwillingness to accept Naaman's gifts, preferring to allow the Aramean God-fearer to remain wholly indebted to Israel's God (2 Kings 5:15-19); his servant Gehazi, however, determined to profit from Naaman and suffered for it (2 Kings 5:20-27). Elisha reminded Gehazi that the current time of spiritual crisis rendered the acquisition of material possessions a vain pursuit (2 Kings 5:26); many early Christians viewed their own time as analogous (1 Cor 7:29-31). A reader of this Gospel would find the most immediate prophetic model in the lifestyle and garb of John (3:4).

On long trips, one typically brought both a change of clothes and money in a bag tied to one's belt or fastened around one's neck (Stambaugh and Balch 1986: 38; cf. 1 Sam 17:40; Prov 7:20); one could even stuff loaves of bread and other food into such pouches (Babrius 86.2). Jesus hence forbids the normal basic apparatus for travel. Jesus' prohibition of the "bag" (10:10; Mk 6:8) prohibits begging (see Deissmann 1978: 108-9), the survival method of the otherwise equally simple Cynics (Liefeld 1967: 247; Meeks 1986: 107; also of priests of Cybele — e.g., Babrius 141.1-6).[16] Mark allows at least staff and sandals, but Matthew's demand for simplicity is still more radical, prohibiting even these.[17] This is not a matter of asceticism but of priorities, as in 6:19-34 (France 1985: 179). At least for the Gospel writers' audiences, these prohibitions would distinguish the disciples from other kinds of wandering preachers (probably similar to Cynics in the Greek world) "whose questionable reputation they did not want to share" (Liefeld 1967: 260; cf. Overman 1996: 146-47; Eddy 1996: 461-62). In contrast to Mark, Matthew not only prohibits taking money on one's journey, but acquiring any money while there (cf. Mk 6:8; Gundry 1982: 186).

The "staff" was an instrument for self-protection (sometimes against robbers, perhaps against wild beasts; cf. Hom. *Od.* 17.236) and perhaps an aid in walking or keeping one's balance on uneven paths (Hom. *Od.* 17.195, 199).[18] Some Jewish teaching forbade the staff, but usually only on the Sabbath (m. Rosh Hash. 1:9), on holy days (2:9), or in the temple (m. Ber. 9:5; Sifre Deut. 258.2.2, which also require the removal of profane dust from one's feet — cf. 10:14). Thus these prohibitions might underline the sacredness of the mission (cf. Schweizer 1975: 239). The point of the prohibitions can hardly be limited to this explanation, however, for this explanation fails to account for details such as "the additional prohibition of two tunics" (Gundry 1982: 187), which applies to discipleship in general (in Lk 3:11). Although Matthew is not endorsing a lifestyle for all disciples, whether itinerant or not, the first disciples' obedience to their calling challenges Matthew's audience to consider what they will sacrifice for the work of God's kingdom (cf. similarly comment on 3:1, 3-4). Even the best Cynics recognized that the significance of their lifestyle was the values it reflected rather than merely the simplicity itself (Julian *Or.* 6.200C-201C in Malherbe 1986: 35; Crates *Ep.* 19; cf. Aul. Gel. 9.2.4-5; Plut. *Isis* 3, *Mor.* 352C; Petron. *Sat.* 14; Diog. *Ep.* 15).

16. Cynics typically wore rough robes (e.g., Epict. *Disc.* 3.22.10; cf. 4.8.12, 15) and carried only a bag and a staff (Epict. *Disc.* 3.22.10; Crates *Ep.* 16, 23, 33; Diog. *Ep.* 6, 7, 13, 19, 26, 30, 46; Diog. Laert. 6.1.13; 6.2.22-23, 33, 76; cf. Anacharsis *Ep.* 5). Many of these references also emphasize that Cynics let their beards grow long, but coins indicate that Palestinian Jews in this period generally already had beards, so this feature of Cynic lifestyle would not be relevant to mention. Liefeld 1967: 167-79 treats the distinctive cloaks of many philosophers and religious figures and notes that some kinds of philosophers — not just Cynics — traveled with only one.

17. Mark very likely toned down the more radical formulation in Q (see Lk 10:4; Boring 1982: 145), yet even Mark is stricter than the Cynics, and the historical Jesus very likely was stricter (cf. Thompson 1985: 182). Pace Mack and Crossan, the likeliest direct point of contact with the Cynics in the Jesus tradition is a contrast, possibly even deliberate, rather than an analogy (e.g., Witherington 1994: 126).

18. Even Cynics carried staffs when traveling, as did beggars (e.g., Aristoph. *Acharn.* 448). Aside from aiding on steep paths, they provided protection against animals like snakes (Schweizer 1975: 239; Gundry 1982: 186) and especially "human attackers," perhaps suggesting that this saying implies pacifism in the face of attack (Davies and Allison 1991: 173, who note that this was more restrictive than the Essenes viewed it — Jos. *War* 2.125 — and so radical that Origen used it as an argument against taking the Bible literally — *De princ.* 4.3.3).

Paul's examples of his qualifications by suffering for true apostleship (1 Cor 4:9-13; 2 Cor 4:8-12; 6:4-10; 11:23-33, presented in terms of philosophers' lists of sufferings) probably reflect the Jesus tradition in view here. Churches provided hospitality for traveling apostles, prophets, and evangelists in the late first century, but Christians had to become wise about hucksters and charlatans (2 Cor 2:17; 4:2; 1 Thess 2:3-6). One early church document advises that prophets and teachers are worthy of their food (Did. 13.1-2), but warns that if a prophet wants to stay more than three days or asks for money, he is a false prophet (Did. 11:5; cf. 2 Cor 11:7-15); Matthew may have had such false teachers in mind as he dictated this warning (Gundry 1982: 186), for receiving the right travelers affects one's reward (10:40-42; 2 Jn 8-11).

Matthew would probably not expect all missionaries in all contexts to follow these specifications exactly (just as Mark apparently toned down Q's instructions for his own community);[19] hospitality might be less dependable in the Diaspora than it was in first-century Jewish Palestine. Nevertheless, in this text he summons his audience to value radically their mission above all possessions, and to live as simply as necessary to devote their resources to evangelism.

Sixth, the disciples can travel light because they trust God to supply their needs where they minister (10:10-11). Ancient Mediterranean peoples emphasized hospitality (e.g., Hom. *Od.* 1.118-20; 3.345-58; 4.26-36; 6.207-8; 9.176; 14.57-58; *Rhet. ad Herenn.* 3.3.4; Cic. *De Offic.* 2.18.64; Epict. *Disc.* 1.28.23; Malherbe 1983: 95), and Jewish people, who avoided inns when possible due to their unsavory moral reputations, particularly stressed this virtue (Gen 19:3; Judg 19:20; Tob 5:10-15; 7:8-9; 10:6-10; Ps-Phocyl. 24; Test. Job 10:1-4; Lk 11:6; Acts 16:15; 1 Tim 3:2; Tit 1:8; Heb 13:2; 1 Pet 4:9; see Koenig 1985).[20] Because strangers could abuse this system, however, Jewish people outside Palestine depended heavily on letters of recommendation showing that the traveler was of good reputation (e.g., Rom 16:1-2; cf. Kim 1972; other sources in Keener 1992: 251). Like the early Christians (2 Jn 10-11; Did. 11–12), most Jewish people would not embrace someone they believed to be a messenger of false teaching (cf. Sir 11:29, 34; t. Dem. 3:9; Sifre Deut. 1.10.1; p. Giṭ. 5:10, §5; cf. perhaps suspicion of strangers in Oakman 1991: 166). Jesus' messengers had better backing than a letter of recommendation, however; the authority of Jesus himself stood behind them (10:40-42; cf. 2 Cor 3:1-6).

Finally, their hearers would be judged by whether they embraced

19. Still, those traveling on foot would probably have carried little besides what they "could carry with ease" (Llewelyn 1994: 88-89).

20. Hospitality implied a potential reciprocal obligation, to be fulfilled when the host himself might be in need; but because they brought a spiritual gift of far greater worth than the hospitality they sought, they fulfilled their reciprocal obligation immediately (cf. Crates *Ep.* 2; Rom 1:11); indeed, the initial burden of obligation lay primarily on the host (1 Cor 9:14; 1 Tim 5:18). Liefeld may be correct that Jewish people disliked the lower-class Greek philosophers' method of simply preaching on streets (a method including but not limited to Cynics); thus Jesus may have encouraged his disciples to work from homes when possible (cf. Acts 18:7; 20:20; Liefeld 1967: 208-9).

Christ's messengers (10:12-15). The missionaries were to use one home as their base of operation for evangelizing the community (10:11-12; cf. Mk 6:10; Lk 10:7). They would find the home first by inquiring around who might hear their message (10:11), then by finding out whether the household welcomed them to stay there (10:12-13). The workers are "worthy" (10:10; cf. Lk 10:7; 1 Tim 5:18) because they have made Jesus their first priority (10:37-38); the question must be whether others would prove worthy to welcome them (10:11-13).[21]

Greetings constituted an essential aspect of social etiquette in Mediterranean antiquity (Soph. *Oed. Rex* 596; Isoc. *Demon.* 20, *Or.* 1; cf. p. Taʿan. 1:4, §1; 4:2, §8), and social convention dictated particular rules for whom to greet and how to do so (23:7; cf. t. Ber. 2:20; p. Ḥor. 3:5, §3; Ketub. 12:3, §6; 2 Jn 10), as they still do today in most Middle Eastern society (Eickelman 1989: 234). But Jewish people also viewed their greetings as "wish-prayers": *Shalom,* "peace," meant, "May it be well with you" (e.g., 1 Chron 12:18; 1QS 2.9; 4 Bar. 7:35; Jas 2:16; also in some other societies; see, e.g., Mbiti 1970: 85). Just as an undeserved curse would not take effect (Prov 26:2), Jesus declares that the blessings will be efficacious only if they prove appropriate (the concept would have been widely understood; cf. *PGM* 4.749-50; Mt 10:34). Disciples thus did not need to fear offering them in good conscience — if they thought the recipient worthy of the blessing — as if such blessings would take effect magically, warranted or not.

Those who received the agents of Christ received Christ himself (10:40-41; cf. 18:5), even if the only hospitality they had available to offer was a cup of water (10:42; cf. 25:35, 42). But those who rejected Christ's agents (or their words — 10:14; cf. 7:26) were to be treated like spiritual pagans (10:14). Just as Jewish people returning to the holy land might shake the dust of Gentile lands from their feet,[22] or those entering the holy temple might shake the relatively profane dust of the land of Israel from their feet (m. Ber. 9:5; t. Ber. 6:19; Sifre Deut. 258.2.2), so Jesus' disciples were to treat as unholy those who rejected their message (Acts 13:51; cf. 18:6; 22:23).[23]

God would treat these nations not merely like Gentiles in general, but as worse than Sodom and Gomorrah (10:15), for they had rejected a greater revelation, a greater opportunity for repentance, than Sodom and Gomorrah had (11:23-24).[24] The prophets had employed Sodom as the epitome of evil, a city

21. By extension Q's "food" of which laborers were worthy could easily become Luke's "wages," but Schwarz 1992 specifically finds behind both the same Aramaic term.

22. Many commentators find this background here: e.g., Manson 1979: 76; Gundry 1982: 190; Nineham 1977: 170; Lake and Cadbury 1979: 160; Anderson 1976: 164; Witherington 1990: 137; Hagner 1993: 273. On the uncleanness of pagan soil, see Jos. *Apion* 2.203; m. Ṭohar. 4:5; Ohol. 18:6.

23. The act was purely symbolic; more prominent Roman roads were paved (Stambaugh and Balch 1986: 37).

24. For the expression "day of judgment," meaning the final judgment here and in 11:22, cf. also Jdt 16:17; 1 Enoch 10:6, 12; 84:4; 94:9; 96:8; 97:3; 98:8; 99:15; Jub. 24:30; 36:10; 1QpHab 12.14; 13.2-3; 1QM 1.11; 7.5; 1 Jn 4:17; 4 Ezra 7:38; 2 Enoch 50:4, 5A; 51:3; Ps. Sol. 15:12; Test. Levi 1:1; cf. Test. Moses 1:18.

that merited judgment (Is 13:19; Jer 50:40; Zeph 2:9) and regularly applied the image to Israel (Deut 32:32; Is 1:10; 3:9; Jer 23:14; Lam 4:6; Ezek 16:46-49; cf. Jub. 20:6).[25] Sodom's rejection of angelic messengers (Gen 19) merited less damnation than Jesus' contemporaries' rejection of him (cf. Mt 12:6, 41-42; 23:35-36).[26]

Persecution Is Promised (10:16-23)

Cf. 24:9-14; Mk 13:9-13; Lk 10:3; 12:11-12; 21:12-19. Matthew's inclusion of material concerning persecution (cf. Mk 13:9-13) in his discourse on the kingdom mission indicates his view that persecution and proclamation are inseparable (Hare 1967: 113; cf. Matthey 1980), as does a brief perusal of Acts or Paul's letters (e.g., Paul's defense of his true apostleship in 2 Cor 11:23-33). For early Christians, true ministry inevitably involved suffering, especially if that ministry was a frontline ministry to nonbelievers.[27] Yet as Jesus reminds the disciples in the next section, the worst persecutors can accomplish is the disciples' death, and disciples die anyway with or without persecution (10:24-33).[28]

First, Jesus promises to empower his followers in the midst of opposition (10:16-20). Jesus "sends" them (10:16), persecution becomes an opportunity for testimony (10:18), and the Spirit of prophecy will provide the words they need (10:20). *Jesus portrays his followers as powerless in their own strength (10:16):* first of all as sheep, like Israel of old (10:6; cf. 9:36). Sheep were notoriously defenseless against such predators as wolves (Sir 13:17; cf. Diog. Laert. 6.5.92; Dion. Hal. 7.11.3; Aelian *Animals* 7.27; Terence *Brothers* 534-35), and

25. Later Jewish texts also employ Sodom as the epitome of immorality (e.g., Sir 16:8; Jub. 36:10; 3 Macc 2:5; t. Sanh. 13:8; Shab. 7:23; Sifra Behuq. par. 2.264.1.3; Sifre Deut. 43.3.5; b. Sanh. 109ab; Pesiq. Rab Kah. 26:2; Gen. Rab. 41:7; 50:5, 7; Song Rab. 8:9, §2; Test. Naph. 4:1; Asher 7:1; Benj. 9:1; cf. *CIJ* 1:417, §567; Katzoff 1987/88; Bodendorfer-Langer 1994); cf. 4Q180.2-4.8.2.7 (Sodom as a burnt offering) in Lange 1993.

26. Judgment for ignorantly rejecting, and blessings for unwittingly accepting, divine messengers occurs frequently in ancient literature, both Greco-Roman (Hom. *Od.* 1.105, 113-35; 17.484-87; Ovid *Metam.* 1.212-13; 2.698; 5.451-61; 6.26-27; 8.621-29; Paus. 3.16.2-3; cf. Acts 14:11-12; other examples of disguised deities approaching mortals abound, e.g., in Hom. *Il.* 4.86-87, 121-24; 13.43-45, 69, 215-16, 356-57; 14.136; 16.715-20; 17.71-73, 322-26, 554-55, 582-83; 20.79-81; 21.284-86, 599-611; *Od.* 1.420; 2.267-68, 382-87, 399-401; 6.21-22; 7.19-20; 8.8, 193-94; Ovid *Metam.* 1.676; 14.765-71) and Jewish (e.g., Heb 13:2; cf. Gen 18; Tob 5:4-6, 12; 9:1-5; Philo *Abr.* 114; the shipwreck victim who turned out to be the king in Qoh. Rab. 11:1).

27. So much was persecution a guarantee for a true disciple (2 Tim 3:12) that the leaders of the apostolic church would probably have questioned the authenticity of the witness of those not experiencing any (cf., e.g., 5:11-12; Acts 5:41; 14:22; Gal 5:11; 1 Thess 3:3; Rev 1:9).

28. One may compare the *peristasis* catalogues, or hardship lists, in Greek philosophic literature and elsewhere (Fitzgerald 1988: 47-49; Hodgson 1983; cf. Jub. 23:13; 4 Macc 18:2-3; Test. Jos. 1:4-7; such catalogues may have roots or an analogy in the earlier Herculean labor tradition — Alexander 1993: 59-60; cf. Epict. *Disc.* 1.6.32-33), which apostles in the Greek world could adapt as a sign of perseverance and genuineness, both for themselves (1 Cor 4:9-13; 2 Cor 4:8-10) and for the church (Rom 8:33-39).

Jewish texts often portray God's people in this manner (Ps. Sol. 8:23; Ex. Rab. 5:20; Pesiq. R. 9:2; cf. Wis 19:9; 2 Clem. 5). While Jewish texts contain similar statements in which the sheep represent Israel or the pious among them (1 Enoch 90.6-17; Tanḥuma Toledot 5; Vermes 1993: 89), Jesus drives home the point still more graphically: his sheep are actually *sent* among the predators (Vermes 1993: 89). People thought of doves and similar birds as weak and timid (Hom. *Od.* 20.243; Soph. *Ajax* 139-40; Phaedrus 1.31; Athenaeus *Deipn.* 11.490d; or inconspicuous, Hom. *Il.* 5.778; or gentle, Chrysostom *Matthew* 12.3, *ACCS,* 13).[29] Matthew's readers, probably in conflict with the Pharisees, might well recall earlier denunciations of the fruitless as wolves (7:15) and of the Pharisees as fruitless (3:7-8; cf. 12:24, 33) in this Gospel. Christians should therefore avoid *unnecessarily* provoking their opponents ("shrewd"), while remaining "guileless" (NRSV; NIV: "innocent").[30]

Disciples must endure physical suffering and shame for Jesus' sake (10:17). The hostility of synagogue officials (cf. Jn 16:2) would extend as far as scourging (10:17; 23:34), recalling the more deadly scourging the Lord himself would undergo (20:19; 27:26). "Sanhedrins" probably also links their judgments with Christ's (26:59), and most hearers would be familiar with them from the tradition.[31] Second-century rabbis expected local "sanhedrins," or judicial assemblies, in every town (t. Sanh. 3:10; cf. Sifra Qed. par. 4.206.2.9), and ruled that local synagogue courts must include at least three or, for capital cases, twenty-three, judges (m. Sanh. 1:1-2; t. Ḥag. 2:9; Sanh. 3:1); it is unlikely that local courts observed these numbers strictly in the first century, but they might suggest an average reflecting something like a normal practice. First-century local courts may have employed an average of seven local elders, with levitical assistants (Jos. *War* 2.571; *Ant.* 4.214, 287). Local councils probably consisted of town elders, with special privileges for local priests.[32]

Many synagogue scourgings probably conformed to the later standard for

29. At least as early as the Neo-Assyrian Empire some used doves in treaties (Begg 1989a). They were, however, hardly heralds of "peace" in all texts; a dove *(peleias),* perhaps meaning the oracle at Dodona, stirred two nations to war (Aelian *On Animals* 11.27); elsewhere a dove could function as a decoy (Aelian *Animals* 13.17).

30. A later rabbi said that Israel was innocent like doves before God but shrewd like serpents before the nations (Song Rab. 2:14, §1); the tradition on which he draws may be later than Jesus. Some ancient Near Eastern cultures viewed serpents as prudent (Carson 1984b: 246), but standing alone the image would not be a pleasant one to Jewish hearers (Gen 3:1-2 LXX). If left to themselves, doves, conversely, could easily be deceived (Hos 7:11; Phaedrus 1.31; Vermes 1993: 90 also cites rabbinic interpretation). Cunning that one viewed as "wisdom" another might envision as deceit, as in traditions about Odysseus (Soph. *Philoct.* 54-55, 107-9, 119, 431, 1228).

31. Warning of beatings in the synagogue likely derives from the earliest stratum of Gospel tradition, when (or before) disciples remained in submission to the discipline of their synagogue communities (Anderson 1976: 293). This is the period when the Jesus tradition would have been transmitted most reliably. Matthew's own audience probably remains subject to this, however (Setzer 1994: 38).

32. Cf. t. Ḥag. 2:9; Sanh. 7:1. Diod. Sic. 40.3.5 supposes that Moses appointed priests to function as judges.

the local *beth din:* a strap of calf leather with interwoven thongs, brought against the condemned person's back 26 times and breast 13 times (m. Mak. 3:10-12; Lane 1974a: 461n.60; cf. Deut 25:3).[33] Those acting as officers stripped the condemned person, binding his hands to a pillar (or with the person lying down — Sifre Deut. 286.4.1). Then a servant of the synagogue would stand on a stone behind the condemned person and administer the multiple straps of animal hide (m. Mak. 3:12) as hard as he could, one-third on the chest and two-thirds on the shoulder (m. Mak. 3:13; Sifre Deut. 286.5.1). Whether they actually read from Deuteronomy 28:58-59 at that time (cf. m. Mak. 3:14) is debatable.

Paul, maintaining his solidarity with the synagogue, suffered this public disgrace at least five times (2 Cor 11:24).[34] Although the fair-minded Pharisees apparently opposed corporal punishment officially for matters of theological disagreement (Hare 1967: 44), it is not difficult to imagine how popular sentiments could yield to violence (cf. Jer 20:1-2; 37:15), and even Pharisees might permit it for disrupting public order (Acts 5:40; Hare 1967: 45-46).[35] That the disciples would be "betrayed" to such hardship underlines their connection with Jesus' sufferings (e.g., 10:4), just as their being "sent" (10:16) symbolizes their solidarity with their predecessors (10:5; 11:10; 15:24; 21:34; 23:34).

God will also empower the disciples to speak his message before Gentile rulers when disciples are on trial before them (10:18-20). Like Jesus (27:21), his followers would face Roman officials. The "governors" refer to propraetors, proconsuls, and procurators, various types of Roman provincial administrators (A. B. Bruce 1979: 163; Nineham 1977: 349; cf. 24:14). That this passage speaks of them in the plural (when Judea had only one governor; cf. Theissen 1991: 56) indicates that Matthew again points beyond the immediate mission of the Twelve

33. Biblical law prohibited more lashes than 40 (cf. also, e.g., 2 Cor 11:24; Jos. *Ant.* 4.238, 248; m. Kil. 8:3; Mak. 1:1-3; 3:3-5; b. Ketub. 33b; Num. Rab. 5:4; Deut. Rab. 2:18; superhuman beings sometimes received 60, as in b. B. Meṣ. 85a; Ḥag. 15a; but contrast 40 in b. Yoma 77a), but whereas Gentiles sometimes used 40 lashes (Petron. *Sat.* 105), they were not always so merciful, assigning even 100 stripes to slaves (Plato *Laws* 9.881C; Petron. *Sat.* 28; *P. Hal.* 1.188-89, 196-99). Later rabbis might allow fewer stripes if someone's physical constitution could not bear 39 (m. Mak. 3:11; p. Nazir 4:3, §1), or in some cases monetary payment in lieu of the flogging (b. Ketub. 32ab).

34. This punishment may have been rarer in Diaspora courts (cf. p. Mak. 1:8, §1). It could apply to technical blasphemy (cursing with God's name, Pesiq. R. 22:6), breaking ritual law (t. Tem. 1:1), including violating festivals (p. Beṣa 5:2, §11; cf. m. Pesaḥ. 7:11), or breaking a Nazirite vow (m. Nazir 4:3), but one could be beaten for more questionable infractions (as Akiba presumably was in Sifra Qed. pq. 4.200.3.3; but the punishment is not corporal in the parallel in Sifre Deut. 1.3.2), including questionable teaching (Pesiq. Rab Kah. 4:3; Gen. Rab. 7:2; Num. Rab. 19:3, 19; Qoh. Rab. 7:23, §4; Pesiq. R. 14:9). At least Hillelite Pharisees may have supported the later custom of making certain the person was warned before flogging him (p. Ter. 7:1) and being conservative on the offenses for which flogging was appropriate (b. Pesaḥ. 24b). The flogging could be repeated more than once if necessary, in extreme cases (b. Ker. 15a; Pesaḥ. 24a).

35. Davies and Allison 1991: 183 note reports of floggings in synagogues (23:24; Acts 22:19; Euseb. *H.E.* 5.16) but suggest that, if rabbinic reports are relevant here, the language may be used loosely (perhaps instrumentally) for discipline at the order of synagogue officials, since it took place outside the synagogue building proper (citing m. Mak. 3:12 on the reasonable assumption that the person was not bound to a pillar and whipped inside).

to the continuing mission of the church among the nations. When disciples are arraigned before them, God is allowing it for a testimony (cf. Mk 13:10-11; Acts 9:15; 23:11; 26:2) and will empower them with the Holy Spirit of prophecy (cf. Rev 19:10; Jn 14:26; Keener 1991b: 69-77), much as God promised to empower Moses (Ex 4:10-12; Kennedy 1980: 127). Thus despite the ancient aristocracy's valuing of rhetorical skills (e.g., Cic. *Brutus* 24.110; Lucian *Teacher of Rhetoric;* Quint. 1, pref. 13, 18; MacMullen 1974: 107) and, when possible, advance preparation (Sir 36:4), disciples need not be anxious about what they will say (cf. Lk 12:11-12; 21:13-15; Jn 16:1-11).

Second, the persecution will divide even families (10:21-22). The hatred of "all" (10:22; Mk 13:12; cf. "all nations," 24:9) on account of Jesus' name (5:11-12; Jn 15:19-21) will extend even to those in closest relation to the disciples; the gospel is offensive to those who reject its demands or whose culture or tradition it challenges. Although Judaism considered betrayal to Gentiles a heinous act (m. Ter. 8:12), even family members would now betray one another to death (10:21; cf. 10:35; 24:9; Mk 13:9, 12; Lk 21:12, 16); slaughter by relatives signaled an especially awful time (Diod. Sic. 17.13.6; Appian *C.W.* 4.4.18; *R.H.* 7.5.28; 1 Cor. 7:16; Lucan *C.W.* 2.148-51; Ovid *Metam.* 1.144-48; Sen. *Benef.* 5.15.3; Jos. *War* 6.208-12). Because only a remnant of many families would be saved (cf. Jer 3:14; contrast Acts 16:31), in the time of judgment personal needs would supplant natural affections (cf. Ezek 5:10). In a culture dominated by honor and shame, in which the opinion of family members was paramount, such a threat demanded an incomparably high allegiance to Christ (10:37-39).

Third, even in Jewish Palestine persecution would be so intense that disciples would have no secure refuge until Jesus' return (10:23). Persecution would cause disciples to flee (cf. 2:13; Acts 14:5-6; 17:14; negatively in Mt 26:56) from one city to another (10:23; 23:34; cf. 10:11, 15). Some regarded flight as undignified (e.g., Jos. *Life* 146, though he fled on other occasions), but most people could distinguish between fleeing and openly denying their faith (e.g., Gen. Rab. 82:8). The expectation of flight suggests that whereas Matthew values martyrdom (as perhaps in Phil 1:20-25), he (as in Mart. Pol. 4) would reject gratuitous martyrdom in the sense in which some might find it in Ign. *Rom.* 3.2–8.3; cf. Ign. *Trall.* 10).

This persecution in Israel would not subside fully until the Son of Man's return (cf. 16:28; 24:27). Their missionary task and its attendant persecution would not be completed until Jesus' return (Kümmel 1957: 61-62); in the end, however, Israel would repent (23:39), just as the prophets had spoken (e.g., Deut 4:30; Jer 31:33; Ezek 37:23; Hos 2:14-23; 11:5-11; 14:1-7; Mal 4:6).

Either judgments (Amos 4:8) or persecution (2 Macc 5:8) might force God's people to flee from one city to another; in one Jewish account, those seeking refuge from persecution finally abandoned Israel's cities altogether and fled to Egypt (2 Macc 5:8; cf. Mt 2:13-14). Although this persecution saying, unlike much of its context, does not appear in Mark's end-time discourse, an analogous Jewish saying confirms that Jesus probably uttered it while speaking of the final testing (m. Soṭa 9:15; cf. Pesiq. Rab Kah. 5:9; Song Rab. 6:10, §1; Pesiq. R. 15:14/15; Bammel 1961; Essame 1961; Witherington 1992: 39). Why does Matthew include sayings about tribulation and Jesus' return in instructions to the Twelve on their short-term mission? Because for Matthew the mission of this discourse, minus the ethnic/geographic restriction of 10:5-6, must continue until the end of the age (24:14; 28:19-20; Ladd 1974: 200). Thus if one place rejects and persecutes disciples (e.g., 23:34), they should move quickly to the next (cf. 7:6; Acts 14:5-7), spreading the gospel as widely as possible in view of the potentially imminent end of the age (France 1985: 184).[36]

Promises for the Persecuted (10:24-33)

Cf. Mk 4:22; Lk 6:40; 8:17; 12:2-9. Since a disciple was to be like a servant (a common observation, e.g., Dalman 1929: 229; see comment on 3:12), he could not be greater than his master (10:24-25; cf. Lk 6:40; Jn 13:16; 15:20); the greatest role to which a disciple could aspire was equality with his teacher (Epict. *Disc.* 1.2.36).[37] Servants were considered part of the household in antiquity; if opponents called the household head "Beelzebul" — or made that the source of his power (9:34; 12:24) — they would not hesitate to apply the charge to those of yet lower social status.[38] (This is a standard Jewish *qal waḥomer,* or "how much more" argument.)

In view of the impending end-time vindication (11:19), Jesus' followers should preach boldly, fearing no shame from their peers in this world (10:26-27). What is now "covered" (hidden, 13:44) will then be revealed; and if God will reveal everything in the end anyway (m. 'Abot 4:4; Targ. Qoh. 12:13 in

36. Schweitzer made this verse central to his eccentric construct of Jesus' eschatology; his interpretation fails to "reckon with the composite character of the chapter" (Ladd 1974: 200; cf. Glasson 1963b: 99). Schweitzer came to this view before critically evaluating the Gospel sources, then continued to endorse it (see Perrin 1963: 32-33). Bultmann, by contrast, saw part of it as a spurious addition in view of the Matthean community's sufferings, ignoring the Mishna parallel (Albright and Mann 1971: 125). Nevertheless, the verse could be authentic and even stem from Q; Luke would probably have dropped the verse (Theissen 1991: 55), though its alleged confidence regarding the Jewish mission (Theissen's argument for pre-Matthean earliness in 1991: 55-56) may also misread the verse, given m. Soṭa 9:15. The interpretations of Jeremias (1958: 20) and Sabourin (1977) fail to interpret the saying properly in the context of the Jesus tradition as a whole.

37. Smith 1951: 153 cites a parallel in Sifra in which God and Israel are the master and servants in this saying; if Jesus' saying depends on the one later recorded in Sifra this passage presents Jesus' deity, but the fact and direction of dependence are unclear (cf. also the later Pesiq. R. 36:2, which applies it to God and the Messiah).

38. Because bilingual readers could render "Beelzebul" as "head of the household" (10:25; cf. MacLaurin 1978; Jeremias 1971: 7; Meier 1980: 111; Hagner 1993: 282), Jesus' lecture here may involve a wordplay, as was common in ancient instruction. His accusers played on the pagan Baal-Zebub, originally a local form of the Baal cult in Ekron (2 Kings 1:2). Stein 1997 thinks Beelzebub here represents the demonized Baal, not the devil per se; proposed associations with "flies" might also link the term with evil (b. Ber. 61a).

Lachs 1987: 185; 4QpNah 3.3; 1 Enoch 38:3; 49:4; b. Soṭa 22b; Ex. Rab. 8:2; Num. Rab. 9:12; 19:6; 2 Clem. 16; cf. 1 Enoch 98:6; Sir 1:30; 1QpHab 10.4-5; 1 Clem. 50), there is no reason to withhold any proclamations now.[39] What Jesus speaks "in darkness" (i.e., in secret — Judg 6:27; 1 Sam 28:8; 2 Kings 25:4; Is 29:15; 45:3, 19; Dan 2:22; 1 Cor 4:5; Pesiq. R. 8:2; Soph. *Antig.* 494; *Electra* 1493-94; Eurip. *Electra* 90; *Iph. Taur.* 1025-26; Ovid *Metam.* 7.192; Lucian *Phalaris* 1), Jesus' messengers (Lk 12:3) should reveal publicly. Because the flat housetops above the streets (24:17) provided easier hearing than the streets themselves, "shouting from the housetops" (10:27) hyperbolically underlines the boldness with which the disciples must make God's message known. A persecuted disciple should not fear (cf. 1:20; 17:7; Jer 1:8) because one would share Christ's sufferings (10:26), because God could destroy far more than the persecutors could (10:28), and because one would face nothing without one's caring Father permitting it (10:31).

Because God is the judge in the end, Jesus' agents should not fear even persecutors who threaten death (10:28). Mortals can destroy only one's body, but God can resurrect the body for damnation and destroy the whole person (for God's destroying "soul and flesh" in judgment on Assyria, cf. Is 10:18; see Gundry 1976).[40] The choice is not between courage and fear but be-

39. I assume an allusion here to the end time due to the context and the sense in Mark, although the saying in its Matthean context could refer merely to making Jesus' words known (cf. 11:25; Mk 4:22; Lk 8:17; 12:2; for varied applications cf. Jeremias 1972: 221n.66; Gundry 1982: 196). Malina and Rohrbaugh 1992: 90 argue that Jesus' audience would have heard the words positively, given villagers' suspicion of secrecy. For the revelation of what is hidden, see 1 Enoch 63:3; Mt 6:4; 11:25; 13:35, 44; Rom 2:16; 1 Cor 4:5; 1 Tim 5:24; for earlier deeds later coming to light, cf. Diod. Sic. 14.1.1-2.

40. Greeks and Romans often distinguished soul and body (e.g., Arist. *N.E.* 1.12.6, 1102a; *Soul* 1.5, 411b; Sall. *Catil.* 1.2, 7; Diog. Laert. *Lives* 3.63; Heraclitus *Ep.* 9, to Hermodorus; Crates *Ep.* 3; Epict. *Disc.* 1.25.21; Diog. *Ep.* 39, to Monimus; Plut. *Plat. Q.* 3.1, *Mor.* 1002B; Sext. Emp. *Pyrrh.* 1.79; Marc. Aur. *Med.* 6.32; *Greek Anth.* 7.109; cf. Long 1974: 171; la Croce 1981; Isaacs 1976: 15), even at times in animals (Arist. *Pol.* 1.2.10, 1254a), and generally believed in the soul's immortality (Herod. *Hist.* 2.123; Porphyry *Life of Pyth.* 19; Plato *Phaedo* 64CE, 80DE; *Phaedrus* 245C; *Rep.* 10.611BC; *Laws* 8.828D; Cic. *Tusc. Disp.* 1.8.18-24; *De Senect.* 20.78; Diog. Laert. *Lives* 6.1.5; 8.1.14, 28; 8.5.83; Dion. Hal. 8.62.1; Plut. *Divine Vengeance* 17, *Mor.* 560B; Sen. *Dial.* 6.26.7; 12.11.7; *Ep. Lucil.* 57.9; Apul. *Metam.* 11.6; Plot. *Ennead* 4.7-8; 7.12, 14; cf. Egyptian Book of Dead, spell 20, T.1.2-3; 30, P-1; 31a, P-1; 35a, P-1; 53, P-1; 79, P-1, S-2; 124; 177, P-1; *PGM* 4.646-48, 748-49; Nilsson 1957: 116-32; Lodge 1928: 394-409; Patterson 1965), with notable exceptions (e.g., Diog. Laert. 10.124-25; Lucretius *Nat.* 3.417-829; cf. Bels 1982). Many Greeks even saw the body as a tomb *(sōma-sēma),* e.g., Plato *Cratylus* 400BC; *Phaedo* 64-67; Plut. *Isis* 5, 28, *Mor.* 353A, 362B; Epict. *Disc.* 1.9.11-12; 3.13.17; 4.7.15; *Fr.* 26; Marc. Aur. *Med.* 3.7; 4:5, 41; 6.28; 11.3; Plot. *Ennead* 1.7.3.20-21; Patterson 1965: 20-21; Guthrie 1966: 154-58; cf. also hellenistic Jewish and Christian authors, e.g., Philo *Som.* 1.138-39; *Virt.* 67; Jos. *War* 2.155; 4 Ezra 7:96; Ep. Diogn. 6; Nock 1964b: 263; Hagner 1971: 85. Contrary to most commentators, most extant early Jewish writers also distinguished body and soul (e.g., Wis 9:15; 2 Macc 7:37; 14:38; Ep. Arist. 139; 236; Jos. *Apion* 2.203; 1 Enoch 22:7; 102:5; Test. Job 20:3; Test. Sim. 2:5; 4:8; Naph. 2:2-3; Asher 2:6; 4 Ezra 7:78; Apoc. Ezek. 1–2; Ps-Philo 3:10; t. Sanh. 13:2, 4; Sifre Deut. 306.28.3; b. Ber. 10a; 60b; Yoma 20b, bar.; Gen. Rab. 14:3, 9; Lev. Rab. 4:8; 34:3; Deut. Rab. 2:37; Qoh. Rab. 6:6-7, §1; Pesiq. R. 31:2; cf. Urbach 1979: 1:218-22, 248-49; Gundry 1976: 87-109) and usually seem to have regarded the latter

tween whom one will fear more (Minear 1950: 169). Judaism regarded the fear of God as an essential mark of piety (e.g., m. 'Abot 1:3; 3:9), although loving God was considered more crucial still (cf. Bonsirven 1964: 28). Jesus may here recall the Jewish martyr tradition, which exhorted its followers not to fear those who think they kill because eternal suffering awaits the soul that disobeys God's command (4 Macc 13:14-15). Although some Jewish teachers spoke of the instantaneous *annihilation* of the wicked at the judgment, "destroy" presumably refers to the same picture of judgment that recurs in the Synoptic tradition: Jesus will burn the wicked with "unquenchable," that is, eternal, fire (see on 3:12).

Jesus assures his disciples that they can trust God's sovereignty in their protection or their death (10:29-31). Often ancient teachers exhorted their hearers to reevaluate matters of worth (Epict. *Disc.* 1.4.16), as Jesus does here (cf. 6:26; 12:12). Sparrows were the cheapest commodity sold in the markets (as food for the poor), probably sold both in pairs and by fives (Deissmann 1978: 272-73); an *assarion* was a small coin that varied in value over time, but in the Roman east sometimes ranked less than one-sixteenth of a denarius, thus equivalent to less than an hour's wage (cf. 5:26; MacDonald 1989; Wheaton 1982: 792). Yet as worthless as sparrows were to people, God watched over them. Even some Jewish teachers who followed the traditional insistence that one should not pray for something as insignificant as a bird's nest (m. Ber. 5:3; Johnston 1982: 208-12) or even think that God's laws really concerned animals (Ep. Arist. 144; cf. 1 Cor 9:9-10) could recognize that God was sovereign over each bird's fate (Pesiq. Rab Kah. 11:16; Gen. Rab. 79:6; Qoh. Rab. 10:8, §1; Esth. Rab. 3:7; cf. Gen. Rab. 33:3; Pesiq. R. 48:2, 4).[41] *Qal waḥomer,* "how much more," then, may disciples be assured that nothing happens to them when God is "not looking" (Ps 121:4; cf. 1 Kings 18:27-29).[42]

This was good Jewish teaching (Bultmann 1968: 107), fitting the biblical perspective of a God sovereign over history. Indeed, he has counted every hair on his people's heads (10:30; cf. Acts 27:34; 1 Sam 14:45; 2 Sam 14:11; 1 Kings 1:52; b. B. Bat. 16a).[43] One may contrast God's gracious providence here and in

---

as immortal, at least for the righteous (Sir 9:12; Jos. *War* 1.84; 2.154-55, 163; 7.341-48; *Ant.* 17.354; 18.14, 18; Philo *Abr.* 258; *Mos.* 2.288; Test. Abr. 1.24-25A; 4, 9B; Ps-Phocyl. 108; Apoc. Mos. 13:6; 32:4; 33:2; Jos. and Asen. 27:10; Wolfson 1968: 395-413), albeit with exceptions (1 Macc 2:63; Jos. *Ant.* 18.16). The departure of the soul meant the body's death (Bar 2:17; Wis 16:14; Qoh. Rab. 5:10, §2; James 2:26; cf. Lucretius *Nat.* 3.121-23, 323-49).

41. Pace Vermes 1993: 86-87, the logion was not "distorted in the process of transmission" (based on divergence from the rabbinic lesson); God's sovereignty is assumed in the saying.

42. In its Matthean context, the line may mean that no sparrow nor disciple may suffer apart from God's plan, just as Jesus died according to God's purposes (16:21; 26:39; Cook 1988).

43. Although I think this interpretation more likely, one should also note Allison 1990, who thinks the text alludes to God in his omniscience counting hairs (Ps 40:12; 69:4), hence knowing rather than protecting. Allusion to a single hair figuratively represented what was tiny (cf. Pub. Syr. 186).

many Jewish texts (e.g., Wis 7:15-16; cf. Sent. Sext. 436)[44] with the more capricious Greek view of Fate or Fortune in pagan texts (e.g., Dion. Hal. 9.25.3; Apul. *Metam.* 10.13). Fate and Fortune play important explanatory roles in Greco-Roman history (e.g., Polyb. 1.4, 58, 62; Dion. Hal. 6.21.1; Diod. Sic. 1.1.3; 31.4.1; Plut. *Fortune of Romans, Mor.* 316C-326C; *Fortune or Virtue of Alexander, Mor.* 326D-345B; *Aemilius Paulus* 36.1) and poetry (e.g., Horace *Ode* 1.7.25; 1.31.10; 1.34.14-16; 1.35.17; 1.37.11-12; 2.1.3; 2.6.9; 2.17.16; 3.1.14-15; 3.24.6; 4.2.38; 4.13.22-23; 4.14.37; *Epode* 4.6; 13.15; *Carmen Saeculare* 25), and as a helpful plot device in novels (e.g., Petron. *Sat.* 29; Char. *Chaer.* 1.13.4; 2.8.4; 5.1.5; 5.5.2; 8.1.2; Ach. Tat. *Clit.* 1.3.2; 4.1.3; 5.11.1; 6.3.1; 7.13.1; Apul. *Metam.* 6.28; 7.16; 9.1; Philost. *V.A.* 4.1).[45]

If one faithfully confesses Jesus in one's witness to others, including earthly tribunals (10:17-20), Jesus will also faithfully confess one before God's tribunal, justifying one before him (cf. 12:36-37; Jn 12:42; 1 Tim 6:12-13; Rev 3:5).[46] He will also deny those who deny or are ashamed to testify boldly of him (10:32-33; Mk 8:38; 2 Tim 2:12; cf. Mt 16:24), though in practice mercy may mitigate this judgment for the repentant (26:34). Thus Tertullian protests that whereas the government tortured other detainees to make them confess their crimes, "the Christians alone you torture to make them deny" (*Apol.* 2.10; LCL

44. Jews were influenced by pagan ideas of Fate and Fortune (e.g., inscription in Carmon 1973: 100, 216; Gersht 1984; Sib. Or. 1.40. 294; 3.502, 513, 517, 571-72; 5.215, 227, 230, 245, 324; 11.221; Ep. Arist. 201), though most undoubtedly viewed these as identical with or executioners of God's purposes (see, e.g., Wis 19:4; Ep. Arist. 17, 195, 197, 210, 227, 231, 237-39, 243, 244, 246, 248, 251, 252, 255, 256, 266-72, 274, 276, 278, 282, 287, 290; Sib. Or. 1.304; 3 Macc 4:21; Ps-Philo 13:6; Test. Moses 12:4; Test. Job 37). For Josephus's historiography, see, e.g., *War* 2.162-65; 6.84, 268; *Ant.* 8.409, 419; 13.172-73; 18.13, 54; Bilde 1979; Martin 1981; Attridge 1986: 327; on Philo, see Winston 1976: 14-15.

45. From the classical period (e.g., Demosth. *Or.* 60, *Funeral Speech* 21; *4th Philippic* 38; *Answer to Philip's Letter* 15; *On the Crown* 289; Isoc. *Demon.* 29, *Or.* 1; *Panegyricus* 26, *Or.* 4) on (e.g., *ILS* 1980 in Sherk 1988: 238; *CIL* 6.32323.90-92 in ibid. 21; Mart. *Epig.* 4.73; 7.47; Juv. *Sat.* 9.135-36; 12.63-65; Plut. *Poetry* 6, *Mor.* 23DE; Dio Chrys. *64th Disc.* 8), the view that Fate or Fortune was sovereign prevailed. Some philosophers probably influenced the growth of this idea, though others contended for free will (cf., e.g., comments in Epicurus *Letter to Menoeceus* 134 in Grant 1953: 160; Lucretius *Nat.* 1.455-58; Cic. *De Fato; Topica* 15.59; Sen. *Dial.* 6.16.5; 7.23.2; *Ep. Lucil.* 54.7; Epict. *Disc.* 1.6; 1.12.25; 3.17; Plut. *On Fate, Mor.* 568B-74F; *Chance, Mor.* 97C-100A; Quint. 5.7.35; Marc. Aur. *Med.* 2.3; 4.2; 12.1.1; Diog. Laert. 1.35; 7.1.149; 9.1.7; 9.7.45; 10.144.16; Philost. *V.A.* 8.31; Plot. 3.1.10; in Stoicism in particular, see Murray 1915: 40-41; Long 1974: 163-70), but eastern astrology probably had a larger influence on the masses. The deities sometimes exercised more autonomy, especially in the earlier period (Paus. 8.37.1), but Fate often reigned even over gods (e.g., Herod. *Hist.* 1.91; Sen. *Dial.* 1.5.8; Jos. *Apion* 2.245); as Fate's dominance grew, many appealed to deities that they believed could free them from it (Horsley 1981: 20; Isis aretalogy in Grant 1953: 133; *PGM* 4.662-73; Apul. *Metam.* 11.6, 15). Burial inscriptions repeatedly emphasize the inevitability of Fate (e.g., Horsley 1987: 20-21, 25, 33-34; *CIL* 2.4313 in Sherk 1988: 168; *CIL* 11.1421 in ibid., 34; cf. Quint. 6.preface 1-2; Sen. *Apocol.* 3).

46. The prophecy of Rev 3:5 reflects the original Jesus tradition rather than the reverse; for Aramaisms in the Gospel saying, see Burkitt 1910: 19-20. Whereas Abrahams (1924: 192) doubts the Jewish use of periphrasis parallel to "angels/God" in Mt 10:32-33//Lk 12:8 (cf. Mt 18:14 with Lk 15:10), McNamara (1972: 95) thinks it common.

13). Jewish people often spoke of "confessing," that is, proclaiming, God (Abrahams 1924: 17; Smith 1951: 153; cf. Mt 12:36-37; Rom 10:9); denial of God and his commands was a heinous offense (Sandmel 1978b: 187). Jesus thus probably calls for a confession of faith in himself here equivalent to confession of faith in God (cf. also Gundry 1975: 214). At the very least, the logion, which may echo Daniel 7:13-14 (including the context of persecution), makes clear Jesus' distinctive soteriology: "it makes Jesus and his proclamation the deciding factors in the coming judgment" (Davies and Allison 1991: 214; cf. Jn 14:6).

Unrivaled Devotion to Jesus (10:34-39)

Cf. Lk 12:51-53; 14:25-27; 17:33; Jn 12:25. Although Jesus values peace (5:9; cf. Lk 2:14) and normally opposes swords (26:52), one should not think (cf. 5:17) that Jesus' mission brings peace rather than a sword (10:34).[47] Given the whole context of Jesus' ministry, the language may even indicate that Jesus' mission would inaugurate the messianic woes, the ultimate tribulation for his followers (Witherington 1990: 123; on the woes, see comment on 24:4-14).[48] The demands of the kingdom are so offensive to a world already convinced of its rightness that they provoke that world's hostility.

Jesus promises the opposition of unconverted family members (10:34-36). Many members of Matthew's audience may well have experienced ostracism from their families because of their commitment to Jesus; by recording this earlier tradition (cf. Lk 12:51-53) Matthew would thus encourage them. Although Jesus values families (5:27-32; 15:4-6; 19:4-9), the division his mission brings appears particularly in families (cf. 10:21).[49] Jesus' example demonstrates

47. Garland 1993: 118 cites Jewish traditions in which the Messiah would establish peace (Is 9:5-7; m. ʿEd. 8:7). The logion is surely authentic; to "cast peace" in the Lukan parallel is also Semitic (Witherington 1990: 121), and "I came" bears marks of authenticity (Semitisms, Qumran parallels — Witherington 1990: 120; Hill 1979: 66-67). Lk 12:51 renders the graphic Semitic idiom in less dramatic Greek ("division").

48. Matthew Black associates the "sword" with the final war against Belial in the Scrolls (1984: 287-94), but because it was standard metonymy for violence and war in Jewish literature (e.g., Gen 27:40; Ex 5:3; Jer 14:12; 15:2; 39:18; 41:2; 42:16-17; Ezek 5:2, 12, 17; 6:3, 8, 11-12; Mic 5:6; 6:14; Nah 2:13; Hag 2:22; Rom 8:35; Rev 6:4; 1 Enoch 14:6; 88:2; 90:19; 91:11-12; Jub. 5:9; 9:15; 20:6; 22:8; 23:22; CD 1.4; 1QM 11.11-12; 12.11-12; 15.3; 16.1; 1QpHab 6.10; 4QpNah 2.5; 2 Bar. 27:3-5; Sib. Or. 3.316, 689; Test. Jud. 23:3; t. B. Qam. 7:6; Sukk. 2:6), the sense need not be so narrow (cf. Tannehill 1975: 141-44, noting also the metaphorical and hyperbolic components of the image). Davies and Allison 1991: 218 list texts in which the sword represents eschatological judgment or suffering (including, e.g., Jub. 9:15; 1 Enoch 90:19; 91:11-12; 4QPsDan Aa; Ps. Sol. 15:7); for other examples, see Witherington 1990: 122.

49. This saying may be attested in a different form among so-called agapha (Jeremias 1964c: 76). Other passages in the Gospel tradition show that Jesus was not antifamily (5:32; 15:4-6; 19:9), but some ancient teachers may have been. Many Stoics, while upholding household codes, also despised relatives who did not share their philosophy (Diog. Laert. 7.1.33; Epict. *Disc.* 3.3.5; 3.15.11); Hesiod *W.D.* 182-85, 188-89 viewed children's ingratitude as a sign of the end time.

how this division is accomplished: although God's agents are "harmless" (10:16; 12:19-20), they proclaim the kingdom uncompromisingly and thus face hostility from others (13:57; cf. 12:46-50; Jn 7:5). Jesus' mission separates disciples from the values of their society, and society responds with persecution. Although strife between father-in-law and son-in-law was also viewed as tragic (Lucan *C.W.* 1.115-18), Jesus selects the specific example of in-laws he does (e.g., mother-in-law and daughter-in-law) because young couples generally lived with the man's family (Malina 1981: 101; Derrett 1973: 38; see comment on 8:14). Relations with mothers-in-law were not always ideal (Plut. *Bride* 35, *Mor.* 143AB; Juv. *Sat.* 6.231-32).

Jewish literature also recognized that one could not always trust friends (Sir 6:7-13; 12:8ff.), and that in the worst of times family members could become enemies (1 Enoch 100:2; Sib. Or. 1.75-76; 5.468-69). Micah 7:6 spoke of Israel's sin before their restoration; some Jewish interpreters thus applied the familial division of this text to the period of messianic woes, the great tribulation that would precede the Messiah's coming (m. Soṭa. 9:15; Pesiq. Rab Kah. 5:9; Song Rab. 2:13, §4; Pesiq. R. 15:14/15; cf. also Edgar 1958: 49). Some other Jewish writers associated familial division with the final tribulation without explicitly referring to Micah's prophecy (Jub. 23:16, 19; cf. 1 Enoch 56:7; Gk. Ezra 3:12-13; 2 Tim 3:2).

Jesus probably knows this tradition (cf. Grelot 1986), hence here indicates that his first coming has initiated that period of travail (24:8), just as his second coming will complete it (10:23; 24:29-31). No less radical grounds could justify the countercultural, apparently counterfamily, stance Jesus' ministry seemed to suggest to outsiders (cf. Hengel 1981b: 13; 1 Cor 7:26-31); those unconvinced that the kingdom was near would not be satisfied even with these grounds. The eschatological Elijah was to reconcile familial differences (Mal 4:6; Sir 48:1, 10), but Jesus here warns his followers to expect the messianic woes first.[50] The kingdom takes precedence over family ties (cf. 4:21-22; 8:21-22; Ex 32:27; Deut 13:6-10).

Jesus matters more than the approval or even civility of one's family (10:37). "Hate" (Lk 14:26) could mean "love less" (Mt 10:37) in both the Hebrew Bible and later Jewish literature (Manson 1979: 131; Ex. Rab. 51:8); Jesus undoubtedly employed the more graphic expression originally as hyperbole, and Matthew has translated more freely. Many viewed honoring one's parents, however, as the highest social obligation (Ep. Arist. 228; Jos. *Apion* 2.206; Ps-Phocyl. 8); even if some spoke of honoring one's teacher more (m. B. Meṣ. 2:11; p. Ḥag. 2:1, §10), no teacher would speak of "hating" one's parents by comparison. God alone was worthy of that role (Deut 13:6; 33:9; 2 Macc 7:22-23; cf. Gen 22:2-12; 4QTest. 16-17; Test. Job 4:5/6; Epict. *Disc.* 3.24.60; 4.1.107, 159; though cf. oaths of allegiance to emperors and the Roman state in *CIL* 2.172;

50. Hill 1972: 194, tentatively following McNeile 1915: 147, suggests that Jesus may have been hinting that he was not the messianic herald Elijah; one must evaluate this interpretation based on its cohesiveness with the rest of the Jesus tradition since the saying may, but need not, be read thus.

IGRR 3.137; *OGIS* 532; *ILS* 190; 8781; Sherk 1988: 31, 78); Jewish texts hence extolled those Gentiles who forsook the acceptance of their families by turning to Israel's God (Jos. and Asen. 12:12/11).

Yet Jesus calls for disciples to love him not only more than their families, but more than their own lives (10:38-39). Then, as today, people understood that the vast majority of people cling desperately to life (cf. Eph 5:29; Epict. *Disc.* 2.22.15-16). But the Gospel tradition emphasizes that once one becomes a follower of Jesus one's own life is forfeited; one chooses a path that could lead any day to one's execution for Christ's name (16:24).[51] In Jesus' day "taking up the cross" meant being forced to bear the instrument of one's execution past a jeering mob to the site of one's imminent death as a condemned criminal (e.g., Tasker 1961: 109; see Hengel 1977; cf. 16:24). The promise of eternal life should be sufficient motivation for one who genuinely believes Jesus' claims (cf. the parallel in Dalman 1929: 228), but disciples sometimes prove less committed than they suppose (26:41). That even the first disciples were not initially prepared for such a demand (26:56) does not mitigate the level of commitment the saying seeks from the Matthean community: if one wants to follow Jesus, one must be ready to *die*.

Honoring Christ's Agents (10:40-42)

Cf. Mk 9:41; Lk 10:16; Jn 13:20. The world persecuted disciples in Jesus' name (10:18, 22, 39; cf. 5:11), but some would welcome them in his name (10:41). One who loses one's own life (10:38-39) becomes a representive of Jesus (10:40-42; cf. 18:5; Mk 9:37; Lk 10:16; Jn 13:20), and one must receive a herald or ambassador in the same way one would receive the one who sent him (for the principle applied to an apostle, cf. 2 Cor 5:20–6:2, 11-13; 7:2-4). An early Jewish saying that may have been circulating in Jesus' day ran similarly: it was reckoned to one who received the sages as if that one had received God himself (Jeremias 1971: 254; Smith 1951: 154);[52] Jewish people viewed Israel as God's representative in a similar manner (b. Sanh. 58b; Bonsirven 1964: 49-50). For Jesus, however, it was not great sages but those who became like children — the epitome of dependence and powerlessness in antiquity — who were his representatives (10:42; 11:25; 18:5-6).[53]

51. In Pauline tradition this initial determination becomes itself a death to one's own right to make selfish choices (e.g., Rom 6:3-4; cf. Col 3:3, 5).

52. This repeats the more general *shaliaḥ* principle, which appears in this chapter (see comment on 10:5), but is most obvious here, with Jesus as God's agent and the disciples as his followers (with Witherington 1990: 136, 143; Davies and Allison 1991: 226-27).

53. Some later teachers said that you should reckon the good you hear from a child as if you had heard it from an adult; from an adult, as if from a sage; from Moses, as if from God (p. Sanh. 10:1, §9). Jesus expresses greater respect for one whose status is that of a child. The Ethiopic Jewish work *Te'ezaza Sanbat,* in which God declares that those who honor his Sabbath honor him and who reject his Sabbath reject him, is probably later (pace Boring 1995: 113).

As one treats God's prophet, so one treats the God who sent the prophet (Ex 16:8; 1 Sam 8:7). Matthew repeatedly emphasizes that disciples as Jesus' agents are his prophets, even greater than the prophets of old (5:11-12; 11:9; 13:17); he thus employs the titles "righteous" and "prophet" interchangeably in this passage (cf. 13:17; 23:29; cf. Deut. Rab. 1:6; not simply a class of teachers; cf. Hill 1965). This passage probably also evokes the Jewish legal image of the appointed agent, who carried the full authority of the one who had authorized him for the specific task on which he was sent (cf. Ladd 1974: 381; Smith 1951: 100; cf. comment on 10:5; for God's agent sending an agent, see Josh 11:15). Disciples were also "little ones," the easily oppressed and powerless who could not or would not defend themselves (10:42), and hence depended solely on God (18:3-6, 10; cf. 11:11, 25; Mk 9:37; 10:14-15).[54]

Receiving Jesus' representatives with even a cup of cold water (10:42; Mk 9:41) probably refers to accepting into one's home the missionaries who have abandoned their own homes and security to bring Christ's message (10:11; cf. also 25:35-40).[55] One must offer some gesture of hospitality to strangers, no matter how humble one's means (e.g., Eurip. *Electra* 357-63). A cup of cold water might be all that a peasant could offer, but hospitality given in faith to a prophet who requested it would be rewarded (cf. 1 Kings 17:12-16; 2 Kings 4:8-17). Although one should ideally offer food if one could (e.g., Hom. *Od.* 1.123-24), everyone would understand the significance of water as a sign of hospitality to a weary traveler; it appears even in pagan myths (Ovid *Metam.* 5.449-50; cf. Hom. *Od.* 15.312; 17.10-12). A Roman historian ridicules an emperor who rewarded a man for something as insignificant as cool water (Suet. *Claud.* 40), but Jesus rejects that sort of aristocratic perspective and values whatever sacrifice one can offer to show that one embraces his messengers. Some Cynics dispensed with cups, but this was rare (Diog. *Ep.* 6, 13). The typical "cup" in Jewish Palestine could not stand upright on a table (Safrai 1974/76b: 742), hence it would have to be passed from the host's hand into that of the guest.

The following narrative may illustrate the point twice: some would not receive a prophet who came in a prophet's name (11:7-19; cf. 10:41); John himself had to continue to "receive" Jesus, to embrace his identity in the midst of challenges to his faith (11:3-6).

54. Davies and Allison 1991: 229 suggest that "little ones" derives from depictions of the oppressed righteous in apocalyptic circles (citing Zech 13:7; 1 Enoch 62:11; 2 Bar. 48:19; the first reference derives from a context significant in early Christian apologetic — cf. comment on Mt 26:31, including eschatological use in the DSS). Vermes 1993: 162n.12 compares Qumran's "simple" ones (1QpHab 12.4; 1QH 2.9).

55. Others suggest that the text applies especially to harboring persecuted church leaders and disciples (Gundry 1982: 201-2). Some hold that "little ones" in Matthew refers especially to the least honored disciples rather than all disciples in general (cf. Agourides 1984).

The Doubts of a Man of God (11:1-6)

Cf. Lk 7:18-23. After Matthew rehearses for his own missionary church Jesus' instructions to his first disciples, he summarizes the actual historical mission as tersely as possible, moving almost directly from the instructions to Jesus' ministry in the cities where disciples had prepared the way (11:1; cf. 10:15, 23). In Luke's narrative concerning the seventy-two the disciples report the amazing victories God has given them in Jesus' name (10:17), and Jesus turns their attention to something greater (10:18-20). But Mark's account of the sending of the Twelve (6:7-13; cf. Lk 9:1-6) inseparably connects the disciples' mission (again summarized tersely — 6:30) with the end of John the Baptist's life, which Mark recounts at great length (6:14-29; cf. Lk 9:7-9). John must contact Jesus through messengers because John is in Herod's prison, soon to face execution for his bold proclamation (14:3-12). Disciples of the kingdom who prepare Jesus' way in power (11:1) need to remember the first one to prepare the way for Jesus (11:10); those who receive Jesus' power (10:7-8) must also bear his cross (10:17-39).

Most modern scholars, including even Bultmann, accept the saying in 11:5-6 as authentic words of Jesus (Davies and Allison 1991: 244). The saying is difficult to dispute: Jesus' roundabout response to John is characteristic of Jesus' responses, fitting both the messianic secret and a Near Eastern teaching style; the gospel for the "poor" coheres with other Q tradition about Jesus (5:3//Lk 6:20); and it exhibits Semitic structure. The setting of the saying also stands a good chance of being authentic.[1] The account is devoid of standard Christian portraits of Jesus (emphasizing atonement or Lordship) and traditional Christian titles ("coming one" hardly qualifies).[2] Further, although Matthew and other early

1. Meier 1994: 130 accepts the sayings, but, noting the divergent wording of the narrative, suspects that the wording for the setting may be secondary. Nevertheless, Matthew and Luke agree on the basic content of the narrative structure (Meier concurs), so either oral tradition or a written narrative must provide the framework for these otherwise isolated sayings; Jesus worded his sayings for memorization and transmission, but traditionaries felt more freedom to retell narratives in their own words (see the Introduction). The narrative structure also makes historical sense (see Davies and Allison 1991: 244).

2. Fitzmyer thinks "Coming One" alludes to Mal 3:1-4 (cf. Lk 3:15-17); Witherington asserts that if this suggestion is correct then Jesus replaces that model with a more Isaianic one, but he also stresses one of Fitzmyer's other suggestions, a background in Zech 9:9 LXX and Qumran texts (1QS 9.11; 4QPBless 3; Witherington 1990: 43). Yet the title appears characteristic to John in the tradition (Mt 3:11; though cf. 11:14).

Christians had reason to stress John's testimony for Jesus (3:14), he here reports John's doubts and does not even conclude with a clear statement of John's renewed faith (Meier 1994: 135). The tradition here is thus authentic, not a creation of early Christian imagination (Witherington 1990: 42-43, 165; Sanders 1993: 94; Wink 1989).[3]

By this narrative, Matthew encourages those whose faith is tested for the work for the kingdom (11:2-3, 6). One could argue that this narrative criticizes John's unbelief. Does not Jesus' response to John's question in 11:4-6 constitute a rebuke? And does not Jesus diminish John's status vis-à-vis that of the disciples in the second half of 11:11? Further, in the time of Matthew's source ("Q") some of John's followers may have been competing for their master's honor vis-à-vis that of Jesus (cf. Acts 18:25; 19:3; later, Daniélou 1964: 62; Ps-Clementine *Recognitions* 1.54); one can therefore see why some early Christian traditions would emphasize his weakness.

But an argument that views John negatively misses the very thrust of the passage. Jesus could confront John's question no more graciously than he does in 11:4-6, quite in contrast with how he addresses his opponents and even wayward disciples (16:23; 23:13-33); far from invoking judgment as on one who had seen much and believed little (11:21-24), he had John's disciples recount to John what they had now seen for the first time (11:4-5) and pronounced a blessing on him if he would persevere (11:6). He calls John his promised forerunner (11:10), Elijah (11:14). He further chides a generation for not receiving that prophet (11:18-19; cf. 10:41), and makes John the greatest figure of history so far (11:11), even if John does not get to hear all the compliments (11:7). ("Those born of women" was idiomatic biblical language for "human beings" in general.) When Jesus announces that disciples of the kingdom are greater than John, he is exalting the disciples, not minimizing John; he uses John for the comparison precisely because he is so significant in God's plan (see comment on 11:11).

John has already recognized Jesus' identity (3:14); now, in prison, he seems discouraged and doubting, but Matthew's biblically literate community might find this less startling than most modern readers. Pursued by Jezebel and finding that even the fire at Mount Carmel had not been sufficient to dislodge idolatry from the land, Elijah asked God to take his life (1 Kings 19:4). Pursued by Saul and frustrated by continual obstacles to God's promises, David nearly committed an act that would have stained the rest of his career, had God not intervened through wise Abigail (1 Sam 25:21-35). Most of his life the only prophet of his generation speaking judgment, torn by the hatred and impending destruction of people he loved, Jeremiah cursed the day of his birth (Jer 20:14-18; cf. 15:10). Dismayed by the long delays in God's promises to Israel, the psalmist protested his people's humiliation (Ps 89:38-51). Matthew shared the early Christian perspective that servants of God were frail like other people (cf.,

3. See Meier 1994: 832-37 for a thorough and convincing case that the claim to raise the dead goes back to Jesus (for the authenticity of the section, see also 130-37).

e.g., Jas 5:16-18; 1 Cor 15:9-10; 2 Cor 4:7-12). Limited weaknesses in generally reliable characters may even facilitate reader identification.

Thus it seems most likely that Matthew recorded John's struggle with doubt not to condemn John, but to encourage subsequent disciples (like the evangelists commissioned from his community) whose faith would be tested by hardships: "Blessed is the one who does not stumble on my account."[4] Yet even for such a prominent servant, Jesus provides a warning: no mortal is incapable of falling. In view of its serious use in the Gospel tradition (e.g., 5:29-30; Mk 9:42-47; cf. especially 21:42-44), the language of stumbling here suggests that one's response to Jesus determines one's place at the final judgment (Witherington 1990: 43-44).

Second, God does not always act the way his servants expect him to act (11:2-3). According to the Gospel tradition, John's expectations of Jesus were correct but incomplete, as would be self-evident to eschatologically oriented followers of Jesus after the completion of his earthly ministry. Some scholars doubt the compatibility of this narrative with the one in Matthew 3; after all, how could John recognize Jesus' Messiahship yet later question his identity (e.g., Kraeling 1951: 130; Mason 1992: 159)? But the narratives make excellent sense together, for Jesus' ministry had so far fulfilled *none* of John's eschatological promises; John had preached that the Coming One would baptize in the Spirit and fire, casting the wicked into a furnace of fire (3:10-12). John's questions arose *when* he heard of Jesus' deeds (11:2-3), not in spite of them. Thus when John asks if they should look for "another," "another" is in an emphatic position and the specific term emphasizes "another of a different kind" (Gundry 1982: 205). In contrast to the expectations of some of his contemporaries, John's expectations about the Messiah's future role were right; but John did not know that Jesus had another mission before the coming judgment. Jesus urged him to believe nonetheless.[5]

Third, Matthew and his tradition contend that the answers to John's questions were already present in Scripture (11:4-6). Jesus may not yet baptize in fire or even in the Spirit, but his signs showed that he was clearly the Spirit-endowed One who would baptize in the Spirit later (3:11, 16). As Jesus performed miracles, he alluded to a passage in the Old Testament, Isaiah 35:5-6, which mentioned some of the same signs he was performing. In so doing he reminded John's disciples that the works he was performing might be less dramatic

4. The narrative may also contribute to the radical distinction between fallible disciples and their Messiah, though Matthew's disciples provide a foil for Jesus less stark than do Mark's.

5. Many of those Jesus touched and healed in these narratives were ceremonially unclean, therefore not to be touched; indeed, even blemishes excluded one from holy service (Lev. 21:23; m. Bek. 7; CD 6-7, 15; 1QM 7; in Greek cults, see Ferguson 1987: 141; Plut. *R.Q.* 73, *Mor.* 281C). Some therefore suspect that John objected to Jesus' violation of ritual purity regulations (cf. Johnson 1977: 133). In view of the narratives themselves, however, most scholars who accept both accounts of John in Matthew believe that it was the discrepancy between John's promise of fire-baptism and Jesus' ministry of "mere" healings that disturbed him (Dibelius 1949: 77; Ladd 1974b: 42; F. F. Bruce 1978: 20; Gundry 1982: 206; Witherington 1990: 43; Davies and Allison 1991: 244; Hagner 1993: 300; Meier 1994: 132)

than a fire-baptism, but Isaiah had already offered them as signs of the messianic era (Goppelt 1964: 77; Jeremias 1972: 116; Borg 1987: 165).[6] The deeds Jesus lists were considered messianic in some streams of Jewish thought (Stanton 1995a: 186-87 cites 4Q521; 11QMelch 18); 4Q521 may blend imagery from Isaiah 35 with that of Isaiah 61 and other precedents, perhaps Elijah's miracles (for discussion, see Wise and Tabor 1992; Tabor and Wise 1992; Collins 1994).

Besides John's messengers' "seeing" Jesus perform the miracles of Isaiah 35, Jesus allowed them to "hear" the good news he preached to the poor (11:4-5), fulfilling Isaiah 61:1 (cf. Lk 4:18).[7] Jesus knew his mission, and John's doubts did not make him insecure; but he knew that John would recognize the words of Scripture. While he is using Isaiah, he reminds John that God himself would be a stumbling stone to Israel and Judah (Is 8:14-15), but not to those who trusted him (Is 8:13; Mt 11:6). Although the phrase derives from Q (Lk 7:22) and is how ancients sometimes expected witnesses to testify of their works (Jos. *Life* 263), it may be significant on the Matthean level that Jesus here uses a characteristic Matthean phrase associated with witness when he instructs John's disciples: "*As you go,* tell John" (cf. 10:7).

Receiving Prophets and More-Than-Prophets (11:7-15)

Cf. Mk 1:2; Lk 7:24-28; 16:16. Those who embraced Jesus' prophets embraced him (10:41); yet most of Israel had accepted neither John the prophet nor Jesus (11:16-19), hence they invited greater judgment than wicked cities that had heard less of God's message (11:20-24). After encouraging John's faith, Jesus praises John's mission (11:7-15). Perhaps he does so only after the messengers' departure (11:7; Lk 7:24) because it is not for a disciple to know the magnitude of his or her service until the final day (10:26; 25:21), but in any case Jesus used the event that had just transpired as an opportunity to provide the crowds an object lesson about the kingdom (11:11-12).[8]

First, John's sacrificial lifestyle proved that he was truly a servant of God (11:7-8). In parallel questions, Jesus begins by affirming what John was not: first, he was not a moral weakling, easily blown by public opinion or human authority (contrast his persecutor in 14:5; cf. 21:46; 22:46). People who proved too weak for the test that awaited them were compared with the weak, tall papyrus reeds, easily moved simply by the wind (1 Kings 14:15; 2 Kings 18:21; 3 Macc

6. Because these verses are likely authentic, Sanders thinks that the historical Jesus did see his miracles in terms of Is 35, hence either that he was fulfilling the prophets' hopes or that their eschatological promises would soon be fulfilled (1993: 168; cf. also Witherington 1990: 44).

7. For "seeing" and "hearing" together, cf., e.g., 13:13; Jer 23:18; Acts 2:33; 4:20; 8:6; 22:15 (the Lukan usages may follow Lk 7:22Q); Rev 22:8.

8. If the Baptist sect later provided competition, Jesus' positive evaluation of the Baptist rather than Christian imagination would seem most likely to stand behind the Gospel tradition praising John (cf. Witherington 1990: 34, following Wink 1968).

2:22; cf. Is 42:3; Ps. Sol. 8:5; Mt 12:20; Babrius 36; a later example in Manson 1979: 68); in this respect he may compare favorably with Jesus' disciples (cf. 8:26). The banks of the Jordan, the site of John's baptism, hosted reeds growing as high as five meters; this may have provided the immediacy of the image (cf., e.g., Gundry 1982: 207; Theissen 1991: 26). John was no easily bent reed.[9]

Second, John was no pampered prince or court prophet who might be tempted to prophesy for hire. Some genuine royal prophets had found a home in royal courts, but only in those few generations when kings were godly enough to welcome their counsel (or when rare kings themselves met the ideal of being prophetically empowered themselves; cf. 1 Sam 10:1, 5-6; 2 Sam 23:2-3). In most generations false prophets outnumbered true prophets there even when they claimed to be Yahweh's prophets, because they were really the king's prophets (1 Kings 22:22-23). In times when true prophets were severely persecuted, some of them lived in the wilderness, as in the days of Elijah (1 Kings 17:3; 18:13; cf. 2 Kings 4:38-44; 6:1-3). John was a prophet in that mold. He had nothing to gain from his prophesying except the approval of his God.[10]

By contrasting John's wilderness lifestyle favorably with the luxury of a royal court, Jesus both praises one model and denigrates the other. Although Herod Antipas was only a tetrarch, he would have been the first "king" to come to most of Jesus' Galilean hearers' minds (Theissen 1991: 36). Similarly his palace, consisting of more than one building, could also be described in the plural as "houses" (Jos. *Life* 66; Theissen 1991: 36); or perhaps Jesus alludes to the fact that Antipas had another fortress palace at Machaerus, where John was imprisoned (14:3; France 1985: 194). Had Jesus' words been reported to Antipas, the latter might have taken them personally whether Jesus intended them that way or not. Although John the Baptist's public denunciation of Antipas's sin led to his imprisonment (14:3-5), John's fate does not lead Jesus to speak much more guardedly.[11]

Second, what makes a servant of God great is the message that servant bears (11:9-10, 13-14). Unlike Elijah and unlike the disciples, John in the Gospel tradition reveals no signs (cf. Jn 10:41), but what made him the greatest

9. Davies and Allison 1991: 247 suggest that the reeds evoke the *yam suph,* Sea of Reeds, in Ex 14–15, hence "Did you go out into the wilderness to see a man repeat the wonders of the exodus?" (cf. people who did so in Jos. *Ant.* 20.97-99); but this, along with their suggestion that royal attire might suggest messianic expectation, makes too specific a potentially broader allusion (tall reeds typically swayed in the wind — Hepper 1992: 70). Still less likely is a misunderstanding of the Aramaic (Schwarz 1996). For a survey of other interpretations (including Aesop's fable *Reed,* later recurring in rabbinic texts), see Theissen 1991: 27. Some views presuppose that Jesus here depicts John as a reed, but the text indicates that Jesus depicts a reed as what John was *not*.

10. This model would also appeal to hellenistic readers mistrustful of mendicant philosophers' motives, hence impressed by simplicity (Liefeld 1967: 246, citing Philost. *V.A.* 1.33; 2.25; 3.50-51).

11. Theissen 1991: 28-41 suggests that even the "reed" is a backhanded allusion to Antipas, arguing for the reed as Antipas's emblem on coins before A.D. 26 (33-34). Although the allusion itself could be broader, the context offers some support for Theissen's proposal, and if he is right, the saying must have originated in Palestine while the memory of Antipas's reed emblem remained fresh — probably in the late 20s, i.e., the time of John's ministry (cf. pp. 39-41).

prophet until that point was that he had the honor of introducing Jesus himself. The greatness of John thus implies something about the greatness of Jesus. At the least this made Jesus the Messiah (Jeremias 1966a: 130). Yet Matthew surely intends much more (1:23). Because the text Jesus cites to prove his case refers to preparing God's way (Mal 3:1), and Jewish tradition *usually* viewed Elijah as preparing God's rather than the Messiah's way (cf. Edgar 1958: 48; Manson 1979: 69; Mal 4:5-6), Jesus dramatically implies his own divine status here (Gundry 1975: 214), although his first disciples probably would not have dared assume he meant that.[12]

Jewish people usually viewed the era of the prophets as ending with Malachi (cf. Keener 1991b: 77-91); Jesus continues it until John, who becomes the pivotal first voice of the new order when those greater than the prophets (5:12; 10:41; 13:17; 23:34) will speak. Thus John's movement represents "the dividing line between the old and the new age" (Dibelius 1949: 50), or at least the first stage of the new age. But Jesus' concern here is hardly neat historical divisions to aid students memorizing time lines;[13] instead he may allude to the Jewish recognition that the law and prophets pointed to the coming messianic era (b. Ber. 34b; Sanh. 99a; Shab. 63a; earlier attested in Acts 3:24), which had now confronted them in his own ministry (12:28).

Jesus' praise of the Baptist in Matthew 11:9-11//Luke 7:26-28 is certainly authentic; the later church, sometimes concerned with John's undue popularity, would hardly have invented it (Hill 1979: 46; Stanton 1995a: 167-68). Yet it is quite easy for those unfamiliar with ancient Jewish rhetorical practices to misunderstand the character of his praise. The suggestion that Jesus denigrates John in 11:11 ("the least in the kingdom is greater than he")[14] rests on inadequate under-

12. The formula quotation resembles those in Qumran (Davies and Allison 1991: 249 cite CD 1.13; 19.16; 16.15; 4QFlor 1.16; 4QCatena a 1-4.7; 5-6.11; 1QpHab 3.2, 13-14; 11QMelch 2.15), which *might* suggest transmission in a source sympathetic toward the Baptist before Q, or may have echoed the language of wilderness sectarians appropriate to speaking of John — or may simply represent one of the standard cultural options preferred here by coincidence or as characteristic of Jesus' style (from Mark; cf. Mt 21:13; 26:31; cf. perhaps "it was said" in 5:21, 27, 31, 33, 38, 43).

13. The debate as to whether John belonged to the old or new order may owe more to the ambiguities of Greek grammar than to either Matthew's or Luke's peculiar constructions of salvation history. Both probably envisioned John as somewhat transitional and viewed the newness of God's kingdom in terms of salvation-historical promise and fulfillment rather than a radical discontinuity with God's past historical acts. One's reading of the rest of the Gospel, rather than grammatical matters, will decide one's reading of this passage: some see here the continuing validity of the law (Barth 1963: 64; Vermes 1993: 20), others its fulfillment and completion (Meier 1980: 123).

14. This is a central argument for Crossan 1991a: 237-38, who thereby seeks to oppose Jesus to John's apocalyptic message. The suggestion that Jesus, the disciple of an apocalyptic seer and the teacher of an eschatological movement, was himself antieschatological, dismisses all available evidence to support a theory without evidence and strains our sense of historical plausibility. Later Christians would not likely have conformed Jesus to John (the competition), but his own contemporaries sometimes compared him with John or with Elijah (16:14), who in Gospel tradition was the background for John (3:4; 11:14; 17:12), *despite* John's lack of signs; they viewed both as prophets (e.g., 21:11, 26, 46).

standing of ancient Jewish speech patterns. The editor of Kings allowed superlative praise of two kings to stand (2 Kings 18:5; 23:25); the editor of Joshua likewise probably spoke hyperbolically in affirming that God had never listened to such a human entreaty before (Josh 10:14; cf. Ex 8:13; 2 Kings 6:18). Jesus' contemporaries and successors developed hyperbolic and superlative praise still further: rabbis called Johanan ben Zakkai "the least" of Hillel's eighty disciples not to demean Johanan but to praise Hillel as a teacher (ARN 28, §57B). Thus Kraeling (1951: 139) comments that 11:11 exemplifies standard Jewish rhetoric:

> In a single passage in the Mekhilta, for instance, we have statements about both Joseph and Moses that use the same expression. About Joseph it is said, "there is not among his brethren one greater than he," and about Moses "there is not in Israel one greater than he." As used in Jewish texts such statements are not to be taken as blanket judgments. . . .

Further, Jesus' division of time into eras hardly means that John would be excluded from the future kingdom; those before the kingdom nevertheless would participate in it (8:11).

John's role was great because of the greatness of the one he introduced. If disciples of the kingdom have a greater role than John, it is not because they are more devout than he was; it is because they proclaim a fuller message of the kingdom, because they can look back and understand what John did not (see above on 11:2-3): the kingdom is not only future but was present in Jesus (11:12; 28:18-20). The "least" in the kingdom is greater than John in the sense that anyone in the kingdom has a fuller message than those who spoke beforehand; but in another sense of the phrase, the "least in the kingdom" is the greatest in the kingdom because God evaluates disciples according to their faithfulness in deferring all honor to him (18:1-4).

Finally, the kingdom belongs to those who contend for it (11:12; cf. Lk 16:16). The gospel tradition agreed with what was probably the prevailing Jewish view of that era: roles may be determined by God's gracious calling, but the calling does not erase human responsibility (cf. Jos. *Ant.* 18.13). Many people thought that the kingdom would come by violent revolution against the Gentile nations, a view that Jesus clearly rejected (5:5, 9, 41). Some think that Jesus is rejecting such a program here, censuring revolutionaries or social bandits (e.g., Cullmann 1956b: 20-21; Betz 1968: 53; Oakman 1992: 121; cf. Moore 1989). Others take the more likely approach that Jesus censures those who opposed Jesus, John, and the kingdom (Catchpole 1978; Thiering 1979; Patte 1987: 161; Blomberg 1992a: 188). On this approach, one might well read "violence" as "forcible acquisition,"[15] in which case Jesus here reprimands those who laid claim to the kingdom but without just, legal claim (Llewelyn 1994: 156). Like

15. E.g., Dion. Hal. 6.81.3; probably Babrius 102.12. Llewelyn 1994: 130-62 shows that this is a frequent sense of the term in legal complaints (e.g., *P. Oxy.* 49.3468; *P. Hal.* 1.col. 8, lines 166-85; *P. Lond.* 1.45; 2.401; *P. Tor.* 3; Athenian law on pp. 147-51).

the wicked tenants of 21:33-43, these people seek to lay claim to the kingdom "without God's consent" (Llewelyn 1994: 156-57, 162).

But especially in its Lukan form the text does not read like censure, and it is not clear that Matthew intends the saying in this sense either.[16] This logion may be a wisdom teacher's riddle (Stein 1978: 18): Jesus regularly borrowed images from his society and applied them in shocking ways, and thus may speak favorably here of *spiritual* warriors who were storming their way into God's kingdom now (10:34-35).[17] One second-century Jewish tradition praises those who passionately pursue the law by saying that God counts it as if they had ascended to heaven and taken the law forcibly, which the tradition regards as greater than having taken it peaceably (Sifre Deut. 49.2.1). These were the people actively following Jesus, not simply waiting for the kingdom to come their way.[18]

Rejecting Diverse Messengers (11:16-19)

Cf. Lk 7:31-35. By a sharp parable Jesus pronounces judgment on his generation that has rejected something greater than the law and prophets rejected by many of their ancestors (cf. 12:39, 41, 42, 45; 23:29-36).[19]

First, Jesus teaches here by means of graphic illustrations, consistent with his usual style (11:16-17). Probably he compares his opponents to spoiled children, but this matter is debated; the parable of complaining children (11:16-17) can fit this context (11:18-19) in one of two ways. (If one speculates on the nature of the saying before it came into the present context — some interpreters assume that the saying was originally handed on independently — one can hypothesize almost any meaning for it. But even in this context, one can defend both views.)

Some interpreters suggest that the children represent Jesus and John, Jesus addressing the generation from the vantage point of joy and John of mourning;

16. Jesus' opening words about the kingdom and "force" may well be in the middle voice ("the kingdom has been forcing its way forward"; cf. Jos. *Ant.* 20.206; see Hunter 1944: 55; Ladd 1974b: 71; Young 1995: 49-55); "violent persons seizing the kingdom," however, must refer, positively or negatively, to human activity in response to God's. In the end, Schnackenburg 1985: 101 rightly observes that the original sense of 11:12-13 is obscure ("dunkel"); for a survey of various views, see Hagner 1993: 306-7.

17. Many see the reference either to disciples storming their way into the kingdom or at times of their "forcing" or "pressing" the kingdom to come (cf. A. B. Bruce 1979: 173; Argyle 1963: 86; Vermes 1993: 140; Papone 1990; Häfner 1992).

18. Scholars frequently object that the language of violence here is always used negatively (France 1985: 195), but Jesus' parables show that he did not scruple to employ shocking images for the advance of God's reign, such as brutal tyrants (Mt 18:25, 34), unjust judges (Lk 18:2), an unexpected thief (Mt 24:42-43), and perhaps a naively benevolent landowner (Mk 12:6).

19. For a defense of the basic authenticity of 11:16-19, cf., e.g., Koenig 1985: 20-21. See also Meier 1994: 150: early Christianity did not seem highly tolerant of "sinners," so one should accept (on the criterion of discontinuity) that Jesus ate with them, hence the probable authenticity of the charge in 11:18-19.

yet the generation rejects both witnesses (e.g., Wimmer 1982: 108; France 1985: 196-97; Witherington 1990: 50). In this context, the identification of the children with Jesus and John is possible, because "children" need not refer back to "generation"; the whole following story, rather than the first noun that followed, could answer parabolic questions like "To what can I compare this generation?" (cf., e.g., 13:24, 45). On this reading, the children's complaint is true: Jesus and John approached the generation from two angles, but the other children would not play either game. Jesus scandalously paints the kingdom in terms of children's play. But this assumes an exact analogy that among other things would require two groups of children, one piping and the other mourning, a picture not explicit in this text (Dodd 1961: 15-16; Schweizer 1975: 264) unless simply assumed from the children's gender (Gundry 1982: 212; see below).

Another interpretation seems more likely. Children in the marketplace complaining that others would not play their games would strike most ancient hearers as spoiled. The children's lines, translated back into Aramaic, seem to exhibit a funeral meter and rhyme, as if they were a mock funeral dirge itself (Jeremias 1971: 26). These spoiled children thus resemble Jesus' opponents, who are dissatisfied no matter what (Dodd 1961: 16; Jeremias 1972: 160-61). They piped to John, and he would not dance (11:17a, 18); they wailed to Jesus, but he refused to mourn (11:17b, 18). This interpretation makes the analogy between the parable and its application less exact, but makes more sense of the image.

In either case, the striking image of the parable is clear: the generation is committed to refusing the truth, even if fickle in its reasons for doing so (cf. Is 29:11-12; less relevant, Eph 4:14).[20] The piping refers to weddings (where men would do the round dance — Jeremias 1972: 161),[21] and the dirge refers especially to the women's role in funeral processions (children sometimes played burying a grasshopper — Jeremias 1972: 161). Matthew's term for "mourning" indicates "beating the breast," a typical eastern Mediterranean expression of grief omitted by Luke (cf. Jeremias 1972: 27). Further, mourners always expected all bystanders to join in funeral processions (Jos. *Apion* 2.205); later rabbis might exempt their students from such duties, but only under special circumstances (ARN 4A; 8, §22B). Most importantly, the parable's point is clear, on either reading: the generation rejects both John and Jesus (11:18-19).

Second, God has different kinds of servants for different missions, but God's people should embrace them all (11:18-19). Whereas neither Jesus nor

20. In a wide variety of ancient texts, both Greek and Jewish, children's games convey the image of inconsistency; see Flusser 1981: 151-53, summarized in Jones 1995: 268. For children's fickleness, see also Epict. *Disc.* 3.15.12.

21. Flutes were, of course, also used for mourning (e.g., 9:23; Sib. Or. 3.488; this would fit the parallel with the dirge) and for workers, e.g., as they treaded grapes with their feet (Lewis 1983: 125; *Select Papyri* 1:64-67). But the conjunction with dancing indicates antithetical rather than synthetic parallelism with the dirge-singers (cf. analogous contrasts in Eccl 3:4; Eurip. *Alcestis* 343-47; Propertius *Eleg.* 2.7.11-12), hence presumably a wedding (cf., e.g., Jer 31:13; b. Ketub. 17a); wedding joy was the opposite of mourning; see comment on 9:15.

John accumulated earthly resources for earthly pleasure, Jesus accepted invitations to urban banquets (cf. 9:10-15; Rom 14:17), while John was a wilderness prophet whose diet was locusts (3:4) and who never banqueted (cf. Jer 16:8). Jesus came partly as God's ambassador to initiate relations with sinners (9:10-13), whereas John primarily took the role of biblical prophets in times of persecution (3:7); Jesus was a missionary within the culture, John a critic from outside it. Both models had biblical precedent (e.g., David versus Jeremiah), but were appropriate for different situations.

Third, Jesus clarifies the inconsistencies behind the world's dogmatic disbelief (11:18-19). Responding to the inconsistencies of critics, thereby suggesting that ill-will rather than logic motivates their criticisms, was acceptable rhetorical practice (Phaedrus 4.7.21-24). John came leading disciples to fast over Israel's sin (9:14; 11:18), but Jesus came celebrating the kingdom like a wedding feast (9:15-17; 11:19; 22:2); each did what was appropriate to his mission (Linton 1976: 178). Yet despite the initial popularity of both prophets, the generation as a whole ultimately rejected both approaches. The charge that John the prophet "has a demon" could suggest "prophetic" madness or an association between recluses and possession (cf. *P. Lond.* 42.9-13), but it may suggest a familiar spirit, such as those that belonged to magicians (Kraeling 1951: 11-12; cf. Aune 1983: 135; idem 1987: 56); although they would not seek to enforce any punishment in the relatively pluralistic Judaism of first-century Palestine, his accusers were slandering him as being guilty of a capital offense. Likewise, the charge that Jesus was a "glutton and a drunkard" alludes to the "rebellious son" of Deuteronomy 21:20 — also a capital offense (cf. Jeremias 1972: 160; though later rabbis severely curtailed the applicability of the text and limited it to minors in a certain age range — cf. m. Sanh. 8:1-2; b. Sanh. 72a, bar.).[22] The charge may have been exaggerated from some maligning him with illegitimate birth (Stauffer 1960: 16; cf. 1:18-20; Jn 8:41); because he did not eat according to Pharisaic purity regulations (Koenig 1985: 18); or more likely because he, though the eldest son, had left his family to minister (cf. 8:21-22; Koenig 1985: 23); or perhaps most likely simply from the fact that he accepted invitations to banquets with those less than scrupulous in the law (9:9-13).

Although other texts speak of prophets condemning their wicked generations (e.g., Jub. 23:14, 15; Sib. Or. 1.199), Jesus specifically condemns his gen-

22. Such a charge shamed the family (Prov 28:7). Greek philosophers, including Plato (cf. Lodge 1928: 27-31, 65, 343-54), also condemned gluttony and enslavement to the belly (Epict. *Disc.* 2.9.4; Sen. *Dial.* 7.20.5; *Ep. ad Lucil.* 60:4; Plut. *Pleasant Life Impossible* 3, *Mor.* 1087D; Diog. Laert. 2.34; Philostr. *V.A.* 1.7; cf. Hor. *Ep.* 1.18.21-25; Juv. *Sat.* 2.114; Mart. *Epig.* 2.40; 3.17.3, 22.1-5; 5.70, 74; 7.20; 11.86; 12.41; Ach. Tat. 2.23.1; gluttony and drunkenness in Plut. *Educ.* 7, *Mor.* 4B), and one of the vices the Diaspora Jewish philosopher Philo condemns most strongly is gluttony and its source, a person accommodating the "belly," the place of irrational desire (e.g., *Opif.* 158-59; *Leg. Alleg.* 3.159; *Migr.* 66; *Som.* 2.155; *Spec. Leg.* 1.192, 281; 4.91; cf. Wolfson 1968: 2:225-37; cf. also 3 Macc 7:10-11; 4 Macc 1:3; Phil 3:19; Syr. Men. *Epit.* 6-8; Test. Mos. 7:4; Apoc. Elijah 1:13); the two forms of gluttony are eating and drinking (Philo *Som.* 2.155; cf. *Spec.* 1.148). Aristocratic Romans were known for gluttony (Barrow 1968: 26).

eration for the ultimate offense: they have consummated the sins of previous generations by rejecting God's ultimate agent (23:31-32, 35). In the very different ministries of Jesus and John, the kingdom confronted that generation from two opposing prophetic models, and the generation as a whole rejected both opportunities.

Finally, true wisdom is vindicated in the eyes of those whose opinions count, that is, the wise (11:19). If some people choose to reject God's message, which he has confirmed by strong evidences, this hardly brings the message into question; it merely brings into question either the sense or the moral honesty of those who reject it. Wisdom's "deeds" here alludes loosely back to Christ's "deeds" in 11:2 (Meier 1980: 124; Gundry 1982: 213; Patte 1987: 157, 202), that is, his miracles (cf. 11:20), paving the way for the identification of Christ and wisdom in 11:28-30. One may compare also Matthew's ready adaptation of Q tradition for wisdom to Christ in 23:24.[23] It is unclear to us whether Matthew's implied audience is familiar enough with the Q tradition to recognize the later change (assuming that Luke reports the earlier form), but the redaction does suggest the perspective of the author. Throughout Matthew, however, Jesus the sage articulates and epitomizes wisdom more fully than any other (13:54; cf. 23:34), and such wisdom would constitute the standard for eschatological vindication or condemnation (7:24-27; 12:37, 42).

Unrepentant Cities Judged (11:20-24)

Cf. Lk 10:12-15. Jesus cries out laments against Jewish cities most exposed to his miracles; none are known to have been particularly hostile to Jesus, but their reception was not close to commensurate with their opportunity. In the logic of Matthew's narrative, these were the cities where Jesus had preached (11:1) after his disciples prepared the way (10:15, 23), carrying on his original mission of preaching the kingdom (9:35).

Those who attribute all oracular activity to the later church may doubt the authenticity of these verses (Boring 1982: 147), but given other evidence that Jesus stands within the Old Testament prophetic tradition that argument for inauthenticity is groundless. The mention of Galilean cities not found in the Old Testament, such as Capernaum and Chorazin (about two miles apart), suggests

23. Jeremias regards Wisdom here as a periphrasis for God, suggesting that Luke's addition of "of God" in 11:49 (par. Mt 23:34) is secondary (1972: 162; 1971: 10). Luke's "children" (7:35) may also be secondary (cf. Sir 4:11), but the sense is much the same as here: wisdom is vindicated by her deeds, i.e., the deeds of her children. Witherington 1990: 51-52 sees pre-Matthean Wisdom Christology here; he may be correct (though I am skeptical of his argument here, revised in his later work, that Matthew does not emphasize Wisdom Christology elsewhere; cf. Deutsch 1990). Pheme Perkins and others argue that in Q Jesus sees himself as Wisdom (Mt 11:19, 25-30; 23:34, 37-39), and that Paul's christological hymns reflect the same Christology (Thompson 1985: 251-52, citing Fuller and Perkins 1983: 55, 63; see Thompson 1985: 261).

an early Palestinian tradition (Burkitt 1910: 14).[24] The prophecy does not reflect later Christian preaching (Theissen 1991: 51n.73)[25] and may reflect signs of an Aramaic origin (Witherington 1990: 166); it may also presuppose the early lack of Christian communities in Tyre and Sidon, in contrast to the situation that obtained by the late 50s at the latest (Acts 21:3-6; 27:3; Theissen 1991: 52).[26] Finally, later Christians might have been loathe to fabricate opposition to Jesus' ministry in his adopted town (Witherington 1990: 166). Indeed, far from testifying that the saying is a later Christian invention (so Bultmann 1968: 112),[27] Capernaum's unrepentance suggests that the saying dates to Jesus' lifetime; Capernaum later became a center of Galilean Christianity (cf., e.g., rabbinic literature's "Jacob of Capernaum").

Following the ancient Near Eastern practice of judgment oracles against other nations, prophets like Isaiah (13–23), Jeremiah (46–51), Ezekiel (25–32), and Amos (1:3–2:3) denounced the sins of various nations in succession; some more recent Jewish oracles had done the same (Sib. Or. 3.295-49; cf. even Plut. *Divine Vengeance* 15, *Mor.* 558F-559C). Like the biblical prophets, however, Jesus prophesies woes against those who claim to be God's people (e.g., Is 22; Jer 2–11; Ezek 24; Amos 2:4–3:8; cf. Mt 18:7; contrast 11:6); God reiterated that he was God of all the earth and would judge Israel as justly as other peoples (Amos 3:2; 9:7; Is 10:9-11). Echoing the language of Isaiah, Jesus prophesies against Capernaum (Is 14:14-15; cf. 5:14; Jub. 24:31; Suet. *Calig.* 22); like the king of Babylon in Isaiah 14, Capernaum thought highly of itself, but God's opinion was quite different (Harrington 1982: 49-50).[28] This passage also suggests that Jesus believed that people's response to him and his message would determine their standing at the coming judgment (Witherington 1990: 167), a confidence appropriate to the prophets (e.g., Num 16:5-11, 28-

24. Theissen 1991: 49 notes that whereas Bethsaida is well known (Mk 8:22, 26; Jos. *Life* 399; *War* 2.168; *Ant.* 18.28; Pliny *N.H.* 5.71; Ptolemy *Geography* 5.16.4), Chorazin is otherwise barely known apart from modern excavations there (Euseb. *Onom.* 333; perhaps b. Menaḥ. 85a, but cf. t. Menaḥ. 9:2). Adinolfi 1994 argues that few Greek and Roman authors except Pausanias know much of the cities around the Lake of Galilee, including Bethsaida; Arav and Rousseau 1993 contend that Bethsaida was forgotten after the Roman destruction. Later Christians would probably not invent such a tradition.

25. Rejection after a miracle may be a form of negative acclamation, but otherwise it is virtually unparalleled outside early Christian texts (Theissen 1983: 72).

26. One should not make too much of the poetic rhythm, which frequently appears in ancient prophecy, including (albeit in specified meter) Pythian utterances (e.g., Diod. Sic. 7.12.1-6; 9.3.1-2; 9.16.1; 9.33.2; 9.36.2-3; 16.91.2; 34/35.13.1) and sayings of the oracle of Dodona (Dion. Hal. 1.19.3); the Odes of Solomon also contain much parallelism.

27. Also pace Bultmann, the prophecy looks back on only the Galilean ministry as completed, and that only in Matthew's redaction (Theissen 1991: 51n.73).

28. Other Jewish texts condemned those who wanted to "ascend to heaven" semiliterally (Gen 11:4; Sib. Or. 3.100) or figuratively (Jer 51:53; Ps. Sol. 1:5; 1 Enoch 45:2; cf. Virg. *Aen.* 7.99-100, 272; 12.795; Sall. *Catil.* 53.1) and promised that the arrogant would be cast to the earth or the grave (Sib. Or. 4.109-11), sometimes explicitly that they would be cast down from heaven (Lam 2:1; Ezek 28:8-10, 17; Jub. 24:31; Sib. Or. 5.72; Gk. Ezra 4:32; Apoc. Elijah 4:11).

34; 2 Chron 20:20; Jer 15:19-21; Ezek 33:33; Amos 7:16-17), but in a manner far more dramatic.

First, God judges peoples according to the opportunities they have had to respond to his truth (11:20). Just as those who rejected both Jesus and John proved their folly (11:11-19), those cities that witnessed many miracles yet did not respond with wholesale repentance demonstrate their folly (11:20-24). Few others had the opportunity for as much evidence as they had had (cf. 13:17), yet many of them took their opportunity for granted, and would be judged far more harshly than those who had had less opportunity (for the principle, cf., e.g., Lk 12:47-48; Rom 2:12-16; 12:19-20; Rev 9:20-21). Tyre may have been known for its oppression of God's people (see comment on 15:21; Ezek 27-28); Sidon was also known for paganism (e.g., Ach. Tat. 1.1.1-2); but neither city had as much opportunity as Israel. One may also note here the evidential value of miracles, but that even such clear evidence is not coercive to the hardened human will (cf. Tannehill 1975: 122-28).

Second, God often judges corporately for corporate sin. When entire cultures perpetuate a hardness against God for generation after generation, judgment may be God's primary means of gaining the people's attention (e.g., Ex 7:5, 17; 9:14; 10:2; Is 26:9-10; 28:9-13; 29:9-14). This case is particularly severe, however, because Jesus has openly revealed himself to cities and they have continued to disbelieve, like Israel in the wilderness. This theme recurs elsewhere in this Gospel (see especially 23:30-38).

Third, those who claim to be God's people are often the most hard-hearted hearers of all. Tyre, Sidon, and Sodom (see comment on 10:15) would have repented, but God's people took the signs for granted; this fits a common enough motif in Matthew as well as the Jesus tradition (cf. 2:4-11). The "sackcloth and ashes" indicate serious mourning and self-humiliation as part of the repentance (Job 42:6; Dan 9:3; Jonah 3:6). Yet just as Capernaum became a center of Galilean Christianity, Chorazin flourished in later centuries (see Yeivin 1983: 75; Goodenough 1953/68: 193-99; Turnheim 1987); these oracles are not later inventions, and, applied to a sinful generation, not to the indefinite future (cf. likewise 27:25). The moral principle, however, is that the exalted are brought low (11:23; cf. 23:12), even to the realm of the dead (cf. comment on Hades in 16:18) Jewish and Greek tradition placed in the underworld (cf. the descent to Hades in Is 5:14; 14:15; cf. Num 16:31-33; Prov 5:5; 30:16).

Rest for the Little Ones (11:25-30)

Cf. Lk 10:21-22; analogous language in Jn 3:35; 10:14-15; 17:2, 25. Just as Israel was wrongly secure in its status before God vis-à-vis the Gentiles (11:20-24), so the "wise" and powerful failed to recognize that God favored the children, the meek (11:25-30). Jesus summons not the mighty or wise to follow him, but the weak laden with heavy burdens (11:28; cf. 23:4), the "weary" like Israel in exile hoping in God alone (Is 40:29-31).[29]

First, God favors the weak, not the arrogant (11:25-26). In words whose Aramaic form may indicate an especially significant saying (cf. Jeremias 1971: 24), Jesus praised the Father (cf. Jn 11:41) as "Lord of heaven and earth," a standard Jewish title for God in prayer (Jeremias 1971: 10, 187-88; Gundry 1982: 216; Aramaic incant. 36.1; also "God of heaven and earth" — 4 Bar. 5:32; Test. Sol. 1:6; cf. for Helios in *PGM* 4.641). Before the Lord of heaven and earth,[30] human wisdom and power were nothing, so no one can protest if it was the Father's purpose (cf. 3:17) to hide these things from the wise (cf. 10:26; 13:11; 1 Cor 2:6-10; Job 12:24-25) and reveal them to the "babes," the "little ones" (10:42; 18:10; cf. to the righteous in 1 Enoch 48:6; to those to whom God "gave" Wisdom in Wis 9:17). One example of the Father so "revealing" these things (11:27) in this Gospel is that of the Father revealing Jesus' Sonship to Peter (16:17), a revelation that had come not so much through a single prior dramatic experience as through learning Jesus' identity while in a relationship of active discipleship.

True wisdom was hidden from those who professed to be wise (Job 12:1, 24-25; Is 19:11-12; 29:14; 47:10; Jer 8:8-9; Ezek 28:3-12; cf. Mt 13:11; Prov 3:7; 26:12, 16; Is 5:21). The "wise" of Jesus' day had careful rules for interpreting the Bible and often rested in the security of the academic consensus of their circle; they prided themselves on their knowledge of traditional interpretations and sayings of the wise who had gone before them; they also emphasized practical piety. Jesus' religious contemporaries stressed humility far more than do most persons of faith who live in modern Western society (Bonsirven 1964: 157-58); yet this passage charges that their humility was inadequate.

Second, in contrast to the "wise and learned" (11:25), Jesus alone is in a position to declare exactly what God is like (11:27). The sages had received traditions from earlier sages, but by using a standard term for passing on tradition (cf. Manson 1979: 79; Jeremias 1971: 59) the Gospels contrast Jesus' revelation, which is directly from the Father (11:27). Although this is not a claim to omniscience (24:36; cf. Vermes 1984: 48), Jesus holds a position of special authority from the Father (28:18; Jn 17:2). Thus the Father has given Jesus the sole prerogative to reveal him, so that anyone who approaches God a different way will not find him. Some scholars object that this passage sounds too much like something the Gospel of John would say (e.g., Jn 1:18; 14:6-9); if Jesus *never* spoke in terms like these, however, it would be more difficult to explain where the Johannine tradition derived its picture of Jesus (so, e.g., Hagner 1993: 317-18; pace Bousset 1970: 83-85). (The summons to "come" in 11:28 can also

29. The Wisdom character of 11:25-27 suggests that these verses constitute a single unit in the Gospel tradition (Witherington 1990: 222).

30. "Before the Father" was not unusual Jewish language; see Jeremias 1971: 10; McNamara 1972: 95; cf. Mt 18:14. "Revealing secrets" is expected Wisdom language even when speaking of human secrets (cf. Sir 27:17; 42:1).

sound Johannine: cf. Jn 6:35; 7:37.) Being part of the early Q tradition (11:25-27//Lk 10:21-22), these words most likely go back to Jesus himself.

Some scholars have objected that this exalted Q picture of Jesus and the language used to describe it is Gnostic or Greek, hence not from Jesus himself.[31] But more recent investigations have shown that it is thoroughly Palestinian Jewish, representing the sort of blend of mystic and apocalyptic thought that clustered around discussions of Israel, divine Wisdom, and the law.[32] "Language, style and structure . . . clearly assign the saying to a Semitic-speaking milieu" (Jeremias 1971: 57; cf. idem 1964a: 45-48; idem 1965: 24). Not all scholars are certain that the saying is authentic, but most today will agree that it is clearly not hellenistic (e.g., Davies and Allison 1991: 283).[33]

But not all scholars who suspect that the saying originated with Jesus agree on its sense; some suggest that Jesus indicates his relationship with God merely by means of analogy with a natural family: "only a father and son really know each other" (Jeremias 1971: 58-61; idem 1965: 25; Borg 1984: 232).[34] The analogy interpretation falters on the inadequacy of the image, however: men were generally closer to their wives and friends than their fathers (Schweizer 1975: 271). Jesus' prayers addressing God as Father and the use of "Son" as a title for Jesus in the indisputably authentic saying in 24:36 also suggest that Jesus here refers to himself as God's unique Son (Gundry 1982: 217-18). Although other images (such as a new Moses — Davies and Allison 1991: 283-87) may also be at work, Jesus describes himself here especially in the language of divine Wisdom (cf. Davies and Allison 1991: 296-97; Deutsch 1987: 143). Witherington (1990: 227) is convinced that

> The claim of exclusivity of mutual knowledge of Father and Son should be compared to the claims that state only Wisdom knows God and vice versa (cf.

31. The Gnostic interpretation falters severely on the phrase, "no one knows the Son but the Father" (Witherington 1990: 224).

32. E.g., Stauffer 1960: 165-66; Grant 1966: 152; Suggs 1970: 71-108; Yamauchi 1973: 35; Witherington 1990: 221-22.

33. Vermes 1993: 162, while agreeing that the Q logion behind 11:25-27 has a Palestinian origin, doubts its authenticity because he says receiving and transmitting revelation (here and in 16:17) are foreign to Jesus' teaching; but if Jesus' contemporaries could apply this language to the mysteries of Wisdom (and Vermes admits they could; cf. also n. 12, where he cites 1QS 1.9; 5.9; 8.1; 9.13; CD 15.13; 1QpHab 2.2-3; 7.5-6; 4Q381 1.1-2), Vermes can exclude the possibility of Jesus the sage speaking likewise only by circularly excluding the evidence of 11:25-27; 16:17. Dunn 1975 allows that Jesus may have spoken 11:27 but remains uncertain.

34. One might appeal here to Wis 2:13, 16, 18 (cf. 7:27), in which Wisdom makes people "sons" of God; but while this may constitute a primary background, it does not limit how Jesus could have reapplied the expression, especially if he functions here as the divine revealer, hence as Wisdom herself. A Jewish audience would recognize Wisdom as God's child; partly because Wisdom was a female figure (cf. the term's gender but also her figurative portrayals, e.g., Prov 8–9), partly because later rabbis usually reserved the "son" image for Israel, Wisdom/Torah became God's "daughter": Sifre Deut. 345.2.2; b. Sanh. 101a; Pesiq. Rab Kah. 26:9; Ex. Rab. 29:4; 33:1; Num. Rab. 12:4; Song Rab. 3:10, §2; 8:11, §2; Pesiq. R. 20:1-2. Hengel rightly regards this personification of Torah as God's daughter as equivalent to Philo's identification of Logos as God's son (1974a: 1:171).

Job 28:1-27; Sir. 1:6, 8; Bar. 3:15-32; Prov. 8:12; Wis. 7:25ff.; 8:3-8; 9:4, 9, 11). The middle two clauses suggest that Jesus sees his relationship to the Father in the light of wisdom ideas, and he may see himself as Wisdom incarnate here.[35]

Third, Jesus offers rest for the broken, and a yoke easier than that of the scholars (11:28-30). People who carried yokes to pull other loads would lay them on their neck and shoulders, with their hands grasping chains or rope attached to each end of the yoke (Jeremias 1972: 194). One would normally expect to find such a burden only on the shoulders of the poor (cf. Test. Job 7:1 with Jastrow 1985: 1:94). Long ago God had lifted the yoke of literal slavery from his people (Hos 11:4), and he promised to do so again at the new exodus (Is 10:27; 14:25). A yoke signified submission to another's rule or authority (e.g., Gen 27:40; 1 Enoch 103:11; Sib. Or. 3.391-92, 448, 508, 537, 567; cf. Fernández 1983). Other teachers in Jesus' day and afterward spoke of accepting the "yoke of God's kingdom," or God's rule, by submitting to the yoke of the law rather than merely human rule.[36]

Yet Jesus speaks here of a figurative bondage of unprofitable labor under an inadequate understanding of God's law (23:4; Acts 15:10; Gal 5:1; cf. Sir 40:1; Did. 6.2; 1 Clem. 16.17). Some teachers spoke figuratively of the "load" of one's teaching a disciple carried (Diog. Laert. 7.170; Boring 1995: 84; cf. Mt 23:4). Like a good sage, Jesus invites his disciples to learn from him (11:29; 24:32; 28:19; cf. Eph 4:20; 5:10). Yet Jesus did not interpret the law, including the law of rest (12:1-14), the same way his contemporaries did; his yoke was "lighter." In contrast to his opponents (23:4), Matthew's Jesus interprets the laws according to their original *purpose,* to which he is privy (5:17-48; 11:27; 12:8), for example, interpreting the Sabbath laws in terms of devotion to God rather than universal rules (12:7) and divorce law in terms of devotion to one's faithful wife rather than a loophole to reject her (19:4-8).

By speaking of God's law as Jesus' own, Jesus implicitly claims authority

35. Suggs 1970 probably did overstate the case in Matthew (see Pregeant 1996), but it should not for that reason be understated. Davies and Allison 1991: 222-25, 231 find the language of "exclusive and reciprocal divine knowledge" in the figure of Moses (Ex 33–34; Num 12; Deut 34; also Allison 1988). They acknowledge the Wisdom language in the context, but seek to keep both backgrounds by noting the idea of the king as embodying a living law (228-29, citing three references in Stobaeus and Moses as living Torah in Philo *Mos.* 1.162; cf. 2.3-5). I suspect, however, that Wisdom language, which is closer and more widespread in this exalted form, would strike Jesus' hearers first. A primary allusion to Is 61 (Charette 1992a) seems even less likely. Tuckett 1966: 280 thinks that in Q Jesus was an envoy of Wisdom, not yet identified with Wisdom, but the identification is surely quite early (1 Cor 8:6).

36. The yoke of God's law or God's kingdom appears throughout ancient Jewish literature in a variety of ways (often in contrast with the yoke of worldly rule); see, e.g., Jer 5:5; Ps. Sol. 7:9; 2 Bar. 41:3; m. 'Abot 3:5; Ber. 2:2; t. B. Qam. 7:5; Sifra Shir. pq. 12.121.2.5; Behar par. 5.255.1.9, 11; Sifre Deut. 344.4.2; b. Ber. 12b, 13b, 14b-15a; Mo'ed. Qat. 16b; p. Qidd. 1:2, §24; Pesiq. Rab Kah. Sup. 1:18; Gen. Rab. 67:7; Ex. Rab. 15:11; Num. Rab. 19:26; Lam. Rab. 3.27, §9; Pesiq. R. 21:16; cf. also Maher 1975: 98-100; Urbach 1979: 1:400-419.

from the Father greater than that of Moses himself (11:27); other Jewish texts would have spoken only of *God's* yoke here (Smith 1951: 153), or of the yoke of Torah (Davies and Allison 1991: 289). Jesus unquestionably models his words directly after the invitation of the sage Joshua ben Sira (Sir 51:23-27):[37]

> Draw near to me, you who are uneducated . . .
> Why do you delay in these matters,
> when your souls thirst so much? . . .
> Place your neck under the yoke,
> and let your soul accept training —
> she is near if you wish to find her.
> Witness with your own eyes that I have labored little,
> yet have found much rest for myself.

Yet the yoke in Matthew is not Ben Sira's, but that of divine Wisdom, and Wisdom elsewhere invites the hearer, "Come to me, you who earnestly desire me," and eat and drink of wisdom (Sir 24:19-21). John is not the only Gospel writer with a "wisdom christology" (Jn 1:1-18; 6:35; 7:37; cf. Hamerton-Kelly 1973: 68; Meier 1980: 127). Obeying God would bring his people "rest for your souls" (Jer 6:16 MT).[38]

Fourth, they would find Jesus' yoke light because they would find him a master who would care for them (11:29). Jesus' yoke is not lighter because he demands less (5:20), but because he bears more of the load with the burdened (23:4; cf. 1 Jn 5:3).[39] In contrast to unconcerned religious teachers who prided themselves on their own position (23:4-7; 24:49), Jesus was going to lay down his life for the sheep (20:25-28). The Gospel tradition repeatedly emphasizes that the Lord of the universe (28:18-20) is humble and prefers to dwell with the humble, the "little ones" (12:19-20). If Jesus is meek, the people in whose lives he rules cannot be proud or self-centered either, for the kingdom belongs only to the meek (5:3, 5).[40]

37. Pace Stanton 1982; idem 1993: 366-77; and Gundry 1982: 220, though Gundry's own evidence points to Matthew's changes of Sirach.

38. Hagner 1993: 323 sees in 11:28 an allusion to Yahweh's giving rest (Ex 33:14) that goes beyond Wisdom. This is possible, but the language can be explained simply as an allusion to divine Wisdom.

39. Making the same point, Garland 1993: 133 emphasizes the impact of the image: "Jesus treats his disciples as yokefellows rather than as camels and donkeys to be loaded down (23:4)."

40. The eschatological survivors will be the "meek and lowly" who submit to God's decrees (Zeph 3:12 LXX, with the same expression; on gentleness, cf. Mt 5:5; 21:5; Zech 9:9; on humility, 18:4, 23:12). Moses provides the model for a meek leader who remains firm because he acts under God's authority (Num 12:3; cf. generosity to enemies in Jos. *Apion* 2.211-13; acting like part of the multitude in *Ant.* 3.212; cf. Sirat and Woog 1992); later rabbis extolled Hillel's gentleness (b. Shab. 31a). Paul's depiction of his own meekness and gentleness in terms of those of Christ seems to allude back to this saying of Jesus (2 Cor 10:1; cf. Eph 4:2).

Conflicting Approaches to Scripture (12:1-14)

Cf. Mk 2:23–3:6; Lk 6:1-11. Matthew writes to disciples who believe their principles of biblical interpretation differ radically from those of the Pharisees (5:20; 9:13), and he has a crucial hermeneutical point to make in this narrative (12:7): transcultural principles and transformation take priority over situation-based rules (cf. 19:8). Whereas Matthew often abbreviates Mark's narratives (e.g., 9:1-8, 18-26), in this case he maintains most of Mark's material and adds some more material to the first debate (12:1-8//Mk 2:23-28).

Matthew uses here two of Mark's Sabbath controversy stories to illustrate the conflict between Jesus' rest and the Pharisees' rest (11:28); this conflict over the nature of the Sabbath further illustrates two different approaches to the law (5:20; cf. similarly Bacchiocchi 1984; Patte 1987: 167; Blomberg 1992a: 195). Jesus undoubtedly agreed with the Pharisees' view that God's law was an excellent yoke to bear (5:17-20), but he also believed that he offered a better interpretation of it than his contemporaries (cf. also Ferguson 1987: 409; cf. Jn 5:17-18): because he is the embodiment of divine wisdom himself, his yoke brings rest (11:28).[41] These Pharisees illustrate the principle that Jesus was hidden "from the wise and learned" (11:25). This narrative illustrates for Matthew's audience various points about biblical interpretation appropriate for Jesus' followers.[42]

First, these Pharisees provide a good example of exegesis if one wants to extrapolate the letter of the law the way a good lawyer might (12:1-2, 14). Josephus emphasizes that the Pharisees were meticulous in interpreting the details of the law (e.g., *War* 2.162; *Life* 191), and the Gospel tradition confirms how critical issues of "lawfulness" were among them (12:4, 10; 19:3) and others (14:4). Those concerned to build a "fence around the law" usually make the law's requirements stricter (see comment on 5:21-48); Jesus instead focused (as other sages did sometimes, e.g., with the *prosbul;* see comment on 6:12) especially on the principles behind the laws.

41. It is highly unlikely that Matthew views himself as relaxing the Sabbath in this passage (Sigal 1986: 158; pace Stanton 1993: 204-5). Matthew is clearer in his affirmation of biblical law here than Mark is (Goulder 1974: 17-18; Overman 1990b: 80-82; Segal 1991: 6-7); such clarity would be important among his community, which probably had to respond to non-Christian Jewish charges of antinomianism.

42. Some suggest that Mark constructed Jesus' conflicts with some of the Pharisees simply on the basis of conflict the early church was experiencing. Yet long before Mark, Jewish Christian writers report conflict between Palestinian Jewish-Christians and some of their contemporaries (e.g., 1 Thess 2:14-16), and we know of at least one Pharisee who actively persecuted Christians (Phil 3:5-6). Acts suggests that conflict with Pharisees decreased for a time, and that with Sadducees increased, after Jesus' resurrection (e.g., Acts 4–5; 15:5; 23:6-9). Matthew and especially John amplified Mark's reports about the Pharisees, but Mark addressed a Diaspora audience that would know the Pharisees *only* from the Jesus tradition. Scholars may question the reliability of such evidence, but when they reject all the evidence we do have and construct a theory without textual evidence that runs against all our textual evidence, one suspects that they value their theory more highly than the data at hand (see more fully the case in Stanton 1995a: 184-85). On a literary level, however, Jesus' conflict with the Jewish authorities is certainly central to Matthew's plot (Kingsbury 1992).

One would not usually expect to find Pharisees in a Galilean wheatfield on the Sabbath;[43] this was hardly their usual habitat (Sanders 1985: 198, 265; idem 1990: 1, 20-21; Anderson 1976: 109) and makes sense only if they were looking for grounds to accuse the disciples (Jeremias 1971: 278-79; Stauffer 1960: 85, 207).[44] But the case against Galilean Pharisees is an argument from silence in Josephus, when the Gospels and some slight strands of evidence (such as Jose the Galilean) may argue the contrary. One could thus argue that more Pharisees lived in Galilee than some of our sources suggest (Witherington 1990: 61, 66, with some evidence in Jos. *Ant.* 20.34-49), a surmise that could be reasonable in view of the limited extant literary sources on both Pharisees and Galilee. One could argue that Mark or his source updated local authorities into "Pharisees" (reasonable in view of Mark's *Tendenz*). One could also argue that these Pharisees were traveling with Jesus or seeking to test him. Perhaps most likely, most resided in Jerusalem, but some were active beyond it (Horsley 1995: 150-52, 256). Aside from the narrative's unusual setting, however, the rest of its portrayal of these Pharisees' reasoning makes sense without much explanation.[45]

Excursus: Conflict Narratives

Although Matthew and John intensify Pharisaic opposition and some scholars attribute conflict stories with the Pharisees only to later Christians (Sanders 1990: 95-96; idem 1993: 217), the substance of these accounts is likely authentic. (1) First of all, the accounts must predate the major Jewish-Christian conflicts to which some wish to attribute them. Mark's accounts clearly precede the major breaches in the post-70 era (Witherington 1990: 60);[46] further, they would not have arisen in a period when

43. Public prayer and study of Torah must have consumed some of each Sabbath (Jos. *Apion* 1.209; 2.175). Even in more hellenized cities, around 6 p.m. Friday evening religious Jews left secular activities, including political assemblies, and began their Sabbath dinner (Jos. *Life* 279). Most Jewish people seem to have observed traditional limits on Sabbath day's journeys (CD 10.20-21; Acts 1:12; cf. Num. Rab. 2:9; Ruth Rab. 6:4; for circumventing by means of Sabbath residences, see, e.g., p. Maʿaś. 2:3; m. ʿErub. passim). Bowker (1973: 39) suggests that the Pharisees made use here of their permitted Sabbath day's journey (something Sadducees apparently prohibited), about 1,100 meters (2,000 cubits, based on Num 35:5; m. Soṭa 5:3; m. ʿErub. 4:3; 5:7; b. ʿErub. 45a; Sukk. 44b; Lake and Cadbury 1979: 10); perhaps seeing Jesus take his disciples to the fields, they confronted them there. Davies and Allison 1991: 307 cite b. Shab. 127a for a rabbi in the field on the Sabbath. Witherington 1990: 67 suggests that Mk 2:24 does not actually identify the Pharisees' location (Matthew is more explicit, but elsewhere abbreviates accounts by omitting clarifying details, e.g., omitting messengers in 8:5-8; 9:18-19). Wheat was ready for harvest and gleaning in April (Stauffer 1960: 84).

44. Powerful Jerusalemites could send aristocratic delegations, which could include Pharisees, to Galilee (Jos. *Life* 21, 28-29, 72-73, 196).

45. Casey 1988 (see especially p. 20) accepts the account as authentic; Sanders 1990: 21; idem 1985: 265 accepts the exchange as authentic, rejecting only its narrative frame.

46. Morton Smith and Jacob Neusner think that Pharisaism was much less significant in the pre-70 period, and that Josephus magnified it in his later *Antiquities,* when Pharisaism was more pop-

Pharisees were not the Christians' primary enemies in the late 40s (Acts 15:5)[47] through the early 60s (Theissen 1991: 230-31),[48] and probably not much in the early period of the Jerusalem church either (cf. Acts 5:17, 33-34). (2) Yet *some* Pharisaic opposition in the early period existed and probably had earlier roots: some Pharisees in the earliest period joined ranks with the Sadducees to persecute Christians (Phil 3:5-6),[49] and it is unlikely that the conflicts simply began shortly after Jesus' cruxifixion.

Together these observations suggest authenticity: Some sort of conflicts appeared in the earliest Jesus tradition, but these were not conformed to the *primary* opponents of Christians in the early years after the resurrection, suggesting that the original opponents in these traditions may have been correctly transmitted. (3) Multiple attestation supports the thesis that Jesus did have Sabbath conflicts (Borg 1984: 139-43; Witherington 1990: 66). They appear in Mark (e.g., Mk 2:23-28), independently in John (Jn 5:1-9), and perhaps independently in special Lukan material (Lk 13:10-17); lack of clear attestation in Q (unless Matthew simply omits the tradition of Lk 13:10-17) is not surprising given how few narratives from Q appear in our Gospels.

One may note that Jesus' teaching more closely resembles that of the Pharisees than that of any of the other "parties" mentioned by Josephus (Sadducees, Essenes, or revolutionaries); yet dissimilarities are also striking (Harvey 1982: 51). But like most of his contemporaries, Jesus undoubtedly did not belong to any of these "parties," and in any case such a marginal kinship would hardly preclude conflict. Social conflict theory illustrates that conflicts become most severe among groups most closely connected (Stanton 1993: 98-102). Josephus faced life-threatening opposition from rivals within his own social class (e.g., *Life* 272-75, 302-3), and both such passages in Josephus and the history of other early Jewish groups such as the Essenes (violent conflicts with the priesthood, e.g., 1QpHab 8.8-12; 9.4-7; 12.5; 4QpNah 1.11)[50] and

---

ular. But cf. *War* 2.163, and note that Josephus may have had apologetic reasons to downplay the Pharisees' role in his earlier *War* (Witherington 1990: 83-84, following Dunn).

47. One could postulate a *Sitz im Leben* for polemic against a Pharisaic faction within the church in the late 40s (Acts 15:5), but would such polemic generate stories about enemies of the earthly Jesus, and if traditionaries took that much liberty, would they not introduce current controversies like circumcision?

48. Theissen's evidence for Pharisaic toleration in the 60s (Jos. *Ant.* 20.200-201; cf. *War* 2.162; *Life* 191) and late 50s (Acts 23:9) is fairly secure, as is his evidence for some hostility in the 30s (Acts 7:54-60; Gal 1:13, 23). His evidence for hostility in the early 40s (Acts 12:2 with Jos. *Ant.* 19.332; 1991: 231-32) is less secure.

49. This is our *earliest* extant Christian mention of Pharisees, unless one dates Mark before the mid-50s. Cf. Acts 9:1-2.

50. The "Wicked Priest" has been identified with Jonathan (Rost 1976: 163), John Hyrcanus (Brownlee 1956-57a: 13-15), or "the false priesthood of the Temple at any time between the Maccabean period and the fall of the Hasmonean dynasty" (Fritsch 1956: 83-84). Some have identified the "Young Lion" of 4QpNah 1.5 with Alexander Jannaeus (Allegro 1956a: 92; Eisenman 1983: 35); others contend that a specific identification is impossible (Rowley 1956a); and still others choose even Pontius Pilate (Thiering 1981a: 70, with little support). As the original teacher of righteousness became a model for the future one (CD 6.10-11) and the title probably applied to all his

Pharisees (conflicts with Sadducees, e.g., Jos. *Ant.* 18.17; m. Yad. 4:7; t. Ḥag. 3:35; Nid. 5:3; ARN 5A; 10B; b. Nid. 33b; Sukk. 48b) indicate the pervasiveness of intra-Jewish strife.

Moses explicitly forbade work on the Sabbath (e.g., Ex 31:13-14; 35:2; Ezek 20:20), and gleaning could certainly be regarded as work, as a form of "reaping" (prohibited in m. Shab. 7:2; though cf. m. Pe'a 2:7-8; Davies and Allison 1991: 307 cite Philo *Vit. Mos.* 2.22; p. Shab. 9c). Essenes (probably the strictest Jewish Sabbath-keepers) forbade so much as scooping up drinking water in a vessel (CD 11.1-2). (Gleaning from another's field was legal on other days — Deut 23:25; Ruth 2:2; most gleaners would have ignored strict regulations on gleaning such as p. Maʿaś. 2:6.) More than Philo, most Pharisees (though see Young 1992: 104 for some evidence for exceptions) must have forbidden picking standing heads of grain (12:1) or at least rubbing them to get to the kernels (Lk 6:1; Albright and Mann 1971: 149).

Yet just as Pharisees could disagree among themselves on some details of Sabbath law (t. Shab. 16:21-22; b. Shab. 5b, bar., 18b; Gen. Rab. 7:2), a Jewish teacher who rejected Pharisaic tradition could have interpreted the law quite differently from the Pharisees, as Jesus did. Whereas the law forbade *preparing* food on the Sabbath (Ex 16:22-30; 35:3; Jos. *War* 2.147; CD 10.9), it certainly did not forbid *eating* it (cf. Jos. *Life* 279), and Jewish people kept the Sabbath with joyous feasting (contrary to pagan views — Strabo 16.2.40; Mart. *Epig.* 4.4.7; Suet. *Aug.* 76; cf. Sevenster 1975: 130-32). Jewish tradition prohibited fasting on the Sabbath (CD 11.4-5; Jub. 50:12-13; Sanders 1990: 13 cites Jdt 8:6; Jos. *Life* 279; m. Taʿan. 1.6), which might leave Jesus' disciples no choice but to glean provided the urgency of their mission had detained them from preparing food the previous day (cf. Borg 1984: 154).

Matthew contends that God's law was not genuinely written in these Pharisees' hearts, emphasizing their hostile response to Jesus' violation of their known tradition (12:10, 14). In Hebrew Scripture, blatant breaches of Sabbath law were punishable by public execution (Ex 31:14; 35:2; Num 15:35); although Rome prohibited its subjects from executing criminals directly, many early Pharisees may have been frustrated by their inability to carry out capital sentences mandated in the Bible (no one forgot the biblical teaching — e.g., p. Meg. 1:6, §2).

---

successors (Buchanan 1977), the identity of the original "Wicked Priest" may have applied to the high priesthood in perpetuity. Overman 1996: 224 cites 4QMMT as a sample of halakic debates at Qumran.

Some scholars find clues of Essene antagonism toward Pharisaism (Roth 1960b: 65; idem 1960c; Dupont-Sommer 1969: 33) or Pharisaic or rabbinic opposition to the Essenes (Lieberman 1951: 396-400). The rabbis nevertheless reflect legal or cultural traditions often shared with Qumran, though reasons for those parallels are debated (e.g., Baumgarten 1958b: 256; Neusner 1973; Schiffman 1983).

The Pharisees may, however, have come to terms with this limitation the way their successors and others in the later rabbinic movement did: by so narrowing the definition of capital offenses that executions were barely ever necessary anyway. The Essenes, though very strict and recognizing the *appropriateness* of capital punishment for even minor infractions like sleeping with one's wife (Jub. 50:8) or fasting (Jub. 50:12-13), in practice punished even intentional Sabbath infringements only with detention (see Sanders 1990: 18-19). Further, most Jews would have required one who transgressed the Sabbath law unintentionally only to offer a sin offering (Stauffer 1960: 205-6; t. Shab. 1:13). Even if these Pharisees are sure that Jesus is wrong, his appeal to Scripture should convince them that his "transgression" is "unintentional" (cf. Sanders 1990: 90).

No sect in early Judaism had rules that would have mandated Jesus' death for his Sabbath practices. Most would have agreed that plotting to kill someone who disagreed with them (12:14; cf. "taking counsel" in 22:15; 26:4; 27:1, 7) was premeditated murder, which the law forbade under penalty of death (Gen 9:5-6; Num 35:29-34; Deut 21:1-9). (By omitting Mk 3:4, Matthew omits the explicit irony of Mk 3:6 in Mt 12:14: it is against the law's intention to kill.) The Pharisees tolerated all sorts of disputes, including concerning varied interpretations of Sabbath law (cf. Riesenfeld 1970: 117-18); Pharisaic theory unequivocally opposed executing people for such disagreements, and Pharisaic practice normally concurred with theory on this matter. Yet these Pharisees are so enraged with Jesus that they resort to plotting his death — *a heinous and obvious breach of the very law they purport to uphold* (12:14).[51] On the Matthean level, even their "accusations" (12:10) foreshadow those of the priestly aristocracy before Pilate (27:12), and perhaps the *delatores* (accusers to the court) who might ultimately betray Matthew's fellow disciples to Roman authorities.

Second, Jesus had based his ethics on Scripture, and Matthew contends that Jesus' ethics reflect a more biblically sensitive approach than those of his opponents (12:3-8). Various sources attest the strictness with which many Jewish pietists guarded the Sabbath; the Essenes, who were especially strict, show us how seriously some Jewish people in antiquity could take the Sabbath (see CD 10.14–11.18; Jub. 50; cf. Finkelstein 1972: 205-11). One could not even speak of work to be done after the Sabbath (CD 10.19), speak secular words (CD 10.18; cf. Is 58:13) or lift dust in one's house (CD 11.10-11). Probably the sectarian Scrolls do not represent common Judaism any more than the more lenient later rabbis do (pace Kimbrough 1966), but they do indicate one option within the Judaism of Jesus' day. Most Jewish people seem to have observed traditional limits on Sabbath day's journeys (CD 10.20-21; t. Shab. 1:3; b. 'Erub. 45a; Sukk. 44b; cf. Acts 1:12). One could not wear soiled garments (CD 11.3; cf. later Ruth Rab. 5:12); later rabbis even threatened divine judgment for playing

51. Sigal 1986: 141-42 suggests that the tradition reflects the Hebrew *lemahrim oto,* "to place him under the ban," misunderstood by the translator in its earlier biblical sense as "destroy." Such a suggestion is not impossible, but is highly speculative.

ball on that day (Lam. Rab. 2:2, §4). Because Gentiles took advantage of the Sabbath to attack Jewish warriors (e.g., Jos. *Ant.* 12.4), exceptions were made for defensive warfare (e.g., Jos. *Ant.* 13.12-13), but pietists differed on how far to press even this exception (cf. Jos. *Life* 159, 161; *Apion* 1.210-12).

Jesus had thought deeply about Scripture, and provides various examples to make his case.[52] But Jesus' growing popularity made his teaching a threat to those who felt that he did not uphold the appropriate academic and religious consensus of their circle. As these Pharisees well knew, a challenge to the behavior of the disciples was a challenge to the teacher who was responsible to train them in proper behavior (cf. Goodman 1983: 79; Daube 1972: 4-6; Harvey 1982: 38). Disciples' behavior reflected on their teachers (e.g., t. ʿEd. 3:4; in Greek circles, cf. Liefeld 1967: 222-24); teachers thus defended their disciples' honor, for their own honor was at stake (ARN 27A; 34, §76B). Yet in this culture dominated by honor and shame, Jesus was quite able to respond to their challenges and defeat them in rhetorical maneuvering. "Have you never read . . . ?" (cf. 19:4; 21:16, 42; 22:31) is a strong insult toward those who claim to be experts in Scripture (so also, e.g., Malina 1993: 99). Jesus proceeds with a line of argument typical in ancient Mediterranean argumentation (cf. Robbins 1988: 21; Mack and Robbins 1989: 140).

Jesus' first example is the story of the breach of the law for David in an emergency — the man of God and his companions were hungry (12:3-4; cf. 1 Sam 21:1-6). Although his opponents may have insisted on beginning with an explicit legal text (cf. Borg 1984: 152-53), Jesus appeals instead to inspired narrative to show how God expected the legal statements to be qualified in practice, "a precedent for allowing hunger to override the law" (Sanders 1990: 20). For the Pharisees to have objected that the David story addressed forbidden food rather than the Sabbath (Borg 1984: 153; cf. ARN 32, §72B) would have missed his point; Jesus challenges not merely their interpretation of the Sabbath but their entire method of legal interpretation.[53] Because the high priest *thought* that David had companions with him (1 Sam 21:2-5), his actions indicate the kind of exceptions that both David and the high priest thought appropriate whether or not David was lying (he probably was). If Jesus uses narrative precedent to qualify legal texts in this way, Matthew surely provides here a hermeneutical key for many of Jesus' nonlegal teachings (radical, succinct statements usually unquali-

52. Jesus' application of traditional Jewish methods of interpretation is generally acknowledged (e.g., Hicks 1984), but some contend that Jesus applied these methods very differently than his trained opponents did; according to this view, Jesus produced analogies they would have rejected and thus provoked their anger (Cohn-Sherbok 1979).

53. The general principle in his illustration also remains relevant whether it contains an implicit claim to Jesus' Davidic descent or not. That no connection between Jesus and David is developed here (pace, e.g., France 1985: 202) suggests authenticity rather than a creation of later Christians (Witherington 1990: 67). Other interpretations also exist: if the view that David's act occurred on the Sabbath (b. Menaḥ. 95b; Yalqut on 1 Sam 21:5) reflects tradition contemporary with Jesus (which is quite uncertain), this tradition might be relevant; Vermes 1993: 24 suggests an extrapolation of hunger to starvation, hence death.

fied); for example, one should compare Jesus' demands with his relative patience in not repudiating his disciples.

Jesus' second example is the law's explicit allowance for the Sabbath activity of priests in the temple (12:5-8; cf. Num 28:9-10). As noted above, the Pharisees probably would have rejected Jesus' argument about David (preserved in Mk 2:25-26) as an invalid analogy; thus Matthew here adds an argument his audience can safely use (Saldarini 1994: 129). After making his argument by example, Jesus proceeds with a *qal waḥomer,* a traditional Jewish "how-much-more" argument (as often noted; see, e.g., Longenecker 1975: 69). Others constructed similar arguments; for instance, an early second-century rabbi contended that saving a human life takes precedence over the Sabbath, for even the temple service overrides the Sabbath (t. Shab. 15:16). Stricter Shammaite Pharisees (who predominated in Jesus' day) accused more lenient Hillelite Pharisees of "working" on holy days; Hillelites defended their behavior by analogy with the priests (Sanders 1990: 90). Others reasoned similarly from the biblical fact that the temple service overrode Sabbath regulations (cf. m. 'Erub. 10:11-15; t. Shab. 15:16; p. Rosh. Hash. 4:3, §3; Sanh. 4:6, §2).[54] The way ancient lawyers argued for exceptions was by showing that at least one exception was already implicit in the law (Quint. 7.6.5).

Yet Jesus ranks not saving a life but his own authority above the temple: if the temple service warrants suspension of the Sabbath, how much more the presence of one greater than the temple (12:6, 41-42; cf. Jn 4:12; 5:46; 8:53), hence a greater locus of God's presence than the temple (cf. Stanton 1993: 130, following A. Schlatter)?[55] For Jesus as Son of Man is Lord of the Sabbath (12:8; cf. 22:44).[56] Jesus' self-claim was veiled enough to prevent accusations of blasphemy — especially since his opponents would not expect him actually to claim what he was claiming — but obvious enough to enrage them (cf. v. 14). (Because the Semitic expression "son of man" usually just means "human being," even many modern commentators have read Jesus' Son of Man statement here as a teaching about persons in general — e.g., Montefiore 1968: 1:44; Borg 1984:

54. Similarly, if slaying the Passover lamb overrides the Sabbath, so also do other Passover preparations (t. Pisha 5:1; some disagreed — 4:13); preparations for Sukkoth override the Sabbath (t. Sukk. 3:1); if circumcision suspends the Sabbath (and it does — t. Shehitat Ḥul. 6:2; Mek. Amalek 3.109-10; Sifra Taz. pq. 1.123.1.8; b. Ḥul. 84b, bar.; p. Ned. 3:9, §2), how much more does saving a life (b. Yoma 85b; cf. Jn 7:22-23; b. 'Arak. 7a). France 1985: 203 notes that some (in m. Menaḥ. 10:3, 9, the Sadducees) rejected the Pharisees' exceptions, too. Davies and Allison 1991: 314 point out that priests "profaning" the Sabbath is apparently traditional language, and list other exceptions in Jos. *Ant.* 14.63; m. Ned. 3:11; Pesaḥ. 6:1-2; t. Pesaḥ. 4:13. Arguments over which commandment takes precedence when two are in conflict were common (Vermes 1993: 22 on Mk 3:4).

55. The use of comparisons in 12:6, 40-42 reflects standard argumentation in Greco-Roman rhetoric (Stanton 1993: 77-80).

56. Saldarini 1994: 131 suggests an allusion to Lev 23:3, a "Sabbath to the Lord," i.e., Yahweh. Equally speculatively, Witherington 1990: 246 (who regards Mk 2:28 par. Mt 12:8 as redactional summary — 67) suggests a contrast with the evil figure who changes times and law in Dan 7:25 (cf. Jos. *Ant.* 10.276).

155.) But in the whole context of Jesus' usage, and certainly in Matthew's usage, it seems more likely as a christological statement, as we have noted.

Jesus' third argument to validate his method of interpretation is an appeal to the prophets' proclamation: the law's principles take precedence over its rituals (12:7; cf. Hos 6:6). Everyone acknowledged that an emergency need, like a human life endangered (CD 11.16-17), especially that of a righteous person (e.g., b. Yoma 35b), warranted an exception to any ritual; but Jesus makes such exceptions the rule. Not merely human life but human need in general takes precedence over regulations. Kindness toward others' genuine need — for example, that of hungry disciples — precedes rules whose purpose was to please the God who values such kindness more highly (12:7; 9:13; cf. 4:2). With this third argument, Jesus has appealed to all three sections of the Old Testament, treating them with equal authority: the law, the prophets, and the writings.[57]

Third, Jesus validates God's approval of his Sabbath activity by healing on the Sabbath (12:9-13). Jesus enters the synagogue (12:9); in this period Jewish people especially congregated in synagogues on Sabbaths (Safrai 1974/76f: 918). Accounts of healing withered or paralyzed hands always suggested great power, both in Jewish (1 Kings 13:6; Test. Sim. 2:12-13) and pagan (Epidauros inscr. 3 in Grant 1953: 56; Bultmann 1968: 233) texts. Jesus heals partly to attest God's endorsement of his ministry (9:4-7); would God heal through him on the Sabbath if God disapproved of his Sabbath ministry? A general rule of thumb among early Jewish teachers was that anything one could as well do before the Sabbath as during it does not override the Sabbath (t. Pisha 5:1).

But this time Jesus not only does not heal the man medically; he does not even lay on hands. Some teachers considered applying medicine to be work justifiable on the Sabbath only if a person's life was in danger (m. Yoma 8:6; cf. p. ʿAbod. Zar. 2:2, §3). But the teachers themselves found ways to circumvent some of their regulations (m. Shab. 14:4; cf. m. Shab. 6:2), and many teachers probably permitted medicine if it had been prepared before the Sabbath (t. Shab. 12:12) or the act was medically urgent (m. ʿEd. 2:5; Shab. 22:6; Yoma 8:6; on saving a life Lachs 1987: 199-200 adds Mek. Shabbata 1, Laut. 3:197-99, on Ex. 31:13), which this act was not (cf. Sanders 1990: 13; idem 1993: 208). But Jesus acted as a man of prayer, not a pharmacist, and in this case (as we have noted) Jesus does not even lay hands on the man, which *some* might have considered work. Instead, he simply orders the man to stretch forth his hand, an act that was not considered work by anyone's standard; God alone performs "work" in this scene (12:13; cf. Danker 1972: 77; Sanders 1990: 21; Rhoads and Michie 1982: 84).

57. Although it appears in Ben Sira's prologue and Cohen 1987: 187 sees it in Josephus and Philo, the three divisions became especially prominent among the rabbis (e.g., ARN 14A; b. B. Bat. 13b, bar.; B. Qam. 92b; Sanh. 90b, 106a; p. Meg. 1:5, §3; Ned. 3:9, §3). Later rabbis also liked to produce proofs from all three divisions (e.g., b. ʿAbod. Zar. 19b; Mak. 10b).

Even the strict majority Pharisaic school in this period, the Shammaites, would have violated their own standards of ethics to have punished Jesus harshly (at most a later rabbinic judge might have fined him or ordered a beating, which one rabbi occasionally — but rarely — levied against another). Although they prohibited prayer for the sick on the Sabbath, they never sought to kill the minority school at the time, Hillelite Pharisees, who permitted prayer on the Sabbath (t. Shab. 16:22; cf. Sanders 1993: 268). Of course, serious and sometimes violent conflicts did occur between Jewish sects (the Qumran Scrolls suggest that the Maccabean period was rife with these, even if Josephus chooses to report as little as possible). Nevertheless, differences in legal interpretation did not constitute highhanded breach of the Sabbath or warrant death. If these Pharisees are upset — contradicting their own Sabbath beliefs — this says more about them in this narrative than it does about Jesus' practice of the Sabbath.

But before healing the man, Jesus offers another "how much more" argument by analogy. Both "sheep" (e.g., 18:12) and "pits" (15:14) were common enough to lend themselves for illustrations.[58] Some people in the Mediterranean world dug camouflaged pits to capture wolves and other predators (cf. Ex 21:33-34; Jos. *Ant.* 4.283-84; Phaedrus 3.2.2; Longus 1.11), but though animals usually avoided pits (Pesiq. Rab Kah. Sup. 3:2), these people sometimes had to rescue their own livestock from the pit, pulling them up by a cord or whatever was available (Longus 1.12; Hock 1988: 140). One's wagon could also fall into a ravine (Babrius 20.1), in which case one should grab the wheels (20.6) and lay the whip on the oxen (20.7). Some animals were accidentally trapped in wells (Phaedrus 4.9.3-12); other animals undoubtedly succumbed to Palestine's naturally rugged inland terrain (perhaps Deut 22:4). In contrast to the stricter Essenes (CD 11.13-14; cf. F. F. Bruce 1969: 73), the Pharisees and most Jewish people accepted the necessity of rescuing an animal on the Sabbath (cf. b. Shab. 128b, bar.; Theissen 1978: 82).[59] Yet "how much more" important is a person than a sheep? Although the hearers would have protested that the withered hand was less urgent (e.g., p. ʿAbod. Zar. 2:2, §3; cf. Barrett 1967: 63) — the man had undoubtedly survived with the problem for some time — their tradition agreed that the man was more important than a sheep (see comment on 6:26). Jesus concludes with a principle that someone less scrupulous could use to justify almost anything he or she wanted on the Sabbath: "Therefore it is lawful to do what is good on the Sabbath" (12:12). (As Athanasius [*Homilies* 28, *ACCS,* 37] recognized, Jesus here reasons from the law itself. Pace modern Protestant antinomianism, however, it is quite doubtful that Jesus himself *would* have justified doing anything and everything on the

58. Assuming that Jesus used the usual halakic example found in rabbinic texts (oxen typically fell into pits, e.g., m. B. Qam. 5:5-6), Hilton and Marshall 1988: 91 suggest that Luke's "ox" is more original and that Matthew changed the illustration to a sheep because it is less likely to die in such a fall than a heavier animal would be.

59. The strict legal teaching in the later sources was not that one might "pull" it out, however; one merely made a way for it to *climb* out (Goulder 1974: 18; Gundry 1982: 227).

Sabbath; cf. the similarly worded Jubilees 50:10-11, which clearly *supports* Sabbath observance.)[60]

If the views of later rabbis provide any indication, many Pharisees would not have accepted miracles as an adequate way to attest divine endorsement for a teaching. Some Jewish teachers reportedly performed miracles to validate their halakah (b. B. Meṣ. 59b; p. Sanh. 6:6, §2; cf. Baumgarten 1983a), though others may often have told stories about such signs simply to praise the teacher's holiness (cf. Dibelius 1971: 145-46; Urbach 1979: 1:108-9). By contrast, however, most teachers regarded their tradition as more authoritative than miracles (e.g., t. Yebam. 14:6; cf. p. Sanh. 11:4, §1; Vermes 1973: 80-81). Unconcerned with the demonstration of God's power before them and simply looking for reasons to accuse Jesus (v. 10; cf. 26:4; 27:12), Jesus' opponents apparently do not listen to what he says.

In fact, for them Jesus' power and growing popularity simply make him all the more dangerous (cf. 12:23-24; Jn 11:48; 12:9-11). In contrast to the predominantly Sadducean aristocracy, the Pharisees were populists, like Jesus; they lacked sufficient political power even to enforce their desire for Jesus' death. That Jesus appeals to the same popular constituency that traditionally followed them probably threatens the sense of religious security and power they would never have admitted they had. But that one might *wish* to execute a capital sentence on one who was gaining the influence to lead Israel "astray" is not hard to believe. The Qumranites apparently believed that a rival sect, perhaps the Pharisees, wanted Qumran's teacher dead (Stanton 1995a: 31, citing 4QMMT; 4Q 171:3-10). Most frequently Jewish aristocrats who sought other Jews' lives did so not for theological reasons but as part of a power struggle (e.g., Jos. *Life* 302).

These Pharisees undoubtedly felt that they had good reason to reject Jesus' claims. If someone were working miracles without God's approval — and how could he have God's approval if he disagreed with God's Word?[61] — then they could only conclude that he was doing supernatural feats as a magician by the devil's power (12:24).

60. The principle here is also somewhat more clearly defined than Mark's "The Sabbath was made on account of humanity, rather than humanity on account of the Sabbath" (Mk 2:27), despite the abundant Jewish parallels to this statement (cf. Smith 1951: 138; Jeremias 1971: 18; Vermes 1993: 24; pace Witherington 1990: 68) and similar logical constructions in Jewish literature (e.g., 2 Macc 5:19; 2 Bar. 14:18; Deut. Rab. 3:1; Pesiq. R. 23:9; cf. Crates *Ep.* 24, to the Thessalians). Witherington 1994: 169 suggests that Jesus' statement in Mark 2:27 may counter the sort of saying that appears in Jub 2:18ff. Matthew may wish to avoid an ambiguity that could be exploited by those charging his community with antinomianism (cf. 5:17).

61. It is questioned today to what extent the Pharisees identified God's Word with their tradition in this period (in contrast to later traditions about the oral law; on today's dispute, e.g., contrast Sanders 1990: 97-130 with Baumgarten 1972). But as in much popular religion today, the line between what Scripture says and what interpreters assume it means may to them have been rather thin.

The Spirit-Anointed Humble Servant (12:15-21)

Cf. Mk 3:7-12; Lk 6:17-19. Rather than contending with the Pharisees further, Jesus withdrew (12:15) and sternly warned those who were beginning to realize his power not to tell others about it (12:16; in the same context in Mk 3:12 it was the demons who recognized his identity and on whom he enjoined silence; the strong term appears in Mt 8:26). Thus Matthew freely renders Isaiah's words to say that Jesus would not "strive." Jesus would not risk extinguishing a wick on the verge of going out, and so far would he go in not breaking a reed (12:20) that he would offer his cheek to those smiting him with one (27:30; cf. Mic 5:1-2). Thus Jesus demonstrated that he preferred not to fight others when it was not necessary (12:19-20; cf. 10:23; Gen 26:14-22). His opponents thought him a youthful upstart, but he knew his identity and his call (cf. 3:17–4:10).

The quotation from Isaiah 42:1-4 in this passage especially looks forward to the conflict in the following narrative: whereas his opponents misinterpret his identity, his empowerment by the Spirit demonstrates that he is the chosen one of Isaiah's prophecy (12:18, 28). Matthew quotes more of the passage than the "Spirit-endowed" or "chosen servant" part, however, to emphasize the lowly character of Jesus' first coming (21:5) and especially the final line, which reinforces Matthew's theme of the Gentile mission (2:1-12; 4:15; 24:24; 28:19): Gentiles will hope in Jesus (12:21; cf. 12:18).

In this passage Matthew reads Jesus as Isaiah's "servant of Yahweh." Although Targum Jonathan (fifth century A.D., including earlier material) calls the servant "Messiah" in Isaiah 42:1; 43:10; and 52:13, though applying the suffering sections to Israel (F. F. Bruce 1963: 143n.1; Moore 1971: 2:327; Lourenço 1990; cf. Edgar 1958: 50 for other late references),[62] Judaism in Jesus' day rarely applied the servant passages to the Messiah. After all, in context Isaiah 42:1-4 refers to *Israel* (44:1, 21; 49:3). But it is not hard to see how Matthew interprets Isaiah 42; despite the skepticism of some of his modern critics, Matthew read the larger context. God's servant Israel failed in its mission (42:18-19), so God chose one person within Israel to restore the rest of his people (49:5-7); this one would bear the punishment (cf. 40:2) rightly due his people (52:13–53:12). As in 12:1-14, Matthew here provides a hermeneutical key for his entire Gospel; his inter-

62. Ådna 1992 argues that this Targum's triumphant Messiah simply follows a traditional Jewish hermeneutic. Doeve 1954: 147-48 links Is 52:13–53:12 with Dan 7:13-14 based on early Jewish hermeneutical methods. Among eighteen people called "servant" in Scripture, one is Messiah, in Is 42:1 (so ARN 43, §121B; cf. Pesiq. R. 31:10; on Targ. Ps-Jon. to Is 53, see Koch 1972); other Jewish sources also portray the Messiah as God's servant (2 Bar. 70:9). For relatively early possible messianic interpretations, including possible application to Qumran's Teacher of Righteousness, see Schoeps 1961b: 134-39; Dupont-Sommer 1973: 361-63; Brownlee 1956/1957a: 18-20; Zimmerli and Jeremias 1957: 57-60. But other views of the Isaianic servant are probably more common; one rabbi saw Moses as the suffering servant, atoning by not entering the land (Davies 1974: 60), and the title "servant" can refer to Israel (Ps. Sol. 12:6; 17:21). That it originates with Jesus seems probable (Taylor 1955; Zimmerli and Jeremias 1957: 93; cf. Schweizer 1963: 257).

pretation of Isaiah may explain the Israel typology predominant in texts cited in the editorial asides of his infancy narratives.

Translating freely from the Hebrew, Matthew conforms the language of Isaiah 42 to God's praise of his Son in Matthew 3:17 ("my beloved . . . in whom I am well pleased").[63] As Matthew pointed out repeatedly earlier in his Gospel (1:1; 2:15, 18; 3:15; 4:1-2), Jesus' mission is not a wholly new event, but one rooted in the history of his people. For Matthew the servant songs greatly define Jesus' identity (3:17; 8:17; 20:28). From this text Matthew reminds his readers that Jesus was not a political or warrior messiah for the present time; he humbled himself as a suffering servant until the time when he would lead "justice to victory" (12:20).

Charges and Countercharges of Sorcery (12:22-45)

Cf. 9:32-34; 16:1-4; Mk 3:22-30; 8:11-12; Lk 6:43-45; 11:14-32; 12:10; Jn 6:30. Convinced that Jesus is not God's agent and annoyed by the popular response to Jesus (12:23; cf. 7:28; 8:27; 9:8),[64] the Pharisees resort to the only other possible explanation for his supernatural power over demons (12:22; cf. 9:32-34): it comes from the devil (12:24). In a lengthy response, Jesus not only refutes their charge, but turns it back on them (12:25-45). People often thought magicians performed their acts through the help of spirit agents (cf. 1 Enoch 65:6; Ps-Philo 34:2-3; Asc. Isa. 2:5; cf. Sib. Or. 1.96; but especially magical papyri, e.g., *PGM* 1.88-89, 164-66, 181-85, 252-53; 2.52-54),[65] hence the charge here is that Jesus was a sorcerer (cf. also Jn 7:20; 8:48; 10:20; Aune 1987: 56). This is no small charge: magic was a capital offense (Meier 1980: 134; cf. 2 Bar. 66:2; p. Ḥag. 2:2, §5; Sanh. 7:13, §2).[66]

The early Christians probably would not invent a charge against Jesus that was not already current (cf. Witherington 1990: 164), but they would surely find the narrative of the charge useful in their own day. This narrative describing Jesus' triumphant response to their charge provides ammunition for Matthew's audience, who undoubtedly confronted the same accusations about their ministry

63. Cf. Gundry 1982: 229; Schweizer 1970: 37-38; Stendahl 1968: 110; on his targumist sort of reading, cf. Tassin 1990.

64. The "Son of David" acclamation might relate to the association of Solomon with exorcism; see Jos. *Ant.* 8.45-49; incant. text 47.1-3; 48.4-5; 50:8; 51; Test. Sol. passim, e.g., 5:10; Pesiq. Rab Kah. 5:3; semipagan texts in *PGM* 4.850-929 (citing "gods" in 4.852-53, 886); 3039-41; cf. also b. Giṭ. 68ab; *OTP* 1:948. Cf. David and exorcism in 1 Sam 16:14-23; 18:10; Ps-Philo 60; Smith 1978: 79 also links Solomon, the "Son of David," and exorcism. But the title's primary usage is messianic (see comment on 1:1).

65. For other possible associations between sorcerers or diviners and demons, cf. CD 12.2-3; b. Sanh. 67b.

66. Essene rules may illustrate the seriousness of the offense: although the Essenes toned down the Bible's capital offense for Sabbath violation (CD 12.4-5), which they nonetheless took quite seriously, they still regarded speaking by demons as a capital offense (CD 12.2-3).

and that of their Lord (cf. Stanton 1993: 173-78, 190).[67] Rather than seeking to deny testimonies of Jesus' miracles, later Jewish sources continued to charge him with sorcery.[68] Because many associated magic with Egypt (e.g., ARN 28A; 48, §32B; b. Qidd. 49b; Ex. Rab. 9:6; 20:19; Hom. *Od.* 4.228-34; Lewis 1983: 95-96), Jesus' youthful stay in Egypt (2:13-19) was also used against him (see Dalman 1973: 33; Plummer 1910: 17). Perhaps equally relevant to Matthew's readers, later Jewish sources also complained that Christians, who were still working miracles well into the second century, were working them by Satan's power (Dalman 1973: 37-38; Herford 1966: 211-15; Bagatti 1971: 95-96). (In one of these later stories, an early second-century rabbi who was dying tried to convince another rabbi to let a Christian enter to pray for him; but the first rabbi died before he could finish his argument, and the second rabbi rejoiced that the first had died without being defiled by a Christian's prayer — Qoh. Rab. 1:8, §3.) But the Gospels nowhere portray Jesus' activity in magical terms (Kee 1983: 214-15); Matthew in fact explicitly argues against it (cf. Keener 1997b: 98-109, 117-18). As Philo and Josephus may have had to rescue the figure of Moses from those who may have exploited it in a magical direction (Gager 1994), some early Christian apologists may have responded to the same charge against Jesus. Matthew's portrayal of Jesus here communicates a number of significant points for his community in their own conflict with synagogue leaders who rejected Jesus as Israel's rightful king.[69]

First, God's enemies may challenge the very activity by which God attests his servants (12:22-24). That Jesus can "know their thoughts" (12:25) further attests his power; but while Jewish teachers normally characterized as a prophet or pious man one who could know others' thoughts (e.g., t. Pisha 2:15;

67. Traveling teachers in the Greek world likewise had to distinguish themselves from charlatans, e.g., Dio Chrysostom from disreputable Cynics and Apollonius from magicians (Liefeld 1967: 285-87); Mark's narrative likewise uses tradition to contrast Jesus' true source of power with the charge (cf. Mansfield 1987: 62).

68. On Jewish accusations that Jesus was a magician, see also Justin *Dial.* 69:7; b. Sanh. 43a; 107b; Klausner 1979b: 27-28, 49-51, 293; Dalman 1973: 45-50; Herford 1966: 50-62; Gero 1978; Yamauchi 1986: 90-91; Horbury 1984: 183-95; Stanton 1995a: 156-58 (Stanton also treats the standard accusation as a form of deviance labeling to maintain social control). The earliest Jewish and pagan sources reflecting this view admittedly date from the second century (Aune 1980: 1525; Flusser 1988: 635), but several reasons suggest that the later charge reflects a first-century one: (1) no *potentially* relevant sources predate the second century anyway; (2) charges of magic are common in societies that accept its existence (see Mbiti 1970: 262); (3) Gospel texts would probably not respond to a nonexistent charge (Sanders 1985: 166); and (4) Mark and Q independently attest the charge (Stanton 1995a: 161-62); (5) fitting Jesus into the ancient category of "magician" would be easy enough if one ignored other features of his ministry, which his opponents did (cf. at length Smith 1978; for critique, e.g., Yamauchi 1986: 95-96; Blomberg 1986: 449). Pagans often viewed Christian exorcism as Egyptian or Jewish trickery (Edwards 1989).

69. Mt 12:28/Lk 11:20, Q material, demonstrates that where Mark depends on an earlier source like Q, Matthew, Luke, or both feel free to add appropriate material from the original source. This multiple attestation also favors the authenticity of the passage. Twelftree 1993: 98-113 regards much of the account as historically reliable.

Mek. Shir. 7.17-18; p. Ḥag. 2:2, §5; Sanh. 6:6, §2; Pesiq. Rab Kah. 4:3; Jos. and Asen. 23:8; *Lives of the Prophets* 17.2), Jesus' enemies here can attribute Jesus' knowledge to the same source as they attributed his exorcisms.

Second, those who truly work against the devil's purposes are doing God's work (12:25-30). Jesus presents a world sharply divided into God's kingdom and the devil's kingdom (12:26, 28), and indicates through various arguments that one cannot be working for both kingdoms at the same time. *Jesus first asks why the devil would work at cross-purposes with himself (12:25-26).* Perhaps the devil might permit a few exorcisms to bring fame to a sorcerer and gain ground in the long run; Jesus' widespread expulsion of demons, however, constitutes no minor strategic retreat, but a wholesale assault on Satan's kingdom on earth. The necessity of concord or harmony for survival (Ps-Phocyl. 74-75; also a common topic of Greek speeches) and warnings about divided kingdoms (Test. Sol. 5:5; 15:8 — perhaps following Jesus; Hom. *Il.* 1.255-58; cf. Livy 2.60.4; 3.66.4; Sall. *Jug.* 73.5; Babrius 44.7-8; 48) represent common wisdom in ancient society.[70] The use of one spirit to drive out another (Lev. Rab. 24:3) was apparently rejected by Jesus (see comment on 8:17).

Jesus next questions why his opponents single out his ministry of exorcism while approving exorcisms performed by their own disciples (12:27). Given the reluctance with which later Christians might wish to emphasize the success of non-Christian exorcists (cf. Acts 19:13-16), this response has a good claim to authenticity (Witherington 1990: 164).[71] Jewish exorcists were common and employed a variety of magical techniques (see comment on 8:17; cf. Meier 1980: 134-35), quite in contrast to Jesus, who merely commanded authoritatively and the demons obeyed in fear (cf. also Taylor 1935: 129). Jesus acted, he claimed, by God's Spirit (12:28), quite in contrast to his opponents who probably did not claim that the Spirit was available in their time (cf. Keener 1991b: 77-84).[72]

Third, if Jesus was driving out demons by God's Spirit, this action constituted proof that the time of the kingdom was upon them (12:28).[73] Most Phari-

70. Davies and Allison 1991: 336 suggest that the words may even be proverbial (cf. Soph. *Antig.* 672; Philo *Decal.* 152; Cic. *Lael.* 7.23; on Satan's "kingdom" they compare 4Q286 10 2.1-13; 4QAmram b fr. 2; Test. Dan 6:1-4).

71. "Sons" (NIV wrongly renders this as "people," but NRSV rightly understands it as "exorcists") could mean "apprentices" or "disciples" (cf. Jeremias 1969: 177). "They will be your judges" (12:27) might mean that these exorcists would testify against Jesus' accusers' inconsistency at the judgment (12:41-42). Although the sources are rare and late, one may note in passing that some later teachers even felt that good demons existed, and those who knew the law well could teach rabbis (Alexander 1980: 36). Shirock 1992 makes a good case in favor of the classical Christian view that the "sons" are Jesus' disciples; but Pharisees would hardly be persuaded by a self-evident appeal to *disciples'* exorcism, and early Christians had polemical reasons to interpret as Shirock does.

72. Beelzebul (cf. 10:25) is probably a corruption of a pagan deity's name (2 Kings 1:2), but he appears as the prince of the demons in the third-century Test. Sol. 3 (perhaps through Christian influence). Davies and Allison 1991: 335 provide parallels for "ruler of the demons" (Jub. 48.15; 1QM 17.5-6; Test. Dan 5:6; b. Pesaḥ. 110a; cf. also our citations under Mt 4:9; Charles 1902: lxxxiii).

73. The authenticity of 12:28 is usually assumed today, and some scholars also hold 12:27 and 12:28 together in the tradition (Davies and Allison 1991: 339).

sees apparently believed that the prophetic Spirit had been quenched when the last biblical prophets had died, and that the Spirit would be restored only in the time of the kingdom (Keener 1991b: 77-84). Although many Pharisees apparently rejected miracles as proof of truth (Bonsirven 1964: 16), Jesus summons them to consider an alternative explanation for his miracles, namely, that the promised time of the Spirit and the kingdom have come on the scene. Indeed, the Greek construction here might be better rendered, "*since* I drive out demons by the Spirit, the kingdom has come on the scene." If the kingdom has not already "come" in some sense in this verse (which is possible; see, e.g., Dodd 1961: 28n.1; Witherington 1990: 202; Meier 1994: 413-23), it is at least quite imminent (cf. Sanders 1985: 134-36; idem 1993: 177).

Q probably envisioned Jesus as God's *shaliaḥ* or agent (Witherington 1990: 214) expelling demons by God's "finger" (Lk 11:20); pace some scholars,[74] Matthew has plenty of reason to add "Spirit" here, and Luke's emphasis on pneumatology makes his omission of "Spirit" here unlikely.[75] Matthew strategically (and for all practical purposes correctly, in view of the ancient Israelite anthropomorphic language) interprets "finger of God" as "God's Spirit," showing that Jesus is the promised harbinger of the Spirit (12:18), the first agent of God's kingdom. This means that the earlier Gospel tradition saw Jesus' exorcisms (not just the Spirit's coming) as a sign of God's impending reign (Ladd 1978a: 48). This end-time interpretation of Jesus' exorcisms lacks parallels in magical exorcism texts (Theissen 1983: 278-79). That it also lacks substantial parallels in Jewish messianic and end-time expectation (cf. Sanders 1985: 134-35; pace Barrett 1966: 59; Betz 1968: 59-60) may support the authenticity of the saying; early Christians had no other available source for the idea than Jesus himself.[76] Yet it makes good sense: as the climax of history approaches, the forces of God's kingdom and the devil's are arrayed in battle against one another.

Fourth, Jesus had defeated the strong man, "binding" him (tying him up) so that he could plunder the possessions in the strong man's house. That is to say, Jesus invaded Satan's domain and defeated him so that Jesus could recapture the human lives that Satan had enslaved through demon-possession or other means (12:29; cf. Augustine *City of God* 20.7; Ladd 1978a: 48; Fenton 1977: 198-99; Jeremias 1971: 94). Far from being authorized by the demons' ruler, Jesus had authority over the devil — one spirit that no mere magical incantation could thwart (cf. Test. Sol. 6:8). Jesus does not speak here as a magician. That "no one plunders a strong man" was common wisdom (Ps. Sol. 5:3; Charlesworth 1985: 79); if Jesus' parable about binding alludes to specific earlier language, it is not to magical terminology but to God as the divine warrior delivering his people in Isaiah 49:24-25 (also Manson 1979: 86; Robinson 1982: 78; Hooker 1983: 37).

74. E.g., Rodd 1961; Dunn 1975: 45-46; Menzies 1991: 186-89.

75. E.g., Gundry 1982: 235; Schweizer 1975: 287; Witherington 1990: 201; Davies and Allison 1991: 340; Allison 1993b: 237.

76. The association of the Spirit with miracles other than prophecy was also rare in early Judaism (Menzies 1991: 57).

Since Jesus claims a specific act of binding prior to his ministry of exorcism, Matthew may expect his audience to recall the most obvious decisive conflict between Jesus and Satan in the Gospel, Jesus' defeat of Satan at the temptation.[77] Although ancient magical texts regularly speak of "binding" or tying up spirits magically so that one can rule them, Jesus' parable does not refer to magical binding.[78] Jesus is saying that his integrity before God in defeating temptation has given him power over Satan (cf. Acts 19:13-20). In establishing the first stage of his kingdom Jesus had *already* defeated the devil and had delegated his authority over evil spirits to those who were truly his followers, those submitted to his reign (Mt 10:8). The final "binding" of Satan in early Jewish and Christian eschatology awaits the devil's future defeat (cf. 13:30; Rev 20:2; Twelftree 1986: 391-92; idem 1993: 117), perhaps suggesting that his binding before the end of the age may have caught him by surprise (cf. 8:29).[79]

Finally, this list of arguments concludes with Jesus' warning that whoever was not on his side was on the other side (12:30). This saying (already located in the comparable section in Q — Lk 11:23; cf. Mk 9:40) also reflects common wisdom in both Greek (cf. Suet. *Julius* 75; Plut. *Sayings of Kings,* Peisistratus 3, *Mor.* 189C) and Jewish (cf. Flusser 1988: 510-11, who wrongly postulates dependence) life. Jesus allows no would-be disciples to straddle the fence: one either follows him or opposes him, just as one does with the devil.

Third, a heart can become so hard against God's evidence that conversion becomes impossible (12:31-32).[80] Jewish teachers acknowledged that deliberate sin against God's law ("sin with a high hand" — cf. Num 15:30-31; Deut

77. So, e.g., Jeremias 1972: 122; Weiss 1971: 81; Rhoads and Michie 1982: 42; pace France 1985: 210.

78. Incantations for warding off demons are at least as old as the Egyptian Book of the Dead (e.g., Spells 40, 41, 136) and Persian sources (Olmstead 1959: 18, citing Vid. 8:21; 20:7). Although "binding" had wider figurative usages (e.g., 22:13; Plato *Cratylus* 403C; cf. sympathetic magic in *PGM* 12.160-78; mummification in *PDM* 14.256) and sometimes referred to demons' present or future imprisonment (1 Enoch 10:4-6, 11-14; 13:1; 14:5; 21:3-4; Jub. 10:7; Test. Levi 18:12; Rev 20:2; cf. 1 Enoch 22:11; 90:23; Deut. Rab. 1:22; Mt 22:13), it became common in magical exorcisms (e.g., Tob 8:1-2; Smith 1978: 127; Twelftree 1986: 385; cf. Test. Sol. 3:7; 18). "Binding" demons appears as part of magical texts in Aram. incant. text 3.2, 7; 5.1-2 ("conquered . . . bound"); 5.3-4 ("I am binding you with the evil and strong spell"); 10.1 ("Wholly bound and sealed and tied in knots . . . that you . . . depart from the house"); 27.2-3; 47.1-3; cf. *PGM* 3.99-100; texts also speak of demons binding persons (e.g., Tob 3:17; Deissmann 1978: 304-7); in Hom. *Il.* 5.385-91 mortals bind Ares in a jar. One could also "bind" demons to manipulate them to do one's will in sorcery (e.g., *PGM* 4.384-85, 2246-48; 101/1-3; cf. also conveniently in Kraemer 1988: 108-9; cf. Alexander 1980: 36-40), or use such demons to "bind" people (e.g., *PGM* 4.355-56, 376-83, 395; 7.912-13; 15.1; 32.1-19; 101.8-9, 16-17, 36; *IG* 3.97.34-41 in Lefkowitz and Fant 1988: 258, §251).

79. Jesus thus believes that his exorcisms prefigure the end, although few texts indicate that eschatological exorcism was a standard expectation (Twelftree 1993: 217-24, 228).

80. For a discussion of the authenticity of the blasphemy against the Spirit saying, see Marshall 1974: 77-78. Apart from its context in the Didache (11:7), none of Boring's arguments that this must be a prophecy later than Jesus himself bears any weight (pace Boring 1982: 159-60; Theissen 1978: 28). Gos. Nic./Acts of Pilate 4:3 (Boring 1995: 88-89) presumably echoes Jesus' saying, though it purports to indicate Jewish tradition.

29:18-20; CD 8.8), such as deliberate blasphemy against God, was unforgivable (Jub. 15:34; 1QS 7.15-17, 22-23; p. Ḥag. 2:1, §9; cf. Heb 6:6); some recognized that atonement could purify even these sins, but only for the genuinely repentant (CD 10.3; Jas 5:19-20; p. Shebu. 1:6, §5; Ruth Rab. 6:4). Even such a sin as Peter's denial of Jesus (26:69-75) does not count in the unforgivable category (28:10-20), however; the context of "blaspheming against the Spirit" here refers specifically to the sin of these Pharisees, who are on the verge of becoming incapable of repentance. The sign of their hardness of heart is their determination to reject *any* proof for Jesus' divine mission, to the extent that they even attribute God's attestation of Jesus to the devil.[81]

Fourth, one's words for or against God's purposes reveal one's character and in the judgment will testify for or against the person who utters them (12:33-37). That one's speech reveals one's heart (also 15:11) may represent conventional wisdom;[82] one ancient story line also apparently recognized that one could ruin one's own defense in court and be convicted by one's own words (Lk 19:22; Num. Rab. 16:21). Jewish wisdom regularly exhorted appropriate use of one's tongue (e.g., Sir 4:29; 20:18; Syr. Men. Sent. 301-13; Ps-Phocyl. 20; m. 'Abot 1:15, 17; 3:13; ARN 1, 26A; Philo *Conf.* 34), and Jewish teachers naturally recognized that one would be accountable for one's words as well as deeds on the day of judgment (Hagner 1993: 350; 1 Enoch 100:9, MSS; b. Sanh. 90a).[83] At least some groups regarded "idle" or "vain" words as profane on a day holy to the Lord (CD 10.18; cf. Is 58:13); others contrasted vain words with discussion of Torah (e.g., ARN 31, §66B; b. Ber. 28b, bar.; cf. Gen. Rab.

81. Blaspheming Jesus directly may not have counted as harshly during his earthly ministry on account of the messianic secret (France 1985: 210). "Will be forgiven" may reflect an Aramaic construction meaning forgiveness in the present rather than only in the future (Gundry 1982: 237). On the Jewish doctrine of two ages, cf., e.g., 13:22; Eph 1:21; Lk 18:30; 4 Ezra 7:50; t. Ta'an. 3:14; Sifre Num. 115.5.7; Sifre Deut. 29.2.3; ARN 12A; 22, §46B; b. Yoma 87a; p. Ḥag. 2:1, §16; Pesiq. Rab Kah. 6:2; 9:1; Gen. Rab. 1:10; 59:6; 90:6; Ex. Rab. 30:19; 47:3; Lev. Rab. 3:1; Deut. Rab. 2:31; Song Rab. 2:2, §6; Pesiq. R. 16:6; 25:2; cf. also Ferch 1977: 135-51. God would punish blasphemy (1 Enoch 96:7); some Jewish circles considered apostasy from the covenant an unforgivable form of blasphemy (Jub. 15:34). Qumran regulations made deliberate rebellion against the community unforgivable (1QS 7.15-17, 22-23); the Watchers, whose rebellion against God had been deliberate and total, were also beyond forgiveness (1 Enoch 12:5). Some later teachers felt that atonement was efficacious for the repentant — hence unavailable to those who cast off the covenant in which repentance was possible (p. Shebu. 1:6, §5; cf. Ḥag. 2:1, §9). Probably reading the blasphemy against the Spirit in light of Heb 6:4-6, some early interpreters understood it as one deliberately rejecting grace, as distinct from falling into error (Origen *First Principles* 1.3), though blasphemy could be forgiven if followed by repentance (Augustine *Sermons on NT Lessons* 21.35, *ACCS*, 46-47; cf. 1 Tim 1:13, 20).

82. For this point, cf. Bultmann 1968: 108n.1; Dalman 1929: 227; Manson 1979: 60; Lachs 1987: 213.

83. Attention to one's speech (often including recommendations to silence) was part of broader Greco-Roman (e.g., *Gnomologium Vaticanum* 459 in Malherbe 1986: 110; *Pythag. Sent.* 14, 16, 22 in ibid. 110-11; Isoc. *Demon.* 34; Sen. *Dial.* 5.10.1; Dio Chrys. *32d Disc.* 2; Plut. *Educ.* 14, *Mor.* 10F; Aul. Gel. 1.15; Diog. Laert. 1.69-70, 87, 92, 104; 7.1.24; 7.5.172; contrast Diog. Laert. 5.40) and ancient Near Eastern (e.g., Ahiqar 98-99, Sayings 15-16; "Ani," *ANET* 420; "Amen-em-opet," *ANET* 424; Prov 12:18; 21:23) wisdom.

91:10; for examples, Qoh. Rab. 1:8, §1; see comment on 9:11). Jesus here indicates that even such careless words spoken without thought will testify concerning one's character on the judgment day. On the day of judgment (cf. 7:22; 10:15; 11:22; 1 Jn 4:17; Jude 6) each person will give account to God (cf. also Rom 14:12), one's words often revealing the character of one's heart (Mt 15:11). In this context, Jesus is saying that one expects people like these Pharisees to be the kind of people who would blaspheme the Holy Spirit because their hearts are so corrupt, though they appeared righteous to most other observers (cf. Lk 16:15). Indeed, in Matthew's narratives, the religious leaders prove utterly duplicitous, expressing their genuine views about Jesus only when speaking among themselves (Powell 1996: 171-76).

Fifth, God has already provided the world sufficient evidence that he has the right to expect faith from those who have heard the truth (12:38-42). The request for a sign (cf. 16:1-4; Jn 6:30) revealed the evil character of that "generation's" hearts (cf. 11:16; 16:4; Deut 32:5; Dalman 1929: 52-53);[84] Jesus had already been providing signs, and his opponents were disputing their validity (12:22-24). The demand for a sign may recall Pharaoh's challenge to Moses for a sign (Ex 7:9; Allison 1993b: 236).[85] The whole of 12:39-45 constitutes Jesus' response to his opponents' charges ("generation" in 12:39, 45, frames the section).

Jesus explains that his generation needs no greater sign that he is from God than his own message. *He first insists that the only sign the sign-seekers would be given was the sign that God supplied the Ninevites:* Jonah's restoration after three days on the edge of death (12:39-40).[86] One should keep in mind, however, that the Ninevites did not witness Jonah's resuscitation for themselves; indeed, there is no evidence that he even recounted it to them (Jonah 3:1-4; cf. 3 Macc 6:8; Justin *Dial.* 107). The Ninevites experienced the effects of a divine sign they never recognized, and this may well be Matthew's point (not clear in Lk 11:29, 32): the Ninevites repented without recognizing a sign, whereas Jesus' opponents were too hard-hearted to repent despite the many signs he had been giving them (cf. 11:20-24; Jonah 1:16; 4:2). All the Ninevites needed was Jonah's

84. "Adulterous" (12:39) could refer to immoral hearts (susceptible to lust and divorce, 5:27-32) or, more likely, as often in the Hebrew Bible, apostasy from their covenant with God (e.g., Is 1:21; Hos 1:2; 2:2; 4:15, 18; 9:1; Jer 2:20; 3:1, 6; Ezek 16:33).

85. Allison 1993b: 237-38 doubts that Matthew wishes to emphasize the allusion strongly given his omission of Q's "finger of God" in 12:28 (cf. Ex 8:18-19), but it may just be that Matthew's need to stress the Spirit took precedence over the Moses allusion there.

86. Jesus' contemporaries seemed more interested in Jonah's experience with the fish than in other features of his book and might therefore understand Jesus as referring to that episode (France 1985: 213); others think that the sign in the Q version meant only Jonah's preaching (Vermes 1993: 57-58). "Three days and three nights" (Jonah 2:1; cf. Hos 6:2) was standard Jewish language covering a period including any parts of three days (references in Gundry 1982: 244-45; Vermes 1993: 58-59). Jewish teachers apparently accepted the witness of one's death only after three days had passed (Dalman 1929: 188); but "three days" may simply represent a short period (e.g., Jos. *Life* 205, 229, 268). Some Jewish sources apply the "heart of the earth" to the realm of the dead (Gundry 1982: 244, who also compares Jonah 2:3; but cf. Ezek 28:2).

preaching of the truth, yet Jesus was greater than Jonah (12:41; cf. 12:6).[87] Jonah's reluctance to see pagans repent lest Israel be condemned by comparison (Mek. Pisha 1.80-82; cf. Jonah 3:10–4:2) underlines the relative responsiveness of Gentiles, fitting Matthew's theme.

Jesus' second example is that Solomon's wisdom[88] was enough to prove his divine appointment, and that a distant queen heard and came to him (as some Gentile seekers had done with Jesus — 2:1-12; 1 Kings 10:1-13).[89] Yet one greater than Solomon was there.[90] The images of the Ninevites and the Queen of Sheba rising up (being resurrected — 16:21) to condemn Jesus' generation in Israel at the judgment would have horrified Jesus' hearers, many of whom expected Israel's final vindication against the nations at that judgment day. Indeed, if God accepted Nineveh's repentance, surely he would accept Israel's (Pesiq. Rab Kah. 24:11).

At the same time, however, some early Jewish readers could respond to the book of Jonah as if it threatened Israel's judgment by Nineveh's comparatively quick repentance (Mek. Pisha 1.81-82). Jewish traditions attested in some rabbinic sources indicate that Gentile converts to Judaism would testify against the nations in the judgment (Lev. Rab. 2:9; Pesiq. R. 35:3); the repentant poor would testify against those who used poverty as an excuse against repentance; the repentant rich and so forth would do likewise (e.g., ARN 6A; 12, §30B; b. Yoma 35b; 3 Enoch 4:3). Jesus employs his people's traditions to show them their own need (cf. 12:27). Matthew here reemphasizes the Gentile mission: those who know little about Israel's God (like the Ninevites or the Queen of Sheba, or the

87. Matthew might also expect his community to recall that Jesus prophesied Jerusalem's destruction (23:38–24:2) as Jonah prophesied Nineveh's, but the specific tradition that Jonah also prophesied Jerusalem's demise (cited by Schmitt 1978) is later and too narrow. Jonah appears more positively in later rabbinic texts than in early ones; see Zucker 1995.

88. Josephus concurs that it was internationally famed (*Apion* 1.111-15; cf. 1 Kings 4:34) but makes Moses the wisest man in history (*Ant.* 4.328); nevertheless, he portrays Solomon very favorably for a hellenistic audience (Feldman 1976).

89. That later Jewish traditions amplify her paganism (Test. Sol. 19:3) is probably irrelevant. Origen and Jerome viewed her as a black African (Felder 1989: 12-13; Snowden 1970: 202-3); Jesus' contemporaries viewed her as African, queen of Egypt and Ethiopia (Jos. *Ant.* 8.159, 165, 175; *Lives of the Prophets* 1.8/12 [Schermann 76.13-14, §24]; Scott 1994: 536n.203); Twelfth Dynasty Egyptian sources reportedly speak of a Saba as capital of Kush, i.e., as Meroe (Adamo 1986: 139; cf. Jos. *Ant.* 2.249). Both Ethiopian and Arabic (Manson 1979: 91) traditions about her claim her for themselves; for further discussion, see Felder 1989: 22-36; Hansberry 1981: 33-58; Adamo 1986: 137-44; C. J. Sanders 1995. In any case, no one disputes that South Arabians and East Africans derive from genetically similar stock (cf., e.g., Rashidi 1988: 23-24). "Queen of the south" may suggest for Nineveh the antithetical title "king of the north," which may recall great evil (Dan 11:6, 8, 11; Theissen 1991: 44-45).

90. Vermes 1993: 61-66 doubts that Jesus often used *pesher* interpretation such as is found in the Scrolls, where its function was (he claims) apologetic rather than didactic; but I believe the *pesharim* include clear didactic elements (even the apologetic was retained within the community, for purposes of self-definition), and Jesus' application of texts to his own (climactic) generation is multiply attested (e.g., Mt 23:35-36//Lk 11:51; Mk 4:11-12; 14:27; Mt 26:54; Lk 4:18-19; 24:44; Jn 15:25).

Magi earlier in his Gospel) are often least arrogant and hence most responsive to the gospel. (The context of the Queen of Sheba in 1 Kings 10, as with the Ninevites in Jonah, is an Israelite's witness to the nations.)

Finally, by rejecting the transformation effected by God's reign Jesus' opponents would become worse than the way they had started (12:43-45). Although this paragraph occurs in the same general context in Luke, Matthew specifically places it within the discussion of "this evil generation" (12:39, 45) and uses it to *conclude* Jesus' response to his opponents. Whatever else the parable might say about exorcism, Jesus' point is what it says to that generation: although Jesus was exorcising the generation, its evil leaders were setting it up to be demonized all the worse by rejecting Jesus' reign (cf. Jeremias 1972: 106; Argyle 1963: 99).

The story includes many clearly Palestinian elements (Jeremias 1972: 197-98; cf. Bultmann 1968: 164), and the story line is quite basic. When an unclean spirit leaves a person and enters the desert seeking a place to dwell (for desert haunts for some demons, cf. 4:1; cf. Is 13:21; Tob 8:3; 2 Bar. 10:8; Test. Sol. 5.11-12; Kraeling 1951: 28; for wandering, cf. the tradition preserved by Yemenite Jewish exorcists in Hes 1964: 375), it finally returns with seven times the original force and the man ends up worse than before his exorcism.[91] If one translates the passage literally, the sentence is conditional: the demons will return *if* the house is left empty (Jeremias 1971: 154). Were Jesus' opponents accusing him of being in league with Satan through his exorcisms (12:24)? Jesus here returns the charge: it is they, not he, who are redemonizing their generation, for they leave the house empty in which God, the only true alternative to the devil, should reign (cf. 23:38-39). (Returning charges was acceptable rhetorical practice, but could intensify one's opposition, e.g., Plato *Apology* 35D; Acts 7:53.)

Jesus' True Family (12:46-50)

Cf. Mk 3:31-35; Lk 8:19-21. Not only the religious leaders (12:24, 38), but Jesus' own family doubted him (Mk 3:21-31, bracketing the Pharisees' attack; cf. Jn 7:5). Given the role of "James the Lord's brother" in the later church (Acts 12:17; 15:13; 21:18; 1 Cor 15:7; Gal 1:19; 2:9; Jude 1), one would rather expect the early Christians to have emphasized his virtues and so avoid the charge of nepotism (cf. Jos. *Ant.* 4.26-28, 34, 58). The stark portrayal here is not apt to reflect an invention of the early Jewish Christians who honored James and provided the bulk of the Matthean community. Nor should we think Matthew would

91. "Sevenfold" represents the rhetoric of amplified punishments (Gen 4:15, 24; Lev 26:18; Ps 79:12) or other amplifications (1 Enoch 72:37; 91:16; cf. Test. Sol. 8:1). For the possibility of demons returning, Davies and Allison 1991: 361 cite Mk 9:25; Jos. *Ant.* 8.45; Philost. *V.A.* 4.20; Acts Thom. 46; for a person as a demon's house, they cite Test. Naph. 8:6; b. Giṭ. 52a. Cf. also magical incantations to make a spirit "dwell" or "remain" (*PGM* 4.709-10).

have invented it (even had he not found it in Mark), as it does not cohere easily, without explanation, with his own portrayal of Jesus' faithful mother (1:18-25) or Jesus' emphasis on honor of parents (15:4). But the account could nevertheless prove encouraging to those facing familial ostracism (10:21, 35-37), and illustrates that Jesus follows the same principles he demands of others (8:21-22).

People often brought reports to teachers (e.g., p. Ḥag. 2:1, §10); here a report is brought to Jesus about his family standing outside wishing to meet with him (12:47). Relatives normally sought to conceal other relatives' behavior that would shame the whole family, hence their concern in Mark 3:20-31 (cf. Malina 1993: 80). Their opposition to or disbelief in Jesus is less clear in Matthew than in Mark, perhaps because of the shame of the family's unbelief, especially after Mary's experiences in Matthew's infancy narratives (1:18–2:23). Whether or not Matthew has intentionally toned down the offense of Jesus' family, Jesus' refusal to place his physical family first is no less clear here than in Mark.[92] Even in traditional Greek (Demosth. *Against Stephanus* 1.53) and Roman (Dupont 1992: 106-8 on clan ties) cultures, family ties were paramount. Being perceived as antifamily was a much greater danger then than it is today (cf. Derrett 1973: 39); yet Jesus followed the practice he had demanded of others (8:21-22; 10:37): the kingdom of God comes first. Allegiance to God's will (7:21; 21:31; 26:42) is what makes one Jesus' true brother, sister, or mother (25:40; 28:10).[93]

92. In contrast to much later tradition, this passage probably refers to Jesus' younger siblings physically (1:25); see most fully and fairly Meier 1991a: 318-32. Benassi 1957 notes that the Semitic expression could mean that Jesus' family members are such not *merely* by human bonds, but especially because they obey the Father. In any case, Jesus is not repudiating his earthly family altogether but declaring priorities graphically (and inescapably offensively). Although Jesus could "stretch forth his hand" to rescue (14:31) or touch the untouchable for healing (8:3), here he does so demonstratively, in typical rhetorical fashion (cf. Acts 26:1; Ap. Rhod. 1.344). Augustine contended that Mary's earthly mothership to Jesus was less important to her than being his disciple (*Letter* 243 to Laetus), and Christians should prefer spiritual kinship to fleshly (*On Virginity* 3; *Tractate* 10.3.2 on *John, ACCS,* 48-49).

93. Saldarini 1994: 120 treats the fictive kinship terminology in terms of congregations functioning as households by meeting in homes, "as did many synagogues in the first century." Many used such kinship terminology in broader Greco-Roman antiquity, e.g., for coinitiates (Burkert 1987: 45), fellow teachers (Sifre Deut. 34.5.3; b. ʿAbod. Zar. 18a, bar.); fellow Jews (Tob 5:10; 6:10; 7:3; 2 Macc 1:1; cf. Acts 9:17), friends (e.g., Marc. Aur. 1.14; Plut. *Many Friends* 2, *Mor.* 93E; Ahiqar 49, col. 4; *CPJ* 3:41, §479), allies (1 Macc 10:18; 12:6, 10, 21; 14:40), or even prospective guests (Test. Abr. 2B); waxing more philosophical, for fellow humans (Diod. Sic. 1.1.3) or sharers in virtue (Diog. Laert. 6.1.12). For mother imagery as expressions of endearment toward older women, see, e.g., Rom 16:13; Diod. Sic. 17.37.6; inscription in Horsley 1987: 34 (toward his stepmother).

The Sower and the Soils (13:1-23)

Cf. Mk 4:1-20; Lk 8:4-15; Jn 9:39; 12:37-40; Acts 28:25-27. That Matthew's central discourse section (13:1-52) contains seven or eight parables depicting the present character of the kingdom until the end is no coincidence. Matthew arranges his work strategically: his final discourse section contains a roughly equal number of end-time kingdom parables (24:32–25:46; Jeremias 1972: 93). As in Mark, Jesus' parables of the kingdom's present state explain why Jesus' kingdom comes first in a hidden way and why Israel's leaders reject Jesus (cf. F. F. Bruce 1972a: 69; Gerhardsson 1972: 36; Ladd 1963a). They dramatically reinforce that Jesus' first coming was coercive neither militarily nor intellectually (11:25-27); he came as the meek burden-bearer (11:28-30), and only the meek could recognize and follow him (11:25, 28).

That the parables in Matthew address his people's acceptance or rejection of the kingdom message follows from the context in Matthew's narrative: Jesus speaks parables "that same day" that he has confronted Pharisaic opposition (12:24-45) and offered a culturally offensive statement about his family (12:46-50). The parables section closes immediately with an account of Jesus' rejection by his hometown (13:53-58), so that rejection by "one's own" frames his kingdom parables (cf. 12:46-50; 10:21, 34-37). This likewise implies that true disciples — those who follow the kingdom message — must be prepared to pay the ultimate price for doing so (13:20-22, 44-46).[1]

What is a parable? The Greek term for "parable" roughly translates the Hebrew *mashal* in biblical Greek (cf. also 1 Enoch 1:2-3); the Septuagint translates *mashal* in different ways, but as *parabolē* in 1 Kings 5:12; Ezekiel 17:2; and Psalm 78:2 (Stern 1991: 290n.10). The *mashal* includes a variety of types of discourse, including stories (e.g., Ezek 24:2-5; cf. fable in Judg 9:7-

1. Scholars have observed different aspects of the chapter's structure. Besides Mark's sower parable, Matthew includes three parables called "parable" and three introduced with "again . . . is like" at the end of each group including an interpretation (Jeremias 1972: 92, 94n.10). Yet if one divides the chapter into two sections (13:1-35; 13:36-52), each shares an analogous structure (setting, parables with excursus, and conclusion — Kingsbury 1969: 12). This chapter is centrally located, and some (including Kingsbury 1969; Ellis 1974: 11) see Mt 13 as the thematically central point of the Gospel. Matthew is not bound to Mark's structure (which bears little resemblance to a typical *chreia,* pace Mack and Robbins 1989: 143-60). Matthew also alternates between crowds with disciples (13:2, 34) and disciples alone (13:10, 36; Heil 1998: 65-66).

15), proverbs (e.g., 1 Sam 24:13), taunt-songs (Is 14:4), and riddles (Ezek 17:2; Jos. *Ant.* 8.148-49; cf. Jesus' questions, e.g., in Mt 21:24, 31).[2] Jewish hearers were thus accustomed to a variety of parables. But in rabbinic literature, the *mashal* specifically includes the kind of story parables told by Jesus (e.g., 21:33; 22:1; 24:32) and later rabbis (Stern 1991: 9-10; cf. Scott 1989: 7-11). This suggests that between the Septuagint and the time of the rabbis, a parable like those Jesus told would already be recognized as a *mashal* (as attested later by the rabbis), which would naturally be rendered into Greek as *parabolē* (as attested by the LXX).[3]

Although Jesus may use "parables" in something related to the Aristotelian sense of analogies (cf. Sider 1981; Quint. 5.11.1), *the source of his storytelling style is plainly not Greek.*[4] When one compares Jesus' parables with many other preachers' illustrations from the Roman period, the frequent illustrations of Paul and Greco-Roman philosophers provide only a relatively distant comparison (cf. *Rhet. ad Herenn.* 4.34.45; 4.49.62; Johnston 1977a: 226).[5] To be sure, rhetoricians also regularly employed metaphor (*Rhet. ad Herenn.* 4.45) and allegory (*Rhet. ad Herenn.* 4.46), and various writers used riddles (e.g., Virg. *Ecl.* 3.104-7). More relevantly, Greeks borrowed the ancient Near Eastern form of story parables called fables (which are attested in the Sumerian period; see Perry 1965: xxviii-xxxiv; Babrius 2.intro. 1-6). Hesiod used animal fables as riddles too obvious to require explanation (*W.D.* 202-11). Aesop's fables were known as early as Aristophanes in the late fifth century B.C. (*Birds* 651-53) and circulated in prose collections before the first century A.D. (e.g., Babrius prol. 15-19), and some speakers employed them to communicate morals in public rhetoric (e.g., Aul. Gel. 2.29.1). Yet the Greeks typically called these stories "fables," not parables (Theon *Progymn.* 3).

Most importantly, our closest parallels to Jesus' parables in form and substance are Jewish, and story parables are a largely Jewish phenomenon (Young 1989: 1). Parables appear in the biblical prophets (2 Sam 12:1-7; Is 5:1-7; Hill 1979: 58-59), in some apocalyptic literature (e.g., 1 Enoch 1:2-3; 37-71; cf. Herm. *Sim.* 3.1-10; Hammershaimb 1975; Witherington 1990: 243), and in other

2. See further Stein 1978: 35-36; Manson 1979: 29; Gerhardsson 1988; Vermes 1993: 90.

3. A variety of forms also appear in Jesus' and rabbinic parables. Johnston 1977b: 520-26 classifies Tannaitic parables into groups including example stories (520-22), short similes and metaphors (522-23; pace Dodd, these usually are called *mashal* and have standard parable formulas), and parabolized fables (523-24). The example stories in the Gospels all appear in Luke (Lk 10:30-37; 12:16-21; 16:19-31; 18:10-14; perhaps 14:7-11, 12-14; Johnston 1977b: 636n.4), and example stories may be distinct from normal parables; but Bultmann's distinction between similitudes and parables is untenable (1977b: 636).

4. Pace Mack 1988: 157-58, who merely summarizes Greco-Roman rhetoric's use of the term and then applies it directly to Jesus' parables. Aristotle used *parabolē* for brief comparisons rhetoricians used as proofs, generally similes; he called genuine stories (like most of Jesus' parables) *logoi* instead, though later rhetoricians also applied the term to narrative illustrations (Stern 1991: 10).

5. This in spite of the fact that Greek models and even story lines (e.g., in Aesop's fables) did affect rabbinic parables (Stern 1991: 7; cf. also Mack 1988: 160n.18).

Jewish texts (e.g., Test. Job 18:7-8) but were especially common property of the sages (Sir 1:24; 3:29; 20:20; 39:2; 47:17; cf. Sir 18:29).

The closest formal and linguistic parallels to Jesus' parables, however, occur in Palestinian rabbinic texts, that is, later records of how Jewish teachers customarily reasoned and taught (e.g., m. Soṭa 9:15; Mek. Pisha 1.82-84; b. Ber. 61b); this seems the consensus of scholars directly familiar with both sets of parables.[6] Although rabbinic parables are later and midrashic, hence more stereotyped, examination demonstrates considerable formal similarities between rabbinic and Gospel parables, especially morphological but often even extending to stock metaphors and characters (Johnston 1977b: 628-33).

Our rabbinic parables are all later than Jesus, but this should not surprise us since all rabbinic literature is later than Jesus, as are most of the sages it cites (Vermes 1993: 97; cf. Young 1989: 3).[7] But because Jesus probably did not influence directly most later rabbis (pace the argument from silence in Jeremias 1972: 12), we may assume that both *Jesus and these rabbis drew on and adapted standard Palestinian Jewish teaching techniques of their day* (Abrahams 1917: 106; Johnston 1977b: 43). Occasionally he probably even developed traditional story lines (Taylor 1935: 104; Johnston 1977b: 635).[8] Whereas the later rabbinic parables often focus on such settings as royal courts, however (cf. 22:2; see comment on Mt 18:23), Jesus most often told stories about agriculture and the daily life of his common hearers (e.g., 20:1; cf. Neusner 1984: 23), a characteristic that supports authenticity. Another contrast with rabbinic parables is that Jesus' parables tend to subvert conventional values, whereas those of the rabbis tend to reinforce them (Johnston 1977b: 633-34).[9] Jesus' parables are also far more apt to emphasize eschatology (Johnston 1977b: 508, but cf. 626), though this might say more about the development of rabbinic Judaism after Bar Kochba than about Jesus.

Except when reporting Jesus' parables, other New Testament writers, usually addressing urban communities outside Palestine, do not employ parables. Because later Christians would therefore not have invented Jesus' parables, this

6. E.g., Stewart 1964; Cave 1965: 387; Johnston 1976: 355; Sandmel 1978b: 105; Barth 1981; de la Maisonneuve 1987; Goulder 1974: 47-69; Scott 1989: 14; Young 1989: 317-18; D'Angelo 1992; Vermes 1993: 97.

7. Our earliest layers of rabbinic texts are quite thin and preserve few parables. Three items attributed to Hillel are not very developed; eleven come from ben Zakkai's generation; thirty-three from the next generation (ten from R. Gamaliel II alone); thirty-nine from the next; and ninety-three from the next (forty-nine of which come from two rabbis); see Johnston 1977b: 498-500; Vermes 1993: 97n.21. Unlike Jesus and perhaps some other early wisdom sages, the rabbis use parables in predominantly midrashic (exegetical) rather than narrative contexts (see Johnston 1977b: 632; Scott 1989: 15-16; Vermes 1993: 114-15; for exceptions, see Johnston 1977b: 503). Even in Aramaic contexts, rabbinic parables appear in Hebrew (except for some vernacular conversation in them; Young 1989: 40-42).

8. Rabbinic parables were sometimes attributed to different authors (Young 1989: 179), probably in part due to their reuse by other rabbis; recycling earlier story lines was a sign of respect for the story's content (e.g., Terence *Eunuch* 30-43 argues that recycling characters is acceptable).

9. As Scott 1989: 39 observes, Jesus' parables employ traditional mythemes but function counterculturally, hence as "antimyth."

supports their authenticity as genuine teachings of Jesus, which most scholars accept.[10]

Authenticity, of course, does not preclude adaptation, although the measure of that adaptation remains open to debate. Later tellers altered characters in earlier rabbinic parables and otherwise adapted them to speak to new situations (Johnston 1977b: 621-24, 639). Likewise, embellishment was natural to the folklorish context in which parables were transmitted (Young 1989: 179). But rabbinic literature preserved and recycled parables primarily because of the story lines themselves, whereas the Gospel tradition preserved parables because they were *Jesus'* parables. As noted in the Introduction, the process of transmission behind our extant Gospels was brief by comparison, and the controlled conditions do not lend themselves to folklorish embellishment. In this early period we should usually think of more conservative adaptations fitting rhetorical principles governing expanding or condensing narratives (compare Matthew's conservative adaptations of Mark 4 in this chapter), allowing, however, for reapplication of parables in new contexts (e.g., Mt 5:15//Mk 4:21). On the authenticity of interpretations for parables, including so-called allegorical interpretations, see comment on 13:18-23 below.

Kinds of parables. If we set aside for the moment morphological categories (e.g., example stories, similes, fables; Johnston 1977b: 520-26), scholars have devised various categorization schemes. For example, Crossan uses Heidegger's time-related scheme of advent, reversal, and action; but not all parables fit such externally imposed structures (Scott 1989: 73). For more reasonable plans based on content, one may examine Scott's organization by social role: parables relating to family, patron-client relations,[11] or daily life artifacts (1989: 73), or, similarly, Vermes' division into countrymen's (rural) parables, daily life episodes, social parables, parables relating to judges and law courts, and parables of wedding feasts (1993: 98). One can determine such divisions by setting inductively, though one cannot thereby create tight, symmetrical categories. One could also distinguish parables according to their main theme or point (of which Vermes 1993: 117 stresses three: *teshubah* — repentance and forgiveness; *'emunah* — trust in God; and superlative trust expressed in high risks for the kingdom).

The setting for the parables is noteworthy (13:1-2). Not every element of the setting is equally critical; mention of the house (13:1) might be part of Matthew's style (cf. 9:28; 13:36; Mk 4:1; 10:46); Jesus also seems to have customarily sat to

10. E.g., Stein 1978: 44-45; Dodd 1961: 11; Vermes 1993: 90-91; see more fully Payne 1980a; Payne 1981a. Pace Mack 1988: 146-47, who resorts to suggesting that most scholars accept authenticity from motives of convenience! Mack 1993: 34 seems correct to observe that few parables (at least in the sense of story parables) appear in Q (unless Mark heavily mined Q's parables, but the evidence, such as Matthew's and Luke's omitting Mk 4:32's "large" branches, is weak), but works from the assumption that only Q (and a hypothetical early layer at that) is largely authentic; yet even his own portrait of Jesus as a wisdom teacher should have allowed parables. (Even the notorious Jesus Seminar accepts many parables — Blomberg 1995: 20.)

11. Although overstating his case on the analogy's primacy, see Malina 1988 for God as patron (and Jesus as broker) in Synoptic theology.

teach (cf. 24:3; comment on 5:1).[12] More significantly, the crowds outside were apparently severe (13:2; cf. Mk 4:1; b. Ber. 6b; Livy 33.33.1-2; ancients would see in this praise of the teacher's rhetorical abilities, e.g., p. B. Meṣ. 2:11, §1; Hor. 3:4, §4; Diog. *Ep.* 2), so Jesus entered into a boat and pushed out slightly from the shore, a technique that had enabled him to speak to large crowds (rather than merely those near him) on other occasions (Lk 5:3, unless the reason Luke omits Mk 4:1's setting in Lk 8:4 is that he used it here). Like a cove near Capernaum, many natural acoustic settings existed in Galilee that would enable thousands to hear the voice of someone properly positioned (Crisler 1976: 134-37).

Bailey 1980: xiii suggests that some of the parable settings may have been transmitted along with the traditions to which they were attached. In rabbinic parables one might expect an attribution and an application, but rarely a description of the setting in which the teaching was uttered; still, rabbinic analogies may break down here since rabbinic texts usually stress the rabbis' teaching more than their person, whereas the Gospel tradition is interested in both. It is thus possible that Jesus may have spoken many parables on specific occasions mentioned in the Gospels. An inductive approach would test this best, and one such study concludes that the Synoptic writers almost invariably claim the same audience for the same parables, with but two exceptions that may represent different parables (Carson 1984b: 409-10, following P. B. Payne's Ph.D. dissertation).

At the same time, it is likely that Jesus spoke parables in a variety of settings (e.g., 18:23-35; 19:30–20:16; 21:28-44; 22:1-14; 24:32–25:46), and many of his parables were collected into arrangements like those in the Gospels; parables tend to occur in bunches in later Jewish texts as well (Johnston 1977b: 502; Perry 1965: xi shows that Greeks had also collected fables for rhetorical purposes by the first century). Also, "Like the gospel parables, the same rabbinic parable may appear in different contexts far removed from one another" (Young 1989: 179; cf. Johnston 1977b: 621-24).

First, Jesus used commonplace images to illustrate kingdom principles (13:3-9). *This "parable of the sower" (13:18) draws from natural agricultural conventions, as one would expect from a teacher sensitive to rural Galilean hearers.* Most Palestinian Jews, like most other Mediterranean people, worked in agriculture (see Jos. *Apion* 1.60; Sanders 1992: 119); perhaps 90 percent of the Roman world was rural (Malina 1981: 72-73; Horsley and Hanson 1985: xii, following Sjoberg 1960/66: 110).[13] With only two large cities, Galilee's population

12. Crosby 1988: 21-75 connects "house" with "church" in Matthew. Theissen 1991: 283 suggests that the "house" reflects later house churches receiving the "additional teachings," but while the tradition might have stressed the house for this reason, we need not suppose that the house was invented. Houses were common places for teaching in Jewish Palestine, and houses where healers stayed might also draw crowds (cf. 8:14-16).

13. Boring 1995: 89 compares Aesop *Fables* 172, but while this example illustrates the widespread use of agricultural images in antiquity, it differs significantly from Jesus' and rabbinic parables. While it offers a moral lesson as any narrative would, it does not provide symbolic correspondences as in Jesus' parables (e.g., the mustard seed represents the kingdom).

primarily resided in agrarian villages and towns (Jos. *Apion* 1.60; Goodman 1983: 27; Freyne 1988: 144-45; Horsley 1995: 189). Although much land was fertile (Jos. *War* 3.42-44), the peasant farmers held few concerns more pressing than harvest (p. Maʿaś. 2:1; Freyne 1988: 246-47; Borg 1984: 31-32). In general in Mediterranean antiquity, farming was a difficult and time-consuming occupation (see, e.g., MacMullen 1974: 32-33), and absentee landlords exploited peasants working on their large estates (MacMullen 1974: 4-6, 39, 48-56; cf. Urbach 1979: 1:632).

Greek and Roman teachers could compare words to seed (Sen. *Ep. Lucil.* 29.2; 38.2; cf. b. Ber. 63a),[14] and though most later rabbinic accounts are farther removed from agricultural images (cf. R. Eleazar's negative view of agricultural occupations in b. Yebam. 63a), Jewish sages like Jesus who moved among agricultural peasants undoubtedly used them. Some writers imply that Jesus (or his later editors) borrowed this style from Greek thinkers (Mack 1988: 159-60), but Jewish tradition supplied Jesus some clear antecedents. Biblical prophets had depicted judgments, especially those of the end time, in agricultural terms (Is 32:13-17; 35:1-2; 44:3-4; Jer 31:28; 51:33; Joel 3:13; Amos 8:1-2; Riesenfeld 1970: 150; Allison 1998: 148). Jewish sources speak of the law bringing forth fruit in Israel (4 Ezra 3:20), God sowing his seed in Israel (4 Ezra 9:31), and the fruit of the law continuing (9:32). God's people should prepare to sow into their minds the fruits of the law (2 Bar. 32:1). Later tradition presents a young Torah scholar as sprouting seed (b. Taʿan. 4a) or speaks of the Torah spreading through a person's body like roots of a tree (Pesiq. R. 3:2).

If 4 Ezra reflects earlier tradition, Jewish sources also provided an eschatological cast for the seed image. 4 Ezra declares that just as not all the seeds a farmer sows survive or put down roots, so not all people will persevere to eternal life (4 Ezra 8:41).[15] But whereas the harvest would be completed in the end time (13:39; 3:12; 21:34; cf. 9:37-38), Jesus portrays the present as a time of sowing to prepare for that harvest.

The sower must sow widely to insure a good harvest. It made more sense, in a field like the one in Jesus' parable, to plow up the ground before sowing, as often in the Old Testament (Is 28:24-25; Jer 4:3; cf. Hos 10:11-12; Gundry 1982: 253; White 1964). On such a reading of the parable, the sower would be "an antihero, not very competent at his job," wasting seed by reversing the sequence (Vermes 1993: 98). Jesus could have used such stark and humorous terms to depict his benevolence in preaching to everyone (18:27; 21:37).

Later literature, however, repeatedly speaks of plowing after sowing (although some plowed both before *and* after sowing); farmers who knew their fields apparently felt comfortable sowing first, then plowing the seed into the

14. Mack 1988: 159 also cites Hippocrates *Law* 3; Antiphon *Fr.* 60; Quint. *Inst. Or.* 5.11.24; Boring 1995: 90 adds Plut. *Lectures* 48.

15. See also Vermes 1993: 98n.23; Hagner 1993: 368; Blomberg 1992a: 214, adding ARN 8:2. Payne 1980b: 568 suggests that the Aramaic of Mark supports *soil* being sown with seed rather than seed being sown in soil, and points to other possible Aramaisms.

ground (Jub. 11:11).[16] Because disciples cannot know the conditions of given hearers' hearts before they preach, Jesus uses the second analogy of sowing before plowing; they must sow as widely as possible and let God bring forth the appropriate fruit (cf. the agricultural counsel in Eccl 11:6).[17]

Not all ground will yield good fruit. The "way" typically meant some sort of road or path (e.g., Test. Job 23:11), but in a field represents one of the footpaths running through or around it (Argyle 1963: 101; A. B. Bruce 1979: 195; perhaps in Virg. *Priapes* 3.21). Some of the grain accidentally fell on (Jeremias 1972: 12n.4) or beside it (cf. 20:30; Gundry 1982: 253); perhaps the farmer plans to plow up the footpath anyway (Jeremias 1972: 12), but until he does he has exposed the seed there to hungry birds, which would devour grain until it was plowed into the soil (Hesiod *W.D.* 469-71), and continue to feed however possible until the harvest (Babrius 13.1-2; 26; 33.1-5; 88). Indeed, when one sowed first and then plowed the seed into the ground, it was not unnatural for birds to consume the seed (Jub. 11:11, where they are sent from the devil; Gundry 1982: 253).

The sower's field in this parable includes some land where the soil is shallow over some rock. Palestine includes much land like this, but though seed springs up quickly on such soil that holds its warmth, the seed readily dies because it cannot sink down roots (Argyle 1963: 101). Even urbanites recognized the disappointment of quick-growing but fruitless grains (Quint. *Inst. Or.* 1.3.5), though some claimed that stony ground in some cases produced better fruit than deep soil (Peleus in Eurip. *Androm.* 636-38, comparing illegitimate children). One kind of thistle *(Silybum marianum)* grows densely around roads, quickly reaching a height of more than one meter (three feet) in April, with small pink or white flowers on its heads (Hepper 1992: 35). The thistles grow up in the field because the farmer had cut them down instead of torn them up by the roots (Argyle 1963: 101).

The fruitful soil yields enough to make up for the useless soil (cf. 5:13-16). Italy and Sicily averaged fivefold or sixfold return on the grain sown; irrigated fields in Egypt averaged around a sevenfold yield for wheat and eightfold or better for barley (Lewis 1983: 121-22). Following the ancient rhetorical technique of praising a land (cf., e.g., Aelius Aristides on Rome), Josephus emphasizes the fruitfulness of Palestine's soil (*Apion* 1.195). The average Palestinian harvest may have yielded seven and a half to ten times the seed sown. Thus while

16. Jeremias 1972: 11; idem 1966b; Nineham 1977: 134; Lane 1974: 153-54; see especially Payne 1978: 128-29, who contends that both practices occurred. Depending on the crop and the region, sowing and plowing could occur around November, anticipating harvest around May (Hesiod *W.D.* 383-84, 448-50).

17. Cf. also 4 Ezra 8:42-45, in which God is the farmer. Following J. B. Payne, some recent scholars suggest that Jesus here applies to himself an OT and Targumic image for God as the sower (Is 61:11; Jer 31:27-28; Targ. Yer. I on Ex 15:17; Witherington 1990: 212). By itself, the evidence cited may be inadequate in view of the frequency of agrarian images; Jesus' self-application of divine language elsewhere may, however, help the case.

even a hundredfold harvest is not "miraculous" for some parts of Palestine (see Payne 1980a:183-86; Hock 1988: 139; pace Jeremias 1972: 30; Hurtado 1983: 58), harvests yielding thirty to a hundred times the seed invested are extraordinarily abundant (Gen 26:12; Jub. 24:15; Sib. Or. 3.264-65), and one rarely exceeded one hundredfold (Payne 1980a:183-84).[18] The fruit from the good soil more than makes up for any seed wasted on the bad soil.

Second, Jesus reveals special truth to his disciples through parables (13:10-17).[19] Jewish teachers used parables as sermon illustrations *to explain a point they were teaching* (e.g., Johnston 1977b: 507). To offer an illustration without stating the point, however, was *like presenting a riddle instead* (cf. Test. Abr. 12-13A). (For this reason some scholars have wrongly thought that Jesus used parables only to reveal and that Mark, the first Gospel writer, misrepresented him — Wrede 1971: 62; cf. Via 1967: 9; Filson 1964: 105.)

Yet *Jesus was not completely alone in such a practice.* Some ancient teachers like Plato wished to keep his teaching obscure to outsiders (Diog. Laert. 3.63 — after all, his mentor Socrates had been martyred); Pythagoras and others sometimes followed the same practice (Diog. Laert. 8.1.15; Boring 1995: 92 adds Iamb. *Life of Pythag.* 23.104). Even most itinerant Greek teachers spent more of their time instructing disciples indoors than lecturing publicly, although members of the general public were welcome to attend (Liefeld 1967: 205-6); unwritten teachings further provided "insiders" a superior status (cf. Botha 1993); some of Epicurus's teachings, while not secret, were penetrable only by his advanced students (Culpepper 1975: 112); philosophers might also choose to communicate in metaphor obvious only to insiders (e.g., Aul. Gel. 13.5.5-12). One might also think of the prophetic aspects of Jesus' calling; in the broader Mediterranean context, oracles often appeared obscure until fulfilled (e.g., Soph. *Oed. Rex* 439; Virg. *Aen.* 6.98-101), though this was less common in the Jewish prophetic tradition; cf. comment on 16:21.

Some Jewish people believed that God had entrusted Israel with special "mysteries" in his law (cf. Test. Levi 2:10; Judah 16:4; t. Qidd. 5:21; Ex. Rab. 19:6; Esth. Rab. 2:4). Sages sometimes spoke of the "hidden things," like the laws of creation, concealed from most of humanity (Deut 29:29; 1 Enoch 4:1-3; 41:1-8; 49:2; 52:2; 59:1-3; 103:2; 106:19; Wis 7:21; 1QH 13:13-14; 1QM 14.14; 2 Bar. 48:3) or "hidden things"/"mysteries" in the teachings of the righteous, concealed from humanity or from the wicked (Wis 2:22; 4 Ezra 14:45-47; Ps-Phocyl. 229; cf. Ps

18. Elsewhere in the Roman world, a hundredfold was quite good and more than that very rare (Pliny *N.H.* 18.21.95; Theophrastus *Hist. Plant.* 8.7.4; Strabo *Geog.* 15.3.11; Columella *Agriculture* 2.9.5-6; Varro *On Agriculture* 1.44.2; Herod. *Hist.* 1.193; see Scott 1989: 357; Davies and Allison 1991: 385 n.50; Garland 1993: 145); real hyperbolic images for eschatological abundance are at least one hundred times this much (Iren. *Haer.* 5.33.3-4; b. Ketub. 111b-12a in Davies and Allison 1991: 385).

19. That the narratives of Matthew and Luke share some features omitted in Mark here suggests that this material also appears in "Q," increasing the likelihood of authenticity by the criterion of multiple attestation (pace Wrede 1971: 63). Even Boring 1982: 152 accepts 13:16-17 as authentic.

25:14; Prov 3:32; conventional wisdom in Job 11:6; 15:8; for the secrets of the wicked, see Wis 14:23; 1 Enoch 16:3; 1QM 14:9; 2 Thess 2:7). The Qumran community believed that God had revealed to its leaders mysteries hidden from other readers of Scripture (1QpHab 7.4-5, 13-14; 1QH 2.13-14; 9.23-24; 11.9-10, 16-17; 12.11-13; 1QS 8.1-2, 12; 9.13, 17-19; cf. 1QS 5.11-12; 11.3-5; 1QM 3.9; 17.9; 4 Ezra 14:45-47).[20] Although most mainstream Jewish teachings were available to the public (cf. Jn 18:20; b. Sukk. 49b; cf. Goodman 1983: 74), many Jewish teachers apparently held particular teachings to be too esoteric for public teaching.[21] Jesus apparently agrees that until the end (10:26), some truths will be communicated to and understood by only a special group (11:25; 16:17; cf. 13:35).

By articulating his principles only in parables, *Jesus offers riddles whose answer can be fathomed only by those who understand the riddles in the context of his own ministry* (e.g., events like the Pharisees' rejection — 12:24-45; some other riddles were comprehensible only in the context of knowledge of the speaker, e.g., Phaedrus 3.1.7) *or who patiently press into his inner circle to wait for the interpretation* (13:12; cf. Iren. *Haer.* 2.27.3). Undoubtedly members of the general public who wished could attend Jesus' private lectures to his disciples, though most would have dispersed after Jesus' public teaching; both situations were normal in Greco-Roman antiquity (Liefeld 1967: 206).

Disciples regularly asked their rabbis questions (e.g., t. Sanh. 7:10; b. Qidd. 31a; Num. Rab. 11:4; Safrai 1974/76a: 966), and sometimes sought a private interpretation after a purposely vague or hostile public statement (e.g., Pesiq. Rab Kah. 4:7; Gen. Rab. 8:9; Num. Rab. 9:48; 19:8; Pesiq. R. 21:2/3; Daube 1973: 141-50; cf. Aul. Gel. 19.1.11-21; for the form of a homily responding to a question, see Aune 1987: 53). Further, whereas parables usually illustrated, even rabbis sometimes used them for secret speech (Stern 1991: 202). Some rabbinic traditions may also link ability to understand with membership in the community of Israel (cf. Stern 1991: 202-4, who cites ARN 15.3 A).

Jesus spoke in parables *because the kingdom was an end-time "mystery" now being revealed to those with ears to hear.*[22] Jesus' parables were revealing

20. Vermes 1993: 116 doubts the authenticity of this Matthean pericope, suggesting that an intention to keep the crowd from fully understanding would make Jesus more Essene or Gnostic, which he is not; he misses rabbinic parallels to the attitude. Wright 1992a: 394 regards Mk 4 as essentially apocalyptic revelation in which Jesus replaces the angelic revealer; but this proposal is again too narrow in view of other forms of revelation mentioned above.

21. Jewish teaching considered too esoteric for popular consumption (in general, e.g., b. Pesaḥ. 119a; Pesiq. R. 22:2) includes especially accounts of the throne-chariot, since no one was to "see" God (t. Ḥag. 2:1; b. Ḥag. 13a, bar.; 14b, bar.; Shab. 80b; p. Ḥag. 2:1, §63-4; cf. 4Qs140) and the creation (m. Ḥag. 2:1; t. Ḥag. 2:1, 7; ARN 39A; b. Ḥag. 15a, bar.; p. Ḥag. 2:1, §15; Gen. Rab. 1:5, 10; 2:4; Pesiq. Rab Kah. 21:5; 2 Enoch 24:3). Later rabbis also preferred teaching in synagogues to public preaching on the streets (Liefeld 1967: 207).

22. This concept of mystery derives from Daniel (future mysteries in 2:18, 19, 22-23, 23, 27-30, 47; 4:9; the mystery involves God's coming *kingdom* in 2:44-45) and possibly 1 Enoch (Nock 1964: 30a; Gibbard 1956: 109; Caragounis 1977: 126); cf. also the Qumran Scrolls dependent on them (cf., e.g., Brown 1958-59; idem 1968; Ellis 1977: 208; Ramirez 1976).

things "hidden from the creation of the world" (13:35; cf. 10:26), but only to a chosen few, who had "ears to hear" (13:9, 16; cf. 11:15; 13:43; Rev 2:7, 11, 17, 29; 3:6, 13, 22);[23] Jesus was making more available to their ears than all that the prophets had heard (13:17).[24] ("Hear" in this context means "understand" — 13:18; cf. 7:24-27.) The disciples are more special than the prophets of old only because they live in a time when they can receive a greater revelation than the prophets of old, as Jesus' blessing on them makes clear. "Happy are those who see" (God's long-awaited blessings on Israel; his Messiah; etc.) was a fairly regular beatitude, a Jewish figure of speech (Ps. Sol. 17:44; Sir 48:11; b. Ḥag. 14b; the Messiah in Ps. Sol. 18:6-7; Pesiq. Rab Kah. Sup. 6:5; Pesiq. R. 37:2). But it was also customary to praise one person by blessing another related to that person; for example, "happy is the one who bore so-and-so" is a means of praising so-and-so (e.g., Lk 11:27; Jub. 25:19; m. 'Abot 2:8; t. Ḥag. 2:1; ARN 13, §32; b. Ḥag. 14b; p. Ḥag. 2:1, §4; Pesiq. R. 37:2; Petron. *Sat.* 94); conversely, declaring unhappiness to one's mother is pronouncing doom on the child (Hom. *Il.* 6.127; Judg 5:28-31; perhaps Lk 2:35).[25] The disciples' eyes and ears were blessed (13:16) because of the greater one among them (13:17; cf. 1 Kings 10:8).

The rest of the hearers, unable to fathom his message, fulfilled the prophecy of Isaiah about penal blindness: *because of Israel's sin, they would be unable to truly "see," "hear," and understand God's message* (13:13-15; 15:8, 14; Is 6:9-10; cf. Is 29:9-10; Jer 4:22; Evans 1981). Rabbinic parables are commonly midrashic or contain biblical allusions (e.g., Vermes 1993: 94), and though Jesus' parables focused far less on Scripture exposition, it is intrinsically likely that he sometimes related his parables to Scripture.[26] Isaiah 6:9-10 is central for the early Christian understanding of why Israel as a whole did not accept Jesus (Mk 4:12; Lk 8:10; Jn 12:37-41; Acts 28:26-27; cf. Mk 8:17-18; for later interpretations see Evans 1982) and reflects a common motif in the prophets (e.g., Is 29:9-10; 42:19-20; 43:8; 44:18-19; Ezek 12:2). Yet those who did turn to the truth would be "healed" (13:15); Jesus' physical healings provided concrete signs of

23. Robbins suggests that Mark modified the prophetic "hear the word of the LORD" to fit Greco-Roman disciple-gathering patterns here (Robbins 1992: 59). But while early Christian prophecy may have borrowed the idiom via Jesus (Rev 2:7), "let one hear" may reflect a wisdom idiom (e.g., Ps 78:1; Prov 4:1; 5:1). Some moralists emphasized the responsibilities of a good audience alongside those of a good speaker (Plut. *Lectures* 14, *Mor.* 45D).

24. The disciples' role was greater than that of the prophets of old because Jesus himself was among them (5:12; 11:9-11; 23:34; especially 10:41, also coupling prophets and "righteous persons"); and the prophets had certainly seen more than hard-hearted outsiders had (13:14-15). In Jewish tradition the prophets of old had not yet seen God (Smith 1951: 154, suggesting that Matthew emphasizes Jesus' deity here) or his messianic redemption (McNamara 1972: 140).

25. For blessings for revelation, besides this Q statement (= Lk 10:23), Davies and Allison 1991: 621 (on Mt 16:17) also cite Jn 20:29; 4 Ezra 10:57; Jos. and Asen. 16:14. As early as 1 Kings 10:8, the Queen on Sheba praises Solomon by declaring how blessed are those with access to his wisdom.

26. Cf. Jones 1995: 71-72, challenging those who a priori assume that biblical allusions in Jesus' parables must be inauthentic.

the spiritual healing of which Isaiah spoke (8:17; cf. Is 6:10; 53:5; Hos 11:3; 14:4; Sir 28:3). For Matthew as for Mark, the parables "conceal truth from some but . . . reveal it to others" (Wenham 1979b: 522; cf. Via 1967: 8-9).[27]

The disciples alone had pressed close enough to Jesus to understand the rest of the teaching he was giving them. That those who had more would receive more was a principle of ancient economics (Stambaugh and Balch 1986: 113; cf. Mt 25:29; Lk 16:10-11; ARN 35, §79B); more to the point, Jewish people recognized that only disciples of wisdom or the law could understand more wisdom or the law (Ps-Phocyl. 89-90; 4 Ezra 7:22-25; cf. ARN 27, §56; 32, §68B; Dalman 1929: 228; Bultmann 1968: 108; Lachs 1987: 219; cf. references in Hagner 1993: 373). Jesus explained that to the disciples, those who had some revelation, more revelation would be given (13:11-12; cf. 12:39; the clarification in Lk 8:18). In other words, the disciples alone proved to be good soil (13:23). Jesus' parable of the sower frames his explanation of the purpose for his parables precisely because it explains the same concept in a different way (cf. Toussaint 1964).[28]

Third, the only conversions that count in the kingdom are those confirmed by a life of discipleship (13:18-23). Jesus sowed the word widely, but not all his hearers persevered in discipleship. What was true of the crowds that followed Jesus would also prove true among subsequent generations of disciples, in ways relevant to Matthew's audience (7:21-22). Whether the message went in one ear and out the other (13:19), whether someone began the Christian life eagerly and then abandoned it because it entailed too much hardship or persecution (13:20-21), whether one accepted the gospel but then backslid into complacency, seduced by other interests (13:22), such crowds are useless to the kingdom. Yet others will more than make up for the seed invested in them, becoming true disciples of the kingdom and spreading the true message of the kingdom to others (13:23).[29]

Some writers attribute many of the parables to Jesus but many of the interpretations of the parables to later editors. Their presupposition for this approach is almost certainly mistaken.[30] Many Greek and Roman fables include explicit

27. It is unlikely that Mt 13:13 softens Mark's point (Mk 4:12), as some have contended (cf., e.g., Stern 1991: 201-2); Matthew's *hoti* (often "because") probably means the same here as Mark's *hina* (often "in order that," though this sense in Mark is often disputed on various grounds; see, e.g., Peisker 1968; Jeremias 1972: 17; cf. Hollenbach 1983). Robbins 1992: 138, suggests irony here similar to that in Plato *Theaetetus* 152C.

28. The "disciples" here are not just the Twelve, but any who had chosen to press in close enough and follow Jesus. (Teachers usually had a close circle, but others could listen in — cf. Safrai 1974/76a: 965. Even if Jesus' circle here is limited to official disciples, however, this group includes more than the Twelve.) Bailey 1976: 61-62 finds a chiasmus in 13:13-17; this structure presupposes Matthean redaction (cf., e.g., Gundry 1982: 258).

29. Gerhardsson 1968: 193 links the various soils to the various expressions of love in the Shema (Deut 6:4-5); despite how commonly the Shema was recited, however, the allusions remain dubious.

30. Davies and Allison 1991: 397-99 represent an exception. Although they tentatively deny authenticity in the tradition of Jeremias, they rightly refute traditional reasons for rejecting authenticity, recognizing that Jewish parables could include interpretations. I believe it likely that Jesus explained the parables to his disciples and that the disciples who preserved the traditions of the parables themselves (it is doubtful that the crowds provide the traditions' source) would have transmitted the interpretations as well.

moral lessons at the beginning[31] or end[32] of the fables; occasionally fables include morals at the beginning and the end (Phaedrus 3.10.1-8, 51-60; 4.13). Some of these are clearly redactional, added by the authors to apply the oral traditions (e.g., Phaedrus 2.2.2; 2.3.4; 3.3.14-17; 3.6.10; 3.19.1). Phaedrus suggests that slaves like Aesop originally used fables because they did not dare to express their views openly (3.prol. 33-40; though this perspective may be somewhat shaped by Phaedrus's experience with Sejanus — 3.prol. 41-44). Other attached lessons, however, may well be part of the original fables (cf., e.g., Babrius 4.6-8; 6.16-17; 11.10-12; 18.15-16).

Of more direct relevance are the Jewish models. Though some are riddles (e.g., perhaps Prov 30:4, 18-19, 21-31; cf. Test. Job 36–38:5), our earliest Israelite parables usually have interpretations (e.g., Judg 9:16-20; 2 Sam 12:7-9), and rabbinic parables nearly always occur alongside the points they illustrate (Johnston 1977b: 561-62, 565-66, 638; Vermes 1993: 92-99).[33] Rabbinic parables typically begin with the point to be illustrated and include the *nimshal* (application or explanation) near the end (Stern 1991: 24). What is unusual about the Gospel parables is not that Jesus interprets them but rather that he usually does *not* do so when telling the parable (13:10). Even the parable of 4 Ezra 4:13-18 includes some sort of explanation in 4:20-21; Enoch's eschatological Similitudes (1 Enoch 37–71) remain more mysterious, however, like most of Jesus' public parables about the kingdom (cf. Vermes 1993: 92).

How many points with significance beyond the story setting can parables contain? Generally unfamiliar with the traditional function of parables in Jesus' Jewish context, many church fathers blatantly allegorized the parables for their own agendas (Young 1989: 317).[34] Clearly, many characters appear in stories for purely literary reasons rather than any function extrinsic to a parable.[35] Many "figures and features . . . are simply 'stage-setting' or

31. E.g., Phaedrus 1.4.1; 1.5.1-2; 1.8.1-3; 1.9.1-2; 1.10.1-3; 1.11.1-2; 1.12.1-2; 1.13.1-2; 1.15.1-3; 1.16.1-2; 1.17.1; 1.18.1; 1.19.1-2; 1.20.1-2; 1.21.1-2; 1.23.1-2; 1.24.1; 1.25.1-2; 1.26.1-2; 1.27.1-2; 1.28.1-2; 1.29.1-3; 1.30.1; 1.31.1-2; 2.2.1-2; 2.5.1-6; 2.6.1-3; 3.1.7; 3.5.1; 3.7.1; 3.8.1; 3.9.1; 3.16.1-2; 4.1.1-3; 4.5.1-2; 4.8.1-2; 4.9.1-2; 4.12.1-2; 4.20.1; 4.23.1; 5.5.1-3; 5.7.1-3.

32. E.g., Phaedrus 1.1.14-15; 1.7.4-5; 1.14.18-19; 1.22.10-13; 2.1.11-12; 2.3.7; 2.4.25-26; 2.6.14-15; 3.2.1; 3.3.1-3; 3.6.10-11; 3.11.7; 3.12.8; 3.14.12-13; 3.17.13; 4.3.5-6; 4.4.12-13; 4.6.11-13; 4.7.25-26; 4.10.4-5; 4.11.14-21; 4.17.7-8; 4.24.3-4; 4.25.23-25; 5.2.14-15; 5.3.11-13; 5.4.7-12; 5.6.7; 5.8.6-7; 5.9.5; 5.10.10.

33. Explanations appear in less than half the parables in the Mishnah, Tosefta, and Babylonian Talmud, but in more cases in other sources, averaging about 76 percent, especially in later Tannaitic strata; but in no stratum are they unknown (Johnston 1977b: 566-67, 637-38). The form of the interpretation in 13:18-23 may deliberately echo Zechariah's vision interpretations (Jones 1995: 79).

34. Jerome was aware of Jewish teachers' skill in using parables, however (*Comm. Matt.* 18.23; Vermes 1993: 91n.14, 95). If Matthew has somewhat more allegorization than Mark (a suggestion the accuracy of which is not always clear), this fits his Jewish context (Goulder 1974: 56-60).

35. Most Tannaitic parables have three characters (41) or fewer (162 with two, 106 with one), but not all the characters are always "absolutely essential," some being "little more than part of the scenery" (Johnston 1977b: 543-44).

'stage props,' there merely because the story requires them" (Johnston 1977b: 601).[36]

Distressed with uncontrolled allegorization of parables among many previous interpreters, such as H. A. W. Meyer (1858), A. B. Bruce (1882), and most influentially Adolf Jülicher rejected allegory in parables, contending for one main point (Young 1989: 21). By contrast, against Jülicher's categorization of parables in Aristotelian terms (following *Rhet.* 2.20; 3.4),[37] Fiebig drew attention to rabbinic parallels that showed weaknesses in Jülicher's line of argument (see history of responses to Jülicher and Fiebig in Johnston 1977b: 27-52). Jülicher began with deductive categories and imposed them on the Gospel data, whereas Fiebig's approach was inductive, based on concrete parables (Johnston 1977b: 119-20). Dodd followed Jülicher, but unfortunately his own work "betrays not the slightest firsthand acquaintance with rabbinic parables" (Johnston 1977b: 75), and Jeremias, who might have known better, admits that he follows Dodd (Johnston 1977b: 77; cf. Young 1989: 25).[38]

Modern interpreters tend to be especially skeptical of Jesus' parable interpretations if the interpretations focus too much on details (cf. Jeremias 1972: 13-14; F. F. Bruce 1977b: 21). But although parables generally exhibit a central thrust and details are sometimes merely part of the story, one cannot exclude some allegory from even their earliest form (pace Jülicher; Dodd 1961: 15; Koester 1982: 2:79; cf. *Rhet. ad Herenn.* 4.34.46); different characters in their narrative world often represent different actors in the real world (e.g., ARN 2A). Biblical parables could include multiple points of contact with the original audience's situation (e.g., 2 Sam 12:1-6); noting these correspondences is legitimate and different from the wanton allegorization practiced in earlier centuries (Bailey 1980: xxi).

Rabbinic parables likewise often have allegorical features (Stern 1991: 11). Vermes 1993: 96, for example, notes that R. Meir took four different men as

36. Johnston, who notes that characters and details often serve as stage props, also observes that in many other cases characters and details correspond to something extrinsic to the story world itself, though these are often ad hoc rather than standard metaphors (1977b: 597). *Most* details, he finds, *are* metaphorical (601). Characters in Matthean parables are "flat," stock figures as in the rabbis, whereas Luke's tend to be "rounder" (cf. Goulder 1974: 55-56, 62, 64).

37. As Johnston 1977b: 578, after a massive analysis of Tannaitic parables, wryly observes against Jülicher, "the rabbis evidently felt no obligation to conform to Aristotelian canons defining parable or allegory. . . ." Witherington 1994: 189 notes that even Aristotle does not truly support the distinction; "What Aristotle in fact says is that the difference between simile and metaphor is slight *(mikron) — The Art of Rhetoric* 3.4, 1406b)!"

38. Funk's structuralist schema for interpretation worked fairly well on the parables he chose but did not work well with Tannaitic parables (Johnston 1977b: 545); for a critique of Funk's parable-as-metaphor view, see Stern 1991: 11-12; cf. Scott 1989: 46 (though Scott 1989: 419 notes that the narrative is "primary and can never be replaced by its supposed meaning"). Against some contemporary writers, subversion is also not implicit in the parable genre itself; rabbinic parables more often reinforce conventional values (Johnston 1977b: 633-34). Witherington among others argues persuasively that Jesus' parables should be examined in the context of other Jewish parables (1994: 183-90) rather than as purely polyvalent literary entities (1994: 147-83; cf. also Gerhardsson 1991).

examples and supplied an interpretation for each, just like Jesus in the Gospels (t. Soṭa 5:9). Johnston 1977b: 601-2 thus complains that "The demand that we must choose between one-point-of-comparison 'parable' and every-feature-must-be-decoded 'allegory' is artificial, arbitrary, and unreasonable." The vast majority of Tannaitic parables "are either allegories, by Jülicher's definition, or mixed forms, to use Fiebig's term" (1977b: 606). One of his dissertation's most important conclusions (1977b: 636-37) bears quotation:

> Most importantly, the study of rabbinic parables renders unusable the distinction between parable and allegory in respect to the parables of the gospels: if the parables of Jesus are generically the same as those of the rabbis, which seems inescapable from the standpoint of morphology and inner structure, then the classical Jülicherian model must be discarded as inapplicable to the gospel parables. . . .

Recent research on metaphor also tends to undermine Jülicher's and Jeremias's skepticism concerning allegory; allegorical language "is no more avoidable in the New Testament parables than it is in the Old Testament prophetic oracles" (Jones 1995: 68). There is thus no historical reason to deny the authenticity of parable interpretations of Jesus based on allegorization or multiple extrinsic referents (Johnston 1977b: 608, 638-39; Witherington 1990: 72; cf. Scott 1989: 44; at greater length, see Blomberg 1990a).

In some cases, the word goes in one ear and out the other; such neglect is the devil's work (13:19). Jewish teachers (who could "sow" Torah, the law — b. Ber. 63a) exhorted students to listen intently and memorize their teachings (e.g., Mek. Pisha 1.135-36; Sifre Deut. 306.19.1-3); they despised those who neglected these teachings (cf., e.g., m. 'Abot 2:8; ARN 36A). One who remembered much would be able to remember more, but one who forgot would forget still more (Sifre Deut. 115.1.1-2; cf. also Mek. Vayassa' 1, Laut. 2:95, on Ex 15.26 in Smith 1951: 135). Yet many who listened to Jesus would forget the message of his kingdom (cf. 21:9; 27:20).

Some embrace the gospel excitedly, but tests ultimately prove the shallowness of their commitment (13:20-21). Rabbinic parables often rehearse the theme of Israel's tribulations (eleven examples in Tannaitic parables; Johnston 1977b: 627). Matthew's Gospel illustrates such failing disciples, both the danger for all disciples (26:41, 56) and for those who truly apostatize permanently (24:9-10).

Some embrace the gospel, but gradually other interests — wealth, security, family, and the like — choke it out of first place (13:22). Ancient moralists sometimes warned that one should bear with hardships so as to be prepared for the tests of ease (Pub. Syr. 218, 220). Like Jesus, some other Jewish teachers believed that the yoke of God's word (in that case the law; here, the gospel) would free one from the cares of this age (m. 'Abot 3:5); Christ's apostles proclaimed that Jesus must hold first place in his followers' lives (cf. 1 Cor 10:31; Col 3:17). (On the deceitfulness or danger of riches, cf. also 6:24; 19:23; Deut 6:10-12; Jub. 23:21; CD 4.17-18; Sen. *Dial.* 10.13.7.) In the Gospel tradition, the warning that they would be fruitless promises severe judgment (21:19). Matthew elsewhere illustrates how desire for money can seduce one to apostasy (26:15).

But some dare to believe the gospel rather than the values they see lived out around them (13:23). These people dare to seek to make other disciples in the world for the name of their Lord Jesus. The fruitful person is the one who *understands* the message (13:23). Jewish teachers emphasized understanding the word; Philo, for example, emphasized reading Scripture with one's understanding rather than one's eyes (*Spec. Leg.* 1.214). Only those who press close to Jesus, persevering until they understand the real point of his teaching, will prove to be long-term disciples (13:10-17; cf. Jn 8:30-47; Marshall 1974: 62-63). By choosing to remain after the "crowds" have dispersed, the truly committed prove themselves to be good ground. Patristic interpreters sometimes recognized Jesus as the sower (Chrysostom *On Temperance*); some seed was then lost through no fault of the sower but because the ground was unwilling (Chrysostom *Gospel of St. Matthew,* Homily 44.5.1–44.6; idem *On Temperance, ACCS,* 51-52). Thus one should work hard and be diligent to *become* good ground (Augustine *Sermons on NT Lessons* 73.3, *ACCS,* 57).

The Future Revelation of the Kingdom People (13:24-43)

Cf. Mk 4:30-34; Lk 13:18-21. Just as Matthew presents the purpose for Jesus' opaque teachings (13:10-17) in the midst of a parable explaining that not all will receive and persevere for him (13:3-9, 18-23), he now presents the parables of the mustard seed and yeast (13:31-33) in the midst of the parable of the weeds (13:24-30, 36-43), with more words about the nature of parables (13:34-35). The parable of the weeds (13:24-30, 36-40) emphasizes the hiddenness of the kingdom in the present: children of the kingdom must coexist with children of the evil one in this world until their vindication at the end. The parable may also reinforce images of conversion, perseverance, and apostasy in the parable of the sower (13:3-9, 18-23): especially in places where disciples can blend into the world (13:22), one cannot be sure who will prove to be God's elect until the final judgment. The parables of the mustard seed and the yeast complement this parable by reminding disciples that the glorious kingdom of the future is present in this age in only an obscure and hidden way, except to those with eyes of faith (13:31-33).

First, Jesus again tells an agricultural story that is relatively realistic (13:24-30).[39] Jesus often utilizes agricultural images familiar to his audience, such as sowing (13:31) and fields (13:31, 44). But while the color is local, the protagonist of the story is not a peasant like many of Jesus' hearers; he is a

39. Realism was appropriate to many kinds of illustration and persuasion. Greco-Roman rhetoric also emphasized making one's images so vivid that it was as if one set them "before hearers' eyes" (Arist. *Rhet.* 2.8.14, 1386a; 3.11.1-3, 1411b; *Rhet. ad Herenn.* 4.55.68; Theon *Progymn.* 7.53-55; Quint. 6.1.31; 8.3.65; 9.2.40; Gal 3:1).

wealthy landowner (13:27), whereas the farmer in the parable of the sower could easily have been a tenant farmer, a fellow peasant. Against some interpreters, peasants would not necessarily resent the figure, although they would not fully identify with him; they might recognize in the protagonist a benevolent local patron on whom they might be dependent. Peasants might even prefer to identify with characters of status greater than their own if those characters were benevolent; we often tell stories as a means of escaping and reflecting on our own social reality.

The protagonist's authority suits him as an analogy for God. A well-to-do man would easily be a "head of a household" (NRSV "householder"; NIV "master"; cf. 10:25; 24:43; Epict. *Disc.* 2.20.20), which figured as an illustration in rabbinic parables (e.g., Sifra Behuq. pq. 3.263.1.8; Marmorstein 1968b: 77-78; cf. the title in Lev. Rab. 6:3; Num. Rab. 13:2; on kings, see comment on 18:23-27), and even Greek philosophers could employ a householder as an analogy for God (Epict. *Disc.* 3.22.4-5).[40] Given the agrarian character of much of ancient life, it should not surprise us that fields figure prominently as settings in rabbinic parables, but that their meaning is entirely ad hoc rather than standard (Johnston 1977b: 596).

Jesus introduces the parable with a standard means of comparison (cf. 7:24; 13:31, 33; 18:23; 22:2; 25:1; 11:16); "the kingdom is like" reflects standard Jewish idiom for "It is this way with the kingdom," rather than implying that the kingdom is equivalent to the first actor stated (Smith 1951: 179; Jeremias 1972: 101).[41] Thus the kingdom need not be the landowner; rather, the situation with wheat and darnel is analogous to the situation with the kingdom. "Tares" or "weeds" here represent darnel *(lolium temulentum),* a poisonous weed organically related to wheat and difficult to distinguish from wheat in the early stages of its growth (Jeremias 1972: 224; A. B. Bruce 1979: 200; Hepper 1992: 88).

40. This parable undoubtedly derives from a source no longer extant; it differs too greatly from Mk 4:26-29 to have been derived from it (A. B. Bruce 1979: 199; pace Gundry 1982: 261) — compare how closely in their essentials Matthew follows the Markan parables he does use (13:1-23, 31-32). Despite the connection of 13:34-35 to the section 13:24-43, Fenton 1966 sees a chiasmus in 13:34-52 (with a smaller such structure in 13:40-50). Despite the pre-Matthean tradition clear at most points, Derrett finds numerous connecting allusions to Mal 3:16–4:3 (1970: 15; many of these appear contrived). Scott 1989: 68-70 suggests 13:24-30 (par. Gos. Thom. 20) is inauthentic because it establishes community boundaries; but does not much of Jesus' authentic teaching do the same?

41. The question "To what shall I compare . . . ?" (11:16; m. 'Abot. 3:17; Sukk. 2:10; t. Ber. 1:11; 6:18; B. Qam. 7:2-4; Ḥag. 2:5; Sanh. 1:2; 8:9; Sifra Shemini Mekhilta deMiluim 99.2.5; Behuq. pq. 2.262.1.9; Sifre Num. 84.2.1; 93.1.3; Sifre Deut. 1.9.2; 1.10.1; 308.2.1; 308.3.1; 309.1.1; 309.2.1; ARN 1, 2, 6, 8, 9, 11, 14, 16, 19, 23, 24, 27, 28, 31A; 2, §10; 4, §14; 8, §24; 9, §24; 12, §29; 13, §§30, 32; 18, §§39-40; 30, §63; 32, §§69, 70B; 35, §77; b. Sanh. 107a; Pesiq. Rab Kah. 1:2; 3:8; 14:5; 27:6; Sup. 1:11; 3:2; 7:3; Qoh. Rab. 9:8, §1; cf. Bultmann 1968: 179; Johnston 1977b: 531, 630) and the statement "So-and-so is like" (13:24; 25:1; t. Sukk. 2:6; Sifra Shemini Mekhilta deMiluim 99.2.2; Behuq. pq. 3.263.1.5, 8; Sifre Num. 84.1.1; 86.1.1; 89.4.2; Sifre Deut. 3.1.1; 11.1.2; 26.3.1; 28.1.1; 29.4.1; 36.4.5; 40.6.1; 43.8.1; 43.16.1; 45.1.2; 48.1.3; 53.1.3; 306.4.1; 306.7.1; 309.5.1; 312.1.1; 313.1.1; 343.1.2; 343.5.2; p. Taʿan. 2:1, §11; Lev. Rab. 27:8; cf. Johnston 1977b: 531; Vermes 1993: 92) were common ways to open a parable.

Given the occasional feuding of rival farmers (Derrett 1973: 43; cf. Virg. *Ecl.* 3.10-11, 17-24; Longus 4.8; two villages in *B.G.U.* 1035), it is not surprising that Roman law would specifically prohibit sowing such poisonous plants in another's field (Hepper 1982: 948), nor that one who found an abundance of such weeds would suspect an enemy's hand (13:28).

Despite their willingness to try (13:28) — workers regularly uprooted weeds before their roots were entangled with those of the wheat (Jeremias 1972: 225; Kümmel 1957: 134-35) — it would be difficult for the workers to root out so many tares without damaging the wheat at this stage (Manson 1979: 193; Meier 1980: 147). They had grown enough that their roots were already intertwined with those of the wheat but not far enough that it would be easy to distinguish them from the wheat; uprooting thus might endanger the wheat (13:29). After the wheat and darnel were grown, they were easily distinguished and reapers could gather the darnel, which did have one use: given the scarcity of fuel, it would be burned (13:30; Jeremias 1972: 225; A. B. Bruce 1979: 200; cf. 3:12).[42] Wheat was normally gathered and bound in sheaves, then transported, probably on donkeys, to the village (or, in this case, the large estate's own) threshing floor (Lewis 1983: 123), then stored.[43]

Second, Jesus insists that the kingdom, though present in a hidden way in the ministry of Jesus and his followers, is the glorious anticipated kingdom of God (13:31-33). These parables most clearly declare that God's kingdom had arrived in some sense in Jesus' ministry, in a hidden and anticipatory way (e.g., France 1985: 225). Far from baptizing the wicked in fire and overthrowing nations at his first coming, Jesus had come as a meek servant (12:18-20), wandering around Galilee with a group of obscure disciples, healing some sick people. The Romans took no notice of him until angry Jewish aristocrats brought him to their attention, and even this did not happen until Jesus attacked the temple system (21:12-17). In a world with governments in turmoil and full of wandering teachers and magicians, Jesus' initial arrival as a meek and politically inconspicuous servant rendered his mission as opaque as his parables, except to disciples bearing the insight of faith. Only those who press into Jesus' circle truly understand his identity.

Jesus first illustrates this principle by comparing the kingdom to a mustard seed (13:31-32). Despite some dispute over which plant Jesus intended, the mustard seed had become proverbial for small size (17:20; commentators cite m. Nid. 5:2; Ṭohar. 8:8; b. Ber. 31a; Antigonus of Carystus 91; Diod. Sic. 1.35.2;

42. Widespread in the Mediterranean, darnel grew each year to between one and two feet (30-60 cm.); later rabbis in Gen. Rab. 28:8 viewed it as false wheat stemming from the sinful period before the Flood. Preserved samples of wheat and barley in Egyptian tombs and excavations in Lachish show inadvertent mixtures of darnel, which can cause sickness and even death (Hepper 1992: 88).

43. Jesus regularly recycles his eschatological agricultural images rather than assigning all details the same sense; thus, e.g., terms for "gather" are positive in 3:12; 13:48; represent judgment here as in Is 13:4; Joel 3:2, 11; Zeph 3:8; Zech 12:3; 14:2; Rev 16:16; and the good and wicked together in Mt 25:32; Is 2:2-4; 66:18.

cf. also p. Ketub. 1:1, §8). That it grew to such a height that birds could "perch" (more likely here than "nest"; cf. Granata 1983) in its branches alludes to the image of God's authority over the mightiest kingdom of a given era (Dan 4:12; cf. Ezek 17:23-24; 31:6; Meier 1980: 149; Gundry 1982: 267; Mounce 1985: 138). Although not literally the smallest of seeds and yielding a shrub rather than a "tree" in the technical botanical sense, the mustard plant hyperbolically conveyed Jesus' point (the inconspicuous becomes mighty) better than any other.[44] This kind of parable is a "similitude" rather than a full story, but it nevertheless exhibits a very basic plot movement that contrasts present obscurity with future greatness (cf. Ladd 1974b: 98).[45]

Jesus next illustrates his point by noting how a little bit of leaven in the beginning can pervade and overtake the whole mixture of dough in the end (13:33). Many writers emphasize leaven's function as a symbol of evil (in Jewish texts, e.g., b. Ber. 17a; cf. Abrahams 1917: 51-53; Schechter 1961: 266; perhaps Philo *Spec. Leg.* 1.293; ARN 9, §25B; Gen. Rab. 17:8; Plut. *R.Q.* 109, *Mor.* 289EF), perhaps here used for shock value (Scott 1989: 328-29), or an analogous but inverted, positive infection (Dodd 1961: 192; Jeremias 1972: 147; in Jewish texts, e.g., b. Ber. 17a; cf. Abrahams 1917: 53), but Scripture had also applied it in other ways (e.g., Gen 19:3; Ex 12:11, 39; Lev 23:17; Deut 16:3; Ladd 1974b: 98; in the rabbis, Young 1989: 210-12). Rather than debating which of many symbolic uses could form the background for the yeast here, we should recognize their common factor: when most women thought of yeast, they contemplated especially its ultimately pervasive character. One leavens unleavened meal until one's finished product is thoroughly leavened. That other sources do not describe this permeation by leaven as "hiding" it need not make this image more "negative" (Scott 1989: 326), but certainly indicates the significance of the tradition's choice of wording: Jesus' kingdom invades the world in a hidden way.

Although Roman cities had bakeries, Galilean women baked their own families' bread (Stambaugh and Balch 1986: 69). The amount of flour involved here (perhaps taken from Gen 18:6) represents roughly fifty pounds, providing

44. One might consider it a "tree" in size, larger than other garden plants. Some commentators remark that it sometimes achieves a height of five meters and rather commonly reaches ten feet around the Lake of Galilee (Jeremias 1972: 148; cf. Vermes 1993: 100); Hepper 1992: 133 argues that the likeliest candidate for Jesus' mustard plant rarely exceeds five feet (1.5 meters). Hepper 1992: 133 suggests that Jesus meant "the smallest of *cultivated* seeds." For more details on reports of the mustard plant's growth, see b. Ketub. 111b; Pliny *N.H.* 19.170; Davies and Allison 1991: 418. For early "tree parables," see Judg 9:8-15; 2 Kings 14:9; cf. Dan 4:11-12.

45. Matthew might read "field" in contrast to Luke's "garden" and Mark's general reference because Palestinian custom located mustard in fields (see m. Kil. 3:2; Gundry 1982: 268). Even if so, however, the planting of mustard seed in a garden was not such an inalienable rule that it would constitute scandal (Scott 1989: 386); indeed, the very ruling in question permitted it if *only* mustard seed was sown and the perimeters of garden were acceptable (see especially Young 1989: 207). Matthew may read "field" only to connect this parable with the preceding one (13:24, 31; cf. Hagner 1993: 386). Ambrose (*The Grain of Mustard Seed, ACCS,* 61) understood the seed as Jesus himself, like the obscure martyrs (probably reading this parable in light of Jn 12:23-26).

enough bread for over one hundred people. A housewife would not normally fix so much meal and could not knead more than this; the unnatural magnitude of the illustration probably suggests that the kingdom far exceeds daily examples to which it may be compared.[46]

Third, Matthew emphasizes that Jesus' parables were to reveal God's long-hidden mysteries (13:34-35). The lesson offered earlier in Jesus' discourse (13:10-17) still applied to the present parables; while the parables were riddles to outsiders, they conveyed God's hidden revelation to his followers (cf. 1 Cor 2:7-10; Col 2:2-3). (Matthew has, however, removed Mark's critique of Jesus' family suggested by "outside" in Mk 3:31 with Mk 4:11.) Matthew cites the psalmist as a prophet in verse 35, recognizing that the psalmists were inspired (cf. 1:7-8; 1 Chron 25:1-3; 2 Chron 29:30; Acts 2:30; Lachs 1987: 226; Keener 1991b: 69-77; idem 1992b: 263-64). He translates the text directly from the Hebrew (Gundry 1982: 270).

Fourth, Jesus explains that God tolerates the wicked in the present for the sake of his elect, but will one day publicly distinguish between the two (13:36-43). That the servants were sleeping may (26:40, 43, 45; Gundry 1982: 263) or may not (cf. 25:5) be significant, but the "enemy" (also, e.g., Lk 10:19; 2 Enoch 70:6) explicitly represents the evil one (13:38-39; cf. 5:37; 6:13; 13:19). The landowner avoids uprooting the young darnel, which still looks like wheat, because he values the wheat; in the same way, God endures the wicked in the present to provide all those who will receive him time to become his followers (Rom 9:22-24). The harvesters differ from the servants (13:30) in part because a harvest's urgency would require extra laborers (9:37-38; 20:1-7) but perhaps in part because the symbolism here may be different: whereas the harvesters represent angels, the servants tending the field may represent disciples (13:39).

Jesus' portrayal of the final judgment is graphic and contains numerous images familiar from contemporary Judaism and early Christianity. One later writer depicts the end time as a harvest when the seed of the evil ones and of the good ones is ripe for harvest (2 Bar. 70:2); a later rabbinic tradition depicts Israel as wheat gathered at the age's end but the wicked nations as the field's straw and stubble to be burned and scattered (Gen. Rab. 83:5). At the final harvest (Rev 16:16; 4 Ezra 4:30-32), the end of the age (Test. Job 4:6; cf. Gk. Ezra 6:1), God will gather his scattered chosen ones for his kingdom (Mt 24:31), but gather the wicked (25:32) to be burned in a furnace of eternal torment (13:42, 50; see comment on 3:10-12; cf. 1 Enoch 54:6; 98:3 MSS; 4 Ezra 7:36) with weeping and gnashing of teeth (8:12; 22:13). The wicked here are the "lawless," those who subvert the true meaning of God's law (5:19; 23:28; 24:12) and seek to bring down the righteous (18:6; cf. 16:23); but the righteous are the "children of the

46. So Jeremias 1972: 147; cf. Meier 1980: 149; Gundry 1982: 268; Hagner 1993: 390; on the precise figures, see Davies and Allison 1991: 423. On women in Jesus' parables, see, e.g., Witherington 1984: 35-37.

kingdom,"[47] who will shine (cf. 5:16; eschatologically, Rom 8:8-19; Col 3:4; 2 Thess 1:10) in their Father's kingdom (13:43).[48] The interpretation includes but does not linger over the striking christological element, where the Son of Man fulfills a divine function (13:41; cf. 24:31; Gundry 1975: 214), albeit through the figure of the reigning Son of Man of Daniel 7:13-14.

Jesus observed these principles when he embraced sinners at table fellowship and denounced the Pharisees; such conflicts with his society's values may have occasioned parables like this one (Jeremias 1972: 224; Gundry 1982: 265). But the principle offers abundant applications for Jesus' followers as well. Matthew himself may have thought specifically of the need for Jewish Christians to remain part of the larger Jewish community rather than withdrawing from it out of resentment against Jewish leaders' opposition (Kingsbury 1969: 75). Jesus' primary point is probably the coexistence of kingdom people with the world's people in this age.[49] Though the context also suggests some application to the church (13:19-23, 47-50; cf. Steinmetz 1993; McIver 1995: 658-59), the point here is not that disciples should abandon efforts to keep the church pure (18:15-20), although that agenda could easily be carried too far (18:7-14, 21-35; cf. Argyle 1963: 105).[50] The point is that the kingdom remains obscure in the present world, and only the final day will bring God's true children into their vindicated glory and banish the wicked from among them (Ladd 1974b: 97; cf. Rom 8:18-21).

Those Who Knew the Kingdom's Value (13:44-52)

The kingdom might be hidden to the world (13:24-43, 47-50) like a hidden treasure or a special pearl that only a merchant searching for it would find (13:44-46; cf. 6:20); but a few people would recognize its value and live accordingly. Such people were those who would relinquish everything they had to obtain it (13:44-46; cf. 6:19-24; 19:21). Having made this point, Jesus returns to his earlier theme about only the final time distinguishing the righteous from the wicked (13:47-50), reminding his hearers that a single sacrifice for the kingdom may be insufficient. Jesus then returns to his theme of knowing the kingdom's value. He con-

47. Jesus' followers, in contrast to Israelites in general in 8:12 (pace Strombeck 1982: 164).

48. The shining of the righteous in the future was a motif in Jewish end-time texts (Wis 3:7-8; Qumran's commentary on Is 54:11-12; Ps-Philo 26:13; 4 Ezra 7:97; 2 Enoch 65:11 A; Sifre Deut. 47.2.1-2; b. Sanh. 100a; Pesiq. Rab Kah. 27:2; Lev. Rab. 30:2; Qoh. Rab. 1:7, §9; Rev 22:5); here it alludes especially to Dan 12:3 (not to Mal 4, pace Derrett 1970: 15) and the language of Jesus' own transfiguration (17:2; cf. Phil 3:21). Smelik 1995 reads the Targumic transformation of the righteous into light as apotheosis; Greeks could describe people shining like stars but noneschatologically (e.g., Ap. Rhod. 1.239).

49. Stern 1991: 198-99 suggests that the parable's purpose is thus theodicy, which fits the rhetorical function of many rabbinic parables.

50. Compare the later rabbi who exhorted an executioner to let God, the garden's owner, root out the garden's thorns himself (Pesiq. Rab Kah. 11:19).

cludes by comparing teachers of the kingdom to well-to-do householders who display or pay out from (cf. 12:35) their new treasure, the kingdom (13:51-52).

First, the kingdom will cost its true followers everything (13:44-46). Most early Christians emphasized that the kingdom is available to disciples only by grace through faith; but most also recognized that genuine faith involves embracing and yielding to God's reign, not simply acknowledging it and then passing it by as if it did not exist. The kingdom is a treasure, and those who really believe it will sacrifice everything else in their lives for the Kingdom's agendas (cf. Ladd 1974b: 99; Fenton 1977: 227; Gundry 1982: 276).[51]

Jesus tells of a man who found treasure hidden in a field (13:44).[52] People in Palestine often hid treasures, which might remain concealed if the hider died before he could retrieve them (Fenton 1977: 227). Thus hidden treasure became a prominent motif in Near Eastern folklore (e.g., 3Q 15; Avianus *Fable* 12; Phaedrus 1.27; 4.21.4; Jeremias 1972: 198; Vermes 1993: 108n.37; for various views on Qumran's Copper Scroll, Goranson 1992; McCarter 1992; Harper 1993; Lehmann 1993), exciting the imagination of peasants for whom it represented the ultimate dream.

Probably the central character of this parable was a peasant working a wealthy landowner's field who when plowing turned up a strongbox or jar containing coins. Once he bought the field the contents of the field legally belonged to him (especially with a contract covering the land "with all that is in it" — m. B. Bat. 4:8-9; Vermes 1993: 107; for later rabbinic texts cf. Lachs 1987: 229; earlier, cf. Gen 23:17), freeing him to "rediscover" the treasure later (Jeremias 1972: 198; cf. Smith 1951: 139). (That the field's original owner sold it to the peasant indicates that the owner had not buried the treasure and was unaware of it, hence was not the treasure's original owner.)[53] Whereas most discovered-treasure stories emphasized the finder's extravagant lifestyle afterward or some compromise between the field's seller and buyer (Gen. Rab. 33:1; Lev. Rab. 5:4; Deut. Rab. 4:8; Jeremias 1972: 200; cf. Menander *Treasure*), Jesus lays the entire emphasis on the price the man was ready to pay to invest in this treasure far greater than any he already owned. Although this treasure, like the kingdom, was

51. That the Son of Man finds the children of the kingdom as a treasure (Burchard 1988) would be consistent with other Gospel pictures of Jesus, but it remains a far less likely interpretation of this parable in this context. Boring 1995: 94-95 cites as examples of sacrificing all possessions for God's purposes Test. Job 18:6-8; Mek. Rabbi Simeon ben Yohai 14:5; see further comments on 4:18-22; 19:21-22.

52. The historical presents, which Matthew usually removes even from Mark, suggest that this parable is pre-Matthean (Jeremias 1972: 198; pace Gundry 1982: 275). The buyer represents not God or Jesus seeking their people, but God's people seeking his blessings, as in Mek. Beshallah 2.142-43 (Blomberg 1992a: 223).

53. Scott 1989: 402 reads too much into the situation to suppose that the field's new owner dare not dig up the treasure "unless he wants to face the rather embarrassing question of whence it came." The situation was legal, from a peasant standpoint surely moral, and finally tangential to the parable's thrust. Compare rabbinic parables in which buyers sell various kinds of property, unaware until too late of the value of what they had lost (Young 1989: 215-19).

hidden to most of the world, the man not only recognized that its value outweighed all he had, but he *acted accordingly*.

After telling of a peasant laborer's discovery, *Jesus tells of a more prosperous merchant seeking pearls.* In contrast to the tenant worker, the protagonist of this story is a merchant, a man with capital, hence a person of greater means. Most merchants and shopkeepers sold single products (e.g., oils, or vegetables, or fruits), though some "general stores" existed as well (Lewis 1983: 136).

Jeremias (1972: 199) notes that divers fished for pearls in the Red Sea (which was proverbial for its wealth, Babrius 115.7), the Persian Gulf, and the Indian Ocean (Virg. *Culex* 67-68 mentions pearls from there); Arrian (*Indica* 8.11) claims that they were often caught by nets (though he also improbably asserts that one must catch the king to catch the other oysters). Normally such pearls were quite valuable (cf. Phaedrus 3.12; p. B. Meṣ. 2:5, §2); the pearls were sold for wealthy women's necklaces, and ancient reports tell of pearls worth tens of millions of dollars in modern currency (Jeremias 1972: 199). This merchant, uniquely sensitive to the value of the pearl, wisely invests all he has to purchase it. Other Jewish accounts of finding expensive pearls typically emphasized the finder's piety; thus a Jewish tailor paid an outrageous price for a fish because he needed it to keep the Sabbath, yet found in it a pearl that supplied his needs the rest of his life (Pesiq. R. 23:6). Jesus, however, instead emphasizes only the value of the pearl and the joy of finding it (Jeremias 1972: 199; cf. Gen. Rab. 39:10). Whereas Jewish teachers sometimes naturally used the pearl as a parable of Torah teaching (ARN 18A) and stressed material sacrifices made to study Torah (Young 1989: 214), Jesus applies these images to the value of the message of the kingdom. One who was unwilling to sacrifice everything else for the kingdom, who did not believe its reality sufficiently to stake all one's future on it, was unworthy of it (19:21).

Second, only the final judgment will reveal who was truly committed to the kingdom, and how wise the committed were to invest their lives in it (13:47-50).[54] Fruits often reveal true and false disciples in the present (7:15-23), but Matthew also emphasizes that some who seem to be genuine today may not persevere to the end, and some who will become believers may not have yet heard the gospel (13:23).

Continuing the practice of parabling in language relevant to his hearers, Jesus applies fishing imagery (cf. 4:18-19). Those who lived around the Lake of Galilee would often have seen fishermen separating the edible and kosher fish from the inedible ones (Harrington 1980: 23). Of at least twenty-four species of fish counted in the Lake of Galilee, many were unclean or inedible, and the net would not discriminate in its catch (just as wheat and darnel appeared similar in the early stages; Jeremias 1972: 226).[55] Jesus probably refers here not to a net

54. Whether or not a direct relationship exists, Gos. Thom. 8 is probably a secondary version of the earlier form preserved in Matthew (see Davies and Allison 1991: 443).

55. For ancient views on various kinds of fish (not all accurate), see, e.g., Pliny *N.H.* 9.16.43–9.45.84.

cast from a single boat but to the still larger seine net either dragged between two boats or drawn to land by long ropes (Jeremias 1972: 225-26).

Although Jesus here draws from the same profession as in 4:19 for his image of gathering fish, the point he is illustrating is quite different. Now he refers not to gathering people into the church, but gathering people to judgment (possibly echoing Ezek 47:10, though we were more skeptical of that allusion in 4:19). Until the final day, Jesus will continue eating with sinners to seek and save the lost (Ladd 1974b: 101). Yet the point here seems less the coexistence of the righteous and the wicked in the church (cf. Kingsbury 1969: 124) than their coexistence in this present age (18:15-20; "the world" in 13:38; cf. "separate" in 25:32). The kingdom had not consumed the wicked with fire (3:10-12) or come "with signs to be observed" (cf. Lk 17:20); it had invaded the world in a hidden way, and would remain hidden until the end. Nevertheless, those who apply the parable to the church are not wholly amiss: the same line between the righteous and the wicked would ultimately divide Jesus' professing disciples (13:20-23).

Finally, true teachers of the kingdom display the kingdom's treasure for all to see (13:51-52). Matthew concludes this central discourse of his Gospel with a final, eighth parable, "a cryptic Wisdom parable, a kind of riddle" that invites further reflection (Jones 1995: 211). If Jesus' disciples have truly understood his teaching (13:51), they are prepared to teach others the value of the kingdom (13:52). Most of Jesus' original disciples were not literal scribes before following Jesus, but the scribes did have the old treasures of God's law, which were still valuable if correctly understood (5:17-20; 23:3; cf. b. Shab. 88b; Pesiq. Rab Kah. 12:11; wisdom in Prov 3:14-15; Isoc. *Demon.* 19, *Or.* 1; Sir 1:24; 41:14; Wis 7:8-14; 8:5; Ep. Arist. 8).[56] Jesus expects his disciples to build on both the biblical teachings that had come before him and on his gospel of the kingdom; the heavy dependence of the earliest Christians, not least the predominantly Jewish Matthean Christians, on both shows that they did so.[57] Matthew emphasizes "understanding" (13:13-14, 19, 23, 51; 15:10, 16; 16:9, 11; 17:13; 22:29; 24:39); because these disciples understand (13:51), they prove that they are the good soil, those who pressed in close enough to Jesus to know him (13:23; cf. 13:11-12, 16).[58]

Many scholars suspect that Matthew's audience included Christians — very possibly including Matthew himself — who had been scribes and brought substantial biblical background with them to the Christian faith; or who viewed

56. Davies and Allison 1991: 445 compare 1QM 10.10 ("schooled in the law and learned in wisdom"). Less convincingly, Lachs 1987: 230 cites various rabbinic parallels; the most convincing is the later rabbinic interpretation of Song 7:13: "The old is the Written Law, the new the words of the Scribes" (b. 'Erub. 21b).

57. Jones 1995: 149-50 suggests that Matthew invites here the vocation of Christian scribes. That Jesus speaks first of "new" treasures and of "old" ones second may suggest the need to understand the kingdom before one may correctly interpret the law (Meier 1980: 154). Derrett 1973: 175 suggests that the image Jesus uses is that of new and old coins, which someone would "pay out."

58. For the centrality of "understanding" in Matthew, especially via "seeing" and "hearing" Jesus, see Kingsbury 1995b: 376.

their Christian vocation as teachers in terms of the Jewish category of scribes.[59] Some suggest that Matthew speaks of Pharisaism's scribes and synagogues as "theirs" in the sense of "theirs as opposed to ours" (e.g., Luz 1989: 78; Overman 1990b: 61). Such Christian scribes (cf. 23:34) would go forth to pass on their new Rabbi's teachings and make disciples for him (28:19; cf. 23:8).[60]

59. E.g., Stendahl 1968: 30; Bonnard 1963; Fenton 1977: 230; F. F. Bruce 1972a: 72; Meeks 1986: 117; cf. Phil 3:5; Acts 15:5; pace Van Tilborg 1972b: 128-41.

60. Orton 1989: 137-76 notes Matthew's scribal compositional and redactional techniques, though he probably overstates them.

A Prophet Visits His Hometown (13:53-58)

Cf. Mk 6:1-6; Lk 4:16-30; Jn 4:44; 6:42; 7:15. Himself greater than a prophet (5:12; 11:11-14), Jesus would face rejection greater than the prophets had (23:29-36). Like Jeremiah (1:1; 11:21-23), Jesus faced the rejection of those closest to him by the ties that usually mattered most in his society — geography and blood (13:53-58; cf. 10:21, 35; 12:46-50). These accounts of breaking traditional ties frame the kingdom parables (12:46–13:58), forcefully illustrating the message of those parables: the kingdom comes in an obscure way like a mustard seed, and only those with the eyes of faith will recognize it. How could anyone believe that God had stepped into history in the person of a young man who had spent most of his life in their own community?

First, the people among whom he had grown up were unprepared to embrace his "wisdom and miraculous powers" (13:54; cf. Jn 6:42; 7:15). John had nearly stumbled over the character of Jesus' mission (11:6); that Pharisees (15:12) or his townspeople (13:57) would do the same is hardly surprising. Jesus did not easily fit any single categories they had for him. In this period, divinely provided wisdom and the power to work miracles usually represented two basically distinct categories of "heroes" in the ancient Mediterranean (e.g., Holladay 1977); like only very rare Jewish figures before him, Jesus combined the two (cf. Jos. *Ant.* 8.42-49; 18.63). Yet his townspeople[1] did not expect *either* model from him; Jesus seemed too ordinary for that; he was just the carpenter's son.[2] Large families were common (e.g., Lewis 1983: 70; on Jesus' siblings, see

1. Davies and Allison 1991: 454 point out that the phrase can mean "hometown" (Philo *Leg. Gai.* 278; Jos. *Ant.* 6.67; 10.114) as easily as "homeland" (Jn 4:44), which in Matthew must mean Nazareth (2:22-23).

2. This is a mark of identification, not of derision; although "carpenter" was not another term for teacher (pace Vermes 1973: 21-22; Borg 1987: 39; see p. Ḥag. 2:1, §8), one could be both; Shammai was a carpenter (stories even equip him with a carpenter's measure to beat an unruly Gentile — cf. b. Shab. 31a), and Herod trained priests as masons for the temple (Jos. *Ant.* 15.390, 421); no one questioned carpenters' (as against, say, shepherds') piety (*Greek Anth.* 6.205), and Greeks could attribute carpentry skills to their heroes (Hom. *Od.* 5.250). The work of "carpenters" varied (see Lewis 1983: 136-37 on varied kinds of construction in Egypt; Gnilka 1997: 69); they were usually woodworking craftsmen who built wooden furniture and utensils (cf. Justin *Dial.* 88), but also constructed roof beams and door frames (Meier 1991a: 280-81); some might have doubled as brick masons as well (Grant 1959: 98; Goodman 1983: 55-56; Nineham 1977: 165). They were artisans, not peasants, fitting into the upper 10 percent of nonaristocratic Galilean society (cf. Hengel 1974b:

comment on 12:46-50). In a town of at most 1,600-2,000 inhabitants (Meyers and Strange 1981: 56) and probably around five hundred inhabitants (Stanton 1993: 112; Horsley 1995: 193), everyone would have assumed that they knew Jesus already (cf. Lk 13:26-28); indeed, Nazareth was a small town from which even Nazarenes, like other Galileans, would not expect a great prophet (2:23; cf. Jn 1:46). They never expected the kingdom to come in a hidden way or to come as close to them as it did; hence, as Matthew continues to reiterate (cf. 2:1-12), those closest to the kingdom did not recognize it, and it passed them by. They questioned the source of his wisdom, but wisdom would be vindicated by her works (11:19), even if those closest to the works rejected them (11:20-24).

Second, Jesus offers a principle that applies to other servants of God, too: prophets will be rejected (13:57; Mk 6:4; cf. Lk 4:24; attested possibly independently in Jn 4:44). As the Johannine tradition underlines, "If the world hates you, you know that it hated me before it hated you" (Jn 15:18). Jesus' contemporaries already knew and emphasized that prophets were rejected (23:37; Acts 7:52, 58),[3] and some recognized the difficulty of accepting a prophet who had grown up in one's community (Jer 1:1; 11:21-23; 12:6; Daube 1973: 10). But whereas Jesus' fellow Nazarenes undoubtedly knew such a principle, they apparently never thought to apply concretely with Jesus what they professed abstractly about the prophets of old. If Gnilka (1997: 69) is correct that many Nazarenes died in the Judean-Roman war, and if Matthew's audience is aware of their demise, the tragic irony of Nazareth's rejection would resemble that with Jerusalem (23:37-38).

Finally, human unbelief limits God's activity (13:58). Mark says that Jesus *could* not do a miracle there because of their unbelief (Mk 6:5; Montefiore 1968: 1:119 regards this admission as a mark of historical accuracy). Mark probably means that Jesus refused to act as a mere magician but demanded faith (Goppelt 1981/82: 1:148; cf. Lane 1974a: 204); elsewhere suppliants came to Je-

26-27; Freyne 1988: 241). That Joseph found employment in carpentry is historically likely: from A.D. 6, Antipas immediately began rebuilding the devastated Galilean capital of Sepphoris (Jos. *War* 2.68; *Ant.* 17.289), from which Nazareth was a distance of only four miles (cf. Schlatter 1929: 455, in Gnilka 1997: 70; Grant 1959: 99; Thurman 1981: 18; pace Batey 1992, however, Sepphoris was probably not a dominant influence in Jesus' early life — cf. Miller 1992; Horsley 1995: 180). That Jesus himself would have labored as a carpenter (Mk 6:3) is also likely; Jewish fathers sought to equip their sons with a trade (Moore 1971: 2:127; Safrai 1974/76a: 958; carpentry in p. Rosh Hash. 1:3, §35; elsewhere in the Mediterranean, MacMullen 1974: 97-98), and most trades were learned by apprenticeship (e.g., Lewis 1983: 135). That Matthew and Luke agree in part against Mark here (Lk 4:22) suggests that Mark reworded an earlier tradition about "the carpenter's son." Mothers commonly bore many children until the very end of childbearing years (see Lewis 1983: 70). Names like "Joses" (Joseph) were common (e.g., *CIJ* 1:89, §126; 1:148, §209; 1:272, §347; 1:399, §538; 1:426, §581; 1:428, §585; 1:492, §681; 2:6, §735; 2:193, §§1052, 1054; 2:237, §1202).

3. E.g., CD 7.17-18; 1 Enoch 89:51; 95:7; 100:10; 4 Bar. 9:31; Jeremiah in *Lives of the Prophets* 2.1-3/Greek 25; Amos in 7.1-2/Greek 14; Micah in 6.1/Greek 17; Pesiq. R. 26:1/2; Urbach 1979: 1:560. Davies and Allison 1991: 460 also compare Dio Chrys. 47.6; Epict. *Disc.* 3.16; Apollonius of Tyana *Ep.* 44; Pindar *Olym.* 12.13-16; Boring 1995: 96 adds Plut. *Exile* 7:13; cf. also Gnilka 1986: 517. They suggest (460) that Gos. Thom. 31 and *P. Oxy.* 1 probably expand Luke's version (pace Crossan) and that Jn 4:44 may be the earliest form.

sus, but here, perhaps out of pride, they may have failed to demonstrate faith by coming (Aune 1980: 1536). Matthew, however, clarifies the wording: Jesus *would* not act because of their unbelief.[4]

A Prophet Martyred (14:1-12)

Cf. Mk 6:14-29; Lk 3:19-20; 9:7-9; Jn 3:24. While dramatically abbreviating Mark's account of John's execution, Matthew retains the primary function of Mark's narrative: John's death foreshadows the imminent martyrdom of Jesus and those who, following him, proclaim righteousness (Mt 5:12; 17:12; cf. Mk 6:7-30; cf., e.g., "seize" and "bind" — 14:3; 21:46; 26:50; 27:2). The parallels between the two missions have been building toward this climax: John introduced Jesus, proclaiming the same message that Jesus would (3:2; 4:17). After Jesus promises persecution and speaks of prophets (10:17-42), he praises John in prison as his ally (11:2-19); narratives about those who reject Jesus follow this account (11:20-25; 12:1-14). But nowhere does John's fate prefigure that of Jesus so clearly as here: if Jesus himself proves to be a "prophet without honor" among his people (13:53-58), what is to keep him (or his followers) from the fate of John the Baptist (14:1-12)? (Ancient literature had long employed various forms of foreshadowing; for example, Agamemnon's death when he returned home built suspense by warning what Odysseus *could* face when returning home — Hom. *Od.* 13.383-85.)

Views of historicity vary. Meier 1994: 171-76 is skeptical of the account, citing Mark's "legendary tone" plus differences with Josephus. But "legendary" is a tricky category; if we allow the Gospels to tell a story about the Herodian court to begin with, many items will support historical verisimilitude (including the character of Herodias in Mark), though some details of the account[5] appear more questionable. Theissen 1991: 81-97 thinks that the story behind Mark was a popular account originally not preserved just among Christians, a tradition also standing behind Josephus. But it appears more likely that Josephus and Mark depend on different traditions of a common event.[6] From a purely historical stand-

4. The issue is the hostility of anti-belief, not a young disciple's struggles with doubt (cf. Moule 1965: 47); sometimes God sovereignly acts on behalf of his own to develop faith, not just to reward it (cf. 17:2-7; 28:5-10, 17; Ex 3:2; Judg 6:12-14). Early Christian interpreters usually attributed the thwarting of God's gifts in Nazareth to God's respect for human freedom (Gregory Nazianzen *Theological Orations,* Oration 30, On the Son 30.10-11; John Cassian *Third Conference of Abbot Chaermeon* 15; Ps-Victor of Antioch *Commentary on Mark* 6; *ACCS,* 79-81).

5. E.g., Herod Philip's name — Theissen 1991: 87; but cf. Hoehner 1972: 155-56.

6. Josephus's sources are probably more Herodian, Mark's more likely from Christians who once circulated among the Baptist's disciples (cf., e.g., Acts 19:3-5), who may have received explanation from contacts within the Herodian court. Given the sheer numbers of early Christian converts, some contacts with the Herodian court are not unlikely (cf. Lk 8:3; Acts 13:1). Although most Palestinian Christians seem to have been from the ranks of the relatively poor (Rom 15:26), there is no reason to doubt some exceptions (cf. Acts 6:7; Jn 18:16; comment on Mt 4:18-22; 10:2-4).

point, we can be certain that Antipas[7] had John executed for preaching that he took as undermining his honor; other details must be debated point by point and on the basis of where one assigns the burden of proof (see the Introduction to this commentary).

First, Herod Antipas remained unsettled about his execution of John (14:1-2). Probably Antipas believes that John has "returned from the dead" in the temporary sense exhibited in some biblical resuscitations (1 Kings 18:21-22; 2 Kings 4:34-36) rather than in the end-time sense of the final resurrection, which Jewish people generally understood as a corporate event (Dan 12:2; cf. Mk 9:10). Although some Jews apparently explained Jewish doctrines to Greeks in terms of reincarnation (Jos. *Ant.* 18.14; *War* 3.374; cf. Plato *Meno* 81BC; Plut. *Divine Vengeance* 32, *Mor.* 567EF; Sallustius, *Concerning Gods and the Universe* 20),[8] the view was not predominant in Judaism and it is unlikely that Herod is thinking in such terms here (John could hardly have been reincarnated and then grown to adulthood again in a few months or even years). Although Antipas had executed John, he knew that John was a righteous man and feared his influence.

Second, the powerful can mistake moral reproof for more disruptive political challenges (14:3-4). Antipas, son of Herod the Great (2:1) and a Samaritan wife, hence Archelaus's full brother (2:22), had functioned as "tetrarch" over Galilee and Perea since about 4 B.C.[9] He had engaged in a politically prudent marriage with a Nabatean princess, perhaps seeking to secure further loyalty from Nabatean subjects within his territory of Perea (Kraeling 1951: 89). (If she held to traditional Nabatean paganism, her faith was far from Jewish; cf. Jones 1989; Schluntz 1998; Lindner 1990.)

Yet Antipas's lust undercut his political prudence. When Antipas planned to divorce his first wife to take his brother's wife (Jos. *Ant.* 18.109-19),[10] he violated not only Matthew's teaching on the moral indissolubility of marriage (5:31-32) but

7. Matthew may preserve the name "Herod," qualified only by "tetrarch," to link this oppressive Herodian with the evil Herod of 2:1-21; but some other writers also called Antipas simply "Herod" (Dio Cassius *R.H.* 60.8.3; for Archelaus as "Herod," see 55.27.6 and Archelaus's coinage; cf. Acts 12:1 for Agrippa I).

8. Matthew's community may have known the doctrine from their broader Greco-Roman context, but it was also certainly not their view; cf. Hoheisel 1984-85.

9. Mark gives him the title "king," perhaps loosely (cf. Jos. *War* 1.208-11; Sanders 1992: 542n.69), but perhaps ironically (6:14). When Antipas, prompted by his new wife Herodias, later sought the title "king" that had been granted Herod Agrippa I (cf. Acts 12:1; Jos. *Ant.* 18.240-44), he was deposed and banished to Gaul for his arrogance (Jos. *Ant.* 18.252-54; Kraeling 1951: 86; Lane 1974a: 211). The source for the story of John's martyrdom could easily be from within Antipas's household, via Joanna or Manaen (probably among Luke's sources — Lk 8:3; 24:10; Acts 13:1); see Hoehner 1972: 303-6. The narrative as a whole seems to derive from a pre-Markan source (see Manson 1961: 40; Lane 1974a: 215).

10. The Gospels call him "Philip," Josephus by the more general title "Herod"; but Herod the Great sometimes gave various sons the same name (if they had different mothers), and elsewhere showed a liking for the name "Philip." Herod Philip was the son of Herod the Great and Mariamne II (Hoehner 1972: 133-36; pace Anderson 1976: 168). Ancient readers would normally have viewed the coalition of evil spouses from previous marriages as a corrupt union (e.g., Dion. Hal. 4.30.1).

the Mosaic law concerning incest (Lev 18:16; 20:21; Jos. *Ant.* 18.136; cf. *Ant.* 17.341); many Greeks also felt that such behavior invited divine wrath (Hesiod *W.D.* 328-29, 333). (Notably Matthew, in contrast to Mark, nowhere recognizes the validity of Antipas's new marriage union.) John thus publicly reproached a public example of immorality. But apart from its political repercussions Antipas was doubtless little concerned about Jewish morality (Jos. *Ant.* 18.38; Horsley 1995: 65), and what John viewed in moral terms, Antipas undoubtedly saw as a potential political threat, undermining the security of his people's allegiance (cf. Jos. *Ant.* 18.118; Kraeling 1951: 85, 90-91, 143-45; Stanton 1995a: 174; Hengel 1981b: 36). The political threat was particularly acute because his affair with Herodias was already destabilizing his kingdom; Antipas's plans to divorce his first wife had provoked trouble with her father, the powerful Nabatean king Aretas (on whom cf. 2 Cor 11:32-33; on the Nabateans, see, e.g., Kraeling 1951: 88-89; Hammond 1991; Matthiae 1989; McKenzie 1988). This trouble later led to war and public humiliation for Antipas (Jos. *Ant.* 18.113-14, 124-25). That many Nabateans in Perea presumably remained loyal to Aretas further extended the embarrassing political implications of Herod's affair. A prophet harping about the tetrarch's misbehavior was therefore politically dangerous.

John's society did not recognize freedom of speech; publicly denouncing a ruler's character was often suicidal (in Rome, even private criticism of some emperors led to executions). Israel had a long-standing tradition exempting prophets from such punishment that only the most vicious rulers ignored; unfortunately for John, Antipas proved to be such a ruler. In another case the government might temporarily act as more sensitive to justice than the masses are (cf. 27:24-25; aristocrats normally viewed themselves as morally superior to the masses), but in this case John's popularity with the people temporarily protects him from the power of a politician (14:5; cf. 21:46). After John's execution, when King Aretas soundly defeated Antipas in war to avenge Antipas's rejection of Aretas's daughter, many people felt that Antipas's loss was divine judgment for the execution of John that by this point had occurred some years before (Jos. *Ant.* 18.116-19).[11]

Third, Antipas ensnared himself in deeper sin because of lust and oaths (14:6-7). In the Greco-Roman world, attendance at birthday celebrations was expected (e.g., *P. Oxy.* 1214; 1676.10-12; *P. Fay.* 114.19-20), especially if thrown by a person of status (Aul. Gel. 19.9.1; cf. *P. Lond.* 1912.29-30). (One may think of Pharaoh's birthday party in Gen 40:20-22, where one of his officials lost his head.) In this period such birthday parties, which normally involved excessive drinking, were a Greek and Roman rather than a Jewish custom, but Antipas readily accommodated the Greco-Roman custom (cf. also Jos. *Apion* 2.204; m. ʿAbod. Zar. 1:3; Safrai 1974/76b: 767; though cf. the interpretation in b. ʿAbod. Zar. 10a); his full-brother Archelaus had also been known for drunken

11. Cf. Meier 1992: 233; see especially F. F. Bruce 1972b: 30 on the timing; cf. Saulnier 1984. As Taylor 1997: 255-56 notes, "Such quarrels could brew for some time before breaking out into hostility."

parties (cf. Jos. *War* 2.29).[12] According to Josephus's briefer account of John's execution, this scene must take place at Herod's famous fortress Machaerus in Perea (see Pliny *N.H.* 5.15.72), where Antipas's first wife had escaped to her father (Glueck 1960: 192), where many Nabateans lived, and near where John had often preached (cf. Kraeling 1951: 9-10, 92-93). This fortress included a dungeon where John was kept, and separate dining facilities for men and women (thus Mark notifies us that Herodias's daughter "went out" to confer with her mother — Mk 6:24; Manns 1981; Riesner 1984b), as readers in the eastern Mediterranean would assume (Corn. Nep. Preface 6-7).

Nearly all Jews would have found Herod's lust disgusting: because the girl was the daughter of a woman with whom Antipas was sleeping, desire for her constituted desire for incest whether or not he was married to her mother (cf. Lev 18:17; Amos 2:7). According to some accounts the girl, Salome, may also have been between six and eight years old; more likely, she was a virgin of marriageable age (twelve to fourteen), but possibly already betrothed or married to Philip the tetrarch (cf. Jos. *Ant.* 18.137; Hoehner 1972: 155-56; Theissen 1991: 90-91; Kraeling 1951: 87). Besides, though dancing was a regular feature of such drinking parties (Babrius 80.1-2), only in a drunken stupor would one invite another member of the royal family to engage in such a sensuous hellenistic dance (cf. Lane 1974a: 221; Nineham 1977: 175; Hoehner 1972: 157; Esth 1:11). Her dance is, as one commentator notes, "an improbably bizarre touch, which could forthwith be dismissed as fictional, were it not a known fact that the excesses of the Herodian court were in most respects quite notorious" (Anderson 1976: 166).[13] Stories of rulers who offered women whatever they wanted (14:7), even part of their kingdom (Esth 5:3; Parthenius *L.R.* 12.1; Soph. *Oed. Rex* 580-81; Mk 6:23 — though Antipas as a Roman client could not actually grant this request; cf. Mk 10:40), indicated how overpowered the ruler was by desire for the woman. (The implied contrast betwen Esther and Salome in Mark underlines how much power this women had, for good or for ill.)

12. Davies and Allison 1991: 472 observe that "'the birthdays of Herod' was a proverbial expression (Persius, *Satura* 5.180)," comparing also Agrippa I's party in Jos. *Ant.* 19.321. Drunkenness and lewd dancing together indicated bad morals even among traditional Greeks (Demosth. *2d Olynthiac Or.* 18-19; on drunkenness, see, e.g., Demosth. *Against Conon* 7; and comments on 24:45-51). For drunkenness and loss of self-control, see e.g., Char. *Chaer.* 4.3.8; sources cited under 24:49. Other kinds of dancing were employed in different settings, including military training (Quint. 1.11.18-19) and worship (Athenaeus 14.631D); for a discussion of forms, see Plut. *Table-Talk* 9.15, *Mor.* 747A-748D. For the dramatic setting, cf. the banquet of the oppressor in Dan 5:1-31, except that in the Gospel vindication of God's name is not immediate.

13. Theissen 1991: 91-99 thinks this is a legendary motif cohering with other attempts to depict the Herodian women's loose morals. His examples, however, may without much difficulty illustrate that such lewdness could and *did* happen at aristocratic banquets (cf. even usual Roman banquets in Dupont 1992: 285; cf. the twelve-year-old boy in Boring 1995: 97), arguing against his own position. That Herodian women's lives were probably "no more corrupt than those of other members of their class" (96) is not saying much (cf. Rawlinson in Hill 1972: 244; for evidence of Herodian women's wealthy lifestyle, cf., e.g., Shoemaker 1991). Indeed, Josephus, *unlike* Mark, notes that Antipas's divorce was Herodias's idea, which Theissen admits fits hellenistic custom (84); that Josephus clearly dislikes strong women is no reason to dispute his report that Herodias was one.

The Greeks and Romans had stories about mortals or deities who regretfully granted deadly requests on account of their oaths (Ovid *Metam.* 2.44-46, 101-2; 3.287-91, 295-98, 308-9). Jewish scholars had devised ways to release people from oaths that would lead to more evil, so most religious teachers would not have faulted Herod for breaking his oath: life took precedence over oaths (cf. 1 Sam 25:22, 34; Ambrose *Duties of the Clergy* 3.12.76-77; *ACCS,* 86). But Antipas was concerned about more than the oath itself. Once Herod has given his oath in front of the dinner guests, his "honor" is at stake (cf. Esth 1:10-19; Jos. *Ant.* 18.299); here short-range political considerations take precedence over long-term ones, but Antipas remained captive to considerations of what others thought (cf. Derrett 1965; idem 1970: 341-42). In this account Matthew graphically illustrates his earlier warnings against the dangers of anger as murder and the evils of lust, divorce, and oaths (5:21-37).

Fourth, Matthew emphasizes that those who speak for righteousness can gain powerful enemies (14:8). John's execution foreshadows Jesus' execution (17:12-13) and the price followers of Jesus must likewise pay (16:24). Antipas and Herodias had wronged Antipas's brother Philip by taking the man's wife; this was an act of adultery in God's sight (5:31-32), and also qualified as incest under the Mosaic law (Lev 20:21; "they will be childless" probably implies their immediate execution). But Herodias wanted vengeance on John for daring to denounce her sin publicly; a member of Herod the Great's royal family would never have tolerated John's audacity (cf. Mk 6:19). (Herod the Great himself executed some Pharisees for instigating the removal of his eagle from the temple in Jerusalem — Jos. *Ant.* 17.160-67.) John must have known that if Antipas's new wife wanted his death, she would ultimately have more influence with Antipas than John would. Naturally Salome, being a minor, would seek her mother's counsel on the gift she should request.

Fifth, John's friends and enemies react in different ways (14:11-12) to his martyrdom (14:9-10). Jewish law forbade execution without trial and would not behead a person (Argyle 1963: 111; Gundry 1982: 289);[14] but the Romans had granted Antipas capital jurisdiction (Stauffer 1960: 209), and he granted execution in the least painful Roman style (cf. O'Rourke 1971: 174; cf. Jos. *Ant.* 17.276).[15] The delivery of John's head on a "platter" provides a grisly conclusion

14. Lachs 1987: 239 and Davies and Allison 1991: 474 cite in favor of Jewish beheading m. Sanh. 7:1, 3, but this was probably not in force. Davies and Allison also cite 1 [sic: 2] Sam 16:9 and 2 Kings 6:30-33, but both are unfulfilled threats based on royal prerogatives and lacking the force of true legal precedent. Rabbinic Judaism's predilection for mercy (see Thoma 1979; contrast Plato *Statesman* 293D; cf. *Crito* 50CE) probably does, however, reflect earlier roots. Traditional Roman law also prohibited execution (Dion. Hal. 7.50.3; cf. Jos. *War* 2.308; Taylor 1966: 87) or other punishments (e.g., Dion. Hal. 5.70.2; Acts 16:37; Sherwin-White 1978: 71-72) without trial, but provincial officials exercised considerably more latitude (see comment on 27:11-26).

15. Roman beheading with a sword, or in the period of the Republic usually with an axe (e.g., Appian *R.H.* 3.9.3; Livy 39.43.2-3; Herodian 3.4.6; 3.7.7; Sen. *Dial.* 3.18.4; O'Rourke 1971: 174), was widely known in Jewish texts (m. Sanh. 7:3; ARN 38A; b. Soṭa 8b; cf. ARN 41, §115 B; b. Sanh. 52b; Gen. Rab. 9:10; 75:1; Ex. Rab. 2:4).

to the feast presupposed by a birthday party (14:6) and dinner guests (14:9). This cavalier treatment of the prophet would have revolted Matthew's audience, as it would have revolted most readers in the Roman world, though it was far from unheard of (Livy 39.42.8-39.43.5; Appian *C.W.* 4.4.20; Tac. *Ann.* 14.57, 59, 64; Suet. *Galba* 20; Dio Cassius *R.H.* 62.14.1) and bringing or displaying a head confirmed an execution (Virg. *Aen.* 9.465-67; Appian *C.W.* 1.8.71-72; 2.12.86; Sall. *Jug.* 12.5; Herodian 3.7.7; 5.4.4; 8.5.9; 8.6.7; 2 Kings 10:6-7). We should not suppose, however, that it would have interfered with the banquet (Carson 1984b: 339, citing Jos. *Ant.* 13.380).

John's disciples, however, risked their own lives to show up and bury John's body (14:12).[16] Unlike John, they would have no populist support, but they were determined to provide the final, basic act of loyalty to their master that they could. (In Mediterranean antiquity, burial was an essential final act; to oppose tyrants in order to perform this act was considered honorable and heroic; cf. comment on 8:21-22; excursus on the burial at 27:57.) With nowhere else to go, John's disciples then find Jesus, the one to whom John had borne witness (3:11-15) and to whom he had sent in prison (11:2-6). The final direct portrayal of John in the Gospel is that of his martyrdom sending his remaining disciples to Jesus, the coming one. This fits any deemphasis on John the Gospel writers felt relevant in their day, but also provides a paradigm for true disciples after John (23:8-11; 28:19).

Feeding Five Thousand in the Wilderness (14:13-21)

Cf. Mk 6:32-44; Lk 9:10-17; Jn 6:1-15. Although Jesus attempted to withdraw to a solitary place (14:13), he was now too popular to escape notice. The aristocracy tended to look down on the "masses," but Jesus has compassion on the needs of the people who have come to him (14:14; 9:36; 20:34), both to heal them (14:14) and to care for their hunger (14:15-20). This narrative probably teaches about the great host at the messianic banquet the feeding foreshadows (5:6; 22:2).[17] Historically and in the text, the narrative includes a christological point: In the context of other attempted signs-workers in the wilderness in Jesus' day, his sign in the wilderness involves a clear messianic statement (Witherington 1990: 91, 100, following Barnett 1977 and citing Jos. *War* 2.261; *Ant.* 20.169). But the narrative especially instructs Matthew's audience concerning God's caring provision for his people in this age (6:11; 7:9-10; 15:25-28, 29-

16. The responsibility normally fell first to the nearest of kin (Jos. *Apion* 2.205), but when no sons were available, disciples might fulfill this filial duty (cf. Diog. Laert. 6.2.78; Diod. Sic. 10.3.4).

17. Some parallels with the last supper may reinforce this image (Hooker 1983: 47); one might also compare Mark's seating by ranks (like an army — cf. Derrett 1973: 31n.3; Hurtado 1983: 93) with Qumran parallels to the seating at the final banquet (CD 13.1-2; cf. Stauffer 1955; Kee 1977: 112; Yadin 1962: 59; pace Derrett 1975). "Reclining" suggests a banquet setting, which some take as an allusion to the messianic banquet (e.g., France 1985: 236).

39). It also stands in deliberate contrast to the drunken feast of the evil ruler Herod Antipas in 14:6-11 (Lane 1974a: 227).[18]

Sanders 1993: 156 doubts the historicity of this narrative, noting the greater public impact of a comparatively small miracle (Mk 1:28). But it is not clear from the Synoptic accounts that the crowds (in contrast to the disciples — Mk 8:19-20) are aware of the miraculous source of their meal; by contrast, the Fourth Gospel, where the crowds *do* know, suggests a considerable impact of this feeding miracle (Jn 6:14-15).[19] Based on multiple attestation (the Johannine account is literarily independent) and coherence, Meier 1994: 950-66 thinks that this story probably goes back to Jesus, at least as a memorable public meal of bread and fish in which the disciples or crowd could have seen eschatological overtones.[20] I would add that nothing would have made the meal so memorable (at least for the disciples who undoubtedly provide the source for the tradition) as a feeding miracle such as this narrative depicts; the disciples undoubtedly ate quite frequently, and even a large meal would probably not have drawn so much comment without early and strong tradition of a feeding miracle.

First, the disciples were right to be concerned about the people's hunger but intended to solve the problem in a purely natural way (14:15, 17). Matthew calls for greater faith when a miracle is needed. Providing food in the wilderness was technically impossible apart from a miracle, but God had used Moses, Elijah, and Elisha for feeding miracles.[21] (The present miracle especially resembles one performed by Elisha — 2 Kings 4:42-44.) If earlier prophets could perform such miracles, why did it not occur to the disciples that Jesus could do the same?

Biblical narrative did not oppose feeding multitudes by natural means (e.g., 2 Kings 6:22), and the disciples who were keeping track of their food supply (the kind of task rabbis often delegated to disciples — cf., e.g., Pesiq. R. 25:2; cf. Liefeld 1967: 228, citing b. ʿAbod. Zar. 35b) were undoubtedly endeavoring to be practical (14:17). But even if many towns lay in this vicinity (given

18. Jesus is a better host than Antipas; one may contrast their motivations (e.g., 14:5, 9, 14) and the different "orders" they give among those reclining (14:9, 19; cf. also 14:28).

19. Sanders suspects that the nature miracles produced less impact than less spectacular healings, and hence are probably unreliable. But when disciples saw Jesus perform such a miracle, they *did* react more dramatically (Mk 4:41//Mt 8:27). As Hagner 1995: 416-17 points out, the primary prejudice against nature miracles (as opposed to healings that can be explained psychosomatically) is antisupernaturalism — a philosophic presupposition, not a datum.

20. Witherington 1990: 98-99 also suggests a possible Q version, noting agreements of Matthew and Luke against Mark here; but Mark may have redacted Q or another source with which Matthew and Luke were familiar.

21. Greco-Roman accounts of miraculous feedings existed (cf. Bultmann 1968: 234-36; Grant 1982), but the Gospel accounts closely resemble and appear to be modeled on OT accounts (Betz 1968: 67; pace Bousset 1970: 103; for Moses parallels specifically, see Allison 1993b: 238-42). Some later Jewish accounts similarly speak of divine provision (Boring 1995: 98 cites b. Taʿan. 24b-25a).

the probable region of this feeding, they did *not*),[22] towns were generally small, accommodating perhaps a few hundred visitors in those of a few thousand people (for instance, at *most* Capernaum and Bethsaida "had only 2000-3000 inhabitants each" — Lane 1974a: 232). Further, most of the day's bread would be consumed by evening (14:15).[23] The "grass" (14:19) also indicates that the time was spring (near Passover — Jn 6:4; Abrahams 1924: 210; Dodd 1965: 211 — before the summer heat had withered the grass), when the previous year's grain stores would be running low (Ramsay 1908: 228-29). If it was impossible for the disciples to feed the crowds, it was *nearly* impossible to imagine perhaps ten thousand people (five thousand men plus women and children — 14:21)[24] fending for themselves in the countryside (pace Freyne 1988: 144-45, who wrongly compares this with the emergency situation of supporting insurgents).

In this light, the disciples' practical objection (14:17) merely recalls that of Elisha's disciple (2 Kings 4:43): the master's command (14:16; 2 Kings 4:42; cf. 1 Kings 17:16) was impossible. But both Elisha's disciple and Jesus' disciples should have been with their master long enough to expect that what the master said, he had power from God to perform. The God of the Exodus, who divided waters (Ex 14:21) and provided manna from heaven (Ex 16:14-18), was at work in history again (2 Kings 2:8-14; 4:38-44; Mt 14:13-33).

Second, like the God of the Hebrew Bible, Jesus takes what his servants bring to him and multiplies it (14:16-19). When Moses insisted that he needed a sign to take with him, God asked Moses what was already in his hand and then transformed it (Ex 4:1-3), using what had been merely a shepherd's rod even to part the sea (Ex 14:16). When a widow needed financial help Elisha asked what she had in her house; she responded that she had only a small amount of oil, so Elisha commanded her to borrow jars into which to pour the oil and multiplied it until all the jars were full (2 Kings 4:1-7). In biblical tradition God frequently transformed the ordinary things of his followers' lives (cf., e.g., Judg 6:14; 15:15-19). The narrative does not even report that Jesus prayed for the food to multiply; confident that he represents the Father's will, he merely "gives thanks" (the meaning of "blessed" the food), which was the standard Jewish custom before and normally after meals (e.g., m. Ber. 6:5-6; Safrai 1974/76c: 802).

22. The exact site is disputed; cf. VanderBroek 1983: 103-4; Bagatti 1981. None of these arguments is conclusive, but Matthew's "lonely place" (14:13) supports our general contention. For crowds running to hear a famous visiting teacher, cf. on a smaller scale, e.g., p. Hor. 3:4, §4; B. Meṣ. 2:11, §1.

23. Carson 1984b: 341 notes the flexibility of the term "evening," which here must mean late afternoon (as in the temple's evening offering), but after sunset in 14:23.

24. Against the charge that the Gospels devalued women and children, they may have simply been reticent to *invent* a number for women and children that their tradition did not supply. It was customary in many circles to number only men (e.g., Ps-Philo 5:7; 14:4), and even the Gospel traditions are thereby no more chauvinistic for using customary language than English-speakers who used masculine pronouns generically were before inclusive language became customary. The proposed allusion to Ex 12:37 (France 1985: 237) is possible, but it actually reads only "besides children"; cf. Jos. *Ant.* 4.309, "with women and children," emphasizing the inclusiveness of this assembly.

He then used his disciples to distribute the food; it is possible that Matthew mentions this means of distribution as a paradigm for subsequent disciples' responsibility (cf. 14:16 with 24:45).

Third, God does miracles only when his people need them (14:20; cf. 2 Kings 4:6). This narrative illustrates the principle of God's provision (6:25; 7:9-10), but it also guards against an abuse of that principle. The miracle depicted here is greater than the manna of the exodus, of which none would be left over (Hooker 1983: 50); but manna was never left over because manna was to be provided every day, whereas this miracle is a rare one.[25] So much was left over that each of the twelve disciples gathered food in his wicker foodbasket (sources may suggest that Jewish workers often carried their meals in these — Lane 1974a: 231; France 1985: 249). The leftovers stress the lavish abundance of God's miraculous power in Christ (cf. Theissen 1983: 67). Many well-to-do persons in the ancient Mediterranean felt that a good host should provide enough food that some was always left over (Plut. *Table-Talk* 7.4, *Mor.* 702D-704B; *R.Q.* 64, *Mor.* 279E). Although other people customarily invited famous teachers over for meals, serving as their patrons, Jesus serves as the host or family head here — and an abundant host he is.

Yet Matthew probably intends the gathering of the leftovers (cf. 2 Kings 4:7, 44; 7:1-2, 16-20; 1 Kings 17:16) to teach more. (John is more explicit that the disciples gather the fragments at Jesus' command — Jn 6:12.) Most moralists condemned the wastefulness of the rich and emphasized saving food or other items (e.g., Cato *Distichs* 3.21; Sall. *Catil.* 5.8; 16.4; Corn. Nep. 7 [Alcibiades], 1.4; Hor. *Sat.* 1.1.101-7; 1.2.62; *Epistles* 1.15.26-27; *Epodes* 1.34; Juv. *Sat.* 1.58-60; Musonius Rufus fr. 8; Diod. Sic. 17.108.4; Ps-Phocyl. 138; t. Pisha 2:15; cf. Johnston 1962: 154; Jn 6:12; Lk 15:13; Sifre Deut. 11.1.2). Jesus likewise trusted that God's provision would always be available when it was needed (cf. 16:9-11), but he refused to squander it; the extra bread, which was more than the amount he started with, could be used for other meals. Matthew's community must trust God to supply their needs (6:25-34; 10:8-10), but they should not thereby neglect what he had already provided.

Fourth, Matthew encourages his audience that God is not intimidated by the magnitude of a problem (14:21).

Extravagant numbers in ancient miracle accounts underlined the greatness of the miracle (Jn 21:11; Theissen 1983: 67 cites also Porphyry *Vit. Pyth.* 25). In this narrative the disciples saw the size of the need and the littleness of the human resources available; Jesus recognizes the size of the need and the greatness of God's resources available.

25. The comparison of Mark's narrative here with Josh 9 (Derrett 1984a) is farfetched; the comparison of leftovers with Ruth (Daube 1956: 342) is likewise too specific. Some claim that Matthew modifies Mark's narrative in a eucharistic direction, but this suggestion is probably too speculative, most of the changes being typically stylistic (Stanton 1993: 42).

Lord of the Sea (14:22-33)

Cf. Mk 6:45-52; Jn 6:16-21. By providing for the crowds, Jesus showed himself greater than a human magician just healing some individuals or turning some stones into bread. At the least, Jesus was a prophet like Moses or Elisha (14:13-21; Ex 16:14-18; 2 Kings 4:42-44). But by treading on the sea, Jesus now takes a role that the Hebrew Bible had reserved for God alone (Job 9:8; cf. also Ps 77:19; Hab 3:15).[26] The same passage in Job had spoken of God's "passing by" (Job 9:11), as in Matthew's source (Mk 6:48); "passing by" could also allude to Jesus' deity by way of Ex 33:22; 34:6. Commentators also often recognize Jesus' deity in his "It is I" in 14:27, which literally declares, "I am."[27] But as in an earlier storm scene, Matthew is interested here in teaching not only Christology but also about the faith required of disciples (8:26). Of all the disciples, Peter alone begins to walk, but Jesus regards even his faith as less than what a disciple should have.

On content-critical grounds, Meier 1994: 905-24 doubts the historicity of the story, despite its multiple attestation. He especially objects that most of Jesus' other miracles help someone in need and proclaim the kingdom rather than authenticating Jesus (1994: 920), and that the epiphany and biblical allusions are central to the story line and not merely part of the story (1994: 921). But one could argue conversely from the same evidence: coming to his disciples during a storm would help them in need, and does one have reason to presuppose that Jesus could not have intended to evoke the biblical allusions? Those who presuppose that Jesus was not who the apostolic church held him to be may dismiss the thought out of hand, whereas those who share the apostolic church's faith have good reason to embrace it; yet from a purely historical standpoint the matter cannot be decided so easily if that question is left aside.

First, the setting for the miracle is intriguing (14:22-24). The setting (again the relative seclusion of a mountain — 17:1; cf. 5:1) presents Jesus as a man of prayer (14:23); it also suggests that just because disciples face difficulties does not mean that Jesus is not the one who sent them (14:22, 24; cf. 10:17-39).

Second, Jesus' coming should bring an end to fear (14:25-27). If the disciples were still struggling against the winds at the fourth watch of the night — the Romans divided the night into four (Livy 36.24.1) instead of the traditional Jewish three watches (b. Ber. 3ab, giving both views; also found in Hom. *Il.* 10.253) — the disciples must have been exhausted. Probably accustomed to awakening around 6 a.m., they instead found themselves still trying to cross the

26. Davies and Allison 1991: 504 also cite here Frag. Targ. Ex. 15:11; Pirqe R. El. 42. Bousset 1970: 101 can offer as a pagan parallel only Lucian *Philopseudes* 13, but the biblical background is more dominant.

27. E.g., Argyle 1963: 115; Lane 1974a: 236-37; Hurtado 1983: 91; cf. 22:32, quoting Ex 3:6 thus. Further, as Davies and Allison 1991: 503 point out, Jewish tradition acknowledges only God as deliverer at sea (citing Ex 14:10–15:21; Ps 107:23-32; Jonah 1:1-16; Wis 14:2-4; 1QH 6.22-25; Test. Naph. 6:1-10; cf. b. B. Bat. 73a).

sea between 3 and 6 a.m. Like modern readers, Matthew's community may have chided the disciples for accepting the popular notion of ghosts,[28] but the biggest offense here is that they still underestimate Jesus' power ("little faith," 14:31; cf. 8:26). It had not occurred to the disciples that Jesus could know their plight, walk on water to come to them, or catch up with them in a storm! To their credit, however, the fear issue seems to be solved once they recognize that their teacher is with them. They knew him enough to know that if he was there, he would bring them through their storm.

Third, Jesus desires disciples to imitate his works, although he is patient with them as they begin to learn (14:28-31). Although the proposal that Peter walk on water was first Peter's idea (14:28), Jesus' response indicates that he approved of it (14:29). Peter is gently reproved not for presumptuously stepping from the boat but for presumptuously doubting in the very presence of Jesus (14:31; cf. 6:30; 8:26; 16:8; 17:20; cf. Manson 1979: 206; France 1985: 239).[29] Disciples were expected to imitate their masters, and Jesus is training disciples who will not simply regurgitate his oral teachings but who will have the faith to demonstrate God's authority in practice as well (see especially 17:19-20; 21:20-22). Stepping into the water on faith presumably recalls the faith of the priests in Joshua's generation (Josh 3:8, 13, 15-17).[30]

Once Jesus had given the command, walking on water was simply a matter of trusting the one who had performed so many miracles in the past. Peter's failure came as he observed the wind (14:30), looking to the natural circumstances rather than to God's power that was sustaining him. Still, Peter knew by this point to whom to cry out; while Jesus is disappointed with Peter's inadequate faith, Peter had acted in greater faith than the other disciples — he was learning through his growing observation of Jesus. Matthew's whole story line progressively develops the disciples' faith, simultaneously inviting his audience to explore deeper realms of faith in their day.

Fourth, Jesus has authority to settle totally any crisis when he is ready

28. A common belief (e.g., Lucan *C.W.* 1.11; cf. Thom 1994: 104-5 for the Pythagorean view), reputed even to route night guards (Dio Cassius *R.H.* 42.11.2-3). The *lilin,* or night spirits, were thought extremely dangerous to night travelers, among others (Alexander 1980: 30-31; cf. Lane 1974a: 237); many pagans also believed that the spirits of those drowned at sea never could descend to the realm of the dead, but wandered endlessly above the waters (Ach. Tat. 5.16.1-2). Yet Matthew's audience would chide the disciples not on the basis of modern antisupernaturalistic presuppositions but because the idea of ghosts contradicted sounder scriptural eschatology (22:31-32).

29. Davies and Allison 1991: 513-14 suggest that this pericope may foreshadow Peter's later overconfidence (26:30-36) and denial (26:69-75), and that Matthew begins here to single Peter out because of Peter's relation to the church (16:15-20). France 1985: 253-54 also notes Peter's prominence from this point (10:2; 14:28-31; 15:15; 17:24-27; 18:21).

30. The suggested Buddhist parallel for walking on water (Stehly 1977; cf. Derrett 1989) lacks close literary correspondences and is chronologically questionable (Gispert-Sauch 1978), not to mention geographically remote. There are closer hellenistic parallels, although about characters of the distant, legendary past (Boring 1995: 99-100 cites Hesiod *Astronomy* 4; Iamb. *Vit. Pythag.* 91; and especially Isoc. *Paneg.* 88-89; Dio Chrys. *3d Disc. Kingship* 30, where it represents a divine power), and second-century Jewish parallels (Mek. Beshallah 6; Betz 1968: 67n.51).

to do so (14:32). As soon as they entered the boat, the wind grew still. Stilling storms was a sign of God's authority in the biblical record.[31] The disciples may have recalled an earlier occasion on which Jesus simply commanded and the storm died down (8:26); this time, however, the storm acts out of respect for him — apparently without so much as requiring a word on his part.

Finally, Jesus' power led his disciples to acknowledge his identity (14:33). Their knowledge would still need to be tested outside the momentary confidence that depended on miracles (16:15), but the disciples had nevertheless offered a correct response, including "worship" (cf. 2:11; 15:25). The acknowledgment that Jesus was God's Son concurs with the divine perspective articulated in 3:17 and is almost identical with the Gentile soldiers' climactic confession in 27:54.[32] One may doubt, however, that the disciples had yet grasped the full implications of Jesus' claim (such as "I am" in 14:27).

Jesus Heals All Who Come (14:34-36)

Cf. Mk 6:53-56; Jn 6:22-25. Jesus had welcomed the crowds (14:13), temporal though their needs may have been (14:14). As word continues to spread, ailing people from throughout Galilee came to Gennesaret (cf. m. Maʿaś. 3:7) seeking the only one who could meet their need (see comment on 4:23-25). Others who had heard of how a woman had been healed by touching a tassel of his tallith, or shawl (9:20), sought to repeat the same act, seeking similar healings for themselves (14:36). Such activity may not have been at the heart of Jesus' mission, but it reflected the heart that motivated his mission: compassion (14:14). After such a description of Jesus gladly providing patronal benevolence for any who needed him (benevolence was a largely positive image in ancient sources), the criticism of the religious leaders in 15:1-20 jars Matthew's audience by its bold relief.

Moral versus Ritual Cleanness (15:1-20)

Cf. Mk 7:1-23; Lk 6:39; 11:37-41. The reader recognizes Jesus as God's Son who not only acts as the prophets of old (14:13-21) but as the Lord of creation himself (14:22-32). The disciples acclaim Jesus as God's Son (14:33), and the masses approach him for healing (14:34-36). In this context the pedantic response of the Pharisees and scribes, members of what we might view as a sort of religious and academic elite, stands in all the starker contrast to reality. Jesus points out that whereas the Pharisees use their traditions as a standard for

31. Most thoroughly, Davies and Allison 1991: 509-10 cite Job 26:11-12; Ps 65:7; 89:9-10; 107:29; Jonah 1:15; Sir 43:23; cf. 4Q 381 and *Sepher Ha-Razim,* 1.226-28; 4.31-32. Cf. Prudentius *A Hymn on the Trinity* 649-79 (*ACCS,* 65).

32. Although *huios tou theou* appears in Mark and Q, *theou huios* (14:33; 27:43, 54) appears to be specifically Matthean redaction where it appears (cf. Mowery 1990).

righteousness, some of their traditions can be extended to contradict the written law. The rhetorical patterns here can be understood as Jewish (Daube 1973: 142-43), but they fit broader Greco-Roman patterns as well, probably because Jewish rhetoric was thoroughly influenced by Greco-Roman rhetoric in this period.[33]

First, members of the religious elite insisted that their custom was right, even though it was based only on their tradition (15:1-2). Again the religious elite object to a practice of Jesus' disciples, implying a deficiency in the training Jesus has supplied to them (see comment on 12:3-8). Other Palestinian Jews recognized that the Pharisees passed on ancestral laws not written in the law of Moses (Jos. *Ant.* 13.297; cf. Baumgarten 1972; Gal 1:14).[34] Hand washing was an extrabiblical Jewish tradition, perhaps originally adopted from foreign Jews (Sib. Or. 3.591-94; Sanders 1990: 39-40, 228, 260-71),[35] concerning which the Pharisees were especially meticulous (see especially Safrai 1974/76d: 801-2; cf. m. Yad. 1:1–2:4; b. Bek. 30b, bar.; Ber. 11b; 15a; 60b).

Because Mark's interpretation of Jesus' comments is so sweeping, some suspect that he created much of the narrative himself (Sanders 1990: 91). But while Mark may join together disparate teachings of and narratives concerning Jesus (as was standard rhetorical practice — cf., e.g., Theon *Progymn.* 4.73-79; 5.388-441), it is likely that his traditions accurately reflect Jesus' own words. After all, if Mark wanted to *create* sayings for Jesus to address questions of his own generation (food laws, circumcision, or keeping holy days — cf., e.g., Rom 14:2-6), he could have done a much better job than he did! He would also have created a more cohesive narrative, as Mark elsewhere demonstrates he can do capably enough. Witherington 1990: 63 defends even Mark 7:15, arguing that the saying did not immediately shape the practice of the earliest Christians (though it did later — Rom 14:14) because they did not understand the saying in the Markan sense; it was ambiguous, and even Mark had to explain it. But Matthew omits

33. The Rhetoric and NT Section discussed Mk 7:1-23 at the Society of Biblical Literature meeting Nov. 22, 1994; of special note were Robbins 1994, presenting significant arguments for a more Greek position; and Basser 1994 and Flesher 1994, providing significant arguments for more rabbinic forms of rhetoric. The dichotomy is probably artificial, especially for Jewish rhetoric written in Greek (such as we find in the Gospels, especially the controversy dialogues).

34. Because they often saw many of their traditions already implicit in the law of Moses (m. 'Abot 1:1; Sifre Deut. 313.2.4; b. Ber. 5a; Meg. 19b), some successors of Pharisaic teachers suggested that the oral traditions even equaled (Sifra Behuq. par. 2.264.1.1; pq. 8.269.2.14; Sifre Deut. 115.1.1-2; 306/25.1; 351.1.2-3; ARN 2, 3, 15A; 29, §§61-62B; Pesiq. Rab Kah. 10:5; 15:5) or outranked (m. Sanh. 11:3; b. ʿAbod. Zar. 35a; ʿErub. 21b; p. ʿAbod. Zar. 2:7, §3; Hor. 3:5, §3; Sanh. 11:4, §1; Num. Rab. 14:4; Song Rab. 1:2, §2; Pesiq. R. 3:2) the written law, although scholars often question whether this was the primary view in the early sources (Sanders 1990: 115-25; Chernick 1980; Landman 1976-77).

35. The images of pure hands and hand washing (often by pouring water over them) are common in Greek texts (see, e.g., Nock 1964a: 18-19; for the Homeric period, Hom. *Il.* 6.266; 9.171, 174; 24.302-5; *Od.* 1.136-38, 146; 2.260-61; 3.338; 4.52-54, 216; 12.336-37; 21.270; Gordon 1965b: 259; for the Greek tragedians, e.g., Dibelius and Conzelmann 1972: 44; elsewhere, Hesiod *W.D.* 724-26, 737-41); for Jewish texts, see, e.g., Ep. Arist. 305-6; Safrai 1974/1976d: 830.

this ambiguous statement (cf. Saldarini 1994: 134, 139), as well as Mark's overly sweeping summary of Jewish practice (cf. Mk 7:3-4).[36]

Some also think that Matthew adapts Mark's language in an anti-Judaic (Meier 1980: 167) or less anti-Judaic (Tilborg 1972b: 16; Goulder 1974: 19) direction. But because Mark himself is no more anti-Judaic than anti-Gentile (Robinson 1982: 113; cf. 106), Mark interprets Jesus' words as challenging only the food laws (Mk 7:19); aside from omitting this challenge Matthew does not modify Mark's point substantially.[37] This difference is significant, however, underlining Matthew's explicit emphasis that Jesus did not violate Torah (5:17; Overman 1990b: 82-84; Segal 1991: 7), an emphasis perpetuated in the immediate context of this passage (see Levine 1988: 161-62).

Second, Jesus challenges their tradition as unbiblical (15:3-11; cf. Test. Asher 7:5, possibly a Christian interpolation). *Jesus begins by showing how easily one of their traditions can conflict with the moral purpose of Scripture (15:3-6).* One could dedicate an object for sacred use, and even if Pharisaic teachers agreed with Jesus that the vow turned out to be inappropriate, they probably would not have used their authority to cancel it. Some scholars contend that the only kind of vow that one school of Pharisaism in Jesus' day would not release was a vow to the temple (Falk 1985: 98-99; cf. Black 1967: 139). A man could also prohibit others from using his property (say, eating his figs) by declaring them dedicated to the temple or perhaps "as if they were" so dedicated, hence, "forbidden to you" (m. Ned. 3:2; Baumgarten 1984-85; Sanders 1990: 54-55). As far away as Alexandria some Jewish teachers could use such vows to keep property from other family members (see Sanders 1990: 57). By laying some commonly held traditional practices against less biblical principles that were less concretely defined legally, an unscrupulous person could have circumvented some biblical principles.[38]

36. They may have washed their hands only for Sabbath or festival meals (m. Ber. 8:1-2; t. Ber. 5:25; Davies 1993: 112).

37. Safrai 1974/76d: 801-2 provides substantial support for Mark's *basic* accuracy here (cf. Jdt 12:7-9; De Jonge 1974/76: 1:40; most concede for at least his statement about the Pharisees; cf. Sanders 1990: 228-31). Mark's description of the "fist" fits later Jewish teachers' regulations (cf. Lightfoot 1859: 2:418; McNamara 1983: 195; Black 1967: 9). But many scholars doubt whether all Palestinian Jews followed the practice (Sanders 1990: 40, 90-91, 185-86; Anderson 1976: 181, 184; Nineham 1977: 193), although Diaspora Jews assumed they did (Ep. Arist. 305). Some debates concerning the appropriate time for hand washing occurred even *within* Pharisaism (see, e.g., Falk 1985: 150 on Lk 11:39). One complication in our evidence is that Jesus dealt primarily with the prevailing, stricter Shammaites, whereas most extant rabbinic texts reflect if anything the more lenient tradition of the later dominant Ḥillelites.

38. Mark has "Korban," an oath meaning "gift" (e.g., Jos. *Apion* 1.167), an offering to God, including what was vowed to the temple (cf., e.g., m. Maʿaś. Sh. 4.10-11; Ned. 1:1-2; 8:7; t. Maʿaś. Sh. 5:2; Ned. 1:1-2; Carmon 1973: 75, §167; Mazar 1980: 59; Fitzmyer 1974: 93-100; McNamara 1983: 200-202; Sanders 1990: 53). Others suggest that this passage refers to vowing not to perform an act (Zeitlin 1968) or an oath uttered by a son in anger from which the Pharisees would not release him (Bligh 1964). Just as Matthew intensifies the Pharisaic interpretation of a Mosaic concession into a commandment (*reductio ad absurdum* — 19:7 vs. Mk 10:4), he here intensifies Jesus' accusation of their unscriptural view into a blatant prohibition of keeping the fourth commandment (15:6 vs. Mk 7:12; Krämer 1981; Gundry 1982: 304), suggesting that Matthew's situation is more polemically advanced than Mark's.

Jesus deliberately picks an issue that will provoke thought and argues from a source that his opponents also held authoritative. A Pharisaic teacher could have offered the same sort of argument Jesus offers here, for the Pharisees could argue by laying one text against the interpretation of another. Judaism heavily stressed honoring[39] and obeying[40] one's parents, as did most Gentile writers.[41] They also highly emphasized the obligation to support one's parents in their old age.[42] Pharisaic tradition also unapologetically criticizes Pharisees who fell short of what they considered appropriate Pharisaic values (ARN 37A; 45, §124B). Jewish teachers who engaged in legal casuistry never contended that such casuistry was the heart of the law nor approved of people exploiting loopholes (cf., e.g., Urbach 1979: 1:576); but that was a natural end result of spending more time debating laws as laws than in teaching ethical principles behind the laws. Jesus is not challenging Pharisaic *views* about parental support, but the danger of evaluating morality on the basis of extrabiblical traditions. The Pharisees often articulated more noble ethical ideals than many Christians do; such ideals, however, were and are often neglected in practice, among Christians as well as others.[43]

Jesus next compares this behavior to Scripture's warning about following human rules rather than an intimate relationship with God (15:7-9, citing Is

39. See Sir 3:8; Syr. Men. Sent. 9-10, 20-24, 94-98; Ps-Phocyl. 8, 180; Ep. Arist. 228, 238; Jos. *Apion* 2.206; Philo *Ebr.* 17; *Spec. Leg.* 2.234-36; *Prob.* 87; Sib. Or. 1.74-75; 2.275-76; Jub. 7:20; 29:14-20; 35:1-6, 11-13; Mek. Pisha 1.28; Bah. 8.28ff.; Sifre Deut. 81.4.1-2; b. Sanh. 66a, bar.; Gen. Rab. 1:15; 36:6; 39:7; Deut. Rab. 1:15.

40. See Sir 3:7; Jos. *Life* 204; Test. Abr. 5B; Test. Jud. 1:4-5; Pesiq. R. 23/24:2; b. Qidd. 31ab.

41. Greco-Roman writers emphasized honoring (Hierocles *On Duties. Toward One's Parents* 4.25.53; *On Fraternal Love* 4.27.20 in Malherbe 1986: 91-94; Hesiod *W.D.* 182-85, 331-32; Isoc. *Demon.* 14, 16, *Or.* 1; Pub. Syr. 8; Cato *Distichs* 3.24; *Collection of Distichs* 2; Appian *R.H.* 3.2; Dion. Hal. 8.53.1; Diog. Laert. *Lives* 1.37, 60; 6.2.65; 7.1.120; 8.1.22-23; 10.1.9; Epict. *Disc.* 3.11.5; Isis aretalogies in Horsley 1981: 11, 17, 20; see further Keener 1991a: 197n.107) and obeying (Isoc. *Nic./Cypr.* 57, *Or.* 3.37; Dion. Hal. 3.23.19; Musonius Rufus 16 in Meeks 1986: 51; Aul. Gel. 2.7; Keener 1991a: 197n.8, and later references there on the authority of the *paterfamilias*) parents.

42. Cf. Sir 3:12-15; Montefiore and Loewe 1974: 500-6; Montefiore 1968: 2:226; Derrett 1970: 110; Pesiq. R. 23/24:2; cf. Prov 28:24; Hesiod *W.D.* 188-89; Quint. 7.6.5; *P. Enteuxeis* 26 (lawsuit against a daughter who failed to provide). Hagner 1995: 431 cites t. Ned. 1.6.4 for a vow taking precedence over a biblical commandment, but notes that in later times honor of parents took precedence over a vow (m. Ned. 9:1).

43. The view that Mark (hence Matthew) misrepresents the spirit of Pharisaism here and hence misrepresents what happened in Jesus' ministry (Parkes 1979: 44) neglects ample other evidence for conflict (cf. on 12:1-14) and the sad reality that ethical theory and practice often differ (in Christian circles as well as early Jewish). Jesus was critiquing not *Judaism,* of which he was a part, but some religious *persons.* The view that Mk 7:15 is too radical for Jesus (Sanders 1985: 266-67; idem 1990: 28) may presuppose too much about Jesus; the view that it must be inauthentic or other Gentile Christians would have appealed to it (Räisänen 1982; cf. Gaston 1970: 93) neglects the facts that (1) it could be interpreted differently than Mark interprets it, and undoubtedly was by the earliest Jewish Christians (cf. Sanders 1990: 28); (2) had it not been susceptible to such interpretation, Mark would not have clarified it; (3) Jesus is rarely quoted *at all* in our extant non-Gospel literature; (4) Mark could have adapted the wording; (5) Matthew sees no reason to modify Mark seriously, except to omit his interpretation.

29:13).[44] One standard part of debate rhetoric included citing an ancient authority, when possible often from the opponent's tradition (Mack 1988: 191); as one of the most commonly cited biblical works in Jesus' day, Isaiah functioned well (cf. Acts 28:25: "The Holy Spirit spoke rightly through Isaiah . . ."). Jesus may here proceed by means of *gezerah shewah,* that is, linking texts on the basis of shared key words: Jesus' interlocutors "honor" God as well as they "honor" their parents — at best in pretense (15:4, 8).

Scribes and Pharisees would have taken offense at the appellation "hypocrites" (6:2; 22:18; 23:13; 24:51); like Jesus, the Pharisees were willing to suspend the letter of the law to uphold its spirit (e.g., m. Sheb. 10:3-4; cf. Strack 1969: 36, 96; Moore 1971: 2:31). But Pharisaic scribes frequently determined morality (where the Torah was unclear) by extrapolating from tradition; by demanding that disciples extrapolate morality instead from biblical principles Jesus takes ethics out of the domain of the academy and courtroom and places it more fully in the daily lives of his followers.

Jesus finally opposes his challengers publicly by declaring a more basic principle (15:10-11). Some Pharisees may have agreed with the principle, but normally stated it only in private (Pesiq. Rab Kah. 4:7; Pesiq. R. 14:14; Jeremias 1971: 211), perhaps due to fear of those who would cease to observe the literal requirements of the law (cf. Philo *Migr. Abr.* 89-93; probably Ps-Phocyl. 228). Although Jesus explains his point in private, he first makes it publicly. In arguing by example (15:4-6) and by citation of accepted authority (15:7-9), Jesus follows standard technique in debate (cf. comment on 12:3-8), but his closing principle is stated bluntly, calculated to retain attention — offensively if need be — rather than persuade by providing an agreeable statement (Tannehill 1975: 91). The concluding principle marks his opponents' rhetorical defeat (which was naturally how narratives about other famous teachers typically also closed).

Third, Matthew presents Jesus as interested in speaking God's truth, not in winning influential allies (15:12-14). Many Greek audiences respected teachers who would publicly deride those of high social status who proved unworthy of it (Epict. *Disc.* 2.4); some brash Jewish teachers like Honi the Circle-Drawer were also known for their lack of respect for worldly status, including that of the sages. Insulting one's accusers as morally or intellectually deficient, so transferring shame from oneself to one's accusers, was customary rhetorical practice (Sall. *Invective against Marcus Tullius* 1). But most Jewish circles and most polite Mediterranean society in general emphasized public respect toward persons of appropriate rank, and most speeches intended to be persuasive began with kind words toward one's audience.

Scholars may debate how much or little political power the Pharisees held in this period (Sanders 1990: 128-29; idem 1992: 388-402, 410-11, 458-90; Co-

44. Early Christian literature regularly cites "the shorter LXX form" (Cope 1976: 56, who thinks "this was [therefore] the form known to the early Christian writers"), but this could be because the Gospel citation was more familiar than its Isaianic context.

hen 1987: 163), but they were highly influential with the people (Jos. *Ant.* 18.17; Sanders 1992: 402-4). Jesus' disciples are thus concerned that he has publicly shamed his influential interlocutors instead of reaching out to them (15:12). Yet Jesus, who elsewhere wishes to avoid causing most people to stumble (17:27), here seems unconcerned about pleasing those who value their elders' traditions too highly.[45] Jesus responds by alluding back to the prophetic image of building or tearing down, planting or uprooting people according to God's message (15:13).[46] Those plants his Father had planted were those who had received the revelation of Jesus' character from the Father — a revelation he had concealed from the "wise and prudent" (11:25-27; 13:11-17; 16:16-17; cf. 14:33). Jesus then graphically compares his self-assured opponents to people who offer to lead the blind but cannot see themselves (15:14; cf. 7:3-5; 13:13-14; 23:16; Rom 2:19).[47] Even were the interpretation of such an image difficult, the disciples should have understood him perfectly well: earlier prophets had also complained that the leaders of God's people were blind (e.g., Is 3:12, 14; 6:10; 9:16; cf. CD 1.9-11). "Let them alone" (15:14) thus carries not a positive sense protecting them (as in 19:14) but a sense more like: Do not waste your pearls on swine (7:6).

Fourth, Jesus is concerned with the state of the heart and what issues from it, not with ritual acts (15:15-20). As was customary with enigmatic, potentially controversial sayings, Peter asks for an interpretation in private, among other disciples already committed to Jesus' message (15:15; see comment on 13:10). But Jesus notes that his words demand little interpretation; they would be obvious if the disciples were not assuming that he could not mean what he had said (15:16-17)! Not food that enters the mouth (Ezek 4:14-15; Acts 10:11-16; Rom 14:1-4; 1 Tim 4:3) but what comes forth (Mt 12:34-37; Eph 4:29; Jas 1:19) renders unclean; alluding to the Isaiah passage he has recently quoted (29:13; cf. 59:13), Jesus emphasizes the heart (cf. 5:21–6:18), as did some of his contemporaries (m. 'Abot 2:9). Matthew does, however, omit Mark's explicit repudiation of the kashrut, which is not explicit in Jesus' own saying (Mk 7:19); as much as

45. Ancient aristocrats' disdain for populists (Isoc. *To Nic.* 48-49, *Or.* 2; *Areopagiticus;* Arist. *Pol.* 4.4.4-7, 1292a; 5.4.1-2, 1304b; 6.2.10-12, 1319b; *Rhet.* 2.20.5, 1393b; Diog. Laert. 4.42; Plut. *Praising Inoffensively* 16, *Mor.* 545C; Diog. *Ep.* 11, to Crates; Martin 1990: 92-116; Gardner 1974: 27-59) provides a partial rhetorical analogy for snubbing others; yet by aristocratic standards both Jesus and the Pharisees were populists. Cynics were among those who regularly snubbed everyone, but Jesus appears far more selective in the objects of his diatribe (note 9:11).

46. Cf. 3:10; Ps 28:5; Jer 1:10; 11:17; 18:7; 24:6; 31:4, 28; 42:10; 45:4; the image of planting and taking root also appears in Jer 12:2, which a midrashic interpreter would connect naturally with Is 29:13, cited earlier in the Gospel pericope. Cf. also disciples in Gen. Rab. 85:5; the Qumran community in F. F. Bruce 1969: 73; cf., e.g., p. Ter. 2:3 for the uprooting of inappropriately planted trees; Test. Asher 1:7 (uprooting sin).

47. Leading the blind may have been a well-known image (Plut. *Bride* 6, *Mor.* 139A); Young 1989: 241-42 cites Plato *Rep.* 8.554B. Certainly the blind required literal guides (Hesiod *Astronomy, Fr.* 5; Soph. *Oed. Rex* 444; *Oed. Col.* 199-201; *Antig.* 989-90). Gundry 1982: 307 cites OT passages showing that "falling in a pit became proverbial for disaster" (Is 24:18; Jer 48:44; Ps 7:15; Prov 26:27).

he likes and often follows Mark, he writes for a very different audience that still values these laws (see summary of background for these laws in Keener and Usry 1997: 213-14n.121).

Jesus illustrates with a vice list, a standard literary form in both Jewish (Wis 14:25-26; 1QS 4.9-11; Philo *Sac.* 32; *Post.* 52; Test. Levi 17:11) and broader Greco-Roman (e.g., Plato *Law* 1.649D; Arist. *E.E.* 2.3.4, 1220b-21; *V.V.* 1249-51b; Epict. *Disc.* 2.8.23; Diog. *Ep.* 36, to Timomachus) circles (Matthew's is somewhat more deliberate than Mark's — Meier 1980: 170). By examining other passages in the Gospel that depict these vices, we can get some sense of how Matthew would have applied this list for his community: evil reasonings (9:4; 16:7; 21:25), murders (2:16; 5:21-26; 14:10; 23:34-35; 27:24-25), adulteries (5:27-32; 14:3-6), sexual immoralities (5:32; 12:39; 21:31; contrast 1:25), theft (27:64), false witness (26:59-61), and slander or blasphemy (cf. 12:31-32). Many of these vices derive from prohibitions in the Ten Commandments; elements that agree with the list in 19:18 follow the same sequence.

A Canaanite Woman's Faith (15:21-28)

Cf. Mk 7:24-30. Placed immediately after a discussion of purity in both Matthew and Mark, Jesus' encounter with this Gentile woman brings out the implications the evangelists find in his view of purity: Gentiles will no longer be separated from Israel (cf. Acts 10:15, 28; 11:9-18). Like an earlier Gentile in Matthew's Gospel (8:10), this woman becomes an illustration of faith. But like that centurion, this woman illustrates not only faith in a general sense but particularly the faith with which Gentiles could approach Jesus, even during his earthly ministry to Israel (as often noted; e.g., cf. Held 1963: 200). This outsider compares favorably with some religious insiders among Jesus' contemporaries (15:1-20; Patte 1987: 220).

Matthew reinforces this point by specifying exactly what Mark's hellenistic Syro-Phoenician woman (Mk 7:26) means.[48] She is a descendant of the ancient Canaanites, the bitter biblical enemies of Israel whose paganism had often led Israel into idolatry (cf. Jub. 22:20-22).[49] Whereas the law granted some respect to Egyptians and some other cultures (Deut 23:7; cf. Is 19:25), Matthew's

48. "Syro-Phoenician" distinguishes her locale from the Carthaginian settlements of Phoenicians in Libya; Phoenicia was now part of the Syrian province, as was Judea (Lane 1974a: 260). She is a "Greek" and a Syro-Phoenician either because Syria was so heavily hellenized in general (Goodman 1983: 64; for Tyre's bilingualism, see Theissen 1991: 68-70) or more likely because she belongs to "the Hellenized citizen class" of Tyre or Sidon (Judge 1960: 15; Theissen 1991: 70-72). One negative association that should not be admitted here is that of Wisdom literature's "strange woman," which referred to prostitutes rather than to foreigners (cf. Witherington 1994: 37).

49. Canaanites and aspects of their culture *had* persisted; see Oden 1976; Flusser 1974/76: 1070-74. Lachs 1987: 248 presents some evidence for applying "Canaanite" to Gentiles in general (m. Qidd. 1:3; Mek. Nezikin 9, Laut. 3:70, 73, on Ex 21:26), such as a Phoenician merchant (Sifre Deut. 306; Yalqut 1.942); at least some of these examples probably refer to descendants of the Canaanites.

Jewish audience may wince at his label for this woman of faith. "Yes," Matthew seems to reply; "God's compassion extends to *all* Gentiles." Matthew cites not only Canaanites, but Magi (2:1-12) and Roman soldiers (8:5-13; 27:54), the most extreme sorts of examples — yet not without biblical precedent (12:41). If "Tyre and Sidon" (15:21) lead some readers to recall Jezebel, others must recall instead the widow who supported Elijah (1 Kings 17:8-24; Lk 4:26). The narrative thus constitutes another Matthean invitation to the Gentile mission (e.g., 2:1-11; 8:5-13), reinforcing the message of 11:21-24 (where Tyre and Sidon were more open to repentance than Chorazin and Bethsaida). The Canaanites Tamar and Rahab in Jesus' genealogy (1:3, 5) especially prepare the reader for positively evaluating this Canaanite woman who, like a few others in this Gospel (9:27), confesses Jesus' Messiahship before Peter does (1:1; 15:22; 16:16). Even in the unlikely event that they are unfamiliar with the Markan tradition, Matthew's ideal audience may experience some cognitive dissonance in the brief narrative's suspense; they know that Jesus cannot ultimately reject this woman for her ethnicity without repudiating two of his ancestors in the genealogy.

The basic account itself is likely authentic. That the best samples of interaction with Gentiles in the Gospel traditions had included some measure of rejection (cf. also 8:7, as a question) indicates that the Gospel writers did not fabricate stories to bolster their appeal to the Gentile mission. It is unlikely that Christians would lightly attribute to Jesus a view they no longer held (Theissen 1991: 63-64). Still, Matthew *increases* the racially polarized tone in Mark, whether because his community knows a stricter tradition that Mark has toned down, or perhaps to appeal to hard-liners in his community with a hard-line Judaic Jesus who finally allows himself to be won over by the woman's persistent faith. Another argument in favor of authenticity, however, is the accurate knowledge of the local situation around Tyre that it presupposes (Theissen 1991: 65, 81).

First, the woman was so desperate that she would not take no for an answer (15:21-25). Modern Western society might consider such a person rude, but Mediterranean judges were sometimes so corrupt that among the poor only a persistent, desperate, otherwise powerless woman could obtain justice from them (Lk 18:2-5; Bailey 1980: 134-35; cf. comment on 20:20-21). Both men and women in the Old Testament (Gen 18:22-32; 32:26-30; Ex 33:12–34:9; 1 Kings 18:36-37; 2 Kings 2:2, 4, 6, 9; 4:14-28) and in the Gospel tradition (Mk 5:28-29; Jn 2:3-5) had shown such courage by refusing to take no for an answer to a desperate need (cf. O'Day 1989; pace Fiorenza 1983: 137).

Second, Jesus reiterates that his mission is specifically for Israel (15:26). Jesus had left Jewish territory because the masses thronged him, and he needed to rest with and teach his disciples (15:21; cf. 16:13); but this stage (cf. 28:19) of his mission remained for Israel alone.[50] Thus when his disciples ask

50. Jeremias 1958: 36 contends that the territory of Tyre and Sidon now extended inland so that Jesus would have to pass through it if heading from Galilee to Caesarea Philippi; he also cites evidence to argue that Jesus could have been working among its many Jewish inhabitants. But Matthew would certainly see the territory as *theologically* Gentile (see 4:15).

him to send her away (15:23),[51] he notes the limitation of his mission (15:24; cf. 10:6; Rom 15:8).[52] Yet neither did he send her away as his disciples requested, which may have encouraged her to persevere in her irritation (cf. 19:13; 20:31). To her own insistent entreaty (15:25) Jesus responds with almost equal firmness (15:26). Some Jewish teachers would have reached out to the woman, hoping to make her a proselyte (cf., e.g., Jos. *Ant.* 20.34-36; *Apion* 2.210; m. 'Abot 1:12; b. Sanh. 99b; Shab. 31a; Goppelt 1964: 54); Jesus simply snubs her.

That the children must be fed "first" (in Mark's account, Mk 7:27) opens the door to a later healing and the coming Gentile mission (Hurtado 1983: 103), but the woman's need is too urgent for that; by omitting the phrase, even if merely to abbreviate the narrative, Matthew reads more harshly. In both Gospels, Jesus probably refers to the children's pet dogs; well-to-do Greeks, unlike most Jews, could raise dogs as pets and not view them as merely troublesome rodents (cf. Ex 22:31; Hom. *Il.* 23.173; *Od.* 2.11; 10.216; 17.290-304; Gordon 1965a: 107; Cary and Haarhoff 1946: 150; Witherington 1984: 170n.103).[53] The image is thus simply one of children's needs (cf. 7:9) taking temporal precedence over those of pets (Lane 1974a: 262; Anderson 1976: 191; Gundry 1982: 314).[54] Such an admission, however, hardly transforms the image into a compliment (cf. 7:6); the image was an unpleasant one (Eurip. *Orestes* 260), and "dog" was an insult in the earliest extant pagan tradition (Hom. *Il.* 8.527; 9.373; 11.362; 20.449; 22.345; *Od.* 17.248; 22.35; cf. "dogfly" in Hom. *Il.* 21.394, 421), as was its female derivative (Hom. *Od.* 11.424; 18.338; 19.91). Dogs were known for their attachment to dung and sniffing other dogs' rear ends (Phaedrus 1.27.10-11; 4.19); more commonly they were linked with birds as scavengers that devoured

51. Whether they are asking him to heal the woman hurriedly or to order her to leave is unclear, but the latter may be more likely given the disciples' earlier counsel in similar words without expecting a miracle (14:15; cf. 19:13; 20:31). They contrast starkly with Jesus, who did not like to send people away with their needs unmet (15:32). Her shouting to them may seek a miracle from them (17:16) or be beseeching them to intercede with the higher patron Jesus.

52. Missing from Mark, the phrase looks suspiciously like Matthean wording (Gundry 1982: 313); but Jeremias 1958: 27 insists that its Aramaic construction suggests its antiquity (cf. also Wilson 1973: 14). A stronger argument in its favor is that it hardly fits Matthew's own perspective (Anderson 1976: 191; cf. Vermes 1984: 55); it would at least seem to belong to his community's tradition which he must answer. The offputting remark about dogs surely predates our extant Gospels (Montefiore 1968: 1:167).

53. Dogs appears as unclean (Is 66:3; Mt 7:6; cf. Hittite *Instructions for Temple Officials* 14, *ANET* 209; Moyer 1969: 96, 106, 127), in part because they are scavengers (Ex 22:31; 1 Kings 14:11; 16:4; 21:19, 23-24; 22:38; 2 Kings 9:10, 36; Jer 15:3; Lk 16:21; Aelian *Animals* 7.19). Schnackenburg 1985: 144 suggests that Jews also knew house dogs.

54. Jesus' image creates distance between his suppliant and the "children," but not in a spiteful sense (Schnackenburg 1985: 144). Some also take note of the diminutive form for "dog" as a reference to pets, but the diminutive had lost most of its force in Greek by this period. An objection that Aramaic lacked the diminutive (France 1985: 247), of course, falters on the likelihood that Jesus would have spoken with the woman in Greek (Matthew's audience may have been unaware of Mark's tradition that she was Greek, but many of them may not have known Aramaic either). Some have related dogs to ancient Phoenician healing rituals (see Stager 1991), but the evidence is in dispute (Wapnish and Hesse 1993).

unburied corpses (Hom. *Il.* 17.127, 255, 272; 22.42-43, 66-70, 335-36, 339, 348, 353; 23.21, 183-87; 24.211, 411; *Od.* 3.258-60; 21.363-64; 22.476; Eurip. *Phoenician Maidens* 1650; Appian *C.W.* 1.8.72; Lucan *C.W.* 7.829). Sometimes dogs could prove vicious (e.g., Hom. *Od.* 14.29-36; Longus 1.21), even assaulting living humans (Aul. Gel. 15.20.9).[55]

Jesus is not cursing the woman, but he *is* putting her off (cf. 8:7). It is possible that he is testing her, as teachers sometimes tested their disciples (Jn 6:6; Lev. Rab. 22:6; cf. p. Sanh. 3:5, §2; Char. *Chaer.* 8.2.13), but he is certainly reluctant to grant her request, and is providing an obstacle for her faith (cf. 8:7; Jn 2:4). Perhaps he is requiring her to understand his true mission and identity, lest she treat him as one of the many wandering magicians to whom Gentiles sometimes appealed for exorcisms. Yet he is surely summoning her to recognize Israel's priority in the divine plan, a recognition that for her will include an admission of her dependent status. As Levine puts it, she receives the miracle "because she accepts her marginal position as a gentile" (1988: 152). One may compare Elisha's requirement that Naaman dip in the *Jordan* despite Naaman's preference for the Aramean rivers Abana and Pharpar (2 Kings 5:10-12), ultimately leading to Naaman's acknowledgment of Israel's God and land (2 Kings 5:17-18).

As a member of the hellenistic citizen class in the Markan account, she belonged to a group that had routinely taken the bread belonging to the impoverished Jews residing in the vicinity of Tyre (Theissen 1991: 66-80; for this region's economic relation with Tyre, cf. Meyers 1988: 74; for the privileged status of a local Greek elite, cf., e.g., Bowan and Rathbone 1992). Now Mark's Jesus reverses the power relations, for the "bread" Jesus offers belongs to Israel first (Theissen 1991: 75); this "Greek" must beg help from an itinerant Jew (Theissen 1991: 78-79; Theissen 1984; cf. Pub. Syr. 172). By instead calling her a Canaanite, Matthew mutes the class issue but focuses on the ethnic issue more relevant to his audience, again underlining the importance of the Gentile mission for his community (cf. Jn 4:7-42).

Third, the woman demonstrates her faith by recognizing Israel's priority in God's plan (15:27-28). She recognizes that Jesus is no mere magician

55. Though Greeks and Romans viewed dogs as faithful to their masters (Aelian *Animals* 6.25; 7.10, 25; *Select Papyri* 3:460-63; Appian *R.H.* 11.10.64), even they viewed them as sexually immoral and shameless (Aelian *Animals* 7.19). Commentators who suggest that Jewish people regularly called Gentiles "dogs" (e.g., Brandon 1967: 172-73; Theissen 1991: 62n.1) probably make too much of relatively scant references (cf. Smith 1951: 167; on associations with Rome, cf. Hayward 1993), but apart from Cynics, who seemed to embrace the title (e.g., *Greek Anth.* 7.63-68, 115-16; Athenaeus *Deipn.* 13.61b; Lucian *Demonax; Dial. of the Dead;* Philo *Plant.* 151; Diog. *Ep.* 2, 7), most people in antiquity would have taken the epithet as an insult related to dogs' ill behavior (cf. 1 Sam 17:43; Prov 26:11; Mart. *Epig.* 1.83; Plut. *Exile* 7, *Mor.* 601DE; Philo *Gig.* 35; Mek. Kaspa 2.23-26; p. Ta'an. 1:6, §8; Pesiq. Rab Kah. 7:6; Gen. Rab. 36:7; Song Rab. 2:13, §4; Pesiq. R. 15:14/15; for dogs' weakness, see 1 Sam 17:43; 24:14; 2 Sam 3:8; 9:8; 2 Kings 8:13; Eccl 9:4). (And people originally meant it as an insult when applying it to the Cynics — cf. Diog. Laert. 6.2.40, 45-46, 60, 77; Mart. *Epig.* 4.53.5; Crates *Ep.* 16.) Theissen 1991: 80 can produce only a single positive example, and that one is irrelevant to the present case.

who performs feats for fame or money. By hailing Jesus as "Lord" (as in, "Your Majesty" — Manson 1979: 200-201), "Son of David" (15:22; cf. Ps. Sol. 17:21), she had already acknowledged him as the rightful king over a nation that had conquered her ancestors (Josh 12:7-24; 2 Sam 8:1-15) — more than many of his own people had done (15:2; 21:15-16; 23:39). Like John's woman at the well (Jn 4:25-29; 6:69), this Canaanite woman publicly acknowledged Jesus' identity before the disciples who wished her to leave had done so (16:16). Now she refuses to dispute that Jesus' mission is to Israel first and that her status is secondary to that of Israel (Jeremias 1958: 30; Rhoads and Michie 1982: 131); nevertheless, she believes that Jesus has so much power that he will have more than enough left over from what Israel does not need or want. Jesus responds to such striking faith.[56] Jesus has enough bread for Israel, but the following narrative reinforces that plenty of scraps remain over for others (15:37).[57] Matthew reminds his community that all, both Jew and Gentile, can approach God only through faith in his Messiah (8:10; cf. Acts 15:8-11; Saldarini 1994: 74; cf. Gundry-Volf 1995).

Feeding Four Thousand in the Wilderness (15:29-39)

Cf. Mk 7:31–8:9. This narrative, like the feeding of the five thousand (14:15-21), teaches Matthew's community about Jesus' power and care for his people. He heals the multitudes (15:29-31), acts out of compassion for their need (15:32; cf. 9:36; 14:14; 20:34), and provides for them (15:33-39).

Many suggest that the two feedings are two versions of a single event (the second may bear signs of Markan composition — see Burkill 1972: 48-70); others contend that two distinct events occurred (Knackstedt 1964; cf. Travis 1977: 160; English 1969). Although Matthew doubles some incidents (9:27-31; 20:29-34), Mark seems more likely to conform two similar accounts to each other and to arrange a systematic structural pattern, suggesting that Mark at least *believed* two events had occurred (cf. 8:19-20; Moule 1965: 60). Many of the parallels between the two accounts are those necessary to depict the multiplying of food (Carson 1984b: 357-58). Possibly Jesus, the tradition, or Mark wanted to parallel an event on Jewish soil with a similar event in a Gentile region (F. F. Bruce

56. For parallels to the praise of "great faith," Davies and Allison 1991: 556 cite Jos. *Ant.* 15.87 and Mek. Beshallah 7 on Ex 14:31. Although the common image of dogs gathering crumbs may be coincidence, Philost. *V.A.* 1.19 (Boring 1995: 104) may be relevant in illustrating how one could turn a negative image to positive application. Ephrem the Syrian (*Commentary on Tatian's Diatessaron, ACCS,* 102) concluded that she received her answer because of persistence and being undeterred by shame.

57. "Master's table" here and "the table of the Lord" (1 Cor 10:21) are the same expression in Greek, and could represent a play on words. As a Greek (Mk 7:26) she could have considered such a wordplay herself, but she had no reason to associate Jesus with patron deities of cultic meals, so, if the parallel language is not coincidence, Matthew has perhaps simply adapted the language himself to make the pun. Puns were standard in Jewish argumentation (Keener 1992: 32, 54n. 101, citing, e.g., CD 8.10-11; Ps-Philo 2:1; Sifre Deut. 306.22.1; 318.4.7; 321.8.6; 345.2.2, 3.1).

1980a: 71; Hagner 1995: 450); more likely they sought to imitate the double feeding miracles of Elijah and Elisha (Blomberg 1992a: 245).

First, after some time alone with his disciples (15:21) Jesus returns to meeting the people's needs (15:29-31). That he sat at a mountain (15:29) may imply that he was teaching (5:1-2), but what is clear from Matthew's language (which may adapt Is 35:5-6; cf. Ryan 1978; Lohse 1955: 58) is that Jesus is meeting people's physical needs (15:30).

Second, Jesus recognizes his followers' need and exercises compassion toward them (15:32). The text does not directly suggest that people were complaining about the food situation. Perhaps Matthew implies that, like his Father, Jesus recognizes his people's need before they ask (6:8, 32).

Third, Jesus acts even though his disciples still fail to understand (15:33-34). In contrast to the multitudes who flock to Jesus for miracles, the disciples seem to miss their significance (cf. Weeden 1971: 28); perhaps they see him too often in his "ordinary" humanness to expect miracles from him *all* the time. Despite Jesus' earlier feeding miracle, they assume again that they must procure bread by purely natural means (15:33). They are still learning, and Jesus does not yet reprove their unbelief — although he will if it continues (16:8-11).

Fourth, Jesus organized his disciples for efficiency (15:35-36). What was not humanly possible, Jesus performed as a miracle; the distribution of the food *was* humanly possible, however, and Jesus organized it efficiently (cf. the principle of delegated responsibility in Ex 18:14-26). See more fully the comments on 14:18.

Fifth, Jesus again supplied more than enough (15:37-39). See the comments on 14:20-21. Matthew provides both a literal lesson taken from the story and its continual retelling in the church, and a figurative lesson based on the context. Figuratively in this context, the leftovers symbolize that plenty of "the children's bread" remains for other seekers (15:26-28, though 15:27 and 15:37 employ different terms for "scraps"). But on the literal level, Matthew instructs his audience about God's limitless power and design in providing for his children's needs. One might think that more food would remain after this feeding miracle than the previous one; this time Jesus started with more food and fewer people (although the kind of baskets used this time may be larger).[58] But such was not the case, reminding the reader that God's design rather than natural considerations determine the magnitude of the miracle.

58. Many commentators associate the baskets in 14:20 with the Jews, and the different term here (15:37) with the Gentiles; France 1985: 249 even thinks the crowd of 15:31 is Gentile, but this is highly improbable (apart from symbolic value noted above in 15:37; cf. also Davies and Allison 1991: 563-64). Had Jesus historically ministered to a crowd of Gentiles the Gospel tradition would have exploited this event, and had Matthew intended us to construe a Gentile audience he would have been far more explicit.

The Sign of Jonah (15:39–16:4)

Cf. 12:38-39; Mk 8:10-13; Lk 11:16, 29; 12:54-56; Jn 6:30. The next scene takes place near "Magadan" (15:39), perhaps the region of Magdala (27:56; cf. Gundry 1982: 322; others are uncertain, e.g., France 1985: 249-50; Davies and Allison 1991: 574) which (if the same Magdala is in view) often appears in later Jewish literature (b. Nid. 33a; Pesiq. Rab Kah. 11:16; Gen. Rab. 5:9; 13:15; 94:4 MSS; Num. Rab. 12:4; cf. the association with promiscuity in the late Lam. Rab. 2:2, §4). Magdala's common Greek name appears to have been Tarichaeae (Avi-Yonah 1974/76b: 96), known as a Galilean city with a fishing industry, elements of Greek culture, but also fierce Jewish patriotism (see Freyne 1988: 172-73; for excavations, see Reich 1989). The passage articulates principles that could prove valuable to Matthew's audience both in defending their devotion to Jesus and in deepening it.

First, asking for a sign after the Lord has already revealed himself is testing him (16:1; cf. Ex 17:7; Ps 78:18-20). Matthew may find here both grounds for challenging opponents of the Christian movement and warning to his own audience. In Mark, only the Pharisees test Jesus here (Mk 8:11), and Jesus later warned against the leaven of the Pharisees and of Herod, whose partisans had teamed up with the Pharisees (with whom they rarely dealt) to confront the urgent problem of Jesus (Mk 3:6; 12:13).[59] Matthew perhaps reapplies the language for his audience, who knew the oppression Christians had suffered from the old Sadducean aristocracy (e.g., Acts 4:1-3; 23:8-9). Pharisees and Sadducees were generally at odds, joining forces only under external duress; Matthew reports that Jesus' mission was one such case of duress (3:7; cf. van Tilborg 1972b).

This passage condemns not those who genuinely fear God yet ask for signs as an assurance of God's promise (Gen 15:6, 8; Judg 6:17, 36-39; 2 Kings 20:8; cf. Ps-Philo 35:7; Is 7:11-14), but those who seek grounds to disbelieve. The religious leaders (there "scribes and Pharisees," here "Pharisees and Sadducees") had challenged Jesus after other miracles (15:1-20); the Gospel's first reference to testing (4:1; cf. 6:13; 19:3; 22:35) may suggest that the devil is their theological source (cf. Robinson 1982: 93).[60] Like the devil and his other mouthpieces in the Gospel (4:3, 6; 12:38; 27:40, 42-44), they want Jesus to demonstrate his power to satisfy their testing, rather than for the sake of those who are in need.

Now they ignore the signs of a prophet already offered (15:21-39; cf. Hooker 1983: 109) and demand instead a sign from heaven (16:1). A "sign from heaven" could mean "from God" ("heaven" often functioned as a circum-

59. *Possibly* Jesus alludes to the "leaven" of Egypt at the Passover, presenting Jesus as a new Moses; but given the more common functions of leaven (see more fully comment on 13:33), this explanation is too specific to be probable.

60. Cf. the common accusation of "testing" God (e.g., Ex 17:2, 7; Num 14:22; Deut 6:16; Ps 78:18, 41, 56; 95:9; 106:14; Jdt 8:12; Test. Mos. 9:4).

locution for God's name — e.g., Lk 15:18; Rom 1:18; Dan 4:26; 1 Enoch 6:2; 13:8; 1QM 12.5; 3 Macc 4:21; m. 'Abot 1:3; t. B. Qam. 7:5; Sifra Behuq. pq. 6.267.2.1; Sifre Deut. 79.1.1; 96.2.2), but in this context it apparently means a sign in the heavens (e.g., Plummer 1910: 221), like those that many people believed presaged the fall of Jerusalem (Jos. *War* 6.288-91) and the end (cf. 24:29-31; 27:45, 51-53). Jewish teachers sometimes debated the interpretation of such signs, for instance, what eclipses at evening predicted versus what eclipses in the morning predicted (t. Sukk. 2:6; for some accurate meteorologic understanding in early Judaism, see Albert and Neumann 1989).[61] Presumably they here ask Jesus to predict a sign in the sky — which could request thunder and lightning (Virg. *Aen.* 8.523-26, especially *signum* in 8.523; 1 Sam 7:10), but, on the less than charitable reading one might assume from Matthew's audience, could reduce them to the level of astrologers or diviners, something forbidden in the Hebrew Bible (Deut 18:10; cf. Jub. 12:16-17). The religious leaders here contrast starkly with some pagan astrologers who came to worship King Jesus (2:1-12)! Jesus' challengers here want him to "show" them a sign (16:1), and he refuses; but later he "showed" his disciples his mission (16:21), suggesting again that those who persevered would always have an advantage over casual or hostile inquirers (13:11).[62]

Second, Jesus was giving them a clearer sign than a sign in heaven would have been (16:3-4). Jesus' questioners could predict many celestial phenomena with no supernatural inspiration at all; a red sky in the morning meant that Mediterranean winds from the west would be bringing rain.[63] But Jesus was not interested in predicting events in the sky or in using such events to predict the future; they were overlooking an explicit sign that was nearer at hand (a matter other ancients would also feel worthy of rebuke — cf. Diog. Laert. *Lives* 6.2.28). Yet the "signs of that time" should have been the only "sign" they needed. Indeed, the sinfulness of that generation was itself a sign, for many Jewish people understood that a sinful generation would immediately precede the coming of God's kingdom (CD 20.14-15; 2 Bar. 26:12; m. Soṭa 9:15; b. Sanh. 97a; Pesiq. Rab Kah. 5:9; Pesiq. R. 15:14/15; cf. Phil 2:15). The description of that generation resembles Moses' complaint against Israel (Deut 32:5), a generation that had

61. If one wishes to construe the Pharisaic request in its worst possible light, which Matthew may have wished his audience to do, magical texts promised signs from the sky for magicians, which signs would become their divine "messengers" or spirit-guides (*PGM* 1.74-76, 154; cf. 4.576). By contrast, some Greek rationalists sought nontheistic explanations for celestial phenomena (Epicurus in Diog. Laert. 10.99).

62. Luke-Acts cites signs as a central propagandistic technique of the early Christians (most pagans also accepted their propagandistic value; see, e.g., Ovid *Metam.* 1.220); John accepts "signs-faith" as ambiguously positive yet inadequate (e.g., 2:23-25; 6:26; 20:29); for Matthew and Mark they remain positive, yet in light of the messianic secret they are not coercive in their effects.

63. The weather signs depicted in the tradition could derive only from a Palestinian milieu (Malina and Rohrbaugh 1992: 111), suggesting authenticity; for an Italian perspective, see Virg. *Georg.* 1.438-60.

repeatedly tested God in the wilderness and rejected his prophet Moses (Ps 78:18-20).[64]

Third, Jesus' own ministry and resurrection constituted the decisive sign to that generation (16:4). With most scholars, the Q reference to the "sign of Jonah" here is probably authentic, Mark having omitted it to retain the messianic secret (Mk 8:11; Witherington 1990: 168). The resurrection was an end-time event (Dan 12:2); Jesus' resurrection was a clear indication that the time of the kingdom was at hand (12:39-40).[65]

Religious Cancer and Doubting Disciples (16:5-12)

Cf. Mk 8:14-21; Lk 12:1. If Jesus' opponents were active in their unbelief (16:1-4), his disciples were passive in their unbelief. Unlike the Pharisees, Jesus' disciples had stayed with him and witnessed the miracles of the loaves; nevertheless, they still fail to understand his power.

First, Jesus warned against testing God as his opponents had just done (16:6, 11-12). Jesus did not disagree with all Pharisaic teaching (23:2), but the context specifies which teaching (16:12) he means. The "Pharisees and Sadducees" had posed challenges intended to discredit Jesus (16:1-4); for Jesus to warn against the yeast of the Pharisees and Sadducees in this context must constitute a warning against the toxic cynicism of these groups. "Yeast" was an appropriate metaphor for something that spreads through the dough (negative, e.g., in Vermes 1993: 103n.31);[66] today we might employ a negative image like cancer. The disciples' passive unbelief (16:8) suggests that the threat of Pharisaic leaven is closer to them than they would have guessed.

Second, the disciples misunderstand his point because they are "of little faith" (16:5, 7-10). *They misunderstand because they are self-absorbed.* Perhaps they were headed for "the sparsely populated east side" of the lake, where bread would be in short supply (Hoehner 1972: 204). At any rate, the disciples had inadvertently neglected their responsibility to bring bread (16:5; see comment on 14:15), and they were so concerned about what their teacher would think about their lapse that they assumed he was addressing their own failure (16:7). Yet Jesus' point had been clear: given what had just transpired (16:1-4),

64. For the textual issue in 16:2-3, see Gundry 1982: 323; Metzger 1971: 41. I think it likely that scribes in Egypt omitted a reference to weather conditions that did not obtain in their own experience. Nevertheless, the textual question for 16:2-3 is difficult to resolve (hence the D rating in the UBS text); despite wide geographical distribution for inclusion (including in the west), some of the earliest manuscripts (Sinaiticus, Vaticanus) and many (though not all) other Egyptian manuscripts omit the lines about the weather, which have also been explained as an interpolation based on Lk 12:54-56. Cf. Metzger 1971: 41.

65. The tradition of refusal to grant a sign is also preserved in Islam (Quran 7.203, in Wansbrough 1977: 7).

66. Blomberg 1992a: 249 suggests an Aramaic wordplay between "teaching" *('amir'a)* and "yeast" *(hamir'a)*. See further comment on 13:33.

how could they assume that the "leaven of the Pharisees and Sadducees" referred to forgetting to take bread? Did they expect Jesus to be instructing them to bake bread from scratch when they had crossed the lake, but to make sure not to borrow any yeast from the spiritually unclean religious elite? The disciples here appear inordinately dense.

But Jesus explains why they cannot understand him. *Spiritual understanding cannot come apart from faith (16:8).* Had they simply forgotten to take bread — a technical rather than a moral failure — Jesus could have provided bread (16:9-10). That Jesus could miraculously supply bread had already eluded them twice (14:15-17; 15:33; cf. 6:11, 25-34; Deut 8:3-5 and Mt 4:4); by this point his disciples should have more faith, so he corrects them. Unconcerned that they had forgotten bread, he was very concerned that they were learning faith so slowly (cf. 15:10, 16). He had serious reason for concern: these were his disciples, by definition apprentices expected to take over his earthly ministry after his departure. Yet the other instances of his "little-faith" rebuke demonstrate that it represents a reproof like that of a concerned parent, not that of a harsh drill-sergeant (cf. 6:30; 8:26; 14:31; 17:20). Some teaching traditions recognized that a few disciples who seemed slow could eventually improve (Plut. *Lectures* 18, *Mor.* 47E), but the ultimate progress of slow disciples was the exception rather than the rule.[67]

Recognition of Jesus' Messiahship as the Foundation (16:13-20)

Cf. Mk 8:27-30; Lk 9:18-21; Jn 1:42; 6:67-71. The religious elite repudiated Jesus (16:1-4); the disciples lacked sufficient faith in him to understand his most basic warnings (16:5-12). But now, informed by Jesus' works (14:33) and perhaps by a new understanding of Jesus' role vis-à-vis that of their people's religious establishment (16:12), the disciples are on the verge of a new level of revelation (16:13-20). Even at this point, however, they do not fully understand his mission (16:21-28). As in Mark, this revelation is pivotal in the development of Matthew's narrative (cf. the growing awareness of disciples in other accounts, e.g., Philost. *V.A.* 2.11-22; Plato in Robbins 1992: 151-52).

Many Protestant interpreters have doubted the authenticity of this section (especially the specifically Matthean blessing of Peter), but more recent interpreters have shown less skepticism. Davies and Allison 1991: 609-15 argue for authenticity on the following grounds: (1) evidence in Paul (especially Gal 1:11-21); (2) Semitisms; (3) indications of Palestinian provenance by comparison with the DSS; (4) the criterion of consistency; (5) the criterion of dissimilarity (gates of Hades, keys of the kingdom, and binding and

67. Quesnell 1969: 108, 111 thinks that Jesus' rebuke in Mark is Markan redaction. But even if Mark has developed earlier tradition, it is unlikely that the tradition would have reported any of the account without including Jesus' response.

loosing are not distinctively Christian;[68] the promise to Peter is not pre-Christian Jewish); (6) geographical setting; and (7) the weakness of the objections to the contrary.

First, the climactic revelation of the gospel occurs in pagan territory (16:13). Jesus has taken his disciples northward from predominantly Jewish territory, presumably to escape the crowds and spend time privately with his disciples. They had journeyed some twenty-five miles (and 1,700 feet uphill) from the Lake of Galilee to the source of the Jordan near the ancient city of Dan, the northern boundary of ancient Israel.[69] The recently renamed Caesarea Philippi was as pagan a territory as one could find: famous for its grotto where people worshiped the Greek god Pan, its earlier name Paneas persisted even in its modern Arabic name Baneas (cf. Pliny *N.H.* 5.15.71; Jos. *War* 1.404; b. B. Bat. 74b; Josephus 1982: 458) and public pagan rites reportedly continued there until a later Christian miraculously demonstrated that Jesus was more powerful (Euseb. *H.E.* 7.17).[70] Following Mark, Matthew emphasizes that God moves where he wills, fitting the theme of Jesus' universal mission in his Gospel (e.g., 1:3, 5-6; 2:1-12; 3:9; 4:15).

Second, outsiders' recognition of Jesus as a prophet is inadequate (16:14); those who truly follow Jesus closely know him as the Christ, God's Son (16:15-16).[71] Herod Antipas thought that Jesus was John (14:2); many Jewish people anticipated the return of Elijah and sometimes other prophets like Baruch (Cullmann 1959: 17-18; Lohse 1955: 47; cf. Sharma 1973). Given Jesus' public activities, it is not surprising that many would have viewed him as a prophet (21:11, 46; Jn 9:17), but while this perspective was correct (cf., e.g., 11:21-24; 24:2-31), it was incomplete. Viewing Jesus in such terms thus managed to fit him into categories of thought that already existed (cf. comment on 4:3-9), rather than letting the Messiah himself redefine their categories by his identity. Peter, the most outspoken of the disciples elsewhere in the tradition (26:35), voices the ultimate confession, though he still has not defined it as Jesus will. "Christ" designates Jesus as the rightful king of Israel (see the Introduction). Matthew does not contradict his source here; although Mark subordinated

68. Duling 1987 doubts the authenticity of "binding and loosing" because it violates the criterion of dissimilarity, though acknowledging that it fits that of a Jewish environment; I believe that the latter criterion ranks higher and here cancels the former out.

69. Because Capernaum was near the Jordan's mouth jutting into the Lake of Galilee, the disciples might not view their location as being so distant from home geographically as culturally.

70. On pagan worship there, see most fully Tzaferis 1992; Tzaferis and Avner 1990. Sacred especially to pastoralists (e.g., Longus 2.26-31; 4.39), Pan was worshiped at other caves (e.g., Paus. 1.32.7) or wooded areas (e.g., Paus. 8.38.5), but caves (Paus. 10.32.6) and wooded areas (Paus. 5.10.1) could also be sacred to other deities; cf. also the second- and third-century-A.D. pagan temple in Upper Galilee in Magness 1990.

71. Asking about his identity might have involved the Mediterranean emphasis on others' view of oneself rather than self-identity (Pilch 1992: 128; Malina and Rohrbaugh 1992: 113), but probably it simply represents Jesus' pedagogic technique, in which questions played a part (as in the rabbis).

Jesus' Messiahship to his suffering, he accepted both (Kingsbury 1983: 91-102, 147; pace Petersen 1978: 63).[72]

Third, this revelation of Jesus' identity was foundational for God's purposes in history (16:17-18). Many scholars doubt the authenticity of this passage (16:17-19), some perhaps for anti-Catholic polemic but others because Matthew alone reports these lines.[73] If one follows Mark's sequence, this material in Matthew may seem intrusive, and one may argue that Matthew himself has placed the earlier tradition of Peter's commendation (the existence of which is probably implied by Peter's central role in the church, e.g., 1 Cor 1:12; 9:5; 15:5; Gal 2:7) in this particular narrative (Cullmann 1968:105). But no other suitable place for commending a Petrine revelation exists in the tradition; certainly after the resurrection commendations on such a revelation would be beside the point.[74] More likely, Luke may simply have followed Mark in omitting it, and Mark's punchy narrative style and emphatic theme of discipleship failure were better served by omitting it (cf. Ellis 1974: 128-29; Weeden 1971: 43; Weber 1961; idem 1962).[75] Matthean wording (Gundry 1982: 330-31) may be more common where Matthew follows oral tradition rather than Mark.[76]

72. Aune 1983: 273 regards Peter's confession as a "recognition oracle," but the prior revelation (16:17; 11:25) need not make the saying oracular per se. Matthew emphasizes the proper sense of "Christ" (Mk 8:29) by adding "God's Son" (cf. Jn 1:49), a title his Gospel has already frequently applied to Jesus (Smalley 1977: 186; Filson 1960: 185; Brown et al. 1973: 86), implied also by "my Father in heaven" (16:17). Luke's adaptation of Mark's "Christ" to "of God" may suggest that Matthew and Luke share a common tradition behind Mark (many of the disciples' reports probably independently preserved this particular event, if it is as decisive as Mark implies), unless both felt the need to expand Mark's christological statement here (cf. Lk 2:26; 23:35; Jn 6:69). Mark may have condensed the tradition or Matthew expanded it; both were rhetorically acceptable options. Matthew could combine Mk 8:29 with Mk 14:61 (cf. also Mt 3:17; 26:53-64), deriving "living God" from elsewhere in the tradition (22:32; 26:63). "Living God" was a frequent Jewish title for God (Jub. 21:4; Marmorstein 1968b: 72). Augustine contrasted Peter's confession "in love" with the demons' confession in fear in 8:29 (*Sermons on New Testament Lessons* 40:8; *On the Gospel of St. John* 6.21; *ACCS*, 22).

73. The polemical basis in arguing for or against authenticity, strictly irrelevant to exegesis or honest historical endeavor, is in any case a moot point. Luz, who is probably wrong to reject the passage's authenticity, is probably correct that the text nowhere implies that Peter would be institutionally succeeded by anyone (1991).

74. Most critical scholars denied the authenticity of this Matthean material (in contrast to its Markan framework — cf. Montefiore 1968: 1:182) until studies confirmed its early Palestinian character; the most common theory then became that it represented a postresurrection saying (Cullmann 1953: 166-67, 180; Meier 1980: 179). Cullmann located it in the passion story (1953: 184); see Gundry's reasoned critique (1964). The debate has somewhat receded, along with the polemics that supported it; most scholars, both Roman Catholic and Protestant, concur that Peter died in Rome but doubt that Mt 16:18 intended the authority later claimed by the papacy (Pelikan 1980: 60). Hagner 1995: 465-66 also supplies arguments for authenticity; on Jesus' intention for the church, cf. also Bowman 1943: 191-225.

75. Feuillet 1991 suggests that Mark omitted it because he depended on Peter, who was too humble to emphasize it.

76. Some scholars cite against the passage's reliability Peter's lack of corresponding prominence in the early church (Beare 1981: 353), an argument that could be turned on its head (why

Jewish teachers often pronounced blessings on those who gave correct responses, as Jesus does here (Young 1995: 199). Peter did not receive his revelation from "flesh and blood" (cf. Gal 1:16, which may reflect this tradition — Wenham 1984a: 26; pace Gundry 1982: 336), a common expression for "mortals" or "humans" (e.g., 1 Cor 15:50; Eph 6:12; Heb 2:14; 1 Enoch 15:4; Test. Abr. 13B; Mek. Pisha 1.120; ARN 32A). Peter's understanding of Jesus' identity came by divine revelation (16:17; 11:25; cf. Gal 1:12; Eph 1:17; 3:5), undoubtedly including God's revelation through Jesus' miraculous acts (14:33; cf. 15:22). Although Peter's father's name *was* the similar "John" (Jn 1:42; 21:15; cf. "Jonah" in *CIJ* 1:483, §671; 2:124, §900), Jesus (at least in Matthew's context) might mean the address "son of Jonah" symbolically as well: Jonah was a preacher to his generation (12:41), and this context specified that Jonah's sign would come to Jesus' generation as well (16:4; cf. Gundry 1982: 332-33).[77]

"You are Peter," Jesus says (16:18), paralleling Peter's "You are the Christ" (16:16). He then plays on Simon's nickname, "Peter," which is roughly the English "Rocky": Peter is "rocky," and on this rock Jesus would build his church (16:18). Scholars have debated precisely what Jesus means by the "rock"; Protestants, following Augustine and Luther, have sometimes contended that the rock in this passage is only Jesus himself (Cullmann 1953: 162n.13).[78] Thus they have sometimes argued that Peter's name in Greek *(petros)* differs from the Greek term for rock used here (*petra;* e.g., Gundry 1982: 334; cf. Lampe 1979; Derrett 1988).[79] But by Jesus' day the terms were usually interchangeable, and the original Aramaic form of Peter's nickname

---

would the early church have created a saying that they knew was untrue in their time?). Other scholars more reasonably find evidence for a measure of Peter's prominence in the early church (1 Cor 1:12; 9:5; Gal 1:18; 2:9; 1 Pet 1:1) and question how he would have obtained this unless he were close to Jesus and somehow appointed to lead the other members of the Twelve (Sanders 1985: 105; see especially Wenham 1984a: 24). Some deny the likelihood of this logion because it differs from other sayings of Jesus (Goppelt 1981/82: 1:213), whereas others find its elements in the earliest strata of Jesus tradition (Michaels 1981: 301-2). Commissionings and beatitudes appear elsewhere in Jesus' words (cf., e.g., 10:5-16; 13:16-17) and certainly elsewhere in early Judaism; e.g., an angel blesses Aseneth for receiving revelation (Jos. and Asen. 16:14/7), and a rabbi would praise his disciples (m. 'Abot 2:8).

The passage has three strophes of three lines apiece (Meier 1980: 179; Gundry 1982: 331). Some attribute the saying's structure to Matthew's love of Semitic parallelism (Gundry 1982: 331); others point to the Semitic language as indicating an early tradition (Ellis 1974: 129-30; Harrington 1982: 68; van Cangh and van Esbroek 1980; Young 1995: 203n.2; cf. Jesus' use of beatitudes, etc., in pre-Matthean tradition). Some who doubt the saying's authenticity nevertheless accept it as pre-Matthean (Carroll 1963; Bornkamm 1995: 111).

77. The imaginative suggestion that "bar-Jona" represents an Akkadian (!) loanword for terrorist identifying Peter as a Zealot or outlaw (cf. Cullmann 1956b: 16; Theissen 1978: 11) has little to commend it (see Brown et al. 1973: 88n.203); the period is too early.

78. Augustine (cf. also Origen and Tertullian) and most of the medieval church thought the rock was Christ, not Peter; the passage was rarely used to debate papal authority before the Reformation (Luz 1994: 60).

79. Caragounis 1990 has probably provided the best argument differentiating Peter and the rock, making a grammatically defensible position.

that Jesus probably used *(kephas)* means simply "rock."[80] Further, Jesus does not say, "You are Peter, *but* on this rock I will build my church"; the weak adversative *de* sometimes means "and," but the copulative *kai* almost always means "and" (exceptions like Tob 4:17 are very rare). Jesus' teaching is the *ultimate* foundation for disciples (7:24-27; cf. 1 Cor 3:11), but here Peter functions as the foundation rock as the apostles and prophets do in Ephesians 2:20-21 (cf. Jeremias 1972: 227). Jesus does not simply assign this role arbitrarily to Peter, however; Peter is the "rock" *because* he is the one who confessed Jesus as the Christ in this context (16:15-16; Cullmann 1953: 162; Ladd 1974b: 110; C. Brown 1978: 386). The Gospel has developed Peter's character to this point, making him a spokesperson for the disciples, hence the prototypical church leader (Overman 1996: 249). Others who share his proclamation also share his authority in building the church (18:18 with 16:19).[81]

Fourth, the community built on such a foundation would prevail against all opposition (16:18). Some scholars doubt that Jesus could have spoken of a "church," of followers after his departure (Boring 1982: 213-14). But this presupposes that Jesus did not expect a period between his initial mission and the end of the age, a view that many of his extant sayings do not support (cf., e.g., 13:3-51; 24:4-51; Witherington 1992). Ancient teachers regularly established communities of followers to perpetuate their teachings (cf., e.g., Culpepper 1975: 123); Albright and Mann (1971: 195; cf. Hunter 1944: 53) go so far as to suspect that confessional polemics are often at work in excluding the passage, noting that "a Messiah without a Messianic Community" would have been "unthinkable" to contemporary Judaism. Other Jewish groups planned communities (cf. Flusser 1988: 35), and culturally relevant evidence (like Jesus' choice

80. Among Protestant scholars, e.g., Cullmann 1953: 18-19; idem 1968: 98, 106; Ladd 1974b: 110; Carson 1984b: 368; France 1985: 254; Blomberg 1992a: 252. Chrysostom *Homilies on St. John,* Homily 19, compared Jesus renaming disciples with God renaming the patriarchs after their trials.

81. That Jesus gave Simon his nickname "Peter," "rock," is likely (due to rabbis' authority, biblical naming traditions, and the independent tradition of Jn 1:42); the name is derived from the term ("rock"), not being a common name (Meier 1980: 182; Gnilka 1997: 86-87; for a possible occurrence in 4Q130.8-9, see Charlesworth 1993), and need not be ironic (pace Stock 1987). The persistence of the Aramaic nickname elsewhere in the NT suggests that Jesus may have been its author (cf. Sanders 1985: 146-47). Although the name "Petros" is attested in some Aramaic Jewish texts (Gen. Rab. 92:2; Ex. Rab. 52:3), Paul's and John's preservation of "Kephas" indicates that Jesus simply gave Peter the Aramaic title (he was speaking Aramaic — hence *bar*-Jona) "Kephas," which was translated into Greek as "Petros" (Cullmann 1953: 19n.14). Although biblical tradition usually called God Israel's "rock," other uses occur, and many scholars point to Abraham's role in Is 51:1-2, as well as to some very late (very possibly *too* late; cf. also Witherington 1992: 89) rabbinic expositions on it (Ford 1965; Cullmann 1968: 106; Ellis 1974: 129-30; F. F. Bruce 1978: 60; Siegal 1978: 108; cf. Chevallier 1982; Manns 1983; the relevance of the rabbinic parallel here is questionable — cf. Arnéra 1984; cf. the perhaps unrelated traditions in Gen. Rab. 44:21; Pesiq. R. 15:2; more relevant for the period, see Ps-Philo 23:4-5); others object that the differences are too great (Hagner 1995: 470). Witherington 1992: 89 suggests the foundation of a new temple, citing the language of m. Yoma 5:2 (cf. Jn 7:37-39). The Qumran sect was also founded on a "rock," a refuge against death (1QH 6.23-28; Driver 1965: 519; Witherington 1992: 89; cf. 1QS 8.7; Hill 1972: 261).

of *twelve* disciples) supports the notion that Jesus did as well.[82] Vermes 1993: 214-15 doubts that Jesus, who expected the kingdom in the near future, could have founded a community; yet Qumran's Teacher of Righteousness, who expected the end of the age in the near future, did just that.

Not only did various leaders plan communities to carry on their work; a Jewish renewal movement might have employed the same language Jesus did. The Essenes described themselves as the *qahal* (Albright and Mann 1971: 121; Brown et al. 1973: 92; Harrington 1982: 29), the Hebrew word for God's congregation in the exodus narrative, which the Greek versions translate as *ekklēsia,* or "church."[83] Jesus likewise depicts his community as the true, faithful remnant of Israel in continuity with the Old Testament covenant community;[84] what marked it as new was Jesus' specific designation, "*my* community" (Ladd 1974b: 110; France 1985: 255). The term would make the most sense in a Jewish setting, where those familiar with the Greek version of the Old Testament would recognize *ekklēsia* and *synagōgē* as translations of the Hebrew term for the community of Israel. Other Greek readers may have scratched their heads, since *ekklēsia* could include any gathering (cf. Deissmann 1978: 112-13), even an army (Dion. Hal. 6.94.1). Most often in regular Greek usage it meant the "citizen assembly" of a local community (e.g., Acts 19:32, 39), including those in Republican Rome (Dion. Hal. 6.87.1; 7.17.2; 11.50.1) and Jerusalem (Jos. *War* 4.162).

Biblical tradition had often spoken of "building up" the community of God (e.g., Ruth 4:11; Ps 51:18; 69:35; 147:2; Jer 1:10; 24:6; 31:4, 28; Ladd 1974b: 109; cf. Prov 9:1); Qumran texts indicate that the usage remained familiar among Jesus' contemporaries (4QpPs 37.3, 16; Jeremias 1971: 168), although there *God* was the builder of his community (Gundry 1982: 336). In the context of the larger Jesus tradition, Jesus may also see himself replacing the "builders" who rejected him (Ps 118:22; Mt 21:42). The "gates of Hades" is a familiar Semitic expression for the threshold of the realm of death (cf. 11:23; Rev 1:18).[85] Pagans

82. See Sanders 1985: 20-22, 104; Borg 1984: 70; Hunter 1966: 38; Witherington 1992: 84-92.

83. Frequently noted; see, e.g., Bultmann 1951: 1:38; Foakes Jackson and Lake 1979a: 327-28; Lake and Cadbury 1979: 54; Richardson 1958: 285; Meeks 1983: 79; Davies and Allison 1991: 629; cf. 1 Macc 2:56.

84. Ridderbos 1975: 328; F. F. Bruce 1963: 84; Klaasen 1981: 112-16; pace Walvoord 1972: 21.

85. The expression appears in the Hebrew Bible (e.g., Ps 9:13; 107:18; Job 38:17; Is 38:10; Ladd 1974b: 116) and in subsequent Jewish literature (Wis 16:13; 3 Macc 5:51; Ps. Sol. 16:2; 1QH 6.24; Sib. Or. 2.228; Ladd 1974b: 116; Schweizer 1975: 342; Betz 1957). Texts likewise can describe Paradise in terms of the gates of the blessed (Sib. Or. 3.770; the "gates of heaven" had more cosmological significance — cf., e.g., 1 Enoch 9:10; 3 Enoch 10.1-2; 3 Bar. 6:13; cf. Hom. *Il.* 5.749). The gates of the realm of the dead appear widely in ancient Near Eastern literature, but the image here may especially evoke Is 28:15-19, where the cornerstone in Zion withstands the assault of water from those in covenant with Sheol (Davies and Allison 1991: 630). The "keys of Hades/the realm of the dead" refer to authorization to admit the dead to their place (Rev 1:18; *PGM* 4.341-42 in Horsley 1981: 33-34). For a history of interpretation, see Lewis 1995; the modern homiletic tradition associating this text with Jesus snatching OT saints from Satan derives from early Christian apocryphal tradition ("Christ's Descent into Hell," trans. F. Scheidweiler, 1:470-76 in Hennecke 1963).

also employed the image of the "gates of Hades" for the realm of death (Hom. *Od.* 14.156; Hesiod *Theog.* 773; Eurip. *Hippol.* 56-57, 1447; *Hecuba* 1; Diog. Laert. 10.126; Char. *Chaer.* 4.1.3; Orphic Hymn 18.15); they often spoke of the house (e.g., Hom. *Il.* 15.251; 20.336; 21.48; 22.52, 213, 425, 482; 23.19, 71, 74, 103, 179; 24.246; *Od.* 14.208; 20.208) or realm (e.g., Soph. *Ajax* 635; Eurip. *Alcestis* 25, 73, 436-37, 457, 626; *Electra* 142-43; *Madness of Heracles* 610, 619; *Children of Heracles* 218, 912-13, 949; *Hippol.* 895; *Androm.* 414; Ap. Rhod. 2.609; 3.810) of Hades as the realm of the dead, as in Jewish texts (Test. Abr. 19A). The words used here suggest that death itself assaults Christ's church, but death itself cannot crush God's people (Ladd 1974b: 116; Jeremias 1968: 927; cf. Heb 2:14; Test. Reub. 4:11).[86] The church will endure until Christ's return, and no opposition, even the widespread martyrdom of Christians or the oppression of the final antichrist (cf. Jeremias 1968: 927), can prevent the ultimate triumph of God's purposes in history. The promise precedes Christ's summons to martyrdom (16:24-25).

Fifth, Jesus gives Peter — and those who share his proclamation of Jesus' identity — authority in the kingdom (16:19; cf. 18:18). The realm of "heaven" here contrasts strikingly with the powers of "Sheol," the realm of the dead thought to lie beneath the earth, in the preceding verse (16:18; cf. Heb 2:14; Rev 1:18). "Keys" opened locked doors or gates,[87] but the carrying of such keys especially symbolized the bearer's authority (cf., e.g., Livy 24.22.14; 24.23.1; 24.37.8). One who bore keys to a royal palace was the majordomo, as in Isaiah 22:22; Revelation 3:7;[88] one may compare supervisors who held the keys to the temple courts among Jesus' contemporaries (ARN 7, §21B; Pesiq. R. 26:6; Jeremias 1969: 165-66).[89] But some later Jewish teachers also applied the image of "keys" to their teaching authority (Davies and Allison 1991: 635 cite Lk 11:52; Sifre Deut. 32:25; b. Shab. 31ab).

Whether Peter thus acts as "prime minister" for the kingdom (cf. Brown et al. 1973: 96-97) or perhaps as a "chief rabbi" making halakic rulings based on Jesus' teachings (Meier in Brown and Meier 1983: 67; Bornkamm 1995: 111), he clearly acts on sufficient delegated authority. Whereas Israel's religious elite was shutting people out of the kingdom (23:13; cf. Lk 11:52; Cullmann 1953: 204; Richardson 1958: 317; Ladd 1974b: 117-18; Schweizer 1975: 343), those who confessed Jesus' identity along with Peter were authorized to usher people into

86. Greek tradition extolled those who brought up an individual from Hades (e.g., Diod. Sic. 4.25.4; 4.26.1); Greeks thus would have heard remarkable claims to power in this passage and Rev 1:18.

87. Marcus 1988 thus contrasts the gates of Hades (which he thinks, probably wrongly, let out demonic forces; Jewish literature associates them primarily with the realm of the dead) and implied gates of heaven (e.g., Lev. Rab. 31:10) here.

88. Commentators generally see in Rev 3:7 an allusion to Is 22 (Montefiore 1968: 2:235; Ellis 1974: 130-31; Meier 1979: 113; idem 1980: 182-83; Gundry 1982: 333; France 1985: 256).

89. Thus, e.g., in Jewish lore prominent angels carried certain keys (e.g., 3 Bar. 1:2), and God reserved for himself certain keys to which angels had no access, including the resurrection (e.g., b. Ta'an. 2a; Pesiq. R. 42:7); presumably God alone would hold the keys to the kingdom.

God's kingdom. Peter may thus function as the representative eschatological missionary, a "fisher of men" par excellence (Davies and Allison 1991: 634). Non-Matthean tradition retains this special role for Peter; thus, for example, Acts indicates that he opened an official door to the Gentiles (Acts 10:44; F. F. Bruce 1951: 227-28; cf. Gal 2:7).

In Jewish texts "binding and loosing" *('asar* and *hittir* or *shera)* could refer to authority to interpret the law, hence to evaluate individuals' fidelity to the law (see comment on 18:18).[90] Some therefore interpret this authority as administrative authority over the church (cf. Bultmann 1968: 138-39n.1).[91] In this context, however, the nuance may be somewhat different than in 18:18: Peter and those who share his role (cf. 18:18) evaluate not those who are in the community, but those who would enter it (a role assigned to the *mebaqqer* of the Qumran community — cf. 1QS 5.20-21; 6:13-14).[92] In both functions — evaluating entrants and those already within the church — God's people must evaluate on the authority of the heavenly court; the verb tenses allow the interpretation that they merely ratify the heavenly decree (see comment on 18:18; cf. Mantey 1973; idem 1981; Keener 1987; see more fully comment on 18:18). Jesus' agents were already exercising this authority in their earlier mission (10:14-15, 40; Jeremias 1972: 217n.42; Ladd 1974b: 118). Peter must thus accept into the church only those who share Peter's confession of Jesus' true identity (cf. Jn 20:22-23).[93]

Finally, Jesus admonished the disciples not to reveal his identity (16:20). The context suggests why: until after the resurrection (17:9) the disciples were unprepared to understand the cross; and apart from the cross, they

90. After surveying views (635-39), Davies and Allison 1991: 638-39 point out that "binding and loosing" apply directly to excommunication only in b. Mo'ed Qaṭ. 16a, and conclude in favor of *teaching* (halakic) authority in this text, seeing Peter as "the authoritative teacher without peer." France 1985: 256 and Lachs 1987: 257 also find legislative authority here. Cf. also comment on Mt 20:23 (e.g., Emerton 1962).

91. A variety of other interpretations exist. Derrett sees the ability to evaluate actions as sinful or not (as in 18:18; 1983a). Basser (1985a) applies the language to releasing death's bonds in the context (those in the church were freed from it). Falk (1974) applies it to dissolving vows, for which the prevailing school of Pharisees exercised less authority than this text suggests. Hiers (1985) suggests that the tradition behind 16:19 originally referred to Jesus' authorization for exorcisms, which Matthew reapplied more generally. Although Smith 1978: 134 finds a parallel to "keys of the kingdom" in *PGM* 3.541-42 (possibly derived from Christian usage), he recognizes (1978: 127) that "binding and loosing" reflect the Jewish legal sense. Disciplinary language for demons is not out of the question; people might also tell demons to get in place of, i.e., "behind," them (incant. text 5:7; cf. Mt 16:23) or put them under the "ban" (e.g., text 14.1-2). But the immediate context of the church's triumph against death does not support this interpretation.

92. Cf. Blomberg 1992a: 254, similar to Korting 1989, whom he follows; rejecting later rabbinic usage, he sees in "binding and loosing" opening and closing (based on the "keys to the kingdom"), hence making the kingdom "available or unavailable to people through their . . . ministry" (see also Wilkins 1995: 196; Hagner 1995: 473).

93. Some scholars think Jn 20:23 reflects the same logion as here (McNamara 1972: 129-30; Claudel 1995; Emerton 1962, albeit admitting that they *might* reflect separate sources, 326), but the sayings are different enough to suggest that they may reflect the same Jesus speaking on different occasions.

could not understand the real nature of Jesus' messianic mission (16:21-28), as Markan scholars often note (e.g., Lambrecht 1980).

The Cost of the Kingdom (16:21-27)

Cf. Mk 8:31-38; Lk 9:22-26; Jn 12:25; perhaps Jn 21:20-23. Many of the points this section emphasizes directly follow those in Mark, with whom Matthew agrees concerning the centrality of the cross. Jesus' opponents wanted him to "show" a sign (16:1); here Jesus instead "shows" his disciples how he will suffer (16:21).

First, the cross is central to Jesus' mission (16:21); the gospel message is incomplete without it. Recognizing Jesus as the Messiah was an important first step (16:13-20), but not very helpful when the disciples' concept of Jesus' Messiahship differed so greatly from his own. Jesus' Messiahship meant that he would suffer and die (16:21); those who wish to follow him must be ready to pay the same price (16:24). The cross was the most scandalous form of criminal execution in Jesus' day (see Hengel 1977: 8-9); texts indicate that even the term sounded terrible to ancient readers (Hengel 1977: 10), and we might not blame the disciples if they hoped that he was speaking metaphorically. Yet Jesus spoke literally for himself — and expected his followers to be prepared to face death for his name literally as well.[94]

Some scholars doubt that Jesus could have predicted his own death (e.g., Wrede 1971: 82-92), but even if one discounts the possibility that God could grant insight to one of his agents concerning his mission (which is merely a philosophical a priori; see Brown 1994: 1468), their doubts are untenable for several reasons. Before providing arguments why their skepticism is ultimately unwarranted, however, we should note that the Gospel writers naturally did have literary and theological reasons to include such predictions in their Gospels: many people believed that prophets and wise men could sense their impending death (see Aune 1983: 178; Boring 1995: 105, 155); further, ancient narratives regularly extol heroes who could face suffering or danger bravely (e.g., Livy 5.46.2-3; Plut. *Sayings of Spartans,* Anonymous 35, *Mor.* 234AB; Dion. Hal. 7.68.2-3; Jos. *Ant.* 3.208; 4.322; 6.126-27).[95] From a literary perspective, one might object to a *deus ex machina* or other denouement not anticipated in the plot itself (Arist. *Poetics* 15.10, 1454ab). Though the opposition Jesus provokes provides such anticipation with or without any explicit passion predictions, they do fit the common classical pattern of explicitly announcing

94. That Matthew would in this context call Jesus "Christ," despite his usual reticence to apply the title in earlier narratives (Metzger 1971: 42-43), is not improbable (Mark merely has a subject implicit in a verb); but while some of our earliest manuscripts support the reading "Jesus Christ" in 16:21, the weight of geographical distribution may support the simple reading "Jesus."

95. Jewish people were known to be particularly committed to martyrdom rather than compromise of their ancestral faith (Jos. *Apion* 1.212; 1.191; 2.218-19, 233-35).

the doom of some characters, which helps build suspense (e.g., Hom. *Od.* 2.163-66).

But good historical reasons also exist for supposing that Jesus foresaw his imminent martyrdom, and probably even viewed it as part of his mission (Brown 1994: 1468-91; Witherington 1990: 250). First, the saying reflects an early Aramaic construction and three characteristics of Jesus' distinctive style (Jeremias 1971: 282; Hill 1979: 61). Second, Jesus taught the Jewish view that sufferings precede the kingdom (cf. 24:8), which renders more understandable his own imminent expectation of suffering. Third, he also accepted the Jewish view, confirmed in John's death, that prophets are martyred (see comment on 23:29-32; cf. Hill 1979: 57; Aune 1983: 157, 159, 173). Fourth, the Gospel tradition reports numerous conflicts Jesus had experienced up to this point, the implications of which should have become clearer as he approached the arena of the political power brokers in Jerusalem.[96] Fifth, some of Jesus' other sayings, such as that about the disciples sharing his cup (20:22-23) and his words at the last supper (26:26-29), point in the same direction (Jeremias 1971: 277-86; Dodd 1961: 57; Stauffer 1960: 171-73).

But finally and most importantly, Jesus could not but have foreknown his death: Jesus ultimately *provoked* his death, showing his control over its timing, by his apparent assault on an institution by which the aristocracy symbolized their power. No one could directly challenge Jerusalem's municipal aristocracy that represented Rome's interests without anticipating severe reprisals, for any such challenge could not but appear as a threat to the state's political security (see comment on 21:12-17). That Jesus' execution as an accused evildoer condemned by the highest court of the land would take place at the hand of the Jewish religious leaders (also Mk 8:31) is one of the striking ironies of the Gospel story that must have made it offensive to Jewish people loyal to the religious establishment (cf. 2:4; 26:57) — hardly the sort of story Jewish Christian apologists would have invented.[97] Yet it is likely that Jesus foresaw it; if he expected a prophet's death in Jerusalem, political conditions being what they were he had to expect the chief priests' Sanhedrin and Romans to play a role ("elders" — e.g., 26:57; 28:12; "high priests" — e.g., 2:4; 26:57; "scribes" — e.g., 2:4; 26:57).

It makes sense that if, like many earlier prophets, Jesus expected to face rejection and death for an offensive message, he might also expect God's vindication in swiftly establishing the kingdom (Brown 1994: 514), hence raising the dead. That Jesus may have expected his own resurrection ahead of that of others

96. Although overstating the case, Adinolfi 1979 is correct that the growing conflicts with his contemporaries could have indicated to Jesus his impending martyrdom (Hill 1979: 61). Adinolfi's appeal to Isaiah's servant tradition, like Schaberg's suggestion concerning Daniel's Son of Man tradition (1985), is less secure.

97. The expression "suffer many things" (16:21; Mk 8:31) summarizes Jesus' preexecution sufferings; the phrase appears occasionally in other texts (cf. Meyer 1964). Despite some tensions, later Christians are also unlikely to have invented such a harsh rebuke of Peter (cf. Schweizer 1970: 165 and Anderson 1976: 213, both overstating the case; pace Weeden 1971).

would be distinctive — I know of no direct precedents for the view — but it is not unreasonable if, as I argued above (on 16:18-19), Jesus expected a community to carry on after him in the intermediate eschatological era. That Jesus *rarely* spoke about his impending passion, especially in public, fits the Gospel picture of his focusing on God's reign rather than on himself in public teaching (Hengel 1981a: 34). That the disciples misunderstood such clear teaching (e.g., 16:22) may imply the strength of the messianic category in light of which they interpreted Jesus' mission; it also suggests that the passion prediction, clear as it was, could function the way oracles in the ancient Mediterranean often functioned, appearing obscure until fulfillment (e.g., Soph. *Oed. Rex* 439; *Women Tr.* 1169-73; Dio Cassius 62.18.4; Diod. Sic. 16.91.2-3; Arrian *Alex.* 7.26.2-3; Jos. *War* 1.80). The foolish often doubt a warning until it comes to pass (e.g., Hom. *Od.* 2.182-82).

Second, promises of the kingdom without the cross come from the devil (16:22-23). After the destruction of the temple, the folly of the military-political paradigm of resistance was at least temporarily obvious; Matthew's audience knew only too well the dangers of the rhetoric of worldly power.

If 16:18-19 grant Peter special authority, this passage qualifies it: his authority functions only when he speaks from God, not when he speaks human and demonic wisdom (cf. Meier 1979: 118).[98] "Never, Lord!" is a vigorous denial, in vehement Septuagintal language (Carson 1984b: 377). When Peter rebuked Jesus, he overstepped his appropriate bounds as a disciple (cf. other wrongful "rebukes" in 19:13; 20:31). Correcting a teacher was rare (ARN 1A), and some sages believed teaching law even in the presence of one's teacher merited death from God (Sifra Shemini Mekhilta deMiluim 99.5.6; b. ʿErub. 63a; Tem. 16a; Lev. Rab. 20:6-7). Disciples "followed" their teachers (4:19-20; 8:22; 9:9-10; 10:38; 16:24; 19:21), literally walking behind them out of respect when they walked (Liefeld 1967: 227-28). Thus, though Jesus "turned" to confront Peter literally behind him (16:23), he now ordered him to "Get behind" him figuratively (16:23), returning to a position of discipleship.[99] It was known that teachers and prophets gave very firm warnings to their disciples (CD 8.20-2).[100]

But Peter was not only out of order; he functioned as the devil's agent. Satan offered Jesus the kingdom without the cross at Jesus' temptation (4:8-9); Pe-

98. Passages such as this one, which underline the weakness of disciples, also point to what Jesus can ultimately accomplish through such weak instruments (cf. Wilkins 1995: 173-216).

99. Some suggest here the mistranslation of a Semitic idiom for "Get *from* behind me," i.e., "You are no longer my disciple" (Smith 1951: 30; cf. Black 1967: 218; in Test. Job 27:1, possibly reflecting the Gospel tradition, such a construction would signal "Stop hiding"); but such a final repudiation leaves no trace either in the Gospel tradition or in subsequent testimony concerning Peter's role in early Christianity. Although "Get behind me" was not a typical rebuke (Smith 1951: 30), "Go" was a fairly typical harsh response to a foolish or hostile statement (e.g., Epict. *Disc.* 3.23.12-13; cf. Jas 4:13; 5:1; Mart. *Epig.* 1.42). Weeden 1971: 65 and Kelber 1979: 47-48 even find in Jesus' rebuke of Peter Markan exorcist language.

100. Thus though one should reject extravagant, overstated praise (on 16:13-20, Boring 1995: 104-5 cites Plut. *Inoffensive Self-Praise* 12, *Mor.* 543DE), the matter here is much stronger.

ter now offers the same temptation and encounters the same title (4:10; Cullmann 1956b: 27). In the early Christian perspective, the devil influenced this world so deeply that the world's values were quite often the devil's values (Jas 3:15; 4:7; Eph 2:1-3; 4:25-27);[101] by valuing the things humans value (such as lack of suffering), Peter shows himself to be in league with the devil (16:23).[102] The religious leaders later echoed Satan's temptation as well (27:42-43). That Peter is a "stumbling block" (16:23; not in Mark) again plays on his name: the "rock" could have negative as well as positive functions (Meier 1979: 117; idem 1980: 185).

Third, if Jesus' mission is death, he expects no less from his disciples (16:24). "Taking up one's cross" in antiquity hardly meant the relatively minor burdens assumed by many popular readers of the text today (though it might lend itself, reasoning from greater demands to lesser, to such application; cf. Caesarius of Arles *Sermons* 159.5; Tert. *On Idolatry* 12; *ACCS,* 112). It meant marching on the way to one's execution, shamefully carrying the heavy horizontal beam (the *patibulum*) of one's own death-instrument through the midst of a jeering mob (Jeremias 1972: 218-19; idem 1971: 242); and under less controlled circumstances, mobs themselves could tear people apart (e.g., Polyb. *R.R.E.* 15.33).[103] Jesus anticipated literal martyrdom for himself and many of his followers by the Romans' standard means of executing lower-class criminals and slaves; his kingdom was ultimately incompatible with Rome's claims (Manson 1979: 131; F. F. Bruce 1972a: 19; Klaasen 1981: 88). If disciples "come after" and imitate their teacher, their lives are forfeit from the moment they begin following him; to "come after" Jesus Peter himself had to return behind him (16:23). Self-denial in this text refers to following Christ to the death (16:24), rather than denying him in the face of persecution (10:33). At the same time, people often recognized the boldness of soldiers and others unafraid to die (e.g., Pub. Syr. 242). Although genuine disciples may fall short on their commitment at times (26:69-75), the Gospel tradition emphasizes that those who wish to follow Jesus must understand from the start that they are surrendering their *lives* to

101. Cf. the parallel with Sitis as Satan's agent in Test. Job 23-25 (Garrett 1998: 77-81). Extant records do not, however, support a parallel with the prevalence of demons (Jub. 10:1, 3, 8-9; 12:20; CD 12.2; 1QS 3.23-24; 1 Enoch 40:9; Test. Sol. 6:4; Test. Zeb. 9:7 MSS; Test. Dan 1:7; possibly 1 Enoch 20:6; in the Amoraim, Num. Rab. 1:5; 12:3; Edersheim: 644) or the pervasiveness of the spirit of error (1QS 3.20-26; cf. Test. Benj. 6:1; Reub. 4:11) in the sins of individual persons found in much of the contemporary folk religion.

102. Although Jewish writers occasionally spoke of "satans" in the plural, i.e., demons (1 Enoch 40:7; 65:6; Gaster 1976: 224, 262n.16; Alexander 1980: 25, 30; repeatedly in the incantation texts, e.g., 23.3-4; 58.1; 60.10; 66.5), Jesus compares Peter to Satan himself because he spoke Satan's lines (cf. Lk 22:31; Jn 13:27; Acts 5:3; Test. Job 26:6/7; 27:1).

103. Nevertheless, crosses also became a natural metaphor for sufferings (e.g., Apul. *Metam.* 7.16, *cruciatibus* [LCL translates more freely]; 10.9; cf. Sen. *Dial.* 1.3.10; 7.19.3) or the pain of grief (Apul. *Metam.* 9.31) or anxiety (Apul. *Metam.* 9.23); for other nonliteral usages, cf. Epict. *Disc.* 3.26.22. Preparing for death (Sen. *Ep. Lucil.* 12.9; 1 Cor 15:30-32; 2 Cor 1:9-10) is closer to the direct point than Paul's application to death to sin (e.g., Rom 6:3-4).

him. From this perspective, most modern Western Christians remain unconverted, a point we should grasp to grapple effectively with the impact Jesus' words would have had on his own contemporaries. A true Christian, Cyprian believed, would not be ashamed of Christ or shrink from suffering for him (*The Lapsed* 28, *ACCS,* 114).

Fourth, Jesus is worth any price a disciple must pay to follow him (16:25-27). Losing one's life in this age would be a small price to preserve it in the eternal age to come (cf. 1 Enoch 108:10; 2 Bar. 51:15-16; m. 'Abot 4:17; ARN 32, §71B; b. Tamid 32a; Lev. Rab. 3:1; Deut. Rab. 11:10; Qoh. Rab. 4:6, §1; Daube 1973: 137).[104] One must decide whether one "wishes" to come after Jesus (16:24) or "wishes" (the same Greek term) to save one's life (16:25); one cannot have it both ways. The cross means death, and nothing less; this point is so important that Matthew redactionally underlines it in an earlier persecution context (10:38-39; cf. Jn 12:25). Jewish teachers regarded a human life as of incomparably great value (Moore 1971: 2:239; Sandmel 1978b: 180); no ransom price would be too great for one's life (or "soul" — the same term in v. 26; 2 Bar. 17:2-3; Char. *Chaer.* 3.3.11-12; Epict. *Disc.* 2.12.21; Marc. Aur. *Med.* 11.1.2; cf. Ex 30:12; Ps 49:7-9).

Yet the only way to preserve one's life is to relinquish it in faith that the Son of Man would someday come with his angels to execute judgment (16:27; cf. 25:31; 2 Thess 1:7-8; Dan 7:9-14) according to each person's works (the principle was widely reported; see, e.g., Ps 62:12; Prov 24:12; Sir 16:12, 14; Rom 2:6; 2 Cor 11:15; Rev 22:12; Pesiq. R. 8:2; cf. Mt 5:26). Those who expected a period of great suffering before the time of the kingdom (24:9-12) would hear in such words a radical call to perseverance (24:13).[105] Disciples may confront death, but such martyrdoms would never crush Jesus' church (16:18).

Multiple attestation supports the authenticity of the logion in 16:27, which may stand, together with (if not part of) 24:30-31, behind 1 Thessalonians 4:15-17. Paul adapts "Son of Man" to "Lord," the preferred title for Jesus in his circles, and the Synoptics, written later, clarify that only "some" would remain alive. That the prediction did not happen, requiring clarification or even revision, further supports its authenticity (Sanders 1993: 181-82). But even in Paul's early writings, it seems clear that Jesus' promise was of a *potentially* imminent parousia, not one that would necessarily arrive immediately (Witherington 1992: 45-58).

104. Cf. the funeral meter rhythm here in Jeremias 1971: 26. Boring 1995: 106 suggests that this call resembles the typical prebattle speech of generals: risking life in battle more often than not yields its preservation (Tyrtaeus *Fr.* 8.11-13).

105. That Matthew (10:33) and Luke (12:9) have "deny" for Mark's "ashamed" in this text (Mk 8:38; Lk 9:26) might suggest a translation variant from Aramaic in the oral tradition (Jeremias 1971: 7n.2) or Markan redaction of Q, supporting the pre-Markan character of this passage (although the sayings may have been circulated independently — see Schweizer 1970: 175). It fits Markan theology so well precisely because Mark constructed his theology from the Jesus tradition he accepted as God's word. Hunter 1966: 35 stresses the solidarity between the suffering Son of Man and his saints in this passage, comparing Paul's "in Christ" formula.

The Son of Man's Glory (16:28–17:13)

Cf. Mk 9:1-13; Lk 1:17; 9:27-36. Had the disciples any doubt that Jesus would someday come to reign in glory (16:27; cf. 24:30; angels in 24:31), he promises them a proleptic vision of his glory in the present (16:28).[106] In a narrative that resembles Moses' revelation on Mount Sinai,[107] some of the disciples become witnesses like Moses of Jesus' divine glory (17:1-8).[108] (Philo's *Life of Moses* similarly places a transfiguration narrative near the middle, as Mack 1988: 289 points out.)[109] The six days (17:1) could be a general literary device for a climactic seventh day after six days of preparation (cf. McCurley 1974: 81), but probably refer specifically to Exodus 24:15-18 (Jub. 1:2-3; ARN 1A; e.g., Mauser 1963: 111; Gundry 1982: 342; Refoulé 1993).[110] Going up to the mountain (17:1; Ex 24:13, 18), the bright cloud (17:5; Ex 24:15; cf. Mt 24:30), and other features of the narrative likewise recall the revelation on Mount Sinai. The appearance of the literal Moses and Elijah in 17:3 (both of whom had experiences with God on Mount Horeb) invites the reader to consider the other

106. Some apply the promise especially to Pentecost (cf. Dunn 1970b: 40), others to Jesus' resurrection (F. F. Bruce 1972a: 25-26); still others contend that it refers to the end of the age and was left unfulfilled (Mattill 1979a: 59-67; cf. Hagner 1995: 485-86). Probably the transfiguration proleptically introduces the whole eschatological sphere, which Jesus' resurrection inaugurates and his return consummates; on the blending of successive future events in prophetic time, cf. 24:3 and the following discourse (cf. Dodd 1980: 33, who suggests that the first disciples understood "resurrection, exaltation, and second advent" as a single, immediate event). For a bibliography of sources on the transfiguration before 1980, see Best 1981. "Taste death" is idiomatic (e.g., Jn 8:52; Heb 2:9; Sib. Or. 1.82; Gen. Rab. 21:5; Lev. Rab. 18:1; Pesiq. R. 48:2; for some other examples of Semitic constructions, see Lane 1991: 49). Although especially prevalent in Jewish texts, the construction would be intelligible to other Greek readers, for whom "taste" could represent "experience" (e.g., Marc. Aur. 9.2; Heb 6:4).

107. Mount Hermon (over 9,200 ft.; but perhaps too rugged, far away, and cold at the top) and Mount Tabor (ca. 1,900 ft.; though a fortress lay on it in Jesus' day; Jos. *War* 2.573; 4.54-55) have been suggested for the mountain here, the former because it is near Caesarea Philippi; one could hardly expect to find the scribes following the disciples into Gentile territory, however (Mk 9:14). Some thus suggest Mount Meron (4,000 ft.), within Israel (Carson 1984b: 384; Blomberg 1992a: 263; Hagner 1995: 492). A range of mountainous country lay between the Jordan Valley and the coastal plain, however, and the actual site is irrelevant to the Gospel writers' point.

108. Many texts indicate transfigurations of deities or light shining on special persons (Boring 1995: 107-8 includes *Homeric Hymns* 2.275-80; Plut. *Fortune of Romans* 10; *Lives of the Prophets* 21; Philo *Virt.* 217); but I suspect that Matthew's biblically literate audience would first identify the allusion most familiar to them, namely, Moses.

109. Mack unfortunately concludes that Mark is therefore mythic, rather than that Mark might draw on Moses motifs earlier in his tradition (Philo, after all, took his point of departure from biblical and early Jewish tradition); and a believer might as easily presuppose that the Gospels and their tradition correctly interpret the revelation as an unbeliever might presuppose that they did not. Allison 1993b: 243-48 shows that Matthew expanded the Moses allusions.

110. Lacking clearly supporting clues, an allusion to the eschatological Sabbath tradition (cf. Mek. Shab. 1.38-40; Jub. 50:9; Test. Abr. 19 A; Life of Adam 51:1-2; Apoc. Mos. 43:2-3; Barn. 15:9; Daniélou 1964: 390-404; in Kabbalah, see Ginsberg 1955: 127) in the six days (Ex 16:5) would probably be too subtle for the implied audience.

allusions to Moses (17:2-5) and the reference to Elijah (17:10-13) later in the narrative.[111]

First, Jesus is the glorious Lord before whom all other heroes of the faith must bow (16:28–17:3). When Jesus again takes some disciples aside for private instruction (15:21; 16:13; 17:1; cf. 20:17; cf. 17:19; see comment on 13:10-17),[112] his transfiguration among them provides a foretaste of his glory when he will return to judge the earth (16:28). One could offer various suggestions for the background for Jesus' proleptic "glorification" here, such as images from apocalyptic texts (Meier 1980: 190). The closest Greco-Roman parallels with divine men would be two who uncovered their golden thighs, which are not at all close (Blackburn 1986: 190); much closer would be the myth in which Zeus reveals his heavenly splendor to Semele, although the effect is quite different here (in that case, Zeus as lightning unhappily vaporized Semele).

Most Jewish parallels are closer in substance and wording.[113] Angels and archangels sometimes appear as brighter than the sun in Jewish texts (28:3; Dan 10:6; Rev 10:1; 2 Enoch 19:1; 3 Enoch 18:25; 22:4-9; 26:2-7; 35:2; Test. Abr. 7, 12A; Apoc. Zeph. 6:11-15). The righteous after death (4 Ezra 7:97) or in the eschatological time (see 13:43; 1 Cor 15:53; Phil 3:21; 2 Bar. 51:3) would shine in the same way, as would Noah (1 Enoch 106:2, 10; 1QapGen col. 2), Abel (Test. Abr. 12A), Enoch (1 Enoch 71:11; 2 Enoch 22:10; 3 Enoch 15:1), Zion in a vision (4 Ezra 10:25), and God himself (Dan 7:9-10; 1 Enoch 14:18-20; 46:1; 71:10; 3 Enoch 28:7).

But a variety of allusions combine to point especially to Moses in the Old Testament. After Moses beheld God's glory, his own face shone with that glory (Ex 34:29-35; cf. Ps-Philo 12:1; 19:16; ARN 13, §32B; b. B. Bat. 75a);[114] most scholars regard this account about Moses as the primary background for the revelation of Matthew 17.[115] Jesus is not only greater than Solomon and the temple (12:6, 42), but greater than Moses as well.

111. It is difficult to say whether Mark first juxtaposed the transfiguration with the saying about seeing the kingdom, but if so Matthew and Luke here concur with Mark's interpretation. Mark's omission of resurrection appearances later could account for including one here (cf. Weeden 1971: 118), but the details of the story and the other two Synoptics' compliance with this arrangement do not favor it. In Mark and Matthew it anticipates the resurrection appearances (Petersen 1978: 65; Kim 1978: 94-97), as well as alluding back to the baptism (cf. Trites 1979).

112. One might keep a small group of only a few friends on hand for the most intimate occasions (e.g., Jos. *Life* 223, four friends). Qumran not only had a special group of twelve, but also a special group of three (1QS 8.1; Hill 1972: 267). In this case, it may be *most* relevant, however, that Moses had three specific companions in Ex 24:1, 9, although they were also joined by the seventy elders (France 1985: 262).

113. Mystics' pursuit of transformation into the divine image (on which see, e.g., Morray-Jones 1992; 2 Enoch 22:8-10) is probably even less relevant here than the Greek mythological parallels, because it appears even further removed from the genre of normal historical narrative.

114. See also commentators on 2 Cor 3, including von der Osten-Sacken 1981; cf. Jn 1:14.

115. Davies 1966b: 20-22; Lane 1974a: 317; Glasson 1963a: 70; Moses 1996: 84-85; for a survey of views on the transfiguration, cf. Liefeld 1992. Davies and Allison 1991: 695 note that Philo *Mos.* 1.57 also applies *metamorphoō* to Moses, and, most importantly, that 2 Cor 3:18 (the context of

The narrative does not state how the disciples recognized Moses and Elijah (it seems most likely that they did so by their conversation), but ancient readers might not have asked (cf. the similar ambiguity in Hom. *Il.* 1.199-200; 2.182, 807, which might allow recognition by statues or more likely previous visitations, neither of which is feasible here). Some see in Moses and Elijah representatives of the law and the prophets (Taylor 1952: 390; Montefiore 1968: 1:207; Origen *Matthew* 12.38; Augustine *Sermons on NT Lessons, ACCS,* 119-20), though some have objected that Elijah appears in the Writings, not in the Prophets per se (Gundry 1982: 343). Others see in them harbingers of the end (Moule 1965: 70; Young 1995: 208). Despite the clear testimony of Deuteronomy 34:5-7 (cf. also 1 Enoch 89:38), some of Jesus' contemporaries doubted that Moses had died (Sifre Deut. 357.10.5; ARN 12A), supposing that he lived on like Elijah and some other figures (cf. 4 Ezra 6:27; pace Jos. *Ant.* 9.28); others at least felt that his death was special in some sense (Philo *Sacrifice of Cain* 8-10; Test. Mos. 11:8; cf. Deut 34:6). The Bible itself claimed that both Elijah (Mal 4:4-5) and a prophet like Moses (Deut. 18:15-19) would return. Most importantly, this literal Moses and Elijah also capture the reader's attention for the figurative new Elijah (17:12) and new Moses — Jesus — of whom this text speaks.

But while the text may present Jesus as a new Moses (especially 17:5), it also presents him as something more. It portrays the disciples as witnesses of his glory on the mountain, just as Moses and Elijah heard God on Mount Sinai (cf. Moiser 1985a). The presence of Moses and Elijah indicates that Jesus is incomparably greater than the prophets with whom some were comparing him (16:14; cf. Thrall 1970: 316).

Second, the Father calls his people to heed Jesus as they would heed God's law (17:4-5). Peter's offer to construct tabernacles so they could stay on the mountain (17:4) need not suggest an allusion to the tabernacle (pace Mauser 1963: 113) or the feast of tabernacles (pace Anderson 1976: 225-26) and does not suggest that the feast of tabernacles was literally at hand. Rather, Peter proposes merely the sort of temporary shelters that feast commemorated, so they may remain on the mountain. Workers erected such shelters of stones, branches, and mats for watchmen in vineyards (cf. 21:33) and for intermittent respite against the sun in the fields (Abrahams 1924: 50); Mediterranean nomads traditionally erected tents for honored guests (Argyle 1963: 132).[116]

But whereas Peter's tabernacles may not reflect biblical significance, God's "tabernacle" may. The description of the bright cloud that "overshadows" them utilizes language reminiscent of the Jewish doctrine of the Shekinah, God's

---

which is a midrash on Ex 33–34) indicates that as early as Paul Christians already applied this term to Moses' experience. Philo *Mos.* 1.70 also compares Moses' radiance to that of the sun (p. 696). For Moses-Sinai and transfiguration themes in Philo, see Moses 1996: 50-57; in Josephus, 57-61; in Qumran, 61-66; in other sources, 66-83.

116. Matthew changes Peter's address of Jesus to "Lord" because he reserves the title "rabbi" (cf. Mk 9:5) for the lips of Judas (26:25, 49; Fenton 1977: 277).

presence, especially recalling God's presence in the tabernacle in the wilderness (Ex 40:34-38; Daube 1973: 30; Davies 1966b: 22-23; Argyle 1963: 132). God then repeats in a *bath qol* (see comment on 3:17) some of the commendation oracle he uttered at Jesus' baptism, revealing Jesus' identity as both Messiah and suffering servant (Ps 2:7; Is 42:1; see comment on 3:17; for the Aramaic, Dalman 1929: 17); to this he adds an allusion that indicates that Jesus is the promised "prophet like Moses" as well, for of that prophet God said, "you must heed him" (17:5; Deut 18:15).[117]

Third, this mighty Jesus does not flaunt his power but cares for his people (17:6-8). The disciples fell on their faces, afraid (17:6). Falling on one's face or being terrified was a customary response to superhuman revelations both in Israel's ancient history[118] and in contemporary Jewish accounts;[119] if the text suggests a more immediate allusion, it is probably the response to the transfigured Moses in Exodus 34:30. As he often did, Jesus crossed barriers and communicated his benevolence by touching (17:7; cf. 8:3, 15; 9:20, 25, 29). He then spoke words of assurance customary for divine and angelic revelations: "Arise, do not be fearful" (17:7; cf. 28:5, 10). The commands to arise and not to fear after an overwhelming revelation have parallels in many Jewish texts.[120]

Finally, God's way is the way of martyrdom not only for prophets but for the Messiah himself (17:9-13). Although scholars disagree concerning how widespread and early was the explicit view of Elijah as the Messiah's forerunner,[121] his end-time function in general is clear from Malachi 4:5-6 (cf. Sir 48:10; see the note on 3:4 above),[122] which also presents him as a "re-

117. Many commentators recognize the allusion to Moses here: Mauser 1963: 114; Davies 1966b: 24; Lane 1974a: 321; F. F. Bruce 1978: 40; Longenecker 1981: 36; Gundry 1982: 343; Young 1995: 211; pace Aune 1983: 272. Sifre Deut. 175.1.3 emphasizes the authority of the prophet in this passage. Jerome *Homily* 80, understood, "Hear *him,*" i.e., more than Moses and Elijah (*ACCS,* 120).

118. Gen 15:12; 28:17; Dan 8:17-18; 10:9; Ezek 1:28; cf. Ex 34:30; *PGM* 4.725.

119. Rev 1:17; Tob 12:16; Jub. 18:10; 1 Enoch 14:13-14; 60:3; 71:2-3, 10-11; 89:30-31; 102:1; 2 Enoch 1:8; 20:2; 21:2; 22:4; 4 Macc 4:11; 4 Ezra 4:12; 5:14; 10:30; Jos. and Asen. 14:10-11; Test. Job 3:4/5; Apoc. Zeph. 6:9-10; cf. Mt 27:54.

120. E.g., Ezek 2:1-2; Dan 8:18; 10:11-12; Rev 1:17; Tob 12:17; 1 Enoch 60:4; 71:3; 2 Enoch 1:8; 20:2; 21:3; 22:5; 3 En. 1:7-9; 4 Ezra 5:15; 2 Bar. 13:1-2; Jos. and Asen. 14:11; cf. *PGM* 1.77-78.

121. Although some scholars have indicated a dearth of evidence from the Tannaitic period about Elijah's future coming (Faierstein 1981; Fitzmyer 1985), other scholars have cited early evidence and argued that it is unlikely that Christian claims would simply have been adopted unmodified by the rabbis (Allison 1984; Milikowsky 1982-83), a position that seems more probable (Mk 9:11; Mt 17:10).

122. Later rabbis typically viewed Elijah as still alive (e.g., ARN 38, §103 B; b. Moʿed Qat. 26; Sanh. 113b; Pesiq. Rab Kah. 9:4), often as a supernatural being like the angels among whom he operated (e.g., b. Ber. 4b; B. Meṣ. 59b). There are a variety of diverse portrayals of Elijah in different texts; for one survey, see Zeller 1986. For an association of Elijah with the end time, see Sifre Deut. 41.4.3, 342.5.2; b. Menaḥ. 63a; Sukk. 52b; Gen. Rab. 71:9; Ex. Rab. 3:4; Song Rab. 8:9, §3; Pesiq. Rab Kah. 5:9; Pesiq. R. 15:14/15; cf. Sir 48:10-11. The context of Sib. Or. 2:187-89 is Christian interpolation, but if it is original, it may testify to belief in an eschatological coming of Elijah. There is

storer."[123] Although some people in antiquity expected literal *redivivus* figures,[124] others employed the *redivivus* image figuratively (e.g., Rev 13:3, 18). The Gospels' portrayal of John the Baptist as Elijah fits the latter category (Lk 1:16-17; see comment on Mt 14:1-2).

Lacking a Mustard Seed of Faith (17:14-23)

Cf. Mk 9:14-32; Lk 9:37-45; Jn 7:1; 14:9. As Moses found that those he had left in charge were unable to control the people (Ex 24:14; 32:1-8; cf. Ps-Philo 12:7), Jesus found that those he had left behind could not cast out a demon. They had cast out demons before, but perhaps they lacked confidence because they felt their commission (10:7-8) was limited to a short-term mission (11:1) or because this demon seemed more powerful than others, requiring more spiritual preparation (cf. Mk 9:29). Jesus casts out the demon immediately, demonstrating how it should be done (17:18; cf. 8:26), but the disciples' inability invites Jesus' reproof of their weak faith twice (17:17, 20).[125]

First, Jesus honors one person's faith on behalf of another. A man brought his son to the one with power to deliver him (17:14-15); love for his son undoubtedly drives his desperation, but Malina 1993: 80 may also be correct in noting the shame associated with having a demonized son. Some of the symp-

---

also later rabbinic evidence of a relationship between Elijah and the Messiah's coming: b. B. Meṣ. 85b; ʿErub. 43b; Ex. Rab. 18:12; Deut. Rab. 6:7; Pesiq. R. 35:4; cf. Gen. Rab. 83:4; Lev. Rab. 34:8; Song Rab. 2:13, §4; Trypho in Justin *Dial.* 8, 49 (on Justin's data, cf. Schneider 1962: 169; Williams 1930: 18nn.5-6). Rabbinic (especially Babylonian Amoraic) texts, which often paint Elijah as a master halakist (ARN 2 A; b. Ber. 3a; Menaḥ. 32a; Qidd. 70a; ʿAbod. Zar. 36a; Ḥag. 9b; Ketub. 106a; Giṭ. 42b; p. Ter. 1:6; Gen. Rab. 71:9; Pesiq. Rab Kah. 11:22; cf. the association of Elijah and the law as early as 1 Macc 2:58), as well as a miraculous messenger who helped rabbis (deliverance or healing in b. Taʿan. 21a; ʿAbod. Zar. 17b; p. Ketub. 12:3, §6; Gen. Rab. 33:3; as a messenger of vengeance, b. Ber. 6b; as a messenger of news, b. Shab. 33b; B. Meṣ. 85b; Yoma 19b-20a; Deut. Rab. 5:15; Pesiq. Rab Kah. 18:5), portrayed his eschatological role of restorer in predominantly halakhic terms (m. ʿEd. 8:7; t. ʿEd. 3:4; Song Rab. 4:12, §5; Teeple 1957: 4-8, on Elijah as restorer of genealogical purity in Israel in the end time; for other eschatological halakic responsibilities, see b. Ber. 35b; B. Meṣ. 3a, 30a; B. Bat. 94b; Menaḥ. 45a). But all this may fit into the rabbinic portrayal of prophets as sages.

123. Malina 1993: 134 suggests that Jesus calls the disciples to keep the matter secret to increase the status of their group as holding private information; but the disciples' lack of understanding may be a more important reason. John the Baptist's being secretly Elijah may parallel the messianic secret about Jesus in Mark (Witherington 1990: 35, following Wink 1968: 110-11).

124. One might compare the widespread expectation for a literal return of Nero (Dio Chrys. *21st Disc., On Beauty* 9-10; Tac. *Hist.* 2.8; Suet. *Nero* 57; Dio Cassius *R.H.* 66.19.3; Sib. Or. 3.63; 4.119-24, 137-39; 5.33-34, 137-54, 361-85; 8.68-72, 139-50; for early Christian texts, see Griffin 1984: 15).

125. Because the church would not invent the disciples' failure and did not update the account in the church's language, and the story may be attested in more than one form, Sterling 1993 contends that this exorcism narrative reflects an actual incident in Jesus' life; cf. further Twelftree 1993: 91-97.

toms depicted here resemble epilepsy (e.g., Alexander 1980: 83), which may imply that demonic forces gaining control over the human central nervous system can cause epileptic-type phenomena; the parallels do not, however, mean that Matthew thinks that epilepsy is always caused by demons (see 4:24). Some contemporary anthropological accounts of spirit-possession also include demons seeking to make people burn themselves (Kaplan and Johnson 1964: 211).[126]

Jesus accepts the father's faith on behalf of his son. Those who support infant baptism have found in this text a principle they believe supports it (Richardson 1958: 359-60); those who emphasize the importance of personal faith at baptism are not persuaded by the analogy. But in either case the early Christians applied the basic principle for many other kinds of prayer (cf., e.g., 10:8; 18:15-20; 1 Jn 5:16), and it encourages disciples in their faith for others' needs (cf. 8:13, 16; 9:2, 18; 12:22; 15:28). As the circumstances of healing would often dictate, various miracle stories include the healer handing the healed person over to relatives (Theissen 1983: 68 cites Lk 7:15; 9:42; 1 Kings 17:23; 2 Kings 4:36-37; Philost. *V.A.* 4.45).

Second, Jesus expected his disciples to have sufficient faith to repeat his miracles by this point (17:16-17, 20; cf. also Held 1963: 271-72). The "unbelieving generation" (17:17) applied generally to Jesus' contemporaries (11:16; 12:39-45; 13:39, 45; 16:4; 23:36; 24:34), but in this case specifically to his disciples who proved unable to stand in for him in his absence (17:16). Disciples were by definition apprentices in training to assume the role of their teachers. Jesus was "able" (literally, "powerful" enough) to bind the strong man (12:29); why were they "unable" (same term) to expel a demon (17:19)? He had already sent his disciples out, and they had healed the sick and driven out demons (10:8). Had they not seen enough to believe (cf. 8:26)? Matthew expected his audience to learn from Jesus' signs that he was recording just as the first disciples did when they witnessed them. As he exposed his audience to more of the character of their risen Lord, he likely expected them to grow in their relationship of faith with Jesus as Jesus expected his first disciples to do.

Third, their inadequacy stemmed from their lack of the most basic level of faith (17:20). Rather than acknowledge their failure in front of others and further risk their honor, the disciples question Jesus privately (17:19; Malina 1993: 118). He explicitly attributes their inability to the smallness of their faith (cf. 6:30; 8:26; 14:21; 16:8), pointing out that even a mustard seed's worth of faith would be sufficient to cast out not only demons but mountains (17:20; 21:21). (The saying is surely authentic; Paul's citation in 1 Cor 13:2 is closer to the Q form related to Mt 17:20 and Lk 17:6 than to the Markan form and its Matthean doublet in Mk 11:23 and Mt 21:21; Richardson and Gooch 1984: 46.) The disciples already recognized how small a mustard seed was (13:32). Ancient peoples thought of mountains as rooted far beneath the earth (Gundry 1982:

126. Some other ancient texts also depict demons wishing to kill their hosts (e.g., the later account of a jealous demon that loves a boy and wishes to slay him in Philost. *V.A.* 3.38).

353), so "moving mountains" was a typical Jewish teacher's image for "doing what was virtually impossible."[127] With this illustration Jesus indicates that even were disciples moving mountains rather than casting out demons, they would only be scratching the surface (employing a mustard seed) of a life of faith.[128] Jesus reproved the disciples because he *expected* them to be able to do his works; their presence with him should have deepened their faith. Matthew encourages his community to go deeper in faith, and such faith arises from intimate attentiveness to their Lord among them.

Finally, a life of faithful obedience to God invites martyrdom as well as God's power (17:22-23). Jesus' own example declares that those who truly have intimate relationships with God in faith act in compassion for others' needs rather than exploiting power frivolously (4:3-10). Like 16:21, this passion prediction reflects some Aramaic expressions that suggest its authenticity (see Jeremias 1971: 295; the expression may also allude to Is 53:6, 12 — Gundry 1982: 354). Disciples may become too infatuated with God's power and protection (17:20), but God often calls disciples to danger. God twice honored Elijah's calling for fire from heaven (2 Kings 1:10-12) but instructed him to accompany the third captain (who by this point, at least, feared God enough to provide the prophet safe passage). Jesus' disciples had preferred the glories of the messianic kingdom to suffering (16:16, 21-22); an important stream of early Christian

127. Jewish teachers often depicted mastering difficult subjects as "moving mountains" (e.g., ARN 6A; 12, §29B; b. Sanh. 24a), e.g., by a bird's scraping off one piece at a time (cf. b. Ber. 63b); presumably they, like Jesus, echo a more popular and generally applicable idiom for what was beyond human power (cf. Ps 46:3; Is 54:10; Hab 3:10). Many scholars note the idiom and its application for doing the impossible (e.g., Manson 1979: 206; Lachs 1987: 263, citing b. B. Bat. 3b; Sanh. 4a; Soṭa 9b; Lev. Rab. 8:2). But while some ancient teachers felt that "nothing would be impossible" for a wise man to endure (Diog. Laert. 6.1.12) and hellenistic writers (cf. also Zech 8:6 LXX; Philo *Creation* 46) acknowledged that deities could do anything (Brown 1994: 175 on Mk 14:36; Soph. *Ajax* 86; cf. Test. Sol. 23:1, which applies the language of mountain moving to a particularly potent demon), Jesus' promise of spiritual power on this level is remarkable.

Matthew's audience might think of the Mount of Transfiguration just mentioned (17:1). Isaiah promised that Israel would be powerful enough to crush mountains (Is 41:15); Zechariah promised that mighty mountains would become like plains before God's Spirit-empowered leaders for his people (Zech 4:6-7), and especially before the Lord himself (Zech 14:3-5). For a thorough discussion of the demands of faith in Mk 11:22-25 (par. Mt 21:20-22), see Dowd 1988. See further comments on Mt 21:21-22; Matthew's repetition underlines his point.

128. 17:21 is missing from some of the best manuscripts. Although its wide geographical distribution could favor its inclusion, it is easily explained as a harmonization with the wording of Mk 9:29, scribes being dissatisfied with Matthew's twofold use of Mk 11:23 (Metzger 1971: 43; on reasons for the double use, cf. Goulder 1974: 37). Matthew omits some Markan material here; e.g., probably due to the danger of false prophets to his community (7:15; 24:24) he omits Mark's account of the exorcist outside their circle (Thompson 1970: 262). Despite the syncretic character of most exorcisms in the magical papyri, many early Christians continued to expel demons immediately by a command (Minucius Felix *Octavius* 24-27) and found fasting an important weapon against more powerful demons (Tert. *On Fasting* 8.8; Jerome *Against Jovinianus* 2.15; the variant reading in Mk 9:29).

thought came to understand that this missed the point of Jesus' triumphant empowerment (cf. 1 Cor 13:2; Lk 10:17-20). The news grieves the disciples (17:23; 18:31; 19:22; 26:22, 37).[129]

Solidarity with Israel, Obedience to Rome (17:24-27)

Since perhaps the end of the Maccabean period (Liver 1963), adult Jewish males throughout the Empire paid an annual two-drachma tax, based on Exodus 30:13-16 (cf. m. Sheqal. passim), used for the upkeep of the Jerusalem temple (cf. Sanders 1992: 156).[130] Before the war of A.D. 66-70, the funds raised by this tax were so enormous that the temple aristocracy had to find what to do with the extra resources, eventually constructing a massive golden vine (cf. Jos. *War* 5.210; Tac. *Hist.* 5.5; Sanders 1992: 84). Although the tax was not compulsory (Garland 1996: 74), collectors undoubtedly did solicit it (though some extant sources are late; cf., e.g., Pesiq. R. 10:1; Nickle 1966: 78-86); because some Jewish groups refused to comply, it is not surprising that they might inquire whether Jesus would (Garland 1996: 69-70). Although the wording may be Matthew's (Gundry 1982: 356), the story apparently predates A.D. 70[131] — before we believe Mat-

129. The third day can mean "after three days," as in Ps-Philo 11:1-3; or *parts* of each of three days (Visotzky 1991; Scott 1995: 260; Ignatius *Trallians* 9; Augustine *On the Trinity* 4.6, 10; *ACCS,* 238); in either case it means "soon" (Gen 40:12-13, 18-19; Ex 3:18). Bousset's hellenistic parallels (1970: 58) are unconvincing (cf. Nock 1964a: 105-6; Jeremias 1971: 304; Fuller 1971: 25); the LXX is a more likely source (Hos 6:2; Jonah 1:17; cf. 1 Cor 15:4; Nock 1964a: 108), though it is unlikely that the early Christians would have noticed elements favoring it had the "third day" not been their initial experience. (Rabbis did, however, somethimes associate Hos 6:2 with the resurrection of the dead; see p. Sanh. 11:6, §1; cf. McArthur 1971: 83-84.) Some later traditions suggest the retention of the soul for three days after death (until the soul sees the body begin to decompose; Gen. Rab. 100:7; Lev. Rab. 18:1; though cf. Dola 1983) or required three days of purgatory before preparation to appear before God (3 Enoch 28:10; cf. Apoc. Zeph. 4:7). Cf. Greek reports of three days for mourning (Ap. Rhod. 1.1059; but Judaism emphasized seven), special funeral rites (Aristoph. *Lysist.* 613; but also the ninth day), purification in the underworld (Eurip. *Alcestis* 1145-46), or a ghost appearing after three days (Eurip. *Hecuba* 32; but this is due to lack of burial).

130. Because many taxes in this period were set at two drachmas (e.g., the tribute for the Great God Suchus in Egypt — Deissmann 1978: 253), Cassidy 1979 thinks that the text refers to a civil tax; the early Christians often applied this text to paying Roman taxes (Horbury 1984b: 265-86), which is at least a natural application of the principle (cf. 22:19, 21; Rom 13:7). But the exemption argument is easier to follow if the Jerusalem temple was originally in view, and most commentators find the temple tax here (e.g., Taylor 1935: 73-74; see especially Davies and Allison 1991: 739-40). Some think that though Matthew wants his readers to pay the tax to avoid offending their Jewish contemporaries, Matthew's audience is outside Judaism (Sandmel 1978a: 58); it seems more likely, however, that Matthew is concerned about offense precisely because his audience sees itself as part of the Jewish community (cf. Hagner 1995: 510-11). The tax was not applied as strictly as possible (i.e., to Judaizing Gentiles) until the reign of Domitian (Gager 1983: 60). Jesus *might* be saying here that he and Peter are true sons of God, unlike most of their people (cf. Sanders 1990: 50; Hagner 1995: 512); but cultural identification is in view at any rate (cf. Acts 21:26; 1 Cor 9:19-23).

131. F. F. Bruce 1980a: 72; Gundry 1982: 355-56; Meier 1994: 880-84; especially Garland 1996: 69-76.

thew was written. It is unlikely that Matthew would have created the story about the temple tax (especially such details as the exemption argument) after A.D. 70, when the temple was destroyed.[132] Even the placement in Matthew's narrative, shortly before the Passover, may be significant (cf. m. Sheqal. 1:1-3).

But taxes remained an issue in Matthew's day, including the two-drachma tax: after 70, the Romans required all Jewish people (including Jewish Christians maintaining allegiance to their Jewish heritage) to pay that tax to the Roman government.[133] For the sake of maintaining public identification with their Jewish heritage, Jewish Christians should join non-Christian Jews in continuing to pay the tax (cf. Grant 1977: 51; Harrington 1982: 73).[134] Similarly, disciples must engage in some otherwise unprofitable pursuits for the sake of upholding their witness as citizens of the communities where God has placed them.[135]

First, Jesus cares about his disciples' social obligations (17:24-26). Various possible reasons exist why the tax gatherers were unsure whether Jesus would pay.[136] Tradition indicates that they did not impose the tax on those living off charity (Derrett 1970: 253); Jesus and his disciples were essentially dependent on monetary sponsors during their period of frequent itinerant ministry (27:55; Lk 8:1-3; cf. 2 Kings 4:42). The Sadducees disapproved of the tax (France 1985: 267), and some ancient pietists, notably wilderness Essenes who regarded the temple as impure, paid the tax only once in a lifetime (4QOrdinances; Derrett 1970: 252; Davies and Allison 1991: 743). Probably they also know Jesus' reputation of conflict with other religious teachers.

Like a good prophet, Jesus knows in advance Peter's question (17:25). He, too, does not regard the poll-tax as binding on himself or Peter (17:25-26), but he recognizes that the tax collectors may (17:24). He thus does not rebuke Peter for committing him (17:25; unless the "yes" simply meant "Yes, I will consult him" — Derrett 1970: 253); he wishes to avoid unnecessary cause for misunderstanding (17:27).

132. Bultmann thinks that 17:25-26 is an early fragment later connected with the temple tax and a fish legend (Bultmann 1968: 34); but for a defense of authenticity (for the fish "legend" as well), see Bauckham 1986: 219-52; Hagner 1995: 510-11. That Matthew alone preserves the story is not surprising, since it is most applicable to a specifically Jewish-Christian audience. The illustration of p. ʿAbod. Zar. 2:7, §1 may be hypothetical, but it suggests the possibility of finding rings and other objects inside an animal.

133. See *CPJ* 1:80-81; 2:119-36, §§160-229; Dio Cassius *R.H.* 65.7.2; Hemer 1973; Carlebach 1975. Appian *R.H.* 11.8.50 claims that Jews paid a higher poll-tax because they rebelled so often.

134. Given the conflict depicted in ch. 23, the suggestion that the tax in this text was for Pharisaic leaders in Jamnia instead is highly unlikely (pace Thompson 1970: 67).

135. Doubting that Matthew reapplies the narrative to taxation in his own day (pace most scholars, 1996: 76-89), Garland finds in the passage solely an object lesson, primarily about relinquishing one's rights to avoid needless offenses (1996: 89-98).

136. Given other economic burdens, Galileans had probably become somewhat lax in tithing to the priesthood (Horsley 1995: 142-43), but the splendor of the temple's golden vine suggests that most Mediterranean Jews were faithful in paying the tax.

Derrett (1970: 256-57) thinks "offend" here means cause the tax gatherers to sin by trying to force Jesus to pay; but it is more likely that Jesus seeks to avoid turning people away from his gospel unnecessarily (cf. 18:6; 5:29-30; 13:41; 16:23). Jesus has offended ("caused to stumble") members of the religious establishment before (15:12-14), but this is an unnecessary "stumbling block" because it addresses one's own rights rather than the truth of God's kingdom (18:6; cf. 1 Cor 8:13; 9:12).

Second, disciples need to be ready to surrender their privileges and "rights" for the sake of the gospel (17:25-26). Jesus' point here is similar to Paul's point in 1 Corinthians 9:3-23; 10:29-33. Head- or poll-taxes (cf. 22:19-21) normally listed specific exceptions who would not have to pay; in Egypt, for instance, the Romans exempted the small minority of Roman citizens, urban Greeks, and some other higher-class residents of Egypt (Lewis 1983: 169; cf. 177). Conquerors subjected conquered peoples, not their own subjects, to taxation (Malina and Rohrbaugh 1992: 116).[137] Nero "freed" Greece, that is, exempted them from taxation (for which the gods were pleased, one Greek writer remarked — Plut. *Divine Vengeance* 32, *Mor.* 568A); Persian officials had earlier reportedly allowed Judeans "freedom" from tribute (1 Esdr 4:49-50). Priests were exempt from the two-drachma tax cited here (Reicke 1974: 168; Sanders 1990: 50); so in later times were rabbis (France 1985: 268).

Most significantly, dependents of a king were naturally exempt from his taxes (Derrett 1970: 255).[138] Jesus will soon tell a story of a king who settles accounts with his servants, tax farmers (18:23-34); but here he speaks in the first-person plural with a disciple who has begun to understand some of mysteries of the kingdom as one of the king's "sons" (cf. 28:10). Unlike some of their Jewish contemporaries, they do not depend at all on the temple or on the atonement some teachers claimed the temple-tax effected for them (Thompson 1970: 57-59).

Third, Jesus supplies needs like these as well as other needs (17:27). The "stater" or "four-drachma coin" of 17:27 probably is a Tyrian stater, precisely enough to pay two persons' temple dues (Avi-Yonah 1974/76a: 60-61). Following an old Greek story, some Jewish stories of uncertain date speak of God blessing pious people by having them find precious objects in fish (e.g., b. Shab. 119a; Bultmann 1968: 238; Jeremias 1971: 87).[139] If Peter knew of such

137. Malina and Rohrbaugh apply Jesus' exemption to all Israel, however, which may or may not be his point.

138. Garland 1996: 92-93 suspects a christological affirmation here, but elsewhere he regards Jesus' disciples also as the "free sons" (94-95). Even Jewish teachers sometimes accorded special privileges to kings' children; other teachers responded, however, that all Israelites were kings' children (m. Shab. 14:4).

139. For other fish miracles, see, e.g., Tob 6:2-5; more distantly, Epidauros inscriptions (47) report a great catch of fish (cf. Lk 5:6-7; Jn 21:5-6) and punishment of the fisher who failed to keep his vow to Asclepius (Theissen 1983: 110). Because the miracle of Mt 17:27 is not fulfilled in the narrative, Meier 1994: 884 doubts the authenticity of the prediction (cf. also France 1985: 268-69). One could argue in the opposite direction, however: the fulfillment's omission shows that the writer

stories, the moral of Jesus causing him to find money in a fish would not be lost on him. This is irony of a sort: the king's children can pay the tax because the king gives them the money to do so (Patte 1987: 247). Matthew encourages his missionary community that Jesus can take care of his people who walk close to him.

---

and/or the transmitters of the tradition were not trying to emphasize the miracle, which was already present in the tradition. Given the fulfillment of Jesus' other predictions in the Gospel, the implied audience would assume the fulfillment of this one (Garland 1996: 93, following Haenchen 1966: 333-34).

The Greatest Is the Child (18:1-5)

Cf. Mk 9:33-37; Lk 9:46-48; Jn 13:20. Here Jesus begins the fourth discourse in Matthew, addressing relationships in the church, which is the community of the kingdom (18:1-35). The disciples are concerned with an issue naturally prominent in status-conscious Mediterranean Judaism (Dalman 1929: 65; Harrington 1982: 73; Anderson 1976: 233): Who will be greatest in the kingdom (18:1; cf. 5:19; 20:26; 23:11)?[1] Jesus declares that the kingdom belongs to children (cf. 19:14) — to those lowly in status.

Early Judaism clearly emphasized humility (cf., e.g., Jos. *Ant.* 3.212; ARN 38A; 41, §111B; b. Soṭa 4b-5a; Gen. Rab. 1:5), both in stories about the early Pharisaic sages (e.g., ARN 15A; 29, §§60-62B; p. Sanh. 6:6, §2) and stories of later rabbis (e.g., p. Taʿan. 4:2, §§8-9; Num. Rab. 9:20; Deut. Rab. 3:6). Such humility was often expressed toward those in positions of greater power (m. ʾAbot 3:12; b. Meg. 28a; Taʿan. 20b), but those in power dare never become too arrogant themselves (e.g., Sifre Deut. 38.1.4; ARN 39A; p. Taʿan. 4:1, §14). At the same time Jesus' example of the child was even more dramatically countercultural than many of these rabbinic sentiments. Some Tannaim opined that one should begin with the greatest when extolling greatness (Sifra Shemini Mekilta deMilium 99.6.1). Scholars often thought that others should serve them (see comment on 23:7-11); for a certainly hyperbolic example, those who did not serve scholars, including serving them food, could warrant death (ARN 27, §56B)! Likewise, any student who was so presumptuous as to offer a legal decision in front of his teacher might be struck dead (Sifra Shemini Mekilta deMilium 99.5.6; Pesiq. Rab Kah. 26:6/7). Matthew's Jesus may not invert all social power structures in practice, but his rhetoric and example certainly challenge his audience to a more radical consideration of humility than was customary.

First, status in the kingdom is often inversely proportional to status in the world (18:1-4). Ancient moralists regularly trotted forth models of heroes and statesmen for their students to imitate; Jesus instead points to a child. More so then than today, children were powerless, without status and utterly dependent

1. Thom 1994: 109-10 points to formal similarities with one kind of Pythagorean question; but this question reflects more directly a live matter of discussion in Jesus' Jewish milieu (see comment on 5:19).

on the parents (Harrington 1982: 74; Hobbs 1990). On one hand, parents loved their children (cf. Arist. *N.E.* 8.12.2-3, 1161b; Diog. Laert. 7.1.120) and townspeople probably showed their "openness" to neighbors by letting other children pass through one's home and workplace (Malina 1981: 77-78; cf. the LCL introduction to Epictetus, p. xix). On the other hand, perhaps due to the high infant mortality rate among rural peasants (cf. *CIJ* passim, e.g., 1:308, §399), ancient Mediterranean parents sometimes may have been slower than are their modern Western counterparts to attach themselves too deeply to their younger children (Dixon 1988: 113). Yet disciples must imitate such people of no status, people who recognize their dependence.[2] To "turn" reflects the Jewish concept of repentance (e.g., Jer 34:15); such a saying about conversion may also stand behind (hence be attested in) John 3:3, 5 (Witherington 1992: 64; cf. Pryor 1991).[3]

Second, by embracing the weak, association with whom can confer no worldly status, disciples embrace Christ himself (18:5). True disciples are "little ones" (10:42; 18:10, 14) "who believe in Jesus" (18:6), out to make Christ alone great.[4] In contrast to false religious leaders (7:22), children who come "in his name" truly represent him (cf. 18:20; 19:29), and other disciples must "re-

2. On the subordination of children in antiquity, see Keener 1991a: 98; cf. idem 1992b: 187-88. Developing Manson's view, Jeremias 1971: 155-56; idem 1972: 190 finds no Jewish parallels for children as images of humility or purity, and hence suggests that "become as children" means "learn how to say 'Abba'" anew, returning to the waiting Father (cf. Lk 15:18-24; Jn 3:3-5; cf. Snodgrass 1993: 193; on conversion as something of a "new birth" in early Judaism, see, e.g., Davies 1980: 119). Gundry counters that this is Matthean composition in Greek rather than dependence on an Aramaic source (1982: 360). Young 1995: 99 suggests that Jesus alludes to children's sense of wonder and faith; Lachs 1987: 265 sees childlike innocence (not humility); for childlike innocence cf. Herm. 3.9.39; many early interpreters felt that infants were infected with humanity's sin but remained exempt from needing repentance because they had not personally sinned — Cyprian *Letters, Epistle* 58; Augustine *Homily* 50; *ACCS,* 137); one could also argue that the passage refers to children's impressionability to learn new matters quickly (Plut. *Educ.* 5, *Mor.* 3E); or conversely (and nonsensically here) as examples of misbehavior (cf. 11:16-17; some texts in Lindemann 1983). Probably, however, "become as children" refers to assuming a child's low status rather than a characteristic like humility (France 1985: 270; Hagner 1995: 518). Jesus' contemporaries could easily enough understand that a radical sacrifice for the kingdom would lead to eternal reward in the future era (e.g., b. B. Meṣ. 85b in Lachs 1987: 266).

3. If so, it is possible that Matthew may have conflated two sayings to produce this one, perhaps using oral tradition; "receiving the kingdom" like a child in Mk 10:15 reflects a typically Jewish phrase (Vermes 1993: 144) that surely did not originate with Mark. "Conversion" was important in hellenistic philosophy (e.g., Diog. Laert. *Lives* 4.16; 6.2.56; Nock 1933a: 164-86; cf. Meeks 1986: 44, 54; Stowers 1986: 37, 112-13; Malherbe 1986: 56-57; for similarities and differences with Christian conversion, see especially MacMullen 1985-1986), but for the Jewish concept see comment on 3:5-9. "Conversion" appears in various cultural contexts, e.g., the shaman's change of behavior in Eliade 1958: 88.

4. First-century sages debated whether or not children needed to be sprinkled with the sin-offering (m. Para 3:4); they were exempted from many duties (e.g., t. Sanh. 9:11; Ter. 10:18; p. Ḥag. 1:1, §4). Some think that "little ones" was a derisive title coined by Jesus' opponents for his low-status disciples (e.g., Borg 1984: 204), or that the rare "believe in me" is a later addition to Jesus' words (Hatch 1917: 22). Historians' and biographers' editorial freedom to interpret and reword sayings allows such possibilities, but the emphasis of Jesus' teachings on servanthood and the centrality of his own servant mission suggest that such phrases were characteristic of Jesus.

ceive" such little ones (10:40). That is, Jesus is modeled best among the most powerless, not among the powerful.[5]

Causing a Little One to Stumble (18:6-9)

Cf. Mk 9:42-50; Lk 17:1-2. Placing a literal stumbling block before an unsuspecting and vulnerable person was illegal (Lev 19:14), but Jesus was hardly the first to reapply the image figuratively; Greek texts use it for obstacles or opposition (cf. Plut. *Cato Younger* 30.2; Marc. Aur. 7.22). Jewish texts developed the Old Testament (Ezek 14:3, 7; 18:30) sense of the term referring to falling into or leading someone into sin to his or her destruction (Sir 9:5; 25:21; 34:7; 1QS 2.12; 3.24; 1QpHab 11.7-8; Jub. 1:9; Test. Reub. 4:7), or like the righteous stumblingstone of Isaiah (Sir 34:15; 39:24). Causing one to "stumble" meant causing the person to fall from the way of Christ and be damned (e.g., Jn 6:61; 1 Cor 8:9), which merited severe judgment (26:24; cf. Prov 28:10; Rev 2:14; Sifre Deut. 252.1.4; Num. Rab. 21:4). Matthew often uses the term in the same manner as here (17:27; 26:31; cf. 5:29-30; 11:6; 13:41; 16:23; Mk 9:42-47).

First, God will avenge the precious little ones, whom he favors (18:6-7). The cruelest legal punishment in Jesus' day was crucifixion, but this image of drowning represents a Roman punishment more horrifying to Jewish hearers than crucifixion and only rarely tolerated among them.[6] When people in a community had much grain to grind they took it to the community mill, pouring it between an upper and lower millstone. Jesus refers here not to the lighter millstone turned by a woman's hand but to the heavier community kind turned by an ass — heavy enough to take one quickly to the bottom (Deissmann 1978: 81; cf. 1 Enoch 48:9).[7] Jesus says that this punishment would be an act of mercy compared to what is in store for those who turn little ones from Christ's way.[8]

5. Though following much of Mark's sequence, Matthew omits Mk 9:38-41. May Matthew do so to avoid permitting the impression that he condones false exorcists in his community (cf. 7:22)?

6. Jeremias 1972: 180; Nineham 1977: 258; Carson 1984b: 398; cf. Livy 1.51.9 (drowned with a crate full of stones); 27.37.5-7 (newborn hermaphrodite); Babrius 27 (weasels); meanwhile, Livy claims that the Romans exercised more humane punishments than other peoples (Livy 1.28.11). For an exception, see Jos. *Ant.* 14.450.

7. Derrett 1985 thinks that the millstone counts as a different kind of stumbling stone, avenging the crime of the lighter stone. A donkey could pull about half the weight a mule could, easily over a hundred pounds (cf. Rapske 1994: 8); at worst, one would use an old horse (Babrius 29.1-2). The image of a "millstone around the neck" may have also become a traditional figure for an encumbrance (b. Qidd. 29b. bar.).

8. The saying has Palestinian Jewish features: woes are characteristic of Jesus (23:13; 24:19); rabbis sometimes described a great burden as a "millstone around the neck" (though Jesus clearly means the language more strongly here — Vermes 1993: 84). Most significantly, "better never to have been born" was also typically Jewish (26:24; 1 Enoch 38:2; 4 Ezra 7:69; 2 Bar. 10:6; ARN 29A; b. Qidd. 40a). Given Jesus' sense of his own mission, we are not surprised that he would declare that the "world" (cf. 5:14) would merit judgment for its oppression of his little ones; "it is better" also fits his (as well as others') usage (5:30; cf. the disciples in 19:10).

Second, avoiding hell is worth *any* price (18:8-9). Here the image shifts from others as the cause of stumbling to personal responsibility; perhaps Matthew's source may have combined disparate material (5:29; Mk 9:42-47; cf. Taylor 1935: 92). Because Judaism so abhorred self-mutilation (Dalman 1929: 227), that injury provided a stark image of the cost one must be willing to pay to avoid spiritual death.[9] "Entering life" was shorthand for "entering the life of the coming age" (19:17).[10] The language of losing limbs was the language of the price martyrs paid for their devotion to God (2 Macc 7:11; 4 Macc 10:20; Lane 1974a: 348). According to a common Jewish belief (e.g., 2 Bar. 50:2-4; Montefiore 1968: 1:222; cf. 2 Macc 7:11; 14:46), a person with missing members would be resurrected in that form before being restored.[11]

Go After the Straying Sheep (18:10-14)

Cf. Lk 15:3-7; on possible translation variants between the two pasasages, cf., e.g., Jeremias 1972: 133. The similar parable in the context of Luke 15:11-24 emphasizes God's pursuit of the lost sheep; in this context, however, the parable summons those who share God's concerns to pursue the lost sheep (Jeremias 1972: 39-40).[12] By his ingenious arrangement of the material, Matthew demonstrates that overbearing leaders unwilling to forgive the repentant fall into the same category as those who caused the stumbling to begin with. As some rabbis did (Marmorstein 1968c: 69), Matthew's audience should be ready to lament leaders in the religious community who are more concerned with their own reputation and position than with the needs of the people (20:25-28; 23:5-12; 24:45-51).

First, Jesus reveals how God feels toward each sheep, even the weakest (18:10, 13-14). Although scholars have proposed various interpretations (e.g., "angels" means the spirits of the little ones after death or the resurrection, as perhaps in Acts 12:15; Mt 22:30; 1 Enoch 104:2; 2 Bar. 51:5, 10, 12; Prayer of Joseph 19; Acts of Paul 3:5; cf. 1 Enoch 51:5; Ps-Phocyl. 104; the view of Carson 1984b:

9. Boring 1995: 113-14, also provides relevant Greek parallels concerning those willing to suffer amputation for a greater good (Plato *Symp.* 204CE; Xen. *Mem.* 1.54; Arist. *E.E.* 7.1; Philo *Worse Attacks Better* 174-75; and especially Porphyry *Letter to Marcella* 34).

10. Cf. the common Jewish expressions "life of the world to come" (e.g., m. 'Abot 2:7; Sifre Deut. 305.3.2-3; *CIJ* 1:474, §661), "eternal life" (= "life of the world"; Ps. Sol. 3:12; 13:11; *CIJ* 1:422, §569; 2:443, §1536; cf. Philo *Fug.* 77), and "life" (Tob 12:9-10; Test. Abr. 11B; Herm. 1.1.1). Compare "entering life" with "entering the kingdom" (5:20; 7:21; 19:24).

11. Addley 1976 and Koester 1978 find behind the original sayings the exclusion of offending members of Christ's body in excommunication. This view also makes some sense of the context, especially in Matthew (cf. also Xen. *Mem.* 1.54), but native Palestinian Jewish images followed above seem more suggestive.

12. For God's people as straying sheep, see, e.g., Ps 119:176; Is 53:6; Jer 23:1-4; Ezek 34:11-16; Mt 9:36; 10:6. Sheep were less prone to stray than most animals (Aelian *Animals* 7.27). Some rabbis also emphasized properly balancing welcome and discipline (b. Sanh. 107b, bar.)

401), the majority view and the most satisfactory interpretation of this passage in light of ancient Jewish ways of speaking would refer to guardian angels (see Davies and Allison 1991: 770-72).[13] The guardian angels of these children were of the highest rank (18:10), indicating their special place before God (cf. Jeremias 1971: 182; Meier 1980: 203-4; cf. perhaps 1 Enoch 43:4; Gen. Rab. 68:12).[14] In Palestinian Jewish idiom, 18:14 even more explicitly reiterates that "it is not God's will for even the very least to be lost" (Jeremias 1971: 10, 39; idem 1972: 39-40; cf. 1 Tim 2:4-5; 2 Pet 3:9; for the emphasis on God's will, e.g., 7:21; 21:31).

Secondly, Jesus summons those who share God's concerns to go after those who stray from his way (18:12). It is not enough simply not to cause stumbling; disciples must also actively seek to prevent anyone from stumbling. Higher-status urban Jews probably looked down on shepherds the way later teachers did;[15] shepherds represented a lower-class occupation in the Empire period in general (MacMullen 1974: 1-2, 15). Yet the image probably does not function totally negatively here (cf. Jos. *Ant.* 1.53); Moses, David, and Amos were shepherds (Ex 3:1; 1 Sam 16:11; 17:15, 28, 34-37; Amos 1:1; 7:14-15),[16] in

13. On guardian angels in Judaism, cf., e.g., Heb 1:14; Ps-Philo 11:12; 59:4; t. Shab. 17:2-3; Sifre Num. 40.1.5; Gen. Rab. 44:3; 60:15; Song Rab. 3:6, §3; Philo *Gig.* 9. Cf. Plotinus 3.4.6 and the Roman *genii* (Malina and Rohrbaugh 1992: 117; cf. Herm. 1.5) for pagan parallels. The step from nations having guardian angels (Dan 10; 12:1) to individuals having them was not large. Guardian angels and deceased spirits are not irreconcilable (in Hesiod *W.D.* 122 deceased members of the golden race now function as guardian spirits) but cannot both be in view simultaneously here.

14. The expression "seeing the face" applied particularly to access to a ruler, only the highest officials of whom had such access "always" (see Gundry 1982: 364). Angels nearest the throne were those of the highest rank, which normally did not include guardian angels (cf. Gaster 1976: 287; Hagner 1995: 526-27; Test. Job 33:2-3), except for Israel's own guardian angel Michael (and sometimes Israel saw itself as God's oppressed "little ones" — 2 Bar. 48:19). Double angels appear under particular circumstances in early Amoraic literature; see *JE* 1: 587; cf. Bonsirven 1964: 36. Cf. connections between the righteous on earth and angels (Jub. 31:14; 1QS 11.8; comment on 5:22.

15. B. Sanh. 25b; Jeremias 1972: 132-33; idem 1971: 110; idem 1975: 304; Bailey 1976: 147; Tooley 1964: 23; Bailey 1976: 147; Malina and Rohrbaugh 1992: 118.

16. "Shepherds" provided a natural analogy for rulers (cf. Anacharsis to Tereus 7; Artem. *Oneir.* 2.12); frequently for leaders in Homer (e.g., *Il.* 1.263; 2.85, 105; 4.296; 5.144, 513; 6.214; 8.81; 10.3, 73, 406; 11.92, 202, 370, 465, 842; 13.411, 600; 15.262; 16.2; 19.386; 20.110; 22.277; 23.389; *Od.* 4.24; 17.109; 18.70; 24.456; especially Agamemnon, *Il.* 2.243, 254; 4.413; 7.230; 19.35, 251; 24.654; *Od.* 3.156; 14.497) and continued later (Hesiod *Theog.* 1000). Natural shepherds like David and Moses easily became "shepherds" of Israel. David became a shepherd of Israel in his generation and the future (2 Sam 5:2; 1 Chron 11:2; Ps 78:70-72; Ezek 34:23; 37:24; in later literature, cf. Ps. Sol. 17:40; Gen. Rab. 59:5). The psalmist calls Moses a shepherd of Israel (Ps 77:20; Is 63:11), as do later texts (1 Enoch 89.35; Ps-Philo 19.3; Sifre Deut. 305.3.1; p. Sanh. 10:1, §9; Soṭa 5:4, §1; Pesiq. Rab Kah. 2:8; Ex. Rab. 2:2; Marmorstein 1968: 100-101). The Davidic Messiah (Mic 5:2-4; cf. Jer 23:1-6; Longenecker 1981: 48-49) and sometimes Jewish teachers (Derrett 1973: 26-28) appear as shepherds. The spiritual leaders God assigned to care for his flock for him were also "shepherds" (Num 27:17; 1 Kings 22:17; Jer 3:15; Mek. Pisha 1.162-63; CD 19.8-9); righteous prophets often ironically labeled Israel's unjust leaders by this title (Is 56:11; Jer 22:22; 23:1-4; 25:34-36; Zech 10:3; 11:5, 15-17; 13:4-7). When God portrays Israel as a scattered or lost flock, his shepherds are often to blame (Jer 10:21; 50:6-7; Ezek 34:1-10). (Some information on shepherds here also appears in my article for InterVarsity Press's *Dictionary of the Later New Testament and Its Developments,* 1090-93.)

the early period the ancient Israelites were mainly shepherds (Gen 46:32; 47:3; Num 14:33; Jos. *Apion* 1.91), and the God of Israel regularly appeared in such terms in the Scriptures (including Ezek 34).[17]

Jesus' portrait of the shepherd is realistic. "One hundred" was common as a round number in Jewish illustrations (Manson 1979: 208), but was also the number of an average-size flock (Jeremias 1972: 133; cf. eighty in *P. Hib.* 33.16); three hundred was large (t. B. Qam. 6:20; cf. Hom. *Od.* 12.129-30; 1 Sam 25:2), and twelve (e.g., *P. Oxy.* 245) small (poor was the widow with but one sheep — Babrius 51.1). Naturally shepherds and goatherds had to keep careful watch to prevent any animals from straying (e.g., Longus 1.10). Contemporary evidence indicates that shepherds and cowherds did leave their flocks or herds to search for lost animals (1 Sam 9:3; Diog. Laert. 1.109; Hock 1988: 139, citing Longus 1.5.1-2; Bultmann 1968: 202; Vermes 1993: 101 citing Gen. Rab. 86:4), as does the practice of more recent Palestinian shepherds (Jeremias 1972: 133); often shepherds would leave sheep with other shepherds (cf. Lk 2:8; Longus 3.29; Bailey 1976: 149; cf. t. B. Qam. 6:20). In rugged terrain, shepherds often became skilled mountaineers (Diod. Sic. 33.1.1); shepherds commonly grazed their flocks in the mountains, as here (e.g., Babrius 91.2). One might bring back a lost sheep or goat by placing it over one's shoulder (Lk 15:5; Ex. Rab. 2:2). Like God, his true shepherd will search for the straying sheep (Ezek 34:4, 11; cf. Riesenfeld 1970: 151).[18]

Addressing Stumbling Blocks Seriously (18:15-20)

Cf. Lk 17:3. Given standard ancient usage for "brother," the sinning "brother" here is a member of one's religious community, the church (Manson 1979: 210).[19] Disciples must pursue the straying sheep (18:10-14), but certain very ex-

17. For God as shepherd, see Ps 23:1-4; 28:9; 74:1-2; 77:20; 78:52; 79:13; 80:1; 100:3; Is 40:11; Jer 13:17; 31:10; Ezek 34:11-17; Mic 7:14; Zech 9:16; 10:3; Sir 18:13; 1 Enoch 89.18; Philo *Agr.* 50-53; Ps-Philo 28.5; 30.5; b. Ḥag. 3b; Pesaḥ. 118a; Ex. Rab. 34:3; Lam. Rab. 1:17, §52; Pesiq. R. 3:2. He carried the young (Ps 28:9; Is 40:11; 46:3-4) and led his flock as in the first exodus (Ps 77:20; 78:52; 80:1; Is 40:11; 63:14; cf. Ex 13:21; 15:13; Deut 8:2; Neh. 9:12; Ps 78:14; 106:9; 136:16; Is 48:21; Jer 2:6, 17; Hos 11:3-4; Amos 2:10). Thus God led and protected his people, for whom he cared. Israel nearly always appears as God's flock; see, e.g., Ps 74:1; 77:20; 78:52; 79:13; 80:1; 100:3; Is 49:9; 63:11; Jer 13:17; 31:10; Zech 9:16; 10:3; 1 Enoch 89-90; 4 Ezra 5:23-24; Ps-Philo 23:12; Mek. Pisha 1.162; Ex. Rab. 24:3; Pesiq. R. 9:2; 26:2. (Sir 18:13 and Philo *Agr.* 50-53 are exceptions.) Again, see my article for the *Dictionary of the Later New Testament*.

18. Textual evidence with wide geographical distribution and patristic support argues for the omission of v. 11. Although it is authentic Jesus tradition (Lk 19:10) and the idea is not foreign to the text of Matthew (cf. 10:6), this verse interrupts the flow of the context here.

19. Brother-sister ties were normally quite close (e.g., Dixon 1988: 19, citing *CIL* 6.9868, 12564, 22423); ancients used "brother" for coinitiates into mysteries (Burkert 1987: 45, citing Andocides 1.132; Plato *Epistles* 7.333E; Plut. *Dio* 56; Sopatros *Rhet. Gr.* 8.123), close friends (Ahiqar 49, col. 4; Plut. *Many Friends* 2, *Mor.* 93E; Marc. Aur. *Med.* 1.14; cf. *CPJ* 3:41, §479), or potential allies (1 Kings 20:32-33; 1 Macc 10:18; 12:6, 10, 21; 14:40). Jewish circles used the title for

ceptional circumstances demand expulsion of wolves in sheep's clothing who may not wish to leave (18:15-20; cf. 7:15-23). In this context of forgiveness to the fullest possible extent (18:21-27), however, even in the case of expulsion the ultimate goal remains restoration (cf. 18:19-20; 1 Cor 5:5; 2 Cor 2:5-11; 1 Tim 1:20; cf. also, e.g., Pfitzner 1982). The unpardonable sin of this context is being a continuing stumbling block to others (18:6-7, 15),[20] unwilling to accept them (18:28-33; cf. 18:1-14) — a sin that results in damnation (18:34-35). Presumably it is an unrepentant and continuing sin against the community or members of the community.

First, a disciple must admonish his or her fellow privately before taking any other steps (18:15). Although Jewish teachers preferred that the offender seek forgiveness first (as many as three times before witnesses if necessary — Edersheim: 378; as long as necessary — cf. b. Ber. 28a; p. B. Qam. 8:7, §1), Jewish law also emphasized proper giving and receiving of reproof (Sifra Qed. pq. 4.200.3.3; Sifre Deut. 1.3.2; b. ʿArak. 16b, bar.; Shab. 119b; Tamid 28a, bar.; Gen. Rab. 54:3; Manson 1979: 210), that admonition must always precede punishment (Sifre Deut. 173.1.2; p. Sanh. 7:6, §2), and it must continue until the offender repents or decisively repulses the reprover (Moore 1971: 2:153).[21] One who reproves must do so with the proper attitude (1QS 5.25; CD 7.2-3).

Like some other ancient moralists (Plut. *Flatterer* 32 in Boring 1995: 115), rabbis emphasized that reproof was to be private (e.g., b. Sanh. 101a) and taken before witnesses only if necessary (Edersheim: 378, cites b. Shab. 119b; Tamid 28a; ʿArak. 16b; see Beer 1988). A sage could hyperbolically rule that publicly shaming one's fellow warrants exclusion from the coming age (m. ʾAbot 3:11; also b. Sanh. 107a; other references in Urbach 1979: 1:253). The Scrolls, which include record keeping of rebukes (for offenses like anger and pride; 4Q477; Eshel 1994), also emphasize this sequence: private reproof, then before witnesses, and finally before the gathered assembly (cf. Schiffman 1983: 97-98; Davies 1966b: 79; Brown 1972: 4); the Qumranites detested disrespect for fellow members of the community (e.g., 1QS 6.26–7.9; 7.15-16). That Josephus adds to Exodus 18:14 this principle of private correction in *Antiquities* 3.67 reinforces the probability that Jewish people expected private reproof. Public admonition thus represented the form of rebuke reserved for the severest of circumstances (cf. Gal 2:14; t. Kip. 4:12).

---

exemplary hospitality toward a stranger (Test. Abr. 2B) and one rabbi's title for another (Sifre Deut. 34.5.3; b. ʿAbod. Zar. 18a, bar.), and Israelites addressed fellow Israelites in such terms (e.g., Tob 5:10; 6:10; 7:3; 2 Macc 1:1). In Matthew the term applies to fellow disciples (23:8-9; 25:40; 28:10; cf. 6:9; 12:49-50).

20. Some of the earliest manuscripts omit the words "against you" in 18:15, but the early geographical distribution favors their inclusion; cf. Metzger 1971: 45.

21. Though to a lesser extent, some Greek and Roman moralists also recognized the importance of reproof (Pub. Syr. 10; Malherbe 1986: 48). This provides a broader context for the rabbinic practice (Hallevy 1982). Hunter 1961: 48 may well be right that Gal 6:1 depends on Jesus' teaching here, but one cannot argue this case based on lack of other available parallels.

Second, although disciples seek reconciliation, they must gather evidence in the proper order in case they later need proof of what transpired (18:16). As community centers, synagogues doubled as local courts, a function they maintained when evaluating internal disputes in Diaspora Jewish communities (cf. Grant 1977: 38; comment on 10:17). Judaism was strict about the need for witnesses (Syr. Men. Sent. 142; t. Sanh. 8:3), and later Jewish teachers regularly echoed the judicial requirement of two witnesses in Deuteronomy 17:6-7 and 19:15 (Jos. *Life* 256; *Ant.* 4.219; CD 9.17-23; 11QTemple 61.6-7; 64.8; Sifre Deut. 148.1.1; 188.2.1-2; 188.3.1-2; b. Sanh. 37b, bar.; p. Giṭ. 4:1, §2; Sanh. 6:3, §3; Smith 1951: 169; cf. Heb 10:28); they required a pair of witnesses even to attest the new moon (m. Rosh Hash. 1:7; 2:6). Under their rules, to speak evil of another without supporting witnesses warranted a public beating (Belkin 1940: 267). The requirement of two witnesses remained standard judicial procedure in early Christianity (2 Cor 13:1-2; 1 Tim 5:19-20). (Because m. Sanh. 1:1 indicates that normal as opposed to capital cases required only three judges, Matthew might suggest that Christian witnesses are competent as judges; but the Mishnah's number of judges may be later than Matthew's period.) Other Jewish groups also required confronting an erring person before witnesses before the matter could be brought before the public assembly (1QS 5.25–6.1; CD 9.3-4).

Third, if all else fails, the messianic community must publicly dissociate itself from a habitually sinning professed disciple (18:17). Neither outsiders nor the sinner should continue under the delusion that this person is truly a follower of Jesus. One should treat such a person as a tax gatherer (cf. 9:9; 21:32) or a Gentile (cf. 5:47; 6:7; 20:25; cf. Pol. *Phil.* 11) — unclean and to be avoided. Although lesser forms of public discipline existed (e.g., 1QS 6.25 vs. 5.16-17; p. Moʿed Qaṭ. 3:1, §§4, 10; 2 Thess 3:6; Edersheim: 407), the discipline urged here was full excommunication, implying spiritual death (1 Cor 5:5; 1 Tim 1:20; Titus 3:10-11).

Fourth, God authorizes the messianic judicial assembly that follows these procedures to act on the authority of heaven (18:18). The verb tenses literally represent the cumbersome "whatever you bind . . . shall have been bound," which grammatically need not but could mean what the context probably suggests: that their earthly action followed the heavenly action.[22] Presumably the "binding and loosing" here (cf. comment on 16:19) mean that "the halakic decisions of the community have the authority of heaven itself" (Davies and Allison 1991: 787).[23] In this context, halakic authority applies to judicial decrees and not merely legal theory. By removing an unrepentant sinner from Jesus' community, believers merely ratify the heavenly court's decree;[24] to borrow Johannine language, they

22. For specific grammatical arguments for either reading of the construction, see Mantey 1973; Marshall 1974; Carson 1984b: 370-72; France 1985: 256; Blomberg 1992a: 255 following Porter 1988.

23. The image would not be unfamiliar to an ancient audience; even in classical Athens, lawbreakers acted lawlessly against the gods, hence a jury might execute justice or vengeance "in place of the gods" (prosecutor in Ps-Demosth. *Or.* 59, *Against Neaera* 126, LCL 6:448-51).

24. For a detailed discussion of the background of the heavenly court here, see Keener 1991a:

merely remove branches already dead on the vine (cf. Jn 15:2, 6). The person has been excluded not only from the community but from salvation (Overman 1990b: 104). "Binding" and "loosing" refer to the judicial authority of gathered Christians to decide cases on the basis of God's law.[25] Most scholars thus recognize that this passage applies to church discipline (Cullmann 1973: 204-5; Fuller 1971: 141).[26]

Fifth, the witnesses are to pray, not to act vindictively (18:19-20). Some suggest that this verse is misplaced from the tradition (Albright and Mann 1971: 221) or that it refers to arbitration rather than prayer (Derrett 1979b), but the verse makes perfect sense in this context. The "two" or "three" gathered for prayer in 18:19-20 must be the "two or three" witnesses of 18:16; the "matter" (cf. the similar forensic use of the general term in 1 Cor 6:1) concerning which they agree is prayer for the offender. Whereas in Deuteronomy 17:6-7 the two or three witnesses were to be the first to cast stones, here they are to be the first to pray. While this could refer to the negative prayer of execration (which may have been more of a curse — cf. 1 Cor 5:5; 1 Tim 1:20; Marshall 1974: 48; cf. 21:19-22; on curse-tablets, cf., e.g., Jordan 1985; Corn. Nep. 7 [Alcibiades], 4.5), in this context of forgiveness the prayer may represent a prayer for ultimate restoration (though cf. 1 Jn 5:16-17). Jewish excommunication even in its long-term form was normally reversible if repentance took place (p. Moʿed Qaṭ. 3:1, §11; though cf. the extreme cases in 1QS 7.1-2, 16-17, 24-25).[27]

Finally, Jesus himself is the presence of God (18:20). An ancient Jewish saying promised God's presence not only for ten males (the minimum prerequisite for a synagogue — b. Ber. 6ab; Meg. 23b; p. Meg. 4:4, §5; Reicke 1974: 121; 1QS 6.3, 6; CD 13.2-3), but for even two or three gathered to study his law (m. 'Abot 3:2, 6; Mek. Bah. 11.48ff.; cf. m. Ber. 7:3).[28] Here Jesus himself fills

141-43. At least some Jewish circles affirmed that the judgments of earthly judges who extrapolated the law properly would always coincide with God's (t. Rosh Hash. 1:18; ARN 2A). Cf. the rabbinic idea in which God ratifies decrees of the *earthly* Beth Din (e.g., on when months occur) — Pesiq. Rab Kah. 5:13; 23:4; p. Rosh Hash. 1:3, §28 (cf. m. Rosh Hash. 3:1; t. Rosh Hash. 1:18; p. Rosh Hash. 3:1, §17). When earthly courts could not execute a requisite death sentence, the heavenly court would do so (t. Sanh. 14:16; Mak. 5:16; ARN 25A; p. Ketub. 3:1, §8; Deut. Rab. 5:5; Midr. Ps 72, §3); for a heavenly "ban" cf. Sifra V. D. Den. pq. 2.2.4.1.

25. In later Jewish literature "binding" and "loosing" signify legislative authority through interpreting the law and mean "prohibiting" and "permitting," respectively, regularly in rabbinic texts (e.g., m. Giṭ. 9:1; t. Sanh. 7:2; b. ʿAbod. Zar. 7a, bar.; ʿErub. 17a; Ḥul. 39b, bar.; Pesaḥ. 42a; p. Ter. 11:7; Beṣa 3:6, §5; 55:2, §13; Gen. Rab. 7:2; 80:9; 85:5; Num. Rab. 20:24; Deut. Rab. 2:19; cf. perhaps Mt 23:4). This legislative authority could be extended judicially, and the terms also naturally apply figuratively to judicial action, given the literal use for detaining and releasing prisoners (e.g., Jos. *War* 1.111; pace Thompson 1970: 190). The neuter *hosa* ("whatever") can include persons (Carson 1984b: 372).

26. The passage does not refer to the ancient practice in the magical papyri of manipulating demons to perform the magician's will, e.g., using a curse and a demon to bind a person from speaking any further against someone (Lefkowitz and Fant 1982: 257; see comment on 12:24). For "divorces" (lit. meaning, "sending away") of demons from people (exorcisms), see Aramaic incant. text 18.1; 19.5-6.

27. Jos. *War* 2.143-44 thinks that in practice the Essenes often mercifully readmitted those expelled.

28. Study of Torah invites the Holy Spirit's presence (b. Mak. 23b). Whenever possible, Jew-

the role of the Shekinah, God's presence, in the traditional Jewish saying (which probably predates this saying, since the rabbis would not likely borrow it from Christian sources; cf. Smith 1951: 152-53; Meier 1980: 206; Barth 1963: 135; Sievers 1984).[29] Jewish teachers often called God "the Place," that is, "the Omnipresent One";[30] Jesus is "God with us" (1:23; 28:20).[31]

Forgiveness (18:21-35)

On Mt 18:21-22, cf. Lk 17:4. This parable employs very Matthean language (Gundry 1982: 371-72). Its point is that one's fellow disciples (18:28-29) are Christ's representatives no less than oneself (18:5-6), and God will avenge their harsh treatment at the hands of those who claim his mercy for themselves.

First, a disciple's forgiveness should be unlimited (18:21-22).[32] Judaism also stressed forgiveness (Ladd 1974b: 130 cites Test. Gad 6:3), though some teachers saw the need to limit forgiveness to three instances of *premeditated* sin, whose repentance was hence not genuine (ARN 40A; cf. Blomberg 1992a: 281,

---

ish disciples studied in groups of two or three (ARN 8A). With the exception of very prominent individuals, later rabbis also disapproved of judging alone (cf. m. 'Abot 4:8; p. Sanh. 1:1, §§4-5; cf. comment on Mt 7:1).

29. Cf. Ziesler 1984, comparing Jesus' presence with Yahweh's in the OT. Davies and Allison 1991: 790, with most scholars (e.g., Stanton 1995a: 60), regard the saying "as an utterance of the risen Lord" (i.e., not "authentic" in the sense of deriving from Jesus before the resurrection). At the same time they concede that they cannot be dogmatic; was Paul the only person to speak "of being spiritually present with others"? But Mt 18:20 means far more than 1 Cor 5:3-5 (which, pace Fee 1987: 205, communicates merely *epistolary* presence — cf. 1 Thess 2:17; Col 2:5; Isoc. *Nic./Cypr.* 51-52, *Or.* 3.37; Sen. *Ep. Lucil.* 32.1; cf. Funk 1967: 264; Hock 1988: 142; Stowers 1986: 58; though contrast Diog. *Ep.* 17 to Antalcides). If Jesus did offer this saying in anticipation of his resurrection, he communicated a point to his disciples the full impact of which they were unprepared to grasp.

30. Although Judaism in general accepted God's omnipresence (Sib. Or. 3.701; sometimes qualified in practice — Mek. Pisha 1), the title especially appears in later rabbinic tradition, e.g., 3 Enoch 18:24; m. 'Abot 2:9, 13; 3:14; t. Pe'a 1:4; 3:8; Shab. 7:22, 25; 13:5; Rosh Hash. 1:18; Ta'an. 2:13; B. Qam. 7:7; Sanh. 1:2; 13:1, 6; 14:3, 10; Sifre Num. 11.2.3; 11.3.1; 42/1/2; 42.2.3; 76.2.2; 78.1.1; 78.5.1; 80.1.1; 82.3.1; 84.1.1; 84.5.1; 85.3.1; 85.4.1; 85.5.1; Sifra V. D. Den. pq. 2.2.4.2; 4.6.4.1; Sifra Sav Mekhilta deMiluim par. 98.7.7; Shemini Mekhilta deMiluim 99.1.4, 5, 7; 99.2.2, 3; 99.3.9, 11; 99.5.13; Sifra Qed. par. 1.195.2.3; pq. 7.204.1.4; Sifra Emor pq. 9.227.1.5; Behuq. pq. 5.266.1.1; Sifre Deut. 1.8.3; 1.9.2; 1.10.4; 2.1.1; 11.1.1; 21.1.1; 24.3.1; 26.4.1; 28.1.1; 32.3.2; 32.5.8; 33.1.1; 37.1.1, 3; 38.1.1, 3; see Keener 1991a: 150n.27 for fuller documentation. Among Greeks, cf. Diog. Laert. 6.2.38.

31. One may exclude this saying from the words of the historical Jesus (e.g., Flusser 1988: 515) only if one a priori assumes that wisdom Christology (here, Shekinah Christology) originated among Jesus' followers after his departure — by excluding a number of Jesus' sayings (e.g., 23:34; 24:36) in favor of this hypothesis. (For the thesis that wisdom Christology originated with Jesus, see Witherington 1994; while the thesis does not match traditional modern theories of Christology's evolution, I believe that it best addresses the evidence of the texts.)

32. Bultmann (1968: 141) thinks that Luke 17:3-4 may preserve the earlier setting; whether Matthew expanded or Luke abbreviated (cf. Lk 16:17-18//Mt 5:18, 32), however, both follow the same original sequence (Mt 18:15, 22).

citing b. Yoma 86b; 87a; Herm. 2.4.1 is stricter, perhaps deliberately). But Jesus here reverses the principle of 490fold (Gen 4:24 LXX; Argyle 1963: 142) or seventy-sevenfold (Gen 4:24, where LXX uses the exact phrase; Carson 1984b: 405; France 1985: 277) vengeance.

Second, the magnitude of God's saving grace is the proper model for forgiveness (18:23-27). Although "the central theme of forgiveness" described here "belongs to the kernel of Jesus' preaching," Vermes 1993: 106 doubts the parable's authenticity; it treats a clearly Gentile court quite different from the Galilean surroundings of most of Jesus' parables. Vermes is right about the court's being Gentile (also Derrett 1970: 35), but he applies the criterion of coherence too narrowly here; the Gentile court provides the requisite suspense for the awfulness of the punishments, and the exaggerations fit Jesus' love for hyperbole and graphic confrontation. Moreover, Galileans were quite aware of some features of royal courts outside Palestine (20:25), and while Jesus usually prefers parables set in the countryside, such is not always the case (e.g., 22:1-14; 25:14-30;[33] Lk 18:10-14). Indeed, examples of Gentile royal authority affected models of royalty in Palestine; even in Palestine rulers had multiple waiting rooms with long benches (Wilkinson 1978: 26), and Antipas, like Herod the Great, accommodated hellenistic models where possible (cf. comment on 14:1-12). Likewise, the language of God's "kingdom" virtually invites a royal comparison. As common as kings become in later rabbinic parables (where they nearly always represent God),[34] we probably should not begrudge Jesus a few.[35]

33. 22:1-14 and 25:14-30 have distant Lukan parallels, the distance of which may suggest a pre-Q oral tradition behind both Matthew and Luke in these cases, or separate parables (possibly somewhat conflated in the tradition) attesting a different *kind* of parable than those that appealed to compilers like Mark or Q.

34. Tos. Ber. 6:18; B. Qam. 7:2, 4; Sanh. 8:9; Suk. 2:6; Mek. Beshallah 6.8-9; Shirata 2.131ff; 3.30, 65; 4.54ff; Amalek 2.22-23; Bahodesh 5.2-3, 82-83; 6.114ff; 8.72ff; Sifra Shemini Mekhilta deMiluim 99.2.2, 5; Behuq. pq. 2.262.1.9; pq. 3.263.1.5; Sifre Num. 84.1.1; 84.2.1; 86.1.1; Sifre Deut. 3.1.1; 8.1.2; 11.1.2; 26.3.1; 27.6.1; 28.1.1; 29.4.1; 36.4.1; 40.6.1; 43.8.1; 43.16.1; 45.1.2; 48.1.3; 53.1.3; 306.4.1; 306.7.1; 312.1.1; 313.1.1; 343.1.2; 343.5.2; 349.1.1; 352.7.1, 4; 355.17.9; 357.18.2; ARN 2; 16; 19; 24; 25A; 2, §10; 8, §24B; 34, §77; b. Ber. 33b; Hag. 16a; Pes. 56a; Sanh. 91a; p. Rosh Hash. 1:3, §§32-34; Ta'an. 2:1, §11; Pesiq. Rab Kah. 1:1-3; 2:7-8; 3:9; 4:2, 8; 5:11, 13; 6:3; 9:5; 11:6; 12:11, 19; 13:11; 14:5; 15:3-4; 16:9; 19:2, 4-5; 21:3; 24:11; 25:4; 26:9; 28:7, 9; Sup. 5:3; 7:3; Gen. Rab. 12:1, 15-16; 28:6; 47:4; 52:5; 56:11; 57:4; 61:6; 62:2; 67:12; Ex. Rab. 2:2; 3:4; 15:9-10, 30-31; 18:10; 19:7; 20:1, 14; 21:8; 29:3-4; 30:9, 20; 43:1, 6; 44:4; 48:3; 52:5; Lev. Rab. 1:13, 14; 2:5; 5:3; 6:5; 10:3; 18:1; 27:10; 31:4, 10; 32:2; Num. Rab. 2:15; 4:1, 20; 8:2; 12:4; 13:2; 15:3; 16:7, 21; 18:9; 19:17; Deut. Rab. 3:3, 7, 10; 4:5; 7:4, 9; 10:4; Ruth Rab. Proem 7; Ruth Rab. 8:1; Lam. Rab. 1:17, §52; 2:1, §3; 3:1, §1; 3:20, §7; Koh. Rab. 1:1, §1; 2:12, §1; 5:10, §2; 5:11, §1; 12:13, §1; Song Rab. 1:9, §5; 3:6, §3; 3:10, §2; 4:12, §1; 5:1, §1; 5:16, §§3, 6; 6:2, §6; 6:11, §1; 6:12, §1; 7:2; 7:14, §1; 8:9, §2; 8:11, §2; Pesiq. R. 8:2; 15.preamble; 15:17, 18; 20:2; 21:9, 15; 29/30:2; 29/30A:9; 31:3; 39:2; 52:6; cf. Test. Abr. 2A; Apoc. Ezek. 1. For one study of five king parables in Mekilta, see Plank 1979. Although most surviving parables are rabbinic, the image of God as king is much wider, e.g., Jdt 9:12; Tob 13:6; 1 Enoch 25:3, 5; 91:13; Sib. Or. 1.73; 3.11, 56, 499, 704; Philo *Prob.* 20; cf. perhaps *PGM* 1.164. In other cultures, cf., e.g., Epict. *Diss.* 1.6.40; Cleanthes' *Hymn to Zeus* in Stob. *Eclogae* 1.1.12; Mbiti 1970: 58-59. Stories often opened with kings (Apul. *Metam.* 4.28).

35. That one does not find *many* examples in Jesus' teaching should not surprise us given his

The parable emphasizes that no one can offend our human moral sensibilities as much as everyone offends the moral sensibilities of a perfect God. The parable accordingly underlines the magnitude of God's forgiveness, a point unlikely to be lost on Jesus' hearers; other Jewish teachers also praised God's forgiveness.[36]

Once the hellenistic aura of the court is taken into account, the setting is realistic, underlining the impossibly unrealistic character of the debt and the characters' absurd folly. A king's "servants" could refer to his higher officials, like provincial satraps (Jeremias 1972: 210, 212; Meier 1980: 208; Via 1967: 138; but contrast Gundry 1982: 373-74). Possibly the "servants" here are tax farmers working for the king; under the old Ptolemaic system in Egypt, tax farmers would bid on collecting taxes for the king and could generally turn a profit — provided everyone paid.[37] Because these tax farmers were responsible to collect the taxes for the king, they could become quite ruthless in their efficiency.[38]

At the appropriate time of year, the king is "settling accounts" with his servants (cf. 25:19; for the phrase, cf. Deissmann 1978: 117, citing *P. Oxy.* 113; *B.G.U.* 775.18-19). Although the extravagant image probably stems from Esther 3:9 (where the talents are, however, of silver) and the talent's worth varied in different periods, 10,000 talents represented between 60 and 100 million denarii (30-100 million days' wages for an average peasant — no small amount of labor). Further, the real worth of the debt in this story may be greater still: 10,000 being the largest single number Greek could express and the talent being the largest unit of currency, Jesus is making the parable particularly graphic. The combined annual tribute of Galilee and Perea just after the death of the repressive Herod the Great came to only 200 talents (Jos. *Ant.* 17.318; Jeremias 1972: 30); the tribute of Judea, Samaria, and Idumea came to 600 talents (Jos. *Ant.* 17.320).[39] This fact starkly reveals the laughably hyperbolic character of the il-

era and his audience. Johnston 1977b: 583 finds the king (nearly always representing God) in over half the Tannaitic parables, noting that this stereotypical feature was often added in the course of developing tradition. Stern 1991: 19-21 gives examples of this transformation, especially from Tannaitic to Amoraic sources: Mek. Beshallah 2 and Pesiq. Rab Kah. 11:3; Mek. Beshallah 4 and Ex. Rab. 21:8; Mek. Bah. 6 and b. ʿAbod. Zar. 54b; Sifre Deut. 356 and 19; b. Sukk. 29a and t. Sukk. 2:6; ARN 1A and 1B. Rabbis also used householders (as Jesus did), albeit less often (e.g., Sifra Behuq. pq. 3.263.1.8), and in view of biblical precedents it is difficult to doubt that Jesus would have viewed God as a king (e.g., 5:35).

36. One very late rabbinic parable even focuses on God's forgiving human debts to him (Ex. Rab. 31:1; Marmorstein 1968b: 63-64). An earlier parable compares sins that squander the merits of one's righteous ancestors to borrowing more and more from a king (Sifre Deut. 349.1.1). Kings were also naturally angry if managers lost any of their money (Ex. Rab. 43:6).

37. Derrett 1970: 37; Scott 1989: 270; cf. *CPJ* 1:16-19; Avi-Yonah 1978: 194; Koester 1982: 1:53.

38. Even in the Roman period papyri speak of peasants with overwhelming tax indebtedness becoming fugitives; see Lewis 1983: 164-65; Avi-Yonah 1978: 216; MacMullen 1974: 51-52; Grant 1992: 90.

39. Davies and Allison 1991: 797-98 think that the figure is Matthean redaction to emphasize God's bountifulness; this is possible (cf. 25:15 with Lk 19:13 if they represent the same parable), but such a hyperbolic image would also not be inconsistent with Jesus' own style (e.g., 19:24).

lustration: the poor man owes the king more money than existed in circulation in the whole country at the time! Jesus' hearers would scoff that the man was a fool to get so far in debt, and that the king had been a fool to let him get away with it.

Selling the man into slavery would recover virtually none of the loss, though it might abate some of the king's anger: the most expensive slave recorded would sell for only a talent, the average being one-twentieth to one-fifth of that (Jeremias 1972: 211). Jewish custom prohibited the sale of women and children, but Jesus' hearers recognized that a pagan king would not care about such just technicalities (cf. m. Soṭa 3:8; t. Soṭa 2:9; Livy 26.34.3).[40] And of course if the story is about a Gentile kingdom and a Gentile slave, there would be no biblical "year of release" to secure the man's freedom later (Ex 21:2; Lev 25:40; Deut 15:12); Jesus' hearers thus recognize the man's impossible plight — not to mention the king's financial shortfall. In all, the king was bound to lose at least 9,999 talents (as much as 99,990,000 denarii — perhaps over 250,000 years' wages for an average worker) despite the sale. Perhaps this was one reason the king canceled the debt at the pitiable sight of the fool offering to pay it all back.[41]

Third, the parable depicts the hubris of unforgiveness toward a fellow servant of Christ (18:28-30). Jesus expects disciples to treat their fellow servants justly (24:49; for the term, cf. also Col 4:7; Rev 6:11), to show mercy as they have received it (5:7). When poor crops or other circumstances forced a ruler to forgive taxes, he did so with the understanding that his people would respect his benevolence; if he released his subordinate ministers' debts, they in turn must release the debts of those indebted to them. In Ptolemaic Egypt no one could bring suit against those who worked for the king, nor could debt collectors arrest them (*P. Hal.* 1.124-27). This principle was widely known, and the first servant should have understood it (Derrett 1970: 42; cf. MacMullen 1974: 35); but as we have seen, this servant was a fool.

Although other ancient creditors were known to have gone so far as to seize debtors by the throat, as here,[42] and creditors could come up with money

40. Cf. Jeremias 1972: 180, 211; Derrett 1970: 38; Via 1967: 138-39. More than in cases of debt (for debt slavery, see, e.g., Varro 7.5.105), conquests often led to the slaughter of male adults and enslavement of women and children (e.g., Dion. Hal. 10.26.3; Paus. 3.23.4; Jos. *Apion* 1.76). Pagan tax collectors in the Roman period still oppressed families of tax fugitives (see Lewis 1983: 161); thus, hearers of Jesus' parable may have thought the king's servant was getting his just due. Cf. debt imprisonment and slavery in the Ptolemaic period (Llewelyn 1994: 218-24; thus Diod. Sic. 1.79.3 may present too idealistic a portrait); cf. Corn Nep. 5 (Cimon), 1.1. Romans no longer imprisoned Romans for it (Livy 8.28.1).

41. "I will repay" was a standard I.O.U. in ancient business documents (Deissmann 1978: 331). Compare with this parable the public gratitude (and economy recovery) when imperial benefactors released the debts of peasants or other economically ravaged people unable to pay (Grant 1992: 88-89; Bowersock 1965: 85). Such a royal release of a city's debt serves as an early third-century parable of God's forgiveness of Israel on Rosh ha-Shanah (Pesiq. R. 51:8); cf. a possibly earlier comparison in Derrett 1970: 46; on ancient bankruptcy, see Derrett 1991.

42. Manson 1979: 213 and Jeremias 1972: 211-12 cite m. B. Bat. 10:8. Lachs 1987: 273 acknowledges this practice but contends that it was especially Roman, because Roman law permitted the creditor to bring the debtor before an official by force (citing also Plautus *Poen.* 3.5.45).

quickly by demanding immediate payment on loans (Stambaugh and Balch 1986: 72), the sum the other man owed the first servant was impossibly small compared to what that higher official owed the king. Perhaps the sum was so small that the first man had previously overlooked it. Yet this first servant, perhaps still determined to repay his debt to the king, has now decided to become ruthlessly efficient in exacting what is owed him — a sum less than one-fifth of the minimum he himself would have fetched on the slave market, and less than one five-hundred thousandth (as little as a millionth) of what he had owed the king. In other words, the forgiven servant has failed to embrace the principle of grace. Once the unforgiven man is jailed, he is unable to settle his own debts with the king (it is still the time of accounting — Derrett 1970: 41); he also is away from his active duties, costing the king more money. Further, he must depend especially on his relatives and political allies — and perhaps the king himself, as his patron — to pay his way out.[43]

Finally, the parable depicts the consequences of human unforgiveness (18:31-35). Although the other servants offer no money to release the imprisoned man, they are "grieved" (17:23; 19:22; 26:22) and do not hesitate to report the forgiven servant's act that has now cost the king (and thus ultimately them) still more money (Manson 1979: 214).[44] Ancient documents indicate that his act was legal — and that officials could severely punish those who abused it (Deissmann 1978: 269-70). The king who was earlier moved with compassion (18:27) is now moved with anger instead (18:34; in both cases his "lord" with a participle).[45] The parable teaches that although God is longsuffering (18:26, 29),

43. The patron-client model was well established in Roman antiquity (e.g., *CIL* 6.1492; Hor. *Sat.* 1.1.9-10; *Epodes* 1.7; *Rhet. ad Heren.* 3.3.4; Juv. *Sat.* 3.122-25; 4.15-18; Mart. *Epig.* 1.112; 2.30.1-5; 2.68; 10.34; Sen. *Benef.* passim; cf. also Friedländer 1965: 1:195-202; Carcopino 1940: 171-73; Crossan 1991a: 59-65), and already applied to imperial benefactions (Lewis 1983: 196-97, citing Virg. *Aen.* 6.851-53). Jewish texts reveal intimate acquaintance with the patron model (e.g., *CIJ* 1:340-41, §462; *CPJ* 2:20-22, §148; Katzoff 1986), which obtained even in the countryside (Macmullen 1974: 47). Benefaction was important in the east (Marc. Aur. *Med.* 1.15.3; Danker 1982; Bowersock 1982: 171; for figurative usages, cf. Philo *Spec. Leg.* 4.58; Epict. *Disc.* 1.4.29), and the concept was familiar in Judaism (Jos. *Ant.* 5.30; 11.253; 15.190; 16.159; 17.109; 20.66; Test. Job 16:6/3; 44:3). Officials (Char. *Chaer.* 4.5.8), rulers (*OGIS* 666; *IGRR* 1.1110 in Sherk 1988: 104; Jos. *Apion* 2.57), and deities (Plut. *Isis* 12, *Mor.* 355E; Kee 1983: 125-28; Otto 1965: 113; Koester 1982: 1:176) could be benefactors; in the east people associated royal benefaction with divinity (Philo *Leg. Gai.* 148) and being a "savior" (*SB* 3924 in Sherk 1988: 61; Jos. *War* 1.530; 7.71; *Life* 244). Jewish texts apply this title to some of the Ptolemaic rulers (Sir prol.; Ep. Arist. 205; Jos. *Apion* 2.48), probably relevant for our parable, as is the fact that Jewish people recognized God as the ultimate benefactor (Wis 3:5; 7:22; 11:13; 2 Macc 6:13; 10:38; Ep. Arist. 190, 210, 281; Philo *Cong.* 97; *Som.* 1.163; *Decal.* 41; *Spec. Leg.* 1.209; 4.187; *Praem.* 122; cf. Epict. *Disc.* 1.6.42; 2.14.13).

44. Scott 1989: 280 thinks that the audience's natural identification with the fellow servants in avenging injustice implicates them, too, in the "systematic evil" of unforgiveness. This reading may fit modern social understanding of guilt, but it is foreign to the text's worldview; the other servants are merely foils to the main action, and the judgment of the unforgiving servant is a just decree analogous to God's justice. The parable is set up to invite condemnation of the wicked servant and those who find themselves in him, which supports the parable's moral summarized in 18:35.

45. Lachs 1987: 273 cites rabbinic parallels for the expression "you wicked servant."

he has his limits ("enraged" in 18:34; 22:7). The first servant's debt is reinstated, and he is handed over to the torturers (for the term, cf. 8:29). Jewish law forbade torture — though exceptionally cruel persons were known to practice it (e.g., Jos. *War* 2.448) — but hellenistic rulers in Egypt and others had customarily tortured tardy officials to extort money from their friends (Jeremias 1972: 212; cf. Livy 3.13.8; 25.4.8-10; 39.41.7; 43.16.5; Appian *R.H.* 2.8.2; Aul. Gel. 16.10.8). Yet who would be so politically naive as to come to the rescue of one who had obviously fallen from the king's favor? The magnitude of the debt was simply unpayable by any means, and the man would *never* escape the torturers.

Forgiveness must issue "from the heart" — it must be sincere (cf. Is 59:13). God has forgiven Jesus' disciples; if they fail to show grace to others who have repented, then this text promises them hellfire (cf. 5:7; 6:12, 14-15; Manson 1979: 214).[46] In Jesus' strongly worded ethical pronouncements characteristic of the Gospel tradition, this parable forces Matthew's audience to interpret the rest of Jesus' ethical teaching in light of grace.

46. For eternal torture by evil angels, cf. 2 Enoch 10:3J, although it is unclear whether the tradition would have been contemporary with the disciples to help them envision Jesus' words in this manner (Rec. A does not specify the angels).

Grounds for Divorce in God's Law (19:1-12)

Cf. Mk 10:1-12; Lk 9:51; 16:18. 19:1 ends the discourse of chapter 18 with Matthew's standard conclusion: "When he had finished these words." The setting is debatable. "Judea" in this verse might refer to "the land of the Jews" in general, as Diaspora writers could apply the term, since Perea (*usually* what was meant by "across the Jordan") was not part of Judea proper (cf. Vander Broek 1983: 128).[1] Alternatively, Matthew may write from a Syrian perspective east of the Jordan (so Theissen 1991: 249-50), or indicate that Jesus had, like some other Galilean pilgrims, crossed into Perea en route to Jerusalem (cf. Jesus' proximity to Jericho in 20:29; Hagner 1995: 543). The crowds who follow Jesus, perhaps for healing (19:2; cf. 8:1), are practicing at least one level of discipleship (cf. 19:21); they provide a stark contrast to the Pharisees who come to "test" Jesus (19:3; cf. 4:1; 16:1; 22:18, 35).

Because most early Christian debates with Jewish contemporaries would have focused on Jesus' mission rather than ethics (unless those ethics distinctively stemmed from Jesus), this debate likely reflects the early Jesus tradition authentically (pace Schweizer 1970: 201).

In this narrative Matthew may suggest that the hard-hearted person who cannot forgive or live in proper relation to others in Christ's body (18:1-35) will also despise weaker people in society — in Jesus' day, people like one's wife (19:1-12; cf. Mal 2:14-16) or anyone's children (19:13-15) — in contrast to Jesus, who is unimpressed by worldly status (19:16-22). It is thus no coincidence that in Matthew Jesus' teaching on marital commitment directly follows his teaching on forgiveness (18:21-35), just as in Mark it follows a discussion of sinning against a "little one" (Mk 9:42-50; cf. Mt 18:7-9). The more intimate the relationship, the deeper the wounds of interpersonal friction sear; intimacy without forgiveness and reconciliation proves difficult. Matthew may expect his audience to find in the passage principles like the following (in addition to the hardheartedness of his community's opponents, which, because the theme is perva-

1. If Mark uses this geographical reference to allude back to the Baptist's primary sphere of influence, he may portray the Pharisees as attempting to lure Jesus into condemning the sort of behavior in which Herodias had engaged (Mk 10:12; 6:17), thus leading Jesus to the same harm as his predecessor (Rhoads and Michie 1982: 87). This thesis questionably presupposes, however, that Mark's audience knew data about Herodias that he had failed to supply them.

sive in the controversy accounts already examined, I will not rehearse in detail; cf. comment on 12:1-14).[2]

First, Jesus summons disciples to work toward God's ideals, his intended purposes for the world (19:4-6). The Pharisees in this pericope have an agenda: they wanted Jesus to enter into a debate currently raging among two schools of Pharisaic thought (19:3, 7).[3] Debate focused on Deuteronomy 24:1, in which a man finds "any matter of indecency" in his wife and hence divorces her. The School of Shammai interpreted Deuteronomy 24 as indicating that a man could divorce his wife for the cause of unfaithfulness ("any matter of *indecency*"); the School of Hillel understood the passage to mean that a man could divorce his wife for any cause, even burning his bread ("*any* matter of indecency" — m. Giṭ. 9:10; Sifre Deut. 269.1.1; cf. m. Ketub. 7:6; Jos. *Ant.* 4.253).[4] In practice both schools agreed that the law often granted the man a right to divorce, regrettable as divorce was (e.g., b. Sanh. 22a; p. Giṭ. 1:1, §4).[5]

Jesus, however, circumvents his interlocutors' focus based on Deuteronomy 24 by appealing to the focus of Genesis 2.[6] The ultimate issue should not be the *right* to divorce, but God's original desire for husbands and wives to be one flesh (cf. Belkin 1940: 231). The principle of Genesis from which Jesus draws this application goes beyond opposing divorce; it opposes marital disharmony altogether (cf. 1 Clem. 6:3). The "beginning" (19:4; cf. 24:21) refers to the creation narrative.[7] Since other Jewish teachers of this period looked to the creation

2. Questions of lawfulness dominate (cf. 12:2; 20:15; 22:17; 27:6). The structure of the argument here seems to reflect that of what later became rabbinic debate (cf. Zimmerman 1962; Fjärstedt 1968). Just as Matthew's citation of Genesis here is more eclectic than Mark's (which is closer to the Septuagint — Stendahl 1968: 59), Matthew also presents an argument that better suits the Palestinian Jewish milieu (and may thus be closer to the way the questions were framed — cf. Keener 1991a: 38).

3. Many commentators note the influence of that first-century debate here (e.g., von Dobschütz 1995: 33; Filson 1960: 206; Argyle 1963: 51-52; Swidler 1976: 231n.225; Gundry 1982: 377; Ilan 1996: 142; Overman 1996: 82, 279; pace Meier 1979: 248-53; idem 1980: 215). For the development of divorce in later Jewish law into the modern period, see Brayer 1968: 18-22.

4. Also p. Soṭa 1:1, §2. The minimum standard of the more liberal Hillelites seems to have accorded more with general practice on this issue, as attested by Sirach (25:26), Philo (*Spec. Leg.* 3.30), and Josephus (*Ant.* 4.253; *Life* 415, 426; cf. Safrai 1974/76b: 790), although these writers may have been accommodating hellenistic practice (Gentile customs prevailed in many respects even among Jewish people near Palestine; see, e.g., *CPJ* 2:10-12, §144; Wasserstein 1989). The coexistence of parties with different views required legal toleration of the more lenient position, hence ultimately securing (along with later Hillelite dominance) the view's broader acceptance.

5. Heth and Wenham rightly suggest (1984: 129) that Jesus must have been stricter than the Shammaites because his disciples said, "Then it is better not to marry" (19:10). Jesus is stricter, however, merely because he called remarriage adultery; Shammaites could not invalidate Hillelite marriages.

6. Sigal 1986: 93 opines that Jesus interprets Deut 24:1 based on Mal 2:14-16; but Gen 2 is clearly the primary basis for Jesus' alternate reading. For various interpretations of Deut 24:1-4 (including LXX; Philo *Spec. Leg.* 3.30-31; Jos. *Ant.* 4.253), see Neudecker 1994.

7. The beginning indicates the creation narrative in Rom 1:20; 4 Ezra 4:30; Ps-Philo 1:1; 32:7; incant. text 20:11-12; Test. Mos. 1:12-13; 12:4; 1 Enoch 69:18; cf. 4 Ezra 6:38; Pryke 1978: 39. As in Greek literature (e.g., Hesiod *Theog.* 452; Diog. Laert. 10.1.75), it refers to the primeval period in general, not always the moment of creation.

narrative for God's ideal purposes (CD 4.20–5:2; 11QTemple 56.18-19, prohibiting royal polygamy),[8] including the Pharisaic schools mentioned above (m. Yebam. 6:6, drawing different applications),[9] Jesus' argument would be difficult to refute, at least without citing another text to resolve the apparent dilemma (as was the practice: Beraita de R. Ishmael pq. 1.7).[10] (Many Jewish speculations about the future kingdom also viewed it as a sort of recapitulation of the beginning, viewing the *Endzeit* in terms of the *Urzeit.*)[11] Indeed, the purpose of the Deuteronomy 24 law itself was probably "to check haste in divorce" (Gundry 1982: 380), hence to provide some legal protection for the wife (Luck 1987: 109; cf. Coiner 1968: 368-69).[12]

According to the Genesis text, a man must leave his parents (19:5). In Jesus' day, early marital residences tended to be patrilocal, with the husband's family of origin (see comment on 8:14); thus citing this text with no further explana-

8. Many have thought that the Qumranites applied this passage to prohibiting divorce as well as polygamy (Schubert 1971: 27; Mueller 1980), but the Qumran texts themselves explicitly prohibit only polygamy here (Keener 1991a: 40-41; cf. Vermes 1974; Nineham 1977: 265; Yadin 1972). A few rabbis, who allowed polygamy but felt that it was not the ideal (cf. m. 'Abot 2:7; b. Yebam. 65a), also appealed to Genesis (ARN 2, §9B; on Jewish polygyny in general, see Ilan 1996: 85-88). In contrast to some other peoples (Diod. Sic. 2.58.1; 1.80.3; Sext. Emp. *Pyrrh.* 3.205, 213), Greeks and Romans mandated monogamy in their society (e.g., Gaius *Inst.* 1.63; Justinian *Codex* 9.18; Dion. Hal. 11.28.4), according to their customs (cf. Eurip. *Androm.* 465-93, 909); the Septuagint and Samaritan Pentateuch reading (the "two" become one) probably supports this practice (Daube 1973: 81; cf. Bowman 1977: 311), and Matthew here concurs with Mark's use of the Greek version.

9. See further Keener 1992: 114-15; Ilan 1996: 125 on Jewish precedents for women drawn from the Eve story.

10. Jesus' "what God joined" would not be controversial; although the rabbis permitted divorce, they agreed that God arranged marriages (Lachs 1987: 326-27; see my comment on 1:1-17), as did many pagan thinkers (Boring 1995: 117 cites Muson. Ruf. *Is Marriage a Handicap for the Pursuit of Philosophy?; SIG* 3.1267). Some have connected Jesus' argument here concerning what God joined together to a traditional Jewish notion that the original human of Gen 1:26-27, being both male and female, was androgynous (Daube 1956: 343, 346; idem 1973: 72; ARN 37, §94 B; b. Ber. 61a; Gen. Rab. 8:1; 14:7), although this was only one tradition (cf. ARN 1A; 8, §23B; Jub. 3:7). For asexuality (not androgynity) in Philo, cf. Baer 1970: 16-35. Meeks 1974: 185 finds the idea of an androgynous progenitor of humanity common in antiquity (suggesting, less plausibly, its assumption in Gal 3:28); in Greek tradition, cf. Guthrie 1966: 101; in Gnosticism, "Eugnostos the Blessed" and "The Sophia of Jesus Christ" (*NHL* 216-17). Although it seems safe to say that neither Matthew nor Mark plays on this concept of an original androgynous man (the rabbis similarly appear more interested in laws concerning the rare situation of hermaphrodites — t. Bik. 2:7; Sifra V. D. Den. pq. 18.31.2.1; Sifra Neg. par. 5.138.1.1; b. Ḥag. 4a; Nid. 28b; p. Ḥag. 1:1, §§5-6; Yebam. 8:6, §3; Lev. Rab. 14:1; in Greek reports, cf., e.g., Diod. Sic. 32.10.2–12.3; Livy 27.11.4; 27.37.5-7; Ovid. *Metam.* 4.368-79), this reading of the Genesis passage they cite may have informed the understanding of some members of their original audiences. Even pagans, however, could think simply of a deity uniting woman and man in marriage (Isis aretalogy in Horsley 1981: 19-20); pagans also spoke of sexual "unions" (e.g., *Alexandrian Erotic Fragment,* col. 1; Arist. *Pol.* 1.2.2, 1253b; cf. 1.2.21, 1255b).

11. See, e.g., Rev 22:1-3; 4 Ezra 8:52-54; Test. Levi 18:10-12; Test. Dan 5:12; m. 'Abot 5:20; cf. 24:21; Russell 1964: 280-84; Arrington 1978: 77-81.

12. Snodgrass 1996: 118 argues that some texts mandated divorce to protect the wife (Ex 21:11; Deut 21:14) and others forbade it for the same reason (Deut 22:19, 29); Jesus thus agrees with the *purpose* in both.

tion might lead hearers to the view that one's marriage must take priority over one's family of origin. (It may be relevant that in Middle Eastern culture, the strength of a woman's ties to her family of origin is proportional to the likelihood of ending her marriage — Eickelman 1989: 175.) Jesus' call to follow and proclaim him come first (10:34-39; 19:27-30), but after that relationship, one's relationship with one's spouse must take priority over any other.

Although they claim Scripture for their purposes, Jesus challenges their actual knowledge of Scripture by showing that they are proof-texting rather than reading it in light of God's entire plan: "Have you never read?" (19:4; cf. 12:3; 21:16, 42; 22:31). Some other radical Jewish thinkers of that era, like Qumran's Teacher of Righteousness, challenged the contemporary religious establishment with their own interpretation of Scripture. Jesus' objection was not to Scripture but to human traditions of interpretation (15:2-9; cf. 5:17-20; 8:4; 22:24, 32); indeed, here he goes so far as to attribute a saying of the biblical narrator directly to God (19:4-5; Wenham 1977: 28; cf. Rom 9:17; Sifre Deut. 45.1.3).[13]

Second, the Pharisees, presumably like the opponents of the Matthean community, interpret the Bible in a way that treats others unjustly (19:7-8). In Scripture, God sometimes allowed what was less than ideal because people's hard hearts made the ideal unattainable (e.g., Ex 13:17; 1 Sam 12:12-13). To be able to exercise some degree of restraint over human injustice, Moses' civil laws regulated some institutions rather than seeking to abolish them altogether: divorce, polygyny, the avengers of blood, and slavery (Keener 1992: 192-96). Jewish lawyers in fact recognized that God had allowed some behavior (marrying a Gentile captive in Deut 21:11-13; according to some, slavery) as a concession to human weakness (Daube 1959); some of their own rulings, such as the *prosbul,* conceded human weakness in hopes of improving the situation of justice (Daube 1959: 10).

Nevertheless, Jesus' opponents here assume that whatever the law addressed it permitted (19:7; cf. ARN 24, §49B); Jesus responds that Moses permitted this merely as a concession to Israel's hard hearts.[14] That his questioners exploit this concession thereby implies their own hardness of hearts, a charge ancients would easily enough apply to those deficient in love toward family members (Epict. *Disc.* 3.3.5). Thus in Matthew (in contrast to Mark), the Pharisees even exploit Moses' concession as a *command* (Gundry 1982: 380). Jesus, by contrast, uses Scripture differently (cf. 12:7), here probably seeking to protect an innocent Jewish wife from her husband wrongfully divorcing her (Kysar 1978:

13. Based on the citation of Scripture in CD 4.20–5.2, Sanders regards the tradition that Jesus cited the creation narrative in defense of his divorce position as likely (1985: 257). Multiple attestation makes Jesus' divorce saying in 5:32, 19:9 one of the most assuredly attested passages, although the precise history of its transmission may be debated; cf. (too recently for inclusion in Keener 1991a), e.g., R. Collins 1992; Keener 1994; Force 1993.

14. This is not to depict the law negatively (cf. 5:17) but to regard the concession as temporary (McConnell 1969: 60).

43; France 1985: 280; Davies 1993: 54).[15] Other Jewish teachers also recognized that by making divorce more difficult they would protect the woman (e.g., t. Ketub. 12:1).[16]

Third, Matthew is careful to include an exception for the innocent party (19:9).[17] This passage addresses which divorces are permitted (Carson 1984b: 412). Although he keeps the focus on Genesis 2, Jesus in Matthew does side more or less with the Shammaites on the issue of narrow exceptions. Roman law permitted either party to divorce the other, regardless of the other's wishes; except in extraordinary circumstances, Jewish law permitted only the husband to divorce the wife, regardless of her wishes (Keener 1991a: 51; Ilan 1996: 143-44; cf. also Diod. Sic. 12.18.1). Matthew permits a disciple divorce only when the disciple's spouse has already irreparably ended the marriage.

Most of Matthew's audience (except his "scribes" for the kingdom, 13:52) may have been unfamiliar with the debate between the Hillelites and Shammaites active among Pharisees of Jesus' day. Nevertheless, when Matthew speaks of "except for the cause of infidelity," his audience would have understood this as a legal charge,[18] interpreting these words in line with the typical meaning of "infidelity" as grounds for divorce, namely, sexual unfaithfulness to the marriage.[19]

15. If one presses the divorce saying literally rather than as hyperbole, however, one could not see it as supporting women, since "the prohibition against remarriage must have been devastating" (Schnackenburg 1996: 253).

16. Some later rabbis also concluded that one unfortunate corollary of remarriage, whether after divorce or widowhood, could be that one might be tempted to compare one former's spouse in bed; there could be "four minds in one bed" (b. Pesaḥ. 112ab, Soncino tr.). Although the Markan form that applies the saying to wives as well could be a subdued criticism of the hellenized Jewish aristocracy (e.g., the actions of Salome, Herod's sister; Herodias; cf. de Vaux 1961: 35; Lane 1974a: 358; Stein 1980: 237; idem 1979: 118n.9; Witherington 1984: 27) and there is support for its rare occurrence in other circles of Jewish Palestine (Stein 1980: 237), it probably represents Markan accommodation to hellenistic Jewish practice (cf., e.g., Elephantine — de Vaux 1961: 35) or Roman custom (Moule 1965: 77; Hardy 1962: 88). (The solution of Herron 1982 — that Jesus refers to desertion rather than divorce here — is less probable textually and also culturally problematic, since leaving without divorce would have been even harder for the woman.)

17. Although the early church viewed Matthew's exception clause as original (Nembach 1970: 171) and some think it authentic from Jesus (Lehmann 1960: 266) or at least preredactional (Guelich 1982: 206-10), more scholars today regard it as Matthean redaction (e.g., Goulder 1974: 25, 39; Gundry 1982: 90; Stenger 1984; note that Paul is unaware of it), though many of us suspect it articulates the implications of the more general saying (e.g., Smalley 1977: 190; Garland 1993: 68). Still, Mark has surely adapted the whole controversy narrative (Mk 10:2-12) for a Gentile audience, and Matthew has re-Judaized it, probably on the basis of Jewish-Christian tradition (cf. Hurtado 1983: 153). (On the textual problem, cf. recently, e.g., Marucci 1990; Holmes 1990).

18. E.g., the wife's adultery exempted the husband from paying the *ketubah* (Safrai 1974/76b: 790); among Romans, she lost much of her dowry (O'Rourke 1971: 182). Cf. Quint. *Inst. Or.* 7.4.11; in older times, Plut. *Romulus* 22.3. Roman and Jewish law mandated divorce for infidelity (e.g., Paulus *Opinions* 2.26.1-17 in Lefkowitz and Fant 1982: 182; Gardner 1986: 89; cf. even Herm. 2.4.1).

19. As held by many interpreters, e.g., Augustine *Tractate on John* 9.2.2; *Adulterous Marriages* 2.9.8 (*ACCS*, 136-37); Hauck/Schulz 1968: 592; Keener 1991a: 31-33; Hill 1972: 125, 281; Schweizer 1975: 124; Christiaens 1983; Carson 1984b: 414, 417; France 1985: 123; Sigal 1986: 102;

Jewish and Roman law, in fact, both *mandated* divorce for these grounds.[20] Mark and Luke probably could assume such an exception without explicitly stating it (Carson 1984b: 418; Garland 1993: 68). As France puts it (1985: 124):

> To repudiate a wife after she had committed adultery was therefore simply the recognition that the marriage had already been terminated by the creation of a new union. . . . The Matthaean exceptive clause is . . . making explicit what any Jewish reader would have taken for granted when Jesus made the apparently unqualified pronouncements of Mark 10:9-12.

Advancing new theories is integral to the culture of the academy, and for this reason among others it is not surprising that, on this matter as on most others, numerous views exist. (I have surveyed these views more fully in Keener 1991a: 28-31; for a more extensive and favorable survey, see Heth and Wenham 1984b; for a recent critique of my own position, see Heth 1995.) Yet in my view many of these arguments seem to evidence little firsthand acquaintance with Matthew's specific cultural setting beyond their immediate proposal. Most views other than the infidelity view imply that Matthew simply permits divorce when the original marriage is not valid. Yet divorce was unnecessary in the case of invalid marriages; further, such marriages were not common enough to warrant Matthew's mention.

Excursus: *Porneia* As Incestuous Unions?

Many alternatives deny that a valid marriage exists (e.g., Leeming and Dawson 1956: 82), for example, that the woman here is a nonmarried sexual partner (Byron 1963); unions after the first in a polygynous marriage (Ramaroson 1971); or, most commonly, an incestuous union (Meier 1979: 256; idem 1980: 52-53; Caron 1982: 312; Schedl 1982; Wambacq 1982; Witherington 1985), though nothing in the context supports such a narrow reading of the term here (if anything, *porneia* should mean *more* than adulterous infidelity; cf. Belkin 1940: 230-31; Luz 1989: 305; Overman 1996: 280).[21]

Luz 1989: 304-5; de la Serna 1989; Wiebe 1989; Blomberg 1990b; Stein 1992a: 195; Davies 1993: 132; Allison 1993a; Carter 1994: 64-65; more tentatively, Davies and Allison 1988: 529-31; idem 1997: 16. For even suspected infidelity as grounds for divorce in Islamic societies today, cf. Delaney 1987: 41. Matthew may use *porneia* instead of "adultery" for rhetorical variation, as in LXX Jer 3:8-9 (Sigal 1986: 97). Because of its association with "playing the prostitute," *porneia* sometimes represents marital infidelity in the LXX (e.g., Jer 2:20; 3:2, 9; Ezek 16:15; Hos 2:2, 4, 6; Amos 7:17; Sir 23:23). For continual rather than momentary misconduct, cf. Leenhardt 1969; Schweizer 1975: 124.

20. Justinian *Dig.* 48.5.1.prol.; Gardner 1986: 131-32; Richlin 1981: 227; Safrai 1974/76b: 762; Bockmuehl 1989.

21. Considine 1956 proposes ecclesiastical annulments here based on rejecting Christ (Considine 1956); Fleming 1963 that Jesus' public view allowed an exception for adultery, but his

The incestuous-marriage interpretation not only demands too narrow a sense for *porneia;* it also requires us to suppose a situation that must have been so rare as barely to warrant mention, especially if we assume a Syro-Palestinian provenance for Matthew. To be sure, many Jewish people suspected Gentiles of widespread incest (Sib. Or. 5:390-91; cf. Gen. Rab. 18:5; 52:11);[22] their suspicions, however, probably misrepresented the actual degree of incidence of the activity. Marriages of full brothers and sisters appear in Egypt (Paus. 1.7.1; Diod. Sic. 1.27.1; Sext. Emp. *Pyrrh.* 1.152)[23] but were widely rejected elsewhere (e.g., Diod. Sic. 10.31.1; Gaius *Inst.* 1.61). Other kinds of incest were condemned throughout the ancient Mediterranean (Diod. Sic. 5.55.6-7; Cic. *De Leg.* 2.9.22; Gaius *Inst.* 1.59-64; Plut. *R.Q.* 108, *Mor.* 289D; *Parallel Stories* 19, *Mor.* 310BC; Juv. *Sat.* 2.32-33; 4.8-9; Tac. *Ann.* 16.8; Suet. *Calig.* 23-24; *Nero* 28; Minucius Felix *Octavius* 31.1; Apul. *Metam.* 10.3; Philost. *V.A.* 1.10; 1 Cor 5:1).[24] Indeed, the incest taboo is almost universal,[25] although the range of forbidden degrees of kinship outside the direct parental line varies considerably from one culture to the next.[26] Further, the term *porneia* does not ap-

---

more private comments later forbade even that; Sabatowich 1987 that one does not cause the unfaithful woman to become adulterous because she already is (this seems too self-evident and tautological to require Matthew to include an exception clause); Lehmann 1960: 265 that the exception is only for Jews.

22. Although Jewish people felt that God tolerated brother-sister marriages in an earlier period (Gen 20:12; p. Sanh. 5:1, §4), Lev 18:9, 11 and Deut 27:22 ruled out subsequent brother-sister marriages (Sifre Num. 90.1.1), except perhaps for Gentile slaves (p. Yebam. 11:2, §3). Jewish people harshly condemned all kinds of incest (Gen 19:30-38; 49:3-4; Jub. 16:8; 33:1-14; 41:23-26; Philo *Spec. Leg.* 3.19; Jos. *Ant.* 17.341; Test. Reub. 1:6-10; Gk. Ezra 4:24; Sifre Deut. 246.1.2; p. Ned. 2:1, §4; Ta'an. 4:5, §8; Deut. Rab. 2:21; cf. Ps-Phocyl. 179-81) and considered the Jewish standard stricter than Gentile practice (e.g., Sifra Qed. par. 4.206.1.2; p. Qidd. 1:1, §2; cf. Jos. *Ant.* 20.18).

23. Cf. also Lewis 1983: 43; Gardner 1986: 36. In Nubia, see Adams 1977: 260; elsewhere, cf. Radcliffe-Brown 1965: 50. Greeks allowed nonuterine, half-sibling unions (e.g., Ach. Tat. 1.3.1-2).

24. Cf. Cohen 1966: 281; Gardner 1986: 35-37, 126-27; for the full horror among Greeks, see, e.g., Soph. *Oed. Rex,* with subsequent allusions (e.g., Epict. *Disc.* 1.24.16; Mart. *Epig.* 10.4.1; cf. Justin *1 Apol.* 27). For rare exceptions, including philosophers and reports about Persians, see Herod. *Hist.* 3.31; Sext. Emp. *Pyrrh.* 1.152, 160; 3.205; Diog. Laert. 7.7.188; Philo *Spec. Leg.* 3.13; Tert. *Apol.* 9.16; Tatian 28; Theophilus 3.6; Beidelman 1971: 190. Claudius married his niece, but many regarded even this as shameful (Dio Cassius *R.H.* 61.31.6; Tac. *Ann.* 12.2; Suet. *Claud.* 39); exceptions were also made for deities (e.g., Burkert 1985: 178).

25. Graburn 1971: 324; Parsons 1971: 410; cf., e.g., Mbiti 1970: 179-80, 192; Evans-Pritchard 1951: 29-48; Firth 1963: 280-97. Incest invites punishment by deities or society (e.g., Wilson 1957: 134-35, 187; Evens 1983; Nukunya 1969: 68; Willner 1983: 152; Fortes 1950: 257; Needham 1971: 27).

26. See, e.g., Farber 1968: 59; Barth 1973: 6; Schapera 1950: 152, 156; cf. Gough 1973a: 433; Pitt-Rivers 94-95. Sometimes degrees of kinship also vary in amount of incest guilt (e.g., Elkins 1968: 171; Evens 1983: 126; Schlegel 1972: 12, 69, 76, 123-24); some cultures also provide rituals for removing incest guilt (e.g., Southall 1971: 159). A few cultures prohibit all first-cousin marriages (Farber 1968: 26-28, 31-32; for parallel cousins, Kuper 1950: 104), but most permit at least cross-cousin marriages (e.g., Mark 1967; Gough 1973b; Murphy and Kasdan 1967: 12). Some societies apply extended sibling terminology to forbidden cousins (e.g., Fields and Merrifield 1980: 27; Farber 1968: 94; on sibling terms, cf. further Goody 1970; Murdock 1968; Nerlove and Romney 1967; Faris 1969), but others apply sibling language to spouses (e.g., Song 4:9-12; 5:1; 8:1; *ANET* 467-68; Haas 1969).

pear in Leviticus 18 LXX, and Jewish law would not require a divorce to dissolve a union it regarded as incestuous (Sigal 1986: 101).

Not only the incestuous-marriage view, but most of the specific proposals for the meaning of *porneia* give it a more restricted sense than it normally bears unless explicitly qualified, which it is not here (as noted by many commentators, e.g., Hagner 1993: 124); they also miss how such a term (used in its unqualified, general sense) would function in a usual legal context (e.g., *B.G.U.* 1052 in Sherk 1988: 243; Suet. *Julius* 6, 74; cf. Safrai 1974/76b: 762).

"Except for infidelity" may modify Jesus' statement about divorce rather than remarriage,[27] but if it does it does so precisely because, in Jesus' graphic statement, it is the validity of the divorce that is in question.[28] No one permitted remarriage if a divorce were invalid, but a valid divorce by definition included the right to remarry, as is attested by ancient divorce contracts (see, e.g., m. Giṭ. 9:3; *CPJ* 2:10-12, §144; Carmon 1973: 90-91, 200-201; cf. *B.G.U.* 1103, cited by Barrett) and the very meaning of the term (besides sources in Keener 1991a, see especially Jos. *Ant.* 4.253; cf. Blomberg 1992a: 111; Hagner 1993: 125). Jesus' point is at any rate not to break up second and third marriages — as if the hyperbolic element in his graphic statement may be missed (even for guilty parties) — but to underline in no uncertain terms the sanctity of marriage and the solemn responsibility of a disciple to preserve it when this is at all possible.[29]

Finally, remaining single is sometimes the price of following Jesus

27. For this grammatical argument see Heth and Wenham 1984b: 117; G. Wenham 1984b; idem 1986; Hagner 1995: 549; Carter 1994: 66-68; cf. against this position Murray 1953: 39-43.

28. Cf. the interesting position in Malina and Rohrbaugh 1992: 121: remarriage is adultery, except in cases of unchastity, if one divorces *in order to remarry;* Young 1995: 115 defends the same position by citing m. Soṭa 5:1. In this case one would not even need to suppose much hyperbole, since desire for another had ended the marriage.

29. Heth and Wenham 1984b helpfully and skillfully summarize various positions, but while they repeatedly (and correctly) point out that none of the other views concurs with the infidelity interpretation (which they characterize as the "Erasmian" and "evangelical" view), I would add that the other views also conflict with one another. Unless one gathers under one heading all interpretations harmonizing exception passages with general statements by minimizing the exception, *all* particular positions are minority positions, but the infidelity position probably claims more adherents than any other individual position. I believe that second- and third-century Christian writers, on whom Heth and Wenham heavily depend, reflect the rise of marital asceticism in the dominant culture and especially the church (cf. examples of the growth of asceticism coupled with misogyny, e.g., in Clark 1993), not the historical situation of the first century; the later view begins in Shepherd of Hermas, a document containing other similar tendencies (cf. my article on "Marriage, Divorce and Adultery" for InterVarsity Press's *Dictionary of the Later New Testament and Its Developments,* ed. R. P. Martin and P. H. Davids, 712-17); patristic opinion against remarriage was "burdened by a less than enthusiastic view of marriage," and it is questionable whether "the later distinction between separation . . . and divorce . . . would have made much sense in Matthew's Jewish environment" (Davies and Allison 1997: 17). Luz argues that the Eastern Orthodox tradition allows remarriage in cases of adultery (1989: 308-9).

(19:10-12). Some doubt the passage's authenticity (Ilan 1996: 62), but if John and Jesus remained unmarried, it is not implausible that Jesus spoke about celibacy, although not necessarily in this context.[30]

Jesus here addresses all disciples "able to bear" his teaching. Some scholars have argued that Jesus here recommends celibacy specifically for all men divorced for the sake of the kingdom,[31] but this reads Jesus' response as if the disciples had not raised an objection in verse 10. Proponents of this position argue, "The antecedent to 'this precept' in verse 11 is not the disciples' words in verse 10 . . . but Jesus' precept in verse 9" (Heth 1990: 106). But one might ask why an interpreter would jump back two verses instead of thinking that Jesus answered his disciples' question immediately preceding in verse 10. To answer this objection, some therefore suggest that 19:26 similarly jumps back. Unfortunately for their argument, 19:26 may refer back to 19:25's question after all; further, Jesus normally answers disciples' questions directly (e.g., 13:10-11, 36-37; 24:3-4), though sometimes impatiently (e.g., 15:15-16).[32]

If 19:9, like 5:32, allows innocent parties in a divorce to remarry, then this text has no more reason to address them than others; if 19:11-12 did refer to divorce, it would also assume the Matthean exception just stated in 19:9. The *general* context is not divorce but family (note children in 19:13-15; Trocmé 1975: 203; Meier 1979: 138-39; cf. also the background of household codes some have suggested here — Anderson 1976: 239; Carter 1994: 203). Further, this passage represents not a command but an exhortation to those with the gift (cf. Meier 1980: 216-17).[33]

30. Following Blinzler, Tannehill suggests that Jesus originally uttered 19:12 in response to accusations about his remaining unmarried (1975: 137-38). Meier 1991a: 343 thinks that 19:12 was originally distinct from the divorce pericope, and that Matthew created 19:10-11 as a transition for it (see also R. Collins 1992: 119-20; cf. Vermes 1993: 145); but Wenham 1984a suggests that the tradition in Mt 19:11 may stand behind 1 Cor 7:7. Hilton and Marshall 1988: 135 suggest that marriage was so standard that Jewish readers would infer Jesus' marriage, rather than his celibacy, from the silence. This burden of proof might normally obtain, yet if Jesus were married one might hope for some indications of provision for his wife in some of our texts (cf. Jn 19:26-27). For sound arguments that Jesus was after all celibate, see Meier 1991a: 332-45.

31. E.g., Gundry 1982: 377; Heth and Wenham 1984b: 88; R. Collins 1992: 127; cf. Côte 1986. By contrast, Davies and Allison 1997: 17 suggest that if one does link 19:10-12 with 19:9, it suggests *freedom* to remarry, because not all get the gift (19:12).

32. Nor is it fair to argue that Jesus would never affirm something his disciples said, except in 16:15-17 (Heth and Wenham 1984b: 61-62). That is also a Matthean insertion into Markan material; Matthew, less negative toward the disciples, omits some of Mark's disciples' foolish questions (Mt 24:1-2//Mk 13:1-2). Cf. partial affirmations of their words in 13:51-52; 17:24-27; Jesus sometimes accepts their premise as partly true and expounds on it (17:10-11) or radicalizes it (18:21-22).

33. In 1 Cor 7:6, Paul also distinguishes command and concession as the rabbis did. Paul was probably unfamiliar with this saying; he neither appeals to it to oppose remarriage — on the other view — or the option of celibacy, on mine. Some complain that Jesus would not utter invitations applicable only to some able to achieve the demand, but this goes against the evidence (e.g., Mt 13:52; 16:17-18, 28); besides, he nowhere else makes such demands to a group such as divorced people (the male members of which did not represent a recognizable group in his culture). They also try to argue that 13:11 and 19:11-12 are parallel (Heth and Wenham 1982: 59, 65), but the context appears to deny this.

If, by contrast, we read the text in sequence, the disciples are concerned about the danger of marrying without an escape clause, and Jesus responds to their question (Carson 1984b: 418-19; France 1985: 282). Ancient marriage contracts typically included arrangements in case of divorce (e.g., *P. Ryl.* 154.28-33), though this was normally expressed as a "just in case"; it was naturally not the outcome for which parties entering a marriage hoped (cf. *P. Oxy.* 1273.25, A.D. 260). If a marriage did not work, divorce was a relatively simple option (Terence *Lady of Andros* 567-69; Keener 1991a: 50-52). Many sages considered it a duty to divorce a "bad" wife (e.g., Sir. 25:26; b. 'Erub. 41b; Yebam. 63b; p. Ketub. 11:3, §2; Gen. Rab. 17:3; Lev. Rab. 34:14); Plutarch ridiculed a man who failed to divorce such a wife as cowardly (Plut. *Virtue and Vice* 2, *Mor.* 100E). Parents arranged marriages, and according to tradition, in Galilee at least, one could not spend time alone with one's prospective spouse until after the wedding (Safrai 1974/76b: 756-57; Finkelstein 1962: 1:45); one could not always know in advance what one's spouse would turn out to be like. To marry without the possibility of divorce in a painful marriage seemed worse than not marrying at all! Responding to this objection, Jesus replied that some would indeed be better off not marrying; perhaps because of the intensity of their callings, it would be difficult for true disciples to find compatible spouses who would share their commitment (cf. the story of Crates and Hipparchia in Keener 1991a: 64; cf. Mt 10:35-37).

Jesus' remark about celibacy is graphic and would certainly seize the attention of Jewish listeners; the first two eunuch images prepare the reader for the "eunuch for the kingdom" (Malina 1981: 5-6). Jewish teachers could distinguish those who were born without sexual organs and those on whom an operation was performed (Manson 1979: 215; cf., e.g., t. Yebam. 10:3; Sifre Deut. 247.1.1-3; p. Yebam. 8:5, §1), but Jewish people were horrified by castration (e.g., Test. Jud. 23:4; Ps-Phocyl. 187; Jos. *Apion* 2.270-71; p. Yebam. 8:1, §11), and those who "made themselves eunuchs" were viewed as morally depraved (Jos. *Ant.* 4.290). Most people looked down on eunuchs for their impotence or effeminity (cf., e.g., Juv. *Sat.* 1.22; Epict. *Disc.* 3.1.31; Ps-Lucian *Affairs of Heart* §21; Babrius 54.4; Lucan *C.W.* 10.133-34; Jos. *Ant.* 4.290-91) and recognized that their desires would never be fulfilled (Sir 20:4; 30:20);[34] some recognized that eunuchs were at a disadvantage (Phaedrus 3.11.4-5) but through no fault of their own (Phaedrus 3.11.6-7; cf. Aul. Gel. 4.2.6-8). "Eunuch" (lit. "half-man") could function as an insult (Virg. *Aen.* 12.99). Whereas some Gentiles equated Jewish circumcision with a form of castration (cf., e.g., Herr 1978; Pesiq. Rab Kah. 3:6), Jewish people did not allow eunuchs into the covenant, based on Deuteronomy 23:1 (though cf. Is 56:4-5).

34. Cf. particular condemnations and ridicule of the Galli, castrated priests of Cybele (Lucretius *Nat.* 2.614-15; *Rhet. ad Herenn.* 4.49.62; Hor. *Sat.* 1.2.120-21; Epict. *Disc.* 2.20.17, 19; Mart. *Epig.* 1.35.15; 3.24.13; Juv. *Sat.* 2.110-16; 6.514-16; Lucian *Syrian Goddess* 50-51; Sext. Emp. *Pyrrh.* 3.217; Heraclitus *Ep.* 9; cf. further Gasparro 1985: 26-28, 53; Vermaseren 1977: 96-101). Eunuchs grew more acceptable in the second through fourth centuries A.D. (Stevenson 1995; cf. the growing asceticism of late antiquity).

The figurative sense of celibacy in which Jesus means the language (cf., e.g., Ach. Tat. 5.22.5; 6.21.3) would have been less jarring, but nonetheless offensive, to most of his contemporaries (see especially Tannehill 1975: 136-37). Although some pietists in the wilderness may have preferred celibacy (Jos. *Life* 11; *War* 2.120; *Ant.* 18.21; Philo *Hypothetica* 11.14; Pliny *N.H.* 5.15.73; CD 12.1-2),[35] mainstream Jewish society regarded marriage and childbearing as solemn responsibilities (Keener 1991a: 72-78).[36] A metaphor of such shame and sacrifice testifies to the value of the kingdom of God for which anyone would pay such a price (Tannehill 1975: 138-40); by embracing both shame and self-control, Joseph to a lesser extent models the nature of this demand (1:25).

The Kingdom Belongs to Children (19:13-15)

Cf. Mk 10:13-16; Lk 18:15-17. Jesus here reiterates his teaching in 18:1-6 — which his disciples have apparently forgotten (cf. again 21:15).[37] Some have argued that peasant parents often avoided undue attachment to infants due to the high mortality rate (Dixon 1988: 113); clearly Greek and Roman fathers often exercised their legal right to discard unwanted infants.[38] Palestinian Jewish society was not so calloused, however (Jos. *Apion* 2.202; Diod. Sic. 40.3.8; Tarn 1974: 102), expressing love for children (cf. Abrahams 1917: 118-20; Falk 1974/1976: 508-9); examples even exist of taking children to prominent men for blessing, as here (cf. Jeremias 1960: 49; Hill 1972: 282; France 1985: 283).[39] It is

35. Cf. also Philo's idealistic depiction of the Therapeutae in *Vit. Con.* 68, 89. A few female skeletons suggest that some women lived in the Qumran community in at least one period (Harrison 1969: 28; Cross 1980: 97); perhaps these were wives of already-married men who were joining the community. Some scholars contend for a larger female presence at Qumran on the basis of references to marriage or descendants (Marx 1970; Hübner 1971; cf. Baumgarten 1983); but these references might reflect the conditions of Essenes in the cities. Thiering 1974 grounds Qumran celibacy in the tradition of Israelite prophets; Buchanan 1963: 399-405 suggests that Qumran may have excluded women for purity considerations.

36. Roman society also emphasized marriage and childbearing (Propertius 4.11; Dion. Hal. 9.22.2; Dio Cassius *R.H.* 54.16.1, 7), though they attributed special power to the Vestal Virgins, the loss of whose virginity was held to warrant capital punishment (e.g., Dion. Hal. 2.67; 9.40.3-4; Dio Cassius *R.H.* 67.3.3-4; Plut. *R.Q.* 83, *Mor.* 284AC; 96, *Mor.* 286EF; *Crassus* 1.2; cf. Dion. Hal. 3.67.3); cf. Greek virgin priestesses (Paus. 2.33.2; 9.27.6); and deities in *Orphic Hymns* 32.7; 42.4 (emphasizing her asexual status). Virginity (both symbolic and literal) is positive in Philo (Boccaccini 1991: 205-12).

37. The present passage abbreviates Mk 10:13-16; school exercises regularly included abbreviating or expanding *chreiae* (Robbins 1988: 18-19). The application of this passage to infant baptism is suspicious (Meier 1980: 218); clear evidence for this practice is too late.

38. E.g., Diod. Sic. 4.64.1; 8.4.1; 19.2.3-5; Juv. *Sat.* 6.602-9; Mus. Ruf. *Rel.* 15B; *P. Oxy.* 744; *B.G.U.* 1210; *ILS* 1486; Paus. 2.26.4; Dixon 1988: 23; Lewis 1983: 54-55; Tarn 1974: 101-2.

39. The evidence cited is not substantial and suggests that the practice was rare. Laying on hands was standard for ordination (Acts 6:6; 1 Tim 4:14; 5:22; 2 Tim 1:6; p. Sanh. 1:2, §13; Jeremias 1969: 235-36; Daube 1973: 207-40, passim; idem 1960: 56-59; cf. Hruby 1970; contrast Hoffman 1979), often on OT precedent (Num 27:18, 23; Deut 34:9; Sifre Deut. 357.17.1; cf. Daube 1973: 238-

doubtful, however, whether the parents who sought Jesus' blessing knew either the power of his hands (3:12) or the power of his prayers (21:21-22).

One was not permitted to oppress minors or other powerless people (e.g., b. Sanh. 25b); the issue is simply that children were expected to be obedient and in their place (cf. Jeremias 1971: 227-28).[40] Children were low-status dependents; they had to trust adults and receive what they provided (cf. Best 1976: 133-34). Low in status, they could not be permitted to deter a teacher like Jesus from "important" matters — at least, this was the view of the disciples (19:13). Disciples, who owed great respect to their teachers, typically sought to avert other interruptions for them (2 Kings 4:27; Diog. Laert. 7.7.182). Jesus responds like Elisha to disciples seeking to shield him from others' supplications: "Let the person alone" (2 Kings 4:27). Later, lest Jesus be delayed in his mission to establish the kingdom in Jerusalem, crowds try to silence blind beggars (20:31). It seems that in both passages, as in the parallel passages in Mark, disciples and crowds alike fail to understand what Jesus' kingdom is really about — caring for the weakest rather than engaging in political triumphalism.

The Cost of Discipleship (19:16-22)

Cf. Mk 10:17-22; Lk 18:18-23. If the kingdom belongs to children (19:13-15), those who receive the kingdom as humble dependents (18:1-6), then someone accustomed to being powerful and supporting dependents might find it difficult to enter life, the kingdom (cf. 5:20; 7:14; 18:8; 25:46).[41] This is the illustration with which 19:16-24 confronts Matthew's community: wealth and status make perfect surrender to God's will more difficult because those who have it think that they have more to lose. Many examples of faith in the Bible are acts of desperation; few are the acts of self-satisfied individuals. Ultimately, one who would receive the kingdom must not only obey like an obedient child, but relinquish one's worldly possessions and cares, acknowledging the absolute authority of the ultimate king (19:16-22).[42]

---

39). Hands were also laid on in sacrifices (e.g., m. Ḥag. 2:2-3). Some evidence does show, however, that the broader OT practice of blessing by laying on hands (Gen 48:14) continued in some subsequent Jewish prayers (1QapGen 20.22, 29; Jos. and Asen. 8:9; 21:6; Acts 13:3; Vermes 1973: 240n.35 cites 2 Kings 5:11 LXX; cf. Flusser 1957); this is what Daube calls the "gentle leaning" (see 1956: 343; cf. Jeremias 1971: 143).

40. Cf. Lindemann 1983. Jesus was not the only wisdom teacher to challenge this practice, however, unless p. Sanh. 10:1, §9 emphasizes only that Israelites as a whole were special to God (hence including the children; cf. also Lam. Rab. 1:5, §32).

41. The "kingdom" and "(eternal) life" here are interchangeable (19:17, 23-24), since Jewish people thought of the latter as the life of the coming age (see Ladd 1978a: 32; cf. also "saved" in 19:25; 1:21).

42. Cope 1976: 119 suggests that in 19:16-22 Matthew draws on Prov 3:35; 4:2, 4; 28:10; however valuable these texts may be in understanding the social picture of the young man, however, they hardly supply an obvious singular background.

Those who want eternal life must obey God's commandments (19:16-20). How to obtain eternal life (19:16; cf. 18:8) was not an uncommon sort of question to address to a religious teacher (b. Ber. 28b, bar.; Tamid 32a; cf. Lk 3:10; Acts 2:37; 16:30). That this young man[43] addresses such a question to Jesus shows great respect; that in Mark he also calls him "good teacher" likewise shows respect (though the rareness of the expression may suggest that he is "overdoing" it; cf. Bailey 1980: 162). In Mark, Jesus shifts the title "good" to God alone, which comports well with Jesus' teaching style whether or not one assumes a high Christology (cf. Lk 12:14; for the emphatic character of the statement and its consistency with some Jewish teaching, cf. Vermes 1993: 159). Traditions emphasize the humility of radical Greek teachers who might deflect praise in very similar manners (Diod. Sic. 10.10.1). Yet such wording allows various interpretations, hence Matthew words the young man's query and Jesus' response differently than Mark; the man calls him simply "teacher" (according to the most likely textual reading; cf. 9:11; 12:38; 17:24; 22:16, 24, 36; 26:18). Matthew elsewhere emphasizes a high Christology in traditional Jewish language (e.g., 1:23; 18:20) and does not wish to risk christological ambiguity here (cf. Gundry 1982: 385; Goulder 1974: 41; Moule 1965: 80). Thus the question becomes, "What good thing shall I do to obtain eternal life?" and Jesus responds with a typical counterquestion: "Why do you ask about what is good?"

Jewish teachers recognized that just as they praised God as good,[44] so also his commandments are good.[45] (Matthew's wording here is good Palestinian idiom: "There is [only] One who is good" employs a typical circumlocution.) Consequently, Jesus tells the man what "good" thing he must do: show his fidelity toward God's covenant by obeying his laws (cf. 5:43; 15:4; 22:39; and the vice list of 15:19). Undoubtedly he even gave to the poor, as Jewish law demanded (see comments on 6:2-4). These laws were part of first-century Jewish culture, and the young man is convinced that he has kept these laws (cf.

43. More specifically than Mark's language (Gundry 1982: 388), this designation probably ranges the man between 24 and 40 years old (Meier 1980: 219).

44. Philo *Mut.* 7; m. Ber. 9:2; b. Ber. 45b, 46a, 48b, 49a, 59b, 60b; Pesaḥ. 50a; p. Ta'an. 2:1, §10; 4:5, §10; Gen. Rab. 13:15; 57:2; cf. Abrahams 1924: 186; Marmorstein 1968b: 85-86; Ep. Diogn. 8; in Philo, Isaacs 1976: 30; in Platonism, Moore 1979: 249-53. Cf. the final benediction of the Eighteen Benedictions, if it is not later (Oesterley 1925: 61).

45. B. Ber. 5a; p. Rosh Hash. 3:8, §5; Pesiq. Rab Kah. 15:5; Abrahams 1924: 186. The issue of the "ultimate good" may have originally been a Greek one. Stoics held that the soul's virtue is the only good (Diog. Laert. 7.1.30) or that God is good (Hierocles 49.24 in van der Horst 1975: 157). This did not, of course, preclude more general Greek uses of the term (Heraclitus *Ep.* 9, to Hermodorus), and the rabbis themselves on occasion applied it more generally (Abrahams 1924: 186). That Matthew means Torah here (Cope 1976: 114) is possible but questionable (leaning heavily on rabbinic sources; in addition, the circumlocution better fits God — Meier 1980: 219; cf. also Mt 20:15); that this was the original sense, which Mark and Luke then misinterpreted (Murray 1985, supposing Matthew's material earlier), is, however, unlikely. Even in Mark, however, "good" quickly becomes an ethical rather than a christological issue (so also Hilary of Poitiers *On the Trinity* 9.2; *ACCS*, 140).

Odeberg 1964: 60).[46] (That he is unwilling to spare all his goods to help the poor will soon bring into question whether he really loves his neighbor as himself, however — 19:19-22.) But if he is really ready to submit to the yoke of God's kingdom, he must also become a follower of Jesus and submit to Jesus' demands.

Jesus summons a person who wants to be a disciple to absolute commitment (19:21-22).[47] Lists of virtues constitute a common rhetorical form (e.g., Theon *Progymn.* 9.15-24; Plut. *Stoic Contradictions* 7, *Mor.* 1034C; Corn. Nep. 15 [Epaminondas], 3.1-3; Philo *Sacrifices of Abel and Cain* 27). The commandments listed in 19:18-19 are humanward, summarized in the decree: "Love your neighbor as yourself" (Lev 19:18); by adding these words from 22:39, Matthew underlines this point. Yet if God alone is "good" (19:17), the man is lacking in some way (he himself admits it in 19:20, allowing Jesus to echo 5:48's call to "perfect obedience" in 19:21). True obedience to God's commandments requires the submission of the heart, abolishing anger, lust, and so forth (5:21-47), but Jesus takes the man at his word that he has kept these humanward commandments. Now the man's allegiance to the Godward love commandment (22:37-38) is tested: Does he serve God or money (6:24)? The loss of one's wealth or fear of how one's needs will be met can test disciples in this way (6:19-34; cf. 13:22); so also can the needs of the poor, as here (19:21). Love for God demands a true love for neighbor that not only avoids harming that neighbor but actively serves that neighbor (cf. comment on 5:40-42). One is also less likely to maintain possessions when one recognizes that disciples are merely stewards or managers to execute the master's will (24:47; 25:14). The young man wanted a "teacher" (19:16); he did not want a Lord who demands sacrifice (20:20-28). No wonder the man was "grieved" (19:22; for the strength of this term, cf. 17:23; 18:31; 26:22, 37).

By "going" (also 8:4; 20:4; cf. 10:6; 28:19) and abandoning all else (cf. especially 13:44), the man could have "followed" Jesus (19:21), that is, become his disciple (cf. 4:19; 8:22; 9:9; 16:24). The kingdom demands more than merely keeping many commandments; if a disciple would recognize Christ as his king, that disciple must surrender to him possessions, life, and even identity (cf. Johnson 1981: 17; Lane 1974a: 367). Whether Jesus then allows the disciple to use some of what the disciple has surrendered is Jesus' choice. Such words would have a jarring effect; mainstream Jewish teachers probably assumed — as later teachers codified — that one should not give away all one's possessions lest one be reduced to poverty oneself (Lane 1974a: 367; Jeremias 1969: 127; one might make an exception if necessary to serve one's parents — Bonsirven 1964: 147).

46. Mark, who does not call him young, emphasizes that he did so "from his youth," perhaps meaning from his coming-of-age ritual in his early teens, when later Jewish tradition argued that a young man became responsible for keeping the commandments (Lane 1974a: 366).

47. The force of Jesus' words may be inferred from the desperate attempts of modern professed disciples to circumvent them, as noted eloquently by Bonhoeffer 1963: 88-91.

Jesus generally called his own chief disciples (Mt 4:19, 21). Yet on some occasions prospective disciples did approach Jesus (8:19); and, as here, Jesus sometimes thrust them aside — probably, like some other ancient teachers, to test the would-be student's real willingness to become a learner. Early Jewish and Greek tradition seems to assume that disciples are responsible for acquiring their own teachers of the law (m. 'Abot 1:6, 16; Socrates *Ep.* 4). But Cynic and Stoic teachers sometimes rejected would-be disciples. Thus, for example, after Diogenes reportedly persisted in following Antisthenes despite the latter's attempts to drive him (and others) away (Diog. Laert. 6.2.21), he apparently adopted this initial rejection as a pedagogical technique for his own would-be disciples (Diog. Laert. 6.2.36); similar stories are told of the early Stoic Zeno repulsing rich young men, unimpressed by their worldly status (Diog. Laert. 7.1.22; cf. Mt 19:21). Such behavior was not simply legendary; an eyewitness reports that one Stoic wittily put a rich challenger in his place (Aul. Gel. 19.1.7-10) but then provided a reasonable private explanation for a more respectful, philosophically inclined inquirer (19.1.12-21).[48]

But in each case, the teachers finally embraced those disciples who persevered despite the rough treatment (Diog. *Ep.* 38; cf. Sifre Num. 115.5.7). Diogenes also successfully exhorted Crates to "throw into the sea any money he had" (Diog. Laert. 6.5.87). Diogenes was happy to attract disciples — provided they were willing to pay the appropriate price for following him, which could include forsaking one's family (Diog. Laert. 6.2.75-76; cf. Mt 4:22; 8:21-22; 10:35-37; for disciples sacrificing materially to follow rabbis, see Young 1989: 214). Would-be philosophers needed to count the cost before getting involved (Epict. *Disc.* 3.15.8-12).

When Jesus turned away prospective disciples with heavy demands, he probably intended his demands much like those of some other teachers: disciples must count the cost, repudiate their prior assets, and recognize the incomparable value of his teaching (cf. Lk 14:26-35 in the context of Lk 15:1-32). Persistent seekers throughout the Jesus tradition display the appropriate response: the Canaanite woman (Mt 15:25-28), the blind men (Mt 20:31-34), the Gentile centurion (Mt 8:7-13), and Jesus' own mother (Jn 2:3-9). Jesus' sorrow over the unwilling disciple (Mk 10:23-25) indicates that he hoped not to turn disciples away, but rather to make them *genuine* disciples, which they could do only by counting the cost and choosing the narrow way of following him. If one accepts Jesus' terms of unconditional surrender to him, however, he promises an unlimited supply of what *truly* matters (19:23-30).

48. Boring 1995: 118 provides an illustration from Diog. *Ep.* 24 to Alexander, which invites the latter to follow Diogenes but recognizes that Alexander will not do so because of his addiction to his boyfriend.

Sacrifice and Reward (19:23-30)

Cf. Mk 10:23-31; Lk 18:24-30. Jesus had promised a man treasure in heaven ("with God" — Jeremias 1971: 9) if he followed him (19:21; cf. 6:20); the young man preferred to keep his treasure on earth (19:22). Those who would follow him must receive the kingdom by grace — as helpless dependents (19:13-15) — but receiving the kingdom also means embracing God's rule, surrendering everything to Jesus without exception (cf. 13:44-46).

First, Jesus warns that the powerful can scarcely enter the kingdom at all (19:23-24). Camels were common beasts of burden among traveling Arabs (Babrius 8), known for their strength (Aelian *Animals* 4.55) but not particularly for gracefulness (Babrius 80.3-4). Jesus apparently employs a common figure of speech when he speaks of a camel passing through a needle's eye. In Babylonia, where the largest land animals were elephants (cf. Ach. Tat. 4.3.5; Lucian *Lover of Lies* 24), Jewish teachers could depict what was impossible or close to impossible as "an elephant passing through a needle's eye" (Abrahams 1924: 208; Dalman 1929: 230; Jeremias 1972: 195; Bailey 1980: 166, citing b. Ber 55b; B. Meṣ. 38b). In Palestine, where the largest land animal and beast of burden was a camel (cf. 23:24; b. Ketub. 67a), describing the impossible as a "camel passing through a needle's eye" may have been a common expression as well.[49] (Some commentators speculate that the "needle's eye" referred to a low gate in Jerusalem peasant homes into which a camel could enter if it cast off its load; there is no evidence, however, for such a gate, and a "needle's eye" meant then essentially what it means today; cf. m. Shab. 6:3.)[50] Despite many interpreters' attempts to evade the force of the saying,[51] toning down the hyperbole robs it of its intended force: the rich and powerful could barely enter the kingdom at all.

Such a statement shocked the sensibilities of the disciples even more than 19:10 had; in the story world of the Gospels, they share the values of Jesus' enemies (Rhoads and Michie 1982: 91-92; Mt 16:23). Presumably because many of their contemporaries viewed wealth as a mark of God's blessing (e.g., Ep. Arist.

49. Jesus may also suggest an Aramaic wordplay here between "camel" *(gamal)* and "acts of charity" (*gemiluth;* Blomberg 1992a: 299, following Derrett 1986). Camels are large; on regular journeys they can bear 400 pounds plus a rider, normally able to travel 28 miles a day or, if bearing only a rider and forced to do so only in extreme circumstances, can traverse as much as 100 miles in 13 hours (Rapske 1994: 7-8). Given the eschatological urgency that adapts the more traditional saying, Vermes 1993: 85 thinks the saying authentic (noting that even Bultmann 1968: 105 accepts it!).

50. See Filson 1960: 210; most fully, Bailey 1980: 166. Some commentators observe that Mark's term for the needle's "eye" can also mean a hole in a rock (Taylor 1952: 431), but the use with a needle is more specific.

51. As Metzger 1971: 169 comments on Lk 18:25, some late scribes changed "camel" to the similar-sounding "rope" "in an attempt to soften the rigor of the statement." Some early Christian interpreters claimed that the text meant only to use wealth rightly (Caesarius of Arles *Sermons* 153.2; Clem. Alex. *Salvation of the Rich Man* 26), or simply not to be controlled by it (Clem. Alex. ibid.); more accurately, Augustine comments (*Sermon* 133), "It is hard to be saved if we have them; it is impossible if we love them" (*ACCS,* 145).

204-5; m. 'Abot 4:9; Qidd. 4:14), the disciples may have assumed that Jesus' standard for people who were not rich was even stricter: "[If not the rich], who then can be saved?" (19:25). Yet because God alone is good (19:17), salvation by merely human means is impossible for anyone; only with God is salvation possible.[52]

Second, Jesus promises the kingdom to whoever follows him (19:25-30). The disciples emphasize that they have forsaken all to follow Jesus, and he does not dispute their claim (19:27-28; 4:22). Nevertheless, the rest of Matthew's narrative casts its shadow back over this pronouncement: even once disciples have committed their lives to him, they must watch and pray to be ready for still other tests. Faced with loss of possessions, the rich young man walked away (19:22); faced with possible death, Jesus' disciples would later abandon him and flee (26:56).[53]

Because families might oppose Christ's call to discipleship, a true disciple must be prepared to abandon not only possessions but family (19:29; cf. 8:21-22; 10:21, 34-37; 19:10-12) for Christ's name (cf. 5:11; 10:22; 24:9). Jesus himself (12:46-50; 13:55-57) and probably many in Matthew's Jewish-Christian audience had suffered rejection by their families, a pain felt much more severely in that culture than in ours. In response to such sacrifices, however, God would multiply the disciples' resources (19:29), precisely because in the kingdom they find a new and larger family than the one they may have left behind, and as a family true believers share their resources with one another (cf. Acts 2:44-45; 4:32-35; Kee 1977: 109-10; Lane 1974a: 372; Tannehill 1975: 147-52; Rhoads and Michie 1982: 92).[54] To at least some degree the second- and third-century church exemplified this ideal (cf. Stark 1998: 30). Matthew seems to assume Mark's stated meaning that part of this reward comes in the present age (cf. also in some Jewish texts, e.g., m. Qidd. 4:14; t. Pe'a 1:2-3; b. Menaḥ. 44a, bar.); this in turn assumes that the church will live like the community of God's kingdom, that his will may be done on earth as it is in heaven (cf. 6:10). While such words may have encouraged early faith missionaries (Trocmé 1975: 203; Rhoads and Michie 1982: 92), they just as readily address a persecuted church (Heb 10:34).

52. Boring 1995: 118 compares Philo *Mos.* 1.31.174, which comments on the promise of God's salvation in Ex 14:13 and declares that what is impossible for humans is possible with God (cf. Mt 17:20; Lk 1:37).

53. It is unlikely that the sharing of "fields" addresses "radical peasant demands for land redistribution" (Oakman 1991: 172), even if many of Jesus' first hearers were peasants who would have longed for more land.

54. For an impoverished person's "wealth" through others' support, see, e.g., Socrates *Ep.* 21-22. Jewish texts also speak of God's reward for righteousness exceeding by many times what the righteous have sacrificed (Sir 35:10-11); the Slavonic text of 3 Bar. 15:2 even speaks of a hundredfold reward in this life, via angels (perhaps based on the Gospels, perhaps related to Gen 26:12; cf. Mt 13:23). The suggestion that Jesus adjusts the traditional "exchange rate" of twofold in Test. Job 4:6-9 (Boring 1995: 119) makes too much of that single reference, which simply reflects Job 42:10.

Specifically to these twelve who forsook their livelihoods to follow Jesus' call he promises that they will sit on thrones judging the twelve tribes of Israel (19:28). Some scholars suggest that this Q promise must be authentic, preceding the betrayal by Judas (Manson 1979: 217). The "Twelve" continued even after Judas's betrayal (1 Cor 15:5), but one would expect any later prediction pretending to be prophecy and addressed to the Twelve to stress the condition of perseverance, given the church's knowledge of Judas's failure (Sanders 1985: 100; idem 1993: 190; Witherington 1990: 140-41). Further, though later Christians might have invented a tradition about their apostles reigning, they certainly would not have limited their rule to Israel (cf. the probable reapplication to the whole church even in Rev 21:12-14). Given Mark's skepticism about the first disciples (perhaps about disciples in general), it is not difficult to see why he would have omitted this promise, even if this is the point at which it appeared in the tradition. Stylistic evidence also favors an early tradition (Martin 1988: 8-9). Although it may also have been a free-floating tradition (22:28-30), it is possible that the promise may have been transmitted as part of Jesus' eschatological discourse (D. Wenham 1984b: 101-34).

That Jesus would reward his loyal followers would not have surprised them; they seem to have expected as much (16:16, 21-22; 20:20-22). Jewish people in Palestine understood that the fate of client kings could rest on their allegiance to the appropriate party in a larger conflict; thus when Mark Antony, Herod the Great's patron, lost to Octavian (Augustus Caesar), Herod recognized his own imminent peril and quickly sought Octavian's pardon for having followed the wrong patron (Jos. *Ant.* 15.161-63, 187-201). When a patron achieved political success, he rewarded his supporters; thus, for example, Sejanus saw to it that Pontius Pilate was prefect of Judea, though Pilate's political fortunes eventually declined with those of Sejanus. Ancient readers also expected such treatment in the divine sphere: Greeks told of Phrygia's destruction for rejecting gods in human disguise (Ovid *Metam.* 8.620-724) and emphasized divine personages like Dionysus who would come unrecognized, punishing those who rejected them (cf. Eurip. *Bacchants*). Judaism maintained its biblical tradition of a future day of judgment that would cut through the ambiguities of present existence.

Thus "when the Son of Man begins to rule from his glorious throne" (19:28; cf. 25:31; for "glory," 24:30), those who had followed him in his humble estate would "rule" (a common sense of "judge"; cf., e.g., Judg 4:4; 10:3; 12:7-14; 15:20; 1 Macc 9:73) Israel's twelve tribes.[55] Indeed, Jesus probably chose twelve disciples with such a connection in mind; see comment on 10:1 (cf. the

55. Witherington 1990: 141-42 also suggests "judging" as in 1 Cor 6:3, however. He also notes (1990: 244) the "Son of Man's" judging function in 1 Enoch 46–62, which moves beyond the imagery in Dan 7:10, 13-14. In early Jewish and Christian thought, the righteous will rule in the world to come (Rom 5:17; 1 Cor 6:2-3; Rev 1:6; 22:5; Wis 3:7-8; 5:16; Jub. 22:11-12; 32:19; 1QM 1.5; 12.16; Sifre Deut. 47.2.8), as in the beginning (Gen 1:26-28; Ps 8:5-8; Sir 17:2, 4; Wis 10:2).

reign of the twelve patriarchs in Test. Jud. 25:1-2; Rev 21:12-14; or of the tribes over the world in Test. Abr. 13A).[56] The language of the "regeneration" could suggest the Stoic idea of a cosmic conflaguration, ending one of the universe's periodic cycles (cf. description in F. F. Bruce 1972b: 44; Philo *Aet.* 85; *Vit. Mos.* 2.65);[57] but in a Jewish context this must refer to the time of the new creation (Acts 3:19-21),[58] applicable especially to the time of Israel's restoration (cf. Jos. *Ant.* 11.66; Acts 1:6-7; 3:21, 25) and the resurrection (cf. Jos. *Apion* 2.218, though cf. also *War* 6.250). From Isaiah (65:17) on, this was a familiar Jewish hope (see, e.g., Black 1961: 135-36; Gaster 1976: 23). Of course, the graphic rather than precise nature of Jewish teachers' language allowed for the superlative exaltation of multiple disciples (e.g., m. 'Abot 2:8; see comment on 5:19; cf. 20:23).

Whatever the original setting of the saying, however, in its Matthean context it emphasizes a point that extends beyond the Twelve: those who sacrifice now and become least in this age will inherit the place of honor in the coming age (19:30–20:16; 19:30 and 20:16 function as an inclusio, bracketing the enclosed parable). The disciples' reward in the kingdom would be commensurate with their sacrifice for that kingdom.

Reversal of Fortunes (19:30–20:16)

The parable in 20:1-16 explicitly illustrates the point that the first will be last and the last first;[59] Matthew uses this principle (19:30; 20:16) to frame the parable (the literary device called inclusio) and hence to summarize its primary point (reversing the elements chiastically). The principle appears at the same point in Mark, ending Jesus' comments about the rich young ruler (Mk 10:31); Luke has

56. "Inherit" (19:29) frequently appears in eschatological contexts (e.g., 5:5; 21:38; 25:34; Ezek 47:13; 1 Macc 2:57; Wis 3:14; 5:5; Rom 8:17; 1 Cor 6:9; Ps. Sol. 12:6; 4 Ezra 7:96; 1 Enoch 40:9; 2 Enoch 50:2; m. 'Abot 3:11; b. Qidd. 40b; p. Qidd. 1:7, §6; Ex. Rab. 2:6; 20:4), evoking a new exodus (e.g., Ex 32:13; Num 33:54; Deut 1:38; 12:10; 1 Macc 2:56; 11QTemple 51:15-16; see Hester 1968: 22-36). For an inheritance in heaven, cf. 1 Pet 1:4; 2 Enoch 55:2; cf. Col 1:5. The wicked "inherit" hell (m. 'Abot 1:5; Pesiq. R. 23/24:2; absent in Mt 25:41). As in the OT, Jewish texts continue to portray Israel as God's inheritance as well (Jub. 1:21; Ps. Sol. 14:5; cf. 1QM 12.12).

57. Cf. also the possibly noncyclical renewal in Pliny and Seneca (Downing 1995); or the seasonal renewal in Longus 3.4. Apocalyptic texts often depicted the *Endzeit* in terms of the *Urzeit* (cf., e.g., Rev 22:1-3; 1QH 6.16-17; 4 Ezra 8:52-54; 9:5-6; Test. Levi 18:10-12; Test. Dan. 5:12; 2 Enoch 8:3; m. 'Abot 5:20; b. Tamid 32b; Tem. 16a; Yoma 87a; Song Rab. 4:12, §3; see further Rissi 1966: 4; Arrington 1978: 77-81), a motif not entirely foreign to Roman readers, who had hoped for a restoration of the primeval Golden Age in the Augustan *Pax Romana* or other events (cf., e.g., Calpurnius Siculus 42-45; cf. Winslow 1971: 239).

58. See Manson 1979: 216; France 1985: 287; Sim 1993b; Hagner 1995: 565; for the "resurrection," see Derrett 1984.

59. The rhyming *kinâ* meter suggests authenticity (see Jeremias 1971: 27; cf. Dalman 1929: 228); for a fuller defense of probable authenticity see Fortna 1990, who also contrasts the realism of 20:1-7 with the unthinkable, hence dramatic, conflict of 20:8-15.

made use of it in a more topical eschatological context addressing Jews and Gentiles (Lk 13:30), perhaps aware that the saying also floated freely in oral tradition. But while Matthew alone includes this parable of laborers in the vineyard, Matthew did not invent the parable; starting with the principle alone, one could have created a parable that would have illustrated it with a closer correspondence than *equal* pay for unequal labor.

In its original setting, the parable may have addressed Israel and the nations (as in 21:33-44; the way Luke employs the detached saying in Lk 13:30). One may compare the parable in Sifra Behuq. pq. 2.262.1.9: a king paid other workers a modest wage, but to an especially hard worker, symbolizing Israel, he provided much pay. God repaid Gentiles for their little good in this life, but would repay Israel all she deserved in the coming world.[60] Still, the parable could also fit Jesus' emphasis on the poor and on embracing sinners (Jeremias 1972: 37), a more Lukan emphasis Matthew included but emphasized less than Luke did. Whether one thinks of Gentiles or other excluded classes, recognizing the exaltation of the socially, ethnically, or morally excluded fits Jesus' emphasis elsewhere (e.g., 22:1-14; 23:12; Lk 14:11; cf. 1 Cor 1:26-31).

In Matthew's context, the parable itself could point to many disciples who have forsaken "all," but also to the fact that even those who had the least to forsake will receive the same reward. More likely, in view of the prominence of the Markan conclusion "the first shall be last . . . ," the emphasis is specifically on disciples who humble themselves, sacrifice much, but are amply rewarded, in contrast to those who only pretend to follow without sacrifice (19:21-30; 23:2-12). Jesus speaks of rank in the day of judgment (5:19).[61]

The story's details fit first-century Galilee. The vineyard (20:1) may represent Israel as in 21:33 (cf. 9:37; 21:28; Is 3:13-15; 5:1-7); but vineyards were common and hence provided a natural setting for parables without a consistent meaning. The parable's point does not in any case hinge on this identification. Rich landowners (Jas 5:1-5), vineyards (Song 8:11; m. Kil. 4:1–8:1), and hirelings (Jn 10:12) were all important features of Galilean life in this period. Other Palestinian texts support the plausibility of various details of the text (e.g., the way idle workers are hired), reflecting an authentic Palestinian source (cf. Manns 1980a). Other Jewish teachers also laid heavy emphasis on fieldowners' showing concern for the poor (cf. m. Pe'a, passim), and, more to the point, could

60. Neusner 3:354; probably the story line is older than its occurrence in this Tannaitic commentary. Matthew's version appears to contradict this older parable deliberately (Smith 1951: 50-51), flouting conventional values (Johnston 1977b: 633-35; cf. Young 1989: 262-66). Jeremias cites a fourth-century parable that he thinks is dependent on Jesus here (1972: 138-39); the parable speaks of laborers receiving equal wages for different tasks, but some (representing a diligent rabbi who died young) had worked harder (1972: 37; cf. Young 1989: 261-62; Vermes 1993: 105-6; Davies and Allison 1997: 70-71). Boring 1995: 120 cites *Tanḥuma Ki teze* and Midr. Ps. 37:13. The proposed midrash here on Jer 31:31-32 (Córeces 1990) is less than obvious.

61. One rhetorically notable feature here is probable preference for beginning words with vowels in one sentence (20:3), with a special play on *agora argous* at the end.

portray God as the master of one's labor, who would pay the reward of one's work (m. 'Abot 2:14).[62]

Many Galileans seem to have owned small homes and worked their own fields or crafts (Goodman 1983: 34, from Tannaitic evidence), but many others were peasants working the estates of a handful of well-to-do absentee landlords (see Horsley and Hanson 1985: 59; Horsley 1995: 207-9).[63] Sometimes workers hired themselves out as servants to work for others for a specified period of time up to six years (Klausner 1979b: 180), but temporary help was cheaper for the employer (MacMullen 1974: 42). The harvest, in late spring, required an influx of extra workers, some to guard both crops in the fields and gathered sheaves against thieves and animals, most to harvest (Lewis 1983: 122), plus a few, lesser-paid donkey drivers, sometimes boys (Lewis 1983: 123). For such workers landowners typically drew on the ranks of the landless — sometimes homeless — poor for such brief and urgent tasks (Goodman 1983: 38-39).

One should not press allegorical significance into all a parable's details; some points may simply provide realism to the story (cf. 20:3 with Prov 26:10). A day officially began at sunset, but Jewish people reckoned hours from sunrise ca. 6 a.m. (Jeremias 1972: 136n.21); the third hour was thus between 8 and 9 a.m. and the eleventh hour (v. 6) between 4 and 5. Twelve-hour workdays were customary only during harvest time (for more details on Mediterranean harvests, see, e.g., Cary and Haarhoff 1946: 108-9).[64] The urgency of the harvest (cf. Babrius 88:11-19; comment on 9:37-38) accounts for the landowner's frequent return to the marketplace to recruit more laborers.

He finds others sitting idle in the marketplace because they have not been hired.[65] Jeremias thinks that, "Because no one has hired us" is a cover for laziness, which 25:24-25 and some later practices in this region might confirm (1972: 37; cf. Acts 17:5; Plut. *Precepts of Statecraft* 2, *Mor.* 798C; b. Ber. 28b, bar.; cf. Pompeiian beggars in MacMullen 1974: 87). But while they intend their response to avoid shame, it could just as easily be because they have spent the morning gathering in the smaller harvest in their own smaller field. Throughout the Empire, many small landholders found part-time employment only during harvest or by serving on larger estates (Finley 1973: 107). During harvest local

62. R. Eleazar ben Arach, a disciple of Johanan ben Zakkai; the "Master of labor" probably serves a function analogous to the "Master of the House" *(ba'al habeyth)* who oversees labor in 2:15, attributed to R. Tarfon; for "hired laborers" as the righteous who would receive rewards, see, e.g., Gk. Ezra 1:14. Jesus uses a "householder" for God in 21:33 but for the hearer in 24:43; the roles of parable characters (limited by the roles visible in society) were usually adaptable.

63. This is not to attribute to Galilee the sort of slave-worked *latifundia* one found in Italy; see Goodman 1983: 33.

64. The popular allegorical interpretation in early Christian centuries, in which the "hours" represented the world's history, probably stemmed from Origen (Tevel 1992). The hours, however, are essential to the story line, without need for allegorization.

65. Jeremias 1972: 136n.21 thinks "stand" is used weakly; from modern village culture he supposes they sat and talked until hired. Malina 1993: 128 suggests that lower-status workers must wait to be asked, rather than seeking work.

shepherds and goatherds might also join in the work (Longus 2.1), though many urban elites did not think highly of them (see comment on 18:12). Unemployed day laborers were common,[66] but most of those were probably hired already in the morning.

The parable contrasts God's mercy with the stinginess of those who oppose his mercy. As in verse 8, employers normally paid wages in the evening (Lev 19:13; Deut 24:14-15; Jeremias 1972: 136; Goodman 1983: 39; cf. m. B. Meṣ. 9:11). This employer provided all the workers the same wages, despite the different lengths of time they had worked.[67] Those who had worked all day lost nothing; justice was served, but mercy was added. Jewish hearers would consider it pious to give wages even to those not expecting it (Test. Job 12:3-4; p. B. Meṣ. 6:1, §2).[68]

Nevertheless, those who had labored all day complained, murmuring (20:11; cf. Ex 16:2; Lk 15:2; Jn 6:41; 1 Cor 10:10);[69] Jesus' hearers may have been shocked that workers would openly react so negatively to a benevolent landowner from whom they might require future favors.[70] But the landowner sets them in their place, politely shaming them by reminding them that they are objecting not to injustice but to generosity. He is "good" (cf. 19:17); they have an "evil eye," that is, are stingy (6:23; Deut 15:9; Prov. 23:6; 28:22; Sir 14:8-10; 34:13; Tob 4:7, 16; m. 'Abot 2:9, 11).[71] In verse 13 he singles out one, perhaps the primary murmurer (Jeremias 1972: 137), but whereas they neglected to greet him with the requisite title (20:12; cf. Lk 15:29), he offers a polite title, "friend" (20:13) — which Matthew always uses to shame one who has presumed on another's grace (22:13; 26:50; also Fenton 1977: 321).[72]

66. See Jeremias 1972: 139; Horsley and Hanson 1985: 58-59; Applebaum 1974/76a: 657; Stambaugh and Balch 1986: 91-92.

67. Further, if some of those hired late had arrived late because they had traveled long distances, it was customary to pay them bonuses (as much as half the standard wage) if they still worked the whole day (Lewis 1983: 122); if any such matter is in view, the justice of the matter is even clearer. But since most Galileans had towns and villages in close proximity, and since the parable does not explain their lateness, this should not be assumed as part of the parable's meaning.

68. Similarly, when 18,000 workers were about to be laid off once the temple was finished, they immediately paid anyone who had worked even an hour (Jos. *Ant.* 20.219-20; Gundry 1982: 399; Young 1989: 259).

69. Those who had labored most of the day would have developed some sense of camaraderie among themselves; singing apparently was customary during the day-long reaping (see, e.g., Theocritus *The Reapers* in *Greek Bucolic Poets,* LCL 130-37; *Select Papyri* 1:64-67). The landowner probably provided food if this was the local custom (m. B. Meṣ. 7:1).

70. "Only" one hour is assumed, as in the undoubtedly underlying Semitic construction (Jeremias 1972: 39n.59).

71. Elliott 1992 focuses on the parable's attack on envy and gives background on types of communities where people believe in an "evil eye." Although both pertain to envy, however, one should distinguish between the more general sense of "stinginess" in this text and the magical danger of the "evil eye" in many cultures.

72. One could use such titles to imply the speaker's generosity and further shame the person addressed (e.g., Demosth. *On the Crown* 318). A hired worker was certainly never a "friend" (the different term *philos*) in its Greek sense of equality (Demosth. *On the Crown* 51). In aristocratic ethics, the poor should not expect favors but count them as "grace" (*charis* — Dion. Hal. 6.81.3).

In later rabbinic parables, the landowner provides one who labored two hours pay equal to that of those who labored all day, because he accomplished more in his two hours than they all day; or he pays a hard worker, symbolizing Israel, much extra.[73] By contrast, the image in Jesus' parable is one of unmerited grace; the owner realizes that an hour's fraction of a day's wage would not sustain a family (Jeremias 1972: 37; France 1985: 289). But a parable of grace also challenges those who operate only on a principle of merit, despising the showing of mercy to others because they felt it unfairly raised others to their own standing (Jeremias 1972: 38, comparing Lk 15:25-32).[74]

Suffering for the Kingdom (20:17-19)

Cf. Mk 10:32-34; Lk 18:31-34. The repeated passion predictions in Matthew, as in Mark, keep the reader focused on the direction of the narrative and color the whole of the narrative. Disciples may sacrifice much and be rewarded (19:21–20:16), but the ultimate sacrifice is martyrdom, the price paid by Jesus and many who would follow him all the way (20:17-19). The placement of this prediction exposes the disciples' selfish conception of the kingdom in 20:20-22, 24: for them, the kingdom is about reigning, but Jesus recognizes that reigning first requires suffering (20:22-28). Significantly, this passion prediction adds the notion of mocking by Gentiles, a horrifying image in a culture emphasizing shame (e.g., Epict. *Disc.* 1.4.10), and diametrically opposed to the picture of a militant Messiah triumphing over the nations.

On passion predictions, see comment on 16:21; 17:22-23; the disciples had managed to ignore Jesus' warnings that did not make sense on their own cultural and theological presuppositions; they presumably felt that other sayings confirmed their predispositions (19:28; Plummer 1910: 276).

73. Cf. the Sifra reference above. Derrett 1974 argues that the landowner paid each the standard minimum wage for laborers; the denarius averaged a day's wage in this period and region (Jeremias 1972: 136; Gundry 1982: 396; and Carson 1984b: 427 cite Pliny 33.3; Tac. *Ann.* 1.17; Tob 5:14). Especially by the second century, the demand for laborers during the harvest allowed day laborers to receive almost the wages of a skilled worker (Lewis 1983: 123; he finds three and a half drachmas in *P. Oxy.* 1049). But in the first century the average harvest wages in Egypt may have been a half drachma or lower (Lewis 1983: 208), and even with wages in Palestine likely being higher than in Egypt, the landowner has probably been generous to all the harvesters (cf. one farm where workers during a normal season were paid only two loaves of bread per day — Lewis 1983: 69). The parable does not mention any other fringe benefits, such as food and drink supplied to the workers (Goodman 1983: 39); but the silence might assume either that it was or was not provided.

74. The parable does not lack an "absolute standard of justice" (pace Scott 1989: 296-97; for the theme of divine impartiality in deuterocanonical literature, see Bassler 1982: 17-44) as much as it points to grace that exceeds justice. But Scott 1989: 296-97 is right that this parable subverts the standard mytheme in the earlier Jewish story line. Emphasizing the criterion of need rather than merit, Rodríguez 1988 favorably titles 20:1-16 "The Parable of the Affirmative Action Employer."

The Reign of a Suffering Servant (20:20-28)

Cf. Mk 10:35-45; Lk 22:24-27. Hearing Jesus' promise of a special place for the Twelve (19:28), they wanted to establish a special place among the Twelve. To accomplish their petition, they enlisted their mother; Jewish tradition accorded aged women a special place of respect younger women did not hold (cf. Judg 5:7; 2 Sam 14:2; 20:16-22; Titus 2:4). Further, women could get away with asking requests men dare not ask, both in Jewish (Lk 18:2-5; 2 Sam 14:1-21; 20:16-22; 1 Kings 1:11-16; 2:17; Bailey 1980: 134) and broader Greco-Roman culture (Dixon 1988: 179; cf. Dion. Hal. 8.44.1–8.54.1; Tac. *Ann.* 16.10).[75] This narrative contrasts starkly with the worship and intercession of a Canaanite mother for her child in 15:25, perhaps inviting "reflection on the differences between the two supplicants" and the nature of appropriate petitions (Davies and Allison 1997: 87). This passage further indicates that the disciples had misunderstood both the preceding passion predictions and Jesus' teaching concerning the kingdom's nature.[76]

To the disciples, recognizing that Jesus was the Messiah and would soon reign was an expression of faith (16:17); unfortunately, they failed to grasp the seriousness of the sacrifice that was the prerequisite for his kingdom (16:21-27). Outsiders recognized Jesus' Davidic rule in truth (15:22; 20:30-31), but James and John at this point may function more like the crowds who recognize Jesus' Davidic role when it is popular (21:9) but do not become disciples submitted to Jesus' rule, preferring a revolutionary (27:17-25). Matthew provides a number of lessons for his community through the negative model of discipleship this passage presents.

First, the Lord evaluates the motivation for disciples' prayers (20:20-21). The sequence of the narrative explicitly contrasts this request for costless glory with a desperate prayer of true need in 20:29-34. Both groups recognized Jesus as the coming king, but the first group sought Jesus for personal advancement, the latter for genuine need.

Second, only those who suffer with Jesus will reign with him (20:22-23). This perspective became the view of the early Christians on the whole (cf. Rom 8:17; 2 Thess 1:5; 2 Tim 2:12) and surely goes back to Jesus himself.[77] A

75. Cf. also appeals to prefects with special concern for women's powerlessness (e.g., *P. Sakaon* 36 in Horsley 1987: 132-33; cf. *P. Oxy.* 261.12-13); despite official laws some women pleaded cases before Roman magistrates (Simon 1990). Neither here nor in 27:56 does Matthew depend on Mark for his knowledge of Zebedee's wife; this suggests either another source — her mediatory function here does not seem theologically significant, at least beyond an immediate community that knew her — or perhaps first- or secondhand acquaintance with information from the sons of Zebedee, especially John (who outlived Acts 12:2). Although her introduction is too incidental for this to be Matthew's point, it may be of interest to us that the fishermen's departure to follow Jesus (4:21-22) had not alienated their mother (hence *probably* not their immediate family).

76. Cullmann 1956b: 17 compares this misunderstanding with the Zealot paradigm of the kingdom; but these disciples may have hoped to avoid even a final war!

77. Because early Christian tradition has John living into the late first century, in contrast to James, the prophecy in 20:23 seems not to arise after the event; hence it is likely authentic

throne's "right" hand was the place of greatest honor (cf. 25:31),[78] but it is possible that Jesus points cryptically to a different throne than the disciples envision: if Jesus was to be enthroned first on a cross, the place reserved for those on either side of *that* throne was for two robbers (27:38). The "cup" the disciples must share is Jesus' death (26:27-28, 39), borrowed from one image for God's wrath in the prophets,[79] an image that continued to be intelligible to early second-century Christians (Mart. Pol. 14; perhaps Mart. Is. 5:13; later, Chrysostom *On the Incomprehensible Nature of God* 8.35; *ACCS,* 150-51). Jesus explicitly connects the cup at the last supper with his impending death (26:27-28; also Lampe 1951: 39).[80] As Cole notes, "this price they will in any case pay, for this is not the price of Christian greatness but the price of following Christ at all" (Cole 1961: 170).

Third, the greatest role in the kingdom is the role of the self-sacrificial servant (20:24-28). James and John were not the only ones with the problem; the other disciples were angry with them because they, too, wanted a high position; competition for status among peers was important in their culture (20:24; see Derrett 1973: 54; Malina 1993: 133).[81] But the world's models for status differ from those in God's kingdom; because honor ultimately belongs to God alone, disciples should seek to humble themselves and serve, allowing God to exalt them if and when he wills. Rank in the day of judgment (5:19) will confound many human expectations (18:4; 23:11). The "first" (cf. 20:16) must be servant of all. The call to enslavement was offensive: it was a commonplace that people, especially those born free, at best endured servitude with difficulty (Dio Cassius *R.H.* 1.5.12; 8.36.3; Philo *Praem.* 137; *Prob.* 36).

The least would be the greatest (20:26-28) as Jesus had just told them (19:30; 20:16). Besides forcefully drawing attention to his teaching by means of antithetical aphorisms in 20:26-27 (Tannehill 1975: 102-7), Jesus argues his point by means of both negative and positive examples. Negatively, one should not be like the pagans (20:25; cf. 5:47; 6:7; 18:17). Some beneficent rulers stressed service (cf. Solon in Diog. Laert. *Lives* 1.60), many Greeks affirmed that power could be either used nobly or abused (Dion. Hal. 5.77.6), and many Dias-

---

(Jeremias 1971: 243-44; Hill 1972: 288; Sanders 1985: 147; pace Theissen 1991: 197, who misses Gal 2:9).

78. For the center as the most important and the right hand as second, Lachs 1987: 337 cites m. Yoma 3:9; t. Sanh. 8:1; b. Yoma 37a; Midr. Ps. 18.

79. Ps 11:6; Is 51:17; Jer 25:15-17; 51:7; Hab 2:16; Zech 12:2; more in Gundry 1982: 402; for later Jewish references, see Lane 1974a: 380; cf., less relevantly but perhaps significant for more peripheral recent Gentile converts in Matthew's audience, Socrates' cup, e.g., in Sen. *Dial.* 1.3.12.

80. Although he implies Jesus' vicarious baptism in 3:6, 11, 14-15, Matthew omits Mark's less obvious picture of this baptism here, the same way Mark omits baptism in fire because he also omits the context that explains it; cf. Lk 12:49-50.

81. Ancient writers rarely view self-subordination to others as a prerequisite for authority, but are more apt to stress benevolent patriarchy; e.g., Diod. Sic. 27.16.2 (who often praises his protagonists' mercy) stresses that mercy is a paramount virtue for leadership. For the exaltation of the least, however, see Test. Jos. 17:8.

pora Jews respected pagan rulers benevolent toward Judaism. Nevertheless, Palestinian Jews, oppressed by a colonial situation in both Jesus' day and Matthew's, would naturally recognize that most rulers exploited power.[82] (Although often deprived of their own rulers, Jewish people also stressed rank — cf. 23:6-7; 1QS 5.23-24; 6.2.) But the tyrants and empires of history confirm the point; absolute power always corrupts precisely because the desire for power over others, to whatever extent one may achieve it, shows that people remain slaves to self-centeredness. Yet even though Christian history has often testified more to Jesus' observation about human depravity than to obedience to his teaching, many have continued to echo his teaching (Chrys. *Matthew* Homily 58; *ACCS,* 127).

Positively, Jesus himself was a suffering servant who laid down his life for his people (20:28; cf. Jn 13:13-15, 31-35).[83] This statement represents a typical *qal waḥomer,* or "how much more" argument: if their master was a servant, how much more should they humble themselves (Phil 2:1-11). Matthew clearly sees in this statement an allusion to the suffering servant of Isaiah (Mt 12:18), particularly in offering his "soul" or "life" (Is 53:12) as a ransom or redemption price (cf. 53:10-11) on behalf of "the many" (Is 53:11-12; cf. Mt 26:28; Rom 5:15). Despite the different paths they have taken into Greek,[84] the numerous correspondences between the first extant appearance of this saying in Mark (Mk 10:45) and the language of Isaiah indicates that Isaiah's servant was in view from the start (pace Hooker 1959: 74-79; idem 1983: 93; Anderson 1976: 257). Certainly by Matthew's day early Christians would recognize the allusion to Isaiah 53 (Lk 22:37; Acts 8:32-35; Jn 12:38; Justin *1 Apol.* 50).[85]

82. Mack 1988: 368-76 charges that the Gospel of Mark's "myth of innocent power" stands behind most of the existential troubles in the United States today (as well as behind Christian anti-Semitism). But Mark teaches disciples to abandon power rather than to seek it (Mk 10:42-45), contrary to Mack's counterreading; what Mack may dislike is the way the oppressed resonate with the way the theme of justice is expressed in apocalyptic vindication, but if so, the rest of his book fails to make his case adequately; pace Mack, Jesus was clearly eschatological.

83. The saying is Semitic and Jewish in its construction; for a defense of authenticity against the (in my view mostly subjective) objections against it, see Morris 1965: 29-33; Cullmann 1959: 65; Page 1980: 137-61; as Hill 1972: 289 observes, the objections to this position are not compelling. Bultmann 1958: 214 took Mk 10:45/Mt 20:28 as a hellenized form of Lk 22:27, but Jeremias 1965a: 46 correctly shows the reverse to be true (cf. Higgins 1964: 44).

84. If this logion originally circulated in Aramaic, an argument against compatibility with the Septuagint text of Is 53 is not particularly relevant for Jesus' ministry. While it may be relevant for Mark, it need not be as relevant for Matthew, who frequently follows Mark's quotations verbatim but elsewhere employs mixed types.

85. Many scholars see Isaiah's servant in the saying (e.g., Taylor 1945: 14; Cullmann 1959: 64-65; Argyle 1963: 154; Higgins 1964: 43; Jeremias 1971: 292-93; Albright and Mann 1971: 243; Ridderbos 1974: 31; Moulder 1977: 127; Gundry 1982: 404; Betz 1991: 73; Hagner 1995: 582; Davies and Allison 1997: 95-97; with less conviction, Kümmel 1957: 73; F. F. Bruce 1978: 29-30), though some, like Hill 1972: 289 and Witherington 1990: 254, find general language from the Isaian servant without Is 53:11-12. The Dead Sea Scrolls later apply "the many" of Isaiah and Daniel to themselves, "the elect" in a sectarian way (1QS 6.6-21; Albright and Mann 1971: 244; Gundry 1982: 404), but the rabbis retain Isaiah's use for the covenant community (Albright and Mann 1971: 245; cf. Lane 1974a: 384). Contrast Schedl 1981, who applies the title to the Gentiles; Greek texts can em-

The language here is that of substitutionary atonement, which (in view of Isaiah and Maccabean texts) need not have been foreign to Jesus himself.[86] Although the sense was Jewish and much of the construction Semitic, the thought would make sense to Mark's Diaspora readers as well: Greeks also regarded dying for others as heroism, and especially shared with them the notion of expiatory sacrifice (Hengel 1981a: 9, 19).[87] As in Philippians 2:1-11, however, the evangelists treat their audiences to this summary of Jesus' mission not to rehearse soteriology but to provide an active model for Christian living.

Persistent Prayer (20:29-34)

Cf. Mk 10:46-52; Lk 18:35-43. Despite the notorious dangers of roads like the one from Jericho to Jerusalem (20:29;[88] cf. Lk 10:30; Jeremias 1972: 203), many beggars would have sought alms from Passover pilgrims there at this season (Lane 1974a: 387).[89] Jericho was a relatively wealthy community with a priestly establishment (see Jos. *War* 4.459-75; Schwartz 1988; Finegan 1969: 81-88; Coughenour 1982: 995-96), boasting also Herod's winter palaces (Gleason 1987; Netzer 1989). Although Matthew, abbreviating Mark's account, omits the label "faith" here (Mk 10:52), he nevertheless illustrates the same principle (Mt 9:29).

---

ploy such phrases to designate the multitudes, as in, e.g., Epict. *Disc.* 1.3.4; 2.1.22; Marc. Aur. 11.23). If Is 53 is at all in view, the ransom would be to satisfy God's own anger (Is 53:10-12); but this may incorporate Is 43:3-4 (Witherington 1990: 254), which specifies "ransom" more clearly, where the price is that of redemption for liberation from captivity (Witherington 1990: 256 suggests "from Satan's grip").

86. See especially Morris 1965: 34; Gundry 1982: 404; Hagner 1995: 579-80; cf. Ladd 1974b: 187-88.

87. Heroic death, particularly in the military service of the state (Epameinondas 2, in Plutarch *Sayings of Kings, Mor.* 192C; inscriptions in *Empire,* ed. Sherk, p. 31, §15, p. 34, §19; Jos. *War* 1.43-44, 58; cf. Deut. Rab. 2:24), was an ideal in Greco-Roman literature, and this ideal extended to laying down one's life for another (Hengel 1981a: 9). One might be called upon to die for a friend (Epict. *Disc.* 2.7.3; Epicurus in Diog. Laert. *Lives* 10.120; Jn 15:13-15), and a sign of loyal friendship might be willingness to die together (Char. *Chaer.* 4.3.5; 7.1.7). But pace Mack 1988: 107, martyrology was not central to the Cynics, who endured torment but rarely martyrdom. In Epitome 22-23 and Sentences 406-7 Syriac Menander praises "friendship which continues to the house of death" (*OTP* 2:591, 604). In early Jewish literature, laying down one's life for another was not considered a norm, but it was nevertheless respected as heroic (Jacobs 1957; on Aqiba's martyrological perspective on love, see ibid., 43-44; Urbach 1979: 1:416-17, 443); "giving one's life" is also Jewish martyrological language (Stanton 1974: 35). 4 Maccabees may provide the closest extrabiblical parallels to atoning martyrdom (cf. Hill 1972: 289; Mack 1988: 105; Witherington 1990: 252).

88. Whether Matthew changes Mark (Mk 10:46) to make clear that the disciples were making a pilgrimage to Jerusalem, hence eager to set up the kingdom, or the two Gospels refer, as some have thought, to different Jerichos in the same proximity (the new one and ruins of the old), the minor change is well within the freedom of ancient biographers and Matthew's own style (cf. Mt 21:12-22// Mk 11:12-25). On the doubling of characters, see 8:28 and the doublet in 9:27.

89. Begging was also common in temples (Jos. *Apion* 1.305; Acts 3:2; cf. Stambaugh and Balch 1986: 109).

While this text does not promote selfish prayers like the one illustrated in 20:20-21, it does provide Matthew's audience principles for one with a desperate, life-affecting need (20:32-33).

First, these suppliants recognized the identity and authority of the one whose help they entreated (20:30). They recognized that Jesus was son of David — rightful ruler in God's coming kingdom (1:1; 15:22; 21:9);[90] they also acknowledged their need of mercy (5:7; cf. 6:2-4 — "alms" originally literally meant "acts of mercy"), humbly depending on his favor rather than their own merit.

Second, they refused to let others' priorities deter them (20:31). The crowd already "following" Jesus (20:29, 31; cf. 8:1; 19:2) did not want the teacher to be interrupted by beggars; many probably wanted him to get on with the business of setting up the kingdom they suspected he would establish (21:9). They did not understand that the agendas of the kingdom involved serving precisely the weakest (20:28; cf. 19:13). But the beggars exercised sufficient faith in the Lord's authority and concern that no one else's impatient dismissal of their need would keep them from persisting in their dependence on the teacher (cf. 8:7; 15:24-26).

Third, Jesus' compassion was the ultimate motivation for his acting (20:34). God knows the pain in his people's lives, and Jesus acted from compassion (cf. 6:8; 9:36; 14:14; 15:32). Biographers might praise the kindness of leaders who admitted to their presence even the lowliest of persons (Corn. Nep. 1 [Miltiades], 8.4), which fits the situation here (20:31-32). The immediacy of the healing is frequently mentioned in ancient healing reports, though Matthew often omits Mark's characteristic "immediately" (Theissen 1983: 66).

Finally, recipients of Jesus' gifts should follow him (20:34). Although Mark's "go" (Mk 10:52) makes their following even more striking, Matthew is equally clear that the formerly blind men, now able to follow Jesus, do just that. When Matthew speaks of "following" he refers especially to following as a disciple (8:19, 22; 19:21), which in this context means following to the cross (20:17-28).

Jerusalem's King Enters Her Gates (21:1-11)

Cf. Mk 11:1-10; Lk 19:28-40; Jn 12:12-19. This narrative both portrays Jesus as a king and reinterprets the significance of his kingship. Because his kingship was so different from worldly models of authority (20:25), Jesus subverts the worldly understanding of kingship to suggest a reign of a different order.

90. Robbins 1973: 241-43 sees Mark here linking the "Son of God" and "Son of David" traditions; but whereas the latter Christology is explicit, the former must be inferred from patterns in the second Gospel. More importantly, Jesus' granting the blind men's request confirms the "Son of David" title they offer him, which, however, is later qualified by a greater title (Mk 12:35-37; Kingsbury 1983: 149-50).

At the same time, although Jesus is not yet explicit about his kingship, with the triumphal entry Jesus begins to relinquish the messianic secret (cf. Burkill 1960).

Some scholars doubt much of the historical substance of this narrative; Catchpole 1984, for instance, notes that Mark 11:1-11 fits the formal pattern of a legend, in this case, of a king entering his city. But historical narrative could be told using the same formal pattern (Witherington 1990: 104). Witherington 1990: 105 argues in favor of the narrative that others commandeered animals; the original acclamation (one coming in the Lord's name) hardly reflects later christological confessions; and Psalm 118:26 was genuinely used during Passover, though later Christians probably would not know this (and hence would not fabricate it; see more fully below; on authenticity, see also Losie 1992). If Jesus entered the city in a memorable way at all (and there was no other reason to preserve the story), he had to acquire the animal by some means;[91] and if he rode an ass, he himself probably intended the allusion to Zechariah (Sanders 1993: 254). And why not, if Jesus both read the Hebrew Bible and knew himself of Davidic descent?

The narrative would convey a number of points to the faithful in the preaching of the church and presumably Matthew's exhortation to his community.

First, disciples' possessions belong to their King (21:1-3). Leaving Jericho (20:29) in the east, one might take the 17-mile Roman road climbing about 3,000 feet to Jerusalem (Carson 1984b: 437; Yamauchi 1972: 104-5). Pilgrims from the east would finally arrive at Bethphage, legally a suburb of Jerusalem but across the Kidron Valley, on the ridge of the Mount of Olives nearest Jerusalem; at this point Jerusalem came into sight (France 1985: 296).[92]

Matthew devotes less space than Mark to Jesus "impressing" or commandeering an animal, but in Matthew as well Jesus exercises a prerogative of authority, in this context suggesting royalty. Although household servants could think of the "lord" as the donkey's absent earthly owner (cf. Lane 1974a: 396; Ross 1984), perhaps implying that the owner already knew Jesus or that the disciples would mislead them, the borrowing more likely testifies to Jesus' status. Whether or not the owner is a disciple (cf. Lane 1974a: 392n.3), he has heard of Jesus, and Jesus foreknows his response. The response testifies first of all to the man's respect for Jesus: rulers (as Jesus is here) and officials could impress animals (Sall. *Jug.* 75.4; Burridge 1994: 54); Jewish teachers (as the man presumably regards Jesus) could also borrow animals among those who respected them (Derrett 1971). More importantly, the passage testifies to Jesus' foreknow-

91. A donkey could cost between two months' and two years' wages, depending on its age and condition, but most peasants who could save enough would buy one, as they were extremely important even in small-scale farming. If a farmer had two, however, he sometimes rented one out (Lewis 1983: 130).

92. If later texts reflect first-century custom here, Jerusalemites could regard Bethphage as an extension of Jerusalem (Lachs 1987: 344 cites m. Menaḥ. 11:2; t. Menaḥ. 11:1; cf. m. Menaḥ. 7:3), and hence domicile paschal pilgrims there.

ledge.[93] Matthew is not so much making a statement about possessions here as one about Christ: as the rightful king, he has the right to anything in creation, certainly among his people (cf. Gundry 1982: 408; Blomberg 1992a: 311-12).[94]

That Matthew includes two animals (e.g., Bratcher 1992) has occasioned considerable discussion. Some scholars (e.g., Sandmel 1978a: 59; Meier 1980: 232) think that Matthew has misunderstood the parallelism in Zechariah 9:9 (which he has also conflated with the similar Is 62:11); if so, Matthew also exploited the Septuagint's more ambiguous translation to convert the Hebrew's "male donkey" in one line into a mother donkey. More likely, however, Matthew attempts to show with what literal detail Jesus fulfilled the prophecy. In view of Matthew's knowledge of Hebrew elsewhere (his citation might *possibly* even presuppose more skilled readers grasping a connection between Jesus' name and the term "salvation" in a part of Zech 9:9 not cited — cf. Mt 1:21; Longenecker 1981: 102), it is quite unlikely that Matthew would be *unfamiliar* with Hebrew parallelism. Even here, where his point is closer to the Septuagint, he translates from the Hebrew more literally than the Septuagint does (Soares Prabhu 1976: 158-59). By reading the text in the manner most useful for his purpose, Matthew was not offering an unusual hermeneutic; his contemporaries regularly read more into a text than it required where it suited their purposes to do so.[95]

Then again, Matthew's mother donkey may fulfill an entirely different function here than the fulfillment of prophecy anyway. She cannot fulfill the prophecy precisely, given the gender in the Hebrew, which his translation shows that Matthew knows. Although Matthew himself does not stress that the colt is unbroken, Matthew's tradition may mention the mother to emphasize that the colt was, indeed, unbroken; such a colt might require the mother's presence to keep it calm amid shouting crowds (Gundry 1975: 199).[96] Citing the sacredness of unused animals in some traditions, some think that the borrowing of an unused animal must be legend here; "but it is just as likely that Jesus deliberately chose an unused donkey for the sacred occasion" (Gundry 1975: 197). As in later Palestine, one would drape the garments (on which Jesus sat) across both the mother

93. That Jesus would have prearranged the situation with the man without the disciples — who would have been his agents — knowing is unlikely (cf. 26:18). Jesus' foreknowledge is clearer in Mk 11:1-6, which parallels Mk 14:13-16 (see Robbins 1976: 23).

94. Lane (1974: 396) finds here a messianic allusion to Gen 49:10-11; while such midrashic allusions are always possible in the tradition, the degree of correspondence between the two texts does not seem adequate to have automatically suggested this allusion to even biblically literate hearers. Some writers have also suggested a possible "public pool of animals" for the Passover season (Gundry 1982: 407, following Derrett).

95. Cope 1976: 87; Goulder 1974: 22-23; cf., e.g., 3 Enoch 18:24; Sifre Deut. 313.1.4; p. Meg. 1:11, §4; Gen. Rab. 51:8; Pesiq. R. 5:3; Gal 3:16.

96. Gundry 1982: 407; Hagner 1995: 594 indicate that a colt would be taken from the mother only after it was broken. This custom makes sense, although some evidence cited in its favor (e.g., m. B. Bat. 5:3, even without the textual variant) is ambiguous. Unbroken animals were worth more (Hom. *Il.* 10.293).

and the colt, although Jesus would ride only one (Gundry 1982: 410; the "them" on which he sat could mean the garments).

It is thus possible that Matthew finds two animals in the text because he had both animals in one of his traditions.[97] At the same time, in view of his doubling of other figures in his narratives, this may simply be Matthew's way of underlining the importance of the event (8:28; 9:27; 20:30). (That Mark and John would independently simplify the narrative by omitting the second animal is not probable, though they could have drawn on a common tradition that had done so.)

Second, Jesus chose to define the kind of King he is (21:4-6). The triumphal entry is undoubtedly historical. Perhaps the Romans waited so long to execute Jesus because they did not know of the entry, perhaps because the acclamations at his entry would have been ambiguous to most Jerusalemites greeting pilgrims and his entrance was accomplished quickly (for the suggestion of a limited-scale event, cf. Catchpole 1984; Sanders 1985: 306). The disciples, however, would have remembered the event in great detail, and what Jesus intended to convey to them through the symbolic act is more critical than the immediate understanding of other bystanders; Jesus would be executed as a messianic pretender soon enough (cf. Sanders 1985: 308; pace Borg 1987: 186n.9).

It is unlikely that the later church would have thought to create a scene based on the authentic character of the Passover season; Mark's account, adapted by Matthew, thus undoubtedly preserves accurate tradition. "Hosanna!" and "Blessed is he who comes in the Lord's name" both reflect Psalm 118, part of the Hallel psalms sung during this season.[98] Although people officially began singing the Hallel apparently the night before the first day of Passover (t. Sukk. 3:2; Pesiq. Rab Kah. Sup. 2:8), many parents would undoubtedly rehearse it with their children before then (second-century rabbis applied to the Hallel the same rules applied to other liturgy — t. Meg. 2:2), and adults would know the Hallel psalms and their association with Passover.

Hopes for redemption ran high in the crowded fervor of Jerusalem near Passover, requiring the Roman governor to increase security during this time. Later Jewish thinkers clearly saw the future redemption prefigured in Passover, the Hallel (Jeremias 1966a: 256-57 and n. 3), and the cry "Hosanna" ("O save!" which had become an acclamation of praise — Moore 1971: 2:48; Lane 1974a: 398). Thus the arrival of a prophet from Galilee already associated with messi-

97. Soares Prabhu 1976: 159; Wenham 1977: 101, following Stendahl 1968: 200; cf. Gundry 1982: 409. Allison 1993b: 251 doubts that Matthew would have taken two animals from Zech 9:8 (the Hebrew has one and the LXX is ambiguous), but thinks that he may allude to Ex 4:20 LXX, which Matthew may have linked with Zech 9:9 via a common key word (252; on 249 he cites some Amoraic passages that link the two).

98. See m. Pesaḥ. 5:7; 9:3; 10:5-7; t. Pisha 8:22; b. Pesaḥ. 117a; cf. 26:30; cf. Moore 1971: 2:42; Jeremias 1966a: 255-56; Barclay 1959b: 42; Safrai 1974/76c: 809; Stendahl 1968: 65; at other feasts, e.g., m. Sukk. 3:10; 4:8; t. Sukk. 3:2; b. Shab. 21b, bar.; Sukk. 38b. On later unawareness of the Hallel here, see, e.g., Augustine *Tractates on John* 51.2; cf. Jerome *Homilies* 94.

anic acts (Mt 14:19-20) could lead crowds to expect the imminent restoration of the Davidic kingdom (Mk 11:10). But viewing Jesus as a mighty prophet proclaiming the kingdom (also Mt 21:11; cf. 21:46) was not the same as explicitly calling him the Son of David (21:9; cf. 16:14). (Unlike the crowds, the reader knows that Jesus was not merely "from Nazareth in Galilee" — 21:11 — but from Bethlehem — 2:1.)

The Sadducean aristocrats' position of power depended on their keeping peace between their people and the Romans (cf. Smallwood 1962; Horsley 1986b; Sanders 1985: 315). That they did not intervene during Jesus' triumphal entry suggests a number of possible factors on the historical level: very likely, the entry happened relatively quickly and the Sadducees, most of whom were busy with duties on the Temple Mount, were unaware of these events while they were transpiring; very likely, many of those greeting the royal party did not recognize the entry as messianic; and possibly the messianic commotion did not spread beyond the portion of the crowd already excited by Jesus' reputation (although Matthew emphasizes the popular acclaim more highly than Mark did — 21:10-11). It is not likely that everyone at the event perceived it in messianic terms; at the same time, the event itself is almost certainly historical, and we must ask what Jesus intended the event to convey. In that vein, it is important to note that the later church or his Jewish contemporaries might have chosen for Jesus a more militant steed, but Jesus chose a beast of burden that would convey the image of Zechariah 9:9 (cf. Judg 10:4; 12:14; 1 Kings 1:44; cf. Sanders 1993: 254; Witherington 1990: 106).[99]

That knowledge of the Zechariah allusion seems lost on Mark and perhaps his tradition (knowledge of Zech 9:9 could have enabled him to avoid a difficult periphrastic expression — Gundry 1975: 197-98) suggests the antiquity of the tradition. But Matthew and John, the Gospels suggesting the most Palestinian flavor and most apt to recognize the source of the allusion, explicitly cite this text. Although later teachers and probably Jesus' contemporaries regarded this prophecy as messianic (b. Sanh. 98a; 99a; Gen. Rab. 75:6; Edgar 1958: 48-49; Lachs 1987: 344), it was not such a popular text that his followers would have grasped the full significance of his actions immediately. Jesus was announcing that he was indeed a king, but not a warrior-king (Moule 1965: 87; Gundry 1982: 409; Sanders 1993: 242; cf. Borg 1987: 174). Jesus was the meek one (11:29; 12:18-21; cf. 5:5), who came to serve rather than be served (20:28).[100]

99. Matthew's first clause may derive from Is 62:11 (France 1985: 298); conflation of texts was common practice. An ass was of lower status than a horse (Babrius 76.18-19); Pesiq. R. 36:1 provides the Messiah with a truly royal mount, namely, the four creatures of Ezek 1.

100. Duff 1992 suggests that Mark employs images from a Greco-Roman king's triumphal entry into a conquered city and Zechariah's images of a divine warrior, but employs them ironically, to show that Jesus is not a warrior-king. A second-century tradition associates the lowly king's entrance on an ass with the rebuilding of the temple (Gen. Rab. 56:2); this could suggest intense irony in Jesus' entry and his following protest in the temple, but the Jewish tradition probably postdates A.D. 70.

Third, even many of those who did not understand the nature of Jesus' kingship paid him royal homage (21:7-11). Matthew specifically upgrades the Christology of Mark's crowd; Jesus' coming not only leads to cries that the Davidic kingdom must be imminent, but to hailing Jesus himself as "Son of David," the promised king (cf. Pope 1988). Essentially they are crying, "God save the king!" (21:9; also Gundry 1982: 411). Jewish tradition sometimes applied Psalm 118's acclamation to the coming king (Hurtado 1983: 185). Yet even in Matthew, Jerusalem itself does not know Jesus (21:10; cf. 8:27; 23:37-39); the crowds of Passover pilgrims (presumably from Galilee) must announce him (21:11).[101] Although the crowds had to honor Jesus by casting something before him (2 Kings 9:12-13) and branches were appropriate to the festal setting (Ps 118:27; cf. Rev 7:9; 2 Macc 10:7), John's specific mention of palm branches (Jn 12:13) is significant, for they normally were more in use at the feast of tabernacles (e.g., Gen. Rab. 41:1).[102]

Whereas Jesus by riding the donkey implies his dismissal of revolutionary aspirations, the crowd's use of palm branches, an allusion to the Maccabean triumphs, implies that they still see him in more revolutionary messianic terms.[103] The garments (21:8) also may function as royal acclamation (2 Kings 9:13).[104] By placing Jesus' prophecy that he would be hailed as the "coming one" after this event (23:39; contrast Lk 13:35; 19:38), Matthew implies that Jerusalem will someday recognize Jesus' true identity and embrace him before the end (cf. Rom 11:26; perhaps Rev 11:13).

Matthew's audience, probably still recalling the brutal events of the Jewish-Roman war, would be familiar enough with the dangers of challenging the political establishment to find another lesson in the story of the triumphal entry. From the perspective of the Gospel writers the entry was virtually an openly messianic claim, hence a challenge to the ruling class to relinquish its power. Such claims invariably led to the arrest and execution of their authors (Overman

101. Galilee was not far as in the Diaspora (only about a three days' journey), and the most pious Galilean pilgrims undoubtedly traveled to feasts frequently the way the Gospels depict (Jos. *War* 2.232; Freyne 1988: 181), even if many did not make all three annual pilgrimage festivals (see arguments in Horsley 1995: 144-46).

102. Although not explicitly mentioning palms, Matthew makes branches more explicit than in Mark, the new language being "more suitable to royalty" (Gundry 1982: 410). Because the branches are thrown down rather than waved, an allusion to the feast of tabernacles is unlikely here (Wilkinson 1978: 116; Lev 23:40); but if the palms are historical rather than part of Johannine symbolism (in favor of the latter, see Schnackenburg 1980: 2:374), they may well have been from Jericho (cf. Deut 34:3; Judg 1:16; 3:13; Jos. *Ant.* 9.7; 14.54; Pliny *N.H.* 5.15.70), hence few in number (cf. Hurtado 1983: 173). Many non-Greeks used branches and wreaths as symbols of peace or alliance (Polyb. *R.R.E.* 3.52).

103. 1 Macc 13:51; 2 Macc 10:7; Rev 7:9; Cullmann 1956b: 38; Stauffer 1960: 110; cf. Pesiq. R. 51:8; Westcott 1950: 179; F. F. Bruce 1980b: 8. Triumphal arrivals were a frequent picture in both Jewish and Greco-Roman texts, usually applying to military triumphs (see Davies and Allison 1997: 112).

104. Cf. also Plut. *Cato the Younger* 12 in Boring 1995: 123; Yalq. Ex. 168 in Lachs 1987: 344. For other honorific uses, one might compare b. Ketub. 66b; Lam. Rab. 1:16 (Lachs 1987: 344).

1996: 291). In the face of the Roman Empire and its local aristocratic allies, Jesus' meek kingship necessarily involved the cross.

When word of a notable visitor spreads quickly in the excited and gossipful crowded atmosphere of the festival (21:10), fanned by possibly growing reports of the entry, the Galilean pilgrims announce to the native Jerusalemites that they are hailing Jesus of Nazareth, a prophet from Galilee (21:11). The division between those who acclaim Jesus and those who seem stunned by the acclaim may represent the traditional division between urban and rural people in the Empire (Malina and Rohrbaugh 1992: 128-29); and, indeed, plenty of evidence substantiates that such divisions existed.[105] But the primary division is probably a regional one; most of Jesus' ministry has taken place in Galilee, which to Jerusalemites seemed far from the cultural corridors of power (see comment on 4:12-16). Jerusalem had been "troubled" at Jesus' birth (2:3), a strong term (reused in 14:26), but Matthew employs even stronger language here (21:10): Jerusalem was "quaked" (27:51; 8:24; 24:7; 28:2).

Jesus now accepts such public homage, which is appropriate (21:16). Nevertheless, the crowds understand the meaning of his messianic identity no more than the disciples had (16:20-22); Son of David remains a true but inadequate Christology (22:41-45).

Judgment on the Temple Establishment (21:12-17)

Cf. Mk 11:15-17; Lk 19:45-46; Jn 2:13-17. Given the large amount of theological controversy in first-century Palestinian Judaism, it was most likely those actions of Jesus that could be interpreted politically that led to his execution (Young 1989: 296; Sanders 1990: 94). Protest actions may be common today in the west, but they often excite little attention because they provoke little danger. When ancient philosophers like the Cynics criticized the authorities, however, they invited both persecution and suspicion of itinerant teachers in general (Liefeld 1967: 162). By challenging nationalism and rulers' policies, the biblical prophets had invited retribution no less frequently (23:30-31).

Against some scholars who have questioned whether Jesus could have predicted his impending death (see comment on 16:21), it seems nearly impossible that he would not have done so: in the events of this narrative, Jesus virtually provoked it.[106] Merely prophesying the temple's destruction invited scourging and the threat of death (Jer 26:11; Jos. *War* 6.300-309; Sanders 1985: 302; see Winkle 1986), and execution was especially the solution if a

105. E.g., m. Meg. 1:3; Oakman 1991: 152-53 cites Hesiod *W.D.* 225-47; Freyne 1988: 146-47 cites Jos. *Life* 177-78, 390-92; see further Finley 1973: 123-49; Applebaum 1974/76a: 663-64; MacMullen 1974: 15, 30-32.

106. This tells against the thesis that the temple cleansing occurred at the feast of tabernacles six months before this Passover (Sanders 1968: 287; Manson 1979: 78); his enemies would not have allowed him to live this long.

leader already had a significant gathering of followers (Sanders 1985: 303). The guardians of law and order in the temple, whose positions depended on keeping peace between the Romans and the people, were permitted to punish violations of the sanctity of the temple — and only this offense — with death (Jos. *War* 6.124-26; *Ant.* 15.417; Carmon 1973: 76, 167-68; cf. O'Rourke 1971: 174; Segal 1989b; pace Rabello 1980: 737-38). If Jesus did not violate the inner sanctuary, nevertheless he provoked the antagonism of those who could hand him over to the Romans as a messianic (royal) pretender, an offense the Romans viewed as treason.[107]

Citing archaeological evidence for shops alongside an adjoining street outside the temple wall, Sanders doubts that buying and selling occurred within the temple precincts (1992: 87). Given strong evidence for the thriving tourist trade in Jerusalem, however (Ep. Arist. 114; Avigad 1983b), these shops outside the temple wall were probably directed toward tourists year round (cf. m. Ber. 9:5; Sanders 1985: 365n.6); for that matter, the ancient Mediterranean urban economy regularly included many small specialized shops (see Lewis 1983: 136). Yet these shops outside the temple were undoubtedly different from the trade Jesus addresses in the Gospel tradition. Authorized money changers and dealers in sacrificial animals would need to be nearer the activity in the temple; further, priests had to examine the animals (also Philo *Spec. Leg.* 1.166).[108] Likewise, if Sanders thinks it absurd that cattle were marched from the outer court into the temple for sacrifice (Sanders 1992: 87-88), how much harder would it have been to have marched them in from *outside* the temple during a crowded festival; the law certainly required offerings of cattle or oxen for some circumstances (cf., e.g., Lev 1:3-9; 4:2-21; 8:2; 22:21; m. Sheqal. 4.7).[109]

Economic exploitation in the temple? Although pilgrims needed money changers in Jerusalem year round (cf. Wilkinson 1978: 118), later reports indicate that the authorities allowed money changers in the temple for only one week, beginning to change money on Adar 25, several days before the temple tax was due (on Nisan 1 — m. Sheqal. 1.3; cf. Abrahams 1917: 86; Jeremias 1969:

107. This is not to say, with Hamilton 1964, that Jesus' act in the temple would have recalled royal appropriation of funds; see the critique by Witherington 1990: 113-14. The mishnaic claim of execution without trial for violating the temple (m. Sanh. 9:6; Segal 1989a) might have been wishful thinking (cf. Acts 21:31); perhaps more likely, Jesus' act in the outer court may have been marginal enough to "violation" to require a hearing. He did not enter a prohibited precinct (a profanation punishable also elsewhere; see, e.g., Hesiod *Astron.* Fr. 3).

108. Later reports amplified and exaggerated the number of pigeons sold there (p. Ta'an. 4:5, §13), but the true numbers must have been enormous nonetheless (e.g., Sanders 1992: 88). Later tradition reports that money changers counted coins on a stool and separated them with a pin, probably to avoid handling them (m. B. Meṣ. 2:4; Kelim 12:5; Goodman 1983: 58).

109. Sanders is, of course, correct that ordinary persons did not normally sacrifice them (1992: 88); but if we suppose that such animals were ever used during this season, there is no reason that a small number of them would not have been kept in a restricted area of the outer court where the priests would have easier access to them (a large number would have required much fodder, as he points out). Sanders cites ancient sources that testify to the temple's quietness (1992: 87), but such reports could at best be propaganda during festivals.

18). Despite later complaints about the chief priestly families,[110] criticisms do not concern their economic exploitation of pilgrims: people seem to have viewed money changers in general as trustworthy and performing a public service (Goodman 1983: 57-58). Even in Galilee the varieties of local currency required money changers who could convert coinage for use in the temple (and local economy); this was necessary, not an option.[111] More importantly, ordinary money changers did not trade in the temple (Abrahams 1917: 86), and the temple money changers made little if any profit (m. Sheqal. 1.6-7), though Jerusalem undoubtedly profited from the resultant trade.[112] Nor is it probable that the priests themselves owned the animals being sold (Sanders 1992: 88); we lack reliable evidence that the priestly aristocracy made a direct profit (pace Reicke 1974: 168).

Because he opposes the buyers as well as the sellers (France 1985: 301), Jesus probably was not criticizing economic exploitation or high prices (Hagner 1995: 600; pace Gundry 1982: 413). But other issues may be at stake. If rabbinic reports are accurate, this practice, originally restricted to the Mount of Olives, had been moved to the temple shortly before Jesus' arrival, undoubtedly drawing considerable opposition (Lane 1974a: 403; Witherington 1990: 110, following Eppstein 1964). The practice would have helped the buyers, reducing the risk of an animal's becoming blemished in transit between the Mount of Olives and the temple, an expensive risk for most people; thus the real problem was paying money in the temple (Chilton 1994: 165). Likewise, treating the outer court of the temple like a hellenistic agora may have seemed reasonable to aristocrats with hellenistic training, but it would have infuriated those committed to contrary traditions. Perhaps this provided one factor in Jesus' challenge to the temple establishment.

A revolutionary challenge. Of all Jesus' acts, his attack on the temple came closest to appearing as a revolutionary challenge to the political order, but

110. E.g., Test. Levi 14:1; t. Menaḥ. 13:21; b. Pesaḥ. 57:1; Avigad 1983a: 71; but cf. Sanders 1993: 324, 336.

111. See Goodman 1983: 57; Sanders 1992: 63-65; cf. Finley 1973: 167; Neusner 1987.

112. Undoubtedly some would unofficially seek profit if it were possible, but were the practice widespread enough to be known, later rabbis had no reason to suppress knowledge of this practice (instead they differed as to the use of the *kollubos* surcharge — see Lachs 1987: 347). Yet some evidence suggests that people could be overcharged for sacrifices (m. Ker. 1:7). Further, later rabbis — whose ideological ancestors were probably Pharisees — felt that God would bless only sellers of Torah scrolls who acted out of devotion to God, not those who acted for profit (t. Bik. 2:15) — implying that the latter did exist. Some religious local families may also have dominated or even monopolized some Jerusalem markets (see Engle 1977: 121-22). But Abrahams 1917: 87 insists that whatever abuses Jesus may have found were not the rule, and he is probably correct; successors of the Pharisees would not have passed up an opportunity to critique a predominantly Sadducean system (cf. more generally Sanders 1992: 90-91 if the aristocracy's practices were widely known). Temples were used as banks (e.g., Juv. *Sat.* 14.261-62; Taylor 1979: 254; Cary and Haarhoff 1946: 126; Koester 1982: 1:90; Yamauchi 1980: 107-8), including the Jerusalem temple (2 Macc 3:6-7; 4 Macc 4:3-7; Goodman 1983: 58; Pesiq. R. 10:1) yet few complaints were directed against the Jerusalem hierarchy's abuse of funds, despite anger against Pilate's action (Jos. *War* 2.175). Most temples tried to keep sacrifices cheap as well to keep people coming (Sanders 1992: 90).

this action was a prophetic declaration rather than the challenge of a Zealot leader seeking a following (Bammel 1984a: 124-26). Revolutionary messianic figures typically drew followings in the wilderness, attempting to build support before striking; Jesus, by contrast, acted under the nose of the Roman authorities and calculated his martyrdom. His act itself was undoubtedly more symbolic than efficacious. Jesus acted against only a small area in the crowded outer court, which was 300 meters by 450 meters (Witherington 1990: 109-10). Further, he neither "recleansed" the temple daily, although the sellers had undoubtedly set up their tables again, nor continued his disruption long enough to permit the intervention of the temple's Levite police or, had a riot begun, the Romans (cf. Borg 1984: 171-73; Sanders 1985: 270).

But while we may question the magnitude of the action, we can doubt neither that it occurred nor that it had profound effects. Many of Jesus' contemporaries criticized the temple and its priesthood, and some expected eschatological judgment there (see Freyne 1988: 187-89; comments on Mt 24:1-3). Thus if Sanders doubts the traditional location of Jesus' action in the temple, he is not similarly dubious of the action itself, which he regards as an "almost indisputable" historical fact (1985: 11). "The action against the buyers and sellers and the frequent accusation that Jesus threatened to destroy the temple are mutually supportive" (1985: 364n.4). Jesus' action also fits his idea of a kingdom established by God's direct intervention (as found in Qumran documents); like some of his contemporaries, Jesus undoubtedly expected a kingdom "in which a temple, whether new or cleansed, would be useful" (1985: 232-33; cf. Brown 1994: 458).[113]

I would add that Jesus probably differed from most of these contemporaries in expecting a future temple that would at least include a spiritual temple (as in other Qumran texts) founded on himself (see evidence for this on 21:42; cf. Aune 1983: 175).[114] Later Christians would not have invented Jesus' act against

113. For the eschatological temple, cf., e.g., Tob 13:10; 14:5; 1 Enoch 90:28-29; 91:13, Eth.; Sib. Or. 3.657-60, 702, 772-74; 11QTemple cols. 30-45 (which depicts a temple much larger than the current Herodian one — Broshi 1987); most extensively, Sanders 1985: 77-90, who emphasizes (86-87) that precise expectations varied. Many expected God to build the sanctuary, however (e.g., Jub. 1:17; 2 Bar. 4:3; 32:4), to the extent that the language is intended literally (cf. Test. Mos. 2:4, which applies this image to the *first* sanctuary; the fourteenth benediction in Oesterley 1925: 65). After the temple's destruction most Palestinian Jews certainly longed for an imminent new one; cf. coins in Carmon 1973: 81, 178; the fourteenth benediction of the Amida; t. Rosh Hash. 2:9; Shab. 1:13; synagogue mosaics as late as the sixth century (Dequeker 1986). Worship may even have continued on the site between 70 and 135 (Clark 1960), and synagogue architecture apparently attempted to symbolize the temple as well (Friedman 1983).

114. For the temple as the community, cf. 1QS 5.5-6; 8.5, 8-9; 9.6; perhaps CD 2.10, 13; 3.19. See, e.g., Flusser 1988: 37-39, 44; Gärtner 1965: 16-46 (who also cites 4QpIsa d, fr. 1; 1QpHab 12.1ff.); Driver 1965: 539; F. F. Bruce 1969: 76; Wilcox 1969: 93-94; Sanders 1985: 376-77; though cf. Caquot 1992. The Temple Scroll even structures the new temple after Israel's camp in the wilderness (cf. Yadin 1984: 42). The same concept may appear in a more individualized form in Philo *Praem.* 123; cf. Herm. *Vis.* 3 (especially if the tower may be identified with the temple by way of 1 Enoch 89:49-50). Gärtner 1965: 30-42 argues for it also in 4QFlor, but this has been seriously challenged (McNicol 1977; Schwartz 1979).

the temple; they maintained their connections with the temple (Acts 2:46; 21:23-26) and wished to avoid the suspicion that they were subversive (which enemies of temples were considered anywhere in the Empire). Attestation by both Markan and Johannine streams of tradition further supports the tradition's antiquity (Witherington 1990: 109-10).

A protest against unholiness? In one interpretation of the temple cleansing, Jesus protested unholiness in the temple and was a scrupulous exponent of holiness (Stauffer 1960: 67; for his known opposition to sin, cf. also *P. Oxy.* 840.34ff.). Certainly later Jewish tradition prohibits entering the temple with staff, sandals, dust on one's feet, or profane clothing, or walking through it for secular purposes (m. Ber. 9:5), so Jesus may have been enforcing a custom already practiced most of the year (Nineham 1977: 304). Borg sets this symbolic sign in the context of his views of Jesus' conflict with his contemporaries over the meaning of holiness (Borg 1983: 171-72; idem 1987: 174-76; cf. 1983: 163-99). Scripture had indeed announced that the temple would be purified (Mal 3:1-4; though cf. the hesitation of Hooker 1983: 79, 83); thus some have viewed Jesus' act as a messianic one but not intended politically (cf. Roth 1960a); messianic figures could claim authority by challenging holy sites (Jerusalem in Jos. *War* 2.261-63; the Samaritan temple site in *Ant.* 18.85-87). This interpretation is not incompatible with the view that Jesus was offering a prophetic sign of the temple's destruction; prophecies of its destruction typically rested on the view that it had already been defiled (cf. 23:38; 24:15). But as Sanders points out, Jesus might have symbolized a *mere* purifying of the temple by pouring out water; overturning tables signified something more ominous (1985: 70).[115]

Jesus could be arguing that the temple is morally and spiritually impure, as the Qumran sect also believed. Because he does not directly charge the Sadducean priestly aristocracy with corruption (as in 1QpHab 9.4-5; 11.6-7; CD 5.6-7; cf. Ps. Sol. 8:11-13; Test. Levi 14:1, if not an interpolation) or false doctrine (cf. later rabbis), his criticisms seem to differ from those of his contemporaries (cf. Sanders 1985: 65-66).[116] But although his action may have offended more than the Sadducees (Sanders 1985: 69), they were the ones he shamed by acting against their control of the temple without their retribution. Jesus clearly rejects the moral authority of those running the temple system (21:24-25, 38-45; Mk 11:29-30; 12:7-12), and his actions, backed by his own growing popularity, could only strike them as a deliberate affront to their own position. His parable about usurping tenants murdering the vineyard's rightful heir virtually constituted a challenge to them to act against him (21:33-45).

A protest against ethnic segregation? That the selling occurred in the

115. But cf. Nehemiah's cleansing in Neh 13:4-9, 12-13 (Witherington 1990: 115) and arguments for the view that Jesus historically sought merely the temple's purification in Evans 1989.

116. If the high priest profited from the temple tax (perhaps, though far from certainly, the *Terumah* and tithe in m. Sheqal. 3:1) and later "the so-called shops of the House of Annas," he may have profited from other business dealings as well (Witherington 1990: 110).

outer court, beyond which Gentiles could not travel, may have been significant (cf. Jos. *Ant.* 12.145; 15.417). Although the front court of the temple was normally to be kept clear as a sacred area (cf. m. Ber. 9.5), the many temporary shops inside it selling animals would have violated this usage even if they consumed but a small part of the temple area. Although scholars dispute whether Jesus actually cited these texts in the temple (Harvey 1982: 132; Sanders 1985: 66),[117] Mark (hence Matthew) claims that he cited two texts, Isaiah 56:7 and Jeremiah 7:11. Because it is unlikely that Jesus would have acted against the temple without citing scriptural precedent, and disciples strove to remember their teachers' sayings, Mark's citation of these texts (albeit in LXX form) may reflect authentic Jesus tradition, hence an accurate interpretation of Jesus' attack on the temple. (Cf. similarly Borg 1983: 173; prophetic acts are normally interpreted, hence the saying is likely authentic.)[118]

In Isaiah 56 God promises to accept foreigners and eunuchs (previously banned — Deut 23:1) as members of his people, declaring that his temple will welcome all peoples; indeed, its purpose had been universalistic from the start (1 Kings 8:41-43; Jos. *Apion* 2.193). But by Jesus' day (in contrast to the ancient Israelite temple) a partition with warning signs segregated Gentiles from the Israelite section of the outer court (Jos. *War* 5.194; 6.124-26; *Ant.* 15.417), probably for purity reasons (Jos. *Apion* 2.102-5; women were similarly considered less pure than men; cf. also 11QTemple 3-48). Although some have inferred too much,[119] concern for the sanctity of this outer court, hence for the worship of the Gentiles, may have been part of Jesus' objection to the current temple order (pace Sanders 1985: 67-68; cf., e.g., MacGregor 1936: 19; Glasson 1963b: 149-50; in Mark, Matera 1982: 147). Whether Jesus protested the architecture of the temple per se (Borg 1984: 175) or primarily the commercial insensitivity to the sacredness of the only part of the temple now available to them may be debated.

Nevertheless, that Matthew, despite his emphasis on the Gentile mission, deletes the words "for all nations" from Mark's quotation may suggest that Mat-

117. That Mark cites the LXX should not surprise us (as he usually does), nor would it be *impossible,* if Jesus wished the crowds from afar to understand or directed his words against the priestly aristocracy, for Jesus himself to have cited a Greek version (though we should probably not think of him having examined various versions and practiced text criticism the way later rabbis did). Although "robbers" in the temple might prefigure the "brigands" who possessed it during the Judean-Roman war (cf. Mt 24:15), the saying no more presupposes that event as past (pace Harvey) than does Jeremiah's statement that it quotes.

118. Some prefer the Johannine tradition, in which they find an allusion to Zech 14:21 (Jn 2:16; Witherington 1990: 114). On the whole, I would prefer Mark to John (the latter seems to extrapolate the tradition considerably where we can examine his method), though it is also possible that both traditions preserve historical substance even at this point.

119. Falk ingeniously but fallaciously argues that Jesus defended Gentiles from Shammaite halakah dominant in the temple (1985: 152), and that the Tosefta's lament that the temple was destroyed for hatred of Gentiles condemns the Shammaite attack on Jesus (1985: 128-29). Likewise, one cannot extrapolate from sectarian documents at Qumran (on which cf. Blidstein 1974) that the Jerusalem temple excluded proselytes (Baumgarten 1982).

thew wishes to lay the emphasis elsewhere — perhaps especially on the next quotation.[120]

A prophetic sign. Although Matthew omits "for all nations" from his quotation of Isaiah 56 in Mark, he does not similarly edit the second quotation from Mark (except by modifying the verb tense). Jeremiah 7 promised judgment on God's people who treated his temple like a safe haven for robbers (perhaps drawing a parallel between ancient temples' function as treasuries and places where robbers stored their loot; robbers could use, for example, a cave in a mountain (Apul. *Metam.* 4.6).[121] Jeremiah warns his contemporaries that the presence of the temple will not stay God's wrath against them; Matthew, probably writing after A.D. 70, wishes to stress the judgment against a temple establishment who rejected Jesus (23:31-36; 24:15; 27:25). Not so much the brigands in the wilderness as the temple authorities are the real bandits.[122]

Beyond Matthew's interpretation, many scholars hold that Jesus himself also meant his act in the temple as a symbolic prophetic sign of impending judgment,[123] and much evidence supports this view.[124] The Qumran community regarded the present temple as defiled and waited for God to purify the temple mount (Flusser 1988: 43); the Old Testament itself predicted such a cleansing in the time of the eschatological Elijah (Mal 3:1-3). Jeremias (1958: 65) is probably correct that Jesus speaks of the eschatological sanctuary not only explicitly (26:61) but in words about the foundation stone (16:18) and perhaps the capstone (26:42).

Blind and Lame (21:14-16)

Like synagogues, the temple courts were often used for teaching,[125] and Jesus begins teaching there. By being a layman rather than a priest, Jesus is already an

120. Like later rabbis, Matthew could have quoted part of a verse and expected his audience to infer its context (e.g., p. Ber. 2:8; Qidd. 4:1, §2); but his deletion from Mark is undoubtedly intentional.

121. Likewise ancients who expected deities to protect those who took refuge in their temples did not expect such protection for temple robbers who fled there (Diod. Sic. 16.58.6).

122. Cf. Herzog 1992: 820; Hanson and Oakman 1998: 155; contrast Buchanan 1959, who thinks Mark may have applied "brigands" literally during the Judean revolt (cf. Borg 1984: 174). Although emphasizing some other texts (particularly 16:14; 17:1-8), cf. Knowles 1993 for Jesus-Jeremiah parallels in Matthew (although Knowles's "rejected-prophet motif" could as easily evoke Moses); the connection in 21:13 is the best (cf. Zucker 1990: 297-98).

123. Recognized by many scholars, e.g., Harvey 1982: 131-32; Aune 1983: 136; Catchpole 1984: 334; Sanders 1985: 70.

124. Prophets often provided symbolic actions as signs of impending judgment (e.g., Is 20:3; Jer 13:10-11; 19:10; Ezek 12:3; 24:17-21; Hos 1:2; cf. Aune 1983: 100); the pointedness of their deeds exceeds the mere shock tactics of many Cynic attacks on convention (cf. Meeks 1986: 54-55 for examples of the latter). We find dubious the anachronistic suggestions that Jesus opposed sacrifice (cf. 5:23; 8:4; Acts 21:26) or that the story prefigures the new sacrifice of the Eucharist (cf. Neusner 1987), a probably post-first-century conception.

125. E.g., m. Ker. 1:7; ARN 38A; b. Pesaḥ. 26a; Liefeld 1967: 191-92, following especially Büchler 1913-14; Safrai 1974/76d: 905; Vermes 1993: 76-77.

outsider to Jerusalem's corridors of power (Meier 1991a: 345); the aristocratic priesthood soon acquires even less reason to feel comfortable with Jesus' approach. The blind and lame came to him in the temple, although Jewish teachers did not require such people to make the journey to the temple (m. Ḥag. 1:1), and at least some traditions excluded them from the temple (2 Sam 5:8 LXX). This exclusion presumably related to purity laws prohibiting the entrance of those with physical abnormalities.[126] Even under Levitical regulations, members of priestly families could not enter the sanctuary as priests if they were blind or lame (Lev 21:17-18); that some carried such rules further by the time of Jesus is likely. Here again Jesus apparently challenges the way the temple hierarchy has conducted the affairs of the old temple (e.g., Hill 1972: 294).[127]

Jesus' deeds are not the only cause for the chief priests' and legal experts' discomfort; Jesus is accepting public praise as the Son of David, and even if the priestly aristocracy were gentler than their opponents' portraits of them suggest, Roman rule left them no choice but to correct him or betray him to the governor. (Assuming that the Roman garrison mainly kept to themselves in the Fortress Antonia, the Romans themselves would notice Jesus as dangerous only when he began to gather a following, which he easily could in the temple, as Paschal hopes ran high. At the same time, the possibility of generating unrest in the temple by arresting a teacher publicly during Passover season was too dangerous to be seriously entertained; if they were forced to deal with him, it would have to be elsewhere — 26:4-5.) This position is logical assuming, of course, that he was *not* the Messiah, a caveat they likely did not consider. To them he was simply another charismatic leader whose reputation had allowed his ego to get out of hand; Josephus provides many examples of such leaders in first-century Palestine.

Jesus, who again defends the receptiveness of children (21:16; cf. 18:1-5; 19:13-15), responds from Scripture (since he now addresses those educated in Scripture): from the lips of children God had ordained "praise." Here some have protested that Matthew's tradition must be later because the Hebrew reads "strength" in contrast to the Septuagint's "praise" (Burkitt 1910: 24).[128] But Greek was the first language of the Jerusalem aristocracy, and Jesus may have been familiar with a Greek text equivalent to the Septuagint at this point. At any

126. 1QSa 2.8-9; 1QM 7.4-6; 12.7-9; Plut. *R.Q.* 73, *Mor.* 281C; *BCH* 7.477.1 in Grant 1953: 7; Soph. *Philoct.* 1032-33.

127. I say "apparently" because direct Sadducean evidence is lacking; the other lines of evidence, however, overwhelmingly suggest that this was the practice (as commentators generally accept — Meier 1980: 235; Gundry 1982: 413). Because Jesus was not forcibly evicted for this practice and because Mark omits healings in Jerusalem, Manson doubts the authenticity of the paragraph (1979: 221). The priestly aristocracy had reason to challenge Jesus only indirectly at this point, however (cf. 26:4-5), and Mark, having reported healings throughout his Gospel, is now focused on the passion narrative. That Matthew has an independent tradition is possible though unproved; given the enmity of Judean leadership (cf. ch. 23), Matthew in either case has occasion to record such flouting of temple tradition, with which he was undoubtedly familiar.

128. Because the object of praise is God himself rather than any mortal (Ps 8:4), the citation could imply a claim to more than humanity (France 1985: 302-3).

rate, Matthew, who knows different text-types well enough to create eclectic texts at times but directly follows Mark's use of the Septuagint, probably follows an earlier tradition here. The text Jesus cites refers to children not yet weaned, hardly those who would shout in the temple (Gundry 1982: 414), but it is close enough to justify Jesus' point: if God can speak through babies, *qal waḥomer,* how much more, children. And if children, *qal waḥomer* — how much more ought the religious leaders to join in.[129] Like many controversy-encounters, this one ends with Jesus' response as the pericope's final statement. Though secondary socially, children could be conduits of divine wisdom (cf. p. Sanh. 10:1, §9; elsewhere cf. Plut. *Isis* 14, *Mor.* 356E).

Then Jesus spent the night in Bethany (21:17), a town whose very name was understood to reflect the abundance of green figs in the region (Lachs 1987: 348).[130] Not only Jesus but many pilgrims would arrive about a week before the festival (see Sanders 1992: 134-35).

Faith to Accomplish the Impossible (21:17-22)

Cf. Mk 11:12-14, 20-26; less relevantly, Lk 13:6-9. Matthew compresses Mark's two accounts into one,[131] thus requiring his "immediately" for the sake of smooth reading. Although admitting their presence in the Hebrew Bible and in Acts, some doubt that punitive miracles fit Jesus' behavior elsewhere (Meier 1993: 884-96), but it should be noted that both destructive miracles in the Gospels (Mk 5:1-20; 11:12-26) are against property rather than people, suggesting consistency with Jesus' teaching as well as his ministry style (cf. Carson 1984b: 446). The passage coheres with Jesus' teaching about impending judgment on the temple, his teachings about radical faith, and his commissioning disciples to carry on his work. It also seems incongruent that Jesus would see himself in the

129. Gundry 1982: 414-15, who agrees that Matthew has children in his tradition, thinks that Matthew cites Ps 8:3 because it speaks of the "Lord's name" like Ps 118:26 cited in 21:9; but that phrase being common, and Matthew not citing the line from Ps 8 relevant for the midrashic connection, the *gezerah shewah* probably falters here. Gundry 1975: 200 also argues that because only Jesus in the NT uses *anaginōskein* in the interrogative (12:3, 5; 19:4; 21:16, 42; 22:31; Mk 2:25; 12:10, 26; Lk 6:3; 10:26), the saying is probably authentic (one conversely inclined could respond, however, that it could imitate Jesus' style).

130. As in Mark, his stay in Bethany provides the setting for his passing a fig tree while approaching Jerusalem the next morning; but Mark has Jesus' attack on the temple that day, not before Jesus spends the night in Bethany. Probably Mark inserts Jesus' attack into a preexisting narrative about the fig tree to connect the examples of judgment (Bultmann 1968: 218); Matthew may revert to it due to tradition or to simplify the connections in the narrative (cf. 12:46-50, which in Matthew follows conflict with the Pharisees over their Beelzebul charge, but in Mark forms the closing half of a narrative about Jesus' family framing the Beelzebul controversy). But because only the Passover meal must be eaten within Jerusalem, Jesus probably lodged with others in Bethany, possibly the family of Lazarus (Jn 11:1; 12:1; on paschal lodgings, see Sanders 1992: 129).

131. Matthew may do so on the basis of prior tradition (as I elsewhere argue that he "re-Judaizes" Mark), if Mark "divided up the original story into two parts using his sandwich technique" to address the act of judgment in the temple (cf., e.g., Witherington 1990: 174).

tradition of biblical prophets like Elijah and yet avoid any judgment miracles. The narrative functions both as an acted parable of judgment and an invitation to prayers of faith (cf. Gardner 1991: 318).

Here Jesus provides an acted parable for his disciples, which symbolized another prophetic act of judgment. Matthew's audience, probably native to Syro-Palestine, is likely aware of what Mark states explicitly: it was not yet the season for figs (Mk 11:13; cf. Epict. *Disc.* 1.15.8).[132] At Passover season in late March or early April, fig trees are often in leaf on the eastern side of the Mount of Olives. At this time of year, such fig trees contained only green early figs (Arabs call them *taqsh*), which ripen around June but often fall off before that time, leaving only green leaves on the tree. Because of their unpalatable taste, these early figs rarely were eaten; but someone too hungry to care about the taste would eat them anyway, as some do today. A leafy tree lacking such early figs, however, would bear no figs at all that year (Lane 1974a: 401; F. F. Bruce 1980a: 73-74; Gundry 1982: 417; France 1985: 303; Witherington 1990: 173).

By his arrangement of the narrative, Mark draws a connection with judgment on the temple (Gaston 1970: 83; Lane 1974a: 400); this symbolic application of the fruitless fig tree's demise makes sense in view of biblical imagery where trees may represent Israel (e.g., Jer 11:16; 24:8; 29:17; Hos 9:10; cf. comment on 3:10; vines in Mt 21:33; Robin 1962: 280-81; Hooker 1983: 82) or their barrenness judgment on Israel's fertility (e.g., Jer 8:13; Joel 1:7, 12; Mic 7:1).[133] While this Markan emphasis on judgment remains in Matthew (cf. Fenton 1977: 336; Harrington 1982: 84) — after all, this is Jesus' only reported judgment miracle[134] — Matthew stresses especially the lesson of faith that Jesus directly drew from the judgment sign.[135] This emphasis is clear both because Matthew

132. One need not hypothesize that Mark has used a story unrelated to Passion Week, hence originally during the season for figs (Hunzinger 1971: 756); in the context of Jesus' teaching on fruit in the Q tradition, an acted parable makes sense, and the early figs (though barely edible) were on the trees even before the leaves. The proposal that Jesus expected the messianic era with its material abundance to begin on his entrance into Jerusalem (Hiers 1968) seems unlikely.

133. The view that Matthew here pronounces judgment on the Roman Empire rather than Israel (cf. Ellul 1992) finds little support in the text. Gregory the Great (*Letters* 39, to Eulogius; *ACCS*, 158) applies the image to the "synagogue," with leaves of the law without the fruit of works; but the same principle might also apply to much of Christendom.

134. "Plucked up" (21:21) represents the same Greek term as appears in the promise of the Jerusalem establishment's overthrow in 21:43, which may be special Matthean material borrowing the term (not frequent in Gospel tradition) from this pericope. Although this verbal parallel would not necessarily carry much weight, the close proximity of the parallel in the sequence of the narrative may suggest that it is intentional. Those unwilling to yield their fruit in this context (21:34-35) also plainly refer to the rebellious Jerusalem leadership.

135. Cf. b. Ta'an. 24a, where one calls forth early fruit on a fig tree, but merits judgment rather than praise for interfering with nature; or "a distant parallel" in b. B. Meṣ. 59b; Bultmann 1968: 235. (At any rate, magical commands, as implied in p. Ber. 13d cited in Alexander 1980: 58, do not fit the narrative illustrations of the Gospels.) Judaism regarded curses as potentially efficacious (e.g., Test. Jud. 11:3-5; b. Ta'an. 23b; Gen. Rab. 74:4; Pesiq. R. 3:4), though normally only if warranted (Prov 26:2). For a thorough examination of Mark's application of faith in Mk 11:23, much of which is relevant both to discussion of Jesus' historical message and to Matthew's use of Mark here, see Dowd 1988.

deemphasizes the connection with the temple by simplifying Mark's sequence, and because the lesson of faith fits other signs as well (17:20; cf. 7:7-11; Jn 14:13-14; 15:7; 16:23). In both Gospels Jesus explicitly answers only the implied question, "How did you do that?" rather than, "What were you trying to communicate?" (cf. also France 1985: 304). Still, even more than in Mark, Matthew's Q material brings out the judgment significance of the acted parable: a generation that falsely claims holiness will face judgment (3:10; 12:44-45; cf. 24:32; Jer 24). Together, these two themes may stress the faith to do miracles in the face of a hostile generation, as in the time of Elijah.

Disciples should exercise faith for what is naturally impossible. "Moving mountains" was a Jewish metaphor for accomplishing what was difficult or virtually impossible (though rabbis, who preserve it, apply it especially to labor in Torah; see, e.g., ARN 6A; 12, §29B; b. Ber. 63b; Sanh. 24a).[136] First-century Jews may have also understood the value of supernaturally authorized commands (e.g., Jos. *Ant.* 2.287 vs. Ex 7:10; Josh 10:12; Acts 3:6)[137] and a call to confidence in God's provision even before they had experienced it (Jos. *Ant.* 3.44-45).

The illustration for "*this* mountain" (21:21) is probably Mount Olivet, plainly visible from where they stood;[138] because one could also see the Dead Sea from its slopes, one might think of Jesus pointing to that sea as the site where the mountain could be cast. In the background may be an allusion to the eschatological leveling of this mountain (Zech 14:4, 10; Lane 1974a: 410), but the background is at best distant; unless Matthew intends us to read this text in view of 24:14 (which seems unlikely), Jesus does not seem to refer to his followers precipitating the eschaton here (see Gundry 1982: 418). Further, few hearers who had not made pilgrimage to Jerusalem would picture the specific mountain enough to reconstruct such an allusion, and Jesus especially uses a more general allusion for the power of faith (undoubtedly belonging to bedrock tradition; cf. 17:20; Lk 17:6; 1 Cor 13:2).

More likely is a direct allusion to Zechariah 4:6-9, where Zerubbabel's obstacles in building the temple are compared to a mountain (perhaps the old Zion); the Spirit of God would bring the obstacles down. In this case Jesus is saying that no challenge to the work God has called his servants to do may stand. The "impossible" task before Jesus himself is the reformation of the Jewish religious system (21:12-13; cf. Richardson 1958: 266, too narrowly). That is, like his Davidic ruling ancestor Zerubbabel (1:12), Jesus was to prepare a new temple (21:42; cf.

136. So also Nineham 1977: 305; Jeremias 1971: 161; cf. Test. Sol. 23:1, possibly derivative.

137. Some later teachers reportedly commanded objects to uproot to validate their halakah, though others rejected the arguments (p. Moʿed Qaṭ. 3:1, §6). Later haggadah also occasionally extols a much earlier character who allegedly could command or curse and it would happen (ARN 25A; b. Taʿan. 23b; Pesiq. Rab Kah. 11:16; Gen. Rab. 74:4; Qoh. Rab. 10:8, §1; Pesiq. R. 3:4).

138. The Temple Mount (Hooker 1983: 84) fits the literary context in Matthew and Mark but probably would have been less obvious geographically to Jesus' original disciples; though see comment below on Zech 4:6-9.

Zech 4:7); more than Zerubbabel, however, he would pay the price for this act of faith with his own life (21:37-39, 42; 26:61).

The Source of Jesus' Authority (21:23-27)

Cf. Mk 11:27-33; Lk 20:1-8. The reader who has witnessed miracles such as the cursing of the fig tree understands that Jesus' authority is from God (21:21-22); the reader who has seen the fate of John the Baptist, an earlier representative of God, also recognizes what Jesus will face (cf. 21:32, 38-39). The political leaders are not, however, privy to the information Matthew's audience shares, and the authority that once excited crowds (7:29) now provokes conflict.

The form Jesus' debate takes here follows what became a standard rabbinic pattern, which probably reflects broader ancient rhetorical conventions as well: a hostile question followed by a counterquestion, admission, and final rejoinder (Daube 1973: 151-55; cf. Jn 2:18-22; Bultmann 1968: 42, 45).[139] Greek controversy-narratives also typically concluded with a wise quip that silenced the opposition (or at least left no reason to report their further response); only the skillful could debate wisely enough to avoid falling into sophistic traps (Epict. *Disc.* 1.7.26-29). The temple courts probably provided a common public location for teaching (ARN 38A; 41, §114B; b. Pesaḥ. 26a; Acts 2:46; Liefeld 1967: 191; Safrai 1974/76d: 905), as in the Greek world.

As far as Matthew is concerned, Jesus' opponents (and those of his community) are hypocritical in their opposition. Undoubtedly they view Jesus as a "populist" (see Rhoads and Michie 1982: 82), the sort of demagogue aristocrats normally despised (Isoc. *Nic.* 48, *Or.* 2; *Areopagiticus;* Arist. *Pol.* 3.6.4-13, 1281a-82b; 3.7.7-9, 1283ab; 3.12.1, 1288a; 4.4.4-7, 1292a; 5.4.1-2, 1304b; 5.5.4-5, 1305b; 6.2.10-12, 1319b; *Rhet.* 2.20.5, 1393b; Arius Didymus *Epitome* in Malherbe 1986: 145-46; Plut. *Praising Inoffensively* 16, *Mor.* 545C; Diog. Laert. *Lives* 4.42; see Martin 1990: 92-116; Gardner 1974: 27-59).[140] Yet like populist politicians themselves, Jesus' adversaries were more interested in making Jesus look bad than in uncovering further truth about Jesus' claims. The Gospel tradition's irony is almost satirical: the aristocrats fear the crowds; later their coconspirators pretend to believe what in fact they do not believe (but what the reader knows to be true), that Jesus defers to no one (22:16). Jesus thus rightly labels his enemies "play actors," "hypocrites" (22:18; on the term, see comment on 6:1-18, 16-18).

Some think that Jesus appeals here to John's baptism as an existential confirmation of his own calling (e.g., Dunn 1975: 64, with Jeremias), but more likely Jesus argues by analogy: he shares the same source of authority as John

139. Matthew rearranges Mark's wording into a chiastic pattern in 21:24 (Gundry 1982: 420).

140. Their failure to "know" need not recall the thoroughgoing agnosticism of some members of the Skeptic school, but it could invite the same sort of criticisms; cf., e.g., Epic. *Disc.* 1.5.

does. In this context, their failure to "believe" John (21:25, 32) distinguishes them from disciples, who ideally act in faith (21:22).

Pretend Obedience versus Delayed Obedience (21:28-32)

Cf. Lk 15:11-32. The three parables in 21:28–22:14 together respond to the Judean leadership, critiquing them harshly (cf. van Tilborg 1972b: 47-52; on the context, see Carter 1998: 148-55). This passage employs customary Jewish rhetoric. "What do you think?" could signal rabbinic-style interrogation (here as a pedagogic technique, or a debate technique as in 22:17); it similarly could request a verdict (26:66). The closing question exploits an ancient parable technique bringing home the emotive force of the parable (Is 5:3-4; Jer 2:21; Lk 7:41-42). Similar story lines appear in later Jewish parables,[141] although characters like a king and peasants usually replace father and sons here (probably reflecting the tendency toward kingly portrayals of God in later rabbinic stories; see comment on 18:23-27). More to the point, Jewish parables sometimes proceeded by contrasting positive and negative characters (Sifre Deut. 349.1.1), including brothers dealing with money from their father (Sifre Deut. 48.1.4; cf. Lk 15:11-13) as here; the basic moral of this story would also not be foreign to Palestinian Judaism (Gen. Rab. 85:3).[142] Ancient Mediterranean culture demanded that sons honor and obey their parents, especially when they still lived on the father's estate (see Keener 1991a: 98, 197).

The vineyard provides a common enough Galilean setting for work (20:1; 21:33),[143] however removed such a site and occupation might be from the daily lives of the Sadducean aristocracy; it is not impossible that Matthew sees more significance in it as well (Is 5:7; cf. Mt 21:33-44). The parable is transparent enough in its Matthean context: the repentant (3:2) son does the father's will (7:21; 12:50);[144] the unrepentant son is unfruitful (3:8), claiming to do but not doing (23:3). Thus the latter stands for Israel's religious leadership, in contrast to the humble who heeded John and Jesus. In its original setting, the parable's "sons" may have alluded to Israel's status (e.g., Ex 4:22), but with a reversal of expectations regarding which part of Israel constituted the "disobedient sons" (Deut 32:20; Hos 11:1-7). (At times Israel had also promised to obey but failed to follow through; see Ex 24:7; Jer 42:6; contrast Ex 4:13.) The issue is not that

141. Bultmann 1968: 201, citing the late Ex. Rab. 27/88a; Johnston 1977b: 635, citing an allegedly earlier tradition in Deut. Rab. 7:4. Scott 1989: 83-84 cites Ex. Rab. on Ex 27 (following Strack-Billerbeck 2:865). Cf. the father's inviting love for his prodigal son Israel in Deut. Rab. 2:24.

142. The story line contrasting two brothers would, as Philo points out, derive ultimately from the Genesis narratives (*Every Good Man Is Free* 57); see Gen 4:1-12; 21:3-10; 25:22-34; 27:1-41; 37:2-28.

143. Here on a family-owned or -tilled plot of land, probably a common arrangement; see Horsley 1995: 203-4.

144. "I" *(egō)* reflects the Septuagintal, "Behold, [it is] I," indicating consent (Hagner 1995: 613).

"tax gatherers and prostitutes"[145] are good (cf. 9:9; 18:17; cf. 19:17);[146] it is that the religious people were worse, were treasonous (22:5-10). Jesus provides a question after a parable (as in Is 5:3-4; Mt 21:40; see Bultmann 1968: 183 for parables ending in questions).

Excursus: Prostitution

For modern readers familiar with the Christian condemnation of prostitution as sin, the inclusion of prostitutes with "tax gatherers" in a category of sinners is not surprising (see comment on 9:9 for tax gatherers). This familiarity should not lead us to neglect a survey of associations prostitution would suggest in an ancient Mediterranean context. Although some rabbinic accounts of prostitutes in Palestine suggest foreigners (e.g., Sifre Num. 115.5.7; b. Menaḥ. 44a; earlier, e.g., Prov 2:16; 5:20; 22:14), prostitutes also existed in Jerusalem in the Second Temple period if Ps. Sol. 2:11 is intended literally. Ilan 1996: 214-21 links both foreign and Jewish prostitutes with Jewish clients; Tannaim seem to have emphasized and resented especially the foreign ones (Goodman 1983: 60).

Scripture forbade Jewish practice of prostitution (Deut 23:17), though it reports that it occurred (e.g., Gen 38:15-16). Jewish teachers generally resented prostitution as immoral and dangerous (Sir 9:6; 19:2; 41:20; Jos. *Ant.* 4.206; Sib. Or. 5.388),[147] and as a primarily Gentile practice (e.g., 2 Macc 6:4; ARN 48, §132). Unattested in other Jewish texts, Philo's claim that prostitution was a capital offense in the law (*Jos.* 43; *Spec. Leg.* 3.51) appears to be idiosyncratic, an apologetic strategy (Belkin 1940: 256).

Many Gentiles also regarded prostitution as shameful (Diod. Sic. 12.21.2; Artem. *Oneir.* 1.78), foolish (Muson. Ruf. *Fr.* 12, *On Sexual Indulgence* in Malherbe 1986: 153; Plut. *Educ.* 7, *Mor.* 5C; Diog. *Ep.* 44; Diog. Laert. 6.2.61, 66), and hurtful (Cato collection of distichs 25; Dio Chrys. *Or.* 7.133-37; Ward 1990: 286). Nevertheless, even moralists regarded prostitution as a better outlet for passion than adultery (Hor. *Sat.* 2.7.46-47; *Greek Anthol.* 7.403; Harrell 1967: 35), some philosophers regarded prejudices against prostitution as merely culturally based (Sext. Emp. *Pyrrh.*

145. Gibson 1981 suggests that Roman soldiers' use of prostitutes also led to the perception that Judean prostitutes collaborated with the Romans as the tax gatherers did. On Roman soldiers and marriage, see comment on 8:5-13.

146. Scott 1989: 84-85 contends that the refusing son shamed his father by publicly refusing to obey him, though he later privately obeyed, whereas the other son publicly honored him but privately shamed him. Scott's insight is helpful in showing that neither son has done completely right, but it may nevertheless read too much into the parable; the text provides no evidence that the refusal was public.

147. Cf. also the references to *zenuth* in 1QS 4.10; CD 4.17; 8.5; if intended more broadly, they certainly imply assumed condemnation of the narrower sense. In later texts, e.g., Ex. Rab. 43:7; Num. Rab. 9:24; 20:7. Taylor 1997: 119-22 thinks the term in Mt 21 denotes anyone sexually immoral, taking the common broader application of the Hebrew term.

3.201; Diog. Laert. 2.69, 74, 99), and the state regulated the practice at a profit wherever possible (*WO* 1157; *OGIS* 674 = *IGRR* 1.1183 in Lewis 1983: 141, 145, 171-72). Roman law did not prosecute an active prostitute unless she had retired and become married, in which case her activity, if she continued in it, constituted legal adultery (Justinian *Codex* 9.20, 22, 29; Gardner 1986: 130, 133).

In the Roman world inns and bars regularly doubled as low-class brothels (Appendix Vergiliana *Copa* 1-6; *CIL* 5.1679 in Sherk 1988: 210-11; Dio Chrys. *Or.* 7.133; Gardner 1986: 32; MacMullen 1974: 86-87; Casson 1974: 206-15). Although some high-class prostitutes became wealthy (e.g., Athenaeus *Deipn.* 13.596B; Sifre Num. 115.5.7), prostitution more often stemmed from economic necessity (e.g., *B.G.U.* 1024.7 in Lewis 1983: 145-46), most often slavery (Mart. *Epig.* 9.6.7; 9.8; Apul. *Metam.* 7.9; ARN 8A; Pomeroy 1975: 140-41, 192).[148]

The interpretation of this parable follows naturally after 21:23-27: Jesus and John represent the same source of moral authority, and those who rejected John's "way of righteousness" showed the hypocrisy of their own claims to be God's servants.[149] The repentance of more openly sinful people did not provoke them to jealousy for their own spiritual status (cf. Rom 11:14).

The Murderous Tenants (21:33-44)

Cf. Mk 12:1-12; Lk 20:9-19. The basic form of the parable, expounding an initial text and concluded by other texts, fits what we know of the form for synagogue sermons (Ellis 1977: 205). **As one expects from Jesus' rural parables, this one is true to life where possible:** the viticulture is accurate enough, although this accuracy stems from the Isaiah allusions (which need not be secondary, pace Nineham 1977: 311; Witherington 1990: 213; 4Q500.1 may conjoin Is 5's vineyard with the temple and possibly even Ps 118, as here — cf. Brooke 1995;

148. Roman tax law penalized those who adopted foundlings, hence encouraging the raising of such discarded infants as slaves instead (Lewis 1983: 54, 58).

149. The phrase means that John "brought the right way" (Jeremias 1971: 46; the interpretation of Kraeling 1951: 81 is, therefore, unnecessary); Gundry 1982: 423 also shows the commonness of the phrase in Palestinian Judaism (Prov 8:20; 12:28; 16:31; Jub. 23:20-21, 26; 25:15; 1 Enoch 92:3; 99:10; cf. b. 'Abot 6:4, bar.). Cf. also Qumran's "way" for the community (1QS 9.17-18, 21; CD 1.13; Zon 1963; Thiering 1981: 65-66; cf. Acts 9:2 and McCasland 1958; Fitzmyer 1966: 240; in later Arab culture, Bishop 1958: 107-8). Finding numerous Mattheanisms, Gundry thinks Matthew composed 21:28-32 from the material in Lk 15:11-32 plus Mt 20:1-16; 21:23-27 (1982: 422); but the story line of Lk 15:11-32 alone is close, and if it does reflect the same story (some of Jesus' other parables recycle related story lines), we should keep in mind that Lk 15 is quite Lukan (cf. the redactional linkage of the three parables) just as this is quite Matthean, suggesting that each has developed the story and not Matthew alone. Although "kingdom of God" could be Matthean (Gundry 1982: 423-24), such rarely Matthean language may indicate prior tradition in this passage.

Baumgarten 1989).[150] The viticultural details would also be recognized throughout the Mediterranean: fences (often a wall of loosely fitted stones) or hedges protected vineyards from animals (Ps 80:12-14; Virg. *Georg.* 2.371-79; Lewis 1983: 125) and watchmen used the tower (2 Chron 26:10; Is 1:8; Gundry 1982: 425), often "a hut of leaf-covered wood or possibly of stone which served both as a look-out . . . and as a shelter for the vinedressers at harvest time" (Anderson 1976: 272; see further Jeremias 1972: 74-75).[151] The one point at which the parable may depart from the most common practice is the leasing of the new vineyard to tenants rather than the use of contract laborers (Llewelyn 1992: 86-105; but cf. Columella *Rust.* 1.7.3; 1.8.6-7). If the parable diverges from standard practice at this point, it may be to underline the degree of trust God invested in Jerusalem's leaders, and therefore the heinous extent of their betrayal.

Probably more telling in favor of its authenticity than its accurate Galilean flavor, many Semitisms appear in the Markan parable (Hengel 1968, followed also by Lane 1974a: 417n.9). It may also adapt some elements of early Palestinian Jewish story lines.[152] It does not distinguish the climactic messenger, the "son," from the earlier messengers as sharply as later Christians would distinguish Jesus from the prophets (Stanton 1995a: 154). Given what we know about Jesus, there is no reason the parable could not stem from him (see further arguments in Hagner 1995: 619).

That the relationship between God and Israel constitutes the most common theme in early rabbinic parables (Johnston 1977b: 625) may be significant here. Because the vineyard probably refers to Israel (Is 5:2; cf. 3:14; Ezek 17:6; Hos 9:10; 3 Bar. 1:2; Mek. Pisha 1.162; Sifre Deut. 15.1.1; Pesiq. Rab Kah. 16:9; Ex. Rab. 30:17; 34:3; Song Rab. 2:16, §1; 7:13, §1; Jeremias 1972: 70, 76-77), the vine growers refer to the nation's religious leadership (Mt 21:45). Thus while Jesus borrows the imagery of Isaiah, he adapts it so that the primary evildoers represent not Israel but her leaders.

150. The absence of this allusion in Gos. Thom. 65 could indicate that the original Jesus tradition lacked this detail, but the Gospel of Thomas may as easily have omitted it — its original point certainly would not fit Thomas's redactional *Tendenz,* whereas Mark had little reason to invent an allusion that was too subtle for most of his own readers to catch (see also Snodgrass 1983; Gundry 1982: 425; Carson 1984b: 452, following Snodgrass 1975, for doubts that the Gospel of Thomas preserves the original form). Still, the *basic* triadic outline of Thomas's parable vindicated Dodd's defense of this form (1961: 100), and Matthew has expanded Mark (cf. Goulder 1974: 61).

151. On the care of vineyards, including irrigation, see more fully Hepper 1992: 96-97; for "digging" (21:33) cf. Babrius 2.1-2 (vineyard trenches); on the danger of animals, see, e.g., Babrius 11.1; 19; Song 2:15; robbers, *CPJ* §21, 1:157-58; Virg. *Priapea* 3.19. People planted vineyards both on hilly and level ground (Virg. *Georg.* 2.273-87; for ideal sites, see Columella *Trees* 4.1-5); some parts of the Empire boasted massive vineyard plantations (see *P. Cairo Zen.* 59736, c. 250 B.C.).

152. Young 1989: 298-301 compares Sifre Deut. 312, in which a king finally expelled wicked tenants from his field after his own son was born; and especially Seder Eliyahu 30/28 (a passage with an early second-century attribution), in which a wicked guardian killed his son (301), depicting God's identification with his people in anthropomorphic terms (304). I suspect that the latter parallel, lacking both tenants and vineyard, is too distant, but Young is right to compare the shock value in the two illustrations (303).

Neither Jesus nor Matthew contends for God's rejection of Israel as a people, but for his rejection of the current religious leadership (23:13-36; cf. Kee 1977: 113; pace Ladd 1974b: 114). Matthew also uses this threat from Jesus' day as a warning for Christian leaders in Matthew's day (24:45-51). The church and many of its leaders who readily condemn Israel's behavior have repeated Israel's frequent disobedience often enough in history and to a great extent continue to do so today; many ministers regard the church as "their" field of ministry, rather than keeping in mind who their Lord is. That the landowner here, rather than being perpetually absent, has "gone on a journey" (21:33; Mk 12:1) alludes to a Jesus tradition Matthew finds directly applicable to Jesus' own professed followers at the second coming (Mt 24:45-51; 25:14-30; Mk 13:34-36). Israel is unprepared for her master because Israel's leaders failed in their stewardship to acknowledge the true Lord of the sheep. When the Lord is absent, the tenants exploit the resources entrusted to them; but a day of reckoning is coming (cf. Prov 7:19, 22-27). The grape vintage here may represent realized eschatology (13:30; cf. 9:37-38), but probably it simply fits the imagery of the parable; the prophets and God's own Son came to collect God's due from the people, but the leaders kept it for themselves (Is 5:2; cf. Ezek 34:2; Hos 10:1-2). If anything remains future for Matthew here, it is the destruction of the leaders and the return of the vineyard to God's care (23:39).

The parable underlines the wickedness of tenants who ignore the vineyard's true owner. Because it normally took vineyards four years before they began yielding profits, it appears that the landowner already has significant wealth (Derrett 1970: 289-90); the hereditary leisured class gained their wealth from owning land that others worked for them. Although small holders may have predominated in Palestine, Galilee boasted many tenant farmers, an occupation numerous in Italy and elsewhere. In the general social structure landowners functioned as patrons, and tenants as clients (Stambaugh and Balch 1986: 64-65; see Foxhall 1990, including details about exploitation), although geographical and social distance was such that tenants had less claim on their patrons' political support than urban clients did. Tenant farmers worked the land for its owners, often absentee landlords, and paid the landowners as much as half the resulting produce.[153] This arrangement was familiar enough that later rabbis also told parables of vineyards tended by tenants (e.g., Pesiq. Rab Kah. Sup. 1:11); they also could tell of an owner uprooting a vineyard that provided no fruit to portray God's judgment on a people who refused to repent (Gen. Rab. 38:9; cf. Lev. Rab.

153. Klausner 1979b: 181; Edersheim 524-25; Anderson 1976: 272; on tenants leasing plots of land, see Stambaugh and Balch 1986: 68, who cite Varro *Agric.* 1.17.2-3; Columella *Agric.* 1.7; Pliny *Ep.* 3.19; 9.37. For examples of tenant farmers elsewhere, e.g., *CIL* 8.25902 (*Empire,* ed. Sherk, 250-51); Deissmann 1978: 33. Grain legally belonged to the landowner until the lessees had paid their rent (Lewis 1983: 123). (Meier 1980: 243 thinks that the landowner here demands *all* the produce in this parable, mirroring the absolute demands of God's reign; but "*his* fruit" simply means the portion the tenants had contracted to deliver to him.) Despite Matthew's eschatological uses for harvest imagery (3:10-12; 13:39) and "drawn near" (4:17), "proper time" (21:41) need not be eschatological (cf. 24:45), probably referring to harvest in early summer (cf. Jos. *Apion* 1.79).

23:3).[154] Ancients valued the benevolence of landowners toward tenants, but even those who recommended that they be less than insistent on timely payment (Columella *Rust.*1.7.1-2) warned them not to neglect collection of payment lest the tenants default (Colum. *Rust.* 1.7.2). Details would be specified in legal contracts (*P. Oxy.* 1631, A.D. 280), and receipts would be issued for rent paid in produce (e.g., *P. Amh.* 104, A.D. 125). Pace Scott 1989: 249-50, the tenants are not "expected" to challenge the landowner's honor; custom demands rather that they accept their socially inferior status and act accordingly.

While ancient Mediterranean peasants undoubtedly enjoyed their plight no more than other peasants in history, they would not have identified with the foolish tenants in this story, nor do the actions of these tenants represent a Galilean peasant revolt (Gundry 1982: 425, following Rostovzeff 1957: 1:269-73; cf. Prov 13:20; 19:7; pace Dodd 1961: 97; Jeremias 1972: 74-75).[155] In antiquity, all sides regarded as treacherous the killing of unarmed messengers, or heralds (cf., e.g., Hom. *Il.* 7.275-82; Appian *R.H.* 8.8.53; although some had killed royal tax collectors — 1 Kings 12:18; Gen. Rab. 42:3; Lev. Rab. 11:7). An audience would hardly expect the violence depicted here, and would undoubtedly have responded with indignation even to hearing the more usual event of a vineyard's loyal guard being beaten by robbers (*CPJ* §21, 1:157-58). The rejected messengers probably depict the biblical prophets (23:29-38; cf. 5:12; 1 Enoch 89:51-53); Jewish tradition not only acknowledged but amplified their sufferings.[156] (The stoning is not, however, a likely allusion to charges of blasphemy.)[157] The slaughter of a group of ambassadors (Jos. *Life* 56-57) or of successive messengers (*Life* 50-52) appeared morally hideous.

154. Johnston 1977b: 594 points out that in rabbinic parables, the landlord always represents God, although the sharecropping tenants variously represent Israel (ARN 16:3A) or groups of the righteous (the patriarchs, tithe payers — Sifre Deut. 312; Ex. Rab. 41:1), or people who should learn Torah (some of whom do and some do not — Deut. Rab. 7:4). Servants in rabbinic parables are more ad hoc: they could represent Israel, Israel's pious, Israel's poor, or Israel's prayerful, but also Gentiles, Egypt, and other referents (Johnston 1977b: 590).

155. Judean rulers before A.D. 66 did need to give attention to the problems afflicting the peasant population, however; see more fully Goodman 1987: 51-75.

156. The killing may allude in the narrative world especially to the Baptist (cf. Petersen 1978: 69); many see in the two sendings the former and latter prophets (cf. Scott 1989: 241). Young 1989: 288 prefers the Lukan and Gospel of Thomas versions, thinking Matthew's (and Mark's) killings represent a later allegorical stage; but Mark is probably our earliest form.

157. Stoning suited blasphemers (Jos. *Ant.* 4.202), and Gundry thinks the stoning (cf. also 23:37) follows killing here to imply execution as false prophets (1982: 426; cf. Lev 20:2, 27; 24:14-16, 23; Deut 13:10; 17:1-5; contrast m. Sanh. 11:1). It is true that criminals who died prior to execution or while under the ban would be posthumously stoned symbolically (m. ʿEd. 5:6; b. Ber. 19a; p. Moʿed Qat. 3:1, §9; cf. Lucian *Syrian Goddess* 52, probably unrelated), presumably on some views to atone for unforgiven sins, whether of the nation (cf. Jub. 30:14-17; 33:13; 41:26) or the individual (m. Sanh. 6:2-3; cf. Ps-Philo 25:7; 27:15). Nevertheless, execution by stoning occurred for other offenses (e.g., Ex 19:13; Num 15:32-26; Deut 21:21; 22:21, 24; Josh 7:25; m. Sanh. 6:4) and here may simply underline the indignity their killers sought to render (cf. Jub. 4:31). Death by stoning was a legal penalty (Sifre Deut. 220.1.2), but stone-throwing also often reflects an enraged mob (e.g., Dion. Hal. 8.59.1; 9.48.2; Paus. 2.23.2; 8.23.7; Jos. *Ant.* 3.21; *Life* 303; Jn 8:59; Acts 7:58-59).

The parable portrays God as *too* patient, but warns that he will eventually judge the abusive leaders. But even had the hearers not recognized the image of God and his prophets here, no one would expect the benevolent landowner to remain benevolent any longer; indeed, landlords sometimes even had their own hit squads to take out troublesome tenants.[158] The state would side with the landlord, and the murderers would die or be enslaved. (Hence in a later Jewish parable, those who have killed a royal — that is, divine — messenger fear retribution — Gen. Rab. 42:3; Lev. Rab. 11:7; cf. Ruth Rab. Proem 7. The Romans likewise enslaved a whole people for killing one of their representatives.)[159] At the very least, the landlord must know that the tenants hate him; in antiquity, the way people treat one's messengers is the way they would treat the sender (cf. 10:40-42; t. Taʿan. 3:2; m. Ber. 5:5; also Scott 1989: 249).[160] By continuing to appeal to their sense of honor, the landowner has made himself appear a fool; to maintain any vestige of honor, he must retaliate against their repeated shaming of him (Scott 1989: 250).

Quite in contrast to expectations, however, the landowner acts with such benevolence that ancient hearers could have regarded his action merely as utter folly: he believes that the murderous tenants will at least respect his son as his own representative. Those who respected an authority figure would respect his son (Herodian 4.1.3); but those who hated that figure might kill his son (Virg. *Aen.* 10.492). Jesus tells us about the death of the father's own son (Matthew omits Mark's "beloved," an explicit allusion to the voice at Jesus' baptism).[161] In the Old Testament, Israel was God's "inheritance" (also Jub. 1:21; Ps. Sol. 14:5; cf. 1QM 12.12), and Israel "inherited" the land (cf. 5:5; 25:34). Here, however, the true heir, God's ultimate representative, comes to receive the fruit due from God's people (3:8); the tenants commit the ultimate act of treachery. Casting him outside the vineyard (cf. Heb 13:13), they kill him.[162] In the final week of his ministry, Jesus is ready to unveil the "messianic secret": more than any prophet

158. For accounts of landholders' use of violence to expand their holdings (the basis for the wealth of the hereditary wealthy), see especially MacMullen 1974: 6-12. They might send slaves or tenants to seize the property of weaker people (MacMullen 1974: 7). Later rabbis did emphasize treating vineyard tenants fairly (b. Ber. 5b).

159. Eustathius, *Paraphrase of Dionysius Periegetes* in *Geographi Graeci Minores* 2, p. 253, lines 8-10, in Sherk 1988: 37; cf. Lk 21:24.

160. This is entirely aside from how peasants in general viewed landowners in general (Oakman 1992: 119); this landowner is so benevolent by contrast to most that in an ancient context he may have appeared favorably.

161. Because "beloved" probably represents "only" (see comment on 3:17), it heightens the story's pathos and suspense; most families had several children, but this father has only one heir (Young 1995: 217-18).

162. "Come, let us kill him" (21:38) reflects Gen 37:20 LXX, hence an allusion to the envy of Joseph's brothers against the one "sent" by their father (Gen 37:13-14), who became their deliverer (cf. Acts 7:9). Matthew probably reverses Mark's sequence to correspond with Jesus' crucifixion outside the city. In the earliest form of the parable, perhaps the tenants threw the corpse out to avoid the risk of ritually defiling the harvest (cf. Lev 11:37-38), which would point to extreme hypocrisy regarding the lighter and weightier matters of Torah (23:23-24; 27:4-6).

before him, Jesus stands in a special relationship with God, and his rejection finally spells doom on the land (cf. Gundry 1982: 427; Kingsbury 1983: 150). Even here, however, his self-revelation may remain obscure until clarified by his death and resurrection; a similar Jewish parable portrays the son as Jacob and thereby Israel (Jeremias 1972: 73).[163]

Israel's leaders were headed for judgment. No law would have granted the vineyard to tenants who had murdered the son; though it might have fallen to them had the landowner been deceased, had no other heirs claimed it, and had they been innocent, the deaths would surely be investigated.[164] Even when done by an Israelite king, the conjunction of murdering and taking possession was astonishingly evil (2 Kings 21:19). (When an owner was murdered, Roman law executed *all* his slaves — e.g., Tac. *Ann.* 14.42; Barrow 1968: 55-56; Roman law likewise treated offenses of the lower class against the higher more severely — Stambaugh and Balch 1986: 113; cf. Gaius *Inst.* 4.183 — and these foolish tenants had left plenty of prior evidence concerning their behavior.) As if asking for a legal ruling, Jesus questions the religious leaders what this patient landowner will finally do to the murderers. Whereas Jesus answers his own question in Mark (12:9), Matthew amplifies Jesus' Jewish teaching style (cf. 21:31; 22:20-21; Lk 19:22; 2 Sam 12:5-7; 14:5-21; 1 Kings 20:40-43; Pesiq. R. 21:2/3), allowing his indignant hearers to pronounce their own judgment (Jeremias 1972: 29).[165] It may be no coincidence that

163. Cf. 21:28-31, above. "Son" usually represents Israel in rabbinic parables (Johnston 1977b: 587; see, e.g., also Ex. Rab. 15:30; Lev. Rab. 2:5; 10:3; Num. Rab. 16:7; Deut. Rab. 7:9; 10:4; Lam. Rab. 1:17, §52; 2; Song Rab. 2:16, §1; 5:16, §3), a natural usage (cf., e.g., Ex. 4:22-23; Hos. 11:1; Is. 1:2; Jer. 3:19-22; Sir. 4:10; Pss. Sol. 13:9; 17:27-30; 18:4; Jub. 1:24-25); but even in rabbinic parables, special servants within Israel are sometimes intended (e.g., Moses in Sifre Deut. 29.4.1; cf. a rabbi in p. Moʿed Qaṭ. 3:1, §6). Stern 1991: 192-95, who doubts that Jesus would have foreseen his death (contrast our comment on 16:21), suggests that the son is John the Baptist, whose death at best foreshadows that of Jesus. But in the context of Jesus' ministry (especially the recent entry and act in the temple) a self-reference is most likely even before interpretation in Christian tradition (cf. also Hagner 1995: 619).

164. Gundry 1982: 427 and Young 1989: 282-83 cite their right of possession if both landowner and son are dead; Meier 1980: 243 and Lachs 1987: 355 note that Jewish law handed land over to the tenants if a proselyte landowner died without an heir (b. Qidd. 17b; on circumstances for inheriting what was deemed ownerless property, see Jeremias 1972: 75; idem 1969: 328). Normally a successor inherits (cf. Dion. Hal. 3.1.4). But the tenants' appeal to any inheritance laws is absurd in view of their illegal behavior, and neither in Matthew nor Mark do the tenants seek to gain *legal* possession of the vineyard.

165. Meier 1980: 244 argues that because their response quotes "a Greek play on words, seen in Sophocles' *Ajax* and repeated by Josephus," this tells against Matthew's Jewish training. Against this we must observe that (1) the respondents include the Sadducean aristocrats (21:23-27, 31-32), who undoubtedly had a good hellenistic education (just like Josephus!); (2) manuals of Greek quotations were easily available to those who read and wrote Greek (e.g., Stambaugh and Balch 1986: 121-22); and finally (3), exaggerated though it may be, the tradition that Gamaliel insisted on teaching Greek as well as Jewish knowledge, as well as plenty of Greek allusions in later Hebrew and Aramaic rabbinic literature (e.g., Pesiq. R. 20:4; Lieberman 1962; Hengel 1974a; Sevenster 1968: 38-61; Manns 1979) and widespread evidence of knowledge of Greek literature and ideas (cf. Goodman 1983: 72-73; Rahmani 1978a; also, e.g., Ep. Arist. 121-22; Jos. *War* 1.353; 2.155-58; *Ant.* 1.222; *Apion* 1.255; Artapanus in Euseb. *P.E.* 9.27.3; Sib. Or. 1.232; 2.15, 19, 337-38; 3.22, 110-13, 121-55, 401-32, 551-54, 588, 814; 5.7-9; 8.43-47; 2 Bar. 10:8; Apoc. Mos. 37:3; Test. Job 51:2/1), considerably weakens the force of the argument.

postexilic interpreters understood Isaiah's parable of the vineyard (Is 5:1-7) on which this parable draws as referring to the temple's destruction (Evans 1984, on 1 Enoch 89).

Jesus concludes by again challenging their knowledge of the Scriptures (which should have made the object of his parable obvious to begin with), as in 12:3; 19:4; 21:16; and 22:31. Here he cites Psalm 118:22 from the Hallel, only a few verses from the praise recently uttered by the children (21:15; cf. 21:9; Ps 118:25-26); not only the religious authorities but the people listening to Jesus' response to their challenge will understand.[166] But the cornerstone or topstone[167] to which Jesus refers is part of the architecture of the temple; hearers may have recognized that he was comparing the elect community to a temple, as in the Dead Sea Scrolls.[168] Most clearly, they would recognize that he was challenging the "builders," here the temple authorities. (On the historical level, this represented especially, though probably not exclusively, the Sadducees.)[169]

Matthew adds a further clarifying comment that expands the reproof to all Israel and loses any vestige of subtlety.[170] Thus, he says, these leaders would no longer administer God's reign among his people as God's stewards (cf. 23:13; 16:19); the "nation" to whom it would be given undoubtedly refers to the holy "nation" of a new exodus (Ex 19:5-6; cf. 1 Pet 2:9).[171] Henceforth they would

166. Although Vermes 1993: 104 characteristically rejects the citation as anti-Jewish church polemic (the saying itself is hardly anti-Jewish), various factors argue strongly for authenticity: Jewish parables typically included a scripture citation (so Stern 1991: 197 on this parable, though many of Jesus' parables lack such allusions); the citation appears in all three Synoptics plus Thomas (Young 1989: 293-94); Jesus draws his citation from the festal liturgy; "stone" may provide a Semitic play on words here with the "son" earlier in the parable (Gundry 1982: 429, following Black); "Have you not read?" is unique to Jesus in the NT (Gundry 1975: 200); and the collection of stone sayings in a variety of disparate early Christian texts supports a common authoritative source for diverse early Christian groups (Acts 4:11; Rom 9:33; 1 Pet 2:6-8; cf. Lk 19:38, 40, 44). Early Christians naturally accommodated the quotation to the LXX (Perrin 1963: 132), although Jesus undoubtedly addressed the Jerusalem aristocracy in Greek. Jesus may read *habonim* ("builders") as if from *bun,* "understand," rather than from *bnh,* "build," and hence apply it to the scribes (Stern 1991: 196); Young 1995: 219 suggests a play among "sons" *(banim),* "builders" *(bonim),* and "stones" *(abanim).* (An allusion back to the tower's "builders" in 21:33 is unlikely because the tower lacks a significant role except to establish the setting.)

167. Cf. McKelvey 1962; Kelly 1981: 94-95 for the former; Gundry 1982: 429; Jeremias 1964a: 792-93 for the latter. For early Jewish haggadah on the temple cornerstone, see, e.g., Sifra Behuq. pq. 3.263.1.9.

168. 1QS 8.5, 8-9; 9.6; CD 2.10, 13; Gärtner 1965: 16-46; Flusser 1988: 37-39; Wilcox 1969: 93-94. That image probably does not appear, however, in 4QFlor (McNicol 1977; Schwartz 1979).

169. A later rabbinic tradition plausibly explains the rejected cornerstone as David, repudiated by Saul (Hilton and Marshall 1988: 60; Young 1995: 219).

170. Some interpreters, e.g., Stern 1991: 191, consider his interpretation anti-Jewish; I would argue that it reflects the same sort of hostility Jewish Essenes reflect against the Jerusalem establishment (and apostate Israel who followed them) in the Dead Sea Scrolls; see further comment on the sermon in ch. 23.

171. Stanton 1993: 331 finds in this Matthean redaction "perhaps the clearest indication" of Matthew's separation from Judaism. But "nation" probably recalls Ex 19:6, and strict Jewish groups that characterized themselves as "righteous remnants" within Israel (e.g., Qumran) could also view

bring forth their "fruits" — the landowner's rightful portion of the vintage — for God (3:10; Lk 13:6-9; Jn 15:1-8).[172] Employing the Jewish hermeneutical technique *gezerah shewah,* which links verses on the basis of key terms they share, the passage develops the cornerstone idea; the prevalence of this linkage in different segments of early Christianity suggests that the image goes back to Jesus (1 Pet 2:6-8; cf. Rom 9:33). The "crushing" probably reflects Daniel 2:44, and the stumbling stone Isaiah 8:15 and 28:16 (for its potentially dual role, cf. Hos 14:9). Neither alternative is intended to be pleasant; *d'* (rather than the stronger adversative *alla*) here probably functions as a simple connective (like the Hebrew *waw*) rather than as a contrast. (Compare the purportedly late-second-century source cited in a still later source, Esth. Rab. 7:10, by Bonsirven 1964: 61; Young 1989: 295: whether Israel, a rock, falls on other nations, which are clay vessels, or the vessels fall on the rock, woe to the vessels.)[173] Finally understanding (15:10) that he was addressing them, the religious leaders looked for a way to seize him (cf. 26:5, 50). Because the Jewish crowds believed he was a prophet, however (21:11), the leaders had to bide their time; they were cowardly politicians (21:45-46).

The Cowardly Politicians (21:45-46)

This character of Jesus' opponents fits their following actions; concerned about the populace's response, they both choose a more advantageous time to seize Jesus (26:4-5, 55; cf. Lk 22:53) and allow Pilate and the Romans to carry out the sentence. Without a degree of favor from the people whom they had to keep quiet as well as from the Romans, the household of Caiaphas could not have stayed in power so long (see fuller comment on 21:23-27).

---

themselves as heirs of the identity of the biblical covenant community. In this period *ethnos* applies to guilds, associations, social classes or other groups, and even orders of priests; urban Greeks used the term for rural Greeks, the LXX for Gentiles, and Greeks for non-Greeks (Saldarini 1994: 59-60). Matthew implies not rejection of Israel but of dependence on any specific group membership, be it synagogue or church (Levine 1988: 193-239).

172. Both biblical (Ex 32:10; Num 14:12) and later Jewish (Ladd 1974b: 114) sources allowed that God could "replace" his people, but no one expected that he would do so (cf., e.g., the late parable in Lev. Rab. 27:6), least of all in the centuries since Israel had renounced idolatry. But by focusing on the wicked leaders (so also Saldarini 1994: 60-62), Matthew's comments, while implying judgment on Israel as a whole, are not as final as some later Christian theology shaped by the anti-Judaism of late Roman antiquity. The idea that Matthew's community has decisively rejected Israel in such words reads second-century theology into Matthew (with Saldarini 1994: 6).

173. I include 21:44 as part of the original text, but it is possible that it was imported from Lk 20:18. The *direct* textual evidence for its omission is weak and may stem from the difficulty of interpreting the verse as it stands.

Scorning the King's Son (22:1-14)

In the context, Jesus' harsh words condemn Israel's leaders. Yet, as often in his Gospel, Matthew apparently uses the community's opponents to warn members of his own community not to be like these opponents. Not only Jesus' enemies but even some of his supposed friends (22:11-14) would betray him.

Scholars differ considerably concerning the original form of this parable and the degree to which Matthew adapted it. Jeremias argues that Matthew has both allegorized and expanded this parable from an earlier version (referring to Lk 14:16-24; Gos. Thom. 64 — 1972: 67-68). Yet it is far from certain that this parable represents the same parable as in Luke 14:16-24; although it shares common motifs, the story's thrust in each represents a common theme in Jesus' teachings in general, and he may have told more than one story about a custom as common as invitations to a banquet. Indeed, if rabbis freely adapted earlier stories for telling in new settings (so, e.g., Johnston 1977b: 621-24, 639), there is no reason that Jesus could not have reused different versions of a similar story line in the hundreds of times he spoke in synagogues or among other crowds (cf. also France 1985: 311). Some have pointed to elements that may be common to many Jewish stories in this period (Bauckham 1996: 482).

The Lukan parable, set amid a Lukan symposium of dinner material (Lk 14:1-24), more realistically depicts an aristocrat inviting others of some social status to a banquet (some thus suppose it more authentic — Goulder 1974: 62; Gundry 1982: 432; Marshall 1978: 584).[174] By contrast, Matthew's parable more closely resembles the format of a standard rabbinic parable in which God as a king throws a wedding banquet for his son, Israel, and his daughter, Torah. (Jeremias thinks that Matthew has adapted Jesus' parable to that format — 1972: 28; I contend, conversely, that it could be a mark of authenticity.)[175] Kings in Jewish para-

174. Seating by rank was not, however, merely a Greek and Roman custom (e.g., Plut. *Table-Talk* 1.3, *Mor.* 619B-F; Lucian *De Mercede conductis* 15; Diog. Laert. *Lives* 2.73; 6.2.34), but far more widespread (e.g., Jos. *Ant.* 20.61), being a Palestinian Jewish custom as well (e.g., 1QS 7.20; Lev. Rab. 1:5; 5:4). Matthew had no *cultural* reason to delete it nor Luke to add it. Some also recommended inviting the virtuous or wise (Ep. Arist. 286) rather than merely those of one's social status. Although most served guests according to rank, evoking displeasure among the slighted (Theissen 1982: 156-58; Friedländer 1965: 1:208; MacMullen 1974: 111; cf. Mart. *Epig.* 3.49; 4.85; 12.28; Juv. *Sat.* 4.24-25, 37-48, 146-58; Plut. *Table-Talk* 1.2.3, *Mor.* 616E; Pliny *Ep.* 2.6), some preferred equal treatment among them (Plut. *Table-Talk* 1.2.5, *Mor.* 618A; Agesilaus 1 in Plut. *Sayings of Spartans, Mor.* 208BC; cf. Athenaeus *Deipn.* 1.12c).

175. Like other Jewish teachers, Jesus historically drew on the familiar image of wedding feasts (9:15; cf. 8:11; Mk 2:19-20; Lk 12:36), and not solely in Matthean material (25:10). In some cases parables simply depict a king (e.g., b. Sukk. 55b; Gen. Rab. 9:10; Song Rab. 8:14, §1) or other important person (b. Sukk. 29a, bar.; Epict. *Disc.* 2.4.8) throwing a banquet for dependents. Many rabbinic parables that depict God as king also depict Israel as his son or daughter (e.g., Sifre Num. 86.1.1; Sifre Deut. 40.6.1; 43.8.1; 45.1.2; 306.4.1; 306.7.1; 352.7.1, 4). If Matthew and Luke have adapted the same parable, Luke may historicize an eschatological banquet by his symposium context (cf. Wilson 1973: 34); later rabbis could, however, also apply present banqueting with a scholar to feasting on God's presence (b. Ber. 64a).

bles almost always represent God (see, e.g., Johnston 1977b: 583; comment on Mt 18:23), and guests at his banquets vary in meaning, though when significant sometimes apply to those facing judgment in the final day (Johnston 1977b: 593-94).

Both the Lukan and Matthean images for God as the host occur elsewhere in Jesus' parables, and the language of each of these two parables differs considerably from that in the other. If they do represent the same original parable (so Gundry 1982: 432-41), one or both evangelists has exercised a quite free hand recasting an originally common oral tradition (the major divergences make a common basis in written Q unlikely).

But especially if Matthew has recast an earlier parable like the one in Luke, one should not lightly pass over his mention that the banquet was for the king's "son" (22:2). Here, though not as explicitly as in 21:37-38 (since the son is merely part of the setting and could be interpreted as Israel), Jesus reveals his hand again; those who dishonor the son shame and dishonor the Father who sent him. It was common for kings or important personages to throw wedding banquets for sons, as expensively as possible, to which they might invite the entire village (cf. Char. *Chaer.* 3.2.10; Diod. Sic. 16.91.4; 16.92.1; Phaedrus 1.6.1; stele in Sherk 1988: 33; Stambaugh and Balch 1986: 119, citing Pliny *Ep.* 10.116; Bailey 1976: 186; for examples of extravagance, cf. Jos. *Ant.* 13.18-21; Terence *Lady of Andros* 450-58). But God's banquet here makes special allusion to the promised messianic banquet of the messianic era (Is 25:6; Manson 1979: 225).[176] In the narrative logic of the Gospel, Jesus is finally ready to unveil his identity in the final week (see Kingsbury 1986: 81-84).

Against whom is the parable directed? In an earlier form it may well have addressed the socially comfortable who despised the marginalized, as in Luke (cf. Jeremias 1972: 128); the calling of the "evil and the good" alike (22:10) may reflect this origin (cf. 13:47-50; 21:31-32). Conversely (or in addition to the previous proposal), the parable may have pronounced judgment on the Jerusalem authorities as it does in the present context. In either case, Matthew would not have been the first Jewish prophet to apply the principle of special accountability to those closest to the word (cf., e.g., Amos 3:2; 9:7). Whether it emphasizes judgment on all Israel (cf. Sandmel 1978a: 60; Mt 27:25), on Israel as a whole but not individual Jews (Hare 1979: 39), or on the Judean leadership in particular (21:43-45) may be debated, but the burning of the city in Matthew plainly refers to the destruction of Jerusalem (Jeremias 1972: 33; Hare 1979: 39; cf. Sib. Or. 4.125-26).[177] In view of the evidence that Jesus expected the impending destruc-

176. The banquet is especially prominent in rabbinic literature; see, e.g., m. 'Abot 3:16; 4:16; t. Ber. 6:21; b. B. Bat. 74b-75a; Ber. 34b; Gen. Rab. 51:8; 62:2; Ex. Rab. 45:6; 50:5; Lev. Rab. 11:2; 13:3; Num. Rab. 13:2; 21:21; Pesiq. R. 41:5; 48:3; Marmorstein 1968a: 46, 59, 120, 135). The meal in 1QSa 2.17-21 may be eschatological and messianic (Priest 1963; Witherington 1990: 75-76), but the matter is disputed (Smith 1958-59: 224).

177. Though Tasker 1961: 208 questions Jesus' identification of the legions with God's armies, biblical prophets did not scruple about portraying Assyrians or Babylonians in these terms; see further below.

tion of the temple (see comment on 24:2; cf. 21:12), that the text employs Old Testament judgment language (Amos 1:4, 7, 12; 2:2, 5; Gundry 1982: 436), that Jerusalemites preferred death to the defilement of Jerusalem (cf. Jos. *Ant.* 18.59, somewhat dramatized), that the Jesus tradition elsewhere speaks of judgment by fire (e.g., 18:8-9), that conquerors regularly burned cities,[178] that kings were known to burn rebellious cities (e.g., Diod. Sic. 33.4.2, on a Syrian king), and that this text omits relevant other details about Jerusalem's demise, one cannot rule out the possibility that Jesus spoke of the city being burned (see especially Robinson 1976: 21-22). Many scholars, however, see it as a Matthean explanation of the judgment the parable implies.

Rejecting God's invitation constitutes a deliberate insult against his dignity. Last-minute notification, such as public lists that drafted people's coming or service, did occur in the ancient world (Arist. *Peace* 1182-84), but that is not likely the problem here. Papyri testify to the practice of double invitations, both among upper classes and in regular village life.[179] Jeremias argues that "those who have been invited" (22:3) is merely a Semitism for "those to be invited" (1972: 68n.74), but this makes Matthew's Greek here more misleading than we would expect from one who might have caught the Semitism himself. Rather, the king had long ago honored the guests with an invitation, and they had appropriately responded with a promise to come; the second invitation in the parable is merely to inform them that the dinner is now ready (22:4).[180] Because weddings required major preparations (Terence *Lady of Andros* 362-65) and the exact time of the completion of preparations was difficult to determine in advance, a second invitation at the appropriate hour was standard procedure, and the lower a person's status, the more punctual the person was expected to be.

Attendance at weddings was a social obligation in Palestinian Judaism (Bonsirven 1964: 151); attendance at a patron's banquet was incumbent on social dependents throughout the Empire (cf. Sir 13:9-10), and one normally accepted banquet invitations even if one did not like the host (Phaedrus 4.26.17-19). Dinner invitations of all sorts were quite common (e.g., *P. Oxy.* 112, 1214, 1485, 1487, 2147). Those invited to some kinds of banquets might need to consider whether they could afford to reciprocate the honor later (Rohrbaugh 1991:141), but clients owed patrons (their social superiors) primarily *honor* (MacMullen 1974: 111; cf. the objection of Sen. *Ep. Lucil.* 4); patrons often based invitations on past flattery (Sen. *Ep. Lucil.* 47.8). To be the only ones of one's social status

178. E.g., Josh 6:24; 8:28; 11:11, 13; 1 Sam 30:1, 3, 14; 1 Kings 9:16; 2 Kings 25:9; 2 Chron 36:19; Neh 1:3; 2:17; 4:2; Ps 74:7-8; Is 1:7; 64:11; Jer 38:23; 39:8; 46:19; 52:13; Amos 1:7, 10, 12; 1 Macc 7:35; 2 Macc 12:6; Paus. 8.27.16; Arrian *Alex.* 3.18.11-12; Corn. Nep. 2 (Themistocles), 4.1-2; cf. Jos. *War* 6.252-53, probably playing down Titus's role. Cf. also suicides in 1 Kings 16:18; Diod. Sic. 16.45.4-5.

179. Scott 1989: 169; Rohrbaugh 1991: 139-41, pace Crossan; cf. also Epict. *Disc.* 2.4.8; Lam. Rab. 4:2, §2; Jeremias 1972: 176.

180. Social custom, rather than an allegory of God sending first the prophets, then Jesus and the apostles (so Manson 1979: 225), or more reasonably John, then Jesus (Sanders 1985: 227), dictates the detail.

not invited to a royal banquet was to feel snubbed (Apoc. Ezek. 1:2, probably first century); in such a society, not inviting the right person, or inviting the wrong person, could have disastrous, even mortal, consequences (b. Giṭ. 55b-56a). Thus, for example, one who invited to a town banquet the townsfolk but not the king merited much severer punishment than one who invited neither (t. B. Qam. 7:2).

By refusing to come, the guests insulted the dignity of the king who had counted on their attendance and graciously prepared food for them. To protect their honor guests might refuse to come to a particular person's (not a king's) banquet if others did (Rohrbaugh 1991: 142). Those invited might reject an invitation if they wished to insult the status of the host or questioned the security of his future; thus guests as well as hosts could play a role in the distribution of honor and shame (Derrett 1973: 43). For *all* the invited guests to refuse to come would shame the host; the absurd excuses given barely disguise what must have been a concerted plan deliberately to insult the host (Scott 1989: 171). But though village life normally continued uninterrupted regardless of who controlled the land (Goodman 1983: 33), rudeness such as is depicted here would never be directed toward a king or someone of extreme power in the community, before whom one could not even expect "safety in numbers." Ignoring a king's proclamation warranted severe punishment (e.g., Ruth Rab. Proem 7).

God will severely judge those who spurn his kindness. For the king graciously to extend the honor of an invitation to a banquet and be rebuffed as if his benefaction were meaningless was a traumatic breach of the social order. The king could salvage some honor only by getting others to eat the banquet and by punishing these who had insulted his kindness; even in less dramatic circumstances, Jewish people could envisage a king avenging his honor by executing those who had insulted him by scorning his invitation to eat (Gen. Rab. 9:10). Rejecting such an invitation was tantamount to a declaration of rebellion (Gundry 1982: 436). Hearers of the parable would marvel at the treasonous foolishness and impudence of those who would insult a king.

The added detail of slaughtered messengers (22:6)[181] exceeded horrendous breach of social custom and constituted a revolutionary act, like Jewish revolutionaries slaying Roman soldiers in blatant violation of a truce. Josephus need only mention the act to explain its invitation of judgment (*War* 2.450-56);[182] elsewhere he recounts how wicked people insulted the messengers of righteous King Hezekiah and killed the prophets, hence warranting their own destruction

181. The term for "mistreating" them (cf. similarly beatings in Acts 14:5; 1 Thess 2:2) further implies public humiliation (cf. Best 1977: 90; F. F. Bruce 1982: 25), of the sort that called for vengeance when possible (cf. Dion. Hal. 10.35.3); thus they explicitly shamed the king by shaming his messengers (cf. 2 Sam 10:4-6). Lk 18:32 applies the term to the passion.

182. The treachery was not without historical parallel (Diod. Sic. 30.4.1; Livy 21.10.9; Appian *R.H.* 6.8.43; 6.9.52; 6.10.60; Corn. Nep. 1 [Miltiades], 4.1). Rulers typically slew those who revolted, though often enslaving some (Arrian *Alex.* 3.25.7), especially women and children (often after conquest, as, e.g., in Ovid *Metam.* 13.497; Appian *R.H.* 3.6.1).

by God (Jos. *Ant.* 9.264-66). The parable's audience would naturally applaud the king's rage (cf. 3:7; 18:34) as just — except those who already felt themselves the object of its lesson (21:45). The language of "seizing" (22:6) is applicable to the fate of John (14:3) and what the authorities wish to do to Jesus (21:46). The violence is both realistic and unrealistic. It is realistic in that after an insult like the one the invitees had made against the king's honor, nothing less than such vengeance as verse 7 depicts would satisfy his honor (Malina and Rohrbaugh 1992: 135).[183] Yet it is unrealistic to suppose that the king would engage in a military expedition while the food was getting cold (Young 1989: 171)! Because the story is meant to climax on the second group of invitees, however, it must narrate the annihilation of the rebels at this point.

The arrogant may spurn him, but God invites the lowly to his banquet. To recoup at least some of his honor, the king must invite other guests (in Matthew's parable, the king has actually recouped quite a bit of his honor by killing those who offended him).[184] In one Jewish story even a wicked tax gatherer, snubbed by all his invited guests, the town's honorable men, invited the poor to keep food from going to waste, and so recouped some lost honor (p. Ḥag. 2:2, §5).[185] The parable's hearer also senses the urgency ("the banquet is ready" — 22:8; cf. Rev 19:7), remembering the importance of freshly prepared food at a banquet. Since the term for "banquet" here refers to a meal taken early in the day (midday at the latest), if Jesus uses the advent of darkness outside (22:13) in a literal as well as figurative way, the meal has been delayed much of the day (cf. Gundry 1982: 434); it cannot retain any semblance of being fresh if delayed any longer. Commentators often suggest that those gathered from outside the destroyed city refer to the Gentiles (Meier 1980: 248; Theissen 1991: 272).[186] Although one could think of the rural peasantry, Mat-

183. In rabbinic parables, military metaphors most frequently depict God as the king and military leader (Johnston 1977b: 593). The depiction of destruction is "topical," including what one expects in any city's destruction; the first temple had been burned (Jos. *Apion* 1.132, 145); and, to be precise, Josephus reports only the *temple* being burned in 70 (Blomberg 1992a: 327). Nevertheless, many view this verse as a post-70 comment on Jerusalem's destruction (e.g., Theissen 1991: 271-72); one may note that the prophecy of the temple's burning in Jos. *Ant.* 4.313 is an *ex eventu* wording of a more general threat. Those who deny that the author could depict God as doing something that historically Titus carried out miss the character of parables; rabbis chose the Roman emperor to symbolize God after the Jewish monarchy ceased (Stern 1991: 94).

184. Scott 1989: 172 notes that the host loses honor by inviting those of much lower social status (though for gifts or invitations to the pious poor, see Tob 2:2; Jn 13:29). It is true that he loses some honor, but not as much as he would lose if the food spoiled. Besides, after 22:7, in Matthew's version these poor are the only people left besides the king!

185. Commentators frequently compare this story about Bar Ma'yan with the story in Mt 22:2-10 (e.g., Vermes 1993: 113).

186. On the streets and lanes, cf. Rohrbaugh 1991:144 (on Lk 14:21). Such imagery is not unnatural, but could it allude to Jesus' ministry on the "highways" (20:30)? Manns 1988 may be right to find a reversal of the Jewish tradition that God offered Torah to Israel only after the Gentiles rejected it; whether it alludes to this specific tradition, certainly the parable announces the reversal of the historic divine order.

thew would know that many of these fled into Jerusalem as the Roman armies advanced, and his Gentile motif elsewhere supports the thesis that Matthew intends them to include Gentiles.

Those inside the church may also dishonor God and warrant death. The parable of the wedding garment, whether originally disparate or connected to this one, probably stems from Jesus the storyteller; it reflects a story line probably already in circulation in Jewish Palestine.[187]

Once the newly chosen guests have begun to dine, the host enters after the banquet has begun, as was customary (Jeremias 1972: 187). Some hold that hosts may have provided wedding garments to guests at the door,[188] for which there is some but slight evidence (Bultmann 1968: 202 cites b. Shab. 152b; cf. 2 Kings 10:22). But most commentators think that "wedding garments" refer simply to clean garments as opposed to soiled ones;[189] to come to a wedding in a soiled garment insulted the host, and this host was in no further mood to be insulted. "How did you enter?" hence means, "How did you manage to slip by the porters at the doors?" (cf. Jeremias 1972: 187; for porters, cf., e.g., Sen. *Ep. Lucil.* 19.11; Treggiari 1975: 51). The question allows for an explanation of misunderstanding; the man's silence, however, indicates that the matter is not merely one of misunderstanding (Bauckham 1996: 486). Patrons invited their social dependents to banquets, expecting in return due honor; this man, like the first guests the king had invited, has responded to grace with a political insult.[190]

Matthew leaves no doubt as to the interpretation: the wedding garment signifies repentance (3:2; 4:17).[191] Just as most of the Jewish leaders were unprepared at Jesus' first coming (cf. 23:13-33), some professing disciples of Jesus

187. A king invited servants to a banquet without announcing the date; the wise waited at the gate, while the foolish kept working; thus the latter, with soiled clothes, ended up having to watch the wise honored with seats at the banquets and themselves relegated to the side. In the latest version of the story, the white garment explicitly represents allegiance to Torah (Jeremias 1972: 188n.71). Attributed to the pre-70 rabbi Johanan ben Zakkai, the story appears in later collections (b. Shab. 153a; possibly from Judah ha-Nasi — Qoh. Rab. 9:8, §1; the parable is cited by Jeremias 1972: 188; Bonsirven 1964: 167; Albright and Mann 1971: 270).

188. See in A. B. Bruce 1979: 272; Gundry 1982: 439.

189. See, e.g., Jeremias 1972: 187-88; Davies and Allison 1997: 204 (citing most early Christian commentators, such as Origen *Hom. Exod.* 11.7; Chrysostom *Hom. Matt.* 69.2; Isaac the Syrian *Asc. Hom.* 2, 76); cf. Meier 1980: 248; Gundry 1982: 439; France 1985: 313. Entering a temple in a dirty garment was thought to merit punishment (Llewelyn 1998: 173, §16). One may compare Qumran rules on clean clothes for entering a house of worship (CD 11.22) and for the Sabbath (CD 11.3-4); cf. Jos. *War* 2.129-31 on their attire for morning worship. Cf. Jos. *War* 2.1; *Ant.* 11.327 for the use of white robes in the temple (cf. comment on 28:2-3). Yet even many villagers in Egypt had a set of special clothes, distinct from their work clothes, for special occasions (Lewis 1983: 69); cf. Diod. Sic. 10.9.6 on the Pythagorean use of "white and clean" garments.

190. That the feast was prepared suggests that the man should have declined if he did not have a clean garment prepared (or should have cleaned it very quickly); but Matthew is more interested in the story's moral than its realism. The story's point at any rate breaks from the bonds of its narrative world in 22:13.

191. So Jeremias 1972: 188; Albright and Mann 1971: 269; Fenton 1977: 350.

will be unprepared at his second (24:45-51).[192] Professing Christians who insult God's grace by presuming on it without truly honoring his Son will be banished to outer darkness (cf. 8:12; 25:30) and weeping with gnashing of teeth (13:42; 24:51; 25:30; cf. Meier 1980: 248-49).[193] As in verse 14, many are "called" or "invited" with the message of repentance (21:32; cf. 9:13), but only those who respond worthily will share the inheritance of the chosen, covenant people (also Jeremias 1971: 131; cf. 24:24); cf. 7:13-23.[194]

Caesar or God (22:15-22)

Cf. Mk 12:13-17; Lk 20:20-26. The next four paragraphs open with leading questions that seek to trap Jesus.[195] Students often asked public questions of various teachers to expose their ignorance on some matter, hence the questioner's superiority (e.g., Aul. Gel. 18.13.7-8; 20.10.1-6). While Mark may not have *purposely* linked four sample representatives of later Jewish types of opening questions (Daube 1956: 343; idem 1973: 158-61) — the categories are too neat and the Gospel tradition's questions do not fit them as well as Daube hopes (Dewey 1980: 61) — Daube's parallels suggest that in general the sort of questions asked may have been characteristic of the developing Jewish schools: halakic (legal; here on tribute to Caesar); *boruth,* mocking questions to ridicule a rabbi's belief (here the resurrection); *derekh 'ereṣ,* principles of successful life (here, the most important commandment); and haggadic (resolving possible contradictions in Scripture, here on Ps 110).[196]

Matthew presents the opposition as conniving. When Matthew announces that the Pharisees "took counsel" to trap Jesus (22:15), the reader may recall the last time the Pharisees "took counsel," when they were plotting his death (12:14). Still more ominously, the Herodians (v. 16) normally constituted unlikely allies for the Pharisees. Josephus's summary statements suggest that

192. Judas is merely a case in point ("friend" in 22:12; 26:50; cf. 20:13); this need not directly allude to Judas, however (pace Crips 1957).

193. The image of binding and casting into darkness the wicked resembles the fate of wicked angels in 1 Enoch (though this might recollect the language generally rather than function as a specific allusion to the text, as Sim 1992 suspects); cf. comment on 8:12.

194. Dalman cites a late parallel to the saying (1929: 228), but it is not particularly close; Davies and Allison 1997: 206 cite Plato *Phaed.* 69C as well as sayings that suggest the salvation of few (4 Ezra 8:1, 3; 2 Bar. 44:15; b. Menaḥ. 29b). Nevertheless, the three-beat rhythm suggests that the saying originated with an Aramaic-speaking teacher, probably Jesus (see Jeremias 1971: 25; Dalman 1929: 228). This militates against van Tilborg's view that Matthew created the saying by combining features of 22:1-10 and 22:11-13 (1972b: 63).

195. Although the evidence cited by Stauffer for watching, catching, and arresting those suspected of subverting the law (1960) reflects rabbinic anachronism of their own practices, it nevertheless suits the general legal process of the period (cf. the Roman use of *delatores* — O'Neal 1978; Hemer 1986: 67).

196. Daube also suggests that the rabbinic style reflects Greek influence (1973: 161-63). Jewish and Greek rhetorical conventions here are not mutually exclusive.

Pharisaic beliefs and those of Judas's revolutionary followers had much in common;[197] Herodians were partisans of the Herodian dynasty, who held their power by Rome's favor and hoped for the full restoration of Herodian authority (cf. Simon 1967: 86).[198] Josephus shows us that the Pharisees cooperated with the aristocracy especially when grave national interests were at stake, providing an essential coalition between populist and institutional leadership (e.g., Jos. *Life* 21-22). Here the extreme situation presented by Jesus brings them together (Smallwood 1976: 164; Bowker 1973: 41). Although Matthew omitted an earlier incident of cooperation (Mt 12:14/Mk 3:6), he retains the cooperation here, which is significant in a political context (cf. Plummer 1910: 304). Together they greet Jesus with the sort of complimentary words with which a rhetorician might seek an audience's favor *(captatio benevolentiae),*[199] but for the purpose of lowering his guard. Ancient moralists frequently condemn the danger of trusting or offering such "flattery."[200]

The coalition here hopes to catch Jesus coming or going: either he will support taxes to Rome, undercutting his popular, messianic support,[201] or he will challenge taxes, thereby aligning with the views that had sparked a disastrous revolt two decades earlier. In the latter case, the Herodians could charge him with being a revolutionary — hence that he should be executed, and executed quickly (cf. Argyle 1963: 168; Harrington 1982: 88; Cullmann 1956b: 34-36). Indeed, given his defiance of the temple authorities and growing following, his opponents undoubtedly felt they had good reason to suspect him of just such sentiments (Filson 1964: 131).

Locally minted copper coins omitted the emperor's portrait due to Jerusalem's sensitivities,[202] but because only the imperial mint (on which in the early

197. Although many follow Josephus's distinction between the two (Jos. *War* 2.118; see also, e.g., Davies 1967a: 18-19; Polish 1970), the revolutionary movement seemed to agree with much of the Pharisees' populist theology (Jos. *Ant.* 18.23; cf. Simon 1967: 44; Sanders 1993: 13-14, 408-10), perhaps as part of common Judaism (cf. Horsley and Hanson 1985: xv).

198. Although Hoehner 1972: 331-42 holds the Herodians to be a religious rather than a political group (identifying them with the Boethusians), Smallwood 1976: 164 contends that the Herodians hoped "for the restoration of Herodian rule in Judaea." Overman 1996: 179-80 thinks that they viewed Herod Agrippa I in quasimessianic terms. On the formation of the -ian suffix (a Latinism) for the Herodians, cf. Lake and Cadbury 1979: 130; Aune 1987: 140-41; Acts 11:28.

199. Not only Gentile rhetoricians (e.g., Quint. 4.1.16; Char. *Chaer.* 5.7.1) but also rabbis were aware of this technique (Sifre Deut. 343.1.2); one may expect it from Jerusalem aristocrats (cf. Acts 24:2).

200. Ancient literature regularly condemns this vice: e.g., Isoc. *Demon.* 30, *Or.* 1; Cic. *De Amicitia* 25.94–26.99; *De Officiis* 1.26.91; Horace *Epodes* 1.16.25-39; Dion. Hal. 1.6.5; Epict. *Disc.* 1.12; 1.9.20, 26; 3.24.45; 4.6.33; 4.7.24; Plut. *Educ.* 17, *Mor.* 13B; *How to Tell a Flatterer from a Friend* 1-37, *Mor.* 48E-74E; Juv. *Sat.* 3.86-87; 4.65-72; Marc. Aur. *Med.* 1.9; 1.16.4; Diog. Laert. 6.1.4; 6.2.51; 6.5.92; Athenaeus 6.236E, 248F; Ps-Phocyl. 91; 1 Thess 2:5.

201. Although Jesus answers prudently, he essentially *does* support taxes to Rome (he simply makes it clear that they do the same). He stood in the prophetic tradition, which appeared traitorous to nationalists (e.g., Jer 26:8-9; 27:6-22; 29:4-9; Ezek 8–9).

202. See Avi-Yonah 1974/76a: 59-60; cf. Smallwood 1976: 95; Sanders 1985: 242-44.

Empire see Jones 1970: 299-305) could legally produce silver and gold coins,[203] Palestine had many foreign coins in circulation (Schürer 1961: 196). The silver denarius of Tiberius, including a portrait of his head and minted especially at Lyon, circulated there in this period; although an earlier coin might be in view, this imperial denarius is most likely (Reicke 1974: 137; Avi-Yonah 1974/76a: 61; Hart 1984). The coin related directly to pagan Roman religion and to the imperial cult in the east: the side bearing his image also included a superscription, namely, "TI. CAESAR DIVI AVG.F.AVGVSTVS" — "Tiberius Caesar, son of the Divine Augustus"; the other side bore a feminine image (perhaps of the Empress Livia personified as the goddess Roma) and read "PONTIF. MAXIM," referring to the high priest of Roman religion (Deissmann 1978: 252n.2; Ferguson 1987: 70-71). The Empire actively used such coins to promote the worship of the emperor (Gardner 1974: xxviii),[204] and while Jews were allowed to honor emperors, they were expected to avoid images (Jos. *Apion* 2.76-77). The emperor controlled the production of the coins, and they were officially his property (Lane 1974a: 424). Yet like it or not, Jews *had* to use this coin; it was the one *required* for the poll tax in all provinces (Lane 1974a: 424). That was, of course, the tax that had provoked Judas the Galilean's famous revolt of A.D. 6 (Jos. *War* 2.118). In the province of Syria, Roman property tax was 1 percent annually; the poll tax was probably one denarius a year for each person (including, in this province, women; Stambaugh and Balch 1986: 78).

Matthew presents Jesus as more than adequate for their rhetorical challenge. But Jesus, as always, knows their thoughts (9:4; 26:10), and responds accordingly. To render to Caesar what was Caesar's was to return his own coin to him (cf. 17:25; Rom 13:6-7; 1 Pet 2:13-14);[205] to render to God what was God's was to render worship to him alone (cf. 4:10).[206] Neither the image nor the superscription on coins in common usage could prevent Jewish people's single-minded devotion to God, nor did the coin have this effect. Further, Jesus undoubtedly challenged the idea that his opponents needed to hold onto the coins at all; why not return them to Caesar? Jerusalemites preferred death to allowing Caesar's image to enter Jerusa-

203. Jews did so only in times of revolt (Avi-Yonah 1974/76a: 60).

204. Some thus think that the pre-Markan tradition points to the issue of iconic idolatry that Judaism debated back then (Finney 1993; on 642-43 he notes that Sepphoris, near Nazareth, was aniconic). Horsley 1995: 120-21 believes that the emperor cult remained a live issue even in predominantly Jewish cities in Palestine (citing, with varying degrees of relevance, Jos. *War* 1.400, 407, 648-55; 2.169-74, 197; *Ant.* 17.149-67; 18.28, 36-38). At the least, the issue of emperor worship informs nationalists' discomfort with the coin and the tax paid with it.

205. Jeremias thinks that Jesus' teaching from the coin in Mk 12:13-17 is probably authentic in view of its echo in Rom 13:7 (1971: 228-29; cf. also F. F. Bruce 1984: 263).

206. Derrett proposes that Jesus was claiming that tithes and the temple tax took precedence over monetary obligations to Caesar (1970: 338); this hardly seems to be the point of the present passage, however; cf. 17:27. A protest against the imperial cult is more probable (Deissmann 1978: 252; Lane 1974a: 424); Herod the Great had constructed temples for Caesar in some of Palestine's Gentile cities (Schürer 1961: 139), a matter of which the Herodians might not wish to be reminded publicly. Later Christians found much of import in this passage (e.g., Justin *1 Apol.* 17), but it fits the issues of Jewish Palestine too well (including hatred of the tax) to be a creation of the Gentile church.

lem on standards (Jos. *Ant.* 18.59), yet they carried it in on coins. One would make such an exception for money only if money were of extreme importance (White 1971: 233; Witherington 1990: 102; cf. 6:19-34); by contrast, surrendering to God "what is God's" implied the surrender of all one was and possessed (Patte 1987: 309-10).[207] In Jesus' teaching elsewhere, possessions have zero value, and those who seek them are not the simple who trust in God (6:19-34). Jesus has not compromised his popular support, but rather embarrassed his challengers; they, not he, are carrying the offensive coin, so scruples against it cannot be their own (Danker 1972: 202-3; Meier 1980: 251-52).[208] In view of this, as well as their shallow sycophancy in pretending to believe that he speaks the "way" of God in truth (22:16, following Jesus' words in 21:32), they rightly earn his derisive title for them: "hypocrites" (6:2; 15:7; 23:13-29; 24:51).[209]

Through others' response to Jesus, Matthew indicates that Jesus was greater than the categories his contemporaries had available for him. Here people marvel at Jesus' response (22:22); elsewhere people marvel at his teaching (7:28), his nature miracles (8:27), his healing (9:8), his exorcism (12:23), and in the Passion Narrative Pilate marvels at Jesus' silence (27:14). In all these cases, Jesus confounds others' expectations.

Proving the Resurrection (22:23-33)

The tradition preserved in this passage has a good claim to authenticity. Later Christians would have little reason to compose a dialogue with Sadducean ideas; although Sadducees persecuted the early Jewish Christians and we might expect traces of that in the tradition, we have no evidence of theological dialogue between them (Witherington 1990: 15n.58).

Levirate marriage and widow inheritance[210] are practiced in many tradi-

207. Gundry 1982: 443 even suggests that the text may imply that "what is God's" is what is stamped with *God's* image — namely, human beings (humans in God's image are thus portrayed here as God's coinage — so Augustine *Sermons on New Testament Lessons* 43; *Tractates on John* 40.9; cf. Tert. *On Idolatry* 15; *ACCS,* 167-68); see more fully Owen-Ball 1993, investigating the rabbinic style of rhetoric here.

208. Jesus may thus have divided the Pharisees and Herodians if the latter were carrying the coin (Malina and Rohrbaugh 1992: 137); but, as noted above, everyone needed it at least to pay their taxes. Lachs 1987: 359 does, however, cite a tradition that R. Nahum b. Simlai was so holy because "he never looked upon the form on a coin" (b. Pesaḥ. 104a).

209. It was customary to insult (particularly with insults like "fool") one's accusers, opponents, or even rhetorical interlocuters if one had the status to get away with it; see, e.g., Demosth. *On the Crown* 209-10; Epict. *Disc.* 2.16.13; 3.13.17; 3.22.85; Mart. *Epig.* 10.100.1; Philo *Cher.* 75; Sifre Deut. 309.1.1; 309.2.1; see further comment on 5:22. Warnings against such speech (5:22; Epict. *Disc.* 1.18.10) were far rarer than the speech itself.

210. On widow inheritance, see Gluckman 1950: 183; Radcliffe-Brown 1950: 26, 64; Fortes 1950: 271; Farber 1968: 74, 91; Gough 1973b: 627. In a custom similar to the practice behind Gen 16, some South African tribes require the relatives of a barren woman to supply her sister to provide her children (Radcliffe-Brown 1950: 64).

tional societies (e.g., Lowie 1968: 58; Abrahams 1973; Evans-Pritchard 1951: 112-15), often as ways to perpetuate the name of the deceased and to provide for the widow in societies where women could not earn sufficient wages for sustenance (e.g., Mbiti 1970: 188-89; Nadal 1950: 350).[211] Always part of Israel's law code (Deut 25:5-6; cf. Gen. 38:8-26), levirate marriage remained a topic of discussion among Jewish teachers (Jos. *Ant.* 4.254-56; m. Yebam.; t. Yebam.),[212] occasionally including attempts to define the law in hypothetical cases like the one the Sadducees propose here (cf. t. Yebam. 2:1; Jeremias 1969: 93-94 on b. Yebam. 15b). In this period in Palestine, one did not simply raise up offspring, but married the widow (Belkin 1970; cf. Ruth 3:12-13). Many ancient hearers would assume dangerous a woman who had outlived seven husbands, blaming her ill fortune or worse (Mart. *Epig.* 9.15; Lucan *C.W.* 3.21-23; Tob 3:7-10; in early Jewish sources see Friedman 1990); some Tannaim even ruled that she should be forbidden to marry after the second or third husband (t. Shab. 15:8). But the Sadducees borrow the story line of a woman with seven husbands especially from the popular Jewish folk tale in Tobit 3:8 (as others note, e.g., Lane 1974a: 427).[213] The Sadducees are interested neither in moral nor in legal questions here, but endeavor to illustrate the impossible dilemmas they believe the doctrine of resurrection creates (one may compare romantic complications in Greco-Roman afterlife scenarios, e.g., Virg. *Aen.* 6.467-76). The Sadducees were known for their opposition to the doctrine of the resurrection (Acts 23:6-8; perhaps Jos. *Ant.* 18.16; *War* 2.164-65; cf. ARN 5; 10A; a reading of b. Shab. 152b; the Palestinian Targum in Isenberg 1970; the alternative hypothesis of Lachs 1977, that the issue was the *character* of the resurrection, is less probable).

In his response Jesus first addresses the nature of the resurrection, arguing by means of analogy with the angels. Other sages (not Sadducees) agreed that the world to come would differ from the present one on some significant points; some later teachers included among the differences no eating, drinking, or begetting children (b. Ber. 17a). Enoch's Similitudes (of possibly but not certainly pre-Christian date) declare that the righteous would dwell with angels (1 Enoch 39:5)[214] and that God originally created people to be like angels, pure and deathless (1 Enoch 69:11; cf. Theophilus 2.24; Israel at Sinai in Num. Rab. 16:24). Others felt that the children of the age to come would be like angels, although

211. Some societies lack the levirate (e.g., Nukunya 1969: 96-97, 116), and incest regulations sometimes prevent it (Schapera 1950: 153); in some cases it leads to permissive sexuality with in-laws (Stephens 1963: 20).

212. Cf. Safrai 1974/76b: 789; Wegner 1988: 99-112; Ilan 1996: 153-57; perhaps Jos. *Ant.* 13.320.

213. In view of the allusion to Tobit, all "had" her may mean that they married her but could not consummate the marriage (Tob 3:7-8); but more likely "have" carries its frequent euphemistic sense in sexual contexts in this period, confronting Jesus with multiple consummated unions (1 Cor 7:2; cf. Tob 8:7).

214. 1 Enoch 51:4-5 may also announce that the righteous will become angels, but note the variations in translation (Knibb 1979: 136 vs. Isaac 1976: 37).

this normally referred to glory rather than specifically to marriage (2 Bar. 51:10-11; cf. also 1 Enoch 104:2, 4).

Many Jewish thinkers also contrasted the nature of humanity with that of the angels (cf. 18:10); most agreed that angels did not eat, drink,[215] or propagate.[216] Propagation is unnecessary since angels do not die (1 Enoch 15:6-7);[217] hence also among the resurrected (cf. b. B. Bat. 58a, no passion in the next world).[218] "Taking in marriage" was the action of a husband (e.g., CD 7.6-7; m. Yebam. 8:6); "giving in marriage" was the action of a father (e.g., Appian *R.H.* 1.1.1). Jesus' statement about lack of marriage and procreation in heaven (22:30) follows from the logic of the resurrection, to which he now turns (22:31-32).

Having defined the nature of the resurrection, Jesus now proceeds to defend the fact of the resurrection, which is the issue really at stake with the Sadducees. Early Jewish teachers regularly argued apart from the Bible with Gentiles or scoffers, but from Scripture for those who knew Scripture (Moore 1971: 2:381). While Jesus may not follow later rabbinic lines of argument (Cohn-Sherbok 1981a), his argument has much in common with the case Pharisees reportedly made for the resurrection (cf., e.g., Lachs 1987: 361; Davies and Allison 1997: 233).[219] When debating the views of Sadducees who doubted the resurrection and demanded proof from the law of Moses, later rabbis found ample proof for this doctrine in the Bible's first five books (b. Sanh. 90b, including a second-century source; cf. Pesaḥ. 68a). Thus, for example, Aaron the priest,

215. Test. Abr. 4, 6 A; ARN 1A; b. Yoma 75b; Gen. Rab. 2:2; 48:11, 14; Ex. Rab. 32:4; Lev. Rab. 34:8; cf. Harrington 1972: 170; Goodman 1986. Greeks (whose deities subsisted on nectar and ambrosia) described as mortals those who ate grain (Hom. *Il.* 13.322).

216. 1 Enoch 15:6-7; ARN 37A; Gen. Rab. 8:11; 14:3; also Moore 1971: 1:405-6; fallen angels, however, did (Jub. 10:5; b. Ḥag. 16a, bar.); good angels lack the evil impulse (Lev. Rab. 26:5). Based on Ps 104:4, many Jewish people held angels to consist of fire (1 Enoch 17:1; 2 Enoch 20:1; 29:3; 4 Ezra 8:22; Pesiq. R. 16:2; Bonsirven 1964: 34; cf. 1 Enoch 14:11-15; Test. Sol. 1:10; 9:4; Cic. *De Re Publ.* 6.15.15; Marc. Aur. *Med.* 4.21). On humanity's mixed character, cf. Philo *Creation* 146.

217. Although God can destroy them, as in b. Sanh. 38b in Moore 1971: 1:406 or with evil angels, e.g., in Num. Rab. 18:22. Thus I refer above specifically to the Enoch tradition; see comment on 8:30-32.

218. Hill 1972: 305 compares 1QH 3.21ff.; 6.13; 1 Enoch 104.4ff., where the righteous are like angels. Sib. Or. 2.328 is probably Christian redaction; the Apocalypse of Zosimus may be Christian as well, but if it is Jewish its teaching about the soul emerging genderless at death (see McNeil 1981) owes more to Greek philosophy (cf. Baer 1970) than Jesus would appeal to, and perhaps even to the hellenistically educated Jerusalem aristocracy. Yet other ideas, such as that of Moses purging food from his body to become like angels and receive revelations (ARN 1A), or those who guard the Sabbath being holy like the angels (Jub. 2:28; cf. 15:27), may support the idea of an angel-like future (Acts 12:15; 23:8; Acts of Paul 3:5; Prayer of Joseph 19; *theoi* in Ps-Phocyl. 104). Some Tannaim even adapted Middle Platonic thought to speak of humans who follow the soul being like angels since it, as opposed to the body, is heavenly (Sifre Deut. 306.28.2; cf. 4 Macc 7:18-19).

219. Bultmann 1968: 26 doubts the tradition's authenticity in Mark because of its supposed rabbinic character; but surely Jesus and the earliest Palestinian tradition that followed him would have more in common with Jewish teachers than Mark would. Many reports of Pharisaic debates with Sadducees and Boethusians are Tannaitic (e.g., m. Yad. 4:7; t. Sukk. 3:1), though their form is stereotypical, and some are clearly inauthentic.

who died before entering the land, must be raised to inherit his portion of the land (b. Sanh. 90b, third-century tradition; cf. Qoh. Rab. 9:5, §1). Others found it in Deuteronomy 32 (Sifre Deut. 329.2.1; cf. also 4 Macc 18:19), Genesis 3 (Gen. Rab. 20:10 — a second-century Tanna), and elsewhere. R. Simai later went so far as to say that all texts implied the resurrection if one simply had the exegetical (modern exegetes would call it eisegetical!) ingenuity to find it (Midr. Tannaim on Deut 32:2, in Moore 1971: 2:383; Sifre Deut. 306.28.3).

Jesus also cites a line of argument intelligible in his culture, as contemporary sources attest: Philo also found in Exodus 3:6 that the patriarchs continued to live (*Abr.* 50-55 in Downing 1982): 4 Maccabees declares that the patriarchs did not die, but live to God (4 Macc 7:18-19; 16:25); some later rabbis also inferred from the promise to the patriarchs (Ex 33:1) that "the righteous are called living even in their death" (Qoh. Rab. 9:5, §1; cf. Ex. Rab. 1:8; Deut. Rab. 3:15). The righteous are lost to their generation at death, but remain the righteous (b. Meg. 15a); sages could also read "living God" as "God of the living" (Pesiq. R. 1:2). Charlesworth is thus right to note that both Jesus' teaching here and 4 Maccabees 7:19 "contain a widespread Jewish notion, namely that the Patriarchs are not really dead" (1985: 78-79).

Jesus may be arguing for God's continuing purposes with an individual after death, which for many Palestinian Jews would imply ultimate resurrection. He implies that God would not claim to be the God of someone who no longer existed (cf. Doeve 1954: 106; Longenecker 1975: 68-69); he also evokes God's covenant faithfulness to his people, which Palestinian Jewish prayers regularly associated with the "God of the fathers," Abraham, Isaac, and Jacob (twice daily, by the second century at the latest; Jeremias 1971: 187; Lane 1974a: 429). Jewish people regularly invoked God as the "God of Abraham, Isaac, and Jacob" (e.g., Mek. *Pisha* 1.23-27; b. Ber. 16b; Gen. Rab. 82:3; Test. Mos. 3:9; the first benediction of the Amida; other nations also addressed the gods of their ancestors, e.g., Virg. *Aen.* 9.247). If God was still God of Abraham, Isaac, and Jacob, and if his power was unlimited, then he would ultimately fulfill his promise to them, not only corporately through their descendants, but personally to them.

As an expert Scripture interpreter, Jesus here exposes his opponents' lack of Scripture knowledge with his standard formula: "Have you not read?" (22:31; cf. 12:3; 19:4; 21:42, 46), which functions as a deliberate challenge. Later rabbis could also question the ignorance of those who doubted the resurrection (Deut. Rab. 3:15); many educated Jews conceded that ignorance of God's law and justice merited judgment (Sib. Or. 3.686-87); denial of eschatology produced immorality (Wis 2:1-24) and invited damnation (m. Ber. 9:5). For Jesus, the problem with the Sadducees comes down to their inadequate faith in Scripture and in God's power to accomplish the resurrection (22:29). When Jesus declares that the Sadducees deny the power of God (cf. 2 Tim 3:5), he may evoke the traditional Jewish view that God expresses his power most visibly in the resurrection of the dead, a view attested in the second of the

Eighteen Benedictions (abbreviated as "Power"; cf. m. Rosh. Hash. 4:5; cf. also Rom 1:4).[220]

In this context, Matthew may also use Jesus' "silencing" of his opponents (22:34; a way of shaming them, e.g., Aul. Gel. 1.2.13; 18.13.7-8) to suggest implications beyond the immediate debate for their standing at the judgment (22:12). The multitudes are again astounded by Jesus' quick wit (22:33; cf. 7:28; 22:22, 46), just as they are by his signs (8:27; 9:8; 12:23).

Loving God and Neighbor (22:34-40)

Cf. Mk 12:28-34; Lk 10:25-28; Jn 13:34-35. "Testing" scholars with riddles (22:35) — and God vindicating the divine wisdom given to his servant — is at least as old as King Solomon (1 Kings 10:1; elsewhere, e.g., Ep. Arist. 187-291). In this context, however, the intent may be more malicious (cf. 16:1; 19:3; 22:18), related to that of the supreme tempter (4:1).

This passage certainly reflects Palestinian Jewish tradition (see most fully Abrahams 1917: 18-29). Some Pharisees ask a question with which they had sufficient practice, since their own teachers debated among themselves which commandment was the "greatest."[221] Although all commandments were equally weighty in one sense (see on 5:19), rabbis had to distinguish between "light" and "heavy" commandments in practice (see on 23:23).[222] Although many opted for the command to obey one's parents as the "greatest," other Jewish teachers stressed love as the preeminent commandment.[223] Judaism continued to stress loving God with one's whole being;[224] love for neighbor had long been a fundamental principle of Jewish ethics (m. 'Abot 1:12, attributed to Hillel; Jub. 36:4, 8).[225]

220. Although his view may be anachronistic, Finkelstein even thinks the Pharisees directed the resurrection benediction against the Sadducees (1972: 266-67). The benediction became quite important (e.g., Gen. Rab. 39:11).

221. The "great" commandment means the "greatest"; Matthew employs "great" as a superlative as in 5:19, following the Koine usage growing more common in his day; Meier 1980: 256 suggests that it is a Semitism. Later rabbis often discussed the question of the "greatest" commandment; see Hagner 1995: 646.

222. The Ten Commandments were heavily stressed on a popular level (Vermes 1959); many rabbis settled on specific commands, such as the prohibition of idolatry (b. Qidd. 40a; p. Ned. 3:9, §3), as particularly heavy.

223. Bonsirven 1964: 29; Smith 1951: 174; for a later example, Montefiore and Loewe 1974: 111.

224. For the idiom "heart and soul" signifying "entirely," cf., e.g., Jub. 1:15-16; 16:25; 19:31; 36:24; also 1QS 1.2 if reconstructed accurately.

225. The closest common analogy in Greek ethics may simply be regarding a friend as oneself (e.g., Hom. *Il.* 18.81-82; Diog. Laert. 7.1.124; 7.23; Diod. Sic. 17.37.6; cf. 1 Sam 18:1, 3) or noting that friends share all things in common (e.g., 1 Macc. 12:23; Plut. *How to Tell a Flatterer from a Friend* 24, *Mor.* 65AB; Diog. Laert. 7.1.124-25; Mart. *Epig.* 2.43.1-16). Cic. *De Amicitia* 21.81 felt that self-love characterized all creatures.

In the late first century R. Akiba, in contrast to some of his colleagues, regarded love of neighbor in Leviticus 19:18 as the greatest commandment in the law (Sifra Qed. pq. 4.200.3.7; Gen. Rab. 24:7); while this is not where Jesus ranked it (Smith 1951: 138), it was close.[226] Other Jewish teachers also conjoined love of God with love of neighbor (Test. Iss. 5:2; 7:6; Dan 5:3; Philo *Decal.* 108-10; cf. Philo *Every Good Man Is Free* 83; Jos. *Ant.* 3.213); following the Jewish interpretive principle *gezerah shewah* (borrowed from hellenism), it was natural to link two commandments on the basis of the common opening word *we'ahabta* ("You shall love" — Diezinger 1978; Flusser 1988: 479). Philo headed the most essential laws under the two categories of Godward and humanward (*Spec. Leg.* 2.63; see more fully Sanders 1990: 70).[227]

Yet Jesus' combination of the two as the greatest commandments, which exercised an authoritative influence on subsequent Christian formulations (including Paul's frequent triad of virtues with love as the greatest — 1 Cor 13:13), is distinctive (cf. Vermes 1993: 43).[228] In the multiplicity of other proposals concerning the greatest commandment in antiquity, only Jesus wielded the moral authority among his followers to focus their ethics so profoundly around a single theme (cf. Meier 1980: 257). The distinctive primacy that love plays in virtually all early Christian ethics would not have been possible had the Christians not derived this primacy from the mouth of the one Teacher who united them. Thence comes the early Christian "law of love" (cf. Rom 13:8-10; Gal 5:14; Jas 2:8; Jn 13:34-35; cf. Manson 1963: 80; on the difference between Matthean and Pauline emphases here, see Mohrlang 1984: 45). This teaching coheres with other extant records of Jesus' ethics (5:43-46; Lk 6:27-35; Nissen 1997).

The first passage Jesus cites in fact portrays the love of God as a summary of the law (Deut 6:1-7); one who loved God would fulfill the whole Torah (Deut 5:29). This passage about loving God was the central and best-known text of Judaism, the Shema. Likewise, the command to love one's neighbor as oneself (Lev 19:18; cf. Mt 5:43; Rom 13:9) expresses a general principle, though its original context applied it to a more specific situation. As in 7:12, Matthew re-

226. The context of Lev 19:18 applies it to foreigners as well as Israelites (19:33-34; cf. also Lk 10:27; Test. Iss. 7:6; perhaps Jub. 7:20; 20:2; 36:4; m. 'Abot 1:12), although not all interpreters applied the principle thus (ARN 16A; such a theme is absent in Greek literature — Boer 1979: 62-72); some sectarians seem to have applied it especially among themselves (CD 6.20-21; Jos. *War* 2.119; cf. Jn 13:34-35); more fully on traditional Jewish interpretations of Lev 19:18, see Neudecker 1992; for love of neighbor in Essene circles, see Södig 1995. One most easily practiced this love with one's most intimate friends (1 Sam 18:1; Test. Sim. 4:6-7). More distant Greek parallels (e.g., Diog. Laert. *Lives* 8.10 in Thom 1994: 111) are not particularly helpful in this instance, since Jesus here directly depends on Torah.

227. Cf. similarly Egyptian piety as reported by Diod. Sic. 1.77.2: the supreme offenses were impiety toward gods and sin against mortals.

228. In Mark the scribe repeats the same words and Jesus appreciates the answer — though the scribe is quoting Jesus. The unnaturalness of the construction may support the Lukan tradition in which the scribe answers directly as being the earlier form (Lk 10:26-27, though some think that this is an artificial link for the Samaritan parable; Vermes 1993: 109); but because it in any case reflects Jesus' own view as well, the scribe might have known it from prior teaching.

minds his audience that these commandments epitomize all the commandments in the Bible.[229] Given Matthew's emphasis on keeping Jesus' commandments (28:20) and Jesus' continuity with Moses' law (5:17-20), two commandments that epitomize the rest are clearly central to his ethics.

David's Son, David's Lord (22:41-46)

While Jesus' teaching could be read as repudiating the Messiah's Davidic descent (so Grant 1943: 193), the real problem here (as Matthew and Luke especially emphasize) is how he can be David's Lord yet at the same time David's son (Schweizer 1975: 427), how he can be younger in age yet superior in rank (Moule 1965: 99; the usual rule seems to have been that the father honors a son of higher rank when in public settings — Aul. Gel. 2.2). Jewish teachers often asked didactic questions that functioned as "haggadic antinomy," in which both sides of a question were correct but their relationship needed to be resolved (Jeremias 1971: 259; France 1985: 321). The Messiah, that is, the "anointed" king, was by definition "Son of David" in various circles of Jewish expectation (Lane 1974a: 435; cf. Ps 89:27; Is 9:7; 11:1; Jer 23:5-6). Yet the title "Lord" describes him far more adequately (Harrington 1982: 90; Argyle 1963: 170; Meier 1980: 260), and this passage supplies the working christological sense of "Lord" elsewhere in Matthew's Gospel (Bornkamm 1963a: 42-43; cf. 12:8).

Because the language about being son of David is ambiguous, however, it is virtually unthinkable that the early Christians would have created a pericope that could be used to challenge Jesus' Davidic descent, hence his Messiahship.[230] Early Judaism may not have applied Psalm 110 in a messianic sense,[231] but the psalm was readily available for Jesus' own use no less than that of his followers, and by speaking of a "lord" of David secondary to Yahweh it naturally enough lent itself to quasimessianic or supermessianic speculation. This passage surely goes back to the historical Jesus.

229. On epitomes, see comment on 7:12. Plutarch thought that all other morals depended on the two basic ones epitomized in the two inscriptions at Delphi (Plut. *Letter to Apollonius* 28, *Mor.* 116CD); the LCL translation assimilates the wording to Jesus' statement more than the Greek warrants, but the two are conceptually parallel as examples of epitomization. In Jewish legal logic, what summarizes other commandments would also permit one to derive the other commandments from it by means of extrapolation (Gundry 1982: 450, citing m. Ḥag. 1:8).

230. So, e.g., Gundry 1975: 200; Witherington 1990: 190; pace Weeden 1971: 133. Witherington 1990: 190-91 responds to arguments against authenticity, noting that the play on words works in Aramaic as well as in Greek (*amar marya le mari;* but is a play on words central in the passage anyway?); there is no clear indication that "Son of God" displaces "Son of David" here (noting the antinomy above); and this is not the only place where Jesus takes the initiative (Mk 8:27-30//Mt 16:13-20) or speaks allusively (cf. Mt 11:5-6//Lk 7:22-23).

231. Whether some Jewish people were interpreting Ps 110 messianically before Jesus is debated (Longenecker 1975: 73 argues that some were), but Jesus' specific application of the psalm here is new in any case, both by allowing "Lord" to bear a meaning much higher than a Davidic king, and by applying it to himself by implication.

That David (accepted by Jesus' contemporaries as the Psalm's author) calls him this "in the Spirit" suggests prophetic inspiration (e.g., Jub. 31:12; 1 Enoch 91:1; Ps-Philo 28:6; 1QS 8.16; Sifre Deut. 22.1.2); of course, most Jews acknowledged that God had inspired Scripture,[232] and ancient Mediterranean society in general viewed songs (like the psalms) as inspired in some manner (cf. Keener 1992: 264-65, 275-77). By reminding his hearers that David speaks by divine inspiration, Jesus indicates that his words are authoritative.

Because Jesus had just cited one text in which the "Lord" was God (22:37), his emphasis on the subordinate "Lord" of Psalm 110 (pronounced as if it read the same in public reading and certainly in Greek, despite the difference in Hebrew) would sound striking, especially given the frequent practice of linking texts on the basis of common key words. If David spoke to a Lord besides Yahweh, a Lord who would be enthroned at God's right hand as his vice-regent, then the eternal king was someone greater than David or merely a descendant of David — perhaps to be understood on the Near Eastern analogy of divine kings (cf. Hanson 1963: 154).[233] Citing "mighty God" (Is 9:6) might have sounded like it violated monotheism, but "Lord" was sufficiently ambiguous to make the point without yet providing the temple authorities words with which to condemn Jesus from his own mouth. Psalm 110 became a widespread messianic testimonium in the early church (e.g., Acts 2:34-35; Eph 1:20; Heb 1:13; Justin *1 Apol.* 45), owing no doubt to Jesus' use here.[234]

Matthew's changes in Mark here are noteworthy; just as Jesus here addresses specifically the Pharisees (22:41; cf. 3:7) rather than the crowds in general (Mk 12:37), Jesus' monologue gives way to questions with answers in typical rabbinic style (Gundry 1982: 450-51). Although technically the question introducing this pericope was Jesus' own, so that Matthew could have followed Mark in announcing "they dare ask him no further questions" earlier in the narra-

232. E.g., 4 Ezra 14:22; Sifra V. D. Den. par. 1.1.3.3; 5.10.1.1; Shemini Mekhilta deMiluim 94.5.12; Behuq. pq. 6.267.1.1; Sifre Deut. 355.17.1.1; a Davidic psalm in Lev. Rab. 5:5; cf. Foerster 1962: 117.

233. Gundry 1975: 214 finds Jesus assuming the role of Yahweh in his teaching, citing examples in Mt 10:32-33; 11:5, 10, 28, 29; 13:41; 16:27; 17:11; 24:31; 25:31, although not all require this interpretation (some, e.g., 11:29, are more naturally susceptible to other interpretations). The NT picture of Jesus' "Lordship" goes back to OT pictures of Yahweh, at perhaps the earliest stage using Ps 110:1; cf. further Marshall 1990: 97-111. Witherington 1990: 276 concurs with Brown 1985 that while Jesus would not have expressed his self-identity in explicit terms of deity (which in a Jewish context would have identified him as the Father), he would have been comfortable even with the Johannine exposition of his identity had he confronted it.

234. Probably against Christian polemic, later rabbis applied Ps 110:1 to Abraham (e.g., b. Ned. 32b; Midr. Ps. 110); cf. Justin's polemic against an application to Hezekiah (*Dial.* 32; perhaps confused with Is 7:14?; cf. Williams 1930: 175; cf. b. Sanh. 94a). Loader 1978 suggests that Christians first applied the passage to Jesus' resurrection, and only later and under hellenistic influence applied "lord" christologically; but it is difficult to think that Christians would fail to notice immediately the title of the exalted one in the text, especially since it is more obvious than any connection to a resurrection (without a *gezerah shewah* connection to Ps 16:8-11 — Acts 2:25-28; cf. Acts 13:33, 35).

tive (Mk 12:34; Lk 20:40), Matthew reserves this "punch" for the end of Jesus' public controversies. He had silenced and shamed his adversaries. Being overawed by a wise speaker's wisdom was a common motif in narratives meant to glorify their protagonist (e.g., 1 Esdr 4:41-42; cf. Ep. Arist. 186, 200, 220, 230, 235, 257, 261, 274, 281, 293); Matthew's audience could see in Jesus their hero who could answer all the objections raised by their opponents.

Religion for Show (23:1-12)

This chapter begins Matthew's final discourse (chs. 23–25). Although a brief amount of narrative interposes a scene change between chapters 23 and 24, the thought of judgment on the religious establishment (23:12-33; 24:24–25:30) and the temple's demise (23:35-38; 24:1-3, 15) continues. Further, this final section approximately balances the first discourse (Mt 5–7) in length, and concludes with the same summary statement as the other discourses: "When Jesus had finished all these words" (26:1). But whereas the first block opened with blessings (5:3-12), this final block opens with woes (Harrington 1980: 100). Perhaps these were together in Q (cf. Lk 6:20-26), like the blessings and curses of the covenant, but Matthew has chosen to frame his summaries of Jesus' teachings with eschatological promises.[1]

Within the logic of Matthew's narrative, the hostility of the Jerusalem elite (21:23; 22:23), including some scribes and Pharisees (19:3; 21:15, 45; 22:15, 34, 41), during Jesus' recent public debates with them, invites the harsh condemnation of them in this chapter.[2] Matthew's audience will naturally hear in such words a vindication of their own spiritual status vis-à-vis that of their opponents; the use of such polemical labels for enemy groups "was always credible, for hypocrisy belongs to the human condition and so can always be found in the enemy camp" (Davies and Allison 1997: 271). Yet while Matthew's specific emphasis on scribes and Pharisees may reflect the intensity of polemic between Jewish Christians and successors of the Pharisees after A.D. 70 (Cohen 1987: 150; cf. Saldarini 1994: 44-67; idem 1992),[3] at numerous points it also reveals its de-

1. Manson 1979: 96 locates the chapter's backbone in M, though he recognizes the conflation of many sayings with Q; I would add the significance of Markan material located here in Mk 12:38-40 before the eschatological discourse (cf. Mt 23:5-6), though it might depend on Q. Matthew may have pulled together diverse sources; some think that the section as a unity stems from the church-synagogue conflicts after 70 (cf. Klein 1978: 68-69), especially since the rabbinate, which they see to be in view here, became far more significant in this period (Davies 1966b: 84-85). While its reapplication in a post–A.D. 70 setting is very probable, pre-70 parallels in Paul (there offered with more hellenistic style) argue that this material existed before 70 (see Dodd 1967: 63-65 for significant evidence for this Jewish-Christian tradition; by contrast, Goulder 1974: 164-65 goes too far, finding dependence on Rom 2 and 1 Thess 2:15-16).

2. Kingsbury 1995a: 179 rightly views the religious leaders as more central to Matthew's plot than the disciples are, because the plot focuses on conflict.

3. Overman 1996: 13, 15 rightly emphasizes that elements of the scribes and Pharisees, already influential before 70, appear to have provided significant roles in the post-70 coalition of lead-

pendence on earlier Jesus tradition (e.g., Mk 12:38-39; Lk 11:39-52). What we can know of Jesus' actions suggests that his ministry would have generated at the least vigorous debate with many of his Pharisaic contemporaries (Falk 1985: 118-27 limits this probably too narrowly to Shammaites). Matthew's narrative structure retains conflict from Mark's plot movement, but particularly intensifies it in this final discourse (23–25). God's Son must face opposition from those who wish to usurp his sovereign role in the world; his followers must expect opposition from the same kind of people.

The harshness of Matthew's language does not imply his alienation from his Jewish heritage — only from rivals for religious power within Syro-Palestinian Judaism. Indeed, more general observation of groups in conflict indicates that the more conflicting groups have in common, the more intense is their conflict (Stanton 1993: 98). Later rabbis themselves were quick to condemn the hypocrisy of some kinds of Pharisees whose motives were less than holy (m. Soṭa 3:4; ARN 37A; 45, §124B; b. Soṭa 22b, bar.; p. Soṭa 5:5, §2),[4] and acknowledged hypocrisy among scholars (b. Yoma 72b) and within Israel (cf. Bonsirven 1964: 58). They regarded hypocrisy in general as morally reprehensible and deserving of judgment (b. Sanh. 103a; Yoma 86b; Moore 1971: 2:190, citing, e.g., b. Soṭa 41b; 42a). Matthew's critiques, like these, are Jewish critiques within Judaism, "no more 'anti-Semitic' than the Dead Sea Scrolls" (Davies and Allison 1997: 260-67), and not intended for exploitation by Gentile anti-Judaism.[5]

The language of these woes reflects the regular conventions of ancient polemical rhetoric (e.g., Ael. Arist. *Plat. Disc.* 307.6; Johnson 1989). Thus, for example, Josephus complains that the accusations of a particular opponent of Judaism merely prove the accuser's ignorance and inferior moral character (*Apion* 2.3); the accuser is like a dog or an ass (2.85). In a detailed study, Overman has demonstrated that the language of Matthew 23 is not ancient anti-Judaic language, but the language of sectarian Judaism like 1 Enoch, 2 Baruch, or 4 Ezra (cf. also Psalms of Solomon) against the establishments of their day, which they viewed as corrupt (1990b: 16-23; cf. McKnight 1993). On our view, Matthew's audience, like much of early Christianity, continued to see itself as part of early Judaism; to be anti-Pharisaic was not to be anti-Jewish (Boccaccini 1991: 215).

At the same time, scribes and Pharisees are hardly the Matthean address's primary audience; despite rhetorical judgments against them, the scribes and Pharisees become a warning, a negative paradigm.[6] The explicit audience, as in

---

ership. Matthew's audience has also already witnessed the judgment of 23:29-39, a judgment Matthew justifies by the woes of 23:13-30 (Garland 1979: 213).

4. See further Moore 1971: 2:193; Sandmel 1978b: 160-61; cf. Rubenstein 1963. For love as a motivation superior to fear, see also b. Soṭa 31a.

5. Davies 1993: 93 (on Mt 12:1-8) rightly notes that Matthew's flat depiction of the Pharisees is "dangerous only when people overlook its literary function and take it to be a true depiction of historical reality."

6. A foil for Jesus, the religious leaders also function "as a negative model for discipleship" (Bauer 1992: 366).

the first discourse section (5:1; 7:28), consists of disciples and crowds (23:1).[7] Some Christian preachers have caricaturized Pharisaic piety to avoid the demands Jesus' condemnations otherwise would make on Christians today (see Odeberg 1964). Matthew, however, appears to apply the warnings directly to his own community. "In comparison with Q, Matthew emphatically turns the conception of judgment 'inward,' i.e., the parenesis of judgment applies to the church" (Luz 1989: 76; cf. Viviano 1990b).

For Matthew, the judgments on Jesus' opposition at his first coming prefigure judgment on the leaders at his second coming (23:12-33; 24:24–25:30); Jesus' own professed servants could belong among the "hypocrites" (24:51; cf. 6:2; 15:7; 22:18). Like Paul in Romans 1–2 and Amos in chapters 1–3, Matthew forces leaders in his own community to see themselves through the prism of a disobedient religious establishment that opposed their Lord, thereby summoning them to take warning.

Excursus on Scribes

The Christian tradition that essentially equates "scribes and Pharisees" with the whole of the Jewish people (e.g., Justin *Dial.* 17) is a wholesale misrepresentation of the evidence. In the villages of the Roman Empire, "scribes" were literate (not always well-educated) professionals who executed legal documents (*CPJ* 1:157, §21; 1:188-89, §43; Lewis 1983: 82). Such persons also existed in Palestine and surrounding territories (cf. Goodman 1983: 59; Sanders 1993: 179).

Yet the Gospels can hardly apply the term in so broad a sense, and ancient views of special education in Judea (cf. Stern 1974: 8-11, 46, 50) suggest that many "literate" professionals did more than execute documents (cf. Ezra 7:10-11; 1 Macc 5:42).[8] Presumably many also instructed children in reciting the law, and the more advanced among them would have had adult disciples (i.e., disciples older than thirteen). Many of the scribes may have been priests (Sanders 1990: 80; idem 1993: 170-71), who may have been better equipped financially to pursue such training. Likewise, some may well have been Pharisees (cf. Sanders 1993: 177-78), given the Phar-

7. Meier 1980: 262 suggests that on the Matthean level the disciples represent the Jewish Christians and the crowds, the *'am haareṣ,* neither group being accepted by the Pharisees. In Brown and Meier 1983: 70, he notes that Matthew responds here to dangerous nascent "clericalism" in the Antioch church.

8. The function of Diaspora synagogue "scribes" (*CIJ* 1:12, §7; 1:18, §18; 1:21, §24; 1:70, §99; 1:84, §121; 1:85, §122; 1:88, §125; 1:100, §142; 1:103, §145; 1:104, §146; 1:106, §148; 1:107, §149; 1:130, §180; 1:158, §221; 1:161, §225; 1:250, §318; 1:275, §351; 1:326, §433; 1:337, §456; perhaps *CIJ* 1:27, §36; cf. *CIJ* 1:545, §22, but probably pagan) is unclear; they could be scholars (cf. "law-t[eacher]" in *CIJ* 1:140, §201; "the wise" in *CIJ* 1:519, §719), secretaries (as in usual Greek usage; see especially Leon 1960: 184-85), or something else (Ferguson 1987: 454-55; cf. *CIJ* 1:XCII-XCIV) — e.g., one could be nineteen years old (*CIJ* 1:196, §279) or, more incredibly (probably honorary), twelve (1:200, §284, but possibly non-Jewish).

isees' popular reputation for skill in the law (see below) and availability for training. Occasionally later rabbis could look ill upon their scribal predecessors, perhaps recognizing their great responsibility to guide Israel rightly (ARN 36A).[9] The scribes should be credited for raising the level of biblical literacy among their people (McNamara 1983: 172-73).

Excursus on Pharisees

"Pharisee" may derive from a term meaning "specifiers," those exact in the law (Baumgarten 1983b); or, considerably less likely, "Persianizers." Most scholars, however, associate the term with a root implying "separatists" (Dalman 1929: 13; Moore 1971: 2:60; Finkelstein 1962: 1:76; Davies 1967: 6; Cohen 1987: 162; Borg 1984: 58).[10] At any rate, their emphasis on tithed food and purity prohibited them from eating with Jews nonobservant in these regards (e.g., t. Shab. 1:15; b. ʿAbod. Zar. 70b, *haberim*). Nevertheless, they constituted primarily a lay rather than a priestly movement (see Sanders 1993: 404), and probably did not eat ordinary food as if they were priests, as some have contended (see Sanders 1990: 131-54, 235-36). They merely agreed to follow a limited number of purity laws (ARN 41A) and were known as "exact" interpreters of the laws who drew on Pharisaic tradition (Jos. *War* 1.110; 2.162; *Ant.* 13.297-98; *Life* 191).

Although they held political power under Salome Alexandra (Jos. *War* 1.110-13; *Ant.* 13.399-405), the families of Herod and the Sadducean priestly aristocracy formed the regional and municipal governments under the Romans in the Herodian period (Sanders 1990: 128-29; Stambaugh and Balch 1986: 101). This is not to say that they were unimportant in this period;[11] from various perspectives, the rabbis, Josephus (especially in the *Antiquities*), and the New Testament (the Gospels; Acts

9. For distinctions between legal scribes and more authoritative rabbis, Overman 1996: 205 cites m. Kelim 13:7; ʿOr. 3:5; Sanh. 11:3; Ṭohar. 4:7; Yad. 3:2. For further documentation on scribalism, see also Keener 1991a: 23, 145-46; Scott 1995: 165-68. In the Tanach, Philo, Josephus, and the rabbis see Orton 1989: 39-61; in ben Sira, 65-75; in apocalyptic literature, 77-120; in the Dead Sea Scrolls, 121-33.

10. Bowker takes the term as generally pejorative and applied by the rabbis descended from the *hakhamim* to their opponents rather than themselves (1973: 15), but this is highly questionable (see Sanders 1985: 50). To confuse matters further, the rabbis did not limit their term *perushim* to pre-70 Pharisees (Rivkin 1969-70; idem 1978: 165; Sanders 1990: 154). They were not always *haberim,* despite significant overlap (Rivkin 1978: 175; Sanders 1985: 187), and often appear as *hakhamim* (scholars; Rivkin 1978: 138, 141); but though many Pharisees, attentive to the law's details, must have been scribes, Rivkin goes too far in identifying them always with the scholar class (1978: 177-79). I have sometimes accepted the identification of Pharisees with *haberim,* but even a Sadducee may appear as a *haber* (b. Nid. 33b).

11. Smith 1978: 29, 50 is too skeptical. Even Sanders 1985: 312-13 probably explains away too much evidence (the Gospels, and some rabbinic and Josephus texts) about Pharisaic presence in the Sanhedrin, although he is almost certainly right to question their dominance vis-à-vis that of the priestly aristocracy.

15:5; 23:6; Phil 3:5) coincide in stressing their prominence (Cohen 1987: 163; cf. Neusner 1984: 45-61; Mason 1990).

They were probably more influential than Josephus allows in *War* (where he may wish to exculpate them from influence in the revolt) but less powerful than many modern scholars have supposed on the basis of his *Antiquities.* By the time he wrote his later *Antiquities,* Pharisaism had become a predominant party within Palestinian Judaism, and Josephus apparently chose to lend greater support (Sanders 1985: 195-96; 1993: 410-11, 488-89; though cf. differently Mason 1992: 140-43; idem 1991; Williams 1993).[12] As Neusner puts it, "Though Josephus exaggerated the extent of their power, the Pharisees certainly exerted some influence" before A.D. 70 (1984: 27).

In this period, the Pharisees' popular influence may have stemmed mostly from popularity with the people rather than official, political power (Jos. *Ant.* 13.298; 18.15, 17; Sanders 1993: 402-4; cf. Rivkin 1978: 38-42).[13] With a total of only 6,000 Pharisees in an earlier period of influence (*Ant.* 17.42; in a population of as many as 500,000, by the older estimate in Simon 1967: 15), their influence derived more from popular respect than from numbers. Later texts typically contrast their views with those of the Sadducees (e.g., t. Ḥag. 3:35; b. B. Bat. 115b; Nid. 33b; Sukk. 48b), with whom they undoubtedly vied for influence (cf. Acts 23:6-9; Jos. *Ant.* 13.297; cf. Mantel 1973).

Nevertheless, Josephus's autobiography suggests that some prominent first-century Pharisees participated in Jerusalem's municipal aristocracy, working together with the leading priests (Jos. *Life* 21). Simon ben Gamaliel, who was wise and powerful (Jos. *Life* 190-92), joins with Ananus the high priest to authorize legates to execute their will in Galilee (Jos. *Life* 216). When the priestly aristocracy sent aristocratic representatives to Galilee, some were Pharisees (Jos. *Life* 196). Thus some have viewed the Pharisees in this period as a political "retainer" class (Overman 1996: 128; Horsley 1995: 149-50). Their influence with the populace was sufficient to allow the criticisms of Matthew 23, the contents of which can therefore reflect pre-70 tradition (Newport 1991).

Pharisaism formed one part of larger Jewish piety in common Judaism, rather than ruling or "normative" Judaism (Sanders 1993: 449; Smith 1961: 355-56); thus they had no choice but to participate with other elements in Judaism for the common society (Sanders 1990: passim, e.g., 12).[14] Later rabbis, who probably included heirs in some sense of earlier Pharisaic scribes,[15] found themselves in a much better posi-

12. Wright 1992a: 212 suggests that the Pharisees wielded considerable populist support but that Josephus may exaggerate their political power to exonerate his own aristocratic class.

13. Certainly they *sought* political influence; Horsley 1995: 149-50 also contends that they functioned as a "retainer" class.

14. Thus some can portray Jesus himself as ideologically a pre-rabbinic Pharisee (Winter 1961: 133).

15. Cf., e.g., Sanders 1993: 422-23; Kugel and Greer 1986: 66; Cohen 1987: 154-59, 227. The earliest Pharisaic layers of rabbinic texts consist of debates rather than rules, suggesting a society in which they participated but did not rule (Sanders 1993: 470-71). Not all agree that the

tion to try to establish a "normative" Judaism, and even they were not wholly successful (cf., e.g., Goodman 1983: 127; Cohen 1987: 223-24).[16] For fuller evidence that the Pharisees did not control Palestine in the time of Jesus, see Sanders 1993: 388-402, 458-90.

Luke correctly distinguishes the scribes and the Pharisees (Lk 11:45), but like many modern preachers, Matthew retells the story in a manner relevant to his own community. In this case he addresses the enemies of his community, of which Pharisaic scribes seem to be the dominant element (cf. Hare 1967: 81). It seems likely that Matthew's community still included some scribes (13:52; 23:34) and possibly Pharisees (Acts 15:5; cf. Acts 23:6) who followed Jesus; because the dominant Pharisaic scribal movement repudiated faith in Jesus, however, a more conciliatory approach like that of James (Acts 21:20-25; Gal 2:12; cf. Jos. *Ant.* 20.200-201) had given way to polemic. Matthew is sensitive to the Jewish orthodoxy of his own constituency, but he is not afraid that his polemic will alienate members of his own community, who have already been marginalized by or in conflict with the Pharisaic leadership.

In this passage Jesus publicly critiques his opponents (23:1), providing a public challenge to their honor that would invite their retaliation (Malina and Rohrbaugh 1992: 141). **Religious leaders must live what they teach (23:2-4).** Jesus agrees that many of the ethical teachings of the scribes and Pharisees are good; the problem is not their teaching but their behavior (23:2-3; Rom 2:21), a dichotomy known to exist among many religious professionals and other religious people today. One could teach what was right but not live accordingly (23:3; cf. Rom 2:21).[17] Josephus testifies that some aristocrats exploited popular piety for personal reasons, and that those who valued popular support dare not appear to fall short in such piety (Jos. *Life* 291).

Pharisees were precursors of the rabbinic movement (e.g., Sigal 1986: 4); although Pharisaic idiosyncrasies may have most often prevailed, Horsley 1995: 95-97 may well be right that later rabbis inherited the mantle of the previous scribal movement as a whole. At least the rabbis inherited the mantle of the scribes' most prominent representatives; but in their eyes this apparently included some significant Pharisees, especially through the influence of Gamaliel II, son of Simon ben Gamaliel.

16. One should note that even in Jesus' day, many people disobeyed laws widely recognized by the pious (Jos. *Life* 65); but synagogues were community centers, and later zodiacs there testify that populist piety (probably including local elders) often differed from the expectations of the legally educated intelligentsia.

17. Ancients generally praised those who lived in accordance with their virtuous teachings (e.g., Diod. Sic. 9.9.1; Diog. Laert. 6.2.64; Herodian 1.2.4; Jos. *Apion* 2.169), a not uncommon demand (e.g., Epict. *Disc.* 1.25.11; 2.9.13; Demosth. *3d Olynthiac* 14; *2d Philippic* 1; Dion. Hal. 7.33.3; 9.10.3; 9.47.4; 11.1.4; 11.58.3; Corn. Nep. *Fr.* 3.1; Sen. *Ep. Lucil.* 20.2; Aul. Gel. 17.19; Jos. *Apion* 2.292); see further citations under Mt 7:24-27. Texts sometimes depicted the whole of behavior by pairing word and deed (e.g., *Homeric Hymn* 2, to Demeter, 65; Hesiod *W.D.* 710; Ap. Rhod. 3.81).

They have seated themselves in Moses' seat,[18] probably meaning that they have adopted the role of the law's interpreters, since instructors sat to teach (cf. 5:1; m. 'Abot 1:1-12; Dodd 1967: 63; Neusner 1972: 74; Rivkin 1978: 83). Carson 1984b: 472 lists many examples showing that the formula "to sit on X's seat" frequently indicates succeeding X.[19] Moses' seat was also a seat for judging the people (Ex 18:13).

Pharisaic ethics emphasized being as lenient or strict with others as one was with oneself (ARN 23, §46B), but in practice the moral authority of a teacher often lends itself to abuse. Jesus accuses them of being too strict with others while too lenient with their own failings (cf. 5:18-20; 15:1-20; Lk 11:46; Gundry 1982: 455); for a contrast between such "burdens" and Jesus' "yoke," see comment on 11:28-30.[20] The Pharisees found ways to circumvent direct teachings of Torah when necessary (v. 4), that their spirit might be more easily fulfilled (e.g., the *prosbul,* attributed to Hillel; cf., e.g., Albright 1963: 8).

Religious leaders must not seek marks of honor (23:5; cf. Mk 12:38). Those who sought their own praise indiscreetly (cf. Plut. *How to Praise Oneself Inoffensively*) invited others' reproach. Epideictic rhetoric dealt with praise and blame, and Jesus here heaps reproach on religious leaders who appear arrogant to Matthew and his audience.

Greek philosophical teachers often wore identifying apparel that provoked respectful greetings (Justin *Dial.* 1; Tert. *De Pallio* 6; Liefeld 1967: 168-70; contrast the apparel of Cynics), and Jewish scribes may have preferred identifying raiment as well, though the evidence here is much weaker (cf. b. B. Bat. 98a).[21]

18. Matthew's opponents, like those of Jesus, cite Moses for their authority (19:7; cf. 22:24); but this does not prevent Jesus or his Matthean followers from depending on Moses as well. Allison 1993b: 275 is correct that Matthew does not denigrate Moses but rather praises him by comparing patterns in his life with those of Jesus.

19. Scholars regularly observe that later Palestinian synagogues often had a special chair for teaching (fitting rabbis' stone chairs known in some literary sources), which came to be known as a "chair of Moses" and thus symbolized the succession of teachers from Moses' day (e.g., Manson 1979: 228; Filson 1960: 243; Yamauchi 1972: 102; Avi-Yonah 1974/76a: 53; Ferguson 1987: 400; Newport 1990; Rahmani 1990; Young 1995: 185-86; especially Pesiq. Rab Kah. 1:7; Song Rab. 1:3). In general, *cathedrae* — armchairs with backs — especially characterized the wealthy and leaders with high status (Safrai 1974/76b: 737). The evidence that the "seat of Moses" was already a literal seat in first-century synagogues, however, is contested (also Meier 1980: 262), as is the presence of many Pharisees in Galilean synagogues (Horsley 1995: 233-35); in any case Jesus applies the expression metaphorically here.

20. France 1985: 324 reads the "binding" here in terms of prohibitive legislation in 16:19; 18:18; if so, the image of "tying" burdens to a person does double duty, a rhetorical strategy not uncharacteristic of Jesus.

21. See further Liefeld 1967: 180; Lane 1974a: 439-40; Hurtado 1983: 197; Goodman 1983: 77; cf. Carson 1984b: 483 on 23:27-28. Cf. also, e.g., the white garments of the Therapeutae in their worship times (Philo *Cont.* 66), and special garments holy only for the festival for which they are provided (Demosth. *Against Meidias* 16), or Pythagoreans offering sacrifice while wearing only simple white garments (Diod. Sic. 10.9.6). Citing Jn 19:23-24, Liefeld 1967: 181 doubts that Jesus wore a philosopher's *pallium.*

Among deeds to be noticed by others (cf. 6:1), Jesus includes the broadening of phylacteries. Although the Greek term applies more broadly to amulets and not merely *tefillin* (Gundry 1982: 456), some of Jesus' contemporaries (and many people in later times) seem to have employed *tefillin* in this manner (Lachs 1987: 366). *Tefillin* were Scripture boxes fixed to one's head and left hand during some prayers (Tigay 1979; pace perhaps Kümmel 1965: 115).[22] A later Jewish teacher could also recognize that "hypocrites" used *tefillin* deceptively (Pesiq. R. 22:5). Whether "broadening" refers to broadening the leather strap that attaches the box to the head or hand, or to wearing them more frequently than during the designated morning and evening times for prayers, is debated (Manson 1979: 230); the critical point is that, whereas phylacteries were supposed to glorify God (Bonsirven 1964: 61), the wearers here draw attention to themselves.

Jewish sources associated *tefillin* with *ṣiṣith* as well as Deuteronomy 6:9's *mezuzoth* (b. Menaḥ. 43b, bar.; Jos. *Ant.* 4.212-13), which appears after the *tefillin* of 6:8. The objects of Jesus' lesson thus also lengthen their tassals, or *ṣiṣith,* the fringes attached to the outer cloak's four corners (Num. 15:38-40; Deut 22:12; see Sandmel 1978b: 152).[23] Matthew takes Mark's "robes" (12:38) as a reference to the *tallith,* then the regular outer garment but eventually the basis for the later prayer shawls. Matthew apparently believes, probably accurately, that Jesus himself wore both *tefillin* and *ṣiṣit* (9:20; 14:36); the issue here is not whether one observes Jewish customs, but whether one seeks honor for oneself rather than for God alone.

Religious leaders must not seek honored treatment (23:6; cf. Mk 12:38-39). Jesus accuses his opponents of seeking the (literally) "*first* seats in the synagogues," a practice that conflicts with dependence on God to exalt when he wills (20:16). Although this discourse focuses on the Pharisees, the practice of coveting the most honored seats was widespread.[24] As in much of the Mediterranean world, Palestinian Jewish society included a heavy emphasis on honor and even hierarchy (e.g., Ahiqar 142-44, sayings 54-55; Ps-Phocyl. 220-22; cf. Bowker 1973: 35), though the Essenes seem to have taken this to an extreme (sometimes praised by outsiders — Jos. *War* 2.150; Philo *Every Good Man Is Free* 87). Young men should rise before elders to offer their seats (Lycurgus 14 in Plut. *Sayings of Spartans, Mor.* 227F), and assemblies often sat according to honor, especially by seniority (Gen 43:33; t. Sanh. 8:1; p. Taʿan. 4:2, §12; b. Hor.

22. Whereas Deut 6:8-9 may have intended them figuratively, they are attested literally at Qumran, Wadi Murabbaʿat, and, e.g., Jos. *Ant.* 4.213; Mek. Pisha 17.106ff., Laut. 1:150ff.; Gen. Rab. 43:9; cf. Ep. Arist. 158; Sandmel 1978b: 151; Finegan 1969: 225; Vermes 1959.

23. Shammaites may have prescribed longer fringes than Hillelites (France 1985: 325), attesting some division of opinion among Jesus' contemporaries on the matter. The *tallith* of a scholar may have been particularly long (b. B. Bat. 57b; Lachs 1987: 367).

24. Horsley 1995: 233-35 doubts the Pharisees' frequent presence in Galilean synagogues, but concurs that when they visited they undoubtedly ranked high socially, being part of the educated elite (234). Local, often hereditary leaders (the village equivalent of municipal aristocracies) undoubtedly dominated (233).

13b, bar.).[25] In the same way esteemed sages were granted special rank (t. Sanh. 7:8; b. Hor. 13b, bar.; p. Sanh. 1:2, §13; Ta'an. 4:2, §§8-9). Seating by rank was the customary practice at banquets (Lk 14:7-11; Plut. *Table-Talk* 1.2.3, *Mor.* 616E; p. Ta'an. 4:2, §§9, 12; Ter. 8:7) and other events (Apul. *Metam.* 10.7; 1QS 2.19-23; 1QSa 2.11-17; p. Ketub. 12:3, §6; Rosh. Hash. 2:6, §9).[26] Those in the Sanhedrin were reportedly seated by rank (m. Sanh. 4:4). Remains of synagogues suggest a similar seating by rank: prominent elders sat on the raised platform with the Torah scroll, facing the congregation (t. Meg. 4:21; Lachs 1987: 367).

Religious leaders must not seek honorary titles (23:7-11). Most of the people respected sages and their disciples (Goodman 1983: 77-78), and honors for rabbis seem to have grown in time (cf., e.g., Neusner 1972: 76, 101; Edersheim 53).[27] In later rabbinic teaching, the whole town must mourn when a sage died (t. Mo'ed Qaṭ. 2:17); disciples served rabbis (ARN 25A; Gen. Rab. 22:2) and could not give legal rulings in the presence of their own teachers (Sifra Shemini Mekhilta deMiluim 99.5.6; Pesiq. Rab Kah. 26:6/7). Still later, one who despised a rabbi despised one's own help (b. Shab. 119b); only those who followed the sages would share eternal life (Pesiq. R. 11:2); one who was stingy with rabbis might inherit hellfire (b. B. Bat. 75a), as would those who spoke negatively of them after their death (b. Ber. 19a).[28] But Jesus was not the only teacher to recognize that one should assume a lower place rather than seek one's own honor (Ben Azzai, early second century, citing Prov 25:7, in ARN 25A; 33, §73; cf. Lk 14:8-11). And whereas disciples were seated by rank in proximity to the sage, rabbis acknowledged that this was irrelevant to heavenly reward (ARN 40A); a sage should also value a disciple's honor (m. 'Abot 4:12). The saying of

25. The Therapeutae reportedly sat in order of their tenure in the community (Philo *Cont.* 66-69). In Jewish society the younger had to respect the elder (Jos. *Apion* 2.206; *Ant.* 3.47; applied to the sages in Sifra Qed. pq. 7.204.3.1; p. 'Abod. Zar. 3:1, §2; Hor. 3:5, §3; Lev. Rab. 11:8), and prominent local leaders tended to be those who were aged, as both literary texts (Jos. *Life* 266; Ep. Arist. 32, 39; Acts 14:23) and inscriptions (*CIJ* 1:294, §378; 1:426, §581; 1:432, §595; 1:433, §597; 2:9, §739; 2:45, §790; 2:46, §792; 2:53, §801; 2:76-77, §828a; 2:77, §828b; 2:79, §829; 2:137, §931; cf. *CIJ* 1: lxxxvi-lxxxvii; Mitten 1966: 65) testify, as do the LXX (e.g., Josh 24:1; Judg 8:14, 16; 11:5-11; 21:16; Ruth 4:2-11; 2 Chron 34:29; Jer 26:17; Jdt 6:16; 7:23-24; 13:12; 1 Macc 1:26; 7:33; 11:23; 12:35; 13:36; 14:20, 28; 2 Macc 13:13; 14:37) and evidence from the Greek world (e.g., Arist. *Pol.* 2.7.5, 1272a; Diod. Sic. 21.18.1; Dion. Hal. 8.15.1). Roman society also demanded giving way to one's elder (Cato *Collection of Distichs* 10; Dion. Hal. 7.47.1).

26. Cf. m. 'Abot 5:15; on order in speaking out, cf. 1 Cor 14:29-30; Jos. *War* 2.132; 1QS 6.9-10.

27. Later rabbis even compared rabbinic authority to that of kings (Gen. Rab. 94:9) and the "seat of Moses" to a royal throne (Pesiq. Rab Kah. 1:7). But whereas rabbis, like some Greek philosophers (cf. Tiede 1972: 55), may have thought they merited such recognition, much of the populace may have disagreed; archaeology attests "unorthodox" practices even in the rabbinic period. They commanded much respect, but not everyone understood or heeded their views.

28. Amoraim warned of deadly judgment for offending rabbis (cf. b. B. Qam. 117a; B. Meṣ. 84a; 'Erub. 63a; Tem. 16a) and promised eternal reward especially to sages (b. Ber. 34b; Sanh. 99a; Lev. Rab. 3:7). For the high honors accorded rabbis, cf. also Aberbach 1966-67, followed by Carson 1984b: 474, with appropriate qualifications for the earlier period.

a later rabbi illustrates the emphasis on humility: if a sage boasts, his wisdom vanishes (b. Pesaḥ. 66b).

Greetings (23:7; cf. 26:49) were virtually mandated by social custom (e.g., Soph. *Oed. Rex* 596); kind greetings softened social relations (Dion. Hal. 8.61.1). Social etiquette dictated the matter of greetings;[29] with the noticeable exception of an urgent prophetic mission (cf. 2 Kings 4:29; Lk 10:4) or during prayer (m. Ber. 5:1), one dare not be silent when greeted (Sir 41:20; cf. b. Ber. 6b). One should greet one's social superior first, which to later rabbis meant one's superior in the knowledge of the law, though the person with superior status could waive the right by greeting the other first (Manson 1979: 99). Later tradition assumes that protocol in greeting rabbis is essential (Goodman 1983: 78, citing t. Ned. 5:1; Sifre Deut. 32, p. 57), and teachers should show respect to one another as well (b. Sanh. 24a), bowing before one another in greeting (Gen. Rab. 33:3).

Fitting this context of public honor and salutations (23:6-7), in Jesus' day "Rabbi" was probably an honorary greeting, "my master" (23:7-8);[30] only gradually did it come to be applied along with someone's name (hence "Rabbi Akiba," but not "Rabbi Hillel"; see Sandmel 1978b: 106). Once teachers whose disciples could make disciples were called rabbis, one with highly praised disciples came to be called "rabban" (t. ʿEd. 3:4). Although Jesus' disciples will teach, they will make disciples for him rather than for themselves (28:19).

Scholars today are more apt to debate the purpose of Jesus' or Matthew's prohibition against calling someone on earth "father" (23:9). It is possible that Jesus originally used the teaching to invite separation from family for the kingdom's sake (cf. Lk 9:58-62; Gnilka 1997: 201-2), but that proposal by itself does not explain its sense in this Matthean context; others have attempted various proposals. One rare view proposes that Jesus here prohibits calling the patriarchs fathers, that is, prohibits trusting in descent from Abraham (Townsend 1961; cf. 3:9). More likely, despite some detractors, is the view that Jesus addresses the custom of using *abba* as a respectful title for older men and other prominent individuals (Jeremias 1971: 68), especially teachers.[31] Sufficient evidence suggests

29. On the importance of appropriate recognition of others' status (lack of which constitutes childishness) in the Middle East, see Eickelman 1989: 236. Although one should greet a superior in the knowledge of Torah first, some texts do praise the humility of scholars (like Johanan ben Zakkai) who greeted others first (b. Ber. 17a; Lachs 1987: 367).

30. For some early use attested on ossuary inscriptions, see Stanton 1989a: 185; cf. *CIJ* 2:337, §1410; for later Diaspora attestation, *CIJ* 1:438-39, §611; 2:7, §736. Some suggest that Matthew's antipathy toward the term reflects discomfort with the growing use of the term in the proto-rabbinic movement (Overman 1996: 322).

31. Rightly noting the rareness of the title, Carson 1984b: 475, following Kohler 1900-1901; Hagner 1995: 661. Blomberg 1992a: 342 sees "father" as reserved especially for the patriarchs of the past (hence, e.g., the tractate 'Abot; Acts 3:13, 25; 5:30; Rom 9:5; 11:28; Moses with Israel in Pesiq. R. 21:6); one might apply it to all esteemed ancestors (Gal 1:14; 1 Cor 10:1; Heb 1:1; Jos. *Ant.* 13.297, 408). France 1985: 325-26 suggests that it may have functioned for very prominent rabbis. Most likely, as I suggest here, it could apply to all elders (Acts 7:2; 22:1; 1 Tim 5:1; 1 Jn 2:13; 4 Bar.

the general use of such fictive kinship terminology in an honorary manner, sometimes in direct address (e.g., 2 Kings 5:13; 13:14; Diod. Sic. 21.12.5).[32] From the earliest period one could address even an older stranger with the title (e.g., Hom. *Il.* 24.362, 371; *Od.* 7.28, 48; 8.145, 408; 17.553; 18.122; 20.199). Various texts apply "father/son" language to teachers and their disciples;[33] this language is also frequent in wisdom texts that would reflect and influence the vocabulary of sages.[34] Some early sages even used the title "abba" in the same way that most came to use "rabbi" (cf. Sandmel 1978b: 106; Manson 1979: 232).[35] This is not unexpected, since rabbis sometimes claimed greater respect than parents (m. B. Meṣ. 2:11; Ker. 6:9; Sifre Deut. 32.5.12; p. Ḥag. 2:1, §10; among Gentiles, Theon *Progymn.* 3.93-97). Jeremias connects this prohibition to Jesus' distinctive use of "abba," which he suggests supports the saying's authenticity (1964a: 43). Jesus emphasizes that with God as their Father, his disciples are all siblings (12:48-50; 18:15; 28:10). The final term for authority has various possible senses but may represent merely a private tutor (cf. Winter 1991); though various levels of tutelage existed, Jesus could be warning against accepting even the simplest titles of respect, all of which disciples must reserve for God's chief representative alone.

5:28; Hom. *Il.* 24.507), some of whom might be dear teachers (1 Cor 4:15; 1 Tim 1:2). One should compare the honorary title "father of a synagogue" (*CIJ* 1:xcv-xcvi; 1:66, §93; 1:250-51, §319; 1:360, §494; 1:372, §§508-9; 1:373, §510; 1:393, §533; 1:397, §535; 1:398, §537; 1:462, §645; 1:463, §646; 1:505, §694; 1:520, §720; 2:9, §739). The title was perhaps "purely an honorary one, probably involving no active duties" (Leon 1960: 186).

32. Cf. "father of the Jews" in 2 Macc. 14:37; "fathers of the world" for the first-century schools of Hillel and Shammai (Gen. Rab. 12:14); and the use of "fathers" for Roman senators (Plut. *R.Q.* 58, *Mor.* 278D; Lucan *C.W.* 3.109; Corn. Nep. 23 [Hannibal], 12.2; Livy 1.8.7; 1.26.5; 2.1.10-11; 2.23.14; 2.24.2; 2.27.3; 2.32.12; 2.34.12; 2.35.3; 2.41.4; 2.48.8; 2.60.3; 3.13.7; 3.16.1; 3.21.1, 3, 4; 3.51.11; 3.52.6; 3.63.8; 4.1.4; 4.2.13; 4.60.1, 3; Sall. *Catil.* 6.6; 31.7; 51.1, 4, 7, 12, 15, 37, 41; 52.2.7, 35; *Jug.* 14.1, 3, 12, 13, 18.25; 24.2; *Speech of Philippus* 1, 17; *Letter of Gnaeus Pompeius* 1, 6; *Letter to Caesar* 11.1; *Invective against Marcus Tullius* 1; Cic. *Invective against Sallustius Crispus* 1.1, 2, 3; 2.5; 4.12; 5.14; 6.16; 8.22), other societal leaders or benefactors (Dion. Hal. 12.1.8; Paus. 8.48.5-6; 8.51.7), older mentors (Hom. *Il.* 9.607, employing a different term; *Od.* 1.308), and leaders in the Mithraic cult (Burkert, *Cults,* 42). Merely being older men, however, was sufficient grounds for showing them respect: see, e.g., 1 Pet. 5:5; t. Meg. 3:24; ʿAbod. Zar. 1:19; 4 Bar. 5:20; Ps-Phocyl. 220-22; Syr. Men. Sent. 11-14, 76-93 (but cf. 170-72); Hom. *Il.* 1.259; 23.616-23; Aul. Gel. 2.15; Diod. Sic. 1.1.4; 2.58.6; Lycurgus 14 in Plut. *Sayings of Spartans, Mor.* 227F; Pythagoras in Diog. Laert. *Lives* 8.1.22-23.

33. E.g., 2 Kings 2:12; 4 Bar. 2:4, 6, 8; 5:5; t. Sanh. 7:9; Sifre Deut. 34.3.1-3, 5; Sifre Deut. 305.3.4; b. Pesaḥ. 112a; Shab. 25b; 31a; Pesiq. R. 51:1; Lucretius *Nat.* 3.9; Epict. *Disc.* 3.22.82; Nock 1964a: 30; Gerhardsson 1979: 17; cf. Jn 13:33; 1 Cor 4:15; 3 Jn 4. Other texts make analogies between fathers and teachers (e.g., t. B. Qam. 9:11).

34. Such wisdom language often occurs in the testamentary genre (even in Proverbs, following models of the Egyptian royal courts) and hence requires such language (e.g., Ahiqar 96, saying 14a; Sir 2:1; 1 Macc 2:50, 64; Jub. 21:21; 1 Enoch 79:1; 83:1; 91:3-4; 92:1; Test. Job 1:6; 5:1; 6:1; Test. Reub. 1:3; Test. Naph. 4:1; Did. 5; Pesiq. R. 21:6).

35. Vermes 1993: 158 doubts that Jesus would polemicize against this rabbinic use of "Abba" because fellow *charismatic* sages like Abba Hilkiah used the name; but were all charismatics agreed on every point?

In any case, if we assume a Syrian provenance and a date for Matthew in the mid-70s to 80s, Matthew's community was well aware of the honor accorded the Pharisaic leadership in Jamnia (rabbis had servant-disciples — Davies 1966b: 134-35). They would hear Jesus' teaching as a warning not to be like their competitors by seeking honorary titles or a position above others.[36]

In short, exalting was God's business alone (23:12; cf. Lk 14:11). Matthew often reports Jesus' sayings about greatness in the kingdom (5:19; 18:4; 20:26), suggesting that the broader culture's emphasis on social status had carried over into his community. The Hebrew Bible (e.g., Is 2:11-12; 5:15-16; Ezek 21:26) and later Jewish sources (Sir 11:5-6; b. 'Abot 6:4, bar.; ARN 11A; 22B; b. 'Erub. 13b; Gen. Rab. 1:5; Der Er. Zut. 9; Moore 1971: 2:274; Lachs 1987: 368) provided a picture of eschatological reversal of the proud and humble, echoed by Jesus here.[37] Jesus emphasizes the model of humility for his own followers here more than the condemnation of outsiders who exalt themselves (cf. 20:25-27; 24:49-51); in antithetic parallelism, one expects the emphasis on the second line (Jeremias 1971: 18-19).

Woes against Human Religion (23:13-32)

Woes such as these would not have commended Jesus to those against whom he directed them, but his teachings on humility and grace would not by themselves have evoked hostility (pace Goppelt 1964: 58-59). Rabbinic Judaism, which probably sprang in large measure from Pharisaism, harshly condemned hypocrisy (e.g., t. Yoma 5:12; b. Soṭa 41b-42a; Pesaḥ. 113b; Esth. Rab. 1:17; Odeberg 1964: 63). Modern Christian readers often think of "Pharisees" as hypocrites,

36. Meier, a Catholic scholar, notes Jesus' prohibition of the title "father" and questions the use of ecclesiastical titles that arose even in Matthew's church in Syria a few decades after his Gospel (Meier 1980: 265); but while Protestants may determine "pecking order" by different means, most Protestant churches offer analogous temptations for personal advancement. Christendom has come a long way from the teachings of Jesus. Matthew probably supports a generally egalitarian approach (18:17-18; 23:8-12) or specifically charismatic authority (10:41-42; 23:34), but he may address a community in which structures have been developing (see Stanton 1993: 103-4 for relevant sociological theory). To what degree the hierarchical system was already developing in the Matthean community (e.g., Overman 1990b: 123) is difficult to determine from the text.

37. For the authenticity of the saying behind Mt 23:12 (focusing on Lk 14:11; cf. Lk 18:14; Jas 1:9; 4:10) and for more parallels, see Jeremias 1972: 107. God's exaltation of the humble may have been a familiar warning of the wisdom tradition (cf. Ahiqar 149, saying 60; Syr. Men. Sent. 116-17; Diog. Laert. 1.69); by the late first century teachers were reportedly claiming that one became exalted over (i.e., proficient in) Torah by humbling oneself before it (as well as the reverse — Gen. Rab. 81:2; cf. ARN 11A; 22, §46B); Hillel reportedly claimed that his humiliation was his exaltation and the reverse, citing Prov 25:7 (Ex. Rab. 45:5), if this is authentic rather than borrowed. For eschatological inversion, see also Wis 5:3; 1 Enoch 46:5-6; 104:2; 1QM 14.10-11, 14-15; 4 Ezra 6:20-24; 2 Bar. 83:5; Test. Jud. 25:4; Sib. Or. 3.350-55; ARN 5; 9; 28A; Sifra Behuq. pq. 3.263.1.8; Sifre Deut. 307.3.2; b. Pesaḥ. 50a; p. Sanh. 6:6, §2; Gen. Rab. 21:1; Lev. Rab. 13:3; 36:2; in Jesus' sayings, cf. Jeremias 1972: 221-22; for the sayings in Luke, Tannehill 1986: 109-10.

and hence do not feel threatened when hearing them denounced, nor do they recognize the scandal Jesus represented to his religious contemporaries. But the Pharisees' contemporaries thought of them as the most devoted practitioners of religion, and of the scribes as Bible experts. One who studies Pharisaic ethics will find them generally comparable with Jesus' teachings (also 23:2-3); it is the human heart, rather than an ethical system, that Jesus here confronts (see Odeberg 1964).

Though a Semitic term, the Greek sense of "woe" can convey a sense lamentation ("Alas") rather than a threat (Argyle 1963: 174; cf. 24:19). Nevertheless, lamentations often functioned as a creative prophetic way of sounding impending judgment (18:7; Is 15:5; 16:11; Jer 48:36; 51:8; Rev 8:13; 18:2); "woe" functions here as a direct pronouncement of judgment, as in the pronouncements against self-satisfied sinners in Isaiah 5:18-23. (Cf. also Hanson 1994 for the possible shame dimension.)

Religious leaders can do more harm than good (23:13-15). Jesus first accuses them of "shutting" off the kingdom, using the image of an authoritative majordomo (16:19; Is 22:22; Rev 3:7; cf. the tragic image in Pesiq. R. 26:6) or perhaps a porter abusing authority to keep welcome guests out. This may allude to the scribes' purported authority of "binding and loosing" by their knowledge of the law (16:19), here used to hinder would-be followers of Christ (Meier 1980: 268-69).[38] Jewish hearers learning of leaders who abused keys God entrusted to them might expect those keys to be taken away by God (2 Bar. 10:18). Thus they are "blind leaders of the blind" (23:16, 24; cf. 23:17, 19; 15:14; Lk 6:39). Textual evidence favors viewing 23:14 as an interpolation (Mk 12:40; Lk 20:47), leaving a total of seven woes (Plummer 1910: 316; though eight woes would come closer to matching the beatitudes, Matthew's sets of seven parables show his predilection toward this number as well); possibly Matthew, who omits the widow (Mk 12:41-44), decides to omit the corresponding warning (Mk 12:40).[39]

They are eager to proselytize, but their converts simply mimic and accentuate their flaws (23:15). Possibly the text warns about Pharisees' making con-

38. Perhaps, if Pauline tradition interprets this Jesus tradition and does so accurately, he also suggests that their behavior discourages others from following Israel's God (cf. Rom 2:17-24; Mt 23:15).

39. "Devouring widows' houses" may refer to sponging off others' hospitality (Lane 1974a: 440-41), or it may refer to exploiting legal loopholes to their own advantage. Because widows might lack powerful legal advocates, their property was more easily seized by persons of status (e.g., the deceased husband's employer who is excused from even showing up for court in *P. Sakaon* 36; cf. *P. Ryl.* 2.114 in Horsley 1983: 20). Jewish hearers would in any case regard it as a terrible crime (e.g., Ps 146:9; Prov 15:25; Is 10:2; 2 Macc 3:10-13; Bonsirven 1964: 96). Jewish law demanded favorable treatment for widows, but some scholars probably did take advantage of them (cf. Pesaḥ. 49b, bar.; Abrahams 1917: 79-81), just as some Christian ministers today have been known to abuse their position. Derrett 1973: 57 suggests that the text addresses trustees spending widows' assets as "expenses." Matthew likewise omits Mark's account of the widow's mite (Mk 12:41-44), perhaps to sustain the section including both chs. 23 and 24–25 as a single discourse addressing judgment on the religious establishment.

verts to Pharisaism, perhaps from among Gentile God-fearers (Carson 1984b: 478; Levinskaya 1996: 36-39),[40] but that would be an unusual use of the term "proselyte." More likely is a reference to seeking Gentile converts to Judaism, although Pharisees would naturally teach them according to their own scrupulous interpretations of Torah (though these varied; cf. the alleged attitudes of Shammai and Hillel toward proselytes). Since Matthew's Jesus challenges their deeds more than their words (23:2-3), he may mean that the Pharisees engender hypocrisy in those who imitate them.

Although Judaism had no central sending agency and hence no "missionaries" in the formal sense (see, e.g., Hoenig 1965: 49; Lake 1979a: 75; Sevenster 1975: 203; Murphy-O'Connor 1992), plenty of evidence, especially in Diaspora Jewish apologetics (e.g., Jos. *Ant.* 20.17, 34-36; *Apion* 2.210)[41] and Gentile criticisms of Jewish conversions (e.g., Tac. *Hist.* 5.5; Dio Cassius *R.H.* 57.18.5; 60.6.7; Hor. *Sat.* 1.4.141-44), testifies to many Jewish people seeking Gentile converts in the course of their other work.[42] Jewish people actively courted the many conversions taking place in the Diaspora until Christian emperors began enforcing earlier Roman laws to shut Jewish proselytism down (cf. Jeremias 1958: 11-12).[43]

The Pharisees were probably no less interested in this process than others, especially if we may judge from the favorable light in which their successors

40. While Jos. *Ant.* 20.34-48, which Carson cites, does describe a stricter and probably Pharisaic teacher tightening the requirements after an earlier proselytizer (much like Paul's opponents in Galatia), Josephus does not suggest that Eleazar seeks to convert the king to *Pharisaism* per se. Josephus himself — at least when writing for a Gentile audience — opposed forced conversions (*Life* 113, 150), in contrast to some of his contemporaries (*Life* 149), but presumably agreed that circumcision was appropriate to conversion where feasible (Ex 12:44, 48; Jdt 14:10; Jos. *Ant.* 20.44; Test. Levi 6:3, 6-7; t. ʿAbod. Zar. 3:12; Ber. 6:13; b. Shab. 135a; Ex. Rab. 30:12), just as it was required for those born in Israel (Gen 17:10-14; Lev 12:3; Josh 5:2; Sir 44:20; cf. Jub. 15:11-14, 25-27, 33-34), a matter on which most Jews refused to compromise (2 Macc 6:10; 4 Macc 4:25; Jos. *Ant.* 12.256), with the rarest exceptions (b. Pesaḥ. 69a). The rabbinic tradition often extols circumcision: e.g., m. Ned. 3:9; t. Ned. 2:5-7; b. ʿErub. 19a; Ned. 32a; Shebu. 13a; Gen. Rab. 11:6; 46:3; Ex. Rab. 5:8; 17:3; 19:5; 38:8; Lev. Rab. 21:6; 31:4; Pesiq. R. 13:8; 23:4; 29/30A:3; 52:4.

41. Cf. Georgi 1986: 83-164, albeit severely overstated; see Boccaccini 1991: 252-56. Jewish proselytism is probably not in view in Horace (cf. Nolland 1979).

42. Certainly rabbinic Judaism continued to emphasize proselytism (e.g., b. Sanh. 99b; Gen. Rab. 47:10; 98:5; Num. Rab. 8:4; Qoh. Rab. 7:8, §1; Pesiq. Rab Kah. Sup. 1:6; see Bamberger 1968: 19-24, 222-30; Urbach 1979: 1:549-54; cf. Goodman 1989, who suggests that Christian successes spurred Jewish efforts) until the Roman government, controlled by Christians and perpetuating previous precedents, suppressed them (cf. also earlier barriers erected by the revolts, e.g., Applebaum 1979: 343; Gager 1975: 137). In later texts proselytism is associated with such figures as Hillel (e.g., b. Shab. 31a; perhaps m. 'Abot 1:12), and Abraham (e.g., Gen. Rab. 39:14; 48:8; Pesiq. R. 43:6); the latter was said to bring Gentiles "under the wings of the Presence" (e.g., Pesiq. R. 14:2) and to "create" them anew (e.g., Gen. Rab. 39:14; 84:8).

43. The case for Jewish "missions" has admittedly been overstated by its adherents at times, but Jewish concern for Gentile conversions has been widely recognized (e.g., Bamberger 1968: 267-73; Moore 1971: 1:323-24; Leon 1960: 250-56; Schoeps 1961b: 220ff.; Blauw 1962: 57; Jeremias 1958: 11, 16; De Ridder 1971a: 120; Daniel 1979: 63; Cohen 1983). Other philosophies also sought converts in the fertile soil of the Empire (see, e.g., Culpepper 1975: 117).

viewed stories of Hillel's openness to converts; one cannot therefore use the lack of ancient Jewish "missionaries" to regard the saying inauthentic (pace Flowers 1961). Presumably by exposing them to the truth of God's standards while allowing hypocrisy through their own bad example (23:3, 13), these proselytizers were leading their converts to be doubly damned. ("Child of gehinnom" was a Semitic way to say "destined for gehinnom"; see, e.g., b. Rosh Hash. 17a.)[44]

Inconsistency in evaluating standards of holiness dishonors God (23:16-22). On 23:16-22, see comments on 5:33-37. Along with Jesus' common use of periphrasis, his abhorrence of oaths that could abuse God's name shows that he not only agreed with, but was among the most devout defenders of, the sanctity of God's name (Jeremias 1971: 179). Oaths involved invoking a deity as witness to the veracity of one's claim. On the popular level, people had begun using many surrogate phrases for God's name, hoping to avoid judgment if they broke the oath; the Pharisees endeavored to distinguish which oath phrases were actually binding, but Jesus rejected such casuistry (Sanders 1990: 55, 91; cf. CD 16.6-13). On blind guides (23:16, 24; cf. 23:17, 19; Lk 6:39), cf. 15:14 and the principles in 7:3-5; 6:22-23; 13:14-17.

Even aside from the fabulous golden vine (e.g., Jos. *War* 5.210; *Ant.* 15.395; cf. another in *Ant.* 14.34-36), the temple boasted much gold, including decorations of the sanctuary (cf. Jos. *Apion* 2.84; *Ant.* 14.72, 106, 110; *War* 5.201-10, 222). As in 23:19, Jewish people viewed the altar as consecrating whatever was offered on it (Bonsirven 1964: 124); although pronouncing judgment on a defiled temple (23:38; 24:15; cf. 21:12; 27:25), Jesus elsewhere respects the sanctity of the temple and its altar (5:23). The Pharisees may have prohibited swearing by the gold of the temple because they felt that it, unlike the temple or the altar, was subject to lien (Gundry 1982: 463); in any case, Jesus rejected the reasoning. Even more than the ancient tabernacle (cf. Haran 1965: 202), early Judaism recognized degrees of holiness (m. Kelim 1:6-9; Neyrey 1991: 278-79); but Matthew charges that they did not behave consistently with this belief. Jesus rails in part against the traditions that have created inconsistent standards of holiness. But Jesus' attack is ultimately directed against the profanation of God's name; because any surrogate oath nevertheless *represents* God's name and implicitly calls him to witness, any breach of truthfulness demands judgment no less severe.

Religion can emphasize holiness in the details while missing more critical matters of holiness (23:23-28). Having remarked on their inconsistency in ritual matters (23:16-22), Jesus now turns to their inconsistency in other respects, beginning with tithing (23:23; cf. Lk 11:42).[45]

44. Interestingly, some Gentiles interested in Judaism also adopted some Jewish practices plainly originally adopted from paganism; see Safrai 1974/76a: 745.

45. Chilton 1994: 118-19 thinks that 23:23-24 reflect Matthew's own social situation, but may include early tradition.

Excursus on Tithing (23:23)

Ancient Israel had been an agrarian society, and they brought one-tenth of their produce into storehouses to care for the landless Levites and priests, and once every third year to provide a major festival, paying the way of the poor who otherwise could not participate (Lev 27:30; Num 18:21-32; Deut 14:22-29; Neh 13:10-12), though early Judaism seems to have included different perspectives on how to harmonize these texts (cf. Jos. *Ant.* 4.68-69; 9.273; *Life* 63, 80; m. Maʿaś. passim; m. Maʿaś Sh. passim; for the data, see Sanders 1990: 43-44).

Jewish teachers highly regarded tithes (cf. Pesiq. R. 25; Safrai 1974/76c: 818-25), esteeming them as a protection for wealth as tradition provided protection (a fence) for Torah (R. Akiba, m. ʾAbot 3:13; cf. Pesiq. Rab Kah. 10:1; Pesiq. R. 5:3). Indeed, one area of piety for which Pharisees were particularly known was their scrupulousness in tithing.[46] Perhaps only the most pious farmers tithed the way the urban Pharisees thought essential; on top of Roman taxes or the share demanded by landlords, economic pressure must have overwhelmed many small farmers (Borg 1987: 85; Stambaugh and Balch 1986: 91; cf. MacMullen 1974: 42). Some scholars (e.g., Sanders 1993: 146-68; Crossan 1991a: 221) are convinced that others (e.g., Horsley and Hanson 1985: 55-59; Oakman 1991: 165) have overstated the amount of taxation; this may be true, but in any case taxes were hard on rural workers throughout the Empire (MacMullen 1974: 34-37). Josephus, perhaps representing an aristocratic perspective, is even harder on the farmers than most rabbis are; but in any case the tithes amounted to 17 to 20 percent of the farmer's income (see Sanders 1990: 44-45). Clearly some people evaded paying the first tithe, as attested by Pharisaic concern to tithe on foodstuffs acquired from those who may not have tithed it (Sanders 1990: 47). Various sources testify that substantial tithes nevertheless reached the temple (e.g., Jos. *Life* 63; Sanders 1990: 46).

Building their fence around the law, the Pharisees were careful about minutiae, about tithing substances where it was disputed whether or not they were foodstuffs, hence debatable whether they were covered under the Old Testament agrarian tithe (cf. Jeremias 1969: 254). Dill (anise) and cummin were aromatic plants;[47] later rabbis settled on dill (probably m. Maʿaś. Sh. 4:5) and cummin

46. E.g., t. Dem. 3:9; ARN 41A; p. Maʿaś. 5:1; Borg 1987: 89; cf. Neusner 1984: 27; McNamara 1983: 203). Tax gatherers appear on the other end of the moral spectrum as making tithes more difficult (e.g., Pesiq. Rab Kah. Sup. 4:2). Among Romans, a tithe to Hercules was common in cases of exceptional luck (Tert. *Apol.* 14.1, where LCL p. 73 n. *d* cites also Cic. *De Nat. Deor.* 3.36.88; Macrob. *Sat.* 3.12.2; Plaut. *Truculentus* 2.7.11); in Eleusis, see Mylonas 1961: 244.

47. Hepper 1992: 132 notes that cummin and dill were used both as spices and as medicinal herbs. Both are annual plants, the former reaching approximately 40 cms. (1 foot 4 inches) and the latter approximately 60 cms. (2 feet) in height.

(m. Dem. 2:1) being tithed but later denied mint (cf. Goulder 1974: 22).[48] First-century Shammaites doubted that black cummin need be tithed, in contrast to Hillelites (m. ʿUq. 3:6; Sanders 1990: 48).[49] In their eagerness to avoid violating any portion of the law, the ultrastrict Pharisees Jesus addresses here (perhaps a hyperbolic, *reductio ad absurdum* construct) tithe even the most disputable of substances. Believing that they were showing their faithfulness to God's law by examining its every detail, they would not have thought of themselves as neglecting the law's broader principles; Jesus, however, insisted that their commendable attention to the former had neglected the latter (see Odeberg 1964: 43). Jesus accepts that they should have kept these biblical laws, but insists that they have missed the forest for the trees (cf. 7:3-5); their neglect of the basic requirements (Deut 10:12-13; Mic 6:8) was inexcusable.[50]

Most Jewish teachers recognized distinctions in the law, such as those between humanward and Godward commandments (e.g., Philo *Spec. Leg.* 2.62-63; Sanders 1992: 192-95; in the rabbis, Sanders 1985: 249). Both philosophers like Philo (Wolfson 1968: 2:277, at length; cf. Epict. 1.26.15) and the rabbis came to regard some commandments as "weightier" — more significant — than others (m. 'Abot 2:1; 4:2; Sifra V. D. Deho. par. 1.34.1.3, par. 12.65.1.3; ARN 1, §8B; cf. Johnston 1982: 207).[51] This practice, too, could lend itself to detailed analysis: Rabbi Meir (second century) regarded the punishment for neglecting the white threads of the *ṣiṣith* as heavier than that for neglecting the blue threads (b. Menaḥ. 43b). Although he, like his contemporaries, regarded no commandment as light,[52] Matthew's Jesus himself taught much about "weightier" matters, even in this context (22:36; 23:5, 17, 19), elsewhere emphasizing justice (e.g., 5:22; 23:33), mercy (e.g., 9:13), and faithfulness (e.g., 8:10).

Jesus illustrates their inconsistency in 23:24 with a witty illustration along the lines of prophetic puns of judgment in Micah 1:10-15 or Jeremiah

48. Hepper 1992: 132-33 argues that the text refers to the horsemint (*M. longifolia;* the traditional spearmint entered this region only later), "a perennial with creeping underground stems, its fragrant lance-shaped leaves borne on the erect stem which is four-cornered and about 60 cm (2 ft) high."

49. Falk 1985: 150-51 regards Jesus' words here as anti-Shammaite (citing m. Maʿaś. 4:5-6). By the second century rabbis exempted "rue" (Lk 11:42) from the requirement to tithe, suggesting that Matthew may preserve the more original wording here (m. Sheb. 9:1; McNamara 1983: 204; Gundry 1982: 463, who usually favors Luke). This saying undoubtedly goes back to an original Aramaic saying of Jesus; Luke's "rue" (Lk 11:42) translates an Aramaic word that resembles the Aramaic term for "dill" (Argyle 1963: 175; Borg 1984: 100). "Cummin" is a Semitic term (Smith 1951: 7).

50. Kaiser 1975: 184 thinks 23:23 refers particularly to Mic 6:8. Allusions to this text appear in 1QS 5.4 and probably 4.5, end.

51. Contrast the Roman belief that only the "ritual prescriptions" of their law were divinely inspired, a distinction not made by Jewish people and perhaps not by Greeks either (Cohen 1966: 1:28-29)

52. See comment on 5:19; cf. Jas 2:10-11; m. 'Abot 4:2; Sifra Qed. pq. 8.205.2.6; Sifra Behar. par. 5.255.1.10; Sifre Deut. 96.3.2; ARN 35, §77B. (Some regarded the laws of purity, menstruation, and bird offerings as essentials of Torah — ARN 27A.)

1:1-12 (especially because in Aramaic the words *gamla* and *kamla* or *kalma* are almost the same — Black 1967: 175-76; Stein 1978: 13; Chilton 1994: 119). Jesus portrays here Pharisees more scrupulous than Pharisaic legal rulings required. If a fly fell into one's drink, they might hope to strain it out before it died, lest it contaminate the drink (cf. Lev 11:34). But Pharisaic legal experts decided that any organism smaller than a lentil (such as a gnat) was exempt (Sanders 1990: 32). Since most of us today would not want a gnat dying in our drink either, we may have sympathy with a Pharisee who for a different reason — in his passion for purity — went beyond the letter of the law (cf. Sanders 1990: 38).[53] These Pharisees were so inconsistent, Jesus said, that they concerned themselves with purity issues as trifling as a gnat but did not mind swallowing a camel whole (cf. Epict. *Disc.* 1.26.16: amateur philosophers incapable of ingesting a morsel instead swallow an entire treatise). Gnats appear in ancient illustrations as the prototypically smallest of creatures (Sifre Deut. 32.2.1; Babrius 84; Ach. Tat. 2.21.4-5; 2.22); by contrast, camels, which were explicitly unclean under biblical law (Lev 11:4), were also the largest land animal in Palestine (see on 19:24).

Although Jesus speaks metaphorically about the inside of a cup (i.e., the human heart) in verses 25 and 26 (cf. Lk 11:39-41), he may allude to a matter of some discussion among his contemporaries. The Mishnah regularly distinguishes between inner and outer parts of vessels with respect to cleanness (McNamara 1983: 197 cites m. Kelim 25:1-9; Para 12:8; Ṭohar. 8:7), and some discussions of cleanness go back to the first-century disputes between the schools of Shammai and Hillel (b. Shab. 14b, bar.). The Shammaite school of Pharisees were less concerned whether one cleansed the inner or outer part first. By contrast the Hillelite Pharisees thought that the outsides of cups were typically unclean anyway and thus, like Jesus, insisted on cleansing the inner part first (Neusner 1976: 492-94; m. Ber. 8:2).[54]

Jesus' statement on the surface challenges Shammaite practice (though for the effect of the metaphor); that the Shammaites predominated in Jesus' time but not after A.D. 70 supports the saying's authenticity.[55] Other matters also support the saying's authenticity. That Luke's version (Lk 11:41) reads "give in charity" rather than "cleanse" again suggests an original Aramaic saying like the one Matthew records; the former (which fits Luke's theology of charity, and might be construed as abrogating purity laws) represents the Aramaic *zakkau,* while the latter (which fits the saying itself) stands for the Ara-

53. Schweizer 1975: 441; Gundry 1982: 464; Lachs 1987: 370 (citing b. Ḥul. 67a; cf. Shab. 20a) also claim that the Pharisees strained everything "through a cloth." While this practice probably occurred, it appears unclear how widespread it was.

54. Cf. b. Ber. 51a; Sanders 1990: 39; but cf. also the skepticism here of Maccoby 1982.

55. Neusner 1976: 495 thinks that the Gospel writers after 70 did not understand the original application. Yet while Matthew probably writes after 70, his own learning in the law probably predates 70 considerably, and he may have known earlier Pharisaic views; more likely, Jesus intended his saying metaphorically, as Matthew infers.

maic *dakkau* (Black 1967: 2; Burney 1922: 9; Argyle 1963: 176).[56] But Jesus' ultimate challenge goes beyond ritual purity practices to the point he illustrates: the heart comes first (15:6-20).

Although dead creatures in one's fluid (23:24) and menstruation produced impurity, corpse uncleanness (23:27-28; Lk 11:44) was more severe, extending seven days (Num 19:11-14; Jos. *Ant.* 18.38; m. Kelim 1:4). If so much as one's shadow touched a corpse or a tomb, one contracted impurity.[57] Although Jesus may have originally alluded to the practice in the spring of using whitewash to warn passersby and Passover pilgrims to avoid unclean tombs lest they become impure and hence barred from the feast (m. Moʿed. Qat. 1:2; Maʿaś. Sh. 5:1; Sheqal. 1:1; b. B. Meṣ. 85b; p. Moʿed. Qat. 1:2, §7; for other warning markers see t. Maʿaś. Sh. 5:13) as in Luke 11:44 (Argyle 1963: 176; Schweizer 1975: 442; Meier 1980: 271; Sanders 1990: 39), Matthew focuses on an incidental effect of the marking. For him, the whitewash was a beautifying agent to cover the tomb's corruption (borrowing the image from Ezek 13:10-12).[58] Their outward appearance (cf. 23:5, 28) merely provided a veneer for the impurity, hence *lawlessness,* of their hearts.[59] To those who prided themselves on obedience to Torah, the charge of lawlessness would be deeply offensive and shaming.[60] In the Septuagint, it involved rebellion against God's will (Meier 1979: 161); to Matthew's audience, it evokes one of the signs inviting end-time judgment (24:12; cf. 2 Thess 2:3, 7-9).

56. By contrast, Gundry 1982: 466 suggests an original play on words by Jesus himself.

57. Sanders 1990: 34, 232; cf. CD 12.15-17 (wood, stone, nails, or dust in a room); for later exceptions, probably following the purported cleansing of Tiberias (on which see, e.g., Levine 1978), cf., e.g., b. Bek. 29b; Ber. 19b; B. Meṣ. 114b. In "cases of doubt" (e.g., Sifra Taz. pq. 1.123.1.6), as in Lk 10:30-32, the priest and Levite might well avoid the possible corpse (cf. Borg 1984: 104-5; Sanders 1990: 41-42), in practice if not in theory (cf. ARN 11A); though cf. p. Nazir 7:1, §§7, 15; Abrahams 1917: 110.

58. Luke's form of the saying is thus probably closer to the original wording (Gundry 1982: 466; Borg 1984: 113-14), although Jesus may originally have alluded to the way first-century Jews treated the exterior of the very common limestone ossuaries to beautify them (Lachs 1975; cf. whitewash to mourn the temple's destruction, b. Yoma 66b; "whitening" by cleaning and restoring a temple's whiteness in Livy 40.51.3). Jesus may also have intended a play on words between the terms for tomb *(qeber)* and inward part (*qereb;* Abrahams 1924: 30, citing similar puns in Ps 5 and Jer 5:16). A wordplay also unites this part of Jesus' diatribe: they build tombs (23:29) and they *are* tombs (23:27).

59. Greek could use the cognate terms for savage, anarchic behavior (e.g., Diod. Sic. 4.70.3; 33.14.1; 34/35.12.1; 36.6.1; 36.11.1) or unjust treatment (Dion. Hal. 8.4.2; *licentius* in Corn. Nep. 10 [Dion], 7.1), and anti-Judaic traditions even applied the label to Israel's customs (Diod. Sic. 34.35.3).

60. This was a charge sectarian communities regularly leveled against those outside (Overman 1990b: 17-18), including Qumran (1QpHab 7.1-5; Overman 1990b: 24-25), 1 Enoch 99:10-12, and Psalms of Solomon (Overman 1990b: 26-27). In 2 Baruch the law reveals who is wicked (41:3; 51:4; 54:14; Overman 1990b: 27), as does 4 Ezra (9:36-37; Overman 1990b: 27-28). Josephus regards the Pharisees as the law's most accurate interpreters (*War* 1.110; 2.162; *Life* 191; *Ant.* 17.41; cf. Acts 22:3; 26:5), further suggesting that this was a focus of debate within post-70 Judaism (Overman 1990b: 68-71). In calling his opponents "lawless," "Matthew has adopted . . . 'the language of sectarianism'" standard among his contemporaries (Overman 1990b: 98). The Greeks also opined that lawlessness merited vengeance from the gods (e.g., Ps-Demosth. *Or.* 59, *Against Neaera* 126).

Bloodguilt for killing God's spokespersons merits divine judgment against God's people (23:29-32; cf. Lk 11:47-48). Jewish tradition emphasized that their ancestors had killed the prophets (Van Tilborg 1972b: 46-72; Amaru 1983; comment on 5:12). More recent prophets, from Onias (rabbinic literature's Honi the Circle-Drawer; Jos. *Ant.* 14.22-24) to Jesus' predecessor John, had shared this very fate. In 23:29-36 Jesus challenges the hypocrisy of those who honor the prophets by caring for their tombs, yet like their ancestors will kill the Prophet who has come to them (so also Jeremias 1971: 146).[61] Their behavior proves that they are spiritually not "descendants of the prophets," but rather "descendants of those who killed them"; Semitic languages can describe a person as being another's son if the person is like the other (Fenton 1977: 376), but descendants who walked in their ancestors' ways would also reap their ancestors' judgments (Ex 20:5). Using the testimony of one's critics against themselves by revealing inherent contradictions was an important rhetorical strategy (Jos. *Apion* 1.219-20; 2.148).

Employing irony in a manner typical of the prophets (who sometimes told the people to go on sinning but to expect God's judgment for it — 1 Kings 18:27; Is 6:9; 29:9; Jer 23:28; 44:25-26; Ezek 3:27; Amos 4:4-5; cf. Eccl 11:9; Rev 22:11; Sib. Or. 3.57-59), Jesus tells his adversaries to fill to the brim the role of prophet-murderers they had inherited, and that the judgment collecting for generations would finally be poured out in their generation (23:36; cf. 2 Kings 21:10-15; 22:16-20; 24:2-4).[62] (The image of "filling up the measure" of suffering should have been a familiar one in ancient Mediterranean culture; cf. Rev 6:11; Hom. *Il.* 8.354; Ap. Rhod. 1.1035, 1323; perhaps Ps 75:8; Is 51:17; Col 1:24.)

Impending Judgment on the Religious Establishment (23:33-39)

Cf. Lk 11:49-51; 13:34-35. Just as members of God's own people had murdered God's spokespeople in the past (23:29-31), so they would do to Jesus (23:32) and

61. The "tombs" of 23:29 may appear here by means of a verbal link with 23:27 (early Christians undoubtedly linked Jesus' sayings as Jewish interpreters linked biblical texts). Veneration of holy persons' and ancestral tombs is an ancient practice in the Middle East (Diod. Sic. 17.17.3; Dion. Hal. 8.24.6; 11.10.1; Argyle 1963: 176; Hill 1972: 313), and tombs of famous persons were, like temples, tourist attractions (Paus. 2.7.2; 8.41.1), but Judean care for prophets' tombs seems to have flourished particularly around Jesus' time (Jeremias 1971: 146n.2; Schweizer 1975: 442-43). Herod's and Hyrcanus's detractors accused them of violating David's tomb (near Jerusalem; Neh 3:16; ARN 35A; t. B. Bat. 1:11; cf. Acts 2:29; see Jos. *Ant.* 7.392-94; 13.249; 16.179-84; *War* 1.61), whereas others reported only his monument for David (Jos. *Ant.* 16.183-84); notable monuments for others who were deceased also appear in this period (*Ant.* 18.108; 20.95; Carmon 1973: 120, 252, §255). Because Matthew elsewhere (10:41) links "prophets" and "righteous," as here, Hill 1965 thinks it applied especially to teachers; but it may simply refer to the "rest of the righteous" besides prophets, or link the two terms as applicable to all the righteous as prophetic witnesses.

62. Although Jesus' style here is more like that of the OT prophets, irony and satire were of course a broader ancient technique (e.g., Plato, *Sophist;* Cic. *De Oratore* 2.58.236; 2.61.251; Dio Chrys. *31st Disc.* 9-10; Marc. Aur. *Med.* 2.6; Ach. Tat. 6.12.1; Jos. *Apion* 1.295; 1 Cor 4:8-10). On satire in Jesus' anti-Pharisee polemic, see, e.g., Boonstra 1980.

his followers (23:34). But whatever judgments past generations might have suffered, the final expression of guilt had been saved up for the climactic murder of this generation — the execution of Jesus (23:32-36; 27:25). The religious establishment of Jesus' day warranted judgment, as had the spiritually irresponsible leaders of previous generations (cf. Is 3:12-14; Hos 5:1; Amos 7:10-17; Mic 3:9-11; Zeph 3:4). Like Matthew 24, this section views the imminent destruction of the temple, due to occur in their generation (23:35-38), in the context of eschatological judgment (23:33, 39).[63]

Like his predecessor John the Baptist, Jesus asks who had warned these offspring of vipers (cf. 3:7; 12:34) to flee the approaching hellfire yet had failed to call them to bear the fruits of repentance (23:33; cf. 3:7-8)? The prophets, wise men (*hokhmim,* sages), and scribes Jesus would send represent the various missions of his own followers (5:12; 13:52; cf. "apostles" in Lk 11:49), whether they came as prophetic or teaching figures (cf. 11:18-19).[64] Jesus here fills a role filled by God in the biblical tradition (e.g., 2 Chron 36:15-16, which also refers to Israel's rejection of the prophets) and some later Jewish sources (Jub. 1:12; Charles 1902: lxxxiii). That Luke (11:49) and probably Q attribute this saying to divine wisdom suggests that Matthew here presents Jesus as deity or divine wisdom (cf., e.g., Hamerton-Kelly 1973: 31, following Suggs).[65] These prophets, like the earlier prophets that Jesus mentioned (23:29-31; cf. 21:35-36) and himself (23:32, 36; cf. 21:39), would face persecution. Matthew's additions to Q here (Lk 11:49) evoke the mission discourse: scourging in the synagogues (10:17) and being hunted from town to town (10:23; Luke probably would not have omitted this — cf. Acts 14:6; 17:13).[66] This suggests that persecution for Jewish Christians remaining in the synagogues could be a live issue for Matthew's community, even if it was not as dramatic as during the editing of Q (probably ca. A.D. 40).

Filling up the cup to the brim refers to meriting all the "blood," that is, bloodguilt, saved up among past generations, never punished as was deserved (cf. Is 40:2; Deut 32:43; Ps 79:10; Rev 6:10; Sifre Deut. 332.2.1). (Jesus may allude here to the Jewish eschatological concept that a predetermined quantity of

63. The Q saying (23:37-39//Lk 13:34-35) may foretell the temple's "abandonment rather than its destruction" (Theissen 1991: 220), but the Matthean application is clear.

64. Jewish tradition continued to affirm that God punished Israel only after warning them in advance (Amos 3:7-8; Sifra Behuq. pq. 5.266.1.1).

65. In favor of Matthew's being earlier is the poor fit of the saying in Luke, which in context reads as if Jesus climaxes this succession of divine representatives (including "apostles"). But Luke rarely emphasizes wisdom Christology, sees Jesus as deity in Acts 2:21, 34-38, and clearly sees the disciples as witnesses sent by Jesus (Acts 1:8); Matthew's change to make Jesus rather than divine wisdom the sender makes more sense. In any case, Thompson 1985: 222 (following H. E. Tödt) is correct to observe that here Q presupposes Jesus' death and resurrection.

66. Davies 1993: 163 reminds us that Nero's execution of Christians included crucifixion, as here (Tac. *Ann.* 15.44.2-8); nevertheless, Jesus' language elsewhere (16:24) may provide the most direct source for Matthew's modification of Q here, by which disciples share Jesus' sufferings (20:19; 27:22; on blood "shed," cf. 26:28).

suffering was prerequisite for the end — Rev 6:10-11; 1 Enoch 47:2-4; 4 Ezra 4:33-37; Meier 1980: 272.) That generation (23:36) would receive the fruit of this judgment (24:34; 11:16; 13:39, 45; 16:4); such warnings in Q material (Lk 11:51) show that the expectation of impending judgment on the generation was not simply a post–A.D. 70 invention of the church.

Jesus uses the Old Testament language of corporate personality, regularly recited in the Passover liturgy: they stood in continuity with their ancestors. Not simply "their ancestors," but they themselves had shed the blood of the righteous. He probably chooses as examples the first and final martyrs of the biblical record (in many arrangements of the Old Testament, the Writings, including 2 Chronicles, was the final section).[67] The blood of Abel, a prototypical martyr[68] and figure for the beginning (Test. Iss. 5:4), had cried for vengeance against his fraternal slayer (Gen 4:10; Heb 11:4; 12:24; Jub. 4:3; 1 Enoch 22:6-7; ARN 31A; Gen. Rab. 22:9; on Heb 11:4, pace Lane 1991: 335). Jewish tradition naturally amplified the judgment on Cain (e.g., Jub. 4:31-32; Test. Benj. 7:3-5; ARN 41A; Gen. Rab. 97 NV). Blood crying out for vengeance becomes an accepted principle (Sib. Or. 3.310-13; Pesiq. R. 24:1; cf. Deut 21:9; Aqhat in *ANET* 154; 1 Enoch 9:1-2).

Jesus' second example probably is the Zechariah of 2 Chronicles 24:20-22, martyred in the temple.[69] (In view of the father's name cited, the tradition here probably conflates this Zechariah with the prophet who wrote the book of Zechariah; see Gundry 1982: 471; pace Wenham 1977: 79.)[70] According to Jewish tra-

67. It is very possible that the order of the Hebrew canon was not yet fixed in this period (though cf. Beckwith 1985: 211-22), but undoubtedly many MSS ended here, presumably including some known to Jesus (cf. Nowell 1988). That this saying thus reflects the Hebrew rather than LXX sequence adopted by later Christians favors the saying's antiquity and probably authenticity.

68. E.g., Ps-Philo 16:2; Test. Abr. 13A; 11B; Life of Adam 23; Apoc. Mos. 2–3; 40:4-5; 1 Clem. 3; Asc. Isa. 9:8. The ancient horror of fratricide (e.g., Cic. *De Offic.* 3.10.41; Hor. *Epode* 7.17-20), as well as chronology, made it an outstanding illustration.

69. So, e.g., Gundry 1982: 471-72; France 1985: 330-31; Urbach 1979: 1:559; Lachs 1987: 372.

70. For a probably accidental conflation, see *Lives of the Prophets* 9 (Obadiah), §§2-4 (in Schermann's Greek text, §15, pp. 53-54); b. Sanh. 39b; for conflation of these two Zechariahs in later Jewish tradition, see Davies and Allison 1997: 319. But that Matthew's conflation here is accidental (cf. Meier 1980: 273) is no more likely than in the transformation of "Amon" and "Asa" into "Amos" and "Asaph" in 1:7-8, 10; for such deliberate allusions, see comment on 27:9. Such conflation of the two figures is attested later, and the early Christians could have conflated the two intentionally to allude to the writing prophet's message (cf. 21:5; 26:31; 27:9-10) or because they assumed their identity, reading "son" in a general sense in one of the passages. Others think that this refers solely to the prophet who wrote the book Zechariah; or to John's father Zechariah in Luke, martyred in later Christian tradition (but the references are too late); suggest an unknown Zechariah (Ross 1987); or follow Chrysostom's view that the text refers to Zechariah son of Bariscaeus whom the zealots murdered in A.D. 67 (Jos. *War* 4.334-44). The last view falters not only because this Zechariah is not known to have been a prophet (Manson 1979: 105) but because either it presupposes that Jesus or Q prophesied this name (and only this name in the tradition) or it dates Q later than 67; further, it supposes that Q would have regarded Zechariah as an apt model for Christians even if he was not one (as a wealthy and outstanding Jerusalemite, he almost certainly was not).

dition, Zechariah's blood, like Abel's, had cried against his murderers for vengeance, this time yielding the massacre of many priests.[71] The bloodguilt for Jesus' death would come on that generation (27:25); as Zechariah's blood had once desecrated the priestly sanctuary and so invited judgment (*Lives of the Prophets* 23:1; Sifra Behuq. pq. 6.267.2.1; p. Ta'an. 4:5, §14; Pesiq. Rab Kah. 15:7; Lam. Rab. 2:20, §23), so would the blood of the priests in A.D. 66 as the "abomination which brings about desolation" (24:15). That the shedding of innocent blood invited judgment was a biblical theme continued in Jewish tradition (Sib. Or. 3.312; Test. Zeb. 2:2; b. Shab. 33a; Yoma 9b), and one had to take special pains to protect the sanctuary from bloodshed (e.g., 2 Chron 23:14-15; cf. Mt 27:6).[72] The murder of Zechariah in the temple (23:35) recalls their murder of the very prophets whose tombs they build (23:29-31)[73] and their profaning the sanctuary with false oaths (23:16-21).

Jesus here utters another lament (the Aramaic fits the rhythm of a funeral dirge — Manson 1979: 126; Minear 1954: 107).[74] In contrast to the woes earlier in the chapter (23:13-29), Jesus' words in 23:37 represent a true lament (cf. Baum 1961: 54). That Jesus laments over Jerusalem is fitting: Judaism never forgot the biblical picture of God's special love for Israel (see, e.g., the sources in Montefiore and Loewe 1974: 58-85), and Jesus elsewhere demonstrates his

71. B. Giṭ. 57b; p. Ta'an. 4:5, §14; Pesiq. Rab Kah. 15:7; Lam. Rab. 2:2, §4; 4:13, §16; Qoh. Rab. 3:16, §1; 10:4, §1; cf. Urbach 1979: 1:559. The tradition appears in later sources, but our largest body of texts (rabbinic literature) includes less haggadah in the earlier collections, and Jesus' words in Q (Matt 23:35; Lk 11:51) most naturally presuppose a tradition like this one. For the image, cf. Paus. 9.33.4; *sanguinis fontem* in Apul. *Metam.* 9.34; Pesiq. R. 24:1.

72. Shrines often functioned as sanctuaries of refuge (Ex 21:14; 1 Kings 2:28-29; Hesiod *W.D.* 327; Eurip. *Madness of Heracles* 48; *Children of Heracles* 61-62, 69-72, 77-78, 123-25, 364-66; *Androm.* 253-54, 260, 411-12, 565, 859; Aristoph. *Knights* 1311-12; Diod. Sic. 11.89.6-8; 16.58.6; 17.41.8; Livy 35.51.1-2; 45.5.3-8, 11-12; Appian *R.H.* 12.1.7; 12.4.23; 12.8.53; Arrian *Alex.* 2.24.5; Corn. Nep. 4 [Pausanias], 4.4-5; 5.2-3; 17 [Agesilaus], 4.6; in Rome, also at the family hearth — Dion. Hal. 8.1.4), and bloodshed there both revealed the wickedness of the killers, inviting judgment (e.g., Eurip. *Daughters of Troy* 69; Virg. *Aen.* 1.349; Appian *C.W.* 5.1.9; Diod. Sic. 13.90.1; 17.13.6; Paus. 7.24.6; Jos. *Apion* 2.57; so also other acts against sanctuaries — e.g., Paus. 3.23.4-5; 9.33.6; Livy 42.28.12; Appian *R.H.* 3.12.2; Phaedrus 4.11; Babrius 78), and desecrated the shrine (e.g., Dio Cassius *R.H.* 51.15.5; Diod. Sic. 14.4.6-7; 38/39.17.1).

73. Typically in the Mediterranean world people honored the sanctity not only of sanctuaries but also of ancestral tombs (Dion. Hal. 11.10.1; Appian *R.H.* 8.12.89); destroying such tombs was hideous (Jos. *Apion* 2.58). Like shrines (see comment on 23:35), tombs could be places of refuge, though not inviolable (Appian *R.H.* 8.7.38).

74. Just as pathos was appropriate in persuasive rhetoric, tears and laments could represent praiseworthy affection in narrative works (e.g., Diod. Sic. 17.69.4; 34/35.11.1; Jos. *Life* 205, 210; *War* 2.402; Test. Abr. 3 A; Test. Mos. 11:2-3; Jn 11:35; Acts 20:37; cf. Gen 31:28, 55; 1 Sam 20:41; Dion. Hal. 3.18.3; 7.7.1; Ep. Arist. 123). Lamentation was part of life (e.g., *Greek Anth.* 7.339-40, 389; Quint. 6, pref.; Pliny *Ep.* 2.1.10-11; see comment on 27:55-66), despite some philosophers' challenges and the stereotypical consolatory exhortation not to grieve beyond measure (Theon *Progymn.* 8.55; Sen. *Dial.* 11.4.1; Epict. *Disc.* 1.9.20; 1.29.65-66; Plut. *Letter of Condolence to Apollonius* 33, *Mor.* 118E; *Consolation to Wife* 2, *Mor.* 608C; 4, *Mor.* 608F-609A; Socrates *Ep.* 21; Ep. Arist. 268; Test. Zeb. 10:1-2; Syr. Men. Sent. 463-69; Stowers 1986: 145-46). See especially Malina 1993: 24-25 and his sources.

special concern for Israel (10:5-6; 15:24-26). That Jesus wished to gather his people under his wings recalls the image of God sheltering his people under his wings (e.g., Ex 19:4; Deut 32:11; Ps 17:8; 36:7; 63:7; 91:4; 1 Enoch 39:7; Sifre Deut. 296.3.1; 306.4.1; 314.1.1-6; b. Soṭa 13b; Pesiq. Rab Kah. 16:1; Pesiq. R. 4:1); Jewish teachers also came to speak of one who converted a Gentile as bringing him or her under the wings of the Shekinah (cf. Ruth 2:12; 2 Bar. 41:4; ARN 12A; Sifra Qed. pq. 8.205.1.4; Sifre Num. 80.1.1; Sifre Deut. 32.2.1; b. ʿAbod. Zar. 13b; Shab. 31a; Gen. Rab. 47:10; Song Rab. 1:1, §10; 1:3, §3; Pesiq. R. 14:2).[75] If Luke's context is original, it also recalls Jesus' physical vulnerability to his enemies on Israel's behalf (Lk 13:32). But as often in the case of God in the Old Testament,[76] Jesus' love for Jerusalem here gives way to the brokenhearted pain of their rejection (for Jerusalem in particular, cf. Rev 11:8 vs. 17:6; for direct address of Jerusalem, e.g., Jer 13:27). God also weeps over his judgment of Israel (e.g., Jer 8:21-22; 9:1, 10), including over the temple's destruction (Lam. Rab. Proem 24; contrast Gentile Christian tradition as early as the second century; cf. Bokser 1973: 205-6). Israel had killed (Jer 26:20-23; here, especially 2 Chron 25:16) and persecuted (Amos 2:12; 7:12-13; Is 30:10) the prophets God had sent; Jewish tradition amplified prophetic martyrology further (Manson 1979: 126-27), as did Christian tradition (the interpolation in Sib. Or. 2.248). After 70, Jewish prayers also confessed that Israel's sins had brought on the calamity of exile (Neusner 1984: 19-20, while disagreeing with their verdict).

For Luke, Jesus' grief and his promise that they will see him later (Lk 13:34-35) precedes, hence is fulfilled in, the triumphal entry (Lk 19:41); Matthew places it among the woes of coming judgment, but in so doing transforms this into a promise of future hope (cf. 10:23; Glasson 1963b: 96-98; Goppelt 1964: 96; Aune 1983: 176; Patte 1987: 329). Perhaps as in some early Jewish teaching (cf., e.g., Ezek 36:33; Amos 9:8-12; Tob 13:6; Jub. 1:15-18; Rom 11:25-27; b. Sanh. 97b), Israel's repentance was the goal of history, and her salvation was contingent on her repentance (cf. Allison 1983).[77] Jesus awaits their

75. For the expression in general, cf. 3 Enoch 7:1. The protective instincts of a mother bird were proverbial, applied at times to human mothers (4 Macc 14:14-17; Eurip. *Madness of Heracles* 71-72; *Androm.* 441, 504-5) or others (Eurip. *Children of Heracles* 10). Boer 1974: 37 believes that 23:37 carries on the rare, but real, OT worship of God's motherly aspects (e.g., Num 11:12). The bird can appear as Israel or as Torah in Tannaitic parables (Sifre Deut. 48), but it is found too infrequently and in too ad hoc a manner to constitute a standard metaphor there (Johnston 1977b: 596).

76. Cf. also God's grief over Israel's judgment, often expressed anthropomorphically, even in Tannaitic parables. There, however, the picture is often apologetic (guaranteeing Israel's restoration), and sometimes God becomes dependent on his people to comfort him (Stern 1991: 126-27).

77. Bultmann 1968: 114-15 argues that 23:37-39 come from a Jewish prophecy based on the wisdom myth with parallels (the dates of which are now known to be questionable) in the Primal Man myth, but allows that the prophecy may have come via either Jesus or the Christian community. Aune 1983: 175, with less speculation, argues that this unit is authentic from Jesus. It fits traditional polemic, noting the biblical pattern of sin-exile-return (Stanton 1993: 250).

cry (cf., e.g., Is 30:19) to enter Jerusalem with acclaim again (cf. 21:9); the Son of Man's appearance will terrify the nations (24:30; cf. 26:64), but a significant proportion of Israel will have returned to the covenant. Israel's restoration was a major theme of the biblical prophets, which reappears at least occasionally in early Christianity (Rom 11:26), though the emphasis of early Christian apologetic came to focus on the Gentile mission.

By itself, the "desolation" of the house could refer to anything from a royal palace (Jer 22:5) to Israel as God's house (Jer 12:7), but in the context of Jesus' teachings, the Gospel tradition, and the immediate context in Matthew it can only mean the destruction of the temple (24:15; see Meier 1980: 274; Baum 1961: 54; Mt 21:13; Jer 12:7; Tob 14:4). Thus the temple is "left" (cf. 24:2) "desolate" (24:15). This interpretation is the most natural in a Jewish context; the temple was also "your house" (Jdt 9:13). The Babylonians had also left the temple (Jos. *Apion* 1.154) and city (*Apion* 1.132) "desolate." Further, later Jewish teachers even used a bilingual play on words to identify Jeremiah's mission with the temple's "desolation" (Pesiq. Rab Kah. 13:12, the same Greek term as here); for them, the house left desolate was plainly the temple (p. Ta'an. 4:5, §11), and exile under a foreign power inevitably followed the "desolation" of their city (4 Bar. 5:28). Israel saw itself rising or falling with its temple (Jer 7:3-15); the restored temple is a symbol of Israel's restoration and glory in Ezekiel 40–44. We cannot read 23:30-39 without viewing it in the light of 24:1-3, 15; Matthew connects the two discrete units of tradition purposefully.

The Temple's Destruction (24:1-3)

The Mount of Olives and Temple Mount were close together, and one could pass directly from one to the other without passing through the rest of Jerusalem (24:3; Gundry 1982: 413; cf. 21:12, 23). Though in Matthew's source (Mk 13:3), this "mountain" balances the mountain in Jesus' first Matthean discourse (Gundry 1982: 453), it might also evoke the new Moses theme again (as probably in 5:1-2; 15:29); many texts portray Moses and figures patterned after him receiving revelations of the future on the mountain (Allison 1993b: 254-55 cites, e.g., Jub. 1:1-4; Ezekiel's *Exag.;* Ps-Philo 19; 4 Ezra 4:5; 2 Bar. 2; Sifre Deut. 357; Targ. Ps-J. Deut. 34:1).

The introduction to the discourse suggests some points that probably would have stood out to the original audience. **First, Jesus is not impressed with splendid buildings and other monuments that impress others (24:1-2).** In ancient literature (at least after the temple's demise), this attitude could evoke praise as **a mark of his different values** (cf. Philost. *V.A.* 1, §30).

The temple was renowned for its beauty (Jos. *War* 6.267; ARN 28A; 48, §132B) and known throughout the Roman world (2 Macc 2:22; Ep. Arist. 84-91; *CIJ* 1:378, §515; Lohse 1978: 151). Perhaps because Judaism's cult was centralized (Sanders 1992: 50), its temple was larger and more magnificent than virtually any other temple of antiquity (Sanders 1992: 55-69; cf. Wilkinson 1978: 76; Patrich 1988).[78] The Pharisees, who generally disliked Herod, were sometimes displeased with his abuse of the temple (especially regarding his golden eagle there — Jos. *Ant.* 17.151-52; *War* 1.651; Schürer 1961: 144, 157); nevertheless, even they regarded the temple as the most holy site in the world's most holy city (e.g., m. Kelim 1:6-9; Mek. Pisha 1.48ff., Laut. 1:4).[79] (In succeeding centuries popular synagogue Judaism seems to have *liked* eagle decorations — Goodenough 1953-68: 8:121-22.) Diaspora Jews were intensely committed to the temple, as attested both by their payment of the annual tax for its upkeep and remarks in Egyptian Jewish literature (e.g., Sib. Or. 3.575-79). A Diaspora Jew like Philo emphasized Jewry's unanimous love for the temple and expected it to remain forever (*Spec. Leg.* 1.76; Sanders 1992: 52); even in the Ptolemaic period, before Herod's grand temple, an Egyptian Jew might view the temple as invincible (Ep. Arist. 100-101).[80] Indeed, if the Greeks believed that gods might fight to defend their temples (e.g., Herod. *Hist.* 8, §37), why should not Israel believe the same about its temple (4 Macc 4:9-12)? Galilean peasants and other Galilean pilgrims like these disciples would certainly have marveled at its grandeur (see Beasley-Murray 1957: 19; Freyne 1988: 181).[81]

Second, God himself would bring swift judgment against the religious establishment (24:2). The temple, as the ultimate symbol of that establishment, which the people took to be the symbol of God's glory (cf. Jer 7:4), would be utterly destroyed. This promise, probably already fulfilled by Matthew's day, would provide a sense of vindication to Matthew's audience; but it probably also accurately recalls Jesus' teaching.

Mack asserts, "apart from Mark's passion narrative, there is no indication that Jesus or his early followers looked for the destruction of the temple" (1988: 10n.4); but few scholars today would find his position consistent with our data.[82]

78. On its massive architecture and how it was built, see Jos. *War* 5.184-227, and for archaeological corroboration Josephus 1982: 346-61. Some recent scholars have also questioned whether the temple proper is under the Dome of the Rock or elsewhere (see Josephus 1982: 364, 426; Vogt 1974; Kaufman 1983; this would be easier politically). In many ancient cities "temple mounts" included palaces and other supremely important buildings as part of the most defensible acropolis (see Rohrbaugh 1991: 134).

79. Long after rabbinic Judaism had adjusted to the loss of the temple, it remained central in Jewish hopes (e.g., Gen. Rab. 14:8; 56:2; 95 MSV); speaking hyperbolically, a later teacher lamented that while pagans pray for the earth, all Israel's prayers were for the temple's rebuilding (Gen. Rab. 13:2).

80. For the general sentiment of its invulnerability, cf. Borg 1984: 165-70. After 70, some revised the claim of invincibility to argue that the western wall would never be destroyed (Num. Rab. 11:2; Song Rab. 2:9, §4; Lam. Rab. 1:5, §31; Pesiq. R. 15:10).

81. Horsley 1995: 145 is probably too skeptical of Galilean devotion to the temple, though he may be right that Galilean pilgrimage was much less frequent than Judean (144-46).

82. Mack 1988: 327 believes that the attribution of Mk 13's eschatological sayings to Jesus is part of Mark's fiction. Kelber 1976a: 168-72 supposes that Mark, being anti-temple, must be post-70; Marxsen, however, believes that Mark sees in the temple's destruction a herald of the imminent end (1969: 168, 189). But while most Jews would have viewed the temple as invulnerable before 66, some thought otherwise (see text). At least Mark's *traditions* are usually dated before 70 (see Allison 1998: 16-17).

That Jesus actually uttered such a judgment against the temple a generation before it happened is difficult to doubt historically. Whereas the later church may have forgotten the significance of some of Jesus' words and deeds against the temple, they nevertheless preserved them: a symbolic act of judgment there (21:12), testimony of witnesses the Christians believed to be false (26:61; cf. Mk 15:29; Jn 2:19; Acts 6:14),[83] and Q material like that of the house being left desolate (Mt 23:38//Lk 13:35). Jewish Christians who continued to worship in the temple (Acts 2:46; 21:26-27) nevertheless remained faithful to a saying of Jesus that they would surely not have created (cf. Hare 1967: 6).

Further, those who question the authenticity of Jesus' more specific threat to destroy and rebuild the temple based on lack of contemporary expectations for the temple's destruction and renewal have not examined contemporary expectations carefully enough (Sanders 1985: 365n.5). Some of Jesus' sectarian contemporaries also predicted judgment on the temple; for instance, if Testament of Levi is pre-Christian at this point, it promises the desolation of the sanctuary on account of the priests' uncleanness (Test. Levi 15:1; cf. 14:6). The Testament of Moses, which accuses priests of polluting the altar (5:4), prophesies judgment against the temple (6:8-9), and because the Roman ruler destroys only part of the temple in the oracle, the prophecy undoubtedly predates A.D. 70. In some texts, enemy rulers may want to destroy the temple (Sib. Or. 3.665), but God will establish it eschatologically (3.657-60). Sanders 1993: 262 cites the repeated expectation in some strands of early Jewish literature that God would bring a new temple down (1 Enoch 90:28-29; 11QTemple 29:8-10; cf. the hope of restoration in the seventeenth benediction of the Amida). Indeed, some interpreters already took 2 Samuel 7:13-14 as messianic (see 4QFlor), which may have supplied ample reason for picturing the messianic Son of David as building the new temple (Witherington 1992: 92, following Juel 1977: 204).

Likewise, that a Qumran document can accurately warn that the Kittim (by whom they mean the Romans) would carry off the Jerusalem priesthood's wealth (1QpHab 9.6-7) hardly makes the prediction, in a document undoubtedly predating A.D. 70, post-70![84] As Hill observes (1979: 62-63),

> that Jesus himself could have made the prediction [of the temple's destruction] is no more improbable than that Jesus ben-Chananiah should have done so in

83. Only Gos. Thom. 71 attributes the statement to Jesus himself, and this version is clearly late and gnosticizing (Aune 1983: 173). Nevertheless Sanders 1985: 73-74 is probably right to suggest that this reflects an authentic (though probably misinterpreted) saying; it is multiply attested and not the sort of threat one would have made up later (also Theissen 1991: 113, 194). If the four-beat rhythm in the proposed Aramaic reconstruction is accurate, it may indicate that Jesus originally offered this teaching privately to the disciples (cf. Jeremias 1971: 22-23).

84. Fritsch thinks that the probable Damascus Essenes were less anti-temple than the Qumran community, based on CD 13.27; 9.46; 8.11ff. (1956: 84); cf. also Davies 1982. Essene opposition sheds light on another point in the Gospels: that Jesus also respected (5:23-24; 23:16-21) and taught in (21:23) the temple does not conflict with his announcement of judgment against it; even Essenes reportedly sent sacrifices to the temple (Jos. *Ant.* 18.19).

AD 62 (Jos. *Bell.* VI.300ff.): indeed, the destruction of the Temple was one of the most important elements in post-Herodian messianism, and not every reference to it requires a date after AD 70.[85]

That the disciples therefore connect the temple's demise with the age's end (24:3) — thus allowing for its imminent rebuilding — fits the sort of expectations known to have existed among some of their contemporaries. Jesus hardly expected his own disciples to tear down the old temple; like some of his contemporaries, he expected God to act (Sanders 1993: 259).[86]

Similarly, Jesus' evocation of the language of the biblical prophets renders superfluous a necessary appeal to prophecy after the event (Robinson 1976: 27, following Dodd; cf. Taylor 1935: 73). That the first temple's previous violations indicated judgment would have made sense to Jesus' contemporaries steeped in biblical tradition (Ps. Sol. 2:1-10; 17:5; cf. Song Rab. 8:12, §1; Lam. Rab. 4:22, §25; Ruth Rab. Proem 7), and many, though not all, Jewish teachers in succeeding centuries recognized the destruction of Herod's temple as judgment (e.g., Jos. *War* 6.288-315; Pesiq. R. 26:6; cf. Apoc. Abr. 27:3-7; Goldenberg 1982).[87]

Finally, those writing a retroactive prophecy after an event might be more likely to report the prophecy with literalistic accuracy rather than with hyperbole; *some* stones were left standing on others (Danker 1972: 198; Kaufman 1981: 115; cf. the language of Hag 2:15). In fact, some of these stones from the retaining wall still remain, and are rather conspicuous, most of them between two and five tons, but one, nearly forty feet long, is close to 400 tons. One "prophesying" after the event might have taken better account of the concrete evidence against one's literal claim (Sanders 1993: 257).

Similarly, one would also never guess from the passage that the temple actually was destroyed by fire (cf. Matthean redaction in 22:7).[88] In a "prophecy" after the event, the sources would probably also have more clearly distinguished between the temple's demise and Jesus' return (cf. Mk 13:2).[89] Similarly, one

85. Making the same point, Aune 1983: 174-75 more thoroughly lists many examples of Jesus' predecessors and contemporaries who prophesied against the temple or made similar claims: e.g., the Egyptian Jewish prophet expected Jerusalem's walls to collapse (Jos. *Ant.* 20.169-70; cf. *War* 2.261-63); Josephus himself claimed to predict the fall of Jotapata (*War* 3.406) and cites an ancient oracle predicting the temple's fall (*War* 6.96-110; 4.388; he may refer to a biblical oracle, however).

86. Strangely, Crossan 1991a: 359, who admits that Jesus' threat against the temple is authentic, doubts that it could have been literal. A "symbolic" threat against the temple is much harder to document among Jesus' contemporaries.

87. Nevertheless, in keeping with prior biblical tradition, they saw the temple's destroyers as ignoble (Jos. *War* 6.95; Gen. Rab. 37:4) and warranting judgment (Urbach 1979: 1:91-92). In contrast to Matthew, Gentile Christians after the first century often saw in the temple's demise God's rejection of Judaism, vengeance for Christ's death, or the present impossibility of fulfilling the law (Lampe 1984: 153-71).

88. See also Beasley-Murray 1957: 24; Meier 1980: 277, 283; Gundry 1982: 475; Davies and Allison 1997: 335.

89. Thus Kümmel 1957: 101-2 sees the temple prophecy as originally referring to the end of

scholar, who doubts that the Synoptics accurately report Jesus' teaching about the imminent end time, complains that if the Synoptics *are* accurate here, Jesus was "mistaken rather than misreported" (Glasson 1963b: 75) — the very sort of conclusion composers of tradition after 70 would have wished to avoid.

Third, this chapter will address two questions: (1) the time of the temple's destruction and (2) the sign indicating his coming and the close of this age (24:3).[90] Commentators draw attention to some contrasts between Matthew and his source. For instance, whereas in Mark the eschatological discourse is esoteric, addressing four disciples (Mk 13:3), Matthew addresses the discourse to all disciples (Mt 13:3; Bornkamm 1963a: 21). Mark suggests that Jesus was teaching while he walked from the temple, in the fashion popularized by Aristotle's school (Mk 13:1; Aune 1983: 186; Robbins 1992: 171, 178, citing Varro *De re rustica* 1.21 and others);[91] Matthew's language may emphasize that Jesus had already departed from the temple, perhaps signifying judgment (Mt 24:1; Minear 1954: 109; Meier 1980: 277-78).[92] More importantly, however, Matthew distinguishes two questions.

Although biblical prophecy often linked events according to the *kind* of event rather than their sequence (e.g., a near locust plague coalesces with eschatological armies in Joel 1:4-7; 2:25; 3:2-17), clarity was essential for Matthew

---

the age rather than a historical event (cf. Ellison 1966: 19ff.). "Since the destruction of the temple and the holy city is a theme of Jewish apocalyptic, Jesus' prophecy is generally and quite correctly regarded as eschatological" (Aune 1983: 175; citing also Bultmann). But Borg may be closer to correct when he suggests that Jesus prophesied judgment rather than constructed an elaborate apocalyptic schema (1984: 181), though he is clearly wrong to deny Jesus' eschatological worldview in other respects (Witherington 1990: 30n.111; see below).

90. Grammatically the coming and close of the age (for *synteleia* see also 13:39-40, 49; 28:20) are linked by the single sign and represent a single question; the single definite article governing them may identify them as well (cf. Gundry 1982: 476; pace Ellis 1974: 87-88). Frost 1924: 22 hopes to distinguish *synteleia* (13:39; 24:3; 28:20) as the end time in a general way, including the tribulation period, from *telos* (24:6, 14), meaning the final end. But despite the intentional connection between 24:6 and 14, *synteleia* and *telos* are interchangeable in this discourse. Other Jewish texts also spoke of "end" both in an eschatological sense (CD 6.11) and as an end-tme "sign" (e.g., 2 Bar. 70:7; cf. Sib. Or. 4.173-76).

91. Gaston 1970: 10-13 thinks the prophecy's original context was a public address; while this suggestion would fit Mark's "mystery" motif, it is improbable that Matthew, who has prior tradition here, would not have changed it back (to correspond to biblical prophets', especially Jeremiah's, public denunciations) if the Palestinian tradition had reported it otherwise.

92. In Jewish tradition, God's presence departs from Israel or the sanctuary when their sin becomes unbearable; cf. 2 Bar. 8:1-2; 64:6; 3 Enoch 5:14; Sifra Qed. pq. 8.205.2.1; par. 4.206.2.6; Sifra Behuq. pq. 6.267.2.6; Sifre Num. 1.10.3; Sifre Deut. 258.2.3; 320.2.1; ARN 34, 38A; b. Ber. 5b; Rosh Hash. 31a; Shab. 33a; 139a; Yebam. 64a, bar.; Yoma 21b; p. Sanh. 8:8, §1; Pesiq. Rab Kah. 1:1; Gen. Rab. 19:7; Deut. Rab. 5:10; 6:14; Ruth Rab. 1:2; Qoh. Rab. 12:7, §1; Lam. Rab. Proem 25; Song Rab. 5:1, §1; Pesiq. R. 5:7; for earlier traditions, see 1 Sam 4:22; Ezek 9:3; 10:4-18; Jn 8:59; Wis 1:4; 6:12-25. (Rabbis regularly associated the Presence with merit — e.g., Sifre Deut. 305.3.1; 313.3.1; 355.6.1; Gen. Rab. 60:16; Ex. Rab. 45:5; Num. Rab. 19:20; Song Rab. 4:5, §2; 7:6, §1; Pesiq. R. 10:2.) Nevertheless, teachers felt that God's presence accompanied Israel into exile (Mek. Pisha 14.87, 100-101; Beshallah 3.82-83; Sifre Num. 84.4.1; p. Ta'an. 1:1, §10; Ex. Rab. 15:16; Num. Rab. 7:10; Lam. Rab. 1:5, §32; Cohen 1982a).

(probably writing after 70) in a way that it was not for Mark (Mk 13:2, probably before 70; cf. F. F. Bruce 1972a: 71; Brown 1979). Jesus' prophecy about the temple's destruction had been fulfilled, yet he had not returned; this situation (the oft-heralded "delay of the parousia") undoubtedly fueled both disillusionment (probably making Christians more susceptible to false prophetic reinterpretations of the parousia, as in 24:23-25) and eschatological speculation.[93] The final prerequisite for Jesus' coming is the evangelization of all nations (24:14), the most quantifiable prerequisite is the temple's desecration (24:15), but the only *sign* of his immediate coming the passage mentions appears in the heavens when or just before (*tote,* "then") Jesus appears (24:30; cf. Wenham 1977: 72; pace Walvoord 1971b).

Not Yet the End (24:4-14)

Although some doubt that Jesus would have spoken eschatological words, particularly in images resembling those often found in apocalyptic literature, their skepticism probably reveals more about their presuppositions about Jesus than about the evidence, as Albert Schweitzer pointed out long ago.[94] An eschatological Jesus pervades the tradition and in a first-century context is hardly inherently incompatible with Jesus the sage or prophet; Gentile Christians would not have introduced such Jewish imagery, and one doubts that Jewish Christians need have been more inclined to it than their teacher (cf. A. B. Bruce 1979: 288; Beasley-Murray 1954; idem 1957: 1-18).[95]

93. Clearly the delay of the parousia appears problematic in some passages (especially 2 Pet 3:3-14). That Jesus seems to have proclaimed only potential imminence minimizes the problem of the parousia's delay (cf. Witherington 1992: 48), but it is doubtful whether in practice this would eliminate it altogether (compare the progressive postponements of expectation in Qumran texts such as 1QpHab 7.7-8, 11-12, and perhaps in OT prophets, e.g., Hab 2:3; Dan 9:2-3; Ps 89:46; Reicke 1964: 179; Vermes 1984: 24, 116-17; for some treatment of imminence in early Qumran texts, cf. Almiñana Lloret 1970). At the same time, we lack evidence for a radical reformulation of early Christian eschatology due to this delay (see Aune 1975); heavily eschatological material (e.g., the Jesus traditions behind 1 Thess 4–5 and some of Revelation) and potentially realized eschatology (the church saying of Mt 16 and John) existed side by side throughout the first century, including in Paul (cf., e.g., Phil 1:23; 3:20-21).

94. See Schweitzer 1968 (original edition 1906); cf. Sanders 1985: 8. Jeremias 1964c: 33-34 doubts the authenticity of agrapha in Papias because they resemble Jewish apocalyptic more than the Gospels (earthly fertility, etc.); but whether or not these agrapha are authentic, such grounds for excluding them are probably unwarranted. Similar imagery appeared in Jesus' Bible (e.g., Amos 9:13; Is 35:1-2; Joel 2:24), and if Jesus could draw on other eschatological images (e.g., Matt 8:11; Is 25:6) and treat the Hebrew Bible as a unified book (Matt 23:35) there is no reason why he could not have embraced biblical images different from those most frequently found in his canonical sayings.

95. Despite their exaggeration, "there is no going back behind Weiss and Schweitzer" (Dunn 1975: 41); those uncomfortable with an eschatological Jesus who fit his milieu, followed John, and left an eschatological church must resort to saying "that everybody misunderstood Jesus completely," based on wishful thinking without evidence (Sanders 1993: 95, 183).

Indeed, the language of the discourse, though thoroughly Palestinian Jewish, is not apocalyptic revelation in the strictest sense, but exhortation based on some end-time motifs characterizing both prophecy and apocalyptic texts (Morris 1972: 88-90).[96] The pre-Synoptic source or sources here reflect motifs common to apocalyptic literature,[97] but also a sober, hortatory realism.[98] Disciples may have assembled elements of the tradition before Mark during a crisis of eschatological significance such as Caligula's public intention to have his statue erected in the temple (e.g., Ford 1979: 23; most fully, Theissen 1991: 125-65).

Jesus' final discourse in Matthew includes Markan, Q, and special Matthean material, but even some elements of Matthew's redaction here (such as the trumpet in 24:31) echo definite Jesus tradition, as the allusions in the earliest extant Christian document indicate (1 Thess 4:13–5:11; cf. 2 Thess 2:1-12): clouds, gathering of the elect, angel(s), lawlessness, apostasy, defilement of God's temple, the parousia (common to Mt 24 and the Thessalonian correspondence), coming as a thief, unknown times and seasons (Acts 1:7), sudden destruction on the wicked, and so on.[99]

96. The genre is technically closer to a testament (cf. Tob 4, 14; 1 Macc 2:49-69; Jub. 36:1-11; 2 Enoch 2:2; Test. 12 Patr.; p. Ketub. 12:3, §§12-13; Ta'an. 4:2, §8; deathbed visions or predictions in p. 'Abod. Zar. 3:1, §2; Soṭa 9:16, §2; Hom. *Il.* 16.853-54, 859; 22.359-60; but on the Testament of Abraham, see rightly Kolenkow 1974; Burnett 1979: 352) or farewell discourse, which often includes eschatological and sometimes apocalyptic features (see Robbins 1992: 175). A sage's imminent death often provides the occasion for parenesis (Perdue 1990; Jos. *Ant.* 4.177-93). On testaments, see Saldarini 1977; Kolenkow 1986; Collins 1986; Endres 1987: 199-201; McNamara 1983: 89-92; on farewell speeches, see also Stowers 1986: 55-56; Kurz 1985. Neusner 1986 is correct, however, that the analogy is largely formal; the Gospels' Christology necessitates radically different content.

97. After commending Beasley-Murray for a brilliant defense of Mk 13's authenticity, Perrin responds that many "non-Markan" terms common to Revelation appear in this chapter (1963: 130-31); but the data he marshals for his objection merely confirm the pre-Markan character of the text and the distinctive vocabulary of Jewish eschatology. Likewise, an argument for prophetic language similar to that of Revelation (Boring 1982: 186-95) does not question authenticity if one concedes (as Boring elsewhere does) that Jesus himself spoke as a prophet.

98. Mark may have combined disparate elements of the Jesus tradition (Beasley-Murray 1983), and may combine apocalyptic with antiapocalyptic motifs (cf. Tagawa 1977). Mark may likewise emphasize suffering for believers too focused on final eschatology (cf. Hooker 1982; Ford 1979: 35; to some degree, Weeden 1971: 101). For connections between predictions and parenesis, see Aune 1983: 185, who, with Hartman, takes this passage as pre-Markan. But imminence and prerequisite signs are hardly incompatible, for they occurred together in apocalyptic texts (Ford 1979: 28); from the earliest sayings of Jesus, imminence would take effect only after the signs were fulfilled (F. F. Bruce 1977c: 230).

99. See especially Waterman 1975 (citing 24 parallels, mostly compelling); D. Wenham 1984b; cf. also Hunter 1961: 49; Stanley 1961: 82; Barrett 1967: 12; Riesenfeld 1970: 13; Minear 1972: 164-65; Mounce 1974; Lane 1974a: 449; Beasley-Murray 1974: 42; Ridderbos 1975: 65; Hill 1979: 130; Plevnik 1979; Robinson 1979: 113-14; Davies 1980: 139; Marshall 1983: 126, 134; Sanders 1985: 144-45; Crossan 1991a: 243-47; cf. Conzelmann 1969: 165; in 2 Thess 2, see besides those above D. Wenham 1984b: 176-80; Milligan 1908: lxi n. 1. The cumulative evidence is, as Ford 1979: 22 puts it, virtually "conclusive." Although it is far from clear, some other material in 1 Thessalonians may also echo the dominical tradition (Riesenfeld 1970: 17; cf. Dibelius

That both Jesus' discourse (see Gundry 1982: 478) and Paul lack many other themes of Jewish apocalyptic (e.g., mutant babies — 4 Ezra 5:8; 6:21; Sib. Or. 2.154-64, following Hesiod *W.D.* 181) strongly supports the view that they share a common source.[100] This coincidence of particular motifs and absence of others also refutes the idea that merely early Jewish-Christian scriptural embellishment rather than Jesus himself would stand behind both the extant Jesus tradition and 1 Thessalonians; the latter probably constitutes our earliest Christian document and derives from a very nonapocalyptic milieu.[101] The same coincidence of motifs refutes the thesis that Paul and the Gospel tradition both depend on an early Christian prophecy.[102] Given the abundance of prophecy in early Christianity (cf. 1 Thess 5:20; 1 Cor 14:26-31) and lack of much concrete evidence for recording such prophecies or, with rare exceptions, for their widespread geographical circulation, why would a particular prophecy or particular set of motifs come to preeminence?[103] The best explanation for the coincidence and the "you yourselves already know" (1 Thess 5:1-2), hence the meaning of Paul's "word of the Lord" (1 Thess 4:15) and "traditions delivered to you" (2 Thess 2:15), is that the earliest dominical tradition stands behind both.

Jesus does not simply seek to stir disciples to short-term eschatological enthusiasm, like some popular modern teachers of prophecy (on whose usual inaccuracy see, e.g., Wilson 1977; Kyle 1998). After listing many of the signs (usually hardships) that characterized the end among contemporary Jewish thinkers and visionaries,[104] Jesus declares that "the end is not yet" (24:6; cf. Rev 6:1-8). Jewish

---

1953: 93). The "catching up" part may be an agraphon (Frame 1912: 171; Morris 1959: 141; Jeremias 1964c: 14; cf. Neil 1950: 97) or a midrashic implication of the explicit gathering (Wenham 1981: 348; cf. Marshall 1983: 130); the descent may derive from OT theophany language (see Scott 1959: 132).

100. Cf. also the early fourth-century-A.D. Egyptian syncretistic text *Asclepius* 72.16-25; 73.5-12, 18-22 (Boring 1995: 135-36), which includes among end-time sufferings not only wars but the pious being considered "insane," wicked angels remaining, atheism prevailing, etc. Some significant parallels remain, but given its date influence from Egyptian Christianity cannot be ruled out.

101. Glasson 1963: 175 and Robinson 1979: 105-7; they rightly find a source for much of the material in the LXX, especially Is 26–27, but miss the one authority behind early Christian eschatology that could combine these particular motifs (cf. similarly Wenham 1981: 348-49). (Note that the Christian tradition also echoes sources like Ps. Sol. 17:11-18.) Goulder 1974: 166 characteristically thinks Matthew derives the trumpet from 1 Thess 4:16 (cf. Dodd 1936: 154-55, on 1 Thess 5:2-8 with Lk 21:34-36), but this gives Paul's correspondence too preeminent and early a role in early Christianity (perhaps before Christians even collected his letters).

102. Pace Koester 1971: 196; Best 1977: 189-93; Boring 1982: 11, 34n.41; Aune 1983: 253-56.

103. Prophecies could be written down and preserved (Test. Job 51:4/3); but it does not appear to have been the norm (cf. Aune 1983: 244). Further, oracles were far more likely to be heavily redacted than didactic traditions were (cf. J. J. Collins in *OTP* 1:320).

104. Cf., e.g., Jub. 23:11-25, especially 23:13; 36:1; 1QM 15.1; Sib. Or. 2.6-33; 3.213-15; 4 Ezra 8:63–9:8; 13:19-20, 30; 2 Bar. 26:1–27:13; 69:3-5; Test. Mos. 7–8; m. Soṭa 9:15; b. Sanh. 97a; Pesiq. Rab Kah. 5:9; Qoh. Rab. 2:15, §2; Lam. Rab. 1:13, §41; Song Rab. 2:13, §4; 8:9, §3; Pesiq. R. 1:7; 15:14/15; 34:1; pace Sanders 1985: 23, who questions the antiquity of the concept. Even the expression is demonstrably pre-Christian if 1QH 3.3-18 refers to the community's eschatological suf-

people sometimes called such events the "birth pangs of the Messiah,"[105] but Jesus declares that these are merely the "beginning of birth pangs" (24:8; cf. Rom 8:22). These are not specifically end-time events, but events that would happen throughout history for which disciples must be prepared (Ladd 1956: 72n.1; pace Frost 1924: 18-19). The end-time discourse presupposes important knowledge about the end time, but its repeated exhortations show that its emphasis is on how to live in light of that reality (see Lane 1974a: 446; Hill 1979: 63).[106]

Jesus' hortatory tone is clear in his "Watch out" (24:4).[107] **One obstacle for which Christians must prepare themselves is false messiahs (24:4-5).**[108] The danger of being misled recurs frequently in this discourse (24:4, 11, 24; cf. Mk 13:5-6, 22),[109] and Matthew elsewhere has cause to report Jesus' warnings against signs-working prophets (7:15, 22; on signs-prophets, see the Introduction), a warning clearly part of the Jesus tradition (2 Thess 2:9).[110] Advance warning (24:25) could help them to distinguish truth from error (for the principle, cf., e.g., Jn 14:29; Is 48:5). But false messianic figures abounded in the first century (e.g., Jos. *War* 2.259-63; 6.285-88; *Ant.* 20.97-98); their attempts at signs, usually failing, may have been attempts "to activate God's eschatological

---

fering (cf., e.g., Black 1961: 149-51; Pryke 1969: 50-51), though the relation to a Messiah is debated (see, variously, e.g., Baumgarten and Mansoor 1955; Silberman 1956; Brownlee 1956-57; Brown 1957; Gordis 1957; Brown 1968).

105. So Morris 1972: 23; Lane 1974a: 459; Ladd 1974b: 201-2; cf. 1QH 3.3-18; 1 Enoch 62:4; b. Sanh. 98b; Shab. 118a. "Birth pangs" draws on OT judgment language (Ps 48:6; Is 13:8; 21:3; 26:17; 42:14; Jer 4:31; 6:24; 13:21; 22:23; 30:6; 31:8; 48:41; 49:22, 24; 50:43; Hos 13:13; also Glasson 1962: 175). Whether Paul in 1 Thess 5:3 also derived it from the dominical tradition (Milligan 1908: 65; Wenham 1981: 353-56) or not (F. F. Bruce 1982: 110) is disputed, since he applies the image quite differently from that tradition. For Paul, cf. the birth pangs in the day of judgment when the Son of Man sits on his throne in 1 Enoch 62:4-5 (Witherington 1990: 245), if it is genuinely non-Christian material, or the birth pangs of final judgment in 4 Ezra 4:42. Similar imagery was applicable to the first creation (Philo *Creation* 43).

106. Matthew and Mark clearly write for the church; this undercuts older dispensational interpretations that deny that the church is addressed (Walvoord 1971a; idem 1976: 73-74; Ware 1981; contrast Beechick 1980: 231-51, who, though supporting pretribulationism, admits that the text addresses the church). Historically, addressing the disciples, Jesus was also addressing the nucleus of the church, no less than in, say, Jn 14–17 (Katterjohn 1976: 17). As Carson 1984b: 490 notes, "Most will agree that no passage in the Bible unambiguously teaches a two-stage return."

107. Robbins 1992: 59 thinks that the Markan hortatory notes represent Greco-Roman adaptations of OT prophetic patterns like "*Behold,* the days are coming." He also notes (176) the frequency of warnings in farewell discourses.

108. The cry "I am (he)" (Mk 13:6; Lk 21:8) may have special messianic or prophetic significance (cf. Daube 1973: 325-27 on the usage for the divine presence; cf. John's "I am" statements); Weeden supposes prophets have identified themselves with Christ in ecstasy (1971: 77-78; cf. Theissen 1991: 152).

109. "Do not be deceived" was standard hortatory language (e.g., Epict. *Disc.* 2.20.7; 2.22.15; 4.6.23; 2 Macc 7:18; 1 Cor 6:9; Gal 6:7; 2 Thess 2:3; Ign. *Eph.* 16). *Planaō* seems an emphasis in Matthew's redaction here (cf. Broer 1993b). For Matthew and the Jesus tradition, those who do not know Scripture or who limit God's power are especially susceptible to being misled (22:29).

110. Sib. Or. 3.63-70 implies that an antichrist figure will work signs, but this may be a Christian interpolation.

salvation" (Barnett 1981: 693). (Roughly a half-century after this Gospel's publication, Jewish Christians rejected the messianic pretensions of Bar Kochba.)

Other obstacles include both human (24:6-7) and natural (24:7) disasters, with Matthew's particular emphasis possibly lying on the former (Gundry 1982: 475-76). Jesus borrows traditional biblical language here (cf. 2 Chron 15:6; Is 19:2; Jer 51:46; for rumors of wars, cf. Dan 11:44), echoed in some early Jewish texts (Sib. Or. 3.636-37; 4 Ezra 13:31-32; cf. Tr. Shem 5:6; 6:13). By saying that these disasters "*must* occur" (24:6), Jesus echoes the biblical and Jewish tradition of God's sovereignty over history and the events of the end time (Dan 2:28-29, 45; Rev 1:1; Hagner 1995: 691).

Pagans also took careful note of omens, or "prodigies," that boded ill for them (the Romans particularly indulged in this pessimistic exercise), usually as signs of hardship within history, in the impending future (e.g., Livy 21.62.1-5; 24.10.6-11; 27.11.2-5; 33.26.7-8; 43.13.3-6; Arrian *Alex.* 4.15.7; Aul. Gel. 4.6.2). Sometimes they called such prodigies "signs" (Arrian *Alex.* 4.15.8). Such prodigies could include familiar images like earthquakes (Ovid *Metam.* 15.798; Livy 32.8.3; Appian *C.W.* 1.9.83), an eschatological vice list (Hesiod *W.D.* 181-201), and signs in the heavens (Livy 25.7.8; 29.14.3; 32.8.2; 41.21.13; Lucan *C.W.* 1.526-43) like comets (Appian *C.W.* 2.10.68; Lucan *C.W.* 1.529). Some standard portents not listed in Matthew 24 appear in early Christian eschatological tradition, such as raining blood or stones (Livy 24.10.7; 25.7.7-8; 26.23.5; 27.37.1; 34.45.7; 35.9.4; 36.37.3; 42.2.4; 43.13.5; 45.16.5; Appian *C.W.* 2.5.36; 4.1.4; but Rev 8:7 depends primarily on Ex 9:23) and fluid turning to gore (Virg. *Aen.* 4.453-63; Livy 24.44.8; Rev 8:8-9 with Ex 7:19).

But they also included many omens not paralleled in biblical tradition, including the howling of dogs in temples (Ovid *Metam.* 15.796-97); animals (e.g., Livy 24.10.10; 27.11.4; 35.21.4; 41.13.2; 41.21.13; 43.13.3; Appian *C.W.* 4.1.4) or infants speaking; weeping, sweating, or bleeding statues (Ovid *Metam.* 15.792; Livy 27.4.14; 40.19.2; 43.13.4; Appian *C.W.* 2.5.36; 4.1.4; Lucan *C.W.* 1.556-57; cf. Eurip. *Iph. Taur.* 1165-67); wailing in sacred groves (Ovid *Metam.* 15.793); animals born malformed or with human parts (Livy 27.4.11, 14; 32.1.11; 40.45.4; Phaedrus 3.3.4-5); or malformed, abnormal, or interspecies births to humans (Livy 27.11.5; 27.37.5; 34.45.7; 35.21.3; 41.21.12; Appian *C.W.* 1.9.83; Herodian 1.14.1; Lucan *C.W.* 1.562-63). As also in later Jewish apocalyptic, some Greek texts portray unusual births as signs of the end (infants with gray hair in Hesiod *W.D.* 180-81).

Other early Jewish texts recognized earthquakes (e.g., m. Ber. 9:2; Sib. Or. 1.187; 3.405 — reapplying Poseidon's title; 3.449, 452, 459, 476; 5.291, 438-39; cf. Tr. Shem 7.19)[111] and famines (e.g., Amos 4:6-9; Ps. Sol. 17:18-19; b. Ber.

111. Poseidon appears regularly as the "earth-shaker" in Greek sources: Hom. *Il.* 7.445; 8.201, 208, 440; 12.27; 13.10, 34, 43, 59, 65, 89, 215, 231, 554, 677; 14.135, 150, 355, 384; 15.41, 173, 184, 205, 218, 222; 20.13, 20, 34, 57-63, 132, 291, 310, 318, 330, 405; 21.287, 435, 462; *Od.* 1.74; 5.282, 339, 366, 375, 423; 6.326; 7.35, 56, 271; 8.354; 9.283, 518, 525; 11.102, 241, 252; 12.107; 13.125, 140, 146, 159, 162; Aristoph. *Acharn.* 510-11.

55a) as God's works of judgment,[112] and included earthquakes (2 Bar. 27:7; 70:8; 4 Ezra 6:13-15; 9:3; Test. Mos. 10:4),[113] famines (Sib. Or. 2.23; 2 Bar. 27:6; 70:8; Pesiq. Rab Kah. 5:9; Gen. Rab. 25:3; 40:3; 64:2; Ruth Rab. 1:4; Pesiq. R. 15:14/15; Rev 6:5-6), pestilence (Sib. Or. 2.23), strife among nations (Sib. Or. 2.22; 3.660-61, 756; 4 Ezra 9:3; 13:30; Gen. Rab. 42:4), and people hating one another (2 Bar. 70:3; cf. 4 Ezra 6:24; Mt 24:7) among the most commonly listed signs of end-time judgment.

Most of the events of 24:5-14 occurred between A.D. 30 and 70 (Blomberg 1992a: 356, following Thompson 1974). False messiahs seem to have arisen toward the end of this period (Jos. *War* 2.444; 7.29; Theissen 1991: 265), and more may have arisen or been expected shortly after it (24:23-24).[114] A Samaritan prophet gained a significant following in A.D. 36 (Jos. *Ant.* 18.85-87; Theissen 1991: 137-38). A major famine struck ca. A.D. 46 (cf. Jos. *Ant.* 3.320; 20.51-53) and earthquakes ca. A.D. 61 (Fenton 1977: 379).[115] When Matthew's audience thinks of nations rising against one another they may recall the recent conflicts of 66-73, when Judea revolted against Rome (Montefiore 1968: 1:299; Meier 1982: 279) and generals vied for power over the Empire in the wake of Nero's death.[116] Some even believe the gospel of the kingdom was proclaimed among the nations in a representative sense (Rom 10:18; Col 1:6; Blomberg 1992a: 356-57; cf. Munck 1967: 98).[117] The data can

112. Tr. Shem 1:1, 5-6, 11; 2:5; 5:1-4; 6:7-11; 7:4-7, 14; 8:6-7; 11:8-9; 12:9 associates food conditions with the zodiac, but as a Jewish document it likely presupposes that God is the one working through such signs. That God authors calamities is also implied but not stated in Syr. Men. Sent. 444-46. Both Epicureans and Stoics found naturalistic causes for earthquakes (Diog. Laert. *Lives* 7.1.154; 10.105), though paganism more frequently attributed them to deities (Orphic Hymn 15.8; Diod. Sic. 15.48.3-4; 16.61-64; Paus. 7.24.6); for plagues as judgment, see, e.g., Diod. Sic. 14.69.4–14.71.4 (but some found naturalistic explanations here as well — Dion. Hal. 7.68.2; or sacrifices could not placate the gods — Dion. Hal. 9.42.1; 10.53.4-6). Some also preferred naturalistic explanations for eclipses (Dio Cassius *R.H.* 60.26.1-5) and thunderbolts (Pliny *N.H.* 2.18.82).

113. One may also compare the ultimate eschatological earthquake (e.g., 1 Enoch 1:6-8; Rev 6:12; cf. Bauckham 1977).

114. Although Josephus reports many false prophets (including in the OT, *Ant.* 8.318), we have little record of messiahs between Jesus and Bar Kochba, which Gundry interprets as supporting the authenticity of the saying that messiahs would come (1982: 477); but Josephus seems to have played down messianic claims wherever possible.

115. Theissen 1991: 277 thinks that Luke's earthquakes, more associated with the final events, reflect events in the 60s (Pompeii, 62-63 — Tac. *Ann.* 15.22.2) and 70s (Pompeii, Corinth, and Cyprus — Pliny *Ep.* 6.16; Dio Cassius 66.21.1-3; Malal. *Chron.* 261; Oros. 7.9.11; Sib. Or. 4.115-44). For a catalogue of earthquakes in Israel from 92 B.C. to A.D. 1994 (including tremors in Jerusalem in A.D. 30, 33, 48), see Amiran, Arieh, and Turcotte 1994.

116. Ancients sometimes recognized civil war as particularly noxious, given its propensity for dividing kin (cf. 24:10); cf. Dion. Hal. 6.79.1; 7.42.3; 10.35.3; Livy 7.60.2; Appian *C.W.* 1.introduction, 5; Corn. Nep. 8 (Thrasybulus), 2.6; 15 (Epaminondas), 10.3; Lucan *C.W.* 1.1; Jos. *Life* 100 (cf. *Life* 26, 128); on lesser forms of civil strife, see Dion. Hal. 11.60.3. Although the Jewish-Roman war was noteworthy (e.g., Tac. *Hist.* 2.4; 5.1-5), other peoples in the east may have retained some nationalistic sentiments (cf. Millar 1987), threatening further potential instability.

117. *Oikoumenē* can mean Roman Empire, but the "representative" sense *began* to be ful-

fit the first generation, just as some contemporary popular "prophecy teachers" fit them to current generations.[118]

The general character of the language prohibits us from *limiting* it to any such events, however (Beasley-Murray 1957: 35, 39). Lists of misfortunes appear in texts referring to the past (e.g., Dion. Hal. 1.23.1-5) as well as in texts warning about the future. Such events occurred throughout the period of A.D. 30-70, and continued to occur afterward. Responding to some who blamed Christians for famines, plagues, earthquakes, and other sufferings, Tertullian retorts that these hardships occurred even more frequently before Christ's coming (*Apol.* 40.2-3, 10, 13, 15)! Theissen's specific parallels for the period before A.D. 40 (1991: 125-61) thus lack adequate conviction, though the Caligula incident may well have provoked the first collection of the material in the apocalyptic discourse around 40, as he suggests (1991: 161; for the history of this view, cf. 127).

Third, disciples should expect persecution and the consequent apostasy of some of their fellow professing disciples (24:9-13; cf. 2 Thess 2:3; 1 Tim 4:1-3; 2 Tim 3:1-9; 2 Pet 3:3; 1 Jn 2:18-19; Rev 13:12-17; Apoc. Pet. Eth. 5.1-2). The "tribulation" to which their persecutors would deliver disciples was especially persecution (24:9; different in 24:21), and this would provide a test of disciples' faith (13:21). Early Christian exhortation regularly portrayed perseverance and apostasy as the alternatives in times of serious testing (Brown 1969: 146). (Cf. Mt 10:17-22, largely borrowed from Mk 13:9-13; 10:22, which is reused in its Markan context in 24:9, 13, making the expectation of universal hatred and the call to persevere emphatic.)[119] Like Mark, Matthew intimately connects the suffering of believers with that of Christ, even by prefacing the passion narrative with the promise of believers' suffering (cf. Feuillet 1980b; Graham 1986; Theissen 1991: 281; more significant than Best 1983: 78 allows).

Mediterranean antiquity regarded loyalty highly and handing over an innocent person negatively (e.g., Apul. *Metam.* 9.41). Hypocrites might join those set apart for God when persecution relents (Dan 11:34), but in times of

---

filled proleptically as early as Acts 2:5-12; in view of the commission in 28:19-20, one might think that 24:14 hopes for a broader evangelization than that. Although Paul spoke of worldwide evangelization (Rom 10:18) before he reached Spain (Rom 15:20-24; Hagner 1995: 696), his use of "every place" was intentionally hyperbolic and perhaps proleptic (1 Thess 1:8). Josephus contended that Jews observed the law "everywhere" (*Apion* 2.282, 284). Those who argue that 24:14 has been fulfilled, however, rightly remind us that the "fulfillment" of this passage is not quantifiable, and hence serves as a motivator but not a predictor.

118. Theissen 1991: 153-54 focuses on the wars shortly before A.D. 40 (Jos. *Ant.* 18.113-14, 124; Tac. *Ann.* 6.31-37), which best fit his dating of the source. See Wilson 1977 for a historical survey of prophecy teachers' (usually errant) applications to current events over a seven-decade period.

119. The hatred of "all humanity" may have been a figure of speech for behavior that was universally odious (e.g., Plut. *Educ.* 14, *Mor.* 11C); Jewish people sometimes used "all the nations" hyperbolically for the whole pagan world, as distinct from Israel (cf. 1 Macc 1:42-43, depicting the sin of both). Mt 24:10-12 seems to reflect pre-Matthean tradition (see Wenham 1980).

persecution many would fall away. Jewish people lamented the danger of apostasy from practicing Judaism,[120] and expected apostasy as one of the tragic signs of the end time[121] as under previous desecrator-oppressors like Pompey (Ps. Sol. 17:13-15) and especially Antiochus IV Epiphanes (1 Macc 2:15, employing the same term as in 2 Thess 2:3). The greatest expression of apostasy was betraying others who intended to remain faithful (cf. 10:21; 1 Jn 3:16; Did. 16.4-5; many people regarded betrayal of friends to death to save one's own life as despicable — e.g., Babrius 138.7-8; cf. m. Ter. 8:12), and the Jewish pietist tradition warned of the necessity to flee into the wilderness when apostates controlled Jerusalem (Ps. Sol. 17.14-17; 1QS 8.13-16). "Lawlessness" (24:12) could characterize especially the outwardly religious (23:28; cf. Jude 4),[122] but probably applies to the society as a whole, including wicked rulers (2 Thess 2:3, 7-8; cf. Mt 13:41).[123] Nevertheless, as a consequence even the hearts of "the many," perhaps the disciples (cf. 20:28) would become loveless (cf. 22:37-39; 5:43; 19:19), hence capable of betrayal (24:10, 12), perhaps aided by false prophets (24:11).[124] Although "enduring to the end" (24:13; cf. v. 22) could refer to survival (cf. 4 Ezra 6:25), the context of apostasy suggests that it here refers to what it does in other NT passages, namely, that only those who continue in the faith will receive salvation at the final day (cf. 7:13-14; Marshall 1974: 73).

120. 1 Macc 1:41-51; see data in Caird 1955: 29-30; Schiffman 1981: 144-46; cf. CD 5.21; Sifre Deut. 318.1.10, 15.

121. E.g., 1 Enoch 91:7; 1QpHab 2.5-6; Test. Iss. 6:1; Naph. 4:1; 3 Enoch 48A:5-6; m. Soṭa 9:15; Pesiq. Rab Kah. 5:9; Pesiq. R. 15:14/15; cf. 4 Ezra 5:1-2; 14:16-18.

122. Schweizer rightly claims that the "lawlessness" here opposed is one that undermines love toward neighbor (1975: 451; cf. 22:39); I would add that it applies to all who reject Jesus' radical interpretation of God's law, including the Pharisees (5:17-20; though it is doubtful that 2 Thess 2:3's "man of lawlessness" was Pharisaism, pace Brunec 1957).

123. Pharaoh is "lawless" in 3 Macc 6:4; Nebuchadnezzar in 4 Bar. 7:25; Nero in Dio Chrys. *21st Disc., On Beauty* 6; wicked priests in Test. Levi 17:11; and antediluvian society in 2 Enoch 71:24-25; among Greeks, revolt against religion was "lawlessness" (Avi-Yonah 1978: 32). Sib. Or. 3.69-70 warns of Beliar's leading astray both the "chosen" (cf. Mt 24:24) and the "lawless" (possibly a Jewish-Christian interpolation, but probably not Christian); Ps. Sol. 1:8 conjoins Jerusalemites' lawlessness with profanation of the sanctuary. Nevertheless, Pompey especially filled the role of "man of lawlessness" for Psalms of Solomon (17:11), as Antiochus IV Epiphanes appears to be the "man of sin" in 1 Macc 2:62. But Antiochus provides the basic model, because he seeks to make Israel forget God's law (1 Macc 1:49). Thus lawlessness *(anomia* and *paranomia)* functions as sin (Test. Job 43:2; Jos. *War* 4.355; cf. Epict. *Disc.* 2.16.44; 4.7.36) and the opposite of piety (Sir. 39:24), but as abandonment of God's law it functions especially as apostasy (Philo *Mos.* 2.165; Test. Dan 6:6; 7:3; Naph. 4:1), as in the Jesus tradition. "Man of lawlessness" may render the Heb. "man of Belial," which also appears in the LXX as man of "apostasy" (F. F. Bruce 1982: 167-68).

124. Although Christians undoubtedly discovered the severity of this temptation during the Neronian persecution, other early Christian texts and the probable Jesus tradition in 2 Thessalonians warn against too specific a referent to that persecution here (as in Taylor 1989). The apostasy of "*the* many" also involves far more widespread (cf. 20:28) apostasy than can be thought to have occurred under Nero.

Finally, true disciples will spread the gospel among all nations (24:14).[125] This is the appropriate response to persecution (cf. Farrer 1956a), probably rooted in the biblical prophets' image of the conversion and tribute of the Gentiles (cf. Thompson 1971). Whereas Jesus says that other phenomena do not mark the end (24:6), in this instance he explicitly declares that universal proclamation *does* mark the end. (Matthew, with his heavy emphasis on the Gentile mission, makes this even more explicit than Mark does — Mk 13:10.) The world controls many other factors, but this is the one factor Jesus' followers may determine: they must complete the commission of discipling all nations before this age will come to a close (28:19-20; cf. Rom 11:25-26; 2 Pet 3:9-15; Acts 1:6-11; cf. Marxsen 1969: 177: "this proclamation helps to hasten the coming of the Parousia"). As in the biblical prophets (e.g., Ezek 36:24-29), the end would accompany Israel's repentance (23:39); but some early Christian texts suggest that this repentance would be completed following the fulfillment of the Gentile mission (Rom 11:25-26).[126] Jesus' claim in 24:14 does not imply that all peoples will be converted, but that the kingdom will not come in its fullness until all peoples have had the opportunity to embrace or reject the King who will be their judge (25:31-32).[127] Jesus' early followers recognized that he would rule a remnant with representatives from all peoples (Rev 5:9; 7:9), just as the world's evil leadership would (Rev 13:7).[128]

125. Jeremias 1958: 22-23 (followed by Barrett 1967: 75) thinks that the Gospel writers meant worldwide evangelism but that Jesus originally referred to an angelic proclamation as in Rev 14:6-7. Yet the logion better fits not only its Markan context but the whole of Jesus' sayings by fitting his sending of disciples, and the primary objection to it is the a priori assumption that Jesus anticipated an immediate appearance of his kingdom. Some of Jesus' other sayings also depict the disciples carrying on in a possible interim after his departure (Mt 10:28; Lk 17:22; Mk 14:58; Goppelt 1981: 217). Against another view, that the Semitic term behind *euangelion* here would not have born a religious sense, see Gundry 1982: 480-81.

126. Many Jewish teachers emphasized that Israel's obedience could hasten the end (e.g., Tob 13:6; Test. Zeb. 9:7; Sifre Deut. 41.4.3; 43.16.3; b. B. Bat.10a; Nid. 13b, bar.; Sanh. 97b; p. Ta'an. 1:1, §7; Ex. Rab. 25:12; Deut. Rab. 3:2; Song Rab. 2:5, §3; 4:8, §3; 5:2, §2; Pesiq. R. 31:5; cf. Acts 3:19; 2 Pet 3:12), whereas others preferred fixed schemes, whether able to be determined or known only to God (e.g., Sifra Behuq. pq. 8.269.2.3; b. 'Abod. Zar. 9ab; Sanh. 97ab; Lev. Rab. 15:1; Lam. Rab. Proem 21). Some reconciled the two by claiming that the redemption was scheduled but would come early if Israel were obedient (Song Rab. 8:14, §1). Later rabbis reported both the multiplicity of dates and prerequisites for the Messiah's coming alongside warnings against speculating when he would come (b. Sanh. 97a-98b). Various texts speak of God delaying death (p. Ta'an. 2:1, §11; Pesiq. Rab Kah. 7:10; Qoh. Rab. 7:15, §1; cf. 4 Ezra 7:82), other judgments (Sib. Or. 1.129; Sifre Deut. 43.14.1; cf. Plut. *Delays of Divine Vengeance, Mor.* 548A-68A), or the end (1 Enoch 60:5; 4 Ezra 7:24; cf. 2 Bar. 85:12) to grant time for repentance.

127. The "entire world" could be hyperbolic, as apparently in some other texts (e.g., Polyb. *R.R.E.* 1.1, 2, 64).

128. The early Christian perspective could thus explain their experience of delay on the analogy of the deferment of God's promise in the earlier biblical record; just as Israel through disobedience ruled the land promised to Abraham only twice in her history (Gen 15:18; 1 Kings 4:21; 2 Chron 34:5-7), so the Lord's return was delayed and the world's suffering prolonged by the church's disobedience to the Great Commission (cf. 2 Pet 3:9-15; Ford 1979: 76).

We should note the context in which this worldwide evangelism occurs: suffering (24:9-13; more explicitly, Mk 13:9-11, earlier applied by Matthew to his fuller discourse on evangelism).[129] Many early Christians recognized suffering as a prerequisite for the end (Rev 6:10-11; Col 1:24; cf. 4 Ezra 4:3-37), because disciples' suffering is inseparable from their witness.

The Tribulation in History (24:15-28)

With 24:15-22, cf. Mk 13:14-20; Lk 21:20-24; with Mt 24:23-28, cf. Mk 13:21-23; Lk 17:23-24. Daniel provides the basis for many motifs in Matthew 24 and its primary source, Mark 13 (Davies and Allison 1997: 332), for instance, the temple's destruction (Dan 9:26); rumors of war (Dan 11:44); the tribulation (Dan 12:1), the Son of Man on the clouds (Dan 7:13), and especially the abomination (Dan 8:13; 9:27; 11:31; 12:11). Various New Testament passages seem to have reapplied Daniel's image of tribulation in different ways; but all agree in warning disciples to be vigilant when they face such testing. In contrast to the false prophets who till the end exhorted Jerusalemites to stand firm and expect sudden deliverance (Jos. *War* 6.285-86),[130] Jesus warns his followers to accept the perils of this age realistically and to escape them when possible. Eusebius reports that the church in Jerusalem responded to true prophets and fled the city before destruction came (Euseb. *H.E.* 3.5.3); probably Jesus' words had guided the Christian prophets to a realistic appraisal of the danger, in contrast to some other Jerusalemites. His words likewise may instruct believers from the Matthean community when they would face peril.

Excursus: The Development of Antichrist Tradition

Antiochus, a typical hellenistic tyrant (see Heininger 1989 on 4 Maccabees), became the ultimate model for the antichrist of Mark 13:14 (F. F. Bruce 1982: xxxvii; cf. Jos. *Ant.* 11.276; Tarn 1974: 214). Bousset's later parallels for the antichrist imagery do not form a unified view (Best 1977: 283; F. F. Bruce 1982: 179-88) and miss three primary features of the New Testament portrayal (cf. also Did. 16.3-4; Iren. *Haer.* 5.25.1-4), which appear in Deuteronomy 13 (Meeks 1967: 49-50; Brown 1982: 335; cf. Giblin 1967: 245), though some of Bousset's features may be early (Flusser 1988:

129. The contextual link might derive from Markan redaction: Mk 13:10 may interrupt its context and bear indications of Mark's special attention (cf. Pryke 1978: 53-54), but this likely suggests that Mark borrowed it from a different context rather than that he composed 13:10 from whole cloth; the idea is too common (and in some cases too early) in early Christianity to have begun with Mark (e.g., 2 Pet 3:9-15; Acts 1:6-11; Rom 11:25-26).

130. Cf. the false prophets of "peace" of Jeremiah's day (e.g., 6:14; 8:11; 14:13; 28:9) and tales of other "deceivers" who led to defeat (e.g., Diod. Sic. 34/35.2.5-6).

207-13; cf. Burgmann 1980). Although some think the Dead Sea Scrolls apply the "Man of the Lie" (CD 20.15; cf. Meeks 1967: 51-52) to Antiochus Epiphanes (Michel 1954) or Simon Maccabee (Burgmann 1978; idem 1980), it probably signifies the Jerusalem high priest (1QpHab 2.1-2; 5.10-12; 10.9-10 in context, e.g., cols. 8-10; 11.4, 12; 12.2, 5-6; cf. CD 2.15) who defiled God's sanctuary (1QpHab 12.8-9), possibly by persecuting the Teacher of Righteousness and his followers (1QpHab 12.6).[131]

But New Testament and some other early Jewish portrayals of an evil eschatological ruler (cf. 2 Bar. 40:1-2) also derive from the Antiochus tradition, developed in the time of desecrators and oppressors like Pompey (Ps. Sol. 2:29; 17:7, 11-14), and Roman emperors (p. Sukk. 5:1, §7), possibly including Nero (Asc. Isa. 4.1-6 in Segal 1981: 261). Rabbinic memories preserved special hatred toward a conqueror like Titus (ARN 1A; 7, §§20-21B; Sifre Deut. 328.1.1-5; Lev. Rab. 20:5; Qoh. Rab. 5:8-9, §4; for the hideousness of the tradition of intercourse on the law scroll see b. Giṭ. 56b; Me'il. 17b; Lev. Rab. 22:3; Num. Rab. 18:22, cf. the halakah in b. Ber. 25b), though Josephus, a Jewish client of the Flavian dynasty, naturally felt differently (Jos. *Ant.* 12.121, 127). Hadrian came in for curses no less severe (Ex. Rab. 51:5; Lam. Rab. 3:58-60, §9), especially because of the massive (and exaggerated — the rabbis report more than the world's population) slaughter at Bethar (p. Taʿan. 4:5, §10; Gen. Rab. 65:21; Song Rab. 2:17, §1); one tradition mentions three and a half years of siege (p. Taʿan. 4:5, §10; Lam. Rab. 2:2, §4), analogous to the period Antiochus Epiphanes held Jerusalem (Jos. *War* 1.19, 32-33).[132]

Caligula's attempt to establish his image in Jerusalem's temple (Jos. *Ant.* 18.259-308; 19.1-20; *War* 2.184-85; Philo *Leg. Gai.* 115-16, 188, 346; Tac. *Ann.* 12.54; cf. Dio Cassius *R.H.* 59.4.4; Bilde 1978; Stern 1974/76b: 354-59; Benko 1971: 51-53) undoubtedly fueled renewed expectations of the final oppressor, and Jewish tradition recalled him harshly (b. Soṭa 33a; Song Rab. 8:9, §3). Philo appropriately charges that Gaius Caligula was zealous for "lawlessness" *(paranomia),* because he regarded himself as law (*Leg. Gai.* 119); some who heard of Caligula's plans sought to rescue themselves from lawlessness (*Leg. Gai.* 190). As Caird observes, while Caligula may not be the antichrist, "he undoubtedly sat for the portrait" in 2 Thessalonians (Caird 1966: 166; for an alternative, neurological reading of his insanity, see Benediktson 1989); Nero and Domitian seem to serve that function in

131. By means of a wordplay Simeon bar Kokhba ("son of a star") became bar Koseba ("son of a lie"); cf., e.g., Lam. Rab. 2:2, §4. The Jewish-Christian avoidance of force contrasts starkly with Bar Kochba's military ideology (Kellner 1988); on his administrative method, see Pileggi 1991. But most Jews would have regarded Hadrian as an antimessiah more than Bar Kochba, who was merely a *false* messiah.

132. The frequent application of "May his bones rot" and similar curses to Titus and especially to Hadrian (Gen. Rab. 10:3; 28:3; 65:21; 78:1; Lev. Rab. 18:1; Deut. Rab. 3:13; Ruth Rab. 3:2; Qoh. Rab. 2:17, §1; Lam. Rab. 3:23, §8) attached to wicked persons in general (probably Tannaitic tradition in Gen. Rab. 49:1), though it probably represents redaction from the editor of Genesis Rabbah and later writers. Again, however, the hatred of him is hardly unanimous (cf. Justin *1 Apol.* 68). Naturally Nebuchadnezzar also featured occasionally in this tradition, though the influence of Jdt 3, 6 on 2 Thess 2 (Mussner 1963) is questionable.

Revelation (see most commentaries). Other evil figures were accused of erecting an idol in the temple (Test. Mos. 2:8-9; m. Taʿan. 4:5; p. Taʿan. 4:5, §6).

Subsequent Christian and Jewish tradition developed this further, including both New Testament motifs and others more familiar from Bousset's portrait (cf. e.g., Apoc. Elijah 1:10). Even in the New Testament the language may be mythological at points. Qumran's probable summation of the Jerusalem high priesthood via the now-mythical image of a "wicked priest" (e.g., 1QpHab 8.8-11; 9.4-7; cf. 1QpHab 11.5-6; 12.5-6 — imperfect verb; van der Woude 1982) suggests the possibility that one antichrist in time became a succession of antichrists (cf. 1 Jn 2:18).

First, no religious symbol, no matter how treasured, provides refuge against judgment that God has decreed. The sanctuary, once desecrated, was doomed (24:15), as Jesus had earlier warned (23:38). The desecration of God's temple (Ps 74:3-4, 7; Is 63:18) undoubtedly constitutes a recurrent judgment motif in Israel's history; it provided the ultimate symbol of national and religious humiliation (cf. 1 Macc 3:45; 3 Macc 1:29; 2:14; 2 Bar. 5:1; Test. Asher 7:2; t. Sukk. 4:28; CD 4.17-18), something Jewish people resisted to death (Philo *Leg. Gai.* 209-10), except in times of national apostasy, when they might cause it (Jos. *Ant.* 10.37-38; Ps. Sol. 1:8; Apoc. Abr. 27:7). The Syrian ruler had defiled the altar in the second century A.D., causing an "abomination" and ruining the sanctuary with "desolation" (1 Macc 4:38; cf. 1:54). Even before the first exile, the prophets recognized scattering and tribulation as a judgment designed to bring God's people to repentance (e.g., Deut 4:26-31; Jer 29:12-14; 31:9). One could also profane the temple by persecuting the righteous there: In Jerusalem, "the Wicked Priest did abominable works and defiled the sanctuary of God" (1QpHab 12.7-9); because this Qumran passage interprets Habakkuk 2:17, which refers to bloodshed, it probably refers to the persecution of the followers of the Teacher of Righteousness (cf. 1QpHab 12.6 and context).

But the language of Jesus' reference to a desolating sacrilege in the sanctuary (24:15) suggests a more specific biblical allusion (cf. Daube 1973: 418-20; Hill 1979: 63; Beale 1984: 5:129). Daniel's language stands behind that of Maccabees and Josephus. When Daniel spoke of the "abomination that would result in desolation," one text referred to the events surrounding Antiochus Epiphanes, who claimed to be deity and oppressed Israel (Dan 8:13; 11:31, 36-39; 1 Macc 1:54-56; 6:7; cf. Jos. *Ant.* 12.253; Jub. 23:21); another text, however, associates the same phenomenon with the cutting off of an anointed ruler, close to the time of Jesus (Dan 9:26; cf. Payne 1962: 146).[133] Further, the end

133. Regardless of the date of Daniel, it cannot be later than the second-century-B.C. manuscript of it among the Dead Sea Scrolls (see Yamauchi 1972: 87-91; Kitchen 1978: 152n.10; Vasholz 1978); nevertheless, calculating the "seventy-sevens" from the time of the decree to which Daniel refers brings one to the early first century. This undoubtedly increased eschatological speculation among Jesus' contemporaries (Beckwith 1981; on Daniel's popularity then, see Jos. *Ant.* 10.268-81;

had not come after Antiochus's desecration of the temple (Dan 11:31; cf. "then" in 12:1), allowing the possibility that another desolation would come (Dan 12:11-12). The image of this final tribulation period was reapplied; in the Dead Sea Scrolls the period of tribulation extended forty years (CD 20.14-15; for reinterpretation after delay, see 1QpHab 7.13-14); other Jewish interpreters provided still other estimates (e.g., seven in b. Sanh. 97a; Pesiq. Rab Kah. 5:9; Song Rab. 2:13, §4; Pesiq. R. 15:14/15; 34:1; 36:1-2; see Bonsirven 1964: 212-13). Jewish speculation concerning the end time regularly reapplied Daniel's figures in various manners (see F. F. Bruce 1956: 177; Russell 1964: 198-201; cf. Ruth Rab. 5:6). Revelation seems to reapply Daniel's tribulation period to the period between Jesus' first and second comings (Rev 12:1-6, 10); some scholars have understood Matthew 24 similarly (Davies and Allison 1997: 369; see discussion below). That hearers of this passage needed to consider its meaning carefully is confirmed by Mark's enigmatic riddle, "Let the reader understand" (Mk 13:14).[134]

Jewish people recognized that shedding innocent blood in the sanctuary would profane it (1 Macc 1:37; Jos. *Ant.* 9.152; so also Mt 23:35; for guilty blood as well, cf. 2 Chron 23:14; cf. perhaps 1 Chron 22:8; 28:3), and some even saw this defilement as a desolation (1 Macc 1:39; 2:12). Josephus indicated that the shedding of priestly blood in the sanctuary (Jos. *War* 4.147-201; 4.343; 5.17-18; cf. 2.424) was the desecration, or "abomination," that invited the ultimate desolation of A.D. 70 (Jos. *War* 5.17-19). Very close to three and a half years after the abomination (cf. *War* 6.93), the temple was destroyed and violated even more terribly. After the temple burned,[135] the Romans erected on the site of the temple their standards, which bore the emperors' images *(imperatorum imagines)* and were housed with idols in the army camps (cf. Josephus 1982: 155; Ferguson 1987: 40; Herodian 8.5.9), then offered sacrifice to them (Jos. *War* 6.316).[136] Jerusalemites had once preferred death to permitting these standards to enter the

---

12.322; Mason 1992: 47), and though Daniel (probably due to its Aramaic portions) appears with Ezra rather than in the prophets, Matthew (24:15; contrast Mk 13:14), like his contemporaries (Jos. *Ant.* 10.266; Mason 1992: 47), considered him a prophet (though cf. also Mt 13:35; Gundry 1982: 482). Many think Daniel applied only to the Maccabean desecration (Aalders 1960; Colunga 1960), but both the Qumran pesharim and texts like *Lives of the Prophets* 12:11 (§ 19 in Schermann, p. 63) indicate that Jesus' contemporaries freely reapplied such images.

134. Cf. the similar call to pesher interpretation in Rev 13:18; typical of Jesus in Mk 4:9, 12. Elsewhere Jesus uses the more general motif of summoning readers to understand (e.g., 21:42), but this instance specifically represents an eschatological riddle (whether because of a politically sensitive reference to Rome, or simply reflecting a Jewish tradition of eschatological mystery — cf. Dan 12:9). Noneschatological riddles belong to the sage tradition (Jos. *Apion* 1.111, 114-15).

135. Although Josephus absolves Titus of personal responsibility (Jos. *War* 6.240-41, 249-66), many ancients considered the burning of temples a hideous act (Diod. Sic. 10.25.1; Livy 31.26.12; 31.30.9-10; 31.31.3; Corn. Nep. 2 [Themistocles], 4.1-2; Jos. *Apion* 2.131).

136. Probably because Titus ordered these standards to be erected, many church fathers held that Titus had erected a statue of himself on the site of the temple, literally fulfilling 2 Thess 2:4 (Lachs 1987: 383, citing Chrysostom and Jerome); but this patristic interpretation is not historically accurate (Ford 1979: 158).

city (Jos. *Ant.* 18.55-59; *War* 2.169-74; cf. also *Ant.* 18.121; 3 Macc 1:29; Philo *Leg. Gai.* 299-308); Qumranites had viewed them as the epitome of idolatry (1QpHab 6.3-4).[137] But Jesus' warning must apply to the earlier rather than the final desecration, because shortly after the Romans surrounded Jerusalem escape became increasingly difficult (e.g., Jos. *War* 5.420-23, 449).[138]

In Matthew, the tribulation seems to begin with the sanctuary's desecration in A.D. 66 and concludes with Jesus' return (24:29). If, as I think most likely, Matthew writes some years after 70, this allows several interpretive options: in Matthew 24 Jesus (1) skips from this tribulation to the next eschatologically significant event, his return (Fuller 1966; cf. Lk 21:24; especially compare Mt 24:21, "nor ever shall," with Dan 12:1; cf. Jos. *War* pref. 1);[139] (2) regards the whole interim between the Temple's demise and his return as an extended tribulation period ("immediately" — 24:29; e.g., Carson 1984b: 507);[140] (3) prophetically blends the tribulation of 66-70 with the final one, which it prefigures (see

137. For bibliography on the incident of Jos. *Ant.* 18.55-59, see LCL 9:45-46. Beasley-Murray (1957: 69ff.) and Payne (1962: 152) believe the desecration referred to was the one of 70 rather than of 66 (cf. Argyle 1963: 182), but the "abomination" probably precedes rather than occurs simultaneously with the "desolation"; see below. Kraeling 1942: 288-89 interestingly notes that Jesus entered Jerusalem in the spring of A.D. 30, three and a half years after Pilate's "abomination" with the standards in Jerusalem, suggesting that eschatological enthusiasm was already high.

138. Some feel the prophecy originated during the time of Caligula's oppression (Gaston 1970: 24-27). But that Jesus predicted an abomination of this or a related nature is, in my mind, indisputable; he could draw directly on Daniel without events directly provoking his words. At the same time, the saying changed through tradition history (cf. Thiselton 1977: 94 on the prophecy's open-endedness). Perhaps reinterpreting Jesus' saying in light of the Caligula crisis of A.D. 40, the long tradition behind Mk 13 seems to imply a personal desecrator in Mk 13:14 (Plummer 1910: 332; Mickelsen 1963: 293; Moule 1965: 106; F. F. Bruce 1972b: 257; Anderson 1976: 296; Lane 1974a: 467; Wenham 1981: 350) — which Matthew, writing after 70, does not (Jeremias 1971: 128; Gundry 1982: 482). 2 Thessalonians (which in view of its image of a literal king enthroned in the temple must be pre-70) likewise interprets the Jesus "tradition" (2 Thess 2:2, 15) as declaring a king who would do what Caligula had previously tried to do (2:3-4). That non-Markan details of Matthew's discourse (e.g., 24:43; the trumpet in 24:31) also appear in 1 Thessalonians in the 50s confirms that the tradition behind Mk 13 is pre-Markan; that Paul draws from Jesus traditions distinct from this discourse, however (cf., e.g., Acts 1:7), indicates that he draws from a body of tradition accepted by the churches as a standard — namely, Jesus tradition — rather than merely from isolated prophecies. For a comparison of James and our passage, cf. Feuillet 1964.

139. Some (e.g., Hagner 1995: 711) argue that Jesus spoke only of Jerusalem's fall, not of his parousia, as imminent (23:36; 24:36). But though the early Christians sometimes understood "coming" language figuratively (Rev 3:3), Jesus' eschatological discourse does seem to imply that his parousia will be unexpected, albeit preceded by some specific prerequisites (like the temple's destruction). Part of the controversy may focus on the sense in which different scholars employ the term "imminent." Harvey 1982: 66-97 suggests that Jesus must portray the end in terms of imminence to retain the crisis's urgency, given the prophetic imagery current in his day.

140. The term bears more weight than in Mark, who uses "immediately" much more loosely (for a transition or starting over, etc. — Ellingworth 1978; though Matthew does use some terms, especially *tote,* transitionally — cf. Buth 1990). Cf. Paul, who believes that Christians are already in the eschatological tribulation (Rom 8:18; 1 Cor 7:26; 1 Thess 3:4; Witherington 1992: 158-59). Option two easily blends into three if one starts the tribulation in 70 but allows an intensification at the end of the age (e.g., Carson 1984b: 495; Blomberg 1992a: 359-60).

Bock 1994: 332-33);[141] (4) begins the tribulation in 66 but postpones the rest of it until the end time; (5) intends his "return" in 24:29-31 symbolically for the fall of Jerusalem.[142]

I currently favor options (1) or (2) with elements of (3). (Against the view of a "spiritual" coming are the many emphatic statements about a personal, visible coming in the context — 24:27; Gundry 1982: 491.) The third option may in fact deserve more attention than my current inclination has given it: certainly the prophetic perspective naturally viewed nearer historical events as precursors of the final events.[143] Early Jewish texts also telescope the generations of history with the final generation (Jub. 23:11-32). As in Mark, the tribulation of 66-70 remains somehow connected with the future parousia (Hare 1967: 179), if only as a final prerequisite. Further, the context may suggest that Jesus employs his description eschatologically, as in some Jewish end-time texts;[144] in this case, the disasters of 66-73 could not have exhausted the point of his words (cf. Harrington 1982: 96). In any case, the view (circulated mainly in current popular circles) that Matthew 24 addresses only a tribulation that even readers after 70 assumed to be wholly future is not tenable; Matthew understands that "all these things" (probably referring to the question about the temple's demise — 24:2; Mk 13:4) will happen within a generation (Mt 24:34), language that throughout Jesus' teachings in Matthew refers to the generation then living (e.g., 11:16; 12:39, 45; 16:4; 23:36; cf. 27:25). Further, Luke dispenses with much of the symbolism and lays the emphasis almost entirely on the Roman conquest of Jerusalem, in which Judean slaves were carried among the nations. For Luke, the "abomination" that brings about desolation becomes simply the Roman armies surrounding Jerusalem, promising desolation (Lk 21:20; A. B. Bruce 1979: 292; Cole 1961: 202).

Second, believers should flee the impending judgment with the greatest of haste (24:16-20). Although John and Matthew's Jesus earlier speak of a warning to flee the coming wrath through the baptism of repentance (3:7; 23:33), the "eschatological" judgment here is the imminent destruction of Jerusalem. Although people fleeing a ravaged countryside normally took refuge in cities, Jesus warns the people of the land to flee from both city and open countryside (cf. Lk 21:21). People could leave Jerusalem safely until the spring of A.D. 68 (Jos. *War*

141. Cf. Frost 1924: 15-19; Meier 1979: 169-70; idem 1980: 282-83; Feuillet 1980; Turner 1989.

142. This last view appears on both sides of the Atlantic but is more common in British than American scholarship; cf. Tasker 1961: 224-26; Wenham 1977: 71; Barclay 1959a; Gaston 1970: 484; France 1985: 333; Hatina 1996.

143. See Ladd 1974b: 196-201 (with OT examples); idem 1978: 36-37; cf. Beasley-Murray 1960; Everson 1974: 337; Bock 1994: 332-33.

144. E.g., some "shorten" particular days (e.g., 1 Enoch 80.2-4, if reading with Knibb against Isaac; perhaps 2 Bar. 20:1; lengthened in Jub. 23:26-28); though here he refers to a shortened *number* of days (cf. Filson 1960: 255; Theissen 1991: 133-34; of a person's life in 3 Bar. 9:7), probably of Daniel's appointed number in Dan 12:11-13 (e.g., Anderson 1976: 296; Gundry 1982: 484).

4.377-80; 410; Lane 1974a: 468). Later deserters to the Romans, suspected of having swallowed jewels to escape with them, were often cut open by Syrian auxiliaries (Jos. *War* 5.550-52); once the city fell, many captured Jerusalemites died entertaining Gentiles in the games (Jos. *War* 7.23-24, 37-40).

The command to flee to the mountains (24:16) makes good sense and is probably authentic. Most scholars today accept Eusebius's report (*H.E.* 3.5.3) that the Christians did indeed flee to Pella.[145] That Pella is not in the Judean mountains (Moule 1965: 106) but in foothills and reached from the Jordan valley thus makes doubtful any suggestion that Jesus' saying was merely conformed to the events of 66-70 (Meier 1980: 283; Gundry 1982: 482).[146] Nevertheless, Palestine's central mountain range provided a natural place to flee (e.g., 1 Sam 23:14; Ezek 7:15-16; Jos. *War* 2.504; cf. Ps-Philo 6:11, 18; 27:11), as mountainous areas with caves often did (Diod. Sic. 34/35.2.22; Dion. Hal. 7.10.3; Appian *C.W.* 4.17.130; Arrian *Alex.* 4.24.2). Although the exhortation is too general to be sure, the language might even allude to the familiar 1 Maccabees 2:28 (cf. Dodd 1968: 82).[147]

The admonitions to leave the rooftop without entering the house (24:17) and to leave the field without returning for one's cloak (24:18) indicate that life matters more than even its basic necessities, which might later be replaced (cf. 1 Macc 2:28; Phaedrus 4.23). Because the flat rooftops were approached by outside staircases, one could descend without entering the house to retrieve possessions.[148] One normally slept in one's outer garment (Deut. 24:13; cf. Mt 5:40) and wore it as one went to the fields[149] and during the cold of morning labor in the fields, but left it at the edge of the field as the day grew warmer (Lane 1974a: 470; Anderson 1976: 296; Meier 1980: 284-85). As essential as this outer cloak was, Jesus declares hyperbolically that the urgency of running at the news of impending destruction was more urgent still. Others also left behind cloaks as they fled in haste (Ovid *Metam.* 4.101; Gen 39:12-13; Mk 14:51-52); some moralists emphasized the priority of saving one's life over possessions in an emergency (Phaedrus 4.23.11-15).

145. E.g., Reicke 1974: 216; Lohse 1978: 49; idem 1955: 79; Sowers 1970; Cole 1961: 203; Schoeps 1960; Pritz 1988: 122-27; pace Brandon 1967: 284; Lüdemann 1980. For some archaeological support, see Smith 1973.

146. Pace Aune 1983: 312, who regards the specific mention of Pella as secondary without stating why, though he accepts the likelihood of an oracle as in Eusebius. Theissen 1991: 160-61 thinks that Christians expected the desolating sacrilege to be set up when this warning was attached to the source, and that this fits the Caligula situation ca. 40 (Philo *Leg. Gai.* 232; but Jos. *Ant.* 18.274 is less clear).

147. David and the Maccabees used such terrain for guerilla warfare, for which tactics such terrain often proved effective (Dion. Hal. 7.10.4-5; those who practiced other kinds of warfare despised this form — Dion. Hal. 3.8.2), but Jesus' words stress flight, not armed resistance. Cf. refuge caves during the Bar Kochba revolt (Patrich 1989).

148. Lane 1974a: 470; Anderson 1976: 296; Meier 1980: 283; Gundry 1982: 483; cf. Stambaugh and Balch 1986: 83.

149. Even for those who lived in villages, but certainly for those who lived in Jerusalem, the fields were sometimes a considerable walk or donkey ride (Lewis 1983: 65).

The "woe" (cf. 18:7; 23:13) over the pregnant and nursing (24:19; cf. Sib. Or. 2.190-92, if pre-Christian) signifies the difficulty of the flight and survival (Lk 23:29; 2 Bar. 10:13-15; cf. Apoc. Elijah 2:35-38); the pregnant may also be more susceptible to death (e.g., Dion. Hal. 9.40.2).[150] But it probably indicates no less the sorrow of losing infants in the trauma (cf. 2 Bar. 10:13-15).[151] Jerusalem's siege did, however, produce worse sorrows than mothers merely lamenting their children: recalling the language of the curses of the law (Lev 26:29; Deut 28:53-57; cf. 2 Kings 6:28-29; 2 Bar. 62:4), Josephus tells us of starved women *eating* their children (*War* 6.208-12; cf. Sifra Behuq. pq. 6.267.2.1; Lam. Rab. 4:9, §12). Conditions provoking a mother's abandonment of her children represented the severest of judgments (1 Enoch 99:5), as did situations producing cannibalism (Diod. Sic. 1.84.1; Appian *R.H.* 12.6.38).[152]

Verse 20 also reveals foresight concerning the Sabbath and winter (whether Mk 13:18 may omit the Sabbath for theological reasons or Matthew may add it to the tradition is debatable). Commentators suggest that on the Sabbath city gates might be shut; one could also not secure animals for transport. Many Jews considered willfully riding horseback on the Sabbath a deathworthy, almost unforgiveable sin (e.g., p. Ḥag. 2:1, §9; 2:2, §6). While Jewish people agreed that one could break the Sabbath to save life (1 Macc 2:41; Montefiore and Loewe 1974: 258),[153] only Jesus' followers recognize the peril of their situation (Gundry 1982: 483).[154] In much of the Mediterranean world winter was the rainy season (Hesiod *W.D.* 450), the cold of which kept men from their fieldwork (Hesiod *W.D.* 494; in Greece, this was especially late January to early February, *W.D.* 504-5). Winter's cold limited both land (Num. Rab. 3:6; cf. Beasley-

150. Cf. Tr. Shem 5.6, of animals; see further Beasley-Murray 1957: 77; Lachs 1987: 383.

151. Ancient sensitivity to mothers' plight typically depicts the execution of pregnant or nursing mothers as horrific (2 Kings 15:16; Hos 13:16; Amos 1:13; 1 Macc 1:61; 2 Macc 6:10; 4 Macc 4:25); the tragedy of nursing mothers epitomizes a public disaster (Eurip. *Suppliants* 1114-64; Dio Cassius *R.H.* 68.25.3-4). The death of adult children also appears in terms of parents' suffering (Hom. *Il.* 22.59-65, 79-90; Judg 5:28; Lk 2:35).

152. With but few exceptions (Sext. Emp. *Pyrrh.* 3.207; Diog. Laert. 7.1.121; 7.7.188; cf. Eliade 1958: 71), inhabitants of the ancient Mediterranean viewed cannibalism as immoral and disgusting (e.g., Herod. *Hist.* 1.73, 119, 123, 129; 3.99; Diod. Sic. 1.14.1; 34/35.12.1; Mart. *Epig.* 10.4.1; 11.31.2; Jn 6:52; cf. Horsley 1981: 20; idem 1987: 57-58). Thus the early slander of cannibalism against Christians (e.g., Athenagoras 3; Theophilus 3.4, 15) proved devastating.

153. Stanton 1989b; idem 1993: 205-6 doubts that Matthew's audience kept the Sabbath this strictly, whereas Wong 1991 responds that they did so. Stanton's view that Mt 12 argues against the Sabbath is not persuasive; the Matthean Jesus upholds Torah (5:17), and even if he did not, the Sabbath precedes the law as part of the creation order (Gen 2:2-3), which Jesus upholds (Mt 19:4-5). While we believe that Matthew's audience maintained the Sabbath, they would be at least as likely as their contemporaries to rank preserving life above observation of a particular Sabbath Day (12:1-14 challenges priorities, not sabbatarianism altogether).

154. The supposed danger of being identified as a Christian by breaking the Sabbath (Gundry 1982: 483; Meier 1980: 284) misses the popularity of law-keeping Jewish Christians in Jerusalem before 66 (Acts 21:20; Jos. *Ant.* 20.200-203; Euseb. *H.E.* 2.23; see Martin 1988: lxii-lxix). A siege during a Sabbatic year would have other consequences (1 Macc 5:49, 53), but the unqualified term in the tradition here means the weekly Sabbath.

Murray 1957: 76) and sea travel;[155] even armies stopped traveling campaigns during this season,[156] and some soldiers who nevertheless marched in "wintry" mountain regions (colder than the Judean hills) reportedly lost their hands and feet (Herodian 6.6.3). Further, cold winter rains could flood the roads and bury them deep in mud (m. Ta'an. 1:3; Jeremias 1969: 58), and the usually dry creekbeds (wadis) were filled with water and difficult to cross (cf. Hom. *Il.* 5.87-88; 13.137; *Od.* 19.205-7; Ap. Rhod. 1.9; Livy 44.8.6-7; Appian *R.H.* 12.11.76; Herodian 3.3.7). Some rivers could, however, flood not only in winter but in spring when mountain snows melted (e.g., Arrian *Alex.* 7.21.2-3; cf. Herodian 8.4.2-3); indeed, in spring 68, because the Jordan was flowing high, Gadarene fugitives were delayed in crossing and slaughtered by the Romans (Jos. *War* 4.433; Davies and Allison 1997: 350). The warning to pray in advance regarding the coming peril (24:20) accords well with Jesus' instructions elsewhere (26:41; cf. 6:13; Prov 22:3; 27:12).

Although Jesus' words specifically and most importantly surround the fall of Jerusalem, the memory of which would remain fresh for Matthew's audience and hence vividly vindicate Jesus' words, they might also provide Matthew's community, and especially its missionaries, with some current principles. Disciples who remember the nature of the time ought not to be attached to worldly possessions; they should value their lives enough to flee immediately. Nor ought they to believe false prophets of peace proclaiming that judgment will not strike their own localities; rather than sparing a locality, God sometimes warns his servants to leave (Gen 19:15-30).

Third, even in the midst of what seems intolerable distress, God has compassion on his own servants (24:21-22). Daniel spoke of the end-time tribulation greater than any that had preceded it (Dan 12:1); other Jewish writers also spoke of eschatological tribulations (1QM 15.1; 2 Bar. 25:3-4). By indicating that no tribulation before *or after* this one would rival it, Mark may allow and Matthew may suggest that the tribulation on which they focus is a tribulation within history, not necessarily the final one (cf. Jos. *War* 1.12, making the same claim for A.D. 66-73), although the language may simply follow an emphatic formula (Jub. 16:8; Ps-Philo 19:16). The memory of Jerusalem's destruction in A.D. 70 seared itself indelibly in early Judaism's memory as the most horrible of times (cf., e.g., Sib. Or. 5.397-413; Pesiq. R. 1:5; 28:1), although the revolt in Egypt of

155. E.g., Longus 2.19, 21; Ach. Tat. 8.19.3; Apul. *Metam.* 11.5; Dion. Hal. 7.2.1; Livy 38.41.15; Herodian 5.5.3; Jos. *War* 1.279-80; 2.203; 4.499; Qoh. Rab. 3:2, §2; Acts 27:9; 2 Tim 4:21; see further Charlesworth 1970: 226; Ramsay 1904b: 376-77. See Rapske 1994: 4-6, 22-29 on exceptions; Virg. *Aen.* 4.309.

156. E.g., 2 Sam 11:1; Polyb. *R.R.E.* 10.40; Diod. Sic. 14.17.12; 15.73.4; 20.113.3; 29.2.1; Livy 5.2.1; 21.58.1-2; 22.22.21; 25.11.20; 32.4.7; 32.32.1; 37.39.2; 38.27.9; 38.32.2; 43.9.3; 45.8.8; Sall. *Jug.* 61.2; 97.3; Corn. Nep. 14 (Datames), 6.1; 17 (Agesilaus), 3.4; 18 (Eumenes), 5.7; 8.1, 4; Appian *R.H.* 7.7.43; 11.3.16; 12.15.101; Lucan *C.W.* 2.648; Arrian *Alex.* 3.6.1; *B.G.U.* 696.3; Jos. *War* 4.442; *Ant.* 18.262; Dio Cassius *R.H.* 55.24.2; cf. Dupont 1992: 199. For exceptions, see, e.g., Dion. Hal. 9.25.1; Livy 43.18.1; 44.1.1; Arrian *Alex.* 1.24.5; 4.21.10. Troops were often quartered in cities and private homes (e.g., Livy 23.18.9-10; 43.7.11; 45.9.1).

115-17 (cf. *CPJ* 2:225-60, §§435-50) — followed by the virtual obliteration of Egyptian Jewry — and the revolt under Hadrian in 132-35 ultimately proved no less devastating (see above). Archaeology has provided some samples of the final moments of horror endured by those within Jerusalem during its fall (especially the burnt house; see Avigad 1980: 120-39; idem 1983a).

Finally, disciples should guard against believing anyone who claims to be Christ, for when the Lord really returns even the sky will declare it (24:23-28; cf. Acts 1:11). When faith is tested, patience may wane (cf., e.g., Gen 16:1-2), but true disciples dare not settle for counterfeit messiahs. The claim "here is Christ" might function as a false prophet's recognition oracle (Aune 1983: 274); "If anyone says to you. . . . Do not believe" may have functioned as a warning formula (cf. p. Taʿan. 2:1, Rabbi Abbahu), and the repetition of the warning not to believe (24:23, 26) makes it emphatic. Although they are sometimes positive (14:29-31; 17:16-17), signs and wonders (24:24) are by themselves inadequate to demonstrate a prophet's authenticity (7:21; 2 Thess 2:9; Deut 13:1-5).[157]

Some later Jewish texts expected the coming of the Messiah in the wilderness, as at the first redemption with Moses (e.g., Passover haggada in Black 1967: 237; Num. Rab. 11:2; Song Rab. 2:9, §3; Pesiq. R. 15:10; cf. Acts 21:38; Jos. *Ant.* 20.189; *War* 2.259-62). The Qumran community likewise illustrates this wilderness expectation, based on Isaiah 40:3 (1QS 8.13-14; F. F. Bruce 1956: 177), though it is quite unlikely that Jesus has them in particular in view (pace Hjerl-Hansen 1959). Whether due to biblical precedent or to the comparative safety of assembling revolutionary followers in the wilderness (also 1 Macc 2:29; 2 Macc 5:27), signs-prophets of first-century Palestine generally gathered in the wilderness (cf. Jos. *War* 2.259, 261-62; cf. Theissen 1978: 48-50). But true disciples of Jesus should not go out to meet them (24:26; cf. 25:6; the warning of ben Zakkai in ARN 31, Bonsirven 1964: 173), for when Jesus himself returned it would not be as another mortal. He would illumine the whole sky, shining like lightning from the east (cf. Ezek 43:2) to the west (cf. eschatological lightning in Gaster's reconstruction of 1QM's prologue in 1976: 399-400, but contrast Vermes 1981: 124).[158] Jesus' "coming" (24:3, 27, 37, 39; 10:23) would be from heaven, and every eye would see him (cf. 2 Thess 1:7; Rev 1:7; 19:11-16).[159]

Although some have taken the "eagles" as an allusion to the eagles on Roman standards, hence as another reference to Jerusalem's fall (Tasker

157. Danger to the elect appears in Sib. Or. 2.169, but this may belong to a Christian interpolation. With the signs Theissen 1991: 266 compares specifically Vespasian's propaganda, which may be one example; cf. Ex 7:11; Jub 48:10; also Sib. Or. 2.165-68 (but this is probably an interpolation).

158. Davies and Allison 1997: 354 rightly emphasize that lightning was widely seen (citing Ps 97:4; Zech 9:14; Ep. Jer. 61; 4Q246 2.1-2; 2 Bar. 53:9) and parallel its use in theophanies or judgments (Ex 19:16; Ps 18:14; 144:6; Philo *Vit. Mos.* 2.56; Ps-Philo 11.4).

159. Schweizer 1983: 260 doubts that contemporary Judaism had a tradition of "a parousia from heaven." Some Jewish tradition did explain the resurrection as uniting the soul from heaven with the body in the earth (e.g., Sifre Deut. 306.28.3; cf. 1 Thess 4:14, 17).

1961: 230), both the biblical language (Ezek 39:17-20; cf. Deut 28:26; 1 Sam 17:44; Ps 79:2; Ezek 32:4) and the context in Luke 17:37 suggest that it refers instead to vultures gathering around the corpses of the wicked slain in judgment.[160] Ancient texts regularly describe the horrible fate of unburied corpses, often after battle, eaten by birds and dogs (Hom. *Il.* 11.395, 454; 22.42-43, 335-36, 353; 24.411; *Od.* 3.258-60; Appian *R.H.* 11.10.64; *C.W.* 1.8.72; Lucan *C.W.* 7.831-35). The clearest source of the wording may be Job 39:30 (Stein 1978: 2; Meier 1980: 286; Gundry 1982: 487), but the eschatological context may also evoke Ezekiel 39:17-20, suggesting that Jesus returns for the final battle (Rev 19:11-21).[161] This is no secretive coming in the wilderness, which false prophets could easily fabricate, but a revelation in glory that the whole world must see (24:29-31; cf. 2 Bar. 29:1). Although the Gospel writers have not revised Jesus' prediction to fit the later situation, his warning may have been helpful in confronting those who already at an earlier date felt that Jesus had returned in some nonphysical sense (cf. 2 Thess 2:2-3; Best 1977: 278).

Jesus' Return (24:29-31)

Cf. Mk 13:24-27; Lk 21:25-28. "Immediately" ties the tribulation of "those days" to the unidentified final tribulation, a tribulation that may follow it by only a few years (as some of Matthew's audience could still have held) or, on a more modern reading, can only be identified as the final one by the fact that the parousia concludes it. Yet the tribulation that dominates much of the chapter is hardly the final word; rather, it is the prelude, the beginning and final "birth pangs" (24:8), of what is to come. Like the day of the Lord in the Old Testament (Amos 5:18-20), however, even Jesus' coming is not good news for everyone.

Assuming that our tentative dating of the Gospel is correct, Matthew's audience already recognizes the accuracy of Jesus' prophecy about the temple's destruction; this should encourage them concerning his prophecies about the future that remain to be fulfilled (assuming a futurist reading of 24:29-31, which again is rejected by a significant stream of scholarship). Ancient documents often would predict events without narrating them, leaving the reader to trust a narra-

160. If Aelian is a reliable guide to a more widespread perspective, eagles were known not to eat prey that they had not killed (*Animals* 2.39; cf. Babrius 137.1-2; they appear positively in Pesiq. R. 23/24:2), whereas vultures were known for consuming carcasses (Aelian *Animals* 2.46; 10.22); some even called vultures "living tombs" (Longinus *Sublime* 3.2). The association of carrion birds with carcasses may have been almost proverbial (see citations in Davies and Allison 1997: 355, including Cornutus *Natura Deorum* 21; Lucian *Navig.* 1).

161. Certainly in context this is not carnage merely during the tribulation (pace Strombeck 1982: 71). The saying could, however, simply declare that Jesus' coming will be as obvious as vultures gathered around corpses (Meier 1980: 286; Gundry 1982: 486-87).

tor who has proved reliable and to accept the fulfillment of such events (e.g., Hom. *Il.* 21.110; 23.80-81; *Od.* 23.266-84).[162]

First, the effects of Jesus' revelation will be cosmic and obvious (24:29). As in some Jewish eschatological texts (cf. Dodd 1980: 83), the Lord himself would intervene to culminate history. One could argue that these signs refer only to those surrounding Jerusalem's destruction, in which Jesus "comes" (cf. Rev 2:16; 3:3) in judgment. Greek and Roman writers recognized heavenly signs as portents of major changes (e.g., Diod. Sic. 1.53.8; Tac. *Ann.* 14.22; Suet. *Nero* 36; Paus. 10.23.1-2; Dio Cassius *R.H.* 56.29.3-6; 57.4.4; Artem. *Oneir.* 2.36; Herodian 1.14.1; cf. Dupont 1992: 185-86), as do Jewish writers (e.g., Jos. *War* 3.404 and Josephus 1982: 242n.404b; LCL 9:124-25), including portents of the end (e.g., 1 Enoch 91:16; 102:2-3; Sib. Or. 1.200-202; 3.82, 800-804; 5.512-31; 8.190-93, 204-5; 4 Ezra 5:4-5; 7:38-42; Test. Mos. 10.5).

More significantly, such signs were reported to have heralded Jerusalem's destruction (Jos. *War* 6.288-310; followed by Tac. *Hist.* 5.13),[163] though these might stem from a tradition circulated by the Flavian emperors (see Saulnier 1989). Moreover, some Jewish texts speak of other historic events in similarly cosmic terms (Jer 4:20-28; Sib. Or. 3.80-83; 4.57-60; cf. Ps 18:7-15 in context; exaggerated language for the Sinai theophany in Ps 68:8; Ps-Philo 11:5; 23:10; cf. Sib. Or. 3.635-56; Petron. *Sat.* 124), so it is possible that Jesus here merely paints Jerusalem's catastrophe in cosmic terms (Borg 1984: 217; France 1985: 333).[164] Nevertheless, biblical (Is 13:10; 24:23; Ezek 32:7-8; Joel 3:14; Zech 14:6) and later Jewish texts (Sib. Or. 2.34-38, if pre-Christian; Rev 6:13), including rabbinic texts (Davies 1980: 330), also speak of heavenly signs heralding what most of Jesus' contemporaries would read as the end; a probably second-century-B.C. Diaspora text lists various signs in heaven and on earth, including warfare in the heavens, as "a very clear sign" (Sib. Or. 3.796-808).[165] This pas-

162. In other cases an apparently unfinished ending may be acceptable because the end is implied; the *Iliad* concludes with Hector's burial (*Il.* 24), but because he was Troy's "last" defender (*Il.* 6.403; 22.506-7) the tragic fall of Troy is implied.

163. Significantly, reports of terrestrial portents that frightened Rome (Dio Cassius *R.H.* 48.43.4-6; 54.19.7) sometimes emphasize disasters to sanctuaries (Dio Cassius *R.H.* 48.43.4; 54.19.7; Appian *C.W.* 1.9.83; Livy 26.23.4; 27.11.2). Some of the portent reports seem incredible (e.g., Dion. Hal. 4.2.1; also 10.2.2-4, though the phenomenon in 10.2.4 might simply be volcanic ash).

164. In Gen 1:14 the sun, moon, and stars themselves are for "signs," though given Deut 13, the Israelite writer undoubtedly did not intend this in an astrological sense. Ancient peoples generally thought gods (Cic. *De Re Publ.* 6.15.15; *De Nat. Deor.* 2.15.39-40; Sen. *De Benef.* 4.23.4; cf. 1 Enoch 80:7-8; Lev. Rab. 31:9; Ps-Phocyl. 71:75) or angels (Philo *Plant.* 12, 14; 1QM 10.11-12; 2 Bar. 51:10; 2 Enoch 4:1; 29:3A; 3 Enoch 46:1; Pesiq. Rab Kah. 1:3; Exod. Rab. 15:6) stood behind celestial powers (cf. demons in Test. Sol. 2:2; 4:6; 5:4; 6:7; 7:6; 8:4; 14:3; ch. 18; links with souls in Plato *Timaeus* 41E; Philo *Gig.* 7-8; perhaps 4 Macc 17:5); Meier thus suggests that 24:29 reflects Christ's cosmic victory over all other spiritual powers (1980: 287; cf. Barrett 1966: 73; Hurtado 1983: 210, 213; Gundry 1982: 487; Eph 1:21; 1 Pet 3:22); on "shaken," cf. Heb 12:27.

165. McCasland 1932: 335 was so impressed with Jewish parallels that he used them to argue for the tradition's antiquity ("within five years after Jesus died"). Herodian reports that some claimed to see the local deity in the sky, and that it might be credible though it may be imagination (8.3.8-9).

sage cites explicitly Isaiah's language (Is 13:10; 34:4, as in Mk 13:24-25). In conjunction with the gathering of the "elect" (22:14; 24:22, 31), this coming most naturally refers to the end of the age (as in Rev 6:12-17).[166] For darkness specifically, see comment on 27:45.

Second, the nations will respond to his coming with terror (24:30). Although such terror appears as a signal of the end in some texts (2 Bar. 25:3; 70:2; cf. Lk 21:26), it naturally fits the context of imminent judgment before an all-powerful executor of divine justice.[167] The nations have good reason to fear. When applied to a king or other prominent dignitary, the term for Jesus' coming *(parousia)* was a quasitechnical expression that implied considerable demands for preparation on the part of the local populace (Ladd 1967: 92; Kreitzer 1989; Deissmann 1978: 368-70; Best 1977: 349-54; for preparation, cf., e.g., Ex. Rab. 29:6).[168] In reference to deities, hellenistic usage applied the term to a theophany (Witherington 1992: 150-51, adapting Kilpatrick 1945; Grayston 1984: 95; cf. Test. Judah 22:2; Test. Abr. 13 A; Test. Job 43:14/11; similarly 1 Enoch 91:7; the Messiah in 2 Bar. 30:1; Old Testament language in Glasson 1963b: 1-7, 177-83).

Here the "sign" may be identified with the Son of Man's appearing itself, referring to Jesus coming in glory (16:27; Meier 1980: 287; Gundry 1982: 488); others suggest an allusion to the "standard" (translated *sēmeion,* "sign," in the LXX) signifying God gathering his people (Is 11:12; 49:22). France 1985: 344-45 mentions both views and concludes that in view of the "apocalyptic symbolism" it is difficult to decide; perhaps the term alludes to the latter and its content to the former.[169] That the Son of Man has authority to dispatch "his" angels to gather "his" elect (24:31; Mk 13:27) portrays Jesus as divine (Meier 1980: 288). (Indeed, early Christian parousia texts regularly reapply to Jesus Jewish eschato-

166. This context implies no secretive coming, as in some popular current North American eschatology (pace Strombeck 1982: 151-53); as Leon Morris warns, "It is difficult to see how he could more plainly describe something that is open and public" (Morris 1959: 145).

167. In some texts, it can be too late to repent (1 Enoch 50:3-4).

168. This is especially true when writers conjoin the term with another quasitechnical expression *apantēsis,* as in 1 Thess 4:17; see Milligan 1908: 62; F. F. Bruce 1963: 68-69; idem 1977a: 527n.26; idem 1982: 102; Best 1977: 199; Marshall 1983: 131; cf. Payne 1962: 68; Jdt 7:15; Pesiq. R. 51:8. Like other NT terms for Jesus' coming, this one is applied "indiscriminately for what [pretribulationists] regard as the two phases of Jesus' return," more likely than not suggesting that the NT picture, like the historic Christian picture till 1830, was of only one return of Jesus, at the very end of the age (Gundry 1973: 158; see also Ladd 1956: 61-70; Katterjohn 1976: 43; pace Strombeck 1982: 147-48, who merely presupposes what he hopes to prove). Correctly noting that only Matthew among the Gospels employs the word *parousia,* Glasson implies that this represents Matthean redaction in an apocalypticizing direction (1963b: 66-69); but whether Matthew here translates pre-Markan tradition or simply applies Pauline language, the eschatological elements of Mark and Q clearly precede Matthew's redaction. The same language appears in the early second-century 2 Bar. 29:3 (revealed); 30:1 *(parousia).*

169. Sib. Or. 12.196-97 speaks of the sign of the great God appearing from heaven, but as a third-century-A.D. text it may include Christian influence. Gundry 1982: 488 renders "sign" here as "ensign," conjoined with the war trumpet of 24:31. Early Christian identification of this "sign" as the cross (Apoc. Pet. 1; Ep. Apost. 16) was speculative (so also Hagner 1995: 713-14).

logical imagery concerning God — Robinson 1979: 140, following Glasson 1962: 162-79.)

As in Mark 13:26, the language of seeing the Son of Man coming with the clouds (presumably of God's glory; cf. 1QM 12.9) alludes to Dan 7:13,[170] but Matthew includes an additional allusion to Zech 12:10, in which the nations mourn (24:30). Other early Christian writers connect these texts in Daniel and Zechariah (Rev 1:7), perhaps suggesting that Matthew here echoes authentic Jesus tradition rather than simply redacting Mark without such tradition; cf. Bauckham 1993: 319-21.[171] (Differences of Greek wording may suggest independent translations of a prior Semitic tradition; cf. Lindars 1961: 123 on the Johannine wording.) But whereas Revelation might apply the Zechariah text, according to its context, to Israel (Rev 1:7; Zech 12:10-14), Matthew generalizes the "tribes" to apply to all nations (pace Fenton 1977: 389). Given the reference to mourning, one may doubt whether Matthew would believe repentance still possible at the final appearing of Christ (as in 1 Enoch 50:2-5; some other Jews believed repentance impossible at the judgment, as in b. ʿAbod. Zar. 3a). The apppearance of "great glory" (24:30) is also eschatological (Sib. Or. 3.282; cf., e.g., Is 40:5; 60:1-2; 2 Thess 1:9).

Finally, Jesus' followers will ultimately be delivered (24:31). Paul likewise observes that deliverance from tribulation in the present age arrives when Jesus comes as king and judges the wicked (2 Thess 1:6-7). The "elect" here can mean only Jesus' community, as in this eschatological tradition (2 Thess 2:13) and usually in early Christian texts (Mt 22:14; Rom 8:33; Col 3:12; 2 Tim 2:10; Tit 1:1; 1 Pet 1:1; 2:9);[172] Paul applies this "gathering" to followers of Jesus (2 Thess 2:1;[173] 1 Thess 4:15-17; cf. also Did. 10.5; 16.6-7).[174] "From one end of heaven to the other" means the whole earth (Mk 13:27; cf. Is 11:12; 1 Enoch 57:2), figuratively viewed, as was common in ancient Mediterranean thought, as a circle surrounded by the dome of heaven (cf. references in Gundry 1982: 489;

170. Clouds are a recurrent motif in early Christian parousia language (Acts 1:9, 11; 1 Thess 4:17; Rev 1:7; 11:12; 14:14; see Rissi 1966: 103n.168); if, as is likely, Paul alludes to Daniel by way of Jesus here, Paul places Jesus' coming for the saints at the end of the tribulation of this age (Mt 24:29-30; 1 Thess 4:17). In a late rabbinic tradition about the eschatological time, clouds would carry Israelites to Jerusalem every Sabbath (Pesiq. R. 1:3); but Matthew's source is primarily Daniel. A king coming in "glory" can imply his royal splendor (1 Macc 11:6).

171. Higgins 1963: 380 thinks Matthew adapted a Christian apocalyptic source and cites (382) Ep. Apost. 16; Did. 16.6; Gos. Pet. 10.39-42; and Apoc. Pet. to argue that the "sign of the Son of Man" is the cross. This common tradition about the cross as the sign may, however, be based on late first-century inference first found in the Didache.

172. So, e.g., Katterjohn 1976: 20; Sandmel 1978a: 38. Walvoord 1971a is forced to argue that the church is removed before the tribulation of 24:15-28, although no such event is mentioned here (nor explicitly mentioned anywhere else in the NT or other Christian literature before 1830).

173. The Granville Sharpe rule links the "gathering" and parousia (Waterman 1975: 112; Best 1977: 274).

174. Patte 1987: 338 suggests that this gathering reverses the scattering of 24:16-20; if his suggestion is correct, it may echo Pentateuchal judgment language about scattering and the Deuteronomic promise of restoration.

also Hom. *Od.* 3.1; 19.434; Arist. *Heavens* 2.4, 286b 10).[175] In biblical and Jewish tradition, the remnant of Israel was "chosen" and would be "gathered" at the end time (e.g., Is 11:12; 43:5; 49:5; 56:8; Pss. Sol. 8:28; 11:2-5; 17:26; 4 Ezra 13:39-40; 4 Bar. 3:11; Test. Asher 7:7; cf. Jesus' long-range desire for Israel in Mt 23:37);[176] but early Christian texts regularly apply the image of Israel's remnant to the church, comprised of all those in covenant relationship with God in Christ, who thereby share in Israel's messianic hope (cf. "gathering" of believers in Jesus in 2 Thess 2:1; Did. 9.4). The gathering here is probably understood as "a rapture to heaven" as in 1 Thess 4:17, but employing language from Jewish eschatology (Davies and Allison 1997: 364). Further, Jesus has been addressing his followers throughout the rest of the discourse (see Payne 1962: 55).

The figure of the trumpet is wholly appropriate, and is one feature of pre-Matthean tradition noted by Matthew but cited earlier by Paul (1 Thess 4:17), who refers to the "last trumpet" at the resurrection of the righteous (1 Cor 15:52) when the final enemy, death, is subdued (1 Cor 15:24-26; recalled in Gk. Ezra 4:36). Biblical tradition employed the trumpet for proclamation, for example, of kingship (2 Kings 9:13), for celebration of triumph (cf. Josh 6:20; for worship in 1 Esdr 5:59, 62, 64-65; 4Q493, Baumgarten 1987; p. Rosh Hash. 4:8, §1), but especially for assembling God's people (e.g., Num 10:1-10; cf. angels in Apoc. Mos. 22:1-3; 37:1), also at the eschatological time (Is 27:12-13; cf. Ps. Sol. 11:1-4; Pesiq. R. 40:7; Goodenough 1954: 4:194).

Most often trumpets assembled God's people for war or alerted them to an attack (e.g., Num 10:9; Josh 6:20; Judg 3:27; 7:20; Is 18:3; Jer 4:19; Ezek 33:3-6; Joel 2:1; Zeph 1:16; Jos. *Ant.* 3.291-94; 4 Bar. 4:2-3); the language could also apply to the coming of God as a triumphant warrior (Zech 9:14). An early commentator on the Qumran texts opined that its portrait of military use of trumpets must stem from the war of 66-70 (Driver 1965: 585), but this position is untenable: the use of trumpets in war figures heavily in all periods throughout the ancient Mediterranean (see especially Maccabean citations in Avi-Yonah 1952: 3, on 1QM 3). Jewish and other armies continued to use trumpets for war (calls to advance, recalling the troops, etc.) in the hellenistic and Roman periods (e.g., 1 Macc 5:31-33; Philo *Spec. Leg.* 2.190; Jos. *War* 3.89-91; 3.265; 5.47; Dion. Hal. 7.59.5; Tac. *Ann.* 1.68; Soph. *Ajax* 291; Char. *Chaer.* 8.2.6; Sen. *Dial.* 4.2.4; Livy 24.46.3; Appian *R.H.* 6.9.52; Lucan *C.W.* 4.750; Arrian *Alex.* 6.3.3; Babrius 76.12; Avianus *Fable* 39.7-16). Significantly for the tradition our text shares

175. For various views on the world's shape, see, e.g., Plut. *fr.* 179 in Euseb. *P.E.* 1.7.16; Diog. Laert. 9.9.57 (perhaps because the sphere was a perfect shape); p. 'Abod. Zar. 3:1, §3. The "four winds" represent the extremities of the four directions; see, e.g., Ezek 5:10; 12:14; 17:21; cf. Deissmann 1923: 248; 1 Enoch 18:2-5; 34:2–36:2; 76:4; Test. Asher 7:2/3.

176. For the *eschatological* elect, see 1 Enoch 1:2. Predestination in its traditional corporate Jewish sense did not raise the question of free will, but in a hellenistic context of cosmic fatalism (cf. Jos. *Ant.* 13.172-73), especially dominant in late antiquity (see comment on 10:29-31), Jewish and Christian apologists had to argue for a sufficient degree of free will to allow moral responsibility (Cook 1981: 151-52, 156).

with 1 Thess 4:16, such a trumpet often occurred with a shout (Virg. *Aen.* 9.503-4; Jos. *War* 3.265; Tac. *Ann.* 1.68; cf. further references in Gaster 1976: 387), or a very shrill and terrifying battle shout could sound like a trumpet (Hom. *Il.* 18.219). In eschatological contexts these images could symbolize the final battle (1QM 8.9-12; cf. 4 Ezra 6:23-25; Knibb 1979: 151; Sib. Or. 4.173-76).[177] Early Jewish texts continue to apply the trumpet image to eschatological salvation, especially in the regularly recited tenth benediction of the Shemoneh Esreh (e.g., in Davies 1980: 82; Bonsirven 1964: 132).[178]

The Day Nor the Hour (24:32-44)

For Mt 24:32-36, cf. Mk 13:28-32; Lk 21:29-33; for Mt 24:37-44, cf. Lk 17:26-36; 12:39-40. Balancing the seven (or eight) parables that teach the presence of the kingdom in Matthew 13, the central discourse, Matthew includes seven parables about Jesus' future coming in 24:32–25:46 (Jeremias 1972: 92-93).

First, the temple's desolation in the first generation constitutes the final visible prerequisite for the kingdom before the cosmic signs of Jesus' return (24:32-35). Because fig trees, unlike most trees in Palestine, lost their leaves seasonally, fruit on fig trees indicated the season; fig trees also produced leaves before other plants like vines (Jeremias 1971: 106; Meier 1980: 288; Harrington 1982: 97; Song 2:13; cf. Hab 3:17; 1 Enoch 2:1–5:3).[179] Given the agrarian character of ancient Israel, the choice of the image of a tree naturally evoked rich biblical imagery (rabbis also applied the fig tree image diversely, e.g., for Torah — b. 'Erub. 54ab; for Abraham — b. Yebam. 63a; Gen. Rab. 53:3; Pesiq.

177. "Shout" appears in various contexts (Lightfoot 67-68), but conjoined with the trumpet may well be a military command (so also Walvoord 1967: 65). The shout was sometimes a war signal (e.g., Dion. Hal. 5.42.3; cf. 5.53.4; Hom. *Il.* 11.15), but troops could also respond to trumpets with battle shouts (Dion. Hal. 6.10.2), employ unified battle shouts when charging to terrify their foes (Appian *R.H.* 4.1.1; 4.8; 7.2.11), shout victory (Livy 36.24.6; Josh 6:5), or shout acclamations for a hero (Dion. Hal. 6.94.2). From the earliest Greek tradition, war cries were typical for exhorting one's side and terrifying the other (Hom. *Il.* 8.92; 11.10-11; 14.146-52; 17.334; Eurip. *Suppliants* 701; Arrian *Alex.* 7.3.6), and "good at the war cry" served as an epithet for strong warriors like Menelaus (Hom. *Il.* 6.37; 10.36, 60; 13.581, 593; 17.237, 656; *Od.* 3.311; 4.307, 609; 15.14, 57, 92; 17.120), Diomedes (Hom. *Il.* 5.114, 596; 6.12, 122, 212; 7.399; 8.91, 145; 9.31, 696; 10.241, 283; 14.109), Hector (Hom. *Il.* 15.671), and others (Hom. *Il.* 24.250). Other instruments were occasionally added to trumpets (Aul. Gel. 1.11).

178. Rissi 1966: 46 cites also Gk. Ezra 4:36 and Samaritan eschatology, but extant texts for both are late and the former probably betrays Christian influence; but for other texts, see Friedrich 1971: 84 (who notes their use in war, worship and coronation, 78-85). The Shemoneh Esreh probably echoes biblical imagery (Mendecki 1983); besides the Shemoneh Esreh Klausner cites later rabbinic texts in which the trumpet signals the gathering of Israel or the resurrection of the dead (1979a: 538-39; cf. Gaster 1976: 436).

179. Cf. also Lachs 1987: 386; Vermes 1993: 99, who tentatively note the possibility of a Semitic pun similar to that between "summer (fruit)" and "end" in Amos 8:2. On planting fig trees, see Columella *Trees* 21.1-2.

R. 42:5; cf. 1QapGen 19.14-23). Some texts compare Israel to a fig tree or other trees (e.g., Hos 9:10; Song Rab. 7:5, §3; Pesiq. R. 15:11), but many either denounce Israel's failure to surrender her fruit to the Lord who owns her (Is 5:1-7; Jer 24:1-10; Hos 10:1, 4, 11-13) — fruitlessness being catastrophic to an agrarian culture (e.g., Deut 28:18; Hab 3:17) — or speak of Israel's fruitfulness in the time of restoration (cf., e.g., Ezek 36:8; Hos 14:6-8; b. Sanh. 98a).[180] Unwilling to offer the vineyard's rightful fruit to its owner (Mt 21:34), the Jewish leaders were fruitless trees meriting destruction (3:8; 12:33).[181] The temple establishment were like fig trees with the veneer of maturity yet without fruit (21:19; cf. Mk 11:12-25).

Whereas the signs Luke mentions mean that the kingdom is near (Lk 21:31; cf. 1 Clem. 23), "these things" in Matthew 24 (cf. 24:2) apply to the desolation of the temple to occur within that generation (24:34).[182] Though some (mentioned in Cullmann 1956a: 151; Mattill 1979a: 97; cf. Bonsirven 1964: 58) wish to take "generation" *(genea)* as "race" (cf. the distinct *genos* in 2 Macc 8:9; Jdt 9:14; 11:10), 23:35-36 leave no doubt that Jesus uses the term as normally (e.g., Jer 7:29) and as elsewhere in Matthew refers to the climactic "generation." Because Jesus' warning of judgment must precede A.D. 70 (see comment on 21:12; 24:2), it is interesting that Jerusalem fell about forty years after Jesus' warning (pace Kidder 1983, who thinks the "generation" follows 70).[183] Once

180. On the vine in the temple, see Jos. *War* 5.211; Tac. *Hist.* 5.5. Texts compare Israel, Jerusalem, or the covenant community to a vineyard (3 Bar. 1:2; Mek. Pisha 1.162; Pesiq. Rab Kah. 16:9; Ex. Rab. 30:17; 34:3; Song Rab. 7:13, §1), a vine (Ps 80:9; 4 Ezra 5:23; 2 Bar. 39:7; Ps-Philo 12:8-9; 23:12; 28:4; b. Ḥul. 92a; Gen. Rab. 88:5; 98:9; Ex. Rab. 44:1; Num. Rab. 8:9), trees in general (Pesiq. Rab Kah. 15:5; Lev. Rab. 30:12; often including vines and fig trees — Gen. Rab. 53:3; Esth. Rab. 9:2), or plants in general (Jub. 1:16; 36:6; 1QS 8.5; 9.8; CD 1.7; see also Fujita 1976; Mussner 1960); cf. the church in Jn 15:1; Rom 11:16-24; 1 Cor 3:6-15; Herm. 3.8. Although the grape cluster features on Jewish coins especially from the Bar Kochba period (Porton 1976), Maccabean coins may portray Israel as a plant (Wirgin 1965: 22-26, despite the uncertain LXX support); cf. artistic tree symbolism in Leon 1960: 146; Goodenough 1953-68: 7:87-134.

181. Those who play down the future aspect in Jesus' teaching naturally apply the original point of this parable to Jesus' earthly ministry (Argyle 1963: 185); but in either case the implied harvest imagery is eschatological (cf. Jeremias 1972: 119). (Historic fig trees, like anything else, could provide noneschatological portents in Roman settings — Tac. *Ann.* 13.58 — but Jesus here applies the image figuratively.) The Jewish tradition applying the fig tree's leaves to seven years of tribulation preceding Messiah's coming might be helpful but is too isolated and late (Song Rab. 2:13); similarly, Rev 6:13 is simply a general image and unrelated to this allusion.

182. There is no need to doubt the prediction's authenticity; if Jesus spoke of the temple's destruction (see comment on 24:2-3), he could also have specified a time (Witherington 1992: 43-44 on Mk 13:30), as did some of his contemporaries, albeit less accurately. Because many early Christians probably took this as a prediction of his return, composing such a prediction after 70 would have complicated matters. Many (Carson 1984b: 507; Blomberg 1992a: 357) argue that the "generation" refers to the time in which all the prerequisites for Christ's return (cf. 24:5-28) were fulfilled; on its Markan and Matthean levels it must include at least the temple's demise.

183. Forty years also appears as an early estimate of the duration of the messianic woes — CD (MS B, 2.15); 1QM 2.6-10; 4QPs 1.7 on Ps 37:10; Pryke 1969: 56; Gaston 1970: 466-67. Cf. also b. Sanh. 99a; Pesiq. R. 1:7, but the rabbis held this view only as one among many estimates (see, e.g., Mek. Amalek 2.189-90, Laut. 2.161).

God has judged the fruitless authorities who dominate the temple, Jesus' return is potentially so imminent ("has drawn near," as in 4:17; 21:34) that he can be described as "at the door" (25:10; Jas 5:9; in a noneschatological sense, cf. Rev 3:20). In declaring that the whole cosmic order would ultimately vanish but his own words would not pass away (24:35), Jesus ranks his words with God's words through the prophets (Zech 1:5-6; Mt 5:18).

Second, the day will catch most people unawares (24:36-44). The "day" in this passage is presumably the day of the Lord (as in 1 Thess 5:2; 2 Pet 3:10; cf. Cullmann 1950: 43).[184] Such a warning prevents those who are suffering from building up undue expectations of the time that would set them up for exploitation (24:23-27); this sort of warning was especially critical in view of the tendency of many of Jesus' contemporaries to predict signs of the end (cf. comment on 24:6-8). Some Jewish futurists set dates (see, e.g., Bonsirven 1964: 178; Morris 1972: 46-47; cf. Test. Abr. 7B; Gk. Ezra 3:3-4), eliciting a strong reaction among the more conservative rabbis (e.g., b. Pesaḥ. 54b, bar.; Sanh. 97a; Num. Rab. 5:6; see Moore 1974: 2:231; Daube 1973: 289-90; cf. 2 Bar. 21:8). Although some rabbis thought that God revealed all things to his angels, rabbis generally doubted that angels knew the time of Israel's deliverance (b. Sanh. 99a; Blau and Kohler 1901: 586), and angels were rarely viewed as omniscient (4 Ezra 4:52).

Jesus here claims that no one knows the day nor the hour, not even himself (24:36), and this saying is surely authentic (pace Bultmann 1968: 159; Vermes 1993: 160).[185] Especially because Scripture already attested that the Lord knows the time (Zech 14:7), the early church would hardly have created a saying limiting divine omniscience to the Father;[186] no circle of first-century Christianity securely known to us could have afforded such a christological concession. Further, had early Christians simply needed a saying to address the delay of the parousia, they would more naturally have created a claim that Jesus denied the imminence of the parousia, not that he was ignorant of its timing (Witherington 1990: 229-30). Because the saying is authentic, however, it incidentally verifies the view that Jesus called himself the Son of God in a distinctive sense, and as-

184. For the possibility that Paul introduced "day of the Lord" here, see Gundry 1987; for the sense of "day of the Lord" in Paul, see Ladd 1974b: 364, 555 (it cannot include the tribulation, pace Walvoord 1967: 81, 117; idem 1972: 160-63; Strombeck 1982: 46-54, which contradict 2 Thess 2:1-4; see F. F. Bruce 1982: 163). But the expression appears in the OT, and the parallel in 2 Pet 3:10 probably suggests that the whole phrase goes back to Jesus or to an early and pervasive midrash on his teaching (though cf. 2 Pet 3:15-16).

185. Vermes 1993: 160 doubts that Jesus believed the Father would hide anything from him; but is it not less likely that the *church* believed he would? Further, his argument that God consults rather than withholds information from his angels (ibid. n. 9) is too sweeping; in Jewish literature God did not reveal everything (including the time of the end) even to them. Thus most accept the verse's point, though some reject its wording (Dunn 1975: 34-35; cf. Barrett 1967: 25).

186. So also Wenham 1977: 46; Gundry 1982: 218, 492; Stanton 1995a: 153; cf. Glasson 1963b: 93.

signs himself a role among or above the angels, that is, similar to divine Wisdom (Witherington 1990: 232).[187]

Like the flood,[188] the Son of Man's coming (Dan 7:13-14) would arrive as sudden and unexpected judgment, without explicit warning (24:37-39; cf. Lk 17:26-27). Jesus' followers might recognize the completion of requisite signs (cf. 1 Thess 5:4-6), but for outsiders events would continue as business-as-usual. The point of the comparison is unexpectedness as well as sudden destruction (Argyle 1963: 186; cf. 1 Thess 5:2-3), a comparison probably followed by 2 Peter (3:5-7; cf. Justin *Dial.* 138).[189] This passage echoes the damnable folly of outsiders repeated throughout the Gospel tradition in general and Matthew in particular (e.g., 13:19; 15:10): they did not understand (24:27, 39). "Eating and drinking" could imply sinful revelry (e.g., 24:49; Lam. Rab., Proem 17),[190] but more than likely it simply indicates life as usual. Two men might be in the field working (cf. 24:18), but only one would be "taken" (24:40). The image of "grinding" together with another woman, presumably at a handmill (24:41; this is the normal sense of the earlier textual reading; further, the larger community mill required the strength of a mule or some other work animal — see comment on 18:6), would be equally familiar, depicting the task of most housewives (m. Giṭ. 5:9).[191] Because Galilean families typically shared both a common courtyard and a common millstone there with other families (Horsley 1995: 192), this picture is not at all surprising.[192] If Je-

187. Perrin 1976: 86 relates the absolute use of "Son" here to the same sayings-source behind Mt 11:25-27/Lk 10:21-22.

188. Matthew alludes to Gen 6–9, which would have been clear to his ideal audience, though other Mediterranean peoples had flood traditions (Diod. Sic. 1.10.4). Noah's flood was "wrath" *(orgē)* in Jos. *Ant.* 1.98; see 1 Thess 1:10; 5:9. Noah proclaimed repentance (Sib. Or. 1.129, 168; 2 Pet 2:5), but his generation was extremely wicked (Sib. Or. 1.171-72; Gen. Rab. 26:5; Urbach 1979: 1:28).

189. Here Luke probably retains a longer Q tradition that includes Lot (Lk 17:26-29); Jewish traditions sometimes connect the generations of Noah and Lot, in view of their similar judgments (e.g., 2 Pet 2:5-7; m. Sanh. 10:3; Mek. Bahodesh 10.20ff., Laut. 2.278; b. B. Meṣ. 49a; Pesiq. Rab Kah. Sup. 4:1; Gen. Rab. 27:3; 49:5), though they also connected one or the other with, e.g., Babel (m. B. Meṣ. 4:2; Sanh. 10:3; cf. Noah and Jonah in 1 Clem. 7). Luke's construction may be more artful (cf. Tannehill 1975: 121-22; I am less persuaded by the chiasmus Aune 1983: 183 finds here); although Luke may preserve the original intention (Tannehill 1975: 122), he may have polished the tradition more here (Gundry 1982: 493; pagans may have recalled the old Greek story preserved, e.g., in Virg. *Georg.* 4.490-91; Ovid *Metam.* 10.50-52, when hearing the looking back implied in Lk 17:32 from Gen 19:26).

190. Cf. Malina and Rohrbaugh 1992: 147, who think "be merry" in "eat, drink and be merry" is euphemistic for sexual relations. "Giving in marriage" (v. 38) refers to the father's role (abolished in the end time; see comment on 22:30). Later rabbis viewed the evil impulse as necessary to allow marriage (e.g., Qoh. Rab. 3:11, §3).

191. Cf. the interpretation of this Gospel passage in Apoc. Zeph. 2.2-4; pace Argyle 1963: 186 (who limits it to a slave girl). Women, including servant women, typically worked at mills (Hom. *Od.* 7.104; 20.105-10) or grinding flour (Goodman 1983: 761).

192. Thus while the women here could be sisters or mother and daughter (so Carson 1984b: 509), they need not be; in Middle Eastern villages, women's daily interaction with one another traditionally tended to be as close as kinship bonds (Eickelman 1989: 163).

sus means "taken in judgment" (Jer 6:11; cf. Jer 8:13 MT; Ps. Sol. 13:11), the taking parallels the different expression in 24:39, where the flood "took" the wicked away (see Lk 17:34-37; contrast Sir 44:16-17).

"Watch" does not mean "look for" or "anticipate immediately," but borrows the image of a night watchman at his post (24:42; 25:13; Ladd 1974b: 208):[193] the disciple must remain prepared for his Lord's coming, remaining alert and awake at his post (26:38, 40-41, 43-46; Did. 16.1).[194] That the time of Jesus' coming is unknown does not therefore preclude that some signs mentioned earlier in the passage will precede it (cf. Gundry 1982: 491-92; Katterjohn 1976: 118-19), any more than such ideas were incompatible in various expressions of Jewish eschatology (cf., e.g., Bonsirven 1964: 53). In one later eschatological tradition, because the final signs are mixed together the earth dwellers will not understand that the end is at hand (2 Bar. 27:15), and will live at peace because they do not recognize the imminence of judgment (2 Bar. 48:32).

The image of a householder's (in parables, e.g., 13:52) being unprepared for a nocturnal thief would catch the attention of uncomfortable homeowners (burglary was common; see, e.g., Lewis 1983: 77; Sib. Or. 3.380); one could not predict the coming of a thief.[195] Although the image is a general one (thieves preferred night and mist; see, e.g., Hom. *Il.* 3.10-11; Phaedrus 1.23.3-4; Job 24:14), the saying may employ the image of a nocturnal thief as divine judgment developed from the biblical prophets (Jer 49:9; Obad 4-6; cf. Joel 2:9). Although Mark does not explicitly report this saying of Jesus (Mt 24:43), it is unquestionably pre-Matthean and came to figure prominently in early

193. In the city of Rome, Romans also knew roving night patrolmen, the *cohortes vigilum* (Dio Cassius *R.H.* 55.26.4-5); see more fully Clarke 1994: 472-73. But Jesus' image more likely presupposes stationary watchmen; like other Mediterranean cultures (cf. Jos. *Ant.* 3.50; Hom. *Il.* 10.159, 164), the Romans respected soldiers who could resist sleep (Dio Cassius *R.H.* 73.3-5; Diod. Sic. 38/39.9.1). The vigilance of sentinels was essential (e.g., Livy 24.28.2; 24.37.4), for entire armies could be destroyed through their failure to watch adequately (Hom. *Il.* 10.309-12, 416-21; Virg. *Aen.* 9.314-66, 375-45; Diod. Sic. 3.55.1; 19.95.5-6; Dion. Hal. 5.47.1; 7.11.2-3; 9.34.4; Livy 24.46.4; 36.23.10–36.24.6; 44.33.8-9; Sall. *Jug.* 58.1; Jos. *Life* 405); warfare typically ended at night (Hom. *Il.* 2.387; 7.282; 8.529-30; 11.209; 14.259-61; Arrian *Alex.* 1.19.2), making night attacks all the more unexpected and deadly (Hom. *Il.* 10.100-101; Arrian *Alex.* 1.4.1).

194. Jeremias 1972: 48n.96 thinks that v. 42 comes from the parable of the doorkeeper (Mk 13:35). See the more detailed analysis of D. Wenham 1984b: 17, 51-52, 96, on the pre-Synoptic source behind both (as well as much of the other material); he thinks Matthew retains only the closing exhortation, Mark an abbreviated form of the parable, and Luke most of the original (ibid., 48-49).

195. Cf. perhaps Apollo's vengeful coming "like the night" (Hom. *Il.* 1.47), though this may refer to nightfall. Manson suggests that "digging through" the house indicates breaking in some other way than through the door (Manson 1979: 116; Gundry 1982: 495), but this would hardly be a quiet invasion even through mudbrick (as opposed to stone) walls (cf. comment on 6:19); perhaps the thief digs beneath, but in any case, a householder who slept through this was neglectful indeed! If crime was half as abundant in Jewish Palestine as in Egypt's villages, where we have fuller evidence (see Lewis 1983: 77, 123), it was quite abundant. Pace Bultmann, Taylor 1935: 108 contends that since as late as Rev 16:15 the utterances of Christian prophets were *distinguished* from the historical Jesus rather than read back into his logia, the saying is authentic.

Christian discussion of the end time (1 Thess 5:2, 4; 2 Pet 3:10; Rev 3:3; 16:15).[196]

Christ's Servants Judged (24:45-51)

Cf. Lk 12:41-46. After Jesus exhorts the disciples to "watch," to stay awake, he illustrates what he means. One stays alert by living in such a manner that one would have no cause for shame if one's master did come unannounced, since he may in fact do so. Paul may echo the warning against living an unexpectant, self-serving life here (cf. 1 Thess 5:3-9).[197]

First, to whom much is given, from that one much is required. The community's ministers have special responsibilities to serve others as well as special standards (Lk 12:41-42; cf. Hos 4:6-9; Jas 3:1; 1 Pet 5:1-4). This parable addresses the teachers, the Matthean community's leaders, showing that the assault on hypocritical leaders in Israel in Matthew 23 is also applicable to those in the church at the second coming, for they would prove equally unprepared (cf. 25:14-30; Jas 3:1; cf. Meier 1980: 293-94; Gundry 1982: 497).[198]

Here the ruling servant exploits the resources meant for others in gluttony and drunkenness (24:49; cf. the demand for sobriety in 1 Thess 5:6-7; Lk 21:34), a biblical image (Is 28:7-8; 29:9-10; 56:10-12). Such banqueting, which sometimes appears as a negative image of excess (cf. Jos. *Ant.* 10.232; Gen. Rab. 39:8; Lev. Rab. 5:3; Pesiq. R. 52:1; 1 Pet 4:3), typically occurred at night (Sen. *Ep. Lucil.* 47.7; Juv. *Sat.* 8.9-12; Jos. *Life* 220, 223; Philo *Cher.* 92-93; Rom 13:12-13; 1 Thess 5:7), probably underlining the contextual contrast with "watching." The false charge against Jesus (11:19) is true with regard to this ser-

196. This is especially significant in favor of its authenticity; although the illustration would make sense (e.g., Juv. *Sat.* 3.302-4; Epict. *Disc.* 1.29.21) I know no other parallels to the expression, and Paul has already told the Thessalonians the saying (1 Thess 5:2); see Jeremias 1972: 50; Wenham 1981: 347; idem 1984: 54-55; cf. Nock 1963: 156; Neil 1950: 110; Marshall 1983: 133; Witherington 1992: 45-46. The more hellenized direction in Gos. Thom. 21 (cf. Gos. Thom. 103) "is surely secondary" (Witherington 1992: 46).

197. One may compare Sifre Deut. 43.15.2 (a parable in which a robber plunders a neglectful householder), as well as the rabbinic parable of preparedness (b. Shab. 153a; Qoh. Rab. 9:8) recounted in Bonsirven 1964: 167; Jeremias 1972: 188. In the Markan form of the parable, a servant would be less likely to expect a householder's return at night since travel then was rare (Jeremias 1972: 54; cf. Gundry 1982: 503 for rare exceptions); the original form may have spoken of only one servant (1972: 55-56, citing Lk 12:45; Mt 24:48). Jeremias does regard various details of non-Markan material here as authentic, however (e.g., the Aramaic rhyme behind Mt 24:48; 1971: 27).

198. Sons and servants could represent Israel in rabbinic parables (Dodd 1961: 151), but the context of Jesus' ministry demands an application to either the first or second comings, and the Matthean context plainly to the latter. Those who deny the possibility that Jesus could have founded a church (but cf. comment on 16:18-19) must see the parable, if authentic, addressing only Israel's leaders, but even if that situation correctly analyzed Jesus' meaning, it misses Matthew's own primary point in context (pace Harrington 1991, who thinks that this text, with 25:1-30, addresses especially the synagogue leadership).

vant, more interested in feeding himself (Ezek 34:2-3) than in watching for his master (cf. 24:38). Biblical tradition condemns the wastefulness of drunkenness (e.g., Prov 20:1; 31:4-7; Is 5:11-14, 22; 28:1; Hab 2:5, 15-16; cf. 1 Kings 16:9-10; 20:16-21), also applying it figuratively to judgment metaphors (Is 29:9; 51:21-23; 63:6; Jer 13:13; Nah 1:10).[199] The image resembles some biblical denunciations of exploitative leaders: "with force and harshness you have ruled [my sheep]" (Ezek 34:4, NRSV).

Second, some servants of Christ at his second coming will be found as unprepared as was much of the religious establishment at his first. The image of sharing hell with the "hypocrites" (24:51) explicitly recalls the false servants of 23:13-29. Like the tenants of 21:35-37 or the shepherds failing to feed the sheep in Ezekiel 34:15 (cf. Mt 24:45), these leaders forgot their true role as servants (23:12) and acted as if they could do as they pleased with what God had entrusted into their care (25:14).[200] Stories were known of servants who had acted in such ways, and precedent inclined Jesus' hearers to expect such servants to face serious consequences (e.g., Jos. *Ant.* 15.205-7, 228-29; cf. Epict. *Disc.* 3.22.3; Jos. *War* 2.481-83; Ep. Arist. 246, 271; Arrian *Alex.* 4.22.4; 6.30.2); the most widely known example would have been in the story of Ahiqar, in which a wicked servant mistreated and, in some versions, killed the other servants (3:2; 4:15 Syr.).[201] A century after Jesus, R. Simeon ben Yohai compared Israel to misbehaving servants whom God then locked off from his storage house (Sifre Deut. 40.6.1). A king, husband, or other master in a distant land was a common parable setting (e.g., ARN 1A; Pesiq. Rab Kah. 11:6) and constituted a temptation for those left behind (Prov 7:19-20; Eurip. *Hippol.* 281; Diod. Sic. 17.108.4; Char. *Chaer.* 1.4.8; Pesiq. Rab Kah. 19:4). Indeed, because they might return unexpectedly early (e.g., Aelian *Animals* 7.25), Roman men, for whatever reasons, normally warned their wives in advance when they were about to return (Plut. *R.Q.* 9, *Mor.* 266A), though some might return unexpectedly at night to check a

199. Whereas Jewish texts praise drinking in moderation (e.g., Sir 31:27-31) and Philo speaks of the intoxication of divine ecstasy (especially in defense of Noah in Gen 9:21-22; see *Plant.* 139-177), Jewish texts more often speak of the dangers of drunkenness (e.g., Philo *Ebr.* passim; Jos. *Apion* 2.195, 204; *Life* 225); the drunk were more susceptible to slaughter or incapacitation (Aqhat in *ANET* p. 155; Jos. *Life* 388; Polyphemus in the *Odyssey;* troops in Polyb. *R.R.E.* 11.3; Dion. Hal. 7.11.3; the enemy general in Jdt 13). For a fuller discussion of ancient views, see Keener 1992: 261-63, 270-72; plus Diod. Sic. 15.74.2. Moralists often recommended sobriety in both literal and figurative ways (Ep. Arist. 209; Anacharsis to Hipparchus *Ep.* 3.6; Marc. Aur. *Med.* 1.16.3; Philo *Cher.* 92-93; 1 Thess 5:6, 8; 1 Tim 3:2, 11; 1 Pet 1:13; 4:7; 5:8).

200. Throughout Mediterranean culture such behavior readily warranted the title "lawless" (Diod. Sic. 40.2.1, on Jerusalem's abusive high priest; 33.14.1; 34/35.12.1, each employing a term cognate to the one in Mt 23:28; 24:12), behavior unfitting for a ruler (Diod. Sic. 34/35.34.1). It may thus provide a stark narrative illustration of this rebellion against God's law of which Jesus warns (23:28; 24:12).

201. Matthew's audience might also think of the sexual abuse tyrants in power sometimes meted out to slaves or subjects, which was viewed extremely negatively (Dion. Hal. 4.36.1; 7.8.1; 11.10.3; Livy 3.44.4–3.48.9; Jos. *Apion* 1.100-101; 2.212; *Life* 259). Women occasionally participated in nocturnal Roman carousals, but it was a predominantly male vice (Friedländer 1965: 1:249).

wife's faithfulness (Phaedrus 3.10.18-20; in a later Arab tale, see Gordon 1989: 86).

Thus the image of the faithful slave is one of readiness (25:14, 21; cf. 6:24). Warnings to stay ready became increasingly important when the end did not materialize as swiftly as many had expected (cf. the similar phenomenon in 1QpHab 2.3-6); continuing tribulation rather than disillusionment may have contributed discontent (Goppelt 1962: 198).

Finally, Jesus calls ministers to serve their fellow servants; those who exploit the flock for their own interests will be damned (cf. 2 Pet 2:3; Mic 3:11-12; 1 Tim 6:5). Those who abused their master's property in his absence had cause for terror at his unexpected return (Diod. Sic. 17.108.6-8). The sort of dismemberment depicted here represents the most horrible sort of fate (e.g., Dan 3:29; Hom. *Od.* 18.339; Livy 8.24.14; Diod. Sic. 16.16.4; 17.83.9; 33.15.1; 34/35.8.1; 34/35.12.1; 34/35.14.1; Paus. 2.2.7). Arrian, for example, declares that his hero Alexander punished Bessus by having his nose and ears cut off before executing him (*Alex.* 4.7.3; the practice could include nose, ears, genitals, hands, and feet, as in Hom. *Od.* 22.474-77), but Arrian disapproves of such "mutilation of extremities" as a practice derived from the barbarians (*Alex.* 4.7.4). More horrible and disgraceful for the corpse was cutting one in pieces and discarding the parts (e.g., Appian *R.H.* 3.6.1; 4.11).[202] Remembering that leaders are not lords but "fellow slaves" (18:29; 23:8-11) keeps their duty in perspective.

Awaiting the Bridegroom (25:1-13)

Cf. Mk 13:33-37; Lk 12:35-38; 13:25. This parable most naturally focuses on the same time of judgment as the preceding one (24:45-51; though the transitional *tote* need not signify so much, being a favorite Matthean particle — cf. Jeremias 1972: 52).

Disciples must watch. Matthew has already emphasized that since the time of Jesus' coming is unknown, disciples must watch and be ready (24:36). Matthew articulates that principle again by means of a parable quite suitable for his Syro-Palestinian Jewish audience. Although some rabbinic parables address the theme of readiness most often in relation to death (cf. Sifre Deut. 43.15.2; b. Shab. 153a), Jesus' parables about the end time especially focus on readiness for

202. Those particularly despised might also be tortured before execution (Dion. Hal. 7.11.3). When other methods of interrogation proved inadequate, torture was sometimes applied (Arist. *Rhet.* 1.15.26, 1376b; Quint. 5.4.1; Apul. *Metam.* 3.8; Pesiq. Rab Kah. 15:7), and much more routinely with slaves (e.g., Demosth. *Against Pantaenetus* 27; *Against Olympiodorus* 18-19; *Against Timotheus* 55-58; *Against Conon* 27; *Against Neaera* 122; *Rhet. ad Herenn.* 2.7.10; Tac. *Ann.* 3.67; 4.29; 14.60; Justin. *Dig.* 48.18.1; Char. *Chaer.* 1.5.1; Apul. *Metam.* 10.28). Amputation of particular members, however, was preferable to execution (Jos. *Life* 147, 173; see comment on 5:30).

the Son of Man (e.g., 24:42–25:13).[203] Although Jewish parables sometimes referred to the wedding of Israel and Torah, the wedding merely provides the setting for the parable; the bridesmaids, rather than the bride herself, constitute the primary characters.[204] Their role might depict Torah scholars in analogous rabbinic parables (Ford 1967), but Jesus addresses all his disciples with this warning. The motif contrasting wise and foolish characters naturally appears in rabbinic literature (Young 1989: 35, citing the king's servants in b. Shab. 152b).

Until the judgment scene, the setting is largely realistic, fitting what Jesus' Galilean hearers knew of weddings, the sort of details Jesus used in other parables (e.g., 9:15; 22:3). Wedding processions from the bride's to the groom's home, accompanied by song and dancing, normally happened at night, hence requiring light. The lamps here are not the small, hand-held Herodian period lamps, which would generate very little light, but torches (as in weddings in the rest of the Mediterranean world — Eurip. *Daughters of Troy* 343-44; Virg. *Aen.* 4.338-39; 7.388; *Culex* 246; *Ecl.* 8.29; Ovid *Metam.* 1.483, 763; 4.758-59; 6.430; 10.6; Lucan *C.W.* 2.356; Plut. *R.Q.* 2, *Mor.* 263F; Ach. Tat. 2.11.1; cf. Safrai 1974/76b: 758). In poorer villages these torches may have been sticks wrapped with oiled rags, as in traditional Arab weddings (Jeremias 1965b; idem 1972: 174-75; followed by Gundry 1982: 498; pace Edersheim 541). Although details differ from one village to the next, traditional Palestinian village weddings in recent centuries climax with women torchbearers leading the bride to the bridegroom's home, and the torchbearers going out to meet the groom and his male friends (Jeremias 1972: 173). Presumably the bridesmaids wait outside the bride's home for his coming, to escort her en route to his home (Argyle 1963: 189; cf. Safrai 1974/76b: 758; pace Fenton 1977: 396; Meier 1980: 295).[205] Greek and Roman weddings also included the torchlit procession to the groom's residence (Ferguson 1987: 55); the groom's residence was usually his parents' home, which would for a time after the banquet become the new couple's residence (Tob 6:13; Derrett 1973: 38; cf. also for other patrilocal cultures, e.g., Mbiti 1970: 182).

In this particular parable (in contrast to 24:42-44), the issue is not that the virgins went to sleep — both the wise and foolish did so; this detail is merely part

203. Although in its Matthean context the parable plainly addresses Jesus' return, some suggest that the original story could address other impending tests of faith (cf. F. F. Bruce 1972a: 71). A sage could demand preparation for such tests, but an eschatological reading of the parable better suits the eschatological content of Jesus' message as a whole. This parable may derive from a pre-Synoptic source collecting much eschatological material (see D. Wenham 1984b: 51-52).

204. This detail, alongside Mk 2:19, supports the authenticity of the parable's present form more than Dodd and Jeremias suppose; see Witherington 1984: 43 (though Gundry 1982: 497, 501, derives the whole wedding setting from the tradition behind Lk 12:36).

205. Conducting someone en route to his or her destination often functioned to honor the person so escorted (e.g., Dion. Hal. 7.7.2; Char. *Chaer.* 4.7.6; Judg 4:18; 11:31, 34; 1 Sam 13:10; 16:4; 21:1; 25:32; Acts 28:15); it appears in royal parousia contexts (e.g., 1 Thess 4:17; cf. 2 Sam 19:25; Jdt 5:4; 7:15; Pesiq. R. 51:8; Moulton and Milligan 1976: 53; Best 1977: 199; F. F. Bruce 1982: 102; Marshall 1983: 131).

of the narrative's setting. The issue is that some were not watchful enough to have sufficient oil (Beare 1981: 482; Schweizer 1975: 467).[206] Some scholars have suggested that the torches could burn only fifteen minutes before being rewrapped with more oiled cloth (e.g., France 1985: 351; Witherington 1984: 43). Some other details, like going to buy the oil, fit the logic of the narrative, although most shops would not have been open at night (though for exceptions see Argyle 1975, retracting idem 1963: 189). In traditional Palestinian Arab weddings, messengers might repeatedly announce the bridegroom's coming,[207] yet it might be delayed for hours (Jeremias 1972: 173); delays occur while the bride's relatives haggle over the value of presents given them, emphasizing the bride's great value and hence the wisdom of the groom's selection (Jeremias 1972: 173-74).[208] That the bridesmaids would be sleepy around midnight is not surprising; because ancient lighting tended to be poorer than today, most people were asleep by midnight (e.g., Ovid *Metam.* 10.368).

All the virgins would have been ready for the groom had he arrived when they expected, but grooms' delays were common enough that they should have anticipated it; this provides clear warning that the parousia might be delayed — perhaps for Jesus' first disciples who expected the kingdom to appear immediately, and surely for those who were disappointed at Jesus' nonreturn at the temple's demise in 70 (cf. 24:22-23, 48; 25:19).[209] The *apantēsis,* or "meeting," "rendezvous" (25:6), often suggested going out to meet someone and forming his escort into the place where he would be honored.[210] The "going out" itself, however, fits the parable's story line and should not be pressed for further significance (cf. 24:26).

Some think that "the calculating self-centredness of the 'wise' virgins" contradicts the piety of Jesus' authentic teaching (Vermes 1993: 113), but this is not quite true. First, the parable represents an analogy arguing that personal

206. Boring 1995: 138 cites Plut. *Precepts of Statecraft* 1 for another analogy with lamps but rightly points out that it is the necessity of oil for lamps that leads both sources to share the same image.

207. The single "cry" of v. 6 may parallel the trumpet call of 24:31, with 1 Thess 4:16 reflecting a tradition including both (Blomberg 1992a: 370); but the "cry" in 1 Thess 4 is probably a war cry and thus might be unrelated to the present image.

208. Cf. Eickelman 1989: 174, where the bride's relatives are engaged in "a farewell celebration . . . at the bride's house," and weep when the groom's relatives arrive to escort the bride to the party that has already begun in his house. The groom has no reason not to delay: he is the central personage of the event, the timing of which will center around him (Malina 1993: 159).

209. Naturally those who think that the delay of the parousia is only a later motif find the parable inauthentic (e.g., reasonably, Vermes 1993: 113), but the delay is already an issue in what is probably our first NT document (1 Thess 4:13), and if the initial disciples expected only a single coming or barely an interval between comings (cf. Dodd 1980), an issue already present in Jesus' ministry could easily translate into this problem by the time of the Gospels. Scott 1989: 70-72 rejects the parable because it describes community boundaries; yet the very selection of the Twelve began that process in Jesus' lifetime.

210. As in 1 Thess 4:17; see Milligan 1908: 62; F. F. Bruce 1963: 68-69; idem 1977a: 527n.26; idem 1982: 102; Best 1977: 199; Marshall 1983: 131; cf. Payne 1962: 68; Jdt 7:15; Pesiq. R. 51:8.

choice determines one's responses to God's gift of the kingdom, an analogy that does not ask all possible moral questions surrounding that determination (cf. 13:44-45). Second, even if the characters exhibited negative features, this hardly precludes their function in the analogy; Jesus characteristically provides unpleasant analogies even for God (as tyrannical or naive; 18:12-14, 23-25; 21:37; Lk 18:1-8) and himself (Mt 24:43-44). But, finally, the image is simply not a negative one: the unwillingness of the wise virgins to share their oil reflects their concern for their friend's wedding. Having only enough for their own torches, sharing would cause *all* the torches to be extinguished, ruining the whole procession (Meier 1980: 295; Gundry 1982: 500).[211]

Bridal processions were so important that later rabbis even suspended their lectures so they could hail the passing bride (ARN 4A; 8, §22B); for the groom and (some held) for the attendants, weddings even took precedence over some ritual obligations (t. Ber. 2:10; b. Sukk. 25b; p. Sukk. 2:5, §1). Later teachers even insisted that God specifically supervised Adam's wedding (ARN 8, §23B; b. B. Bat. 75a; Gen. Rab. 8:13; 18:1; Qoh. Rab. 8:1, §2). In short, Palestinian Jewish people regarded weddings as critical events (contrast Romans — O'Rourke 1971: 181), and a breach of etiquette was therefore serious.

Those who fail to watch will suffer shame. The host or groom excludes the foolish virgins as a punishment, not merely because the bolt on the door was cumbersome (cf. Meier 1980: 296).[212] Doors could be bolted or barred shut (e.g., Aristoph. *Wasps* 154-55), but the door would hardly be locked throughout the feast, which lasted seven days.[213] New guests sometimes arrived during those days, requiring the repeating of the blessings (Safrai 1974/76b: 760; cf. b. Ketub. 7b-8b; p. Ketub. 1:1, §6); elsewhere in the first-century Mediterranean world doorkeepers watched the doors during weddings (Demetrius *On Style* 3.167). The foolish virgins were not excluded simply because the door was locked (25:10-11), nor because the host actually did not recognize them (25:12), but because they had insulted the bride and groom, as well as all their relatives! The expression "I do not know you" was sometimes used when one wished to treat others as strangers and keep them from approaching (Blomberg 1992a: 371n.76, following Green 1975: 205). This was an offense they would never be allowed to forget.[214]

211. For another bold request for oil, cf. Diog. Laert. *Lives* 7.1.17; but there the boldness is that of Cynic impudence in begging, whereas here it stems from desperation.

212. The bridegroom image in the OT represented God (Is 49:18; 54:5-7; Jer 2:2; Ezek 16:8-14; Hos 2:16-23; Witherington 1990: 212, following Payne 1981b); the banquet host in Jewish parables is typically God as well. Yet while the parable may assume christological implications (Matthew's audience would certainly apply the image to Jesus), they remain secondary or tertiary to the parable's focus.

213. Judg 14:12, 17; Tob 11:19; Jos. and Asen. 21:8/6; Sifra Behuq. pq. 5.266.1.7; b. Ketub. 8b; p. Ketub. 1:1, §6; Meg. 4:4, §3; probably Pesiq. Rab Kah. 28:9; Lam. Rab. 1:7, §34; Safrai 1974/76b: 760; cf. fourteen days in Tob 8:19-20.

214. Vermes 1993: 113 thinks that this "heartless refusal of the 'bridegroom' to admit those who failed to be properly prepared" speaks against authenticity; but what then of Jesus' many other images of damnation (e.g., Mk 9:42-48; Mt 8:12//Lk 13:28; Mt 22:13; 24:39-41) or deadly judgment (Mk 12:9; Mt 22:7)?

To participate in their friend's wedding was a great honor; as virgins, these young women were in a sense practicing for their own impending weddings around the ages of twelve to sixteen. But to have spoiled the wedding for her by failing to do their appropriate part was a great insult to their friend and to the groom and guests. That they would be shut out of the feast in punishment suits their case, but the language used to depict this nightmare points beyond itself to more severe, eternal judgment, probably echoing the sayings in 7:21-23 (Jeremias 1972: 175 compares a rabbi's temporary ban). Wedding feasts involved great joy;[215] thus the transgressors will mourn because they have been shut out from it.

The Industrious and the Lazy Managers (25:14-30)

Cf. Lk 19:11-27; perhaps Mk 13:34.[216] Many aspects of the parable depict social reality in a wealthy household. Householders going on long journeys might entrust their estate to slaves to oversee (cf. 24:45-51), since household slaves often held managerial roles (Treggiari 1975: 49; Stambaugh and Balch 1986: 66; Judge 1960: 38). The Lukan version depicts a master who entrusts to slaves a much smaller sum (especially given the price of slaves themselves), but Matthew paints the story in much grander terms (portraying sixty to one hundred times Luke's sum; cf. Goulder 1974: 62; Gundry 1982: 503). Although Jesus might have reapplied a similar story line on several occasions,[217] Jeremias may be right to suggest that Matthew and Luke (or, more likely, their sources) have both expanded the figures in an original parable in distinct ways (1972: 27).[218]

215. B. Ber. 6b; 30b-31a; p. Ketub. 1:1, §6; Mk 2:19; Jn 3:29; also feasts in general (Ep. Arist. 294). Thus tragedies at weddings were particularly noteworthy; cf. 1 Macc 9:39-41; Jos. *War* 6.301; Lev. Rab. 20:3; Qoh. Rab. 2:2, §4.

216. Fitzmyer believes that parallels show that the Matthean and Lukan versions reflect the same original parable; Young 1989: 165, holds that all three Synoptic accounts reflect a single original Hebrew source behind the Gospels. I suspect that Mk 13:34 reflects a shortened version of an oral tradition preserved in Matthew; the Lukan parable could be a variant oral recension but may as easily reflect a separate parable (see comment on 22:1-14). Malina and Rohrbaugh 1992: 150 think the Gospel of Nazoreans version (in Euseb. *Theophania* on Mt 25:14-15) is older than Matthew's version because of its "peasant" point of view. But the Nazorean report is *not* clearly more peasantlike; most people, including urban moralists, despised squandering (e.g., Juv. *Sat.* 1.58-60; t. Pisha 2:15), and the squandering allusion here may be borrowed from Lk 15:13-14; 16:1; the Gospel of Nazoreans may be a secondary expansion of Matthew into Aramaic (see Meier 1991a: 116).

217. Even in his first telling Jesus could have adapted a familiar story line; Tannaim told a parable of a king whose servants improved the property he gave them, referring to the patriarchs' treatment of the land (Sifre Deut. 8.1.2). Scott 1989: 230-31 compares a story in ARN 14A, in which God deposited Torah with his servants, and those who kept it and returned it undefiled by their sin would be rewarded; Jesus, he says, demands more than merely *keeping* the trust (cf. Davies and Allison 1997: 404).

218. The differences between the Matthean and Lukan reports are substantial; some therefore conclude that they derive from separate sources (e.g., Lachs 1987: 340-41). Because Matthew and Luke are normally so close when following Q, one suspects that if they used the same source the tradition in this case must have been mediated to them by other means.

Because Luke's figures for the money are probably more accurate and he says that each received the same amount, Matthew may here make a special point in noting that the master gave "each according to his ability" — he already knew which slaves would be most industrious, but expected all to show *some* industry. In the Roman Empire, slaves could earn wages and bonuses and could acquire property (Apul. *Metam.* 10.13; p. Yebam. 7:1, §2; Buckland 1908: 187-238; Finley 1973: 64; Cohen 1966: 179-278), hence they would have more incentive to look out for the master's property than slaves in many cultures do. Thus the servants understand very well what is required of them.

As in 24:45-51, readiness for Jesus' return here demands faithfulness in doing the work he has called one to do. This warning applies to all disciples, but perhaps most severely to church leaders: "A Christian leader who does not lead is damned" (Meier 1980: 300). That the householder is on a journey and will return unexpectedly may imply a possible "delay" of the parousia, although it is clearer in Luke ("far" country — Lk 19:12). "Settling accounts" again becomes a figure for the time of judgment (cf. 18:23).

The rewards were commensurate with their faithfulness in pursuing the master's interest (25:20-23). Elsewhere one encounters the principle that one untrustworthy in what was his own would not be trustworthy in what concerns others (Lk 16:10-12; m. Dem. 2:2; *Rhet. ad Herenn.* 4.18.25); here one encounters the principle that only those proved in small leadership positions would be prepared for bigger ones.[219] Similarly, only those who were wise would receive further instruction (Sir 21:12), for as a later rabbi put it, God pours more into a full vessel but not into an empty one (b. Ber. 40a). Although Matthew may know that the Aramaic word translated into Greek as "joy" can also mean "feast" or "wedding feast" (Jeremias 1972: 60n.42; Gundry 1982: 506), purely Greek-speaking readers would lose very little: the term "joy" can connote banqueting with the master (cf. 25:10), and the context of the preceding parable supports this interpretation. Some of Jesus' contemporaries stressed the "joy" of the righteous in the world to come.[220]

The lazy servant does nothing with his resources because he does not

219. Ep. Arist. 264; t. Ḥag. 2:9; Sanh. 7:1; Sheqal. 3:27; 1 Tim 3:10; cf. Plut. *Compliancy* 7, *Mor.* 531DE; in household leadership, e.g., Isoc. *Demon.* 35, *Or.* 1; *Nic./Cypr.* 41, *Or.* 3.35; Plut. *Bride, Mor.* 144CD; Diog. Laert. *Lives* 1.70. Cf. ARN 35, §79B, praising a poor person who handles a deposit trustworthily; Davies and Allison 1997: 407 cite m. 'Abot 4:2, which they render, "The reward of duty [done] is a duty [to be done]"; the greater are judged more strictly in b. Ta'an. 8a.

220. Tob 13:10, 13-14; 1QM 17.7; 1 Enoch 5:7; 25:6; 47:4; 103:3; Jub. 23:30; Sib. Or. 3.619; Ps. Sol. 11:3; Test. Jud. 25:4; cf. Sifra Shemini Mekhilta deMiluim; at death in 4 Ezra 7:91; cf. 2 Bar. 14:13; *CIJ* 1:472, §656. Greek philosophers emphasized that true happiness followed virtue rather than vice (Cic. *Par. Stoic.* 16-19; *De Leg.* 1.23.60; *Tusc. Disp.* 5.7.19-20; 5.25.70; Sen. *Ep. Lucil.* 23; 59.10; *Dial.* 7; *De Benef.* 7.2.3); Jewish writers often found joy in virtuous behavior as well (Ep. Arist. 261; Jos. *Apion* 2.189; Jub. 36:6), usually recognized as joy in God's law (Ps 19:8; 119:14; b. Yoma 4b; Pesiq. Rab Kah. 27:2; Lev. Rab. 16:4; Song Rab. 4:11, §1; Pesiq. R. 21:2/3; 51:4; cf. Wis 8:16) or prayer (Tob 13:1; cf. Jos. and Asen. 3:4). For "joy" in sacrificially embracing the kingdom, see 13:44; cf. 13:20; at news of the resurrection, 28:8.

care about the master's agendas. Temples, including the Jerusalem temple, functioned as banks,[221] and moneylenders were also common elsewhere in the Gentile world. Most people lacked capital, but those who had it could multiply their investment fivefold or even tenfold (Lk 19:16-18); doubling one's investment (Mt 25:20, 22) might be regarded as a reasonable minimum return to expect in the ancient economy (Derrett 1970: 24, though citing here Hammurabi; cf. Hock 1988: 140).[222] Burying money (Mt 25:18; cf. Hor. *Sat.* 1.1.41-42) at least kept that capital safe; ancient law viewed merely wrapping it in a napkin, however, as disrespecting its safety altogether (Lk 19:20; Derrett 1970: 24; Jeremias 1972: 61). But the money would have been no less safe with bankers (m. B. Meṣ. 3:11; Gundry 1982: 509; on ancient bankers, see Lewis 1983: 147-48). When the lazy servant declares, "Here is your own money back!" he refuses to acknowledge responsibility (see Derrett 1970: 25 on a possibly corresponding mishnaic phrase); by failing the master's trust, he insults the master.[223] His excuse is hardly acceptable: knowing the master's reputation for sternness, he was paralyzed with fear (25:24-25).[224] The master rightly responds, "On the assumption that I *am* hard and merciless, you should have been all the *more* diligent!" (25:26-27).

Disciples who neglect the resources entrusted to them in this life will be damned. As in the preceding parable, the exclusion of the unfaithful, who insult their patron's trust in them, is explicit: hell's darkness (8:12; 22:13) and wailing (22:13). The master accepts the servant's portrait of his severity — supplying both a mark of the parable's authenticity (the church would hardly have portrayed Jesus thus; Gundry 1982: 508) and, more importantly, a warning not to take the impending judgment lightly. Whereas the other servants are rewarded by the master's benevolence, this servant, fearing the master's harshness but unaware of his benevolence (cf. Patte 1987: 346), experiences the very wrath he

221. E.g., Lucan *C.W.* 9.515-16; Corn. Nep. 23 (Hannibal), 9.3; Herodian 1.14.3. Only the most impious robbers would risk violating their sanctity (e.g., 2 Macc 3:12; 4 Macc 4:3-7; Jos. *War* 2.175; *Ant.* 4.207; Pesiq. R. 10:1; Diod. Sic. 14.63.1-2; 14.69.4; 14.76.3; 27.1; 27.4.3; 28.3.1; 34/35.9.1; 34/35.28.1-3; *P. Tebt.* 5.5; Livy 32.1.8; 36.20.3; 42.3.8; 42.28.12; 43.7.10; Appian *R.H.* 3.12.1-2; 8.20.133; Corn. Nep. 17 [Agesilaus], 4.8; Arrian *Alex.* 1.17.11; 6.30.2; Strabo 17.1.43; Phaedrus 4.11.1-13; Babrius 78; Juv. *Sat.* 14.261-62; Paus. 3.23.4; 9.25.10; 9.33.6; Taylor 1979: 254; Trebilco 1994: 325; Goodman 1983: 58; cf. comments on 21:12).

222. Despite biblical prohibitions of usury, Jewish teachers had found ways to allow interest (Carson 1984b: 517), which may have reflected current practice (cf. Neh 5:10); see comment on 6:12.

223. For an opposite interpretation, cf. Malina 1993: 143, who contends that the third servant (in Lk 19:11-27) fulfilled the values of the culture (by maintaining things and avoiding risks; cf. Scott 1989: 232). But deposits with banks involved little risk. I thus find doubtful the suggestion that Jesus may have condemned the *master's* viewpoint and appealed to peasant support for the viewpoint of the third servant (Rohrbaugh 1993).

224. The word often translated "lazy" *(oknēros),* in fact, normally means "fearful," suggesting that fear was the source of the slave's passivity (Nielsen 1990). However Jesus intended the parable (and he himself may have directed it toward disciples), Matthew warns the lazy within the church rather than using this passage to criticize the Pharisees (pace Harrington 1991; Dietzfelbinger 1989).

knew about. This is the punishment for a professed disciple who failed to invest all his or her resources in the work of the kingdom.

The Division of the Sheep and the Goats (25:31-46)

This parable is unique to Matthew in our extant sources, but that neither Matthew nor Luke uses every detail of Mark warns us against rejecting material not documented more than once in extant sources. Those who deny that Jesus could have planned the admission of Gentiles naturally see the parable as inauthentic (e.g., Sanders 1985: 111), but the premise presupposes the exclusion or a particular interpretation of some Jesus material some scholars, including myself, regard as authentic (cf., e.g., comment on 8:11-12). The parabolic form, the "Son of Man," the use of *Amēn* (25:40, 45), and similar features recall Jesus' own style. Generally "Matthean" features may suggest that Matthew has more freely recast oral tradition here than he often adapts Mark, but some purportedly "Matthean" features (like parallelism) make just as much sense in Jesus' Palestinian milieu. The parallels to many of Jesus' other sayings (Robinson 1962: 88-89) can argue either for a Matthean construction from other materials or, as I prefer, authenticity on the basis of coherence with authentic Jesus tradition.[225]

Jesus is the final judge. This parable assumes a high Christology consonant with Matthew's Christology in general (Luz 1996: 308). This observation need not render the parable inauthentic: that Jesus should claim to be King (25:34) fits his actions (see 21:7-8); that he should claim to be the final judge fits some Q tradition (see 7:21-23). But this parable probably goes so far as to assume, in appropriate Matthean imagery, Jesus' *deity* (cf. 18:20). To be sure, others sometimes fill the role of final judge in Jewish tradition (e.g., Abel, with Enoch's help, in Test. Abr. 12-13A; 11B;[226] Enoch in 3 Enoch 16:1; the son of man in 1 Enoch 69:27 [Similitudes], all on the model of the Greek Minos and Rhadamanthys, Hom. *Od.* 11.568-71; Eurip. *Cyclops* 273; Virg. *Aen.* 6.431-33, 566-69; Lucian *Zeus Catechized* 18; *Menippus* 10-13; *On Funerals* 7; *Dialogues of the Dead* 24/450-54); the saints also join in the judgment (1QpHab 4.4; 1 Cor 6:2), and the rule of the Son of Man (Dan 7:13-14; Mt 25:31) could be understood in such terms. Nevertheless, the central biblical and Jewish role of eschatological judge that Jesus here assumes normally belongs to God himself (cf., e.g., Sib. Or. 4.183-84; 1 Enoch 9:4; 60:2; 62:2; 47:3 with 46:2; Test. Abr. 14A); as noted earlier, the king in rabbinic parables is nearly always God. Coming with

225. In favor of authenticity, see further Broer 1970. Other imagery may derive from the Similitudes of Enoch (cf. Catchpole 1979), if they are early enough, or the broader judgment scene tradition on which both are based, and the OT, especially Is 58:7, but also Ezek 18:7 (cf. Gundry 1982: 513, 516).

226. For comparison of the two recensions of Testament of Abraham's judgment scene, see Nickelsburg 1972: 29-40; in a later Christian text, MacRae 1972. Davies and Allison 1997: 421 also cite among judges besides God Melchizedek in 11QMelch 2.13.

"all the angels" (25:31; cf. 13:41; 16:27; 24:31; 2 Thess 1:7) alludes to various versions of Zechariah 14:5 (see Gundry 1982: 511), where God is in view.

Although in biblical and Jewish tradition shepherds could represent Moses, David, and others, the chief shepherd was God himself.[227] In the Matthean context, this background may be significant. The sheep, of course, almost always stand for the people of God (e.g., 1 Enoch 90:32-33; Pesiq. R. 9:2; 26:2). In the earlier work 1 Enoch, the "Lord of the sheep" who was judge at the day of judgment (1 Enoch 90:20) was God himself (1 Enoch 89:16, 20, 26, 33, 50, 52, 54, 70). Similarly, Jesus' claim that whatever others have done to his servants they have done to him fits a rabbinic perspective about God (Smith 1951: 154, citing Midr. Tannaim 15.9), though both cases might simply echo the Jewish custom of a *shaliaḥ,* an appointed agent or representative (see comment on 10:5). Whether Jesus in this passage claims deity or merely an exalted role as God's Davidic agent ("in his name" — cf. 1 Enoch 55:4), he clearly becomes the focus of the final judgment, spelling disaster to those who ignore him on this side of the day of judgment.

In Jewish texts, God judges the nations after raising them from the dead (cf. 4 Ezra 7:37); the judgment among nations was an ancient Israelite hope (e.g., Mic 4:3, *beyn,* between peoples). The same time frame is in view here: as in both the context and the Daniel passage that initially supplied the "Son of Man" title, Jesus here returns after the tribulation (25:31; 24:29-30; Dan 7:13-14), "in glory" (cf. 16:27; 24:31; 2 Thess 1:10; 2:8), "in his kingdom" (16:28), enthroned (cf. 20:23; 22:44). The parable's "throne of glory" (cf. 25:31) appears frequently in Jewish texts (most frequently of God's throne), those addressing the final judgment being of special significance here (e.g., 1 Enoch 45:3; 47:3; 60:2; 62:2).

The "nations" or "Gentiles" in Jewish literature would be judged according to how they treated Israel (4 Ezra 7:37; Klausner 1979b: 200). As in other word pictures, here they are "gathered" (cf. 13:40; Is 2:4; Rev 16:16)[228] and separated (13:30, 49), in this instance the way a shepherd would separate sheep from goats (cf. Ezek 34:17), to keep the goats warm at night while keeping the sheep in open air as they preferred (Jeremias 1972: 206).[229] The parable's portrayal of the righteous as sheep and the wicked as goats may stem from their relative value to the owner. Goats were sometimes disobedient to the goatherd (Babrius 3.2-3), probably more often than sheep to the shepherd. Moreover, sheep cost more than

227. E.g., Ezek 34:11-17; Zech 10:3; Ps 23:1-4; 74:1-2; 77:20; 78:52; Is 40:11; Jer 13:17; 31:10; Mic 7:14; Sir 18:13; 1 Enoch 89:18; Philo *Agr.* 50-53; Ps-Philo 28.5; 30.5. See further comment on the imagery in 18:12.

228. Jeremias 1972: 206 points out that *synagō,* "gather," is a common shepherd's term; nevertheless, its technical connotations are suspect: the term is common enough that one wonders what term shepherds might have used had they not used this.

229. Regardless of whether all shared the same owner, Greek goatherds and shepherds often grazed near each other (e.g., Theocritus *The Goatherd and the Shepherd* in *Greek Bucolic Poets,* LCL 62-81; *P. Ryl.* 114.10; Longus 1.8). Sheep and goats usually got along (Aelian *Animals* 5.48; 7.27).

goats did (Jeremias 1972: 206), and because of their greater utility and value, they were nearly always held in greater quantity.[230]

Jesus portrays the judgment scene in masterful ways.[231] Ancients, most of whom, like most people today, were right-handed, generally preferred the right side to the left (e.g., Plut. *R.Q.* 78, *Mor.* 282E — the left side is physically weaker; Eccl 10:2; b. Ber. 61a, bar.); in one Jewish tradition the angel on the right of the throne recorded good deeds while the one on the left recorded evil ones (Test. Abr. 12A; more fully on right and left in early Judaism and Christianity, cf. Court 1985; Lachs 1987: 394).[232] More significantly, Davies and Allison 1997: 424 note that in Plato *Rep.* 10.614C the righteous are sent right and up to heaven while others are sent to the left; likewise, in Virg. *Aen.* 6.540-43 the road to the right leads to Elysium but the road to the left to Tartarus. Also, the vindication of the righteous on specific grounds will leave the wicked after them without excuse: in later rabbinic tradition, the converts to Judaism from among the nations would indict the nations on the day of judgment, proving that conversion had been a viable option (Pesiq. R. 161a in Davies 1980: 65); cf. more fully the comment on 12:38-42.

Who are the sheep, goats, and siblings?[233] The older dispensational scheme viewed this as the judgment of the nations based on their treatment of Israel, a view that could fit Jewish perceptions of the judgment (cf. Manson 1979: 249-50). But this hardly fits Jesus' own designation of his "brothers" elsewhere (12:50; 28:10; see below), and perhaps not the shift from the neuter "nations" to the masculine pronoun, suggesting individual judgment of Gentiles (cf. Gundry 1982: 512). Because the passage explicitly declares that this judgment determines people's *eternal* destinies (25:46), it cannot refer to a judgment concerning who would enter the millennium, as in some older dispensational schemes (Ladd 1977: 38; cf. idem 1978b: 98-102).

Nor is the popular view that this text refers to treatment of the poor or those

230. Often ten to fifty times as many, by the same owner; see Lewis 1983: 131-32, citing *P. Lond.* 1171; *P. Strassb.* 24; *P. Oxy. 807; P. Hamb.* 34. Sheep were preferred for wool, the milk of both preferred to that of cows, and goatskins preferred for leather containers (ibid. 132). Jeremias 1972: 206 notes that sheep are white whereas goats are black, but this is not always true (see, e.g., Aelian *Animals* 3.32; 16.33). Whether white or black (though *especially* white), sheep in dreams are auspicious; whether white or black (but especially black), goats were inauspicious (Artem. *Oneir.* 2.12). Some of Matthew's hearers might have thought of white sheep here through recalling 1 Enoch 90:32.

231. Mani later adapted these speeches in a Gnostic direction (Hutter 1991), but Jesus adapts a tradition of judgment scenes that appear in some form at least as early as the Egyptian Book of the Dead 125 (Herrmann 1991). The motif of divine messengers arriving in disguise was also frequent; see comment on 10:12-15.

232. The tradition persisted in the Near East and East Africa; thus, e.g., left-handedness as a sign of the demonic in the chronicles of Lebna Dengel, emperor of Ethiopia, in October 1531 (Pankhurst 1967: 62). The evil angel Sammael in later Jewish texts bears a *samech,* not a *sin,* hence is technically unrelated to the Hebrew word for "left"; but a wordplay might be possible (Derrett 1997: 178).

233. For a fuller history of interpretation see Gray 1989; Luz 1996: 271-86.

in need (e.g., Gross 1964; Hare 1967: 124; Feuillet 1980a; Lapoorta 1989; Jones 1995: 247-49; Davies and Allison 1997: 428-29) exegetically compelling, although that view would on other grounds be entirely consonant with the Jesus tradition (e.g., Mk 10:21; Lk 16:19-25) and biblical ethics as a whole (e.g., Ex 22:22-27; Prov 17:5; 19:17; 21:13; Gardner 1991: 363).[234] Jewish lists of loving works include showing hospitality and visiting the sick, though not visiting prisoners.[235] Such acts were found praiseworthy in the day of judgment (2 Enoch 63:1-2; b. Ned. 39b-40a; Jeremias 1972: 207-8; cf. Bonsirven 1964: 151-52). Some rabbis felt that when Israel fed the poor, God counted it as though Israel had done it for God (Midr. Tann. on Deut 15:9, in Jeremias 1972: 207); a first-century teacher reportedly claimed that charity could atone for the nations' sins (b. B. Bat. 10b, bar., in Jeremias 1972: 208). Those who cared for the poor would be saved (Lachs 1987: 394 cites b. Ned. 40a; Midr. Ps. 118:19). One could thus understand Jesus' disciples as bringers of healing (10:8), caring for the least (Heil 1998a: 203).

But in the context of Jesus' teachings, especially in the context of Matthew (as opposed to Luke), this parable probably addresses not serving the poor on the whole but receiving the gospel's messengers. Elsewhere in Matthew, disciples are Jesus' "brothers" (12:50; 28:10; cf. also the "least" — 5:19; 11:11; 18:3-6, 10-14); likewise, one unwittingly treats Jesus as one treats his representatives (10:40-42), who should be received with hospitality, food, and drink (10:8-13, 42). Imprisonment could refer to detention until trial before magistrates (10:18-19), and sickness to physical conditions stirred by the hardship of the mission (cf. Phil 2:27-30; perhaps Gal 4:13-14; 2 Tim 4:20). Being "poorly clothed" appears in Paul's lists of sufferings (Rom 8:35), including his most detailed extant apostolic *peristasis* catalogue (1 Cor 4:11); it may also recall the public humiliation of Jesus' crucifixion (27:35), although the impossibility of "clothing" Jesus at that point weighs against the allusion.

The king thus judges the nations based on how they have responded to the gospel of the kingdom already preached to them before the time of his kingdom (24:14; 28:19-20). True messengers of the gospel will successfully evangelize the world only if they can also embrace poverty and suffering for Christ's name

234. Cf. Stark 1991a: 202 and 1991b on how Christians cared for the sick, nursing them back to health in a plague of ca. A.D. 260, though others in antiquity regularly fled from the sick during epidemics. For a more recent example, see Jones and Allen 1794. Boring 1995: 143-44 compares *Left Ginza* 3.19 in which care for the poor determines the fate of one's soul en route to its home in the heavens; though admitting that the texts do not predate A.D. 500, he thinks that "some traditions may reach back to" the first century!

235. On the positive requirements, see, e.g., Sir 7:35; 4 Bar. 5:22-23; 7:37; Test. Iss. 5:2; ARN 30; 41A; Sifre Deut. 32.5.12; Gen. Rab. 13:16; p. Ḥag. 2:1, §10; Apoc. Zeph. 7:4-5; Jeremias 1972: 207; Van Unnik 1954: 96-97; Jones 1995: 258-59; for a comparative chart of lists, see Davies and Allison 1997: 426; cf. Tob 1:16-17; 4:16-17; Sir 18:21; Jas 1:27; outside Jewish circles, cf. Diog. Laert. *Lives* 1.70; Babrius 103.6-8; Friedländer 1965: 1;210-11; on hospitality, see Keener 1991a: 97, 196; in general, Koenig 1985. Presumably Jewish tradition would advocate visiting prisoners, too, in times of persecution when the pious were detained for their faith.

(cf. Matthey 1980). That the "siblings" are here "disciples" is the majority view in church history and among contemporary New Testament scholars, although those who hold "siblings" to be disciples divide sharply over whether they are specifically missionaries or poor fellow disciples in general.[236] This interpretation fits the function of analogous eschatological discourses (e.g., 1 Enoch 62; 103–4; 4 Ezra passim; 2 Bar. 72), which often encourage repressed minorities that God will judge the world on the basis of how it treated them (Stanton 1993: 223-28).

Blessing (Gen 12:3), inheritance (Mt 5:5; 19:29; 21:38), and kingdom relate to the promised land concept of the exodus, and had become components of Israel's eschatological hope by the time of Jesus (see on 5:3-12; in Paul, cf. 1 Cor 6:9-10; Gal 3:14; 5:21; Eph 1:3, 14). The paragraph in 25:41-46 repeats the literary pattern of 25:34-40, but because it follows it functions climactically (contrast the reverse sequence in judgment in Sib. Or. 4:183-92). The horrifying conclusion is the damnation of people who did not actively embrace the messengers of the gospel but nevertheless were oblivious to how they had offended God. The goats thus depart (7:23) into eternal fire (the worst possible conception of hell; see comment on 3:8, 10, 12), but God had not originally created them for the fire or the fire for them (cf. 4 Ezra 8:59-60; contrast b. ʿErub. 19a; perhaps Rom 9:22; Prov 16:4). Rather, it had been "prepared" (cf. 25:34), that is, by God for the devil and his angels (cf. 2 Pet 2:4; 1QM 13.11-12; 15.13-14).[237]

But in the context of the surrounding parables, "receiving" Christ's messengers probably involves more than *only* initially embracing the message of the kingdom: it means treating one's fellow servants properly (24:45-49). Unless disciples "receive" one another in God's household, they reject Christ whose representatives their fellow disciples are (18:5-6, 28-29). Paul likewise reminds the Corinthians that to be reconciled to him is to be reconciled to God himself (2 Cor 5:11–7:1).[238]

236. See, e.g., Michaels 1965; Grassi 1965b: 46; Cope 1969; Ladd 1974a: 191-99; Harrington 1982: 101; Gundry 1982: 511-14; France 1985: 355; Akano 1992; Blomberg 1992a: 377-78; Hagner 1995: 745; Overman 1996: 349-51; most fully, Gray 1989.

237. Prepared by God: Tob 6:17; Wis 9:8; the expression especially applies to eschatological reward or judgment (cf. 20:23; Rom 9:23; 1 Enoch 22:3; 54:1-2; 4 Ezra 8:60; 2 Bar. 21:17; 2 Enoch 9:1; ARN 12A). For eternal blessedness in Roman literature, one might compare Macrob. *Comm.* 1.4.4 in van der Horst 1973: 223. For the devil's angels, though of questionable date, see, e.g., Life of Adam 14:3; Test. 'Asher 6:4; Asc. Isa. 1:3; 2:2. Later rabbinic tradition frequently contrasts Eden and Gehinnom (m. 'Abot 5:20; b. Ber. 28b; ʿErub. 19a; Yoma 87a; Gen. Rab. 65:22; Ex. Rab. 7:4; Lev. Rab. 32:1; Qoh. Rab. 7:14, §3).

238. Judgment for ignorantly rejecting, and blessings for unwittingly accepting, divine messengers occurs frequently in ancient literature, both Greco-Roman (Ovid *Metam.* 8.621-29; Paus. 3.16.2-3; cf. Acts 14:11-12) and Jewish (e.g., Heb 13:2; cf. Gen 18; Tob 5:4-6, 12; 9:1-5; Philo *Abr.* 114; the shipwreck victim who turned out to be the king in Qoh. Rab. 11:1).

How Much Is Jesus Worth? (26:1-16)

Cf. Mk 14:1-11; Lk 7:36-50; 22:1-6; Jn 11:47-53; 12:1-8. Matthew concludes his grand eschatological vision of the exalted Son of Man with the harsh reality of present suffering (25:35-36), leading directly into the Passion Narrative. As Mark intimately connects Jesus' suffering (Mk 14–15) with that of the disciples (Mk 13) in a climax that fits the rest of his narrative, so for Matthew the Passion Narrative reminds disciples in this age of their present testing until their eschatological deliverance (e.g., 24:42-43; 25:13; 26:41). Because the Passion story provides the historical record of their once-for-all redemption, it reveals in intimate detail both the concrete expression of God's love for his people and the awfulness of their rebellion against his will. Matthew thus expands the irony already latent in the Passion Narrative: the travesties of justice, the confessions of Gentiles like Pilate and Roman soldiers, the recollections of Satan's testing in the words of the religious leaders at the cross, and so forth. But whereas Matthew teaches about the historic passion of Jesus, this is not his only concern. Because Jesus' sacrifice becomes the model for that of his disciples (16:24), it invites Matthew's audience to count the cost of discipleship in a world hostile to God's purposes and agendas.[1]

Excursus: Historical Tradition in the Passion Narrative

Because both address the unjust death of the righteous, the Passion Narratives repeat some themes also appearing in martyr stories (e.g., 2 Macc 6–7; Wis 2:12-20; cf. Sisti 1977; *Acts of the Alexandrian Martyrs* in *CPJ* 2:55-107, §§154-59), as many scholars have properly emphasized (e.g., Dibelius 1971: 201; Donahue 1976: 65-66; Weeden 1976: 66; Nickelsburg 1980; Aune 1987: 52-53; Robbins 1992: 173, 188).[2]

1. Although the Passion Narrative is critical to Matthew, his Gospel is not simply "a Passion Narrative with an extended introduction," as some characterize Mark; the speech sections are too significant (Dahl 1995: 64-65).

2. A stock arsenal of motifs may have been applied when expanding stories for dramatic purposes; one may thus compare the mother in Maccabean accounts with the Spartan mother Argileonis in Plut. *Sayings of Spartan Women, Mor.* 240C. Cf. Robbins 1992: 185, following Nickelsburg 1980: 156 on the tradition of a righteous sufferer vindicated by God, but note that while similar story lines

But important as this observation is for analysis of the texts, apart from the fact that both martyr stories and Gospel Passion Narratives involve a righteous person's unjust death, the parallels may be inadequate to place the Gospel Passion stories *fully* in this genre, especially given the differences.[3] Some features characteristic of martyr stories, such as betrayal, refusal to compromise, and sentencing (Boring 1995: 152), reflect the common pattern of ancient law and Jewish resilience, rather than the borrowing of motifs (though recording such details augments the hortatory value of the narratives).[4]

Of the other motifs both share, many are no more distinctively characteristic of martyr stories than of other ancient literature. For example, where possible, Diogenes Laertius ends his discussions of the lives of eminent philosophers with their death, for example, with Cleanthes in 7.5.176. Martyr stories of course could vindicate their protagonist's devotion and so packed more impact than other death accounts; a legendary figure might even receive a legendary martyrdom (cf. *Life of Aesop,* end, in Drury 1976: 29).

Nevertheless, we can hardly suppose that Jesus' execution was merely fabricated to fit this genre (most biographies that reported their subjects' death did not conclude with martyrdom, and nearly all scholars concur with good reason that the basic kerygma arose shortly after Jesus' execution). Jewish accounts stress martyrdom as an example of commitment, but despite the use of Jesus' death as a model in the Gospel narratives (16:24), summaries of the earliest gospel (e.g., 1 Cor 15:3-4) suggest their very early kerygmatic function as well. In other words, martyr stories may explain the form in which some cohesive Passion Narrative or Narratives circulated, but they would not indicate their composition as fiction. Theissen 1991: 123 concludes, "There is no analogy to the Passion narrative in all of ancient literature. Elements of Hellenistic acts of the martyrs and Jewish tales of martyrdom have been melded into something quite new." If he overstates their uniqueness from a formal

---

illustrate the nuances with which an ancient audience would have heard the story, they do not demonstrate dependence or genetic relationship. Those who take moral (or immoral) stands against the status quo often invite repression, and did so even more often in antiquity; and presupposing that no deity would ever vindicate those aligned with that deity's cause is no more historically "neutral" than presupposing the reverse. The tradition places Jesus especially within the rejected prophet tradition (cf. Robbins 1992: 186).

3. Boring 1995: 156 lists contrasts with the Maccabean martyr accounts: the Gospels avoid sensationalistic details, interpretive speeches by Jesus, a Stoic lesson contrasting reason with emotions (Plut. *Whether Vice Is Sufficient to Cause Unhappiness* 2; 4 Macc 8:15; though this feature says more about the social context of the Maccabean audience than about any larger genre per se), and "vengeful threats."

4. E.g., though Greek thought readily supplied intelligibility to an atoning martyr tradition (cf. Robbins 1992: 187 following Williams 1975: 137-254), early Jewish Christians could have drawn on the Isaian servant songs (see comment on 20:28). The concept of atonement in general appears in the Hebrew Bible and is widespread in apparently unrelated cultures, and the ancient Mediterranean champion tradition appears in the Hebrew Bible (1 Sam 17; 2 Sam 2:14-16; cf. Yamauchi 1972: 64-65; Gordon 1965b: 262) just as e.g., with Aias and Hector in the *Iliad* bk. 8, or with Menelaos and Alexandros (Paris) in bk. 3. On the diversity of Jewish martyr stories, see van Henten 1985.

standpoint, he nevertheless corrects an overemphasis on parallels that explains less than is sometimes claimed. The vast majority of ancient biographies concluded with the subject's death, funeral, and related events (Burridge 1992: 146-47, 179-80); the roughly 15 percent of Matthew's narrative devoted to the passion is comparable to the length devoted to such matters in contemporary biographies (Burridge 1992: 197-98).[5]

Mack at times substitutes suspicion of motives (suggesting that scholars have gone easy on the Passion Narratives from faith prejudice) for actual evidence that the narratives are unreliable (1988: 249; for arguments, see 249-68). Despite this confidence, he cites Jeremias (a "conservative" scholar, 254) only three times, and never Blinzler, Stauffer, Hengel, or other more conservative continental scholars. In contrast to Mack and his naive dismissal of previous scholarship on the Passion Narratives as uncritical (Perry wrote as early as 1920; cf. Lietzmann's skepticism on some points in 1931), we have no record of any Christianity where the basic structure of the kerygma was missing, whether or not Christians had yet constructed full Passion Narratives.[6] Other narratives may have figured as much in early Christian ethical preaching, but it is likely that the early Christians would have told and retold the Passion story, which lay at the heart of their kerygma, and that the Gospel writers would have here a variety of oral and perhaps written traditions from which to draw.[7] Paul has a sequence similar to Mark's (1 Cor 11:23; 15:3-5; cf. Jewish and Roman responsibility in 1 Thess 2:14-15; 1 Cor 1:23), and if, as is probable, John represents an independent tradition (e.g., Dodd 1965: 45, 150), it is significant that his Passion Narrative again confirms the outline Mark follows, suggesting a pre-Markan Passion Narrative (Brown 1994: 53-55, 77-80). In preaching one could flesh out the full sequence or omit some of the stories, but the basic outline remained the same (Brown 1994: 54).

But more specific evidence favors the substantial reliability of the Passion Narratives. Theissen 1991: 166-99 argues for the most part (and sufficiently) persuasively that the pre-Markan Passion Narrative as a whole was in use by A.D. 40 in Jerusalem and Judea. Thus, for example, Mark preserves names (such as the sons that identify the second Mary and Simon) that serve no recognizable function in his own narrative — but which may well have been recognizable to the traditionaries of his early Jerusalem source (Mk 15:40, 43; Theissen 1991: 176-77). Place names like Nazareth, Magdala, and Arimathea would mean nothing to audiences outside Palestine (Theissen 1991: 179; I should add here that the Galilean names may have meant little to the Jerusalem church as well, who may have preserved them for the same reasons that Mark did). Although one normally identifies local persons through their fa-

5. While the rest of the Gospels foreshadow this climax, that is also the case in some contemporary biographies (Burridge 1992: 199).

6. Dibelius 1971: 178-217 thinks that "the Passion story is the only piece of Gospel tradition which in early times gave events in their larger connection."

7. Thus Jewish scholars with no faith commitment to the narratives may also suggest that other Gospels draw on pre-Markan Passion material (e.g., Flusser 1988: 575-87, though his particular reconstruction may presuppose Lukan priority).

thers' names, most persons in the Passion Narrative (which identifies more people "than elsewhere in the synoptic tradition") are identified by their place of origin instead. This practice makes the most sense in the church's first generation in Jerusalem, when (and where) it consisted of people from elsewhere (Theissen 1991: 180). Mark presumes his audience's prior knowledge of Pilate and (more significantly) Barabbas and other insurrectionists, despite Pilate's numerous confrontations with such revolutionaries (Theissen 1991: 171, 182-83).[8] Finally, some central characters in the account remain anonymous, probably to protect living persons who could face criminal charges in Jerusalem, fitting other ancient examples of protective anonymity (Theissen 1991: 186-88).[9] Taken together, these arguments seem persuasive.[10]

Markan editing of the Passion Narrative (for Markan structuring, see, e.g., Beavis 1987) also does not challenge the authenticity of the prior tradition;[11] thus, for example, Matthew and Luke may agree against Mark at points (e.g., Mk 14:72; Dewey 1976: 102-3). Independent tradition drawn on by Matthew, Luke and John preserves the name of the high priest, but Mark may follow the oldest Passion account in omitting his name for political prudence, though Pilate, now deposed and despised, could easily be named in this period (Theissen 1991: 172-74; cf. Philo *Leg. Gai.* 299-304). One should see most fully Soardes 1994, who makes a strong case both that Mark uses a source and that we probably cannot separate the tradition from the redaction.

The Passion Narrative fits what we know of the period in question. Thus Craig Evans (1995: 108) compares Josephus's account of Jesus ben Ananias, who similarly entered the temple area during a festival (Jos. *War* 6.300-301). Like Jesus, he spoke of doom for Jerusalem, the sanctuary, and the people, even referring (again like Jesus) to the context of Jeremiah's prophecy of judgment against the temple (Jer 7:34 in *War* 6.301; cf. Jer 7:11 in Mk 11:17).[12] The Jewish leaders arrested and beat Jesus

8. Whether in following a source incompletely or for other reasons, writers occasionally cite as familiar a name not previously mentioned (e.g., Livy 40.55.2); but it is not the usual practice.

9. Some view the fleeing young man of Mk 14:51-52 only in terms of his symbolic significance in the narrative (Crossan 1976: 147-48; Fleddermann 1979; Kelber 1979: 77), but Theissen is probably right to find genuine tradition from the early Palestinian church here (1991: 186; cf. Dibelius 1971: 182-83; Stauffer 1960: 121).

10. Some of Theissen's other arguments (1991: 189-97) are weaker. Pesch 1991 argues at length for a pre-Markan passion narrative, especially the very early last supper material, but Hengel 1991: 209-10 may be correct that Pesch is overly optimistic about his ability to reconstruct sources.

11. Brown 1994: 56 suspects that Mark may have acquired some of his style from frequent recitation of the Passion Narrative, the way some modern evangelists acquire their style from the KJV; further, Mark may have rephrased the narrative in his own words, especially where his sources were oral. Brown 1994: 554 also emphatically challenges some earlier redaction-critical studies on the trial narrative in Mk 14:55-64 (perhaps Donahue 1976), complaining that though "Mark used earlier material . . . *our best methods do not give us the ability to isolate confidently that material in its exact wording, assigning pre-Markan verses and half-verses* from the existing, thoroughly Markan account" (emphasis his).

12. On the opposition Jeremiah faced for his "unpatriotic" prophecies, cf., e.g., Jer 26:6-24; Jos. *Ant.* 10.89-90; angry crowds could also vent their rage on anyone they felt brought them misfortune (Jos. *Life* 149). A man inside Tyre likewise reportedly prophesied its judgment and faced the charge of being a traitor (Diod. Sic. 17.41.7-8, which may be legendary or repeat Alexander's propaganda). A Cynic might be flogged for speaking out and apparently ignore it (Diog. Laert. 6.5.91).

ben Ananias (*War* 6.302) and handed him over to the Roman governor (*War* 6.303), who interrogated him (*War* 6.305). He refused to answer the governor (*War* 6.305), was scourged (6.304), and — in this case unlike Jesus (though cf. Mk 15:9) — released (6.305). The different outcome is not difficult to account for: unlike Jesus ben Ananias, Jesus of Nazareth was not viewed as insane and already had a band of followers, plus a growing reputation that could support messianic claims (cf. Sanders 1993: 267). Jesus ben Ananias could simply be punished; Jesus of Nazareth had to be executed.

Matthew's Passion Narrative starts with the events of the last supper. Because 51 percent of his words follow Mark, some scholars, like Taylor, suppose that Matthew simply embellished Mark with popular stories, lacking other sources (Taylor 1935: 54; cf. Senior 1987). That Matthew calculated that much of his manuscript remained and would have followed standard rhetorical techniques for amplification (which could draw on sources) is quite likely; but given Matthew's dependence on other Palestinian sources elsewhere, one need not suppose that his sources here — admittedly largely oral — are unreliable. One would expect much of the Passion Narrative (those parts with many witnesses) to have been the best-remembered part of Jesus' ministry, especially given the plurality of disciples. While strictly oral sources might lend themselves to freer adaptation, Matthew's familiarity with Palestinian views and language that elsewhere allows him to "re-Judaize" (or, more accurately, "re–*Palestinian* Judaize") Markan accounts also suggests to us that he retained Palestinian traditions about his Lord's passion.

The extravagant anointing at Bethany (26:6-13) is framed by a plot to arrest Jesus (26:3-5, 14-16).[13] The disciples, who elsewhere in the Gospels can appear less wise than the women they seek to silence (e.g., 15:23; cf. Lk 24:11), protest the extravagant anointing of Jesus. One disciple, Judas, who realizes that Jesus advocates servanthood rather than conquest, decides that following Jesus will not be profitable and determines to gain at least some profit. By contrasting characters, Matthew teaches about Jesus and the life of discipleship he demands.

First, knowing that death was his mission, Jesus faced God's calling obediently (26:1-2). By adding another passion announcement here (contrast Mk 14:1-2), Matthew reminds his audience that whatever the power of those who plotted against Jesus (26:3-5), Jesus moved according to his Father's plan and not theirs. Matthew may thereby also encourage his community that no matter how strong the forces arrayed against them, God would ultimately fulfill *his* purposes among them (cf. 16:21-26). In contrast with Judas in this passage (26:14-16), Jesus obeys God's calling at great cost to himself, and pro-

13. Kelber 1976a: 173 rightly notes that women seeking to anoint Jesus frames Mark's Passion section (Mk 14:3-9; 16:1-8); although Matthew cuts the second anointing, he preserves the frame involving women's devotion.

vides a model for those who would follow him. (That Jesus' death would coincide with the Passover — 26:2 — was also significant, on which see comment on 26:17-30.)[14]

Second, not all those who are supposed to lead God's people follow the rules (26:3-5). Matthew's audience may have experienced repression from a sociopolitical elite, but anyone in the ancient Mediterranean could recognize this narrative's abuse of power. In Matthew's view, the Jerusalem aristocracy (21:46) as well as Pilate (27:24) concern themselves more with political prudence and crowd control than with justice (26:5). Matthew can employ the expression "take counsel" (26:4) for unjust "plotting" (12:14; 28:12; cf. 27:1, 7). A first-century audience would respond to this sort of "taking counsel" as negatively as most audiences today would (Jos. *Life* 236).

Although the plan to arrest Jesus away from the crowds was politically prudent, it was the stratagem of those who could not win by persuasion or demonstrations of God's power. Throughout the Mediterranean, the wealthy, especially those wealthy by heredity, formed a ruling class; Judean tradition bestowed this role especially on aristocratic priests (Sanders 1990: 79). The high-priestly office constituted the most powerful religious, and one of the most powerful political, positions in Jewish Palestine (see excursus, below).[15] Romans were fond of reminding local aristocracies that they held their power with Rome's blessing and were themselves subject to Roman authority (cf., e.g., Plut. *Praec. Ger. Reip.* 813EF, in Trebilco 1994: 346), and the Judean priestly aristocracy was no exception (Stauffer 1960: 102; Winter 1961: 43; Vermes 1984: 12).

Annas held power from A.D. 6 to 15 and retained considerable political influence until his death in 35; he may have dominated the two high priests (his successors included a son-in-law and five sons) who followed (Reicke 1974: 142-43; Jos. *Ant.* 20.198). The current high priest, Joseph Caiaphas, was Annas's son-in-law; that he remained in office nineteen years (A.D. 18-36) — longer than any other first-century high priest — suggests his political acumen in keeping the Romans content (Schnackenburg 1980: 2:348; Sanders 1993: 265). In the case of threats to the political stability of Jerusalem, of course, that would mean dealing with them swiftly and efficiently. And someone who caused a commotion in the temple in the dangerously crowded period just before Passover was clearly a threat to the public order (so Vermes 1993: ix-x, though he doubts that Jesus saw himself in messianic terms, 5). Despite his otherwise high opinion of Caiaphas, Sanders 1993: 265 thinks the high priest probably wanted Jesus "dead for the same reason Antipas wanted John dead": public order. That Caiaphas and Pilate would have cooperated in the matter is likely; "That is the way the gospels describe the events, and that is the way

14. For how positively this courage would sound to first-century hearers (and how this narrative would thus function epideictically), see comment on 16:21.

15. The Romans probably used public religious offices for politics even more so; cf. Taylor 1966: 90-95.

things really happened, as the numerous stories in Josephus prove" (Sanders 1993: 269).[16]

Excursus: High Priests

Elsewhere in the Roman Empire, the title did not always bear the prestige it held in Palestine (cf. Lewis 1983: 47; Reicke 1974: 147). Perhaps under foreign influence, Jewish writers came to speak of the priestly aristocracy or high-priestly family as high priests, rather than merely the ruling chief priest, the *kohen hagadol* of the Old Testament (e.g., 1QM 2:1; Jos. *War* 2.243, 316, 320, 342, 410-11; 4.151, 315; *Life* 197; Mk 2:26; Acts 4:6; Stern 1974/76a: 601, 603; Sanders 1993: 327-32; Jeremias 1964c: 51).

Even Pharisaic tradition respected the office of high priest (m. Hor. 3:1; p. Sanh. 2:1, §2; Acts 23:5-6), though Sadducees dominated it. The priesthood as a whole reportedly included both those committed to extrabiblically stringent purity rules (probably Pharisees or their sympathizers) and those who were not (p. Ter. 6:1). Jewish high priests held considerable political authority (Smallwood 1962), recognized even among Gentiles (Diod. Sic. 40.3.5-6). Contrary to Israelite law, however, Roman officials freely gave and revoked the office of high priests; thus Quirinius installed Annas (Jos. *Ant.* 18.26); Vitellius retired Caiaphas after Pilate's recall to Rome (Jos. *Ant.* 18.95).

Josephus experienced the opposition of high priests he considered corrupt (*Life* 216). He especially regards the chief priests as corrupt during the period of Agrippa II (A.D. 59-65; Sanders 1993: 324), but this specification may reflect his own uncomfortable experiences and suggest broader corruption within the aristocratic ranks from which such priests were drawn.[17] Qumran and others opposed the priestly aristocracy that controlled the temple (e.g., 1QpHab 9.4-5); "For many marginalized groups in this period the problem, in short, was the local leaders and politicians in Roman Palestine" (Overman 1996: 329).

---

16. Rome held the high priests responsible for controlling the masses (Jos. *War* 2.232-44), and the high priests moved against potential threats to public order when they thought it best to do so (Jos. *War* 6.300-309; *Ant.* 20.199-203; Sanders 1993: 266-67).

17. Perhaps in part because I find myself more skeptical that religion often changes human nature, I am less sympathetic to their piety than is Sanders 1993: 336. They probably acted in their own self-interest, as well as for the peace, in relations with the Romans (Horsley 1986b). The charges may be stylized, sectarian polemic, as Sanders suggests (and against the priesthood in general he may be right — 1992: 182-89), but one should not dismiss too readily the reasons for the polemic, which appear widely (cf. 1QpHab 9.4-5; Test. Levi 14:1; 2 Bar. 10:18; t. Minhot 13.21 in Avigad 1980: 130; idem 1983: 71; Hengel 1974b: 23); corrupt priesthoods were common targets of polemic in the ancient Near East through the first century (Crocker 1990). Cf., e.g., the servants of the later Ananias who beat poorer priests to seize their tithes (Jos. *Ant.* 20.181, 206).

Excursus: The Sadducees

Though some aristocrats were not Sadducees (some, like Gamaliel, were Pharisees), nearly all the Sadducees belonged to the aristocracy (see Sanders 1992: 318, 332). Probably a priestly sect, they were likely the well-to-do priests who had remained loyal to the Zadokite line during the Maccabean era (while other Zadokites fled to Qumran and elsewhere — cf. 1QS 5.2; 6.3-4; CD 5.5), returning to positions of power under the Romans (see Baumbach 1971).[18]

Later rabbinic tradition links them with "Boethusians" under the special charge that they denied the resurrection from the dead (ARN 5 A; 10 B; cf. m. Ber. 9:5; Bowker 1973: 53-76).[19] Many Jews besides the Pharisees felt that a denial of such future hope led to wickedness (Wis 2:1-24). Other grounds also separated these aristocrats from the dominant views that became rabbinic practice (m. Nid. 4:2; Yad. 4:7; t. Nid. 5:2; Sukk. 3:1). Probably claiming to take Scripture as their only authority, the Sadducees felt no obligation to embrace Pharisaic traditions (Jos. *Ant.* 18.16; cf. Neusner 1984: 27-28; Sanders 1990: 107). Nevertheless, powerful Pharisees and others had to work alongside them before 70.[20]

Excursus: The Sanhedrin

Although Matthew describes the assembly of representatives from the ruling class as a "sanhedrin" only in 26:59 (cf. Mk 14:55; 15:1), the group likely overlaps with what we otherwise know as Jerusalem's Sanhedrin. A *synedrion* was a ruling council, equivalent to a *boulē,* or a senate.[21] Cities like Tiberias had their own ruling senates composed of the leading citizens (Jos. *Life* 64, 69, 169, 313, 381); such assemblies were distinguishable from the larger citizen assembly (Jos. *Life* 300).[22] The Jerusa-

18. Manson 1961: 16 derives "Sadducees" from a cognate of "Sanhedrin," but the Zadokite explanation seems more probable (with Lohse 1978: 74 and others).

19. Medieval tradition sometimes links them with Karaites (Jacobs 1973: 10), perhaps for polemical purposes against the Karaites; others (aside from those scholars who once dated the Scrolls to the medieval period) have found for the Karaites predecessors in the Essenes (early after the discovery of the Scrolls; cf., e.g., Ginsberg 1953: 81; Kahle 1953; Wieder 1956-57; Fritsch 1956: 86-89).

20. Pace Eppstein 1966, even had Pharisaism exercised adequate control to effect excommunication, the Sadducees could not have been excommunicated almost a decade before the temple's destruction. Worse still, Jeremias 1969: 264-65 takes later rabbinic sources at such face value that he supposes that Pharisaic (proto-rabbinic) authority had stripped the Sadducees of power (cf. Finkelstein 1962: 2:659).

21. "Sanhedrin" is a broad rather than restrictive term, applicable also in Greek texts to an informal assembly of advisors (Diod. Sic. 13.111.1) or, frequently, to Rome's "senate" (e.g., Diod. Sic. 40.1.1; Dion. Hal. 5.70.5; 6.30.2; 6.81.1; 6.85.2; 8.69.2; 9.32.5; 10.2.6; 12.1.14; 12.6.2 [4]; in these texts it appears interchangeably with *boulē,* a more common term, e.g., in Dion. Hal. 5.71.1; 6.1.1; 6.21.1; 6.81.4).

22. Officials could also assemble their own administrative "councils" from among their friends (e.g., Jos. *Life* 368).

lem Sanhedrin was in a sense the municipal aristocracy of Jerusalem; but just as the Roman senate wielded power far beyond Rome because of Rome's power, Jerusalem's Sanhedrin wielded some influence in national affairs, to the degree that Roman prefects and Herodian princes allowed.[23]

The Sanhedrin may well have held seventy-one members, as tradition indicates;[24] it is, however, doubtful that all members were expected to be present on all occasions (especially an emergency meeting on the night when people had eaten the Passover).[25] The Sanhedrin included the high priest, who according to tradition could break ties (cf. Ferguson 1987: 453). Again according to tradition, they met in the Chamber of Hewn Stone on the Temple Mount (t. Sheqal. 3:27; Sifre Deut. 152.1.2; b. Yoma 25a; Gen. Rab. 70:8; Num. Rab. 19:26; Qoh. Rab. 1:1, §1); otherwise they met close to the Temple Mount (cf. Jos. *War* 5.144).[26] Our first-century sources, the New Testament and Josephus, include Sadducees and other groups in the Sanhedrin, under high-priestly control; later rabbis portray the Sanhedrin as an assembly of rabbis (Cohen 1987: 156). The later portrayals should not surprise us; rabbinic portraits of the Sanhedrin include more striking anachronisms than this, depicting leaders of the Sanhedrin in biblical times (e.g., b. Ber. 3b; Gen. Rab. 74:15; Ex. Rab. 1:13; Pesiq. R. 11:3).[27]

According to rabbinic (and probably Pharisaic) ideals, judges who proved themselves locally could be promoted to the Sanhedrin (t. Sheqal. 3:27), but in actuality the Sanhedrin in Jesus' day probably consisted largely of members of the Jerusalem aristocracy and wealthy landowners in the vicinity. Rulers could use

23. Overman 1996: 372-73, 385 regards the Sanhedrin as a Roman political institution, although conceding that "some of the local Jewish elite may have been involved." Yet in cities like Jerusalem Rome ruled through municipal aristocracies — here, pro-Roman Jewish aristocrats.

24. M. Sanh. 1:6; cf. Josephus's Galilean council of A.D. 70 in *War* 2.570; *Life* 79, and that of the Zealots in *War* 4.336, both undoubtedly following the standard contemporary model; the models probably derive ultimately from Mosaic tradition (Exod 24:9; Num 11:16, 24; cf. Ezek 8:11). Josephus also assumed a council of seven judges as a lower court in every city (*War* 2.571; *Ant.* 4.214). An odd number to break a tie made sense; as in Roman law (Dion. Hal. 7.64.6), a tie vote would yield acquittal.

25. Brown 1994: 348-49 doubts that an exact list of 71 members existed in the first century, suggesting that it merely included elders from distinguished families alongside chief priests, representatives of whom were expected to appear.

26. For bibliography on the Sanhedrin, see Safrai 1974/76e: 418 (the section on the Sanhedrin is on 379-400). Josephus generally prefers the term "sanhedrin," "assembly," in *Antiquities,* and *boulē,* "council," in *War.* Later rabbis believed that God supported the decrees of the rabbinic *beth din hagadol,* great assembly (Ex. Rab. 15:20), on which Israel rightly depended (Song Rab. 7:3, §1; Lam. Rab. 2:4, §8).

27. Brown 1994: 58 suggests that Matthew as a former scribe (Mt 13:51-52) may play down scribal opposition, hence in contrast to Mark has chief priests 15 times, elders 7 times, but scribes only 2 times here. This is improbable, however, given his excoriation of scribes with Pharisees in 23:13-36; Matthew may instead simply wish to emphasize that the priestly aristocracy largely engineered the execution, a conclusion our other data for the most part support. Some of the "scribes" may have been Pharisees, but the Pharisees, though represented (Acts 23:6-9), probably were not dominant in the Sanhedrin (Brown 1994: 350-52), despite Josephus's possible favoritism toward them (Jos. *Ant.* 18.15, 17; cf. *Life* 1, 12 and *Ant.* passim; Brown 1994: 353-56).

sanhedrins, or assemblies, the way some politicians today use committees: to secure the end one wants without taking full responsibility for that decision. In Josephus, rulers like Herod appointed the Sanhedrin members they wished and consequently obtained the results they wished (see Sanders 1993: 482-83; cf. *Ant.* 15.173; 20.216-18). Before Herod came to power, the Jerusalem Sanhedrin exercised significant authority (Jos. *Ant.* 14.177). In Pilate's time, without Herod the Great's interference and with the Romans expecting local aristocracies to administer the business they could (cf. Jos. *War* 2.331, 405; *Ant.* 20.11), we should not be surprised that the chief priests would convene a sanhedrin (Jos. *Ant.* 20.200), especially since the priestly aristocracy constituted a large portion of it (cf. Sanders 1993: 484-87; Jos. *War* 2.331, 336; *Ant.* 17.160, 164; 20.216-17; probably the municipal aristocracy in *Ant.* 14.91, 163, 167, 180; *Life* 62). We should also not be surprised if the Sanhedrin sought to please Rome (cf. Kennard 1962).

Less than four decades after the events the Gospels describe, Jerusalem's aristocracy continued to act as a body. When the high priest and the leading Pharisee allegedly acted without the approval of the rest of the assembly, they provoked that assembly's anger (Jos. *Life* 309).

A small minority of scholars, wishing to preserve both the later rabbinic portrait of the Sanhedrin and the one found in Josephus and early Christian sources, have opted for two Sanhedrins — the religious Sanhedrin of the rabbis and the political Sanhedrin attested in first-century sources. Some of these scholars came to argue that the political Sanhedrin tried Jesus, thereby exonerating the religious Sanhedrin of the rabbis. One scholar favoring the rabbinic picture has even argued that the Gospels and Acts are late sources on this matter, with changes into the fourth century (Mantel 1961). Nevertheless, even apart from textual evidence to the contrary, evidence within the early Christian texts refutes this theory: later writers fail to clear up conflicts and to impose later theology (Sutcliffe 1963). In the final analysis, it is simply anachronistic to reject all our first-century portraits on the basis of later, idealized rabbinic accounts, although reliable tradition may remain in the latter at points. Few scholars have therefore accepted the double Sanhedrin thesis (see Blinzler 1959: 15, 140; Brown 1994: 343-48).

After examining Josephus's three mentions of "Sanhedrin" and five of *boulē* (Jos. *War* 2.331, 336; 5.142-44, 532; *Ant.* 20.11, 200-201, 216-17; *Life* 62), Brown 1994: 342-43 concludes that Josephus's portrait of the Sanhedrin is quite close to that of the Gospels and Acts. They judge, consist of "chief priests, scribes, and rulers or influential citizens (= elders)," sentence those found guilty of crimes, and constitute the leading Jewish body with which Roman rulers would deal. Clearly they "played a major administrative and judicial role in Jewish self-governance in Judea."

Some commentators have observed the incongruity between the leaders' stated intention not to arrest Jesus at the feast and their arrest of him before the festival has ended (e.g., Anderson 1976: 304-5). From the Gospel writers' perspective, these leaders may not have known Jesus' God well, but they knew the Romans and their people (cf. Jn 11:48)[28] and were concerned to time matters in a politically expedient manner (21:46; 27:24). Because the city's population (we follow a median estimate of 50,000, but this is only a guess) may have quintupled during Passover season and hopes for redemption ran high during this season,[29] crowd control became especially difficult (cf. Lane 1974a: 490).[30] The Roman prefect thus spent time in Jerusalem, strengthening with additional troops the garrison in the fortress Antonia (Jos. *War* 2.223-27; *Ant.* 20.105-12; on the fortress, see further Wightman 1990). *He* would make the matter public, but only after the more delicate arrest. The leaders do not intend to defer arresting him until the festival is over — Jesus would then have returned to Galilee with the other pilgrims — but during the "festal assembly," that is, while the crowds are gathered during the day (Gundry 1982: 519). Execution during a festival was in some ways ideal, as a deterrent to others (cf. Jeremias 1971: 78; Hill 1979: 52; Stauffer 1960: 209; m. Sanh. 11:4).

Third, Jesus is worth the best that disciples can offer (26:6-13). Matthew forces his audience, grieved by the failure of every one of their male spiritual predecessors to stand with their Lord in his time of testing (26:40-56), to find solace in the love shown Jesus by the women disciples (26:7; 27:61; 28:1; cf. Mk 15:40-41). Although the threat to their safety may have been less grave, the devotion of women in the Passion Narrative nevertheless puts the male disciples to shame for their cowardice. Although disciples are supposed to let their "good works" shine (5:16), Jesus commends only this woman for a "good work" (26:10).[31]

Indeed, it is male disciples here who actively oppose the woman (more emphatically than in Mark, who does not call the opposers here "disciples"); the disciples become "indignant" (26:8), as they did in 20:24 (there following Mark). Their objection to her behavior in 26:8-9 recalls Jesus' opponents' charges against his disciples earlier in Matthew's narrative (12:2; cf. 9:11, 14; 17:24;

28. Jn 11:48 probably reflects earlier tradition (see Winter 1961: 37; Vermes 1973: 50).

29. Cf. Mek. Pisḥa 14 (Laut. 1:115) on Ex 12:42 (one of several views) in Lane 1974a: 500; traditions in the Passover haggadah in Black 1967: 237; interpretation of the Hallel in t. Ber. 1:10-11; Pesiq. Rab Kah. 27:5; Lev. Rab. 30:5; Pesiq. R. 2:1. Bokser 1985 argues that redemption is more central in early (m. Pesaḥ. 10) than in later texts.

30. Some, relying more on (though lowering — cf. Jos. *War* 6.420) Josephus's estimates, propose a population of over 200,000 for metropolitan Jerusalem (Byatt 1973); but obviously no one, including Josephus, was counting. Based on water supply, estimates settle between 40,000 and 80,000 (Wilkinson 1974a; Broshi 1975; idem 1978:14; Stambaugh and Balch 1986: 97); modern sociological studies may suggest no more than 35,000 (Rohrbaugh 1991: 133; cf. Jeremias 1969: 77-82, estimating 25,000). During Passover perhaps 300,000 to 500,000 people were present (Sanders 1993: 125-27); Josephus's estimates (Jos. *War* 6.423-25) are too high and rabbinic estimates (e.g., t. Pisha 4:15; Lam. Rab. 1:1, §2) are patent exaggerations, but pilgrimage cities today demonstrate how many people can be packed into a city during festivals (e.g., Jochim 1986: 152).

31. The supposed relevance of "prodigies-at-meals" to the anointing (Boring 1995: 146 cites Suet. *Vesp.* 4) falters both because prodigies-at-meals did not constitute a recognizable category of prodigies and because the anointing, while unusual, remains within the bounds of the natural order.

21:16). Particularly in contrast to Judas, who seeks only what he can get from Jesus (26:14-16), this woman seeks what she can offer to Jesus. The extravagance of a disciple's love is but infinitesimal compared to the price of his love for his followers (cf. 26:26-29, again expressed symbolically), but Jesus both accepts it and grants such devoted disciples all the more (26:10, 13).

Hosts of banquets customarily provided oil to anoint the heads of guests of notable social status (Lk 7:46; Bailey 1980: 8; Lachs 1987: 400), but the outpouring of love here is more costly than the mere use of oil in customary acts of hospitality. People often used expensive alabaster bottles, which were semitransparent and resembled marble, to store the most costly ointments (commentators cite texts like Pliny *N.H.* 13.3.19; 36.23.60; see Argyle 1963: 195; Lane 1974a: 492).[32] They would seal the ointment to prevent evaporation, requiring the long neck of the jar to be broken and the ointment to be expended at once (Meier 1980: 312). Archaeologists have uncovered such long-necked flasks in first-century tombs near Jerusalem, suggesting the frequent once-for-all expenditure of this expensive perfume at the death of loved ones (Stanton 1995a: 117). Nard was a costly ointment imported from India (Lane 1974a: 492) or elsewhere in the east (Hor. *Ode* 2.11.16), and its expense might suggest an heirloom passed from one generation to the next (Lane 1974a: 492).

Because people anointed kings on their heads (e.g., 2 Kings 9:6), some scholars suspect that Matthew and Mark or, more arguably, a stage in the tradition they report, may have seen a royal anointing, alongside Jesus' emphasis on an anointing for burial (which probably appears independently in Mark and John; cf. Dibelius 1949: 96; Hooker 1983: 98). In any case, the disciples did not catch either possible christocentric nuance of the anointing (Fenton 1977: 412). That Jesus knew he would not be anointed later may suggest that he would be executed as a criminal (Lane 1974a: 494), although the Gospels suggest that Joseph circumvented custom on such matters (27:58), and women came to anoint him appropriately after the Sabbath (Mk 16:1).[33] We may contrast Jesus' response to that of the disciples; he honors this obscure woman — not even named in the Markan tradition followed by Matthew (cf., however, Jn 11:2, which presupposes the audience's familiarity with an anointing by one of the Marys in the tradition) — more highly than any of the male disciples: her act would henceforth be preserved as part of the passion tradition relating to Jesus' burial (cf. Jdt 14:7), recounted "in the whole world" (26:13), that is, wherever the good news would

32. For hints of the high cost sometimes expended even on normal unguents and perfumes, see Lachs 1987: 401; for ointments used in burials, see, e.g., m. Shab. 23:5 and below on Jesus' burial.

33. If the phrase usually translated "in memory of her" represents a subjective genitive, it could suggest "her memorial" for *Jesus* (Greenlee 1960), although this is not the most obvious way to take the phrase. Closer is the Jewish expression "of blessed memory" or "May their memory be blessed" (Sir 45:1; 46:11; cf. Gaius *Inst.* 1.53) and the formula echoed in rabbinic texts — "May so-and-so be remembered [before God] for good" (Lachs 1987: 401 cites b. B. Bat. 21a; Shab. 13b; cf. m. Yoma 3:9; *Tan. Ha'azinu* 1) — also attested in late inscriptions (Carmon 1973: §§184, 186, pp. 83, 86, 186-87, 192-93; Levine 1982: 8-9).

be preached (24:14). This did not mean, of course, that every individual would know about her, but that her fame would become widespread, as Ovid hopes for himself at the conclusion of his work (Ovid *Metam.* 15.877-79) or others who had acted heroically could expect their memory to be preserved in epics (Virg. *Aen.* 9.446-49; 11.846-47).[34]

Different versions of the anointing story occur in the four Gospels (Mk 14:3-9; Lk 7:36-50; Jn 12:1-8), where the mixture of different traits suggests that the various writers may have conflated two different anointing stories,[35] with Luke's story being the most distinctive (and characteristically Lukan). Moule, for instance, provides a basic summary comparison of some key elements (1965: 112):

Mk	**Matthew**	**Luke**	**John**
Bethany	Bethany	—	Bethany
Simon	Simon	Simon	(Lazarus [Eleazar])
the leper	the leper	a Pharisee	—
a woman	a woman	a sinful woman	Mary
head	head	feet	feet
anointing for burial	anointing for burial	gratitude for forgiveness	anointing for burial

As Sanders observes, "These stories probably rest on memories, though details have been exchanged and possibly confused" (1993: 127). It would have been only natural that in the oral tradition some conflation between two anointing stories would occur; it would be equally natural that each evangelist, reporting only one incident, would employ the most suitable features of the anointings for his own account.[36]

From Matthew's account, we might not guess that the woman is known to Jesus; but in any case, his host's home was probably open for other people from the village to enter and leave at will (Lk 7:36-38; cf. Malina 1981: 78; Koenig 1985: 16-17; Witherington 1984: 55; Talbert 1982: 86). Especially in the Lukan

34. One may compare honorific inscriptions, which could enjoin public mourning in a prominent woman's honor (Horsley 1987: 10-17).

35. Origen harmonized accounts by suggesting three separate anointings (Origen *Matthew* 77; Wiles 1960: 16); but variations likely arose during oral transmission (Dodd 1965: 172). The two stories I propose would be either divergent traditions stemming from one event (e.g., Mack 1988: 200), or a second event in which a second woman probably followed the example of the first (cf. similarly 9:20; 14:36). In view of the likely pre-Markan divergence (except in his programmatic scene at Nazareth, Luke rarely takes such liberties as to rewrite an entire Markan narrative from scratch, and the Johannine account probably confirms the independent antiquity of some of its details), and in view of what most often seems accurate preservation of tradition in the early period (though this pattern would not preclude exceptions transmitted in different circumstances), two distinct anointings eventually conflated in the tradition seem more likely. Following a custom of hospitality, another woman may have followed the example of an earlier woman's anointing.

36. Sanders 1993: 126-27 thinks that Jn 12 may represent a composite of Lk 7 and the accounts in Mt 26/Mk 14, or the traditions associated with them. In any case, he considers it "evident that Jesus attracted women who were not 'followers', but who admired him."

and Johannine versions, where the woman lets down her hair (Lk 7:38; Jn 12:3), her action would appear sexually loose to outsiders, making Jesus look bad for embracing it (cf., e.g., Jeremias 1972: 126; Witherington 1984: 113; Mack 1988: 200-201). (Ancient stories could combine women's heroism with traditional feminine qualities like meekness and modesty, as in Wiersma 1990; despite her submissive act, however, letting down her hair would appear immodest.) But Matthew follows the shorter Markan version, which focuses on her sacrifice and Jesus' anointing in advance for burial.

When Matthew emphasizes that Jesus responds because "he knew the [male disciples'] thoughts" (26:10, rightly interpreting Mark's "said to themselves" in Mk 14:4), readers will recall that Jesus elsewhere had to respond to the religious leaders on the same basis (22:18). As in the final Matthean discourse, Jesus here speaks to disciples who have the potential to become like the very establishment that was hostile to Jesus. Some modern readers take Jesus' reproof in 26:9-11 as playing down the priority of the poor. (That the disciples would actually have thought of the needs of the poor shortly before Passover fit their culture's custom — m. Pesaḥ. 9:11; 10:1; Jeremias 1966a: 54; Jn 13:29; cf. Tob 2:2). Jesus never played down that priority, however (e.g., 5:42; 19:21), and his very words about the poor remaining with them allude to Deuteronomy 15:11, where the context demands caring for the poor (Deut 15:1-10).[37] (Matthew may also intentionally omit some of Mark's words to avoid leaving the impression that believers' obligation to the poor was optional — Gundry 1982: 521.) This woman supplied something for Jesus shortly before his death that no one else can exactly repeat (hence 26:13), but she provides a model of sacrificial love. Subsequent disciples show that sacrificial love to Jesus now by using all their resources for the work of his kingdom (13:44-46), including serving the poor (6:2, 19-24; cf. Lk 12:33-34).

Finally, Judas provides an example of those who follow Jesus for what they can get out of him rather than for how they can serve him (26:14-16). Ancient narrators sometimes contrasted positive and negative moral examples; as Judas contrasts with Peter in 26:69–27:10, he contrasts here with the woman who displays extravagant love in 26:6-13. Judas's motivation for "silver" links him with the deceitful guards (28:12), a disciple who does not care for the master's funds (25:18), or a disciple who worries about preserving one's own (6:19-24; 10:9). Ancients despised those who would betray a tie of loyalty for the sake of a bribe (e.g., in the case of loyalty to one's people, Demosth. *For the Liberty of the Rhodians* 23; *On the Crown* 46-49; *On the Embassy* 120).[38] Loyalty to

37. At least some later rabbis interpreted the passage so literally that they doubted that the poor would even cease in the days of the Messiah (Lachs 1987: 401 cites b. Shab. 63a). Even if this interpretation obtained in Jesus' day, however, it appears irrelevant to his use of the allusion.

38. Cohn 1977: 83 links Judas's betrayal with the tradition that the priestly aristocracy engaged in "undercover activity," a tradition that Cohn insists originated only after the lifetime of Jesus. Against Cohn, the initiative here lies with Judas, and even Romans without interest in pursuing crimes were forced to investigate once a *delator* (accuser) brought activity to their attention (on Christians, see, e.g., Pliny *Ep.* 10.97).

one's people was one of the highest values (Corn. Nep. 13 [Timotheus], 4.4); traitors were widely hated (e.g., Babrius 138.7-8), usually even by family members (Livy 2.5.7-8; Corn. Nep. 4 [Pausanias], 5.3), thought to be hated by the gods (Virg. *Aen.* 6.621), and often despised even by those to whom they betrayed those who trusted them (Livy 1.11.6-7; 5.27.6-10; though not always — Livy 4.61.8-10).

Jesus has continued to discuss his death (26:2, 12), and perhaps at least Judas has now caught on. But when Judas finds that Jesus' kingdom will not profit him materially (and may even cost him his life),[39] he chooses to get what he still can from his lengthy investment in Jesus: he sells him for the price of a slave in the Mosaic legislation (26:15; Ex 21:32; contrast the more lucrative betrayal in Judg 16:5).[40] No less significantly for Matthew, thirty pieces of silver was the wages of Zechariah's faithful shepherd, God or his agent, who sought to rescue Israel from worthless shepherds but was rejected (Zech 11:12-13); that Matthew intends this allusion is clear from his deliberate citation of it when the money goes to the "potter" in 27:9-10 (Zech 11:13). Like another disciple of old (2 Kings 5:26-27), Judas abandoned his spiritual birthright for better material conditions, and in saving his own life lost it for eternity (Mt 16:24-27; 27:1-10).

The Meaning of Jesus' Death (26:17-30)

Cf. Mk 14:12-26; Lk 22:7-20, 39; Jn 13:1, 21-30; 1 Cor 11:23-26. As Jesus' death approaches, he instructs his disciples more fully regarding the meaning of his mission. The disciples could not guess that their teacher's death was part of God's sovereign plan, and would scatter in fear once it came; but by reinterpreting a familiar ritual Jesus gave them a new way of looking at God's purposes that would make sense to them once he had risen.

39. Cullmann 1956b: 39 suggests that Judas had materialistic ideas concerning Messiahship into which Jesus' teachings (especially those concerning vicarious suffering and the new covenant from Isaiah, presented more directly in the next paragraphs) could not fit. (Brandon suggests that Judas sought to betray *Jesus'* revolutionary intentions, but this speculation hardly fits the extant evidence about Jesus; more likely, he betrayed the inner circle's view that Jesus was a "king" — Sanders 1985: 309.)

40. Although Gen 37:28 reports that Joseph's brothers sold him for twenty shekels (the correct average price of slaves in the era in which Joseph lived), most manuscripts of Test. Gad 2:3 have thirty (*OTP* 815 n. a suggests that this is either from Ex 21:32 or a Christian interpolation; I suspect the latter). Hagner 1995: 761 is impressed that "thirty shekels" reflects a Sumerian idiom for a very small sum (following Reiner 1968); but it is hardly likely that first-century Jews would have any contact with Sumerian idioms. Thirty silver coins was not a small sum; by 100 B.C. a silver drachma was worth about 500 copper ones (*Select Papyri* 2:xxxiii).

Excursus: Was Jesus Executed on Passover?

Whereas in the Fourth Gospel Jesus is executed on the day of the Passover sacrifice (18:28), the Synoptics present the last supper as a Passover meal, presupposing that the lamb has already been offered in the temple. Both traditions — a paschal last supper and a paschal crucifixion — are theologically pregnant (cf., e.g., Byron 1993; Boring 1995: 147), but I suspect that Jesus, followed by the earliest tradition, may have intended the symbolism for the last supper, whereas John has applied the symbolism more directly to the referent to which the last supper pointed.

Many scholars have argued that John is historically correct (e.g., Oesterley 1925: 158-67; Blinzler 1959; Stauffer 1960: 143; Grappe 1985; Meier 1991a: 395-401; Brown 1994: 1351-73), noting that the last supper narrative mentions no lamb and that an execution on the first day of the feast was inconceivable, and suggesting that the disciples could have celebrated Passover early, according to a sectarian calendar (Reicke 1974: 179-82; Meier 1991a: 396), or that Mark inserted Passover references for theological reasons (Jewett 1979: 27; cf. Meier 1980: 316). Other details of the Passion Narrative behind Mark, such as the Sanhedrin's originally wishing to kill Jesus before the feast (Mk 14:1-2), Simon's coming from the fields (15:21, which some take as coming from work), or burial on a "preparation day" (which in Mk 15:42 is preparation for the Sabbath, but some take as preparation for Passover; Theissen 1991: 167), can support the Johannine chronology.

But the priestly aristocracy might act even on Passover to preserve public order, Pilate would care little for calendrical matters, and an execution on the day on which the lamb had been eaten would deter crowds no less than the day on which they were being slaughtered, if the site of execution were not far outside Jerusalem's walls. The minor details "behind" Mark's Passion Narrative could also be explained in other ways that fit the narrative equally well. Mark could simply be correct that the preparation was for the Sabbath;[41] Simon could come "from the fields" because he has spent the night in a suburb like Bethphage; and on the Sanhedrin's wishing to kill Jesus before the feast, see comment on 26:1-2, above. The main argument against the Johannine chronology in a conflict between John and the Synoptics is that on most points Mark's narrative seems more dependable for historical detail, John's more expository (although many hold John's chronology to be an exception, especially regarding the duration of Jesus' ministry).

Thus many scholars suggest that the Synoptics are historically correct; the Synoptics certainly portray the last supper as a Passover meal, even on details that their audiences would no longer have recognized as relevant (Jeremias 1966a: 20-23, 62-84; Hagner 1995: 772-73; cf. Hill 1972: 336-37).[42] As scholars commonly note

41. Despite disagreement on the relation to the festival, most commentators agree that the crucifixion occurred on a Friday (Brown 1994: 1350-51). Even by the third century rabbis were not unanimous about trying and executing someone on a Sabbath (p. Sanh. 4:6, §2).

42. Those favoring the Johannine dating respond that, whereas the Synoptics regard the meal as a Passover meal (this is "challenged by no one"), this does not decide the *historical* question

(e.g., Higgins 1955: 208-9), John certainly had theological reasons to place the death of God's lamb (Jn 1:29) on Passover (Jn 19:36).

One attempt to harmonize the Johannine and Synoptic dating, originally associated with a proposal of Annie Jaubert in 1957 (Jaubert 1965), has commended itelf to a number of scholars. According to this proposal, Jesus followed a solar calendar like the one used at Qumran, but Jerusalem's official Passover, and the one followed by John, occur afterward. Given sectarian calendars (cf. Jub. 49:10, 14; Herr 1974/76)[43] and even calendrical differences among rabbis due to different witnesses regarding the new moon (m. Rosh Hash. 2:9), it is not *impossible* that Jesus' disciples followed an Essene, sectarian date for the Passover (cf. Driver 1965: 330, 335; Simon 1967: 151; Stauffer 1960: 115; F. F. Bruce 1980a: 57; F. F. Bruce 1969: 78; Morris 1971: 785).

But would such an important disagreement with the temple authorities have gone unnoted in the tradition (cf. Benoit 1973: 1:87-93)? It is also possible that John followed a Palestinian and the Synoptics the Diaspora reckoning of Passover (Shepherd 1961),[44] but this fails to explain the paschal character of the last supper tradition, the accommodation of Diaspora pilgrims at the festival, and again the inadequacy of supporting evidence in the tradition. Calendrical differences may allow us to harmonize John and the Synoptics, but most likely John has simply provided a theological interpretation of Jesus' death, considering the way he *opens* Jesus' ministry with the temple cleansing so that the shadow of passion week may cover the whole period. If the two accounts must be harmonized, however, the simplest solution would be the best: "Jesus, knowing that he would be dead before the regular time for the meal, deliberately held it in secret one day early" (France 1985: 365).[45]

(Bornkamm 1969: 132); but then how do Mark and Paul, writing for largely Gentile audiences, conform the narrative so closely to Passover traditions? And if the Synoptics report the disciples actually keeping the Passover but on a "sectarian" date, would sectarians have observed as many other paschal customs as the text suggests? Jeremias admittedly depends on later traditions, but what evidence we do have fits the Gospel narratives and can hardly have derived from them.

43. The calendar of Jubilees may have had some impact on public policy in the second century B.C. (Wirgin 1965: 12-17, 42-43) and has some parallels with later rabbinic calendrical halakah (Grintz 1972: 325), but in contrast to what became mainstream Judaism it preserves the older solar calendar (Morgenstern 1955; cf. Marcus 1956: 12), which is why some even (probably wrongly) label it pre-Hasmonean (Zeitlin 1957-58: 224; cf. idem 1939: 8-16). Opposition to the lunar calendar is implied even in the creation narrative (Jub. 2:9-10; cf. 6:36). This places Jubilees much closer to Qumran thought than to Pharisaism (e.g., Brownlee 1951: 32; Baumgarten 1958a; Grintz 1972: 324); Rivkin 1982 even thinks that Jubilees writes polemically against the Pharisaic calendar.

44. Some Diaspora Jews may have ignored Palestinian rules (*CPJ* 3:27-29, §467). Carson 1984b: 529 also mentions the proposal that Pharisees and Sadducees followed divergent calendars (Strack-Billerbeck) or that the Galileans followed the Pharisaic (and Synoptic) one and Judeans the Sadducean (and Johannine) one. But I suspect that a major difference in *observance* in the temple would have left more trace in extant first-century sources concerning feasts (sources like Josephus).

45. One cannot argue this, however, from the lack of mention of purification or lamb; these elements of Passover ritual would be taken for granted (everyone in the Roman Empire expected animal sacrifices and purifications for festivals), and it would be their *omission* that would have required comment (Sanders 1993: 251).

First, Jesus' mission signifies a new Passover (26:17-20, 26). The "first day of unleavened bread" (26:17) had come to be applied in popular parlance to the Passover as well (see Gundry 1982: 524); popular religion had combined Passover proper and the following feast of unleavened bread (cf. Philo *Spec. Leg.* 2.150). Passover pilgrims tried to find refuge with Jerusalemites during the actual Passover celebration, to eat the Passover within the city walls as tradition demanded (m. Pesaḥ. 7:9; Lane 1974a: 497). Although Mark is relatively clear that Jesus' selection of the host, as with the donkey for the triumphal entry (Mk 11:2-3), represents prophetic revelation (14:13-16; pace Anderson 1976: 310), a reader of Matthew could be forgiven for thinking that Jesus was simply presuming on the hospitality of someone he already knew there, a disciple (Argyle 1963: 198), and the response of the host suggests that this might be the case (Edersheim 555).[46] In contrast to Mark, Matthew particularly emphasizes disciples carrying out Jesus' commands, Jesus' authority, and Jesus' ominous, "My time is at hand" (26:18; cf. 26:2; Meier 1980: 182).[47]

If the home's owner had already had the lamb taken for slaughter in the temple, the disciples sent to prepare the Passover would make ready the bitter herbs and other food, bring out the bread and wine already purchased by their host, and perhaps roast the lamb (Lane 1974a: 500; Stauffer 1960: 115-16). Otherwise, two of them would also need to slaughter the lamb in the temple (which merely required being clean, as, e.g., in CD 11.18-21). Since the lambs were being slaughtered continually to accommodate the large crowds, we cannot narrow down the time to the afternoon offering ca. 2:30 p.m. (pace Edersheim 556-57); the three groups of m. Pesaḥim 5:5 may also be suspect as too orderly. Worshipers probably brought lambs continuously (Sanders 1992: 136). Ten to twenty people shared each lamb, gathering together as households for the purposes of the festival (Jeremias 1966a: 47; Reicke 1974: 167).[48] (Although some ancient Mediterranean aristocrats thought that an ideal banquet setting welcomed no more than nine people due to the risk of disorder, as in Aul. Gel. 13.11.2-3, the

46. Perhaps because slaves (Gen. Rab. 53:13; 93:6; in Rome, Carcopino 1940: 38-39), especially female slaves, often carried water (Test. Job 21:2-3; cf. Jn 2:7; Gen. Rab. 53:13; 93:6; cf. Eurip. *Electra* 55, 140; in Rome, Carcopino 1940: 38-39), the disciples could readily recognize the particular man in Mk 14:13. Matthew's abbreviating technique here also omits the fact that the disciples met in an "upper room" (Mk 14:15), the sort of place scholars sometimes met (cf. Dalman 1929: 114). For so many disciples to have met there would have required that the house was in the well-to-do Upper City (cf. Avigad 1976). People could eat in walled courtyards (Safrai 1974/76b: 730), and sometimes they may have eaten Pesaḥ on rooftops (Safrai 1974/76b: 732).

47. Jesus' "appointed time" here (26:18) is also the fateful "hour" (26:45; cf. Jn 2:4; 7:30; 8:20; 12:23).

48. Stauffer probably reads too much into the lack of mention of lamb at the last supper, suggesting that Jesus did not have one and associating the later prohibition of lamb — but not the other paschal food — to apostates (1960: 113); but he also believes (following the Johannine chronology) that they celebrated the Passover a day early (ibid. 115). He suggests that they ate roast kid instead (116-17, referring to m. Pesaḥ. 4:4, which does not directly support his case).

paschal meal was an occasion for festivity but not drunkenness, and Jesus' eating with the Twelve as in 26:20 fits Jewish practice.)

Whereas supper normally fell in late afternoon, one meal in the "evening" (26:20; cf. 1 Cor 11:23; Jn 13:30) was Passover (m. Pesaḥ. 10:1; t. Pisha 5:2; b. Pesaḥ. 107b; Jeremias 1966a: 44-46; cf. b. Ber. 9a), starting after sunset around 6 p.m. (Stauffer 1960: 115); likewise, Jewish people customarily sat for normal meals, but by this period normally reclined at banquets (e.g., Sifre Deut. 41.2.5; t. Ber. 4:20; b. Ber. 37a, 42b-43a), including Passover (m. Pesaḥ. 10:1; b. Ḥag. 14b; Pesaḥ. 108a; Ex. Rab. 20:18; cf. Daube 1963: 45), in typical Greek fashion (e.g., Ep. Arist. 183; Plato *Rep.* 2.372D; Mart. *Epig.* 3.30.1; Athenaeus *Deipn.* 1.18ab; Jeremias 1966a: 48-49; Horsley 1981: 9; idem 1982: 75); Luke is explicit that this is a Passover meal (Lk 22:15). Men would normally recline on their side, supporting themselves by their left elbow; the couches were arranged so that one's head was nearest and one's feet furthest from the table (Cary and Haarhoff 1946: 96; Brown 1970: 551). When women dined in the same room, they would sit (Dupont 1992: 98-99).[49]

Because traditions like those that developed into the Passover liturgy probably remained fairly stable, it is likely that the celebration included most of the following elements: The father or host offered the blessing for the festival and the first cup of wine (m. Pesaḥ. 10:2);[50] after reciting traditions later incorporated into the Passover Haggadah, participants might sing early portions of the Hallel (like Psalms 113 or 114) and the *paterfamilias* or equivalent (father, host, or other head of the group) would bless the bread and explain its significance.[51] This household head would lift most elements as he explained them except for the lamb (b. Pesaḥ. 116b). Participants would eat the bitter herbs, fruit and unleavened bread, and later the lamb, which they must finish by midnight (m. Pesaḥ. 10:3, 9). At least in later tradition and for gathered families, one son would ask about the feast and the father would explain about their deliverance from slavery (m. Pesaḥ. 10:4-6). The prayer over the third cup concluded the feast; they recited the rest of the Hallel (like Psalms 115–18 or 116–18); then the

49. Although dinners worked well for a symposium format (e.g., Plato *Symp.;* Plut. *Dinner of Seven Wise Men; Table-Talk;* Athenaeus *Deipn.;* Trimalchio's dinner in Petron. *Sat.;* symposium section of Ep. Arist.; Lk 14:1-24), the Synoptics do little with the possibility at the last supper.

50. At a few months' remove from the grape vintage, *all* wine (the meaning of "fruit of the vine" in Jewish blessings — 26:29; cf. p. Ned. 7:1, §6; Whitacre 1992: 867) had some alcohol content, although ancients could not yet artificially increase it beyond natural limits through distillation; nonalcoholic grape juice for the Lord's Supper arose from nineteenth-century concern for recovering alcoholics. We should note, however, that at most meals ancients watered down wine at least two parts water to every part wine (Plut. *Poetry* 1, *Mor.* 15E; *Bride* 20, *Mor.* 140F; *Table-Talk* 1.4.3, *Mor.* 621CD; Diog. Laert. 7.7.184; Casson 1974: 213; Ruck 1978: 41; in Jewish texts, see Sifra Shir. par. 1.100.1.3; b. ʿAbod. Zar. 30a; Num. Rab. 10:8; Safrai 1974/76b: 748), unless they specifically wished to get drunk (Diog. Laert. 10.1.15; Apul. *Metam.* 7.12; Ferguson 1987: 80); in the latter case, Greeks may also have added some other intoxicants (Wasson, Hoffmann and Ruck 1978: 89).

51. Although the antiquity of the *afikomen* may be questioned, one should note Daube's interpretation, followed by Carmichael 1991, of the *afikomen* (symbolically reuniting the Messiah, a fragment of Israel, with his people).

host offered praise for the fourth cup (m. Pesaḥ. 10:7; Stauffer 1960: 116-17; Lane 1974a: 501-2; Lohse 1978: 156). That Jesus blesses the bread before the wine fits the sequence of the Passover, in contrast to normal Jewish meals in which the household head blessed the wine first.[52]

Second, even some who now claim to follow Christ may ultimately betray him (26:21-25). Scripture indicated that the Son of Man's destiny included betrayal, but this did not relieve from responsibility the particular betrayer, who acted from personal choice (26:24). Jesus' "woe" (cf. 18:7) that the betrayer would have been better left unborn resembles both biblical (Job 3:3-26; Jer 20:14-18) and Greek (e.g., Hom. *Il.* 18.86-90; 22.481; *Od.* 8.312; 18.79; *Contest of Homer and Hesiod* 315, end; Eurip. *Daughters of Troy* 636-37; perhaps Hom. *Il.* 3.40) lamentations; other Jewish teachers also uttered such sayings; for example, if one's first words after waking are not from Torah, "it would have been better for him if the afterbirth in which he lay had been turned over his face, and he had never been born and beheld the world" (ARN 29A, trans. p. 120; cf. Lev. Rab. 35:7). "Better never to have been born" was a pronouncement of frightful judgment (b. Qidd. 40a; Urbach 1979: 1:253; 1 Enoch 38:2; 4 Ezra 7:69; 2 Bar. 10:6; 2 Enoch 41:2; Gk. Ezra 1:6, 21; cf. perhaps Sib. Or. 3:310). The woe to "that *man*" might contrast Judas with the "son of *man*" whom he betrays, underlining the heinousness of betraying a fellow human being. In any case, Matthew clarifies Mark to show that Jesus here foreknows the specific betrayer (26:25).[53]

The language of interchange between Judas and Jesus is significant. In contrast to Jesus' true disciples who consistently address him as "Lord" (e.g., 26:22), Judas calls Jesus "Rabbi" (26:25); although "my *rab*" and *mari,* "my lord," may have been interchangeable in popular parlance, the Matthean nuance here is significant (cf. Bornkamm 1963a: 41): Judas regards Jesus *only* as a teacher. Also significant is Jesus' roundabout manner of reply (26:25), characteristic of responses given to his opponents on that night (26:64; 27:11). (Judas's greeting "Hail" in v. 49 may likewise link him with those who ridicule Jesus in 27:29 — Gundry 1982: 537.)

52. Jeremias 1966a: 49-50; Lane 1974a: 497; pace Meier 1980: 318. Less probable is the suggestion (Flusser 1973) that the bread-then-wine sequence (Mt 26:26-27; Mk 14:22-23; 1 Cor 11:23-25) follows Essene versus standard Jewish practice, whereas Lk 22:17-19 and Did. 9–10 follow the more common Jewish sequence (1QapGen 22.14-15 even omits bread and wine in Gen 14); Crossan 1991a: 365 differently finds in the wine-after-supper practice Greco-Roman custom for a formal meal. Contrast Oesterley 1925: 164, who argues that the Gospel sequence implies that the meal preceded the blessings, which is not true of the Pesaḥ meal. But the Gospels simply do not narrate the meal.

53. Because the early Christians would hardly have invented the disciples' failure and certainly not a betrayer — rabbis were esteemed for the loyalty of their followers, not their apostasy! — these traditions, especially that of the betrayal, are surely authentic (cf., e.g., Robbins 1976: 30). The emphasis on Jesus' foreknowledge of the betrayer (26:20-25; cf. Jn 6:64; 13:18-30) may be counterpolemic against opponents who employed this aspect of the tradition to question Jesus' prophetic aptitude — underlining the "problem" the betrayer presented to early Christian tradition and how dangerous it would have been for Christians to have invented it.

Yet Judas would not alone betray Jesus; the betrayal of all the disciples serves as a warning to Matthew's community about the weakness of potential disciples, despite their own disclaimers (26:33, 35; 26:69–27:10). The joyous occasion of Passover here becomes a sorrowful one (26:22; cf. 17:23; 18:31; 19:22) through the announcement of betrayal (more like the solemn Samaritan Passover, merely repeating the exodus rather than celebrating liberation — cf. Jeremias 1966a: 205; cf. also Pesiq. Rab Kah. Sup. 2:8, but this may be ad hoc explanation of a tradition). By dipping his hand with Jesus in the bowl containing the sauce of bitter herbs (26:23), the betrayer had shown himself a treacherous person indeed; rising against one with whom one had eaten violated the sanctity of tradition (cf. Ps 41:9).[54]

Third, Jesus' body and blood provide a new covenant, the ultimate act of redemption (26:26-30). Disciples who experience redemption freely by God's kindness must not forget the great cost of that redemption; Jesus had become the new Passover lamb.

Excursus: The Context of the Last Supper

Some have compared the Lord's Supper to pagan cult meals (e.g., Bousset 1970: 131) or suggested that the hellenistic sacramental meals were read back into the Jewish last supper tradition (Bultmann 1958: 153). Some (cf. Moffatt 1938: 170) have drawn connections with the Greco-Roman cult of the dead (e.g., *CIL* 6.911; *ILS* 4966 in Sherk 1988: 234; Plut. *R.Q.* 86, *Mor.* 285A), which honored departed ancestors;[55] one must especially placate spirits who had died a violent death (Paus. 1.34.5; Aune 1983: 26).[56] Among the most remote suggestions is Smith 1978: 122-23, who con-

54. E.g., Hom. *Il.* 21.76; *Od.* 4.534-35; 11.414-20; 14.404-5; Hesiod *W.D.* 327; Eur. *Cycl.* 126-28; *Hec.* 25-26, 710-20, 850-56; Ap. Rhod. 3.377-80; Livy 25.16.6; 39.51.12. Some have also compared the Qumran custom in which members partook of a meal in sequence by rank (1QS 6.4-5; cf. Jos. *War* 2.130-31), suggesting that we read "dip with me" temporally: by stretching out his hand simultaneously with Jesus, Judas deliberately indicated his rebellion (Fensham 1965; Albright and Mann 1971: 321; cf. Gundry 1982: 527). While this view is plausible (cf. how one respects others by allowing them to grab first — Sir 31:14-18; for other gestures, see, e.g., 1QS 2.19-23; 1QSa 2.11-17; Jos. *War* 2.132; Ta'an. 20b), it does leave one to question why no one seems to have noticed such an act where it bore this significance (26:22).

55. More relevant would be comparison with teachers like Epicurus who instituted monthly memorial meals in their honor (Diog. Laert. 10.18 in Boring 1995: 149-50), *minus* the pagan associations with sacrifices for the dead. More distantly, cf. rabbinic phrases used in naming the deceased: "May so-and-so be remembered [before God] for good" (Lachs 1987: 401 cites b. B. Bat. 21a; Shab. 13b; cf. m. Yoma 3:9), probably relevant to 26:13.

56. Against this thesis is the antiquity of the resurrection tradition (i.e., disciples were not simply "remembering" a departed loved one), and the closer parallel in the biblical paschal tradition to "commemorating" rather than simply retaining in one's memory (e.g., F. F. Bruce 1971: 111-12; Gregg 1979; Davies 1980: 252; Martin 1982: 147). The language of the Passover celebration assumed the participation of current generations in the exodus event (e.g., m. Pesaḥ. 10:4-5; t. Pisha 8:18; b. Ber. 14b).

nects rare magical traditions in which recipients feeding on the substance of a magician are united with him.

Greek associations (sometimes burial clubs or guilds) regularly met for common meals (Angus 1925: 127; Wilken 1971: 280-81; Theissen 1982: 131-32; Willis 1985: 14), normally dedicated to the association's patron deity but celebrated with attention on the banquet itself (Willis 1985: 47-61). Some associations gathered for specifically religious purposes (e.g., Cic. *De Senec.* 13.45; Horsley 1981: 5-9; Cole 1984: 36-37), and cultic meals were also standard in pagan festivals (e.g., Burkert 1985: 107). Greek meal practice did affect contemporary Jewish banquets, including Passover customs (Bokser 1977: 6-7; cf. Pines 1974), hence they did indirectly influence some customs at the last supper; in some respects the hellenistic church also assimilated the Lord's Supper to, and interpreted it in the light of, hellenistic meals (cf. Justin *1 Apol.* 66; Tert. *Apol.* 39.15; Pliny *Ep.* 10.96).[57] These do not provide the most immediate parallels for the earliest form of the Lord's Supper tradition, however. Most scholars also recognize that before the spread of Christianity, hellenistic meals were not sacramental[58] and did not communicate mystical elements of the deity (Nock 1964a: 74; Willis 1985: 18-46, 62; Kane 1979: 349-51; pace Willoughby 1929: 85, 136-37, 161; Goodenough 1970: 22; Godwin 1981: 28).

Others have compared Qumran meals (Fritsch 1956: 123-24; Cross 1980: 235), which may themselves evince some hellenistic influence (cf. Culpepper 1975: 168; Donceel-Vouté 1993). Some think these meals followed rules for sacerdotal purity (Gnilka 1961; Gärtner 1965: 10), were sacrificial sacred meals (Delcor 1968; cf. 1QapGen 21.20-22), were annual and sacramental (Groh 1970), or foreshadowed eschatological meals (Harrison 1969: 32-33; Schiffman 1979; idem 1983: 191-210; Simon 1967: 77-78; Harrington 1980: 41-42). But the sacral character may be no more than in most Jewish meals (Sutcliffe 1960c; Schiffman 1983: 191-97), and the eschatological interpretation also remains unclear: 1QSa's messianic banquet could simply evoke the common practice of the community rather than the latter evoking the former. The meal in 1QS 6 is "pure" because consecrated by the community and the priestly blessing, but not the ceremonial food; the text merely indicates that a newcomer cannot partake until he has surrendered his own wealth and labor to the community, preventing free handouts.

The proposed parallels between the Qumran meals and the Lord's Supper are not strong: the claim that only men participated at each is based on inference about Qumran practice in general, not just meals, and an inference about the last supper that

57. Minor assimilation begins as early as the Pauline churches (Guthrie 1966: 268; cf. Caird 1955: 96). Paul's *kyriakos,* "of the Lord," may allude to typical Roman usage for "imperial" (Deissman 1978: 357). But early attestation of parallels often comes from early Christian writers who interpreted the Mysteries through the grid of their own experience (cf. Campbell 1968: 323), as an "imitation demoniaque du Christianisme" (Benoit 1975: 79-81), and the rites remained quite distinct (Metzger 1955: 15).

58. A small following of Dionysus (Henrichs 1982: 160) and Mithraism (which gained prominence in the Empire after Paul; Nock 1964a: 133; Metzger 1955: 13-15) may have been the exceptions that ultimately affected other Mysteries and the later Christian sacramental view.

probably would not have obtained in house churches. The leader presiding over the meal and blessing the bread and wine fits all Jewish meals (see below) — like most other characteristics of the meal (Van der Ploeg 1957; Driver 1965: 506-16; Lach 1958). Certainly special rules obtained in the Qumran order (1QS 6.4-5, 20-21), but their meals merely show that a concept related to the sacred meal was already present in Palestinian Judaism and that one need not appeal to geographically distant parallels to explain the Lord's Supper. One may also compare the sacred communal meals of the Therapeutae (Philo *Cont.* 82).

Some think that Jesus' final meal resembles more the regular weekly gatherings of the *haburoth* (Oesterley 1925: 167), whose Pharisaic purity rules, some think, may have bound them to eating especially among themselves (see Neusner 1984: 27). Among schools of sages in Palestine, study companions often ate together as well (ARN 18, §40B), though perhaps partly to save time (ARN 14, §34B). But again, are meals of associates or students of the sages distinctive enough as meals to warrant special attention in connection with the last supper? Palestinian Jewish families probably celebrated the more common weekly Sabbath Kiddush very early (Oesterley 1925: 79, citing t. Ber. 5:1);[59] one could also share Sabbath meals with other families (e.g., p. B. Bat. 1:5, §2). Diaspora Jews apparently also assembled for communal meals at times (*Ant.* 14.215-16; cf. 14.260-61; Sanders 1990: 78; idem 1993: 202; Rabello 1980: 707).

Jeremias contends that Essene meals are more different than similar and that *haburoth* meals are undocumented (Jeremias 1966a: 29-36). Many of the Passover traditions are undoubtedly early, although some scholars have overstated the case (Segal 1963; Finkelstein 1942-43; Wright 1966: 417; Safrai 1974/76c: 809; at the opposite end, Stemberger 1987 doubts that any of the Pesach Haggadah predates A.D. 70). Many of those features of the last supper that are distinguishable from regular Jewish meals parallel the Passover meal, a correspondence not surprising in view of the night on which Jesus was betrayed.[60] That Jesus followed the more common practices regarding Passover cannot be proved, but it is likely, especially in view of the correspondences on points that can be tested.[61]

---

59. Jeremias 1966a: 28 doubts this, but one may compare echoes of the Kiddush blessing in Did. 9, which far more likely betray Jewish liturgical influence than influence later rabbinic tradition; cf. Jos. *Life* 279.

60. Jeremias 1966a: 50-51 contends that Jewish people drank wine only on special occasions, but he appears incorrect here; even if one merely factors in the regular Sabbath Kiddush meals (e.g., t. Ber. 3:8; Tannaitic tradition in b. B. Qam. 69b; Pesaḥ. 102a, bar.; later, b. Shab. 23b; Taʿan. 24a; Safrai 1974/76b: 747; cf. Jub. 2:21), which he concedes, they drank it quite regularly (cf. blessings over wine in meals in 1QS 6.4-5; b. Ber. 33a; 51a). He is, however, probably correct to emphasize that of the many kinds of wines available (on which cf., e.g., b. ʿAbod. Zar. 30a; Paul 1975), *red* wine was used on Passover, augmenting Jesus' symbolism (1966a: 53, 290; t. Pesaḥ. 10:1).

61. The generally stricter Shammaite school (regarding Passover, e.g., b. Shab. 18b, bar.) prevailed in his day, but our records were preserved by more lenient, rather than stricter, practitioners. For some source-critical suggestions on the Pesaḥ Haggadah, see Finkelstein 1972: 13-120.

On the grounds of multiple attestation (Paul as well as the Synoptic tradition) Jesus' paschal language is among the most secure elements of the Jesus tradition (Sanders 1993: 263; cf. Bornkamm 1969: 135; Pesch 1991). Paul's claim that he "received" and "delivered" to the Corinthian church the Lord's Supper tradition (1 Cor 11:23) reflects Jewish language for the passing on of traditions (Jos. *Ant.* 13.297, 408; m. 'Abot 1:1), also intelligible in a broader milieu (Socrates *Ep.* 20; Cornutus in Van der Horst 1981: 168-69; cf. Sen. *Ep. Lucil.* 40.3; Conzelman 1975: 195-96), though the hellenistic world rarely joined the terms together (Metzger 1955: 17-18n.84). Other Jewish teachers would claim to receive a *halakah* from Sinai even though it was mediated via other authorities,[62] so Paul's claim to have received the tradition "from the Lord" (Jesus) does not diminish the claim to Palestinian tradition here (Gerhardsson 1961: 321; De Beus 1968; Davies 1980: 248; cf. Cullmann 1956a: 73). Although variations in the tradition (see, e.g., Sanders 1985: 15) fit the sort of development one might expect on the basis of liturgical and rhetorical usage, a partly recoverable common Aramaic tradition may remain behind the Markan and Pauline versions (Jeremias 1966a: 187).[63]

The last supper was a symbolic act, like the triumphal entry and Jesus' act in the temple (Sanders 1993: 263). Whether the specific act of *breaking* bread foreshadowed Jesus' death is difficult to decide; it was customary for the head of the household to break bread so he could distribute it (14:19; cf. Safrai 1974/76c: 802). (Not merely nuclear families but associations of people could band together for one Passover offering — t. Pisha 9:1.) Interpreting the elements of the Passover feast (the bread, bitter herbs, etc.) was a standard part of paschal tradition (Jeremias 1966a: 56), but instead of using standard explanations Jesus interprets the two elements (the two elements representative of food and drink in blessings at Jewish meals) in a strikingly new way. Some scholars even suggest that early Christians recited the Passion Narrative in this context as a new Passover Haggadah, recalling Paul's phrase: "proclaim the Lord's death until he comes" (F. F. Bruce 1971: 113; idem 1972a: 16).[64]

Whatever this early tradition preserves, therefore, likely tells us much about Jesus' view of his mission. Jesus elsewhere spoke of the pouring out of martyrs' blood (23:35) in terms of death, guilt, and impending judgment, a theme Matthew develops further in 27:4, 25. But even if the Gospel tradition also plays on the atoning value of martyrs' deaths (especially attested in 4 Maccabees) here,

62. E.g., m. 'Ed. 8:7; ARN 25A; b. Qidd. 30a; Meg. 19b; Nazir 56b; Pesaḥ. 110b; Shab. 108a, bar.; Qoh. Rab. 1:10, §1; cf. Hillel as a disciple of Ezra in Sanh. 11a, bar.; Soṭa 48b; Song Rab. 8:9, §3.

63. Paul may even draw the Last Supper tradition from a larger Passion story already available to him (see Borgen 1986-87), although scholars must examine the evidence for this possibility more thoroughly. The appearance of *agrapha* (Justin *Dial.* 35; Syr. *Didaskalia* 6.5.2 in Jeremias 1964c: 76) in Paul's context (1 Cor 11:19) may support this thesis.

64. The genre of a teacher's departing instructions may be relevant here, but it is much more relevant to the preceding eschatological discourse (cf. Socrates in Xen. *Mem.* 4.7.1-10; Robbins 1992: 172 on Mk 13); cf. comment there.

Jesus' death appears as more than that of a *mere* martyr in this earliest tradition. Jesus' probable allusions to Isaiah 52–53 (e.g., Cullmann 1956b: 64-65; Gundry 1982: 528; pace Hooker 1959: 80-82) tell us a great deal about how Jesus viewed his own death.

Even more probably, many of Jesus' words (such as "flesh," "blood," "poured out") suggest sacrificial terminology, especially since crucifixion itself technically required no blood (Romans sometimes fixed criminals to crosses with rope; Jeremias 1966a: 220-22);[65] "for the remission of sins" appears in Targum Neofiti with reference to sacrifices (McNamara 1972: 129).[66] Whether Paul's "new covenant" midrashically interprets the "blood of the covenant" allusion to Exodus 24:8 in light of Jeremiah 31:31 (cf. Heb 8:8; farther removed, Justin *Dial.* 11), or the most likely textual tradition in Mark and Matthew suppresses "new" to heighten the Exodus allusion, the tradition probably implies the suggestion of a "new" covenant, a prophetic image current in Jesus' day among the Qumran sect (e.g., CD 6.4-5, 19; 8.21; 20.12; Flusser 1988: 44-50; Black 1961: 91; cf. Gemés 1969) and probably others (e.g., Sifra Behuq. pq. 2.262.1.13).

That the bread "is" his body means that it "represents" it;[67] we should interpret his words here no more literally than the disciples would have taken the normal words of the Passover liturgy, related to Deuteronomy 16:3 (cf. Stauffer 1960: 117): "This is the bread of affliction which our ancestors ate when they came from the land of Egypt." (By no stretch of the imagination did anyone suppose that they were re-eating the very bread the Israelites had eaten in the wilderness.) Those who ate of this bread participated by commemoration in Jesus' affliction in the same manner that those who ate the Passover commemorated in the deliverance of their ancestors. The language of Passover celebration assumed the participation of cur-

65. Some scholars think that the "cup" rather than the "blood" is the earlier form of wording (e.g., Dibelius 1971: 207), whereas others defend the reverse position (e.g., Davies 1980: 244-50). Crossan 1991a: 366 compares "poured out" with the language of libation; a common Mediterranean practice, it appears in the OT (for a metaphorical usage with blood, cf. 2 Sam 23:16-17). For its sacrificial connotations (e.g., Lev 1–7, 16) relevant to Passover, see, e.g., Gundry 1982: 528; Carson 1984b: 537; Hagner 1995: 773. On "the many," see comment on 20:28.

66. Missing in the parallels (including 1 Cor 11:23-25), however, "for remission of sins" may represent Matthean interpretation (Sanders 1985: 112), probably transferred from John's baptism (Mk 1:4, where Matthew, unlike Luke, omits the phrase; cf. also Meier 1979: 184). Although the LXX expresses the phrase differently, "poured out" may translate the Hebrew in Is 53:12; the phrase surely represents the event of violent death (Hurtado 1983: 223 cites Gen 4:10-11; 9:6; Deut 19:10; 2 Kings 21:16; Ps 106:38; Jer 7:6; Mt 23:35). "For many," a Semitism that very likely dates to the first decade of Jesus tradition (see Jeremias 1965a: 45), may represent *rabbim* in this section of Isaiah (Jeremias 1966a: 227), which Jeremias applies not only to Israel but to the nations (1966a: 230-31; cf. Is 52:14-15). "Blood of the covenant" seems to suit first-century Palestinian Aramaic (Emerton 1964).

67. Martin 1982: 153 argues this from the Greek and Aramaic, though McNamara 1972: 127-28 is surely right that the words here derive from Ex 24:8 and are possible in Palestinian Aramaic (cf. Gundry 1982: 528; pace Deissmann 1978: 337, who reads the term for covenant here primarily in light of Greco-Roman usage for wills). M. Pesaḥ. 10:6 uses the Passover wine as a metaphor for the blood of the covenant in Ex 24:8 (e.g., Hill 1972: 339; Carson 1984b: 537). And while allusions to Jer 31:31-34 and Is 53:11-12 are probable in this narrative, the Ex 24:8 allusion is the most explicit (Allison 1993b: 257-58).

rent generations in the exodus event (e.g., m. Pesaḥ. 10:4-5; t. Pisha 8:18; b. Ber. 14b).[68] That Jesus was also *in* his body at the time he uttered the words further militates against interpreting the bread as literally equivalent to his body (Moffatt 1938: 168). Nevertheless, one can see how Jewish people would have revolted against even the metaphor (Jn 6:52; 1 Enoch 98:11; Vermes 1993: 16),[69] and how outsiders could have construed the language as cannibalism (cf. Athenag. *Plea* 3; Theoph. 3.4, 15; Tert. *Apol.* 4.11; 7.1; Visotzky 1987).

The head of the household, who had been reclining, would now sit up to bless (give thanks for) the bread before the meal; after the meal, Jesus interprets the third or fourth cup (see, e.g., Cohn-Sherbok 1981; though Sigal 1983 argues for the second).[70] If later codified customs continued earlier basic practice, as is probable in the case of an annual festal tradition, Jesus may have lifted the cup with both hands, holding it in his right hand about a handbreadth above the table (see Jeremias 1966a: 110; Pesiq. R. 9:1). But after partaking of this cup, Jesus utters what resembles a traditional vow of abstention (cf. Num 6:4; 30:2; 11QTemple 53-54),[71] in this case vowing not to drink wine until the coming of his reign (Jeremias 1966a: 182-85; Kümmel 1957: 31; Palmer 1973; cf. Ziesler 1973). Many Jewish people viewed the kingdom as a banquet (cf. comment on 8:11-12; cf. 9:17) and thought of an eschatological abundance of wine (Amos 9:13; Sib. Or. 3.622; 1 Enoch 10:19; 2 Bar. 29:5). 1 Corinthians 11:26 probably recalls this eschatological signficance in the Lord's Supper, related to the implications of future redemption many Jewish people saw in the Passover (F. F. Bruce 1971: 114).[72]

68. For various conceptions of the memorial value of Jewish rituals among various ancient Jewish groups, see Boccaccini 1991: 231-39 (Josephus on 242-45).

69. Also most Greeks and Romans: Herod. *Hist.* 1.123, 129; Mart. *Epig.* 10.4.1; 11.31.2; Isis aretalogy in Grant 1953: 132; Guthrie 1966: 40. Like a good Skeptic, Sext. Emp. *Pyrrh.* 3.207 regards abhorrence of cannibalism as culturally conditioned and gives examples of toleration (cf. also Stoics in Diog. Laert. *Lives* 7.1.121, 188; reports in Herod. *Hist.* 1.73, 119; 3.99; Otto 1965: 113).

70. The tradition of the four cups (e.g., m. Pesaḥ. 10:1; t. Ber. 4:8; b. Pesaḥ. 108a-9a; Gen. Rab. 88:5; Ex. Rab. 6:4; Safrai 1974/76b: 748) may precede the superstitious practice of avoiding drinking an even number of cups, though later teachers harmonized these practices (b. Pesaḥ. 109b). (One *could* drink more than the four required cups — b. Pesaḥ. 107b-8a; p. Meg. 3:5, §1.) The custom probably borrows or is related to the Greek use of cups to signal stages in banquets (Boring 1995: 147 cites Diod. Sic. 4.3.4; *IG* 12 3.330, 670).

71. By this period people often promised by God to abstain from something for a specified period (cf. Acts 23:12; m. 'Abot 3:13; conjoined with mourning in Gen. Rab. 92:5). One had to specify the precise parameters of one's vow, however: one who vowed not to use light, e.g., was not even allowed to use starlight (b. Pesaḥ. 2a, bar.). On kinds of vows, cf. McNamara 1983: 197.

72. Lane 1974a: 508 suggests that Jesus abstained from the fourth cup, having participated in and interpreted the third cup that signified redemption in the Passover liturgy (cf. Lachs 1987: 408; also Stauffer 1960: 117, though he places the vow after the first cup — 115). Fredriksen 1988: 115 thinks Jesus' meal with his disciples possible because gospel traditions sometimes depict the kingdom as a messianic banquet and because Essenes and others reportedly celebrated meals of eschatological import. But that Jesus would keep the Passover fits what we may surmise from his loyalty to Torah in the traditions, and his special interpretation of it is consistent with what we may surmise about his deliberate provocation of his martyrdom (see comment on 16:21).

After what was normally a few hours of discussion, here perhaps abbreviated, the household sang the remaining hymns of the Hallel, undoubtedly the "hymn" to which the text refers (26:30),[73] antiphonally if they could.[74] That discussion should focus on the significance of Passover would fit what we know of later Passover tradition and conform to the desires of the sages for edifying talk (Sir 9:15; m. 'Abot 3:2; ARN 26, 29A; 32, §68B; p. Ta'an. 3:11, §4; cf. CD 11.4), including at meals (Ps. 154:14; p. Ḥag. 2:1, §9; 2:2, §5; Safrai 1974/76a: 968-69). The singing of the Hallel also fits what we know about most ancient Mediterranean banquets; most banquets with means emphasized music over lectures (Sir 35:3-4; cf. Plut. *Table-Talk* 1.1.5, *Mor.* 614F-615A).

Jesus' Turmoil and the Disciples' Weakness (26:31-46)

Cf. Mk 14:27-42; Lk 22:31-34, 39-46; Jn 13:36-38; 18:1. Brown 1994: 12 may well be right that the demands of narrative forced the Passion Narrative's omniscient narrators to fill in details. He allows that the tradition probably knew that Jesus "cried out to God when facing death (Heb 5:7)"; but he thinks that the early Christians fleshed out the authentic references to the "hour" and the "cup" with language from biblical psalms and the style of prayer they had learned from Jesus (Brown 1994: 12, 225). Yet the substance of the prayer is more than plausible; it meets the authenticity criterion of embarrassment.[75] It may be easier to think that Peter, James, or John overheard parts of Jesus' prayer while drifting in and out of sleep than to surmise that the early Christians would have composed a prayer so exposing Jesus' vulnerability (Gundry 1982: 533; Witherington 1990: 219).[76]

73. With Daube 1963: 45; Ellington 1979; Meier 1980: 321; Carson 1984b: 538; Hagner 1995: 774; cf. Philo *Spec. Leg.* 2.148. Probably pilgrims also sang en route to festivals (Sanders 1992: 128-29, especially citing Herodotus).

74. Brown 1994: 123 thinks Mark's and Matthew's audiences would think instead of Christian hymns (Eph 5:19; Col 3:16); but it seems likely that at least Matthew's community would recognize the use of hymns in the paschal context, especially if the community was, as I think, located near Palestine. Even if most of the later paschal liturgy was not in use or common use in this period, praise was standard in eating the Passover (Jub. 49:6; cf. Philo *Spec. Leg.* 2.148). The exact sequence of the Hallel in the liturgy was probably not standardized by Jesus' day (cf. the differences among rabbis in t. Pisha 10:9; b. Pesaḥ. 118a).

75. See Brown 1994: 217 especially on the scandal the account would represent to "educated Greco-Roman pagans," whose models of martyrdom included Socrates and others facing death calmly; but also among Jews (the Maccabean martyrs; also Jos. *War* 1.653; 2.153; 7.417-18). That Mark elsewhere mentions prayer only at 1:35 and 6:46 suggests that this prayer is not a Markan creation (Brown 1994: 150). Sanders 1993: 264 also regards the prayer the tradition attributes to Jesus as "perfectly reasonable"; hoping to escape death, he nevertheless was ready to face whatever God wished. For further discussion of the historicity of the Gethsemane tradition, see Green 1992b.

76. The threefold repetition of the prayer (26:44) may be stylistic or derived by inference from Mk 14:41; an echo of the threefold test in 4:1-11 (cf. Thiemann 1989: 336n.13) is less likely.

Matthew's narrative suggests that even in events that seem as hideous and disastrous as Jesus' arrest and execution seemed to the first disciples, God may be preparing his sovereign purposes. Nevertheless, disciples have their part to play — and in this case, all of the disciples failed, despite their protestations to the contrary (26:31-34); indeed, in their failure to be ready for the test by prayerfulness, they had failed it before it arrived (26:40-45). Matthew acknowledges that his Lord is exalted (28:18), and hence no longer depends on his friends the way he did at Gethsemane. Yet is it possible that Matthew still intends his community to hear the plaintive cry of the Lord of harvest in this narrative? The sleep of the first disciples would speak forcefully to a community needing to be more involved in their Lord's agendas.

The disciples may have descended into the Kidron Valley by an ancient stairway (since recovered, Yamauchi 1972: 106; Jn 18:1) en route to the Mount of Olives. This "mountain" had three summits parallel to Jerusalem for about two and a half miles on the east; it rose three hundred feet higher than the elevated Temple Mount. The narrative may refer specifically to the central summit, for which the title was often used (Mount Scopus being the northern and the Mount of Offense the south-southwestern summits; Brown 1994: 125). As David prayed for deliverance from a betrayer on this mountain (2 Sam 15:30-31), this site would provide a suitable location for an analogous prayer by David's descendant (Davies and Allison 1997: 565).[77] The name "Gethsemane" suggests an olive press, and hence was probably the name for an olive orchard at the base of Mount Olivet, most likely enclosed on one side by the road from the Kidron Valley and by stone walls on the rest (Argyle 1963: 203; Lane 1974a: 515; Meier 1980: 323). If the press originally belonged to an individual estate rather than a local village, the estate must have been sizeable (cf. Lewis 1983: 127). Although Jesus had spent the preceding nights in Bethany (21:17), Jewish tradition (interpreting Deut 16:7) insisted that Passover pilgrims spend the Passover night within the district of Jerusalem. Although Gethsemane and Bethphage counted as part of that district, Bethany did not (Jeremias 1966a: 55).

First, Jesus knows better than his disciples do what his disciples are made of (26:31-32, 34, 41). Jesus thus tells them what it will take for them to succeed in his mission (26:41) — for testing *must* come (26:45-46; Tert. *Baptism* 20, in Jeremias 1964b: 73). When Jesus warns that they would "fall" because of him (cf. Is 8:14), he probably refers to apostasy (cf. 5:29-30; 13:41; 16:23; 17:27; 18:6-9). Despite Peter's objection that he would not stumble (cf. Test. Job 4:2; 5:1), Jesus responds that Peter will do so, and three times at that (26:34; cf.

77. Brown 1994: 125 believes that Zech 14:4 is the direct background for Acts 1:9, 12; Mk 13:3 but that the Passion Narrative echoes David's ascent in 2 Sam 15:16, 23, 30; his connection between David's ascent and the "house of David" in Zech 13 (128) may be more strained. If the location on the Mount of Olives in our passage (26:30) recalls for the reader the location of Jesus' end-time discourse, it appropriately sets the scene for his impending suffering in the context of the world's powerlessness and his ultimate triumph (cf. Zech 14:4).

Jn 13:36-38)[78] — hardly a merely preventive measure (pace Dewey 1976: 107). The cockcrowing, which generally lasted no more than five minutes (and which Mark alone mentions twice) may mark the third Roman watch, which was punctuated with such rooster crows (reportedly ca. 12:30, 1:30, and 2:30 a.m.; Argyle 1963: 201; Lane 1974a: 543; Carson 1984b: 542).[79] Yet most people slept through that cockcrowing and especially identified the rooster crow with dawn (e.g., Virg. *Moretum* 1-2; Hor. *Sat.* 1.1.9-10; Apul. *Metam.* 2.26; 3 Macc 5:23; b. Ber. 60b; cf. m. Yoma 1:8; Tamid 1:2). After surveying diverse cockcrowings based on varied observations by M. J. Lagrange, H. Kosmala, and W. M. Ramsay (*ExpT* 28: 280), Brown 1994: 607 rightly concludes:

> Despite all this, Cicero (*De Divinatione* 2.26.56) may well be right: "Is there any time, night or day, that cocks do not crow?" The evangelists are imagining the early hours of the morning before dawn; nothing more definite can be concluded.[80]

Still, in a local area, a rooster might let its owner know how long remained until dawn and other times (Babrius 124.12-18). In any case, the denial would happen before daybreak — that is, this Peter who was vigorously protesting that he would never deny Jesus was already on the verge of renouncing him.

The scattering of the flock when the shepherd was struck (26:31) stems from Zechariah 13:7, which in its immediate context could refer to false prophets (Zech 13:2-6), but given the singular and the shepherd image of Zechariah 11:9-13, to which Matthew alluded in 26:15, he may understand it messianically. Then again, he may simply use the language of Zechariah 13:7 to point out that sheep are quickly scattered without a shepherd (cf. Jn 16:32, which, lacking the citation, probably testifies to a common tradition of this shepherd logion). The Qumran community did, however, interpret this text eschatologically (CD 19.5-

78. The Johannine parallel provides multiple attestation, probably independent of the Markan account (Dewey 1976: 106; Brown 1994: 611-13); for a full defense of the authenticity of the denials, see Brown 1994: 614-21, noting especially that the earliest Christians would not have invented a negative story about Peter (615). Brown suspects that the basic historical fact is retold in an imaginative way (620-21). Given other sets of three in the Passion Narrative (e.g., he finds them sleeping three times), the three denials *could* fit an early storytelling pattern (Brown 1994: 11-12) but are probably authentic (Brown 1994: 613-14).

79. Many follow here Kosmala 1963. Later rabbis' claim that no fowl existed in Jerusalem (m. B. Qam. 7:7; Lachs 1987: 412) is fanciful nostalgia. Most references to cockcrowing in antiquity, including the context in the Gospels, omit connection with night spirits (although for superstition and cockcrowing, cf. Petron. *Sat.* 74); hence we may reject the suggestion of Derrett 1983b. And though "cockcrow" was the name of the third Roman night watch (customary signals marked night watches — Sall. *Jug.* 99.1), it is unlikely that Jesus would have referred to the more obscure trumpet blast at the 3 a.m. changing of the Fortress Antonia guard than to a rooster (pace Hunter 1965: 169; cf. Mounce 1985: 259); in any case, one could not expect Matthew's audience to catch this allusion.

80. Cf. Brown 1994: 137, noting that Mark's "second" cockcrow would be associated with the dawn, as the second cockcrow normally was (citing Aristoph. *Ecclesiazusae* 30-31, 390-91; Juv. *Sat.* 9.107-8; Ammianus Marcellinus *Res Gestae* 22.14.4).

9; Longenecker 1981: 49), perhaps testifying to a broader eschatological reading in Matthew's day of which he could make apologetic use. In either case, it illustrates the principle that a flock scatters without its shepherd (see comment on 9:36, where the allusion is probably to Ezek 34:5, with which Matthew probably connects Zech 13 midrashically). It was understood that when leaders fell, human troops usually scattered (e.g., Arrian *Alex.* 4.27.2; 4.24.4-5).[81]

Yet in promising to go to Galilee (which normally has positive associations in Matthew — 4:12, 23; 10:5) after he has risen (28:7, 16), Jesus promises a restoration beyond their apostasy (26:32; cf. Petersen 1978: 76);[82] his "going before" them may carry forth the shepherd analogy of the preceding verse (Jeremias 1971: 297). Jesus' demands are high (10:33), but he does not automatically repudiate those who fail. Given Jesus' radical rhetoric, his merciful example would encourage subsequent disciples in Matthew's audience not to give up (cf. 26:69–27:10) while working toward the standard Jesus' teaching made for them.

Second, one's best intentions (26:33, 35) cannot protect one in the time of severest testing unless one has learned how to seek God in prayer (26:41). The three disciples worthy of special censure here (26:37, 40) are the three who had witnessed his glory on the mountain (17:1), including the disciple most adamant about his faithfulness (26:33, 35, 40; cf. Kelber 1976b: 47). The willing "spirit" here refers to the purpose of the human spirit versus the weakness of mortal humanity (in contrast to Paul's usual contrast between God's Spirit and human flesh; e.g., Rom 8:4-13; but cf. 2 Cor 7:1); cf. the similar statement in Phaedrus 5.10.8 (an old dog weak not in spirit but in strength) or admonitions to discipline the body that it might submit to the mind (Sen. *Ep. Lucil.* 8.5).[83] In later Jewish tradition the Israelites confess to God that they have been asleep with regard to righteous works, but their hearts are awake with willingness to do them (Song Rab. 5:2, §1); later Christians might likewise identify with the failure of these disciples.

The language of the passage probably suggests an application for the whole eschatological period in which disciples are tested. Jesus had already warned his disciples to pray lest they succumb to the test, a warning applicable to

81. Matthew may conform the reading to his reading of the LXX (cf. Gundry 1982: 530) or scribes may have conformed that version of the LXX to Matthew.

82. Marxsen views this promise in Mark as the parousia, related to but not identical with the resurrection (in Mk 14:28; 16:7; cf. 1969: 75, 90, 111-16); objections to his position are summarized in VanderBroek 1983: 55-65.

83. As such, it does not reflect much "Persian or Hellenistic influence" (pace Meier 1980: 325), although hellenistic influence elsewhere affected early Jewish and Christian language ("flesh" indicated weakness and consequent susceptibility, e.g., in Plut. *Pleasant Life Impossible,* 6, *Mor.* 1090EF; 1QS 11.9, 12; see Best 1965: 52). This is no radical contrast between body and soul, as in Plut. *Isis* 78, *Mor.* 382F; cf. Epict. *Disc.* 2.23.20; 3.7.2-3; Marc. Aur. *Med.* 2.2; the components in Sifre Deut. 306.28.2. Even Paul's usual usage reflects biblical and Jewish tradition in which humanity *is* flesh (Ps 78:39; Jub. 5:2; Sir 28:5; Test. Job 27:2/3; Test. Jud. 19:4; Zeb. 9:7) and wholly distinct from God's Spirit (Gen 6:3; Is 31:3; Jub. 5:8; see Flusser 1988: 64-65).

all disciples (6:13); his admonitions to "watch" likewise apply to all disciples subsequent to the first ones (24:42-43; 25:13).[84] Perhaps even the expression that Jesus "found them" sleeping (26:40) recalls some language in the eschatological parable in 24:46, though it is difficult to imagine what other expression Matthew should have used in either instance (the wording in this latter instance is borrowed directly from Mark). The lesson of Gethsemane is for Matthew's generation as well as Peter's.

Guards who fell asleep on duty (cf. 28:13) and so allowed the entrance of enemies were severely punished (e.g., Eurip. *Rhesus* 812-27; see comment on 24:42). The disciples' failure reminds the reader that they were people of flesh and blood just like subsequent disciples (Acts 3:12-13; Jas 5:16-18), and that Jesus called and transformed ordinary people — who sometimes failed him. (This may facilitate reader identification with these disciples.) That they would fall asleep on this night of all nights underlines their failure. Most people in the ancient Mediterranean were asleep by midnight (Ovid *Metam.* 10.368), but this was a special night. A household had to finish eating the Passover lamb by midnight (m. Pesaḥ. 10:9) or earlier (Jub. 49:12), but the disciples may have reached Gethsemane as early as 10 p.m., a few hours after sunset. Even the big meal should not have put them to sleep so quickly, however; it was customary to discuss God's redemptive acts for a few hours after the meal before singing the Hallel (t. Ketub. 5:5; Lane 1974a: 509). Some Jewish tradition suggested that those who fell asleep to the point that they could not even answer thereby dissolved their Passover group — which the disciples inexplicably did by the time Jesus had finished praying (Daube 1956: 342). If staying awake on this one night was a test (as in initiatory rituals in many cultures, Eliade 1958: 14-15), the disciples failed it. In prayer with him this one night, Jesus offered a better rest (11:28).

Third, God's call may lead his followers through unbearable pain (26:37-39, 42, 44), as it did with Jesus. The disciples' disobedience provides a foil that illumines the contrasting obedience of Jesus. By describing his sorrow as "to the point of death" (language familiar from Jonah 4:9), Jesus underlines the intensity of his grief, that of itself the very grief could kill him (Meier 1980: 323).[85] When a person experiences such pain, he or she typically needs the strength of others' presence. Jesus' disciples provide a stark contrast in this narrative, a foil that reveals his own sacrifice all the more plainly.

The "cup" refers to Jesus' sufferings and death on the cross (20:22; 26:27-

84. Cf. 1 Pet 4:7; 5:8; F. F. Bruce 1972a: 71n.14; Jeremias 1972: 44, 55; Garrett 1998: 91-94; pace Barrett 1967: 47. But Brown 1994: 196, following Lövestam, is right to find "the combination of watching and praying in Psalms" (e.g., Ps 63:6; 77:6; 119:148; also 1QS 6.7-8; Lk 2:37; Acts 16:25).

85. Brown 1994: 154 relates Mk 14:34 (Mt 26:38) to Ps 42:6-7 (LXX Ps 41), which 1QH 8.32 also echoes; Davies and Allison 1997: 565 point out that Jewish tradition assigned this psalm to David in the context of Absalom's betrayal. Dodd 1965: 71 suggests multiple attestation for Ps 41 in Mk 14:36; Jn 12:27; and Heb 5:7. The "troubling" of the soul, however, is idiomatic; if Ps 41:11; 42:5 LXX (Ps 42:11; 43:5 MT) reflect the exact wording of the text, analogous wording appears in Ps 6:3; Gen 41:8 (cf. Jn 12:27).

28; cf. 27:48), possibly alluding, like his interpretation of the cup at dinner, to the Hallel's "cup of salvation" (Ps 116:13; cf. Gen. Rab. 88:5).[86] The image probably alludes as well to the frequent biblical picture of God's "cup of wrath" against the nations.[87] Thus Jesus may shrink not merely from death but from dying as a sacrifice under his Father's wrath (Gundry 1982: 533; Is 53:10).

Jewish texts occasionally designate God as "my Father" (Sir 23:1, 4); probably the corporate emphasis in extant prayer texts indicates why it is no more frequent than it is. "*Our* Father" becomes quite common in Jewish prayers; Jeremias 1971: 62-65 thus excludes too much Jewish material calling God "Father." He also lacks adequate proof that "Abba" generally stands behind Jesus' use of "Father" in prayer in the Gospels, but Mark (14:36) demonstrates that, in this case at least, "Abba" does stand behind our extant translation "Father" (26:39). Perhaps like a good scribe, Matthew translates Mark's Semitic terms into the vernacular (Goulder 1974: 23), but this does not obscure the basic sense of intimacy that stands behind the more formal and acceptable Matthean expression. Because the Greek-speaking church must have gotten "Abba" (Rom 8:15; Gal 4:6) from the Aramaic-speaking church, who would not have learned it from Jewish culture in general (note the paucity of examples; see Witherington 1990: 217-18) and probably not have dared to use it regularly without the authority of Jesus, most scholars concur that Jesus sometimes used the informal and intimate title "Abba" (Mk 14:36; Martin 1982: 34-35).[88] This is a term of special intimacy (cf. Jeremias 1964b: 59-60; F. F. Bruce 1963: 56).[89] While Jeremias's claim that no Jewish evidence suggests anyone called God "Abba" (Jeremias 1964: 57, 60, 109-10; F. F. Bruce 1978: 21-22) is an overstatement (Vermes 1973: 42, 210-13), the exceptions are quite rare (see Klausner 1979b: 378; Stanton 1995a: 153). Even the "charismatic rabbi" Vermes cites (followed by Borg 1987: 45) alludes

86. Kiley 1986 also finds an allusion in the Markan form of the prayer to Ps 116:4's entreaty, "Save my life," but the verbal allusions by themselves, at least, are inadequate.

87. Ps 11:6; 60:3; 75:8; Is 29:9-10; 51:17, 21-23; 63:6; Jer 25:15-29; Lam 4:21; Zech 12:2; cf. Ps. Sol. 8:14-15; in the ancient Near East, Albright and Mann 1971: 327. The image could signify death in general as in texts betraying more hellenistic influence, perhaps alluding to Socrates' execution: Test. Abr. 1:10; 16A; Cic. *Tusc. Disp.* 1.40.96; *Greek Anth.* 7.96. But this source was less available to the early Christians than the LXX and far less available to Jesus (though Brown 1994: 169 also finds the cup of suffering in Targ. Neof. Deut 32:1; Neof. Yer. II, and Fr. Targ. Gen 40:23; Mart. Is. 5:13; he also notes "taste death" in Heb 2:9; Jn 8:52; 4 Ezra 6:26, but this was idiomatic — e.g., Sib. Or. 1.82; cf. Marc. Aur. *Med.* 9.2; Gen. Rab. 21:5; Lev. Rab. 18:1; Pesiq. R. 48:2; Lane 1991: 49). On the nature of literal cups at banquets, see Varro 5.26.121; Athenaeus *Deipn.* 11.781c-503f; Safrai 1974/76b: 742-43.

88. That the Gentile churches may have treated it as an ecstatic palindrome (Aune 1980: 1550) is rendered less probable by the translation accompanying it (Rom 8:15; Gal 4:6); for early Christian liturgical usage, see Jeremias 1964b: 64-65. The supposition that it goes back to the Lord's Prayer (e.g., Hunter 1961: 50; Ridderbos 1953: 158), however, remains undemonstrated (see, e.g., Lull 1980: 67; comment on 6:9).

89. "Abba" is not exclusively children's language (Vermes 1993: 182), although the frequency of its use in that domain produces nuances of affectionate intimacy (Witherington 1990: 218). It provides some insight into Jesus' relationship with his Father (see Dunn 1975: 21-26).

to God as "Abba" parabolically rather than directly addressing him as such in a prayer (also Witherington 1990: 216-17, though the messianic sense he cites in Targ. Mal. 2:10 is also too narrow to fit all the data).

Fourth, no matter what their suffering, God's servants must obey the mission he has given them (26:39, 42, 44). Jesus had lived his life in filial obedience to his Father's will; now he chooses the Father's plan over his own desire.[90] Jesus' obedience is an example for disciples (12:50; cf. 7:21). Loving God does not always mean that they *want* to face what God calls them to face; it does mean that they choose to face it anyway. Thus when the test arrives, Jesus summons all his disciples to "arise" to face it — ready or not (26:46).[91] Other Jewish sages also emphasized choosing God's will over one's own will, or conforming one's will to his will (m. 'Abot 2:4; cf. m. 'Abot 3:7; 1QS 5:9; CD 3.11); some tradition even applied this to dying for God (1 Macc 3:59-60; Test. Iss. 4:3; ARN 32, §71B; cf. Acts 21:14; Mart. Pol. 7.1).[92] In biblical tradition, one could ask God to change his mind, though there was no guarantee that he would do so (Brown 1994: 166-67 cites Ex 32:10-14; 2 Kings 20:1-6; cf. David's submission in the context of the Mount of Olives in 2 Sam 15:25-30). Still, it is doubtful that the early Christians would have invented a prayer in which Jesus distinguished his will from the Father's, especially regarding the cross (Witherington 1990: 219).

Jesus' submission to the Father's final authority is evident in his call to his disciples to arise to face the betrayer (26:46); regardless of what opponents of the early Christians claimed, their Messiah acted fully in line with the Father's will. From this point forward, passive verbs depicting Jesus' suffering and actions done to Jesus dominate most of the Passion Narrative (Perrin 1976a: 91); having labored until his hour, he now relinquishes his destiny to the Father. Yet even in his surrender, he remains in majestic control; only his own words (26:64) will allow his accusers to condemn him (cf. Rhoads and Michie 1982: 88). The reli-

90. In the terms of traditional Christian theology, by becoming fully human, Jesus experienced the full human dread of death; because the Son is distinct from the Father, his own desire might differ from the Father's, though he was ready to submit to the Father. The text probably tends, however, more toward a so-called "monothelite" interpretation than much of later Christendom adopted. Some philosophers emphasized leaving decisions to deities rather than praying as one wanted, as in popular piety (Burkert 1985: 75; van der Horst 1995), but resignation to God's will was a Jewish conception no less (1 Sam 3:18; 2 Sam 10:12; 16:10-12). Even some nonphilosophers regarded praying for one's life as less than heroic (Longinus *Sublime* 9.10). Meanwhile, the element of the Son's choice conflicts with the frequent Greek tradition that stressed the futility of trying to escape one's prophesied appointed fate (Diod. Sic. 15.74.3-4; cf. Sen. *Ep. Lucil.* 27.3); on Fate, see comment on 10:29-31.

91. Moule 1965: 118 suggests that this is military language summoning soldiers to advance (also Gundry 1982: 536); while this suggestion is too specific, it does reflect the strength of the summons. As in Jn 14:31, the summons is to join Jesus in his mission of suffering according to the Father's will.

92. Stoics could also suggest resigning oneself to God's will, though this was intended in the sense of fate (e.g., Epict. *Disc.* 2.16.42; 2.17.22). One should compare Jesus' prayer with the ancient praise of courage in the face of death (see comment on 16:21).

gious establishment had complained that Jesus ate with "sinners" (9:11), but at this point in the Markan and Matthean narratives the reader first hears Jesus apply the title to leaders of the Jerusalem establishment (26:45; cf. Judas in 27:4).

The Betrayal (26:47-56)

Cf. Mk 14:43-52; Lk 22:47-53; Jn 18:2-12; 1 Cor 11:23 probably also refers to the "betrayal" to the chief priests (Fee 1987: 549), although "handing over to the Romans" was also dramatic enough that it could figure in the tradition (e.g., Mk 10:33-34). (Harvey 1982: 24-25 thinks "handing over" in Rom 4:25 reflects Is 53:12 LXX, which the Gospels may have used if they had no information to contradict it; but in context Is 53 reads more naturally as if *God* handed the servant over.) In this passage, everyone who was close to Jesus — from Judas to the disciples who planned to follow to the death — either betrayed or abandoned him to his opponents. As Jesus faced injustice alone as a victim, he also showed his disciples the depth of his love: when not another human being stood with him, their Lord nevertheless continued in the Father's plan to save them.

The guards Judas led to Jesus probably belonged to the Levite temple guard (hence "not in the temple" — 26:55; cf. Lk 22:4, 52; Jn 7:32; Jeremias 1969: 210) and the armed auxiliary police who worked for them (Lane 1974a: 524); the captain of the temple guard was a high officer who on occasion even rose to the office of high priest (see Reicke 1974: 148).[93] Such a police battalion was customary for municipalities throughout the Empire (Stambaugh and Balch 1986: 34). Jewish soldiers did use swords (m. Shab. 6:4), and the high priest's servants were notorious for their use of clubs in the temple, as was the use of clubs in quieting unrest.[94] Contrary to many proposals,[95] it is unlikely that Pilate, who probably had recently arrived and knew little of Jesus, would have dispatched *Roman* troops from the Fortress Antonia at their request, especially with Jewish officers at their head. Although some military terms in the Passion story (see especially Jn 18:3) are Roman, Greek and Roman military

93. On the temple watch, see Safrai 1974/76d: 872-73; Cadbury 1979: 300; on their captain, the *segan,* and his authority and high-priestly connections, see, e.g., b. Pesaḥ. 14b; 47a; Tamid 27b-28a; Acts 4:1; possibly "the king's captain" in Jos. *War* 1.652.

94. Klausner 1979b: 337; Lane 1974a: 524, citing b. Pesaḥ. 57a, bar.; t. Menaḥ. 13:21; for use by Pilate's soldiers, cf. Jos. *War* 2.176; *Ant.* 18.61; other Romans, Jos. *War* 2.326. Stauffer 1960: 120 thinks that carrying nonadorning weapons violated Sabbath law (m. Shab. 16:4), hence that the expedition does not occur after the Passover meal. Even assuming that the Levite police would normally have observed this rule (which is unlikely), however, military emergencies suspended normal Sabbath regulations (1 Macc 2:40-41), and the chief priests may have been willing to construe the potential revolutionary Jesus in these terms.

95. Cf., e.g., Stauffer 1960: 119; Winter 1961: 30, 44; Hunter 1965: 166; Anderson 1976: 327; Cohn 1977: 78; F. F. Bruce 1980b: 9; Blomberg 1992a: 397; Brown 1994: 248-51; cf. Jn 18:3, 10, 31. Blinzler 1959: 9 complains about critics who suppress (as inauthentic) evidence "inconvenient" for the thesis.

terms had long before been transferred to Jewish soldiers (e.g., Jos. *Life* 242).[96]

They came armed as if Jesus were a *lēstēs* (26:38, 55), usually translated "robber," the term Josephus most frequently applies to those many viewed as revolutionaries, such as those who violated the temple (Moule 1965: 119; cf. Mart. Pol. 7), perhaps a "social bandit" (e.g., Malina and Rohrbaugh 1992: 157). They did not understand that Jesus' real threat was quite different. Their secretive capture resembled the way authorities had long dealt with guerilla revolutionaries (Stauffer 1960: 119). In the context of the whole Gospel, however, their assumption appears ironic: Jesus had compared *them* with "robbers" who invited God's judgment on the temple (21:13).

First, disciples may betray Jesus with the very sort of acts that outwardly symbolize devotion (26:47-49). Matthew must report the betrayal, which is an integral part of the Passion Narrative; yet one may guess that he also drew from this account moral instruction for his audience. Persecution often presented disciples an opportunity to betray others in their own interests (e.g., 24:10).

Brown 1994: 255 is correct that we cannot historically establish or refute the historicity of Judas's kiss; but it does make sense. Except when obscured by clouds, the moon would illumine the countryside during Passover (on moonlight's adequacy, cf., e.g., Virg. *Aen.* 7.9); yet others around Jesus, the shade of olive trees, and the importance of getting the right person immediately (before resistance or flight could allow his escape) demanded that Judas specify the right person (cf. Gundry 1982: 537). Yet visibility was probably less to the point than trying (however vainly) to make the expedition look more peaceful than it was; the authorities needed to capture mainly the ringleader and wished to minimize confrontation and bloodshed (cf. Lk 22:38).[97] By having a disciple trusted by his colleagues approach the group, the priests could hope to catch the disciples off guard; and the high priests undoubtedly considered Judas expendable if the ploy failed (cf. 27:3-10).

The emphatic point of the narrative, however, is that it was a *disciple* who betrayed Jesus. One's current commitment is no guarantee of one's perseverance, for even disciples can become traitors (24:10). Disciples often greeted rabbis

96. See further Catchpole 1971: 149; Blinzler 1959: 64-65; Bammel 1984c: 439-40; cf. Wilkinson 1978: 126-27. Some have argued that the Synoptic trial narratives increase Jewish guilt as against Roman (cf. Townsend 1979: 77, on John; Zeitlin 1962; Winter 1961), others that some historical data point to the Jewish leaders' responsibility (cf. Bammel 1984c: 445; Betz 1988); for a full summary of views, see Blinzler 1959: 3-21; and especially Catchpole 1971. The narratives make the most sense if both Jewish leaders and Romans were involved (so also Brown 1994: 250, though basing this view partly on the involvement of Roman troops in the arrest; cf. 1 Thess 2:15). Cohn 1977: 75 doubts that any but people of the "lower strata" would have joined this mission; but I suspect that the temple police would have followed the orders of the *sagan,* a member of the priestly aristocracy.

97. In cases of lesser danger, Romans often settled for executing ringleaders of a revolt rather than a whole populace (e.g., Dion. Hal. 3.40.3; 5.43.2); the Jewish officials would probably be still more inclined toward mercy to fellow Jews.

with a kiss as a sign of intimacy and respect (e.g., Lane 1974a: 525; Wilkinson 1978: 126; Anderson 1976: 323).[98] That Judas should betray Jesus with an outward gesture of devotion makes the act all the more heinous, and an ancient audience might grasp something of the depth of such betrayal's pain (Lk 22:48; cf. 2 Sam 20:9; Prov 27:6).[99] "Hail!" *(Chaire)* was simply the normal Greek salutation (e.g., Char. *Chaer.* 4.5.8; Kim 1972: 10-20), possibly translating an original *shalom* (Brown 1994: 254; cf. Jub. 12:29; 18:16; 19:29; 21:25; 1QS 2.9; Bar Kochba letters; Gen. Rab. 100:7), although it would likely have been original had the interchange been in Greek (e.g., 2 Macc 1:1; 3 Macc 7:1; Test. Abr. 16A; 13B; cf. 2 Bar. 78:2-3). Jesus responds by confronting him with his crime — after addressing him as "Friend," an appropriate title for a disciple (A. B. Bruce 1979: 316) but earlier applied in Matthew to those behaving in a shameful manner (20:13; 22:12; cf. also Suggit 1988).

Second, disciples often wish to fight the kingdom's battles the traditional mortal way or not at all (26:50-54, 56). Protecting Jesus was a paramount issue, yet Jesus did not want his disciples to protect him (cf. 5:44). For Matthew, Jesus came to conquer by way of suffering on the cross, not by way of wielding the sword. Yet it is easier, in human terms, for disciples to fight for their cause than simply to embrace martyrdom for it without resistance; once they realized that martyrdom without resistance was the price of following Jesus, the disciples fled (26:56).[100] Greek and Roman historians often mentioned leaders who shamed their retreating troops by charging into the battle themselves, which normally sallied their troops again (e.g., Appian *R.H.* 10.4.20). Likewise, pietists

98. The early Christians probably extended to one another (Rom 16:16; 1 Cor 16:20; 2 Cor 13:12; 1 Thess 5:26; 1 Pet 5:14; Justin *1 Apol.* 65; cf. Acts of Jn 78) the practice of (generally) lip-kissing (light, not passionate; e.g., Eurip. *Phoenician Maidens* 1671; Virg. *Aen.* 12.434; Ovid *Metam.* 2.356-57, 430-31; 10.362) as a matter of familial intimacy (Gen 33:4; Song 8:1; Tob 7:6; 10:13; Jub. 22:10-11; 26:21; 31:21; Lk 15:20; Test. Sim. 1:2; Jos. and Asen. 8:4/3 in view of 7:8/11; Num. Rab. 9:9; Song Rab. 8:1, §1; Eurip. *Androm.* 416; Virg. *Georg.* 2.523; Ovid *Metam.* 4.222, 334; 10.525; Longus 4.22-23; Dion. Hal. 7.7.1; Plut. *R.Q.* 6, *Mor.* 265B; Ach. Tat. 1.7.3; cf. Dupont 1992: 285). It was also extended to close friends (Hom. *Od.* 21.224-27; Ovid *Metam.* 2.430-31; Artem. *Oneir.* 2.2) and respected teachers or others (even pupils) who brought one great joy (1 Esdr 4:47; t. Ḥag. 2:1; ARN 6A; 13, §32B; b. Ḥag. 14b; p. Ḥag. 2:1, §4; Hor. 3:5, §3; Rosh Hash. 2:9, §2; Soṭa 13a; Pesiq. Rab Kah. 1:3; Qoh. Rab. 6:2, §1; 9:5, §1; Pesiq. R. 23/24:2; Ap. Rhod. 1.313; Arrian *Alex.* 4.11.3; Epict. *Disc.* 1.19.24; Char. *Chaer.* 2.7.7). Serious kissing could indicate more, however (Jos. and Asen. 8:5-7/4-7), and Roman custom did limit even marital kissing in public (Plut. *Bride* 13, *Mor.* 139E; cf. Dupont 1992: 112-13; Brown 1994: 255; Median custom in b. Ber. 8b). Because *phileō* could mean "love" as well as "kiss," one could play on both nuances (Diod. Sic. 9.37.1).

99. Robbins 1992: 189 cites Dio Chrys. *Or.* 3.86, 114: the king depends on his friends' loyalty, and discovering that they are his enemies is his greatest pain. Greek and Roman texts often enough regard the treachery of deceitful betrayal as deplorable (e.g., Polyb. *R.R.E.* 1.7; 3.52; Jos. *War* 2.450-54).

100. Cf. Cullmann 1956b: 40-41: At last the disciples realized that Jesus was not a revolutionary Messiah and would not fight. Flight is not always wrong (10:23), but abandonment of Jesus was apostasy (10:28, 32-33). Davies and Allison 1997: 566 helpfully compare Ahithophel's plan to make David's troops flee (2 Sam 17:2), but the Gospel tradition probably depends on a broader principle here (see Matt 26:31).

often fought and died for causes (e.g., Jos. *Ant.* 17.157-59). By contrast, for disciples to abandon their teacher in this way was a betrayal of their bond of intimacy, and would have shamed Jesus deeply in the social order of the day (Malina 1993: .18).[101] Betrayal by one's own troops, whom one ought to have been able to trust, was tragic (Corn. Nep. 18 [Eumenes], 10.2). Abandonment by one close to a person (such as a relative) would create scandal and generate mass abandonment (Corn. Nep. 14 [Datames], 6.3), and in time of great danger such traitors merited death (Corn Nep. 14 [Datames], 6.8; 9.5). The abandonment could reflect badly on Jesus in terms of status and clearly reflects badly on the disciples; it is surely not the invention of the later church.

Jesus was voluntarily doing the Father's will (26:39, 42), and the Father still would have granted him twelve legions of angels (one for himself and each disciple) had he asked;[102] but the Father had called him to face death for the very ones who had just abandoned him. In Matthew's world angels will assist at the end (cf. 13:41-42; 16:27; 24:30-31), but in the present time dependence on them for deliverance without God's permission would yield to Satan's test (cf. 4:5-7).

That a disciple (named only in John) cut off the high priest's servant's ear probably does not imply that he hoped to render the man ceremonially unfit for service in the temple (cf. Daube 1960: 59), nor that he was satisfied with such disfigurement (cf. Diog. Laert. 9.5.26). Rather, the disciple was probably aiming for a more substantive target (like the man's neck) and missed because he had no practice striking at what rapidly became a moving target.[103] Jesus' response to the disciple — and to the Matthean community who has survived the crises of a Judean-Roman war (cf. Borg 1984: 194-95; for the Markan community, cf. McVann 1986) — provides three reasons for rejecting violence (26:52-54; cf.

101. Josephus praises himself by emphasizing the loyalty of the Galileans to him (Jos. *Life* 84), though as an aristocrat he would have disdained "populist" support had he lacked it.

102. Angels can fight for saints (Davies and Allison 1997: 513 cite 2 Kings 6:15-17; 1QM 7.6; 13.10; Ps-Philo 27:10; 61:8; 2 Bar. 63:5-11; 4 Macc 4:10) and sometimes appear with swords (ibid. cite Num 22:23; Josh 5:13; 1 Chron 21:16, 30; 3 Enoch 22:6). Some Jewish texts portray angelic armies arranged in ranks (see, e.g., 1 Enoch 69:3; 75:1; 3 Enoch 5:2; Gk. Ezra 1:7; cf. Jos. and Asen. 14:7; Test. Abr. 1.13; 2.1; 14A; 14B; Test. Mos. 10:2; 3 Bar. 11:4, 6, 8; 2 Enoch 22:6 J; 33:10 A, J; Gk. Ezra 1:4; 4:24; Apost. Const. 8.12.27; Delcor 1955: 374; cf. the armies of heaven in 2 Kings 6:16-17; Josh 5:13-14; 1QM 7.6; 12:8; the alleged apparitions in 2 Macc 5:2-4; Jos. *War* 6.298-99; Tac. *Hist.* 5.13). Cf. the common Jewish notion of guardian angels in, e.g., Ps-Philo 11:12 *(custodes);* 59:4; Sifre Num. 40.1.5; Gen. Rab. 44:3; Philo *Gig.* 9; cf. Sent. Sext. 32. Matthew lays special stress on angels (20 times in his Gospel; Brown 1994: 276).

103. Brown 1994: 268-29 finds little evidence in the text to explain why a disciple would have a sword, except Lk 22:35-38, which may derive from a source; he notes that Essenes carried weapons during travel because of bandits (Jos. *War* 2.125). After the temple cleansing, it is logical to think that some disciples expected trouble (Lk 22:27-28). Given the *Lex Iulia de maiestate* (Justinian *Dig.* 48.4.1, cited in Brown 1994: 274), Jesus may have allowed the presence of swords to facilitate his rapid conviction as one dangerous to the public order (Lk 22:37). That Matthew and John independently agree (without Mark) on the command to sheath the sword suggests that this command derives from pre-Gospel tradition (Brown 1994: 86; unless John depends on *very* recent oral tradition derived solely from Matthew).

5:39-42): violence destroys those who employ it (26:52); Jesus trusts the Father's ability to protect him (26:53); and Jesus recognizes that his Father's will for him includes suffering (26:54; Meier 1980: 328). Jesus' warning about those taking a sword perishing by it resembles a Jewish proverb found in a targum of Isaiah 50:11 (Gundry 1982: 539) and Syriac Menander's Sentences 15-19.[104]

Third, Jesus confronts injustice but submits to Scripture's plan (26:54-56). The authorities act unjustly as well as in political cowardice, and Jesus does not hesitate telling them so (26:55). But Scripture dictated his own mission, so he submitted to the Father's will (as in 4:1-11). Jesus' model of confronting injustice contrasts starkly with that of his disciples (cf. 5:39; 26:51).

The Political and Religious Leaders versus Jesus (26:57-68)

Cf. Mk 14:53-65; Lk 22:54-71; Jn 18:13-24. The trial scene, heavily laden with ironies, exemplifies Jesus' teaching about the hiddenness of the kingdom (13:31-33). Apart from those who share the correct presuppositions, the kingdom's presence remains ambiguous to those it confronts (e.g., 26:64). Ironically, the kingdom remained obscure even to many of those providing religious and political leadership to others.

Excursus: Historicity of the Trial Narratives

Some have assailed the historicity of the "trial" that occurs here (e.g., Winter 1961; idem 1964; Cohn 1977: 98; Grant 1964; Zeitlin 1962); others have shown that the arguments against authenticity are at best inconclusive and at worst fallacious (Goppelt 1964: 84ff.; Sherwin-White 1978: 34ff.; cf. idem 1965; Catchpole 1971: 271; Corley 1992; cf. Keener 1998). Although elements of the later Mishnaic code of legal conduct are probably early (Abrahams 1924: 129), and I cautiously employ some of the material below, it is tenuous to dispute the historicity of the earlier Gospel accounts of the trials (with traditions more contemporary than those on which the Mishnah is based) based on conflicts with those rules. First, the Mishnah reports Pharisaic idealizations of the law in its own day, at a period over a century later than Jesus' trial (Brown 1994: 357-63; Blinzler 1959: 138-43), and the council in Jesus' day was hardly dominated by Pharisees (cf. Anderson 1976: 326; pace Cohn 1977: 105).

Second, rabbinic sources themselves indicate that the aristocratic priests did not always play by the rules (cf. Klausner 1979b: 337; see my excursus on "high

104. On like-for-like repayment of misdeeds, cf., e.g., Demosth. *Against Zenothemis* 6; Diod. Sic. 20.65.2; 20.101.3; Aul. Gel. 7.4.4; Sir 27:25-27; Jub. 4:32; 35:10-11; 37:5, 11; 1QpHab 11.5, 7, 15; 12.5-6; Ps-Philo 44.9-10; m. 'Abot 2:7; Mek. Nez. 18.55-58; Sifre Deut. 238.3.1; ARN 27, §56; b. 'Abod. Zar. 17b; Sanh. 108b; Bonsirven 1964: 110; Finkelstein 1972: 219; for another, unrelated culture, see, e.g., Whisson 1964: 289.

priests" at 26:1-16); in fact, because elements of proper legal procedure were standard throughout Mediterranean antiquity, the Gospel writers may expect us to *notice* significant breaches of procedure. Unless one presupposes that the aristocratic priests (like later rabbis) would follow careful procedure even in explosive political situations — which is unlikely — an argument from Mishnaic technicalities does not work against the Gospel narrative (cf. Sanders 1985: 317). Sanders puts the matter best (1992: 487):

> The gospel accounts do present problems, but disagreement with the Mishnah is not one of them. . . . The system *as the gospels describe it* corresponds to the system that we see in Josephus. The trial of Jesus agrees very well with his stories of how things happened.

Further, the Matthean/Markan "trial" account probably represents what was more technically a preliminary inquiry in which Jesus' interrogators would be even less likely to regard the rules as constraining (cf. Jn 18:19-24, 28).[105] Finally, the Gospel writers probably *intended* to convey breach of procedure, not to pretend that the mock trial and abuse they depict were standard Jewish custom (cf. Hooker 1983: 86; Rhoads and Michie 1982: 120-21).[106]

While one cannot prove by historical means the veracity of the contents of the trial narrative at this remove, skepticism that the first followers of Jesus would have had access to such information (e.g., Sanders 1985: 299) also assumes too much. Sources for the trial narrative may derive from Joseph of Arimathea (Mk 15:43), from connections within the high priest's household (Jn 18:15-16), others who later became disciples or sympathizers (Jn 19:39; cf. perhaps Acts 6:7), or Jesus himself (cf. Acts 1:3); it is unthinkable at least that the early Palestinian tradition would have neglected the witness of anyone like Joseph who could have had contacts present at the trial. That leaks from within the Jerusalem council occurred on other occasions in the first century (Jos. *Life* 204; among other peoples, e.g., Corn. Nep. 4 [Pausanias], 5.1; 14 [Datames], 5.3) does not prove that such a leak occurred in Jesus' case, but it does challenge the claims of those who suppose such a leak implausible.

Even though Mark may have crafted the material in his own words and for his own purposes (see Donahue 1973: 98-99; idem 1979: 62-65; Dewey 1976: 97-100), substantial evidence remains that he accurately preserves "the decisive elements of Jesus' examination before the Sanhedrin in their correct order" (Schubert 1984: 401; see 385-402). Some believe that the Romans would have acted without some sort of session from leaders of the municipal aristocracy (Cohn 1977: 109; Flusser 1988: 589), but this does not fit the Roman manner of delegating preliminaries to local officials.

105. See Cullmann 1956b: 42, 46; Argyle 1963: 206; Reicke 1974: 146; France 1985: 377; Hagner 1995: 797; cf. Harvey 1982: 31; Meier 1980: 330; Sanders 1993: 67.

106. Brown 1994: 433 observes that "ancient literary accounts of famous trials" usually include polemic or bias (he would not, however, call the narrative as a whole a "fiction," as in Mack 1988: 295). Trial scenes can also provide suspense in a plot, e.g., in Chariton *Chaereas,* toward the beginning, and later before the king of Persia.

Together the cleansing of the temple (which would offend the Sadducean aristocracy) and crucifixion by the Romans suggest the intermediary step of arrest by the priestly authorities; as Sanders observes, conflict with the Romans, crowds, or Pharisees would not explain subsequent events, but the continuing enmity of the chief priests against Jesus' followers (e.g., Acts 4:1-7; 5:17-18; 9:1-2) points to the priestly aristocracy as the main source of opposition (1985: 286).[107] Given high-priestly involvement, the Gospel writers are not so generous as to have alleged even the pretense of a hearing if in fact they had no tradition that one occurred. Like the best modern preachers, the Gospel writers were more interested in applying their text than in creating a wholly new source to be applied.[108]

Anti-Semites have often exploited the negative portrayal of the aristocracy in Jesus' trial; but their abuse of this narrative attributes to the whole Jewish people blame for the behavior of a political elite other Jewish minorities also complained about (see the excursus on "high priests" on 26:1-16). Despite Matthew's denunciations of Pharisees elsewhere, he adds them to his passion narrative only in 27:62; the miscarriage of justice he recounts is attributed only to the sociopolitical elite.

Most people in mainstream Jewish society presumably respected their law teachers, elders, and priesthood as their spiritual leaders (representatives of these groups constituted the Sanhedrin — see the excursus on the Sanhedrin above), but here most of these spiritual leaders prove too hostile to Jesus to concern themselves with legal ethics. Although exceptions historically existed,[109] the overwhelming picture of religious leaders in the Gospels provides a warning to Matthew's own community. It is common practice to follow those in eminent positions, and if those in positions of authority in the church dare forget whose servants they are, they can easily become enemies of their own Lord, vying for the power and honor that rightfully belong to him alone (21:38; 24:45-51).

First, the high priest and council ignore proper judicial procedures (26:57-61). Although we know the rules primarily from later Pharisaic sources that would not reflect the views of most aristocratic priests (the rabbinic portrait of the Sanhedrin itself is severely distorted; cf. Doeve 1954: 37-38, 46), parallels

107. Rabbinic attestation of a religious trial of Jesus (Stauffer 1960: 225; cf. Herford 1966: 78-83) is late and probably derivative, hence I do not admit it as independent evidence; but a Jewish hearing is essential. Even Winter, who emphasizes an arrest and agenda set by the Romans (1961: 30, 147), recognizes that Pilate would have expected the high priest's aides to prepare the case (1961: 29).

108. Weeden's thesis that the pre-Markan trial tradition belonged to Mark's "divine man" Christology opponents (Weeden 1976: 129) is fanciful; no trial narrative leading to execution (contrast Apollonius of Tyana's disappearance) would easily fit such a Christology.

109. According to the Mishnah, only a portion of the Sanhedrin need have been present; cf. Mk 15:43; but contrast Mt 27:57, underlining the extent of the opposition perhaps in a manner more relevant to Matthew's audience. The absence of a defending attorney for Jesus despite rabbinic practice (Blinzler 1959: 135) could represent violation of the rules, but it probably reflects the lateness of the rules (cf. Blinzler 1959: 142-43).

between extant Jewish and Roman laws (cf. Cohen 1966) suggest that some procedures the leaders ignore here were standard. Given the reports about the aristocratic priesthood from their Pharisaic and Essene enemies, the improprieties of the priesthood should hardly surprise us. Arguments based solely on the reports of a group's enemies are weaker than evidence from the group itself, but in the absence of other evidence should weigh more than arguments from pure silence. The rest of history testifies that power and dogmatic certainty that one's cause is right prove a deadly combination for those who do not feel constrained to play by the rules, for whom the supposedly just end justifies the means, no matter how religious they may be.

To the extent that the later sources provide a reliable picture of legal ethics that the Sanhedrin would have respected, probable breaches of legality include the following. First, judges must conduct and conclude capital trials during daylight (m. Sanh. 4:1; cf. Roman practice in Aul. Gel. 14.7.8); this may, however, explain a late, brief, more official meeting around 5:30 a.m., before conducting Jesus to Pilate (cf. 27:1; Lk 22:66-71). Further, trials should not occur on the eve of a Sabbath or festival day (cf. m. Sanh. 4:1; Yom Tob 5:2; t. Yom Tob 4:4; Philo *Migr. Abr.* 91; cf. Blinzler 1959: 143-44), but officials may have regarded this as an emergency situation, and a festival was the one sort of occasion when one *could* most gather the Sanhedrin, if members came from outside Jerusalem (Reicke 1974: 145; but as I argued above, the Sanhedrin was *largely* drawn from the municipal aristocracy). Even Pharisaic interpretation supported executing an extraordinary offender on a pilgrimage festival to warn others not to repeat the crime (m. Sanh. 11:4; t. Sanh. 11:7; Dalman 1929: 98; Lane 1974a: 529-30); the offenders included those regarded as false prophets, among others (Hill 1979: 52).

Other possible breaches of legal custom occur. Pharisaic rules also required a day to pass before issuing a verdict of condemnation (m. Sanh. 4:1; Wilkinson 1978: 131-32). Still, the Sadducees may generally have preferred speedier executions than the Pharisees thought appropriate (cf. m. Mak. 1:6; the Sadducees did prefer stricter punishments — Jos. *Ant.* 20.199). Further, the Sanhedrin should not meet in the high priest's palace (Cohn 1977: 98 cites b. ʿAbod. Zar. 8b; Sanh. 41b; Shab. 15a); they would soon move, however, most likely to their normal meeting place (probably what rabbinic sources call "the chamber of hewn stone") on or near the temple Mount (m. Midd. 5:5; Sanh. 11:2; Jos. *War* 5.144; Wilkinson 1978: 86-87; Brown 1994: 350).

Most obviously, Jewish law opposed false witnesses. The biblical penalty for false witnesses in a capital case was execution (Deut 19:16-21), and later Jewish ideals, at least, continued to regard this penalty as appropriate (Jos. *Ant.* 4.219; 11QTemple 61.7-11; m. Mak. 1:7; t. Sanh. 6:6; Sifre Deut. 190.5.1), as did Roman law (Ferguson 1987: 51).[110] Cross-examination of wit-

110. So also reportedly Egyptian custom (Diod. Sic. 1.77.2). Diod. Sic. 12.12.2 thus considers particularly merciful a law that merely shames false witnesses so much that they flee a city. Cf. also the distaste for perjury in Sall. *Catil.* 16.2; *Speech of Philippus* 15; *Invective against M. Tullius* 2; Cic. *Invective against Sallust* 5.14; Propertius *Eleg.* 3.6.20.

nesses was standard in Jewish law (e.g., Sus 48–62; m. 'Abot 1:9; Sanh. 5:1-4; tos. Sanh. 6:3, 6; Sifre Deut. 93.2.1; 149.1.1-2; 189.1.3), and apparently the examiners did their job well enough here to produce contradictions they did not expect.[111] In the end, these witnesses could provide only a garbled account of Jesus' proclamation of judgment against the temple (cf. Jn 2:19; Acts 6:14), which could have seemed to the Sanhedrin political reason enough to convict him (cf. comment on 21:12-17; Lane 1974a: 534; Brown 1994: 458; Stanton 1995a: 180-83).[112]

On the claim in 26:61, see comment on 24:1-3.[113] While later Christians might have invented the story of a general charge of blasphemy, they would hardly have invented this charge that Jesus threatened to destroy the temple (Sanders 1985: 71-74; Theissen 1991: 113, 194; Brown 1994: 454-60).[114] While Pharisees might dispute the nature of Sabbath law with Jesus (cf. 12:2), the Sanhedrin would hardly assemble to address such an offense (pace Stauffer 1960: 122-23; Tert. *Spec.* 30; Hill 1985 also thinks the Sanhedrin tried Jesus as a "seducer"); the real charge is profaning the temple, hence by implication insulting or blaspheming God (cf. comment on 21:12-17). From their vantage point after 70, Matthew's audience (in contrast to earlier disciples) may well wonder if the false witnesses did not utter words that proved partly truthful. But at any rate, the high priest must choose another tack; even a court as slanted as this one will not admit evidence from witnesses whose testimony was inconsistent (see Trites 1977: 186; Stauffer 1960: 123-24). Thus for the Jewish court (as opposed to Pilate) the chief priest seeks a new charge in 26:62-68: blasphemy (Blinzler 1959: 170).

Second, when the truth is revealed, it often merely increases the opposition of the powerful predisposed to reject it (26:62-68). The high priest stood (following biblical legal custom — see Trites 1977: 187; but cf. Stauffer 1960: 123) and gave Jesus the opportunity to defend himself, as Jewish law demanded (26:62), but Jesus chose to remain silent (26:63; cf. Is 53:7; Stauffer

111. Gentile sages also admonished checking out all claims (e.g., Phaedrus 3.10.5-6). Stauffer 1960: 206 contends that Jewish law permitted the use of "secret witnesses" only in the case of a "misleader"; but it remains doubtful whether the Sanhedrin's leaders would have observed this rule.

112. Greek rhetoric often preferred arguments from probability and internal consistency (which were frequent; see, e.g., Demosth. *On the Embassy* 120; *Against Pantaenetus* 23; Arist. *Rhet.* 1.15.17, 1376a; Dion. Hal. 3.35.5-6; 11.34.1-6; Jos. *Apion* 1.219-20, 267, 286; 2.8-27, 82, 148; *Life* 342, 350; Acts 26:8) to witnesses (see Kennedy 1980: 20-21), but the effective testimony of witnesses was nevertheless adequate to convict (Dion. Hal. 8.78.3). Any proofs were, however, better than mere assertions (Jos. *Ant.* 17.131).

113. Jn 2:19 could represent a more original form of the saying; "raise up" *(egeirein)* fits the image of building a temple (Sib. Or. 3.290).

114. Pace Weeden 1976: 121-29, who links it to purveyors of a proposed divine man Christology. What Jesus meant by the new temple in the logion is more problematic; Brown 1994: 438-43 classifies the main positions as follows: (1) the Christian community (Cullmann, Donahue, Gaston, Juel, Sweet, Vielhauer; 440-41); (2) an eschatological sanctuary (Jeremias, Pesch, Sanders; 441-43); (3) the body of Christ raised on the third day (Cole, Gärtner, Gaston again, Lamarche, Nineham, Simon; 443).

1960: 125-26; Argyle 1963: 207).[115] Perhaps exasperated, the high priest seeks to place Jesus under the curse of an oath, crying "I adjure you." This was the beginning of an oath formula often used to secure testimony (m. Shebu. 4:5-13) or to produce other action (e.g., 2 Tim 4:1).[116]

Here the high priest explicitly asks Jesus if he claims messianic authority (26:63). Some doubt that the high priest would have asked such a question, skeptical that Jesus' ministry had hinted at this role (Sanders 1985: 297) or supposing that such a charge would have been invented by later Christian dogmatics (Bousset 1970: 73). But given his earlier hints in public parables in Jerusalem (21:37-39; Kingsbury 1986: 87) and the charge on which Pilate executed him (27:11, 29, 37), some question of this nature is not unlikely. Nor is the answer incongruent with Jesus' self-identity reflected in actions like the triumphal entry and act in the temple on one hand, and eschatological teaching about the Son of Man (see Introduction) on the other.[117] Because Matthew added "Son of the living God" to Peter's confession in 16:16, the high priest's demand may recall that passage for Matthew's audience: Jesus concurred when Peter correctly confessed Jesus' identity, although Peter did not understand the full ramifications of the title; Jesus will surely concur now that another openly confronts him with the matter of his identity.

When Jesus responds, "You said," he may speak ironically for them (cf. Soph. *Antig.* 576-77). Jesus' answer is probably "affirmative in content, and reluctant or circumlocutory in formulation" (Catchpole 1971: 226; see also Marshall 1990: 86). Jesus' response may not be so much evasive (cf. Cullmann 1956b: 28) as implying that the title was more their choice of wording than his (cf. F. F. Bruce 1972b: 176n.45). Such a response forces his questioner to take responsibility for the claim (26:25; 27:11) — something the priestly aristocracy will ultimately refuse to do (27:43). In a sense, the narrative has allowed the high priest himself to reveal Jesus' identity correctly — though ironically and unintentionally (Hooker 1983: 101-2; cf. Jn 11:50-52). The need to delay the messianic secret now ended, Jesus reveals publicly that he is God's Son

115. It is doubtful that first-century Jewish custom prescribed that "the examining judge," here the president of the Sanhedrin, "had the right and even the duty to intimidate the defendant" to make him lose composure (so Stauffer 1960: 123-24, citing p. Soṭa 1:16d; b. Soṭa 1:4). If the high priest's motives are less than noble, it is in violation rather than fulfillment of Jewish custom. Bowker 1973: 49-50 thinks that Jesus' refusal to cooperate corroborates their opinion that he is a "rebellious elder."

116. Cf. also Trites 1977: 187. This is a "testimonial oath"; Judaism later borrowed the custom of swearing on the Bible from the Roman-Christian practice (see Cohen 1966: 710-33). The supposed exorcistic link here (e.g., van Tilborg 1972b: 79) represents too narrow an application of the term and is without merit (Gundry 1982: 544; even in Mk 5:7 it is the demon rather than the exorcist who employs it).

117. Witherington 1990: 258-59 also defends the saying by the criterion of dissimilarity (later Christians did not combine Ps 110:1 with Dan 7:13-14), by the criterion of embarrassment (the prophecy was unfulfilled in that they did *not* see him exalted in their lifetimes), and, in my opinion a much stronger argument here, the criterion of consistency: Jesus elsewhere uses both texts cited here (Mk 12:36; 13:26).

(again, 27:54).[118] But Jesus must also define the nature of that Sonship; by responding in scriptural allusions (26:64), he defines his mission in terms his interrogators could not misapprehend: he is both Son of Man coming on the clouds (cf. Dan 7:13-14; Mt 24:30) and *Lord* (Ps 110:1; Mt 22:44).[119] The older Greek version of Daniel and second-century rabbinic tradition attest that some viewed Daniel's "Son of Man" in superhuman, almost divine terms (F. F. Bruce 1972b: 198), but the allusion to Psalm 110's "Lord" is considerably clearer, especially for those who knew Jesus' teaching that this represented one greater than a son of David (22:44).

By declaring that "from this point forward"[120] Jesus would reign, Jesus may seem to the Sanhedrin to claim that he is going to rule politically despite their power over him. But undoubtedly he means that his reign opens not with power but with the cross. In the words of the Fourth Gospel, the time had come for the Son of Man to be lifted up and glorified (Jn 12:23, 32-33; cf. Is 52:13 LXX). Yet the ultimate fulfillment would occur when even his enemies would see him at his coming in triumph as heavenly ruler (26:64; cf. 24:30; Rev 1:7); that is, though they claimed to judge Jesus now, he would ultimately prove *their* judge (cf. Kingsbury 1983: 124) — a claim certain to enrage unbelieving leaders who demand honor.[121] Nevertheless, Jesus still regards his Father as greater than himself, entitling the Lord at whose right hand he would sit with a standard respectful Jewish circumlocution for God, "power" (Heb. *Geburah*).[122]

118. Cf. further here Kingsbury 1983: 122; Perrin 1976a: 95; Hooker 1983: 58-59. Stauffer 1960: 125 and Schoeps 1961b: 161 suggest from the Markan version that Jesus may have originally uttered the sacred name "I am" *(ani [we] hu),* leading to the condemnation of blasphemy and echoing (Schoeps) "the assertion of His divine sonship . . . behind the 'I am' sayings." While explaining the charge of blasphemy (a mere claim to Messiahship cannot — Ladd 1974b: 168), this proposal does require an interpretive leap on the part of the high priest, especially given the absence of this formula at most points (Sanders 1990: 65). Nor does a variant reading of the LXX explain the blasphemy charge here (see Pace 1984, against F. F. Bruce).

119. That Dan 7 and Ps 110 are here in view, see Dodd 1961: 91; Ellis 1977: 203.

120. The phrase could refer to the future (cf. Betz 1968: 90) but probably, as in Luke, begins in the present in some sense (cf. Tasker 1961: 256; F. F. Bruce 1972b: 176; Glasson 1962: 54-59; Brown 1994: 500-504). Thus (pace Meier 1979: 192, who thinks the phrase addresses the Matthean community in particular) Matthew and Luke probably share a common oral (hence the smooth paraphrase) tradition here apparently unknown to Mark (given his theology of the cross, Mark *probably* would have retained it had he known it). The language ultimately demands the parousia, however, and not merely a heavenly exaltation (Cullmann 1950: 149; McArthur 1958: 158; Argyle 1963: 207; Gundry 1982: 546).

121. Although some read Jesus' "from this time forth" statement and other evidence as a denial that Jesus foresaw an interim between his comings (cf., e.g., Barrett 1967: 74, against Kümmel), Jesus' presence-of-the-kingdom parables (ch. 13), mission for his disciples, and other factors militate against this suggestion (cf., e.g., Goppelt 1964: 92). Jeremias notes that Jesus rejected forecasts of dates and allowed that God could shorten or lengthen times of distress (Lk 13:6-9; 18:7-8; Mk 13:20; Jer 18:7-10; Jeremias 1971: 139); against "consistent eschatology," Cullmann notes that the completed victory of the past produces rather than replaces futurist anticipation (1950: 87).

122. This title is widely recognized, e.g., by Moore 2:355; Klausner 1979b: 197; Marmorstein 1968b: 161; Smith 1951: 35n.2; Barrett 1966: 72; Jeremias 1971: 10; more references are found in

Such a claim might have been offensive, but at least later the Pharisees, careful to err on the side of leniency in capital cases (contrast the Sadducees — Jos. *Ant.* 20.199), would not have construed it as technically blasphemous (m. Sanh. 7:5).[123] Uninfluenced by Pharisaic details, the high priest might be far less cautious about what he would admit as blasphemy, but messianic claims were not themselves blasphemous (Sanders 1985: 298; idem 1990: 64; Mack 1988: 294). Because the priestly aristocracy perceives Jesus as a political threat to the temple establishment and the peace of the nation, however, and because the charge of threatening the temple (which could also function as blasphemous; cf. 1 Macc 7:35, 38) remained unproved by strict standards of investigation, they need a charge quickly.[124] Thus choosing (probably correctly) to construe Jesus' words as associating himself with God's majesty, they may imply that Jesus has lowered God's majesty to his own level (cf. Sanders 1990: 64-67; b. Sanh. 63a).[125] Most uses of "blasphemy" in fact were nontechnical (Brown 1994: 522-23; see comment on Mt 9:3). Then again, this may simply represent another example of twisting the rules to get the job done, so frequent in the rest of the narrative; it does fit what we know about some ancient aristocracies dealing with potential troublemakers (cf., e.g., Hanson and Oakman 1998: 94-95).

One could reasonably argue that the Gospels emphasize a Sanhedrin trial so that Jesus dies for religious rather than political reasons (Fredriksen 1988: 117); but the admission of claiming Messiahship in some form would naturally lend itself to the Roman charge of treason; Roman authorities would understand the messianic category in political terms. A messianic claim could be construed as a threat to Rome (cf. Sanders 1985: 55; Schneider 1984: 414); if the Gospels do portray the leaders of the aristocracy as seeking a charge that was more religious than political, their portrait may err by portraying these leaders as *more* pious (at least outwardly) than they actually were at the trial, rather than less so (a portrait that may fit Matthew's understanding of his own community's opposition; cf. 27:6).

By whatever means they construe his words as blasphemy, the high priest stands to rend his cloak as custom required when one heard blasphemy (m. Sanh. 7:5; cf. b. Moʿed Qaṭ. 25b-26a; Sanh. 60a; p. Moʿed Qaṭ. 3:7, §§7-8; Sanh. 7:6, §7), following a traditional behavior for mourning (e.g., Gen 37:34; 44:13; 1 Esdr 8:71; 1 Macc 2:14; 4:39-40; 5:14; 11:71; ARN 4, 25A; Char. *Chaer.* 1.3.4; 3.5.6; 3.10.3;

Davies and Allison 1997: 529. The NIV's "Mighty One" captures the sense; Lk 22:69 adds "of God" to "power," retaining but clarifying the circumlocution (cf. Test. Abr. 4A).

123. Perhaps guarding against convictions based merely on dominant legal interpretations, later rabbis distinguished between violations of Torah, which could be capital offenses, and those of scribal teachings, which could not be (Sifre Deut. 154.2.1). But his hearers would surely regard Jesus' words as at least presumptuous (Davies and Allison 1997: 534 parallel Test. Job 33:3-9).

124. Overman 1996: 388 suggests that "son of God" had political connotations, as a title of the emperor. Matthew's audience could thus have associated this claim with the impending charge of treason.

125. Greek culture also understood that human courts had to prosecute those who insulted the gods or their laws (e.g., Ps-Demosth. *Or.* 59, *Against Neaera* 126).

5.3.4; 7.1.5; Sifre Deut. 43.3.8; p. B. Meṣ. 2:11, §1; Sanh. 2:1, §4);[126] Matthew shifts Mark's undergarments to an outer cloak, perhaps implying the sacerdotal robe (Tasker 1961: 256; but historically cf. Lane 1974a: 538). Whether Josephus merely dramatizes or accurately reports the scenes, he provides evidence that leaders donning sackcloth or rending garments performed a persuasive rhetorical function for the people (Jos. *War* 2.237, 316), an activity matching Roman custom as well (Dio Cassius *R.H.* 48.31.6). Dramatic action augmented rhetorical force (Cic. *Brutus* 55.203; cf. Cic. *Verr.* 5.62.161; Quint. 6.1.31).[127]

If he followed what later records deem standard procedure, Caiaphas may have "opened the voting by asking the members to give their verdict." Again, if the court followed the procedure known to us from later sources, in capital cases the clerk began with the votes of the youngest, probably so that they would not be intimidated by their elders (m. Sanh. 4:2; Stauffer 1960: 126; Blinzler 1959: 135; but cf. p. Rosh Hash. 2:6, §9; seated in a semicircle: Ex. Rab. 5:12); but such formality is improbable at this mock trial.[128] The spirit of Jewish law opposed condemning a criminal on his own admission (Cohn 1977: 98 cites t. Sanh. 9:1), but the Sanhedrin treats Jesus' words here not as admission of a crime, but as a crime itself, that is, blasphemy, to which they themselves are witnesses, obviating the need for other witnesses (Blinzler 1959: 137; Stauffer 1960: 125; cf. Jer 26:11; Barrett 1978: 528). (For some, one's self-accusation was no less incriminating than capture in the act — Ach. Tat. 7.11.1.) The Mishnah apparently prohibited witnesses from participating in sentencing the accused (Blinzler 1959: 135, citing m. Sanh. 5:4, which does not make his case),[129] but given the political urgency of the moment, it is doubtful that the Sanhedrin would observe such a technicality. Just as their charge of blasphemy is itself blasphemous (12:31-32), so the unjust verdict that Jesus merited death (26:66) ironically visits the same sentence on his judges (5:21-22).

Whatever else may have been illegal, the physical mistreatment of a prisoner certainly was; this behavior would have shamed Jesus as well, for such treatment was inappropriate to the status he had claimed. By ridiculing his prophet status (26:68) — challenging him to fulfill a child's game of guessing —

126. Brown 1994: 517 shows that non-Jews would also understand, citing the examples of Licinius Regulus and Augustus, who tore clothes in mourning (Dio Cassius *R.H.* 54.14.1-2; 56.23.1).

127. 27:51 may perhaps represent God's rending for true blasphemy as opposed to human rending for false blasphemy in 26:65, but had Matthew intended the connection to be obvious, he may have more likely used the same word.

128. The rabbinic practice may respond to the earlier Roman custom by which the elders voiced their views first (Dion. Hal. 7.47.1; though this changed — Aul. Gel. 4.10; 14.7.9); but the Sanhedrin, not constrained by later Mishnaic rules, may well have followed general Mediterranean practice (cf. 1QS 6.10).

129. Although the Mishnah itself is later (Blinzler 1959: 142-43), this rule does suit the spirit of Jewish law in general. Rabbinic rules prohibited convicting one of blasphemy until he had first been warned, but teachers of the law were exempt from requiring such warning (Blinzler 1959: 136, following Strack-Billerbeck); this particular rule, however, sounds much like later rabbinic leniency toward the accused rather than a common Jewish custom of the first century.

they may imply that they have condemned him as a false prophet according to the rules of Deuteronomy 18:20 (Hill 1979: 52). His very condemnation and likely imminent execution disproved for them his prophecies about the temple and his own imminent enthronement (26:61, 64; Gundry 1982: 547; Brown 1994: 575, 580). The informed reader, by contrast, sees Jesus as the truest prophet of all (Deut 18:15-18; cf. Mt 2:16; 4:2; 5:1; 17:1-5), meaning that his *accusers* merited judgment (Deut 18:19; cf. Mt 5:22). Yet when they treat Jesus as a false prophet, unrequited blows to the cheek (cf. 5:39; 26:53) demonstrate Jesus' integrity to the audience familiar with his teachings (contrast 23:3); earlier prophets had also been struck on the cheek for their prophecies (1 Kings 22:24; Is 50:6; cf. Mt 5:12; b. Soṭa 13a). Jesus' opponents mock him "as a false prophet at the very moment when his prophecy about Peter is being fulfilled" (26:69-75; Donahue 1976: 78-79 on Mk 14:65-66).

Because mocking follows both the Jewish and Roman trials in Matthew (following Mark), most scholars think that one account (usually the Jewish) was created from the other (usually the Roman). But the details of the abuse are different in each case, and all four Gospels include the Jewish abuse (Brown 1994: 569); all four also have the Romans mock Jesus as "King of the Jews" before or after the trial. It is thus possible that both mockings have a historical basis, and that Mark has assimilated them to one another and arranged them in such a way as to draw attention to the shameful parallel between the behavior of the religious leaders and the Romans (Brown 1994: 572).[130] Jewish holders offered the same kind of beating to Jesus ben Ananias in Jos. *War* 6.302 before handing him over to the Romans (Brown 1994: 586).[131]

The political and religious leaders condemn Jesus for blasphemy for claiming simply what God had claimed about him all along (3:17; 17:5; cf. Kingsbury 1983: 151). From Jesus' condemnation as "God's Son" (26:63-68) to the centurion's recognition that Jesus really is God's Son (27:54), the dominant christological title will be "King of the Jews" (so Kingsbury 1983: 151). This title constitutes a double irony in that those who apply it intend it ironically, but the Gospel tradition ironically inverts the irony so that they have described him accurately (cf. 21:5; 27:11, 29, 37).

The First Response to Betrayal (26:69-75)

Cf. Mk 14:66-72; Lk 22:54-71; Jn 18:25-27. The burden of proof rests heavily against those skeptical of the historical substance of Matthew's account in this

130. Jewish men could mock their enemies no less thoroughly than Romans; cf. Jos. *Life* 323.

131. Matthew follows Mark on the beating by the Sanhedrin (who are *ultimately* responsible), but despite other reports of abuse by high priests, Winter 1961: 21 believes that Luke's account of beating by jailers may more accurately reflect a pre-Markan Passion Narrative (Lk 22:63-65), although Luke probably also takes over material from Mark here, which he then rearranges (Lk 22:67-71).

passage. The earliest Christians, facing hostility from their environment, would not likely have created a story so unflattering to themselves as the abandonment of Jesus by his disciples or denial of Peter (Overman 1996: 369).

Matthew anticipates this section in 26:58 (cf. the "courtyard" in 26:58, 69). A reader unfamiliar with the Gospel tradition might find in Peter's "following" (4:20) a sign of hope that at last one of the male disciples will honor Jesus; but most of Matthew's community has probably heard the stories of Peter's betrayal before and instead would react with some apprehension at the forthcoming further example of apostasy.

The primary point of the denial account in Mark is to warn the community about apostasy in the face of persecution (Taylor 1952: 572), and given the threat of severe opposition, the same naturally holds for Matthew as well. By placing two responses to betrayal side by side, Matthew also points out how disciples should respond to their failures in discipleship. Peter wept with remorse (26:75); Judas killed himself (27:5). Only the former was able to return to Jesus.[132] The narrative may contain another contrast as well: Peter's denial contrasts starkly with Jesus' faithful confession (France 1985: 382; Theissen 1991: 196).[133] The high priest's home, like other homes of the priestly aristocracy in the Upper City, was quite large and wealthy (on the wealth of the priestly aristocracy, see, e.g., Hachlili and Killebrew 1983: 46), hence the massive "gateway" (26:71; cf. Filson 1960: 284; Beare 1981: 524).

First, Peter cared more about his own life than about his Lord's honor (26:69-74) — behavior unacceptable for a disciple (10:32-33). Peter sought to be a disciple; while Jesus' enemies "gathered" (cf. 13:40), Peter "followed" (cf. 4:19; 8:22), but from a distance, to see the "end" (*telos* — 26:58).[134] Denying that one knew another was shameful if the claim was false (e.g., Terence *Phormio* 392-94). That he would renounce his faith before one of minimal social status (though the high priest's servants wielded considerable power, a "slave girl" would have quite little, and Matthew, unlike Mark, underlines this point with *two* servant girls — 26:69, 71) increases the heinousness of the denial.[135] Peter's wording does the same; "I do not know what you say" and similar formulas represent the emphatic form standard in Jewish law "for formal, legal denial"

132. Brown 1994: 641 believes that the contrast between Peter and Judas emphasizes that Judas was guilty of Jesus' blood but Peter was not guilty. But why would Matthew need to stress this?

133. Theissen's parallel with Acts 12, however, is fatally flawed; as Theissen admits, Peter did not deny his faith under Agrippa I. Indeed, there remains no evidence that anyone supposed that he had; rather, that account fits Acts's theme of miraculous escapes (Acts 5, 16).

134. Given the other eschatological connotations in the language of the disciples' testing (e.g., 26:41), the "outcome" here may point beyond Jesus' suffering to the birth pangs of the Messiah to be suffered by Jesus' followers preceding his return (24:6). This is, however, somewhat speculative; the expression is perfectly good Greek.

135. Naturally she could accuse him to others, and Jewish tradition seems to have suspected women in particular of gossip (b. Qidd. 49b; Gen. Rab. 70:11). But the witness of women was also more suspect (e.g., Jos. *Ant.* 4.219; see further below), and she had less direct power to hurt him than did other actors in the narrative.

(e.g., m. Shebu. 8:3, 6; Smith 1951: 35).[136] Denials with cursing imply not profanity but invoking a curse upon himself if he were lying (Beare 1981: 524; cf. Meier 1980: 335; e.g., b. Shab. 16b-17a); because he was lying, he was directly violating Jesus' teaching in 5:33-37, but more significantly, he was denying the Lord he had promised never to deny (10:33; 26:35).[137] Whereas Jesus fearlessly confessed his identity under oath (26:63), Peter under oath denied *knowing* Jesus (26:72).

If Daube is right (1969), Peter's denials may increase in intensity. His first denial may simply be an evasion designed to save his life (26:69-70); Judaism considered such an evasion acceptable. (In contrast to Mark, however, Matthew's report of even this first denial is plainly public.) Peter's second denial involves a false oath and is a direct denial (26:72), and his third involves much swearing (26:74). Nearly all Jewish hearers would regard the final form of denial, if it would shame one's allegiance to God, as wrong.

That Peter's speech inadvertently betrays him (cf. Judg 12:6) is not surprising.[138] Jewish texts report that Galileans failed to distinguish their gutturals properly (Dibelius 1949: 40). The commonly cited modern idea that Galileans were particularly prone to revolution, however, is questionable; the regional prejudice of Judeans against Galileans is more to the point. Zeitlin and others have argued that Josephus used "Galilean" as a revolutionary rather than geographical title (Zeitlin 1974; Loftus 1975; cf. idem 1977), but this approach omits a significant body of evidence (see Armenti 1981; Freyne 1980; Bilde 1980). At least Cumanus apparently thought that Galilean villagers were sympathetic toward revolutionaries (Jos. *War* 2.228-29), and Judas the Galilean, leader of the infamous and ill-fated tax revolt during Jesus' childhood, was certainly Galilean.[139] Nevertheless, when Josephus's rhetoric is taken into account (e.g., Jos. *War* 3.41), Galilee was clearly unprepared at the time of the first revolt; it hardly proved an ideal base for Zealot sympathizers (Freyne 1988: 162). Sepphoris, in fact, refused to join the revolt of 66-70, perhaps recalling its earlier destruction under Varus. Further, the messianic uprisings of the Samaritan Theudas and the Egyptian prophet that Josephus reports neither transpired near Galilee nor boasted explicit Galilean support (Freyne 1988: 195). Galilean leaders generally respected Jerusalem's representatives as leaders of their nation (Jos. *Life* 198). Finally, Jesus hailed from Lower Galilee, which participated in

136. The supposed Aramaic mistranslation here is untenable (see Boyd 1956).

137. Malina and Rohrbaugh 1992: 160-61 contend that Peter's deception to maintain his honor comported with Mediterranean values, and the difficulty is that Peter gave his word to Jesus that he would not deny him (26:35). But another problem is that Jesus demands that his followers honor him publicly, so gaining honor before his Father's tribunal, and that this must take absolute precedence over honor in this world (cf. 10:32-33). Cf. even ARN 27A: The honor of one's master (and one's disciple) should be as dear to one as one's own.

138. Analogously, lack of fluency in a second language could give someone away (see Horsley 1989: 31).

139. For Upper Galilee as a hotbed of revolutionary fervor, cf. Vermes 1973: 46-48; Vermes 1984: 4-5. Jesus ministered especially in Lower Galilee.

Judean and broader Mediterranean commerce, not from the isolated hills of Upper Galilee or from Judas's Gamala on the other side of the Jordan (Witherington 1990: 88-89, following Meyers 1976; see comment on 4:12-16). Jesus' Galilee was probably no more revolutionary than Judea was.

Nevertheless, the primary significance of Peter's being a Galilean is that he did not belong to the high priest's household, having instead followed the Galilean prophet. Judean regional prejudice against Galilee (cf. Davies 1974: 243) probably contributed to the noteworthiness of this observation. Peter had hoped to follow a Messiah whose kingdom did not involve the cross (16:22); thus he proved unprepared when the time came to take up his cross and follow the Lord (16:24; cf. Dewey 1976: 111). That Peter illustrates Jesus' teaching about discipleship in 16:24-27 indicates Peter's function as a paradigm for disciples: only by counting the cost of following Jesus, only by watching and praying, will disciples be ready when the hour comes for them to share the sufferings of their Lord for his name's sake.

Second, the exposure of disciples' weakness is cause for repentance (26:75; cf. 26:31-32), not sorrow unto death (27:5; cf. 2 Cor 7:10). By juxtaposing two responses to betrayal (26:69-75 with 27:1-10), Matthew forces his audience to confront the appropriate ways to address human failure as disciples. Peter's example warns Matthew's audience to be ready for testing; but it also summons those who have stumbled to return to the kingdom way, and calls upon the community to show mercy to those who have already stumbled but wish to return to the way of Christ (cf. 18:10-35).

The Other Response to Betrayal (27:1-10)

Like Peter, Judas is guilty of apostasy, but unlike that of Peter, Judas's apostasy was premeditated. Whereas Peter's remorse leads to repentance, Judas's leads to terminal despair. This narrative also further indicts the heartlessness of the priestly leadership, who value laws of ritual purity more highly than their God-given responsibility as shepherds of other lives among their people. Lest modern Christians be tempted to conceive these leaders in ethnic rather than political and religious terms, we should take note how many churches today seem more concerned about petty church rules than about the life-and-death needs in the communities around them, and recall that the various groups competing for religious leadership in Jesus' day probably could have justified more of their rules from Scripture than modern religious leaders tend to do. As one scholar opines, "it seems that past attempts by Christians to interpret the Passion in such a way as to condemn modern Jews exemplify the very attitudes the Passion-narratives were designed to challenge" (Wilkinson 1978: 144). Finally, Matthew emphasizes in this narrative that even to the smallest details, the events of the passion fulfilled God's purposes previously revealed in his Scriptures.

Matthew reworks his traditions to emphasize his case. Although this narrative contains prior tradition (cf. Acts 1:18-19), Matthew has clearly reworked it to emphasize a point found in this form in neither Markan nor Johannine traditions. Judas's end (27:3-10) is full of Matthean vocabulary, following the liberty he could take in putting an oral tradition into writing (cf. Van Tilborg 1972b: 83-84).

Although Matthew does not create the story, he may fill in its gaps on the basis of biblical prophecy (Hill 1972: 348). Matthew quotes Zechariah 11:13 as if *yoṣer* ("potter") could be read *'oṣer* ("treasury"), revocalizing to provide a new interpretation, as we know later Jewish interpreters often did (Longenecker 1975: 150; cf. Burkitt 1907: 125; Lindars 1961: 118). If the priests prevented the money from making it to the "treasury," Scripture would be fulfilled when it reached the "potter"; "One way or another the prophetic Scriptures must reach fulfillment" (Gundry 1982: 556; cf. Mt 5:18). In its original context (with which Matthew appears familiar), the prophecy referred to how cheaply (at the price of a slave) Israel had valued their shepherd, the prophet (or perhaps God himself), and how he would therefore give them a foolish shepherd so that they might learn by contrast how benevolent the prophet (or God) had been to them (Zech 11:4-17; cf. 13:7-9; Edgar 1958: 50).

By appealing to "Jeremiah" rather than to Zechariah, however, Matthew makes clear that he intends his biblically literate audience to link an analogous passage in Jeremiah (32:6-14) and to interpret them together (as in the *gezerah shewah* of Mk 1:2-3, which Matthew recognizes and modifies in Mt 3:3).[140] In so doing, Matthew reapplies Zechariah's prophecy with a message of Israel's coming restoration in Jeremiah. Matthew may well allude to Jeremiah 18–19 (regarding the potter; cf. Meier 1980: 339; Gundry 1982: 556; Upton 1982) as well; in this case he evokes a prophecy of the impending destruction of Jerusalem (Jer 19:10-13; Mt 27:25).[141]

The betrayal of innocent blood is central to the narrative. The phrase "innocent blood" reflects substantial LXX influence (it appears there fifteen times; Gundry 1982: 554).[142] Ancient Eastern peoples regarded very seriously the guilt of innocent blood, sometimes viewed in terms of corporate responsibil-

140. Cf. Lindars 1961: 120; Gundry 1982: 556-57; Meier 1980: 339; Brown 1994: 651. Jerome cites an apocryphal copy of Jeremiah that included these words (cf. Lachs 1987: 423), but some Jewish Christians had undoubtedly created that document to address the "problem" in Mt 27:9. Luther felt that Matthew's "error" here was inconsequential (Stanton 1995a: 8), but while Matthew may have been capable of such an error, it is unlikely that one occurred in this case. Given his ability to retranslate the entire Hebrew text based on revocalization (I have examined only the point most germane to the sense of our passage), it is unlikely that Matthew simply got his attribution wrong.

141. But cf. Gundry 1975: 202: "The connection with and the typological interpretation of Jer 19 would never have suggested itself apart from a prior tradition of the potter's field."

142. Overman 1996: 382 finds a specific allusion to 1 Sam 26:11; 2 Sam 1:16 (opposing killing "the Lord's 'christ'"), but if Matthew intended so narrow an allusion, one would expect clearer echoes of that phrase here.

ity.[143] Like Pilate (27:24), the priestly officials want nothing further to do with the situation (27:4), and likewise understand that the blood was innocent (27:6). Meanwhile, leading characters in the narrative who foreshadow oppressors of Matthew's community try to pass off responsibility (cf. Jer 38:5); both aristocratic priests and Pilate declare, "See to that yourself" (27:4, 24, the "you" being emphatic). But contrary to their own interpretation (27:4, 24),[144] the whole generation that betrayed Jesus shared in Judas's guilt (27:25). In accepting the blood "upon" them (27:25), they accepted the bloodguilt (cf. Acts 5:28), and hence merited Jesus' pronouncement of vengeance in 23:35. In Matthew's narrative world, their own words have ironically condemned them (12:37).

According to the story line, Judas gets what he deserves. Jewish law prescribed for false witnesses the penalty they had wished to inflict on others (Deut 19:16-21; 11QTemple 61.7; Ferguson 1987: 51; cf. Sifre Deut. 190.5.1); since the chief priests refuse to serve the cause of justice, Judas has to see to his own execution (Meier 1980: 338-39).[145] Roman society, as well as many others in Mediterranean antiquity, regarded suicide as an honorable and noble way to die,[146] and in some circumstances many Jews in this period concurred.[147] Some

143. E.g., Gen 4:10; 9:5-6; Num 35:33; 2 Sam 3:28-29; 4:11; 21:1; 1 Kings 2:5-6; *Middle Assyrian Laws* Tablet A 10 in *ANET* 181; see on 23:35-36; for the guilt of locales, cf. Deut 21:1-9; Paus. 10.5.3; Aqhat in *ANET* p. 154; Hammurabi 24; Moyer 1969: 67-69, 120. See other references in Brown 1994: 641, including Philo *Spec. Leg.* 1.204. Van Unnik 1974: 44-57 rightly notes the betrayal of innocent blood here, but less probably he argues that Judas's hanging himself resolved the curse because the priests would not let him atone for his sin by sacrifice. Philonenko 1993 finds in righteous blood an allusion to 1 Enoch 47:1, 4.

144. Van Tilborg 1972b: 88 regards 27:4 as Matthew's most significant contribution to the tradition here, painting the authorities as more guilty than Judas; Gundry 1982: 558 concurs with the increase of their guilt but denies the reduction of Judas's. Stauffer's conclusion that the recantation of a witness could not alter an established verdict (1960: 128, citing m. Sanh. 6:23 [perhaps he means m. Sanh. 5:5, though its point is somewhat different]; b. Sanh. 43a) is undoubtedly irrelevant to the thought of first-century Sadducean officials.

145. This may be implied in their "see to it"; cf. Marc. Aur. *Med.* 5.25. In at least some Jewish traditions, a suicide could turn away God's wrath from the person on whom God had pronounced judgment (Qoh. Rab. 7:12, §1; 9:10, §3).

146. Regularly in the texts, e.g., Acts 16:27; Soph. *Women Tr.* 721-22; Demosth. *3d Philippic* 62; Diod. Sic. 12.19.2; 16.45.4-5; 25.17.1; Tac. *Ann.* 1.61; 3.42; 4.25; 6.23-26, 38-40; 11.37-38; 12.8, 22; 13.1, 25, 30; 15.57, 63-64, 69; 16.11, 14-15, 17; Suet. *Aug.* 27, 53, 67; *Tib.* 45, 61; *Nero* 49; *Otho* 9, 11; Dio Cassius *R.H.* 17.15.4; 18.4.6; 19, fr. in Zonaras 9.21; 48.44.1; 51.15.3; 57.18.10; Appian *C.W.* 1.8.74; 1.10.94; 2.14.98-99; Livy 26.15.13-15; 41.11.4-6; Corn. Nep. 20 (Timoleon), 1.6; 23 (Hannibal), 12.5; Epict. *Disc.* 2.1.19; 3.8.6; Paus. 9.17.1-2; 9.25.1; Jos. *Apion* 1.236. Taylor 1966: 167 also cites Plut. *Cato Min.* 66-72. Though (at least for Romans) falling on a sword was often preferred, hanging oneself appears in various localities (e.g., Diod. Sic. 2.6.10; 20.71.4; Philo *Mut.* 62; Apul. *Metam.* 1.16).

147. 4 Macc 17:1; cf. the analogous b. Giṭ. 57b (Montefiore and Loewe 1974: 260); Jos. *Life* 137; the Sicarii at Masada (Jos. *War* 7.320-406); cf. Goodblatt 1995. Although the narratives portray Judg 9:54; 1 Sam 31:4; 2 Sam 17:23 as shameful deaths of wicked men, the doers probably perceived their suicides as tragic acts of valor in keeping with the heroic horror at dishonor of the epic age (Soph. *Ajax* 864-65, 898-99, 907-8; *Oed. Rex* 1237-66; Eurip. *Androm.* 811-13; *Helen* 136, 200-202; *Hippol.* 776-81; Virg. *Aen.* 10.681-82; Ovid *Metam.* 13.388-92) or its romantic pathos (Soph. *Antig.*

therefore think that Judas's suicide, perhaps coupled with his "repentance" (27:3), may suggest his forgiveness (cf. Van Unnik 1974; Moeser 1992; Whelan 1993; tentatively, Davies and Allison 1997: 561-63).[148] Admittedly the narrative emphasizes the continuing guilt of the priests more than of Judas, but it hardly absolves Judas of responsibility. Bribery was common enough (Jos. *Life* 73; *War* 2.273; Qoh. Rab. 11:1, §1; Acts 24:26), but considered reprehensible;[149] ancients particularly despised those who would betray a tie of loyalty for the sake of a bribe (e.g., Demosth. *For the Liberty of the Rhodians* 23; *On the Crown* 46-49; *On the Embassy* 120; Appian *R.H.* 8.3.17; Corn. Nep. 1 [Miltiades], 7.5-6). Further, Judas's suicide is a death of despair, a dishonorable suicide;[150] even Romans generally regarded hanging oneself as a dishonorable death that might preclude burial (Livy 42.28.11-12) or invite a shameful one (Aul. Gel. 15.10.2); and most Jews opposed suicide, at least under most circumstances (Jos. *War* 3.374-82).

The hanging may well recall the story of Ahithophel's end after his betrayal of David (2 Sam 17:23; Meier 1980: 338; Gundry 1982: 553; Brown 1994: 656-57), which fits some other David/Jesus parallels in the pre-Matthean passion tradition (Davies and Allison 1997: 565-66). But in any case the absence of Judas in either Christian or anti-Christian accounts thereafter confirms that historically he met a speedy end. The account of Judas's speedy death and the "field"[151]

1175-77, 1234-36, 1282-83, 1315-16; *Women of Trachis* 891, 923-35; Ap. Rhod. 1.1063-65; Virg. *Aen.* 4.663-65; Ovid *Metam.* 4.119-20, 147-66; 6.271-72; 10.378-81; 11.783-84; 14.80-81; Parthenius *L.R.* 10.4; 11.3; 31.1-2; cf. Hom. *Il.* 18.33-34; Eurip. *Phoenician Maidens* 1455-57; Appian *R.H.* 6.2.12).

148. Cf. the prayer of the condemned, "May my death atone for all my sins" (m. Sanh. 6:3; cf. Ps-Philo 25:7; 27:15; t. Ber. 6:17; Kip. 4:8-9; 6:17; Sifra A.M. par. 2.176.1.5-6; ARN 29; 39A; b. Ber. 60a; Shebu. 13a; p. Sheb. 1:6, §5; Pesiq. Rab Kah. 11:23; 25:3).

149. E.g., Hesiod *W.D.* 221; Livy 40.19.11; Longinus *Sublime* 44.9; Appian *C.W.* 2.3.23; 2.4.24; Sall. *Speech of Philippus* 6; *Speech of Macer* 5; Corn. Nep. 6 (Lysander), 3.2; 15 (Epaminondas), 4.1-3; Dio Cassius *R.H.* 54.16.1; Quint. 4.1.21; Ex 23:8; Deut 16:19; 27:25; 11QTemple 51.16-18; Jos. *Apion* 2.207; *Life* 79, 196; Pesiq. Rab Kah. 15:9. People in authority, especially judges, were expected to be impartial (Demosth. *On the Crown* 1-2; Isoc. *To Nicocles* 18, *Or.* 2; Cato the Elder 13 in Plut. *Sayings of Romans, Mor.* 198F; Sir 42:2; 1 Esdr 4:39; Ps-Phocyl. 9-12, 137; ARN 36A; on deities, Plato *Alcib.* 2.150A), and God's impartiality was often extolled (Sir 35:12-13; Wis 6:7; 2 Bar. 13:8; 44:4; Ps-Philo 20:4; Test. Job 4:7-8; 43:13/10; Sifre Num. 42.1.2; Sifre Deut. 304.1.1; Rom 2:11; see most fully Bassler 1982: 7-119).

150. Cf. similarly the hangings in Philo *Mut.* 61-62 and Ovid *Metam.* 10.378-81; Parthenius *L.R.* 11.3; 31.1 (though this was a common method — Soph. *Antig.* 1221-22; *Oed. Rex* 1237-66; Ap. Rhod. 1.1063-65; Virg. *Aen.* 12.600-603; Aul. Gel. 15.10.1-2; Herodian 7.9.4); Brown 1994: 644 cites Jos. *War* 3.369; m. Sanh. 10:2; *Semahot* 'Ebel Rabbati 2.

151. The field in the tradition may suggest Matthew's use of the "potter's field" from Zech 11:13 and possibly Jer 19:6 (Gundry 1982: 556). Surprisingly, Benoit 1973: 189-207 concludes that where Matthew's and Luke's accounts diverge, Matthew is more apt to be correct. Cf. Papias *Fg.* 3 (from Oecumenius), possibly dependent on the Acts account but perhaps attesting a fuller tradition. Those who wish to harmonize the accounts can point to ropes breaking in unsuccessful suicide attempts (e.g., the spoof in Apul. *Metam.* 1.16; cf. Petron. *Sat.* 94; hopefully no one will appeal to the possibility of one's surviving his innards being spattered — b. Ḥul. 56b-57a), though hanging and

in Acts (1:18-19) indicates that Matthew depends here on prior tradition, but adjusts the telling of the story midrashically (see the discussion of midrash in the infancy narratives; cf. Cope 1976: 88; Manns 1980b; Gundry 1982: 553; but cf. also the more conservative conclusions of Moo 1983:157-75 on the entire pericope). Judas presumably died without atonement (cf. Jn 17:12), and the narrative underlines that he received his just due (Boring 1995: 154 appropriately cites Suet. *Julius* 89).

The priestly aristocracy is also guilty. Matthew especially plays on the hypocrisy of the chief priests — willing to pay out blood money for Jesus' capture, willing to allow Judas's suicide,[152] but too pious to accept their own blood money into the temple treasury (cf. 23:23-32).[153] (Money from the temple treasury apparently paid for all the needs of the city, including water maintenance [Jeremias 1969: 16, citing m. Sheqal. 4:2; b. Beṣa 29a, bar.], though Pilate's use of such money for an aqueduct was viewed as misappropriation [Jos. *War* 2.175-76; cf. *Ant.* 18.60; *The Suda* in Sherk 1988: 75, §39B].[154] Just as ancients in general viewed plundering a temple treasury or stealing an idol as terrible sacrilege,[155] so early Judaism viewed plundering their temple as an invitation to judgment [e.g., 4 Macc 4; cf. comment on 25:16].)

Hanging oneself in a place (Diog. Laert. 6.2.61), especially in a sanctuary (Temple Chron. of Lindus in Rhodes D 60-93 in Grant 1953: 12), would defile it,

---

falling are normally distinguished (Lucan *C.W.* 2.154-58). Bowels coming out represents a horrid fate (2 Macc 9:5-9; Jos. *Ant.* 9.103; cf. Acts 12:23; Herod. *Hist.* 4.205; Jos. *War* 1.656; *Ant.* 17.167; 19.346, 350; Test. Job 20:8-9; b. 'Erub. 41b). That the wicked bought a field with Jesus' bloodprice (27:7) might suggest an ironic contrast with 13:44, where one gives up all one has to acquire the kingdom (though buying fields was common and the language could be coincidental).

152. Ancients would regard offering money as a bribe to falsify another's witness as despicable (Demosth. *Against Meidias* 107); for this offense, Athenian law prescribed being stripped of one's citizenship and property (Demosth. *Against Meidias* 113), and current Roman law removed officeholders who had achieved office through bribery (Dio Cassius *R.H.* 54.16.1). The high priests repeat the offense in 28:12-15.

153. Ancients were sensitive to such portrayals of hypocrisy (e.g., posthumous concern for another one injured while alive — Babrius 14.5) and would negatively regard the hypocrisy of religious pretense coupled with irreligious motives (e.g., Jos. *Life* 75; Juv. *Sat.* 2, 4 in Stewart 1994).

154. Roman governors were noted for gaining wealth, sometimes at their clients' expense (Stambaugh and Balch 1986: 65). The older Roman tradition of avoiding taxes to pay for public works (Badian 1972: 30) or displeasure at Julius Caesar's spending public monies on a purpose different from that for which they were allotted (Appian *C.W.* 2.6.41) might have given him pause to consider his decision, but he probably assumed that he followed safe Roman precedent: Augustus and others paid for workers on aqueducts from public and imperial treasuries (Frontinus *De aquis* 2.89-101, 116-18, in Jones 1970: 207), and the use of public money would have been expected (Jos. *Life* 199) had it not been from the *temple* treasury.

155. Plato *Euthyphro* 5; Diog. Laert. *Lives* 6.2.72-73; Paus. 6.11.2-3; Artem. *Oneir.* 3.3; Lucian *Phalaris* 1; *Zeus Catechized* 18; *Zeus Rants* 25; Apul. *Metam.* 11.10; Char. *Chaer.* 1.5.25; Athenaeus *Deipn.* 12.523; Tert. *Apol.* 15.7; cf. Polybius 9.28-39; Strabo *Geog.* 4.1.13; Tac. *Ann.* 15.45; Suet. *Nero* 32; Dio Chrys. *31st Disc.* §148; for Jewish attitudes against desecrating pagan shrines, see Ex 22:27 LXX; Sib. Or. 2.14; Jos. *Ant.* 4.207; *Apion* 2.237; Philo *Mos.* 2.205; *Spec. Leg.* 1.53; ARN 31, §66B; b. Sanh. 64a, bar.; cf., somewhat less tolerantly, Deut 7:25-26; p. Giṭ. 5:9, §8. On temple robbery, see also comment above on 25:14-30.

and while Judas left the temple to perform his own execution, the leaders' blatant unconcern for justice or for his life contrasts starkly with their attention to purity on details. By sentencing Judas to take care of his own guilt, they have unconsciously sentenced themselves before God (12:34-37). They do the same by acknowledging that the money is in fact "blood money," and thus that they have paid for the murder of an innocent man (Patte 1987: 377). Although the authorities were careful how they used the blood money (cf. Deut 23:18's prohibition of wages from prostitution), most ancient readers would still assume that its curse remained on them (see Test. Zeb. 3:1-3, where judgment for use of blood money obtains despite precautions).

Pilate and others who allow the wrong judgments of others participate in their guilt (27:1-2). By framing Judas's end with the account of Jesus being brought before Pilate (27:1-2, 11), Matthew contrasts Judas not only with Peter but also with the courageous Lord he had betrayed. The theme of shedding innocent blood connects Judas, Pilate, the high-priestly authorities, and the people (27:4-6, 24-25): like Pilate (27:24) the priestly officials wish nothing further to do with the situation (27:4), and likewise understand that the blood was innocent (27:6). The modern Western dichotomy between personal and societal responsibility was foreign both to Matthew and to his Jewish contemporaries.

The "taking counsel" in the morning (27:1) may represent a second hearing of sorts that actually would carry the semblance of legality (also Mk 15:1; Reicke 1974: 146; the syntax here probably reflects a Latin judicial expression, *consilium capere* — Carson 1984b: 559). Local authorities typically interrogated the prisoner first, preparing the legal charge before bringing the accused before a Roman provincial official (Dodd 1961: 91n.1); in the same manner, the Roman administration permitted the Sanhedrin to charge and hand over one suspected of treason (Winter 1961: 27).[156]

Ancient readers would not be surprised that the authorities brought Jesus "early," and hence would not be as skeptical as some modern commentators about the eventful night that had preceded that morning. Winter doubts that so much could have occurred in as little time as the Gospel record indicates (1961: 7), but the events fit fairly well into ancient chronology. Like other Roman officials and patrons,[157] Pilate would be available from dawn until ca. 11 a.m.; the committee thus had to have the charges settled overnight (Wilkinson 1978: 133; Lane 1974a: 549).[158] Winter's doubt that the high priests could gain

156. Thus the repetition of the death sentence in 27:1 is hardly merely a haggadic echo of the repetition in Jer 26:8, 11 (pace Doeve 1954: 187-88).

157. Cf. Hor. *Sat.* 1.1.9-10 — at cockcrow; *Epodes* 2.1.103-5; Mart. *Epig.* 3.26.1-3; Plut. *R.Q.* 84, *Mor.* 284D; 3 Macc 5:26; Carcopino 1940: 151; Friedländer 1965: 1:86-93, 207; Cary and Haarhoff 1946: 149; Clarke 1994: 475.

158. Prefects in Roman Egypt visited local municipalities only a few days a year, and addressed 700 to 750 petitions in a ten-hour day, better than one a minute, though clerks processed many of these (Lewis 1983: 190). Since he was present primarily to bolster security during the festi-

access to Pilate without advance notice (1961: 29) likewise misses the custom of local leaders visiting Roman officials, the prominent role of the high priests, and the urgency of the charge against Jesus during the crowded conditions of Passover.

Political Expediency versus Justice (27:11-26)

This segment of the narrative has less to do with Jesus than with Pilate; for those reading or hearing Matthew, it is not Jesus but the character of Pilate that is on trial.[159] As one proverb observed, *Tam de se iudex iudicat quam de reo*: "A judge passes judgment on himself as much as on the accused" (Pub. Syr. 698, LCL 106-7). Though Pilate knows the unjust motivation of the charges ("envy" — 27:18; cf. Mk 15:10; Acts 5:17)[160] and receives a divine warning (27:19), political expediency takes precedence over justice.

But the narrative does not try Pilate alone: the insistent people, blindly following their blind religious leaders (27:20; cf. 15:14; 23:16), embrace the moral responsibility Pilate seeks to evade. (Perhaps in view of his community's conflict with Jewish authorities or the greater responsibility adhering to those who should know the most, Matthew portrays Pilate as *less* guilty than Jesus' own people. Washing hands most obviously constituted a repudiation of responsibility for innocent blood in Jewish tradition, as in Deut 21:6-7; Ps 26:6; Is 1:15-16; Ep. Arist. 306; cf. Gos. Peter, fr. 1:1.)[161] In the narrative world of Matthew, their acceptance of guilt for Jesus' blood on themselves and

---

val, it is doubtful whether Pilate would make himself that available. I omit here discussion of attempts to harmonize the Markan and Johannine chronologies, the latter of which probably fits into John's theological Passover motif; for discussion, see Brown 1994: 958-59.

159. Although Pilate may well have taken counsel with his *accessores* and *comites,* as in Acts 25:12 (Brown 1994: 716; cf. O'Rourke 1971: 174-75; Ferguson 1987: 51), the Gospels omit them as unworthy of mention; the governor issued the final decision and stood responsible for it (his responsibility appears also in Tac. *Ann.* 15.44.3). Yet despite designations of authority consistently applied to Pilate in this Gospel, his submission to the crowds ironically underlines his powerlessness (Weaver 1996: 191-95).

160. Attributing the motive of envy to opponents (in stories, e.g., 3 Macc 6:7; Test. Dan 1:6; Acts of Paul 3:15; b. Yoma 71b) does double duty rhetorically: it praises or exonerates the one they accuse while diminishing the opponents' status. Josephus charges that some Gentile writers ignored Israel due to envy (*Apion* 1.213, 222, 225), that his fellow aristocrats opposed him due to envy (*Life* 204), and that his own good fortune produced jealousy (*Life* 423), though God protected him (*Life* 425). Political biography regularly lists envy as a motive for hostility (e.g., Herodian 3.2.3; Corn. Nep. 5 [Cimon], 3.1; 8 [Thrasybulus], 4.1-2; 12 [Chabrias], 3.3; 14 [Datames], 5.2; 15 [Epaminondas], 7.1; 18 [Eumenes], 7.2; 10.2; 23 [Hannibal], 1.2). Given Jesus' populist support, however, the alleged motive is not implausible.

161. Although some (e.g., Meier 1980: 342) therefore assume that the gesture is not historical — Pilate was probably not so culturally sensitive as to adopt a Jewish gesture — it remains quite possible, because pagans also used it. (Blinzler 1959: 217-18 cites Virg. *Aen.* 2.719; Soph. *Ajax* 654; Herod. *Hist.* 1.35. Brown 1994: 834 adds Hom. *Il.* 6.266-68.) Pilate's protestation of his innocence echoes the wording of the righteous Daniel in Sus 46 (Gundry 1982: 565).

the generation of their children (27:24-25) directly invites the catastrophic events of 66-70 (23:29-39).[162]

The responsibility of freeing Jesus or consenting to the Sanhedrin's condemnation of him fell to Pilate. That Jesus appeared before Pilate[163] is an inescapably historical datum; only the governor could order him crucified, and if he wished to follow some semblance of order, he would provide at least a brief hearing. Likewise, Jesus' own countrymen would normally perform the function of *delatores,* or accusers, to charge him with sedition (Harvey 1982: 16; see Sherwin-White 1978: 47). (The "governor" in Judea in this period was technically a "prefect," rather than the later "procurator," as in Tac. *Ann.* 15.44; the Gospels simply use the general title "governor," which could have covered either.)[164]

That Jesus was crucified by the Romans is likewise inevitably historical;[165] the Christians would hardly have invented execution at all, but certainly not *Roman* execution, which would have painted them thereafter as subversives in the Roman world.[166] Pilate often went to great lengths to quell so much as public complaints, including violent suppression of a crowd, leading to many deaths (Jos. *War* 2.176-77; *Ant.* 18.60-62). Under strict Roman law (sometimes ignored), Roman citizens could not be crucified, but slaves and provincials could be (Stauffer 1960: 131). Although slaves (e.g., Suet. *Dom.* 10) and dangerous criminals (Suet. *Julius* 4) were regularly crucified, crucifixions of free persons in Palestine usually involved the charge of rebellion against Rome.[167]

162. Matthew probably wrote after A.D. 70, when many Jewish pietists struggled with the question, "Why has God so punished us?"; Matthew intends to supply a response (Brown 1994: 29). Later anti-Semites abused a text whose proclamation of judgment focused on the generation of the temple's destruction, i.e., Matthew's own (Hare 1979: 38).

163. See Sherk 1988: 40, §39A; Smallwood 1976: 145; Brown 1994: 336-37. Although scholars once thought that the officials brought Jesus to Pilate in the Fortress Antonia, most now concur that Pilate was residing in Herod's palace (Schürer 1961: 181; Lane 1974a: 548; Wilkinson 1978: 140; Brown 1994: 705-10), as ancient sources suggest (Pilate in Philo *Leg. Gai.* 299; Florus in Jos. *War* 2.301, 328). Herod's palace is farther from the temple but not a difficult trek.

164. For the responsibilities of a governor, see, e.g., Justin. *Dig.* 1.16.4-13 in Jones 1970: 180-83.

165. The Docetic idea of a wraith as substituted for Jesus on the cross, followed in a popular interpretation of the Qur'an, derives from hellenistic mythology, e.g., Eurip. *Helen* (following the *Recantation of Stesichorus*); Hom. *Il.* 5.449-53.

166. Although the severest form of execution Pharisaic law acknowledged on the basis of the Hebrew Bible was stoning (b. Sanh. 49b-50a), Jewish rulers had used crucifixion before the Roman period. Under Roman rule, however, all official, public executions belonged to the Romans. Even the Essenes toned down capital sentences from Moses' law (CD 12.2-5), while also destesting Gentile executions in the holy land (CD 9.1). The apparently Jewish execution in b. Sanh. 43a depends on Christian tradition, though preserving the crucifixion's association with the Passover season.

167. Harvey 1982: 12; Overman 1996: 380-81, 387; e.g., Jos. *War* 2.75, 241, 253, 306; 3.321; 5.449; *Ant.* 20.102. It also appears as a fitting end for other military enemies (e.g., Diod. Sic. 2.1.10; 25.5.2; Jos. *Ant.* 12.256; 13.380) and for the most horrid crimes (Apul. *Metam.* 3.9).

Excursus: The Sanhedrin and the Sword

The local aristocracy would prepare the charges and suggest action, but Pilate had to pronounce sentence. The governor held the power of life and death in a province (Jos. *War* 2.117; cf. b. Shab. 108a). Some scholars think that the Sanhedrin could execute capital sentences (Winter 1961: 10-15; Smallwood 1976: 150), but this does not fit what we know of the way the Romans administered their provinces. Acts 23:1-10 constitutes a preliminary inquiry to formulate a charge (22:30; 23:28-29), *not* evidence for capital authority (pace Winter 1961: 75-90), even though profanation of the temple (cf. 21:28-29) was the one charge for which the Romans permitted local executions (cf. O'Rourke 1971: 174; Sanders 1992: 61).[168]

Some rabbinic tradition traces the loss of Jewish courts' capital authority to A.D. 70 (Sifre Deut. 154.1.1; b. Sanh. 37b), other tradition to no later than A.D. 30 (p. Sanh. 1:1, §3; 7:2, §3; Safrai 1974/76e: 398 also cites b. Shab. 15a; ʿAbod. Zar. 8b; cf. Abrahams 1917: 73). Although Josephus does not report any precedents unfavorable toward Jewish autonomy, this loss of sovereignty (for so it would be viewed — Ep. Jer. 14) must have begun much earlier. Although Rome delegated the right of the sword to Herod and other client rulers,[169] it withheld that right from municipal aristocracies who could employ it against citizens loyal to Rome. Although councils of subject territories could pronounce a death sentence, they had to bring their sentence before the governor for ratification (Blinzler 1959: 164-68; Ramsay 1897: 293). Most scholars thus currently recognize that the Sanhedrin had no capital authority in this period (Jos. *Ant.* 20.200; Benoit 1973: 1:135; Lane 1974a: 530; Stewart 1975; Sanders 1990: 17; F. F. Bruce 1980b: 12-13). As Roman legal scholar Sherwin-White notes (1978: 36; see more fully 32-43),

> When we find that capital power was the most jealously guarded of all the attributes of government, nor even entrusted to the principal assistants of the governors, and specifically withdrawn, in the instance of Cyrene, from the competence of local courts, it becomes very questionable indeed for the Sanhedrin.

The Sanhedrin could sentence offenders and recommend them for execution, but apart from violating the temple few Jewish religious charges would receive an auto-

168. An intermediate position is that Romans rarely delegated capital authority, but that the Roman governors were authorized to do so (O'Rourke 1971: 174-75); but whatever governors of some provinces may have wished to do, it is inconceivable that Pilate would have shared this authority with the Sanhedrin. Brown 1994: 339 correctly observes that executions required ratification by the Sanhedrin in Jos. *Ant.* 14.167; while this datum is undoubtedly relevant, we should note that it describes the time of Herod the Great, not direct Roman rule.

169. Theissen 1991: 189-93 thinks that the Passion Narrative presupposes that the Sanhedrin had capital authority, and thus reads its own milieu's circumstances of A.D. 41-44, under Agrippa I, into the narrative. This proposal falters on two counts: First, the logic of the Passion Narrative actually presupposes that the Sanhedrin lacks capital authority; why else would they hand Jesus over to Pilate? Second, Agrippa I was a client king who would hold capital authority — but he was not the Sanhedrin. Besides, Johannine tradition preserves the Sanhedrin's lack of capital authority in the last decade of the first century (Jn 18:31-32).

matic capital sentence from the Romans (e.g., the case of Jesus ben Ananias; Brown 1994: 363-72).

As in normal judicial procedure (e.g., Char. *Chaer.* 5.4.9; Apul. *Metam.* 10.7; t. Sanh. 6:3),[170] the accusers speak first (27:11-13). Pilate's initial interrogation of Jesus clarifies the charge the Sanhedrin has brought to Pilate: Jesus claims to be a king, which Rome, like the priestly aristocracy, would understand in revolutionary terms (27:11). Whatever the possible religious motivations behind the charge, the charge against Jesus is political: by claiming to be a king, Jesus implied a worldly kingdom that would challenge Rome (e.g., F. F. Bruce 1972b: 199). The political charge in Luke 23:2 accurately summarizes the gist of the charge in Mark and Matthew: Jesus was a revolutionary (Schneider 1984; cf. similarly the Johannine charges — Robinson 1984). This is easily the charge of *lese majesty* (Blinzler 1959: 213, citing *Dig.* 48.4.1, 3-4; cf. Bammel 1984b: 357), for which the normal punishment in the provinces was crucifixion (Blinzler 1959: 238). Because Pilate had authority to conduct his inquiry without a jury or dependence even on the Roman *ordo,* the hearing was merely a *cognitio* to determine the facts and inform his decision (F. F. Bruce 1980b: 13; Ferguson 1987: 50). Jesus' only answer (27:11; cf. 26:25, 64) in the context affirms the charge (Wrede 1971: 47).

Pilate preferred political expediency to justice, but the political leaders of Jesus' own people appear even guiltier. The narrative portrays those who brought the charge as quite insistent that Jesus be executed, and this behavior is hardly surprising given the situation portrayed. What is instead striking is Pilate's reticence to pronounce sentence; if no Roman citizens were involved, one would expect most governors to act quickly at the local aristocracy's request (cf. Harvey 1982: 17; Sanders 1993: 274; for an impoverished provincial condemned to death without trial, cf., e.g., Apul. *Metam.* 9.42). The Gospels show that Pilate did indeed act quickly, but they also report his reluctance to do so.

Thus some scholars question whether the Pilate of the Gospels is "in character" with the Pilate known to us from other sources (Winter 1961: 54-55, 60; Borg 1987: 179). Pilate executed people without trial, and excessive use of capital punishment ultimately cost him his office (Philo *Leg. Gai.* 302; Jos. *Ant.* 18.88-89; Sanders 1993: 274).[171] From what Philo and especially Josephus show us of Pilate's character, any reticence to accept the local leaders' recommendation would be more out of spite for them than concern for justice (cf. Benoit 1973/74: 1:141-42).

170. Later rabbinic rules allowed the defendant to speak first in a capital case (t. Sanh. 7:2), but even if some Jewish teachers held this view in Jesus' day, Pilate would have operated under Roman procedure.

171. On governors being tried for abusing power, especially executing innocent people (particularly Roman citizens), see Pliny *Ep.* 2.11, in Jones 1970: 192-95.

Yet this reticence need not be unhistorical. As corrupt as the later governor Albinus was, he dismissed Jesus ben Hananiah from further punishment (after a scourging reportedly bared his bones) once he took him to be insane, hence harmless (Jos. *War* 6.305). Philo and especially Josephus are ill disposed to report good of Pilate (cf. Brown 1994: 697; Krieger 1995; Thatcher 1995); they seem to have felt that the unrest in Judea was better blamed on deceased prefects like Pilate (once supported by the corrupt Sejanus, still despised, e.g., in Juv. *Sat.* 10.66, 76, 89-90, 104; Phaedrus 3, prol., 41-44; cf. also Brown 1994: 694 on Philo *Flacc.* 1; *Leg. Gai.* 160-61) than left with the Judeans themselves. Even as governor, Pilate seems to have been quite unpopular (cf. rumors circulating in Lk 13:1 and Bailey 1980: 75).[172]

Still, the narratives go to great lengths to emphasize that Pilate cooperated with Jesus' execution against his own preference, and this emphasis is understandable for apologetic reasons. Minority sects often validate themselves through reports of praises by those respected among their oppressors; those writing in socially delicate situations must also show proper deference to officials. Thus, for example, Josephus repeatedly excuses Roman rulers' motives; for instance, Titus wished to spare the temple, but some soldiers failed to cooperate (*War* 6.254, 258, 260-66), or Titus allowed his soldiers to torture Jews only for good reason (*War* 5.449-51). The Epistle of Aristeas likewise defends the Ptolemaic ruler's motives against the Jews (Ep. Arist. 14), and Josephus claims that Ptolemy Philadelphus praised Jewish law (*Apion* 2.45-47). In the same manner, early Christians commending themselves to an audience in the broader Roman world might wish to exonerate the Roman prefect (cf. Sanders 1985: 298; Cohn 1977: 326-27) or even cite in their own defense Roman officials' reticence to condemn them (e.g., Acts 13:12; 18:14-15). Matthew probably writes for a largely Jewish-Christian rather than Gentile audience, but nevertheless has ample reason to emphasize the guilt of Jewish rather than Roman leaders whom he views as predecessors of his own community's opponents. Matthew may use historical tradition yet emphasize what best fits his purposes.

Historically, Pilate may have had good reason for political concern if he erred in judgment. Philo notes Pilate's patron, Sejanus, for his anti-Jewishness (Philo *Flacc.* 1). If Sejanus was executed on October 19, A.D. 31 (Stauffer 1960: 132; Lane 1974a: 556-57n.34; cf. Sherk 1988: 75-77, §40), some premonitions of his impending weakness might have been felt a year and a half earlier at the more likely time of Jesus' trial near Passover of A.D. 30. (Some, e.g., Jewett 1979: 29, prefer a trial in A.D. 33, but it seems more problematic on other grounds.) Such premonitions are admittedly at best a guess rather than a direct inference from our sources, which, unanimously hostile to Sejanus, suggest that most of those who disagreed with him in Rome would have been more circumspect than to *say* so. More clearly Pilate, like most provincial officials (see

172. Brown 1994: 695-705 ultimately concludes, as I do, that most of the Gospel portrait fits what we know of Pilate from the other sources once all has been taken into account.

Reicke 1974: 138, 175), was probably politically ambitious and hence could ill-afford bad reports about himself (cf. Malina 1993: 115-16). In contrast to many of his peers in office, Pilate was only an equestrian, and that left him especially vulnerable apart from Sejanus's patronage (on that order, see Jones 1970: 134-40). More to the point, Pilate had incurred the hatred of the Jewish people (e.g., Jos. *War* 2.169-77; *Ant.* 18.55-62), and on some other occasions he had backed down to pacify them (Philo *Leg. Gai.* 301-2; Jos. *War* 2.171-74; *Ant.* 18.59). Thus Pilate was not only cruel but, like many bullies, fearful of exposure to those in authority over him (Winter 1961: 53-54).

If anything, this situation would probably require Pilate in time to become more rather than less cooperative with the more powerful of his subjects (cf. Jn 19:12-13); failure to prosecute a potential revolutionary, accused by the leaders of his own people, could lay Pilate himself open to the charge of *maiestas* (Blinzler 1959: 236; Smallwood 1972: 169). Even the suspicion of treason could be fatal under Tiberius, and despite Sejanus's patronage he likely would not risk it.[173] Further, although Jesus may have proved politically innocuous (Cullmann 1956b: 46-47), cooperation with the local aristocracy would be more advantageous politically; that he survived as governor until A.D. 36, long after his patron's demise, suggests that he had belatedly acquired some political savvy.[174] Pilate's wife's dream (27:19) thus makes some sense of the hesitation depicted in the four Gospels,[175] although we should note that divine intervention by dreams is a specifically Matthean technique (1:20; 2:12, 13, 19, 22; cf. Soares Prabhu 1976: 167),[176] and Pilate's wife may become another prototype of Gentile sympathizers (2:2, 11; 8:10-11; 15:28; Gundry 1982: 562; Brown 1994: 806). In any case, the hearing before Pilate is brief, and the execution swift (a few hours later).

Fortified through Gethsemane, Jesus now faces death heroically for his people. The hearing was swift not only because Pilate was unconcerned with justice, but because Jesus refused to defend himself, probably in submission to his Fa-

173. Tiberius reportedly viewed even negative remarks as *maiestas* (e.g., Dio Cassius *R.H.* 57.9.2; 57.19.1; 57.23.1-2; cf. Caligula — 59.11.6), leading to many false accusations (57.4.5-6); some later emperors also suffered paranoia (Herodian 1.13.7). Among Romans treason was the greatest crime (Dion. Hal. 8.80.1; see comment on 26:15 regarding traitors).

174. Reasons for his dismissal in A.D. 36 are debated; Krieger 1992b rejects Josephus's explanation.

175. In Roman tradition ideal matrons were unobtrusive, but many privately influenced their husbands to appropriate public action, often more effectively than Pilate's wife here (Stambaugh and Balch 1986: 111; cf. negatively p. Sukk. 5:1, §7). After Augustus (cf. Suet. *Aug.* 24) Roman governors could take wives with them (cf. Tac. *Ann.* 1.40; 2.54-55; 3.33-34; contrast Severus in Herodian 3.2.5), and many prominent women were interested in Judaism (Jos. *War* 2.560; *Ant.* 20.195; cf. Acts of Pilate 2.1; *CIJ* 1:384, §523; Blinzler 1959: 217; Brown 1994: 804; Leon 1960: 256). Jewish people also told stories of women who influenced powerful relatives not to punish God's people (Lachs 1987: 428 cites b. Ta'an. 24b). On dreams, see excursus on Mt 1:20.

176. Elsewhere in early Christianity, cf. Acts 2:17, but Luke's narrative emphasizes the more dramatic "visions" (e.g., Acts 7:55; 9:3-4; 10:3, 10; 18:9; 22:6-7, 17-18; 26:19; cf. Acts 27:23; 2 Cor 12:1).

ther's plan, though this did not reduce the perpetrators' responsibility (18:7; 26:24; Acts 2:23; 4:27-28; cf. Esth 4:14; Is 10:5-19). According to Roman law, a defendant who refused to make a defense had to be assumed guilty (Lane 1974a: 551; cf. Appian *R.H.* 11.7.41); Roman officials typically offered "a defendant three opportunities to respond before convicting by default" (France 1985: 389, following Sherwin-White 1978: 25-26), and Pilate offers Jesus at least two here (27:13). It is no wonder, therefore, that Pilate is amazed by the silence (27:14), an amazement that characterizes some other pagans in Jewish martyr stories (4 Macc 17:16) — and may suggest that Matthew links Jesus' opponents with the enemies of his people. From a literary perspective, Matthew can underline Jesus' heroism: such astonishment of judges characterizes Jewish accounts of defiant martyrs who — in contrast to their judges — value God's kingdom more than their lives (Stanton 1974: 36); others also praised courage in the face of death (e.g., Plut. *Sayings of Spartans,* Anon. 35, *Mor.* 234AB).[177] Matthew's audience might also recall that Jesus had used silence to express initial disdain for another Gentile (15:23, with slightly different wording; cf. Lk 23:9-10).

Pilate could not evade responsibility by passing it off on someone else. Pilate's only way to avoid the situation is to put forward Jesus as the one to be freed at the paschal amnesty. With others (e.g., Cohn 1977: 166), Brown 1994: 814-19 doubts the adequacy of any of the proposed analogies, hence (819) the custom itself, though it is multiply attested in the Gospels (793-95).[178] Although current evidence is insufficient to prove that the custom existed, denying its existence argues from silence (in a narrative that can be confirmed at many other points), and, if we weigh the burden of proof in favor of the Gospels' usual authenticity (see the Introduction), various factors support the likelihood of the custom. Like *most* customs of the Roman administration in Palestine, this one is currently unattested, but parallels from other Roman administrations and the Gospel writers' assumption that their audiences were familiar with this practice in the Gospel tradition support it.

Later Roman law dictated that judges should not ignore laws, decrees, or custom (*legibus . . . constitutionibus . . . moribus* — Justin. *Inst.* 4.17). Nevertheless, Roman provincial officials were not bound by "precedents of their predecessors or local customs" (Ferguson 1987: 50);[179] thus Pilate's offer of amnesty (27:15) might be a custom Pilate himself initiated, though it is more likely an earlier one he merely de-

177. For ancient literary portrayals of heroism, see comment on 16:21. Cohn 1977: 328-29 thinks that Jesus was innocent but pleaded guilty, perhaps to earn martyrdom and fulfill his prophecies. Some church fathers compared Jesus' silence to that of an innocent lamb (Gregory Nazianzen *Oration* 29, *On the Son* 20; Augustine *Tractates on John* 116.4; *ACCS,* 222-23; cf. Is 53:7).

178. Theissen 1991: 196 links this story with the Caligula crisis, when he thinks more of the populace would have sided with the "bandits" than with Christians (citing Tac. *Ann.* 12.54.1; Jos. *Ant.* 20.5, 97, 102); but this is hardly the *only* period in the first century in which that would be the case, and Jesus would be less popular than Barabbas to those prone to revolution (22:21) and, probably more to the point here, less popular with most of the Jerusalem masses than the priestly authorities were.

179. This freedom may call into question the supposed official report cited by Eusebius (*H.E.* 2.2) and Tertullian (*Apol.* 21:24; cf. 5:2), which may depend on an earlier Christian forgery that the Christians assumed to be accurate (probably as in Justin *1 Apol.* 35, 48; pace Stauffer 1960: 145-46).

cided to continue (Jn 18:39).[180] His offer may suggest that he thought himself indulgent on special occasions; his otherwise brutal disposition, however, colors all the other brief Jewish reports of his activity that remain extant. Romans sometimes deferred to local custom in forgiving an offense (e.g., Plut. *R.Q.* 83, *Mor.* 283F); they also sometimes performed mass amnesties on local feasts (Livy 5.13.8; Blinzler 1959: 206), a custom known in various other ancient Near Eastern and Mediterranean cultures (Merritt 1985). Sometimes they also released captives due to the people's demands.[181] Roman law permitted two kinds of amnesty: *abolitio* (acquitting a prisoner before trial — *Codex* 9.42; *De Abolitionibus; Dig.* 48.16) and *indulgentia* (pardoning a convicted criminal — *Codex* 9.43.3; Blinzler 1959: 207-8). Since Pilate had not yet pronounced sentence against Jesus (27:26), an *abolitio* allowed him to circumvent the whole matter placed before him.

Why would Pilate have sought to release Jesus? Possibly because it was safer to release Jesus, the "so-called Christ" (27:17, 22), than alternatives like Barabbas, who, like those ultimately executed with Jesus, was a "robber" (27:38, 44; Mk 15:7),[182] the aristocracy's derisive title (shared by Josephus) for insurrectionists. Pilate probably saw Jesus in the terms suggested in John 18:36-38: as the sort of relatively harmless wandering philosopher-king known to him from Greco-Roman tradition (see Keener 1993: 309; Epict. *Disc.* 3.22.49; Plut. *Flatterer/Friend* 16, *Mor* 58E).[183] Roman officials were generally not inclined to ex-

180. Pilate could have abolished a preexisting custom, but given previous conflicts with the people (e.g., Jos. *War* 2.174, 177) and the dangers of popular unrest at festivals (e.g., Jos. *War* 2.224) he probably would not have done so (though its lack of attestation in Josephus may suggest that someone eventually abolished the custom). Politically prudent rulers in the east presumably often continued festival traditions begun by their predecessors (e.g., Diod. Sic. 17.16.3).

181. P. Florentinus 61.59ff., in Deissmann 1978: 269; Blinzler 1959: 207; Lane 1974a: 553; also Livy 8.35.1-9; the later practice of pardoning criminals at Easter (*Cod. Theod.* 9.38.3-4, 8), however, is probably dependent on the Gospels (Cohn 1977: 167). Blinzler 1959: 207, 218-21 argues for the custom of a paschal release of a prisoner in m. Pesaḥ. 8:6 (following Chavel's 1941 article; cf. also Schnackenburg 1982: 3:252); but see Bammel 1984c: 427, who argues more persuasively that the text merely indicates the special Jewish desire to free prisoners at this time. Because we have little evidence for the customs of the period and because Roman governors were not required to continue previous customs (Ferguson 1987: 50; hence probably abolishing this one in time), it is not surprising that we have little direct evidence for the practice. Governors might also release prisoners in acceding to terrorist demands (Jos. *Ant.* 20.208-10). Ancient Mediterranean officials could even proclaim selective mass amnesties if they wished (*P. Tebt.* 5.1-13, 118 B.C.).

182. Matthew or a later scribal tradition may heighten the contrast by including Barabbas's real name ("Barabbas" is Aramaic for "son of the father"), "Jesus" (a common Jewish name in the period — Acts 13:6; Col 4:11; Jos. *Ant.* 6.129; 12.239; 20.234; *Life* 66-67, 134; Ep. Arist. 49; R. Joshua in Tannaitic texts; etc.); so Meier 1980: 341; Gundry 1982: 561. The reading's difficulty may favor its authenticity (see Metzger 1971: 67-68), though the best texts omit it and geographical distribution seems slightly against it; the matter is not easily decided.

183. Philosophers considered themselves most fit to rule (e.g., Quint. 2.17.28; Diog. Laert. 7.1.122; cf. CD 6.6; ARN 44, §124B; Gen. Rab. 93:2; Deut. Rab. 2:33), and many philosophers and moralists writing on the *topos* of kingship emphasized the ruler's need for wisdom (e.g., Plato *Rep.* 5.472; Isoc. *To Nicocles* 10-11, 29, *Or.* 2; Plut. *Sayings of Romans,* Cato the Elder 8, *Mor.* 198F; cf. Prov 8:15; the Epistle of Aristeas's symposium section; Sifre Deut. 161.2.1).

ecute (hence, perhaps, make martyrs of) those they saw as harmless fools (cf. Jos. *War* 6.305). By contrast, the Jerusalem aristocrats appear more sensitive to the sort of political threat a populist leader like Jesus might actually pose to their power base.

Jesus' contemporaries shared the guilt of his execution (cf. 23:30-36). Perhaps because the high priests have reported Jesus' popular appeal along with the charge, Pilate gambles that the people will prefer Jesus to Barabbas; if so, his hope is disappointed. Although Jesus' following may have been large, the high priests represented the temple system respected by most local and foreign Jews, and they could more easily inflame a general mob in their favor, by mob pressure silencing any of Jesus' core supporters who might be present. Ancient literature is replete with examples of masses being easily swayed by leaders (e.g., many who voted for Aristides' banishment allegedly did not know the charge, Corn. Nep. 3 [Aristides], 1.4), including by these priests (Jos. *War* 2.237-38, 316-17, 321-25; cf. 2.406), and being fickle in the populist favor they bestowed on various figures (Tac. *Ann.* 2.41; *Hist.* 1.32, 45; 3.85; Ps-Phocyl. 95-96; Philo *Embassy to Gaius* 120; Jos. *Life* 87, 97, 143-44, 313-17, 333; Livy 31.34.3; Lucan *C.W.* 3.52-58; Corn. Nep. 10 [Dion], 10.2; 13 [Timotheus], 4.1; 1 Sam 18:16; 25:10; 2 Sam 5:2; 15:6).[184] Further, the outdoor hearing at Pilate's bema (Jn 19:13; Jos. *War* 2.175-76, 301, 308; cf. Acts 18:12; 2 Cor 5:10)[185] undoubtedly took place at Herod the Great's old palace (Wilkinson 1978: 140; Gnilka 1997: 309; Jos. *War* 2.301); although still in the Upper City dominated by the priestly aristocracy, it was some distance from the temple, where Jesus' popular following had been growing and where most Galileans would be found, and perhaps earlier than most of Jesus' supporters would have returned to the temple area anyway after a late night Passover.

On a literary and theological level, Pilate may be offering that particular generation of Israel the "two ways," one of life and the other of death (7:13-14; cf. Deut 30:15-19). Nevertheless, the apparent inconsistency between the crowds that favored Jesus and those who opposed him may have less to do with the Gospel writers adjusting the traditions (cf. Sandmel 1978a: 39) than with their failure to explain the diversity of crowds in their traditions more thoroughly (including diversity based on locales, above). Although this lack of differentiation seems prejudicial to modern readers, understanding a literary device may increase our familiarity with their technique: ancient writers, especially those influenced by the

184. Cf. also references in Meeks 1986: 57: Epicurus *Fr.* 43; Themistius *Oration* 26; *Vatican Sayings* 58; Ex 4:30-31; 5:21-23; fickleness was negative (Sall. *Jug.* 56.5). The ruling class usually could sway the masses (Saldarini 1994: 38), although deep-rooted popular convictions were no more easily removed then than today (Paus. 2.23.6; Jos. *Ant.* 13.298; 18.17). Contrast the motif of being well-liked by the people, who advocate one's case, as a sign of one's great nobility (e.g., Char. *Chaer.* 1.1.10; 1 Sam 14:45; Jos. *Ant.* 6.128; *Life* 303). Switching sides was sometimes a matter of political discretion, however (e.g., Jos. *Ant.* 15.193; Bowersock 1965: 85).

185. Jn 19:13 necessarily occurs at the bema; capital sentences, unlike others, had to be pronounced from there (Blinzler 1959: 240, following Mommsen). It was natural to go outside if one were to speak with the multitude (Jos. *War* 2.172).

chorus tradition of Greek drama, often allowed a corporate body to speak as if in unison (e.g., Virg. *Aen.* 11.122-31; Dion. Hal. 6.10.1; 6.87.1; Acts 4:24; cf. 1 Sam 11:4; 2 Sam 5:1-2).[186] These crowds can function on a literary level to underline the ambivalence of God's own people swayed by various competing voices. Given the dangers of riots, Pilate's acquiescence to the masses at the Passover (27:24; cf. 26:5) was likely (also Albright and Mann 1971: 345; Brown 1994: 722).

Finally, Matthew underlines in obvious ways that the crowds shared the guilt for Jesus' execution — though he also refuses to let Pilate absolve himself from guilt as easily as he desires. Pilate, who hands Jesus over to the crowds' wishes, is no less guilty than weak-willed Zedekiah, who hands over Jeremiah in Jeremiah 38:5. By accepting the bloodguilt on themselves and their children, however (cf. 2 Sam 3:28-29), Matthew's crowds directly fulfill Jesus' warning in Matthew 23:29-36, thereby inviting the destruction of their temple at the end of the generation, in their children's days. They ironically invite a curse against themselves (cf. Jer 42:5).[187] Because later professing Christians abused this passage in an anti-Jewish manner[188] (forgetting the ethnic Jewishness of Matthew's own community), interpreters have frequently charged Matthew with vicious anti-Semitism. Others have sought various ways to absolve him of the charge (e.g., Caprile 1960): for example, Matthew meant that Jesus' blood would cover them salvifically, as in Jewish traditions about Exodus 24 (cf. Bowman 1974; Smith 1990; Cargal 1991; Sullivan 1992; but the context is bloodguilt); only the Jewish leaders are indicted here (Vandone 1964); or the leaders represented all of sinful humanity (Stephens 1964). How subsequent interpreters have applied Matthew in anti-Jewish ways is an important issue,[189] but it is quite different from what Matthew intended; for Matthew, the curse invoked in this verse was fulfilled in the year 70, "children" in this instance referring to the generation immediately following from that multitude (23:36–24:2; 24:34).[190]

186. Some also venture a chronological explanation for the transformation of the crowds, namely, the passage of six months between Jesus' act in the temple (at Sukkoth) and his arrest (at Pesach); so Manson 1961: 79. Yet it seems inconceivable that the authorities would have allowed Jesus to survive in public six months after the act in the temple.

187. Contrast the Roman people's swearing (hence involving curses against themselves) specifically for an institution to be ordained forever (Dion. Hal. 6.89.4).

188. See, e.g., the laments of Schnackenburg 1996: 263; Garland 1993: 258. Although guilt could be communicated transgenerationally (Ex 20:5; 34:7; Deut 5:9; 23:3-4; 1 Sam 15:2-3; 2 Sam 21:1-9), people were not to effect transgenerational punishments except under direct divine orders (Deut 24:16; 2 Kings 14:6; 2 Chron 25:4; Dion. Hal. 8.80.1).

189. Although many contemporary scholars overplay the Gospels' emphasis on "Jewish" guilt (e.g., Brandon 1967: 282), all four Gospels do emphasize the Jerusalem leadership's responsibility more than that of Pilate. This apologetic works, however, because they present the leaders' hostility as an internal Jewish dispute — which requires that the texts be read as the Gospel writers assumed they would be, Jesus and the Christians comprising a movement *within* Judaism. Cf. Reicke 1974: 184n.44 on the anachronism of the modern question: "it was Jews [Judeans] and Romans who killed him, not Israelis and Italians."

190. So, e.g., Albright and Mann 1971: 345; Matera 1989; Saldarini 1994: 33; Overman 1996: 383-84. Even the second century letter of Mara bar Serapion associates the exile of Israel with

The Romans torture Jesus. Pilate decrees the sentence, as his position required him to do (27:26). A Roman court had to pronounce the method of execution, which for sedition in the provinces was normally crucifixion; the sentencer normally declared, *"Ibis in crucem"* (You will mount the cross) (Blinzler 1959: 238, citing Petron. *Sat.* 137.9; Plaut. *Mostell.* 3.2.63, §850). That Pilate "delivered" him up to carrying the cross fits customary language (Char. *Chaer.* 4.2.7).

The preliminary scourging here (27:26) is more serious than the maximum thirty-nine lashes administered by synagogue communities (10:17; cf. 2 Cor 11:23)[191] and more severe than most Roman public corporal disciplines as well (cf. Acts 16:22; 2 Cor 11:25; Test. Jos. 2:3; *Dig.* 47.21.2);[192] sometimes this kind of scourging caused death itself (F. F. Bruce 1977a: 445). Unlike the lesser *fustigatio* (beating), the severer disciplines of *flagellatio* (flogging) and especially *verberatio* (scourging) accompanied the death sentence (Brown 1970: 2:874; but Brown concedes in 1994: 851 that the Gospel writers and their audiences probably did not recognize these distinctions); whereas Romans used rods on freemen and sticks on soldiers, they used scourges on slaves or provincials of equivalent status (*Dig.* 48.19.10; 68.28.2; Blinzler 1959: 222).[193] Thus Pilate here orders the preliminary scourging that, whether with rods or whips, generally preceded crucifixion and other forms of capital punishment.[194]

Probably stripped and tied to a pillar or post (Plaut. *Bacchides* 4.7.25; Artem. *Oneir.* 1.78 in Blinzler 1959: 222; see similarly m. Mak. 3:12),[195] Jesus was beaten with *flagella* — leather whips "whose thongs were knotted and interspersed" with pieces of iron or bone, or a spike (Apul. *Metam.* 7.30.154; *Cod.*

---

the condemnation of Jesus. Although not from a Christian (Boring 1995: 124-25), it undoubtedly testifies to a view circulated by Christians. Rabbinic texts often connect the suffering of A.D. 70 with judgment for sins, but never with Jesus' execution (Cohn 1977: 219-20).

191. Romans did not limit the number of lashes, hence sometimes victims not even sentenced to death died or were disabled under cruel supervisors (Cic. *Verr.* 2.4.39.85; Philo *Flacc.* 75); Josephus had opponents scourged "until their entrails were visible" (*War* 2.612) and reports a procurator laying bare a man's bones, though the man survived (*War* 6.304; Blinzler 1959: 223).

192. For *coercitio* as part of preliminary examinations, cf. Lake and Cadbury 1979: 282-83. Josephus adapts such discipline (*Life* 335).

193. Independently attested by Jn 19:1, although the sequence there differs (Brown 1994: 852). Some argue that Jn 19:1 represents a lesser form of scourging (cf. F. F. Bruce 1980b: 15; Blinzler 1959: 224; Bammel 1984c: 440-41, though Blinzler and Bammel go too far in separating this from the crucifixion historically). Blinzler distinguishes forms of scourging thus: "an inquisitional torture [Acts 22:24; probably Jos. *War* 4.304], as a death sentence (*fustuarium,* primarily a military punishment [Hor. *Sat.* 1.2.41-42], as an independent police chastisement [*P. Flor.* 61; Jos. *War* 2.269; cf. *Dig.* 48.2.6; Philo *Flacc.* 75], and as the introductory stage to execution after the sentence of death [*War* 2.306, 308; 5.449; 7.200, 202; Livy 33.36]" (Blinzler 1959: 223). But these distinctions may have eluded Matthew's audience anyway (Brown 1994: 851).

194. E.g., Jos. *War* 2.306-8; 5.449; Livy 2.5.8; 9.24.15; 10.1.3; 26.40.13; 33.36; 41.11.8; Appian *R.H.* 3.9.3; Cic. *Verr.* 5.62.162; Dion. Hal. 3.40.3; 5.43.2; 7.69.1; 9.40.3-4; 12.6.7; 20.16.2; 20.17.2; Arrian *Alex.* 3.30.5; Klausner 1979b: 350; cf. Lucian *Dead to Life/Fishermen* 2.

195. One could also be scourged while bound to the cross itself (Dio Cassius *R.H.* 49.22.6), though this may have worked best with the upright stake lacking a crossbeam. Victims were normally stripped naked before being beaten (Longus 2.14).

Theod. 8.5.2; 9.35.2; Goguel 1948: 527; Blinzler 1959: 222); it left skin hanging from the back in bloody strips (Klausner 1979b: 350; Blinzler 1959: 222). Various texts (e.g., Hor. *Sat.* 1.3.119; Cic. *In Defense of Rabirius* 5.15-16; Brown 1994: 851) attest the horror with which this punishment was viewed. Soldiers normally executed this task in the provinces (cf. Suet. *Calig.* 26; Blinzler 1959: 222). Some felt that the *flagellum* was merciful because it so weakened the prisoner as to hasten his death on the cross (Wilkinson 1978: 151). That the Gospels mention but do not describe the practice makes them read more like official reports than rhetorical documents with a heavy element of pathos at this point (Goguel 1948: 527); nevertheless, Matthew's audience would undoubtedly understand the procedure, for floggings and executions were generally public affairs in the Roman Empire.

That Pilate "delivers" Jesus up (27:26) to the soldiers (perhaps foreign auxiliaries) links him to Judas and the chief priests, who had also "delivered" Jesus over (26:48; 27:2-3; cf. Patte 1987: 376); far from escaping responsibility, Pilate forms the next link in the chain of guilt in which members of all involved parties participated.

The World Ridicules God's Son (27:27-44)

Cf. Mk 15:16-32; Lk 23:26-43; Jn 19:2-3, 17-27. Following Jesus to the cross means that disciples follow a road that may quite well cost them their lives physically (16:24); it also means sacrificing their own honor for Christ's along the way. Ridicule often provided the social backdrop of public executions, especially naked crucifixion, which constituted the ultimate form of shame (cf., e.g., Epict. *Disc.* 3.26.22; Cic. *Pro C. Rabirio* 5.10).[196]

This section rings with tragicomic irony (as noticed also by early interpreters, e.g., Cyprian *The Good of Patience* 7; Cyril of Jerusalem *Sermon on the Paralytic* 12; *ACCS,* 226-27). The Roman soldiers mocked Jesus' kingship (27:27-31), not for a moment considering the possibility that they were abusing a king greater than any the world had ever known. That Jesus submitted to such abuse reminds the reader that power does not function in the kingdom the way it does in the world (20:25-28). In the next section, Jesus bears public humiliation in front of and from the crowds he had come to save (27:32-40). The soldiers drafted a bystander to suffer with Jesus (27:32), a bystander who performed the role disciples should have been performing (16:24). As Jesus participated with humanity in its suffering under injustice in the world, he summoned his disciples to endure the unjust treatment visited on them for his name's sake (5:10-11). Also, Jesus possibly refused a narcotic meant to dull

196. On the shame of crucifixion, see further Brown 1994: 946-47, and especially Hengel 1977. The "equally negative portrayal" of Roman mockers here with Jewish mockers earlier invalidates the modern "claim that the Gospels excuse the Gentiles but condemn the Jews" (Brown 1994: 877).

the pain; he came to embrace the world's pain, and he would accept nothing less than the full impact of his bloody death (27:34). Further, the crowds invite Jesus to prove his divine Sonship by escaping the death of the cross (27:39-40) — thereby acting as Satan's final mouthpieces to turn Jesus from his divine mission (4:3-10; 16:21-23). In the final section of this unit, the religious authorities (at the top of the Jewish social order) and the dying robbers (at the bottom) join the crowds in functioning as Satan's mouthpieces. In Matthew's narrative world, neither outward piety nor being oppressed necessarily guarantees a heart obedient to God.

The soldiers mock Jesus' kingship and beat him. Although one would expect to find a larger contingent of soldiers in the Fortress Antonia (Anderson 1976: 335), Pilate brought soldiers with him at Passover and would keep his own temporary residence heavily guarded (hence, "the prefect's soldiers"). Although *speira* often means "cohort" (up to 600 troops), it can signify the Roman *manipulus,* roughly one-third that number (Liddell-Scott loc. cit.), and Matthew probably uses the term loosely here (Gundry 1982: 566).[197]

That soldiers would take the opportunity to taunt a captive for entertainment should not surprise us; although one cannot prove that they did so on this occasion, evidence suggests that such events were not unusual (see Brown 1994: 877; Davies and Allison 1997: 600). Public abuse of prisoners, even adorning one as a king and beating him, occurred on other occasions.[198] Games of mockery included the game of king (Livy 36.14.4; Corn. Nep. 14 [Datames], 3.1-4; Pollux *Onomasticon* 9.110; cf. Herod. *Hist.* 1.114; Hor. *Odes* 1.4.18), and theatrical mimes were common as well (Brown 1994: 874-77). Most daily entertainment was less dramatic. Soldiers usually had to entertain themselves with games like tossing coins or dice;[199] tossing knucklebones seems to have been common (Mart. *Epig.* 14.14-17; Diog. Laert. 9.1.3). The earliest Christian tradition indicates that Jesus was abused and humiliated (Johnson 1996: 120 cites Ps 69:9 in Rom 15:3), a tradition validated by the criterion of embarrassment.

The Gospels reveal Jesus' status as a servant-king in part by revealing how unlike a king the world thought him to be: if Jewish opponents ridiculed his claim to be a prophet (26:68), Roman ones mock his pretentious claim to royalty (27:29). Syrian or other eastern auxiliaries, who may have predominated here (France 1985: 393; Davies and Allison 1997: 601), but also Romans stationed in Palestine, might be happy to ridicule the notion of a Jewish king

197. Matthew's "whole" and "around" might also intentionally echo Ps 22:16 (Cope 1976: 103), though the correspondences are too few to be sure.

198. Commentators cite Philo *Flacc.* 36-39; *CPJ* 154, 158; Plut. *Pomp.* 24; Dio Cassius *R.H.* 15.20-21; cf. also Winter 1961: 102-3. Robbins 1992: xxvi, 189 helpfully supplies another parallel from Persian behavior at the Sacian festival (Dio Chrys. *Or.* 4.67-70), but lays too much emphasis here to the exclusion of other parallels.

199. Cary and Haarhoff 1946: 149; cf. in general Mart. *Epig.* 4.14; 11.6.2; Carcopino 1940: 250-53; Grant 1977: 82-83.

— thereby also ridiculing the people among whom they were stationed (Malina and Rohrbaugh 1992: 163).[200] The abuse of Jesus' captivity to disdain the Jerusalemites strikes a note of irony that Matthew might have seen carried into 70. Those in the east who worshiped Caesar or hellenistic rulers would kneel and cry *"Ave,"* or "Hail, Caesar!" (Blinzler 1959: 227; Brown 1970: 2:875); the soldiers here offer the same to Christ, but the irony of the narrative is that it inverts their own irony: he is the person whom they sarcastically claim him to be.

The "scarlet" robe (27:28) is undoubtedly a faded red soldier's cloak, which Mark (15:17) and John (19:2) apparently independently describe as "purple,"[201] reflecting the color of garments worn by hellenistic princes, hence the soldiers' mockery. The soldiers provide Jesus with this "purple" *chlamys,* a sceptre (probably from a bamboo cane used for military floggings), and a crown of thorns (probably woven from the branches of an available shrub like acanthus; Blinzler 1959: 227). The crown recalls the garlands worn by hellenistic vassal princes, since only the highest ruler wore a diadem with white wool.[202] The long thorns may thus have turned outward to imitate contemporary crowns rather than inward to draw blood, and the soldiers probably removed it along with the other mocking regalia before leading him to crucifixion (Blinzler 1959: 244-45; Gundry 1982: 567). (Luke's white robe in Lk 23:11 characterized Jewish kings as well — Hill 1979: 52.) The reed provides "a mock staff or sceptre" (Anderson 1976: 339).

Some suggest that the soldiers' spittle (27:30) may also parody the kiss of homage with which eastern subjects greeted their rulers (Blinzler 1959: 227; cf. Phaedrus 5.1.5), but the spitting comes at the end of the mockery, when they have begun beating him with the rod. Now they are abusing him physically, though the blows remain insulting as well as painful (cf. comment on 5:39; Dupont 1992: 126-27), and spitting was one of the severest expressions of disgust, as well as one of the severest experiences of disgust for its recipient (cf. Num 12:14; 4 Ezra 6:56; 2 Bar. 82:5; Ps-Philo 7:3; 12:4; ARN 35A; 19,

200. Anti-Judaism was common in parts of the Greek East, especially Greek-speaking Egypt (e.g., *CPJ* 1:24-25; 2:36-55, §153; 3:119-21, §520; Philo *Flacc.* 1, 47, 85; Jos. *Apion* bk. 2; Sib. Or. 3.271-72), and also at times in Rome, especially in response to Jewish successes in attracting Roman converts (Hor. *Sat.* 1.5.100-101; Juv. *Sat.* 14.96-106; Quint. 3.7.21; Tac. *Hist.* 5.1-5; Persius *Sat.* 5.179-84; for more general Roman xenophobia, cf., e.g., *Rhet. ad Herenn.* 3.3.4; Cic. *De Leg.* 2.10.25). For more detail, see Whittaker 1984: 85-91; Sevenster 1975; Daniel 1979; Meagher 1979; Gager 1983.

201. "Purple" could mean scarlet (e.g., Rev 17:4; 18:16; Appian *C.W.* 2.21, §150; Brown 1994: 866; cf. Dupont 1992: 260), though the Gospel tradition probably preserves it for its symbolic value, both to the soldiers and Jesus' later followers. Egyptian gentry in nome capitals purchased green, red, and especially blue apparel (Lewis 1983: 52-53). Derrett 1990 improbably suggests an allusion to Is 1:18, but somewhat more likely (although the LXX employs a different term) also to Is 63:2, which depicts God coming in red.

202. See, e.g., Blinzler 1959: 226-27; Jeremias 1971: 78; Lane 1974a: 559; Anderson 1976: 339; Hill 1979: 52; Carson 1984b: 573; Brown 1994: 866; citing 1 Macc 10:20, 62, 69; 11:58; 14:43-44. A person of status who loses prestige may then be insulted by cowards (Phaedrus 1.21.1-2).

§42B; Sifre Num. 106.1.1; Pesiq. Rab Kah. 10:8; Jews would regard Gentile spittle as particularly unclean).

The soldiers must draft a bystander (27:32) to do what the disciples were unwilling to do (16:24). Matthew's primary point is striking, reinforcing the negative portrayal of the disciples his audience has experienced in his recitation of the Gethsemane tradition. While Jesus suffered for them, his own disciples, who should have borne his cross (16:24), abandoned him, forcing the Romans to impress a foreigner.[203]

Normally a condemned prisoner carried his own *patibulum,* or transverse beam of the cross, to the site of the execution, where soldiers would fix the *patibulum* to the upright stake *(palus, stipes, staticulum),* which they regularly reused for executions.[204] Both Jewish people (Lev 24:14; Num 15:35-36; Deut 17:5; 1 Kings 21:13; Jos. *War* 4.360; Ant. 4.264) and Romans (Artem. *Oneir.* 2.53; Plaut. *Soldier* 2.4.6-7, §359-60) performed executions outside a town (Blinzler 1959: 251; Lane 1991: 2:541). In this case, a proposed site for the execution is only about 1,000 feet north to northeast of Herod's palace, where Pilate pronounced the sentence (Reicke 1974: 185). The soldiers presumably led Jesus through part of the upper city and out the Garden Gate, near the Hippicus tower of Herod's old palace (Gnilka 1997: 309).

Given the unlikehilood that the soldiers would simply show mercy to a condemned prisoner, scholars are probably correct to suppose that Jesus was too weak to carry the cross, and that his executioners preferred to have him alive on the cross rather than dead on the way (cf. Goguel 1948: 530-31; Lane 1974a: 562; Davies 1993: 197; Brown 1994: 914). Although soldiers sometimes scourged prisoners en route to the crucifixion, the practice is not mentioned here, probably because Jesus was already scourged (Valerius Maximus 1.7.4; Dion. Hal. 7.69.1; Blinzler 1959: 244), perhaps also because he was too weak already. Since crucifixion sometimes lasted days (Jos. *Life* 420-21), the quickness of Jesus' death (multiply attested: Mk 15:44; Jn 19:31) reinforces the notion that Jesus was already quite weak (Klausner 1979b: 353), probably partly from the scourging, perhaps partly exhausted from the Gethsemane experience (26:38) and partly wishing to surrender his own life as quickly as possible (12:40; 16:21; 17:22-23; 20:18-19, 28; 26:26-28). In such circumstances, that the soldiers would have drafted a bystander is not improbable;[205] one would not expect them

203. With Matthew's "led away" here (27:31), cf. also Dion. Hal. 12.6.7, where one is *apēchthēsan* for crucifixion.

204. Artem. *Oneir.* 2.56; Plut. *De Sera Numinis Vindicta* 9, *Mor.* 554AB; Char. *Chaer.* 4.2.7; 4.3.10; Stauffer 1960: 135; Reicke 1974: 185; Brown 1994: 913.

205. That Simon was coming in from the "field" (Mk 15:21) cannot mean that he was coming from work — first, work was prohibited on the feast day (Lev 23:7-8) and, second, one would hardly finish working in the fields at 9 a.m. The expression may thus mean that Simon had miscalculated his transportation and arrived from Cyrene late for the feast (cf., e.g., Acts 20:16; Sen. *Ep. Lucil.* 53.1-3; 57.1; though the most difficult season — cf., e.g., Acts 27:9; Jos. *War* 1.279-80; 2.203; 4.499; Ach. Tat. 8.19.3 — had probably ended a month before); more likely, it simply means "from outside the city" (Dalman 1929: 100-101), where he had spent the night, perhaps in a nearby town.

to carry the beam themselves if they could "impress" another into service (see comment on 5:41).[206]

Most scholars agree that Simon of Cyrene is a historical figure (Brown 1994: 913). It does not seem simply part of Markan predictions of scripture fulfillment, and Simon does not bear the cross willingly as a mere invention to fulfill a disciple paradigm would (B. Sanders 1995: 56-57). Archaeologists have uncovered the grave of an "Alexander son of Simon," a Cyrenian Jew, near Jerusalem (Lane 1974a: 563), which would fit the Jerusalem-based Passion Narrative Theissen suggests behind Mark, where Simon's sons seem to have been familiar (Mk 15:21; Theissen 1991: 176-77; some cite Rom 16:13 for Rome). Given the commonness of names like "Alexander"[207] and "Simon,"[208] we cannot be sure that the same Cyrenian is in view, but it remains possible. ("Rufus" was a common Roman name, especially among slaves, but naturally less known in the Greek East; for Roman Jews, see *CIJ* 1:103, §145; cf. 1:52, §79; 1:401, §541.)

Simon's ancestral ethnicity also remains uncertain. Boykin Sanders (1995: 62-63) makes a reasonable case for Simon's ancestry being native Cyrenian rather than immigrant Jewish Cyrenian, showing how frequently early Christian narratives designate characters' ethnicity. Yet at Jerusalem's festivals, full of pilgrims from other parts of the world (Acts 2:5-11; Jos. *War* 1.253; *Ant.* 17.254; Safrai 1974/76d: 898), one might simply identify oneself by one's place of origin. This would also be true if Simon or his sons remained part of the Christian community (many believe the tradition recalls his name because he became a Christian — e.g., France 1985: 395; Brown 1994: 913) in Jerusalem, which probably traditioned the Passion Narrative (see Theissen 1991: 166-99). Cyrene was as much as a quarter Jewish (Jos. *Ant.* 14.115-18; cf. *Apion* 2.44; Caird 1955: 21; Brown 1994: 915), and its Jewish community is well known (Acts 2:10; 13:1; see especially Applebaum 1979; Yamauchi 1992). "Simon" is also a frequent (though not exclusively) Jewish name, but we currently lack adequate evidence to decide whether Simon was of fully Jewish descent or may have been descended from proselytes. Soldiers would march the prisoner through crowds of spectators (Reicke 1974: 185); crowds normally gathered to watch executions, especially if near the city (Morris 1971: 807).

Jesus deliberately endured the full physical pain of the cross. The passion tradition not only employs Simon carrying Jesus' cross to underline the horrendous failure of disciples to share Jesus' cross, but it juxtaposes this failure

206. Brown 1994: 914 questions whether the Romans would force someone when Josephus says they did not force subjects to break their own laws (*Apion* 2.73), but this objection lays too much weight on Josephus's propaganda; Josephus employs legal precedents apologetically (cf. Rajak 1984).

207. Including a Jewish name in Acts 4:6; *CIJ* 1:lxvii; 1:59, §85; 1:149, §210; 1:157, §219; 1:288, §370; 2:27, §764; 2:249, §1217; 2:274, §1284; *CPJ* 1:xix; 3:168-69; in the feminine, *CIJ* 1:13, §8; 1:102, §144; 1:436, §606.

208. E.g., 10:2, 4; 13:55. Fitzmyer (1974: 105-12) regards it as the most popular name of the period. The Greek "Simon" readily matches the biblical and later Jewish "Simeon" (cf. Cullmann 1968: 100; Dalman 1929: 5).

with Jesus' willingness to suffer. The wine mixed with gall (27:34) may have been intended to dull his pain (cf. Prov 31:4-7). Mark's "myrrh" (Mk 15:23)[209] had many uses, among them narcotic properties that may induce sleep (scholars cite Dioscorides Pedanius *Materia Medica* 1.44.3); it is reported that Jerusalem's respected women provided (financially or in person) a narcotic to men being executed to diminish their pain (b. Sanh. 43a; Jeremias 1971: 225; Lane 1974a: 564; Blinzler 1959 252-53 and n. 27).[210] Whether or not Matthew's implied audience would find such a narcotic implied in his "gall,"[211] they would expect the wine itself to serve a pain-killing function (Prov 31:6-7). Once he tasted the wine and its additive, Jesus may have refused it, in part because of his vow in 26:29 (Moule 1965: 126; cf. 27:48; Num 6:4); but Jesus apparently refused it also because he had come to share humanity's pain, and had to experience it in full.

Jesus' crucifixion by the Romans outside Jerusalem is an "almost indisputable" historical fact (Sanders 1985: 11); Christians would not have invented the crucifixion. The full horror of that mode of execution (e.g., Apul. *Metam.* 3.9; 6.32; Char. *Chaer.* 3.3.12) remained vivid enough in the first century that all four evangelists hurry by the event itself quickly, Matthew "disposing of it in a participial clause" (A. B. Bruce 1979: 328). It was established rhetorical practice to hurry most quickly over points that might disturb the audience (Theon *Progymn.* 5.52-56).

Although some features of crucifixions remained common, executioners could perform them in a variety of manners, limited only by the extent of their sadistic creativity (Hengel 1977: 25).[212] Executioners usually tied victims to the

209. Matthew changes the myrrh to "gall" to connote the taste depicted in Ps 69:21 (Blinzler 1959: 252-53n.27), possibly under the influence of an Aramaic wordplay (Gundry 1982: 569). The generic Hebrew and Greek sense of "gall" as covering whatever is poisonous or (in this case) bitter (e.g., Hom. *Il.* 16.203) may allow Matthew to make this change (Gundry 1975: 202). The righteous sufferer of Psalm 69 apparently represents Israel in exile (Ps 69:33-36), which is appropriately applicable to Jesus in Matthew (cf. 2:15-18).

210. But pace Bammel 1984c: 442, it need not follow that "This detail . . . points to a Jewish execution"; actual Jewish executions were undoubtedly rare, and if some showed special mercy during a Jewish execution, how much more during a Roman one? Cf. the Christian allusion in Gk. Ezra 2:25.

211. Because myrrh had multiple uses, others doubt that the tradition's audiences would take the soporiferous effect for granted (so Brown 1994: 941) and interpret the action as part of the mockery, based on its bad taste (e.g., Carson 1984b: 575; Brown 1994: 943). Matthew's "gall" would probably be less clear whether or not his audience would recall Markan tradition. In any case, noting that ancients sometimes mixed bitter substances with their wine (Pliny *N.H.* 14.19, §109), Brown 1994: 943 observes that "the Matthean picture is not absurd, even if its readers would recognize the action in the present context as hostile." Myrrhed wine may also imply expensive scented wine (Pliny *N.H.* 14.15.92), perhaps seized from a well-to-do paschal pilgrim. That ancient Greeks were aware of narcotics is clear, e.g., in Hom. *Od.* 4.219-26; cf. Ruck 1978: 42.

212. Thus, e.g., one man is bound to a fig tree and anointed with honey so that the ants devour him, but this, too, is called a cross *(cruciatum);* Apul. *Metam.* 8.22; cf. Prometheus's fetters (Mart. *Epig.* 7; Lucian *Prometheus* 2). Thus positions varied, but for evidence for one probably common position, see Tzaferis 1985: 52-53. Before the Roman conquest, following hellenistic (e.g., Jos. *Ant.* 12.256) and Persian (Esth 9:25; De Vaux 1961: 159) practice, Jewish executions had also adopted hanging by crucifixion (e.g., Jos. *War* 1.97; *Ant.* 13.380; 4QpNah 1.7-8; Sifre Deut. 221.1.1; p. Sanh.

cross, but in some cases hastened their death by nailing their wrists as well (Jn 20:25).[213] Romans crucified their victims naked;[214] although some later rabbis explaining the proper way to carry out theoretical executions allowed men a loincloth (m. Sanh. 6:3; Blinzler 1959: 253), it is unlikely that Pilate's soldiers would have accommodated their sensitivities.[215] Further, other tradition indicates that most teachers allowed men to be executed naked (m. Sanh. 6:3; Soṭa 3:8; b. Sanh. 45a, bar.). Public nakedness could cause shame in other settings (e.g., Juv. *Sat.* 1.71; Plut. *R.Q.* 40, *Mor.* 274A; Diog. Laert. 2.73; but contrast Plato *Rep.* 5.452C; Dio Chrys. *13th Disc.* §24), but especially for Palestinian Jews (e.g., Gen 3:7, 10-11; Jub. 3:21-22, 30-31; 7:8-10, 20; 1QS 7.12; t. Ber. 2:14; Sifre Deut. 320.5.2). One being executed on the cross could not swat flies from one's wounds, nor withhold one's bodily wastes from coming out while hanging naked for hours and sometimes days (Klausner 1979b: 350).

The specific mention of divided clothing (27:35) may well recall Psalm 22:18 (e.g., Cope 1976: 103), but it can hardly be a mere accommodation to it without historical substance (cf. Freed 1965: 101);[216] Roman law allowed the execution squad to seize the few possessions the condemned might have on his person (*Dig.* 48.20.6;[217] Dibelius 1971: 188; Sherwin-White 1978: 46; against the Jewish custom, e.g., b. Sanh. 48b, bar.).[218] The Roman army's basic unit was a

---

6:6, §2; cf. 11QTemple 64); though some read the later practice back into earlier times (Ps-Philo 55:3), however, the Israelites originally hanged corpses posthumously (cf. Gen 40:19) and only till nightfall, limiting the shame (Deut 21:23; m. Sanh. 6:4).

213. See Artem. *Oneir.* 2.56; Plaut. *Mostell.* 2.1.12-13; Lucan *C.W.* 6.545, 547; m. Shab. 6.10; Lane 1974a: 564; Jn 20:25; cf. Lk 24:39. Cf. Diod. Sic. 25.5.2 (if *prosēloō* here means "nailed," as it often does); also the skeleton recovered at Givat ha-Mivtar — F. F. Bruce 1980b: 18, though original reports about the ankle nail(s) have been revised (Stanton 1989a: 148; Kuhn 1978); on the wrists, see Yamauchi 1982: 2; Tzaferis 1985: 52.

214. Artem. *Oneir.* 2.61; Brown 1994: 870 adds Dion. Hal. *Rom. Ant.* 7.69.2; Val. Max. *Fact.* 1.7.4; Jos. *Ant.* 19.270.

215. Brown 1994: 870 thinks that the Gospels may "reflect a local concession," noting that Jos. *War* 2.246 and *Ant.* 20.136 do not mention Celer's disrobing; but this would be an argument from silence. (Brown, citing Melito of Sardis *On the Pasch* 97 in favor of nakedness and Acts of Pilate 10.1 in favor of a loincloth, ultimately doubts that we can know either way — 953.) Nakedness was probably the rule of thumb (in public Roman punishments, e.g., in Dion. Hal. 7.69.2; in non-Roman executions, e.g., in Jos. *Apion* 1.191; 2.53).

216. Edersheim: 608 insists that ancient Judaism did interpret Ps 22 messianically (citing Yalq. on Is 60); cf. also Pesiq. R. 36:2; 37:1. Whether this interpretation existed before the time of Jesus is unclear (Longenecker 1975: 156 notes its use five times in 1QH to suggest that it may be messianic, but this is not absolutely clear), and certainly other interpretations existed (e.g., Midr. Ps. 22:6 applies to Esther — Bowman 1975: 136); in any case, though many parallels with Ps 22 in the Passion Narrative are noteworthy, they also correspond with what we genuinely know of crucifixion.

217. Brown 1994: 955 notes that the law itself exempts the clothing the condemned is wearing, but acknowledges that such rules may not have been followed in the first century. I would add doubts that anyone would have restrained provincial soldiers from such seizure (especially given the abuses of requisitioning from persons not condemned).

218. This practice stemmed from the custom of plundering the slain on the battlefield (cf., e.g., 1 Sam 31:8; Joel 3:2-3; 2 Macc 8:27-28; Virg. *Aen.* 11.193-94; Polyb. *R.R.E.* 9.26; Dion. Hal. 3.40.3; 3.56.4; 6.29.4-5; and throughout ancient literature).

contubernium, eight men who shared a tent; normally half of such a unit would be dispatched for a work detail like a crucifixion (Jones 1971: 193-94; see Jn 19:23). The casting of lots (27:35) may involve the guessing of another's hidden fingers (Brown 1994: 955), but the bored soldiers may as easily have brought dice to entertain themselves (cf. Cary and Haarhoff 1946: 149).

The charge posted above Jesus' head[219] reveals the irony of the situation: Jesus is executed for being king of Israel (27:37). Yet for all the charge's irony, it is historically quite probable (so even Winter 1961: 108-9).[220] Jesus' triumphal entry (21:6-11) marked him as a royal aspirant; the priestly aristocracy would arrest and the Romans execute anyone who offered the slightest grounds for suspicion of treason against Rome (see 27:11-13, 29, 37, 42). The title is not a traditional Christian confession; Jesus' "you say" (27:11) suggests that it is not the title he would have emphasized, and Romans crucified many self-proclaimed kings and their followers under the *Lex Iulia de maiestate* (Jos. *Ant.* 17.285, 295; Brown 1994: 968). Other Jewish rebels apparently hoped for kingship (Jos. *War* 2.443-44; *Ant.* 17.285; Harvey 1982: 13n.12), but unless they *desired* repression Christians would hardly have invented the claim that Jesus was crucified on these grounds (Harvey 1982: 13-14; Stanton 1995a: 173; cf. Acts 17:7); surely the apolitical Markan community would have been an unlikely source for the invention (cf. Kee 1980: 120-21).

A further datum supports the plausibility of the account: on other known occasions a member of the execution squad would carry in front of or beside the condemned a small tablet *(tabula)* declaring the charge *(titulus),* the cause of execution *(causa poenae),* which he might later post on the cross.[221] That Matthew and Luke (perhaps Q; "this is") and Matthew and John ("Jesus") share some

219. The location of the charge identifies the shape of the cross as in Christian tradition, rather than the T or X-shaped crosses also used; mass executions sometimes simply employed scaffolds (on various forms of crucifixion, Brown 1994: 948 cites, e.g., Sen. *Consol.* 20.3; Jos. *War* 5.451; on the four-armed cross, the *crux immissa,* see Iren. *Haer.* 2.24.4; Tert. *Ad Nationes* 1.12.7). The upright stakes were ten feet at the highest, more often closer to six or seven feet so that the man hung barely above the ground, with a seat *(sedile)* in the middle (Blinzler 1959: 249; Reicke 1974: 186); animals sometimes assaulted the feet of the crucified. The Romans could employ high crosses to increase visibility for significant public executions (Suet. *Galba* 9.1), and given the reed here (27:48; Mk 15:36), Jesus may have been slightly higher than usual (Blinzler 1959: 249); Brown 1994: 948-49 guesses seven feet.

220. Boring 1995: 151-52 compares *Acta Appiani* 33 (second or third century A.D.), in which the martyr receives the mark of distinction "he claims, even if only mockingly." Whereas many details of martyr stories may be relevant, however, this one is not; in view of the many acts of martyrs with which Jesus' passion could be compared, a minor parallel involving such ridicule is easily enough coincidental.

221. Cullmann 1956b: 42-43; Reicke 1974: 186; Brown 1994: 963 cite Suet. *Calig.* 32.2; *Dom.* 10.1; Dio Cassius *R.H.* 54.3.7; 54.8; Tert. *Apol.* 2.20; Euseb. *H.E.* 5.1.44; cf. b. Sanh. 43a. The posting of the accusation on the cross is not well-attested, either because those describing crucifixion had already mentioned its being carried (Bammel 1984b: 353) or because the practice was not in fact standard, although, given the variations among executions, in no way improbable (Harvey 1982: 13). Blinzler 1959: 254 thinks the tablet was "in black or red letters on a white ground."

common elements against Mark suggests the prominence of this memory in the common passion tradition.

Jesus endures the mocking of those present. Jewish people could view mockery, which often accompanied executions, as a final test martyrs had to endure (Boring 1995: 158 cites Asc. Isa. 5:2-3). The "robbers" on either side, one on the left and one on the right (27:38; cf. Jn 19:18), could recall the promise to those enthroned on either side of Jesus (20:23); crowned with thorns (27:29) as "King of the Judeans" (27:37), Jesus had a cross for a throne (as in Mark — cf. Perrin 1976a: 93). That Jesus would be hung between "robbers" is not surprising; the Roman charge against him is that of treason, viewing him as a revolutionary or a "social bandit" (Oakman 1992: 121; cf. 26:55). Because the "robbers" are probably revolutionaries (e.g., Malina 1981: 77) who may have sought to facilitate the establishment of God's earthly kingdom,[222] the irony and pathos of their ridicule become all the clearer.

Both lay and aristocratic mockers pass by, perhaps along a road,[223] "wagging their heads" (Ps 22:7),[224] repeating the slanderous charge of 26:61 (cf. Jn 2:19), seeking a sign (cf. 16:1), and serving as mouthpieces for Satan's desire for a kingdom without the cross (cf. 4:3, 7). Perhaps they were mocking in order to demand appropriate vindication of the court's sentence; at least in later tradition an executed person was to confess his sins in order to receive God's mercy (cf. m. Sanh. 6:2-3; Num. Rab. 8:5; Ps-Philo 25:6-7; 27:15; in view of death in general, t. Ber. 6:17). While uttering the sort of derision one might expect at an execution of a misled pietist, the mockers from the Sanhedrin[225] (27:41-43) unwittingly cite Psalm 22:8 (Matthew presumably conforms their mockery to

222. Josephus usually uses "robbers" of revolutionaries (e.g., Jos. *War* 4.138); Jn 18:40 probably also uses it thus. The term can elsewhere retain its usual sense, of course (e.g., Jn 10:1; *CPJ* 1:157-58, §21; Ach. Tat. 2.16.2; 2.18.5; 3.9.3; 3.10.1; cf. Epict. *Disc.* 1.18.5; MacMullen 1966: 255). The conjunction of these terms via Josephus's aristocratic language suggests support for the thesis of "social bandits"; see under Revolutionaries in the Introduction.

223. Because crucifixions were intentionally public events, passersby were historically certain to be there. The Romans crucified near highways for optimum warning value (*Dig.* 48.19.28.15; Harvey 1982: 12; Brown 1994: 1026-27); those passing by would often learn of the grounds for execution from the other spectators.

224. "Pass by" may here recall such sorrowful predicaments as in LXX Lam 1:12; 2:15 (Wilkinson 1978: 154). "Wagging heads" reflects Ps 22:7 and Lam 2:15 (so also, e.g., France 1985: 396).

225. That members of the Sanhedrin would want to see that what they had set in motion was plausible, and Joseph of Arimathea's testimony could strengthen the claim for a reliable source (Brown 1994: 1027-28). Brown doubts, however, that they would show up on Passover; certainly on the eve of Passover even the aristocratic priests would be occupied in the temple while lower priests slaughtered the lambs. But I have argued that this is the day *after* the slaughter of lambs, and would the priestly aristocracy have considered viewing an execution (which they had devised earlier the same day) to be "work" improper on a feast day? (Even by the third century rabbis were not unanimous about trying and executing someone on a Sabbath — p. Sanh. 4:6, §2.) In any case, however, we should not think that they were present *long* after being up most of the night.

correspond clearly with that text)[226] — showing themselves enemies of God's anointed servant, hence of God himself.

The language of the priestly mockers probably also echoes Wisdom 2:18 in the Septuagint: "For if the righteous man is a son of God, God will help him, and deliver him from the hand of those who resist him." In the Wisdom of Solomon, those who utter these words are the wicked who want to condemn the righteous to death unjustly, because he claims to be a child of God and to have a good future (2:16-20). In other words, by their own words Jesus' enemies are condemned (Mt 12:37; cf. Lk 19:22). The King of the Judeans refuses to respond (5:39; cf. Is 53:7).

Again irony saturates the narrative: they are right that he cannot save himself if he would save others (27:42). That they offer to believe if he will come down, just as Satan offered him the kingdom if he would bow down, tests Jesus: he can have people's allegiance if he will just forsake the Father's way of getting it (26:39, 42). But Jesus himself models the sacrificial life of discipleship for Matthew's community: whoever wishes to save his or her life will lose it (10:39; 16:25).

Signs at Jesus' Death (27:45-54)

Cf. Mk 15:33-39; Lk 23:44-49; Jn 19:25-30. The pious priestly aristocrats would not have waited for Jesus to die and may well have left for the afternoon liturgy in the temple (Stauffer 1960: 138). Like Pilate (Mk 15:44-45), they may not have anticipated his death so quickly. Crucified persons could survive several days, depending on their constitution and whether ropes or nails were used (Sen. *Ep.* 101.10-13; Jos. *Life* 420-21; Brown 1994: 1222).

Jesus' suffering elicits a plaintive cry of final dependence on God. Given subsequent Christian Christology, the early church would hardly have invented Jesus' cry of despair in uttering a complaint about alienation from God, quoting Psalm 22:1 (e.g., Stauffer 1980: 140; Gundry 1975: 203; Jeremias 1971: 189).[227] Jesus' contemporaries recognized in the psalm a plea for mercy (cf. Mek. Shir. 3.75ff., Laut. 2:28), which accords with Jesus' most recent recorded prayer (26:39, 42). Mark records the prayer in its fully Aramaic form, perhaps following an early Palestinian tradition that conformed Jesus' cry to the Targum; Matthew re-Hebraizes the address (changing "Eloi" to "Eli"), either to conform to frequent early synagogue practice of using Hebrew prayers (though this Hebra-

226. Gundry 1975: 203 cites Edersheim's view that Jewish teachers cited Scripture loosely enough that a genuine citation of Ps 22:8 is possible; but Gundry's other solution, adapting a different text to recount others' perspective (ibid., following R. Gordis in *HUCA* 22), is more likely.

227. Boring 1995: 157-60 rightly contrasts Jesus' pain here with the standard traditions of glad martyrs (2 Macc 6:18–7:42; Jos. *War* 2.119-20; b. Ber. 61b), adding that Matthew's signs, Luke's psalm of trust (Lk 23:46 citing Ps 31:5), and certainly John alleviate some of the starkness of the Markan portrait.

ism had come over into Aramaic; cf. also the use of "Eli" in Qumran's hymns), or to explain (probably correctly, cf. Layton 1996: 611-12; pace, e.g., Cope 1976: 104) how listeners thought they heard "Elijah" (*Eliyahu;* Jeremias 1971: 5n.2; cf. Anderson 1976: 346).

That Jesus utters the complaint of the righteous sufferer (Ps 22:1)[228] might well suggest to early Christians that he participated in humanity's ultimate alienation from God in experiencing the pain of death (27:46).[229] Although Christians are not likely to have invented such a cry, they undoubtedly found great significance in the use of Psalms 22 and 69 in the Passion Narrative. Jewish Christians, like other Jews, recited these psalms identifying with the oppressed; to hear Jesus in terms of these psalms invited them to contemplate how fully Jesus had embraced their condition of suffering.

The cry does not imply collapse of faith in what he had already prophesied; "my God" implies continuing trust (Kingsbury 1983: 130). Neither for the Gospels, nor necessarily for their sources, do Jesus' abandonment and despairing "Godforsakenness" (Kelber 1979: 81) necessarily imply doubt of ultimate triumph.[230] Jesus had to know that Psalm 22 went on to declare the psalmist's vindication (22:22-24; cf., e.g., Meier 1980: 349).[231]

Still, his own people did not recognize what was happening. When some of the bystanders think that Jesus is calling Elijah, the Gospels reinforce the picture that their smug assurance is folly (as in the philosophers' misinterpretation of Paul's "deities" in Acts 17:18; cf. Haenchen 1971: 518), although it is hardly unlikely that Judeans might mishear a weakened Galilean's utterance (Albright and Mann 1971: 350). They may have known the tradition that rabbis in distress sometimes looked to Elijah for help,[232] and assumed that Jesus was doing likewise. He had failed to "save himself" (27:40, 42), so now perhaps Elijah would (27:49); they mock Jesus as a deluded visionary (cf. 1 Cor 1:23; comment on 4:5-6). Clearly they expected no supernatural intervention, expectations seem-

228. Gundry 1975: 210; Hurtado 1983: 264, and others are probably right that the Ps 22 and 69 allusions reflect a typological application to Jesus as the righteous sufferer. For a fuller discussion of the use of Ps 22 in the Passion Narratives, see Brown 1994: 1455-64. Augustine insightfully suggests that Jesus adopts the psalmist's voice, identifying with humanity fully here (*Letters,* 140 to Honoratus 5-6; *ACCS,* 233-34).

229. Cf., similarly, e.g., Hagner 1995: 844. But contrast the explicit Johannine emphasis that Jesus' Father remains with him in his passion (Jn 16:32).

230. The psalm portrays the righteous sufferer, not specifically identified as the Messiah (though cf. Soggin 1965 on corporate suffering of a king for his people). God could turn away from viewing the defiled (Philo *Spec. Leg.* 1.167). Translating the Aramaic "praised" instead of "forsaken" (cf. Cohn-Sherbok 1982) misses the context as well as demanding too much knowledge of early audiences concerning the Aramaic rendering of Ps 22:1.

231. Given the practice of Jewish Scripture citations, Jesus may actually have quoted more than the sample preserved (cf. Stauffer 1960: 140).

232. Rabbinic tradition, which could here reflect ideas already current in the first century, emphasizes that Elijah (who had never died in the OT — 2 Kings 2:11) would periodically rescue sages in distress or aid them in their needs (cf. b. ʿAbod. Zar. 17b; Taʿan. 21a; p. Ketub. 12:3, §6; Pesiq. Rab Kah. 18:5; Gen. Rab. 33:3; Dalman 1929: 205-6; cf. Bamberger 1969: 308).

ingly confirmed because Elijah would not come (27:47-49). The narrative again bristles with irony: far from being able to help Jesus, "Elijah" was his forerunner in martyrdom (17:10-13; Hooker 1983: 79; Kingsbury 1983: 130).

Jesus yielded his life for the many (20:28). Whereas the bystanders assume that a misled pietist is calling for help to survive, Jesus has in fact relinquished his life. The wine vinegar[233] (27:48) was probably an attempt to revive him (Reicke 1974: 187), perhaps to prolong the torment, probably in mocking pretense that Elijah had come to relieve him.[234] Jesus had come to drink the cup of suffering (26:39), the cup of God's wrath (Jer 25:15-29). That Jesus "gave up his spirit" simply means that he died (cf. Test. Abr. 17A; Life of Adam 27:1; 45:3; 2 Enoch 70:16; Sen. *Dial.* 7.20.5; cf. Quint. *Inst. Or.* pref. 12), but it may imply an element of his choice (cf. 4 Macc 9:25; 12:20; Tert. *Apol.* 21). Jesus is both his followers' model, obedient and uncomplaining as he serves the Father no matter what the cost, and their savior, who offers himself for the sins of the world.

By expiring at 3 p.m., Jesus died close to the official time of the evening lamb offering in the temple, especially significant in a paschal context (m. Pesaḥ. 5:1; Reicke 1974: 166 — though I would argue that the final Passover lambs were being slaughtered the preceding day). Earlier studies argued that because of the position of their bodies, victims of crucifixion eventually became unable to lift their diaphragms and normally died by asphyxiation (Reicke 1974: 187). Some more recent studies suggest that dehydration and loss of blood are more plausible causes (Brown 1994: 1092). In any case (various factors undoubtedly weakened the body, whichever factors ultimately proved decisive in inviting death), Jesus died more quickly than expected (Mk 15:44-45; see comment above). Jesus' dying "cry" may echo the Greek version of Psalm 22:2, 5, 24 (Ps 21 LXX; France 1985: 400).

God confirms Jesus' righteousness by signs in nature. But whereas Elijah did not come to rescue Jesus, the sort of signs that Judaism regularly expected to accompany the death of the righteous (because the prayers of the righteous sustained the world)[235] *did* follow Jesus' death (27:51-53). These signs would indicate divine approval of Jesus and disapproval of his executioners to both pagan and Jewish audiences (see Kee 1983: 189; Best 1965: 98, citing, e.g., Virg. *Georg.* 1.466ff.; cf. also Macrobius *Comm.* 2.2.3 in van der Horst 1973: 224).[236]

233. Laborers and soldiers in the ancient Mediterranean found wine vinegar better for quenching thirst than water (Ruth 2:14; Plut. *Cato Major* 1.13; *P. Lond.* 1245.9; Lane 1974a: 573; Blinzler 1959: 255). Reed mace *(Typha)* was probably not accessible or strong enough, but most true reeds *(Arundo* and *Phragmites)* would have served the purpose of the "reed" here (Hepper 1992: 70).

234. Some used pennyroyal or mint stored in vinegar to revive those who had fainted (Pliny *N.H.* 20.54.152); but these were probably not available.

235. E.g., m. Soṭa 9:15; p. ʿAbod. Zar. 3:1, §2; Pesiq. Rab Kah. 27:1; Gen. Rab. 59:4; 62:4; Dalman 1929: 220; with less spectacular signs for "ordinary" persons, see ARN 25A.

236. Brown 1994: 1113-14 adds 4 Macc 9:20 (cf. the analogous Mart. Pol. 16.1); Jos. *Ant.* 17.167 (eclipse of the moon); b. Ber. 61b; ʿAbod. Zar. 18a; and on 1043, 1114 cites considerable Greco-Roman evidence as well (Virgil *Georg.* 1.472-90 — including earthquakes; Plut. *Romulus* 27.6; *Caesar* 69.4; Ovid *Fasti* 2.493; Cic. *De Re Publ.* 6.22; Pliny *N.H.* 2.30, §97; Dio Cassius *R.H.* 51.17.4-5; 60.35.1; Jos. *Ant.* 14.309; one may add Hom. *Il.* 16.459; Ovid *Metam.* 11.44-47). The Py-

Although Matthew does not borrow these signs from Mark, the style of these verses suggests that he follows a different pre-Matthean source "circulating in popular circles" (Brown 1994: 1138, who doubts its historical accuracy).

The darkness (Mk 15:33) could stem simply from heavy cloud cover, but the Gospel writers use it to convey a more profound theological point. For many Jewish people, the darkness would recall the three-day plague immediately preceding the sacrifice of the first paschal lamb (Ex 10:21-23; Wis 17),[237] as well as judgment imagery (Sib. Or. 4.56-58; 11.45; 2 Enoch 7:1-2; Gen. Rab. 28:1), especially eschatological (4 Ezra 7:38-42; Ps-Philo 3:10; Sib. Or. 3.800-804; Test. Mos. 10:5; cf. 4 Ezra 5:4-5; Pesiq. Rab Kah. 9:1). Fierce darkness worthy of mention might also recall ancient views concerning eclipses. Although many ancients understood that the moon passing in front of the sun caused a solar eclipse (Diog. Laert. *Lives* 7.1.145-46; 10.96; Pliny *N.H.* 2.6.47; Dio Cassius *R.H.* 60.26.1-5; Livy 44.37.6-7), eclipses normally constituted a bad omen (Diod. Sic. 20.5.5; Plut. *Aemilius Paulus* 17.5; Arrian *Alex.* 3.7.6; 3.15.7), in Jewish tradition signifying divine judgment (t. Sukk. 2:5-6; cf. b. Sukk. 29a). An eclipse at midday (as here, the sixth hour, 27:45) seemed particularly noteworthy (Livy 37.4.3). On at least one occasion in Greek tradition a lunar eclipse signified nature's sympathy for the decease of a great man (Diog. Laert. *Lives* 4.64, on Carneades, ca. 213-129 B.C.); more frequently, they at least saw unexpected darkness as the activity of deities (cf. Plut. *Timoleon* 28.2).[238]

As noted above, Jewish hagiography typically listed signs at a righteous person's decease (Dalman 1929: 220), perhaps in conjunction with the view that the merit of the righteous sustained the world.[239] That Matthew should add signs to those mentioned by Mark is hardly surprising, both given Matthew's expansion from Palestinian traditions consistent with contemporary Jewish thought and Mark's specialized emphasis on the cross and hidden revelation. (That some cosmic signs, such as darkness, remain even in Mark may suggest that the tradition had more signs, which Mark and John had theological reasons not to emphasize.)

Matthew provides an astute theological observation in the raising of dead

---

thagoreans attributed earthquakes to "a mass meeting of the dead" (Thom 1994: 104-5), but the context cited above is closer. Consistent with his antisupernaturalism, Bultmann 1968: 282 regards all these as "pure novelistic motifs."

237. Also recalled in later texts: Pesiq. Rab Kah. 5:9; Ex. Rab. 14:3; Lev. Rab. 6:6; Num. Rab. 15:12; Song Rab. 2:13, §1; Pesiq. R. 17:7; cf. Rev 8:12; 16:10.

238. Already objecting to the Gospel tradition some two decades after the event, one Thallus reportedly attributed the darkness to a coincidental eclipse, which Julius Africanus (ca. 221) disputes (Goguel 1948: 91-92; F. F. Bruce 1980a: 113). The darkness could be local ("the whole land"; Hill 1972: 354 prefers the "whole earth," but all Mediterranean antiquity would have recalled a three-hour worldwide solar eclipse, and no early Christians could have gotten away with fabricating one). An unanticipated solar eclipse for three hours (most last a few minutes at most, like one eclipse for under two minutes in A.D. 29 — Brown 1994: 1041-42) is improbable, but the report suggests that Diaspora Christians were circulating this tradition of the Passion Narrative even before the early 50s.

239. For this view, cf. Ps-Philo 44:6-8; m. 'Abot 1:2, 18; b. Ned. 32a, bar.; b. Sanh. 113b, bar.; p. 'Abod. Zar. 2:1, §1; Ta'an. 4:2, §13; Pesiq. Rab Kah. 19:6; Pes. Rab Kah. Sup. 1:11.

persons at Jesus' death (27:52-53): by refusing to save himself, Jesus *did* save others (27:42). Yet by mentioning only "many" of the saints, Matthew clearly intends this sign merely to prefigure the final resurrection, proleptically signified in Jesus' death and resurrection (Cullmann 1956a: 168).[240] Popular folk religion venerated the tombs of saints (Meyers and Strange 1981: 162), and the very people who sought Jesus' death built those tombs (23:29-32); but Jesus, the holiest saint of all, had power to raise them.[241] Appearances of shades of the dead at night (Ovid *Metam.* 15.797) functioned as portents like earthquakes (15.798) that could terrify Romans; but Matthew is clear that these are not merely apparitions of the dead, but actual resuscitations prefiguring the eschatological resurrection at Jesus' return. Signs "in the city" would be especially terrifying (2 Macc 5:2, 4). Like the resuscitations, the earthquake likely has proleptic eschatological significance (1 Enoch 1:6-8; 2 Bar. 27:7; 70:8; 4 Ezra 6:13-15; 9:3; Rev 6:12; cf. Bauckham 1977), as well as connecting the cosmic implications of Jesus' death with those of the resurrection triumph in the context of the earthquake in 28:2.[242]

The rending of the veil, however, already appears in Mark, probably admitted because it is a "hidden" sign (more public in later tradition such as, e.g., Sib. Or. 8.305). Scholars dispute whether the rending of the veil refers to the inner (cf. Ex 26:33) or outer[243] (cf. Lane 1974a: 574-75; Blomberg 1992a: 421) veil of the temple; if the former (as I prefer, given theological capital possibly drawn from it in early Christian tradition — Heb 6:19-20; 9:3; 10:19-20),[244] the rending would have occurred at the time of the evening sacrifice (27:45-46), when it would be obvious to the attending priests (Edersheim: 614). In either case, the rending could symbolize the departure of God's presence that preceded God's judgment against the temple.[245] Perhaps the old veil was "rent" because

240. While affirming the historical core of the signs tradition (1995: 750), Hagner 1995: 851 thinks that the resucitation of the saints makes better theological than historical sense. He suggests that the tradition may have stemmed from some tombs in the area opened by the earthquake.

241. The Messiah apparently leads white-robed, resurrected saints into Jerusalem in the Dura Europos synagogue panel on Ezekiel (Grassi 1965a: 163; cf. also the earthquake in that scene; cf. Ezek 37).

242. Some patristic and later interpreters reported these two earthquakes as if they were one (see Swart 1993). For adding earthquakes, cf. Jos. *Ant.* 6.27 (though cf. the list of Jerusalem tremors in Amiran, Arieh, and Turcotte 1994).

243. Though the outer veil appears in postbiblical sources (see the evidence in Faber van der Meulen 1985), it surely existed in Herod's temple; but would sources later than the earliest Jerusalem Passion Narrative know this? In my opinion, the specification of *"the"* curtain (27:51) strongly favors the inner curtain, the OT one; the outer curtain was less prominent than the barricade.

244. Mark's interpretation may represent a theophany, the unveiling of the hidden God near the cross; cf. Chronis 1982.

245. As in Ezek 9:3; 10:4-18; cf. 2 Bar. 8:1-2; 64:6; 3 Enoch 5:14; Sifra Qed. pq. 8.205.2.1; par. 4.206.2.6; Sifra Behuq. pq. 6.267.2.6; Sifre Num. 1.10.3; Sifre Deut. 258.2.3; 320.2.1; ARN 34, 38A. For judgment on the temple here in Mark (cf. 13:2; 14:58; 15:29), cf. Hurtado 1983: 257; Kingsbury 1983: 132; Matera 1982: 139; undoubtedly Matthew continues this motif. Daube 1973: 25 seeks a parallel with Elijah, supposing that the rending of the veil responds to the crowd's mockery; but the parallel is not obvious enough to carry much weight.

the new order would not fit it (cf. 9:16 — *schisma*). That the rocks were likewise "rent" (not in Mark) amplifies the impact of the rending (27:51).

Some commentators believe that this description is merely symbolic, perhaps deduced from symbolic comments on fresh access to God. They note that Josephus fails to mention clearly this extraordinary sign (Moule 1965: 127), and that only priests (and a small number of them at that) would be privy to the rending of the veil, which leads one to question how the Passion Narrative's source would *know* what happened (Beare 1981: 536). But some rabbinic sources may report a garbled account of a similar tradition, though the evidence is not clear.[246] Josephus may know a related tradition about a heavy gate to the inner court opening by itself presaging Jerusalem's destruction, though he or his source place it closer to the latter event (Jos. *War* 6.293-96); likewise, the priestly aristocracy would certainly not have publicized a rending of the inner veil at Jesus' death (which they might regard as coincidence — cf. the Sadducean view in Jos. *Ant.* 13.173), but early "leaks" to the Christians unconfirmed by the hierarchy would be possible (Acts 6:7). Modern readers who wish to settle their view of the event's historical probability may need to resort to presuppositions about the possibilities of the miraculous and about the reliability of the Gospel traditions as a whole.

The Gentiles present — Jesus' own brutal executioners — recognize his identity. Whereas his own people had not believed, the supervising centurion[247] and (in Matthew) those with him (presumably the other Gentile soldiers) recognized Jesus' identity the way Peter had some time before (16:16). In contrast to Peter, however, these Gentiles recognize Jesus' Sonship *in* the cross, rather than by ignoring it (16:21-22), all the more remarkable because this defied Gentile models of leadership (20:25).[248] These were among the very men who had beaten him (27:30), providing also an example of repentance (3:2). The Gospel has come full circle: again the religious leaders of Israel have missed the significance of Jesus, whereas the pagans one would expect most hostile to Christ have understood and embraced his true identity (2:1-12). Matthew's message to his

246. Dibelius 1971: 195 cites the tradition that the temple doors miraculously opened forty years before the temple's destruction (Jos. *War* 6.293-96; b. Yoma 39b; p. Yoma 43c; cf. Tac. *Hist.* 5.13), although he thinks the tradition circulated only after 70 (ibid. 195n.3; cf. Carson 1984b: 580; France 1985: 400n.2). Rabbinic legend also laments blood found on the veil after Jerusalem's fall, though these may simply be stains from the Yom Kippur sprinkling (t. Kip. 2:16; cf. m. Yoma 5:4). Perhaps more relevant theologically, as one tore one's clothes on hearing blasphemy or mourning the temple's defilement (m. Sanh. 7:5; cf. b. Moʿed Qaṭ. 25b-26a; p. Moʿed Qaṭ. 3:7, §§7-8; Sanh. 7:6, §7), God rent the veil in response to the blasphemy involved in crucifying his Son (cf. 26:65). Some have also proposed a connection with the rending of heavens in 3:16 (on Mk 1:9-11; 15:38, cf. Motyer 1987).

247. For a centurion supervising even an execution by a swordsman, see, e.g., Sen. *Dial.* 3.18.4.

248. The emphasis on recognition in the cross remains clearer in Mark; Matthew's signs (omitted in Mark) might actually lead a Gentile to recognize Jesus as a son of God (Boring 1995: 160 cites Plut. *Agis and Cleomenes* 39; Suet. *Julius* 88-89).

community is clear: regardless of the response of the Jewish religious leaders, you must evangelize the Gentiles. Jesus is for Israel first (15:26-28), but he does not belong only to their own ethnic community.

Ironically, the Roman centurion, a participant in Jesus' torments, recognizes without prompting what the Sanhedrin had denied: Jesus is God's Son (27:54). Fellow members of Jesus' own ethnic community ridicule Jesus' Sonship (27:40, 43) based on a statement they themselves elicited (26:64); by contrast this Gentile persecutor becomes the first person after Jesus' death to concur with Jesus' identity announced by God in 3:17 and by Peter in 16:16.[249] Matthew's signs offer more reason for this confession than Mark had, but the specific title remains unexpected (apart from hearers' familiarity with the tradition). Whereas a centurion might intend the title in the sense of a divine man (Moule 1965: 128; Lane 1974a: 576; cf. Dan 3:25, where the narrative suggests an angel, Dan 3:28), on the narrative level it fulfills the Son of God motif in both Mark and Matthew.[250] Although less clearly than in Mark, it remains the cross that declares Jesus' Sonship (cf. 4:3; 27:40), as in 8:8-12 the astonishing first confession in the holy land comes from a Gentile centurion,[251] and as in 2:1-12 those who first acknowledge Jesus as King of Israel are those outside God's household. Matthew reinforces this picture by indicating that not only Mark's centurion but apparently the other members of the Gentile execution squad recognized his identity (27:54).

Guardians of Jesus' Body (27:55-66)

Cf. Mk 15:40-47; Lk 23:50-56; Jn 19:38-42. The identities of the actors in this narrative are significant. Because John's disciples took great risk and buried their teacher (14:12), the reader may expect at least as much courage from Jesus' disciples here (Rhoads and Michie 1982: 133). But Jesus' disciples disappoint us, leaving the task to characters readers would not anticipate apart from having heard the story before.[252]

249. "Truly" echoes 14:33 (which Matthew may have derived from the parallel to this text in Mk 15:39); "this was" derives from Mark ("this man was") but on the Matthean level echoes Matthean redaction in 3:17; 27:37. Sim 1993 ingeniously suggests that the soldiers' "confession" is actually only a recognition of their own sin and defeat, anticipating sorrow at the day of judgment; but this proposal misses the greater emphasis on the Gentile mission in Matthew.

250. In Mark, it sends the same message as the rent veil, ending the messianic secret (F. F. Bruce 1972a: 21) and climaxing Mark's probable christological introduction (1:1; F. F. Bruce 1980a: 45), associating Sonship with the cross. "Son" is not articular but (whatever the centurion's intention) the evangelists hardly mean it in a watered-down pagan sense (Martin 1972: 131; Bratcher 1956); predicate nominatives often lacked definite articles (Metzger 1952: 125; in Diognetus, cf. Meecham 1952), though one wishing to *emphasize* the article would include it (Harner 1973: 87).

251. The centurion in Mk 15:39 points to the conversion of Gentile Christians (Stock 1978).

252. The centrality of the women and the guards closely connects this passage with the resurrection narrative in 28:1-15 (see Reeves 1993: 11).

First, whereas the male disciples feared for their lives and were nowhere to be found, the women followed all the way to the tomb. In that culture women were relegated to a marginal role in discipleship at best, and not permitted to be disciples of rabbis (cf. Swidler 1976: 97-111; Keener 1992: 83-84; Gnilka 1997: 179); but these women had followed Jesus as disciples in whatever ways they could (the rabbis and Matthew both applied "follow" to discipleship — cf. Davies 1966b: 134-35), even ways that would have appeared scandalous in that culture (27:55; cf. Stanton 1989a: 202; Stambaugh and Balch 1986: 104).[253] Their "ministry" to Jesus' needs (27:55) probably largely followed the roles assigned their gender and social rank in their culture (8:15), but this narrative evaluates and bestows honor on the basis of their courage and faithfulness rather than their social prominence.[254]

This potential for scandal militates against the invention of this tradition by later Christians (Witherington 1984: 117; Sanders 1993: 109); multiple attestation also supports the tradition (Mk 15:40; Lk 8:1-3; Jn 19:25).[255] The situation is also historically likely: the culture allowed family members to gather around the person being crucified (Lane 1974a: 576, citing t. Giṭ. 7:1; p. Giṭ. 48c; Witherington 1984: 94, 187n.103; cf. also Sifre Deut. 308.2.1; pace Barrett 1978: 551), and women were granted greater latitude in mourning (Soph. *Ajax* 580; Eurip. *Madness of Heracles* 536; *Medea* 928; Livy 26.9.7; Diod. Sic. 17.37.3; Dion. Hal. 7.67.2; 8.39.1; Jos. *Ant.* 4.320; Pomeroy 1975: 44; Dupont 1992: 115). Finally, although some rulers executed women under extreme circumstances, such punishment was rare,[256] and women, unlike men, would not be

253. Cf. Liefeld 1967: 240: "A preacher who enjoyed the association of women was thus open to suspicion and criticism" (cf. Iren. *Haer.* 1.13.1, 3; 1.23.2.4; Lucian *Runaways* 18, on pp. 239-41). Perhaps because of their weaker ties to the established social order, women were often thought more susceptible to various religious movements (e.g., Dion. Hal. 8.39.1; Juv. *Sat.* 6.540-50); Greek culture also provided them more participation in the religious sphere (Gould 1980: 50). Women could support religious movements as patrons (cf., e.g., Pomeroy 1975: 200-201; Gardner 1986: 239-40; perhaps *CIJ* 1:384, §523; 2:10, §741; 2:20, §756); but their support tended to reflect negatively on those movements among their critics, including with early Pharisaism (Sanders 1993: 109; Ilan 1995).

254. Strength and courage were typically masculine traits (Hom. *Il.* 20.251-551; Phaedrus 4.17.6). Ancient texts regularly praise women's courage when it appears (e.g., Appian *R.H.* 2.5.3), but usually remark on how unusual it is (4 Macc 15:30; Arist. *Pol.* 3.2.10, 1277b; Dion. Hal. 4.82.3; 6.92.6; Diod. Sic. 5.32.2; 10.24.2; Livy 2.13.6; 28.19.13; Appian *R.H.* 7.5.29), or depict women's courage as "manliness" (2 Macc 7:21; 4 Macc 15:23; 16:14; Diod. Sic. 17.77.1; 32.10.9; Apul. *Metam.* 5.22); conversely, cowardly men were taunted as "women" (Hom. *Il.* 7.96; 8.163; 11.389; 16.7-8; Virg. *Aen.* 9.617; 12.52-53; Dion. Hal. 9.7.2; 10.28.3; Diod. Sic. 12.16.1; 34/35.2.22; Aul. Gel. 17.21.33; cf. Hom. *Il.* 22.124-25; Aristoph. *Lysistr.* 98). "Courage" is literally "manliness" (e.g., 1 Macc 2:64; Arist. *E.E.* 3.1.2-4, 1228ab; Dio Cassius *R.H.* 58.4.6; Diod. Sic. 17.45.6; 40.3.6; Theon *Progymn.* 9.22; Crates *Ep.* 19; Char. *Chaer.* 7.1.8). On women as economic patrons (as here), see note above.

255. Wire 1991 suggests that women were marginalized even in Matthew's "scribal" community, but Perkins 1991 responds that Matthew's community may not be wholly scribal, and objects to Wire's use of Chinese examples to interpret Pharisaic/Matthean scribalism.

256. The rabbis allow it in theory (e.g., m. Sanh. 6:3), but one incident proved so noteworthy that it recurs, in legendary form, in many later texts (e.g., Sifre Deut. 221.1.1; p. Sanh. 6:6, §2). Reported capital charges for women most often involved adultery (Ilan 1996: 159-62). Men were crucified far more frequently (e.g., Diod. Sic. 17.46.4; Jos. *Apion* 2.267).

suspected as disciples and hence potential coconspirators with Jesus (Klausner 1979b: 354).

Yet the special role accorded women among Jesus' disciples,[257] in addition to the loyalty with which they responded to him, is significant. The Gospels note that the women were watching the burial (Mk 15:47); although many tombs existed in the Judean hills, these women must return by themselves early Sunday morning to the same site. This is hardly simply Christian apologetic to cover up the women's ignorance of the site (pace Crossan 1976: 152); immediately after claims of resurrection appearances, others would have checked the tomb. But it does underline the care that was taken to locate the right site, albeit initially for later expressions of mourning. "Salome" (Mk 15:40) may be the name of Zebedee's wife (Mt 27:56); the wife of Alphaeus and mother of James the Less (10:3; 27:56; Mk 15:40, 47) also was part of the group.

Second, Joseph of Arimathea models one of the few wealthy allies of the Jesus movement (27:57).[258] Although Matthew omits mention of Joseph's membership in the Sanhedrin,[259] he mentions that he was "rich" — the sort of people who rarely showed up among Jesus' disciples, especially when pressure became serious (19:24; 26:18). Given early Christian experiences with and feelings toward the Sanhedrin, the invention of a Sanhedrist acting piously toward Jesus (Mk 15:43) is not likely (Brown 1994: 1240; Davies and Allison 1997: 647). Brown is certain that pious Jews, given their views of burial, would not have allowed Jesus to go unburied (1994: 1240; cf. also Davies and Allison 1997: 648). He doubts that Joseph was a disciple (27:57, not noted in Mark), thinking that this is why the women did not cooperate with him in the burial (1994: 1218); but we may well question to what degree the women would have *trusted* a Sanhedrist at this point. Acts 13:29 could suggest burial by hostile leaders, but this may simply represent summary language. The preservation of his name and other details may suggest that Joseph either followed Jesus at this time (as I think more likely) or, as Brown 1994: 1230 thinks, that

257. See, e.g., Witherington 1984; cf. Stanton 1974: 147; Harrington 1985; Borsch 1990; Kopas 1990; Schineller 1992; Knoch 1994.

258. Matthew may connect a righteous Joseph protecting Jesus at the beginning and end of his Gospel (Davies and Allison 1997: 656). But even if Matthew had written his Gospel first and started the tradition about Joseph reported elsewhere in Gospel tradition, one should not think that he derived the name from the Joseph of 1:19–2:23 or that the tradition was borrowed by Joseph from Genesis (50:7-8). "Joseph" was a relatively common Jewish name in the Roman period (e.g., *CPJ* 3.182-83; in a Jerusalem ossuary, *CIJ* 2:281, §1291; see more fully Davies and Allison 1988: 182).

259. Arimathea, from Ramathaim-zophim (1 Sam 1:1), was about 20 miles northwest of Jerusalem (Euseb. *Onomasticon* 32; Lane 1974a: 579); given the proximity, Joseph would certainly have been present at Jerusalem for the whole feast even if still residing in Arimathea; but the expression probably denotes merely his place of origin, allowing him to function in Jerusalem's council. Insufficient information exists to demonstrate whether the high priests would have welcomed him to the trial (Anderson 1976: 350 thinks he belonged only to a local "council," though this was certainly not the impression Mark wished to offer in 15:43), or why he would have preferred this tomb nearer to Jerusalem than to the residence of his ancestors.

Joseph became a disciple later. In Matthew, however, Joseph is already a "disciple," a model to be imitated, one of the few rich men who squeezed through a needle's eye by God's grace (19:24-26). Many people liked generous rich people (Hom. *Il.* 6.12-19; Prov 19:6), but the issue with Joseph is more than generosity. He squeezed through the needle's eye because he risked all his wealth and status to stand with the condemned Jesus — something Jesus' other male disciples failed to do.

Excursus: The Importance of the Burial

If Jesus died at 3 p.m. and Joseph stopped to seek Pilate's permission, perhaps only an hour remained before sundown and the prohibition of work. Although anointing and washing the corpse was permissible even on the Sabbath (m. Shab. 23:5),[260] some other elements of the burial (see Safrai 1974/76b: 776-77 for samples of these) could be conducted only in the most preliminary manner for the moment, though undoubtedly hastened considerably through the agency of Joseph's servants. One could not move the corpse or its members on the Sabbath (m. Shab. 23:5). In a Jewish setting, linen shrouds were part of honorable burial (Mt 27:59; Finegan 1969: 213), specifically for the righteous (Test. Abr. 20A; Life of Adam 48.1; Apoc. Mos. 40.1-3; b. Ber. 18b; cf. white wrappings in Ps-Philo 64:6; Gen. Rab. 96:5). Although the plural form of linen strips in John 19:40; 20:7 could tell against the authenticity of the traditional shroud (so Brown 1970: 2:941-42),[261] others have argued that the plural could be idiomatic for "grave clothes" (Thompson 1985: 240).[262] Joseph or his agents had purchased the linen before the Sabbath (Mk 15:46), but the women either purchased or more likely prepared the spices only after the Sabbath (Mk 16:1; Lk 23:56; 24:1; Dalman 1929: 101).[263] (When spices were used they were important, not to preserve

260. Washing the corpse was standard preburial practice in Mediterranean antiquity (e.g., Hom. *Il.* 18.345; 24.582; Virg. *Aen.* 6.219; 9.487; Eurip. *Phoenician Maidens* 1667; Ovid *Metam.* 13.531-32; Apul. *Metam.* 9.30; Acts 9:37), and anointing appears to be frequent as well (e.g., Hom. *Il.* 18.350-51; 24.582; Virg. *Aen.* 6.219; Mart. *Epig.* 3.12; Test. Abr. 20A; for ointments in embalming, Hagner 1995: 758 cites *P. Oxy.* 736.13; Artemidorus 1.5; Gen 50:2 LXX); for incense, e.g., Virg. *Aen.* 6.224-25; Ovid *Metam.* 2.626.

261. Although the radiocarbon dating seems against it (Stanton 1995a: 119-20, noting the three independent carbon 14 tests, each claiming 95% certainty) and the colors are known from medieval artists' pigments (cf. Thompson 1985: 238-43, who surveys both sides), traces of Palestinian plant fibers and early first-century Judean burial customs suggest elements of accurate portrayal in the Shroud of Turin. For a thorough and well-documented survey of scientific data for the latter, as well as scientific evaluations on the contamination of the radiocarbon sample, see Borkan 1995. If the Shroud dates from 1260 to 1390 as the radiocarbon tests suggest, it points to remarkable technology.

262. In 1994: 1264-65, Brown argues that the Synoptics probably think of a single cloth whereas John has multiple wrappings.

263. Taylor believes that the Markan chronology confirms the Johannine tradition here (1952: 601); Jeremias observes that one could buy necessary food for Passover even on the Sabbath, but pay later (Jeremias 1966a: 77; m. Shab. 23:1).

the corpse but to diminish the stench[264] and, in practice, to pay final respects to the deceased.)[265]

Although reports existed of cultures that did not bury (Sext. Emp. *Pyrrh.* 3.226-28), burial was an essential duty both in Jewish (Gen 23:3-20; 50:12-14, 25-26; Sir. 38:16-17; Tob 1:17-20; 2:7-10; 4:3-4; 6:14; 1QM 7.2; Acts 8:2; Jos. *Apion* 2.205, 211; Ps-Phocyl. 99-101) and broader Mediterranean culture (Diod. Sic. 20.84.3; Plut. *Nicias* 6.5-6; Diog. Laert. 6.2.52; Paus. 1.32.5; Char. *Chaer.* 4.1.3; cf. Plut. *Solon* 21.1). Like most of their contemporaries (e.g., Eurip. *Suppliants;* Diod. Sic. 15.35.1),[266] the Jews regarded lack of burial as a horrible fate (Eccl 6:3; Jub. 23:23; Jos. *War* 5.514; Sib. Or. 3.643; Qoh. Rab. 3:2, §2). Burial societies ensured that even poor people would receive proper burial (e.g., *ILS* 7360a; Sherk 1988: 234; Cary and Haarhoff 1946: 151-52; for slaves, cf. Buckland 1908: 74), whereas the rich and well known had elaborate public funerals (Polyb. *R.R.E.* 6.53; Dion. Hal. 6.96.1; Corn. Nep. 10 [Dion], 10.3; Herodian 4.2.2; Apul. *Metam.* 2.27; 1 Macc 2:70; Jos. *Ant.* 9.166; 13.406; Mart. Pol. 17) and other honors (Theon *Progymn.* 9.4-5; cf. Jos. *Ant.* 4.320; b. Shab. 153a; Gen. Rab. 100:2; Qoh. Rab. 7:12, §1; 9:10, §3). Even those considered morally reprehensible normally permitted burials of their enemies (2 Macc 4:49; Jos. *Ant.* 4.264-65); it was honorable behavior (e.g., Hom. *Il.* 7.79, 84, 409-10; Virg. *Aen.* 11.100-7; Livy 38.2.14; Corn. Nep. 18 [Eumenes], 13.4), and sometimes constituted a dead or dying person's final request (Hom. *Il.* 23.65-71; *Od.* 11.71-76; Eurip. *Children of Heracles* 588-90; *Hecuba* 47-50; *Phoenician Maidens* 1447-50).[267] Authorities or very angry enemies might prohibit burial (Hom. *Il.* 17.126-27, 255, 272; Eurip. *Phoenician Maidens* 1627-30; Diod. Sic. 16.16.4; 18.67.6; Dion. Hal. 3.21.8; 4.40.5-6; 6.9.4; 20.16.2; Appian *R.H.* 3.9.3; 12.8.52; 12.16.107; *C.W.* 1.8.73; Herodian 1.13.4-6; 8.8.7; Char. *Chaer.* 1.5.25; 1 Enoch 98:13; 2 Macc 13:7) or public mourning (m. Sanh. 6:6; Eurip. *Phoenician Maidens* 1631-34; cf. Jos. *Ant.* 9.104) in the case of a particularly heinous crime. Still, such occasions were sometimes disputed (cf. Soph. *Ajax* 1130-41; *Antig.* 21-30, 43-48),

264. Weeden doubts that women would seek to anoint a corpse decomposing this long (1971: 104), but see Craig 1981: 184: "In point of fact, Jerusalem, being 700 meters above sea level, can be quite cool in April" (cf. also Jn 18:18); the body remained in the tomb only a day and two nights, and "a rock-hewn tomb in a cliff side would stay naturally cool"; *perhaps* some aromatic spices had already been left with the body as well.

265. Spices would diminish the stench and could be sprinkled on the bier or burned during the funeral procession (Meyers and Strange 1981: 97-98), but they were not used as preservatives. Jewish burials in this period did not seek to preserve the corpse; rather, they expected the flesh to rot off the bones for one year, after which the person responsible would inter the corpse in an ossuary (cf. m. Sanh. 6:6; m. Pesaḥ. 8:8; Mo'ed Qat. 1:5; Meyers and Strange 1981: 28). For the use of spices at funerals, see Jos. *Ant.* 17.199; *War* 1.673; m. Ber. 8:6; Safrai 1974/76b: 776; among Gentiles, Herodian 4.2.8.

266. Many Greek philosophers constituted notable exceptions (Epict. *Disc.* 4.7.31; Diog. Laert. 6.2.79; Stowers 1986: 142-43), though even their own disciples often disobeyed their instructions (Socratics *Ep.* 14; Diog. Laert. 6.2.78).

267. In pagan thought, the dead could not enter Hades without burial (Hom. *Il.* 23.71; Virg. *Aen.* 6.365-66; cf. Lucan *C.W.* 1.11), and some thought unburied corpses more susceptible to abuse by witches (Lucan *C.W.* 6.626).

prohibitions were not always permanent (fragments of the bodies in Lucan *C.W.* 2.166-68; 2 Sam 21:13), those who could not be buried by free persons when executed for treason could be buried by slaves (Corn. Nep. 19 [Phocion], 4.4), in practice some Roman leaders might grant burial even to enemies (Appian *R.H.* 12.9.60), and, most widely attested, withholding burial was viewed as impious (e.g., Hom. *Il.* 24.22-137; Soph. *Ajax* 1326-69; *Antig.* 278-79, 450-55, 692-95, 1348-53; Eurip. *Suppliants* 19; Lucan *C.W.* 7.809-11).

The Romans normally preferred having the bodies of condemned criminals rot on crosses (Petron. *Sat.* 112; Brown 1994: 962, 1208 cites also Phaedrus *Fables of Aesop,* Perotti's Appendix 15.9; Hor. *Epodes* 1.16.48), but Jewish custom prohibited this final indignity, demanding burial even for the condemned by sunset (Deut 21:23; Jos. *War* 4.317; see further Safrai 1974/76b: 774). The Jewish people may ordinarily have buried condemned criminals in a common grave reserved for that purpose (cf. m. Sanh. 6:5; t. Sanh. 9:8; Daube 1973: 311; Daube 1956: 342; elsewhere, e.g., Corn. Nep. 4 [Pausanias], 5.5), a purposely shameful burial (especially if a Jewish court rather than a Roman one rendered the verdict — cf. Jos. *Ant.* 5.44; b. Sanh. 47b).[268] Although Roman custom in this period officially prohibited burying the executed (Tac. *Ann.* 6.29; cf. Petron. *Sat.* 112), the Romans sometimes surrendered the corpse to friends or relatives who sought permission to bury them (Philo *Flacc.* 83-84; Taylor 1952: 600; Lane 1974a: 578 also cites Cic. *Orationes Philippicae* 2.7.17; Plut. *Antonius* 2).[269] Pilate would hardly cooperate with Jesus' accusers (historically likely, as we noted above, because consistent with the way matters were handled in the provinces), then suddenly defy the religious scruples of his subjects, which Pilate had previously learned the hard way could be intense (Jos. *Ant.* 18.59). Governors usually seem to have accommodated Jewish requests for the body, exceptions being noteworthy (Philo *Flacc.* 83-84; Gnilka 1997: 314). But unless Joseph already held special favor before Pilate (cf. Jos. *Life* 420-21), which is unlikely, *only a courageous ally would identify himself before the governor as "friend" or patron of one condemned for conspiracy against Rome* (cf. Chrys. *Matthew,* Homily 88; *ACCS,* 238; cf. also Brown 1994: 1217).[270]

268. If the Mishnah reflects general first-century Jewish practice here, Jewish courts granted criminals obscure burials in a common place, but then expected the gathering of the bones to the place of one's ancestors a year later (m. Sanh. 6:6), meaning that the bones were kept track of even in the common place, not scattered (Brown 1994: 1209-11). Dishonorable burial was burial nonetheless (Jos. *Ant.* 4.202, 265).

269. Brown 1994: 1207-8 shows that Justin. *Dig.* 48.24 reports Roman law as early as Augustus allowing relatives to bury the corpse, but refusing it for *maiestas* (treason); but he rightly observes that magistrates made these decisions themselves in the provinces (cf. Cic. *Verr.* 2.5.45, §119; Philo *Flacc.* 83-84). Brown doubts that Pilate would hand over the corpse if he admits the charge of *maiestas,* which he may not personally do (1208-9). The Jewish officials would probably not object to the burial, however (unlike later in Mart. Pol. 17.2; but even then bones might be handed over — Mart. Pol. 18.1-2), and without opposition Pilate was free to act as he pleased. He had settled matters adequately for the chief priests.

270. Burying the dead despite prohibitions against this practice (Eurip. *Suppliants;* Demosth. *Or.* 60, *Funeral Speech* 8; Tob 1:17-20; 2:8) or in the face of danger (Dio Cassius *R.H.* 57.18.1) functions as a model of courage in ancient texts.

To be sure, one might expect Joseph's status, like the women's gender, to afford him some protection; but from an aristocratic perspective, social prominence could invite closer scrutiny and hostility (Phaedrus 2.7.14-15; 3.5.1; 4.6.11-13; Babrius 4.6-8; 31.23-24; 64.10-11; Corn. Nep. 1 [Miltiades], 7.5-6; 2 [Themistocles], 8.1-7; 3 [Aristides], 1.1-5; 7 [Alcibiades], 4.1-2; 12 [Chabrias], 3.3; 19 [Phocion], 4.3). In any case, being associated with one condemned for treason was a dangerous matter (e.g., Herodian 1.13.6; 3.5.6; 4.6.1); though Pilate would not view Jesus as a major political threat, Joseph could not be sure of this in advance, and much of Matthew's audience may not have known governors' leniency toward Sanhedrists' requests. Thus the tradition prefers Joseph's devotion at this point to that of the long-term disciples, though perhaps Joseph's status (like the women's gender) would in the end render him less vulnerable to retaliation. That Jesus was buried is also attested in pre-Pauline tradition known to Paul's readers in his own and other congregations (Rom 6:4; 1 Cor 15:4). A tradition that admitted Jesus' execution as a public enemy had no reason to invent for him a burial to remove shame, and had it invented one it might have invented more time for greater honors.

Only Matthew explicitly notes the use of Joseph's own family tomb, fulfilling Isaiah 53:12, but the tradition behind Mark 15:46 probably presupposes it (pace Brown 1994: 1252); how else would Joseph acquire a tomb so quickly? To bury Jesus in his own tomb (27:60) fits the situation of haste and location, but also suggests a special love normally reserved for family members or those equally esteemed (cf. 1 Kings 13:30-31). Further, archaeological evidence for the tombs in this area may suggest that the tomb belonged to a person of some material substance (Craig 1995: 148). The "newness" of the tomb (27:60; b. Sanh. 47b) may suggest that wealth had come into his family only in his own generation, or that rising prominence had led him to move closer to Jerusalem from another home.[271]

The earliest Christians preserved the accurate site of the tomb. Most Judean burial sites were private family tombs scattered around Jerusalem and elsewhere (Safrai 1974/76b: 779-80). Often these were caves with an opening covered by a large stone rolled in a groove; such stones could not be removed from within (Reicke 1974: 187; Yamauchi 1972: 112; Anderson 1976: 351; cf. m. ʿErub. 1:7; Nazir 7:3; Ohol. 2:4). Indeed, such stones would be cumbersome to move from the outside; people generally moved them only for reburials or new burials (Thompson 1962: 318; cf. examples in Josephus 1982: 283, 393). Because Joseph was well-to-do he probably owned a more ornate tomb, whose disk-shaped stone would be too large (a yard in diameter) for a single man to

271. A rock-hewn tomb might be particularly expensive (Hagner 1995: 858 cites Is 22:16 LXX). As noted above (Excursus on the burial), extravagant burials were reserved for the most noble and wealthy. For historical data on Jesus' burial, see in greater detail Green 1992a.

move even from outside (Thompson 1962: 318-19; Lane 1974a: 581). The practice of secondary burial — in which the corpse rots in an antechamber in the tomb for a year, then the bones are gathered in a box slid into a niche in the wall — is a largely first-century custom.[272] Such burial involved no shoveling of dirt as today, and often no coffin (Meyers and Strange 1981: 98; Safrai 1974/76b: 780-81, 786; Carmon 1973: 121).[273]

That Jesus' followers would forget the site of the tomb (or that officials who held the body would not think it worth the trouble to produce it after the postresurrection Jesus movement arose) is extremely improbable. James and the Jerusalem church could easily have preserved the tradition of the site in following decades (Brown 1994: 1280-81), especially given Middle Eastern traditions of pilgrimage to holy sites (though admittedly evidence for early veneration there is lacking, perhaps because the body was not there — Craig 1995: 148-49, 152). The traditional Protestant "Garden Tomb" is a much later tomb and cannot represent the site of Jesus' burial;[274] by contrast, the Catholic Holy Sepulchre and tombs in its vicinity date to the right period.[275] The tradition of the latter vicinity is as early as the second century (when Hadrian erected a pagan temple there; he defiled many Jewish holy sites in this manner — cf. Finegan 1969: 164), and probably earlier. Good evidence exists, in fact, that this site dates to within the first two decades after the resurrection. This is because (1) Christian tradition is unanimous that Jesus was buried outside the city walls, and no one would make up a site inside (cf. Heb 13:12; Jn 19:41); (2) Jewish custom made it common knowledge that burials would be outside the city walls (4 Bar. 7:13; Wilkinson 1978: 146); (3) the traditional vicinity of the Holy Sepulcher is *inside* Jerusalem's walls; (4) Agrippa I expanded the walls of Jerusalem sometime in the 40s A.D.[276]

272. Hachlili 1980: 239; Hachlili and Killebrew 1983a suggest a window perhaps as narrow as A.D. 10-70 (cf. p. Mo'ed Qaṭ. 1:5, §§4-5). But some evidence suggests a less significant use for more than a century later (Goodenough 1953: 1:114; cf. Rahmani 1982; idem 1986). For Jewish loculi in Rome, cf. Leon 1960: 59.

273. That he was buried fits the culture as well as pre-Pauline tradition (1 Cor 15:4). It is quite difficult to account for the view attributed to Crossan (respected cochairman of the Jesus Seminar) by Ostling 1994 as cited in Craig 1995: 142, namely, that Jesus' corpse was merely covered with a little dirt and probably eaten by wild dogs, a view that not only runs counter to the consensus of scholarship (no crime in itself) but appears to reflect inadequate familiarity with Jewish burial customs of the period. Even among Greeks, it could seem unthinkable that one would not at least have provided mass graves to enemies slain in battle (Paus. 1.32.5); dogs and birds normally ate the unburied (Hom. *Il.* 22.42-43, 71-76, 335-39, 353; 23:21; 24:211, 411; *Od.* 21.363-64; 22.476; Soph. *Antig.* 697; Eurip. *Phoenician Maidens* 1650; Virg. *Aen.* 9.485; Lucan *C.W.* 7.825-35; 2 Sam 21:10; in a crucifixion, see Llewelyn 1998: 1-3, §1), but as I have noted, even among pagans public sympathy often favored burial and Jews would require it.

274. Tomb architecture changed radically after Jerusalem's fall (Goodenough 1953: 1:84-89), and the Protestant site's skull shape postdates the first century (Brown 1994: 938-39).

275. On the latter, see Brown 1970: 899; idem 1994: 1279-83; cf. Blinzler 1959: 251-52; Smith 1967; Ross 1976; Riesner 1985.

276. See, e.g., Brown 1994: 1282; cf. Blinzler 1959: 251-52; for archaeological data, see the notes in Josephus 1982: 338-40, on Jos. *War* 5.148-55.

In contrast to the women and Joseph, the other participants in the tomb narrative have quite different motives: they want Jesus to stay buried lest his promises to reign stir hope. They want the whole Jesus movement to stay buried in the tomb (27:62-66).[277] This paragraph inaugurates a contrast between the alleged deceitfulness of Jesus (27:63) and of his disciples (27:64) and, not long after, the actual deceitfulness of his enemies (28:13-15; cf. Gundry 1982: 582; Mt 24:4; on the possible relation to a charge before the Sanhedrin of being a "misleader," see Stauffer 1960: 230). Most early Christians, presumably frustrated with the power structures of their day, would likely have resonated with the portrait of the authorities wielding raw power. But while the religious leaders appear to have the power of life and death, the following resurrection narrative (and story line already known to Matthew's implied audience) reveals that God's power subverts the apparent power of such human initiative (see Weaver 1992: 399).

But the primary focus of this paragraph and its conclusion in 28:11-15 is the incontrovertible evidence Matthew apparently wishes to present for Jesus' resurrection. Sealing the stone (27:66) made it impossible for anyone to enter the tomb while the guards slept and then replace the stone (cf. Dan 6:17; Filson 1960: 299). Although Jesus has already left the tomb, the stone is first removed at 28:2. Because Matthew would hardly create a charge that did not exist, we may be sure that the primary polemic against the Christian claim concerning Jesus' resurrection was theft of the body (cf. Craig 1984; Meier 1980: 356).

Some think that Matthew's response about the guards is a Christian invention to counter that story (Schweizer 1975: 519);[278] while this proposal is possible (would the authorities have taken Jesus' promises to reign more seriously than the disciples did?), it is also possible that the sources that betrayed information about Jesus' trials and perhaps about the temple veil would have had inside information about the guards. If Pilate did grant the priests a small contingent of guards, probably a *quaternion* (cf. Acts 12:4; Lake and Cadbury 1979: 134),[279] Joseph of Arimathea would surely have learned of it and reported the incident. At the same time, if the charge of disciples stealing the body to which Matthew responds included the claim of the guards' witness (and the story would have more credibility if it claimed witnesses), the early Christians would not have needed "inside information." Based on firsthand knowledge of their own inno-

277. That they call Pilate "Lord" or "Sir" (26:63) is to be expected, but the contrast between this title that suppliants apply to Jesus (e.g., 8:2, 6, 8, 21) and their portrait of Jesus as a deceiver (27:63-64) may also sustain the conviction that many Judeans after 70 might share, that the priestly aristocracy were too beholden to the Romans.

278. The opposite suggestion of France 1985: 409, that a fiction created too long after the event for anyone to refute it would have little apologetic value, is equally weak.

279. The chief priests would not need Pilate's approval merely to station their own guards (Gundry 1982: 584; France 1985: 405; cf. Brown 1994: 1295). Using Roman guards rather than their own would leave the Jewish authorities less open to the charge of tampering with evidence; for Matthew, this conveniently provides another example of collaboration between the Jerusalem authorities who opposed Jesus and the Romans.

cence and the resurrection appearances, as well as their acquaintance with high-priestly treachery in conjunction with Judas's betrayal, they could have reconstructed a basic account similar to the one Matthew preserves. The other Gospels could have suppressed the negative witness just as easily as Matthew could have created it. Officials would have posted guards to prevent theft of the corpse, as the story declares, rather than because they feared Jesus might reign and wished to detain him in the tomb!

Brown 1994: 1311 regards as a particularly strong argument against the historicity of the guards that the women could not hope to enter the tomb. But first of all, we cannot be certain that the guards would have prevented the women from paying respects to the body; after all, the guards were there to prevent theft and would hardly suspect these women of stealing the body under their noses. Perhaps they might even help in removing the stone (the real problem for access — Mk 16:3), which the women could not do by themselves; men generally treated women more gently than they treated other men (see comment on 20:20-28; the opening paragraphs under 27:55-66). Second and more important, however, the narrative's own logic counters this argument. If the guards were posted on the Sabbath as the narrative indicates (perhaps to indict the Sanhedrin's selective piety again — cf. 27:4-6), the women did not know that the guards were there.[280]

The Report of the Women (28:1-10)

Cf. Mk 16:1-8; Lk 24:1-12; Jn 20:1-18; Mk 16:9-11. The various resurrection narratives vary considerably in length, focus, and detail. If Q included a resurrection narrative, most of the Gospel writers treated it as one among many; given the many witnesses of the risen Christ (1 Cor 15:6), it is hardly surprising that numerous accounts would exist and different Gospel writers would draw on different accounts. The four Gospels differ in detail, but in all four the women become the first witnesses, and Mary Magdalene is explicitly named as one witness among them (also Gos. Pet. 12:50–13:57). Sanders 1993: 280 may be right to argue that "a calculated deception should have produced greater unanimity. Instead, there seem to have been *competitors:* 'I saw him first!' 'No! I did.'" But the divergent details suggest independent traditions, thereby underlining the likelihood of details the accounts share in common (e.g., Boyd 1995: 277-78). This fits what we should expect of eyewitness traditions. (Thus, for example, though two eyewitnesses who accompanied Alexander agreed that Callisthenes was in-

280. Brown 1994: 1301-10 contends for a pre-Matthean popular story about the guards that Matthew has interwoven with the story of the women at the tomb; he believes that the Gospel of Peter, which uses the same story, includes more oral development. Meier 1991a: 117 finds in Gos. Peter 30 the same phrase as in Mt 27:64b and notes that "disciple" is particularly Matthean (73 times in Matthew; 2 times in the Gospel of Peter; not at all in Crossan's supposed Cross Gospel) — strongly suggesting the Gospel of Peter's direct dependence on Matthew here.

dicted, publicly scorned, and died, and though their accounts could be called entirely trustworthy [*pany pistoi*], they differ even on whether he died by sickness or hanging — Arrian *Alex.* 4.14.3. The variation in the Gospel accounts is far less significant than this.)

The variation in length of the Gospels' resurrection narratives (Lk 24 is long though recapitulated briefly in Acts 1; Mt 28 is quite brief) may represent the desire to make optimum use of scroll length rather than leaving a blank space at the end (as sometimes happened — Diog. Laert. 6.2.38). Josephus once seems caught unexpectedly by the end of his scroll (Jos. *Apion* 1.320); Matthew, approaching the length limit of his standardized scroll (see the Introduction), may hasten to his conclusion. He surveys the testimony of the women (28:1-10), the testimony of the guards (28:11-15), and finally the testimony of the church (28:16-20) related to that of the women.

The Gospel narratives agree that the revelation of Christ's resurrection began on the first day of the week, after the Sabbath (Mt 28:1; Mk 16:1; Lk 24:1; Jn 20:1; cf. 20:19, 26). Especially in Mark and Matthew, this language makes it clear that the earliest Christians regarded Sunday as a special day celebrating the resurrection (cf. Acts 20:7; 1 Cor 16:2; Justin *1 Apol.* 67; Iren. frg. 7), perhaps even "the Lord's day" (cf. Rev 1:10; Did. 14.1; Vanni 1978; but note Strand 1967; Lewis 1968), but *not* as a new Sabbath (this developed in the second century and later; cf. Ign. *Magn.* 9.1; Barn. 15.8-9; Chadwick 1967: 128; Bacchiocchi 1977), which among the earliest Jewish Christians remained on the last day of the week. The tradition is too early to be influenced by Mithraism (pace Cary and Haarhoff 1946: 344), which did not spread widely in the Roman world until the next century (Grant 1986: 40-41);[281] this simply was the day Jesus' followers found the empty tomb, the day after the Sabbath. Sunday became the "Lord's Day" because of the discovery of the empty tomb rather than the reverse.

First, the narrative demonstrates that those of whom society thinks the least are often those whom God sends with his message. Not all testimony was regarded as being of equal merit; the trustworthiness of witnesses was considered essential (CD 9.21-22; 10.1). Most of Jesus' Jewish contemporaries held little esteem for the testimony of women;[282] this reflects a broader Mediterra-

281. It already existed in other areas, such as the northern coast of the Black Sea (Blawatsky and Kochelenko 1966) or farther to the east (cf. Cumont 1975; Francis 1975); it later spread widely in the Roman army (Daniels 1975; Gager 1975: 134; Serban and Baluta 1979; Koester 1982: 1:372-74; Burkert 1987: 7, 42), but even then it remained limited to particular parts of the Empire (Frank 1932: 49-50; Nock 1937: 113; Daniels 1975: 273; Bianchi 1979: 879).

282. See, e.g., Jos. *Ant.* 4.219; m. Yebam. 15:1, 8-10; 16:7; Ketub. 1:6-9; t. Yebam. 14:10; Sifra V. D. Deho. pq. 7.45.1.1; cf. Lk 24:11; Keener 1992: 162-63; Baumgarten 1957; Hooker 1983: 119. Some, though not all, condemned listening to women more generally (e.g., Jos. *Ant.* 18.255; Syr. Men. Sent. 118-21, 336-39; Maccini 1996: 63-97 rightly notes that the responses are more diverse than in legal contexts). Ilan 1996: 227 thinks that in practice the non-Pharisaic legal system "often" required women's witness; even if this is overstated, women could testify concerning various matters, and some views of 1QSa 1.10-11 suggest that Qumran was more open to the practice than the Pharisees were (Ilan 1996: 163-66).

nean limited trust of women's speech and testimony also enshrined in Roman law.[283] By contrast, the guards' report that the disciples had stolen the body (28:11-15) might command much greater respect then,[284] and in an antisupernaturalistic culture like much of modern academia as well. Indeed, even the disciples in the late tradition in Mark 16:11 did not believe the women — a tradition that may reflect historical reality at this point (Vermes 1973: 40-41; cf. Ps-Philo 9:10). For the early Christians, neither the empty tomb nor the testimony of the women was adequate evidence by itself (cf. Lk 24:22-24); they also depended on the testimony of men for the public forum (1 Cor 15:5-8; cf. Stauffer 1960: 151; Dunn 1975: 126).[285] No one had apologetic reason to invent the testimony of these women, but the Gospel writers may have a profound theological purpose in preserving it.

Matthew lays these two reports, the true and the false, side by side, forcing his audience to declare their choice. The testimony of the women thus becomes a model for the disciples who will follow them (28:16-20). Jesus commissions them as his *shaliaḥim* — agents or apostled ones (see comment on 10:5) — to bring news of his resurrection to his own disciples. Their faithfulness, like Joseph's (27:55-61), is laid over against the authorities' deceitful accusation of deceit (27:62-66); Matthew thereby calls his audience to suffer rejection and dishonor at the hands of the hostile authorities of their own day.[286] In ancient literature, one woman's wrong behavior could be held against her gender (Hom. *Od.* 11.432-34, 436-39, even though Clytemnestra also slew Cassandra in 11.422; Eurip. *Orestes* 1153-54);[287] likewise, a woman's prowess or courage could shame men into acts of valor (Virg. *Aen.* 11.734; Ovid *Metam.* 8.380-89, 392, 401-2), though they might also allow the woman's honor (Virg. *Aen.* 11.846-47; Ovid *Metam.* 8.425-27). Such examples

283. Hesiod *W.D.* 375; Livy 6.34.6-7; Babrius 16.10; Phaedrus 4.15; Avianus *Fables* 15-16; Justin. *Inst.* 2.10.6 (though contrast the earlier Gaius *Inst.* 2.105); Plut. *Publicola* 8.4; Gardner 1986: 165; Kee 1980: 89. Many men regarded women as gullible (cf. Philo *Prob.* 117; Juv. *Sat.* 1.38-39).

284. Corpses were used for magic (Lewis 1983: 96), and people suspected that witches sometimes stole bodies for magic (see especially the tale of Telephron in Apul. *Metam.* bk. 2; in other cultures, e.g., Mbiti 1970: 261); corpses that died violent deaths were considered particularly potent for magic (*PGM* 1.248-49; 2.49-50; 4.342-43, 1390-95, 1402-3, 2211-17; 57.5-6; 58.5-9; 67.21; 101.1-3; Ap. Rhod. 4.51-53; Lucan *C.W.* 6.538-68). If Jesus' enemies considered him a magician (12:24), some Jewish leaders may even have anticipated the theft of the body as in 27:64. In less severe cases, tombs generally settled for divine threats against robbers (e.g., *IG* 3.1417 in Grant 1953: 9). Both tying rope from a cross (Pliny *N.H.* 28.11.46) and iron that had been pounded through the hands (Lucan *C.W.* 6.545-47) were used in witchcraft (as a superstitious cure in m. Shab. 6:10).

285. Dunn also notes the tradition that stresses Peter first (1 Cor 15:5; cf. Lk 24:34), which Farmer and Kereszty 46 regard as a pro-Petrine tradition.

286. The sudden reintroduction of Pharisees in Matthean material charging Jesus as a "deceiver" (27:62-64) undoubtedly fits a charge of Matthew's time (Stanton 1993: 178-79). Their knowledge of his resurrection claim presumably alludes to 12:40 (likewise involving Matthean redaction; see Stanton 1993: 82).

287. The subtext of the *Iliad,* probably the most widely circulated literary work in the ancient Mediterranean, was that male warriors were fighting because of women, such as Helen and Briseis; cf. especially *Il.* 9.339-42.

suggest that ancient readers generally noticed the gender of heroes when they were female; it is thus not unreasonable to suppose that Matthew expects the positive performance of these women to reflect favorably on their gender. But more importantly, as female examples could provoke both women and men, the women in Matthew's narrative function as a model for disciples, male or female.

Although Matthew is less explicit than Mark about unfinished business in the burial (Mk 16:1), the approach of the Sabbath with sundown (Mt 27:57)[288] and the return of the women after the Sabbath had ended Saturday at sundown and Sunday's morning light had come suggest that this was the purpose for which the women came in the first Gospel as well.[289] (Gundry 1982: 585-86 thinks that the women in Matthew arrive Saturday evening, but against this interpretation, *epiphōskō* in Mt 28:1 means "grow toward dawn.") Jewish custom permitted women to attend to corpses of either gender, although men could not tend women's corpses, and women were often permitted to engage in such preparatory burial rituals (for comparison with the Greek world, see Abrahamsen 1986: 121-22).

Second, the narrative reveals God's power (28:2-3). The angelic revelation exhibits points of contact with biblical theophanies. The description of glory recalls Jesus' own in 17:2 (cf. Dan 7:9; 10:5-6). In 4 Ezra, the heavenly Zion (10:25-27) has a countenance that flashes "like lightning" (10:25) and at its voice the earth quakes (10:26). Elsewhere, lightnings flash from the fiery face of a mighty angel and earthquakes accompany him (3 Enoch 22:9). (On such appearances see comment on 17:6-8.)[290]

The white clothes could allude to a variety of functions. Priests generally wore linen, including Egyptian priests (Appian *C.W.* 4.6.47; Plut. *Isis* 3-4, *Mor.* 352C; Apul. *Metam.* 11.10, 23; Lewis 1983: 92), those at the temple of Artemis (Acts of Jn 38), and Jewish priests (Jos. *War* 5.229; Pesiq. R. 33:10; Yadin 1962: 219). Worshipers wore white or linen in other worship settings (Eurip. *Bacch.* 112; Paus. 2.35.5; 6.20.3; Diog. Laert. 8.1.33; *SEG* 11.923 in Sherk 1988: 58; Ramsay 1904a: 386; cf. the change of garments in Olmstead 1959: 511), including the Jerusalem temple (Jos. *War* 2.1; *Ant.* 11.327; Safrai 1974/76d: 877) and that of the Therapeutae during worship (Philo *Cont.* 66). A philosopher like Pythagoras might wear white wool (replaced in later times with linen — Diog.

288. Lachs 1987: 436 notes that "evening" can mean "about evening" and that burial on the day of death was essential (b. Mo'ed Qat. 28a; Sifre Deut. 221).

289. Noting the tradition in Semahot 8:1, Longstaff 1981 suggests that relatives often observed the tomb for three days to be sure the person was genuinely dead (cf. Safrai 1974/76b: 784-85; but could the practice have arisen from anti-Christian polemic?); given the brutality of crucifixion, however, this should not have been necessary. Final acts of devotion the next morning would not be uncommon (Char. *Chaer.* 3.3.1; cf. t. Shab. 17:19 in Safrai 1974/76b: 774; Pesiq. Rab Kah. 11:23).

290. Some features of Jesus' appearances may also be theophanic (Smyth 1975, although some of his material, like the Moses parallel, may be overstated). Some ancients also had nonsupernaturalistic explanations for lightning (Stoics in Diog. Laert. 7.1.153). But *all* the canonical accounts are restrained by comparison with second-century apocryphal accounts (e.g., Gos. Peter 9:35–11:44; Carson 1984b: 588).

Laert. 8.1.19). Perhaps because white could signify good and black evil (Diog. Laert. 8.1.34; Ovid *Metam.* 2.832),[291] converts might wear linen (Jos. and Asen. 14:12/13; cf. Rev 3:4-5; 4:4; 19:8, 14). Pagan deities could appear in white garments (e.g., *PGM* 4.637-38, 698-99; inscr. in Grant 1953: 16); Jewish angels likewise appeared in linen (Ps-Philo 9:10; Rev 15:6) or white garments (1 Enoch 71:1; 87:2;[292] 90:31-33; 2 Macc 3:26; 11:8; Jannes and Jambres fragments in Chester Beatty Papryrus 16; cf. the exception in late Pesiq. R. 20:4), or clothed in glory (3 Macc 6:18; 1 Enoch 71:1; cf. Adam in Gen. Rab. 20:12). In this context, the angelic or theophanic functions are paramount.

That the angel "sits" on the stone (28:2; cf. Mk 16:5, likely seated elsewhere) is itself a dramatic statement of supernatural triumph since the stone, probably disk-shaped, would not naturally accommodate one sitting on it; single-handedly rolling away the stone also indicated great strength (cf. Gen 29:8, 11). Ancients had other traditions of becoming "like the dead" before a deity's holiness (Diod. Sic. 4.24.5), but 28:4 reflects the biblical tradition (Rev 1:17; see comment on Mt 17:6; for the idiom more generally, cf. Jos. *Ant.* 6.306). Although the guards feared for their lives, God had no intention of slaying them. Yet despite this manifestation of his power, they failed to believe (28:15).

Matthew abbreviates Mark's account yet heightens the miraculous;[293] in Mark, even the angel can be mistaken for a young man, who is less explicit about the resurrection (Montefiore 1968: 1:402 thus surmises that the Markan account may be historically accurate). Some attribute this heightening of the miraculous to haggadic elaboration of Mark (Beare 1981: 542), but Mark may as easily have toned down other features to condense his conclusion (like his introduction in Mk 1:1-13 or 1:1-15) and focus on vindication by the resurrection sign alone.[294]

291. White also signified joy (p. Rosh Hash. 1:3, §27; cf. Gregory the Great *Homilies* 21; *ACCS*, 243) and black mourning (Jos. and Asen. 10.8-9/10; 14:12; Aristoph. *Frogs* 1337; Dupont 1992: 260; Ovid *Metam.* 8.777-78; Herodian 4.2.3; but cf. Plut. *R.Q.* 26, *Mor.* 270DE) or death (Hom. *Od.* 11.32-33), hence the burial clothes of the righteous (Ps-Philo 64:6; cf. Test. Abr. 20A; Life of Adam 48.1; Apoc. Mos. 40.1-3; b. Ber. 18b); black is negative in Hom. *Il.* 1.103; Marc. Aur. *Med.* 4.28.

292. Ephraim Isaac, an Ethiopian translator of 1 Enoch, points out that in 1 Enoch 87:2 white suggests the image of purity in Ethiopic (*OTP* 1:63n.) Against some modern assumptions, these associations with color derive from day/night divisions (e.g., night magic in Lucan *C.W.* 6.624; the netherworld in Hesiod *W.D.* 154-55), not human pigment (e.g., Philo *Creation* 29 views air as black without light). White is associated positively with the spirit world in various traditional African societies (Mbiti 1970: 73, 277; Isichei 1995: 64).

293. Some details, like the invitation to "see the place where he lay" or "they laid him" (functioning to bolster the eyewitness claim), are essentially the same in both (28:6; Mk 16:6); Greek regularly used *keitai* for lying in a tomb, often in Diaspora Jewish tomb inscriptions (e.g., *CIJ* 1:8, §4; 1:12, §§6-7; 1:14, §§10-11; 1:15, §§12-13; 1:16, §§14-15; 1:17, §17; 1:19, §20; 1:21, §23; 1:23, §28; 1:24, §30; 1:26, §35; 1:30, §42; 1:31, §45; 1:32, §§46-47; 1:35, §§51-52; 1:36, §53; 1:37, §§55-56; 1:38, §58; 1:39, §§62-63; 1:49, §78; 1:52, §79; 1:56, §81; 1:60, §86; 1:62, §88; 1:66, §93; 1:69, §97; 1:70, §§99, 100; 1:74, §105; etc.).

294. The literary connection some draw between Mk 14:50-52 and 16:5 (e.g., Jenkins 1983) lacks adequate foundation (Brown 1994: 299-300).

Various non-Markan material here recurs in John and Luke-Acts (e.g., 28:6; cf. Lk 24:6), suggesting access to non-Markan resurrection traditions or material in a now-lost ending of Mark (Wenham 1973; Gundry 1982: 590-91).[295] It is, in fact, difficult to doubt that such other traditions would have existed, given the large number of witnesses to the resurrection (cf. 1 Cor 15:5-7). Some scholars are convinced that one can completely harmonize the stories of the women at the tomb if we grant that the Gospel writers reported only data essential to their distinctive accounts (Hodges 1966); others, while acknowledging that the conviction of the resurrection is early, doubt that our current Easter stories belong to the earliest stratum of tradition (Dibelius 1949: 139). While harmonization approaches become strained when they misunderstand the liberties literary historians sometimes took in recounting secondary details (see the Introduction), they do work harder than more skeptical approaches to make the best possible sense of the data we have. On any account, two matters are plain: (1) the differences in accounts demonstrate that the Gospel writers were aware of a variety of *independent* traditions; (2) these divergent traditions overlap significantly, hence independently corroborate the basic outlines of the story.

Third, the narrative shows that God is selective in his revelation (28:4-9). Although the guards witnessed God's power, the angel spoke only to the women; often when people fell before a revelation as if they were dead, the revealer declared, "Fear not."[296] But here the angel says "Fear not" to the women, not to the guards who had fainted before him (28:4-5; cf. 28:10; 17:7; Mk 16:6; Dan 10:11-12). Jesus appears directly to the women as well, but not to those who did not believe (28:8-10; cf. Acts 10:41). In view of the prejudice against women's testimony in antiquity (see above), no one would have invented the testimony of the women attested in all four Gospels; indeed, Paul even omits it.

The initial dependence of the men on the testimony of the women reflects the gospel's power to transcend gender restrictions (Thompson 1985: 233). When the women met Jesus, they worshiped (28:9) — finally responding as the

295. The sudden ending of Mk 16 with 16:8 may be original, however, fitting some ancient narration patterns; though in some cases, e.g., Ps-Philo, the ending may be lost, one may also compare abrupt original endings, e.g., in some of Plutarch's speeches (*Fame of Athenians* 8, *Mor.* 351B; *On the Fortune of Alex.* 2.13, *Mor.* 345B; *Fortune of Romans* 13, *Mor.* 326C; *Uneduc. Ruler* 7, *Mor.* 782F); Isoc. *Demon.* 52, *Or.* 1; Demetrius *On Style* 5.304; Lucan *C.W.* 10.542-46; Herodian 8.8.8. See especially Magness 1986 for more ancient literary parallels; for consistency with Markan style, especially a final *gar,* cf. Boomershine and Bartholomew 1981; Mus. Ruf. 12 (van der Horst 1974: 308). An abbreviated conclusion allows Mark to retain the centrality of the cross without actually playing down the resurrection (cf. also Thompson 1985: 225). (Mark nevertheless points to resurrection appearances beyond his narrative; e.g., Anderson 1976: 353; Rhoads and Michie 1982: 42; Hooker 1983: 120; pace Weeden 1971: 44-45; Kelber 1979: 87.) Farmer 1974 even makes a noteworthy case on external (3-75) and internal (79-103) grounds that Mk 16:9-20 has more support for being the original ending than often accepted; though it runs counter to scholarly consensus, his thesis is well-supported and worthy of more attention than it has received.

296. Raphael reveals himself and says "Fear not" in Tob 12:17; for other parallels, see comment on 17:7. In this passage, the women not only should not fear but should receive news of great joy (28:8), which fits discovery of or entrance into the kingdom (13:44; 25:21, 23; cf. 2:10).

wise Gentiles had (2:2, 11), yet — again with an ironic touch — before the male disciples did (28:17).[297] Nevertheless, Jesus does not cast off the male disciples here; he identifies the disciples to whom he is sending them as his "brothers" (12:50; 25:40; cf. a similar tradition in Jn 20:17, via Mary Magdalene).[298]

Because Paul explicitly reports only resurrection *appearances,* some suppose that the empty tomb tradition was a myth;[299] Mack, for example, suggests that before the Gospels we have only Paul's account of "visions" (Mack 1988: 308).[300] But while Paul's language could include visionary experiences,[301] he is reporting earlier Palestinian tradition in 1 Corinthians 15:3-7,[302] and Palestinian Jews did not speak of nonbodily resurrections.[303] (Dibelius 1971: 191, who

297. "Worship" or "prostration" could be offered not only to deities or spirits (e.g., *PGM* 13.704-5; to God in 3 Macc 5:50) but to humans in this period, not only by Gentiles (e.g., Polyb. *R.R.E.* 15.1; Char. *Chaer.* 5.2.2) but by Jews as well (Ruth 2:10; Jos. and Asen. 5:7; Test. Jos. 13:5); but at this point in Matthew, the term clearly connotes worship of Jesus as divine (cf. 1:23; Jn 9:38).

298. Eastern Christian tradition regarded Mary Magdalene as *isapostolos,* "equal to the apostles" (Davies and Allison 1997: 637). That both the angel (28:7) and Jesus (28:9) offer the same commission to Galilee probably represents the weaving together of two traditions (not necessarily challenging the reliability of either), though the second could represent pro-Galilean redaction of tradition.

299. Weeden 1971: 102 is among those who doubt that the empty tomb tradition precedes Mark; his claim that there is no "hard evidence that the early church ever knew of Jesus' grave's being empty" suggests that it did not occur to him that anyone would have checked — an idea as unlikely in Roman antiquity as today. Boyd 1995: 275 rightly questions whether Mark was inventing 16:1-8 as apologetic — aside from pre-Markan Semitic expressions in the passage, its conclusion with the women's fear and silence is hardly apologetic, and it lacks mention of corroborating attestation from Joseph of Arimathea or others.

300. Likewise, against the unanimous witness of extant evidence, from earliest to latest, he supposes that the resurrection was a late myth originated by Christians not in Jewish Palestine but in northern Syria and Asia (1993: 2). Evidence for early tradition for the site of the tomb (see comment on 27:57), the largely Palestinian evidence for Jewish belief in the resurrection, the extreme unlikelihood of a Diaspora movement becoming more Palestinian or Judaized in the anti-Judaism of parts of the Greek East, and so forth render his suggestion incredible.

301. Deities periodically "manifested" themselves to mortals in Greek tradition, sometimes in sleep and sometimes as apparitions (e.g., Eurip. *Bacch.* 42, 53-54; Ael. Arist. *Or.* 48.41; Apul. *Metam.* 11.3; Ach. Tat. *Clit.* 7.12.4; Char. *Chaer.* 2.2.5; 2.3.5; reports in Grant 1953: 9-13, 123); in unrelated cultures, see Wolf 1958; Mbiti 1970: 105-12 passim; for more concrete effects of angelic manifestations in hellenistic Jewish tradition see Tob 12:19, 22; 2 Macc 3:24-26 (cf. God in 2 Macc 3:30). Paul's language in 1 Cor 15 applied in the LXX especially to revelations of God or angels (cf. Bar. 3:37; Sib. Or. 1.200; Bartsch 1980). But from the late hellenistic age "epiphanies" of Greek gods usually meant the activity of a deity rather than its appearance (Nilsson 1948: 106; Diod. Sic. 5.62.4; 11.14.3-4; Dion. Hal. 8.56.1-3; it is primarily these that witnesses attest — cf. Grant 1986: 66, 54-55, 64-65), though appearances in personal dreams and visions occur (e.g., *PDM* 14.74-9195, 98-102, 169); further, Jesus "appeared" to his followers in Acts 1:3 but there provided concrete proofs of his physicality (cf. Lk 24:39-40). Finally, Paul himself distinguishes between the Easter appearances and mere visions (cf. 1 Cor 9:1; 15:8; 2 Cor 12:1-4; Goppelt 1980: 18-19).

302. See, e.g., Dibelius 1971: 18-20; Gerhardsson 1961: 299-300; Barrett 1967: 1-2; Conzelmann 1975: 251; Hunter 1961: 15-17; Fuller 1971: 10-11; Webber 1983; Fee 1987: 722.

303. Nor is there historical merit to the old "swoon" theory (that Jesus was not yet dead, hence revived enough to act "resurrected" but then died somewhere unknown); crucified persons did

doubts that Paul had the empty tomb tradition because he does not mention it, nevertheless recognizes that Paul would have to assume it based on Jewish premises about the nature of the resurrection. But if early disciples assumed it they would have checked, and given the availability of traditions concerning the resurrection apearances, Paul had no reason to mention the far more ambiguous evidence of the empty tomb.) Nor would anyone have persecuted them for simply affirming that they had seen someone who had been dead; apart from the *bodily* character of the resurrection — the sort that would leave an empty tomb — people would merely assume that they claimed to see a ghost, a noncontroversial phenomenon (cf. comment on 14:26; note on 1:20).[304] Ghosts were "phantasms" that appeared especially at night (Plut. *Brutus* 36), but this is not what the resurrection narratives report (Lk 24:40; Sanders 1993: 278). Further, very little evidence suggests the plausibility of successive and mass, *corporate* visions (e.g., Schweizer 1971: 48-49; see especially 1 Cor 15:5-7).[305] Those inventing an empty tomb tradition would hardly have included women as the first witnesses (see above), and "Jesus' resurrection could hardly have been proclaimed in Jerusalem if people knew of a tomb still containing Jesus' body" (Schweizer 1971: 48).[306]

---

not simply revive: Josephus had three friends taken from crosses, and despite medical attention, two died (Jos. *Life* 420-21). Apul. *Metam.* 10.11 cites a drug to simulate death (cf. also Diog. Laert. *Lives* 8.2.61), but his book is full of magic herbs that can do almost anything, here accommodating the story line (cf. the similar plot device in Ach. Tat. 3.15-21; 5.18.2; 7.6.2). Further, if one could revive, one would still be trapped within the tomb, which would lead to death (Char. *Chaer.* 1.4.11-12; 1.8).

304. Conditions in first-century Judea and Galilee were not those that produced the seventeenth-century Messiah Sabbetai Zevi, many of whose followers failed to be deterred by his apostasy (Grayzel 1961: 516; Bamberger 1962: 240), and some even by his death (Scholem 1973: 920; Greenstone 1906: 225-30). Aside from different social conditions, knowledge of the Christian belief in Jesus' resurrection and redefinition of Messiahship could provide later messianic movements a model for redefining the messianic mission in a manner that did not exist prior to Jesus.

305. Some less than persuasive parallels could be adduced. Jos. *War* 6.297-99 reports that people saw heavenly chariots moving through the clouds and surrounding cities (cf. 2 Kings 6:17; 2 Macc 3:24-26; 4 Macc 4:10-11; Sib. Or. 3.805-8), and priests heard voices in the temple; Horsley and Hanson 1985: 182-84 regard these as collective fantasies, but they could also be (1) true (which we regard as unlikely but which a Post-Enlightenment perspective cannot simply dismiss) or (2) the sun playing tricks on eyes at dusk or (3) borrowed from Flavian propaganda (Saulnier 1989) or (4) Josephus' own propaganda (he is the only extant witness concerning witnesses apart from sources dependent on him). Other reports of such prodigies are almost standard and stereotypical (e.g., Appian *C.W.* 4.1.4; Livy 24.10.10; 24.44.8), and often include the warning that imagination may be involved (e.g., Herodian 8.3.8-9) or that the apparitions remained only in the distance (Livy 21.62.5); some opined that such reports tended to circulate and multiply among the superstitious (Livy 21.62.1; 24.10.6; 29.14.2). Some reports imply celestial phenomena we would consider natural (Livy 25.7.8; 29.14.3; 32.8.2; 41.21.12-13; 43.13.3), and the most striking accounts of such apparitions are poetry recycling literary motifs and citing no witnesses (Lucan *C.W.* 1.572-73). In any case, this phenomenon is quite different from meeting again a person one had personally known, which the Gospel accounts stress (probably authentically, though developed further in later tradition; see, e.g., *Epistula Apostolorum* passim).

306. For a fuller defense of the empty tomb traditions, see Craig 1981; idem 1985; idem 1995: 146-52; Ladd 1963; on the bodily character of the resurrection, see Craig 1980: 47-74.

Those who witnessed Jesus alive from the dead (e.g., 1 Cor 15:1-8; virtually all the narrative accounts also suggest significant conversation with him, rather than fleeting appearances) were so convinced of the veracity of their claims that many devoted their lives to proclaiming what they had seen, and some died for it; clearly their testimony was not fabricated (Sanders 1993: 280).[307] Supposed pagan parallels to the resurrection stories are weak (see Aune 1981: 48).[308] Most pagans would have preferred to play down a savior's human death (Boring 1995: 151, comparing Philost. *V.A.* 7:14).

Excursus on Mysteries, Resurrection, and Salvation

The Mysteries appear to have been less popular than was once thought (Rives 1998). They apparently influenced some Palestinian Jewish thought in late antiquity, though the exact date of the evidence is unclear. Numismatic evidence indicates some presence of the Mysteries in Palestine (Avi-Yonah 1974/76a: 60; Flusser 1974/76: 1,065-1,100); the influence of a third-century-A.D. Mithraeum in Caesarea (on the Mithraeum see Bull 1974; Lease 1975; Flusser 1974/76: 1099) is unclear, since Caesarea was of mixed population and the date is much later than our period (cf. Charlesworth 1985: 82). Mystery language did infiltrate some forms of Judaism (Philonenko 1975; idem 1965),[309] but pagan accusations that confused Judaism and the Mysteries (Russell 1932: 338; cf. Reitzenstein 1978: 174-84) do not constitute good evidence that Judaism as a whole made that confusion; Reitzenstein's claim that "Even in Trajan's time the Roman Jewish community still . . . either altogether or in large part worshiped the *Zeus Hupsistos Ouranios* and the Phrygian Attis together with Yahweh" (1978: 125) lacks the support of subsequent research into Roman Judaism.

The language of the Mysteries clearly infiltrated Christian writers of the second century and later. Tertullian claims that Christianity has the true Mysteries, of

307. Ancients also recognized that willingness to die proved one's commitment to what one testified and that it did not spring from ulterior motives (e.g., Dio Cassius *R.H.* 63.11.2–12.1; 58.4.5-6). Josephus cites Jews' willingness to die for the law (*Apion* 1.42-43).

308. Admitting historical evidence favoring Jesus' resurrection is not purely the domain of Christian apologetic; e.g., orthodox Jewish scholar Pinchas Lapide, while doubting that the resurrection proves Jesus' messianic or divine identity (connected though this has traditionally been to the resurrection; see Rivkin 1971: 398), nevertheless finds the evidence for his resurrection compelling (see the review in Kennedy 1985). Without addressing Jesus' resurrection appearances, Vermes 1973: 41, another Jewish scholar closely acquainted with the primary evidence, opines that "the only conclusion acceptable to the historian" must be that the women actually found the tomb empty. "Those scholars who are unable to believe in an actual resurrection of Jesus admit that the disciples believed it" (Ladd 1974: 320).

309. Willoughby 1929: 225-62 tries to compare Philonic language with the conversion language of the Mysteries, but like Godwin 1981: 78-83, he tends to generalize too much. More nuanced is the approach of Wolfson 1968: 1:27-36, cf. 1:101 (Philo adapts their language but denounces them as religious alternatives).

which others are poorer and later copies (*Apol.* 47.14). Such language becomes much more prevalent in the third and fourth centuries A.D. (Eliade 1958: 120).[310] Yet it is possible that some features of the Mysteries derive from Christianity. As they began to lose devotees to Christians in a later period, the Mysteries could have adopted some features of Christianity; many of the "parallels" in the Mysteries occur only in the later period (Metzger 1955: 10-11; Eliade 1958: 115). That the church fathers understood the Mysteries as "imitation demoniaque du Christianisme" (Benoit 1975: 79-81) may suggest that they, like many early modern students of these cults, read them through the grid of their own Christian background, and the ready-to-hand explanation of demonic imitation may have led them to heighten rather than play down the similarities between the two.

Much of the most specifically Mystery vocabulary is lacking in earliest Christianity: Metzger, following Nock, lists such terms as *mystēs, mystikos, mystagōgos, katharmos, katharsia, katharsis, teletē,* and so on (1955: 11). What is perhaps more significant is the different perspective on the events described by the two kinds of religions. As Metzger points out (1955: 20),

> . . . the Mysteries differ from Christianity's interpretation of history. The speculative myths of the cults lack entirely that reference to the spiritual and moral meaning of history which is inextricably involved in the experiences and triumph of Jesus Christ.[311]

Regarding the apostolic and subapostolic literature Metzger (1955: 15) asserts,

> In all strata of Christian testimony concerning the resurrection of Jesus Christ, "everything is made to turn upon a dated experience with a historical Person," [citing Nock] whereas nothing in the Mysteries points to any attempt to undergird belief with historical evidence of the god's resurrection.

To be aware of this is perhaps to notice the different cultural matrixes in which these religions took root; it would be difficult indeed for a cult rooted in Israelite biblical piety to have ignored a *heilsgeschichtliche* perspective on history. In this perspective, God's acts might be celebrated annually in cultic ritual, but they were viewed as unique events secured by the testimony of witnesses and grounded in corporate piety.[312]

310. Others have pointed to similarities between Mithraism and Christianity (cf. Gervers 1979, though qualifying on 598; cf. Gager 1975: 132-34; note the contrast stressed by Mattingly 1967: 5). For example, Deman 1975 notes the later link between the twelve apostles and the twelve signs of the zodiac; but the twelve apostles in earliest Christian tradition stem from the twelve tribes (though Judaism had already linked the tribes with the zodiac in that period). The closest true parallels address only later Gentile Christianity, as it assimilated into the guise of a broader Roman cultural context.

311. Manson 1963: 64-65 stresses the moral contrast between the Mysteries (where moral ideals were irrelevant) and Christianity (cf. Carcopino 1940: 138-39).

312. Cf. Nock 1933b: 136 for Christianity's "Oriental" nature but lack of "Oriental" trappings. This is not to suggest that many other Greco-Roman cults could not be distinguished from one another, but rather to point out that the originating cultural matrix of Christianity was different enough, and earliest Christianity's monotheism rigorous enough, to disallow the degree of assimilation that could characterize most of the cults.

Nock points out that, while many of Paul's hearers may have understood him in terms of the Mysteries, most of the early Jewish-Christian missionaries like Paul had probably had little firsthand exposure to the Mysteries and reflected instead a broader milieu of which the Mysteries were only a part (cf. Nock 1964a: 31; Cadbury 1955: 28).

One area of special comparison between the two, especially in early twentieth-century literature, involves the matter of salvation and dying and rising gods. The motif of dying and rising gods certainly predates the time of Jesus. Just as fertility fled the earth during Demeter's search for Persephone in the Eleusinian myth,[313] so it flees during the absence of the Hittite deity Telepinus (*ANET* 126-28), the Canaanite Baal (*ANET* 129-42; Bright 1981: 118), and perhaps the man Aqhat (*ANET* 149-55, especially Ginsberg on 155). The same theme appears in the late-second-millennium-B.C. story of Ishtar's descent to the netherworld (*ANET* 108 lines 76ff.; cf. reverse 34ff.). It seems likely that a much older story line or lines stand behind all the regional variations.

Descent to the underworld in such texts need not be permanent. In the epic of Gilgamesh (*Gilgamesh* 6.97-99; *ANET* 84), Ishtar forces Anu to comply with her demands by threatening to smash the doors of the netherworld and to raise up the dead so that they outnumber the living, and similarly addresses the gatekeeper of that world with the tale of her descent there (*ANET* 107, *Descent* lines 12ff.). In a tale perhaps dating to the first half of the second millennium B.C. or earlier, Inanna is put to death (though she is a goddess), but after three days and nights she is restored, as the food and water of life are sprinkled sixty times on her corpse (*ANET* 52-57, especially 55).[314]

But the parallels remain problematic. While there is widespread pre-Christian evidence for the account of Osiris's resuscitation (cf. also Plut. *Isis* 35, *Mor.* 364F), he is magically revivified, not transformed into an eschatological new creation; his corpse is awakened through the same potencies as exist in procreation, and he remains in the netherworld, still needing protection by vigilant gods and replacement on earth by his heir (Wagner 1967: 119; on Nile water, see 127-35). Adonis's death was mourned annually (e.g., Plut. *Nicias* 13.7; Ovid *Metam.* 10.710-39), but his rising is not documented prior to the middle of the second century A.D. (Wagner 1967: 171-207, especially 195).[315] Attis, too, was mourned as dead, but there is no possible

313. E.g., Ovid *Metam.* 5.564-71. Burkert argues that Persephone's connection with the nature cycle must go back to pre-Greek, perhaps Neolithic times, because the real facts of Mediterranean vegetation suggest an interpretation earlier than the one the Greeks themselves held (Burkert 1985: 160). Whether or not his argument is accepted as persuasive, it is clear that Persephone's return from the underworld precedes the apostolic proclamation of Christ's resurrection by many centuries.

314. Some have likewise claimed that Marduk died and rose again in some sense (Klausner 1979a: 103, though I have not noticed this in *Enuma Elish* in Heidel 1951: 18-60).

315. The Adonis tradition itself was Semitic and imported into Greek religion from an early period (Burkert 1985: 176-77 thinks perhaps as early as the sixth century B.C.). Apart from the resuscitation it is clearly early; in the Greek bucolic poets, cf., e.g., *Women at the Adonis Festival* (third century B.C.), a lament for Adonis perhaps by Bion, and *The Dead Adonis* (*Greek Bucolic Poets,* LCL 176-95, 386-95, 480-83).

evidence for his resurrection before the third century A.D., and aside from the testimony of the Christian writer Firmicus Maternus, no clear evidence exists before the sixth century A.D. (Wagner 1967: 219, 229; for the typical story, see Vermaseren 1977: 91).

Dionysus's return from death (cf. Otto 1965: 79-80, 103-19) is clear enough, but perhaps in the same category as Heracles' apotheosis or the wounding of Ares in the *Iliad;* mortals could be deified and deities could suffer harm.[316] Even Persephone was taken down to the underworld alive, and Orpheus descended alive to rescue his beloved Eurydice. Frazer's scheme of the "dying and rising god" has thus come under heavy criticism in recent times (see documentation in Gasparro 1985: 30n.16).

Many Christian writers have asserted, again perhaps through the grid of their own religious understanding, that the Mysteries must have provided salvation through union with dying-and-rising gods (e.g., Conzelmann 1969: 11; cf. Case 1975: 111; Bultmann 1956: 158-59; Ridderbos 1975: 22-29). While there may be some truth in the idea that ancients accepted that a god not subject to death could grant immortality, Burkert cautions that "This multiplicity of images can hardly be reduced to a one-dimensional hypothesis, one ritual with one dogmatic meaning: death and rebirth of 'the' god and the initiand" (1987: 100). Much of the evidence is late (e.g., Apuleius, whom Dunand 1975: 58 interprets thus) and/or specifically Christian (e.g., Firmicus Maternus *De Errore Profanarum Religionum* 22 in Grant 1953: 146). More recent writers are therefore generally more cautious about connecting spiritual salvation (when it appears in the Mysteries) with the dying deity motif (e.g., Davies 1980: 91).

In the Eleusinian rites, the *mystēs* received the promise of a happy afterlife, but by being pledged to the goddess rather than by being reborn or by dying and rising with the deity (Wagner 1967: 87). The cult of Cybele also does not support the common conclusion, as Gasparro notes (Gasparro 1985: 82). The main problem with the view that many members of the old *Religionsgeschichte* school, eager to produce "parallels" to primitive Christianity, adduced is that most of the people who turned to the Mysteries already believed in some afterlife in the netherworld anyway; it was merely a happier afterlife in that world that the gods could guarantee.

Those like Bousset who drew such connections (1970: 57) did not take adequate account of the vegetative, cyclical, and seasonal nature of most of the resuscitation rituals (for the vegetative association see, e.g., Gasparro 1985: 29, 43-49; Ruck 1978: 44-45; Guthrie 1966: 55-56). This is a far cry from the earliest Christian picture of Christ's *bodily* resurrection rooted in explicit Jewish eschatological hopes — a perspective on the resurrection that Paul affirms is guaranteed by hundreds of eyewitnesses, including himself, and argues, despite his hellenistic audience, is a necessary understanding of resurrection for a true follower of Jesus (1 Cor 15). One would

316. E.g., Hom. *Il.* 5.382-404; 5.388; on the death of Pan in Plut. *Mor.* 419.17, see Borgeaud 1983. Dionysus returns in the spring in poetic fragments (ca. 1 B.C.) in *Select Papyri* 3:390-93.

not think that earlier Palestinian Christianity held a less rigorously Jewish perspective than Paul did (cf. Metzger 1955: 19-20; Ring 1944: 228).

While the third day is used for resurrection in the later ritual for Attis and perhaps for Adonis, these may be based on Christian precedents. The third day in the cult of Osiris is most significant, but the traditional Jewish view about the corpse, the use of a "third day" for an interval between two events in close succession in the Hebrew Bible, and the inherent likelihood of some coincidence between a brief period in early Christian tradition and one in the Mysteries qualify its significance considerably. The fixing of the third day in the pre-Pauline formula in 1 Corinthians 15:3, however, weights the case in favor of a Palestinian Jewish-Christian tradition for Jesus' resurrection prior to any exposure to the cult of Osiris in the hellenistic world (Metzger 1955: 18-19). And while gods could often die in the Mysteries, their deaths were not portrayed as triumphant or meaningful as in many strands of early Christian tradition.

Because Greek religion in general, like *many* religions in the world,[317] addressed the survival of the soul after death (e.g., Herod. *Hist.* 2.123; Plato *Phaedo* 64CD; 80DE), it should not surprise us that the Eleusis cult promised a happy life in the underworld (Burkert 1987: 21; Grant 1962: 11-12; Mylonas 1961: 268-69; Wagner 1967: 87), that Isis promised patronage and protection (Wagner 1967: 112), and that the Dionysiac Mysteries may have indicated a happy afterlife (Burkert 1985: 293-95; idem 1987: 21-22). But there is little evidence for any future hopes in the cult of Cybele, and certainly not linked with Attis (Gasparro 1985: 84-106, 125; Wagner 1967: 255-56). When the early Christian picture of bodily resurrection derives directly from Jewish eschatological teaching, one casts the net rather widely to make all human hopes for afterlife parallel to it.[318]

The arguments for deification in the Mysteries (cf. Angus 1925: 108-9; Reitzenstein 1978: 200; Avi-Yonah 1978: 42; Tarn 1974: 354-55) would not add much to the idea in hellenistic religion in general, given the apotheosis of famous philosophers (e.g., Cic. *De Opt. Gen. Orat.* 6.17; *De Leg.* 3.1.1; *De Nat. Deor.* 2.12.32) and heroes (Cic. *Tusc. Disp.* 1.12.28; 2.7.17; *De Nat. Deor.* 2.29.62; 3.15.39; Herod. *Hist.* 1.65-66) or the divinization of good men in philosophy (e.g., Plato *Rep.* 10.611DE; Philost. *V.A.* 3.18, 29; 8.5; Plotinus 1.2.7, *On Virtue;* Epict. *Disc.* 1.intro.12; 1.9.6-11, 22; 1.14.6; 1.17.27; 2.8.10-11; 2.19.26-28; Cic. *Par. Stoic.* 14; *De Re Publ.* 6.24.26; *De Leg.* 2.9.22; 2.22.55; *Tusc. Disp.* 1.24.56–26.65; *De Divin.*

317. Some utterly unrelated cultures also supply examples of resurrection legends (e.g., the Sonjo myth in Mbiti 1970: 251), although without the sort of historical attestation surrounding the case of Jesus. But *given the transcultural interest in life after death,* one need not suppose an organic connection among all such accounts except when they are geographically close and the story line is substantially similar.

318. Cumont's view of astral immortality (Cumont 1922: 91-109; cf. Reitzenstein 1978: 64-65; Dahl 1977: 17; Avi-Yonah 1978: 40-41) is much broader than the Mysteries and thus should not be directly linked to them (Gasparro 1985: 98). On regeneration in the Mysteries and Christianity, see Keener 1997b: 143-46. The doctrine of bodily resurrection also appears in the Hebrew Bible earlier than it is attested in Persian texts (Yamauchi 1990: 456-57, 461; cf. 409; for immortality, however, cf. Olmstead 1959: 40, 100-101).

1.37.80; Sen. *Dial.* 1.1.5; *Ep. Lucil.* 32.11; 48.11; Marc. Aur. *Med.* 2.13, 17; 3.5-6, 12, 16.2; 4.16; 5.10.2; 5.27; 12.26). But while the doctrine comes to figure highly in Gnostic and Hermetic systems (cf., e.g., Ménard 1980: 149; Jonas 1963: 44-45), it is lacking in early Judaism and Christianity (cf. 1 Cor 3:4).[319]

Excursus on Jewish Resurrection Theology

Pagan notions of the afterlife and myths of risen deities did provide Gentiles a handle for apprehending aspects of early Christian teaching about the resurrection (cf. Lewis 1983: 100), but the Christian teaching remains distinctly Jewish in its origin.[320] Although it is not the emphasis there (cf. Schuller 1989), the teaching appears in some Old Testament texts (Is 26:19; Dan 12:2; Ferguson 1987: 439) and probably has early antecedents in Israel's history, though personalized eschatology appears in texts only after the exile (cf. Wifall 1978). Jesus' Jewish contemporaries regarded that resurrection as collective and future (Collins 1997: 97).

Not all streams of early Judaism clearly articulate a doctrine of bodily resurrection. The Sadducees denied it (Jos. *Ant.* 18.16-17; *War* 2.165),[321] while the evidence we do have from Qumran supports the likelihood that they accepted it, though we lack concrete evidence (see Puech 1993; Sanders 1992: 370; cf. Ulrichsen 1977).[322] Clearly the Pharisees and their probable successors in the rabbinic movement (e.g., Stemberger 1973; in the Targums, see McNamara 1972: 136) affirmed the doctrine of the bodily resurrection,[323] almost equating belief in it with belief in the

319. Though the language appears in some Jewish sources (e.g., Philo *Mos.* 1.279), the same authors advocate monotheism, and other Jewish texts may polemicize against divinization (Jub. 3:19; 10:20, following Genesis; Ep. Arist. 211, 263; Sib. Or. frg. 1.1-2; especially Philo *Virt.* 172; Ex. Rab. 8:2; cf. Urbach 1979: 1:252). The second-century church, like Gnosticism, came much closer to accommodating such language than first-century Christians could (cf. Tatian 7; Taylor 1945: 206, citing Irenaeus and, more to the point though later, Athanasius).

320. Mack makes Jesus' resurrection purely mythical (1988: 112-13) by wrongly equating immortality in the Wisdom of Solomon with "resurrection" in 2 Maccabees, wrongly interpreting eschatological *narratives* about Christ's resurrection as if they were eschatological allegory, and wrongly taking the Spirit in a purely hellenistic sense instead of its Jewish usage in the NT (on this, see Keener 1997b: 7-8 with ibid. 8-13).

321. Rabbinic texts often emphasize that the Sadducees, unlike the Pharisees, denied the teaching and hence held no place in the coming world (e.g., m. Sanh. 10:1; ARN 5A; 10, §26B; cf. b. Sanh. 90b). The doctrine of the resurrection was particularly relevant in the context of martyrdom (2 Macc 7:9, 11; 14:46); those inclined to defend the honor of martyrs hence would take serious offense at the denial (rabbinic texts also suggest moral consequences for denying resurrection and judgment, which they viewed together).

322. The supposed resurrection of the Teacher of Righteousness is based on inference from a reconstructed text (cf. 4QpPs 37 fr. 2.2-4 in Dupont-Sommer 1973: 272), which other scholars have reconstructed quite differently.

323. This is true though Josephus, adapting his depiction of Jewish "sects" to Greek schools like Pythagoreans and Middle Platonists, portrays Pharisaic confidence in more acceptable hellenistic terms suggesting reincarnation (Jos. *Ant.* 18.14; *War* 2.163; 3.374; *Apion* 2.218).

afterlife.[324] But the doctrine was much more widely held than among the Pharisees, representing common Judaism, as widespread attestation indicates (e.g., Ps. Sol. 3:12; 15:12-13; 1 Enoch 22:13; 2 Bar. 30:1; Ps-Philo 3:10; Test. Abr. 7B; cf. Test. Jud. 25:1-4; Test. Zeb. 10:2; Apoc. Ezek. intro.), and as the widespread use of Daniel (especially in the LXX) would almost require (Dan 12:2). The Second Benediction of the Amida undoubtedly obtained beyond Pharisaic circles. The use of ossuaries for secondary burial in the first century likely also supports the widespread character of belief in the bodily resurrection (Rahmani 1978; cf. Goodenough 1953: 1:164-77).[325] Sanders is probably right that nearly everyone but the Sadducees affirmed the doctrine (1985: 237; cf. Wright 1992a: 320-34).

The belief was probably less widely held initially in the Diaspora, though some evidence exists.[326] Some hellenistic Jewish writers, while accommodating the idea to hellenistic notions of immortality (e.g., Ps-Phocyl. 105) and the language of deification (104), also allude to the doctrine of bodily resurrection (102-4). Perhaps after rabbinic Judaism consolidated its influence, the doctrine of a literal, bodily resurrection also became standard in much of the Diaspora (see Garte 1973).

All our early Christian sources unanimously affirm the doctrine of the bodily resurrection of Jesus,[327] although 1 Corinthians 15 attests that Paul had to deal with Gentiles who could assimilate the Palestinian Jewish doctrine only with difficulty and did not wish to accept it beyond the case of Jesus. Within earliest Christianity, however, there remains no debate about the received tradition that Jesus himself rose bodily, unless one is inclined to count inferences by some modern scholars without explicit supporting evidence. By some point in the second century, however, Gnostics and others who found the notion of a bodily resurrection of any sort incompatible with Platonic metaphysics sought to interpret the early Christian tradition differently (cf., e.g., in Iren. *Haer.* 2.29).

---

324. They condemned a few others for its denial besides explicit Sadducees (e.g., p. Sanh. 10:2, §11). Other texts regularly defend the resurrection long after the Sadducees themselves had ceased to be an issue (e.g., Lev. Rab. 27:4; Lam. Rab. 3:23, §8), but that the rabbis would engage in "textbook apologetics" (not uncommon in some more traditional religious circles today) would not be surprising, given the variety of hypothetical legal situations they also surveyed.

325. Cf. also the graffito in Greek at Beth She'arim: "Good fortune in your resurrection" (Finegan 1969: 208). Ossuaries belong especially to the Roman Imperial period and the pre-Israelite Chalcolithic period (see Silberman 1991).

326. Some evidence exists in contemporary Egyptian Judaism, but Philo himself never mentions the doctrine (Wolfson 1968: 1:404). The Samaritans may well have accepted it, though our evidence here is late (see McDonald 1964: 376).

327. One cannot cite the widespread use of crosses on early ossuaries, which probably are simply markings for the placement of the lids (R. H. Smith 1974). Is Gustafsson 1956 more helpful?

Ancients commonly reported apparitions of deceased persons (e.g., Apul. *Metam.* 8.8; 9.31; ARN 40A; see comment on Mt 1:20) or deities, and hence occasionally those of persons who had become immortal (e.g., Plutarch's reports of Romulus more than half a millennium earlier, in Talbert 1977: 41),[328] but these are not *resurrection* appearances. Even the appearance of Apollonius of Tyana, which exhibits some parallels with the Gospel accounts (Philost. *V.A.* 8.31; Sanders 1985: 320), is not an exception. This story appears in a third-century source — after Christian teaching on the resurrection had become widely disseminated; further, Apollonius proves that he has not died, not that he has risen (Blackburn 1986: 193). Most cultures believe in some form of life after death, and such cultures frequently accept some form of contact with the spirits of the dead or some of the dead. Such phenomena may help explain how ancient Mediterranean hearers may have conceived of Jesus' resurrection appearances; but to cite them as "parallels" to those appearances, as if they define the latter, stretches the category of parallel too far to be useful. If Jesus rose again, how would the disciples know it and proclaim it if he failed to appear to them?

Ancients could depict the soul as rising to heaven (e.g., Test. Abr. 20A; 7, 14B), and told stories of newly divinized immortals ascending to heaven (e.g., Diog. Laert. 8.2.68; cf. Talbert 1975), as well as traditions about Enoch, Elijah, Ezra, and others thought to have escaped death (e.g., 1 Macc 2:58; 1 Enoch 39:3; 2 Enoch 67:1-3; Gk. Ezra 5:7; Palatty 1986), and on a more regular basis angels (e.g., Tob. 12:20-22; Jos. and Asen. 17:8, MSS; Test. Abr. 4, 8, 9-10, 15, 20A; 4, 7-8, 10B; cf. Jub. 32:20-21). Some early Christian traditions (not Matthew) recounted as a climactic resurrection appearance Jesus' spatial remove from his disciples in these terms (Lk 24:51; Acts 1:9-11; cf. Jn 20:17; Mk 16:19).[329] But the difference again concerns the resurrection. To most ancient Mediterranean peoples, the concept of corporal resurrection was barely intelligible; to Jewish people, it was strictly eschatological. Yet once one grants the possibility of a bodily resurrection of Jesus within past history, the appearances follow naturally with or without parallels. In a Jewish framework, Jesus' resurrection within history must also signify the arrival of the eschatological era in some sense (e.g., Acts 1:3-6; "from among the dead ones" — Rom 1:4; 1 Cor 15:20; Heb 6:5).

328. Boring 1995: 163-64 cites Romulus's apotheosis appearance to Proculus Julius in Livy 1.16.2-8; Plut. *Romulus* 28; *Numa* 11.3; Ovid *Fasti* 2.500-9, and notes that Justin *1 Apol.* 21 made an apologetic comparison between Jesus' resurrection appearances and pagan understanding of imperial apotheosis.

329. Because of Heracles' apotheosis people searched only vainly for his corpse (Diod. Sic. 4.38.3-5); other deified persons like Aeneas also "disappeared" (*ēphanisthē,* Diod. Sic. 7.5.2), as did Moses in Jos. *Ant.* 4.326. Boring 1995: 162-63 also compares the first-century-B.C. traditions of Romulus's ascension (Ovid *Metam.* 14.805-51; *De Viris Illustr.* 2.13; Plut. *Numa* 11.2), even by horses and carriage (Ovid *Fasti* 2.475-510; cf. 2 Kings 2:11-18), and Job's children in Test. Job 39:8–40:4.

The Report of the Guards (28:11-15)

See comment on the guards on 27:55-66, especially 27:62-66. Just as Josephus's response to the anti-Jewish polemic of *Apion* has inadvertently preserved the basic outline of anti-Jewish polemic in his day, Matthew's response to arguments against the early Christian claims about the resurrection preserves what must have been the basic charge of his day: the disciples stole the body (cf. later sources in Stauffer 1960: 144-45; Tert. *Apol.* 21).[330] Matthew would hardly invent anti-Christian polemic of this nature, but he would respond to what was already in circulation. Scholars therefore often concur that this story was circulating among his contemporaries (e.g., Overman 1996: 401).

Indirectly this charge testifies that the opponents of Christianity conceded that the body of Jesus was missing and that no simpler explanation (such as the body's getting lost by deposition in the wrong tomb) was available (also Craig 1984; Meier 1980: 356). Although Paul does not appeal to the empty tomb tradition in 1 Corinthians 15, his account necessarily implies it. Many people in antiquity claimed to see "ghosts," but for Palestinian Jews "resurrection" meant bodily resurrection and nothing else.[331] Against some commentators, it is quite difficult to imagine that the disciples would have begun proclaiming the resurrection and the authorities begun opposing them without someone checking the tomb (Craig 1995: 151). Yet the church depended on the testimony of witnesses of the risen Christ, not simply on an empty tomb (Ladd 1974b: 325); the empty tomb tells us about the *nature* of the resurrection (and of the body and history), but the witnesses attest to its facticity.

Yet the report of the guards is not credible. Graves, especially with expensive contents, were often robbed eventually (Arrian *Alex.* 6.29.4); stones were rolled away so that graves could be robbed (Char. *Chaer.* 3.3.1), but not with guards posted (at least not without subduing the guards, normally fatally). Further, whereas tomb robbers normally carried off wealth, carrying off the body was so rare that it would shock those who heard of it (Char. *Chaer.* 3.3). If the disciples did not protect Jesus while he was alive, surely they would not have risked their lives to rob his tomb after his death (grave robbing was not only impious — e.g., Plut. *Mor.* 173B — but a capital offense — e.g., *SEG* 8.13 in Sherk 1988: 52, §27); nor could they have rolled away the massive stone without waking the guards.[332] Penalties for falling asleep on guard duty could be severe, and

330. Departing from Mark, Matthew exercises more literary freedom in the narrative about the guards, which he alone includes; the language is particularly Matthean (Fenton 1977: 451). Four times in the Gospel Gentiles use the term "Jews" here used by Matthew (28:15; Saldarini 1994: 34-35); but Matthew, like Josephus, applies it to part of his people, often applying "the gentile designation 'Jews' for that part of the people he opposes" (Saldarini 1994: 36); Jews regularly call other Jews by this title in Diaspora inscriptions (Overman 1996: 401).

331. I do not deny that some may have conceived of various forms of afterlife in different terms; but the term "resurrection" indicated a bodily phenomenon.

332. Other factors also militate against supposing that the disciples stole the body. Jewish scholar Geza Vermes notes (1973: 40) that "From the psychological point of view, they would have

guards who claimed to have slept through the stealing of the body, yet suffered no harm, would sound very suspicious. (Thus, for example, a soldier assigned to guard corpses hanging on crosses to prevent burial found the body stolen, and preferred suicide to court martial and execution — Petron. *Sat.* 112.)[333] Under normal circumstances, people might suppose that they and those who failed to punish them had collaborated in the disappearance of the body, but in this situation those who failed to punish them had too much to lose for anyone to suppose that.[334]

One might argue that someone took the body, but that guards were not actually present. But then why would the ruling establishment circulate a rumor (to which Matthew must respond) that guards were present? The testimony of guards who slept through the theft would be no more credible than the guesses of investigators after a theft. The story makes the most sense if guards had been present, somehow failed to protect the body, and the officials had to strike a deal to cover their embarrassment.

The narrative's irony announces both God's power and human weakness. Guards who saw an angel (rather obviously *not* a disciple) were ready, like Judas (26:15), to betray the truth for money (28:12); like Peter (26:69-75), they were ready to deny the unbelievable to protect their lives (28:14).[335] At the same time,

---

been too depressed and shaken to be capable of such a dangerous undertaking. But above all, since neither they nor anyone else expected a resurrection, there would have been no purpose in faking one."

333. For keeping watch over corpses, often to prevent burial, see also Soph. *Antig.* 217; Plut. *Agis and Cleomenes* 39; cf. 2 Sam 21:10. Guards who fell asleep could be scourged or beheaded (Eurip. *Rhesus* 812-19, 825-27). Roman soldiers who fell asleep during night watch were normally beaten; if a soldier survived, he was banished from family and country and deeply shamed (Dupont 1992: 126). One could sometimes strike deals, however, and some careless sentries escaped execution (Tac. *Hist.* 5.22; Brown 1994: 1311, though he does not argue for historicity). The punishment for falling asleep at night watch was so dreadful that some might desert to escape it (Assyrians in Diod. Sic. 2.18.8), though Roman custom also made desertion of one's post a capital offense (Polyb. *R.R.E.* 1.17; Livy 24.37.9; similarly, for desertion in battle, cf. Dio Cassius *R.H.* 48.42.1-2; Dion. Hal. 3.30.7; 6.9.4; Livy 30.43.13; though less severely, Appian *R.H.* 7.7.43; peoples who showed mercy to deserters were apparently exceptional — Diod. Sic. 1.78.1; 12.16.1).

334. Roman guards from whom a prisoner escaped could be executed (Justinian *Cod.* 9.4.4; Lake and Cadbury 1979: 139; cf. Acts 16:27-28; 27:42), and while the priests would not execute guards (Acts 5:22-24), some Jewish authorities followed that stricter practice (Acts 12:19). Later tradition reports that the chief of the temple police was authorized to beat or even set aflame any watchmen found sleeping (m. Mid. 1:2, where one rabbi testifies that the latter actually happened to his uncle; b. Tamid 27b-28a). Beare 1981: 543 is correct that Roman guards would not normally first report to Jewish officials, but Gundry rightly responds that they would do so in this extraordinary circumstance if Pilate had placed them under the priests' supervision on this assignment (Gundry 1982: 592).

335. Because sleeping on duty was a punishable offense, one would doubt that the guards normally would publicly admit it (Beare 1981: 543); but because the missing body could spell their execution either way, they have reason to please the authorities, who promise conditional amnesty (Gundry 1982: 585). Further, Matthew emphasizes that the authorities paid a *substantial* sum of money; the narrative probably means a "large" sum, but whether it refers to large (heavy, hence expensive) *coins,* cf. Thompson 1962: 310. "Persuading" Pilate could easily mean bribing him (*Embassy to Gaius* 38; Gundry 1982: 593), though if high priests used temple funds rather than their own it would represent serious hypocrisy (Jos. *Ant.* 18.60-62; *War* 2.175-77).

the guards pretend to have slept through the Messiah's deliverance (28:15), whereas when Jesus needed them the most, his disciples *had* slept through his time of testing (26:40-45). Disciples and enemies alike proved weak, but Jesus' resurrection was an act of *God's* power.

The Report of the Church (28:16-20)

Cf. Lk 24:47-49, Acts 1:8, Jn 20:21, and Mk 16:14-18 in Jerusalem; Jn 21:1-23 in Galilee.[336] In this closing pericope, Matthew recapitulates and develops the most important themes of his Gospel (Bauer 1988: 109-28): because Jesus is the rightful king, his followers must make disciples for him among the nations.[337]

The "mountain" (28:16) recalls the other sites of revelation in the Gospel (5:1; 17:1), and various other features indicate that Matthew has heavily reworked the tradition behind the closing scene of his Gospel to conclude with an important theological message. Some doubt that the commission in the Gospels stems from the risen Jesus (cf., e.g., Bultmann 1968: 289; Bornkamm 1969: 15; S. Brown 1980), but others argue for the authenticity of this passage (e.g., White 1960: 338-45; Beasley-Murray 1962: 77-92), although recognizing that Matthew has heavily redacted his prior tradition to emphasize the focal themes of his Gospel (see Meier 1977b; Brooks 1981; cf. Harrison 1973; Hubbard 1974; Davies and Allison 1992). (That Luke himself is free to vary the wording in his two accounts illustrates the degree of freedom permitted on such matters — Lk 24:47-49; Acts 1:8.) Certainly the Lukan, Johannine, and Matthean commissions, as well as the missionary spirit of Pauline and Markan Christianity, leave little evidence of a Christianity *without* missionary impetus; that Christianity's unanimous urge for missions derives from its founder seems inherently likely. And the different forms of the commission suggest its essential accuracy by multiple attestation (cf. Guillet 1982, though perhaps overplaying divergences).

The women offered a true report (28:1-10) and the guards a false one (28:11-15); Matthew's closing paragraph announces that disciples of both genders in his own community, like the first women disciples, must offer a true report and resist temptations like money and protection to which the guards succumbed.

First, the narrative teaches about faith and unbelief (28:16-17). Matthew does not report the resurrection appearances in Jerusalem (Lk 24:36-49; Jn

336. Sanders 1993: 278 suggests that the disciples "fled to Galilee and then returned to Jerusalem"; Luke-Acts is Jerusalem-centered, so Luke had reason to omit the Galilean pilgrimage. Marxsen 1969: 111-16 thinks that Mk 16:7-8 (the rendezvous in Galilee — 28:10) refers to the parousia rather than resurrection appearances in Mark, but this is hardly likely (cf. Lüdemann 1980: 166-67).

337. Michel 1995: 49 emphasizes totality in the closing lines: "all" authority (28:18), nations (28:19), Jesus' precepts (28:20), always (28:20).

20:19-29; probably 1 Cor 15:2, 5, 7); within the logic of his narrative, the disciples believe the women enough to proceed to Galilee without them (although his audience is probably so familiar with the resurrection tradition that they know other events intervened). The resurrection experiences came especially to those who had followed Jesus before (Acts 10:41), but also to some who had been skeptics (1 Cor 15:8-9; Gal 1:14-16; cf. also James in 1 Cor 15:7). Perhaps also due to space limitations, Matthew omits the inability of some of Jesus' followers to recognize him initially (Lk 24:16; Jn 20:14-15; cf. Tob 5:4-6, 12; 12:19; Ps-Philo 12:1; 61:9; 64:4).

Those who see him (cf. 1 Cor 15:5, 7) worship him (cf. 28:9), which suggests that they recognize him for who he is — the "God with them" (1:23; 28:18-20). Some of them, however, *despite* seeing him, still doubt (cf. Lk 24:40), although in this context the expression may connote troubled indecision — "littleness of faith" (8:26) — rather than opposition and unbelief (Garland 1993: 266).[338] Although Matthew stresses this theme less than Mark, he agrees with Mark that disciples often are foolishly unbelieving (6:30; 14:31; 17:20), even after the resurrection. If even seeing is not necessarily believing, disciples ought not to wait to see before they will believe, as if God has not provided enough evidence already.

Second, the narrative teaches about Jesus' identity (28:18-20). As Daniel 7's Son of Man, Jesus holds "all authority" (28:18; cf. 7:29; 9:6; Jn 17:2; Dan 7:13-14).[339] One may contrast here Satan's offer in 4:8-9; by pursuing obedience Jesus received more than Satan offered (France 1985: 413). Jewish teachers felt that confessing the one Lord by means of the Shema expressed submission to God's royal authority (m. Ber. 2:5); this passage indicates that such submission requires confession of Jesus (cf. 10:32). Making disciples for Jesus alone and not for themselves (23:8-10) also portrays Jesus as more than a normal rabbi (28:19).

Disciples baptize not only in the name of the Father and the Holy Spirit, whom biblical and Jewish tradition regarded as divine,[340] but also in the name of the Son. Placing Jesus on the same level as the Father and Spirit makes even

338. Parkhurst 1979 suggests that the object of doubt is the high Christology implied in worshiping him (for another nontraditional reading cf. Grayston 1984); while this makes sense of the following context, it lacks sufficient clarity in its immediate context. In any case, ancients viewed skepticism with regard to deities or holy men as potentially dangerous (b. B. Bat. 75a; Pesiq. Rab Kah. 18:5) or at least humiliating (Epidauros inscr. 3-4 in Grant 1953: 56-57); doubtlessness was virtuous (Sifra Shemini Mekhilta deMiluim 99.5.13).

339. Most scholars recognize the influence of Dan 7 here (e.g., Fuller 1971, also comparing Mt 11:27; Jn 3:35; Michel 1995: 45-46; Ellis 1974: 22; Meier 1980: 369; Garland 1993: 267); despite notable differences between the two texts, the allusion seems likely (cf. 9:6; 24:30; 26:64; pace Vögtle 1964; Gundry 1982: 595). If *edothē* is an ingressive aorist, it suggests that Jesus' reign began at the resurrection (Jeremias 1971: 310). Malina and Rohrbaugh 1992: 24 find an echo of 2 Chron 36:23, which closes the Hebrew Bible, just as Mt 1:1 echoes Genesis; the allusion seems strongest in v. 18, but closer verbal parallels elsewhere make the connection at best hypothetical.

340. Jewish tradition did not articulate a doctrine of the Spirit's personality or distinction from the Father, as Christian theology came to do (e.g., Jn 14:16-17, 26; 15:26; 16:7-15; see Keener 1991b: 233-65). Baptism "in the name of the Spirit" may remind believers that this baptism alluded to an experience greater than any that accompanied John's (cf. 3:11).

more explicit what is implicit in Acts's "baptism in Jesus' name" (Acts 2:38; 8:16; 10:48; 19:5; cf. 22:16)[341] — that is, that Jesus is divine (28:19). While many doubt the authenticity of this baptismal formula (e.g., Bultmann 1985: 252; its specific form could be a Matthean or traditional construct summarizing what they felt was Jesus' idea), it certainly climaxes Matthew's emphasis on Jesus' deity (1:23) and authority (28:18).[342]

Still, even the formula could go back to prior Christian tradition or to Jesus himself (cf. Did. 7:1-3).[343] Albright and Mann (1971: 362) point out that the trinitarian formula is established by the period of our first extant Christian documents (1 Cor 12:4-6; 2 Cor 13:14; see especially Fee 1994: 839-42) and widespread in the church (1 Pet 1:2; 1 Jn 3:23-24; Did. 7:1, 3; Odes Sol. 23:22);[344] Mark already pairs "Father" and "Son," as do Q (Mt 16:27) and Johannine tradition; and "For all we know, such a saying may have stood in the now-lost ending of Mark."[345] The formula distinguishes Christian from other forms of Jewish proselyte baptism (see comments on 3:5-9).

341. Jesus' divinity is explicit in Luke's theology of baptism in Jesus' name, Acts 2:38 fulfilling Joel's prophecy recorded in 2:21. Lachs 1987: 442 compares "into the name" with the Heb. *leshem,* "for the purpose of," but rabbinic evidence for "baptism in the name of heaven [i.e., God]" may be more fruitful (Abrahams 1917: 45). Cf. repentance "in the name of the Most High God" (Jos. and Asen. 15:7); salvation "in the name of the Lord of Spirits" (1 Enoch 48:7); for a summary of various uses of "name" in the Tenach, see, e.g., Keener 1993: 299-300. Our earliest evidence for Christian communities shows that initiatory baptism was already in place (see Meeks 1986: 99).

342. Davies 1993: 207 misses this motif, regarding Jesus' inclusion here as merely that of a human being whose Sonship was "exemplary for other human beings."

343. Schaberg 1982: 335-36 finds it in a traditional midrash behind Matthew's redaction, based on the triad of Ancient of Days, one like a son of man, and angels in Dan 7. She doubts, however, that it is fully trinitarian, even in Matthew, thinking the Spirit is assimilated to angels and a human but heavenly figure accepted into the divine council (336-37); Dan 7 does, after all, appear in v. 18 (Allison 1993b: 265-66). Meier 1980: 371 more plausibly accepts the trinitarian sense in Matthew, though also viewing the formula as pre-Matthean (probably from his community's liturgy); trinitarian language certainly predates this Gospel (e.g., in Paul). France 1985: 415 argues from the baptism in Jesus' name in Acts that the explicit trinitarian formula is the church's language (cf. Carson 1984b: 598, who also doubts that this represents the *ipsissima verba*); but if trinitarian language is as early as Paul (see Fee 1994: 839-42) there is no reason why it cannot have originated with the risen Christ, so the question of the language's origin should remain open.

344. Cf. Athenag. *Plea* 24; Acts of Jn 94.1-2; in Justin, Kaye 1912: 54; Chadwick 1964: 287; much later, Sib. Or. prol. 15-16. Though regarding both as deity, the early Christians did not confuse Jesus with the Father the way that many forms of ancient mysticism could coalesce persons (e.g., *PDM* 14.349). Proposed earlier pagan trinities (e.g., Diop 1974: 194) are just subgroups within polytheistic pantheons (e.g., Book of Dead Spells 1; 142), which could as easily come to more or less than three in other cases. The Christian doctrine can hardly derive from such sources; those who formulated the established Christian doctrine did so inductively from NT texts that in many cases had not themselves emphasized the triadic nature so clearly. Later Judaism accommodated the Christian trinity for Gentile Christians as *shittuf,* partnership, while denying it to Jews for whom they claimed God held a higher standard (Schoeps 1963: 16-17; Berger and Wyschogrod 1978: 33; Jocz 1979: 13; Borowitz 1980: 32; Falk 1985: 33-35).

345. This assumes, of course, that Mk 16 did not originally end with 16:8; it may have done so, however (for abrupt endings, see, e.g., Ps-Philo; Isoc. *Demon.* 52, *Or.* 1; Plut. *Fame of Athenians* 8, *Mor.* 351B; and other references above).

One other aspect of this pericope emphasizes Matthew's high Christology. Jesus' continuing presence with his followers even after his departure (28:20) suggests his omnipresence — an attribute limited to deity alone (see comment on 1:23; 18:20).

Finally, the narrative teaches the Matthean community about its mission (28:18-20).[346] Because Jesus has all authority, because he is king in the kingdom of God, his disciples must carry on the mission of teaching the kingdom (10:7).[347] Jesus' instructions include an imperative surrounded by three participial clauses: one should make disciples for Jesus by going, baptizing, and "teaching." Conjoined with "discipling," the "teaching" involves instruction no less serious than Jewish sages customarily provided their students. In the full context of Matthew, it includes making the kind of disciples Jesus made, to carry on his mission of proclaiming and demonstrating his kingdom or rulership.

Jesus' "authority" (28:18) includes authority to tell his subordinates to "go" (cf. 8:9); the probably independent attestation of the phrase in Mark 16:15 suggests that this was part of Jesus' final commission. Making disciples involves "going" (28:19), as it had before (10:7). Because "going" is a participle, we could read, "as you go," essentially, "on your way," implying that one need not cross cultural boundaries to fulfill this commission (Culver 1968).[348] But this suggestion misses the parallel between the final commission and the model mission in chapter 10: even while remaining within Galilee, the disciples had to proclaim the kingdom to those who had not yet heard the message (10:7; cf. Mk 1:38). Further, the participle is aorist: perhaps "having gone," the going being presupposed in the commission; the aorist participle "going" may represent part of the command, the aorist imperative "make disciples," whereas the two present participles explain how to make disciples (Rogers 1973; cf. White 1960:

346. Jewish teachers, who heavily emphasized traditioning through disciples (e.g., ARN 1A; 1, §2B) and disciples replacing them (Pesiq. R. 51:2, bar.), recognized that prophets, like teachers, trained disciples to succeed them (Sir 46:1; 48:12; Test. Mos. 1:7; 10:15; Mek. Pisha 1.150-53; even patriarchs, in Jub. 19:17), though they did not always succeed in maintaining the same level of power (Pesiq. Rab Kah. 24:18). Smith 1978: 113 parallels Jesus' sending his disciples (e.g., 10:1) with magic being taught and its powers imparted to others, but this ignores the abundance of nearer parallels. Drawing parallels between characters was standard practice (e.g., Polyb. *R.R.E.* 10.2; Plut. *Theseus* 1.2), and those who did so normally located parallels in their abundant data or traditions rather than inventing them (Plut. *Sertorius* 1.1).

347. They continue Jesus' message earlier in the Gospel (4:17; Scaer 1991). Some scholars find in the sequence (preamble, demand, promise) a covenant format, or echoes of biblical commissioning language (De Ridder 1971a: 178; Hubbard 1974; Smyth 1975; Carson 1984b: 591-92). Additional precedents for authorization-commission are also possible, though probably more distant; e.g., in the final form of the Pentateuch God commissions Adam and Noah to "subdue" the earth (Gen 1:28) because all was *beyedkem nitanu,* "given into your hands" (Gen 9:2), which prefigures Israel's commission for conquering the promised land (cf. perhaps Jub. 6:5). For comments on farewell discourses (directed toward Mk 13), see Robbins 1992: 174-75.

348. Cf., e.g., "Going, learn what . . ." Hos 6:6 means (Mt 9:13), but contrast, "I coming will heal him" (8:7), where the participle is significant whether one reads the sentence as a statement or a question.

127n.3). But this does not require us to subordinate "going" excessively since Matthew often uses this participle in a sense coordinate with the main verb (cf. 2:8; 11:4; 17:27; 28:7; Blomberg 1992a: 431). Thus "going" may be one of the three components here of "making disciples" for Jesus, one that helps explain discipling the *nations*.

Greek tradition could praise those who made many disciples (e.g., Diog. Laert. 8.1.16); Greek philosophers thought in terms of "conversion" to philosophy (see Nock 1933a) and various cults were propagated by travelers in antiquity (Stambaugh and Balch 1986: 42; for Christians, cf. Acts 8:4; Liefeld 1967: 151; Malherbe 1983: 65). Judaism also spoke of sages with disciples (cf. comment on 4:19; 19:21-22), spoke of discipleship to earlier stages in transmission of the Torah like Moses or Ezra (e.g., Philo *Spec. Leg.* 1.345; 2.88; b. Sanh. 11a, bar.; Soṭa 48b; Song Rab. 8:9, §3), emphasized sages raising up many disciples (m. 'Abot 1:1), and sometimes even spoke of persuading large numbers of people to become more peripheral students of Torah (e.g., ARN 26, §54; Qoh. Rab. 11:6, §1); they also separately recognized the conversion of Gentiles (cf. on 23:15; see De Ridder 1971a; idem 1971b). But ancient hearers would, and modern hearers should, recognize a drastic innovation in a command to disciple "nations." To be sure, the discipling of nations is carried out through baptizing and teaching individuals in those nations; although exceptions to grammatical consistency in antiquity abound, it is probably significant that the object "them" attaching to baptizing and teaching (28:19-20) is masculine *(autous)* rather than neuter *(auta),* although "nations" *(ta ethnē)* is neuter. Nevertheless, the stark command to disciple "nations" implies more than producing disciples for any ancient teacher would, and in contrast to other disciplers Jesus' followers would not disciple others to themselves (23:8).

All "nations" probably signifies "all peoples," rather than the modern concept of "nation-states" (McGavran and Arn 1977: 38; for people-groups see rightly Piper 1993: 169-81). Also far from abandoning the mission to his own people, Matthew's commission represents "peoples" and not simply "Gentiles" (De Kruijf 1993; Saldarini 1994: 59-60, 78-81; cf. Meier 1977a). When Matthew adds "all nations" to a Markan logion (Matt 24:9), he clearly includes Jewish participation (10:17-18; Stanton 1993: 158). Those who prefer to translate "Gentiles," however (e.g., Hre Kio 1990; Luz 1992), are correct that Gentile peoples are where the emphasis lies, because this statement extends the commission in chapter 10, which was explicitly limited to Jews (see Levine 1988: 191).

On either translation, therefore, what is important to remember is that the Gentile mission extends the Jewish mission — not replaces it; Jesus nowhere revokes the mission to Israel (10:6), but merely adds a new mission revoking a previous prohibition (10:5).[349] Given the context of his whole Gospel it is most rea-

349. Simply because Jewish-Christians perhaps could not witness in some *synagogues* after 85 would not end their witness among their acquaintances (see Hagner 1996: 43). It is doubtful that Matthew would think that the church proclaims the kingdom as the "new Israel" (as in Roux 1956: 294).

sonable to suppose that Matthew lays the emphasis here on Gentile peoples, whom his predominantly Jewish-Christian community most needs to be encouraged in evangelizing; they were already deeply engaged with the needs of their own ethnic communities. Matthew elsewhere emphasizes the nations (1:3-5; 2:1-2; 3:9; 4:15; 8:5, 11, 28; 11:21-22; 12:41-42; 15:22; 16:13; 27:54), including the importance of their hearing the message of the kingdom before the kingdom and judgment come (24:14; 25:31-32; perhaps Rom 1:5; 16:26 indirectly reflect the tradition Matthew preserves here).

But wherever God leads particular disciples to carry out this commission ("going"), the text is clear on the other ways one makes disciples. First of all, one baptizes them under the rulership of Christ. Baptism was an act of initiation and conversion (see comment on 3:6), and this text suggests that disciples initiate others into the faith. Baptism was part of Christian practice universally and from the first, and it is unlikely that the early Jewish Christians borrowed John's practice of proselyte-baptizing fellow Jews without some sort of approval from Jesus (cf. Jn 4:1-2); thus a command of Jesus to baptize is historically likely (Taylor 1997: 299).[350] But once they are initiated, mature disciples must also build the new disciples into stronger discipleship by teaching them Jesus' message. The summaries of Jesus' teachings earlier in Matthew's Gospel (chs. 5–7; 10; 13; 18; 23–25) work well as a discipling manual for young believers. Various passages in fact epitomize Jesus' commandments (7:12; 12:7; 22:37-40; 23:23), but the community still requires specific articulation of the older commandments in light of the kingdom (5:17-19; 13:52). Few Jewish teachers would admit proselytes without basic instruction in the demands of Judaism; Jesus' command to teach his message is at least implicit in sending his followers, and was probably explicit as well (see De Ridder 1971a: 108); here, as in Jewish instruction in Judaism, the process of teaching continues subsequent to the initiation.

The Gospel closes with a promise. As his disciples carry out the great commission, Jesus will be with them to the end of the age (28:20).[351] The text probably specifies the end of the age because at that time the Son of Man would return in his kingdom — after the nations had heard the good news of the kingdom (24:14), and hence been prepared for the judgment (25:32-36). Until his coming, the disciples would thus need to exemplify Jesus' reign on earth as it is in heaven (cf. 6:10). If many Christians today have lost a sense of

350. Cf. likewise Argyle 1963: 222, arguing from the universality of the early Christian practice; pace Bultmann 1958: 153, who improbably attributes the practice to the hellenistic church (ignoring the common function between Christian and proselyte baptism shared via the Baptist; see comment on 3:5-6).

351. Unlike Luke (Lk 24:51; Acts 1:9-11), Matthew does not narrate the ascension (though implied in Mt 24:30; 26:64; Mk 13:26; 14:62; Jn 20:17) because he stresses Jesus' continuing presence and reign; cf. Kingsbury 1975: 32. The final pericope of his Gospel proleptically anticipates the parousia (Meier 1979: 37-38); "until the termination of the age" could imply imminence (cf. Sib. Or. 3.756-57) as easily as delay.

Jesus' presence and purpose among them, it may be because they have lost sight of the mission their Lord has given them. Those who would be his disciples must prepare the way for his future coming and his kingdom, as John the Baptist did for his first (3:1-3).

Bibliography of Secondary Sources Cited

Aalders, G. C.

1960 "De 'gruwel der verwoesting.'" *Gereformeerd Theologisch Tijdschrift* 60: 1-5. (*New Testaments Abstracts;* hereafter *NTA* 5:26)

Aalen, L.

1957/1958 "Lysets begrep i de synoptiske evangelier [The Nation of Light in the Synoptic Gospels]." *Svensk Exegetisk Årsbok* 22-23: 17-31. (*NTA* 3:237)

Aalen, Sverre.

1962 "'Reign' and 'House' in the Kingdom of God in the Gospels." *New Testament Studies* 8: 215-40.

Abelson, Joshua.

1969 *The Immanence of God in Rabbinical Literature.* 2d ed. New York: Hermon.

Aberbach, Moses.

1966-1967 "The Relations between Master and Disciple in the Talmudic Age." 1:1-24 in *Essays Presented to Chief Rabbi Brodie.* 2 vols. Edited by H. J. Zimmels. London: Soncino Press.

Abogunrin, Sanuel O.

1980 "The Modern Search of the Historical Jesus in Relation to Christianity in Africa." *Africa Theological Journal* 9: 18-29.

1987 "The Synoptic Gospel Debate: A Re-Examination in the African Context." *African Journal of Biblical Studies* 2: 25-51.

Abrahams, I.

1917 *Studies in Pharisaism and the Gospels.* 1st series. Cambridge: Cambridge University Press.

1924 *Studies in Pharisaism and the Gospels.* 2d series. Cambridge: Cambridge University Press.

Abrahams, R. G.

1973 "Some Aspects of Levirate." Pp. 163-74 in *The Character of Kinship.* Edited by Jack Goody. New York: Cambridge University Press.

BIBLIOGRAPHY OF SECONDARY SOURCES CITED

Abrahamsen, Valerie Ann.

1986 "The Rock Reliefs and the Cult of Diana at Philippi." Th.D. dissertation, Harvard Divinity School.

Abramowski, Luise.

1991 "The 'Memoirs of the Apostles' in Justin." Pp. 323-35 in *The Gospel and the Gospels.* Edited by Peter Stuhlmacher. Grand Rapids: Eerdmans.

Achtemeier, Paul J.

1976 "Jesus and the Disciples as Miracle Workers in the Apocryphal New Testament." Pp. 149-86 in *Aspects of Religious Propaganda in Judaism and Early Christianity.* Edited by Elisabeth Schüssler Fiorenza. University of Notre Dame Center for the Study of Judaism and Christianity in Antiquity 2. Notre Dame: University of Notre Dame Press.

Adamo, David Tuesday.

1986 "The Place of Africa and Africans in the Old Testament and Its Environment." Ph.D. dissertation, Baylor University Press.

Adams, William Y.

1977 *Nubia: Corridor to Africa.* Princeton: Princeton University Press.

Adan-Bayewitz, David, and Isadore Perlman.

1990 "The Local Trade of Sepphoris in the Roman Period." *Israel Exploration Journal* 40: 153-72.

Addley, W. P.

1976 "Matthew 18 and the Church as the Body of Christ." *Biblical Theology* 26: 12-18.

Adinolfi, M.

1979 "Il servo di Jhwh nel logion servizio e del riscatto (*Mc.* 10,45)." *Bibbia e Oriente* 21: 43-61. (*NTA* 24: 24)

1994 "Il lago di Tiberiade e le sue città nella letteratura greco-romana." *Studii Biblici Franciscani Liber Annuus* 44: 375-80. *(NTA)*

Ådna, J.

1992-1993 "The Attitude of Jesus to the Temple: A critical examination of how Jesus' relationship to the temple is evaluated within Israeli scholarship, with particular regard to the Jerusalem School." *Mishkan* 17-18: 65-80. *(NTA)*

1992 "Herrens tjener i Jesaja 53 skildret som triumferende Messias, Profettargumens gjengivelse og tolkning av Jes 52,13-53,12." *Tidsskrift for Teologi og Kirke* 63 (2,1992): 81-94.

Agourides, Savas.

1984 "'Little Ones' in Matthew." *Bible Translator* 35: 329-34.

1992 "The Birth of Jesus and the Herodian Dynasty: An Understanding of Matthew, Chapter 2." *Greek Orthodox Theological Review* 37: 135-46.

Akano, Y.

1992 "The Ethical Teaching of Matthew 25:31-46." [In Japanese.] *Katorikku Kenkyu* 31: 141-65. (*NTA* 37:352)

Aland, Kurt, editor.

1980-1982 *Synopsis of the Four Gospels: Greek-English Edition of the Synopsis Quattuor Evangeliorum.* 4th/5th ed. New York: United Bible Societies.

Albert, P., and J. Neumann.

1989 "An Ancient 'Correlation' between Streamflow and Distant Rainfall in the Near East." *Journal of Near Eastern Studies* 48: 313-14.

BIBLIOGRAPHY OF SECONDARY SOURCES CITED

Albright, William Foxwell.

1946 *From the Stone Age to Christianity: Monotheism and the Historical Process.* Baltimore: Johns Hopkins University Press.

1963 *The Biblical Period from Abraham to Ezra.* New York: Harper & Row.

1968 *Yahweh and the Gods of Canaan.* The Jordan Lectures 1965, delivered at the School of Oriental and African Studies, University of London. Garden City, NY: Doubleday and Company.

Albright, William Foxwell, and C. S. Mann.

1971 *Matthew.* Anchor Bible. Garden City, NY: Doubleday and Company.

Aleixandre, Dolores.

1987 "En torno a la cuarta petición del padrenuestro." *Estudios Bíblicos* 45: 325-36. (*NTA* 33:22)

Alexander, Loveday C. A.

1993 "Acts and Ancient Intellectual Biography." Pp. 31-63 in *The Book of Acts in Its Ancient Literary Setting.* Edited by Bruce W. Winter and Andrew D. Clarke. Vol. 1 in The Book of Acts in Its First Century Setting. Grand Rapids: Eerdmans; Carlisle: The Paternoster Press.

1998 "Ancient Book Production and the Circulation of the Gospels." Pp. 71-112 in *The Gospels for All Christians: Rethinking the Gospel Audiences.* Edited by Richard J. Bauckham. Grand Rapids: Eerdmans.

Alexander, P. S.

1995 "Bavli Berakhot 55a-57b: The Talmudic Dreambook in Context." *Journal of Jewish Studies* 46: 230-48.

Alexander, William Menzies.

1980 *Demonic Possession in the New Testament: Its Historical, Medical, and Theological Aspects.* Grand Rapids: Baker; reprint from Edinburgh: T & T Clark, 1902.

Allegro, J. M.

1956a "Further Light on the History of the Qumran Sect." *Journal of Biblical Literature* 75: 85-95.

1956b "Further Messianic References in Qumran Literature." *Journal of Biblical Literature* 75: 174-87.

1964 "An Astrological Cryptic Document from Qumran." *Journal of Semitic Studies* 9: 291-93.

Allen, Lloyd.

1992 "The Sermon on the Mount in the History of the Church." *Review and Expositor* 89: 245-62.

Allen, Willoughby C.

1977 *A Critical and Exegetical Commentary on the Gospel according to S. Matthew.* 3d ed. International Critical Commentary. Edinburgh: T & T Clark.

Allison, Dale C., Jr.

1983 "Matt. 23:39 = Luke 13:35b as a Conditional Prophecy." *Journal for the Study of the New Testament* 18: 75-84.

1984 "Elijah Must Come First." *Journal of Biblical Literature* 103: 256-58.

1987a "The Eye Is the Lamp of the Body (Matthew 6.22-23 = Luke 11.34-36)." *New Testament Studies* 33: 61-83.

1987b "Jesus and Moses (Mt 5:1-2)." *The Expository Times* 98: 203-5.

1988 "Two Notes on a Key Text: Matthew 11:25-30." *Journal of Theological Studies* 39: 477-85.

1989 "Who Will Come from East and West? Observations on Matt 8.11-12–Luke 13.28-29." *Irish Biblical Studies* 11: 158-70.

1990 "'The hairs of your head are all numbered.'" *The Expository Times* 101: 334-36.

1992 "The Baptism of Jesus and a New Dead Sea Scroll." *Biblical Archaeology Review* 18 (2, 1992): 58-60.

1993a "Divorce, Celibacy and Joseph (Matthew 1.18-25 and 19.1-12)." *Journal for the Study of the New Testament* 49: 3-10.

1993b *The New Moses: A Matthean Typology.* Minneapolis: Fortress Press.

1993c "What Was the Star That Guided the Magi?" *Bible Review* 9: 20-24, 63.

1994 "A Plea for Thoroughgoing Eschatology." *Journal of Biblical Literature* 113: 651-68.

1998 *Jesus of Nazareth: Millenarian Prophet.* Minneapolis: Fortress Press.

Almiñana Lloret, V. J.

1970 "Proximidad de los tiempos escatológicos y sus signos según los escritos de Qumrán." *Estudios Eclesiásticos* 45: 153-72. (*NTA* 15:103)

Alsup, John E.

1981 "Type, Placement, and Function of the Pronouncement Story in Plutarch's *Moralia.*" *Semeia* 20: 15-27.

Amaru, Betsy H.

1983 "The Killing of the Prophets: Unraveling a Midrash." *Hebrew Union College Annual* 54: 153-80.

1988 "Portraits of Biblical Women in Josephus' Antiquities." *Journal of Jewish Studies* 39: 143-70.

Ambrozic, Alcysius M.

1990 "Reflections on the first beatitude." *Communio/International Catholic Review* 17: 95-104.

Amiran, D. H. K., E. Arieh, and T. Turcotte.

1994 "Earthquakes in Israel and Adjacent Areas: Macroseismic Observations since 100 B.C.E." *Israel Exploration Journal* 44: 260-305.

Ancient Near Eastern Texts Relating to the Old Testament.

1955 Edited by James Pritchard. 2d ed. Princeton: Princeton University Press.

Anderson, Hugh.

1976 *The Gospel of Mark.* New Century Bible. London: Oliphants (Marshall, Morgan & Scott).

Anderson, Janice Capel.

1985 "Double and Triple Stories, the Implied Reader, and Redundancy in Matthew." *Semeia* 31: 71-89.

1994 *Matthew's Narrative Web: Over, and Over, and Over Again.* Journal for the Study of the New Testament Supplement 91. Sheffield: JSOT Press, Sheffield Academic Press.

1996 "Matthew: Sermon and Story." Pp. 233-250 in *Treasures New and Old: Recent Contributions to Matthean Studies.* Edited by David R. Bauer and Mark Allan Powell. Society of Biblical Literature Symposium Series 1. Atlanta: Scholars Press.

Andiñach, P.

1990 "Una antigua barca del Mar de Galilea." *Revista Bíblica* 52: 178-84. (*NTA* 36:225)

Angus, S.

1925 *The Mystery-Religions and Christianity.* New York: Charles Scribner's Sons.

BIBLIOGRAPHY OF SECONDARY SOURCES CITED

Anthonysamy, S. J.

1980 "The Gospel of Mark and the Universal Mission." *Biblebhashyam* 6: 81-96.

Applebaum, Shim'on.

1971 "The Zealots: The Case for Reevaluation." *Journal of Roman Studies* 61: 155-70.

1974/1976a "Economic Life in Palestine." Pp. 631-700 in *The Jewish People in the First Century: Historical Geography, Political History, Social, Cultural and Religious Life and Institutions.* 2 vols. Edited by S. Safrai and M. Stern with D. Flusser and W. C. van Unnik. Section 1 of Compendia Rerum Iudaicarum ad Novum Testamentum. Vol. 1: Assen: Van Gorcum & Co., B.V.; Vol. 2: Philadelphia: Fortress Press.

1974/1976b "The Organization of the Jewish Communities in the Diaspora." Pp. 464-503 in *The Jewish People in the First Century: Historical Geography, Political History, Social, Cultural and Religious Life and Institutions.* 2 vols. Edited by S. Safrai and M. Stern with D. Flusser and W. C. van Unnik. Section 1 of Compendia Rerum Iudaicarum ad Novum Testamentum. Vol. 1: Assen: Van Gorcum & Co., B.V.; Vol. 2: Philadelphia: Fortress Press.

1979 *Jews and Greeks in Ancient Cyrene.* Studies in Judaism in Late Antiquity 28. Leiden: E. J. Brill.

Arai, S.

1983 "Individual und Gemeindeethik bei Lukas." *Annual of the Japanese Biblical Institute* 9: 88-127. (*NTA* 28:250)

Arav, Rami.

1991 "Bethsaida, 1989." *Israel Exploration Journal* 41: 184-85.

Arav, R., and J. Rousseau.

1993 "Bethsaïde, ville perdue et retrouvée." *Revue Biblique* 100: 415-28.

Argyle, A. W.

1956 "An Alleged Semitism." *Expository Times* 67: 247.

1963 *The Gospel According to Matthew.* Cambridge: Cambridge University Press.

1969 "The Meaning of *exousia* in Mark I:22, 27." *Expository Times* 80: 343.

1973 "Greek among the Jews of Palestine in New Testament Times." *New Testament Studies* 20: 87-89.

1975 "Wedding Customs at the Time of Jesus." *Expository Times* 86: 214-15.

Armenti, Joseph R.

1981 "On the Use of the Term 'Galileans' in the Writings of Josephus Flavius: A Brief Note." *Jewish Quarterly Review* 72: 45-49.

Arnéra, G.

1984 "Du rocher d'Esaïe aux douze montagnes d'Hermas." *Etudes Théologiques et Religieuses* 59: 215-20. (*NTA* 29:20)

Arnold, Clinton E.

1989 *Ephesians: Power and Magic. The Concept of Power in Ephesians in Light of Its Historical Setting.* Society for New Testament Studies 63. Cambridge: Cambridge University Press.

Arrington, French L.

1978 *Paul's Aeon Theology in 1 Corinthians.* Washington, D.C.: University Press of America.

Ashton

1991 *Understanding the Fouth Gospel.* Oxford: Clarendon Press.

BIBLIOGRAPHY OF SECONDARY SOURCES CITED

Assmann, Jan.

1992 "When Justice Fails: Jurisdiction and Imprecation in Ancient Egypt and the Near East." *Journal of Egyptian Archaeology* 78: 149-62.

Attridge, Harold W.

1986 "Jewish Historiography." Pp. 311-43 in *Early Judaism and Its Modern Interpreters.* Edited by Robert A. Kraft and George W. E. Nickelsburg. Society of Biblical Literature Bible and Its Modern Interpreters Series 2. Atlanta: Scholars Press.

Aune, David Edward.

1972 *The Cultic Setting of Realized Eschatology in Early Christianity.* Supplements to Novum Testamentum 28. Leiden: E. J. Brill.

1975 "The Significance of the Delay of the Parousia for Early Christianity." Pp. 87-109 in *Current Issues in Biblical and Patristic Interpretation: Studies in Honor of Merrill C. Tenney Presented by His Former Students.* Edited by Gerald F. Hawthorne. Grand Rapids: Eerdmans.

1980 "Magic in Early Christianity." *Aufstieg und Niedergang der römischen Welt.* 2.23.1.1507-57.

1981 "The Problem of the Genre of the Gospels: A Critique of C. H. Talbert's *What Is a Gospel?*" 2:9-60 in Gospel Perspectives. 6 vols. Edited by R. T. France and David Wenham. Sheffield: JSOT Press, 1980-1986. Vol. 2: *Studies of History and Tradition in the Four Gospels.* Sheffield: JSOT Press.

1983 *Prophecy in Early Christianity and the Ancient Mediterranean World.* Grand Rapids: Eerdmans.

1987 *The New Testament in Its Literary Environment.* Library of Early Christianity 8. Philadelphia: Westminster Press.

1988 "Greco-Roman Biography." Pp. 107-26 in *Greco-Roman Literature and the New Testament: Selected Forms and Genres.* Edited by David E. Aune. Society of Biblical Literature Sources for Biblical Study 21. Atlanta: Scholars Press.

Avigad, Nahman.

1976 "How the Wealthy Lived in Herodian Jerusalem." *Biblical Archaeology Review* 2: 1, 23-35.

1980 *Discovering Jerusalem.* Nashville: Thomas Nelson.

1983a "The Burnt House Captures a Moment in Time." *Biblical Archaeology Review* 9 (6, November-December): 66-72.

1983b "Jerusalem Flourishing — A Craft Center for Stone, Pottery, and Glass." *Biblical Archaeology Review* 9: 48-65.

Avi-Yonah, Michael.

1952 "The 'War of the Sons of Light and the Sons of Darkness' and Maccabean Warfare." *Israel Exploration Journal* 2: 1-5.

1974/76a "Archaeological Sources." Pp. 46-62 in *The Jewish People in the First Century: Historical Geography, Political History, Social, Cultural and Religious Life and Institutions.* 2 vols. Ed. S. Safrai and M. Stern with D. Flusser and W. C. van Unnik. Section 1 of Compendia Rerum Iudaicarum ad Novum Testamentum. Vol. 1: Assen: Van Gorcum & Co.; Vol. 2: Philadelphia: Fortress Press.

1974/76b "Historical Geography." Pp. 78-116 in *The Jewish People in the First Century: Historical Geography, Political History, Social, Cultural and Religious Life and Institutions.* 2 vols. Ed. S. Safrai and M. Stern with D. Flusser and W. C. van Unnik. Section 1 of Compendia Rerum Iudaicarum ad Novum

Testamentum. Vol. 1: Assen: Van Gorcum & Co.; Vol. 2: Philadelphia: Fortress Press.

1978 *Hellenism and the East: Contacts and Interrelations from Alexander to the Roman Conquest.* Jerusalem: Institute of Languages, Literature and the Arts, The Hebrew University; University Microfilms International.

Bacchiocchi, Samuele.

1977 *From Sabbath to Sunday. A Historical Investigation of the Rise of Sunday Observance in Early Christianity.* Rome: Gregorian University Press.

1984 "Matthew 11:28-30: Jesus' Rest and the Sabbath." *Andrews University Seminary Studies* 22: 289-316.

Badian, E.

1972 *Publicans and Sinners: Private Enterprise in the Service of the Roman Republic.* Ithaca, NY: Cornell University Press.

Baer, Richard A., Jr.

1970 *Philo's Use of the Categories Male and Female.* Arbeiten zur Literatur und Geschichte des hellenistichen Judentums 3. Leiden: E. J. Brill.

Bagatti, Bellarmino.

1971 *The Church from the Circumcision.* Jerusalem: Franciscan Printing Press.

1981 "Dove avvenne la moltiplicazione dei pani?" *Salmanticensis* 28: 293-98. (*NTA* 26:131)

Bailey, Kenneth Ewing.

1976 *Poet and Peasant: A Literary-Cultural Approach to the Parables in Luke.* Grand Rapids: Eerdmans.

1979 "The Manger and the Inn: The Cultural Background of Luke 2:7." *Near East School of Theology Theological Review* 2: 33-44. (NTA 24:244)

1980 *Through Peasant Eyes: More Lucan Parables, Their Culture and Style.* Grand Rapids: Eerdmans.

1991 "Informal Controlled Oral Tradition and the Synoptic Gospels." *Asia Journal of Theology* 5: 34-54.

Baines, William.

1987 "The Rotas-Sator Square: A New Investigation." *New Testament Studies* 33: 469-76.

Baker, J. A.

1963 Review of T. F. Glasson. *Greek Influence in Jewish Eschatology: With Special Reference to the Apocalypses and Pseudepigraphs.* S.P.C.K. Biblical Monographs 1 (London: S.P.C.K., 1961). *Journal of Theological Studies* 14: 120-21.

Balch, David L.

1991 "The Greek Political Topos περὶ νόμων and Matthew 5:17, 19 and 16:19." Pp. 68-84 in *Social History of the Matthean Community: Cross-Disciplinary Approaches.* Edited by David L. Balch. Minneapolis: Fortress Press.

Bamberger, Bernard J.

1962 *The Story of Judaism.* New York: The Union of American Hebrew Congregations.

1968 *Proselytism in the Talmudic Period.* 2d ed. Foreword by Julian Morgenstern. New York: KTAV.

1969 "The Changing Image of the Prophet in Jewish Thought." Pp. 301-23 in *Interpreting the Prophetic Tradition: The Goldman Lectures 1955-1966.* Edited by Harry M. Orlinski. Cincinnati: Hebrew Union College Press; New York: KTAV.

Bammel, Ernst.

1961 "Matthäus 10:23." *Studia Theologica* 15: 79-92.

1984a "The Poor and the Zealots." Pp. 109-28 in *Jesus and the Politics of His Day.* Edited by Ernst Bammel and C. F. D. Moule. Cambridge: Cambridge University Press.

1984b "The *titulus.*" Pp. 353-64 in *Jesus and the Politics of His Day.* Edited by Ernst Bammel and C. F. D. Moule. Cambridge: Cambridge University Press.

1984c "The Trial before Pilate." Pp. 415-51 in *Jesus and the Politics of His Day.* Edited by Ernst Bammel and C. F. D. Moule. Cambridge: Cambridge University Press.

1984d "The revolution theory from Reimarus to Brandon." Pp. 11-68 in *Jesus and the Politics of His Day.* Edited by Ernst Bammel and C. F. D. Moule. Cambridge: Cambridge University Press.

Bandstra, Andrew J.

1981 "The Original Form of the Lord's Prayer." *Calvin Theological Journal* 16: 15-37.

Barclay, William.

1959a "Great Themes of the NT — VI. Matthew xxiv." *Expository Times* 70: 326-30, 376-79.

1959b *Train Up a Child: Educational Ideals in the Ancient World.* Philadelphia: Westminster Press.

1978 "The One, New Man." Pp. 73-81 in *Unity and Diversity in New Testament Theology: Essays in Honor of George E. Ladd.* Edited by Robert A. Guelich. Grand Rapids: Eerdmans.

Barnard, Leslie William.

1957 "Matt. III.11//Luke III.16." *Journal of Theological Studies* 8: 107.

1964 "The Old Testament and Judaism in the Writings of Justin Martyr." *Vetus Testamentum* 14: 395-406.

1967 *Justin Martyr: His Life and Thought.* Cambridge: Cambridge University Press.

Barnett, Paul.

1977 "The Jewish Eschatological Prophets." Ph.D. dissertation, The University of London.

1981 "The Jewish Signs-Prophets — A.D. 40-70: Their Intentions and Origin." *New Testament Studies* 27: 679-97.

1986 *Is the New Testament Reliable? A Look at the Historical Evidence.* Downers Grove, IL: InterVarsity Press.

Barnouw, Victor.

1955 "Eastern Nepalese Marriage Customs and Kinship Organization." *Southwestern Journal of Anthropology* 11: 15-30.

Barrett, C. K.

1961 *The New Testament Background: Selected Documents.* New York: Harper & Row; London: S.P.C.K., 1956.

1966 *The Holy Spirit and the Gospel Tradition.* London: S.P.C.K.

1967 *Jesus and the Gospel Tradition.* London: S.P.C.K.

1978 *The Gospel according to St. John: An Introduction with Commentary and Notes on the Greek Text.* 2d ed. Philadelphia: Westminster Press.

Barrett, D. S.

1981 "'One-Up' Anecdotes in Jewish Literature of the Hellenistic-Roman Era." *Prudentia* 13: 119-26.

BIBLIOGRAPHY OF SECONDARY SOURCES CITED

Barrow, R. H.

1968 *Slavery in the Roman Empire.* New York: Barnes & Noble; London: Methuen & Co. Reprint of 1928 ed.

Barth, Frederik.

1973 "Descent and Marriage Reconsidered." Pp. 3-19 in *The Character of Kinship.* Edited by Jack Goody. New York: Cambridge University Press.

Barth, Gerhard.

1963 "Matthew's Understanding of the Law." Pp. 58-164 in *Tradition and Interpretation in Matthew.* By Günther Bornkamm, Gerhard Barth, and Heinz Joachim Held. Philadelphia: Westminster Press.

Barth, M.

1981 "Autonome statt messianische Ethik?" *Judaica* 37: 220-33. Review of David Flusser, *Die rabbinischen Gleichnisse und der Gleichniserzähler Jesus. 1. Teil.*

Barthell, E. E., Jr.

1971 *Gods and Goddesses of Ancient Greece.* Miami: University of Miami Press.

Bartnicki, Roman.

1988 "Die Jünger Jesu in Mt 9,35–11,1." *Collectanea Theologica* 58: 39-56.

Barton, John.

1984 *Reading the Old Testament: Method in Biblical Study.* Philadelphia: Westminster Press.

Barton, Stephen.

1998 "Can We Identify the Gospel Audiences?" Pp. 173-94 in *The Gospels for All Christians: Rethinking the Gospel Audiences.* Edited by Richard J. Bauckham. Grand Rapids: Eerdmans.

Bartsch, Hans W.

1980 "Inhalt und Funktion des urchristlichen Osterglaubens." *New Testament Studies* 26: 180-96.

Basser, Herbert W.

1985a "Derrett's 'Binding' Reopened." *Journal of Biblical Literature* 104: 297-300.

1985b "The Meaning of 'Shtuth', Gen. R. 11 in Reference to Matthew 5.29-30 and 18.8-9." *New Testament Studies* 31: 148-51.

1994 "Jesus and the Pharisees: Interpretation of Form and Content." Paper presented to the Rhetoric and New Testament Section of the Society of Biblical Literature 1995 Annual Meeting, Chicago.

Bassler, Jouette M.

1982 *Divine Impartiality: Paul and a Theological Axiom.* Society of Biblical Literature Dissertation 59. Chico, CA: Scholars Press.

Batey, Richard A.

1971 *New Testament Nuptial Imagery.* Leiden: E. J. Brill.

1984 "Jesus and the Theatre." *New Testament Studies* 30: 563-74.

1992 "Sepphoris, An Urban Portrait of Jesus." *Biblical Archaeology Review* 18 (3, 1992): 50-62.

Bauckham, Richard.

1976-1977 "Synoptic Parousia Parables and the Apocalypse." *New Testament Studies* 23: 162-76.

1977 "The Eschatological Earthquake in the Apocalypse of John." *Novum Testamentum* 19: 224-33.

1983 "The Liber Antiquitatum Biblicarum of Pseudo-Philo and the Gospels as

'Midrash.'" 3:33-76 in Gospel Perspectives. 6 vols. Edited by R. T. France, David Wenham, and Craig Blomberg. Sheffield: JSOT Press, 1980-1986. Vol. 3: *Studies in Midrash and Historiography.* Edited by R. T. France and David Wenham. Sheffield: JSOT Press.

1986 "The Coin in the Fish's Mouth." Pp. 219-52 in *The Miracles of Jesus.* Edited by David Wenham and Craig Blomberg. Vol. 6 in Gospel Perspectives. Sheffield: JSOT Press.

1993a "The Acts of Paul as a Sequel to Acts." Pp. 105-52 in *The Book of Acts in Its Ancient Literary Setting.* Edited by Bruce W. Winter and Andrew D. Clarke. Vol. 1 in The Book of Acts in Its First Century Setting. Grand Rapids: Eerdmans; Carlisle: The Paternoster Press.

1993b *The Climax of Prophecy: Studies on the Book of Revelation.* Edinburgh: T. & T. Clark.

1996 "The Parable of the Royal Wedding Feast (Matthew 22:1-14) and the Parable of the Lame Man and the Blind Man *(Apocryphon of Ezekiel).*" *Journal of Biblical Literature* 1996: 471-88.

1998a "For Whom Were Gospels Written?" Pp. 9-48 in *The Gospels for All Christians: Rethinking the Gospel Audiences.* Edited by Richard J. Bauckham. Grand Rapids: Eerdmans.

1998b "Introduction." Pp. 1-9 in *The Gospels for All Christians: Rethinking the Gospel Audiences.* Edited by Richard J. Bauckham. Grand Rapids: Eerdmans.

Bauer, David R.

1988 *The Structure of Matthew's Gospel: A Study in Literary Design.* Journal for the Study of the New Testament Supplement 31. Sheffield: Sheffield Academic Press, Almond Press.

1992 "The Major Characters of Matthew's Story: Their Function and Significance." *Interpretation* 46: 357-67.

1996 "The Literary and Theological Function of the Genealogy in Matthew's Gospel." Pp. 129-59 in *Treasures New and Old: Recent Contributions to Matthean Studies.* Edited by David R. Bauer and Mark Allan Powell. Society of Biblical Literature Symposium Series 1. Atlanta: Scholars Press.

Bauer, David R., and Mark Allan Powell.

1996 "Introduction." Pp. 1-25 in *Treasures New and Old: Recent Contributions to Matthean Studies.* Edited by David R. Bauer and Mark Allan Powell. Society of Biblical Literature Symposium Series 1. Atlanta: Scholars Press.

Baum, Gregory.

1961 *The Jews and the Gospel: A Re-examination of the New Testament.* London: Bloomsbury Publishing Company.

Baumbach, Günther.

1965 "Zeloten und Sikarier." *Theologische Literaturzeitung* 90: 727-40.

1971 "Das Sadduzäerverständnis bei Josephus Flavius und im Neuen Testament." *Kairos* 13: 17-37.

Baumgarten, Albert I.

1983a "Miracles and Halakah in Rabbinic Judaism." *Jewish Quarterly Review* 73: 238-53.

1983b "The Name of the Pharisees." *Journal of Biblical Literature* 102: 411-28.

1984-1985 "*Korban* and the Pharisaic *Paradosis.*" *Journal of Ancient Near Eastern Studies* 16-17: 5-17.

Baumgarten, Joseph M.

1957 "On the Testimony of Women in 1QSa." *Journal of Biblical Literature* 76: 266-69.

1958a "The Beginning of the Day in the Calendar of Jubilees." *Journal of Biblical Literature* 77: 355-60.

1958b "Qumran Studies." *Journal of Biblical Literature* 77: 249-57.

1972 "The Unwritten Law in the Pre-Rabbinic Period." *Journal for the Study of Judaism* 3: 7-29.

1982 "Exclusions from the Temple: Proselytes and Agrippa I." *Journal of Jewish Studies* 33: 215-25.

1983 "4Q 502, Marriage or Golden Age Ritual?" *Journal of Jewish Studies* 34: 125-35.

1987 "The Sabbath Trumpets in *4Q493 M*[c]." *Revue de Qumran* 12: 555-59.

1989 "4Q500 and the Ancient Conception of the Lord's Vineyard." *Journal of Jewish Studies* 40: 1-6.

1990 "The 4Q Zadokite Fragments on Skin Disease." *Journal of Jewish Studies* 41: 153-65.

1992 "A 'Scriptural' Citation in 4Q Fragments of the Damascus Document." *Journal of Jewish Studies* 43 (1, 1992): 95-98.

Baumgarten, Joseph, and Menahem Mansoor.

1955 "Studies in the New *Hodayot* (Thanksgiving Hymns) — II." *Journal of Biblical Literature* 74: 188-95.

Beale, Gregory K.

1984 "The Use of Daniel in the Synoptic Eschatological Discourse and in the Book of Revelation." Pp. 129-53 in *The Jesus Tradition outside the Gospels.* Vol. 5 in Gospel Perspectives. Edited by David Wenham. Sheffield: JSOT Press.

Beare, Francis Wright.

1967 "Sayings of the Risen Jesus in the Synoptic Tradition: An Inquiry into Their Origin and Significance." Pp. 161-81 in *Christian History and Interpretation: Studies Presented to John Knox.* Edited by William R. Farmer, C. F. D. Moule, and R. R. Niebuhr. Cambridge: Cambridge University Press.

1981 *The Gospel according to Matthew.* San Francisco: Harper & Row.

Beasley-Murray, G. R.

1954 *Jesus and the Future: An Examination of the Criticism of the Eschatological Discourse, Mark 13, with Special Reference to the Little Apocalypse Theory.* London: Macmillan & Company.

1957 *A Commentary on Mark Thirteen.* London: Macmillan & Company.

1960 "The Eschatological Discourse of Jesus." *Review and Expositor* 57: 153-66.

1962 *Baptism in the New Testament.* Grand Rapids: Eerdmans.

1974 *The Book of Revelation.* The New Century Bible. Greenwood, SC: Attic Press; London: Marshall, Morgan & Scott.

1983 "Second Thoughts on the Composition of Mark 13." *New Testament Studies* 29: 414-20.

Beavis, Mary Ann L.

1987 "The Trial before the Sanhedrin (Mark 14:53-65): Reader Response and Greco-Roman Readers." *Catholic Biblical Quarterly* 49: 581-96.

Beck, Robert.

1976a "Interpreting the Ponza Zodiac." *Journal of Mithraic Studies* 1: 1-19.

1976b "A note on the scorpion in the tauroctony." *Journal of Mithraic Studies* 1: 208-9.
1976c "The Seat of Mithras at the Equinoxes: Porphyry, *De Antro Nympharum* 24." *Journal of Mithraic Studies* 1: 95-98.

Becker, Jürgen.
1978 "Jesu Frohbotschaft und Freudenmahl für die Armen." *Bibel und Kirche* 33: 43-47.

Beckwith, Roger T.
1981 "Daniel 9 and the Date of Messiah's Coming in Essene, Hellenistic, Pharisaic, Zealot and Early Christian Computation." *Revue de Qumran* 10: 521-42.
1985 *The Old Testament Canon of the New Testament and Its Background in Early Judaism.* Grand Rapids: Eerdmans.

Beechick, Allen.
1980 *The Pre-Tribulation Rapture.* Denver: Accent Books.

Beer, M.
1988 "'l lykwdm hhbrty sl hz'l [On Solidarity among the Sages]." *Zion* 53:149-66. (*NTA* 33:218)

Begg, Christopher.
1988 "The Death of Josiah: Josephus and the Bible." *Ephemerides Theologicae Lovanienses* 64: 157-63.
1989a "Doves and Treaty-Making: Another Possible Reference." *Biblische Notizen* 48: 8-11.
1989b "Josephus's Zedekiah." *Ephemerides Theologicae Lovanienses* 65: 96-104.
1993a "Filling in the Blanks: Josephus' Version of the Campaign of the Three Kings, 2 Kings 3." *Hebrew Union College Annual* 64: 89-109.
1993b "Josephus's Version of Jehu's Putsch (2 Kgs 8,25–10,36)." *Antonianum* 68 (4, 1993): 450-84.
1994 "The Gedaliah Episode and Its Sequels in Josephus." *Journal for the Study of the Pseudepigrapha* 12: 21-46.
1995a "Ahaziah's Fall (2 Kings 1). The Version of Josephus." *Sefarad* 55: 25-40.
1995b "Amaziah of Judah according to Josephus (*Ant.* 9.186-204)." *Antonianum* 70: 3-30.
1995c "Hezekiah's Illness and Visit according to Josephus." *Estudios Bíblicos* 53: 365-85.
1995d "Jehoahaz, King of Israel, according to Josephus." *Sefarad* 55: 227-37.
1995e "Jehoshaphat at Mid-Career according to *AJ* 9,1-17." *Revue Biblique* 102: 379-402.
1995f "Josephus and Nahum Revisited." *Revue des études juives* 154: 5-22.
1995g "Josephus' Portrait of Jehoshaphat Compared with the Biblical and Rabbinic Portrayals." *Biblische Notizen* 78: 39-48.
1995h "Uzziah (Azariah) of Judah according to Josephus." *Estudios Bíblicos* 53: 5-24.
1996 "Jotham and Amon: Two Minor Kings of Judah according to Josephus." *Bulletin for Biblical Research* 6: 1-13.

Beidelman, T. O.
1971 "Some Kaguru Notions about Incest and Other Sexual Prohibitions." Pp. 181-201 in *Rethinking Kinship and Marriage.* Edited by Rodney Needham. Association of Social Anthropologists Monograph 11. New York: Tavistock Publications.

Beitzel, Barry J.
1971 "The *Via Maris* in Literary and Cartographic Sources." *Biblical Archaeologist* 54 (2, 1991): 64-75.

Belkin, Samuel.
1940 *Philo and the Oral Law: The Philonic Interpretation of Biblical Law in Relation to the Palestinian Halakah.* Harvard Semitic Series 11. Cambridge: Harvard University Press.
1970 "Levirate and Agnate Marriage in Rabbinic and Cognate Literature." *Jewish Quarterly Review* 60: 275-329.

Bels, Jacques.
1982 "La survie de l'âme, de Platon à Posidonius." *Revue de l'Histoire des Religions* 199: 169-82.

Benassi, V. M.
1957 "'Chi è mia madre, chi sono i miei fratelli?' (Mt. 12,48ss)." *Marianum* 18: 347-54. *(NTA)*

Benediktson, D. T.
1989 "Caligula's Madness: Madness or Interictal Temporal Lobe Epilepsy?" *Classical World* 82: 370-75.

Benko, Stephen.
1971 "The History of the Early Roman Empire." Pp. 37-80 in *The Catacombs and the Colosseum: The Roman Empire as the Setting of Primitive Christianity.* Edited by Stephen Benko and John J. O'Rourke. Valley Forge: Judson Press.

Bennett, Thomas J.
1987 "Matthew 7:6 — A New Interpretation." *Westminster Theological Journal* 49: 371-86.

Benoit, A.
1975 "Les Mystères Païens et le Christianisme." Pp. 73-92 in *Mystères et Syncrétismes.* Études d'Histoire des Religions 2. Edited by M. Philonenko et M. Simon. Paris: Librairie Orientaliste Paul Geuthner.

Benoit, Pierre.
1973/1974 *Jesus and the Gospels.* 2 vols. Translated by Benet Weatherhead. Vol. 1: New York: Herder & Herder; London: Darton, Longman & Todd. Vol. 2: New York: The Seabury Press (Crossroad); London: Darton, Longman & Todd.

Berger, David, and Michael Wyschogrod.
1978 *Jews and "Jewish Christianity."* New York: KTAV.

Bernegger, P. M.
1983 "Affirmation of Herod's Death in 4 B.C." *Journal of Theological Studies* 34: 526-31.

Best, Ernest.
1965 *The Temptation and the Passion: The Markan Soteriology.* Society for New Testament Studies Momograph 2. Cambridge: Cambridge University Press.
1976 "Mark 10:13-16: The Child as Model Recipient." Pp. 119-34 in *Biblical Studies: Essays in Honor of William Barclay.* Edited by J. R. McKay and J. F. Miller. Philadelphia: Westminster Press.
1977 *A Commentary on the First and Second Epistles to the Thessalonians.* Black's New Testament Commentaries. London: Adam & Charles Black.
1983 *Mark: The Gospel as Story.* Studies of the New Testament and Its World. Edinburgh: T & T Clark.

Best, Thomas F.

1981 "The Transfiguration: A Select Bibliography." *Journal of the Evangelical Theological Society* 24: 157-61.

Betz, Hans Dieter.

1979 "The Sermon on the Mount: Its Literary Genre and Function." *Journal of Religion* 59: 285-97.

1980 "Fragments from a Catabasis Ritual in a Greek Magical Papyrus." *History of Religions* 19: 287-95.

Betz, Otto.

1957 "Felsenmann und Felsengemeinde. (Eine Parallele zu Mt 16,17-19 in den Qumran psalmen)." *Zeitschrift für die Neutestamentliche Wissenschaft* 48: 49-77.

1968 *What Do We Know about Jesus?* Philadelphia: Westminster; London: SCM.

1988 "The Temple Scroll and the Trial of Jesus." *Southwestern Journal of Theology* 30: 5-8.

1990 "Was John the Baptist an Essene?" *Bible Review* 6 (6, 1990): 18-25.

1991 "Jesus' Gospel of the Kingdom." Pp. 53-74 in *The Gospel and the Gospels.* Edited by Peter Stuhlmacher. Grand Rapids: Eerdmans.

Bianchi, Ugo.

1979 "Epilegomena." Pp. 873-79 in *Mysteria Mithrae.* Edited by Ugo Bianchi. Études Préliminaires aux Religions Orientales dans l'Empire Romain tome 80. Publiées par M. J. Vermaseren. Leiden: E. J. Brill.

Bianquis, T.

1988 "Egypt from the Arab conquest until the end of the Fatimid State (1171)." Pp. 163-93 in *Africa from the Seventh to the Eleventh Century.* Vol. 3 in *General History of Africa.* Edited by M. El Fasi; assistant editor I. Hrbek. UNESCO International Scientific Committee for the Drafting of a General History of Africa. Berkeley: University of California Press; London: Heinemann Educational Books; Paris: United Nations Educational, Scientific, and Cultural Organization.

Bietenhard, Hans.

1967 "ὄνομα." 5:242-83 in *Theological Dictionary of the New Testament.* 10 vols. Edited by Gerhard Kittel and Gerhard Friedrich. Grand Rapids: Eerdmans, 1964-1976.

Bilde, Per.

1978 "The Roman Emperor Gaius (Caligula)'s Attempt to Erect His Statue in the Temple of Jerusalem." *Studia Theologica* 32: 67-93.

1979 "The Causes of the Jewish War according to Josephus." *Journal for the Study of Judaism* 10: 179-202.

1980 "Galilaea og galilaeerne på Jesu tid." *Dansk teologisk tijdsskrift* 43: 113-35. (*NTA* 28:177)

Bindemann, Walther.

1991 "Das Brot für morgen gib uns heite. Sozialgeschichtliche Erwägungen zu den Wir-Bitten des Vaterunsers." *Berliner Theologische Zeitschrift* 8: 199-215.

Bishop, Eric Francis Fox.

1958 *Apostles of Palestine: The Local Background to the New Testament Church.* London: Lutterworth Press.

1964 "Bethlehem and the Nativity: Some Travesties of Christmas." *Anglican Theological Review* 46: 401-13.

Bivin, D.
1991 "A Measure of Humility." *Jerusalem Perspective* 4: 13-14.
1992 "Prayers for Emergencies." *Jerusalem Perspective* 5: 16-17.

Black, David Alan.
1988 "Jesus on Anger: The Text of Matthew 5:22a Revisited." *Novum Testamentum* 30: 1-8.

Black, Matthew.
1957 "The Recovery of the Language of Jesus." *New Testament Studies* 3: 305-13.
1961 *The Scrolls and Christian Origins.* London: Thomas Nelson.
1967 *An Aramaic Approach to the Gospels and Acts.* Oxford: Clarendon Press.
1984 "'Not peace but a sword': Matt. 10:34ff.; Luke 12:51ff." Pp. 287-94 in *Jesus and the Politics of His Day.* Ed. Ernst Bammel and C. F. D. Moule. Cambridge: Cambridge University Press.

Blackburn, Barry L.
1986 "'Miracle Working ΘΕΙΟΙ ΑΝΔΡΕΣ' in Hellenism (and Hellenistic Judaism)." 6:185-218 in Gospel Perspectives. 6 vols. Edited by R. T. France and David Wenham. Sheffield: JSOT Press, 1980-1986. Vol. 6: *The Miracles of Jesus.* Edited by David Wenham and Craig Blomberg. Sheffield: JSOT Press.

Blank, Josef.
1989 "Schwört überhaupt nicht." *Orientierung* 53: 97-99.

Blau, Ludwig, and Kaufmann Kohler.
1901-1906 "Angelology." 1:583-97 in *The Jewish Encyclopedia.* 12 vols. Edited by Isidore Singer. New York: Funk & Wagnalls.

Blauw, Johannes.
1962 *The Missionary Nature of the Church.* Grand Rapids: Eerdmans.

Blawatsky, W., and G. Kochelenko.
1966 *Le culte de Mithra sur la côte septentrionale de la Mer Noire.* Études préliminaires aux religions orientales dans l'empire romain tome 8. Leiden: E. J. Brill.

Blidstein, Gerald.
1974 "4QFlorilegium and Rabbinic Sources on Bastard and Proselyte." *Revue de Qumran* 8: 431-35.

Bligh, J.
1964 "'Qorban!'" *Heythrop Journal* 5: 192-93. (*NTA* 9:49)

Blinzler, Josef.
1959 *The Trial of Jesus: The Jewish and Roman proceedings against Jesus Christ described and assessed from the oldest accounts.* Translated by Isabel and Florence McHugh. Westminster, MD: The Newman Press.

Blomberg, Craig L.
1984 "Tradition and Redaction in the Parables of the Gospel of Thomas." 5:177-205 in Gospel Perspectives. 6 vols. Edited by R. T. France, David Wenham, and Craig Blomberg. Sheffield: JSOT Press, 1980-1986. Vol. 5: *The Jesus Tradition outside the Gospels.* Edited by David Wenham. Sheffield: JSOT Press.
1986 "Concluding Reflections on Miracles and Gospel Perspectives." Pp. 443-57 in *Gospel Perspectives: The Miracles of Jesus.* Gospel Perspectives, vol. 6. Edited by David Wenham and Craig Blomberg. Sheffield: JSOT.
1987 *The Historical Reliability of the Gospels.* Downers Grove, IL: InterVarsity Press.

1990a *Interpreting the Parables.* Downers Grove, IL: InterVarsity Press.

1990b "Marriage, Divorce, Remarriage, and Celibacy: An Exegesis of Matthew 19:3-12." *Trinity Journal* 11: 161-96.

1991 "The Liberation of Illegitimacy: Women and Rulers in Matthew 1-2." *Biblical Theology Bulletin* 21: 145-50.

1992a *Matthew.* The New American Commentary 22. Nashville: Broadman Press.

1992b "On Wealth and Worry: Matthew 6:19-34 — Meaning and Significance." *Criswell Theological Review* 6: 73-89.

1995 "Where Do We Start Studying Jesus?" Pp. 17-50 in *Jesus under Fire.* Edited by Michael J. Wilkins and J. P. Moreland. Grand Rapids: Zondervan.

Blue, Bradley.

1994 "Acts and the House Church." Pp. 119-222 in *The Book of Acts in Its Graeco-Roman Setting.* Edited by David W. J. Gill and Conrad Gempf. Vol. 2 in The Book of Acts in Its First Century Setting. Grand Rapids: Eerdmans; Carlisle: The Paternoster Press.

Boccaccini, Gabriele.

1991 *Middle Judaism: Jewish Thought 300 B.C.E. to 200 C.E.* Foreword by James H. Charlesworth. Minneapolis: Fortress Press.

Bock, Darrell L.

1994 *Luke.* The IVP New Testament Commentary Series. Downers Grove, IL: InterVarsity Press.

1995 "The Words of Jesus in the Gospels: Love, Jive, or Memorex?" Pp. 73-99 in *Jesus under Fire.* Edited by Michael J. Wilkins and J. P. Moreland. Grand Rapids: Zondervan.

Bockmuehl, Klaus.

1988 *The Unreal God of Modern Theology. Bultmann, Barth, and the theology of atheism: A call to recovering the truth of God's reality.* Translated by Geoffrey W. Bromiley. Colorado Springs: Helmers & Howard.

Bockmuehl, Marcus N. A.

1989 "Matthew 5.32; 19.9 in the Light of Pre-rabbinic Halakah." *New Testament Studies* 35: 291-95.

Bodendorfer-Langer, G.

1994 "'Und die Hand des Armen und Elenden machte sie nicht stark' (Ez 16,49). Zur Parteilichkeit der Bibel und der unterschiedlichen Wertung in jüdischer und christlicher Auslegung." *Protokolle zur Bibel* 3:9-23.

Boelter, Francis W.

1977 "Sepphoris — Seat of the Galilean Sanhedrin." *Explorations* 3: 36-43.

Boer, P. A. H. de.

1974 *Fatherhood and Motherhood in Israelite and Judean Piety.* Leiden: E. J. Brill.

Boer, W. Den.

1979 *Private Morality in Greece and Rome: Some Historical Aspects.* Mnemosyne: Bibliotheca Classica Batava. Leiden: E. J. Brill.

Bokser, Baruch.

1977 "Philo's Description of Jewish Practices." *The Center for Hermeneutical Studies in Hellenistic and Modern Culture Colloquy* 30. Berkeley, CA: The Center for Hermeneutical Studies in Hellenistic and Modern Culture.

1985 "Changing Views of Passover and the Meaning of Redemption according to the Palestinian Talmud." *American Jewish Studies Review* 10 (1, 1985): 1-18.

Bokser, Ben Zion.
1973 "Justin Martyr and the Jews." *Jewish Quarterly Review* 64: 97-122, 204-11.

Bonhoeffer, Dietrich.
1963 *The Cost of Discipleship.* Rev. ed. New York: Macmillan & Company; London: SCM Press.

Bonnard, Pierre.
1963 *L'Évangile selon Saint Matthieu.* Commentaire du Noveau Testament 1. Neuchâtel: Delachaux & Niestlé.

Bons, Eberhard.
1995 "Psaume 2. Bilan de recherche et essai de réinterprétation." *Revue de Sciences Religieuses* 69: 147-71.

Bonsirven, Joseph.
1964 *Palestinian Judaism in the Time of Jesus Christ.* New York: Holt, Rinehart & Winston.

Boomershine, Thomas E., and Gilbert L. Bartholomew.
1981 "The Narrative Technique of Mark 16:8." *Journal of Biblical Literature* 100: 213-23.

Boonstra, Harry.
1980 "Satire in Matthew." *Christianity and Literature* 29: 32-45.

Borg, Marcus J.
1971 "The Currency of the Term 'Zealot.'" *Journal of Theological Studies* 22: 504-12.
1984 *Conflict, Holiness and Politics in the Teachings of Jesus.* Studies in the Bible and Early Christianity 5. New York: The Edwin Mellen Press.
1987 *Jesus: A New Vision (Spirit, Culture, and the Life of Discipleship).* San Francisco: Harper & Row.

Borgeaud, Philippe.
1983 "The Death of the Great Pan: The Problem of Interpretation." *History of Religions* 22: 254-83.

Borgen, Peder.
1986-1987 "Nattverdtradisjonen i 1. Kor. 10 og 11 som evangelietradisjon." *Svensk Exegetisk Årsbok* 51-52: 32-39. (*NTA* 31:179)

Boring, M. Eugene.
1972 "How May We Identify Oracles of Christian Prophets in the Synoptic Tradition? Mark 3:28-29 As a Test Case." *Journal of Biblical Literature* 91: 501-21.
1982 *Sayings of the Risen Jesus: Christian Prophecy in the Synoptic Tradition.* Society for New Testament Studies Monograph 46. Cambridge: Cambridge University Press.

Boring, M. Eugene, Klaus Berger, and Carsten Colpe, editors.
1995 *Hellenistic Commentary to the New Testament.* Nashville: Abingdon Press.

Borkan, Mark.
1995 "Ecce Homo? Science and the Authenticity of the Turin Shroud." *Vertices: The Duke University Magazine of Science, Technology, and Medicine* 10 (2, Winter): 18-51.

Bornkamm, Günther.
1963a "End-Expectation and Church in Matthew." Pp. 15-51 in *Tradition and Interpretation in Matthew.* By Günther Bornkamm, Gerhard Barth, and Heinz Joachim Held. Philadelphia: Westminster Press.
1963b "The Stilling of the Storm in Matthew." Pp. 52-57 in *Tradition and Interpre-*

tation in Matthew. By Günther Bornkamm, Gerhard Barth, and Heinz Joachim Held. Philadelphia: Westminster Press.

1969 *Early Christian Experience.* New York: Harper & Row; London: SCM Press.

1978 "Der Aufbau der Bergpredigt." *New Testament Studies* 24: 419-32.

1995 "The Authority to 'Bind' and 'Loose' in the Church in Matthew's Gospel (1970)." Pp. 101-14 in *The Interpretation of Matthew.* 2d ed. Edited by Graham Stanton. Edinburgh: T & T Clark.

Borowitz, E. B.

1980 *Contemporary Christologies: A Jewish Response.* New York: Paulist Press.

Borsch, Frederick H.

1990 "Jesus and Women Exemplars." *Anglican Theological Review Supplement* 11: 29-40.

Botha, F. J.

1967 "Recent Research and the Lord's Prayer." *Neotestamentica* 1: 42-50.

Botha, Pieter J. J.

1993 "Living voice and lifeless letters: Reserve towards writing in the Greco-Roman world." *Hervormde Teologiese Studies* 49: 742-59.

Bourgoin, Henri.

1979 "Epiousios expliqué par la notion de préfixe vide." *Biblica* 60: 91-96.

Bourke, Myles M.

1960 "The Literary Genius of Matthew 1–2." *Catholic Biblical Quarterly* 22: 160-75.

Bousset, William.

1970 *Kyrios Christos: A History of the Belief in Christ from the Beginnings of Christianity to Irenaeus.* Translated by John E. Steely. Nashville: Abingdon Press.

Bouttier, Michel.

1978 "Hésiode et le sermon sur la montague." *New Testament Studies* 25: 129-30.

Bowan, A. K., and D. Rathbone.

1992 "Cities and Administration in Roman Egypt." *Journal of Roman Studies* 82: 107-27.

Bowers, Paul.

1980 "Paul and Religious Propaganda in the First Century." *Novum Testamentum* 22: 316-23.

Bowersock, G. W.

1965 *Augustus and the Greek World.* Oxford: Clarendon Press.

1982 "The Imperial Cult: Perceptions and Persistence." 3:171-82 in *Jewish and Christian Self-Definition.* 3 vols. Edited by E. P. Sanders. Philadelphia: Fortress Press, 1980-1982.

Bowker, John.

1973 *Jesus and the Pharisees.* Cambridge: Cambridge University Press.

Bowman, John.

1974 "The Significance of Mt. 27:25." *Milla wa-Milla* 14: 26-31. (*NTA* 20:27)

1975 *The Fourth Gospel and the Jews: A Study in R. Akiba, Esther and the Gospel of John.* Pittsburgh Theological Monograph Series 8. Pittsburgh: Pickwick Press.

1977 Translator and editor. *Samaritan Documents Relating to Their History, Religion, and Life.* Pittsburgh Original Texts and Translations Series 2. Pittsburgh, PA: Pickwick Press.

Bowman, John Wick.
1943 *The Intention of Jesus.* Foreword by Walter Marshall Horton. Philadelphia: Westminster Press.

Bowsher, Julian M. C.
1987 "Architecture and Religion in the Decapolis: A Numismatic Survey." *Palestine Exploration Quarterly* 119: 62-69.

Boyd, Gregory A.
1995 *Cynic Sage or Son of God?* Wheaton, IL: BridgePoint.

Boyd, W. J. Peter.
1956 "Peter's Denials — Mark xiv.68, Luke xxii.57." *The Expository Times* 67: 341.

Brandon, S. G. F.
1967 *Jesus and the Zealots.* New York: Charles Scribner's Sons.

Branham, R. Bracht.
1993 "Authorizing Humor: Lucian's *Demonax* and Cynic Rhetoric." *Semeia* 64: 33-48.

Brant, Jo-Ann A.
1996 "Infelicitous Oaths in the Gospel of Matthew." *Journal for the Study of the New Testament* 63: 3-20.

Bratcher, Robert G.
1956 "A Note on *huios theou* (Mark xv.39)." *Expository Times* 68: 27-28.
1992 "That Troublesome Καί in Matthew 21:5." *Notes on Translation* 6: 14-15.

Braun, F. M.
1956 "La vie d'en haut." *Revue des Sciences Philosophiques et Théologiques* 40: 3-24.

Brawley, Robert L.
1987 *Luke-Acts and the Jews: Conflict, Apology and Conciliation.* Society of Biblical Literature Monograph 33. Atlanta: Scholars Press.

Brayer, Menachem M.
1968 "The Role of Jewish Law Pertaining to the Jewish Family, Jewish Marriage and Divorce." Pp. 1-43 in *Jews and Divorce.* Edited by Jacob Freid. Commission on Synagogue Relations of the Federation of Jewish Philanthropies of New York. New York: KTAV.

Brennan, Joseph P.
1964 "Virgin and Child in Isaiah 7:14." *Bible Today* 1: 968-74.

Bricker, Daniel P.
1995 "The Doctrine of the 'Two Ways' in Proverbs." *Journal of the Evangelical Theological Society* 38: 501-17.

Bright, John.
1981 *A History of Israel.* 3d ed. Philadelphia: Westminster Press.

Brocke, M.
1967 "Tun und Lohn im nachbiblischen Judentum. Ein Diskussionsbeitrag." *Bibel und Leben* 8: 166-78. *(NTA)*

Broer, Ingo.
1970 "Das Gericht des Menschensohnes über die Völker: Auslegung von Mt 25,31-46." *Bibel und Leben* 11: 273-95.
1993a "Die Antithesen der Bergpredigt. Ihre Bedeutung und Funktion für die Gemeinde des Matthäus." *Bibel und Kirche* 48: 128-33.
1993b "Redaktionsgeschichtliche Aspekte von Mt. 24:1-28." *Novum Testamentum* 35: 209-33.

1993c "Zur Wirkungsgeschichte des Talio-Verbots in der Alten Kirche." *Biblische Notizen* 66: 23-31.
1994 "Das Ius Talionis im Neuen Testament." *New Testament Studies* 40: 1-21.

Brooke, George.
1984 "The Feast of New Wine and the Question of Fasting." *The Expository Times* 95: 175-76.
1989 "The Wisdom of Matthew's Beatitudes (4QBeat and Mt. 5:3-12)." *Scripture Bulletin* 19: 35-41.
1995 "4Q500 1 and the Use of Scripture in the Parable of the Vineyard." *Dead Sea Discoveries* 2: 268-94.

Brooks, Oscar S.
1981 "Matthew xxviii 16-20 and the Design of the First Gospel." *Journal for the Study of the New Testament* 10: 2-18.
1995 "4Q500 1 and the Use of Scripture in the Parable of the Vineyard." *Dead Sea Discoveries* 2: 268-94.

Brooks, Stephenson H.
1987 *Matthew's Community: The evidence of his special sayings material.* Journal for the Study of the New Testament Supplement 16. Sheffield: JSOT, Sheffield Academic Press.

Broshi, Magen.
1975 "La population de l'ancienne Jérusalem." *Revue Biblique* 82: 5-14.
1978 "Estimating the Population of Ancient Jerusalem." *Biblical Archaeology Review* 4: 10-15.
1987 "The Gigantic Dimensions of the Visionary Temple in the Temple Scroll." *Biblical Archaeology Review* 13: 36-37.

Brown, Colin.
1976 "The Form of the Lord's Prayer." 2:869-73 in *The New International Dictionary of New Testament Theology.* 3 vols. Edited by Colin Brown. Grand Rapids: Zondervan, 1975-1978.
1978 "'Rock' in Matt. 16:18." 3:385-88 in *The New International Dictionary of New Testament Theology.* 3 vols. Edited by Colin Brown. Grand Rapids: Zondervan.

Brown, Raymond E.
1957 "The Messianism of Qumran." *Catholic Biblical Quarterly* 19: 53-82.
1958-1959 "The Semitic Background of the New Testament *Mysterion* (II)." *Biblica* 39: 426-48; 40: 70-87.
1966 "J. Starcky's Theory of Qumran Messianic Development." *Catholic Biblical Quarterly* 28: 51-57.
1966-1970 *The Gospel according to John.* 2 vols. Anchor Bible 29 and 29A. Garden City, NY: Doubleday & Company.
1968 *The Semitic Background of the Term "Mystery" in the New Testament.* Philadelphia: Fortress Press.
1972 "The Dead Sea Scrolls and the New Testament." Pp. 1-8 in *John and Qumran.* Edited by James H. Charlesworth. London: Geoffrey Chapman.
1977 *The Birth of the Messiah.* Garden City, NY: Doubleday & Company.
1982 *The Epistles of John.* Anchor Bible 30. Garden City, NY: Doubleday & Company.
1985 "Did Jesus Know He Was God?" *Biblical Theology Bulletin* 15: 74-79.
1994 *The Death of the Messiah: From Gethsemane to Grave. A Commentary on*

the Passion Narratives in the Four Gospels. 2 vols. New York: Doubleday & Company.

Brown, Raymond E., Karl P. Donfried, and John Reumann, eds.

1973 *Peter in the New Testament.* New York: Paramus; Toronto: Paulist Press; Minneapolis: Augsburg Publishing House.

Brown, Raymond E., and John P. Meier.

1983 *Antioch and Rome: New Testament Cradles of Catholic Christianity.* New York: Paulist Press.

Brown, Schuyler.

1968 "Deliverance from the Crucible: Some further reflexions on 1QH iii.1-18." *New Testament Studies* 14: 247-59.

1969 *Apostasy and Perseverance in the Theology of Luke.* Rome: Pontifical Biblical Institute.

1978 "The Mission to Israel in Matthew's Central Section (Mt 9:35–11:1)." *Zeitschrift für die Neutestamentliche Wissenschaft* 69: 73-90.

1979 "The Matthean Apocalypse." *Journal for the Study of the New Testament* 4: 2-27.

1980 "The Matthean Community and the Gentile Mission." *Novum Testamentum* 22: 193-221.

Brownlee, William H.

1950 "A Comparison of the Covenanters of the Dead Sea Scrolls with Pre-Christian Jewish Sects." *Biblical Archaeologist* 13: 50-72.

1951 "Light on the Manual of Discipline (DSD) from the Book of Jubilees." *Bulletin of the American Schools of Oriental Research* 123: 30-32.

1956/1957a "Messianic Motifs of Qumran and the New Testament." *New Testament Studies* 3: 12-30.

1956/1957b "Messianic Motifs of Qumran and the New Testament, II." *New Testament Studies* 3: 195-210.

Bruce, Alexander Balmain.

1979 "The Gospel According to Matthew." 1:61-340 in *The Expositor's Greek Testament.* 5 vols. Edited by W. Robertson Nicoll. Reprint ed. Grand Rapids: Eerdmans.

Bruce, F. F.

1951 *The Acts of the Apostles: The Greek Text with Introduction and Commentary.* Grand Rapids: Eerdmans.

1956 "Qumrân and Early Christianity." *New Testament Studies* 2: 176-90.

1963 *The Books and the Parchments.* Old Tappan, NJ: Fleming H. Revell.

1966 "Holy Spirit in the Qumran Texts," *The Annual of Leeds University Oriental Society* 6: 49-55.

1969 "Jesus and the Gospels in the Light of the Scrolls." Pp. 70-82 in *The Scrolls and Christianity: Historical and Theological Significance.* Edited by Matthew Black. London: S.P.C.K.

1971 *1 & 2 Corinthians.* New Century Bible 38. Greenwood, SC: The Attic Press; London: Marshall, Morgan & Scott.

1972a *The Message of the New Testament.* Grand Rapids: Eerdmans.

1972b *New Testament History.* Garden City, NY: Doubleday & Company.

1977a *Commentary on the Book of the Acts: The English Text with Introduction, Exposition, and Notes.* New International Commentary on the New Testament. Grand Rapids: Eerdmans.

1977b "The History of New Testament Study." Pp. 21-59 in *New Testament Inter-*

pretation: Essays on Principles and Methods. Edited by I. Howard Marshall. Grand Rapids: Eerdmans.

1977c *Paul: Apostle of the Heart Set Free.* Grand Rapids: Eerdmans.

1978 *The Time Is Fulfilled.* Grand Rapids: Eerdmans.

1980a *The New Testament Documents: Are They Reliable?* 5th ed. Grand Rapids: Eerdmans.

1980b "The Trial of Jesus in the Fourth Gospel." Pp. 7-20 in *Gospel Perspectives: Studies of History and Tradition in the Four Gospels.* Edited by R. T. France and David Wenham. Vol. 1 in Gospel Perspectives. Sheffield: JSOT Press.

1982 *1 & 2 Thessalonians.* Word Biblical Commentary 45. Waco, TX: Word Books.

1984 "Render to Caesar." Pp. 249-63 in *Jesus and the Politics of His Day.* Edited by Ernst Bammel and C. F. D. Moule. Cambridge: Cambridge University Press.

Brunec, M.

1957 "De 'Homine Peccari' in 2 Thes 2:1-12." *Verbum Domini* 35: 3-33. (*NTA* 2:38)

Bruns, J. Edgar.

1961 "The Magi Episode in Matthew 2." *Catholic Biblical Quarterly* 23: 51-54.

Buchanan, George Wesley.

1959 "Mark 11.15-19: Brigands in the Temple." *Hebrew Union College Annual* 30: 169-77.

1963 "The Role of Purity in the Structure of the Essene Sect." *Revue de Qumran* 4: 397-406.

1970 *The Consequences of the Covenant.* Novum Testamentum Supplements 20. Leiden: E. J. Brill.

1977 "The Office of the Teacher of Righteousness." *Revue de Qumran* 9: 241-43.

Büchler, Adolf.

1913-1914 "Learning and Teaching in the Open Air in Palestine." *Jewish Quarterly Review* n.s. 4: 485-91.

Buckland, W. W.

1908 *The Roman Law of Slavery: The Condition of the Slave in Private Law from Augustus to Justinian.* Cambridge: Cambridge University Press.

Bull, R.

1974 "A Mithraic Medallion from Caesarea." *Israel Exploration Journal* 24: 187-90.

Bultmann, Rudolf.

1951 *Theology of the New Testament.* 2 vols. Translated by Kendrick Grobel. New York: Charles Scribner's Sons.

1956 *Primitive Christianity in Its Contemporary Setting.* Translated by Reginald H. Fuller. New York: Meridian Books.

1958 *Jesus and the Word.* Translated by Louise Pettibone Smith and Erminie Huntress Lantero. New York: Charles Scribner's Sons.

1968 *The History of the Synoptic Tradition.* 2d ed. Translated by John Marsh. Oxford: Basil Blackwell.

1984 *New Testament Mythology and Other Basic Writings.* Edited by Schubert M. Ogden. Philadelphia: Fortress Press.

1985 *The Second Letter to the Corinthians.* Translated by Roy A. Harrisville. Minneapolis: Augsburg Publishing House.

Burchard, C.
1988 "Senfkorn, Sauerteig, Schatz und Perle in Matthäus 13." *Studien zum Neuen Testament und seiner Unwelt* 13: 5-35.

Burge, Gary M.
1987 *The Anointed Community: The Holy Spirit in the Johannine Tradition.* Grand Rapids: Eerdmans.

Burgmann, Hans.
1978 "Der Gründer der Pharisäergenossenschaft. Der Makkabäer Simon." *Journal for the Study of Judaism* 9: 153-91.
1980 "Antichrist — Antimessias. Der Makkabäer Simon?" *Judaica* 36: 152-74.

Burkert, Walter.
1985 *Greek Religion.* Translated by John Raffan. Cambridge: Harvard University Press.
1987 *Ancient Mystery Cults.* Carl Newell Jackson Lectures. Cambridge: Harvard University Press.

Burkill, T. A.
1960 "Strain on the Secret: An Examination of Mark 11:1–13:37." *Zeitschrift für die Neutestamentliche Wissenschaft* 51: 31-46.
1972 *New Light on the Earliest Gospel: Seven Markan Studies.* Ithaca: Cornell University Press.

Burkitt, F. Crawford.
1907 *The Gospel History and Its Transmission.* Edinburgh: T. & T. Clark.
1910 *The Earliest Sources for the Life of Jesus.* Boston and New York: Houghton Mifflin Company.
1932 *Church and Gnosis: A Study of Christian Thought and Speculation in the Second Century.* The Morse Lectures for 1931. Cambridge: Cambridge University Press.

Burnett, Fred W.
1979 *The Testament of Jesus-Sophia: A Redaction-Critical Study of the Eschatological Discourse in Matthew.* Washington, D.C.: University Press of America.

Burney, C. F.
1922 *The Aramaic Origin of the Fourth Gospel.* Oxford: Clarendon Press.

Burridge, Richard A.
1992 *What Are the Gospels? A Comparison with Graeco-Roman Biography.* Society for the Study of the New Testament Monograph Series 70. Cambridge: Cambridge University Press.
1994 *Four Gospels, One Jesus?* Grand Rapids: Eerdmans.
1998 "About People, by People, for People: Gospel Genre and Audiences." Pp. 113-46 in *The Gospels for All Christians: Rethinking the Gospel Audiences.* Edited by Richard J. Bauckham. Grand Rapids: Eerdmans.

Burrows, Millar.
1955 *The Dead Sea Scrolls.* New York: The Viking Press.
1958 *More Light on the Dead Sea Scrolls.* New York: The Viking Press.

Buse, S. Ivor.
1956 "The Markan Account of the Baptism of Jesus and Isaiah LXIII." *Journal of Theological Studies* 7: 74-75.

Buth, Randall.
1990 "Matthew's Aramaic Glue." *Jerusalem Perspective* 3: 10-12.

Byatt, Anthony.

1973 "Josephus and Population Numbers in First Century Palestine." *Palestine Exploration Quarterly* 105: 51-60.

Byrne, M.

1982 "No Room for the Inn." *Search* 5: 37-40. (*NTA* 27:143)

Byron, Brian.

1963 "The Meaning of 'Except It Be for Fornication'." *Australasian Catholic Record* 40: 90-95.

1993 "The Last Supper a Passover? The Theological Response." *Australasian Catholic Record* 70: 233-39.

Cadbury, Henry J.

1955 *The Book of Acts in History.* London: Adam & Charles Black.

1968 *The Making of Luke-Acts.* London: S.P.C.K.

1979 "Roman Law and the Trial of Paul." 5:297-338 in *The Beginnings of Christianity.* 5 vols. Edited by F. J. Foakes Jackson and Kirsopp Lake. Grand Rapids: Baker. Reprint ed.

1980 "Four Features of Lucan Style." Pp. 87-102 in *Studies in Luke-Acts.* Edited by Leander E. Keck and J. Louis Martyn. Philadelphia: Fortress Press.

Caird, George B.

1955 *The Apostolic Age.* London: Gerald Duckworth & Company.

1965 "Expounding the Parables: I — The Defendant (Matthew 5.25f.; Luke 12.58f.)." *The Expository Times* 77: 36-39.

1966 *A Commentary on the Revelation of Saint John the Divine.* Harper's New Testament Commentaries. New York: Harper & Row.

Cameron, Peter S.

1990 "'Lead us not into temptation.'" *The Expository Times* 101: 299-301.

Campbell, Kenneth M.

1978 "The New Jerusalem in Matthew 5.14." *Scottish Journal of Theology* 31: 335-63.

Campbell, Leroy A.

1968 *Mithraic Iconography and Ideology.* Études Préliminaires aux Religions Orientales dans l'Empire Romain 11. Published by M. J. Vermaseren. Leiden: E. J. Brill.

Canevet, Mariette.

1986 "Remarques sur l'utilisation du genre littéraire historique par Philon d'Alexandrie dans la *Vita Moysis* ou Moïse général en chef-prophète." *Revue de Sciences Religieuses* 60: 189-206.

Caprile, G.

1960 "La responsabilita del popolo ebreo nella morte di Gesù." *Palestro del Clero* 39: 969-76. (*NTA* 5:154)

Caquot, André.

1992 "La secte de Qoumrân et le temple (Essai de synthèse)." *Revue d'Histoire et de Philosophie Religieuses* 72: 3-14.

Caragounis, Chrys C.

1977 *The Ephesian Mysterion: Meaning and Content.* Coniectanea Biblica, New Testament 8. Lund: Gleerup.

1990 *Peter and the Rock.* Beihefte zur Zeitschrift für die Neutestamentliche Wissenschaft 58. Berlin and New York: Walter de Gruyter.

Carcopino, Jérôme.

1940 *Daily Life in Ancient Rome: The People and the City at the Height of the*

Empire. Edited by Henry T. Rowell. Translated by E. O. Lorimer. New Haven: Yale University Press.

Cargal, Timothy B.

1991 "'His Blood Be upon Us and upon Our Children': A Matthean Double Entendre?" *New Testament Studies* 37: 101-12.

Carlebach, A.

1975 "Rabbinic References to Fiscus Judaicus." *Jewish Quarterly Review* 66: 57-61.

Carlston, Charles E.

1980 "Proverbs, Maxims, and the Historical Jesus." *Journal of Biblical Literature* 99: 87-105.

Carmichael, Deborah Bleicher.

1991 "David Daube on the Eucharist and the Passover Seder." *Journal for the Study of the New Testament* 42: 45-67.

Carmignac, Jean.

1955 "Les Kittim dans la «Guerre des fils de lumière contre les fils de ténèbres.» *La Nouvelle Revue Théologique* 77: 737-48.

1977 "The Meaning of Parthenos in Luke 1.27 — A reply to C. H. Dodd." *Bible Translator* 28: 327-30.

1980 "Pré-pascal et post-pascal. Sens et valeur de ces expressions." *Esprit et Vie* 90: 411-15.

Carmon, Efrat, ed.

1973 *Inscriptions Reveal: Documents from the Time of the Bible, the Mishna and the Talmud.* Translated by R. Grafman. Jerusalem: Israel Museum.

Caron, Gerard.

1982 "Did Jesus Allow Divorce? (Mt. 5:31-32)." *Africanae Fraternae Ephemerides Romance* 24: 309-16.

Carroll, Kenneth L.

1963 "'Thou Art Peter.'" *Novum Testamentum* 6: 268-76.

Carson, D. A.

1980 *The Farewell Discourse and Final Prayer of Jesus.* Grand Rapids: Baker.

1981 *Divine Sovereignty and Human Responsibility: Biblical Perspectives in Tension.* New Foundations Theological Library. Atlanta: John Knox Press, 1981.

1984a *Exegetical Fallacies.* Grand Rapids: Baker.

1984b "Matthew." 8:3-599 in *The Expositor's Bible Commentary.* Edited by Frank Gaebelein. Grand Rapids: Zondervan.

1987 *When Jesus Confronts the World: An Exposition of Matthew 8–10.* Grand Rapids: Baker.

Carson, D. A., Douglas J. Moo, and Leon Morris.

1992 *An Introduction to the New Testament.* Grand Rapids: Zondervan.

Carter, Warren.

1994 *Households and Discipleship: A Study of Matthew 19–20.* Journal for the Study of the New Testament Supplement 103. Sheffield: JSOT Press.

1996 *Matthew: Storyteller, Interpreter, Evangelist.* Peabody: Hendrickson.

1998a "The Parables in Matthew 21:28–22:14." Pp. 147-76 in *Matthew's Parables: Audience-Oriented Perspectives.* By Warren Carter and and John Paul Heil. Catholic Biblical Quarterly Monograph 30. Washington, DC: Catholic Biblical Association of America.

1998b "Toward an Imperial-Critical Reading of Matthew's Gospel." Paper presented at the annual Society of Biblical Literature meeting, Orlando 1998.

Carter, Warren, and John Paul Heil.
1998 *Matthew's Parables: Audience-Oriented Perspectives.* Catholic Biblical Quarterly Monograph 30. Washington, DC: Catholic Biblical Association of America.

Cary, M., and T. J. Haarhoff.
1946 *Life and Thought in the Greek and Roman World.* 4th ed. London: Methuen & Company.

Case, Shirley Jackson.
1975 *The Social Origins of Christianity.* New York: Cooper Square Publishers. Reprint of 1923 ed.

Casey, P. Maurice
1988 "Culture and Historicity: the Plucking of the Grain (Mark 2:23-28)." *New Testament Studies* 34:1-23.

Cassidy, Richard J.
1979 "Matthew 17:24-27 — A Word on Civil Taxes." *Catholic Biblical Quarterly* 41: 571-80.

Casson, Lionel.
1974 *Travel in the Ancient World.* London: George Allen & Unwin.

Catchpole, David R.
1971a "The Answer of Jesus to Caiaphas (Matt. XXVI.64)." *New Testament Studies* 17: 213-26.
1971b *The Trial of Jesus: A Study in the Gospels and Jewish Historiography from 1770 to the Present Day.* Studia Post-Biblica (volumen duoetvicesimum). Leiden: E. J. Brill.
1978 "On Doing Violence to the Kingdom." *Journal of Theology for Southern Africa* 25: 50-61.
1979 "The Poor on Earth and the Son of Man in Heaven: A Re-Appraisal of Matthew xxv.31-46." *Bulletin of the John Rylands University Library of Manchester* 61: 355-97.
1984 "The 'Trumphal' Entry." Pp. 319-34 in *Jesus and the Politics of His Day.* Edited by Ernst Bammel and C. F. D. Moule. Cambridge: Cambridge University Press.
1992 "The Beginning of Q: A Proposal." *New Testament Studies* 38: 205-21.
1993 *The Quest for Q.* Edinburgh: T. & T. Clark.

Cave, Cyril H.
1965 "The Parables and the Scriptures." *New Testament Studies* 11: 374-87.

Chadwick, Henry.
1964 "Justin Martyr's Defence of Christianity." *Bulletin of the John Rylands Library* 47: 275-97.
1967 *The Early Church.* New York: Penguin.

Chance, J. Bradley.
1991 "Fiction in Ancient Biography: An Approach to a Sensitive Issue in Gospel Interpretation." *Perspectives in Religious Studies* 18: 125-42.

Charbel, A.
1983 "Mt 2,1-12: Os Magos no ambiente do Reino Nabateu." *Revista de Cultura Biblica* 7: 90-100. (*NTA* 28: 128)

Charette, Blaine.
1992a "'To Proclaim Liberty to the Captives': Matthew 11.28-30 in the Light of Old Testament Prophetic Expectation." *New Testament Studies* 38: 290-97.
1992b *The Theme of Recompense in Matthew's Gospel.* Journal for the Study of the

New Testament Supplement 79. Sheffield: JSOT Press, Sheffield Academic Press.

Charles, J. Daryl.

1992 "The Greatest or the Least in the Kingdom?: The Disciple's Relationship to the Law (Matt 5:17-20)." *Trinity Journal* 13: 139-62.

Charles, R. H.

1902 *The Book of Jubilees or The Little Genesis.* London: Adam & Charles Black.

Charlesworth, James H.

1977 "Jewish Astrology in the Talmud, Pseudepigrapha, the Dead Sea Scrolls, and Early Palestinian Synagogues." *Harvard Theological Review* 70: 183-200.

1981 *The Pseudepigrapha and Modern Research with a Supplement.* Society of Biblical Literature Septuagint and Cognate Studies 7-S. Chico, CA: Scholars Press.

1985 *The Old Testament Pseudepigrapha and the New Testament: Prolegomena for the Study of Christian Origins.* Society for New Testament Studies Monograph 54. Cambridge: Cambridge University Press.

1993 "Has the Name 'Peter' Been Found among the Dead Sea Scrolls?" *Qumran Chronicle* 2: 105-6.

1997 "The Son of David: Solomon and Jesus (Mark 10.47)." Pp. 72-87 in *The New Testament and Hellenistic Judaism.* Edited by Peder Borgen and Søren Giversen. Peabody: Hendrickson Publishers.

Charlesworth, M. P.

1970 *Trade-Routes and Commerce of the Roman Empire.* 2d rev. ed. New York: Cooper Square Publishers.

Chen, Doron.

1980 "The Design of the Ancient Synagogues in Judea: Masada and Herodium." *Bulletin of the American Schools of Oriental Research* 239: 37-40.

1986 "On the Chronology of the Ancient Synagogue at Capernaum." *Zeitschrift des Deutschen Palästina-Vereins* 102: 134-43.

Chernick, Michael.

1980 "Some Talmudic Responses to Christianity, Third and Fourth Centuries." *Journal of Ecumenical Studies* 17: 393-406.

Chevallier, Max-Alain.

1982 " 'Tu es Pierre, tu es le nouvel Abraham' (Mt 16/18)." *Etudes Théologiques et Religieuses* 57 (3, 1982): 375-87.

Chilton, Bruce.

1981 "Announcement in Nazara: An Analysis of Luke 4:16-21." 2:147-72 in Gospel Perspectives. 6 vols. Edited by R. T. France and David Wenham. Sheffield: JSOT Press, 1980-1986. Vol. 2: *Studies of History and Tradition in the Four Gospels.* Sheffield: JSOT Press, The University of Sheffield.

1988 "Jesus and the Repentance of E. P. Sanders." *Tyndale Bulletin* 39: 1-18.

1994 *Judaic Approaches to the Gospels.* University of South Florida International Studies in Formative Christianity and Judaism 2. Atlanta: Scholars Press.

Christiaens, M.

1983 "Pastoraal van de echtscheiding volgens Matteüs. Vragen rond de 'ontuchtclausule.' " *Tijdschrift voor Theologie* 23: 3-23. (*NTA* 27:255)

Chronis, Harry L.

1982 "The Torn Veil: Cultus and Christology in Mark 15:37-39." *Journal of Biblical Literature* 101: 97-114.

Clark, Gillian.

1993 *Women in Late Antiquity: Pagan and Christian Lifestyles.* Oxford: Clarendon Press.

Clark, Kenneth W.

1960 "Worship in the Jerusalem Temple after A.D. 70." *New Testament Studies* 6: 269-80.

Clarke, Andrew D.

1994 "Rome and Italy." Pp. 455-81 in *The Book of Acts in Its Graeco-Roman Setting.* Edited by David W. J. Gill and Conrad Gempf. Vol. 2 in The Book of Acts in its First-Century Setting. 6 vols. Edited by Bruce W. Winter. Grand Rapids: Eerdmans; Carlisle: The Paternoster Press.

Claudel, G.

1995 "Jean 20,23 et ses parallèles matthéens." *Revue de Sciences Religieuses* 69: 71-86.

Clavier, Henri.

1957 "Matthieu 5:39 et la non-résistance." *Revue d'Histoire et de Philosophie Religieuses* 37: 44-57.

Cóbreces, Ignacio R.

1990 " 'Los obreros de la viña.' Elementos midr shicos en la par bola de Mt 20,1-16." *Studium* 30: 485-505.

Cohen, Boaz.

1966 *Jewish and Roman Law: A Comparative Study.* 2 vols. New York: The Jewish Theological Seminary of America.

Cohen, M. S.

1992 "The Tallit." *Conservative Judaism* 44 (3, 1992): 3-15.

Cohen, Norman J.

1982a "Shekhinta ba-Galuta: A Midrashic Response to Destruction and Persecution." *Journal for the Study of Judaism* 13: 147-59.

1982b "Structural Analysis of a Talmudic Story: Joseph-Who-Honors the Sabbaths." *Jewish Quarterly Review* 72: 161-77.

1992 "Taryag and the Noahide Commandments." *Journal of Jewish Studies* 43 (1, 1992): 46-57.

Cohen, Shaye J. D.

1983 "Conversion to Judaism in Historical Perspective: From Biblical Israel to Postbiblical Judaism." *Conservative Judaism* 36: 31-45.

1986 "Pagan and Christian Evidence on the Ancient Synagogue." Pp. 159-81 in *The Synagogue in Late Antiquity.* Edited by Lee I. Levine. Philadelphia: The American Schools of Oriental Research.

1987 *From the Maccabees to the Mishnah.* Library of Early Christianity 7. Philadelphia: Westminster Press.

Cohn, Haim.

1977 *The Trial and Death of Jesus.* New York: KTAV. First English translation from the Hebrew, 1967.

Cohn-Sherbok, D. M.

1979 "An Analysis of Jesus' Arguments concerning the Plucking of Grain on the Sabbath." *Journal for the Study of the New Testament* 2: 31-41.

1981a "Jesus' Defense of the Resurrection of the Dead." *Journal for the Study of the New Testament* 11: 64-73.

1981b "A Jewish Note on *to potērion tēs eulogias.*" *New Testament Studies* 27: 704-9.

1982 "Jesus' Cry on the Cross: An Alternative View." *The Expository Times* 93: 215-17.

Coiner, H. G.

1968 "Those 'Divorce and Remarriage' Passages (Matt. 5:32; 19:9; 1 Cor. 7:10-16)." *Concordia Theological Monthly* 39: 367-84.

Cole, R. A.

1961 *The Gospel according to St. Mark.* Tyndale New Testament Commentaries. Grand Rapids: Eerdmans.

Cole, Susan Guettel.

1984 *Theoi Megaloi: The Cult of the Great Gods at Samothrace.* Études Préliminaires aux Religions Orientales dans l'Empire Romain 96. Published by M. J. Vermaseren. Leiden: E. J. Brill.

Collins, Adela Yarbro.

1997 "Apotheosis and Resurrection." Pp. 88-100 in *The New Testament and Hellenistic Judaism.* Edited by Peder Borgen and Søren Giversen. Peabody: Hendrickson Publishers.

Collins, John J.

1972 *The Sibylline Oracles of Egyptian Judaism.* Society of Biblical Literature Dissertation Series 13. Missoula, MT: Society of Biblical Literature.

1986 "The Testamentary Literature in Recent Scholarship." Pp. 268-85 in *Early Judaism and Its Modern Interpreters.* Edited by Robert A. Kraft and George W. E. Nickelsburg. Society of Biblical Literature Bible and Its Modern Interpreters, Series 2. Atlanta: Scholars Press.

1992 "The Son of Man in First-Century Judaism." *New Testament Studies* 38: 448-66.

1993 "A Pre-Christian 'Son of God' among the Dead Sea Scrolls." *Bible Review* 9 (3, 1993): 34-38, 57.

1994 "The Works of the Messiah," *Dead Sea Discoveries* 1: 98-112.

Collins, Marilyn F.

1972 "The Hidden Vessels in Samaritan Traditions." *Journal for the Study of Judaism* 3: 97-116.

Collins, Raymond F.

1974 "The Temptation of Jesus." *Melita Theologica* 26: 32-45. (*NTA* 19:320)

1992 *Divorce in the New Testament.* Good News Studies 38. Collegeville, MN: The Liturgical Press, Michael Glazier.

Colunga, A.

1960 "La abominación de la desolación (Mat. 24,15)." *Cultura Bíblica* 17: 183-85. (NTA 5: 153)

Considine, T.

1956 "Except It Be for Fornication." *Australasian Catholic Record* 33: 214-23. (NTA 1:177)

Conzelmann, Hans.

1969 *An Outline of the Theology of the New Testament.* New York: Harper & Row.

1975 *1 Corinthians: A Commentary on the First Epistle to the Corinthians.* Translated by James W. Leitch. Bibliography and references by James W. Dunkly. Edited by George W. MacRae. Philadelphia: Fortress Press.

Cook, John G.

1988 "The Sparrow's Fall in Mt 10:29b." *Zeitschrift für die Neutestamentliche Wissenschaft* 79: 138-44.

Cook, Michael.
1981 *Early Muslim Dogma: A source-critical study.* Cambridge: Cambridge University Press.

Cook, Michael J.
1983 "Interpreting 'Pro-Jewish' Passages in Matthew." *Hebrew Union College Annual* 54: 135-46.

Cope, O. Lamar.
1969 "Matthew xxv 31-46: 'The Sheep and the Goats' Reinterpreted." *Novum Testamentum* 11: 32-44.
1976 *Matthew: A Scribe Trained for the Kingdom of Heaven.* Catholic Biblical Quarterly Monograph 5. Washington, D.C.: The Catholic Biblical Association of America.

Corbo, Virgilio C.
1989 *Herodion I: Gli Edifici della Reggia-Fortezza.* Studium Biblicum Franciscanum, Collecto Major 20. Jerusalem: Franciscan Printing Press.

Corley, B.
1992 "Trial of Jesus." Pp. 841-54 in *Dictionary of Jesus and the Gospels.* Edited by Joel B. Green, Scot McKnight, and I. Howard Marshall. Downers Grove, IL: InterVarsity Press.

Corpus Inscriptionum Iudaicarum: Recueil des Inscriptions Juives qui vont du IIIe Siècle de Notre Père.
1936-1952 3 vols. Edited by P. Jean-Baptiste Frey. Roma: Pontificio Istituto di Archeologa Cristiana.

Corpus Papyrorum Judaicarum.
1957-1964 3 vols. Edited by Victor A. Tcherikover, with Alexander Fuks. Vol. 3 edited by Victor A. Tcherikover, Alexander Fuks, and Menahem Stern, with David M. Lewis. Cambridge: Harvard University Press, for The Magnes Press, The Hebrew University.

Côté, Pierre-Rene.
1986 "Les eunuchues pour le Royaume (Mt 19,12)." *Église et Théologie* 17: 321-34.

Cotton, H. M.
1995 "The Archive of Salome Komaise Daughter of Levi: Another Archive from the 'Cave of Letters.'" *Zeitschrift für Papyrologie und Epigraphik* 105: 171-207.

Cotton, H. M., and J. Geiger.
1989 "Yyn lhwrdws hmlk (Wine for Herod)." *Cathedra* 53: 3-12. (*NTA* 34:211)

Coughenour, R. A.
1982 "Hasmonean and Herodian Jericho." 2:995-96 in *The International Standard Bible Encyclopedia.* 4 vols. Edited by Geoffrey W. Bromiley. Grand Rapids: Eerdmans, 1979-88.

Court, J. M.
1985 "Right and Left: The Implications for Matthew 25.31-46." *New Testament Studies* 31: 223-33.

Couturier, Guy.
1984 "La vision du conseil divin: étude d'une forme commune au prophétisme et à l'apocalyptique." *Science et Esprit* 36: 5-43.

Craig, William Lane.
1980 "The Bodily Resurrection of Jesus." Pp. 47-74 in *Studies of History and Tra-*

dition in the Four Gospels. Vol. 1 in Gospel Perspectives. Edited by R. T. France and David Wenham. Sheffield: JSOT Press.

1981 "The Empty Tomb of Jesus." Pp. 173-200 in *Studies of History and Tradition in the Four Gospels.* Edited by R. T. France and David Wenham. Vol. 2 in Gospel Perspectives. 6 vols. Sheffield: JSOT Press, University of Sheffield.

1984 "The Guard at the Tomb." *New Testament Studies* 30: 273-81.

1985 "The Historicity of the Empty Tomb of Jesus." *New Testament Studies* 31: 39-67.

1986 "The Problem of Miracles: A Historical and Philosophical Perspective." 6:9-48 in Gospel Perspectives. 6 vols. Edited by R. T. France and David Wenham. Sheffield: JSOT Press, 1980-1986. Vol. 6: *The Miracles of Jesus.* Edited by David Wenham and Craig Blomberg. Sheffield: JSOT.

1995 "Did Jesus Rise from the Dead?" Pp. 141-76 in *Jesus under Fire.* Edited by Michael J. Wilkins and J. P. Moreland. Grand Rapids: Zondervan.

Craigie, Peter C.

1978 *The Problem of War in the Old Testament.* Grand Rapids: Eerdmans.

Cranfield, C. E. B.

1955 "The Baptism of Our Lord — A Study of St. Mark 1.9-11." *Scottish Journal of Theology* 8: 53-63.

Cranford, Lorin L.

1992 "Bibliography for the Sermon on the Mount." *Southwestern Journal of Theology* 35: 34-38.

Crapanzaro, Vincent, and Vivian Garrison.

1977 *Case Studies in Spirit Possession.* New York: John Wiley & Sons.

Crips, K. R. J.

1957 "A Note on Matthew 22:12." *The Expository Times* 69: 30.

Crisler, B. Cobbey.

1976 "The Acoustics and Crowd Capacity of Natural Theaters in Palestine." *Biblical Archaeologist* 39: 128-41.

Croatto, J. Severino.

1979 "Los oprimidos poseerán la tierra (Recontextualización de un tema bíblico)." *Revista Bíblica* 41: 245-48.

Crocker, P. T.

1987 "Sepphoris. Past History and Present Discoveries." *Buried History* 23 (4, 1987): 64-76.

1990 "Corrupt Priests — A Common Phenomenon." *Buried History* 26: 36-43.

1991 "Nets, Styli and Ophthalmology — a mystery solved." *Buried History* 27: 59-63.

Crosby, Michael H.

1988 *House of Disciples: Church, Economics, and Justice in Matthew.* Maryknoll, NY: Orbis Books.

Cross, Frank Moore.

1980 *The Ancient Library of Qumran and Modern Biblical Studies.* Rev. ed. Grand Rapids: Baker. Originally Garden City, NY: Doubleday & Company, 1961.

Crossan, John Dominic.

1976 "Empty Tomb and Absent Lord (Mark 16:1-8)." Pp. 135-52 in *The Passion in Mark: Studies in Mark 14–16.* Edited by Werner H. Kelber. Philadelphia: Fortress Press.

1986 "From Moses to Jesus: Parallel Themes." *Bible Review* 2: 18-27.

1991a *The Historical Jesus: The Life of a Mediterranean Jewish Peasant.* San Francisco: HarperSanFrancisco.

1991b "Open Healing and Open Eating. Jesus as a Jewish Cynic." *Biblical Research* 36: 6-18.

Crouzel, H.

1978 "L'imitation et la 'suite' de Dieu et du Christ dans les premiers siècles chrétiens, ainsi que leurs sources gréco-romaines et hébraïques." *Jahrbuch für Antike und Christentum* 21: 7-41. (*NTA* 23:319)

Cullmann, Oscar.

1950 *Christ and Time.* Translated by Floyd V. Filson. Philadelphia: Westminster Press.

1953 *Peter: Disciple, Apostle, Martyr.* Philadelphia: Westminster Press.

1956a *The Early Church.* Edited by A. J. B. Higgins. London: SCM Press.

1956b *The State in the New Testament.* New York: Charles Scribner's Sons.

1959 *The Christology of the New Testament.* Philadelphia: Westminster Press; London: SCM Press.

1968 "Πέτρα." 6:95-99. "Πέτρος, Κηφᾶς." 6:100-112 in *Theological Dictionary of the New Testament.* 10 vols. Edited by Gerhard Kittel and Gerhard Friedrich. Grand Rapids: Eerdmans, 1964-1976.

Culpepper, R. Alan.

1975 *The Johannine School: An Evaluation of the Johannine-School Hypothesis Based on an Investigation of the Nature of Ancient Schools.* Society of Biblical Literature Dissertation Series 26. Missoula, MT: Scholars Press.

Culver, Robert D.

1968 "What Is the Church's Commission? Some Exegetical Issues in Matthew 28:16-20." *Bibliotheca Sacra* 125: 239-53.

Cumont, Franz.

1922 *After Life in Roman Paganism: Lectures Delivered at Yale Unversity on the Silliman Foundation.* New Haven: Yale University Press.

1975 "The Dura Mithraeum." 1:151-214 in *Mithraic Studies: Proceedings of the First International Congress of Mithraic Studies.* 2 vols. Edited by John R. Hinnells. Manchester: Manchester University Press.

Cunningham, Scott, and Darrell L. Bock.

1987 "Is Matthew Midrash?" *Bibliotheca Sacra* 144: 157-80.

Custance, Arthur C.

1975 *Noah's Three Sons: Human History in Three Dimensions.* The Doorway Papers, vol. 1. Grand Rapids: Zondervan.

Dahl, Nils Alstrup.

1977 *Studies in Paul: Theology for the Early Christian Mission.* Minneapolis: Augsburg Publishing House.

1995 "The Passion Narrative in Matthew (1955)." Pp. 53-67 in *The Interpretation of Matthew.* 2d ed. Edited by Graham Stanton. Edinburgh: T & T Clark.

Dahl, Nils A., and Alan F. Segal.

1978 "Philo and the Rabbis on the Names of God." *Journal for the Study of Judaism* 9: 1-28.

Dahms, John V.

1974 "'Lead Us Not into Temptation.'" *Journal of the Evangelical Theological Society* 17: 223-30.

Dalman, Gustaf.

1929 *Jesus-Jeshua: Studies in the Gospels.* New York: Macmillan & Company.

1973 *Jesus Christ in the Talmud, Midrash, Zohar and the Liturgy of the Synagogue.* New York: Arno. Originally Cambridge: Deighton, Bell, 1893.

D'Angelo, T. P.

1992 "The Rabbinic Background of the Parables of Jesus." *Catholic World* 235: 63-67.

Daniel, Constantin.

1969 " 'Faux Prophètes': surnom des Esséniens dans le Sermon sur la Montagne." *Revue de Qumran* 7: 45-79.

Daniel, Jerry L.

1979 "Anti-Semitism in the Hellenistic-Roman Period." *Journal of Biblical Literature* 98: 45-65.

Daniélou, Jean.

1964 *The Theology of Jewish Christianity.* Translated and edited by John A. Baker. The Development of Christian Doctrine before the Council of Nicaea 1. London: Darton, Longman & Todd; Chicago: The Henry Regnery Company.

Daniels, C. M.

1975 "The Role of the Roman Army in the Spread and Practice of Mithraism." 2:249-74 in *Mithraic Studies: Proceedings of the First International Congress of Mithraic Studies.* 2 vols. Edited by John R. Hinnells. Manchester: Manchester University Press.

Danker, Frederick W.

1972 *Jesus and the New Age.* St. Louis: Clayton Publishing House.

1982 *Benefactor: Epigraphic Study of a Graeco-Roman and New Testament Semantic Field.* St. Louis: Clayton Publishing House.

1992 "God with Us: Hellenistic Christological Perspectives in Matthew." *Currents in Theology and Mission* 19: 433-39.

Dar, Shimon, and Nikos Kokkinos.

1992 "The Greek Inscriptions from Senaim on Mount Hermon." *Palestine Exploration Quarterly* 124: 9-25.

Daube, David.

1956 "The Gospels and the Rabbis." *The Listener* 56: 342-46.

1959 "Concessions to Sinfulness in Jewish Law." *Journal of Jewish Studies* 10: 1-13.

1960 "Three Notes Having to Do with Johanan ben Zaccai." *Journal of Theological Studies* 11: 53-62.

1963 *The Exodus Pattern in the Bible.* All Souls Studies 2. London: Faber & Faber.

1969 "Limitations on Self-Sacrifice in Jewish Law and Tradition." *Theology* 72: 291-304.

1972 "Responsibilities of Master and Disciples in the Gospels." *New Testament Studies* 19: 1-15.

1973 *The New Testament and Rabbinic Judaism.* New York: Arno. Originally University of London Press, 1956.

Dauphin, C.

1993 "A Greco-Egyptian Magical Amulet from Massuvah." *'Atiqot* 22: 145-47. (*NTA* 38:245)

Davids, Peter H.

1980 "The Gospels and Jewish Tradition: Twenty Years after Gerhardsson." 1:75-99 in Gospel Perspectives. 6 vols. Edited by R. T. France and David

Wenham. Sheffield: JSOT Press, 1980-1986. Vol. 1: *Studies of History and Tradition in the Four Gospels.* Edited by R. T. France and David Wenham. Sheffield: JSOT Press.

1982 *The Epistle of James: A Commentary on the Greek Text.* New International Greek Testament Commentary. Grand Rapids: Eerdmans.

Davies, Margaret.

1993 *Matthew.* Readings: A New Biblical Commentary. Sheffield: JSOT Press, Sheffield Academic Press.

Davies, Philip R.

1982 "The Ideology of the Temple in the Damascus Document." *Journal of Jewish Studies* 33: 287-301.

Davies, Stevan L.

1983 "John the Baptist and Essene Kashruth." *New Testament Studies* 29: 569-71.

Davies, W. D.

1964 *The Setting of the Sermon on the Mount.* Cambridge: Cambridge University Press.

1966a *Invitation to the New Testament: A Guide to Its Main Witnesses.* Garden City, NY: Doubleday & Company.

1966b *The Sermon on the Mount.* Cambridge: Cambridge University Press.

1967a *Introduction to Pharisaism.* Philadelphia: Fortress Press.

1967b "Reflexions on Tradition: The Aboth Revisited." Pp. 129-37 in *Christian History and Interpretation: Studies Presented to John Knox.* Edited by W. R. Farmer, C. F. D. Moule, and R. R. Niebuhr. Cambridge: Cambridge University Press.

1974 *The Gospel and the Land: Early Christianity and Jewish Territorial Doctrine.* Berkeley: University of California Press.

1980 *Paul and Rabbinic Judaism: Some Rabbinic Elements in Pauline Theology.* 4th ed. Philadelphia: Fortress Press.

Davies, W. D., and Dale C. Allison, Jr.

1988 *A Critical and Exegetical Commentary on the Gospel according to Saint Matthew.* International Critical Commentary. 3 vols. Vol. 1: *Introduction and Commentary on Matthew I-VII.* Edinburgh: T & T Clark.

1991 *A Critical and Exegetical Commentary on the Gospel according to Saint Matthew.* International Critical Commentary. 3 vols. Vol. 2: *Introduction and Commentary on Matthew VIII–XVIII.* Edinburgh: T & T Clark.

1992 "Matt. 28:16-20: Texts behind the Text." *Revue d'Histoire et de Philosophie Religieuses* 72: 89-98.

1997 *The Gospel according to Saint Matthew.* Vol. 3. Edinburgh: T & T Clark.

Davis, J. J.

1958 "The Age of Saint Joseph at the Time of His Marriage." *Cahiers de Joséphologie* 6: 47-66. (*NTA* 3:16)

Davison, James E.

1985 "Anomia and the Question of an Antinomian Polemic in Matthew." *Journal of Biblical Literature* 104: 617-35.

Dawes, Stephen B.

1991 "*'anāwâ* in translation and tradition." *Vetus Testamentum* 41: 38-48.

Dawson, John.

1964 "Urbanization and Mental Health in a West African Community." Pp. 305-42 in *Magic, Faith, and Healing: Studies in Primitive Psychotherapy Today.*

Edited by Ari Kiev. Introduction by Jerome D. Frank. New York: The Free Press; A Division of Macmillan Publishing Company.

De Beus, C.

1968 "Paulus en de traditie over de opstanding in I Cor. 15:3 vlg." *Nederlands Theologisch Tijdschrift* 22: 185-99. *(NTA)*

Deissmann, G. Adolf.

1923 *Bible Studies: Contributions Chiefly from Papyri and Inscriptions to the History of the Language, the Literature, and the Religion of Hellenistic Judaism and Primitive Christianity.* Translated by Alexander Grieve. Edinburgh: T & T Clark. Reprint: Winona Lake, IN: Alpha Publications, 1979.

1978 *Light from the Ancient East.* Grand Rapids: Baker. Reprint from 4th ed., 1922.

De Jonge, Marinus.

1966 "The Use of the Word 'Anointed' in the Time of Jesus." *Novum Testamentum* 8: 132-48.

1974/1976 "The New Testament." Pp. 37-43 in *The Jewish People in the First Century: Historical Geography, Political History, Social, Cultural, and Religious Life and Institutions.* 2 vols. Edited by S. Safrai and M. Stern with D. Flusser and W. C. van Unnik. Section 1 of Compendia Rerum Iudaicarum ad Novum Testamentum. Vol. 1: Assen: Van Gorcum & Co., B.V.; Vol. 2: Philadelphia: Fortress Press.

De Kruijf, Theo C.

1993 "Go Therefore and Make Disciples of All Nations: Mt 28,19." *Bijdragen* 54: 19-29.

De La Maisonneuve, D.

1987 "The Parables of Jesus and the Rabbinic Parables." *Service International de Documentation Judéo-Chrétienne* 20: 8-15. (*NTA* 32:17)

De la Serna, Eduardo.

1989 "¿Divorcio en Mateo?" *Revista Bíblica* 51: 91-110. *(NTA)*

Delaney, Carol.

1987 "Seeds of Honor, Fields of Shame." Pp. 35-48 in *Honor and Shame and the Unity of the Mediterranean.* Edited by David D. Gilmore. American Anthropological Association 22. Washington, D.C.: American Anthropological Association.

Delaygue, M.-P.

1995 "Les Grecs connaissaient-ils les religions de l'Inde à l'époque hellénistique?" *Bulletin de l'Association Guillaume Budé* 54: 152-72.

Delcor, Matthias.

1955 "La guerre des fils de lumière contre les fils de ténèbres." *Nouvelle Revue Théologique* 77: 372-99.

1968 "Repas cultuels esséniens et thérapeutes. Thiases et Haburoth." *Revue de Qumran* 6: 401-25.

1971 "La portée chronologique de quelques interprétations du Targoum Néofyti contenues dans le cycle d'Abraham." *Journal for the Study of Judaism* 1: 105-19.

Delling, Gerhard.

1967 "Παρθένος." 5:826-37 in *Theological Dictionary of the New Testament.*

Delorme, J.

1974 "La mission de Douze en Galilée. Mc 6,7-13." *Assemblées du Seigneur* 46: 43-50. (*NTA* 19: 30)

Deman, A.

1975 "Mithras and Christ: Some iconographical similarities." 2:507-17 in *Mithraic Studies: Proceedings of the First International Congress of Mithraic Studies.* Edited by John R. Hinnells. 2 vols. Manchester: Manchester University Press.

Deming, Will.

1990 "Mark 9.42–10.12, Matthew 5.27-32 and *B. Nid.* 13b: A First Century Discussion of Male Sexuality." *New Testament Studies* 36: 130-41.

De Nazareth, M.

1956 "La maison de saint Joseph à Nazareth." *Cahiers de Joséphologie* 4: 243-72. (*NTA* 2:171)

Dequeker, Luc.

1986 "Le Zodiaque de la Synagogue de Beth Alpha et le Midrash." *Bijdragen* 47: 2-30.

De Ridder, Richard R.

1971a *Discipling the Nations.* Grand Rapids: Baker.

1971b *The Dispersion of the People of God: The Covenant Basis of Matthew 28:18-20 against the Background of Jewish, Pre-Christian Proselyting and Diaspora, and the Apostleship of Jesus Christ.* Kampen: J. H. Kok.

Derrett, J. Duncan M.

1965 "Herod's Oath and the Baptist's Head." *Biblische Zeitschrift* 9: 49-59, 233-46.

1966 "The Light under a Bushel: The Hanukkah Lamp?" *The Expository Times* 78: 18.

1970 *Law in the New Testament.* London: Darton, Longman, & Todd.

1971 "Law in the New Testament: The Palm Sunday Colt." *Novum Testamentum* 13: 241-58.

1973 *Jesus' Audience: The Social and Psychological Environment in Which He Worked.* New York: Seabury Press.

1974 "Workers in the Vineyard: A Parable of Jesus." *Journal of Jewish Studies* 25: 64-91.

1975 "Leek-beds and Methodology." *Biblische Zeitschrift* 19: 101-3.

1979a "Contributions to the Study of the Gerasene Demoniac." *Journal for the Study of the New Testament* 3: 2-17.

1979b "'Where two or three are convened in my name . . .': a sad misunderstanding." *The Expository Times* 91: 83-86.

1980 "Esan gar halieis (Mk. I.16). Jesus's Fishermen and the Parable of the Net." *Novum Testamentum* 22: 108-37.

1982 "The Merits of the Narrow Gate (Mt. 7:13-14, Lk. 13:24)." *Journal for the Study of the New Testament* 15: 20-29.

1983a "Binding and Loosing (Matt 16:19; 18:18; John 20:23)." *Journal of Biblical Literature* 102: 112-17.

1983b "The Reason for the Cock-crowings." *New Testament Studies* 29: 142-44.

1984a "Crumbs in Mark." *Downside Review* 102: 12-21.

1984b "Palingenesia (Matthew 19.28)." *Journal for the Study of the New Testament* 20: 51-58.

1985 "*Mylos onikos* (Mk 9:42 par.)." *Zeitschrift für die Neutestamentliche Wissenschaft* 76: 284.

1986 "A Camel through the Eye of a Needle." *New Testament Studies* 32: 465-70.

1988 “‘Thou Art the Stone, and upon This Stone . . .’” *Downside Review* 106: 276-85.

1989 “Der Wasserwandel in christlicher und buddhistischer Perspektive.” *Zeitschrift für Religions- und Geistesgeschichte* 41: 193-214.

1990 “Ecce homo Ruber (John 19.5 with Isaiah 1:18; 63:1-2).” *Bibbia et Oriente* 32: 215-29.

1991 “Bankruptcy and the New Testament.” *Downside Review* 109: 173-82.

1997 “Unfair to Goats (Mt 25:32-33).” *Expository Times* 108.6: 177-78.

Deutsch, Celia.

1987 *Hidden Wisdom and the Easy Yoke: Wisdom, Torah and Discipleship in Matthew 11.25-30.* Journal for the Study of the New Testament Supplement 18. Sheffield: JSOT Press, Sheffield Academic Press.

1990 “Wisdom in Matthew: Transformation of a Symbol.” *Novum Testamentum* 32: 13-47.

1991 “Torah, Jesus and Discipleship in the Gospel of Matthew.” *Service International de Documentation Judéo-Chrétienne* 24: 43-52.

De Vaux, Roland.

1961 *Ancient Israel: Its Life and Institutions.* Translated by John MacHugh. New York: McGraw-Hill.

Dewailley, Louis M.

1980a “‘Donne-nous notre pain’: quel pain? Notes sur la quatrième demande du Pater.” *Revue des Sciences Philosophiques et Théologiques* 64: 561-88.

1980b “Vilket bröd avses i Fader vår?” *Svensk Exegetisk Årsbok* 45: 77-89. (*NTA* 25:130)

Dewey, Joanna.

1973 “The Literary Structure of the Controversy Stories in Mark 2:1–3:6.” *Journal of Biblical Literature* 92: 394-401.

1980 *Markan Public Debate: Literary Technique, Concentric Structure, and Theology in Mark 2:1–3:6.* Society of Biblical Literature Dissertation Series 48. Chico, CA: Scholars Press.

Dewey, Kim E.

1976 “Peter’s Curse and Cursed Peter (Mark 14:53-54, 66-72).” Pp. 96-114 in *The Passion in Mark: Studies in Mark 14–16.* Edited by Werner H. Kelber. Philadelphia: Fortress Press.

Dibelius, Martin.

1949 *Jesus.* Translated by Charles B. Hedrick and Frederick C. Grant. Philadelphia: Westminster Press.

1953 *Paul.* Edited and completed by Werner Georg Kümmel. Philadelphia: Westminster Press.

1956 *Studies in the Acts of the Apostles.* London: SCM Press.

1971 *From Tradition to Gospel.* Translated from the 2d (1933) German ed. by Bertram Lee Woolf. Cambridge: James Clarke & Company.

1976 *James: A Commentary on the Epistle of James.* Revised by Heinrich Greeven. Translated by Michael A. Williams. Edited by Helmut Koester. Hermeneia. Philadelphia: Fortress Press.

Dibelius, Martin, and Conzelmann, Hans.

1972 *The Pastoral Epistles: A Commentary on the Pastoral Epistles.* Translated by Philip Buttolph and Adela Yarbro. Edited by Helmut Koester. Hermeneia: A Critical and Historical Commentary on the Bible. Philadelphia: Fortress Press.

Dickie, M. W.

1991 "Heliodorus and Plutarch on the Evil Eye." *Classical Philology* 86: 17-29.

Dietzfelbinger, Christian.

1989 "Das Gleichnis von den anvertrauten Geldern." *Berliner Theologische Zeitschrift* 6: 222-33.

Diezinger, Walter.

1978 "Zum Liebesgebot Mk xii,28-34 und Parr." *Novum Testamentum* 20: 81-83.

Dihle, Albrecht.

1991 "The Gospels and Greek Biography." Pp. 361-86 in *The Gospel and the Gospels.* Edited by Peter Stuhlmacher. Grand Rapids: Eerdmans.

Dillon, John.

1977 *The Middle Platonists: 80 B.C. to A.D. 220.* Ithaca, NY: Cornell University Press.

Dillon, Richard J.

1991 "Ravens, Lilies, and the Kingdom of God (Matthew 6:25-33/Luke 12:22-31)." *Catholic Biblical Quarterly* 53: 605-27.

Dimant, Devorah.

1983 "The Biography of Enoch and the Books of Enoch." *Vetus Testamentum* 33: 14-29.

Diop, Cheikh Anta.

1974 *The African Origin of Civilization.* Translated by Mercer Cook. Westport, CN: Lawrence Hill & Company.

Di Segni, Leah.

1991 "A Fragmentary Greek Inscription from the Giv'at Seled Burial Cave." *'Atiqot* 20: 164-65.

Dix, Gregory.

1947 *The Apostolic Ministry.* Edited by Kenneth E. Kirk. London: Hodder & Stoughton.

Dixon, Suzanne.

1988 *The Roman Mother.* Norman, OK: Oklahoma University Press.

Dodd, Charles Harold.

1935 *The Bible and the Greeks.* London: Hodder & Stoughton.

1961 *The Parables of the Kingdom.* London: Nisbet & Company. Rev. ed. (First ed. 1936). New York: Charles Scribner's Sons.

1965 *Historical Tradition in the Fourth Gospel.* Cambridge: Cambridge University Press.

1967 *New Testament Studies.* Manchester: Manchester University Press.

1968 *More New Testament Studies.* Grand Rapids: Eerdmans.

1980 *The Apostolic Preaching and Its Developments.* Grand Rapids: Baker. Originally, London: Hodder & Stoughton, 1936.

Doeve, J. W.

1954 *Jewish Hermeneutics in the Synoptic Gospels and Acts.* Assen: Van Gorcum & Company.

Dola, T.

1983 "Antropologiczna interpretacja formuly 'zmartwychwstal dnia trzeciego' (Die anthropologische Interpretation der Formel 'auferweckt am dritten Tag nach der Schrift')." *Collectanea Theologica* 53: 37-52. (*NTA* 28: 239-40)

Donahue, John R.

1973 *Are You the Christ? The Trial Narrative in the Gospel of Mark.* Society of

Biblical Literature Dissertation 10. Missoula, MT: Society of Biblical Literature.
1976 "Temple, Trial, and Royal Christology (Mark 14:53-65)." Pp. 61-79 in *The Passion in Mark: Studies in Mark 14–16.* Edited by Werner H. Kelber. Philadelphia: Fortress Press.

Donaldson, Terence L.
1990 "Rural Bandits, City Mobs and the Zealots." *Journal for the Study of Judaism* 21 (1, 1990): 19-40.

Donceel-Vouté, P. H. E.
1993 "'Coenaculum' — La salle à l'étage du *locus* 30 à Khirbet Qumrân sur la Mer Morte." *Res Orientales* 4: 61-84.

Doohan, Leonard.
1988 "Mission and Ministry." *Bible Today* 26: 243-47.

Dover, K. J.
1984 "Classical Greek Attitudes to Sexual Behaviour." Pp. 143-58 in *Women in the Ancient World: The Arethusa Papers.* Edited by John Peradotto and J. P. Sullivan. Suny Series in Classical Studies. Albany, NY: State University of New York Press.

Dowd, Sharyn Echols.
1983 "The Theological Function of Petitionary Prayer in the Thought of Philo." *Perspectives in Religious Studies* 10: 241-54.
1988 *Prayer, Power, and The Problem of Suffering: Mark 11:22-25 in the Context of Markan Theology.* Society of Biblical Literature Dissertation Series 105. Atlanta: Scholars Press.

Down, M. J.
1978 "The Matthaean Birth Narratives: Matthew 1:18–2:23." *Expository Times* 90: 51-52.
1984 "The Sayings of Jesus about Marriage and Divorce." *Expository Times* 95: 332-34.

Downing, F. Gerald.
1982 "The Resurrection of the Dead: Jesus and Philo." *Journal for the Study of the New Testament* 15: 42-50.
1985 "Philo on Wealth and the Rights of the Poor." *Journal for the Study of the New Testament* 24: 116-18.
1988a "Compositional Conventions and the Synoptic Problem." *Journal of Biblical Literature* 107: 69-85.
1988b "Quite Like Q. A Genre for 'Q': The 'Lives' of Cynic Philosophers." *Biblica* 69: 196-225.
1988c "A bas les aristos. The Relevance of Higher Literature for the Understanding of the Earliest Christian Writings." *Novum Testamentum* 30 (3, 1988): 212-30.
1991 "Actuality versus Abstraction: The Synoptic Gospel Model." *Continuum* 1: 104-20.
1995 "Common Strands in Pagan, Jewish and Christian Eschatologies in the First Century." *Theologische Zeitschrift* 51: 196-211.

Draper, H. Mudie.
1956 "Did Jesus Speak Greek?" *Expository Times* 67: 317.

Draper, Jonathan
1984 "The Jesus Tradition in the Didache." 5:269-287 in Gospel Perspectives. 6 vols. Edited by R. T. France, David Wenham, and Craig Blomberg. Shef-

field: JSOT Press, 1980-1986. Vol. 5: *The Jesus Tradition outside the Gospels.* Edited by David Wenham. Sheffield: JSOT Press.

Driver, G. R.
1965 *The Judaean Scrolls: The Problem and a Solution.* Oxford: Basil Blackwell.

Drury, John.
1976 *Tradition and Design in Luke's Gospel: A Study in Early Christian Historiography.* London: Darton, Longman & Todd.

Dschulnigg, Peter.
1989 "Gleichnis vom Kind, das zum Vater flieht (JosAs 12.8)." *Zeitschrift für die Neutestamentliche Wissenschaft* 80: 269-71.

Duff, Paul Brooks.
1992 "The March of the Divine Warrior and the Advent of the Greco-Roman King: Mark's Account of Jesus' Entry into Jerusalem." *Journal of Biblical Literature* 111: 55-71.

Duling, Dennis C.
1987 "Binding and Loosing: Matthew 16:19; Matthew 18:18; John 20:23." *Forum* 3: 3-31.

Duling, Dennis C., and Norman Perrin.
1994 *The New Testament: Proclamation and Parenesis, Myth and History.* 3d ed. Fort Worth: Harcourt Brace College Publishers.

Dunand, Françoise.
1975 "Les Mystères Egyptiens." Pp. 11-62 in *Mystères et Syncrétismes.* Études d'Histoire des Religions 2. Edited by M. Philonenko et M. Simon. Paris: Librairie Orientaliste Paul Geuthner.

Dunn, James D. G.
1970a *Baptism in the Holy Spirit: A Re-examination of the New Testament Teaching on the Gift of the Spirit in Relation to Pentecostalism Today.* Studies in Biblical Theology, 2d series, 15. London: SCM Press.
1970b "Spirit and Kingdom." *The Expository Times* 82: 36-40.
1975 *Jesus and the Spirit: A Study of the Religious and Charismatic Experience of Jesus and the First Christians as Reflected in the New Testament.* London: SCM Press.
1978a "Prophetic 'I'-Sayings and the Jesus Tradition: The importance of testing prophetic utterances within early Christianity." *New Testament Studies* 24: 175-98.
1978b "Spirit." 3:688-707 in *The New International Dictionary of New Testament Theology.* Edited by Colin Brown. Grand Rapids: Zondervan.
1983 "The Incident at Antioch (Gal. 2:11-12)." *Journal for the Study of the New Testament* 12.

Du Plessis, I. J.
1967 "The Ethics of Marriage according to Matt. 5:27-32." *Neotestamentica* 1: 16-27.

Dupont, Florence.
1992 *Daily Life in Ancient Rome.* Translated by Christopher Woodall. Oxford: Basil Blackwell.

Dupont, Jacques.
1966 "L'origine du récit des tentatons de Jésus au désert." *Revue Biblique* 73: 30-76.

Dupont-Sommer, André.

1969 *Les Manuscrits de la Mer Morte et la Problème des Origines Chrétiennes.* Paris: Éditions Estienne.

1973 *The Essene Writings from Qumran.* Translated by G. Vermes. Gloucester, MA: Peter Smith.

Durston, Chris.

1988 "Historical Interpretations of the Sermon on the Mount." *Scripture Bulletin* 18: 42-49.

Dvorjetski, E., and R. Last.

1991 "Gadara — Colony or Colline Tribe: Another Suggested Reading of the Byblos Inscription." *Israel Exploration Journal* 41: 157-62.

Easton, Burton Scott.

1940 "Divorce in the New Testament." *Anglican Theological Review* 22: 78-87.

Edelstein, Gershon.

1990 "What's a Roman Villa Doing outside Jerusalem?" *Biblical Archaeology Review* 16 (6, 1990): 32-42.

Edersheim, Alfred.

n.d. *The Life and Times of Jesus the Messiah.* Reprint: Peabody: Hendrickson.

Eddy, Paul Rhodes.

1996 "Jesus as Diogenes? Reflections on the Cynic Jesus Thesis." *Journal of Biblical Literature* 115: 449-69.

Edgar, S. L.

1958 "The New Testament and Rabbinic Messianic Interpretation." *New Testament Studies* 5: 47-54.

Edwards, James R.

1987 "The Use of *Proserchesthai* in the Gospel of Matthew." *Journal of Biblical Literature* 106: 65-74.

Edwards, M. J.

1989 "Three Exorcisms and the New Testament World." *Eranos* 87: 117-26.

Edwards, Richard A.

1975 *A Theology of Q: Eschatology, Prophecy, and Wisdom.* Philadelphia: Fortress Press.

1985 *Matthew's Story of Jesus.* Philadelphia: Fortress Press.

Efird, James M.

1985 *Marriage and Divorce: What the Bible Says.* Nashville: Abingdon Press.

Ehrhardt, Arnold.

1958 *The Apostolic Ministry.* Scottish Journal of Theology Occasional Papers 7. Edinburgh: Oliver & Boyd.

Eickelman, Dale F.

1989 *The Middle East: An Anthropological Approach.* 2d ed. Englewood Cliffs, NJ: Prentice Hall.

Eisenman, Robert.

1983 *Maccabees, Zadokites, Christians and Qumran: A New Hypothesis of Qumran Origins.* Studia Post-Biblica. Leiden: E. J. Brill.

Eliade, Mircea.

1958 *Rites and Symbols of Initiation: The Mysteries of Birth and Rebirth.* Translated by Willard R. Trask. New York: Harper & Row.

Elkins, Richard E.

1968 "Three Models of Western Bukidnon Manobo Kinship." *Ethnology* 7: 171-89.

Ellington, John.

1979 "The Translation of *humnéo* 'Sing a Hymn' in Mark 14.26 and Matthew 26.30." *Bible Translator* 30: 445-46.

Ellingworth, Paul.

1978 "How Soon Is 'Immediately' in Mark?" *Bible Translator* 29: 414-19.

Elliott, John H.

1988 "The Fear of the Leer. The Evil Eye from the Bible to Li'l Abner." *Forum* 4 (4, 1988): 42-71.

1992 "Matthew 20:1-15: A Parable of Invidious Comparison and Evil Eye Accusation." *Biblical Theology Bulletin* 22: 52-65.

Ellis, E. Earle.

1975 "The Composition of Luke 9 and the Sources of Its Christology." Pp. 121-27 in *Current Issues in Biblical and Patristic Interpretation: Studies in Honor of Merrill C. Tenney Presented by His Former Students.* Edited by Gerald F. Hawthorne. Grand Rapids: Eerdmans.

1977 "How the New Testament Uses the Old." Pp. 199-219 in *New Testament Interpretation: Essays on Principles and Methods.* Edited by I. Howard Marshall. Grand Rapids: Eerdmans.

1991 "Gospels Criticism: A Perspective on the State of the Art." Pp. 26-52 in *The Gospel and the Gospels.* Edited by Peter Stuhlmacher. Grand Rapids: Eerdmans.

Ellis, Peter F.

1974 *Matthew: His Mind and His Message.* Collegeville, MN: Liturgical Press.

Ellison, H. L.

1966 *The Mystery of Israel: An Exposition of Romans 9-11.* Grand Rapids: Eerdmans; London: Paternoster Press.

Ellul, Danielle.

1990 "Le Testament d'Abraham: mémoire et source d'imaginaire. La pesée des âmes." *Foi et Vie* 89 (5, 1990): 73-82.

1992 "Dérives autour d'un figuier: Matthieu 21,18-22." *Foi et Vie* 91: 69-76.

Emerton, John A.

1962 "Binding and Loosing — Forgiving and Retaining." *Journal of Theological Studies* 13: 325-31.

1964 "Mark XIV.24 and the Targum to the Psalter." *Journal of Theological Studies* 15: 58-59.

Endres, John C.

1987 *Biblical Interpretation in the Book of Jubilees.* Catholic Biblical Quarterly Monograph 18. Washington, D.C.: Catholic Biblical Association of America.

Engle, Anita.

1977 "An Amporisk of the Second Temple Period." *Palestine Exploration Quarterly* 109: 117-22.

English, E. Schuyler.

1969 "A Neglected Miracle." *Bibliotheca Sacra* 126: 300-305.

Enz, Jacob J.

1976 "Origin of the Dualism Expressed by 'Sons of Light' and 'Sons of Darkness.'" *Biblical Research* 21: 15-18.

Eppstein, Victor.

1964 "The Historicity of the Gospel Account of the Cleansing of the Temple." *Zeitschrift für die Neutestamentliche Wissenschaft* 55: 42-58.

1966 "When and How the Sadducees Were Excommunicated." *Journal of Biblical Literature* 85: 213-24.

Erickson, Richard J.

1996 "Divine Injustice? Matthew's Narrative Strategy and the Slaughter of the Innocents (Matthew 2.13-23)." *Journal for the Study of the New Testament* 64: 5-27.

Eshel, Esther.

1994 "4Q477. The Rebukes by the Overseer." *Journal of Jewish Studies* 45: 111-22.

Essame, William G.

1961 "Matthew X.23." *The Expository Times* 72: 248.

Evans, Craig A.

1981 "A Note on the Function of Isaiah, VI." *Revista Biblica* 88: 234-35.

1982 "Isaiah 6:9-10 in Rabbinic and Patristic Writings." *Vigiliae Christianae* 36: 275-81.

1984 "On the Vineyard Parables of Isaiah 5 and Mark 12." *Biblische Zeitschrift* 28: 82-86.

1989 "Jesus' Action in the Temple: Cleansing or Portent of Destruction?" *Catholic Biblical Quarterly* 51: 237-70.

1995 "What Did Jesus Do?" Pp. 101-15 in *Jesus under Fire.* Edited by Michael J. Wilkins and J. P. Moreland. Grand Rapids: Zondervan.

Evans-Pritchard, E. E.

1951 *Kinship and Marriage among the Nuer.* Oxford: Clarendon Press.

Evens, T. M. S.

1983 "Mind, Logic, and the Efficacy of the Nuer Incest Prohibition." *Man* 18: 111-33.

Everson, A. Joseph.

1974 "The Days of Yahweh." *Journal of Biblical Literature* 93: 329-37.

Faber van der Meulen, Harry E.

1985 "One or two veils in front of the holy of holies?" *Theologica Evangelica* 18: 22-27.

Fabry, Heinz-Josef.

1977 "Umkehr und Metanoia als monastisches Ideal in der 'Mönchsgemeinde' von Qumran." *Erbe und Auftrag* 53: 163-80.

1993 "Neue Texte aus Qumran." *Biblische Kirche* 48: 24-27.

Faierstein, Morris M.

1981 "Why Do the Scribes Say That Elijah Must Come First?" *Journal of Biblical Literature* 100: 75-86.

Falk, D.

1994 "4Q393: A Communal Confession." *Journal of Jewish Studies* 45: 184-207.

Falk, Harvey.

1985 *Jesus the Pharisee: A New Look at the Jewishness of Jesus.* New York: Paulist Press.

Falk, Ze'ev W.

1974 "Binding and Loosing." *Journal of Jewish Studies* 25: 92-100.

1974/1976 "Jewish Private Law." Pp. 504-34 in *The Jewish People in the First Century: Historical Geography, Political History, Social, Cultural, and Religious Life and Institutions.* 2 vols. Edited by S. Safrai and M. Stern with D. Flusser and W. C. van Unnik. Section 1 of Compendia Rerum Iudaicarum ad Novum

Testamentum. Vol. 1: Assen: Van Gorcum & Co., B.V.; Vol. 2: Philadelphia: Fortress Press.

Fallaize, E. N.

1918 "Purification: Introductory and Primitive." 10:455-66 in *Encyclopedia of Religion and Ethics.* 13 vols. Edited by James Hastings. Edinburgh: T & T Clark.

Farber, Bernard.

1968 *Comparative Kinship Systems: A Method of Analysis.* New York: John Wiley & Sons.

Faris, James C.

1969 "Sibling Terminology and Cross-Sex Behavior: Data from the Southeastern Nuba Mountains." *American Anthropologist* 71: 482-88.

Farmer, William R.

1964 *The Synoptic Problem: A Critical Analysis.* New York: Macmillan & Company.

1974 *The Last Twelve Verses of Mark.* Society of New Testament Studies Monograph 25. Cambridge: Cambridge University Press.

Farmer, William R., and Roch Kereszty.

1990 *Peter and Paul in the Church of Rome: The Ecumenical Potential of a Forgotten Perspective.* Studies in Contemporary Biblical and Theological Problems. New York; Mahwah, NJ: Paulist Press.

Farrer, Austin.

1956a "An Examination of Mark XIII.10." *Journal of Theological Studies* 7: 75-79.

1956b "Q." *Theology* 59: 247-48.

Fee, Gordon D.

1987 *The First Epistle to the Corinthians.* New International Commentary on the New Testament. Grand Rapids: Eerdmans.

1994 *God's Empowering Presence: The Holy Spirit in the Letters of Paul.* Peabody, MA: Hendrickson.

Feiler, Paul F.

1983 "The Stilling of the Storm in Matthew: A Response to Günther Bornkamm." *Journal of the Evangelical Theological Society* 26: 399-406.

Felder, Cain Hope.

1989 *Troubling Biblical Waters: Race, Class, and Family.* The Bishop Henry McNeal Turner Studies in North American Black Religion 3. Maryknoll, NY: Orbis Books.

Feldman, Louis H.

1976 "Josephus as an Apologist of the Greco-Roman World: His Portrait of Solomon." Pp. 69-98 in *Aspects of Religious Propaganda in Judaism and Early Christianity.* Edited by Elisabeth Schüssler Fiorenza. UNDCSJCA 2. Notre Dame: University of Notre Dame Press.

1982 "Josephus' Portrait of Saul." *Hebrew Union College Annual* 53: 45-99.

1985 "Josephus as a Biblical Interpreter: The *'Aqedah.*" *Jewish Quarterly Review* 75: 212-52.

1988a "Josephus' Portrait of Jacob." *Jewish Quarterly Review* 79 (2-3, 1988-1989): 101-51.

1988b "Josephus' Version of Samson." *Journal for the Study of Judaism* 19: 171-214.

1989a "Josephus' Portrait of David." *Hebrew Union College Annual* 60: 129-74.

1989b "Josephus's Portrait of Joshua." *Harvard Theological Review* 82: 351-76.

1991 "Josephus' Portrait of Manasseh," *Journal for the Study of the Pseudepigrapha* 9 (1991): 3-20.

1992a "Josephus' Interpretation of Jonah." *Association for Jewish Studies Review* 17: 1-29.

1992b "Josephus' Portrait of Ahab." *Ephemerides Theologicae Lovanienses* 68: 368-84.

1992c "Josephus' Portrait of Daniel." *Henoch* 14: 37-96.

1992d "Josephus' Portrait of Hezekiah." *Journal of Biblical Literature* 111: 597-610.

1992e "Josephus' Portrait of Joseph." *Revue Biblique* 99: 379-417, 504-28.

1992f "Josephus' Portrait of Moses. Parts One and Two." *Jewish Quarterly Review* 82: 285-328; 83: 7-50.

1992g "Josephus' Portrait of Nehemiah." *Journal of Jewish Studies* 43: 187-202.

1992h "Josephus' Portrait of Samuel." *Abr-Nahrain* 30: 103-45.

1993a "Josephus' Portrait of Ezra." *Vetus Testamentum* 43: 190-214.

1993b "Josephus' Portrait of Isaac." *Rivista di Storia e Letteratura Religiosa* 29 (1, 1993): 3-33.

1993c "Josephus' Portrait of Jeroboam." *Andrews University Seminary Studies* 31 (1, 1993): 29-51.

1993d "Josephus' Portrait of Josiah." *Louvain Studies* 18 (2, 1993): 110-30.

1993e "Josephus' Portraits of the Pharaohs." *Syllecta Classica* 4: 49-63.

1994a "Josephus' Portrait of Ahasuerus." *Australian Biblical Review* 42: 17-38.

1994b "Josephus' Portrait of Asa." *Bulletin for Biblical Research* 4: 41-59.

1994c "Josephus' Portrait of Jehoram, King of Israel." *Bulletin of the John Rylands University Library of Manchester* 76 (1, 1994): 3-20.

Feldmeier, Reinhard.

1991 "The Portrayal of Peter in the Synoptic Gospels." Pp. 252-56 in *The Gospel and the Gospels.* Edited by Peter Stuhlmacher. Grand Rapids: Eerdmans.

Fensham, F. Charles.

1960 "The Legal Background of Mt vi 12." *Novum Testamentum* 4: 1-2.

1965 "Judas' Hand in the Bowl and Qumran." *Revue de Qumran* 5: 259-61.

1967 "The Good and Evil Eye in the Sermon on the Mount." *Neotestamentica* 1: 51-58.

Fenton, J. C.

1966 "Expounding the Parables. IV. The Parables of the Treasure and the Pearl (Mt 13:44-46)." *The Expository Times* 77: 178-80.

1977 *Saint Matthew.* Philadelphia: Westminster Press.

Ferch, A. J.

1977 "The Two Aeons and the Messiah in Pseudo-Philo, 4 Ezra, and 2 Baruch." *Andrews University Seminary Studies* 15: 135-51.

Ferguson, Everett.

1987 *Backgrounds of Early Christianity.* Grand Rapids: Eerdmans.

Fernández, E. López.

1983 "El yugo de Jesús (Mt 11,28-30). Historia y sentido de una metáfora." *Studium Ovetense* 11: 65-118. (*NTA* 31:287)

Feuillet, André.

1964 "Le Sens du mot Parousie dans l'Evangile de Matthieu. Comparison entre Matth. xxiv et Jac. v.1-11." Pp. 261-80 in *The Background of the New Testament and Its Eschatology: Essays in Honor of Charles Harold Dodd.* Edited by W. D. Davies and D. Daube. Cambridge: Cambridge University Press.

1979 "Die Versuchungen Jesu." *Internationale Katholische Zeitschrift Communio* 8: 226-37.

1980a "Le caractère universel du jugement et la charité sans frontières en *Mt* 25,31-46." *Nouvelle Revue Théologique* 102: 179-96.

1980b "La signification fondamentale de Marc XIII. Recherches sur l'eschatologie des Synoptiques." *Revue Thomiste* 80: 181-215.

1988 "Observations sur les deux généalogies de Jésus Christ de saint Matthieu (1,1-17) et de saint Luc (3,23-38)." *Esprit et Vie* 98: 605-8, 294.

1991 "La primauté et l'humilité de Pierre. Leur attestation en Mt 16,17-19, dans l'Evangile de Marc et dans la Première Epître de Pierre." *Nova et Vetera* 66: 3-24.

Fields, Harriet L., and William R. Merrifield.

1980 "Mayoruna (Panoan) Kinship." *Ethnology* 19: 1-28.

Filson, Floyd V.

1960 *A Commentary on the Gospel according to St. Matthew.* New York: Harper & Row.

1964 *A New Testament History.* Philadelphia: Westminster Press.

Finegan, Jack.

1952 *The Archaeology of World Religions.* Princeton: Princeton University Press.

1969 *The Archeology of the New Testament.* Princeton: Princeton University Press.

Finkel, Asher.

1981 "Yavneh's Liturgy and Early Christianity." *Journal of Ecumenical Studies* 18: 231-50.

Finkelstein, Louis.

1942-1943 "Pre-Maccabean Documents in the Passover Haggadah." *Harvard Theological Review* 35: 291-332; 36: 1-38.

1962 *The Pharisees: The Sociological Background of Their Faith.* 2 vols. 3d ed. Philadelphia: The Jewish Publication Society of America.

1970 *Akiba: Scholar, Saint and Martyr.* New York: Atheneum.

1972 *Pharisaism in the Making: Selected Essays.* New York: KTAV.

Finley, M. I.

1973 *The Ancient Economy.* Sather Classical Lectures 43. Berkeley: University of California Press.

Finney, Paul Corby.

1993 "The Rabbi and the Coin Portrait (Mark 12:15b, 16): Rigorism Manqué." *Journal of Biblical Literature* 112: 629-44.

Fiorenza, Elisabeth Schüssler.

1983 *In Memory of Her: A Feminist Theological Reconstruction of Christian Origins.* New York: Crossroad Publishing Company.

Firth, Raymond.

1963 *We, the Tikopia: A Sociological Study of Kinship in Primitive Polynesia.* 2d ed. Preface by Bronislaw Malinowski. Boston: Beacon Press.

Fischer, Moshe L., and Alla Stein.

1994 "Josephus on the Use of Marble in Building Projects of Herod the Great." *Journal of Jewish Studies* 45: 79-85.

Fitzgerald, John T.

1988 *Cracks in an Earthen Vessel: An Examination of the Catalogues of Hardships in the Corinthian Correspondence.* Society of Biblical Literature Dissertation Series 99. Atlanta: Scholars Press.

Fitzmyer, Joseph A.

1961 "The Use of Explicit Old Testament Quotations in Qumran Literature and in the New Testament." *New Testament Studies* 7: 297-333.

1965 "The Aramaic 'Elect of God' Text from Qumran Cave IV." *Catholic Biblical Quarterly* 27: 348-72.

1966 "Jewish Christianity in Acts in Light of the Qumran Scrolls." Pp. 233-57 in *Studies in Luke-Acts: Essays in Honor of Paul Schubert.* Edited by Leander E. Keck and J. Louis Martyn. Nashville: Abingdon.

1971 *The Genesis Apocryphon of Qumran Cave 1: A Commentary.* 2d rev. ed. Biblica et Orientalia 18A. Rome: Biblical Institute Press.

1974 *Essays on the Semitic Background of the New Testament.* 2d ed. Studies in Biblical Theology 5. Missoula, MT: Scholars Press,

1985 "More about Elijah Coming First." *Journal of Biblical Literature* 104: 295-96.

1993 "4Q246. The 'Son of God' Document from Qumran." *Biblica* 74 (2, 1993): 153-74.

Fjärstedt, B.

1968 "Fråga och svar i Matt. 19,3-12." *Svensk Exegetisk Årsbok* 33: 118-40. (*NTA* 14:37)

Fleddermann, Harry.

1979 "The Flight of a Naked Young Man (Mark 14:51-52)." *Catholic Biblical Quarterly* 41: 412-18.

Fleming, Thomas V.

1963 "Christ and Divorce." *Theological Studies* 24: 106-20.

Flesher, Paul V. M.

1994 "Mark 7:1-23 and Rabbinic Rhetoric." Paper presented in the Rhetoric and New Testament Section, Society of Biblical Literature 1994 Annual Meeting, Chicago.

Flowers, Harold J.

1953 "En pneumati hagiō kai puri." *Expository Times* 64: 155-56.

1961 "Matthew xxiii.15." *Expository Times* 73: 67-69.

Flusser, David.

1957 "Healing through the Laying-On of Hands in a Dead Sea Scroll." *Israel Exploration Journal* 7: 107-8.

1960 "Blessed Are the Poor in Spirit . . ." *Israel Exploration Journal* 10: 1-13.

1973 "The Last Supper and the Essenes." *Immanuel* 2: 23-27.

1974/1976 "Paganism in Palestine." Pp. 1065-1100 in *The Jewish People in the First Century: Historical Geography, Political History, Social, Cultural, and Religious Life and Institutions.* 2 vols. Edited by S. Safrai and M. Stern with D. Flusser and W. C. van Unnik. Section 1 of Compendia Rerum Iudaicarum ad Novum Testamentum. Vol. 1: Assen: Van Gorcum & Co., B.V.; Vol. 2: Philadelphia: Fortress Press.

1981 *Die rabbinischen Gleichnisse und der Gleichniserzähler Jesu. 1. Teil. Das Wesen der Gleichnisse.* Bern: Lang.

1986 "Abraham and the Upanishads." *Immanuel* 20: 53-61.

1988 *Judaism and the Origins of Christianity.* Jerusalem: Magnes Press, The Hebrew University.

1989 "Die Versuchung Jesu und ihr jüdischer Hintergrund." *Judaica* 45: 110-28.

Foakes Jackson, F. J., and Kirsopp Lake.

1979a "The Development of Thought on the Spirit, the Church, and Baptism."

1:321-44 in *The Beginnings of Christianity.* 5 vols. Ed. F. J. Foakes Jackson and Kirsopp Lake. Grand Rapids: Baker.

1979b "The Internal Evidence of Acts," 2:121-204 in *The Beginnings of Christianity.* 5 vols. Ed. F. J. Foakes Jackson and Kirsopp Lake. Grand Rapids: Baker.

Foerster, Werner.

1962 "Der heilige Geist im Spätjudentum." *New Testament Studies* 8: 117-34.

Force, Paul.

1993 "Encore les incises de Matthieu!" *Bulletin de Littérature Ecclésiastique* 94: 315-28.

Ford, Desmond.

1979 *The Abomination of Desolation in Biblical Eschatology.* Washington, D.C.: The University Press of America.

Ford, J. M.

1965 "'Thou Art Abraham' and Upon This Rock . . .'" *Heythrop Journal* 6: 289-301. (*NTA* 10:190-91)

1966 "The Meaning of 'Virgin.'" *New Testament Studies* 12: 293-99.

1967 "The Parable of the Foolish Scholars (Matt. xxv 1-13)." *Novum Testamentum* 9: 107-23.

Foresti, F.

1984 "Maria, genitrice del sabato escatologico. Considerazioni sul significato di *Mt.* 1,1-17." *Biblia e Oriente* 26: 31-43. (*NTA* 29:16)

Fortes, Meyer.

1950 "Kinship and Marriage among the Ashanti." Pp. 252-84 in *African Systems of Kinship and Marriage.* Edited by A. R. Radcliffe-Brown and Daryll Forde. New York: Oxford University Press.

Fortna, Robert T.

1990 "'You have made them equal to us!' (Mt 20:1-16)." *Journal of Theology for Southern Africa* 72: 66-72.

Fox, J. Robin.

1964 "Witchcraft and Clanship in Cochiti Therapy." Pp. 174-200 in *Magic, Faith, and Healing: Studies in Primitive Psychotherapy Today.* Edited by Ari Kiev. Introduction by Jerome D. Frank. New York: The Free Press: A Division of Macmillan Publishing Company.

Foxhall, L.

1990 "The Dependent Tenant: Land Leasing and Labour in Italy and Greece." *Journal of Roman Studies* 80: 97-114.

Frame, James Everett.

1912 *A Critical and Exegetical Commentary on the Epistles of St. Paul to the Thessalonians.* International Critical Commentary. Edinburgh: T & T Clark.

France, R. T.

1976 "The Authenticity of the Sayings of Jesus." Pp. 101-43 in *History, Criticism, and Faith.* Edited by Colin Brown. Downers Grove, IL: InterVarsity Press.

1977 "Exegesis in Practice: Two Examples." Pp. 252-81 in *New Testament Interpretation: Essays on Principles and Methods.* Edited by I. Howard Marshall. Grand Rapids: Eerdmans.

1979 "Herod and the Children of Bethlehem." *Novum Testamentum* 21: 98-120.

1981a "The Formula-Quotations of Matthew 1 and the Problem of Communication." *New Testament Studies* 27: 233-51.

1981b "Scripture, Tradition and History in the Infancy Narratives of Matthew." 2:239-66 in Gospel Perspectives. 6 vols. Vol. 2: *Studies of History and Tra-*

dition in the Four Gospels. Edited by R. T. France and David Wenham. Sheffield: JSOT, University of Sheffield.

1985 *Matthew.* Tyndale New Testament Commentaries. Grand Rapids: Eerdmans.

1986 *The Evidence for Jesus.* Downers Grove: InterVarsity Press.

1989 *Matthew: Evangelist and Teacher.* Grand Rapids: Zondervan; n.p.: Paternoster.

Francis, E. D.

1975 "Mithraic graffiti from Dura-Europos." 2:424-45 in *Mithraic Studies: Proceedings of the First International Congress of Mithraic Studies.* 2 vols. Edited by John R. Hinnells. Manchester: Manchester University Press.

Francis, Fred O.

1973 "Humility and Angelic Worship in Col 2:18." Pp. 163-95 in *Conflict at Colossae: A Problem in the Interpretation of Early Christianity Illustrated by Selected Modern Studies.* Edited and translated by Fred O. Francis and Wayne A. Meeks. Sources for Biblical Study 4. Missoula, MT: Society of Biblical Literature.

Frank, Tenney.

1932 *Aspects of Social Behavior in Ancient Rome.* Cambridge: Harvard University Press.

Frankfurter, D.

1994 "The Magic of Writing and the Writing of Magic: The Power of the Word in Egyptian and Greek Traditions." *Helios* 21: 189-221.

Fredriksen, Paula.

1988 *From Jesus to Christ: The Origins of the New Testament Images of Jesus.* New Haven: Yale University Press.

Freed, Edwin D.

1965 *Old Testament Quotations in the Gospel of John.* Supplements to Novum Testamentum 11. Leiden: E. J. Brill.

1987 "The Women in Matthew's Genealogy." *Journal for the Study of the New Testament* 29: 3-19.

Frei, Hans.

1989 "Apologetics, Criticism, and the Loss of Narrative Interpretation." Pp. 45-64 in *Why Narrative? Readings in Narrative Theology.* Edited by Stanley Hauerwas and L. Gregory Jones. Grand Rapids: Eerdmans.

Freund, R. A.

1991 "Lying and Deception in the Biblical and Post-Biblical Judaic Tradition." *Scandinavian Journal of the Old Testament* 5: 45-61.

Freyne, Sean.

1980 "The Galileans in the Light of Josephus' *Vita.*" *New Testament Studies* 26: 397-413.

1981 "Galilean Religion of the First Century C.E. against Its Social Background." *Proceedings of the Irish Biblical Association* 5: 98-114. (*NTA* 26:175-76)

1987 "Galilee-Jerusalem Relations according to Josephus' *Life.*" *New Testament Studies* 33: 600-609.

1988 *Galilee, Jesus and the Gospels: Literary Approaches and Historical Investigations.* Philadelphia: Fortress Press.

1994 "The Ethos of First-Century Galilee." *Proceedings of the Irish Biblical Association* 17: 69-79.

Friedländer, Ludwig.

1965 *Roman Life and Manners under the Early Empire.* 4 vols. Translated from the 7th rev. ed. by Leonard Magnus, J. H. Freese, and A. B. Gough. New York: Barnes & Noble.

Friedman, M. A.

1990 "Tamar, A Symbol of Life: The 'Killer Wife' Superstition in the Bible and Jewish Tradition." *Association for Jewish Studies Review* 15 (1, 1990): 23-61.

Friedman, T.

1983 "Some Unexplained Features of Ancient Synagogues." *Conservative Judaism* 36: 35-42.

Friedrich, Gerhard.

1971 "Σάλπιγξ." 7:71-88 in *Theological Dictionary of the New Testament.* 10 vols. Edited by Gerhard Kittel and Gerhard Friedrich. Grand Rapids: Eerdmans, 1964-1976.

Fritsch, Charles T.

1956 *The Qumran Community: Its History and Scrolls.* New York: Macmillan Company.

Frontisi-Ducroux, Francoise, and Jean-Pierre Vernant.

1983 "Figures du masque en Grece ancienne." *Journal de Psychologie Normale et Pathologique* 80: 53-69.

Frost, Henry W.

1924 *Matthew Twenty-Four and the Revelation.* New York: Oxford University Press.

Fry, C. George, James R. King, Eugene R. Swanger, and Herbert C. Wolf.

1984 *Great Asian Religions.* Grand Rapids: Baker.

Frye, Richard N.

1996 *The Heritage of Central Asia: From Antiquity to the Turkish Expansion.* Princeton, NJ: Markus Wiener Publishers.

Fuchs, Stephen.

1964 "Magic Healing Techniques among the Balahis in Central India." Pp. 121-38 in *Magic, Faith, and Healing: Studies in Primitive Psychotherapy Today.* Edited by Ari Kiev. Introduction by Jerome D. Frank. New York: The Free Press; A Division of Macmillan Publishing Company.

Fujita, Shozo.

1976 "The Metaphor of Plant in Jewish Literature of the Intertestamental Period." *Journal for the Study of Judaism* 7: 30-45.

Fuller, Daniel P.

1980 *Gospel and Law: Contrast or Continuum?* Grand Rapids: Eerdmans.

Fuller, George C.

1966 "The Olivet Discourse: An Apocalyptic Timetable." *Westminster Theological Journal* 28: 157-63.

Fuller, Reginald H.

1956 "The Virgin Birth: Historical Fact or Kerygmatic Truth?" *Biblical Research* 1: 1-7.

1971 *The Formation of the Resurrection Narratives.* New York: Macmillan Company.

Fuller, Reginald H., and Pheme Perkins.

1983 *Who Is This Christ?: Gospel Christology and Contemporary Faith.* Philadelphia: Fortress Press.

Funk, Robert W.

1967 "The Apostolic *Parousia:* Form and Significance." Pp. 249-68 in *Christian*

History and Interpretation: Studies Presented to John Knox. Edited by W. R. Farmer, C. F. D. Moule, and R. R. Niebuhr. Cambridge: Cambridge University Press.

Funk, Robert W., Roy W. Hoover, and the Jesus Seminar.

1993 *The Five Gospels: The Search for the Authentic Words of Jesus.* New York: Polebridge Press, Macmillan Publishing Company.

Gärtner, Bertril.

1965 *The Temple and the Community in Qumran and the New Testament: A Comparative Study in the Temple Symbolism of the Qumran Texts and the New Testament.* Cambridge: Cambridge University Press.

Gangemi, A.

1977 "La manna nascosta e il nome nuovo." *Revista Biblica* 25: 337-56. (*NTA* 23:185)

Gager, John G.

1975 *Kingdom and Community: The Social World of Early Christianity.* Prentice-Hall Studies in Religion. Englewood Cliffs, NJ: Prentice-Hall.

1979 Review of *Early Christianity and Society: Seven Studies* by R. M. Grant; *Social Aspects of Early Christianity* by A. J. Malherbe; and *Sociology of Early Palestinian Christianity* by Gerd Theissen. *Religious Studies Review* 5: 174-80.

1983 *The Origins of Anti-Semitism: Attitudes toward Judaism in Pagan and Christian Antiquity.* New York: Oxford University Press.

1994 "Moses the Magician: Hero of an Ancient Counter-Culture?" *Helios* 21: 179-88.

Gagnon, Robert A. J.

1994 "The Shape of Matthew's Q Text of the Centurion at Capernaum: Did It Mention Delegations?" *New Testament Studies* 40: 133-42.

Gamoran, Hillel.

1976 "Talmudic Usury Laws and Business Loans." *Journal for the Study of Judaism* 7: 129-42.

García Martínez, F.

1993 "Nuevos Textos Mesiánicos de Qumrán y el Mesías del Nuevo Testamento," *Communio* 26: 3-31. *(NTA)*

Gardner, Jane F.

1974 *Leadership and the Cult of Personality.* London: J. M. Dent & Sons; Toronto: Hakkert.

1986 *Women in Roman Law and Society.* Bloomington: Indiana University Press.

Gardner, Joseph L., editor.

1981 *Reader's Digest Atlas of the Bible: An Illustrated Guide to the Holy Land.* Pleasantville, NY: Reader's Digest Association.

Gardner, Richard B.

1991 *Matthew.* Believer's Church Bible Commentary. Scottsdale, PA: Herald Press.

Garland, David E.

1979 *The Intention of Matthew 23.* Novum Testamentum Supplements 52. Leiden: E. J. Brill.

1993 *Reading Matthew: A Literary and Theological Commentary on the First Gospel.* New York: Crossroad Publishing Company.

1996 "Matthew's Understanding of the Temple Tax." Pp. 69-98 in *Treasures New and Old: Recent Contributions to Matthean Studies.* Edited by David R.

Bauer and Mark Allan Powell. Society of Biblical Literature Symposium Series 1. Atlanta: Scholars Press.

Garnet, Paul.

1980 "The Baptism of Jesus and the Son of Man Idea." *Journal for the Study of the New Testament* 9: 49-65.

Garrett, Susan R.

1998 *The Temptations of Jesus in Mark's Gospel.* Grand Rapids: Eerdmans.

Garte, Edna.

1973 "The Theme of Resurrection in the Dura-Europos Synagogue Paintings." *Jewish Quarterly Review* 64: 1-15.

Gasparro, Giulia Sfameni.

1985 *Soteriology and Mystic Aspects in the Cult of Cybele and Attis.* Études Préliminaires aux Religions Orientales dans l'Empire Romain, tome 103. Publiées par M. J. Vermaseren. Leiden: E. J. Brill.

Gaster, Theodor H.

1976 *The Dead Sea Scriptures.* Garden City, NY: Doubleday & Company.

Gaston, Lloyd.

1970 *No Stone on Another: Studies in the Significance of the Fall of Jerusalem in the Synoptic Gospels.* Novum Testamentum, Supplements 23. Leiden: E. J. Brill.

Gelfand, Michael.

1964 "Psychiatric Disorders as Recognized by the Shona." Pp. 156-73 in *Magic, Faith, and Healing: Studies in Primitive Psychotherapy Today.* Edited by Ari Kiev. Introduction by Jerome D. Frank. New York: The Free Press; A Division of Macmillan Publishing Company.

Gemés, I.

1969 "Aliança no Documento de Damasco e na Epístola aos Hebreus. Uma contribuiçâo à questâa: Qumrân e as origens do Cristianismo." *Rivista Cultura Bíblica* 6: 28-68. (*NTA* 15:105)

Gempf, Conrad.

1993 "Public Speaking and Published Accounts." Pp. 259-303 in *The Book of Acts in Its Ancient Literary Setting.* Edited by Bruce W. Winter and Andrew D. Clarke. Vol. 1 in The Book of Acts in Its First Century Setting. 6 vols. Grand Rapids: Eerdmans; Carlisle: The Paternoster Press.

Genot-Bismuth, Jacqueline.

1981 "Pacifisme pharisien et sublimation de l'idée de guerre aux origines du rabbinisme." *Etudes Théologiques et Religieuses* 56: 73-89.

George, A.

1966 "Ne nous soumets pas à la tentation . . . Note sur la traduction nouvelle du Notre Père." *Bible et Vie Chrétienne* 71: 74-79. (*NTA* 11:205)

Georgi, Dieter.

1986 *The Opponents of Paul in Second Corinthians.* Philadelphia: Fortress Press.

Gerhardsson, Birger.

1961 *Memory and Manuscript: Oral Tradition and Written Transmission in Rabbinic Judaism and Early Christianity.* Acta Seminarii Neotestamentici Upsaliensis 22. Uppsala: C. W. K. Gleerup.

1963 "The Seven Parables in Matthew XIII." *New Testament Studies* 19: 16-37.

1966 *The Testing of God's Son (Matt 4:1-11 & Par.): An Analysis of an Early Christian Midrash.* Coniectanea Biblica, New Testament 2.1. Lund: C. W. K. Gleerup.

1968 "The Parable of the Sower and Its Interpretation." *New Testament Studies* 14: 165-93.

1978 "Fader vår i Nya testamentet." *Svensk Teologisk Kvartalskrift* 54: 93-102. (*NTA* 23:145)

1979 *The Origins of the Gospel Traditions.* Philadelphia: Fortress Press.

1988 "The Narrative Meshalim in the Synoptic Gospels. A Comparison with the Narrative Meshalim in the Old Testament." *New Testament Studies* 34: 339-63.

1991a "If We Do Not Cut the Parables out of Their Frames." *New Testament Studies* 37: 321-35.

1991b "The Path of the Gospel Tradition." Pp. 75-96 in *The Gospel and the Gospels.* Edited by Peter Stuhlmacher. Grand Rapids: Eerdmans.

Gero, Stephen.

1978 "Jewish Polemic in the Martyrium Pionii and a 'Jesus' Passage from the Talmud." *Journal of Jewish Studies* 29: 164-68.

Gersht, Rivka.

1984 "The Tyche of Caesarea Maritima." *Palestine Exploration Quarterly* 116: 110-14.

Gervers, Michael.

1979 "The Iconography of the Cave in Christian and Mithraic Tradition." Pp. 579-99 in *Mysteria Mithrae.* Edited by Ugo Bianchi. Études Préliminaires aux Religions Orientales dans l'Empire Romain tome 80. Publiées par M. J. Vermaseren. Leiden: E. J. Brill.

Gibbard, S. M.

1956 "The Christian Mystery." Pp. 97-120 in *Studies in Ephesians.* Edited by F. L. Cross. London: A. R. Mowbray & Company.

Giblet, Jean.

1974 "Un mouvement de résistance armée au temps de Jésus?" *Revue Théologique de Louvain* 5: 409-26.

Giblin, Charles H.

1967 *The Threat to Faith: An Exegetical and Theological Re-Examination of 2 Thessalonians 2.* Analecta Biblica 31. Rome: Pontifical Biblical Institute.

Gibson, J.

1981 *"Hoi Telōnai kai hai Pornai." Journal of Theological Studies* 32: 429-33.

Giese, Ronald L.

1993 "Compassion for the Lowly in Septuagint Proverbs." *Journal for the Study of the Pseudepigrapha* 11: 109-17.

Gill, David.

1991 "Socrates and Jesus on Non-Retaliation and Love of Enemies." *Horizons* 18: 246-62.

Gill, David W. J., and Conrad Gempf.

1994 *The Book of Acts in Its Graeco-Roman Setting.* Vol. 2 in The Book of Acts in Its First Century Setting. Grand Rapids: Eerdmans; Carlisle: The Paternoster Press.

Gilmore, David D.

1987 "Introduction: The Shame of Dishonor." Pp. 2-21 in *Honor and Shame and the Unity of the Mediterranean.* Edited by David D. Gilmore. American Anthropological Association 22. Washington, D.C.: American Anthropological Association.

Ginsberg, Christian D.

1955 *The Essenes: Their History and Doctrines; The Kabbalah: Its Doctrines, Development and Literature.* London: Routledge and Kegan Paul. The Kabbalah section was first published in 1863; the Essenes section in 1864.

Ginsberg, H. L.

1953 "The Cave Scrolls and the Jewish Sects: New Light on a Scholarly Mystery." *Commentary* 16: 77-81.

Gispert-Sauch, G.

1978 "St. Peter Walking on the Ganges?" *Vidyajyoti* 42: 468-72. (*NTA* 23: 281)

Glasson, T. Francis.

1961 *Greek Influence in Jewish Eschatology: With Special Reference to the Apocalypses and Pseudepigraphs.* S.P.C.K. Biblical Monographs 1. London: S.P.C.K.

1963a *Moses in the Fourth Gospel.* Studies in Biblical Theology. Naperville, IL: Alec R. Allenson.

1963b *The Second Advent: The Origin of the New Testament Doctrine.* 3d rev. ed. London: Epworth.

1976 "The Son of Man Imagery: Enoch XIV and Daniel VII." *New Testament Studies* 23 (1, October 1976): 82-90.

Gleason, Kathryn L.

1987 "Garden Excavations at the Herodian Winter Palace in Jericho, 1985-7." *Bulletin of the Anglo-Israel Archaeological Society* 7: 21-39.

Gluckman, Max.

1950 "Kinship and Marriage among the Lozi of Northern Rhodesia and the Zulu of Natal." Pp. 166-206 in *African Systems of Kinship and Marriage.* Edited by A. R. Radcliffe-Brown and Daryll Forde. New York: Oxford University Press.

Glueck, Nelson.

1960 *Rivers in the Desert: A History of the Negev.* New York: Grove Press.

Gnilka, Joachim.

1961 "Das Gemeinschaftsmal der Essener." *Biblische Zeitschrift* 5: 39-55.

1986-1988 *Das Matthäusevangelium.* 2 vols. Herders theologischer Kommentar zum Neuen Testament. Freiburg: Herder.

1988 "Selig, die reinen Herzens sind." *Internationale Katholische Zeitschrift/Communio* 17: 385-91.

1997 *Jesus of Nazareth: Message and History.* Translated by Siegfried S. Schatzmann. Peabody, MA: Hendrickson.

Gnuse, Robert K.

1989 "Dream Reports in the Writings of Flavius Josephus." *Revue Biblique* 96: 358-90.

1990a "Dream Genre in the Matthean Infancy Narratives." *Novum Testamentum* 32: 97-120.

1990b "The Jewish Dream Interpreter in a Foreign Court: The Recurring Use of a Theme in Jewish Literature." *Journal for the Study of the Pseudepigrapha* 7: 29-53.

1993 "The Temple Experience of Jaddus in the *Antiquities* of Josephus: A Report of Jewish Dream Incubation." *Jewish Quarterly Review* 83: 349-68.

Godwin, Joscelyn.

1981 *Mystery Religions in the Ancient World.* San Francisco: Harper & Row.

Goergen, D. J.

1986 *The Mission and Ministry of Jesus.* Wilmington, DE: Michael Glazier.

Goetz, Stewart C., and Craig L. Blomberg.

1981 "The Burden of Proof." *Journal for the Study of the New Testament* 11: 39-63.

Goguel, Maurice.

1948 *The Life of Jesus.* Translated by Olive Wyon. New York: Macmillan Company.

Goldberg, Michael.

1989 "God, Action, and Narrative: *Which* Narrative? *Which* Action? *Which* God?" Pp. 348-65 in *Why Narrative? Readings in Narrative Theology.* Edited by Stanley Hauerwas and L. Gregory Jones. Grand Rapids: Eerdmans.

Goldenberg, Robert.

1982 "Early Rabbinic Explanations of the Destruction of Jerusalem." *Journal of Jewish Studies* 33: 517-25.

Goldingay, John.

1977 "Expounding the New Testament." Pp. 351-65 in *New Testament Interpretation: Essays on Principles and Methods.* Edited by I. Howard Marshall. Grand Rapids: Eerdmans.

Goldstein, Bernard R., and David Pingree.

1979 "Astrological Almanacs from the Cairo Geniza, Parts I and II." *Journal of Near Eastern Studies* 38: 153-76, 231-56.

Goldstein, Jonathan.

1984-1985 "The Central Composition of the West Wall of the Synagogue of Dura-Europos." *Journal of Ancient Near Eastern Studies* 16-17: 99-142.

Good, Deirdre.

1990 "The Verb ἀναχωρέω in Matthew's Gospel." *Novum Testamentum* 32: 1-12.

Goodblatt, David.

1995 "Suicide in the Sanctuary: Traditions on Priestly Martyrdom." *Journal of Jewish Studies* 46: 10-29.

Goodenough, Erwin R.

1953-1968 *Jewish Symbols in the Greco-Roman Period.* 13 vols. Bollingen Series 37. New York: Pantheon for Bollingen Foundation. Vol. 13: Princeton University for Bollingen Foundation.

1962 *An Introduction to Philo Judaeus.* 2d ed. Oxford: Basil Blackwell.

1970 *The Church in the Roman Empire.* New York: Cooper Square Publishers.

Goodman, David.

1986 "Do Angels Eat?" *Journal of Jewish Studies* 37: 160-75.

Goodman, Felicitas D.

1974 "Disturbances in the Apostolic Church: A Trance-Based Upheaval in Yucatán." Pp. 227-364 in *Trance, Healing, and Hallucination: Three Field Studies in Religious Experience.* By Felicitas D. Goodman, Jeannette H. Henney, and Esther Pressel. New York: John Wiley & Sons.

1988 *How about Demons? Possession and Exorcism in the Modern World.* Bloomington, IN: Indiana University Press.

Goodman, Martin.

1983 *State and Society in Roman Galilee, A.D. 132-212.* Oxford Centre for Postgraduate Hebrew Studies. Totowa, NJ: Rowman & Allanheld, Publishers.

1987 *The Ruling Class of Judaea: The Origins of the Jewish Revolt against Rome A.D.* 66-70. Cambridge: Cambridge University Press.

1989 "Proselytising in Rabbinic Judaism." *Journal of Jewish Studies* 40: 175-85.

Goody, Jack.

1970 "Cousin Terms." *Southwestern Journal of Anthropology* 26: 125-42.

Goppelt, Leonhard.

1962 "The Existence of the Church in History according to Apostolic and Early Catholic Thought." Pp. 193-209 in *Current Issues in New Testament Interpretation: Essays in Honor of Otto A. Piper.* New York: Harper & Row.

1964 *Jesus, Paul and Judaism.* Translated by Edward Schroeder. New York: Thomas Nelson.

1980 *Apostolic and Post-Apostolic Times.* Translated by Robert Guelich. Grand Rapids: Baker.

1981/1982 *Theology of the New Testament.* 2 vols. Translated by John E. Alsup. Edited by Jürgen Roloff. Grand Rapids: Eerdmans.

Goranson, Stephen.

1992 "Sectarianism, Geography, and the Copper Scroll." *Journal of Jewish Studies* 43: 282-87.

Gordis, Robert.

1957 "The 'Begotten' Messiah in the Qumran Scrolls." *Vetus Testamentum* 7: 191-94.

Gordon, Cyrus H.

1965a *The Ancient Near East.* New York: W. W. Norton & Company.

1965b *The Common Background of Greek and Hebrew Civilizations.* New York: W. W. Norton & Company.

1977 "Paternity at Two Levels." *Journal of Biblical Literature* 96: 101.

1978a "The Double Paternity of Jesus." *Biblical Archaeology Review* 4: 26-27.

1978b "Two Aramaic Incantations." Pp. 231-44 in *Biblical and Near Eastern Studies: Essays in Honor of William Sanford LaSor.* Edited by Gary A. Tuttle. Grand Rapids: Eerdmans.

Gordon, Murray.

1989 *Slavery in the Arab World.* New York: New Amsterdam Books. Originally published as *L'Esclavage dans le monde arabe.* Paris: Editions Robert Laffont, 1987.

Gottlieb, Isaac B.

1990 "Pirqe Abot and Biblical Wisdom." *Vetus Testamentum* 40: 152-64.

Gough, Kathleen.

1973a "Mappilla: North Kerala." Pp. 415-42 in *Matrilineal Kinship.* Edited by David M. Schneider and Kathleen Gough. Berkeley: University of California Press.

1973b "Variation in Preferential Marriage Forms." Pp. 614-30 in *Matrilineal Kinship.* Edited by David M. Schneider and Kathleen Gough. Berkeley: University of California Press.

Gould, John.

1980 "Law, Custom and Myth: Aspects of the Social Position of Women in Classical Athens." *Journal of Hellenic Studies* 100: 38-59.

Goulder, M. D.

1963 "The Composition of the Lord's Prayer." *Journal of Theological Studies* n.s. 14: 32-45.

1964 *Type and History in Acts.* London: S.P.C.K.

1974 *Midrash and Lection in Matthew.* The Speaker's Lectures in Biblical Studies 1969-71. London: S.P.C.K.

1978 "On Putting Q to the Test." *New Testament Studies* 24: 218-34.

Graburn, Nelson.

1971 "Introduction to 'Incest Taboos: Origins and Functions.'" Pp. 324-25 in *Readings in Kinship and Social Structure.* Edited by Nelson Graburn. New York: Harper & Row.

Graham, Helen R.

1986 "A Passion Prediction for Mark's Community: Mark 13:9-13." *Biblical Theology Bulletin* 16: 18-22.

Granata, Giovanni.

1983 "Some more information about mustard and the Gospel." *Bibbia e Oriente* 25: 105-6.

Grant, Frederick C.

1943 *The Earliest Gospel.* New York: Abingdon-Cokesbury.

1953 *Hellenistic Religions: The Age of Syncretism.* The Library of Liberal Arts. Indianapolis: The Bobbs-Merrill Company, The Liberal Arts Press.

1959 *Ancient Judaism and the New Testament.* New York: Macmillan Company.

1962 *Roman Hellenism and the New Testament.* New York: Charles Scribner's Sons.

1964 Review of A. N. Sherwin-White's *Roman Society and Roman Law in the New Testament. Journal of Theological Studies* 15: 352-58.

1965 "Turning Back the Clock." *Interpretation* 19: 352-54.

Grant, Michael.

1992 *A Social History of Greece and Rome.* New York: Charles Scribner's Sons; Oxford: Maxwell Macmillan International.

Grant, Robert M.

1966 *Gnosticism and Early Christianity.* 2d ed. New York: Columbia University Press.

1977 *Early Christianity and Society: Seven Studies.* San Francisco: Harper & Row.

1978 "The Sermon on the Mount in Earliest Christianity." *Semeia* 12: 215-31.

1982 "The Problem of Miraculous Feedings in the Greco-Roman Period." *Center for Hermeneutical Studies Protocol* 42: 1-15. (*NTA* 27: 177).

1986 *Gods and the One God.* Library of Early Christianity 1. Philadelphia: Westminster Press.

Grappe, Christian.

1985 "Essai sur l'arrière-plan pascal des récrits de la dernière nuit de Jésus." *Revue d'Histoire et de Philosophie Religieuses* 65: 105-25.

Grassi, Joseph A.

1965a "Ezekiel XXXVII.1-14 and the New Testament." *New Testament Studies* 11: 162-64.

1965b *A World to Win: The Missionary Methods of Paul the Apostle.* Maryknoll, NY: Maryknoll Publications.

1977 "The Last Testament-Succession Literary Background of Matthew 9:35–11:1 and Its Significance." *Biblical Theology Bulletin* 7: 172-76.

1989 "Matthew as a Second Testament Deuteronomy." *Biblical Theology Bulletin* 19: 23-29.

Gray, Sherman W.

1989 *The Least of My Brothers: Matthew 25.31-46: A History of Interpretation.* Society of Biblical Literature Dissertation 114. Atlanta: Scholars Press.

Gray, V.
1987 "*Mimesis* in Greek Historical Theory." *American Journal of Philology* 108: 467-86.
Grayston, Kenneth.
1984a *The Johannine Epistles.* New Century Bible Commentary. Grand Rapids: Eerdmans; London: Marshall, Morgan & Scott.
1984b "The Translation of Matthew 28.17." *Journal for the Study of the New Testament* 21: 105-9.
1993 "The Decline of Temptation — and the Lord's Prayer." *Scottish Journal of Theology* 46: 279-95.
Grayzel, Solomon.
1961 *A History of the Jews.* Philadelphia: Jewish Publication Society of America.
The Greek Bucolic Poets.
1912 Translated by J. M. Edmonds. The Loeb Classical Library. Cambridge: Harvard University Press; London: William Heinemann.
Green, Elliot A.
1991-1992 "Did Pythagoras Follow Nazirite Rules?" *Jewish Bible Quarterly* 20: 35-42, 60.
Green, H. B.
1975 *The Gospel according to Matthew.* Oxford: Clarendon Press.
Green, Joel B.
1992a "Burial of Jesus." Pp. 88-92 in *Dictionary of Jesus and the Gospels.* Edited by Joel B. Green, Scot McKnight, and I. Howard Marshall. Downers Grove, IL: InterVarsity Press.
1992b "Gethsemane." Pp. 265-68 in *Dictionary of Jesus and the Gospels.* Edited by Joel B. Green, Scot McKnight, and I. Howard Marshall. Downers Grove, IL: InterVarsity Press.
Greene, Wallace.
1976 "Extra-legal Juridical Prerogatives." *Journal for the Study of Judaism* 7: 152-76.
Greengus, Samuel.
1991 "Filling Gaps: Laws Found in Babylonia and in the Mishna but Absent in the Hebrew Bible." *Maarov* 7: 149-71.
Greenlee, J. Harold.
1960 "Εἰς μνημόσυνον αὐτῆς, 'For her Memorial': Mt xxvi.13, Mk xiv.9." *Expository Times* 71: 245.
Greenspoon, Leonard.
1981 "The Pronouncement Story in Philo and Josephus." *Semeia* 20: 73-80.
Greenstone, Julius H.
1906 *The Messiah Idea in Jewish History.* Philadelphia: Jewish Publication Society of America.
Gregg, David W. A.
1979 "Hebraic Antecedents to the Eucharistic ἀνάμνησις Formula." *Tyndale Bulletin* 30: 165-68.
Grelot, Pierre.
1979 "La Quatrième Demande du 'Pater' et son Arrière-Plan Sémitique." *New Testament Studies* 25: 299-314.
1986 "Michée 7,6 dans les évangiles et dans la littérature rabbinique." *Biblica* 67: 363-77.
1989 "L'épreuve de la Tentation." *Esprit et Vie* 99: 280-84.

Grenz, Stanley J.
1992 *The Millennial Maze: Sorting Out Evangelical Options.* Downers Grove, IL: InterVarsity Press.
Griffin, Miriam T.
1984 *Nero: The End of a Dynasty.* New Haven: Yale University Press.
Grintz, Yehoshua M.
1972 "Jubilees, Book of." 10:324-26 in *Encyclopaedia Judaica.* 16 vols. Jerusalem: Keter Publishing House.
Groenewald, E. P.
1967 "God and Mammon." *Neotestamentica* 1: 59-66.
Groh, John E.
1970 "The Qumran Meal and the Last Supper." *Concordia Theological Monthly* 41: 279-95.
Gross, G.
1964 "Die 'geringsten Brüder' Jesu in Mt 25,40 in Auseinandersetzung mit der neueren Exegese." *Bibel und Leben* 5: 172-80.
Grudem, Wayne A.
1982 *The Gift of Prophecy in 1 Corinthians.* Lanham, MD: University Press of America.
Guelich, Robert A.
1973 "Mt 5 22: Its Meaning and Integrity." *Zeitschrift für die Neutestamentliche Wissenschaft* 64: 39-52.
1976 "The Antitheses of Matthew v.21-48: Traditional and/or Redactional?" *New Testament Studies* 22: 444-57.
1982 *The Sermon on the Mount: A Foundation for Understanding.* Waco, TX: Word Books.
1991 "The Gospel Genre." Pp. 173-208 in *The Gospel and the Gospels.* Edited by Peter Stuhlmacher. Grand Rapids: Eerdmans.
Guenther, Heinz.
1989 "Greek: Home of Primitive Christianity." *Toronto Journal of Theology* 5: 247-79.
Guillemette, P.
1980 "La forme des récits d'exorcisme de Bultmann. Un dogme à reconsidérer." *Église et Théologie* 11: 177-93.
Guillet, Jacques.
1982 "Les récits évangéliques de la résurrection." *Quatres Fleuves* 15-16: 7-21.
Gundry, Robert H.
1964 "The Narrative Framework of Matthew xvi 17-19. A Critique of Professor Cullmann's Hypothesis." *Novum Testamentum* 7: 1-9.
1973 *The Church and the Tribulation.* Grand Rapids: Zondervan.
1974 "Recent Investigations into the Literary Genre 'Gospel.'" Pp. 97-114 in *New Dimensions in New Testament Study.* Edited by Richard N. Longenecker and Merrill C. Tenney. Grand Rapids: Zondervan.
1975 *The Use of the Old Testament in St. Matthew's Gospel: With Special Reference to the Messianic Hope.* Supplements to Novum Testamentum 18. Leiden: E. J. Brill.
1976 *Sōma in Biblical Theology: With Emphasis on Pauline Anthropology.* Cambridge: Cambridge University Press.
1982 *Matthew: A Commentary on His Literary and Theological Art.* Grand Rapids: Eerdmans.

1987 "The Hellenization of Dominical Tradition and Christianization of Jewish Tradition in the Eschatology of 1-2 Thessalonians." *New Testament Studies* 33: 161-78.

1991 "A Responsive Evaluation of the Social History of the Matthean Community in Roman Syria." Pp. 62-67 in *Social History of the Matthean Community: Cross-Disciplinary Approaches.* Edited by David L. Balch. Minneapolis: Fortress Press.

1996 "ΕΥΑΓΓΕΛΙΟΝ: How Soon a Book?" *Journal of Biblical Literature* 115: 321-25.

Gundry-Volf, Judith

1995 "Spirit, Mercy, and the Other." *Theology Today* 51: 508-23.

Gurney, O. R.

1977 *Some Aspects of Hittite Religion.* Oxford: Oxford University Press for the British Academy.

Gustafsson, Berndt.

1956 "The Oldest Graffiti in the History of the Church?" *New Testament Studies* 3: 65-69.

Guthrie, Donald.

1990 *New Testament Introduction.* Rev. ed. Downers Grove, IL: InterVarsity Press; Leicester: Apollos.

Guthrie, W. K. C.

1966 *Orpheus and Greek Religion: A Study of the Orphic Movement.* 2d ed. New York: W. W. Norton & Company.

Guy, Harold A.

1959 "The Golden Rule." *Expository Times* 70: 184.

Haas, Mary R.

1969 "Sibling Terms as Used by Marriage Partners." *Southwestern Journal of Anthropology* 25: 228-35.

Habermas, Gary R.

1995 "Did Jesus Perform Miracles?" Pp. 117-40 in *Jesus under Fire.* Edited by Michael J. Wilkins and J. P. Moreland. Grand Rapids: Zondervan.

Hachlili, Rachel.

1977 "The Zodiac in Ancient Jewish Art: Representation and Significance." *Bulletin of the American Schools of Oriental Research* 228: 61-77.

1980 "A Second Temple Period Jewish Necropolis in Jericho." *Biblical Archaeologist* 43: 235-40.

Hachlili, Rachel, and Ann Killebrew.

1983a "Jewish Funerary Customs during the Second Temple Period, in the Light of the Excavations at the Jericho Necropolis." *Palestine Exploration Quarterly* 115: 109-39.

1983b "The Saga of the Goliath Family." *Biblical Archaeology Review* 9 (1, January): 44-53.

Hadas, Moses, editor and translator.

1951 *Aristeas to Philocrates (Letter of Aristeas).* New York: Harper & Brothers, for The Dropsie College for Hebrew and Cognate Learning.

Hadas-Lebel, Mireille.

1984 "Jacob et Esaü ou Israël et Rome dans le Talmud et le Midrash." *Revue de l'Histoire des Religions* 201: 369-92.

1993 "Les mariages mixtes dans la famille d'Hérode et la *Halakha* prétalmudique sur la patrilinéarité." *Revue des Études Juives* 152: 397-404.

Häfner, Gerd.

1992 "Gewalt gegen die Basileia? Zum Problem der Auslegung des 'Stürmerspruches' Mt 11,12." *Zeitschrift für die Neutestamentliche Wissenschaft* 83: 21-51.

1993 "'Jene Tage' (Mt 3,1) und der Umfang des matthäischen 'Prologs.' Ein Beitrag zur Frage nach der Struktur des Mt-Ev." *Biblische Zeitschrift* 37: 43-59.

Haenchen, Ernst.

1966 *Der Weg Jesu: Eine Erklärung des Markus-Evangeliums und der kanonischen Parallelen.* Berlin: Alfred Töpelmann.

1971 *The Acts of the Apostles: A Commentary.* Philadelphia: Westminster Press.

Hagner, Donald A.

1971 "The Vision of God in Philo and John: A Comparative Study." *Journal of the Evangelical Theological Society* 14: 81-93.

1993 *Matthew 1–13.* Word Biblical Commentary 33A. Dallas: Word Books.

1995 *Matthew 14–28.* Word Biblical Commentary 33B. Dallas: Word Books.

1996 "The *Sitz im Leben* of the Gospel of Matthew." Pp. 27-68 in *Treasures New and Old: Recent Contributions to Matthean Studies.* Edited by David R. Bauer and Mark Allan Powell. Society of Biblical Literature Symposium Series 1. Atlanta: Scholars Press.

1997 "Balancing the Old and the New. The Law of Moses in Matthew and Paul." *Interpretation* 51: 20-30.

Hall, Robert Givin.

1986 "Revealed History: A Jewish and Christian Technique of Interpreting the Past." Ph.D. dissertation, Duke University.

Hallevy, A. A.

1982-83 "Mhsbt ysr'l wmhsbt ywn (Jewish Thought and Greek Thought)." *Jerusalem Studies in Jewish Thought* 2: 497-514. (*NTA* 29:68-69)

Hamerton-Kelly, R. G.

1973 *Pre-Existence, Wisdom, and the Son: A Study of the Idea of Pre-existence in the New Testament.* Cambridge: Cambridge University Press.

Hamilton, Neill Q.

1964 "Temple Cleansing and Temple Bank." *Journal of Biblical Literature* 83: 365-72.

Hammershaimb, E.

1975 "Om lignelser og billedtaler i de gammeltestamentlige Pseudepigrafer." [On Parables and Figurative Sayings in the Old Testament Pseudepigrapha.] *Svensk Exegetisk Årsbok* 40: 36-65. (*NTA* 20:342)

Hammond, P. C.

1991 "Nabataean Settlement Patterns inside Petra." *Ancient History Bulletin* 5 (1-2, 1991): 36-46.

Hansberry, William Leo.

1981 *Pillars in Ethiopian History.* The William Leo Hansberry African History Notebook, vol. 1. Edited by Joseph E. Harris. Washington, D.C.: Howard University Press.

Hanson, John S.

1980 "Dreams and Visions in the Graeco-Roman World and Early Christianity." *Aufstieg und Niedergang der Römischen Welt* 2 (Principat). 23.2.1395-1427.

Hanson, K. C.

1989 "The Herodians and Mediterranean Kinship. Part I: Genealogy and Descent." *Biblical Theology Bulletin* 19 (3, 1989): 75-84.

1990 "The Herodians and Mediterranean Kinship. Part III: Economics." *Biblical Theology Bulletin* 20 (1, 1990): 10-21.

1994 "How Honorable! How Shameful! A Cultural Analysis of Matthew's Makarisms and Reproaches." *Semeia* 68: 81-111.

Hanson, K. C., and Douglas E. Oakman.

1998 *Palestine in the Time of Jesus: Social Structures and Social Conflicts.* Minneapolis: Fortress Press.

Hanson, Stig.

1963 *The Unity of the Church in the New Testament: Colossians and Ephesians.* Lexington, KY: The American Theological Library Association.

Haran, Menahem.

1965 "The Priestly Image of the Tabernacle." *Hebrew Union College Annual* 36: 191-226.

Hardy, W. G.

1962 *The Greek and Roman World.* Cambridge: Schenkman Publishing Company.

Hare, Douglas R. A.

1967 *The Theme of Jewish Persecution of Christians in the Gospel according to St. Matthew.* Cambridge: Cambridge University Press.

1979 "The Rejection of the Jews in the Synoptic Gospels and Acts." Pp. 27-47 in *Anti-Semitism and the Foundations of Christianity.* Edited by Alan T. Davies. New York: Paulist Press.

Harner, Philip B.

1973 "Qualitative Anarthrous Predicate Nouns: Mark 15:39 and John 1:1." *Journal of Biblical Literature* 92: 75-87.

Harper, James E.

1993 "26 Tons of Gold and 65 Tons of Silver." *Biblical Archaeology Review* 19 (6, 1993): 44-45, 70.

Harrell, Pat Edwin.

1967 *Divorce and Remarriage in the Early Church: A History of Divorce and Remarriage in the Ante-Nicene Church.* Austin: R. B. Sweet.

Harrelson, Walter.

1969 *From Fertility Cult to Worship.* Garden City, NY: Doubleday & Company.

Harrington, Daniel J.

1972 "Abraham Traditions in the Testament of Abraham and in the 'Rewritten Bible' of the Intertestamental Period." Pp. 165-72 in *Studies on the Testament of Abraham.* Edited by George W. E. Nickelsburg. Society of Biblical Literature Septuagint and Cognate Studies 6. Missoula, MT: Scholars Press.

1980 *God's People in Christ.* Philadelphia: Fortress Press.

1982 *The Gospel according to Matthew.* Collegeville, MN: The Liturgical Press.

1986 "The Bible Rewritten (Narratives)." Pp. 239-47 in *Early Judaism and Its Modern Interpreters.* Edited by Robert A. Kraft and George W. E. Nickelsburg. Society of Biblical Literature and Its Modern Interpreters, Series 2. Atlanta: Scholars Press.

1989a "A Dangerous Text: Matthew and Judaism." *Canadian Catholic Review* 7: 135-42.

1989b "'Not to abolish, but to fulfill.'" *Bible Today* 27: 333-37.

1991 "Polemical Parables in Matthew 24–25." *Union Seminary Quarterly Review* 44: 287-98.

Harrington, Wilfrid.

1985 "Jesus and Women." *Religious Life Review* 24: 168-75.

Harris, J. G.

1965 "Aspects of the Ethical Teaching of the Qumran Covenanters." *Evangelical Quarterly* 37: 142-46.

Harris, Murray J.

1986 "'The Dead Are Restored to Life': Miracles of Revivification in the Gospels." Pp. 295-326 in *The Miracles of Jesus.* Vol. 6 of Gospel Perspectives. Edited by David Wenham and Craig Blomberg. Sheffield: JSOT Press.

1992 *Jesus as God: The New Testament Use of Theos in Reference to Jesus.* Grand Rapids: Baker.

Harrison, E. F.

1973 "Did Christ Command World Evangelism?" *Christianity Today* 18: 210-14.

Harrison, R. K.

1969 "The Rites and Customs of the Qumran Sect." Pp. 26-36 in *The Scrolls and Christianity: Historical and Theological Significance.* Edited by Matthew Black. London: S.P.C.K.

Hart, H. St. J.

1984 "The coin of 'Render unto Caesar . . .' (A note on some aspects of Mark 12:13-17; Matt. 22:15-22; Luke 20:20-26)." Pp. 241-48 in *Jesus and the Politics of His Day.* Edited by Ernst Bammel and C. F. D. Moule. Cambridge: Cambridge University Press.

Harvey, A. E.

1982 *Jesus and the Constraints of History.* Philadelphia: Westminster Press.

Haslam, J. A. G.

1985 "The Centurion at Capernaum: Luke 7:1-10." *The Expository Times* 96: 109-10.

Hata, Gohei.

1975 "Is the Greek Version of Josephus' *Jewish War* a Translation or a Rewriting of the First Version?" *Jewish Quarterly Review* 66: 89-108.

Hatch, William Henry Paine.

1917 *The Pauline Idea of Faith in Its Relation to Jewish and Hellenistic Religion.* Harvard Theological Studies. Cambridge: Harvard University Press. Reprint, New York: Kraus Reprint Co., 1969.

Hatina, Thomas R.

1996 "The Focus of Mark 13:24-27: The Parousia, or the Destruction of the Temple?" *Bulletin for Biblical Research* 6: 43-66.

Hauck, Friedrich, and Siegfried Schulz.

"Πόρνη, πόρνος, πορνεία, πορνεύω, ἐκπορνεύω." 6:579-95 in *Theological Dictionary of the New Testament.* 10 vols. Translated by Geoffrey W. Bromiley. Grand Rapids: Eerdmans, 1964-1976.

Hauerwas, Stanley.

1988 "The Sermon on the Mount, Just War and the Quest for Peace." *Concilium* 195: 36-43.

Hayman, P.

1989 "Was God a Magician? Sefer Yesira and Jewish Magic." *Journal of Jewish Studies* 40: 225-37.

Hayward, R.

1993 "Targum Pseudo-Jonathan to Genesis 27:31." *Jewish Quarterly Review* 84: 177-88.

Healey, John F.

1989 "Models of Behavior: Matt 6:26 (//Luke 12:24) and Prov 6:6-8." *Journal of Biblical Literature* 108: 497-98.

Heidel, Alexander.

1951 *The Babylonian Genesis.* Chicago: University of Chicago Press.

Heil, John Paul.

1991 "The Narrative Roles of the Women in Matthew's Genealogy." *Biblica* 72: 538-45.

1993 "Ezekiel 34 and the Narrative Strategy of the Shepherd and Sheep Metaphor in Matthew." *Catholic Biblical Quarterly* 55: 698-708.

1998a "Final Parables in the Eschatological Discourse in Matthew 24–25." Pp. 177-209 in *Matthew's Parables: Audience-Oriented Perspectives.* By Warren Carter and John Paul Heil. Catholic Biblical Quarterly Monograph 30. Washington, DC: Catholic Biblical Association of America.

1998b "Narrative Progression of the Parables Discourse in Matthew 13:1-52." Pp. 64-95 in *Matthew's Parables: Audience-Oriented Perspectives.* By Warren Carter and John Paul Heil. Catholic Biblical Quarterly Monograph 30. Washington, DC: Catholic Biblical Association of America.

1998c "Parable of the Wise and Foolish Builders in Matthew 7:24-27." Pp. 23-35 in *Matthew's Parables: Audience-Oriented Perspectives.* By Warren Carter and John Paul Heil. Catholic Biblical Quarterly Monograph 30. Washington, DC: Catholic Biblical Association of America.

Heinen, Heinz.

1990 "Göttliche Sitomatrie: Beobachtungen zur Brotbitte des Vaterunsers." *Trierer Theologische Zeitschrift* 99: 72-79.

Heininger, Bernhard.

1989 "Der böse Antiochus. Eine Studie zur Antiochus. Eine Studie zur Erzähltechnik des 4. Makkabäerbuchs." *Biblische Zeitschrift* 33: 43-59.

Held, Heinz Joachim.

1963 "Matthew as Interpreter of the Miracle Stories." Pp. 165-299 in *Tradition and Interpretation in Matthew.* By Günther Bornkamm, Gerhard Barth, and Heinz Joachim Held. Philadelphia: Westminster Press.

Hellestam, S.

1990 "Mysteriet med saltet." *Svensk Exegetisk Årsbok* 55: 59-63. *(NTA)*

Hemer, Colin J.

1973 "The Edfu *Ostraka* and the Jewish Tax." *Palestine Exploration Quarterly* 105: 6-12.

1984 "Epiousios." *Journal for the Study of the New Testament* 22: 81-94.

1986 *The Letters to the Seven Churches of Asia in Their Local Setting.* Journal for the Study of the New Testament Supplement 11. Sheffield: Department of Biblical Studies, University of Sheffield.

Hengel, Martin.

1961 *Die Zeloten. Untersuchungen zur jüdischen Freiheitsbewegung in der Zeit von Herodes I. bis 70n. Chr.* Arbeiten zur Geschichte des Spätjudentums und Urchristentums Band I. Leiden, Cologne: E. J. Brill.

1968 "Das Gleichnis von den Weingärtnern Mc 12,1-12 im Lichte der

Zenonpapyri und der rabbinischen Gleichnisse." *Zeitschrift für die Neutestamentliche Wissenschaft* 59: 9-31.

1969 "War Jesus Revolutionär? Sechs Thesen eines Neutestamentlers." *Evangelische Kommentare* 2: 694-96.

1974a *Judaism and Hellenism: Studies in their encounter in Palestine during the early Hellenistic period.* 2 vols. Translated by John Bowden. Philadelphia: Fortress Press.

1974b *Property and Riches in the Early Church: Aspects of Social History of Early Christianity.* Philadelphia: Fortress Press.

1976 *Son of God.* Translated by John Bowden. Philadelphia: Fortress Press.

1977 *Crucifixion in the Ancient World and the Folly of the Message of the Cross.* Philadelphia: Fortress Press.

1980 *Acts and the History of Earliest Christianity.* Translated by John Bowden. Philadelphia: Fortress Press. London: SCM Press (1979).

1981a *The Atonement: The Origins of the Doctrine in the New Testament.* Translated by John Bowden. Philadelphia: Fortress Press.

1981b *The Charismatic Leader and His Followers.* Edited by John Riches. Translated by James Greig. New York: Crossroad Publishing Company.

1985 *Studies in the Gospel of Mark.* Translated by John Bowden. Philadelphia: Fortress Press.

1991 "Literary, Theological, and Historical Problems in the Gospel of Mark." Pp. 209-51 in *The Gospel and the Gospels.* Edited by Peter Stuhlmacher. Grand Rapids: Eerdmans.

1994 "Aufgaben der neutestamentlichen Wissenschaft." *New Testament Studies* 40: 321-57.

1996 "Tasks of New Testament Scholarship." *Bulletin for Biblical Research* 6: 67-86.

Hennecke, Edgar.

1963/1965 *New Testament Apocrypha.* Edited by Wilhelm Schneemelcher and R. McL. Wilson. 2 vols. Philadelphia: Westminster Press.

Henney, Jeannette H.

1974 "Spirit-Possession Belief and Trance Behavior in Two Fundamentalist Groups in St. Vincent." Pp. 1-111 in *Trance, Healing, and Hallucination: Three Field Studies in Religious Experience.* By Felicitas D. Goodman, Jeannette H. Henney, and Esther Pressel. New York: John Wiley & Sons.

Henrichs, Albert.

1982 "Changing Dionysiac Identities." Pp. 137-60 in *Self-Definition in the Greco-Roman World.* Edited by Ben F. Meyer and E. P. Sanders. Vol. 3 in *Jewish and Christian Self-Definition.* Philadelphia: Fortress Press.

Hepper, F. N., et al.

1982 "Plants." Pp. 945-48 in *New Bible Dictionary.* 2d ed. Edited by J. D. Douglas and Norman Hillyer. Leicester, Eng.: InterVarsity Press.

Hepper, F. Nigel.

1992 *Baker Encyclopedia of Bible Plants.* Grand Rapids: Baker; Leicester: Inter-Varsity Press.

Herford, R. Travers.

1966 *Christianity in Talmud and Midrash.* Library of Philosophical and Religious Thought. Clifton, NJ: Reference Book Publishers; reprint of 1903 edition.

Herr, M. D.

1974/1976 "The Calendar." Pp. 834-64 in *The Jewish People in the First Century: His-*

torical Geography, Political History, Social, Cultural, and Religious Life and Institutions. 2 vols. Edited by S. Safrai and M. Stern with D. Flusser and W. C. van Unnik. Section 1 of Compendia Rerum Iudaicarum ad Novum Testamentum. Vol. 1: Assen: Van Gorcum & Co., B.V.; Vol. 2: Philadelphia: Fortress Press.

1978 "Sybwtyw sl mrd br-kwkb." *Zion* 43: 1-11. (*NTA* 24: 169).

Herrenbrück, Fritz.

1981 "Wer waren die 'Zöllner'?" *Zeitschrift für die Neutestamentliche Wissenschaft* 72: 178-94.

Herrmann, Volker.

1991 "Anmerkungen zum Verständnis einiger Paralleltexte zu Mt 25,31ff aus der altägyptischen Religion." *Biblische Notizen* 59: 17-22.

Herron, Robert W.

1982 "Mark's Jesus on Divorce: Mark 10:1-12 Reconsidered." *Journal of the Evangelical Theological Society* 25: 273-81.

Herzog, W. R., II.

1992 "Temple Cleansing." Pp. 817-21 in *Dictionary of Jesus and the Gospels.* Edited by Joel B. Green, Scot McKnight, and I. Howard Marshall. Downers Grove, IL: InterVarsity Press.

Hes, Jozef Ph.

1964 "The Changing Social Role of the Yemenite *Mori.*" Pp. 364-83 in *Magic, Faith, and Healing: Studies in Primitive Psychotherapy Today.* Edited by Ari Kiev. Introduction by Jerome D. Frank. New York: The Free Press: A Division of Macmillan Publishing Company.

Hester, James D.

1968 *Paul's Concept of Inheritance: A Contribution to the Understanding of Heilsgeschichte.* Scottish Journal of Theology Occasional Papers 14. Edinburgh: Oliver & Boyd.

Heth, William A.

1990 "Divorce, but No Remarriage." Pp. 73-129 in *Divorce and Remarriage: Four Christian Views.* Edited by H. Wayne House. Downers Grove, IL: InterVarsity Press.

1995 "Divorce and Remarriage: The Search for an Evangelical Hermeneutic." *Trinity Journal* n.s. 16: 63-100.

Heth, William A., and Gordon J. Wenham.

1984 *Jesus and Divorce: The Problem with the Evangelical Consensus.* Nashville: Thomas Nelson.

Hicks, John M.

1984 "The Sabbath Controversy in Matthew: An Exegesis of Matthew 12:1-14." *Restoration Quarterly* 27: 79-91.

Hiers, Richard H.

1968 "'Not the Season for Figs.'" *Journal of Biblical Literature* 87: 394-400.

1985 "'Binding' and 'Loosing': The Matthean Authorizations." *Journal of Biblical Literature* 104: 233-50.

Higgins, A. J. B.

1953 "Priest and Messiah." *Vetus Testamentum* 3: 321-36.

1955 "The Origins of the Eucharist." *New Testament Studies* 1: 200-209.

1963 "The Sign of the Son of Man (Matt. XXIV.30)." *New Testament Studies* 9: 380-82.

1964 *Jesus and the Son of Man.* Philadelphia: Fortress Press.

1966-1967 "The Priestly Messiah." *New Testament Studies* 13: 211-39.

Hill, David.

1965 "DIKAIOI as a Quasi-Technical Term." *New Testament Studies* 11: 296-302.

1972 *The Gospel of Matthew.* New Century Bible. Grand Rapids: Eerdmans; London: Marshall, Morgan & Scott.

1974 "On the Evidence for the Creative Role of Christian Prophets." *New Testament Studies* 20: 262-74.

1976 "False Prophets and Charismatics: Structure and Interpretation in Matthew 7,15-23." *Biblica* 57: 327-48.

1977 "On the Use and Meaning of Hosea VI.6 in Matthew's Gospel." *New Testament Studies* 24: 107-19.

1979 *New Testament Prophecy.* New Foundations Theological Library. Atlanta: John Knox Press.

1980 "Son and Servant: An Essay on Matthean Christology." *Journal for the Study of the New Testament* 6: 2-16.

1984 "The Figure of Jesus in Matthew's Story: A Response to Professor Kingsbury's Literary-Critical Probe." *Journal for the Study of the New Testament* 21: 37-52.

1985 "Jesus before the Sanhedrin — On What Charge?" *Irish Biblical Studies* 7: 174-86.

Hilton, Michael, with Gordian Marshall.

1988 *The Gospels and Rabbinic Judaism: A Study Guide.* Hoboken, NJ: KTAV.

Hirsch, E. D., Jr.

1967 *Validity in Interpretation.* New Haven: Yale University Press.

Hirschfeld, Yizhar, and Giora Solar.

1980 "Hmrhs'wt hrwmyym sl hmt-gdr — slws 'wnwt-hpyrh (The Roman Thermae at Hammath-Gader — Three Seasons of Excavations)." *Qadmoniot* 13: 66-70. (*NTA* 25: 279)

1984 "Sumptuous Roman Baths Uncovered near Sea of Galilee: Hot Springs Drew the Afflicted from Around the World." *Biblical Archaeology Review* 10: 22-40.

Hjerl-Hansen, Börge.

1959 "Did Christ Know the Qumran Sect? Jesus and the Messiah of the Desert: An Observation Based on Matthew 24,26-28." *Revue de Qumran* 1: 495-508.

Hladik, Joe.

1992 "Geld(ver)leih im Imperium Romanum zur Zeit Jesu. Seine Praxis und die dadurch verursachte Not der SchuldnerInnen." *Protokolle zur Bibel* 1: 115-33.

Hobbs, T. Raymond.

1990 "Crossing Cultural Bridges: The Biblical World." *McMaster Journal of Theology* 1: 1-21.

Hock, Ronald F.

1980 *The Social Context of Paul's Ministry: Tentmaking and Apostleship.* Philadelphia: Fortress Press.

1988 "The Greek Novel." Pp. 127-46 in *Greco-Roman Literature and the New Testament: Selected Forms and Genres.* Edited by David E. Aune. Society of Biblical Literature Sources for Biblical Study 21. Atlanta: Scholars Press.

Hodges, Zane C.

1966 "The Women and the Empty Tomb." *Bibliotheca Sacra* 123: 301-9.

Hodgson, Robert.
1983 "'Paul the Apostle and First Century Tribulation Lists.'" *Zeitschrift für die Neutestamentliche Wissenschaft* 74: 59-80.

Hoehner, Harold W.
1972 *Herod Antipas.* Society for New Testament Studies Monograph 17. Cambridge: Cambridge University Press.

Hoenig, Sidney B.
1965 "Conversion during the Talmudic Period." Pp. 33-66 in *Conversion to Judaism: A History and Analysis.* Edited by David Max Eichhorn. New York: KTAV.

Hoffman, L. A.
1979 "L'ordination juive à la veille du christianisme." *Maison Dieu* 138: 7-47.

Hofius, Otfried.
1991 "Unknown Sayings of Jesus." Pp. 336-60 in *The Gospel and the Gospels.* Edited by Peter Stuhlmacher. Grand Rapids: Eerdmans.

Hoheisel, Karl.
1984/1985 "Das frühe Christentum und die Seelenwanderung." *Jahrbuch für Antike und Christentum* 27-28: 24-46.

Holladay, Carl R.
1977 *Theios Aner in Hellenistic Judaism: A Critique of the Use of This Category in New Testament Christology.* Society of Biblical Literature Dissertation 40. Missoula, MT: Scholars Press.

Holladay, John S.
1970 "Assyrian Statecraft and the Prophets of Israel." *Harvard Theological Review* 63: 29-51.

Hollenbach, Bruce.
1983 "Lest they should turn and be forgiven: irony." *Bible Translator* 34: 312-21.

Hollenbach, P. W.
1981 "Jesus, Demoniacs, and Public Authorities: A Socio-Historical Study." *Journal of the American Academy of Religion* 49: 567-88.

Holmes, Michael W.
1990 "The Text of the Matthean Divorce Passages: A Comment on the Appeal to Harmonization in Textual Decisions." *Journal of Biblical Literature* 109: 651-64.

Honeyman, A. M.
1954 "Matthew V.18 and the Validity of the Law." *New Testament Studies* 1: 141-42.

Hooke, Samuel H.
1957 "Jesus and the Centurion: Matthew viii.5-10." *The Expository Times* 69: 79-80.

Hooker, Morna D.
1959 *Jesus and the Servant.* London: S.P.C.K.
1982 "Trial and Tribulation in Mark XIII." *Bulletin of the John Rylands Library* 65: 78-99.
1983 *The Message of Mark.* London: Epworth Press.

Horbury, William.
1982 "The Benediction of the *Minim* and Early Jewish-Christian Controversy." *Journal of Theological Studies* 33: 19-61.
1984 "Christ as brigand in ancient anti-Christian polemic." Pp. 183-95 in *Jesus*

and the Politics of His Day. Edited by Ernst Bammel and C. F. D. Moule. Cambridge: Cambridge University Press.

1984b "The temple tax." Pp. 265-86 in *Jesus and the Politics of His Day.* Edited by Ernst Bammel and C. F. D. Moule. Cambridge: Cambridge University Press.

1985 "Extirpation and Excommunication." *Vetus Testamentum* 35: 13-38.

1997 "The Hebrew Text of Matthew in Shem Tob Ibn Shaprut's *Eben Bohan.*" Pp. 729-38 in *The Gospel according to Saint Matthew.* Vol. 3. By W. D. Davies and Dale C. Allison, Jr. Edinburgh: T & T Clark.

Horsley, G. H. R., editor.

1981 *New Documents Illustrating Early Christianity: A Review of the Greek Inscriptions and Papyri Published in 1976.* Vol. 1. North Ryde, N.S.W.: The Ancient History Documentary Research Centre, Macquarie University.

1982 *New Documents Illustrating Early Christianity: A Review of the Greek Inscriptions and Papyri Published in 1977.* Vol. 2. North Ryde, N.S.W.: The Ancient History Documentary Research Centre, Macquarie University.

1983 *New Documents Illustrating Early Christianity: A Review of the Greek Inscriptions and Papyri Published in 1978.* Vol. 3. North Ryde, N.S.W.: The Ancient History Documentary Research Centre, Macquarie University.

1987 *New Documents Illustrating Early Christianity: A Review of the Greek Inscriptions and Papyri Published in 1979.* Vol. 4. North Ryde, N.S.W.: The Ancient History Documentary Research Centre, Macquarie University.

1989 *New Documents Illustrating Early Christianity.* Vol. 5: *Linguistic Essays.* North Ryde, N.S.W.: The Ancient History Documentary Research Centre, Macquarie University.

Horsley, Richard A.

1985 "'Like One of the Prophets of Old': Two Types of Popular Prophets at the Time of Jesus." *Catholic Biblical Quarterly* 47: 435-63.

1986a "Ethics and Exegesis: 'Love Your Enemies' and the Doctrine of Non-Violence." *Journal of the American Academy of Religion* 54: 3-31.

1986b "High Priests and the Politics of Roman Palestine. A Contextual Analysis of the Evidence in Josephus." *Journal for the Study of Judaism* 17: 23-55.

1988 "Liberating Christmas." *Christianity and Crisis* 48: 436-38.

1993a *The Liberation of Christmas: The Infancy Narratives in Social Context.* New York: Continuum.

1993b "Palestinian Jewish Groups and Their Messiahs in Late Second Temple Times." *Concilium* (1, 1993): 14-29.

1995 *Galilee: History, Politics, People.* Valley Forge, PA: Trinity Press International.

Horsley, Richard A., and John S. Hanson.

1985 *Bandits, Prophets, and Messiahs: Popular Movements in the Time of Jesus.* Minneapolis: A Seabury Book, Winston Press, 1985.

Hort, Fenton John Andrew.

1894 *Judaistic Christianity.* Edited by J. O. F. Murray. Reprint ed. Grand Rapids: Baker, 1980.

Hoskyns, Edwyn Clement.

1947 *The Fourth Gospel.* Edited by Francis Noel Davey. 2d rev. ed. London: Faber & Faber.

Houk, Cornelius B.

1966 "Peirasmos, the Lord's Prayer, and the Massah Tradition." *Scottish Journal of Theology* 19: 216-25.

Howell, David B.

1990 *Matthew's Inclusive Story: A Study in the Narrative Rhetoric of the First Gospel.* Journal for the Study of the New Testament 42. Sheffield: JSOT Press, Sheffield Academic Press.

Hre Kio, Stephen.

1990 "Understanding and Translating 'Nations' in Mt 28.19." *Bible Translator* 41: 230-38.

Hruby, Kurt.

1970 "La notion d'ordination dans la tradition juive." *Maison-Dieu* 102: 30-56.

Hubbard, Benjamin Jerome.

1974 *The Matthean Redaction of a Primitive Apostolic Commissioning: An Exegesis of Matthew 28:16-20.* Society of Biblical Literature Dissertation 19. Missoula, MT: Society of Biblical Literature.

Hübner, Hans.

1971 "Zölibat in Qumran?" *New Testament Studies* 17: 153-67.

Hummel, Reinhart.

1963 *Die Auseinandersetzung zwischen Kirche und Judentum im Matthäusevangelium.* München: Kaiser Verlag.

Humphreys, Colin J.

1992 "The Star of Bethlehem, a Comet in 5 B.C. and the Date of Christ's Birth." *Tyndale Bulletin* 43: 31-56.

Hunter, Archibald M.

1944 *The Message of the New Testament.* Philadelphia: Westminster Press.

1961 *Paul and His Predecessors.* Rev. ed. Philadelphia: Westminster Press; London: SCM Press.

1965 *The Gospel according to John.* The Cambridge Bible Commentary. Cambridge: Cambridge University Press.

1966 *The Gospel according to St. Paul.* Philadelphia: Westminster Press.

Hunzinger, Claus-Hunno.

1971 "Συκή, σύκον, ὄλυνθος, συκάμινος, συκομορέα, συκοφαντέω." 7:751-59 in *Theological Dictionary of the New Testament.* 10 vols. Edited by Gerhard Kittel and Gerhard Friedrich. Grand Rapids: Eerdmans, 1964-1976.

Hurtado, Larry W.

1983 *Mark.* Good News Commentary. San Francisco: Harper & Row.

Hutter, Manfred.

1984 "Ein altorientalischer Bittgestus in Mt 9:20-22." *Zeitschrift für die Neutestamentliche Wissenschaft* 75: 133-35.

1991 "Mt 25:31-46 in der Deutung Manis." *Novum Testamentum* 33: 276-82.

Ilan, Tal.

1987 "Lhbdly ktyb sl smwt btqwpt byt sny." *Lesonénu* 52: 3-7.

1995 "The Attraction of Aristocratic Women to Pharisaism during the Second Temple Period." *Harvard Theological Review* 88: 1-33.

1996 *Jewish Women in Greco-Roman Palestine.* Tübingen: J. C. B. Mohr; Peabody: Hendrickson.

Isaacs, Marie E.

1976 *The Concept of Spirit: A Study of Pneuma in Hellenistic Judaism and Its Bearing on the New Testament.* Heythrop Monographs 1. London: Heythrop College.

Isbell, Charles D.
1975 *Corpus of the Aramaic Incantation Bowls.* Society of Biblical Literature Dissertation 17. Missoula, MT: Scholars Press.
Isenberg, Sheldon R.
1970 "An Anti-Sadducee Polemic in the Palestinian Targum Tradition." *Harvard Theological Review* 63: 433-44.
Isichei, Elizabeth.
1995 *A History of Christianity in Africa from Antiquity to the Present.* Lawrenceville, NJ: Africa World Press; Grand Rapids: Eerdmans.
Ito, Akio.
1991 "The Question of the Authenticity of the Ban on Swearing (Matthew 5.33-37)." *Journal for the Study of the New Testament* 43: 5-13.
1992 "Matthew and the Community of the Dead Sea Scrolls." *Journal for the Study of the New Testament* 48: 23-42.
Jackson, Bernard S.
1971 "Liability for Mere Intention in Early Jewish Law." *Hebrew Union College Annual* 42: 197-225.
Jacobs, Louis.
1957 "Greater Love Hath No Man . . . The Jewish Point of View of Self-Sacrifice." *Judaism* 6: 41-47.
1973 *Jewish Biblical Exegesis.* New York: Behrman.
Jacobson, David M.
1988 "King Herod's 'Heroic' Public Image." *Revue Biblique* 95: 386-403.
Jastrow, Marcus.
1985 *A Dictionary of the Targumim, the Talmud Babli and Yerushalmi, and the Midrashic Literature.* New York: The Judaica Press.
Jaubert, Annie.
1965 *The Date of the Last Supper.* Staten Island: Alba House.
Jenkins, Allan K.
1983 "Young Man or Angel?" *Expository Times* 94: 237-40.
Jennings, Theodore W., Jr.
1990 *Good News to the Poor: John Wesley's Evangelical Economics.* Nashville: Abingdon, 1990.
Jeremias, Joachim.
1958 *Jesus' Promise to the Nations.* Translated by S. H. Hooke. The Franz Delitzsch Lectures for 1953. Studies in Biblical Theology 24. London: SCM Press.
1960 *Infant Baptism in the First Four Centuries.* Philadelphia: Westminster Press.
1963 *The Sermon on the Mount.* Translated by Norman Perrin. Philadelphia: Fortress Press.
1964a "Γωνία, ἀκρογωνιαῖος, κεφαλῆ γωνίας." 1:791-93 in *Theological Dictionary of the New Testament.* 10 vols. Edited by Gerhard Kittel and Gerhard Friedrich. Grand Rapids: Eerdmans, 1964-1976.
1964b *The Prayers of Jesus.* Philadelphia: Fortress.
1964c *Unknown Sayings of Jesus.* 2d English ed. Translated by Reginald H. Fuller. London: S.P.C.K.
1965a *The Central Message of the New Testament.* New York: Charles Scribner's Sons.
1965b "LAMPADES: Mt 25:1.3f.7f." *Zeitschrift für die Neutestamentliche Wissenschaft* 56: 196-201.

1966a *The Eucharistic Words of Jesus.* Philadelphia: Fortress.
1966b "Palästinakundliches zum Gleichnis vom Säemann (Mark. IV.3-8 Par.)." *New Testament Studies* 13: 48-53.
1968 "Πύλη." 6:921-28 in *Theological Dictionary of the New Testament.* 10 vols. Edited by Gerhard Kittel and Gerhard Friedrich. Grand Rapids: Eerdmans, 1964-1976.
1969 *Jerusalem in the Time of Jesus.* Philadelphia: Fortress Press. London: SCM Press.
1971 *New Testament Theology.* New York: Charles Scribner's Sons.
1972 *The Parables of Jesus.* 2d rev. ed. New York: Charles Scribner's Sons.

Jewett, Robert.
1979 *A Chronology of Paul's Life.* Philadelphia: Fortress Press.

Jochim, Christian.
1986 *Chinese Religions: A Cultural Perspective.* Prentice-Hall Series in World Religions. Englewood Cliffs, NJ: Prentice-Hall.

Jocz, Jakob.
1979 *The Jewish People and Jesus Christ: The Relationship between Church and Synagogue.* 3d ed. Grand Rapids: Baker. London: S.P.C.K., 1962.

Jörns, Klaus Peter.
1987 "'Armut, zu der Geist hilft' (Mt 5,3) als *nota ecclesiae.*" *Theologische Zeitschrift* 43: 59-70.

Johnson, Luke Timothy.
1977 *The Literary Function of Possessions in Luke-Acts.* Society of Biblical Literature Dissertation Series 39. Missoula, MT: Society of Biblical Literature.
1981 *Sharing Possessions: Mandate and Symbol of Faith.* Philadelphia: Fortress Press.
1986 *The Writings of the New Testament: An Interpretation.* Philadelphia: Fortress Press.
1989 "The New Testament's Anti-Jewish Slander and Conventions of Ancient Rhetoric." *Journal of Biblical Literature* 108: 419-41.
1996 *The Real Jesus: The Misguided Quest for the Historical Jesus and the Truth of the Traditional Gospels.* San Francisco: HarperSanFrancisco.

Johnson, M. D.
1985 "Introduction to the Life of Adam and Eve." 2:249-57 in *The Old Testament Pseudepigrapha.* 2 vols. Edited by James H. Charlesworth. Garden City, NY: Doubleday & Company.
1988 *The Purpose of the Biblical Genealogies: With Special Reference to the Setting of the Genealogies of Jesus.* 2d ed. Society of New Testament Studies Monograph 8. Cambridge: Cambridge University Press.

Johnson, Norman B.
1948 *Prayer in the Apocrypha and Pseudepigrapha.* Journal of Biblical Literature Monograph 2. Philadelphia: Society of Biblical Literature and Exegesis.

Johnston, Edwin D.
1962 "The Johannine Version of the Feeding of the Five Thousand — An Independent Tradition?" *New Testament Studies* 8: 151-54.

Johnston, George.
1992 "Should the synoptic evangelists be considered as theologians?" *Studies in Religion/Sciences Religieuses* 21: 181-90.

Johnston, Robert Morris.
1976 "The Study of Rabbinic Parables: Some Preliminary Observations." Pp.

337-57 in *Society of Biblical Literature Seminar Papers, 1976.* Edited by George MacRae.

1977a "Greek Patristic Parables." Pp. 215-29 in *Society of Biblical Literature Seminar Papers, 1977.* Edited by Paul Achtemeier.

1977b "Parabolic Interpretations Attributed to Tannaim." Ph.D. dissertation, Hartford Seminary Foundation. Ann Arbor, MI: University Microfilms International, 1978.

1982 "'The Least of the Commandments': Deuteronomy 22:6-7 in Rabbinic Judaism and Early Christianity." *Andrews University Seminary Studies* 20: 205-15.

Jonas, Hans.

1963 *The Gnostic Religion: The Message of the Alien God and the Beginnings of Christianity.* 2d rev. ed. Boston: Beacon Press.

Jones, Absalom, and Richard Allen.

1794 *A Narrative of the Proceedings of the Black People during the Late Awful Calamity in Philadelphia in the Year 1793.* Philadelphia pamphlet, pp. 3-13. Reprinted as pp. 20-27 in *Afro-American History: Primary Sources.* Edited by Thomas R. Frazier. Shorter ed. New York: Harcourt Brace Jovanovich.

Jones, A. M. H.

1970 *A History of Rome through the Fifth Century.* Vol. 2: *The Empire.* New York: Walker and Company.

Jones, James L.

1971 "The Roman Army." Pp. 187-217 in *The Catacombs and the Colosseum: The Roman Empire as the Setting of Primitive Christianity.* Edited by Stephen Benko and John J. O'Rourke. Valley Forge, PA: Judson Press.

Jones, Ivor H.

1995 *The Matthean Parables: A Literary and Historical Commentary.* Novum Testamentum Supplements 80. Leiden: E. J. Brill.

Jones, Richard N.

1989 "A New Reading of the Petra Temple Inscription." *Bulletin of the American Schools of Oriental Research* 275: 41-46.

Jordan, David R.

1985 "A Survey of Greek Defixiones Not Included in the Special Corpora." *Greek, Roman and Byzantine Studies* 26: 151-97.

Josephus.

1982 *The Jewish War.* Edited by Gaalya Cornfeld with Benjamin Mazar and Paul L. Maier. Grand Rapids: Zondervan.

Jospe, Raphael.

1990 "Hillel's Rule." *Jewish Quarterly Review* 81: 45-57.

Judge, E. A.

1960 *The Social Pattern of the Christian Groups in the First Century: Some Prolegomena to the Study of New Testament Ideas of Social Obligation.* London: Tyndale House.

Juel, Donald.

1977 *Messiah and Temple.* Missoula, MT: Scholars Press.

Käsemann, Ernst.

1980 *Commentary on Romans.* Grand Rapids: Eerdmans.

Kahane, Henry and Renée.

1957 "Pearls before Swine? A Reinterpretation of Matt. 7.6?" *Traditio* 13: 421-24.

Kahle, P.

1953 "The Karaites and the Manuscripts from the Cave." *Vetus Testamentum* 3: 82-84.

Kaiser, Walter C., Jr.

1973 "The Ugaritic Pantheon." Ph.D. dissertation, Brandeis University Department of Mediterranean Studies.

1975 "The Weightier and Lighter Matters of the Law: Moses, Jesus and Paul." Pp. 176-92 in *Current Issues in Biblical and Patristic Interpretation: Studies in Honor of Merrill C. Tenney Presented by His Former Students.* Edited by Gerald F. Hawthorne. Grand Rapids: Eerdmans.

Kaplan, Bert, and Dale Johnson.

1964 "The Social Meaning of Navaho Psychopathology and Psychotherapy." Pp. 203-29 in *Magic, Faith, and Healing: Studies in Primitive Psychotherapy Today.* Edited by Ari Kiev. Introduction by Jerome D. Frank. New York: The Free Press; A Division of Macmillan Publishing Company.

Katterjohn, Arthur D., with Mark Fackler.

1976 *The Tribulation People.* Carol Stream, IL: Creation House.

Katz, Steven T.

1984 "Issues in the Separation of Judaism and Christianity after 70 C.E.: A Reconsideration." *Journal of Biblical Literature* 103: 43-76.

Katzoff, Louis.

1987-1988 "Sodom: Manners, Morals, Misdeeds." *Dor le Dor* 16: 211-13.

Katzoff, Ranon.

1986 "*Suffragium* in Exodus *Rabbah* 37.2." *Classical Philology* 81: 235-40.

Kaufman, Asher F.

1981 "The Eastern Wall of the Second Temple at Jerusalem Revealed." *Biblical Archaeologist* 44: 108-15.

1983 "Where the Ancient Temple of Jerusalem Stood." *Biblical Archaeology Review* 9.2: 42-59.

Kaufmann, Y.

1994 "The Messianic Idea: The Real and the Hidden Son-of-David." *Jewish Bible Quarterly* 22 (3, 1994): 141-50.

Kaunfer, Alvan.

1995 "Who Knows Four? The *Imahot* in Rabbinic Literature." *Judaism* 44: 94-103.

Kaye, John.

1912 *The First Apology of Justin Martyr.* Edinburgh: John Grant.

Keck, Leander E.

1966 "The Poor among the Saints in Jewish Christianity and Qumran." *Zeitschrift für die Neutestamentliche Wissenschaft* 57: 54-78.

1974 "On the Ethos of Early Christians." *Journal of the American Academy of Religion* 42: 435-52.

Kee, Howard Clark.

1968 "The Terminology of Mark's Exorcism Stories." *New Testament Studies* 14: 232-46.

1977 *Community of the New Age: Studies in Mark's Gospel.* Philadelphia: Westminster Press.

1980 *Christian Origins in Sociological Perspective: Methods and Resources.* Philadelphia: Westminster Press.

1983 *Miracle in the Early Christian World: A Study in Sociohistorical Method.* New Haven: Yale University Press.

Keegan, Terence J.

1982 "Introductory Formulae for Matthean Discourses." *Catholic Biblical Quarterly* 44: 415-30.

Keener, Craig S.

1987 "Matthew 5:22 and the Heavenly Court." *Expository Times* 99: 46.

1991a . . . *And Marries Another: Divorce and Remarriage in the Teaching of the New Testament.* Peabody, MA: Hendrickson.

1991b "The Function of Johannine Pneumatology in the Context of Late First-Century Judaism." Ann Arbor: University Microfilms International; Ph.D. dissertation, Duke University Graduate School.

1992 *Paul, Women and Wives: Marriage and Women's Ministry in the Letters of Paul.* Peabody, MA: Hendrickson.

1993 *The IVP Bible Background Commentary.* Downers Grove, IL: InterVarsity Press.

1994 "Review of *Divorce in the New Testament.* By Raymond F. Collins." *Critical Review of Books in Religion 1993.* Vol. 6. Atlanta: Scholars Press.

1995 "A Critique of Burton Mack's *Lost Gospel.*" Theological Research Exchange Network, P.O. Box 30183, Portland, OR 97294-3183.

1996a "'I've Got You Covered': The Cultural Background for Veiling Women." *Priscilla Papers* 10 (1, Winter 1996): 7-8.

1996b "Review of *Windows on the World of Jesus: Time Travel to Ancient Judea.* By Bruce J. Malina. Louisville, KY: Westminster/John Knox, 1993." *Critical Review of Books in Religion 1994.* Vol. 7. Atlanta: Scholars Press.

1997a *Matthew.* The IVP Commentary Series. Downers Grove, IL: InterVarsity Press.

1997b *The Spirit in the Gospels and Acts.* Peabody: Hendrickson.

1998 "Mistrial of the Millennium." *Christian History* 59: 38-40.

Keener, Craig S., and Glenn J. Usry.

1997 *Defending Black Faith.* Downers Grove, IL: InterVarsity Press.

Kelber, Werner H.

1976a "Conclusion: From Passion Narrative to Gospel." Pp. 153-80 in *The Passion in Mark: Studies in Mark 14–16.* Edited by Werner H. Kelber. Philadelphia: Fortress Press.

1976b "The Hour of the Son of Man and the Temptation of the Disciples (Mark 14:32-42)." Pp. 41-60 in *The Passion in Mark: Studies in Mark 14–16.* Edited by Werner H. Kelber. Philadelphia: Fortress Press.

1979 *Mark's Story of Jesus.* Philadelphia: Fortress Press.

Kellner, Wendelin.

1988 "Bar Kochba und die Gemeinde der christlichen Juden. Zwei Versuche einer Politik auf biblischer Grundlage." *Bibel und Kirche* 43 (4, 1988): 140-46.

Kelly, J. N. D.

1981 *A Commentary on the Epistles of Peter and Jude.* Thornapple Commentaries. Grand Rapids: Baker Book House.

Kennard, J. Spencer, Jr.

1962 "The Jewish Provincial Assembly." *Zeitschrift für die Neutestamentliche Wissenschaft* 53: 25-51.

Kennedy, George A.

1980 *Classical Rhetoric and Its Christian and Secular Tradition from Ancient to Modern Times.* Chapel Hill: University of North Carolina Press.

1984 *New Testament Interpretation through Rhetorical Criticism.* Chapel Hill, NC: University of North Carolina Press.

Kennedy, Kieran A.

1985 "The Resurrection of Jesus." *Studies* 74: 440-54.

Kensky, Allan.

1993 "Moses and Jesus: The Birth of the Savior." *Judaism* 42: 43-49.

Kern-Ulmer, Brigitte.

1991 "The Power of the Evil Eye and the Good Eye in Midrashic Literature." *Judaism* 40: 344-53.

Kertelge, Karl.

1991 "'Selig die Trauernden . . .' (Mt 5,4)." *Internationale Katholische Zeitschrift/Communio* 20: 387-92.

Keyser, P. T.

1994 "On Cometary Theory and Typology from Nechepso-Petosiris through Apuleius to Servius." *Mnemosyne* 47: 625-51.

Kidder, S. Joseph.

1983 "'This Generation' in Matthew 24:34." *Andrews University Seminary Studies* 21: 203-9.

Kiev, Ari, editor.

1964 *Magic, Faith, and Healing: Studies in Primitive Psychotherapy Today.* Introduction by Jerome D. Frank. New York: The Free Press; A Division of Macmillan Publishing Company.

Kiley, Mark.

1984 "Why 'Matthew' in Matt 9,9-13?" *Biblica* 65: 347-51.

1986 "'Lord, Save My Life' (Ps 116:4) as Generative Text for Jesus' Gethemane Prayer (Mark 14:36a)." *Catholic Biblical Quarterly* 48: 655-59.

Kilpatrick, George D.

1945 "Acts 7.52 *ELEUSIS.*" *Journal of Theological Studies* 46: 136-45.

Kim, Chan-Hie.

1972 *Form and Structure of the Familiar Greek Letter of Recommendation.* Society of Biblical Literature Dissertation Series 4. Missoula, MT: Society of Biblical Literature.

Kim, Deuk-Joong.

1978 "Mark — A Theologian of Resurrection." Ph.D. dissertation, Drew University Graduate School.

Kimbrough, S. T.

1966 "The Concept of Sabbath at Qumran." *Revue de Qumran* 5: 483-502.

Kimelman, Reuven.

1981 "*Birkath Ha-Minim* and the Lack of Evidence for an Anti-Christian Jewish Prayer in Late Antiquity." 2:226-44 in *Jewish and Christian Self-Definition.* 3 vols. Edited by E. P. Sanders. Philadelphia: Fortress Press, 1980-1982.

Kingdon, H. Paul.

1972 "The Origin of the Zealots." *New Testament Studies* 19: 74-81.

Kingsbury, Jack Dean.

1969 *The Parables of Jesus in Matthew 13.* London: S.P.C.K.

1975 *Matthew: Structure, Christology, Kingdom.* Philadelphia: Fortress Press.

1978 "Observations on the 'Miracle Chapters' of Matthew 8–9." *Catholic Biblical Quarterly* 40: 559-73.

1983 *The Christology of Mark's Gospel.* Philadelphia: Fortress Press.

1984 "The Figure of Jesus in Matthew's Story: A Literary-Critical Probe." *Journal for the Study of the New Testament* 21: 3-36.

1986 *Matthew as Story.* Philadelphia: Fortress Press.

1988a "On Following Jesus: The 'Eager' Scribe and the 'Reluctant' Disciple (Matthew 8.18-22)." *New Testament Studies* 34: 45-59.

1988b "Reflections on 'the Reader' of Matthew's Gospel." *New Testament Studies* 34: 442-60.

1991 "Conclusion: Analysis of a Conversation." Pp. 259-69 in *Social History of the Matthean Community: Cross-Disciplinary Approaches.* Edited by David L. Balch. Minneapolis: Fortress Press.

1992 "The Plot of Matthew's Story." *Interpretation* 46: 347-56.

1995a "The Developing Conflict between Jesus and the Jewish Leaders in Matthew's Gospel: A Literary-Critical Study (1987)." Pp. 179-97 in *The Interpretation of Matthew.* 2d ed. Edited by Graham Stanton. Edinburgh: T & T Clark.

1995b "The Rhetoric of Comprehension in the Gospel of Matthew." *New Testament Studies* 41: 358-77.

Kipgen, Kaikhohen.

1983 "Translating *Kataluma* in Luke 2.7." *Bible Translator* 34: 442-43.

Kirchschläger, W.

1976 "Exorzismus in Qumran?" *Kairos* 18: 135-53.

Kirk, J. Andrew.

1975 "Apostleship since Rengstorf: Towards a Synthesis." *New Testament Studies* 21: 249-64.

Kirk, Kenneth E.

1934 *The Vision of God: The Christian Doctrine of the Summum Bonum.* The Bampton Lectures for 1928. Abbr. ed. New York: Longmans, Green & Company.

Kirschner, Robert.

1986 "Imitatio Rabbini." *Journal for the Study of Judaism* 17: 70-79.

Kitchen, Kenneth A.

1978 *The Bible in Its World: The Bible and Archaeology Today.* Downers Grove, IL: InterVarsity Press. Exeter: Paternoster Press, 1977.

Klaasen, Walter, ed.

1981 *Anabaptism in Outline: Selected Primary Sources.* Scottsdale, PA: Herald Press.

Klausner, Joseph.

1979a *From Jesus to Paul.* Translated by W. Stinespring. New York: Menorah Publishing Company. Reprint from n.p.: Macmillan Company, 1943.

1979b *Jesus: His Life, Times, and Teaching.* Translated by Herbert Danby. Foreword by Sidney B. Hoenig. New York: Menorah; n.p.: Macmillan Company, 1925.

Klein, Charlotte.

1978 *Anti-Judaism in Christian Theology.* Translated by Edward Quinn. Philadelphia: Fortress Press.

Knackstedt, J.

1964 "Die beiden Brotvermekrungen im Evangelium." *New Testament Studies* 10: 309-35.

Knibb, Michael A.

1979 *The First and Second Books of Esdras.* Cambridge: Cambridge University Press.

Knoch, O.

1994 "Die 'andere' Maria. Eine von den 'Frauen um Jesus.'" *Bausteine* 34: 3-6. *(NTA)*

Knowles, Michael P.

1989 "Moses, the Law, and the Unity of 4 Ezra." *Novum Testamentum* 31: 257-74.

1993 *Jeremiah in Matthew's Gospel: The Rejected-Prophet Motif in Matthaean Redaction.* Journal for the Study of the New Testament Supplement 68. Sheffield: JSOT Press, Sheffield Academic Press.

Kobelski, Paul Joseph.

1978 "Melchizedek and Melchiresa: The Heavenly Prince of Light and the Prince of Darkness in the Qumran Literature." Ph.D. dissertation, Department of Theology at Fordham University.

Koch, K.

1972 "Messias und Sündenvergebung in Jesaja 53 — Targum. Ein Beitrag zu der Praxis der aramäischen Bibelübersetzung." *Journal for the Study of Judaism* 3: 117-48.

Köhler, Konrad.

1919 "Zu Mt 5,22." *Zeitschrift für die Neutestamentliche Wissenschaft* 19: 91-95.

Koenig, John.

1985 *New Testament Hospitality: Partnership with Strangers as Promise and Mission.* Overtures to Biblical Theology 17. Philadelphia: Fortress Press.

Koester, Helmut.

1971 "One Jesus and Four Primitive Gospels." Pp. 158-204 in *Trajectories through Early Christianity.* By James M. Robinson and Helmut Koester. Philadelphia: Fortress Press.

1978 "Mark 9:43-47 and Quintilian 8.3.75." *Harvard Theological Review* 71: 151-53.

1982 *Introduction to the New Testament.* 2 vols. Hermeneia Foundations and Facets Series. Vol. 1: *History, Culture, and Religion of the Hellenistic Age.* Vol. 2: *History and Literature of Early Christianity.* Philadelphia: Fortress Press.

1990 *Ancient Christian Gospels: Their History and Development.* Philadelphia: Trnity Press International; London: SCM Press.

1992 "Jesus the Victim." *Journal of Biblical Literature* 111: 3-15.

1994 "Written Gospels or Oral Tradition?" *Journal of Biblical Literature* 113: 293-97.

Kohler, Kaufmann.

1900-1901 "Abba, Father: Title of Spiritual Leader and Saint." *Jewish Quarterly Review* 13: 567-80.

Kolenkow, Anitra Bingham.

1974 "What Is the Role of Testament in the Testament of Abraham?" *Harvard Theological Review* 67: 182-84.

1986 "The Literary Genre 'Testament.'" Pp. 259-67 in *Early Judaism and Its Modern Interpreters.* Edited by Robert A. Kraft and George W. E.

Nickelsburg. Society of Biblical Literature Bible and Its Modern Interpreters Series 2. Atlanta: Scholars Press.

Kollmann, Bernd.

1994 "Göttliche Offenbarung magisch-pharmakologischer Heilkunst im Buch Tobit." *Zeitschrift für die Alttestamentliche Wissenschaft* 106: 289-99.

1996 "Das Schwurverbot Mt 5,33-37/Jak 5,12 im Spiegel antiker Eidkritik." *Biblische Zeitschrift* 40: 179-93.

Kopas, Jane.

1990 "Jesus and Women in Matthew." *Theology Today* 47: 13-21.

Korting, Georg.

1989 "Binden oder lösen: Zu Verstockungs- und Befreiungstheologie in Mt 16,19; 18,18.21-35 und Joh 15,1-17; 20, 23." *Studien zum Neuen Testament und seiner Umwelt* 14: 39-91.

Kosch, D.

1997 "Das Gesetz der Freiheit. Zum Toraverständnis von Jesus und Matthäus." *Protokolle zur Bibel* 6: 47-71.

Kotansky, R.

1995 "Remnants of a Liturgical Exorcism on a Gem." *Muséon* 108: 143-56.

Kosmala, Hans.

1963 "The Time of the Cock-Crow." *Annual of the Swedish Theological Institute* 2: 118-20.

Kraeling, Carl H.

1942 "The Episode of the Roman Standards at Jerusalem." *Harvard Theological Review* 35: 263-89.

1951 *John the Baptist.* New York: Charles Scribner's Sons.

Krämer, Helmut.

1981 "Eine Anmerkung zum Verständnis von Mt 15,6a." *Wort und Dienst* 16: 67-70.

Kraemer, Ross Shepard.

1988 *Maenads, Martyrs, Matrons, Monastics: A Sourcebook on Women's Religions in the Greco-Roman World.* Philadelphia: Fortress Press.

Kraft, Robert A., translator and commentary writer.

1965 *Barnabas and the Didache.* Vol. 3 in *The Apostolic Fathers: A New Translation and Commentary.* New York: Thomas Nelson.

Kraybill, Donald B., and Dennis M. Sweetland.

1983 "Possessions in Luke-Acts: A Sociological Perspective." *Perspectives in Religious Studies* 10: 215-39.

Kreitzer, Larry.

1989 "Sibylline Oracles 8, the Roman Imperial *Adventus* Coinage of Hadrian and the Apocalypse of John." *Journal for the Study of the Pseudepigrapha* 4: 69-85.

Krieger, Klaus-Stefan.

1992a "Zur Frage nach der Hauptquelle über die Geschichte der Provinz Judäa in den Antiquitates Judaicae des Flavius Josephus." *Biblische Notizen* 63: 37-41.

1992b "Die Problematik chronologischer Rekonstruktionen zur Amtszeit des Pilatus." *Biblische Notizen* 61: 27-32.

1994 "War Flavius Josephus ein Verwandter des hasmonäischen Königshauses?" *Biblische Notizen* 73: 58-65.

1995 "Pontius Pilate — ein Judenfeind? Zur Problematik einer Pilatusbiographie." *Biblische Notizen* 78: 63-83.

Kronholm, Tryggve.
1989 "Den Kommande Hiskia." *Svensk Exegetisk Årsbok* 54: 109-17. (*NTA* 34: 161)

Küchler, Max.
1989 "'Wir haben seinen Stern gesehen . . .' (Mt 2,2)." *Bibel und Kirche* 44: 179-86.

Kugel, James L., and Rowan A. Greer.
1986 *Early Biblical Interpretation.* Library of Early Christianity 3. Philadelphia: Westminster Press.

Kuhn, Heinz W.
1978 "Zum Gekreuzigten von Giv'at ha-Mivtar. Korrektur eines Versehens in der Erstveröffentlichung." *Zeitschrift für die Neutestamentliche Wissenschaft* 69: 118-22.

Kümmel, Werner George.
1957 *Promise and Fulfilment: The Eschatological Message of Jesus.* Translated by Dorothea M. Barton. Studies in Biblical Theology 23. Naperville: Alec R. Allenson.
1965 *Introduction to the New Testament.* London: SCM Press.
1973 *The Theology of the New Testament According to Its Major Witnesses — Jesus, Paul, John.* Translated by John E. Steely. Nashville: Abingdon Press.

Kuper, Hilda.
1950 "Kinship among the Swazi." Pp. 86-110 in *African Systems of Kinship and Marriage.* Edited by A. R. Radcliffe-Brown and Daryll Forde. New York: Oxford University Press.

Kurz, William S.
1985 "Luke 22:14-38 and Greco-Roman and Biblical Farewell Addresses." *Journal of Biblical Literature* 104: 251-68.

Kürzinger, J.
1963-1964 "Irenäus und sein Zeugnis zur Sprache des Matthäusevangeliums." *New Testament Studies* 10: 108-15.

Kuzenzama, K. P. M.
1980 "La préhistoire de l'espression 'pain de vie' (Jn 6,35b, 48). Continuité ou émergence?" *Revue Africaine de Théologie* 4: 65-83.

Kyle, Richard.
1998 *The Last Days Are Here Again: A History of the End Times.* Grand Rapids: Baker.

Kysar, Myrna and Robert.
1978 *The Asundered: Biblical Teachings on Divorce and Remarriage.* Atlanta: John Knox Press.

Lach, J.
1958 "Uczta Zrzeszenia z Qumran a Ostatnia Wieczerza (Convivium congregationis Quomranensis cum ultima cena comparatur)." *Ruch Biblijny i Liturgiczny* 11: 489-97. *(NTA)*

Lach, Jan.
1987 "Die Pficht zur Versöhnung und Liebe (Mt 5,43-48)." *Collectanea Theologica* 57 (1987): 57-69.

Lachs, Samuel Tobias.
1975a "On Matthew VI.12." *Novum Testamentum* 17: 6-8.

1975b "On Matthew 23:27-28." *Harvard Theological Review* 68: 385-88.
1977 "The Pharisees and Sadducees on Angels: A Reexamination of Acts XXIII.8." *Gratz College Annual of Jewish Studies* 6: 35-42.
1987 *A Rabbinic Commentary on the New Testament: The Gospels of Matthew, Mark, and Luke.* Hoboken, NJ: KTAV; New York: Anti-Defamation League of B'nai B'rith.

La Croce, Ernesto.
1981 "El origen del concepto de alma en la tradicion occidental." *Psicopatologia* 1: 311-16. (PsycLIT Database)

Ladd, George Eldon.
1956 *The Blessed Hope.* Grand Rapids: Eerdmans.
1963a "The Life-Setting of the Parables of the Kingdom." *Journal of Bible and Religion* 31: 193-99.
1963b "The Resurrection and History." *Religion in Life* 32: 247-56.
1967 *The New Testament and Criticism.* Grand Rapids: Eerdmans.
1974a "The Parable of the Sheep and the Goats in Recent Interpretation." Pp. 191-99 in *New Dimensions in New Testament Study.* Edited by Richard N. Longenecker and Merrill C. Tenney. Grand Rapids: Zondervan.
1974b *A Theology of the New Testament.* Grand Rapids: Eerdmans.
1977 "The Historic Premillennial View." Pp. 17-40 in *The Meaning of the Millennium: Four Views.* Edited by Robert G. Clouse. Downers Grove, IL: InterVarsity Press.
1978a *The Gospel of the Kingdom.* Grand Rapids: Eerdmans; reprint of Exeter: Paternoster, 1959.
1978b *The Last Things.* Grand Rapids: Eerdmans.

Ladouceur, David J.
1980 "Hellenistic Preconceptions of Shipwreck and Pollution as a Context for Acts 27–28." *Harvard Theological Review* 73: 435-49.

Lake, Kirsopp.
1979a "Proselytes and God-Fearers." Pp. 74-96 in *The Beginnings of Christianity.* 5 vols. Edited by F. J. Foakes Jackson and Kirsopp Lake. Grand Rapids: Baker. Reprint ed.
1979b "The Twelve and the Apostles." 5:37-59 in *The Beginnings of Christianity.* 5 vols. Ed. by F. J. Foakes Jackson and Kirsopp Lake. Grand Rapids: Baker, 1979, reprint ed.

Lake, Kirsopp, and Henry J. Cadbury.
1979 *English Translation and Commentary.* Vol. 4 in *The Beginnings of Christianity.* 5 vols. Edited by F. J. Foakes Jackson and Kirsopp Lake. Reprint ed. Grand Rapids: Baker.

Lambrecht, Jan.
1980 "A Man to Follow: The Message of Mark." *Revue Africaine de Théologie* 4: 37-53. (*NTA* 25: 238-39)

Lampe, G. W. H.
1951 *The Seal of the Spirit.* New York: Longmans, Green & Company.
1984 "A.D. 70 in Christian Reflection." Pp. 153-71 in *Jesus and the Politics of His Day.* Edited by Ernst Bammel and C. F. D. Moule. Cambridge: Cambridge University Press.

Lampe, Peter.
1979 "Das Spiel mit dem Petrusnamen — Matt. xvi.18." *New Testament Studies* 25: 227-45.

Lampe, Peter, and Ulrich Luz.

1991 "Overview of the Discussion." Pp. 387-404 in *The Gospel and the Gospels.* Edited by Peter Stuhlmacher. Grand Rapids: Eerdmans.

Landman, H.

1976-1977 "Some Aspects of Traditions Received from Moses at Sinai. *Halakhah le-Mosheh mi-Sinai.*" *Jewish Quarterly Review* 67: 111-28.

Lane, William L.

1974a *The Gospel according to Mark.* New International Commentary on the New Testament. Grand Rapids: Eerdmans.

1974b "*Theios Anēr* Christology and the Gospel of Mark." Pp. 144-61 in *New Dimensions in New Testament Study.* Edited by Richard N. Longenecker and Merrill C. Tenney. Grand Rapids: Zondervan.

1982 "Paul's Legacy from Pharisaism: Light from the Psalms of Solomon." *Concordia Journal* 8.4: 130-38.

1991 *Hebrews.* Word Biblical Commentary 47A and B. Dallas: Word Books.

Lange, Armin.

1993 "Eine neue Lesart zu 4Q180: *Kllh* vice *klh.* Die Vernichtung von Sodom und Gomorrha als Ganzopfer." *Zeitschrift für Althebraistik* 6: 232-34.

Langer, G.

1991 "Pflanzen, Schützen und Bewahren — eine ökologische Ethik der Rabbinen." *Bibel und Liturgie* 6 (2, 1991): 86-91.

Lapide, Pinchas E.

1984 *Hebrew in the Church: The Foundations of Jewish-Christian Dialogue.* Translated by Erroll F. Rhodes. Grand Rapids: Eerdmans.

1991 "Das Vaterunser — ein jüdisches oder ein christliches Gebet?" *Renovatio* 47: 108-10.

Lapoorta, Japie J.

1989 "'. . . whatever you did for one of the least of these . . . you did for me' (Matt. 25:31-46)." *Journal of Theology for Southern Africa* 68: 103-9.

LaSor, William Sanford.

1956 "'The Messiahs of Aaron and Israel.'" *Vetus Testamentum* 6: 425-29.

1987 "Discovering What Jewish Miqva'ot Can Tell Us about Christian Baptism." *Biblical Archaeology Review* 13 (1, 1987): 52-59.

Latourette, Kenneth Scott.

1970 *The First Five Centuries.* Vol. 1 in *A History of the Expansion of Christianity.* 5 vols. New York: Harper & Row; Grand Rapids: Zondervan.

Laughlin, John C. H.

1993 "Capernaum: From Jesus' Time and After." *Biblical Archaeology Review* 19 (5, 1993): 55-61.

Laurin, Robert B.

1958 "The Question of Immortality in the Qumran Hodayot." *Journal of Semitic Studies* 3: 344-55.

1963 "The Problem of Two Messiahs in the Qumran Scrolls." *Revue de Qumran* 4: 39-52.

LaVerdiere, Eugene.

1985 "No Room for Them in the Inn." *Emmanuel* 91: 552-57.

Lavery, Gerard B.

1994 "Plutarch's *Lucullus* and the Living Bond of Biography." *Classical Journal* 89 (3, 1994): 261-73.

Laws, Sophie.
1980 *A Commentary on the Epistle of James.* Harper's New Testament Commentaries. San Francisco: Harper & Row.
Layton, Scott C.
1996 "Leaves from an Onomastician's Notebook." *Zeitschrift für die Alttestamentliche Wissenschaft* 108: 608-20.
Leaney, A. R. C.
1958 *A Commentary on the Gospel according to St. Luke.* London: Adam & Charles Black.
Lease, Gary.
1975 "The Caesarea Mithraeum: A Preliminary Announcement." *Biblical Archaeologist* 38: 2-10.
Lee, Edwin Kenneth.
1962 *The Religious Thought of St. John.* London: S.P.C.K.
Leeming, Bernard, and R. A. Dawson.
1956 "Except It Be for Fornication?" *Scripture* 8: 75-82.
Leenhardt, Franz J.
1969 "Les femmes aussi . . . à propos du billet de répudiation." *Revue de Théologie et de Philosophie* 19: 31-40.
Lefkowitz, Mary.
1996 *Not Out of Africa: How Afrocentrism Became an Excuse to Teach Myth as History.* New York: Basic Books, HarperCollins.
Lefkowitz, Mary R., and Maureen B. Fant.
1982 *Women's Life in Greece and Rome.* Baltimore, MD: Johns Hopkins University Press; London: Gerald Duckworth & Company.
Légasse, S.
1976 "Baptême juif des prosélytes et baptême chrétien." *Bulletin de Littérature Ecclesiastique* 77: 3-40. *(NTA)*
Lehmann, Manfred R.
1960 "Gen 2.24 as the Basis for Divorce in Halakhah and New Testament." *Zeitschrift für die Neutestamentliche Wissenschaft* 72: 263-67.
1975 "New Light on Astrology in Qumran and the Talmud." *Revue de Qumran* 8: 599-602.
1993 "Where the Temple Tax Was Buried." *Biblical Archeology Review* 19 (6, 1993): 38-43.
Leivestad, Ragnar.
1972 "Exit the Apocalyptic Son of Man." *New Testament Studies* 18: 266-67.
Lemcio, E. E.
1978 "External Evidence for the Structure and Function of Mark iv.1-20, vii.14-23 and viii.14-21." *Journal of Theological Studies* 29: 323-38.
Leon, Harry J.
1960 *The Jews of Ancient Rome.* The Morris Loeb Series. Philadelphia: The Jewish Publication Society of America.
Levine, Amy-Jill.
1988 *The Social and Ethnic Dimensions of Matthean Salvation History: "Go nowhere among the Gentiles . . ." (Matt. 10:5b).* Studies in the Bible and Early Christianity 14. Lewiston, NY: Edwin Mellen Press.
1996 "Discharging Responsibility: Matthean Jesus, Biblical Law, and Hemorrhaging Woman." Pp. 379-97 in *Treasures New and Old: Recent Contributions to Matthean Studies.* Edited by David R. Bauer and Mark Allan

Powell. Society of Biblical Literature Symposium Series 1. Atlanta: Scholars Press.

Levine, Lee I.

1976 "R. Simeon b. Yohai and the Purification of Tiberias: History and Tradition." *Hebrew Union College Annual* 49: 143-85.

1982 "Excavations at the Synagogue of Horvat 'Ammudim." *Israel Exploration Journal* 32: 1-12.

1986 "The Second Temple Synagogue: The Formative Years." Pp. 7-31 in *The Synagogue in Late Antiquity.* Edited by Lee I. Levine. Philadelphia: The American Schools of Oriental Research.

1996 "The Nature and Origin of the Palestinian Synagogue Reconsidered." *Journal of Biblical Literature* 115: 425-48.

Levinskaya, Irina.

1996 *The Book of Acts in Its Diaspora Setting.* Vol. 5 in The Book of Acts in Its First Century Setting. Grand Rapids: Eerdmans; Carlisle: Paternoster Press.

Levison, John R.

1991 "Josephus's Version of Ruth." *Journal for the Study of the Pseudepigrapha* 8: 31-44.

Lewis, Bernard.

1975 *History Remembered, Recovered, Invented.* New York: Simon & Schuster.

1990 *Race and Slavery in the Middle East: An Historical Enquiry.* New York: Oxford University Press.

Lewis, I. M.

1971 *Ecstatic Religion: An Anthropological Study of Spirit Possession and Shamanism.* Baltimore: Penguin.

Lewis, Jack P.

1995 "'The Gates of Hell Shall Not Prevail against It' (Matt 16:18): A Study of the History of Interpretation." *Journal of the Evangelical Theological Society* 38: 349-67.

Lewis, John J.

1974 "The Wilderness Controversy and Peirasmos." *Colloquium* 7: 42-44.

Lewis, Naphtali.

1983 *Life in Egypt under Roman Rule.* Oxford: Clarendon Press.

Lewis, Richard B.

1968 "Ignatius and the 'Lord's Day.'" *Andrews University Seminary Studies* 6: 46-59.

Liddell, Henry George, and Robert Scott.

1968 *A Greek-English Lexicon.* Rev. Henry Stuart Jones and Roderick McKenzie. Oxford: Clarendon Press.

Lieberman, Saul.

1951 "Light on the Cave Scrolls from Rabbinic Sources." *Proceedings of the American Academy for Jewish Research* 20: 395-404.

1962 *Hellenism in Jewish Palestine: Studies in the Literary Transmission, Beliefs and Manners of Palestine in the I Century B.C.E.–IV Century C.E.* 2d ed. Texts and Studies of the Jewish Theological Seminary of America, 18. New York: The Jewish Theological Seminary of America.

1987 "A Mesopotanian Background for the So-Called *Aggadic* 'Measures' of Biblical Hermeneutics?" *Hebrew Union College Annual* 58 (1987): 157-225.

Liefeld, Walter L.

1967 "The Wandering Preacher as a Social Figure in the Roman Empire." Ph.D.

dissertation, Columbia University. Ann Arbor: University Microfilms International, 1976.

1992 "Transfiguration." Pp. 834-41 in *Dictionary of Jesus and the Gospels.* Edited by Joel B. Green, Scot McKnight, and I. Howard Marshall. Downers Grove, IL: InterVarsity Press.

Lietzmann, Heinrich.

1931 "Der Prozess Jesu." *Sitzenberichte der Akademie der Wissenschaft* 14 (1931): 310-22.

Lightfoot, J. B.

n.d. *Notes on the Epistles of St Paul (I & II Thess, 1 Cor 1–7, Rom 1–7, Eph 1:1-14).* Winona Lake, IN: Alpha Publications; reprint ed.

1869 *St Paul's Epistle to the Galatians.* 3d ed. London: Macmillan & Company.

Lightfoot, John.

1859 *A Commentary on the New Testament from the Talmud and Hebraica.* Oxford: Oxford University Press. Reprint: Hendrickson Publishers.

Limbeck, Meinrad.

1970 "Der Lobpreis Gottes als Sinn des Daseins." *Theologische Quartalschrift* 150: 349-57.

1971 *Die Ordnung des Heils. Untersuchungen zum Gesetzesverständnis des Frühjudentums.* Kommentare und Beiträge zum Alten und Neuen Testament. Düsseldorf: Patmos.

Lincoln, Andrew T.

1981 *Paradise Now and Not Yet: Studies in the role of the heavenly dimension in Paul's thought with special reference to his eschatology.* Society for New Testament Studies Monograph 43. Cambridge: Cambridge University Press.

1990 *Ephesians.* Word Biblical Commentary 42. Dallas: Word Books.

Lindars, Barnabas.

1961 *New Testament Apologetic.* London: SCM Press.

1975 "Re-Enter the Apocalyptic Son of Man." *New Testament Studies* 22: 52-72.

1983 *Jesus Son of Man: A Fresh Examination of the Son of Man Sayings in the Gospels in the Light of Recent Research.* Grand Rapids: Eerdmans.

Lindemann, A.

1983 "Die Kinder und die Gottesherrschaft. Markus 10,13-16 und die Stellung der Kinder in der Späthellenistischen Gesellschaft und im Urchristentum." *Wort und Dienst* 17: 77-104.

Lindner, Manfred.

1990 "Ein nabatäisches Heiligtum oberhalb der Nischenklamm *(Sidd el-Ma'āgīn)* von Petra (Jordanien)." *Zeitschrift des Deutschen Palästina-Vereins* 106: 145-54, plates 14-19.

Lindsey, Robert L.

1990 *Jesus: Rabbi and Lord. The Hebrew Story of Jesus behind Our Gospels.* Oak Creek, WI: Cornerstone Publishing.

1992-1993 "A New Approach to the Synoptic Gospels." *Mishkan* 17-18: 87-106. *(NTA)*

Linnemann, Eta.

1990 *Historical Criticism of the Bible: Methodology or Ideology?* Translated by Robert W. Yarbrough from *Wissenschaft oder Meinung? Anfragen und Alternativen.* Grand Rapids: Baker.

1992 *Is There a Synoptic Problem? Rethinking the Literary Dependence of the First Three Gospels.* Translated by Robert W. Yarbrough from *Gibt es ein synoptisches Problem?* Grand Rapids: Baker.

1996 "The Lost Gospel of Q — Fact or Fantasy?" *Trinity Journal* 17: 3-18.

Linton, Olof.

1976 "The Parable of the Children's Game." *New Testament Studies* 22: 156-79.

Liver, Jacob.

1963 "The Half-Shekel Offering in Biblical and Post-Biblical Literature." *Harvard Theological Review* 56: 173-98.

Llewelyn, Stephen.

1989 "Mt 7:6a: Mistranslation or Interpretation?" *Novum Testamentum* 31: 97-103.

Llewelyn, S. R., with R. A. Kearsley.

1992 *New Documents Illustrating Early Christianity: A Review of the Greek Inscriptions and Papyri Published in 1980-81.* Vol. 6. North Ryde, N.S.W.: The Ancient History Documentary Research Centre, Macquarie University.

1994 *New Documents Illustrating Early Christianity: A Review of the Greek Inscriptions and Papyri Published in 1982-83.* Vol. 7. North Ryde, N.S.W.: The Ancient History Documentary Research Centre, Macquarie University.

1998 *New Documents Illustrating Early Christianity: A Review of the Greek Inscriptions and Papyri Published in 1984-85.* Vol. 8. North Ryde, N.S.W.: The Ancient History Documentary Research Centre, Macquarie University. Grand Rapids: Eerdmans.

Loader, W. R. G.

1978 "Christ at the Right Hand — Ps. CX.1 in the New Testament." *New Testament Studies* 24: 199-217.

Lodge, Rupert C.

1928 *Plato's Theory of Ethics: The Moral Criterion and the Highest Good.* New York: Harcourt, Brace & Company; London: Kegan Paul, Trench, Trubner & Company.

1953 *Plato's Theory of Art.* New York: The Humanities Press; London: Routledge and Kegan Paul.

Loffreda, S.

1971 "Recenti scoperte a Cafarnao." *Rivista Biblica* 19: 221-29. (*NTA* 16:349)

Loftus, Francis.

1975 "A Note on *syntagma tón Galilaión* B.J. iv 558." *Jewish Quarterly Review* 65: 182-83.

1977 "The Anti-Roman Revolts of the Jews and the Galileans." *Jewish Quarterly Review* 68: 78-98.

Lohse, Eduard.

1955 *Mark's Witness to Jesus Christ.* New York: Association Press.

1971 *Colossians and Philemon.* Translated by William R. Poehlmann and Robert J. Karris. Hermeneia. Philadelphia: Fortress Press.

1978 *The New Testament Environment.* Translated by John E. Steely. Nashville: Abingdon Press.

Long, A. A.

1974 *Hellenistic Philosophy: Stoics, Epicureans, Sceptics.* New York: Charles Scribner's Sons.

Longenecker, Richard N.

1975 *Biblical Exegesis in the Apostolic Period.* Grand Rapids: Eerdmans.

1976 *Paul, Apostle of Liberty.* Grand Rapids: Baker.

1981 *The Christology of Early Jewish Christianity.* Grand Rapids: Baker; from London: SCM Press, 1970.

Longstaff, Thomas R. W.

1977 *Evidence of Conflation in Mark? A Study in the Synoptic Problem.* Society of Biblical Literature Dissertation 28. Missoula, MT: Scholars Press.

Losada, D.

1979 "Bienaventurados los mansos porque ellos heredar n la tierra." *Revista Bíblica* 41: 239-43. *(NTA)*

Losie, L. A.

1992 "Triumphal Entry." Pp. 854-59 in *Dictionary of Jesus and the Gospels.* Edited by Joel B. Green, Scot McKnight, and I. Howard Marshall. Downers Grove, IL: InterVarsity Press.

Lourenço, J.

1990 "Targum de Is 52,13–53,12. Pressupostos históricos e Processos literários." *Didaskalia* 20: 155-66. (*NTA* 36:401)

Lowe, Malcolm, and David Flusser.

1983 "Evidence Corroborating a Modified Proto-Matthean Synoptic Theory." *New Testament Studies* 29: 25-47.

Lowie, Robert H.

1968 "Relationship Terms." Pp. 39-59 in *Kinship and Social Organization.* Edited by Paul Bohannan and John Middleton. Garden City, NY: The Natural History Press.

Lown, J. S.

1986 "The Miraculous in the Greco-Roman Historians." *Forum* 2: 36-42.

Luck, William F.

1987 *Divorce and Remarriage: Recovering the Biblical View.* San Francisco: Harper & Row.

Lüdemann, Gerd.

1980 "The Successors of Pre-70 Jerusalem Christianity: A Critical Evaluation of the Pella-Tradition." Pp. 161-73 in *The Shaping of Christianity in the Second and Third Centuries.* Vol. 1 in Jewish and Christian Self-Definition. 3 vols. Edited by E. P. Sanders. Philadelphia: Fortress Press.

Lull, David John.

1980 *The Spirit in Galatia: Paul's Interpretation of* Pneuma *as Divine Power.* Society of Biblical Literature Dissertation 49. Chico, CA: Scholars Press.

Luz, Ulrich.

1989 *Matthew 1–7: A Commentary.* Translated by Wilhelm C. Linss. Minneapolis: Fortress Press.

1991 "The Primacy Text (Mt. 16:18)." *Princeton Seminary Bulletin* 12: 41-55.

1992 "Matthew's Anti-Judaism: Its Origin and Contemporary Significance." *Currents in Theology and Mission* 19: 405-15.

1994 *Matthew in History: Interpretation, Influence, and Effects.* Minneapolis: Fortress Press.

1995 "The Disciples in the Gospel according to Matthew (1971)." Pp. 115-48 in *The Interpretation of Matthew.* 2d ed. Edited by Graham Stanton. Edinburgh: T & T Clark.

1996 "The Final Judgment (Matt 25:31-46): An Exercise in 'History of Influence' Exegesis." Pp. 271-310 in *Treasures New and Old: Recent Contributions to Matthean Studies.* Edited by David R. Bauer and Mark Allan Powell. Society of Biblical Literature Symposium Series 1. Atlanta: Scholars Press.

Lyons, George.
1985 *Pauline Autobiography: Toward a New Understanding.* Society of Biblical Literature Dissertation 73. Atlanta: Scholars Press.
McArthur, Harvey K.
1958 "Mark XIV.62." *New Testament Studies* 4: 156-58.
1971 "'On the Third Day.'" *New Testament Studies* 18: 81-86.
McCane, Byron R.
1990 "'Let the Dead Bury Their Own Dead': Secondary Burial and Matt 8:21-22." *Harvard Theological Review* 83: 31-43.
1991 "Bones of Contention? Ossuaries and Reliquaries in Early Judaism and Christianity." *Second Century* 8: 235-46.
McCarter, P. Kyle.
1992 "The Mysterious Copper Scroll, Clues to Hidden Temple Treasure?" *Bible Review* 8 (4, 1992): 34-41, 63-64.
McCasland, Selby Vernon.
1932 "Portents in Josephus and in the Gospels." *Journal of Biblical Literature* 51: 323-35.
1958 "'The Way.'" *Journal of Biblical Literature* 77: 222-30.
Maccini, Robert Gordon.
1996 *Her Testimony Is True: Women as Witnesses according to John.* Journal for the Study of the New Testament 125. Sheffield: Sheffield Academic Press.
Maccoby, H. [Hyam]
1982 "The Washing of Cups." *Journal for the Study of the New Testament* 14: 3-15.
McConnell, Richard S.
1969 "Law and Prophecy in Matthew's Gospel: The Authority and Use of the Old Testament in the Gospel of St. Matthew." Th.D. dissertation, University of Basel.
McCurley, Foster R., Jr.
1974 "'And after Six Days' (Mark 9:2): A Semitic Literary Device." *Journal of Biblical Literature* 93: 67-81.
MacDonald, D.
1989 "The Worth of the Assarion." *Historia* 38: 120-23.
McDonald, John.
1964 *The Theology of the Samaritans.* Philadelphia: Westminster Press.
McEleney, Neil J.
1979 "The Principles of the Sermon on the Mount." *Catholic Biblical Quarterly* 41: 552-70.
1985 "Does the Trumpet Sound or Resound? An Interpretation of Matthew 6:2." *Zeitschrift für die Neutestamentliche Wissenschaft* 76: 43-46.
McGavran, D. A., and W. C. Arn.
1977 *Ten Steps for Church Growth.* San Francisco: Harper & Row.
MacGregor, G. G. C.
1936 *The New Testament Basis of Pacifism.* London: James Clarke & Company. Reprinted in *The New Testament Basis of Pacifism and the Relevance of an Impossible Ideal.* Nyack, NY: Fellowship Publications.
McIver, Robert K.
1995 "The Parable of the Weeds among the Wheat (Matt 13:24-30, 36-43) and the Relationship between the Kingdom and the Church as Portrayed in the Gospel of Matthew." *Journal of Biblical Literature* 114: 643-59.

McKelvey, R. J.

1962 "Christ the Cornerstone." *New Testament Studies* 8: 352-59.

Mack, Burton L.

1988 *A Myth of Innocence: Mark and Christian Origins.* Philadelphia: Fortress Press.

1993 *The Lost Gospel: The Book of Q and Christian Origins.* San Francisco: HarperSanFrancisco.

Mack, Burton L., and Vernon K. Robbins.

1989 *Patterns of Persuasion in the Gospels.* Sonoma, CA: Polebridge Press.

McKenzie, Judith S.

1988 "The Development of Nabataean Sculpture at Petra and Khirbet Tannur." *Palestine Exploration Quarterly* 120: 81-107.

McKnight, Scot.

1992 "Matthew, Gospel of." Pp. 526-41 in *Dictionary of Jesus and the Gospels.* Edited by Joel B. Green, Scot McKnight, and I. Howard Marshall. Downers Grove, IL: InterVarsity Press.

1993 "A Loyal Critic: Matthew's Polemic with Judaism in Theological Perspective." Pp. 55-79 in *Anti-Semitism and Early Christianity: Issues of Polemic and Faith.* Edited by Craig A. Evans and Donald A. Hagner. Minneapolis: Fortress Press.

MacLaurin, E. C. B.

1978a "Beelzeboul." *Novum Testamentum* 20: 156-60.

1978b "The Divine Fishermen." *St. Mark's Review* 94: 26-28. (*NTA* 23:27)

MacMullen, Ramsay.

1966 *Enemies of the Roman Order: Treason, Unrest, and Alienation in the Empire.* Cambridge: Harvard University Press.

1974 *Roman Social Relations: 50 B.C. to A.D. 284.* New Haven: Yale University Press.

1985-1986 "Conversion: A Historian's View." *Second Century* 5: 67-81.

McNamara, Martin.

1968 "Were the Magi Essenes?" *Irish Ecclesiastical Record* 110: 305-28. *(NTA)*

1972 *Targum and Testament.* Grand Rapids: Eerdmans.

1983 *Palestinian Judaism and the New Testament.* Good News Studies 4. Wilmington, DE: Michael Glazier.

McNeil, Brian.

1981 "Asexuality and the Apocalypse of Zosimus." *Heythrop Journal* 22: 172-73.

McNeile, A. H.

1915 *The Gospel according to St. Matthew.* London: Macmillan & Company.

McNicol, Allan J.

1977 "The Eschatological Temple in the Qumran Pesher 4QFlorilegium 1:1-7." *Ohio Journal of Religious Studies* 5: 133-41.

MacRae, George.

1972 "The Judgment Scene in the Coptic Apocalypse of Paul." Pp. 285-88 in *Studies on the Testament of Abraham.* Edited by George W. E. Nickelsburg, Jr. Society of Biblical Literature Septuagint and Cognate Studies 6. Missoula, MT: Scholars Press.

McVann, Mark.

1986 "Conjectures about a Guilty Bystander: The Sword Slashing in Mark 14:47." *Listening* 21: 124-37.

Maddox, Robert.
1982 *The Purpose of Luke-Acts.* Edinburgh: T & T Clark.

Madson, William.
1964 "Value Conflicts and Folk Psychotherapy in South Texas." Pp. 420-40 in *Magic, Faith, and Healing: Studies in Primitive Psychiatry Today.* Edited by Ari Kiev. Foreword by Jerome D. Frank. New York: Free Press.

Magness, J. Lee.
1986 *Sense and Absence: Structure and Suspension in the Ending of Mark's Gospel.* Society of Biblical Literature Semeia Studies. Atlanta: Society of Biblical Literature.
1990 "Some Observations on the Roman Temple at Kedesh." *Israel Exploration Journal* 40: 173-81.

Maher, Michael.
1975 "'Take My Yoke Upon You' (Matt. XI.29)." *New Testament Studies* 22: 97-103.
1979 "The Merit of the Fathers and the Treasury of the Church." *Irish Theological Quarterly* 46: 256-75.
1981 "Service of the Heart: The Quest for Authentic Prayer in Judaism." *Review of Religion* 40: 40-47. (*NTA* 25:286)
1983 "Humble of Heart: The Virtue of Humility in Rabbinic Literature." *Milltown Studies* 11: 25-43. (*NTA* 28:66)

Maier, Johann.
1978 *Jesus von Nazareth in der Talmudischen Überlieferung.* Erträge der Forschung, Band 82. Darmstadt: Wissenschaftliche Buchgesellschaft.

Maillot, A.
1978 "Quelques remarques sur la Naissance Virginale du Christ." *Foi et Vie* 77: 30-44.

Malan, F. S.
1976 "The relationship between apostolate and office in the theology of Paul." *Neotestamentica* 10: 53-68.

Malherbe, Abraham J.
1967 "Life in the Graeco-Roman World." Pp. 4-36 in *The World of the New Testament.* Edited by Abraham J. Malherbe. Austin, TX: R. B. Sweet.
1970 "'Gentle as a Nurse': The Cynic Background to I Thess ii." *Novum Testamentum* 12: 203-17.
1983 *Social Aspects of Early Christianity.* 2d ed. Philadelphia: Fortress Press.
1986 *Moral Exhortation, A Greco-Roman Sourcebook.* Library of Early Christianity 4. Philadelphia: Westminster Press.

Malina, Bruce J.
1981 *The New Testament World: Insights from Cultural Anthropology.* Atlanta: John Knox.
1988 "Patron and Client. The Analogy behind Synoptic Theology." *Forum* 4: 2-32.
1993 *Windows on the World of Jesus: Time Travel to Ancient Judea,.* Louisville, KY: Westminster/John Knox.

Malina, Bruce J., and Richard L. Rohrbaugh.
1992 *Social Science Commentary on the Synoptic Gospels.* Minneapolis: Augsburg Fortress Press.

Malinowski, Francis X.

1980 "Torah Tendencies in Galilean Judaism according to Flavius Josephus with Gospel Comparisons." *Biblical Theology Bulletin* 10: 30-36.

Mánek, Jindrich.

1967 "On the Mount — On the Plain (Mt. v 1–Lk. vi 17)." *Novum Testamentum* 9: 124-31.

Manns, Fréderic.

1979 "Une source de l'aggadah juive: la littérature grecque." *Studii Biblici Franciscani Liber Annuus* 29: 111-44.

1978 "La Halakah dans l'Évangile de Matthieu." *Antonianum* 53: 3-22.

1980a "L'arrière-plan socio-économique de la Parabole des ouvriers de la onzième heure et ses limites." *Antonianum* 55: 258-68.

1980b "Un midrash chrétien: le récit de la mort de Judas." *Revue des Sciences Religieuses* 54: 197-203.

1981 "Marc 6,21-29 à la lumière des dernières fouilles du Machéronte." *Studii Biblici Franciscani Liber Annuus* 31: 287-90.

1983 "La Halakah dans l'évangile de Matthieu. Note sur *Mt.* 16,16-19." *Bibbia e Oriente* 25: 129-35.

1988 "Une tradition rabbinique réinterprétée dans l'évangile de Mt 22,1-10 et en Rm 11,30-32." *Antonianum* 63: 416-26.

Mansfield, M. Robert.

1987 *"Spirit and Gospel" in Mark.* Peabody, MA: Hendrickson.

Manson, T. W.

1961 *The Servant-Messiah.* Cambridge: Cambridge University Press.

1963 *On Paul and John: Some Selected Theological Themes.* Studies in Biblical Theology 38. Edited by Matthew Black. London: SCM Press.

1979 *The Sayings of Jesus.* Grand Rapids: Eerdmans; reprint from London: SCM Press, 1957.

Mantel, Hugo.

1961 *Studies in the History of the Sanhedrin.* Harvard Semitic Studies 17. Cambridge: Harvard University Press.

1967 "The Nature of the Great Synagogue." *Harvard Theological Review* 60: 69-91.

1973 "The Dichotomy of Judaism during the Second Temple." *Hebrew Union College Annual* 44: 55-87.

Mantey, Julius R.

1973 "Evidence That the Perfect Tense in John 20:23 and Matthew 16:19 Is Mistranslated." *Journal of the Evangelical Theological Society* 16: 129-38.

1981 "Distorted Translations in John 20:23; Matthew 16:18-19 and 18:18." *Review and Expositor* 78: 409-16.

Marcus, Joel.

1988 "The Gates of Hades and the Keys of the Kingdom (Matt 16:18-19)." *Catholic Biblical Quarterly* 50: 443-55.

Marcus, Ralph.

1956 "The Qumran Scrolls and Early Judaism." *Biblical Research* 1: 9-47.

Marguerat, Daniel.

1982 "L'avenir de la loi: Matthieu á l'épreuve de Paul." *Etudes Théologiques et Religieuses* 57: 361-73.

Mark, Linda Li.

1967 "Patrilateral Cross-Cousin Marriage among the Magpie Miao: Preferential or Prescriptive." *American Anthropologist* 69: 55-62.

Marmorstein, A.

1923 "The Attitude of the Jews towards Early Christianity." *The Expositor* 49: 383-89.

1968a *The Doctrine of Merits in Old Rabbinical Literature.* New York: KTAV. Reprint of 1920 ed.

1968b *The Old Rabbinic Doctrine of God: Essays in Anthropomorphism.* New York: KTAV. Reprint of 1937 ed.

1968c *The Old Rabbinic Doctrine of God: The Names and Attributes of God.* New York: KTAV. Reprint of 1927 ed.

Marshall, I. Howard.

1966 "The Synoptic Son of Man Sayings in Recent Discussion." *New Testament Studies* 12: 327-51.

1969 "Son of God or Servant of Yahweh? A Reconsideration of Mark i.11." *New Testament Studies* 15: 326-36.

1970 *Luke: Historian and Theologian.* Exeter: Paternoster Press.

1974 *Kept by the Power of God: A Study in Perseverance and Falling Away.* Minneapolis: Bethany Fellowship; originally London: Epworth Press, 1969.

1977 "Historical Criticism." Pp. 126-38 in *New Testament Interpretation: Essays on Principles and Methods.* Edited by I. Howard Marshall. Grand Rapids: Eerdmans.

1978 *Commentary on Luke.* New International Greek Testament Commentary. Grand Rapids: Eerdmans.

1983 *1 and 2 Thessalonians.* New Century Bible. Grand Rapids: Eerdmans.

1990 *The Origins of New Testament Christology.* 2d ed. Downers Grove: InterVarsity Press.

1991 "Luke and His Gospel." Pp. 273-92 in *The Gospel and the Gospels.* Edited by Peter Stuhlmacher. Grand Rapids: Eerdmans.

Martin, Dale B.

1990 *Slavery as Salvation: The Metaphor of Slavery in Pauline Christianity.* New Haven: Yale University Press.

Martin, Luther H.

1981 "Josephus' Use of *Heimarmene* in the *Jewish Antiquities* XIII, 171-3." *Numen* 28.2: 127-37.

1987 *Hellenistic Religions: An Introduction.* New York: Oxford University Press.

1991 "Artemidorus: Dream Theory in Late Antiquity." *Second Century* 8: 97-108.

Martin, Ralph P.

1972 *Mark: Evangelist and Theologian.* Grand Rapids: Eerdmans.

1977 "Approaches to New Testament Exegesis." Pp. 220-51 in *New Testament Interpretation: Essays on Principles and Methods.* Edited by I. Howard Marshall. Grand Rapids: Eerdmans.

1978 "The Pericope of the Healing of the 'Centurion's Servant/Son (Matt 8:5-13 par. Luke 7:1-10): Some Exegetical Notes." Pp. 14-22 in *Unity and Diversity in New Testament Theology: Essays in Honor of George E. Ladd.* Edited by Robert A. Guelich. Grand Rapids: Eerdmans.

1982 *The Worship of God.* Grand Rapids: Eerdmans.

1988 *James.* Word Bible Commentary 48. Waco, TX: Word Books.

Martin, W. H. Blyth.

1956 "The Indispensability of Q." *Theology* 59: 182-88.

Marucci, C.

1990 "Clausole matteane e critica téstuale. In merito alla teoria di H. Crouzel sul testo originale di Mt 19,9." *Rivista Biblica* 38: 301-25. (*NTA* 35:160)

Marx, A.

1970 "Les racines du célibat essénien." *Revue de Qumran* 7: 323-42.

Marxsen, Willi.

1969 *Mark the Evangelist: Studies on the Redaction History of the Gospel.* Translated by James Boyce, Donald Juel, and William Poehlmann with Roy A. Harrisville. Nashville: Abingdon Press.

Mason, Steven.

1990 "Pharisaic Dominance before 70 CE and the Gospels' Hypocrisy Charge (Matt 23:2-3)." *Harvard Theological Review* 83: 363-81.

1991 *Flavius Josephus on the Pharisees.* Studia Post-Biblica 39. Leiden: E. J. Brill.

1992 *Josephus and the New Testament.* Peabody, MA: Hendrickson.

Massaux, Édouard.

1990 *The First Ecclesiastical Writers.* Vol. 1 in *The Influence of the Gospel of Saint Matthew on Christian Literature before Saint Irenaeus.* 3 vols. Translated by Norman J. Belval and Suzanne Hecht. Edited by Arthur J. Bellinzoni. New Gospel Studies 5/1-3. Macon, GA: Mercer University Press.

1990-1992 *The Later Christian Writings.* Vol. 2 in *The Influence of the Gospel of Saint Matthew on Christian Literature before Saint Irenaeus.* 3 vols. Translated by Norman J. Belval and Suzanne Hecht. Edited by Arthur J. Bellinzoni. New Gospel Studies 5/1-3. Macon, GA: Mercer University Press.

1993 *The Apologists and the Didache.* Vol. 3 in *The Influence of the Gospel of Saint Matthew on Christian Literature before Saint Irenaeus.* 3 vols. Translated by Norman J. Belval and Suzanne Hecht. Edited by Arthur J. Bellinzoni. New Gospel Studies 5/1-3. Macon, GA: Mercer University Press.

Matera, Frank J.

1982 *The Kingship of Jesus: Composition and Theology in Mark 15.* Society of Biblical Literature Dissertation 66. Chico, CA: Scholars Press.

1989 "'His blood be on us and on our children.'" *Bible Today* 27: 345-50.

Matthews, Victor H., and D. C. Benjamin.

1991a "The Leper." *The Bible Today* 29: 292-97.

1991b "The Stubborn and the Fool." *The Bible Today* 29: 222-26.

Matthey, Jacques.

1980 "The Great Commission according to Matthew." *International Review of Mission* 69: 161-73.

Matthiae, Karl.

1989 "Die Nabatäer. Ein antikes Handelsvolk in der Wüste." *Das Altertum* 35: 222-31.

Mattill, Andrew J., Jr.

1979a *Luke and the Last Things: A Perspective for the Understanding of Lukan Thought.* Dillsboro, NC: Western North Carolina Press.

1979b "'The Way of Tribulation.'" *Journal of Biblical Literature* 98: 531-46.

Mattingly, Harold.
1967 *Christianity in the Roman Empire.* New York: W. W. Norton & Company.
Mauser, Ulrich.
1963 *Christ in the Wilderness.* Studies in Biblical Theology 39. London: SCM Press.
Maxwell-Stuart, P. G.
1979 "'Do not give what is holy to the dogs.' (Mt 7:6)." *Expository Times* 90: 341.
May, Herbert Gordon.
1944 "Synagogues in Palestine." *Biblical Archaeologist* 7: 1-20.
Mayer, Günter.
1972 "Aspekte des Abrahambildes in der hellenistisch-jüdischen Literatur." *Evangelische Theologie* 32: 118-27.
Mayer, Reinhold.
1981 "Der Anfang des Evangeliums in Galiläa." *Bibel und Kirche* 36: 213-21.
Mazar, Benjamin.
1980 "Excavations near Temple Mount Reveal Splendors of Herodian Jerusalem." *Biblical Archaeology Review* 6: 44-59.
Mbiti, John S.
1970 *African Religions and Philosophies.* Garden City, NY: Doubleday & Company.
Meadors, E. P.
1992 "The Orthodoxy of the 'Q' Sayings of Jesus." *Tyndale Bulletin* 43: 233-57.
Meagher, John C.
1979 "As the Twig Was Bent: Antisemitism in Greco-Roman and Earliest Christian Times." Pp. 1-26 in *Anti-Semitism and the Foundations of Christianity.* Edited by Alan T. Davies. New York: Paulist Press.
Mealand, David L.
1975 "Community of Goods at Qumran." *Theologische Zeitschrift* 31: 129-39.
1978a "Dissimilarity Test." *Scottish Journal of Theology* 31: 41-50.
1978b "Philo of Alexandria's Attitude to Riches." *Zeitschrift für die Neutestamentliche Wissenschaft* 69: 258-64.
1985 "The Paradox of Philo's Views on Wealth." *Journal for the Study of the New Testament* 24: 111-15.
Meecham, H. G.
1952 "The Anarthrous θεος in John i.1 and 1 Corinthians iii.16." *Expository Times* 63: 126.
Meeks, Wayne A.
1967 *The Prophet-King: Moses Traditions and the Johannine Christology.* Supplements to Novum Testamentum 14. Leiden: E. J. Brill.
1974 "The Image of the Androgyne: Some Uses of a Symbol in Earliest Christianity." *History of Religions* 13: 165-208.
1983 *The First Urban Christians: The Social World of the Apostle Paul.* New Haven: Yale University Press.
1986 *The Moral World of the First Christians.* Library of Early Christianity 6. Philadelphia: Westminster Press.
Meier, John P.
1976 *Law and History in Matthew's Gospel: A Redactional Study of Mt. 5:17-48.* Analecta Biblica 71. Rome: Biblical Institute Press.
1977a "Nations or Gentiles in Matthew 28:19?" *Catholic Biblical Quarterly* 39: 94-102.

1977b "Two Disputed Questions in Matt 28:16-20." *Journal of Biblical Literature* 96: 407-24.

1979 *The Vision of Matthew: Christ, Church, and Morality in the First Gospel.* Theological Inquiries. New York: Paulist Press.

1980 *Matthew.* New Testament Message 3. Wilmington, DE: Michael Glazier.

1991a *A Marginal Jew: Rethinking the Historical Jesus.* Vol. 1: *The Roots of the Problem and the Person.* The Anchor Bible Reference Library. New York: Doubleday & Company.

1991b "Matthew and Ignatius: A Response to William R. Schoedel." Pp. 178-86 in *Social History of the Matthean Community: Cross-Disciplinary Approaches.* Edited by David L. Balch. Minneapolis: Fortress Press.

1992 "John the Baptist in Josephus: Philology and Exegesis." *Journal of Biblical Literature* 111: 225-37.

1994 *A Marginal Jew: Rethinking the Historical Jesus.* Vol. 2: *Mentor, Message, and Miracles.* The Anchor Bible Reference Library. New York: Doubleday & Company.

Ménard, Jacques E.

1980 "Normative Self-Definition in Gnosticism." Pp. 134-50 in *The Shaping of Christianity in the Second and Third Centuries.* Vol. 1 in Jewish and Christian Self-Definition. 3 vols. Edited by E. P. Sanders. Philadelphia: Fortress Press.

Mendecki, Norbert.

1983 "Die zehnte Bitte des Achtzehngebets." *Collectanea Theologica* 53 (special edition): 161-66.

Mendels, D.

1988 "'Creative History' in the Hellenistic Near East in the Third and Second Centuries BCE: The Jewish Case." *Journal for the Study of the Pseudepigrapha* 2:13-20.

Menzies, Robert P.

1991 *The Development of Early Christian Pneumatology with Special Reference to Luke-Acts.* Journal for the Study of the New Testament Supplement Series 54. Sheffield: Sheffield Academic Press.

Merkel, Helmut.

1984 "The opposition between Jesus and Judaism." Pp. 129-44 in *Jesus and the Politics of His Day.* Edited by Ernst Bammel and C. F. D. Moule. Cambridge: Cambridge University Press.

Merritt, Robert L.

1985 "Jesus Barabbas and the Paschal Pardon." *Journal of Biblical Literature* 104: 57-68.

Metzger, Bruce M.

1952 "On the Translation of John i.1." *Expository Times* 63: 125-26.

1955 "Considerations of Methodology in the Study of the Mystery Religions and Early Christianity." *Harvard Theological Review* 48: 1-20.

1957 "How Many Times Does 'Epiousios' Occur outside the Lord's Prayer?" *Expository Times* 69: 52-54.

1968 *The Text of the New Testament.* New York: Oxford University Press.

1971 *A Textual Commentary on the Greek New Testament.* New York: United Bible Societies.

Meyer, Dieter.

1964 "Πολλαπαθεῖν." *Zeitschrift für die Neutestamentliche Wissenschaft* 55: 132.

Meyers, Eric M.
1976 "Galilean Regionalism as a Factor in Reconstruction." *Bulletin of the American Schools of Oriental Research* 221: 93-101.
1980 "Ancient Synagogues in Galilee: Their Religious and Cultural Setting." *Biblical Archaeologist* 43: 97-108.
1986 "The Current State of Galilean Synagogue Studies." Pp. 127-37 in *The Synagogue in Late Antiquity.* Edited by Lee I. Levine. Philadelphia: The American Schools of Oriental Research.
1988 "Early Judaism and Christianity in the Light of Archaeology." *Biblical Archaeologist* 51: 69-79.

Meyers, Eric M., Ehud Netzer, and Carol L. Meyers.
1986 "Sepphoris 'Ornament of All Galilee.'" *Biblical Archaeologist* 49: 4-19.
1988 "Byt-mydwt snhsp b'qrwpwlys sl sypwry wbmrkzw psyps mpw'r." *Qadmoniot* 21: 87-92. (*NTA* 34:78)

Meyers, Eric M., and James F. Strange.
1981 *Archaeology, the Rabbis, and Early Christianity.* Nashville: Abingdon Press.

Michaels, J. Ramsey.
1965 "Apostolic Hardships and Righteous Gentiles." *Journal of Biblical Literature* 84: 27-38.
1976 "Christian Prophecy and Matthew 23:8-12: A Test Exegesis." Pp. 305-10 in *Society of Biblical Literature Seminar Papers 1976.*
1981 *Servant and Son: Jesus in Parable and Gospel.* Atlanta: John Knox.

Michel, A.
1954 *Le Maitre de Justice d'apres les documents de la Mer Morte, la Litterature Apocryphe et Rabbinique.* Avignon: Maison Aubunel Pere.

Michel, Otto.
1932 *Prophet und Märtyrer.* Gütersloh: Verlag Bertelsmann.
1995 "The Conclusion of Matthew's Gospel (1950)." Pp. 39-51 in *The Interpretation of Matthew.* 2d ed. Edited by Graham Stanton. Edinburgh: T. & T. Clark.

Mickelsen, A. Berkeley.
1963 *Interpreting the Bible.* Grand Rapids: Eerdmans.

Milik, J. T.
1959 *Ten Years of Discovery in the Wilderness of Judaea.* London: SCM Press.

Milikowsky, Chaim.
1982/1983 "'lyhw whsyh (Elijah and the Messiah)." *Journal for the Study of the New Testament* 2: 491-96. (*NTA* 29:70).
1988 "Which Gehenna? Retribution and Eschatology in the Synoptic Gospels and in Early Jewish Texts." *New Testament Studies* 34: 238-49.

Millar, Fergus.
1981 "The World of the *Golden Ass.*" *Journal of Roman Studies* 71: 63-75.
1987 "Empire, Community and Culture in the Roman Near East: Greeks, Syrians, Jews and Arabs." *Journal of Jewish Studies* 38: 143-64.

Miller, James E.
1990 "Dreams and Prophetic Visions." *Biblica* 71: 401-4.

Miller, Robert J.
1988 "The Rejection of the Prophets in Q." *Journal of Biblical Literature* 107: 225-40.

Miller, Stuart S.
1992 "Sepphoris, the Well Remembered City." *Biblical Archaeologist* 55: 74-83.

1993 "The *Minim* of Sepphoris Reconsidered." *Harvard Theological Review* 86: 377-402.

Milligan, George.

1908 *St Paul's Epistles to the Thessalonians: The Greek Text with Introduction and Notes.* London: Macmillan & Company.

Minear, Paul S.

1950 *The Kingdom and the Power: An Exposition of the New Testament Gospel.* Philadelphia: Westminster Press.

1954 *Christian Hope and the Second Coming.* Philadelphia: Westminster Press.

1960 *Images of the Church in the New Testament.* Philadelphia: Westminster Press.

1972 *Commands of Christ.* Nashville: Abingdon Press.

Minor Latin Poets.

1935 2 vols. Translated by J. Wight Duff and Arnold M. Duff. LCL 284 and 434. Cambridge: Harvard University Press; London: William Heinemann.

Mitten, David Gordon.

1966 "A New Look at Ancient Sardis." *Biblical Archaeologist* 29.2: 38-68.

Moeser, Annelies G.

1992 "The Death of Judas." *Bible Today* 30: 145-51.

Moffatt, James D.

1938 *The First Epistle of Paul to the Corinthians.* The Moffatt New Testament Commentary. London: Hodder & Stoughton.

Mohrlang, Roger.

1984 *Matthew and Paul: A Comparison of Ethical Perspectives.* Society for the Study of the New Testament Monograph 48. Cambridge: Cambridge University Press.

Moiser, Jeremy.

1985a "Moses and Elijah." *Expository Times* 96: 216-17.

1985b "The Structure of Matthew 8–9: A Suggestion." *Zeitschrift für die Neutestamentliche Wissenschaft* 76: 117-18.

Molldrem, Mark J.

1991 "A Hermeneutic of Pastoral Care and the Law/Gospel Paradigm Applied to the Divorce Texts of Scripture." *Interpretation* 45: 43-54.

Momigliano, Arnaldo.

1977 *Essays in Ancient and Modern Historiography.* Middletown, CT: Wesleyan University Press; Oxford: Basil Blackwell.

Monson, J., consultant.

1979 *Student Map Manual: Historical Geography of Bible Lands.* Grand Rapids: Zondervan; Jerusalem: Pictorial Archive (Near Eastern History).

Montefiore, C. G.

1968 *The Synoptic Gospels.* 2 vols. Library of Biblical Studies. New York: KTAV; reprint of 1927 ed.

1979 "The Spirit of Judaism." 1:1-34 in *The Beginnings of Christianity.* 5 vols. Edited by F. J. Foakes Jackson and Kirsopp Lake. Grand Rapids: Baker.

Montefiore, C. G., and Herbert Loewe.

1974 *A Rabbinic Anthology.* New York: Schocken; originally London: Macmillan & Company, 1938.

Montefiore, Hugh W.

1956 "God as Father in the Synoptic Gospels." *New Testament Studies* 3: 31-46.

Moo, Douglas J.
1983 "Tradition and Old Testament in Matthew 27:3-10." Pp. 157-75 in *Studies in Midrash and Historiography.* Vol. 3 in Gospel Perspectives. Edited by R. T. France and David Wenham. Sheffield: JSOT Press.

Moore, Clifford H.
1979 "Life in the Roman Empire at the Beginning of the Christian Era." 1:218-62 in *The Beginnings of Christianity.* 5 vols. Edited by F. J. Foakes Jackson and Kirsopp Lake. Grand Rapids: Baker.

Moore, W. Ernest.
1989 "Violence to the Kingdom: Josephus and the Syrian Churches." *Expository Times* 100: 174-77.
1991 "'Lead us not into temptation.'" *Expository Times* 102: 171-72.

Moore, George Foot.
1911 "The Definition of the Jewish Canon and the Repudiation of the Christian Scriptures." Pp. 99-125 in *Essays in Modern Theology and Related Subjects: Gathered and Published as a Testimonial to Charles Augustus Briggs on the Completion of His Seventieth Year, January 15, 1911.* New York: Charles Scribner's Sons.
1971 *Judaism in the First Centuries of the Christian Era.* 2 vols. New York: Schocken Books, 1971. Reprint from Cambridge: Harvard University Press, 1927.

Morgenstern, Julian.
1955 "The Calendar of the Book of Jubilees, Its Origin and Its Character." *Vetus Testamentum* 5: 34-76.

Morosco, Robert E.
1979 "Redaction Criticism and the Evangelical: Matthew 10 A Test Case." *Journal of the Evangelical Theological Society* 22: 323-31.
1984 "Matthew's Formation of a Commissioning Type-Scene Out of the Story of Jesus' Commissioning of the Twelve." *Journal of Biblical Literature* 103: 539-56.

Morray-Jones, C. R. A.
1992 "Transformational Mysticism in the Apocalyptic-Merkabah Tradition." *Journal of Jewish Studies* 43: 1-31.

Morris, Leon.
1959 *The First and Second Epistles to the Thessalonians.* New International Commentary on the New Testament. Grand Rapids: Eerdmans.
1965 *The Apostolic Preaching of the Cross.* 3d ed. Grand Rapids: Eerdmans.
1971 *The Gospel according to John: The English Text with Introduction, Exposition and Notes.* New International Commentary on the New Testament. Grand Rapids: Eerdmans.
1972 *Apocalyptic.* Grand Rapids: Eerdmans.
1974 *The Gospel according to St. Luke.* Grand Rapids: Eerdmans.

Morton, A. Q., and G. C. H. MacGregor.
1964 *The Structure of Luke and Acts.* New York: Harper & Row.

Moses, A. D. A.
1996 *Matthew's Transfiguration Story and Jewish-Christian Controversy.* Journal for the Study of the New Testament Supplement 122. Sheffield: Sheffield Academic Press.

Mosley, A. W.

1965 "Historical Reporting in the Ancient World." *New Testament Studies* 12: 10-26.

Motyer, Stephen.

1987 "The Rending of the Veil: A Markan Pentecost?" *New Testament Studies* 33: 155-57.

Moulder, James.

1978 "Who Are My Enemies? An exploration of the semantic background of Christ's command." *Journal of Theology for Southern Africa* 25: 41-49.

Moulder, W. J.

1977 "The Old Testament Background and the Interpretation of Mark X.45." *New Testament Studies* 24: 120-27.

Moule, C. F. D.

1939 "Matthew v.21, 22." *Expository Times* 50: 189-90.

1965 *The Gospel according to Mark.* Cambridge: Cambridge University Press.

1969 "Uncomfortable Words — I. The Angry Word: Matthew 5.21f." *Expository Times* 81: 10-13.

1974 "An Unsolved Problem in the Temptation-Clause in the Lord's Prayer." *The Reformed Theological Review* 33: 65-75.

Moulton, James Hope, and George Milligan.

1976 *The Vocabulary of the Greek New Testament.* Grand Rapids: Eerdmans. Reprint of 1930 ed.

Mounce, Robert H.

1974 "Pauline Eschatology and the Apocalypse." *Evangelical Quarterly* 46: 164-66.

1985 *Matthew.* A Good News Commentary. San Francisco: Harper & Row.

Mowery, Robert L.

1990 "Subtle Differences: The Matthean 'Son of God' References." *Novum Testamentum* 32: 193-200.

Moxnes, Halvor.

1991 "Patron-Client Relations and the New Community in Luke-Acts." Pp. 241-68 in *The Social World of Luke-Acts: Models for Interpretation.* Edited by Jerome H. Neyrey. Peabody, MA: Hendrickson.

Moyer, James.

1969 "The Concept of Ritual Purity among the Hittites." Ph.D. dissertation, Brandeis University.

Mueller, James R.

1980 "The Temple Scroll and the Gospel Divorce Texts." *Revue de Qumran* 10: 247-56.

Mull, K. V., and C. S. Mull.

1992 "Biblical Leprosy — Is It Really?" *Biblical Archaeology Review* 8 (2, 1992): 32-39, 62.

Müller, Mogens.

1992 "The Gospel of St Matthew and the Mosaic Law — A Chapter of a Biblical Theology." *Studia Theologica* 46: 109-20.

Munck, Johannes.

1967 *Christ and Israel: An Interpretation of Romans 9–11.* Foreword by Krister Stendahl. Philadelphia: Fortress Press.

Murdock, George P.

1971 "Cross-Sex Patterns of Kin Behavior." *Ethnology* 10: 359-68.

Murphy, Frederick J.

1988 "Retelling the Bible: Idolatry in Pseudo-Philo." *Journal of Biblical Literature* 107: 275-87.

Murphy, Jane M.

1964 "Psychotherapeutic Aspects of Shamanism on St. Lawrence Island, Alaska." Pp. 53-83 in *Magic, Faith, and Healing: Studies in Primitive Psychiatry Today.* Edited by Ari Kiev. Foreword by Jerome D. Frank. New York: Free Press.

Murphy, Robert F., and Kasdan, Leonard.

1967 "Agnation and Endogamy: Some Further Considerations." *Southwestern Journal of Anthroplogy* 23: 1-14.

Murphy-O'Connor, Jerome.

1992 "A First-Century Jewish Mission to Gentiles?" *Pacifica* 5 (1, 1992): 32-42.

Murray, A. Gregory.

1984 "Mark the Conflator." *Downside Review* 102: 157-62.

1985 "The Rich Young Man." *Downside Review* 103: 144-46.

Murray, Gilbert.

1915 *The Stoic Philosophy.* New York: G. P. Putnam's Sons.

Murray, John.

1953 *Divorce.* Philadelphia: The Committee on Christian Education, The Orthodox Presbyterian Church.

Mussies, G.

1976 "Greek in Palestine and the Diaspora." Pp. 1040-64 in *The Jewish People in the First Century: Historical Geography, Political History, Social, Cultural, and Religious Life and Institutions.* 2 vols. Edited by S. Safrai and M. Stern with D. Flusser and W. C. van Unnik. Section 1 of Compendia Rerum Iudaicarum ad Novum Testamentum. Vol. 1: Assen: Van Gorcum & Co., B.V.; Vol. 2: Philadelphia: Fortress Press.

1983 "Greek as the Vehicle of Early Christianity." *New Testament Studies* 29: 356-69.

Mussner, Franz.

1960 "1QHodajoth und das Gleichnis von Senfkorn (Mk 4.30-32 Par.)." *Biblische Zeitschrift* 4 (1960): 128-30.

1963 "Das Buch Judith und die neutestamentliche Antichristidee." *Trierer Theologische Zeitschrift* 72: 242-45. (*NTA* 8:228)

Mylonas, George E.

1961 *Eleusis and the Eleusinian Mysteries.* Princeton: Princeton University Press.

Nadal, S. F.

1950 "Dual Descent in the Nuba Hills." Pp. 333-59 in *African Systems of Kinship and Marriage.* Edited by A. R. Radcliffe-Brown and Daryll Forde. New York: Oxford University Press.

Nanan, Madame.

1994 "The Sorcerer and Pagan Practices." Pp. 81-87 in *Our Time Has Come: African Christian Women Address the Issues of Today.* Edited by Judy Mbugua. Grand Rapids: Baker; Carlisle, U.K.: Paternoster Press/World Evangelical Fellowship.

Narkiss, Bezalel.

1986 "Pagan, Christian, and Jewish Elements in the Art of Ancient Synagogues." Pp. 183-88 in *The Synagogue in Late Antiquity.* Edited by Lee I. Levine. Philadelphia: American Schools of Oriental Research.

National Conference of Catholic Bishops
1986 *Economic Justice for All: Pastoral Letter on Catholic Social Teaching and the U.S. Economy.* Washington, D.C.: National Conference of Catholic Bishops.

Needham, Rodney.
1971 "Remarks on the Analysis of Kinship and Marriage." Pp. 1-34 in *Rethinking Kinship and Marriage.* Edited by Rodney Needham. Association of Social Anthropologists Monograph 11. New York: Tavistock Publications.

Neil, William.
1950 *The Epistle of Paul to the Thessalonians.* The Moffatt New Testament Commentary. London: Hodder & Stoughton.
1976 "Five Hard Sayings of Jesus." Pp. 157-71 in *Biblical Studies: Essays in Honor of William Barclay.* Philadelphia: Westminster Press.

Neirynck, Frans.
1988 "ΑΠΟ ΤΟΤΕ ΗΡΞΑΤΟ and the Structure of Matthew." *Ephemerides Theologicae Lovanienses* 64: 21-59.

Nembach, Ulrich.
1970 "Ehescheidung nach alttestamentlichem und jüdischem Recht." *Theologische Zeitschrift* 26: 161-71.

Nepper-Christensen, Poul.
1958 *Das Matthäusevangelium. Ein judenchristliches Evangelium?* Aarhus: Universitetsforlaget.
1991 "Apostlen Matthaeus og Matthaeusevangeliet." *Dansk Teologisk Tidsskrift* 54: 95-112. *(NTA)*

Nerlove, Sara, and A. Kimball Romney.
1967 "Sibling Terminology and Cross-Sex Behavior." *American Anthropologist* 69: 179-87.

Nettelhorst, R. P.
1988 "The Genealogy of Jesus." *Journal of the Evangelical Theological Society* 31: 169-72.

Netzer, Ehud.
1983 "Searching for Herod's Tomb." *Biblical Archaeology Review* 9: 31-51.
1989 "Jericho und Herodium: Verschwenderisches Leben in den Tagen der Hasmonäer und Herodes des Grosses." *Judaica* 45: 21-44.

Neudecker, Reinhard.
1992 "'And You Shall Love Your Neighbor as Yourself — I Am the Lord' (Lev 19.18) in Jewish Interpretation." *Biblica* 73: 496-517.
1994 "Das 'Ehescheidungsgesetz' von Dtn 24.1-4 nach altjüdischer Auslegung. Ein Beitrag zum Verständnis der neutestamentlichen Aussagen zur Ehescheidung." *Biblica* 75: 350-87.

Neusner, Jacob.
1970 *Development of a Legend.* Studia Postbiblica. Leiden: E. J. Brill.
1972 *There We Sat Down: Talmudic Judaism in the Making.* Nashville: Abingdon Press.
1973 "'By the Testimony of Two Witnesses' in the Damascus Document IX,17-22 and in Pharisaic-Rabbinic Law." *Revue de Qumran* 8: 197-217.
1975 *First-Century Judaism in Crisis: Yohanan ben Zakkai and the Renaissance of Torah.* Nashville: Abingdon Press.
1976 "'First Cleanse the Inside.'" *New Testament Studies* 22: 486-95.
1984 *Judaism in the Beginning of Christianity.* Philadelphia: Fortress Press.

1986 "Death-Scenes and Farewell Stories: An Aspect of the Master-Disciple Relationship in Mark and in Some Talmudic Tales." *Harvard Theological Review* 79: 187-96.

1987 "I cambiavalute nel tempio: la spiegazione della Mishnah." *Rivista Biblica* 35: 485-89. *(NTA)*

1998 "Foreword." Pp. xxv-xlvi in *Memory and Manuscript: Oral Tradition and Written Transmission in Rabbinic Judaism and Early Christianity,* with *Tradition and Transmission in Early Christianity.* By Birger Gerhardsson. Grand Rapids: Eerdmans.

Newport, Kenneth G. C.

1990 "A Note on the 'Seat of Moses' (Matthew 23:2)." *Andrews University Seminary Studies* 28: 53-58.

1991 "The Pharisees in Judaism Prior to A.D. 70." *Andrews University Seminary Studies* 29: 127-37.

Neyrey, Jerome H.

1991 "The Symbolic Universe of Luke-Acts: 'They Turn the World Upside Down.'" Pp. 271-304 in *The Social World of Luke-Acts: Models for Interpretation.* Edited by Jerome H. Neyrey. Peabody, MA: Hendrickson.

1994 "Josephus' *Vita* and the Encomium: A Native Model of Personality." *Journal for the Study of Judaism* 25 (2, 1994): 177-206.

Nicholson, E. W.

1965 "The Meaning of the Expression *'m h'rs* in the Old Testament." *Journal of Semitic Studies* 10: 59-66.

Nickle, Keith F.

1966 *The Collection: A Study in Biblical Theology.* Studies in Biblical Theoogy 48. Naperville, IL: Alec R. Allenson.

Nickelsburg, George W. E., Jr.

1972 "Eschatology in the Testament of Abraham: A Study of the Judgment Scene in the Two Recensions." Pp. 23-64 in *Studies on the Testament of Abraham.* Ed. George W. E. Nickelsburg, Jr. Society of Biblical Literature Septuagint and Cognate Studies 6. Missoula, MT: Scholars Press.

1980 "The Genre and Function of the Markan Passion Narrative." *Harvard Theological Review* 73: 153-84.

1981 *Jewish Literature between the Bible and the Mishnah.* Philadelphia: Fortress Press.

Niedner, Frederick A.

1989 "Rereading Matthew on Jerusalem and Judaism." *Biblical Theology Bulletin* 19: 43-47.

Nielsen, Helge Kjaer.

1990 "Er den 'dovne' tjener doven? Om oversaettelsen af ὀκνηρός i Matth 25,26." *Dansk Teologisk Tidsskrift* 53: 106-15. (*NTA* 35:27).

Nilsson, Martin Persson.

1948 *Greek Piety.* Translated by Herbert Jennings Rose. Oxford: Clarendon Press.

1957 *The Dionysiac Mysteries of the Hellenistic and Roman Age.* Skrifter Utgivna Av Svenska Institutet I Atheen, 8°, V. Lund: C. W. K. Gleerup.

Nineham, D. E.

1977 *Saint Mark.* Pelican New Testament Commentaries. Philadelphia: Westminster Press; London: SCM Press.

Nissen, Johannes.

1997 "The Distinctive Character of the New Testament Love Command in Relation to Hellenistic Judaism: Historical and Hermeneutical Reflections." Pp. 123-50 in *The New Testament and Hellenistic Judaism.* Edited by Peder Borgen and Søren Giversen. Peabody: Hendrickson.

Noack, Bent.

1957-1958 "Qumran and the Book of Jubilees." *Svensk Exegetisk Årsbok* 22-23: 191-207.

Nock, Arthur Darby

1933a *Conversion: The Old and the New in Religion from Alexander the Great to Augustine of Hippo.* Oxford: Clarendon Press.

1933b "The Vocabulary of the New Testament." *Journal of Biblical Literature* 52: 131-39.

1937 "The Genius of Mithraism." *Journal of Roman Studies* 27: 108-13.

1963 *St. Paul.* New York: Harper & Row.

1964a *Early Gentile Christianity and Its Hellenistic Background.* New York: Harper & Row.

1964b "Gnosticism." *Harvard Theological Review* 57: 255-79.

Nolland, John.

1979 "Proselytism or Politics in Horace *Satires* I.4, 138-143?" *Vigiliae Christianae* 33: 347-55.

1996 "What Kind of Genesis Do We Have in Matt 1.1?" *New Testament Studies* 42: 463-71.

1997 "The Four (Five) Women and Other Annotations in Matthew's Genealogy." *New Testament Studies* 43: 527-39.

North, Robert.

1958 "'Kittim' War or 'Sectaries' Liturgy?" *Biblica* 39: 84-93.

Nortjé, S. J.

1989 "John the Baptist and the Resurrection Traditions in the Gospels." *Neotestamentica* 23: 349-58.

Nowell, Irene.

1988 "Canonical Order." *The Bible Today* 26: 220-21.

Nukunya, G. K.

1969 *Kinship and Marriage among the Anlo Ewe.* London School of Economics Monographs on Social Anthropology 37. New York: Humanities Press.

Nun, Mendel.

1993 "Cast Your Net upon the Waters: Fish and Fishermen in Jesus' Time." *Biblical Archaeology Review* 19 (6, 1993): 46-56, 70.

Oakman, Douglas E.

1991 "The Countryside in Luke-Acts." Pp. 151-79 in *The Social World of Luke-Acts: Models for Interpretation.* Edited by Jerome H. Neyrey. Peabody: Hendrickson.

1992 "Was Jesus a Peasant? Implications for Reading the Samaritan Story." *Biblical Theology Bulletin* 22 (1992): 117-25.

Oberhelman, S.

1979 "A Survey of Dreams in Ancient Greece." *Classical Bulletin* 55: 36-40. (*NTA* 23:209)

O'Day, Gail R.

1989 "Surprised by Faith: Jesus and the Canaanite Woman." *Listening* 24: 290-301.

Odeberg, Hugo.
1964 *Pharisaism and Christianity.* Translated by J. M. Moe. St. Louis: Concordia. Swedish ed., 1943.

Oden, Robert A., Jr.
1976 "The Persistence of Canaanite Religion." *Biblical Archaeologist* 39.1: 31-36.

Oden, Thomas C., and Christopher A. Hall.
1998 *Mark.* Edited by Thomas C. Oden and Christopher A. Hall. Vol. 2 in *Ancient Christian Commentary on Scripture: New Testament.* Downers Grove, IL: InterVarsity Press. [cited in text as *ACCS*]

Oepke, Albrecht.
1967 "Ὄναρ." 5:220-38 in *Theological Dictionary of the New Testament.* 10 vols. Edited by Gerhard Kittel and Gerhard Friedrich. Grand Rapids: Eerdmans, 1964-1976.

Oesterley, William Oscar Emil.
1925 *The Jewish Background of the Christian Liturgy.* Oxford: Clarendon Press.

Olmstead, A. T.
1959 *History of the Persian Empire.* Chicago: Phoenix Books, The University of Chicago Press.

Omanson, Roger L.
1991 "A question of harmonization — Matthew 9.18-25." *Bible Translator* 42: 241.

O'Neal, W. J.
1978 "Delation in the Early Empire." *Classical Bulletin* 55: 24-28.

O'Neill, J. C.
1993 "The Lord's Prayer." *Journal for the Study of the New Testament* 51: 3-25.

Onwu, Nlenanya.
1988 "Righteousness and Eschatology in Matthew's Gospel: A Critical Reflection." *Indian Theological Studies* 25: 213-25.

O'Rourke, John J.
1971 "Roman Law and the Early Church." Pp. 165-86 in *The Catacombs and the Colosseum: The Roman Empire as the Setting of Primitive Christianity.* Edited by Stephen Benko and John J. O'Rourke. Valley Forge, PA: Judson Press.

Orton, David E.
1989 *The Understanding Scribe: Matthew and the Apocalyptic Ideal.* Journal for the Study of the New Testament Supplement 25. Sheffield: JSOT Press, Sheffield Academic Press.

Osborne, Robert E.
1973 "The Provenance of Matthew's Gospel." *Studies in Religion/Sciences Religieuses* 3: 220-35.

Osborne, Grant R.
1991 *The Hermeneutical Spiral: A Comprehensive Introduction to Biblical Interpretation.* Downers Grove: InterVarsity Press.
1992 "Redaction Criticism." Pp. 662-69 in *Dictionary of Jesus and the Gospels.* Edited by Joel B. Green, Scot McKnight, and I. Howard Marshall. Downers Grove, IL: InterVarsity Press.

Osten-Sacken, Peter von der.
1981 "Geist im Buchstaben. Vom Glanz des Mose und des Paulus." *Evangelische Theologie* 41 (3, 1981): 230-35.

Oster, Richard.
1982 "Numismatic Windows into the Social World of Early Christianity: A Methodological Inquiry." *Journal of Biblical Literature* 101: 195-223.
Ostling, Richard N.
1994 "Jesus Christ, Plain and Simple." *Time,* January 10: 32-33.
O'Toole, Robert F.
1978 *Acts 26: The Christological Climax of Paul's Defense (Acts 22:1–26:36).* Analecta Biblica 78. Rome: Biblical Institute Press.
Ottey, J. L.
1986 "'In a stable born our brother.'" *Expository Times* 98: 71-73.
Otto, Walter F.
1965 *Dionysus: Myth and Cult.* Translated by Robert B. Palmer. Bloomington: Indiana University Press.
Overman, John Andrew.
1989 "Matthew's Gospel and Formative Judaism: A Study of the Social World of the Matthean Community." Ph.D. dissertation, Boston University Graduate School. Ann Arbor, MI: University Microfilms, 1990.
1990a "Deciphering the Origins of Christianity." Review of *A Myth of Innocence: Mark and Christian Origins,* by Burton L. Mack. *Interpretation* 44: 193-95.
1990b *Matthew's Gospel and Formative Judaism: The Social World of the Matthean Community.* Minneapolis: Fortress Press.
1996 *Church and Community in Crisis: The Gospel according to Matthew.* The New Testament in Context. Valley Forge: Trinity Press International.
Owen-Ball, David T.
1993 "Rabbinic Rhetoric and the Tribute Passage (Mt. 22:15-22; Mk. 12:13-17; Lk. 20:20-26)." *Novum Testamentum* 35: 1-14.
Pace, Sharon.
1984 "The Stratigraphy of the Text of Daniel and the Question of Theological *Tendenz* in the Old Greek." *Bulletin of the International Organization for Septuagint and Cognate Studies* 17: 15-35.
Page, Sydney H. T.
1980 "The Authenticity of the Ransom Logion (Mark 10:45b)." Pp. 101-36 in *Gospel Perspectives: Studies of History and Tradition in the Four Gospels.* Edited by R. T. France and David Wenham. Vol. 1 in Gospel Perspectives, 6 vols. Sheffield: JSOT Press.
Palatty, Paul.
1986 "The Ascension of Christ in Lk-Acts (An exegetical critical study of Lk 24,50-53 and Acts 1,2-3, 9-11)." *Biblebhashyam* 12: 100-117.
Palmer, D.
1973 "Defining a Vow of Abstinence." *Colloquium* 5: 38-41.
Palmer, Darryl W.
1993 "Acts and the Ancient Historical Monograph." Pp. 1-29 in *The Book of Acts in Its Literary Setting.* Edited by Bruce W. Winter and Andrew D. Clarke. Vol. 1 in The Book of Acts in Its First Century Setting. Grand Rapids: Eerdmans; Carlisle: The Paternoster Press.
Pankhurst, Richard K. P., editor.
1967 *The Ethiopian Royal Chronicles.* Addis Ababa: Oxford University Press.
Papone, Paolo.
1990 "Il regno dei cieli soffre violenza? (Mt 11,12)." *Rivista Biblica* 38: 375-76. (*NTA* 35:159)

Parker, David.
1993 "The Early Traditions of Jesus' Sayings on Divorce." *Theology* 96: 372-83.
Parker, S. Thomas.
1975 "The Decapolis Reviewed." *Journal of Biblical Literature* 94: 437-41.
Parkes, James.
1979 *The Conflict of the Church and the Synagogue: A Study in the Origins of Antisemitism.* New York: Atheneum, Temple Books.
Parkhurst, L. G.
1979 "Matthew 28:16-20 Reconsidered." *Expository Times* 90: 179-80.
Parshall, Phil.
1983 *Bridges to Islam: A Christian Perspective on Folk Islam.* Grand Rapids: Baker.
Parsons, Talcott.
1971 "Kinship and the Associational Aspect of Social Structure." Pp. 409-38 in *Kinship and Culture.* Edited by Francis L. K. Hsu. Chicago: Aldine Publishing Company.
Paterson, J. H.
1982 "Galilee, Sea of." Pp. 403-4 in the *New Bible Dictionary.* 2d ed. Ed. J. D. Douglas and N. Hillyer. Downers Grove, IL: InterVarsity Press.
Patrich, Joseph.
1988 "Reconstructing the Magnificent Temple Herod Built." *Bible Review* 4 (5, 1988): 16-29.
1989 "Hideouts in the Judean Wilderness." *Biblical Archaeology Review* 15 (5, 1989): 32-42.
Patte, Daniel.
1975 *Early Jewish Hermeneutic in Palestine.* Society of Biblical Literature Dissertation Series 22. Missoula, MT: Scholars Press.
1976 *What Is Structural Exegesis?* Philadelphia: Fortress Press.
1987 *The Gospel according to Matthew: A Structural Commentary on Matthew's Faith.* Philadelphia: Fortress Press.
Patterson, Robert Leet.
1965 *Plato on Immortality.* University Park, PA: The Pennsylvania State University Press.
Paul, S. M.
1975 "Classifications of Wine in Mesopotamian and Rabbinic Sources." *Israel Exploration Journal* 25: 42-45.
Pawlikowski, John T.
1970 "The Pharisees and Christianity." *Bible Today* 49: 47-53.
Payne, J. Barton.
1962 *The Imminent Appearing of Christ.* Grand Rapids: Eerdmans.
Payne, Philip Barton.
1978 "The Order of Sowing and Ploughing in the Parable of the Sower." *New Testament Studies* 25: 123-29.
1980a "The Authenticity of the Parable of the Sower and Its Interpretation." 1:163-207 in *Gospel Perspectives: Studies of History and Tradition in the Four Gospels.* 6 vols. Edited by R. T. France, David Wenham, and Craig Blomberg. Sheffield: JSOT Press, University of Sheffield.
1980b "The Seeming Inconsistency of the Interpretation of the Parable of the Sower." *New Testament Studies* 26: 564-68.
1981a "The Authenticity of the Parables of Jesus." 2:329-44 in *Gospel Perspec-*

tives: Studies of History and Tradition in the Four Gospels. 6 vols. Edited by R. T. France, David Wenham, and Craig Blomberg. Sheffield: JSOT Press, University of Sheffield.

1981b "Jesus' Implicit Claim to Deity in His Parables." *Trinity Journal* n.s. 2: 3-23.

1983 "Midrash and History in the Gospels with Special Reference to R. H. Gundry's *Matthew.*" 3:177-215 in Gospel Perspectives. 6 vols. Edited by R. T. France, David Wenham, and Craig Blomberg. Sheffield: JSOT Press, 1980-1986. Vol. 3: *Studies in Midrash and Historiography.* Edited by R. T. France and David Wenham. Sheffield: JSOT Press.

Peachey, Claire.

1990 "Model Building in Nautical Archaeology. The Kinneret Boat." *Biblical Archaeologist* 53 (1, 1990): 46-53.

Pearlman, Moshe.

1967 *The Zealots of Masada.* New York: Charles Scribner's Sons.

Peisker, Carl Heinz.

1968 "Konsekutives ἵνα in Markus 4:12." *Zeitschrift für die Neutestamentliche Wissenschaft* 59: 126-27.

Pelikan, Jaroslav.

1980 "The Two Sees of Peter." Pp. 57-73 in *The Shaping of Christianity in the Second and Third Centuries.* Edited by E. P. Sanders. Philadelphia: Fortress Press. Vol. 1 in Jewish and Christian Self-Definition. 3 vols. Philadelphia: Fortress Press, 1980-1982.

Penney, Douglas L., and Michael O. Wise.

1994 "By the Power of Beelzebub: An Aramaic Incantation Formula from Qumran (4Q 560)." *Journal of Biblical Literature* 113: 627-50.

Pentecost, J. Dwight.

1958 "The Purpose of the Sermon on the Mount." *Bibliotheca Sacra* 115: 128-35, 212-17, 313-19.

Perdue, Leo G.

1990 "The Death of the Sage and Moral Exhortation: From Ancient Near Eastern Instructions to Greco-Roman Paraenesis." *Semeia* 50: 81-109.

Perkins, Pheme.

1991 "Gender Analysis: A Response to Antoinette Clark Wire." Pp. 122-26 in *Social History of the Matthean Community: Cross-Disciplinary Approaches.* Edited by David L. Balch. Minneapolis: Fortress Press.

Perrin, Norman.

1963 *The Kingdom of God in the Teaching of Jesus.* Philadelphia: Westminster Press.

1976a "The High Priest's Question and Jesus' Answer (Mark 14:61-62)." Pp. 80-95 in *The Passion in Mark: Studies in Mark 14–16.* Edited by Werner H. Kelber. Philadelphia: Fortress Press.

1976b *Jesus and the Language of the Kingdom: Symbol and Metaphor in New Testament Interpretation.* Philadelphia: Fortress Press.

Perry, Alfred Morris.

1920 *The Sources of Luke's Passion Narrative.* Chicago: University of Chicago Press.

Perry, Ben Edwin.

1965 "Introduction." Pp. xi-cii in Babrius and Phaedrus. Translated by Ben Edwin Perry. Loeb Classical Library. Cambridge: Harvard University Press.

Pesch, Rudolph.
1991 "The Gospel in Jerusalem: Mark 14:12-26 as the Oldest Tradition of the Early Church." Pp. 106-48 in *The Gospel and the Gospels.* Edited by Peter Stuhlmacher. Grand Rapids: Eerdmans.

Petersen, Norman R.
1978 *Literary Criticism for New Testament Critics.* Philadelphia: Fortress Press.

Petit, M.
1976 "À propos d'une traversée exemplaire du désert du Sinaï selon Philon (*Hypothetica* VI, 2-3.8): texte biblique et apologétique concernant Moïse chez quelques écrivains juifs." *Semitica* 26: 137-42.

Petrie, C. Stewart.
1959 "'Q' Is Only What You Make It." *Novum Testamentum* 3: 28-33.

Petrotta, Anthony J.
1985 "A Closer Look at Matt 2:6 and Its Old Testament Sources." *Journal of the Evangelical Theological Society* 28: 47-52.
1990 "An Even Closer Look at Matt 2:6 and Its Old Testament Sources." *Journal of the Evangelical Theological Society* 33: 311-15.

Petuchowski, Jacob J.
1968 "The Concept of 'Teshuvah' in the Bible and the Talmud." *Judaism* 17: 175-85.

Petuchowski, Jacob J., and M. Brocke, editors.
1978 *The Lord's Prayer and Jewish Liturgy.* New York: The Seabury Press.

Pfitzner, V. C.
1979 "The School of Jesus: Jesus-Traditions in Pauline Paranesis." *Lutheran Theological Journal* 13 (2, 1979): 22-36.
1982 "Purified Community — Purified Sinner, Expulsion from the community according to Matthew 18:15-18 and 1 Corinthians 5:1-5." *Australian Biblical Review* 30: 34-55.

Philonenko, Marc.
1965 "Initiation et mystère dans Joseph et Asénath." Pp. 147-53 in *Initiation: Contributions to the Theme of the Study-Conference of the International Association for the History of Religions,* held at Strasburg, September 17th to 22nd 1964. Edited by C. J. Bleeker. Studies in the History of Religions, Supplements to Numen 10. Leiden: E. J. Brill.
1975 "Un Mystère Juif?" Pp. 65-75 in *Mystères et Syncrétismes.* Études d'Histoire des Religions 2. Edited by M. Philonenko et M. Simon. Paris: Librairie Orientaliste Paul Geuthner.
1992 "La troisième demande du 'Notre Père' et l'hymne de Nabuchodonosor." *Revue d'Histoire et de Philosophie Religieuses* 72: 23-31.
1993 "Le sang du Juste (*1 Hénoch* 47,1.4; Matthieu 27,24)." *Revue d'Histoire et de Philosophie Religieuses* 73: 395-99.

Pilch, John J.
1989 "Reading Matthew Anthropologically: Healing in Cultural Perspective." *Listening* 24: 278-89.
1991 "Sickness and Healing in Luke-Acts." Pp. 181-209 in *The Social World of Luke-Acts: Models for Interpretation.* Edited by Jerome H. Neyrey. Peabody, MA: Hendrickson.
1992 "Lying and Deceit in the Letters to the Seven Churches." *Biblical Theology Bulletin* 22: 126-35.
1995 "The Bible's Sense of Humor." *Bible Today* 33: 353-58.

Pileggi, David.
1991 "The Bar-Kochva Letters." *Jerusalem Perspective* 4 (1, 1991): 9-11.
Pilgaard, Aage.
1997 "The Hellenistic *Theios Aner* — A Model for Early Christian Christology?" Pp. 101-22 in *The New Testament and Hellenistic Judaism.* Edited by Peder Borgen and Søren Giversen. Peabody: Hendrickson Publishers.
Pines, Shlomo.
1974 "From Darkness into Great Light." *Immanuel* 4: 47-51.
Piper, John.
1993 *Let the Nations Be Glad! The Supremacy of God in Missions.* Grand Rapids: Baker.
Pitt-Rivers, Julian.
1973 "The Kith and the Kin." Pp. 89-105 in *The Character of Kinship.* Edited by Jacky Goody. New York: Cambridge University Press.
Plank, K. A.
1979 "Reigning Victim, Threatened King: An Explanation of the King Parables of Shirata." *Judaica* 35: 172-83.
Plevnik, Joseph.
1979 "1 Thessalonians 5,1-11: Its Authenticity, Intention and Message." *Biblica* 60: 71-90.
Plummer, Alfred.
1910 *An Exegetical Commentary on the Gospel according to S. Matthew.* London: Elliot Stock.
Polag, Athanasius.
1991 "The Theological Center of the Sayings Source." Pp. 97-105 in *The Gospel and the Gospels.* Edited by Peter Stuhlmacher. Grand Rapids: Eerdmans.
Polish, David.
1970 "Pharisaism and Political Sovereignty." *Judaism* 19: 415-22.
Pomeroy, Sarah B.
1975 *Goddesses, Whores, Wives, and Slaves: Women in Classical Antiquity.* New York: Schocken Books.
Pope, Marvin H.
1988 "Hosanna — What It Really Means." *Bible Review* 4: 16-25.
Porter, Stanley E.
1988 "Vague Verbs, Periphrastics, and Matt 16:19." *Filologia Neotestamentaria* 1: 155-73.
1993 "Did Jesus Ever Teach in Greek?" *Tyndale Bulletin* 44: 199-235.
1994 "Excursus: The 'We' Passages." Pp. 545-74 in *The Book of Acts in Its Graeco-Roman Setting.* Edited by David W. J. Gill and Conrad Gempf. Vol. 2 in The Book of Acts in its First Century Setting. Grand Rapids: Eerdmans; Carlisle: The Paternoster Press.
Porton, Gary G.
1976 "The Grape-Cluster in Jewish Literature and Art of Late Antiquity." *Journal of Jewish Studies* 27: 159-76.
1981 "The Pronouncement Story in Tannaitic Literature: A Review of Bultmann's Theory." *Semeia* 20: 81-99.
Poulos, Paula Nassen.
1981 "Form and Function of the Pronouncement Story in Diogenes Laertius' *Lives.*" *Semeia* 20: 53-63.

Powell, Mark Allan.

1992 "Toward a Narrative-Critical Understanding of Matthew." *Interpretation* 46: 341-46.

1993 "Expected and Unexpected Readings of Matthew: What the Reader Knows." *Anglican Theological Review* 48.2: 31-52.

1995 *God with Us: A Pastoral Theology of Matthew's Gospel.* Minneapolis: Fortress Press.

1996 "Characterization on the Phraseological Plane in the Gospel of Matthew." Pp. 161-177 in *Treasures New and Old: Recent Contributions to Matthean Studies.* Edited by David R. Bauer and Mark Allan Powell. Society of Biblical Literature Symposium Series 1. Atlanta: Scholars Press.

Pregeant, Russell.

1996 "Wisdom Passages in Matthew." Pp. 197-232 in *Treasures New and Old: Recent Contributions to Matthean Studies.* Edited by David R. Bauer and Mark Allan Powell. Society of Biblical Literature Symposium Series 1. Atlanta: Scholars Press.

Pressel, Esther.

1974 "Umbanda Trance and Possession in São Paulo, Brazil." Pp. 113-225 in *Trance, Healing, and Hallucination: Three Field Studies in Religious Experience.* By Felicitas D. Goodman, Jeannette H. Henney, and Esther Pressel. New York: John Wiley & Sons.

Priest, John F.

1962 "Mebaqqer, Paqid, and the Messiah." *Journal of Biblical Literature* 81: 55-61.

1963 "The Messiah and the Meal in 1QSa." *Journal of Biblical Literature* 82: 95-100.

Prince, Raymond.

1964 "Indigenous Yoruba Psychiatry." Pp. 84-120 in *Magic, Faith, and Healing: Studies in Primitive Psychiatry Today.* Edited by Ari Kiev. Foreword by Jerome D. Frank. New York: Free Press.

Pritz, Ray A.

1988 *Nazarene Jewish Christianity: From the End of the New Testament Period until Its Disappearance in the Fourth Century.* Studia Postbiblica. Jerusalem-Leiden: Magnes Press, The Hebrew University, E. J. Brill.

1991 "'He Shall Be Called a Nazarene.'" *Jerusalem Perspective* 4: 3-4.

Pryke, E. J.

1978 *Redactional Style in the Marcan Gospel: A Study of Syntax and Vocabulary as Guides to Redaction in Mark.* Cambridge: Cambridge University Press.

Pryke, John.

1964 "John the Baptist and the Qumran Community." *Revue de Qumran* 4: 483-96.

1969 "Eschatology in the Dead Sea Scrolls." Pp. 45-57 in *The Scrolls and Christianity: Historical and Theological Significance.* Edited by Matthew Black. London: S.P.C.K.

Pryor, John W.

1991 "John 3.3, 5. A Study in the Relation of John's Gospel to the Synoptic Tradition." *Journal for the Study of the New Testament* 41: 71-95.

Przybylski, Benno.

1974 "The Role of Mt 3:13–4:11 in the Structure and Theology of the Gospel of Matthew." *Biblical Theology Bulletin* 4: 222-35.

1980 *Righteousness in Matthew and His World of Thought.* Society for New Testament Studies Monograph 41. Cambridge: Cambridge University Press.

Puech, Emile.

1993 *La croyance des Esséniens en la vie future: Immortalité, resurrection, Vie éternelle? Histoire d'un croyance dans le judaïsme ancien. II. Les données qumraniennes et classiques.* École biblique 22. Paris: Gabalda.

Puiggali, J.

1983 "La démonologie de Philostrate." *Revue des Sciences Philosophiques et Théologiques* 67: 117-30.

Pusey, Karen.

1984 "Jewish Proselyte Baptism." *Expository Times* 95: 141-45.

Quesnell, Quentin.

1969 *The Mind of Mark: Interpretation and Method through the Exegesis of Mark 6,52.* Analecta Biblica 38. Rome: Pontifical Biblical Institute.

Rabe, Virgil W.

1976 "Origins of Prophecy." *Bulletin of the American Schools of Oriental Research* 221: 125-28.

Rabello, Alfredo Mordechai.

1980 "The Legal Condition of the Jews in the Roman Empire." *Aufstieg und Niedergang der Römischen Welt* 2.13.662-762. Berlin: Walter de Gruyter.

Rabin, Chaim.

1956 "Alexander Jannaeus and the Pharisees." *Journal of Jewish Studies* 7: 3-11.

Radcliffe-Brown, A. R.

1950 "Introduction." Pp. 1-85 in *African Systems of Kinship and Marriage.* Edited by A. R. Radcliffe-Brown and Daryll Forde. New York: Oxford University Press.

1965 "Taboo." Pp. 72-83 in *Reader in Comparative Religion: An Anthropological Approach.* 3d ed. Edited by William A. Lessa and Evon Z. Vogt. New York: Harper & Row.

Rahmani, L. Y.

1978a "An Ancient Cast of a Cameo." *Israel Exploration Journal* 28: 83-85.

1978b "Glwsqmwt wlyqwt 'snwt bslhy tqwpt byt sny [Ossuaries and Bone-Gathering in the Late Second Temple Period]." *Qadmoniot* 11: 102-12. (*NTA* 24:53)

1981 "A Magic Amulet from Nahariyya." *Harvard Theological Review* 74: 387-90.

1982 "Ancient Jerusalem's Funerary Customs and Tombs. Part Four." *Biblical Archaeologist* 45: 109-19.

1986 "Some Remarks on R. Hachlili's and A. Killebrew's 'Jewish Funerary Customs.'" *Palestine Exploration Quarterly* 118: 96-100.

1990 "Stone Synagogue Chairs: Their Identification, Use and Significance." *Israel Exploration Journal* 40: 192-214, plates 19-21.

Räisänan, Heikki.

1982 "Jesus and the Food Laws: Reflections on Mark 7.15." *Journal for the Study of the New Testament* 16: 79-100.

Rajak, Tessa.

1978 "Moses in Ethiopia: Legend and Literature." *Journal of Jewish Studies* 29: 111-22.

1983 *Josephus: The Historian and His Society.* London: Gerald Duckworth & Company. Reprinted by Philadelphia: Fortress Press, 1984.

1984 "Was There a Roman Charter for the Jews?" *Journal of Roman Studies* 74 (1984): 107-23.

Rajak, Tessa, and D. Noy.

1993 "*Archisynogogoi*: Office, Title and Social Status in the Greco-Jewish Synagogue." *Journal of Roman Studies* 83: 75-93.

Ramaroson, Leonard.

1971 "Une nouvelle interprétation de la 'clausule' de Mt 19,9." *Science et Esprit* 23: 247-51.

1991 "'Notre part de nourriture' (Mt 6,11)." *Science et Esprit* 43: 87-115.

Ramirez, J. M. Casciaro.

1976 "El 'Misterio' divino en los escritos posteriores de Qumran." *Scripta Theologica* 8: 445-75. *(NTA)*

Ramsay, William M.

1897 *The Church in the Roman Empire.* 5th ed. London: Hodder & Stoughton. Reprinted by Grand Rapids: Baker, 1979.

1898 *Was Christ Born at Bethlehem? A Study on the Credibility of St. Luke.* Grand Rapids: Baker, 1979; originally, London: Hodder & Stoughton, 1898.

1904a *The Letters to the Seven Churches of Asia.* London: Hodder & Stoughton. Reprint: Grand Rapids: Baker, 1979.

1904b "Roads and Travel (in NT)." 5:375-402 in *The Dictionary of the Bible.* 5 vols. Edited by James Hastings. Edinburgh: T. & T. Clark; New York: Charles Scribner's Sons, 1898-1923.

1906 *Pauline and Other Studies in Early Church History.* New York: A. C. Armstrong & Son. Reprinted by Grand Rapids: Baker, 1979.

1908 *Luke the Physician and Other Studies in the History of Religion.* London: Hodder & Stoughton. Reprinted by Grand Rapids: Baker, 1979.

Rapske, Brian M.

1994 "Acts, Travel and Shipwreck." Pp. 1-47 in *The Book of Acts in Its Graeco-Roman Setting.* Edited by David W. J. Gill and Conrad Gempf. Vol. 2 in The Book of Acts in Its First Century Setting. 6 vols. Edited by Bruce W. Winter. Grand Rapids: Eerdmans; Carlisle: The Paternoster Press.

Rashidi, Runoko.

1988 "Africans in Early Asian Civilizations: A Historical Overview." Pp. 15-52 in *African Presence in Early Asia.* Edited by Ivan Van Sertima and Runoko Rashidi. New Brunswick, NJ: Transaction Books (Rutgers)/Journal of African Civilizations.

Rathey, Markus.

1991 "Talion im NT? Zu Mt 5,38-42." *Zeitschrift für die Neutestamentliche Wissenschaft* 82: 264-66.

Rawson, Beryl.

1986a "Children in the Roman *Familia.*" Pp. 170-200 in *The Family in Ancient Rome: New Perspectives.* Edited by Beryl Rawson. Ithaca, NY: Cornell University Press.

1986b "The Roman Family." Pp. 1-57 in *The Family in Ancient Rome: New Perspectives.* Edited by Beryl Rawson. Ithaca, NY: Cornell University Press.

Ray, Charles A., Jr.

1992 "The Beatitudes: Challenging Worldviews." *Theological Educator* 46: 97-104.

Raynor, D. H.
1984 "Moeragenes and Philostratus: Two Views of Apollonius of Tyana." *Classical Quarterly* 34: 222-26.

Reeves, Keith Howard.
1993 *The Resurrection Narrative in Matthew: A Literary-Critical Examination.* Lewiston, NY: Mellen Biblical Press.

Refoulé, François.
1993 "Jésus, nouveau Moïse, ou Pierre, nouveau Grand Prêtre? (Mt 17,1-9; Mc 9,2-10)." *Revue Théologique de Louvain* 24: 145-62.

Reich, Ronny.
1984 "A Miqweh at 'Isawiya near Jerusalem." *Israel Exploration Journal* 34: 220-23.
1989 "H'rh lpsyps hrwmy mmgdl 'sr lhwp ym-kynrt." *Qadmoniot* 22: 43-44. (*NTA* 34:213)
1991 "A Note on the Roman Mosaic at Magdala on the Sea of Galilee." *Studii Biblici Franciscani Liber Annuus* 41: 455-58.

Reicke, Bo.
1964 *The Epistles of James, Peter, and Jude.* The Anchor Bible 37. Garden City, NY: Doubleday & Company.
1974 *The New Testament Era: The World of the Bible from 500 B.C. to A.D. 100.* Translated by David E. Green. Philadelphia: Fortress Press.

Reiner, Erica.
1968 "Thirty Pieces of Silver." *Journal of the American Oriental Society* 88: 186-90.

Reinhold, Meyer.
1983 *Diaspora: The Jews among the Greeks and Romans.* Sarasota and Toronto: Samuel Stevens & Company.

Reitzenstein, Richard.
1978 *Hellenistic Mystery-Religions: Their Basic Ideas and Significance.* Translated by John E. Steely. Pittsburgh Theological Monograph Series 15. Edited by Dikran Y. Hadidian. Pittsburgh: The Pickwick Press.

Remus, Harold E.
1982 "'Magic or Miracle'? Some Second-Century Instances." *Second Century* 2: 127-56.

Renehan, Robert.
1973 "Classical Greek Quotations in the New Testament." Pp. 17-46 in *The Heritage of the Early Church: Essays in Honor of the Very Reverend Georges Vasilievich Florovsky.* Orientalia Christiana Analecta 195. Rome: Pontificium Institutum Studiorum Orientalium.

Rengstorf, Karl Heinrich.
1969 *Apostolate and Ministry.* St. Louis: Concordia Publishing House.

Rhoads, David M.
1992 "The Gospel of Matthew. The Two Ways: Hypocrisy or Righteousness." *Currents in Theology and Mission* 19: 453-61.

Rhoads, David, and Donald Michie.
1982 *Mark As Story: An Introduction to the Narrative of a Gospel.* Philadelphia: Fortress Press.

Richardson, Alan.
1958 *An Introduction to the Theology of the New Testament.* New York: Harper & Brothers.

Richardson, Peter, and Peter Gooch.
1984 "Logia of Jesus in 1 Corinthians." Pp. 39-62 in *The Jesus Tradition outside the Gospels.* Edited by David Wenham. Vol. 5 in Gospel Perspectives. Sheffield: JSOT Press.

Richlin, Amy.
1981 "Approaches to the Sources on Adultery at Rome." *Women's Studies* 8: 225-50.

Ridderbos, Herman N.
1953 *The Epistle of Paul to the Churches of Galatia.* Grand Rapids: Eerdmans.
1974 *Paul and Jesus.* Translated by David H. Freeman. Philadelphia: Presbyterian and Reformed Publishing Company.
1975 *Paul: An Outline of His Theology.* Translated by John Richard De Witt. Grand Rapids: Eerdmans.

Riesenfeld, Harald.
1964 "The Mythological Background of New Testament Christology." Pp. 81-95 in *The Background of the New Testament and Its Eschatology: Essays in Honor of Charles Harold Dodd.* Edited by W. D. Davies and D. Daube. Cambridge: Cambridge University Press.
1970 *The Gospel Tradition.* Philadelphia: Fortress Press.

Riesner, Rainer.
1982a "Education élémentaire juive et tradition évangélique." *Hokhma* 21: 51-64.
1982b "Der Ursprung der Jesus-Überlieferung." *Theologische Zeitschrift* 38.6: 493-513.
1984a *Jesus als Lehrer: Eine Untersuchung zum Ursprung der Evangelien-Überlieferung.* 2d ed. Wissenschaftliche Untersuchungen zum Neuen Testament. 2d series, 7. Tübingen: J. C. B. Mohr.
1984b "Johannes der Täufer auf Machärus." *Bibel und Kirche* 39: 176.
1985 "Golgotha und die Archäologie." *Bibel und Kirche* 40: 21-26.
1987 "Neues vom See Gennesaret." *Bibel und Kirche* 42: 171-73.

Riggans, Walter.
1987 "Romans 11:17-21." *Expository Times* 98: 205-6.

Ring, George C.
1944 "Christ's Resurrection and the Dying and Rising Gods." *Catholic Biblical Quarterly* 6: 216-29.

Ringgren, Helmer.
1963 *The Faith of Qumran.* Philadelphia: Fortress Press.

Rissi, Mathias.
1966 *Time and History: A Study on the Revelation.* Translated by Gordon C. Winsor. Richmond, VA: John Knox Press.

Rives, James B.
1998 "How Popular Were the 'Oriental Cults'?" Paper presented at the Society of Biblical Literature Convention, Orlando.

Rivkin, Ellis.
1969-1970 "Defining the Pharisees: The Tannaitic Sources." *Hebrew Union College Annual* 40-41: 205-49.
1971 "The Meaning of Messiah in Jewish Thought." *Union Seminary Quarterly Review* 26: 383-406.
1978 *A Hidden Revolution.* Nashville: Abingdon Press.
1982 "The Book of Jubilees — An Anti-Pharisaic Pseudepigraph?" *Erets-Yisrael* 16: 193-98.

Robbins, Vernon K.

1973 "The Healing of Blind Bartimaeus (10:46-52) in the Markan Theology." *Journal of Biblical Literature* 92: 224-43.

1976 "Last Meal: Preparation, Betrayal, and Absence (Mark 14:12-25)." Pp. 21-40 in *The Passion in Mark: Studies in Mark 14–16.* Edited by Werner H. Kelber. Philadelphia: Fortress Press.

1981 "Classifying Pronouncement Stories in Plutarch's *Parallel Lives.*" *Semeia* 20: 29-52.

1988 "The Chreia." Pp. 1-23 in *Greco-Roman Literature and the New Testament: Selected Forms and Genres.* Edited by David E. Aune. Society of Biblical Literature Sources for Biblical Study 21. Atlanta: Scholars Press.

1992 *Jesus the Teacher: A Socio-Rhetorical Interpretation of Mark.* Minneapolis: Augsburg Fortress Press.

1994 "Jewish and Greco-Roman Modes of Argumentation in Mark 7:1-23." Paper presented at the Society of Biblical Literature 1994 Annual Meeting, Chicago.

Roberts, J. J. M.

1970 "A New Parallel to I Kings 18$_{28\text{-}29}$." *Journal of Biblical Literature* 89: 76-77.

Roberts, R. L.

1963 "An Evil Eye (Matthew 6:23)." *Restoration Quarterly* 7: 143-47.

Robin, Arthur de Quetteville.

1962 "The Cursing of the Fig Tree in Mark XI. A Hypothesis." *New Testament Studies* 8: 276-81.

Robinson, James M.

1982 *The Problem of History in Mark and Other Marcan Studies.* Philadelphia: Fortress Press.

Robinson, John A. T.

1962 *Twelve New Testament Studies.* Studies in Biblical Theology 34. London: SCM Press.

1976 *Redating the New Testament.* Philadelphia: Westminster Press; London: SCM Press.

1977 *Can We Trust the New Testament?* Grand Rapids: Eerdmans.

1979 *Jesus and His Coming.* 2d ed. Philadelphia: Westminster Press.

1984 "'His witness is true': A test of the Johannine claim." Pp. 453-76 in *Jesus and the Politics of His Day.* Edited by Ernst Bammel and C. F. D. Moule. Cambridge: Cambridge University Press.

Rochberg-Halton, Francesca.

1984 "New Evidence for the History of Astrology." *Journal of Near Eastern Studies* 43: 115-40.

1988 "Elements of the Babylonian Contribution to Hellenistic Astrology." *Journal of the American Oriental Society* 108: 51-62.

1989 "Babylonian Horoscopes and Their Sources." *Orientalia* 58: 102-23.

Rodd, Cyril S.

1961 "Spirit or Finger." *Expository Times* 72: 157-58.

Rodríguez, José D.

1988 "The Parable of the Affirmative Action Employer." *Currents in Theology and Mission* 15: 418-24.

Rogers, Cleon.

1973 "The Great Commission." *Bibliotheca Sacra* 130: 258-67.

1993 "The Promises to David in Early Judaism." *Bibliotheca Sacra* 150: 285-302.

Rohrbaugh, Richard L.

1991 "The Pre-Industrial City in Luke-Acts: Urban Social Relations." Pp. 125-49 in *The Social World of Luke-Acts: Models for Interpretation.* Edited by Jerome H. Neyrey. Peabody, MA: Hendrickson.

1993 "A Peasant Reading of the Parable of the Talents/Pounds: A Text of Terror?" *Biblical Theology Bulletin* 23: 32-39.

Romaniuk, K.

1980 "'Józef, maz sprawiedliwy . . .' (Mt 1,19) ('Joseph, son époux, qui était un homme juste et ne voulait pas la dénoncer . . .' [Mt 1,19])." *Collectanea Theologica* 50: 25-34. (*NTA* 25:129)

Rook, John.

1990 "The Names of the Wives from Adam to Abraham in the Book of *Jubilees.*" *Journal for the Study of the Pseudepigrapha* 7 (1990): 105-17.

Ropes, James Hardy.

1916 *A Critical and Exegetical Commentary on the Epistle of St. James.* International Critical Commentary. Edinburgh: T & T Clark.

Rosner, Brian S.

1993 "Acts and Biblical History." Pp. 65-82 in *The Book of Acts in Its Ancient Literary Setting.* Edited by Bruce W. Winter and Andrew D. Clarke. Vol. 1 in The Book of Acts in Its First Century Setting. 6 vols. Grand Rapids: Eerdmans; Carlisle: Paternoster Press.

Ross, John M.

1978 "Epileptic or Moonstruck?" *Bible Translator* 29: 126-28.

1984 "Names of God: A comment on Mark 11.3 and parallels." *Bible Translator* 35: 443.

1987 "Which Zachariah?" *Irish Biblical Studies* 9: 70-73.

Ross, J.-P. B.

1976 "The Evolution of a Church — Jerusalem's Holy Sepulchre." *Biblical Archaeology Review* 2 (3, September): 3-8.

Rost, Leonhard.

1976 *Judaism outside the Hebrew Canon: An Introduction to the Documents.* Translated by David E. Green. Nashville: Abingdon Press.

Rostovzeff, Mikhail I.

1957 *The Social and Economic History of the Roman Empire.* 2d ed. Oxford: Clarendon Press.

Roth, Cecil.

1960a "The Cleansing of the Temple and Zechariah xiv 21." *Novum Testamentum* 4: 174-81.

1960b "The Subject Matter of Qumran Exegesis." *Vetus Testamentum* 10: 51-68.

1960c "A Talmudic Reference to the Qumran Sect?" *Revue de Qumran* 2: 261-65.

Roth, Wolfgang.

1992 "Moses and Matthew." *Bible Today* 30: 362-66.

Rousselle, Robert.

1985 "Healing Cults in Antiquity: The Dream Cures of Asclepius of Epidauros." *Journal of Psychohistory* 12 (3, Winter 1985): 339-52.

Roux, Hébert.

1956 *L'Evangile du Royaume: Commentaire sur l'Evangile selon saint Matthieu.* 2d ed. Genève: Editions Labor et Fides.

Rowley, H. H.

1940 "Jewish Proselyte Baptism and the Baptism of John." *Hebrew Union College Annual* 15: 313-34.

1956a "4QpNahum and the Teacher of Righteousness." *Journal of Biblical Literature* 75: 188-93.

1956b "The Kittim and the Dead Sea Scrolls." *Palestine Exploration Quarterly* 88: 92-109.

Rubenstein, Richard L.

1963 "Scribes, Pharisees and Hypocrites. A Study in Rabbinic Psychology." *Judaism* 12: 456-68.

Ruck, Carl A. P.

1978 "Solving the Eleusinian Mystery." Pp. 35-50 in *The Road to Eleusis: Unveiling the Secret of the Mysteries.* By Robert Gordon Wasson, Albert Hofmann, and Car A. P. Ruck. New York: A Helen and Kurt Wolff Book, Harcourt Brace Jovanovich.

Rüger, Hans Peter.

1969 "'Mit welchem Mass ihr messt, wird Ruch gemessen werden.'" *Zeitschrift für die Neutestamentliche Wissenschaft* 60: 174-82.

Runnalls, Donna.

1983 "Moses' Ethiopian Campaign." *Journal for the Study of Judaism* 14: 135-56.

Russell, D. S.

1964 *The Method and Message of Jewish Apocalyptic.* Philadelphia: Westminster Press.

1993 "Countdown: Arithmetic and Anagram in Early Biblical Interpretation." *Expository Times* 104 (4, 1993): 109-13.

Russell, Elbert.

1932 "Possible Influence of the Mysteries on the Form and Interrelation of the Johannine Writings." *Journal of Biblical Literature* 51: 336-51.

Rutenbar, Culbert Gerow.

1946 "The Doctrine of the Imitation of God in Plato." Ph.D. dissertation. University of Pennsylvania Press. Published by Columbia University Press.

Ryan, Thomas J.

1978 "Matthew 15:29-31: An Overlooked Summary." *Horizons* 5: 31-42.

Sabatowich, Jerome J.

1987 "Christian Divorce and Remarriage." *Bible Today* 25: 253-55.

Sabourin, Leopold.

1977 "'You will not have gone through all the towns of Israel, before the Son of Man comes' (Mat 10:23b)." *Biblical Theology Bulletin* 7: 5-11.

Sachs, Abraham J., and C. B. F. Walker.

1984 "Kepler's View of the Star of Bethlehem and the Babylonian Almanac for 7/6 B.C." *Iraq* 46: 43-55, plates 1-2. (*NTA* 32:301)

Safrai, S.

1974/1976a "Education and the Study of the Torah." Pp. 945-70 in *The Jewish People in the First Century: Historical Geography, Political History, Social, Cultural, and Religious Life and Institutions.* 2 vols. Edited by S. Safrai and M. Stern with D. Flusser and W. C. van Unnik. Section 1 of Compendia Rerum Iudaicarum ad Novum Testamentum. Vol. 1: Assen: Van Gorcum & Co., B.V.; Vol. 2: Philadelphia: Fortress Press.

1974/1976b "Home and Family." Pp. 728-92 in *The Jewish People in the First Century: Historical Geography, Political History, Social, Cultural, and Religious Life and Institutions.* 2 vols. Edited by S. Safrai and M. Stern with D. Flusser and W. C. van Unnik. Section 1 of Compendia Rerum Iudaicarum ad Novum Testamentum. Vol. 1: Assen: Van Gorcum & Co., B.V.; Vol. 2: Philadelphia: Fortress Press.

1974/1976c "Jewish Self-government." Pp. 377-419 in *The Jewish People in the First Century: Historical Geography, Political History, Social, Cultural, and Religious Life and Institutions.* 2 vols. Edited by S. Safrai and M. Stern with D. Flusser and W. C. van Unnik. Section 1 of Compendia Rerum Iudaicarum ad Novum Testamentum. Vol. 1: Assen: Van Gorcum & Co., B.V.; Vol. 2: Philadelphia: Fortress Press.

1974/1976d "Religion in Everyday Life." Pp. 793-833 in *The Jewish People in the First Century: Historical Geography, Political History, Social, Cultural, and Religious Life and Institutions.* 2 vols. Edited by S. Safrai and M. Stern with D. Flusser and W. C. van Unnik. Section 1 of Compendia Rerum Iudaicarum ad Novum Testamentum. Vol. 1: Assen: Van Gorcum & Co., B.V.; Vol. 2: Philadelphia: Fortress Press.

1974/1976e "The Synagogue." Pp. 908-44 in *The Jewish People in the First Century: Historical Geography, Political History, Social, Cultural, and Religious Life and Institutions.* 2 vols. Edited by S. Safrai and M. Stern with D. Flusser and W. C. van Unnik. Section 1 of Compendia Rerum Iudaicarum ad Novum Testamentum. Vol. 1: Assen: Van Gorcum & Co., B.V.; Vol. 2: Philadelphia: Fortress Press.

1974/1976f "The Temple." Pp. 865-907 in *The Jewish People in the First Century: Historical Geography, Political History, Social, Cultural, and Religious Life and Institutions.* 2 vols. Edited by S. Safrai and M. Stern with D. Flusser and W. C. van Unnik. Section 1 of Compendia Rerum Iudaicarum ad Novum Testamentum. Vol. 1: Assen: Van Gorcum & Co., B.V.; Vol. 2: Philadelphia: Fortress Press.

1991a "Literary Languages in the Time of Jesus." *Jerusalem Perspective* 4 (2, 1991): 3-9.

1991b "Spoken Languages in the Time of Jesus." *Jerusalem Perspective* 4 (1, 1991): 3-8, 13.

Safrai, S., and David Flusser.

1976 "The Slave of Two Masters." *Immanuel* 6: 30-33.

Saldarini, Anthony J.

1977 "Last Words and Deathbed Scenes in Rabbinic Literature." *Jewish Quarterly Review* 68: 28-45.

1991 "The Gospel of Matthew and Jewish-Christian Conflict." Pp. 38-61 in *Social History of the Matthean Community: Cross-Disciplinary Approaches.* Edited by David L. Balch. Minneapolis: Fortress Press.

1992 "Delegitimation of Leaders in Matthew 23." *Catholic Biblical Quarterly* 54: 659-80.

1994 *Matthew's Christian-Jewish Community.* Chicago Studies in the History of Judaism. Chicago: The University of Chicago Press.

Salerno, A.

1980 "Un nuovo aspetto del primato di Pietro in Mt. 10,2 e 16, 18-19." *Rivista Biblica* 28: 435-39. *(NTA)*

Saller, Richard P.

1987 "Men's Age at Marriage and Its Consequences in the Roman Family." *Classical Philology* 82: 21-34.

Salomonsen, Børge.

1964 "Nogle synspunkter fra den nyere debat omkring zeloterne." *Dansk Teologisk Tidsskrift* 27: 149-62. *(NTA)*

1966 "Some Remarks on the Zealots with Special Regard to the Term 'Qannaim' in Rabbinic Literature." *New Testament Studies* 12: 164-76.

Sánchez, S.

1976 "Los 'daimones' del mundo helénico." *Biblia y Fe* 2.4: 47-59. (*NTA* 20:345)

Sanders, Boykin.

1995 "In Search of a Face for Simon the Cyrene." Pp. 51-63 in *The Recovery of Black Presence: An Interdisciplinary Exploration, Essays in Honor of Dr. Charles B. Copher.* Nashville: Abingdon Press.

Sanders, Cheryl J.

1995 "Black Women in Biblical Perspective: Resistance, Affirmation, and Empowerment." Pp. 121-43 in *Living the Intersection: Womanism and Afrocentrism in Theology.* Edited by Cheryl J. Sanders. Minneapolis: Fortress Press.

Sanders, E. P.

1969 *The Tendencies of the Synoptic Tradition.* Society for New Testament Studies Monograph 9. Cambridge: Cambridge University Press.

1977 *Paul and Palestinian Judaism.* Philadelphia: Fortress Press.

1985 *Jesus and Judaism.* Philadelphia: Fortress Press.

1990 *Jewish Law from Jesus to the Mishnah: Five Studies.* London: SCM Press; Philadelphia: Trinity Press International.

1992 *Judaism: Practice and Belief, 63 BCE–66 CE.* London: SCM Press; Philadelphia: Trinity Press International.

1993 *The Historical Figure of Jesus.* New York: Allen Lane, Penguin Press.

Sanders, E. P., and Margaret Davies.

1989 *Studying the Synoptic Gospels.* London: SCM Press; Philadelphia: Trinity Press International.

Sanders, J. N.

1968 *A Commentary on the Gospel according to St. John.* Edited and completed by B. A. Mastin. Harper's New Testament Commentaries. New York: Harper & Row.

Sandmel, Samuel.

1958 *The Genius of Paul.* New York: Farrar, Straus & Cudahy.

1978a *Anti-Semitism in the New Testament?* Philadelphia: Fortress Press.

1978b *Judaism and Christian Beginnings.* New York: Oxford University Press.

Satterthwaite, Philip E.

1993 "Acts against the Background of Classical Rhetoric." Pp. 337-79 in *The Book of Acts in Its Ancient Literary Setting.* Edited by Bruce W. Winter and Andrew D. Clarke. Vol. 1 in The Book of Acts in Its First Century Setting. 6 vols. Grand Rapids: Eerdmans; Carlisle: Paternoster.

Saulnier, Chritiane.

1984 "Hérode Antipas et Jean le Baptiste. Quelques remarques sur les confusions chronologiques de Flavius Josèphe." *Revue Biblique* 91: 362-76.

1989 "Flavius Josèphe et la propagande flavienne." *Revue Biblique* 96: 545-62.

1991 "Flavius Josèphe et la propagande flavienne." *Revue Biblique* 98 (2, 1991): 199-221.

Saunders, Ernest W.
1977 "Christian Synagogues and Jewish-Christianity in Galilee." *Explorations* 3: 70-77.
Sawyer, George S.
1858 *Southern Institutes; or, An Inquiry into the Origin and Early Prevalence of Slavery and the Slave-Trade.* Philadelphia: J. B. Lippincott.
Scaer, Donald P.
1991 "The Relation of Matthew 28:16-20 to the Rest of the Gospel." *Concordia Theological Quarterly* 55: 245-66.
Schaberg, Jane.
1982 *The Father, the Son and the Holy Spirit: The Triadic Phrase in Matthew 28:19b.* Society of Biblical Literature Dissertation 61. Chico: Scholars Press.
1985 "Daniel 7.12 and the New Testament Passion-Resurrection Predictions." *New Testament Studies* 31: 208-22.
Schäfer, Peter.
1975 "Die Sogenannte Synode von Jabne: zur Trennung von Juden und Christen in ersten/zweiten Jh. n. Chr." *Judaica* 31: 54-64.
Schapera, Isaac.
1950 "Kinship and Marriage among the Tswana." Pp. 140-65 in *African Systems of Kinship and Marriage.* Edited by A. R. Radcliffe-Brown and Daryll Forde. New York: Oxford University Press.
1966 *Married Life in an African Tribe.* Evanston: Northwestern University Press.
Schattenmann, Johannes.
1979 "Jesus und Pythagoras." *Kairos* 21: 215-20.
Schechter, Solomon.
1900 "Some Rabbinic Parallels to the New Testament." *Jewish Quarterly Review* 12: 415-33.
1961 *Aspects of Rabbinic Theology.* New York: Schocken Books; originally, n.p.: Macmillan Company, 1909.
Schedl, Claus.
1981 "Fragen zur revidierten Einheits Übersetzung. Nochmals 'für 'die Vielen' oder 'für alle'?" *Bibel und Liturgie* 54: 226-28.
1982 "Zur Ehebruchklausel der Bergpredigt im Lichte der neugefundenen Tempelrolle." *Theologische-Praktische Quartalschrift* 130: 362-65.
Schierling, Marla J.
1980 "Women as Leaders in the Marcan Communities." *Listening* 15: 250-56.
Schiffman, Lawrence H.
1979 "Communal Meals at Qumran." *Revue de Qumran* 10: 45-56.
1981 "At the Crossroads: Tannaitic Perspectives on the Jewish Christian Schism." 2:115-56 in *Jewish and Christian Self-Definition.* 3 vols, 1980-1982. Edited by E. P. Sanders. Philadelphia: Fortress Press.
1983 *Sectarian Law in the Dead Sea Scrolls: Courts, Testimony and the Penal Code.* Brown Judaic Studies 33. Chico: Scholars Press.
1985 *Who Was a Jew? Rabbinic and Halakhic Perspectives on the Jewish Christian Schism.* Hoboken, NJ: KTAV.
1986 "The Dead Sea Scrolls and the Early History of Jewish Liturgy." Pp. 33-48 in *The Synagogue in Late Antiquity.* Edited by Lee I. Levine. Philadelphia: The American Schools of Oriental Research.
1993 "*4QMysteries*^{b}, A Preliminary Edition." *Revue de Qumran* 16: 203-23.

Schineller, Peter.

1992 "Women in the Gospels." *Emmanuel* 98: 256-61.

Schlatter, Adolf.

1929 *Der Evangelist Matthäus.* Stuttgart: Calwer.

Schlegel, Alice.

1972 *Male Dominance and Female Autonomy: Domestic Authority in Matrilineal Societies.* Foreword by Raoul Naroll. N.p.: Human Relations Area Files Press.

Schlier, Heinrich.

1961 *Principalities and Powers in the New Testament.* New York: Herder & Herder.

Schluntz, Erika L.

1998 "'Protectress of Petra': Isis and Popular Cult in Nabataean Petra." Paper presented to the Society of Biblical Literature, Orlando 1998.

Schmeller, Thomas.

1992 "Der Weg der Jesusbotschaft in die Städte." *Bibel und Kirche* 47: 18-24.

Schmidt, K. E.

1964 "Folk Psychiatry in Sarawak: A Tentative System of Psychiatry of the Iban." Pp. 139-55 in *Magic, Faith, and Healing: Studies in Primitive Psychotherapy Today.* Edited by Ari Kiev. Introduction by Jerome D. Frank. New York: The Free Press; A Division of Macmillan Publishing Company.

Schmidt, K. L.

1923 "Die Stellung der Evangelien in der allgemeinen Literaturgeschichte." Pp. 59-60 in *ΕΥΧΑΡΙΣΤΗΡΙΟΝ: Studien zur Religion und Literatur des Alten und Neuen Testaments,* Festschrift für Hermann Gunkel. Edited by K. L. Schmidt. Forschungen zur Religion und Literatur des Alten und Neuen Testaments 19.2. Göttingen: Vandenhoeck & Ruprecht.

Schmidt, Thomas Ewald.

1983 "Hostility to Wealth in Philo of Alexandria." *Journal for the Study of the New Testament* 19: 85-97.

1988 "Burden, Barrier, Blasphemy: Wealth in Matt 6:33, Luke 14:33, and Luke 16:15." *Trinity Journal* 9: 171-89.

Schmidt, V.

1982 "Apuleius *Met.* III 15f. Die Einweihung in die falschen Mysterien (Apuleiana Groningana VII)." *Mnemosyne* 35: 269-82.

Schmithals, Walter.

1969 *The Office of Apostle in the Early Church.* Translated by John E. Steely. Nashville: Abingdon Press.

Schmitt, Götz.

1978 "Das Zeichen des Jona." *Zeitschrift für die Neutestamentliche Wissenschaft* 69: 123-29.

Schnackenburg, Rudolf.

1968-1982 *The Gospel according to St John.* 3 vols. Vol. 1: Translated by Kevin Smyth. Edited by J. M. Ford and Kevin Smyth. New York: Herder & Herder, 1968. Vol. 2: New York: The Seabury Press, A Crossroad Book, 1980. Vol. 3: New York: Crossroad Publishing Company, 1982.

1985 *Matthäusevangelium 1,1–16,20.* Die Neue Echter Bibel. Kommentar zum Neuen Testament mit der Einheitsübersetzung, Band 1. Würzburg: Echter-Verlag.

1996 "Matthew's Gospel as a Test Case for Hermeneutical Reflection." Pp. 251-

69 in *Treasures New and Old: Recent Contributions to Matthean Studies.* Edited by David R. Bauer and Mark Allan Powell. Society of Biblical Literature Symposium Series 1. Atlanta: Scholars Press.

Schneider, Gerhard.

1984 "The political charge against Jesus (Luke 23:2)." Pp. 403-14 in *Jesus and the Politics of His Day.* Edited by Ernst Bammel and C. F. D. Moule. Cambridge: Cambridge University Press.

Schneider, H. P.

1962 "Some Reflections on the Dialogue of Justin Martyr with Trypho." *Scottish Journal of Theology* 15: 164-75.

Schniedewind, W. M.

1994 "King and Priest in the Book of Chronicles and the Duality of Qumran Messianism." *Journal of Jewish Studies* 45: 71-78.

Schoedel, William R.

1991 "Ignatius and the Reception of the Gospel of Matthew in Antioch." Pp. 129-77 in *Social History of the Matthean Community: Cross-Disciplinary Approaches.* Edited by David L. Balch. Minneapolis: Fortress Press.

Schoeps, Hans Joachim.

1950 "Die jüdischen Prophetenmorde." Pp. 126-43 in *Aus frühchristlichen Zeit: Religionsgeschichtliche Untersuchungen.* Tübingen: J. C. B. Mohr.

1960 "Ebionitische Apokalyptik im Neuen Testament." *Zeitschrift für die Neutestamentliche Wissenschaft* 51: 101-11.

1961a *Israel und Christenheit.* Munich: Ner Tamid.

1961b *Paul: The Theology of the Apostle in the Light of Jewish Religious History.* Philadelphia: Westminster Press.

1963 *The Jewish-Christian Argument: A History of Theologies in Conflict.* Translated by David E. Green. New York: Holt, Rinehart & Winston; London: Faber & Faber, 1965.

Scholem, Gershom.

1973 *Sabbatai Sevi: The Mystical Messiah.* Princeton: Princeton University Press.

Schottroff, Luise.

1991 "Wanderprophetinnen. Eine feministische Analyse der Logienquelle." *Evangelische Theologie* 51: 332-44.

Schroer, S.

1986 "Der Geist, die Weisheit und die Taube. Feministischkritische Exegese eines neutestamentlichen Symbols auf dem Hintergrund seiner altorientalischen und hellenistich-frujüdischen Traditionsgeschichte." *Freiburger Zeitschrift für Philosophie und Theologie* 33: 197-225.

Schubert, Kurt.

1971 "Ehescheidung im Judentum zur Zeit Jesu." *Theologische Quartalschrift* 151: 23-27.

1981 "Sacra Sinagoga — Zur Heiligkeit der Synagoge in der Spätantike." *Bibel und Liturgie* 54.1: 27-34.

1984 "Biblical criticism criticized: with reference to the Markan report of Jesus' examination before the Sanhedrin." Pp. 385-402 in *Jesus and the Politics of His Day.* Edited by Ernst Bammel and C. F. D. Moule. Cambridge: Cambridge University Press.

Schürer, Emil.

1961 *A History of the Jewish People in the Time of Jesus.* Edited by Nahum Glatzer. New York: Schocken Books.

Schürmann, Heinz.

1960 "'Wer daher eines dieser geringsten Gebote auflöst . . .' Wo fand Matthäus das Logion Mt 5,19?" *Biblische Zeitschrift* 4: 238-50.

Shuler, Philip L.

1982 *A Genre for the Gospels: The Biographical Character of Matthew.* Philadelphia: Fortress Press.

Schuller, Eileen.

1989 "Ideas of Resurrection in Intertestamental Sources." *Bible Today* 27 (3, 1989): 140-45.

Schwank, Benedikt.

1987 "Die neuen Grabungen in Sepphoris." *Erbe und Auftrag* 63: 222-25; *Bibel und Kirche* 42: 75-79.

Schwartz, Daniel R.

1979 "The Three Temples of 4QFlorilegium." *Revue de Qumran* 10: 83-91.

Schwartz, Joshua.

1988 "On Priests and Jericho in the Second Temple Period." *Jewish Quarterly Review* 79: 23-48.

Schwarz, Günther.

1980 *"Prostheinai epi ten helikian autou pechyn hena." Zeitschrift für die Neutestamentliche Wissenschaft* 71: 244-47.

1981 *"Aphes tou nekrous thapsai tous heauton nekrous." Zeitschrift für die Neutestamentliche Wissenschaft* 72: 272-76.

1992 "'Seiner Nahrung' oder 'seines Lohnes'? (Mt 10,10e/Lk 10,7c)." *Biblische Notizen* 65: 40-41.

1996 "'Ein Rohr, vom Wind bewegt'? (Matthäus 11,7 par. Lukas 7,24)." *Biblische Notizen* 83: 19-21.

Schweizer, Eduard.

1955 "Discipleship and Belief in Jesus as Lord from Jesus to the Hellenistic Church." *New Testament Studies* 2: 87-99.

1963 "The Son of Man Again." *New Testament Studies* 9: 256-61.

1970 *The Good News according to Mark.* Atlanta: John Knox Press.

1971 *Jesus.* Translated by David E. Green. New Testament Library. London: SCM Press.

1975 *The Good News according to Matthew.* Translated by David E. Green. Atlanta: John Knox.

1995 "Matthew's Church (1974)." Pp. 149-77 in *The Interpretation of Matthew.* 2d ed. Edited by Graham Stanton. Edinburgh: T & T Clark.

Schweitzer, Albert.

1968 *The Quest of the Historical Jesus.* Introduction by James M. Robinson. Translated by W. Montgomery from 1906 ed. New York: Macmillan & Company.

Schwienhorst-Schönberger, L.

1990 "'Auge um Auge, Zahn um Zahn.' Zu einem antijüdischem Klischee." *Bibel und Liturgie* 63: 163-75.

Scobie, Charles H. H.

1969 "John the Baptist." Pp. 58-69 in *The Scrolls and Christianity: Historical and Theological Significance.* Edited by Matthew Black. London: S.P.C.K.

Scott, Bernard Brandon.

1989 *Hear Then the Parable: A Commentary on the Parables of Jesus.* Minneapolis: Augsburg Fortress Press.

Scott, Bernard Brandon, and Margaret E. Dean.

1996 "A Sound Map of the Sermon on the Mount." Pp. 311-78 in *Treasures New and Old: Recent Contributions to Matthean Studies.* Edited by David R. Bauer and Mark Allan Powell. Society of Biblical Literature Symposium Series 1. Atlanta: Scholars Press.

Scott, David.

1986 "Buddhist attitudes to Hellenism: A review of the issue." *Studies in Religion/Sciences Religieuses* 15: 433-41.

Scott, James M.

1994 "Luke's Geographical Horizon." Pp. 483-544 in *The Book of Acts in Its Graeco-Roman Setting.* Edited by David W. J. Gill and Conrad Gempf. Vol. 2 in The Book of Acts in Its First Century Setting. 6 vols. Edited by Bruce W. Winter. Grand Rapids: Eerdmans; Carlisle: The Paternoster Press.

Scott, J. Julius.

1990 "Gentiles and the Ministry of Jesus: Further Observations on Matt 10:5-6; 15:21-28." *Journal of the Evangelical Theological Society* 33: 161-69.

1995 *Customs and Controversies.* Grand Rapids: Baker.

Scott, R. B. Y.

1959 "'Behold, He Cometh with Clouds.'" *New Testament Studies* 5: 127-32.

Scroggs, Robin.

1980 "The Sociological Interpretation of the New Testament: The Present State of Research." *New Testament Studies* 26: 164-79.

Seccombe, David.

1978 "Was There Organized Charity in Jerusalem before the Christians?" *Journal of Theological Studies* 29: 140-43.

Segal, Alan F.

1981 "Ruler of This World: Attitudes about Mediator Figures and the Importance of Sociology for Self-Definition." 2:245-68 in *Jewish and Christian Self-Definition.* 3 vols, 1980-1982. Edited by E. P. Sanders. Philadelphia: Fortress Press.

1985 "Covenant in rabbinic writings." *Studies in Religion/Sciences Religieuses* 14: 53-62.

1991 "Matthew's Jewish Voice." Pp. 3-37 in *Social History of the Matthean Community: Cross-Disciplinary Approaches.* Edited by David L. Balch. Minneapolis: Fortress Press.

Segal, J. B.

1963 *The Hebrew Passover from the Earliest Times to A.D. 70.* London Oriental Series 12. New York: Oxford University Press.

Segal, Peretz.

1989a "The 'Divine Death Penalty' in the Hatra Inscriptions and the Mishnah." *Journal of Jewish Studies* 40: 46-52.

1989b "The Penalty of the Warning Inscription from the Temple of Jerusalem." *Israel Exploration Journal* 39: 79-84.

Seitz, Oscar Jacob Frank.

1969 "Love Your Enemies." *New Testament Studies* 16: 39-54.

Select Papyri.

1932-1935 Translated by A. S. Hunt and C. C. Edgar. 5 vols. The Loeb Classical Library. Cambridge: Harvard University Press.

Selvidge, Marla Schierling.
1984 "Mark 5:25-34 and Leviticus 15:19-20: A Reaction to Restrictive Purity Regulations." *Journal of Biblical Literature* 103: 619-23.

Senior, Donald.
1983 *What Are They Saying about Matthew?* New York: Paulist Press.
1987 "Matthew's Special Material in the Passion Story: Implications for the Evangelist's Redactional Technique and Theological Perspective." *Ephemerides Theologicae Lovanienses* 63: 272-94.

Serban, Ioan, and Closca L. Baluta.
1979 "On Mithraism in the Army of Dacia Superior." Pp. 573-78 in *Mysteria Mithrae*. Edited by Ugo Bianchi. Études Préliminaires aux Religions Orientales dans l'Empire Romain tome 80. Publiées par M. J. Vermaseren. Leiden: E. J. Brill.

Setzer, Claudia J.
1994 *Jewish Responses to Early Christians: History and Polemics, 30-150 C.E.* Minneapolis: Fortress Press.

Sevenster, J. N.
1968 *Do You Know Greek? How Much Greek Could the First Jewish Christians Have Known?* Supplements to Novum Testamentum 19. Leiden: E. J. Brill.
1975 *The Roots of Pagan Anti-Semitism in the Ancient World.* Supplements to Novum Testamentum 41. Leiden: E. J. Brill.

Shanks, Herschel.
1984 "Synagogue Excavation Reveals Stunning Mosaic of Zodiac and Torah Ark." *Biblical Archaeology Review* 10: 32-44.

Sharma, A.
1973 "Matthew 16:13-16 — An Exegetical Study." *Jeevadhara* 3: 187-94. *(NTA)*

Shaw, Brent D.
1987 "The Age of Roman Girls at Marriage: Some Reconsiderations." *Journal of Roman Studies* 77 (1987): 30-46.

Shedinger, R. F.
1997 "The Textual Relationship between P^{45} and Shem-Tob's Hebrew Matthew." *New Testament Studies* 43: 58-71.

Shepherd, Massey H.
1961 "Are Both the Synoptics and John Correct about the Date of Jesus' Death?" *Journal of Biblical Literature* 80: 123-32.

Sherk, Robert K., editor and translator
1988 *The Roman Empire: Augustus to Hadrian.* Translated Documents of Greece and Rome, 6. New York: Cambridge University Press.

Sherwin-White, A. N.
1965 "The Trial of Christ." Pp. 97-116 in *Historicity and Chronology in the New Testament.* Essays by D. E. Nineham, et al. London: S.P.C.K.
1978 *Roman Society and Roman Law in the New Testament.* Grand Rapids: Baker. Originally, Oxford: Oxford University Press, 1963.

Shimoff, Sandra R.
1993 "David and Bathsheba: The Political Function of Rabbinic Aggada." *Journal for the Study of Judaism* 24: 246-56.

Shirock, Robert J., Jr.
1992 "Whose Exorcists Are They? The Referents of οἱ υἱοὶ ὑμῶν at Matthew 12.27/Luke 11.19." *Journal for the Study of the New Testament* 46: 41-51.

Shoemaker, Michael T.

1991 "Herod's Lady's Earring?" *Biblical Archaeology Review* 17 (4, 1991): 58-59.

Shotwell, Willis A.

1965 *The Biblical Exegesis of Justin Martyr.* London: S.P.C.K.

Sider, John W.

1981 "The Meaning of *Parabole* in the Usage of the Synoptic Evangelists." *Biblica* 62: 453-70.

Sider, Ronald J.

1979 *Christ and Violence.* Scottsdale, PA: Herald Press.

1990 *Rich Christians in an Age of Hunger.* 3d ed. Foreword by Kenneth Kantzer. Dallas: Word Books.

Siegal, Seymour.

1978 "The Meaning of Israel in Jewish Thought." Pp. 98-118 in *Evangelicals and Jews in Conversation on Scripture, Theology, and History.* Edited by Marc H. Tanenbaum, Marvin R. Wilson, and James A. Rudin. Grand Rapids: Baker.

Sievers, J.

1984 "'Where Two or Three . . .': The Rabbinic Concept of Shekhinah and Matthew 18:20." *SIDIC* 17: 4-10.

Sigal, Phillip.

1983 "Another Note to 1 Corinthians 10.16." *New Testament Studies* 29: 134-39.

1986 *The Halakah of Jesus of Nazareth according to the Gospel of Matthew.* Lanham, MD: University Press of America.

Siker, Jeffrey S.

1987 "Abraham in Graeco-Roman Paganism." *Journal for the Study of Judaism* 18: 188-208.

Silberman, Lou H.

1955 "The Two 'Messiahs' of the Manual of Discipline." *Vetus Testamentum* 5: 77-82.

1956 "Language and Structure in the Hodayot (1QH 3)." *Journal of Biblical Literature* 75: 96-106.

1961-1962 "Unriddling the Riddle. A Study in the Structure and Language of the Habakkuk Pesher." *Revue de Qumran* 3: 323-64.

1989 "From Apocalyptic Proclamation to Moral Prescript: Abot 2,15-16." *Journal of Jewish Studies* 40: 53-60.

Silberman, Neil Asher.

1991 "Ossuary: A Box for Bones." *Biblical Archaeology Review* 17 (3, 1991): 73-74.

Silver, Daniel J.

1973 "Moses and the Hungry Birds." *Jewish Quarterly Review* 64: 123-53.

Sim, David C.

1992 "Matthew 22.13a and 1 Enoch 10.4a: A Case of Literary Dependence?" *Journal for the Study of the New Testament* 47: 3-19.

1993a "The 'Confession' of the Soldiers in Matthew 27:54." *Heythrop Journal* 34: 401-24.

1993b "The Meaning of παλιγγενεσία in Matthew 19.28." *Journal for the Study of the New Testament* 50: 3-12.

1996 *Apocalyptic Eschatology in the Gospel of Matthew.* Society for New Testament Studies Monograph 88. Cambridge: Cambridge University Press.

Simon, Marcel.

1958 *St Stephen and the Hellenists in the Primitive Church.* The Haskell Lectures delivered at the Graduate School of Theology, Oberlin College, 1956. New York: Longmans, Green & Company.

1967 *Jewish Sects at the Time of Jesus.* Philadelphia: Fortress Press.

Simon, S. J.

1990 "Women Who Pleaded Causes before the Roman Magistrates." *Classical Bulletin* 66 (3-4, 1990): 79-81.

Sinclair, Patrick.

1993 "The *Sententia* in *Rhetorica ad Herennium*: A Study in the Sociology of Rhetoric." *American Journal of Philology* 114: 561-80.

Sirat, René-Samuel, and Agnès Woog.

1992 "Moïse 'notre maître', prince des prophètes." *Vie Spirituelle* 146: 625-32.

Sisti, A.

1977 "La figura del giusto perseguitato in *Sap.* 2,12-20." *Bibbia e Oriente* 19: 129-44. *(NTA)*

Sjoberg, G.

1960-1966 *The Preindustrial City.* New York: The Free Press.

Small, J. P.

1995 "Artificial Memory and the Writing Habits of the Literate." *Helios* 22: 159-66.

Smalley, Stephen S.

1977 "Redaction Criticism." Pp. 181-95 in *New Testament Interpretation: Essays on Principles and Methods.* Edited by I. Howard Marshall. Grand Rapids: Eerdmans.

Smallwood, E. Mary.

1962 "High Priests and Politics in Roman Palestine." *Journal of Theological Studies* 13: 14-34.

1976 *The Jews under Roman Rule: From Pompey to Diocletian.* Studies in Judaism in Late Antiquity 20. Leiden: E. J. Brill.

Smelik, Willem F.

1995 "On Mystical Transformation of the Righteous into Light in Judaism." *Journal for the Study of Judaism* 26: 122-44.

Smith, Christopher R.

1997 "Literary Evidence of a Fivefold Structure in the Gospel of Matthew." *New Testament Studies* 43: 540-51.

Smith, Derwood.

1982 "Jewish Proselyte Baptism and the Baptism of John." *Restoration Quarterly* 25: 13-32.

Smith, Morton.

1951 *Tannaitic Parallels to the Gospels.* Philadelphia: Society of Biblical Literature.

1958-1959 "'God's Begetting the Messiah' in 1QSa." *New Testament Studies* 5: 218-24.

1959 "What Is Implied by the Variety of Messianic Figures?" *Journal of Biblical Literature* 78: 66-72.

1961 "The Dead Sea Sect in Relation to Ancient Judaism." *New Testament Studies* 7: 347-60.

1963 "A Comparison of Early Christian and Early Rabbinic Tradition." *Journal of Biblical Literature* 82: 169-76.

1971 "Zealots and Sicarii, Their Origins and Relation." *Harvard Theological Review* 64: 1-19.

1978 *Jesus the Magician.* San Francisco: Harper & Row.

Smith, Robert Houston.

1967 "The Tomb of Jesus." *Biblical Archaeologist* 30: 74-90.

1973 "A Sarcophagus from Pella: New Light on Earliest Christianity." *Archaeology* 26: 250-56.

1974 "The Cross Marks on Jewish Ossuaries." *Palestine Exploration Quarterly* 106: 53-66.

1990 "Matthew 27:25: The Hardest Verse in Matthew's Gospel." *Currents in Theology and Mission* 17: 421-28.

1992a "Interpreting Matthew Today." *Currents in Theology and Mission* 19: 424-32.

1992b "Matthew's Message for Insiders. Charisma and Commandment in a First-Century Community." *Interpretation* 46: 229-39.

Smith, Robert H., Anthony W. McNicoll, and J. B. Hennessey.

1981 "The 1980 Season at Pella of the Decapolis." *Bulletin of the American Schools of Oriental Research* 243: 1-30.

Smyth, Kevin.

1975 "Matthew 28: Resurrection as Theophany." *Irish Theological Quarterly* 42: 259-71.

Snodgrass, Klyne R.

1975 "The Parable of the Wicked Husbandman: Is the Gospel of Thomas Version the Original?" *New Testament Studies* 21: 142-44.

1983 *The Parable of the Wicked Tenants.* Wissenschaftliche Untersuchungen zum Neuen Testament 27. Tübingen: J. C. B. Mohr/Paul Siebeck.

1992 "Matthew's Understanding of the Law." *Interpretation* 46: 368-78.

1993 "That Which Is Born from ΠΝΕΥΜΑ Is ΠΝΕΥΜΑ: Rebirth and Spirit in John 3:5-6." Pp. 181-205 in *Perspectives on John: Method and Interpretation in the Fourth Gospel.* Edited by Robert B. Sloan and Mikeal C. Parsons. National Association of Baptist Professors of Religion Special Studies Series 11. Lewiston, NY: Edwin Mellen Press.

1996 "Matthew and the Law." Pp. 99-127 in *Treasures New and Old: Recent Contributions to Matthean Studies.* Edited by David R. Bauer and Mark Allan Powell. Society of Biblical Literature Symposium Series 1. Atlanta: Scholars Press.

Snowden, Frank M., Jr.

1970 *Blacks in Antiquity: Ethiopians in the Greco-Roman Experience.* Cambridge: Harvard University Press.

Soards, Marion L.

1994 "Appendix IX. The Question of a Premarcan Passion Narrative." Pp. 1492-1524 in *The Death of the Messiah: From Gethsemane to Grave. A Commentary on the Passion Narratives in the Four Gospels.* 2 vols. New York: Doubleday & Company.

Soares Prabhu, George M.

1976 *The Formula Quotations in the Infancy Narrative of Matthew: An Enquiry into the Tradition History of Mt 1–2.* Rome: Biblical Institute Press.

1980 "The Dharma of Jesus: An Interpretation of the Sermon on the Mount." *Biblebhashyam* 6: 358-81. (*NTA* 26:16)

Södig, Thomas.
1995 "Feindeshass und Bruderliebe. Beobachtungen zur essenischen Ethik." *Revue de Qumran* 16: 601-19.

Soggin, J. A.
1965 "Appunti per l'esegesi cristiana della prima Parte del Salmo 22." *Bibliotheca Orientalis* 7: 105-16. (*NTA* 10:35-36)

Songer, Harold S.
1992 "The Sermon on the Mount and Its Jewish Foreground." *Review and Expositor* 89: 165-77.

Southall, Aidan.
1971 "Ideology and Group Composition in Madagascar." *American Anthropologist* 73: 144-64.

Sowers, Sidney.
1970 "The Circumstances and Recollection of the Pella Flight." *Theologische Zeitschrift* 26: 305-20.

Speidel, M. A.
1992 "Roman Army Pay Scales." *Journal of Roman Studies* 82: 87-106.

Spencer, F. Scott.
1993 "Acts and Modern Literary Approaches." Pp. 381-414 in *The Book of Acts in Its Ancient Literary Setting.* Edited by Bruce W. Winter and Andrew D. Clarke. Vol. 1 in The Book of Acts in Its First Century Setting. Grand Rapids: Eerdmans; Carlisle: The Paternoster Press.

Spivey, Robert A., and D. Moody Smith.
1982 *Anatomy of the New Testament: A Guide to Its Structure and Meaning.* 3d ed. New York: Macmillan Publishing Company; London: Collier Macmillan Publishers.

Stager, Lawrence E.
1991 "Deities and Dogs — Their Sacred Rites." *Biblical Archaeology Review* 17 (3, 1991): 40-42.

Stambaugh, John E., and David L. Balch.
1986 *The New Testament in Its Social Environment.* Library of Early Christianity 2. Philadelphia: Westminster Press.

Stanley, David Michael.
1961 *Christ's Resurrection in Pauline Soteriology.* Analecta Biblica 13. Rome: Pontifical Biblical Institute.

Stanton, Graham N.
1974 *Jesus of Nazareth in New Testament Preaching.* Cambridge: Cambridge University Press.
1982 "Salvation Proclaimed: X. Matthew 11:28-30: Comfortable Words?" *Expository Times* 94: 3-9.
1984 "The Gospel of Matthew and Judaism." *Bulletin of the John Rylands Library of Manchester* 66: 254-84.
1989a *The Gospels and Jesus.* Österreichische biblische Studien. Oxford: Oxford University Press.
1989b "'Pray that your flight may not be in winter or on a Sabbath' (Matthew 24:20)." *Journal for the Study of the New Testament* 37: 17-30.
1991 "Matthew as a Creative Interpreter of the Sayings of Jesus." Pp. 257-72 in *The Gospel and the Gospels.* Edited by Peter Stuhlmacher. Grand Rapids: Eerdmans.
1992a "The Communities of Matthew." *Interpretation* 46: 379-91.

1992b "Matthew: ΒΙΒΛΟΣ, ΕΥΑΓΓΕΛΙΟΝ, or ΒΙΟΣ?" Pp. 1187-1201 in *The Four Gospels 1992: Festschrift for Franz Neirynck.* Edited by F. Van Segbroeck, C. M. Tuckett, G. Van Belle, and J. Verheyden. Leuven: Leuven University Press.

1993 *A Gospel for a New People: Studies in Matthew.* Louisville: Westminster Press/John Knox. Edinburgh: T & T Clark, 1992.

1995a *Gospel Truth? New Light on Jesus and the Gospels.* Valley Forge, PA: Trinity Press International.

1995b "Introduction: Matthew's Gospel in Recent Scholarship (1994)." Pp. 1-26 in *The Interpretation of Matthew.* 2d ed. Edited by Graham Stanton. Edinburgh: T & T Clark.

Stark, Rodney.

1991a "Antioch as the Social Situation for Matthew's Gospel." Pp. 189-210 in *Social History of the Matthean Community: Cross-Disciplinary Approaches.* Minneapolis: Fortress Press.

1991b "Epidemics, Networks, and the Rise of Christianity." *Semeia* 56: 159-75.

1998 "Live Longer, Healthier, & Better." *Christian History* 57: 28-30.

Stassen, Glen H.

1992 "Grace and Deliverance in the Sermon on the Mount." *Review and Expositor* 89: 229-44.

Stauffer, Ethelbert.

1955 "Zum apokalyptischen Festmahl in Mk 6,34ff." *Zeitschrift für die Neutestamentliche Wissenschaft* 46: 264-66.

1960 *Jesus and His Story.* Translated by Richard and Clara Winston. New York: Alfred A. Knopf.

Stefanovic, Zdravko.

1992 "'One Greater than the Temple' — The Sermon on the Mount in the Early Palestinian Liturgical Setting." *Asia Journal of Theology* 6: 108-16.

Stegner, William R.

1985 "The Baptism of Jesus: A Story Modeled on the Binding of Isaac." *Bible Review* 1: 36-46.

1990 "The Temptation Narrative: A Study in the Use of Scripture by Early Jewish Christians." *Biblical Research* 35: 5-17.

Stehly, R.

1975 "Une citation des Upanishads dans Joseph et Aséneth." *Revue d'Histoire et de Philosophie Religieuses* 55: 209-13.

1977 "Bouddhisme et Nouveau Testament à propos de la marche de Pierre sur l'eau (Matthieu 14.28c)." *Revue d'Histoire et de Philosophie Religieuses* 57: 433-37. (*NTA* 22: 265)

Stein, Bradley L.

1997 "Who the Devil Is Beelzebul?" *Bible Review* 13.1: 42-45, 48.

Stein, Robert H.

1978 *The Method and Message of Jesus' Teachings.* Philadelphia: Westminster Press.

1979 "'Is It Lawful for a Man to Divorce His Wife?'" *Journal of the Evangelical Theological Society* 22: 115-21.

1980 "The 'Criteria' for Authenticity." 1:225-63 in Gospel Perspectives. Vol. 1: *Studies of History and Tradition in the Four Gospels.* Edited by R. T. France and David Wenham. Sheffield: JSOT Press, 1980.

1992a "Divorce." Pp. 192-99 in *Dictionary of Jesus and the Gospels.* Edited by

Joel B. Green, Scot McKnight, and I. Howard Marshall. Downers Grove, IL: InterVarsity Press.

1992b "The Matthew-Luke Agreements against Mark: Insight from John." *Catholic Biblical Quarterly* 54: 482-502.

1992c "Synoptic Problem." Pp. 784-92 in *Dictionary of Jesus and the Gospels.* Edited by Joel B. Green and Scot McKnight. Downers Grove, IL: InterVarsity Press.

Steinhauser, Michael G.

1976 "The Patch of Unshrunk Cloth (Mt 9:16)." *The Expository Times* 87: 312-13.

Steinmetz, Franz-Josef.

1993 "'Umkraut unter dem Weizen' (Mt 13,24-30). Ein aktuelles, aber nichtssagendes Gleichnis?" *Geist und Leben* 66: 1-9.

Stemberger, Günter.

1973 "Zur Auferstehungslehre in der rabbinischen Literatur." *Kairos* 15: 238-66.

1977 "Die sogenannte 'Synode von Jabne' und das frühe Christentum." *Kairos* 19: 14-21.

1987 "Pesachhaggada und Abendmahlsberichte des Neuen Testaments." *Kairos* 29 (3-4, 1987): 147-58.

Stendahl, Krister.

1962 "Hate, Non-Retaliation, and Love. 1QS x,17-20 and Rom. 12:19-21." *Harvard Theological Review* 55: 343-55.

1968 *The School of St. Matthew and Its Use of the Old Testament.* Philadelphia: Fortress Press.

1995 "Quis et Unde? An Analysis of Matthew 1–2 (1960)." Pp. 69-80 in *The Interpretation of Matthew.* 2d ed. Edited by Graham Stanton. Edinburgh: T & T Clark.

Stenger, Werner.

1984 "Zur Rekonstruktion eines Jesusworts anhand der synoptischen Ehescheidungslogien (Mt 5,32; 19,9; Lk 10,11f; Mk 10,11f)." *Kairos* 26: 194-205.

Stephens, G. H.

1964 "The Jews and the Crucifixion." *Christianity Today* 9: 290-92.

Stephens, William N.

1963 *The Family in Cross-Cultural Perspective.* New York: Holt, Rinehart & Winston.

Sterling, Gregory E.

1993 "Jesus as Exorcist: An Analysis of Matthew 17:14-20; Mark 9:14-29; Luke 9:37-43a." *Catholic Biblical Quarterly* 55: 467-93.

Stern, David.

1991 *Parables in Midrash: Narrative and Exegesis in Rabbinic Literature.* Cambridge: Harvard University Press.

Stern, Menahem.

1974/1976a "Aspects of Jewish Society: The Priesthood and Other Classes." Pp. 561-630 in *The Jewish People in the First Century: Historical Geography, Political History, Social, Cultural, and Religious Life and Institutions.* 2 vols. Edited by S. Safrai and M. Stern with D. Flusser and W. C. van Unnik. Section 1 of Compendia Rerum Iudaicarum ad Novum Testamentum. Vol. 1: Assen: Van Gorcum & Co., B.V., 1974; Vol. 2: Philadelphia: Fortress Press, 1976.

1974/1976b "The Province of Judaea." Pp. 308-76 in *The Jewish People in the First Century: Historical Geography, Political History, Social, Cultural, and Religious Life and Institutions.* 2 vols. Edited by S. Safrai and M. Stern with

D. Flusser and W. C. van Unnik. Section 1 of Compendia Rerum Iudaicarum ad Novum Testamentum. Vol. 1: Assen: Van Gorcum & Co., B.V.; Vol. 2: Philadelphia: Fortress Press.

1974/1984 *Greek and Latin Authors on Jews and Judaism: Edited with Introductions, Translations and Commentary.* Vol. 1: *From Herodotus to Plutarch.* Jerusalem: The Israel Academy of Sciences and Humanities, 1974. Vol. 2: *From Tacitus to Simplicius.* Jerusalem: The Israel Academy of Sciences and Humanities, 1980. Vol. 3: *Appendixes and Indexes.* Jerusalem: The Israel Academy of Sciences and Humanities, 1984.

Stevens, Gerald L.

1992 "Understanding the Sermon on the Mount: Its Rabbinic and New Testament Context." *Theological Educator* 46: 83-95.

Stevenson, W.

1995 "The Rise of Eunuchs in Greco-Roman Antiquity." *Journal of the History of Sexuality* 5: 495-511.

Stewart, Roy A.

1964 "The Parable Form in the Old Testament and the Rabbinic Literature." *Evangelical Quarterly* 36: 133-47.

1975 "Judicial Procedure in New Testament Times." *Evangelical Quarterly* 47: 94-109.

Stewart, Roberta.

1994 "Domitian and Roman Religion: Juvenal. *Satires* Two and Four." *Transactions of the American Philological Association* 124: 309-32.

Stieglitz, Robert R.

1981 "The Hebrew Names of the Seven Planets." *Journal of Near Eastern Studies* 40: 135-37.

Stock, Augustine.

1986 "Jesus, Hypocrites, and Herodians." *Biblical Theology Bulletin* 16: 3-7.

1987 "Is Matthew's Presentation of Peter Ironic?" *Biblical Theology Bulletin* 17: 64-69.

Stock, Klemens.

1978 "Das Bekenntnis des Centurio. Mk 15,39 im Rahmen des Markusevangeliums." *Zeitschrift für Katholische Theologie* 100: 289-301.

Stone, G. R.

1989 "The Galilee Boat — A Fishing Vessel of New Testament Times." *Buried History* 25 (2, 1989): 46-54.

Stowers, Stanley K.

1986 *Letter Writing in Greco-Roman Antiquity.* Library of Early Christianity 5. Philadelphia: Westminster Press.

1988 "The Diatribe." Pp. 71-83 in *Greco-Roman Literature and the New Testament: Selected Forms and Genres.* Edited by David E. Aune. Society of Biblical Literature Sources for Biblical Study 21. Atlanta: Scholars Press.

Strack, Hermann L.

1969 *Introduction to the Talmud and Midrash.* New York: Atheneum.

Strand, Kenneth A.

1967 "Another Look at 'Lord's Day' in the Early Church and in Rev. I.10." *New Testament Studies* 13: 174-81.

Strange, James F., and Hershel Shanks.

1982 "Has the House Where Jesus Stayed in Capernaum Been Found?" *Biblical Archaeology Review* 8.6: 26-37.

1983 "Synagogue Where Jesus Preached Found at Capernaum." *Biblical Archaeology Review* 9: 25-31.

Strauss, Heinrich.

1973 "Jüdische Quellen frühchristlicher Kunst-optische oder literarische Anregung." *Zeitschrift für die Neutestamentliche Wissenschaft* 64: 323-24.

Strecker, Georg.

1966 *Der Weg der Gerechtigkeit: Untersuchung zur Theologie des Matthäus.* 2d rev. ed. Göttingen: Vandenhoeck & Ruprecht.

1978 "Die Antitheses der Bergpredigt (Mt 5 21-48 par)." *Zeitschrift für die Neutestamentliche Wissenschaft* 69: 36-72.

1995 "The Concept of History in Matthew (1966)." Pp. 81-100 in *The Interpretation of Matthew.* 2d ed. Edited by Graham Stanton. Edinburgh: T & T Clark.

Streeter, B. H.

1925 *The Four Gospels.* New York: Macmillan & Company.

Strombeck, J. F.

1982 *First the Rapture.* Foreword by Warren W. Wiersbe. Eugene, OR: Harvest House Publishers.

Stuhlmacher, Peter.

1991a "The Pauline Gospel." Pp. 149-72 in *The Gospel and the Gospels.* Edited by Peter Stuhlmacher. Grand Rapids: Eerdmans.

1991b "The Theme: The Gospel and the Gospels." Pp. 1-25 in *The Gospel and the Gospels.* Edited by Peter Stuhlmacher. Grand Rapids: Eerdmans.

Suder, R. N.

1982 "Epiphany Texts and the Akedah." *Lutheran Theological Seminary Bulletin* 62: 3-7. (*NTA* 27:144)

Suggit, John N.

1988 "Comrade Judas: Matthew 26:50." *Journal of Theology for Southern Africa* 63: 56-58.

Suggs, M. J.

1970 *Wisdom, Christology and Law in Matthew's Gospel.* Cambridge: Harvard University Press.

Sullivan, D.

1992 "New Insights into Matthew 27:24-25." *New Blackfriars* 73: 453-57.

Sutcliffe, Edmund Felix.

1960a "Baptism and Baptismal Rites at Qumran?" *Heythrop Journal* 1: 179-88.

1960b "Hatred at Qumran." *Revue de Qumran* 2: 345-56.

1960c "Sacred Meals at Qumran?" *Heythrop Journal* 1: 48-65.

1963 Review of H. Mantel, *Studies in the History of the Sanhedrin. Heythrop Journal* 4: 283-87.

Swart, G. J.

1993 "Twee aardbewings of een? Die assosiasie van literêre motiewe in die eksegese van Matteus 27:51-54 and 28:2-4." *Hervormde Teologiese Studies* 49: 255-65. *(NTA)*

Sweet, J. P. M.

1984 "The Zealots and Jesus." Pp. 1-9 in *Jesus and the Politics of His Day.* Edited by Ernst Bammel and C. F. D. Moule. Cambridge: Cambridge University Press.

Swidler, Leonard.

1976 *Women in Judaism: The Status of Women in Formative Judaism.* Metuchen, NJ: Scarecrow Press.

Syon, Danny.
1992 "Gamla: Portrait of a Rebellion." *Biblical Archaeology Review* 18 (1, 1992): 20-37, 72.

Syreeni, Kari.
1990 "Between Heaven and Earth: On the Structure of Matthew's Symbolic Universe." *Journal for the Study of the New Testament* 40: 3-13.

Tabor, James D.
1992 "4Q521 'On Resurrection' and the Synoptic Gospel Tradition: A Preliminary Study." *Journal for the Study of the Pseudepigrapha* 10: 149-62.

Tagawa, Kenzo.
1977 "Marc 13. La tâtonnement d'un homme réaliste éveillé face à la tradition apocalyptique." *Foi et Vie* 76: 11-44.

Talbert, Charles H.
1975 "The Concept of Immortals in Mediterranean Antiquity." *Journal of Biblical Literature* 94: 419-36.
1977 *What Is a Gospel? The Genre of the Canonical Gospels.* Philadelphia: Fortress Press.
1982 *Reading Luke: A Literary and Theological Commentary on the Third Gospel.* New York: Crossroad Publishing Company.

Tannehill, Robert C.
1975 *The Sword of His Mouth.* Society of Biblical Literature Semeia Supplements 1. Missoula, MT: Scholars Press.
1986 *The Narrative Unity of Luke-Acts: A Literary Interpretation.* 2 vols. Vol. 1: *The Gospel according to Luke.* Philadelphia: Fortress Press.

Tarn, W. W.
1974 *Hellenistic Civilisation.* 3d rev. ed. Revised by W. W. Tarn and G. T. Griffith. New York: New American Library.

Tasker, R. V. G.
1961 *The Gospel according to St. Matthew.* Tyndale New Testament Commentaries. Grand Rapids: Eerdmans.

Tassin, Claude.
1990 "Matthieu 'targumiste?' L'exemple de Mt 12,18 (= Is 42,1)." *Estudios Bíblicos* 48: 199-214.

Taussig, Hal.
1988 "The Lord's Prayer." *Forum* 4: 25-41.

Taylor, Joan E.
1989 "Capernaum and Its 'Jewish-Christians': A Re-examination of the Franciscan Excavations." *Bulletin of the Anglo-Israel Archaeological Society* 9: 7-28.
1997 *The Immerser: John the Baptist within Second Temple Judaism.* Grand Rapids: Eerdmans.

Taylor, Justin.
1989 "'The Love of Many Will Grow Cold': Matt 24:9-13 and the Neronian Persecution." *Revue Biblique* 96: 352-57.

Taylor, Lily Ross.
1966 *Party Politics in the Age of Caesar.* Berkeley: University of California Press.
1979 "Artemis of Ephesus." 5:251-56 in *The Beginnings of Christianity.* Part I: *The Acts of the Apostles.* 5 vols. Edited by F. J. Foakes Jackson and Kirsopp Lake. Reprint ed. Grand Rapids: Baker.

Taylor, T. M.
1956 "The Beginnings of Jewish Proselyte Baptism." *New Testament Studies* 2: 193-98.

Taylor, Vincent.
1935 *The Formation of the Gospel Tradition.* 2d ed. London: Macmillan & Company.
1945 *The Atonement in New Testament Teaching.* London: Epworth Press.
1952 *The Gospel according to St. Mark.* London: Macmillan & Company.
1955 "The Origin of the Markan Passion-Sayings." *New Testament Studies* 1: 159-67.

Teeple, Howard M.
1957 *The Mosaic Eschatological Prophet.* Journal of Biblical Literature Monograph Series 10. Philadelphia: Society of Biblical Literature.

Ten Kate, R.
1978 "Greef ons heden ons 'dgelijks' brood." *Nederlands Theologisch Tijdschrift* 32: 125-39. (*NTA* 23:23)

Testuz, Michel.
1955 "Deux fragments inédits des manuscrits de la mer morte." *Semitica* 5: 37-39.

Teugels, G.
1991 "De kuise Jozef. De receptie van een bijbels model." *Nederlands Theologisch Tijdschrift* 45: 193-203. (*NTA* 36:92)

Tevel, J. M.
1992 "The Labourers in the Vineyard: The Exegesis of Matthew 20,1-7 in the Early Church." *Vigiliae Christianae* 46: 356-80.

Thapar, Romila.
1966 *A History of India.* Vol. 1. Baltimore: Penguin Books.

Thatcher, Tom.
1995 "Philo on Pilate: Rhetoric or Reality?" *Restoration Quarterly* 37: 215-18.

Theissen, Gerd.
1978 *Sociology of Early Palestinian Christianity.* Philadelphia: Fortress Press.
1982 *The Social Setting of Pauline Christianity.* Edited and translated by John H. Schütz. Philadelphia: Fortress Press.
1983 *The Miracle Stories of the Early Christian Tradition.* Translated by Francis McDonagh. Edited by John Riches. Philadelphia: Fortress Press.
1984 "Lokal- und Sozialkolorit in der Geschichte von der syrophönikischen Frau (Mk 7.24-30)." *Zeitschrift für die Neutestamentliche Wissenschaft* 75: 202-25.
1991 *The Gospels in Context: Social and Political History in the Synoptic Tradition.* Translated by Linda M. Maloney. Minneapolis: Fortress Press.

Thiemann, Ronald.
1989 "The Promising God: The Gospel as Narrated Promise." Pp. 320-46 in *Why Narrative? Readings in Narrative Theology.* Edited by Stanley Hauerwas and L. Gregory Jones. Grand Rapids: Eerdmans.

Thiering, Barbara E.
1974 "The Biblical Source of Qumran Asceticism." *Journal of Biblical Literature* 93: 429-44.
1979 "Are the 'Violent Men' False Teachers?" *Novum Testamentum* 21: 293-97.
1980 "Inner and Outer Cleansing at Qumran as a Background to New Testament Baptism." *New Testament Studies* 26: 266-77.

1981a *The Gospels and Qumran: A New Hypothesis.* Australian and New Zealand Studies in Theology and Religion. Sydney: Theological Explorations.

1981b "Qumran Initiation and New Testament Baptism." *New Testament Studies* 27: 615-31.

Thiselton, Anthony C.

1977 "Semantics and New Testament Interpretation." Pp. 75-104 in *New Testament Interpretation: Essays on Principles and Methods.* Edited by I. Howard Marshall. Grand Rapids: Eerdmans.

Thom, Johan C.

1994 "'Don't Walk on the Highways': The Pythagorean *Akousmata* and Early Christian Literature." *Journal of Biblical Literature* 113: 93-112.

Thoma, Clemens.

1979 "The Death Penalty and Torture in the Jewish Tradition." *Concilium* 120: 64-74.

Thompson, J. A.

1962 *The Bible and Archaeology.* Grand Rapids: Eerdmans.

Thompson, James W.

1971 "The Gentile Mission as an Eschatological Necessity." *Restoration Quarterly* 14: 18-27.

Thompson, Michael B.

1991 *Clothed with Christ: The Example and Teaching of Jesus in Romans 12.1–15.13.* Journal for the Study of the New Testament Supplement 59. Sheffield: JSOT Press.

1998 "The Holy Internet: Communication between Churches in the First Christian Generation." Pp. 49-70 in *The Gospels for All Christians: Rethinking the Gospel Audiences.* Edited by Richard J. Bauckham. Grand Rapids: Eerdmans.

Thompson, William G.

1970 *Matthew's Advice to a Divided Community: Mt. 17,22–18,35.* Analecta Biblica 44. Rome: Pontifical Biblical Institute.

1974 "An Historical Perspective in the Gospel of Matthew." *Journal of Biblical Literature* 93: 243-62.

Thompson, William M.

1985 *The Jesus Debate: A Survey and Synthesis.* New York: Paulist Press.

Thorley, John.

1981 "When Was Jesus Born?" *Greece and Rome* 28: 81-89.

Thrall, Margaret.

1970 "Elijah and Moses in Mark's Account of the Transfiguration." *New Testament Studies* 16: 305-17.

Thurman, Howard.

1981 *Jesus and the Disinherited.* Richmond, IN: Friends United Press. Reprint from Nashville: Abingdon Press, 1949.

Tiede, David Lenz.

1972 *The Charismatic Figure as Miracle Worker.* Society of Biblical Literature Dissertation 1. Missoula, MT: Society of Biblical Literature.

Tigay, Jeffrey H.

1979 "On the Term Phylacteries (Matt 23:5)." *Harvard Theological Review* 72: 45-53.

Tödt, Heinz Eduard.

1965 *The Son of Man in the Synoptic Tradition.* Philadelphia: Westminster Press.

Tompkins, Jane P., editor.

1980 *Reader-Response Criticism: From Formalism to Post-Structuralism.* Baltimore: Johns Hopkins University Press.

Tooley, Wilfred.

1964 "The Shepherd and Sheep Image in the Teaching of Jesus." *Novum Testamentum* 7: 15-25.

Tosato, Angelo.

1979 "Joseph, Being a Just Man (Matt 1:19)." *Catholic Biblical Quarterly* 41: 547-51.

Toussaint, Stanley D.

1964 "The Introductory and Concluding Parables of Matthew Thirteen." *Bibliotheca Sacra* 121: 351-55.

Townsend, John T.

1961 "Matthew xxiii.9." *Journal of Theological Studies* 12: 56-59.

1971 "Ancient Education in the Time of the Early Roman Empire." Pp. 139-63 in *The Catacombs and the Colosseum: The Roman Empire as the Setting of Primitive Christianity.* Edited by Stephen Benko and John J. O'Rourke. Valley Forge: Judson Press.

1979 "The Gospel of John and the Jews: The Story of a Religious Divorce." Pp. 72-97 in *Anti-Semitism and the Foundations of Christianity.* Edited by A. T. Davies. New York: Paulist Press.

Trapnell, D. H.

1982 "Health, Disease and Healing." Pp. 457-65 in *New Bible Dictionary.* 2d ed. Edited by J. D. Douglas and N. Hillyer. Downers Grove, IL: InterVarsity Press.

Travis, Stephen H.

1977 "Form Criticism." Pp. 153-64 in *New Testament Interpretation: Essays on Principles and Methods.* Edited by I. Howard Marshall. Grand Rapids: Eerdmans.

Trebilco, Paul.

1994 "Asia." Pp. 291-362 in *The Book of Acts in Its Graeco-Roman Setting.* Edited by David W. J. Gill and Conrad Gempf. Vol. 2 in The Book of Acts in Its First Century Setting. 6 vols. Edited by Bruce W. Winter. Grand Rapids: Eerdmans; Carlisle: Paternoster Press.

Treggiari, Susan.

1975 "Jobs in the Household of Livia." *Papers of the British School at Rome* 43: 48-77.

Treves, Marco.

1958 "The Date of the War of the Sons of Light." *Vetus Testamentum* 8: 419-24.

Trifon, D.

1989-90 "H'm 'brw msmrwt hkwhnym myhwdh lglyl 'hry mrd br-kwkb'?" *Tarbiz* 59: 77-93. (*NTA* 36:239)

Trites, Allison A.

1977 *The New Testament Concept of Witness.* Society for New Testament Studies Monograph Series 31. Cambridge: Cambridge University.

1979 "The Transfiguration of Jesus: The Gospel in Microcosm." *Evangelical Quarterly* 51: 67-79.

1992 "The Blessings and Warnings of the Kingdom (Matthew 5:3-12; 7:13-27)." *Review and Expositor* 89: 179-96.

Trocmé, Etienne.

1975 *The Formation of the Gospel according to Mark.* Translated by Pamela Gaughan. Philadelphia: Westminster Press.

Tuckett, Christopher M.

1984 "On the Relationship between Matthew and Luke." *New Testament Studies* 30: 130-41.

1988 "A Cynic Q?" *Biblica* 70: 349-76.

1993 "Les logia et le Judaïsme." *Foi et Vie* 92: 67-88.

1996 *Q and the History of Early Christianity: Studies on Q.* Peabody, MA: Hendrickson.

Tuñí, J. O.

1972 "La tipología Israel-Jesús en Mt 1–2." *Estudios Eclesiásticos* 47: 361-76. (*NTA* 18:24-25)

Tupper, E. Frank.

1991 "The Bethlehem Massacre — Christology against Providence?" *Review and Expositor* 88: 399-418.

Turner, David L.

1989 "The Structure and Sequence of Matthew 24:1-41: Interaction with Evangelical Treatments." *Grace Theological Journal* 10: 3-27.

Turner, Nigel.

1964 "Second Thoughts — VII. Papyrus Finds." *Expository Times* 76: 44-48.

Turnheim, Yehudit.

1987 "Some Observations on the Decoration of the Chorazin Pilaster." *Palestine Exploration Quarterly* 119: 152-55.

Tuttle, Gary A.

1977 "The Sermon on the Mount: Its Wisdom Affinities and Their Relation to Its Structure." *Journal of the Evangelical Theological Society* 20: 213-30.

Twelftree, Graham H.

1986 "'EI DE . . . EGO EKBALLO TA DAIMONIA . . .'" 6:361-400 in Gospel Perspectives. 6 vols. Vol. 6: *The Miracles of Jesus.* Edited by David Wenham and Craig Blomberg. Sheffield: JSOT Press.

1993 *Jesus the Exorcist: A Contribution to the Study of the Historical Jesus.* Peabody, MA: Hendrickson; Tübingen: J. C. B. Mohr.

Tzaferis, Vassilios.

1985 "Crucifixion — The Archaeological Evidence." *Biblical Archaeology Review* 11 (1, January): 44-53.

1989 "A Pilgrimage to the Site of the Swine Miracle." *Biblical Archaeology Review* 15 (2, 1989): 44-51.

1992 "Cults and Deities Worshipped at Caesarea Philippi-Banias." Pp. 190-201 in *Priests, Prophets and Scribes: Essays on the Formation and Heritage of Second Temple Judaism in Honour of Joseph Blenkinsopp.* Edited by Eugene Ulrich et al. Journal for the Study of the Old Testament Supplement 149. Sheffield: JSOT Press.

Tzaferis, V., and R. Avner.

1990 "Hpyrwt b'ny's." *Qadmoniot* 23 (3-4, 1990): 110-14. (*NTA* 36:228-29)

Ulrichsen, Jarl H.

1977 "Troen på et liv etter døden i Qumrantekstene [Belief in a Life after Death in the Qumran Texts]." *Norsk Teologisk Tidsskrift* 78: 151-63. *(NTA)*

Uprichard, R. E. Henry.

1981 "The Baptism of Jesus." *Irish Biblical Studies* 3: 187-202.

Upton, John A.
1982 "The Potter's Field and the Death of Judas." *Concordia Journal* 8: 213-19.

Urbach, Ephraim E.
1979 *The Sages: Their Concepts and Beliefs.* 2d ed. 2 vols. Translated by Israel Abrahams. Jerusalem: Magnes Press, The Hebrew University.
1980/1982 "Self-Isolation or Self-Affirmation in Judaism in the First Three Centuries: Theory and Practice." 2:269-98 in *Jewish and Christian Self-Definition.* 3 vols. Edited by E. P. Sanders. Philadelphia: Fortress Press.

Urman, Dan.
1993 "The House of Assembly and the House of Study: Are they one and the same?" *Journal of Jewish Studies* 44: 236-57.

Usry, Glenn J., and Craig Keener.
1996 *Black Man's Religion: Can Christianity Be Afrocentric?* Downers Grove, IL: InterVarsity Press.

Vale, Ruth.
1987 "Literary Sources in Archaeological Description: The Case of Galilee, Galilees, and Galileans." *Journal for the Study of Judaism* 18: 209-26.

Valler, Shulamit.
1995 "The Number Fourteen as a Literary Device in the Babylonian Talmud." *Journal for the Study of Judaism* 26: 169-84.

Van Beek, Gus W.
1960 "Frankincense and Myrrh." *Biblical Archaeologist* 23: 70-94.

Van Boxel, P. W.
1988 "You have heard that it was said." *Bijdragen* 49: 362-77.

Van Cangh, J.-M., and M. van Esbroek.
1980 "La primauté de Pierre (Mt 16,16-19) et son contexte judaïque." *Revue Théologique de Louvain* 11: 310-24. (*NTA* 25:131)

VanderBroek, Lyle D.
1983 *The Markan Sitz im Leben: A Critical Investigation into the Possibility of a Palestinian Setting for the Gospel.* Ph.D. dissertation, Drew University, 1983. Ann Arbor, MI: University Microfilms International.

Van der Horst, Pieter W.
1973 "Macrobius and the New Testament: A Contribution to the Corpus Hellenisticum." *Novum Testamentum* 15: 220-32.
1974 "Musonius Rufus and the New Testament." *Novum Testamentum* 16: 306-15.
1975 "Hierocles the Stoic and the New Testament." *Novum Testamentum* 17: 156-60.
1978 "Seven Months' Children in Jewish and Christian Literature from Antiquity." *Ephemerides Theologicae Lovanienses* 54: 346-60.
1981 "Cornutus and the New Testament." *Novum Testamentum* 23: 165-72.
1992 "Jewish Funerary Inscriptions. Most Are in Greek." *Biblical Archaeology Review* 18 (5, 1992): 46-57.
1994 "Silent Prayer in Antiquity." *Numen* 31: 1-25.
1995 "Maximus van Tyrus over het gebed. Een geannoteerde vertaling van Eἰ δεῖ εὔχεσθαι (Maximus of Tyre on Prayer)." *Nederlands Theologisch Tijdschrift* 49: 12-23.

VanderKam, James C.
1978 "Enoch Traditions in Jubilees and Other Second-Century Sources." *SBL*

1978 Seminar Papers 13, vol. 1. Missoula, MT: Scholars Press for the Society of Biblical Literature.

1981 "Intertestamental Pronouncement Stories." *Semeia* 20: 65-72. (*NTA* 26:64)

1992 "Jubilees — How It Rewrote the Bible." *Biblical Archaeology Review* 8 (6, 1992): 32-39.

Van der Minde, Hans-Jürgen.

1988 "Die Absonderung der Frommen. Die Qumrangemeinschaft als Heiligtum Gottes." *Bibel und Liturgie* 61: 190-97.

Van der Ploeg, J.

1957 "The Meals of the Essenes." *Journal of Semitic Studies* 2: 163-75.

1959 *Le Rouleau de la Guerre: Traduit et Annoté Avec une Introduction.* Studies on the Texts of the Desert of Judah 2. Edited by J. Van der Ploeg. Leiden: E. J. Brill.

Van der Woude, A. S.

1982 "Wicked Priest or Wicked Priests? Reflections on the Identification of the Wicked Priest in the Habakkuk Commentary." *Journal of Jewish Studies* 33: 349-59.

Vandone, L. M.

1964 "Responsabilità giudaica." *Palestra del Clero* 43: 1276-81. (*NTA* 9:338)

Van Henten, Jan Willem.

1985 "Einige Prolegomena zum Studien der jüdischen Martyrologie." *Bijdragen* 46: 381-90.

Van Tilborg, Sjef.

1972a "A Form-Criticism of the Lord's Prayer." *Novum Testamentum* 14: 94-105.

1972b *The Jewish Leaders in Matthew.* Leiden: E. J. Brill.

Van Unnik, Willem C.

1954 "The Teaching of Good Works in I Peter." *New Testament Studies* 1: 92-110.

1974 "The Death of Judas in Saint Matthew's Gospel." Pp. 44-57 in *Anglican Theological Review* supplement 3.

Van Veldhuizen, Milo.

1985 "Moses: A Model of Hellenistic Philanthropia." *Reformed Review* 38: 215-24.

Van Zyl, H. C.

1982 "'n Moontlike verklaring vir Matteus 7:6." *Theologia Evangelica* 15: 67-82. (*NTA* 27:137-38)

Vanni, U.

1978 "Il 'Giorno del Signore' in Apoc. 1,10, giorno di purificazione e di discernimento." *Rivista Biblica* 26: 187-99. *(NTA)*

Vardaman, E. J.

1975 "Herodium: A Brief Assessment of Recent Suggestions." *Israel Exploration Journal* 25: 45-46.

Vasholz, Robert I.

1978 "Qumran and the Dating of Daniel." *Journal of the Evangelical Theological Society* 21: 315-21.

Veghazi, E. N.

1979 "La idea de la 'imitación de Dios' en el judaísme." *Revista Biblica* 41: 91-95. (*NTA* 24:154)

Verdenius, W. J.

1949 *Mimesis: Plato's Doctrine of Artistic Imitation and Its Meaning to Us.*

Philosophia Antiqua: Monographs on Ancient Philosophy 3. Leiden: E. J. Brill.

Vermaseren, Maarten J.

1977 *Cybele and Attis: The Myth and the Cult.* Translated by A. H. H. Lemmers. London: Thames & Hudson.

Vermes, Geza.

1959 "Pre-mishnaic Jewish worship and the phylacteries from the Dead Sea." *Vetus Testamentum* 9: 65-72.

1973 *Jesus the Jew: A Historian's Reading of the Gospels.* Philadelphia: Fortress Press.

1974 "Sectarian Matrimonial Halakah in the Damascus Rule." *Journal of Jewish Studies* 25: 197-202.

1981 *The Dead Sea Scrolls in English.* 2d ed. New York: Penguin Books.

1984 *Jesus and the World of Judaism.* Philadelphia: Fortress Press, 1984; London: SCM Press, 1983.

1993 *The Religion of Jesus the Jew.* Minneapolis: Augsburg Fortress Press.

Verner, David C.

1983 *The Household of God: The Social World of the Pastoral Epistles.* Society of Biblical Literature Dissertation Series 71. Chico, CA: Scholars Press.

Via, Dan Otto, Jr.

1967 *The Parables: Their Literary and Existential Dimension.* Philadelphia: Fortress Press.

1975 *Kerygma and Comedy in the New Testament: A Structuralist Approach to Hermeneutic.* Philadelphia: Fortress Press.

Villalón, José R.

1972 "Sources vétéro-testamentaires de la doctrine qumrânienne des deux Messies." *Revue de Qumran* 8: 53-63.

Villiers, P. G. R.

1978 "The Messiah and messiahs in Jewish Apocalyptic." *Neotestamentica* 12: 75-100.

Visotzky, Burton L.

1987 "Overturning the Lamp." *Journal of Jewish Studies* 38: 72-80.

1991 "Three Syriac Cruxes." *Journal of Jewish Studies* 42: 167-75.

Viviano, Benedict T.

1979 "Where Was the Gospel according to St. Matthew Written?" *Catholic Biblical Quarterly* 41: 533-46.

1990a "The Genres of Matthew 1–2: Light from 1 Timothy 1:4." *Revue Biblique* 97: 31-53.

1990b "Social World and Community Leadership: The Case of Matthew 23.1-12, 34." *Journal for the Study of the New Testament* 39: 3-21.

1992 "Beatitudes Found among Dead Sea Scrolls." *Biblical Archaeology Review* 18 (6, 1992): 53-55, 66.

1993a "Eight Beatitudes at Qumran and in Matthew? A New Publication from Cave Four." *Svensk Exegetisk Årsbok* 58: 71-84.

1993b "Eight Beatitudes from Qumran." *Bible Today* 31: 219-24.

1996 "The Movement of the Star, Matt 2:9 and Num 9:17." *Revue Biblique* 103: 58-64.

Vogt, Ernst.

1974 "Vom Tempel zum Felsendom." *Biblica* 55: 23-64.

Vögtle, A.
1964 "Das christologische und ekklesiologische Anliegen von Mt 28,18-20." *Studia Evangelica* 2: 266-94.

Von Dobschütz, Ernst.
1995 "Matthew as Rabbi and Catechist (1928)." Pp. 27-38 in *The Interpretation of Matthew.* 2d ed. Edited by Graham Stanton. Edinburgh: T & T Clark.

Von Lips, Hermann.
1988 "Schweine füttert man, Hunde nicht — ein Versuch, das Rätsel von Matthäus 7:6 zu lösen." *Zeitschrift für die Neutestamentliche Wissenschaft* 79: 165-86.

Wächter, Ludwig.
1969 "Astrologie und Schicksalglaube im rabbinischen Judentum." *Kairos* 11: 181-200.
1976 "Jüdischer und christlichen Messianismus." *Kairos* 18 (2, 1976): 119-34.

Wachsmann, Shelley.
1988 "The Galilee Boat: 2,000-Year-Old Hull Recovered Intact." *Biblical Archaeology Review* 14 (5, 1985): 18-33.

Wagner, Günter.
1967 *Pauline Baptism and the Pagan Mysteries: The Problem of the Pauline Doctrine of Baptism in Romans VI.1-11, in Light of Its Religio-Historical "Parallels."* Translated by J. P. Smith. Edinburgh: Oliver & Boyd.

Walker, Michael B.
1962 "Lead Us Not into Temptation." *Expository Times* 73: 287.

Walker, Norman.
1963 "The Alleged Matthaean Errata." *New Testament Studies* 9: 391-94.

Walker, Rolf.
1964 "Allein aus Werken. Zur Auslegung von Jakobus 2.14-26." *Zeitschrift für Theologie und Kirche* 61: 155-92.

Walker, William O., Jr.
1982 "The Lord's Prayer in Matthew and in John." *New Testament Studies* 28: 237-56.

Walvoord, John F.
1967 *The Thessalonian Epistles.* Grand Rapids: Zondervan.
1971a "Christ's Olivet Discourse on the End of the Age." *Bibliotheca Sacra* 128: 109-16.
1971b "Christ's Olivet Discourse on the End of the Age: Signs of the End of the Age." *Bibliotheca Sacra* 128: 316-26.
1972 *The Rapture Question.* Grand Rapids: Zondervan.
1976 *The Blessed Hope and the Tribulation.* Grand Rapids: Zondervan.

Wambacq, B. N.
1982 "Matthieu 5,31-32. Possibilité de divorce ou obligation de rompre une union illégitime." *Nouvelle Revue Théologique* 104: 34-49.

Wansbrough, John.
1977 *Quranic Studies: Sources and Methods of Scriptural Interpretation.* London Oriental Studies 31. School of Oriental and African Studies, University of London. Oxford: Oxford University Press.

Wapnish, Paula, and Brian Hesse.
1993 "Pampered Pooches or Plain Pariahs? The Ashkelon Dog Burials." *Biblical Archaeologist* 56: 55-80.

Ward, Roy Bowen.
1990 "Musonius and Paul on Marriage." *New Testament Studies* 36: 281-89.
Ware, Bruce A.
1981 "Is the Church in View in Matthew 24–25?" *Bibliotheca Sacra* 138: 158-72.
Warry, J. G.
1962 *Greek Aesthetic Theory: A Study of Callistic and Aesthetic Concepts in the Works of Plato and Aristotle.* New York: Barnes & Noble.
Wasserstein, A.
1989 "A Marriage Contract from the Province of Arabia Nova: Notes on Papyrus Yadin 18." *Jewish Quarterly Review* 80 (1-2, 1989): 93-150.
Wasson, Robert Gordon, Albert Hoffmann, and Carl A. P. Ruck.
1978 *The Road to Eleusis: Unveiling the Secret of the Mysteries.* New York: Harcourt Brace Jovanovich.
Waterman, G. Henry.
1975 "The Sources of Paul's Teaching on the Second Coming of Christ in 1 and 2 Thessalonians." *Journal of the Evangelical Theological Society* 18: 105-13.
Watson, Frances.
1998 "Toward a Literal Reading of the Gospels." Pp. 195-217 in *The Gospels for All Christians: Rethinking the Gospel Audiences.* Edited by Richard J. Bauckham. Grand Rapids: Eerdmans.
Weaver, Dorothy Jean.
1990 *Matthew's Missionary Discourse: A Literary Critical Analysis.* Journal for the Study of the New Testament Supplement 38. Sheffield: JSOT Press.
1992 "Matthew 28:1-10." *Interpretation* 46: 398-402.
1996 "Power and Powerlessness: Matthew's Use of Irony in the Portrayal of Political Leaders." Pp. 179-96 in *Treasures New and Old: Recent Contributions to Matthean Studies.* Edited by David R. Bauer and Mark Allan Powell. Society of Biblical Literature Symposium Series 1. Atlanta: Scholars Press.
Weber, Beat.
1992 "Schulden erstatten — Schulden erlassen. Zum matthäischen Gebrauch einiger juristischer und monetärer Begriffe." *Zeitschrift für die Neutestamentliche Wissenschaft* 83: 253-56.
Webb, Robert L.
1991 "The Activity of John the Baptist's Expected Figure at the Threshing Floor (Matthew 3.12 = Luke 3.17)." *Journal for the Study of the New Testament* 43: 103-11.
Webber, Randall C.
1983 "A Note on 1 Corinthians 15:3-5." *Journal of the Evangelical Theological Society* 26: 265-69.
Weber, J.-J.
1961 "Notes exégétiques sur le texte 'Tu es Petrus.'" *Bulletin Ecclésiastique du diocèse de Strasbourg* 80: 541-60. *(NTA)*
1962 "Notes exégétiques sur le texte 'Tu es Petrus.'" *Ami du Clergé* 72: 113-21. (*NTA* 6:313)
Weeden, Theodore J., Sr.
1971 *Mark — Traditions in Conflict.* Philadelphia: Fortress Press.
1976 "The Cross as Power in Weakness (Mark 15:20b-41)." Pp. 115-34 in *The Passion in Mark: Studies in Mark 14–16.* Edited by Werner H. Kelber. Philadelphia: Fortress Press.

Wegner, Judith Romney.
1988 *Chattel or Person? The Status of Women in the Mishnah.* New York: Oxford University Press.
Weiss, Johannes.
1971 *Jesus' Proclamation of the Kingdom of God.* Edited by Richard Hyde Hiers and David Larrimore Holland. Philadelphia: Fortress Press.
Weiss, Z., and Ehud Netzer.
1991 "Sty 'wnwt-hpyrh bsypwry." *Qadmoniot* 24 (3-4, 1991): 113-21. (*NTA* 36:393)
Wenham, David.
1973 "The Resurrection Narratives in Matthew's Gospel." *Tyndale Bulletin* 24: 21-54.
1979a "Jesus and the Law: An Exegesis on Matthew 5:17-20." *Themelios* 4: 92-96.
1979b "The Structure of Matthew XIII." *New Testament Studies* 25: 516-22.
1980 "A Note on Matthew 24:10-12." *Tyndale Bulletin* 31: 155-62.
1981 "Paul and the Synoptic Apocalypse." Pp. 345-75 in *Gospel Perspectives: Studies of History and Tradition in the Four Gospels.* Edited by R. T. France and David Wenham. Vol. 2 in Gospel Perspectives. 5 vols. Sheffield: JSOT Press, University of Sheffield.
1984a "Paul's Use of the Jesus Tradition: Three Samples." Pp. 7-37 in *The Jesus Tradition outside the Gospels.* Edited by David Wenham. Vol. 5 in Gospel Perspectives. Sheffield: JSOT Press.
1984b *The Rediscovery of Jesus' Eschatological Discourse.* Gospel Perspectives, vol. 4. Sheffield: JSOT Press.
Wenham, Gordon J.
1984 "Matthew and Divorce: An Old Crux Revisited." *Journal for the Study of the New Testament* 22: 95-107.
1986 "The Syntax of Matthew 19.9." *Journal for the Study of the New Testament* 28: 17-23.
Wenham, John W.
1977 *Christ and the Bible.* Downers Grove, IL: InterVarsity Press.
Wernberg-Møller, P.
1956-1957 "A Semitic Idiom in Matt. V.22." *New Testament Studies* 3: 71-73.
Westcott, B. F.
1950 *The Gospel according to St. John: The Authorized Version with Introduction and Notes.* Grand Rapids: Eerdmans. Reprint of 1881 edition.
Westerholm, Stephen.
1982 "Jesus, the Pharisees, and the Application of Divine Law." *Eglise Théologie* 13: 191-210.
Wheaton, D. H.
1982 "Money." Pp. 790-93 in *New Bible Dictionary.* 2d ed. Edited by J. D. Douglas and Norman Hillyer. Leicester, Eng.: InterVarsity Press.
Wheeler, Sir Mortimer.
1971 *Rome beyond the Imperial Frontiers.* Westport, CN: Greenwood.
Whelan, Caroline F.
1993 "Suicide in the Ancient World: A Re-examination of Matthew 27:3-10." *Laval Théologique et Philosophique* 49: 505-22.
Whisson, Michael G.
1964 "Some Aspects of Functional Disorders among the Kenyan Luo." Pp. 283-304 in *Magic, Faith, and Healing: Studies in Primitive Psychotherapy To-*

day. Edited by Ari Kiev. Introduction by Jerome D. Frank. New York: The Free Press; A Division of Macmillan Publishing Company.

Whitacre, Rodney A.

1982 *Johannine Polemic: The Role of Tradition and Theology.* Society of Biblical Literature Dissertation 67. Chico, CA: Scholars Press.

1992 "Vine, Fruit of the Vine." Pp. 867-68 in *Dictionary of Jesus and the Gospels.* Edited by Joel B. Green, Scot McKnight, and I. Howard Marshall. Downers Grove, IL: InterVarsity Press.

White, K. D.

1964 "The Parable of the Sower." *Journal of Theological Studies* 15: 300-307.

White, L. Michael.

1991 "Crisis Management and Boundary Maintenance: The Social Location of the Matthean Community." Pp. 211-47 in *Social History of the Matthean Community: Cross-Disciplinary Approaches.* Edited by David L. Balch. Minneapolis: Fortress Press.

White, R. E. O.

1960 *The Biblical Doctrine of Initiation.* Grand Rapids: Eerdmans.

White, William, Jr.

1971 "Finances." Pp. 218-36 in *The Catacombs and the Colosseum: The Roman Empire as the Setting of Primitive Christianity.* Edited by Stephen Benko and John J. O'Rourke. Valley Forge, PA: Judson Press.

Whittaker, C. R.

1969 "Introduction." 1:ix-lxxxvii in Herodian's *History.* 2 vols. Translated by C. R. Whittaker. Loeb Classical Library. Cambridge: Harvard University Press; London: William Heinemann.

Whittaker, Molly.

1984 *Jews and Christians: Graeco-Roman Views.* Cambridge Commentaries on Writings of the Jewish and Christian World 200 BC to AD 200, 6. Cambridge: Cambridge University Press.

Wiebe, Phillip H.

1989 "Jesus' Divorce Exception." *Journal of the Evangelical Theological Society* 32: 327-33.

Wieder, N.

1956-1957 "The Qumran Sectaries and the Karaites." *Jewish Quarterly Review* 47: 269-92.

Wiersma, S.

1990 "The Ancient Greek Novel and Its Heroines: A Female Paradox." *Mnemosyne* 43: 109-23.

Wifall, Walter R.

1978 "The Status of 'Man' as Resurrection." *Zeitschrift für die Alttestamentliche Wissenschaft* 90: 382-94.

Wightman, Gregory J.

1990 "Temple Fortresses in Jerusalem. Part II: The Hasmonean *Baris* and Herodian Antonia." *Bulletin of the Anglo-Israel Archaeological Society* 10: 7-35.

Wilcox, Max.

1969 "Dualism, Gnosticism, and Other Elements in the Pre-Pauline Tradition." Pp. 83-96 in *The Scrolls and Christianity: Historical and Theological Significance.* Edited by Matthew Black. London: S.P.C.K.

Wild, Robert A.

1981 *Water in the Cultic Worship of Isis and Sarapis.* Études Préliminaires aux Religions Orientales dans l'Empire Romain 87. Leiden: E. J. Brill.

Wiles, Maurice F.

1960 *The Spiritual Gospel: The Interpretation of the Fourth Gospel in the Early Church.* Cambridge: Cambridge University Press.

Wilken, Robert L.

1971 "Collegia, Philosophical Schools, and Theology." Pp. 268-91 in *The Catacombs and the Colosseum: The Roman Empire as the Setting of Primitive Christianity.* Edited by Stephen Benko and John J. O'Rourke. Valley Forge, PA: Judson Press.

Wilkins, Michael J.

1995 *Discipleship in the Ancient World and Matthew's Gospel.* 2d ed. Grand Rapids: Baker. First edition in Novum Testamentum Supplements. Leiden: E. J. Brill, 1988.

Wilkinson, John.

1964 "Apologetic Aspects of the Virgin Birth of Jesus Christ." *Scottish Journal of Theology* 17: 159-81.

1974a "Ancient Jerusalem: Its Water Supply and Population." *Palestine Exploration Quarterly* 106: 33-51.

1974b "The Mission Charge to the Twelve and Modern Medical Missions." *Scottish Journal of Theology* 27: 313-28.

1978 *Jerusalem as Jesus Knew It.* London: Thames & Hudson.

Williams, A. Lukyn.

1930 *Justin Martyr: The Dialogue with Trypho. Translation, Introduction, and Notes.* Translations of Christian Literature Series I — Greek Texts. New York: Macmillan Company.

Williams, D. S.

1993 "Morton Smith on the Pharisees in Josephus." *Jewish Quarterly Review* 84: 29-41.

Williams, Sam K.

1975 *Jesus' Death as a Saving Event: The Background and Origin of a Concept.* Harvard Dissertations in Religion 2. Missoula, MT: Scholars Press.

Williamson, H. G. M.

1982 *1 and 2 Chronicles.* New Century Bible Commentary. Grand Rapids: Eerdmans; London: Marshall, Morgan & Scott.

Willis, Geoffrey G.

1975 "Lead Us Not Into Temptation." *Downside Review* 93: 281-88.

Willis, John T.

1978 "The Meaning of Isaiah 7:14 and Its Application in Matthew 1:23." *Restoration Quarterly* 21: 1-18.

Willis, Steve.

1993 "Matthew's Birth Stories. Prophecy and the Magi." *Expository Times* 105: 43-45.

Willis, Wendell Lee.

1985 *Idol Meat in Corinth: The Pauline Argument in 1 Corinthians 8 and 10.* Society of Biblical Literature Dissertation 68. Chico, CA: Scholars Press.

Willner, Dorothy.

1983 "Definition and Violation: Incest and the Incest Taboos." *Man* 18: 134-59.

Willoughby, Harold R.

1929 *Pagan Initiation: A Study of Mystery Initiations in the Graeco-Roman World.* Chicago: University of Chicago Press.

Wilson, Dwight.

1977 *Armageddon Now!* Grand Rapids: Baker.

Wilson, Marvin.

1978 "An Evangelical Perspective on Judaism." Pp. 2-33 in *Evangelicals and Jews in Conversation on Scripture, Theology, and History.* Edited by Marc H. Tanenbaum, Marvin R. Wilson, and James A. Rudin. Grand Rapids: Baker.

Wilson, Monica.

1957 *Rituals of Kinship among the Nyakyusa.* London: Oxford University Press.

Wilson, Stephen G.

1973 *The Gentiles and the Gentile Mission in Luke-Acts.* Society for New Testament Studies Monograph 23. Cambridge: Cambridge University Press.

Wimmer, Joseph F.

1982 *Fasting in the New Testament: A Study in Biblical Theology.* New York: Paulist Press.

Wink, Walter.

1968 *John the Baptist in the Gospel Tradition.* Society for the Study of the New Testament Monograph 7. Cambridge: Cambridge University Press.

1989 "Jesus' Reply to John. Matt 11:2-6/Luke 7:18-23." *Forum* 5: 121-28.

1991 "Neither Passivity nor Violence. Jesus' Third Way (Matt 5:38-42//Luke 6:29-30)." *Forum* 7: 5-28.

1992 "Beyond Just War and Pacifism: Jesus' Nonviolent Way." *Review and Expositor* 89: 197-214.

1993 "Jesus and the Nonviolent Struggle of Our Time." *Louvain Studies* 18: 3-20.

Winkle, Rose E.

1986 "The Jeremiah Model for Jesus in the Temple." *Andrews University Seminary Studies* 24: 155-72.

Winslow, Donald.

1971 "Religion and the Early Roman Empire." Pp. 237-54 in *The Catacombs and the Colosseum: The Roman Empire as the Setting of Primitive Christianity.* Edited by Stephen Benko and John J. O'Rourke. Valley Forge, PA: Judson Press.

Winston, David.

1976 "Freedom and Determinism in Philo of Alexandria." The Center for Hermeneutical Studies in Hellenistic and Modern Culture, Colloquy 20. Berkeley: Center for Hermeneutical Studies.

Winter, Bruce W.

1991 "The Messiah as the Tutor: The Meaning of καθηγητής in Matthew 23:10." *Tyndale Bulletin* 42: 152-57.

Winter, Paul.

1961 *On the Trial of Jesus.* Studia Judaica Forschungen zur Wissenschaft des Judentums, band. 1. Berlin: Walter de Gruyter & Company.

1964 "The Trial of Jesus and the Competence of the Sanhedrin." *New Testament Studies* 10: 494-99.

Wintermute, Orval S.

1985 "Introduction to Jubilees." 2:35-50 in *The Old Testament Pseudepigrapha.* 2

vols. Edited by James H. Charlesworth. Garden City, NY: Doubleday & Company.

Wire, Antoinette Clark.

1991 "Gender Roles in a Scribal Community." Pp. 87-121 in *Social History of the Matthean Community: Cross-Disciplinary Approaches.* Edited by David L. Balch. Minneapolis: Fortress Press.

Wirgin, Wolf.

1965 *The Book of Jubilees and the Maccabaean Era of Shmittah Cycles.* Leeds University Oriental Society Monograph 7. N.p.: Leeds University Press.

Wise, Michael O., and James D. Tabor.

1992 "The Messiah at Qumran." *Biblical Archaeology Review* 18 (6, 1992): 60-63, 65.

Witherington, Ben, III.

1984 *Women in the Ministry of Jesus: A Study of Jesus' Attitudes to Women and Their Roles as Reflected in His Earthly Life.* Society for New Testament Studies Monograph 51. Cambridge: Cambridge University Press.

1985 "Matthew 5.32 and 19.9 — Exception or Exceptional Situation?" *New Testament Studies* 31: 571-76.

1990 *The Christology of Jesus.* Minneapolis: Augsburg Fortress Press.

1992 *Jesus, Paul and the End of the World: A Comparative Study in New Testament Eschatology.* Downers Grove, IL: InterVarsity Press.

1994 *Jesus the Sage: The Pilgrimage of Wisdom.* Minneapolis: Augsburg Fortress Press.

1995 *The Jesus Quest: The Third Search for the Jew of Nazareth.* Downers Grove, IL: InterVarsity Press.

Wojciechowski, Michal.

1988 "Mt 2,20: Herod and Antipater? A Supplementary Clue to Dating the Birth of Jesus." *Biblische Notizen* 44: 61-62.

Wolbert, Werner.

1988 "'Wer seinem Bruder ohne Grund zürnt.' Zu einer Lesart der 1. Antithese." *Theologie und Glaube* 78: 160-70.

Wolf, Eric.

1958 "The Virgin of Guadalupe: A Mexican National Symbol." *Journal of American Folklore* 71: 34-39.

Wolfson, Harry Austryn.

1968 *Philo: Foundations of Religious Philosophy in Judaism, Christianity, and Islam.* 2 vols. 4th rev. ed. Cambridge: Harvard University Press.

Wong, Eric Kun-Chun.

1991 "The Matthaean Understanding of the Sabbath: A Response to G. N. Stanton." *Journal for the Study of the New Testament* 44: 3-18.

Wrede, William.

1971 *The Messianic Secret.* Translated by J. C. G. Greig. Cambridge: James Clarke & Company.

Wright, Addison G.

1966 "The Literary Genre Midrash." *Catholic Biblical Quarterly* 28: 417-57.

Wright, G. Ernest.

1962 *Biblical Archaeology.* Philadelphia: Westminster Press.

Wright, N. T.

1992a *The New Testament and the People of God.* Vol. 1 in Christian Origins and the Question of God. Minneapolis: Fortress; London: S.P.C.K.

1992b *Who Was Jesus?* Grand Rapids: Eerdmans.

Yadin, Yigael.

1962 *The Scroll of the War of the Sons of Light against the Sons of Darkness.* Translated by Batya and Chaim Rabin. Hertford, Herts: Stephen Austin & Sons, for Oxford University Press.

1966 *Masada: Herod's Fortress and the Zealots' Last Stand.* New York: Random House.

1972 "L'attitude essénienne envers la polygamie et le divorce." *Revue Biblique* 79: 98-99.

1984 "The Temple Scroll." *Biblical Archaeology Review* 10: 32-49.

Yamauchi, Edwin M.

1966 "The 'Daily Bread' Motif in Antiquity." *Westminster Theological Journal* 28: 145-56.

1972 *The Stones and the Scriptures: An Introduction to Biblical Archaeology.* Grand Rapids: Baker.

1973 *Pre-Christian Gnosticism: A Survey of the Proposed Evidences.* Grand Rapids: Eerdmans.

1978 "Concord, Conflict, and Community: Jewish and Evangelical Views of Scripture." Pp. 154-196 in *Evangelicals and Jews in Conversation on Scripture, Theology and History.* Edited by Marc H. Tannenbaum, Marvin R. Wilson, and James A. Rudin. Grand Rapids: Baker.

1980 *The Archaeology of New Testament Cities in Western Asia Minor.* Grand Rapids: Baker.

1982 "The Crucifixion and Docetic Christology." *Concordia Theological Quarterly* 46: 1-20.

1986 "Magic or Miracle? Diseases, Demons and Exorcisms." Pp. 89-183 in Gospel Perspectives. 6 vols. Edited by R. T. France and David Wenham. Sheffield: JSOT Press, 1980-1986. Vol. 6: *The Miracles of Jesus.* Edited by David Wenham and Craig Blomberg.

1990 *Persia and the Bible.* Foreword by Donald J. Wiseman. Grand Rapids: Baker.

1992 "The Archaeology of Biblical Africa: Cyrene in Libya." *Archaeology in the Biblical World* 2 (1, 1992): 6-18.

Yeivin, Ze'ev.

1983 "Has Another Lost Ark Been Found?" *Biblical Archaeology Review* 9: 75-76.

Young, Brad H.

1989 *Jesus and His Jewish Parables: Rediscovering the Roots of Jesus' Teaching.* New York: Paulist Press.

1995 *Jesus the Jewish Theologian.* Forewords by Marvin R. Wilson and Rabbi David Wolpe. Peabody, MA: Hendrickson.

Young, J.

1992 "The Unspoken Premise." *Homiletic and Pastoral Review* 93: 55-58.

Zakowitch, Yair.

1975 "Rahab also Mutter des Boas in der Jesus-Genealogie (Matth. I 5)." *Novum Testamentum* 17: 1-5.

Zatelli, Ida.

1991 "The Rachel's Lament in the Targum and Other Ancient Jewish Interpretations." *Rivista Biblica* 39: 477-90.

Zeitlin, Solomon.
1939 "The Book of Jubilees, Its Character and Its Significance." *Jewish Quarterly Review* 30: 1-31.
1957-1958 "The Book of 'Jubilees' and the Pentateuch." *Jewish Quarterly Review* 48: 218-35.
1962 "The Trial of Jesus." *Jewish Quarterly Review* 53: 85-88.
1968 "Korban: A Gift." *Jewish Quarterly Review* 59: 133-35.
1974 "Who Were the Galileans? New Light on Josephus' Activities in Galilee." *Jewish Quarterly Review* 64: 189-203.
1975 "Dreams and Their Interpretation from the Biblical Period to the Tannaitic Time: An Historical Study." *Jewish Quarterly Review* 66: 1-18.

Zeller, Dieter.
1986 "Elija und Elischa im Frühjudentum." *Bibel und Kirche* 41: 154-60.

Zias, Joseph.
1989 "Lust and Leprosy: Confusion or Correlation?" *Bulletin of the American Schools of Oriental Research* 275: 27-31.

Ziesler, J. A.
1973a "The Removal of the Bridegroom: A Note on Mark II.18-22 and Parallels." *New Testament Studies* 19: 190-94.
1973b "The Vow of Abstinence Again." *Colloquium* 6: 49-50.
1984 "Matthew and the Presence of Jesus (2)." *Epworth Review* 11: 90-97.

Zimmerli, W., and J. Jeremias.
1957 *The Servant of God.* Naperville, IL: Alec R. Allenson.

Zimmerman, H.
1962 "*Mē epi porneia* (Mt 19,9) — ein literarisches Problem. Zur Komposition von Mt 19,3-12." *Catholica* 16: 293-99.

Zolli, Eugenio.
1958 "Nazarenus Vocabitur." *Zeitschrift für die Neutestamentliche Wissenschaft* 49: 135-36.

Zon, A.
1963 "Droga w Regule Wspólnoty. 1QS 9.18 (De notione viae in Qumranensi Regula)." *Ruch Biblijny i Liturgiczny* 16: 187-96. (*NTA* 8:430)

Zucker, David J.
1990 "Jesus and Jeremiah in the Matthean Tradition." *Journal of Ecumenical Studies* 27: 288-305.
1995 "Jonah's Journey." *Judaism* 44: 362-68.

Zumstein, Jean.
1980 "Antioche sur l'Oronte et l'évangile selon Matthieu." *Studien zum Neuen Testament und seiner Umwelt* 5: 122-38.

[illegible]

Robert A. Guelich [illegible]

[illegible]

Index of Selected Subjects

(especially excursuses and extended topical treatments in the Introduction)

Index of Authors

INDEX OF AUTHORS

INDEX OF AUTHORS

Index of Ancient Sources

(Note: pseudonymous authors like Ps-Cicero will appear under their alleged author.)

APOCRYPHA

1. Sirach references may vary according to recensions.

NEW TESTAMENT

DEAD SEA SCROLLS and related collections

TANNAITIC COLLECTIONS

2. We include in this list even those portions of Pirke 'Abot which are not in the Mishnah.

INDEX OF ANCIENT SOURCES

OTHER RABBINIC LITERATURE

INDEX OF ANCIENT SOURCES

EARLY CHRISTIAN AND GNOSTIC LITERATURE[3]

3. In some cases the distinction between early Christian and other early Jewish texts is debatable; some texts in the "early Jewish" category include Christian interpolations or redaction, or may be Jewish-Christian works.

4. We cite here only those entries not cited under other collections.